Introduction to

Knowledge Systems

Mark Stefik

M K *Morgan Kaufmann Publishers, Inc.*
San Francisco, California

Sponsoring Editor   Michael B. Morgan
Production Manager   Yonie Overton
Production Editor   Elisabeth Beller
Editorial Coordinator   Marilyn Uffner Alan
Text Design, Project Management,
  Electronic Illustrations, and Composition   Professional Book Center
Cover Design   Ross Carron Design
Copyeditor   Anna Huff
Printer   Quebecor

Brand and product names referenced in this book are trademarks or registered trademarks of their respective holders and are used here for informational purposes only.

Morgan Kaufmann Publishers, Inc.
Editorial and Sales Office
340 Pine Street, Sixth Floor
San Francisco, CA 94104-3205 USA
Telephone   415/392-2665
Facsimile   415/982-2665
Email   mkp@mkp.com
WWW   http://www.mkp.com

Library of Congress Cataloging-in-Publication Data
Stefik, Mark.
  Introduction to knowledge systems / Mark Stefik.
    p.   cm.
  Includes bibliographical references and index.
  ISBN 1-55860-166-X
  1. Expert systems (Computer science)   I. Title.
QA76.76.E95S83   1995
006.3'3—dc20   95-16537

This book is dedicated to all those people in my life
who have helped me to see the light in others,
so that I can now more easily see it in myself.

Contents

Foreword

Edward A. Feigenbaum

The AI enterprise is justly famous for a long series of brilliant conceptualizations that have informed our understanding of thinking and problem solving. The AI enterprise is justly infamous for its inability to turn these powerful ideas into powerful, thinking artifacts that have achieved widespread use in human affairs. Why?

AI's nearest approach to powerful, thinking artifacts are the expert systems; and it is no accident that expert systems to date have been the major knowledge-based systems. It is enlightening that the dictionary definition of intelligence incorporates knowledge as a major, defining concept. The lexicographers apparently understood what it took our discipline a decade to discover—that intelligence is essentially applied knowledge.

At the risk of oversimplification, let me divide the knowledge-based system (KBS) into two parts: the reasoning or problem-solving processes (R) and the knowledge base (K). The experience of building tens of thousands of expert systems to date has shown that building the R part is by far the simpler task. In fact, reasoning engines are available off-the-shelf in many software tools. But there are no off-the-shelf knowledge bases. It is in the very nature of the expert system that it is knowledge intensive, since it is a model of human expertise in a domain, and expertise is based on broad, often deep, knowledge of a domain. Each knowledge base is built *de novo* and is domain-specific, and often task-specific. The jobs of acquiring the knowledge and representing it are, more often than not, time consuming, arduous, and reach deep into a domain. To paraphrase the famous saying, God is in the details, not in general theorems or high-level abstractions.

Expert systems are knowledge-centric, but knowledge is distributed. From a university perspective, knowledge is distributed across different schools and departments. From a larger perspective, the knowledge to perform all kinds of tasks is spread out among the people who do them. The building of expert systems must continue to move beyond computer science departments. Importantly, the teaching about expert systems must reach out from computer science departments as well.

This is where *Introduction to Knowledge Systems* comes in. A field is established and in some ways defined by its first great textbook. For example, Fred Terman's book on radio electronics defined the field of electrical engineering. Every department has one or two courses, based on such textbooks, that become part of the general curriculum for all students. For mathematics departments, the main course offered to other departments is calculus. Computer science departments have traditionally offered a course in programming. The publishing of *Introduction to Knowledge Systems* marks an important event: computer science now has a second course that is timely and appropriate for general education—knowledge systems.

The spreading of knowledge systems, especially into the various specialities of engineering, medicine, and business, coincides with the explosive growth of the Internet. The increasing number of people active on the Internet opens up possibilities for knowledge sharing and eventually commerce in knowledge services on the network. Imagine thousands of individuals and groups preparing and making available by gift or sale portions of a large, common, distributed KB in the same way that people today write textbooks. In the space of shared information, we already see the growth of free and for-sale information on the Internet and World Wide Web (WWW).

The technological enablers for this information sharing are the hardware and software technologies of the Internet, WWW, Mosaic, and the other find-and-retrieve systems of the Internet. For knowledge sharing, a knowledge-based software infrastructure must be added to the existing information infrastructure.

The spirit of the enterprise is: "If you build it, they will come." Build what? Better tools for representing knowledge. Practical languages and associated protocols for moving knowledge across the Internet. Tools enabling communities on the network to build shared ontologies, the terms and concepts of a cognitive domain. I look for an Internet-like explosion of sharing of KBs among a large number of KBSs in the next decade or two.

AI is as much an engineering discipline as it is a scientific one. Mark Stefik anticipated the appearance of networked knowledge services in his paper, "The Next Knowledge Medium," that appeared in *AI Magazine* a few years ago. To move from journal articles to more and better practical KBS artifacts, an important enabler is an integrated, comprehensive treatment of the KBS science and technology. *Introduction to Knowledge Systems* now provides that enabler. It is insightful and practical—a textbook of science and engineering from which we can learn, and with which we can teach the principles of knowledge-based systems to a new generation of scientists and technologists. This new generation of students will build the new generation of knowledge services—on the network.

Preface

Every year more people use personal computers, personal digital assistants, or some other form of digital information system. They want their digital systems to operate simply, seamlessly, and intelligently. My word processing program should know about spelling, punctuation, and word choice; my spreadsheet should come pretailored to my financial interests; my interactive database should have a profile of the things I want to include and exclude; my calendar manager should know about the people I interact with; my communications system should know how to reach my friends and associates by phone, fax, and electronic mail.

Digital systems cannot act reliably and intelligently in ignorance. They need to *know how* to act intelligently. Computer systems that use knowledge are called knowledge-based systems, or simply knowledge systems.

Knowledge systems are used in engineering, the sciences, medicine, and business. Like numerical computer systems, they model situations and solve problems. Knowledge systems provide representation and reasoning capabilities for which purely numerical methods are unsuitable. They use representations based on symbols and graphs. To understand numeric tasks, we analyze numerical convergence and use approximation methods. To understand knowledge tasks, we analyze patterns of knowledge use and use search methods and nonmonotonic reasoning.

So what are the principles behind knowledge systems? What are knowledge systems useful for? How are they built? What are their limitations? How can they connect with human activities for creating and using knowledge? Addressing these questions is the purpose of this book.

A Textbook on Knowledge Systems

"Knowledge systems," as it is usually taught, is not a coherent field. The main cause of this incoherence is a confusion of intimacy with the subject matter of the applications of knowledge systems. Many knowledge engineering conferences are organized as sessions titled "Knowledge Systems in X," where X might be shop-floor planning, medicine, or civil engineering. In creating this book, Ive tried to pull out the core topics that cross those application boundaries, without losing the power with which applications drive invention in the field. Ideally, the relationship between knowledge engineering and its applications is like the relationship between the invention of calculus and early physics and mechanics.

This book explains how knowledge systems are used and what assumptions they depend on. It is a roadmap to what is known about building and using knowledge systems.

The book is organized in three parts: foundations, the symbol level, and the knowledge level. The foundations part discusses symbols, search, and knowledge. The symbol-level part discusses concepts for representation and reasoning. The knowledge-level part discusses and analyzes models for tasks such as classification, configuration, and diagnosis.

Each chapter begins with the main concepts and covers their application, their assumptions, and their limitations. Each chapter closes with a brief tour of research topics and open issues. This is the pattern for all of the chapters: first the basics and then the "relativistic corrections" and open issues. In this way I hope to convey not only the best understood concepts of knowledge systems, but also the limitations of our understanding and the excitement that attracted us to the field in the first place.

An Academic Course on Knowledge Systems

In a university setting, this book is intended for use at the advanced undergraduate levels and beginning graduate levels. For students outside of computer science, this book provides an introduction that prepares them for using and creating knowledge systems in their own areas of specialization. For computer science students, *Introduction to Knowledge Systems* provides a deeper treatment of knowledge systems than is possible in a general introduction to artificial intelligence (AI). It fills a gap between general introductions and graduate seminars. Rated exercises follow every section and answers are given at the back of the book.

For many students, an introduction to knowledge systems has been a short course about one of the knowledge-representation tools, a course presenting case studies of expert systems, an overview of business applications of artificial intelligence, or a general course about AI. Courses about particular knowledge-representation tools focus attention on the details of passing technologies, such as the syntax and idiosyncratic features of particular production-rule languages. Courses based on case studies are exemplary along some dimensions but not along others.

My goal is to provide more enduring foundations. This book is for those who want to understand how a computational medium can represent knowledge, reason with it, and create it. It is for those who want to automate some knowledge-intensive task and who expect to use knowledge systems throughout their careers.

Introduction to Knowledge Systems covers both basic and advanced topics. Advanced sections of the book are indicated with "ADVANCED" next to the section head. In many cases, these sections introduce concepts that are used in other advanced sections later in the text. Students seeking a basic understanding and working under time pressure may safely choose to skip these sections at the first reading.

For the Professional

Introduction to Knowledge Systems provides organized access to the state of the art in knowledge systems. The practice of building knowledge systems requires an understanding of methods and approaches from several disciplines. This text brings together key results, illustrates them with concrete examples, and explains the assumptions and limitations of each method. Exercises at the end of each section and selected answers at the back help a reader to check understanding of topics not traditionally discussed in computer science classes. The text presents fundamentals of symbol-level representations including representations for time, space, uncertainty, and vagueness. Its coverage of search methods goes beyond the basic methods to include the more efficient hierarchical methods for large search spaces. The text also compares the knowledge-level organizations for three common knowledge-intensive tasks: classification, configuration, and diagnosis.

Preparation and Assumed Background

The presentation in *Introduction to Knowledge Systems* is introductory but not elementary. A background in programming, set theory, and logic is helpful but is not required. For some of the material, a background in calculus and discrete mathematics is useful. No previous background in AI is required. Those who have taken an AI overview course will find some overlap of material such as search methods, but there is a substantial shift of emphasis and deepening of coverage.

The programming-language features discussed in this book are now available in a wide variety of commercially available knowledge-representation tools. Since commercial knowledge-programming shells and languages are undergoing rapid change, any attempt to describe them in detail would become quickly dated. A person with a firm grasp of the fundamentals should have no difficulty using whatever tools are convenient.

The Social and Technical Context for Knowledge Systems

Beyond computer literacy is "knowledge literacy," which implies an interest and awareness in how information becomes knowledge. The explicit representations and reasoning methods used in knowledge systems make knowledge tangible. When communities and companies begin using knowledge systems, they become more aware of how knowledge enables them to do their work. They become interested in methods for creating, debugging, and using knowledge. These organizations learn, evolve, and create and use knowledge.

The "information superhighway" is coming to pass, bit by bit, as technology and social practice dance into the digital age. New services of all kinds arise when there are improvements in the production economies of scale and changes in technologies for storing, retrieving, transmitting, and displaying information. Knowledge systems are part of the blending of computers, televisions, and books into new, integrated forms that are changing the ways we work, play, and learn. Today's students in engineering, science, and business will be among the major consumers and creators of the next generations of knowledge systems.

Acknowledgments

This book started out to be the textbook that I wished I had had as a graduate student at Stanford University. It began as a two-year, part-time project but ultimately took more than five years to write. As it took shape, I discovered that the field was changing quickly. I needed to catch up in areas outside my own sphere.

My point of view has been heavily influenced by close colleagues and friends, especially Daniel Bobrow, Sanjay Mittal, and Lynn Conway. Lynn Conway challenged me to reach beyond the AI community to graduate students in science and engineering. For many years she has been observant and curious about the creation and propagation of cultural forms. She challenged me to pay more attention to processes of knowledge creation and propagation.

No one can succeed at an effort of this size without benefit of advice from mentors. Several people have stepped in with encouragement and help at different stages of the project. I especially thank Daniel Bobrow, Bruce Buchanan, Lynn Conway, and Edward Feigenbaum, as well as my patient editor, Michael Morgan.

I have relied extensively on the goodwill of colleagues who found the time to discuss the ideas, to read drafts, and to offer much advice and encouragement. They offered pointers to papers and points of view beyond my experience. They critiqued the chapters, uncovering confusions and offering suggestions and fresh perspectives. They answered questions about theory and practice concerning the knowledge systems they have built. Some of them taught courses from draft versions of the text. Of course, I accept responsibility for whatever inaccuracies remain. Thanks to Shoshana Abel, Phil Agre, Agustin Araya, James Bennett, Hans Berliner, William Birmingham, Daniel Bobrow, Susan Bridjes, Bruce Buchanan, Stuart Card, Robert Causey, William Clancey, Jan Clayton, Lynn Conway, James Coombs, Greg Cooper, Harley Davis, Randall Davis, Rina Dechter, Johan deKleer, Tom Dietterich, Richard Duda, Clive Dym, Larry Eshelman, Brian Falkenhainer, Edward Feigenbaum, Felix Frayman, Eugene Freuder, Marcus Fromherz, Dan Greene, Anurag Gupta, Frank Halasz, Walter Hamscher, Pat Hayes, Frederick Hayes-Roth, Tadd Hogg, Gary Kahn, Kenneth Kahn, Jonathan King, Johan deKleer, Stanley Lanning, David McAllester, John McDermott, Sandra Marcus, Sanjay Mittal, Richard Neapolitan, Ramesh Patil, Judea Pearl, James Reggia, Daniel Russell, Jim Schmolze, Mark Shirley, Edward Shortliffe, Daniel Siewiorek, Jeffrey Mark Siskind, John Sowa, Deborah Tatar, Eric Tribble, Sholom Weiss, Daniel Weld, Brian Whatcott, Brian Williams, and Colin Williams.

The duration of this project outlived several management changes at Xerox Palo Alto Research Center (PARC). One fixed point in all of that change was John Seely Brown, who encouraged me to write this book and who waited much longer than he wanted to. I am deeply grateful to the Xerox Corporation for granting me the means to bring this project to a successful conclusion.

Thanks to Mimi Gardner, who supported me during a hectic beginning period when I was managing the Knowledge Systems Area at Xerox PARC and writing this book. Thanks also to Giulianna Lavendel and her staff at Xerox PARC's Technical Information Center. Their ingenuity in obtaining books, papers, and sometime obscure materials for me was greatly appreciated.

I also thank my students. I taught courses based on the evolving book over a five-year period and the book got better with time. The students still tell me, "Speak up. Slow down." Finally, I thank my family for years of patience, and Barbara Tropiano, who is taking the path of life with me and who helps to illuminate the path with light, wisdom, love, and understanding.

Notes on the Exercises

It is difficult to master a subject without practicing it. Reading about ideas is not nearly as important for learning as working with ideas. For this reason exercises are the heart of a good course and essential for a good textbook. This book has exercises for every section of every chapter. The exercises provide an opportunity to work with the concepts and to test understanding. Designed for either self-study or guided courses, they range from simple questions to research problems. The exercises are integral to the presentation of the material.

Rating symbols are provided to suggest the relative difficulty of the exercises. Different people require different amounts of time to do exercises. As one student who used a draft version of this book remarked, "The numbers indicate how many minutes the exercises should take if you are Einstein and already know the answer." In any case, the rating "00" indicates a warm-up exercise whose answer is immediate. More difficult exercises have higher numbers on a roughly linear scale.

The labels *T* and *R*, mean that exercises are appropriate for a *term* project in a class or that they are posed as a *research* problem whose solution is unknown to me at the time of this writing. This rating of exercises was inspired by Donald Knuth's rating system for the exercises in his books *The Art of Computer Programming*.

Some exercises are preceded by a ■. They are especially instructive and recommended.

Some of the exercises have proven especially suitable for class discussions. Exercises preceded by the label CD have been successfully used for this purpose in my own classes.

Summary of Exercise Codes

■	Recommended
L	Logic
M	Discrete mathematics

CP	Computer programming
!	Discovery exercise
CD	Class discussion
00	Immediate
05	Simple
10	Easy
30	Moderately hard
60	Difficult
T	Term project
R	Research project

This book is written for students with varying amounts of experience in computer science and mathematics. Some exercises require a formal background in logic, concrete mathematics, or programming. A rating is preceded by an L if a background in logic is assumed. It is preceded by an M if substantial use of mathematical concepts is required. For example, some exercises require that the reader be familiar with calculus or with discrete mathematics. A rating is preceded by CP if substantial computer programming experience or a computer science background is assumed.

Exercises in the early chapters anticipate material that is discussed in later chapters. For example, exercises in the first chapter introduce the backward chaining of rules, interacting assumptions, and simple models of diagnosis—all topics of later chapters. This practice is intended to offer students the pleasure and opportunity of discovering these concepts and to give extra ways to understand the material.

Exercises that lead to a discovery or insight beyond the material in the section are marked with an exclamation point (!). These discovery exercises are not necessarily difficult, but they do require initiative. They raise questions that can provide the basis for an extended class discussion.

If you do not have time to work through all of the exercises, start with the recommended ones and easy ones. If you are using this book outside of a course, you are strongly advised to read through all of the exercises. Notes are interspersed occasionally with the exercises to indicate the relationships between the exercises and the text.

I sometimes make a small effort at humor in the exercises, presenting silly true/false questions or asking apparently outrageous questions. Professor Digit and his graduate student Sam are often featured in the exercises. Professor Digit is a sometimes bungling but ever hopeful professor at a university of uncertain location. Both are entirely fictitious. Any resemblance to the names of professors, students, or other esteemed colleagues is entirely a coincidence. Some of my students have started to refer to the professor as "ol' Digit" and to make generalizations about his character based on repeated encounters with him throughout a course. Be forewarned, however, that Digit is not always wrong!

Exercise

■   **Ex. 1**   [*00*] What does the rating CP-20 mean?

Introduction and Overview

The Building of a Knowledge System to Identify Wild Plants

There is always a tension between top-down and bottom-up presentations. A top-down presentation starts with goals and then establishes a framework for pursuing the parts in depth. Bottom-up presentations start with fundamental and primitive concepts and then build to higher-level ones. Top-down presentations can be motivating but they risk lack of rigor; bottom-up presentations can be principled but they risk losing sight of goals and direction.

Most of this book is organized bottom-up. This reflects my desire for clarity in a field that is entering its adolescence, metaphorically if not chronologically. The topics are arranged so a reader starting at the beginning is prepared for concepts along the way. Occasionally I break out of the bottom-up rhythm and step-at-a-time development to survey where we are, where we have been, and where we are going. This introduction serves that purpose.

The following overview traces the steps of building a hypothetical knowledge system. Woven into the story are some notes that connect it with sections in this book that develop the concepts further. Many of the questions and issues of knowledge engineering that are mysterious in a bottom-up presentation seem quite natural when they are encountered in the context of building a knowledge system. In particular, it becomes easy to see why they arise.

I made up the following story, so it does not require a disclaimer saying that the names have been changed to protect the innocent. Nonetheless, the phenomena in the story are familiar to anyone who has developed a knowledge system. Imagine that we work for a small software company that builds popular software packages including knowledge systems. This is a story of a knowledge system: how it was conceived, built, introduced, used, and later extended.

To Build a Knowledge System

It all began when we were approached by an entrepreneur who enjoys hiking and camping in the hills, mountains, and deserts of California. Always looking for a new market opportunity, he noticed that campers and hikers like to identify wild plants but that they are not very good at it. Identifying wild plants can be useful for survival in the woods ("What can I eat?") and it also has recreational value. He was convinced that conservationists, environmentalists, and well-heeled hikers have a common need.

The entrepreneur proposed that we build a portable knowledge system for identifying wildlife. He had consulted a California hiking club and a professional naturalist. He suggested that we begin by constructing a hypertext database about different kinds of plants, describing their appearance, habitats, relations to other wildlife, and human uses. Our initial project team is as follows:

- A hiker representing the user community and customer.
- A naturalist, our domain expert on wildlife identification.
- A knowledge engineer, our expert in acquiring knowledge and knowledge representation.
- A software engineer, the team leader having overall responsibility for the development of software.

After some discussion within the company we agreed to develop a prototype version of the knowledge system using the latest palmsize or "backpack" computers. If the technical project seemed feasible, we would then consider the next steps of commercialization. We planned to use the process of building the prototype to help us determine the feasibility of a larger project. We recruited the naturalist and a prominent member of one of the hiking clubs to our project team. We called the group together and started to learn about each other's ideas and terminology.

Notes   The participants are just getting started. They need to size up the task, develop their goals, and determine their respective roles on the project. They need to consider many questions about the nature of the knowledge system they would build. They ask "Who wants it?" because the situation and people matter for shaping the system. They also ask "What do these people do?" and "What role should the system play?" because these issues arise in all software engineering projects.

Connections   See Chapter 3 for a discussion of the initial interview concepts and background on software engineering.

Our Initial Interviews

Our naturalist tells us he wants to focus on native trees of California. We begin with the famous California redwood trees, the *Sequoia sempervirens* or coastal redwood and the *Sequoiadendron giganteum* or giant redwood that thrives in the Sierras. Our naturalist is a stickler for completeness. He also adds the *Metasequoia glyptostroboides* or dawn redwood, which grew in most parts of North America. The dawn redwood was thought to have become extinct until a grove was discovered in China in 1944. At a blackboard he draws a chart of plant families as shown in Figure I.1. He tells us about the history of the plant kingdom:

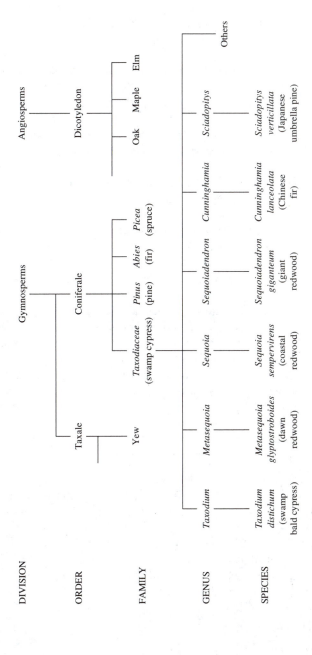

FIGURE I.1. A partial taxonomy showing relations among plants closely related to California redwood trees. In our scenario and thought experiment, the naturalist was asked about redwoods and started lecturing about plant families.

Plants evolved on Earth from earlier one-celled animals. About 200 million years ago was the age of conifers, the cone-bearing trees. Redwoods are members of the conifers, which were the dominant plant species at that time. They are among the gymnosperms, plants that release their seeds without a protective coating or shell.

Our naturalist is a gifted teacher but he tends to slip into what we have started to call his "lecture mode." After an hour of exploring taxonomies of the plant kingdom we begin to get restless. One of the team members interrupts him to ask the proper location in the taxonomy for the "albino redwoods," which are often visited in Muir Woods. This question jars the naturalist. Albinos do not fit into the plant taxonomy because they are not a true species, but rather a mutated parasite from otherwise normal coastal redwoods. Redwoods propagate by both seeds and roots. Sometimes something goes wrong in the root propagation, resulting in a tree that lacks the capability to make chlorophyll. Such rare plants would normally die, except a few that continue to live parasitically off the parent. Albino trees have extra pores on their leaves that make them efficient for moving quantities of water and nutrients from their host and parent trees.

At this point another member of the group, a home gardener, wants to know about trees she had purchased at a local nursery called *Sequoia sempervirens soquel* and *Sequoia sempervirens aptos blue*. Again, the naturalist explains that these trees are not really species either. Rather, they are clones of registered individual coastal redwoods, propagated by cuttings and popular with nurseries because they grow to be predictable "twins" to the parent tree, having the same shape and color. These registered clones are sometimes called cultivars. They would be impossible to identify reliably by visual examination alone and they are not found in the wild.

This leads us to a discussion of exactly what a taxonomic chart means, what a species is, what the chart is useful for, and whether it is really a good starting place for plant identification. Clearly the chart does not contain all the information we need about plants because some plants of apparent interest do not appear in it. We also have learned that there are some plants about which there is debate as to their lineage. After discussion we decide that the information is interesting and that it would be a good base for establishing names of plants, but that it would not be appropriate for us to proceed by just filling out more and more of the taxonomic chart. We decide to focus on actual cases of plant identification at our next session.

Notes   In this part of the story the participants are beginning to build bridges into each other's areas to understand how they will work together. They bring to the discussion some preexisting symbol structures or representations, such as the plant taxonomic chart. Often there needs to be discussion about just what the symbols mean and whether those meanings are useful for the task at hand. As in this story, it sometimes turns out that these symbols and representations need to be modified. When the end product includes a knowledge system, then conventions about symbol structures must be made precise enough for clear communication and also expressive enough for the distinctions made in performing the task.

Connections   See Chapter 1 for an introduction to symbols and symbol structures and the assignment of meaning to them. See Chapter 3 for a discussion of tools and methods for incremental formalization of knowledge.

1. The specimen is tall,
2. I'd guess about 30 or 35 feet tall.
3. So it's a tree . . .
4. symmetrical in shape.
5. From the needles in the foliage, it's obviously a pine,
6. but not one of the coastal pines since we're at too high an elevation in these mountains.
7. Could be either a *Pinus ponderosa*, a *jeffreyi*, or a *torreyana*.
8. Let's see (walking in closer) . . . dark green needles, not yellow-green,
9. about 7 inches long, and
10. in clusters of three.
11. Rather grayish bark, not cinnamon-brown.
12. Medium-sized cones.
13. Seems to be a young tree. Others like it are near, reaching heights of over a hundred feet tall.
14. It's probably a *Pinus jeffreyi*, that is, a Jeffrey pine.

FIGURE I.2.   Transcription of our naturalist talking through the identification of one of the plants.

The Naturalist in the Woods

We prepare to study the naturalist's classification process on some sample cases. One member of the group sets up portable video and audio recorders at a local state park. Our hiking club member is our prototype user. We define his job as walking into the woods and selecting a plant to be identified. In this way we hope to gain insight into what plants he finds interesting and to test the relevance of the plant taxonomy. We ask the naturalist to "think out loud" as he identifies plants. Recording such a session is called taking a protocol. This results in verbal data where the naturalist talks about the bark coloration, surface roots, and leaf shapes. After these dialogs are recorded and pictures of the plants are taken, we transcribe all of the tapes. Figure I.2 shows a sample transcript.

After the session in the park, we go over the transcripts carefully with the naturalist, trying to reconstruct any intermediate aspects of his thought process that were not verbalized. We ask him a variety of questions. "What else did you consider here? How did you know that it was not a manzanita? Why couldn't it have been a fir tree or a digger pine? Why did you ask about the coloring of the needles?" Our goal is not so much to capture exactly what his reasoning was in every case, but rather to develop a set of case examples that we could use as benchmarks for testing our computer system. As it turns out, the naturalist does different things on different cases. He does not always start out with exactly the same set of questions, so his method is not one of just working through a fixed decision tree or discrimination network.

Notes   At this point the group has begun a process of collecting knowledge about the task in terms of examples of problem-solving behavior. As we will see below, it is possible to make some false starts in this, and it is also possible to recover from such false starts.

Connections   See Chapter 3 for discussion of the assumptions and methods of the "transfer of expertise approach."

Characterizing the Task

The knowledge engineer begins a tentative analysis of the protocols. He tells us he might need to analyze these sessions several different ways before we are done. He wants to characterize the actions of the naturalist in terms of problem-solving steps. His approach is to model the problem-solving task as a search problem, in which the naturalist's steps carry out different operations in the search. Figure I.3 shows his first tentative analysis of the session from Figure I.2. In this, he

---

Collect Initial Data
Determine height of plant: Plant is more than 30-feet tall. (1)
Shape is symmetrical. (4)
Foliage has needles. (5)

Determine General Classification
Infer: Plant is a tree. (3) Plant is a pine tree or a close relative.
Knowledge: Only pines and close relatives have needle-shaped leaves. (5)

Collect Data about Location
Mountain location.
Knowledge: Trees from the low areas and the coast do not grow in the mountains. (6)
Rule out candidates that do not grow in this region.

Form Specific Candidate Hypotheses
Mountain pine trees include the *Pinus ponderosa*, the *jeffreyi*, and the *torreyana*. (7)

Determine Data to Discriminate among Hypotheses
Knowledge: The hypotheses make different predictions about needle color and bark color.

Species:	*ponderosa*	*jeffreyi*	*torreyana*
Bark color:	cinnamon-brown	grey	brown
Needle color:	yellow-green	dark green	dull green
Needle clusters:	three	three	five
Needle length:	8"	7"	10"

Collect Discriminating Data
Needles are dark green. (8)
Needles are 7 inches long. (9)
Needles are clustered in threes. (10)
Bark is grayish. (11)
Cones are medium-size. (12)

Consider Reliability of Data
There are other trees in the area of the same character. (13)
Mature height of others is more than 100 feet. (13)
Infer that the specimen is representative but not yet full grown. (13)

Determine Whether Unique Solution Is Found
Only a *Pinus jeffreyi* fits the data. (14)

Retrieve Common Name
Knowledge: A *Pinus jeffreyi* is commonly called a Jeffrey pine.

FIGURE I.3. Preliminary analysis of the protocol from the transcript in Figure I.2. The numbers in parentheses refer to the corresponding steps in Figure I.2.

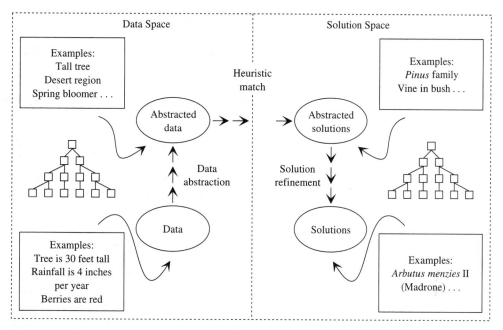

FIGURE I.4. The search spaces for classification. This method reasons about data, which may be abstracted into general features. The data are associated heuristically with abstracted solutions and ultimately specific solutions.

characterized operations such as "determining the general classification," "collecting data," "forming specific candidate hypotheses," and so on. These operations constitute a sketch of a computation model for the plant identification, which searches through a catalog of possible answers.

This tentative analysis of the protocol is consistent with a computational model that the knowledge engineer calls "classification." Someone in the group objects, arguing that the naturalist was not "classifying." Instead, he was merely "identifying" plants because the classes of possible plants were predetermined. The knowledge engineer agrees but explains that this is exactly what classification systems do. He draws Figure I.4 to illustrate the basic concepts used in this method.

To use this method, we needed to identify the kinds of data that could be collected in the field—the data space—as well as the kinds of solutions—the solution space. Data consist of such observations as the number of needles in a cluster. A final solution is a plant species. Classification uses abstractions of both data and solutions. A datum such as "3 inches of rain falls in the region annually" might be generalized to "this is a dry, inland region." A solution and species description such as *Pinus contorta murrayana* (lodgepole pine) might be generalized to pine tree. There are variations of classification, but they all proceed by ruling out candidate solutions that do not fit the data. Further analysis of protocols on multiple cases would be needed to determine what kinds of knowledge were being used and how they were used.

The knowledge engineer now has some questions for the naturalist. Suppose the solution space is given by a catalog of possibilities, such as the charts in the botany books we used on the project. The protocol analysis in Figure I.3 shows that the naturalist quickly ruled out the coastal varieties of the pine tree. But how about the many other species of pine that grow in the mountains? With book in hand, he asks why the naturalist had not considered a coulter pine (*Pinus coulteri*). The naturalist is taken aback. He answers that the coulter pine actually is a plausible candidate and asks to see the pictures of the specimen. After looking at it, he says the pine cones are too small and that the specimen does not have a characteristic open tree shape like an oak tree. Continuing, the knowledge engineer asks about the sugar pine. The naturalist answers that the cross-examination ferls like "lesson time," but that sugar pines are the tallest pine trees in the world, being more than 200 feet tall and that you would know immediately if you were in a sugar pine forest. However, the idea of systematically going through the catalog to analyze the protocols is appealing, so the two of them start working over them. The naturalist suggests that all of this post-protocol explanation and introspection might make him more systematic about his own methods.

As we continue to work on this, the significant size of the search space becomes clearer to everyone. One could be "systematic" by asking leading questions about each possible plant species. However, there are about 50 common species of just pine trees in California. Species of trees represent only a small fraction of the native plants. A quick check of some catalogs suggests that there are about 7,000 plant species of interest in California, not counting 300 or 400 species of wildflowers that are often discounted as weeds. It is clear that any identification process needs a means to focus its search, and that we need to be economical about asking questions. We begin to examine the protocols for clues about search strategy. We want to understand not only what he knows about particular plants, but also how he narrows the search, using knowledge about the families of plants and other things to quickly focus on a relatively small set of candidates.

Notes   The group is developing a systematic approach for gathering and analyzing the domain knowledge. The protocol analysis has led to a framework based on heuristic classification. Usually protocol analysis and selection of a framework are done together. It is not unusual for the analysis to reveal aspects that were not articulated. Experts sometimes forget to say things out loud and sometimes make mistakes. For these reasons, it is good practice to compare many examples of protocols on related cases. Knowledge needed for a task is seldom revealed all at once.

Connections   See Chapter 2 for characterizations of problem solving as search and for the terminology of data spaces, search spaces, and solution spaces. This chapter focuses on basic methods for search. To build a computational model of a task domain, we need to identify the search spaces and to determine what knowledge is needed and how it is used. See Chapter 3 for a discussion about approaches and psychological assumptions for the analysis of protocols. See Chapters 7, 8, and 9 for examples of the knowledge-level analysis and computational models for different tasks.

A "Naturalist in a Box"

As we build up a collection of cases and study the transcripts, we become aware of some difficulties with our approach. The first problem is that the naturalist is depending a great deal on properties of the plants that he can see and smell. Much of the knowledge he is using in doing this is not articulated in the transcripts.

Our hiking club representative kids the naturalist, saying he is "cheating" by just looking at the plants. We decide to take this objection seriously, and then notice three specific kinds of problems in the collected protocols. The first problem is that the naturalist makes his visual observations very quickly and often neglects to verbalize what he is doing at that point. Second, the naturalist does not articulate what guides his processes of perception. We need a systematic way of knowing where he is looking and then gathering the characterizations and inferences from what is seen. Third, we realize that the situation in which our system will be used introduces a new aspect of the task outside of the naturalist's field experience: communicating as though blind with an inexperienced observer. In short, the taking and analyzing of protocols seemed to be a good approach, but our approach was providing us with data for solving the wrong problem.

These problems mean that we have more work to do. For example, some additional "definitions" need to be captured, such as just what a "mottled pattern" is and what color is "cinnamon-brown." In using terms to refer to things in the world, we need to be sure that another observer can interpret the description and find the same thing. We call this the "reference" problem. We become nervous about the perceptual aspects of the naturalist's thinking because our "portable classifier" would not have capabilities for machine perception: In our projected system our users will need to observe the plants themselves. In addition, much technical vocabulary appeared in the protocols. We are becoming familiar with the naturalist's vocabulary as a result of working on the project. However, we recognize that our potential users and customers will not be comfortable with a question such as "Does it have radical leaves?" or "How many stamens and stigma are there?"

Again, we need a new approach to create a product that our potential customers will find usable. After a few hours of brainstorming, one of the group members proposes a knowledge acquisition set up that we later called "our naturalist in a box," as shown in Figure I.5.

In our setup the naturalist sits at a working table in a tent in the forest with whatever books and pictures he needs. The user walks off into the woods with a portable television. Each has a headset that allows them to speak by radio. In addition, the naturalist can show pictures from his books or drawings over the video link. This setup approximates the storage and display functions we would have with a portable hypermedia system, where the computer and stored images might perform the role of the "naturalist in the box." The voice communication would substitute for a pointing device and keyboard. All communications on the audio and video links are recorded for our later analysis. In addition, pictures of the plants and the user are taken, but not shown to the naturalist until later when we analyze the sessions.

At first the naturalist feels quite confined and hampered by the setup. A crucial question was whether the naturalist could properly identify the plants without seeing them. Soon, however, it becomes clear that the naturalist is able to function in this mode and that the setup is suitable for obtaining the information we need. We begin to discover specific requirements about the interactions with the user.

Along the way there are some interesting surprises. One fall day, a user wants to identify a brilliant red shrub at the side of the trail. As he describes the bush, the naturalist starts to ask whether it has shiny leaves organized in groups of three originating from the same point on the

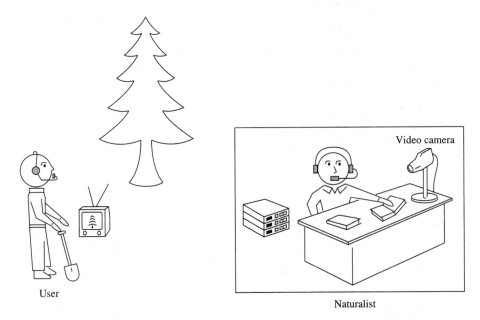

FIGURE I.5.   Our "naturalist in a box" setup for gathering realistic problem-solving protocols.

stem. Suddenly the naturalist becomes alarmed and says, "No, don't touch that! It's probably *Rhus diversiloba*, I mean, poison oak!" This leads us to recognize the need for additional functionality in the performance program, beyond the simple drive to classify.

We begin to record various images of the plants from our cases and organize them for computer-controlled retrieval in a catalog of digitized images. The naturalist begins to use these images in his conversations with the "users." With a few keystrokes, he can retrieve an image and display it on the user's television. We make a simple interface to switch from general views of a plant to close-up views of its foliage, bark, or seeds. We also make it easy to arrange image arrays of similar plants next to each other for visual comparison. Together with the naturalist we experiment with different ways of retrieving and displaying images.

From the many video sessions it becomes apparent that our users are not willing to answer "20 questions" in order to identify plants. For one thing, they often do not understand words such as *pollen cones* or *deciduous*. Over a few weeks of experimenting with the setup, we begin to understand more about the flexibility inherent in the information exchanged in a session between the naturalist and a user. We notice that a user might volunteer some basic constraints at the beginning. For example, once it is determined that the region was "high desert" there is no point in considering plants that could grow only in less arid regions. Once it is determined that it is winter, there is no point asking questions about deciduous leaves that would no longer be on the plant. If the user is interested in shrubs, it is not necessary to enter that constraint for every specimen.

Our programmers create a template of constraints that can be carried over from problem to problem, without the need to reenter them or infer them from new data. To avoid tailoring our interactive approach to the requirements and idiosyncrasies of a single user, we rotate through a collection of users and test whether the vocabularies and kinds of interactions can be easily understood.

As we broaden our activities to different parts of the wilderness, our naturalist suggests that we enlist the help of other naturalists who specialized in those regions. The naturalists work alternatively as a team and as individuals checking each other's work. We find that they differ in their approaches. This raises general issues about combining expertise. We collect the interesting cases for staff discussion.

As we begin to use the system, we need a name for it. Someone proposes calling it SEQUOYAH, after the Cherokee for whom the redwoods are thought to be named. Born in 1760, Sequoyah was known for developing a written alphabet for Native American languages. His goal was to enable the tribes to communicate and to preserve their Indian dialects. We thought that the name was appropriate for honoring the Native Americans who lived in and knew so much about the wilderness. We also saw the knowledge system as a new kind of writing medium or active documentation, that would be an appropriate tool for a modern-day Sequoyah.

Notes   The group has had some false starts. They needed to define the task better to focus their process of finding and formulating the relevant knowledge. The term *process* keeps coming up in the context of building and using knowledge systems. Knowledge systems for specific tasks must be designed to fit the processes in those tasks. In this example, the group discovered that it had made a crucial error in its assumptions about the way that the system would be used. In particular, it had implicitly assumed that the user would have the same observational skills as the naturalist. Addressing this exposed the need for different protocols.

Connections   Chapter 3 considers general points from software engineering about defining tasks and about involving potential users and multiple experts in early stages of system design. When multiple experts are available, there is an opportunity for them to check each other's work, to find idiosyncrasies and gaps, and to develop alternative reasoning models. Chapter 1 discusses the use of multiple models in reasoning.

Developing Formal Representations

Working from the protocols and other background material, we begin to develop formal relations for modeling the identification of plants. These relations need to make distinctions adequate for representing the reasoning in our sample cases. For example, we need to define a "color" relation that would map consistently to a range of colors and color mixtures. Furthermore, we know that the bark, leaves, and cones could all be different colors. This leads us to formalize a vocabulary of standard "parts" for plants. Following the biologist's lead, we select standard terms for parts and use the same names for particular relations throughout our database.

The knowledge engineer develops an example of a frame for our consideration, as shown in Figure I.6. As he explains it, the frame is a representation that would be used for the reasoning done internally by SEQUOYAH and externally for our discussions of what SEQUOYAH could and should do. Internally, SEQUOYAH might employ multiple and different representations for some parts of its task, but we would define our understanding and view of them largely through the **vocabulary** made visible in frames. Externally, user interfaces would specify how we viewed

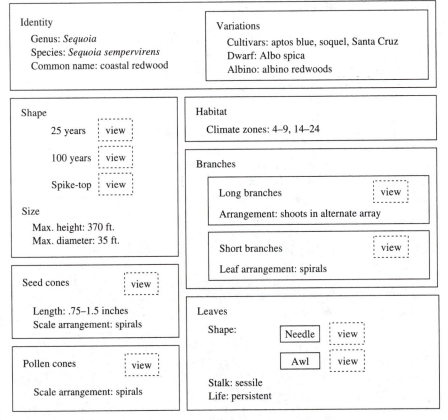

FIGURE I.6.   Example of a composite frame tried for data entry. In designing these we seek ways that would ensure the use of a uniform vocabulary in the database.

and interacted with the frames. His purpose at this setting is to consider some of the meaning and vocabulary that we would use in creating SEQUOYAH. The general idea is that we will choose a uniform vocabulary to the extent that it is possible.

The first thing he explains about the frame in Figure I.6 is that it contains many different kinds of information. For example, the boxes marked "view" are intended to link to digitized photographs that can be shown to the user. They are not intended for interpretation by SEQUOYAH itself. The second point is that many of the entries have further elaborations elsewhere in the data base. For example, there is a frame for pollen cones, a frame for the *Sequoia* genus, a frame for climate zone 14, a general frame for leaves, and so on. Using the frames, we define vocabulary and relations for plants, their parts, their botanical classifications, their habitats, as well as observations and tests that could be carried out by our users. In addition we develop criteria for choosing what to observe, choosing what candidates to consider, combining constraints, and developing warnings about hazards.

We then discuss the different data fields, with an eye toward specifying more precisely what they should mean. The naturalist says that separating the common name from the botanical name is a good idea. In the case of the redwood, several other trees are commonly called red-woods that are not related. In Brazil, the Amazonia is often called a redwood. It has light red and orange wood. In Burma, there is a tree called the Andaman redwood. It has red or crimson wood streaked with red. In Europe, the wood from *Pinus sylvestris* or Scots pine is often called red-wood. The naturalist suggests that we provide means for retrieving descriptions and comparing trees with similar names.

We then talk about descriptions of climate zones. We decide to use the zones established in the *Sunset New Western Garden Book*, which is widely used in the western states. However, there is an important issue about the meaning of *habitat*. Do we mean the places where the tree could be grown or the places where it grew naturally? Do we mean the places where it survives or the places where it thrives? Naturalists sometimes define habitat as the regions where the species will propagate naturally. It becomes clear that we needed to be able to distinguish several differ-ent meanings of habitat, both for consistent reasoning by the system and for consistent encoding of the database. The naturalist offers to provide a candidate set of standard terms and relations for the knowledge base.

Climate zones delineate places on the map. We notice in the protocols that the naturalist makes substantial use of information about location. If SEQUOYAH knew where the user was located, it could automatically take that information into account in its analysis, ruling out or de-emphasizing plants that would not be expected to grow there naturally. This leads us to consider representations of map data, relating information about climate, latitude, longitude, and eleva-tion. We also decide to include information about parks, towns, lakes, and so on. We recruit a specialist to the team who can investigate the availability and possible formats of map informa-tion.

A question comes up about the choice of units of measurement. In talking about length or width, should we use inches and miles or metric units? That issue turns out not to matter much because the computer can convert the information between different units of measurement.

One of the important uses of the frames is to represent the possible solutions to the classifi-cation task. Ideally, a solution corresponds to a single species. In going over the cases we had obtained from the "naturalist in a box" protocols, however, we find a few cases that challenge our representational capabilities. Some of the most interesting (and at first perplexing) cases are ones where several plants were growing so closely together that the observer did not realize that the "specimen" was actually two or more different plants. For example, vines can become so intertwined with their host plants that their leaves appear to belong to the host. To enable SEQUOYAH to reason about such cases, we decide to admit "composite solutions," generated by appropriately mixing together the attributes of plants that grow in this way. In cases such as this, decisions about what the system can represent determine the coverage of its problem-solv-ing abilities.

Finally, we notice that we need to model some data about the seasons. Plants appear differ-ently in different seasons. This is especially true for plants that show bursts of spring growth, plants that lose their leaves, and flowers with a limited blooming period.

Over the next few weeks, we build up a knowledge base about the domain. As the knowl-edge base becomes more complete, we compare its performance on test cases with that of our naturalist. Our goal is not so much to replicate the precise sequence of his steps as much as to approximate his skill and expertise over a range of cases.

Notes   At this point the group is beginning to develop formal symbolic representations to model the domain, as in the example of the redwood tree frame. To judge adequacy of representations, the group needs to keep the task in mind. The world is quite open-ended, and every project needs to determine the bounds on the knowledge that it will formalize. Different designs for representation have different capabilities for making distinctions. Different choices for symbol structures can also have a large impact on the practicality of making different kinds of inferences. For example, before picking representations for space (map data) and time (seasonal data), we need to know what kinds of inferences we expect the system to make and which ones must be made quickly.

One powerful advantage of computer systems over books as knowledge media is that they can be executed. That is, the models can be run and debugged on cases. This encourages the systematic development and testing of models in an experimental mode.

Connections   Chapter 1 introduces concepts about symbols and meaning with examples of objects and relations used in building models. Issues about representation and reasoning about space and time are considered in Chapters 4 and 5.

Testing the System with Users

Over the next few weeks we get ready to work with what we called our "beta-test" users. By "beta-test," we mean the first people outside of our working group to try out our system. Given our operational version of SEQUOYAH, we knew that people could give us quite specific feedback about what they thought about it. Our goal is to collect information that will enable us to improve our product, bringing it closer to our customers' needs.

We use a variety of approaches to gather information. One is to work with hiking clubs to observe their use of the system. We collect detailed records of their interactions with the system, including video records, trying to identify those places where SEQUOYAH confused them. We also interview them about the system and collect questionaires and suggestions. This process reveals bugs, proposed changes, and proposed new features, which we then consider in the meetings of our development staff.

One thing we discover is that our customers often have very good ideas. We decide that we need a way to encourage customers to send us new ideas and bug reports on a regular basis. This leads to a "message" feature that we add to our system. At any time during a session, a user can push a message key and type in a short message with a suggestion or bug report. This creates a file on the computer with the user's name, the version of the system, the context in the session, and so on. At some later time, the user can plug his or her computer into a modular telephone and it would dial an 800-number that passed the information to us. The information gathered automatically in this way enables us to reproduce the situation where the problem arose. To encourage contributions, we offer rewards for suggestions that we later incorporate into our products.

Notes   Testing the early version of a system in realistic settings is a crucial part of every knowledge-system project. Custom systems that are tailored for a single group of users can be developed with those users from the beginning. Companies that try to market to a large set of users need to have effective ways to probe those markets and to assess the products. These studies can involve a joint effort between marketing and development staff.

Connections   Marketing and testing are not major themes in this text. We mention them here to fill in some of the larger commercial context of knowledge systems. However, Chapter 3 contains some suggestions for approaches for developing systems jointly with user groups.

Add-on Systems

We now skip forward in the story. SEQUOYAH is in its second release in the market. Several organizations have approached us about "opening" our knowledge base so it can be extended.

One idea that provokes a lot of interest is extending SEQUOYAH to act as a "digital trail guide" to the hiking trails in the state and national parks. Several well-known hikers express an interest in collaborating on add-on systems, which would provide an interactive interface for hikers in choosing and selecting hiking trails. Different tour promoters specialize in different kinds of hikes. Some focus on challenges. Some focus on nature walks. Some would like to exchange "hiking instructions" that connect with each other and into the extensive map and plant database that we have already built. For example, software for guiding a nature walk could draw the hiker's attention to a particularly interesting redwood on a trail and could provide backup for questions drawing on our general database about wildlife. We see that by providing facilities for extending and exchanging databases, we can extend our market. One of the hiking magazines proposes to work with us to develop digital trail guides that they would distribute with their quarterly magazine. They would like to have a partnership arrangement with us for developing the software and also to give special agreements to their members for purchasing our systems. The simpler proposals for a digital trail guide would build on our map database by overlaying trail information, showing the distance between points, the altitudes, the slope of trails. Other more elaborate proposals include systems that would design day hikes for campers on demand, given constraints about distance, what they want to see, and so on.

In addition, a group of California nurseries approaches us about extending SEQUOYAH to advise on landscaping with native plants. With the difficulties created by drought in California, they have seen much greater interest in the horticultural use of water-efficient native plants. One nursery wants to extend our database of native plants and to develop a design assistant for landscapes. The database would be extended to include information about layout, planting, fertilizing, pruning, ecology, and forest management. They want to extend the plant selections to include plants overlooked by hikers, such as native grasses used for controlling erosion. They observe that many horticulturists are trying to catch up in their understanding about native plants. In an arrangement similar to one of the hiking clubs, one professional nursery proposes to create quarterly "digital feature reports" that recommend newly available plants and to extend the database and ideas into new areas.

We convene some company meetings to assess the commercial prospects and managment and technical issues for these proposals. One of the issues that we see is that there will suddenly be many different versions of our system. What will the maintenance issues be when someone is using last year's version of our plant database with a new digital trail guide from the hiker's club? We want the software to work together as well as possible, accessing the latest versions.

We also discover that the landscaping advisor system would need representation and reasoning capabilities beyond those that we had used in SEQUOYAH. One member of the development sketches out a mockup of the user interface in conjunction with one of the landscape specialists, a horticulturalist. The mockup, which is shown in Figure I.7, shows the system reasoning about plants and maps. The map representations are more detailed than the ones that we used for SEQUOYAH, but about the same as would be needed for the trail guide applications. They would, however, need to represent additional elements, such as water systems and lighting. Furthermore, the preliminary examination of the search processes for landscape design suggested that the methods used by SEQUOYAH, heuristic classification, would not be adequate. The landscaping system has a much more complex space of possible solutions. For example, a solution might include compatible plant selections; layout; land contouring; and the construction of sheds, patios, water sytems, and so on. There are quite a range of functions that the system could perform, including creating perspective drawings of the landscape, projecting plant growth over time using parameterized fractal drawings of plants, and comparsion views that show the effects of different choices. In general, it appears that the landscape advisor would be much more complex than SEQUOYAH to build. We need to identify software from other vendors that we could incorporate in the product. We recognize that a preliminary study is needed to determine what features would be desirable and what is affordable.

As we explore the technical and policy issues for our product, we recognize that there is not just the one business of selling "boxes" to hikers, but rather that there are many different businesses for providing data and services in our "knowledge medium." Some of the businesses could build on each other, and some of them require expertise beyond the means of our company. We need to understand which businesses make sense strategically and what the conditions are for making them commercially viable. If we turn our knowledge system into an "open system," we need to consider what protections would be required for our software.

As we consider the changes we are seeing in technologies and concepts for publication and communication, we realize that our products are examples of a new kind of writing for people who enjoy the wilderness. The products are enabling such people to make their ideas and expertise active in a way that is more adaptable than books. Reflecting back on the Cherokee Sequoyah's work to introduce an alphabet as a symbol system for American Indians, we feel that the selection of a name for our system is even more appropriate.

Notes   As knowledge systems become larger, the issues for managing, updating, and sharing information become more crucial. In the current state of the art, people have not yet confronted the issues of making knowledge bases that can be used for multiple tasks. Although this point is not emphasized in the story, there are many open issues about copyright and distribution of electronic publications and electronic services. The first generation of electronic networks discouraged commercial participation and sidestepped the opportunity (and effort) to shape or inform enduring public policies. Many policy-makers now believe that even the research networks seem likely to benefit from the use of market mechanisms to foster the creation and administration of new services.

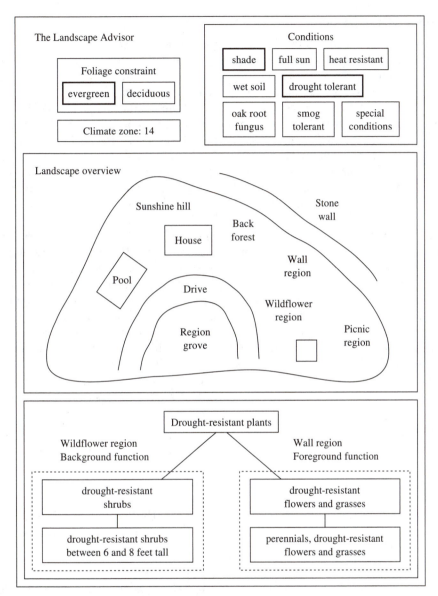

FIGURE I.7. Mockup of a user interface for a landscape advisor. This system needs to accept as input a description of a landscape, including details about land contours, existing vegetation and trees, and uses for different areas. It needs a vocabulary to identify different uses of plants in yards, such as for erosion control, screening, shade, and so on. It needs to represent a variety of constraints about kinds of foliage desired, soil condition, and user needs. A "solution" is an expression of any of the plantings, changes to land contours, or physical structures that make up the elements of a landscape.

The Story and This Book

The preceding story is a tour through topics relevant to building knowledge systems. It emphasizes the social and product issues over the technical issues of building them, which are the primary topics of this book.

The SEQUOYAH story is intended to "make the strange more familiar." We seek an integrated perspective on diverse topics: protocol analysis from information-processing psychology, project organization concepts from software engineering, search methods from artificial intelligence and operations research, and representation and reasoning concepts from computer science and graph theory. To understand about knowledge systems — from what knowledge is to how it is represented, or from how systems are built to how they are used — requires that we wear several different hats. For everyone, some of these hats fit better than others. This introductory story provides an orientation for why there are so many hats. We refer back to it occasionally in the text.

As you read this book, these increasingly familiar topics will reinforce each other. Protocol analysis may seem familiar as the art of conversation or the art of interview, but when applied in knowledge engineering it rests on models of problem solving as search and psychological assumptions. Choosing a data structure may seem like the art of programming, but in the context of knowledge engineering, the engineering choices depend on requirements for the reasoning and search. Building a model of a classification task or a configuration task may seem like formalizing common sense, but in the context of knowledge engineering it rests on foundations about search methods and solution spaces. In this book, I hope to sharpen our perceptions of the "unexamined familiar." People who participate in knowledge engineering in their own areas of expertise report a deeper sense about what they know and how they use it. They also gain new perspectives on the nature of knowledge, and the processes for creating it, using it, debugging it, and communicating it.

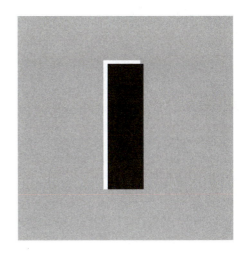

FOUNDATIONS

This chapter introduces symbol structures, representation, meaning, modeling, inference, and computation. It presumesonly a modest familiarity with programming and logic.

Symbol Systems

In their 1975 Turing Award paper, Allen Newell and Herbert Simon presented what they called the physical symbol system hypothesis:

> **The Physical Symbol System Hypothesis**. A physical symbol system has the necessary and sufficient means for general intelligent action.

By *necessary*, Newell and Simon meant that an analysis of any system exhibiting general intelligence would show that the system is a physical symbol system. By *sufficient*, they meant that any physical symbol system of sufficient complexity could be organized to exhibit general intelligence. By *general intelligent action*, they meant the same order of intelligent and purposeful activity that we see in people, including activities such as planning, speaking, reading books, or composing music. This hypothesis puts symbols at the core of intelligent action. Roughly, it says that intelligent systems are subject to natural laws and that the natural laws of intelligence are about symbol processing.

Symbols are central and familiar elements of natural language, mathematics, logical formalisms, and programming languages. As suggested by the physical symbol system hypothesis, they have also been traditionally associated with dominant theories of mind and intelligence. In recent years, symbolic and representational theories of mind have been challenged by other accounts based on nonsymbolic and subsymbolic structures. To pursue these topics here would defer us from our primary interest in knowledge systems and is deferred to the quandaries section of this chapter.

Whatever the case for natural systems and general intelligence, symbols are central to knowledge systems. We can build and study knowledge systems without resolving the issue of whether they are intelligent. However, we cannot build them or understand them without using symbols or without understanding the nature of symbols. This chapter is about symbols, what they are, how they acquire meaning, and how they are used in creating computational models.

1.1 *Symbols and Symbol Structures*

Symbols are the elements of our spoken and written languages. Here are some examples of symbols:

> Paige
> infers
> 3.141592654
> computer
> a-very-long-hyphenated-word

Symbols can be arranged into larger structures that we call **symbol structures** or simply **expressions**. Figure 1.1 shows several examples of symbol structures.

When we refer to symbols in the context of knowledge systems, we usually mean words, numbers, and graphics. These symbols appear on computer displays, are represented in computer memories, and are manipulated by our programs. Symbols and symbol structures are so familiar that we seldom pause to examine their nature. In the following, however, we define symbols and introduce terminology that will enable us to be precise about the properties that we attribute to them.

1.1.1 *What Is a Symbol?*

The dictionary defines a **symbol** as a written or printed mark that stands for or represents something. A symbol may represent an object, a quality, a process, or a quantity as in music, mathematics, or chemistry.

For us the dictionary definition of symbol is preliminary. It conveys basic intuitions about the term. Symbols are marks in a medium. They are used to represent things. Although this definition seems simple enough, it raises some questions: Is any marking a symbol? Does the notion of "write" include electronic or biological encodings? Can we determine from a symbol itself what it represents? Can two people disagree about what a symbol represents? Can a symbol represent itself?

Although these questions may seem obscure, simple confusions about symbols and representation repeatedly lead to difficulties in creating and using knowledge systems. Symbols are fundamental to creating and using computational models. Through a series of examples, this section develops terminology and a framework for understanding and answering these questions.

The dictionary definition suggests that two basic themes concern the nature of symbols: (1) What is a marking, and (2) What is representation or reference? Markings and reference are the topics of this section.

We begin with **registration**, which is about recognizing and identifying markings. Consider Figure 1.2. What symbols are in the figure? One person might say that there are two overlapping squares arranged so that part of one square is occluded by the other. Another person might say simply that there is a set of eight horizontal and vertical lines. There is nothing about

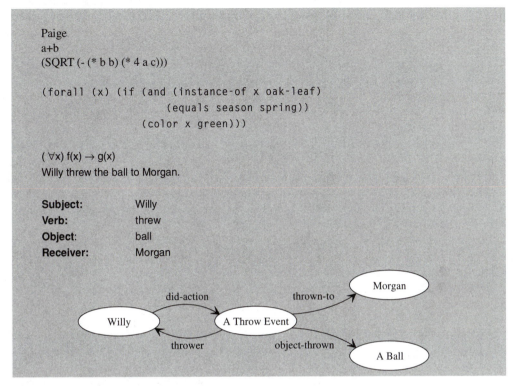

Paige
a+b
(SQRT (- (* b b) (* 4 a c)))

```
(forall (x) (if (and (instance-of x oak-leaf)
                     (equals season spring))
                (color x green)))
```

$(\forall x)\ f(x) \rightarrow g(x)$
Willy threw the ball to Morgan.

Subject: Willy
Verb: threw
Object: ball
Receiver: Morgan

FIGURE 1.1.   Examples of symbol structures. A symbol is a pattern in a physical medium recognizable by some interpreter. A symbol structure is a physical arrangement of symbols.

the figure itself that makes one person right and the other wrong. These different accounts of what symbols are in the figure are called different **registrations** of the figure. When different people look at markings they may disagree about what symbols are present. They may use different conventions about notation to identify symbols in particular kinds of documents, such as musical scores, books of poetry, or architectural drawings.

The issue of what markings constitute a symbol is intimately bound up in however a person or machine *recognizes* it. When we say that something is a symbol, we imply the choice of a recognizer. Typically, a recognizer has an associated alphabet or set of symbols that it can recog-

FIGURE 1.2.   The registration of symbols: This example shows marks on a page. There they might be recognized as a single symbol, or as two overlapping squares, or as a set of horizontal and vertical lines. Each different registration corresponds to a recognition process for a different interpreter.

nize. It can tell whether some set of markings constitutes a symbol in the set, and also, identify the symbol. We use the terms **token** and **type** to distinguish individual physical symbols (tokens) from classes of symbols that are recognized by the recognizer as equivalent (types). For example, if a recognizer was designed to recognize the alphabet letters used in English as printed in a particular font, then not counting numerals and punctuation there would be 52 types — one for each upper and lowercase character. On a printed page in this font, each occurrence of the letter "a" corresponds to a token. Two tokens are equivalent for the purposes of recognition if they are of the same type.

We now give a definition of symbol that takes recognizers into account. A **symbol** is a physical marking or pattern, which can be read, recognized, and written by a recognizer. A **symbol structure** is an arrangement of one or more symbols in a physical medium. We also use the simpler term expression to refer to a symbol structure. So far, our definition of symbol mentions markings but not representation. We postpone discussing representation, that is, the assignment of meaning to symbols.

Not every piece of matter or energy is a symbol. The wind blows leaves across the ground and leaves markings, but these are not symbols. When we identify certain patterns as symbols, there must always be a recognizer that identifies the symbols. The recognizer can determine where each symbol starts and stops, can tell them apart, and can determine the salient features of the arrangement of symbols. Sometimes the recognizer is part of a larger system that can retrieve and sense symbols, compare them, write new symbols, and do various kinds of reasoning. Sometimes we use the somewhat vague term **interpreter** to refer to various kinds of larger systems that include a recognizer.

The registration issue even arises in mundane contexts such as interpreting text symbols written on a page. Consider the symbols in the following sentences on this page.

Willy lives across the street. He threw a ball to Morgan. (1)

In the typical account, the symbols in (1) are the images of the eleven printed words, and the symbol structures are the sentences, which are composed of adjacent words. Other registrations are possible. For a theory of English spelling and grammar, the symbols are the printed characters, that is, images of letters of the alphabet and the symbol structures are words composed of letters; the sentences in turn are composed of words. For a theory of typography and font design, the symbols could be printed strokes or dots and the symbol structures the letters that they form. Different registrations correspond to different recognizers.

The modifier *physical* is intended to emphasize the concrete physical realizability of symbols, and to preclude any confusion with "ideal" symbols that have no tangible existence, such as perfect letters of an alphabet. The patterns can be almost anything. They can be arrangements of electrical charge in a computer memory, arrangements of organic compounds in brain cells connected by nerves, patterns of electromagnetic waves with intensities arranged in time, patterns of brightness on a display screen, patterns of nucleotides in a gene, dark marks on white paper, or scratches and paintings on ancient Indian pottery. When we say that genes are symbols, we could have in mind recognizers that are either automatic machines that read genes from DNA, or naturally occurring biological mechanisms that read genes to build proteins. The symbols in a symbol structure can be adjacent in a medium or linked together in some other way.

A **physical symbol system** is a machine such as a computer that operates on symbol structures. It can read, recognize, and write symbols. A symbol system creates new expressions, modifies old expressions, makes new copies of expressions, and destroys expressions. Symbols may be communicated from one part of a symbol system to another in order to specify and control activity. Over time, a physical symbol system produces a changing collection of symbol structures.

Our definition of symbol admits a very wide variety of techniques for realizing symbols. They need to persist long enough to be useful for a symbol system.

1.1.2 *Designation*

In some branches of theoretical computer science and mathematics, symbols are taken as primitive and undefined terms. In these theoretical studies of computation, ideal machines with various kinds of finite and infinite memories read and write symbols. Turing machines with finite control stores and infinite tapes are examples of ideal machines of this sort. Like other such abstract machines, they are used for discussing formal theories about computability.

These theories are concerned with fundamentals of formal languages and mathematical objects. Not only are they removed from finite and physical implementations, but they are also removed from practical uses and familiar settings.For example, these theories are not concerned with issues involved in creating physical patterns and arranging for their flexible and reliable manipulation. They treat computers as isolated systems. Symbols go in. An idealized computer munches on them and then other symbols come out.

However, knowledge systems are built from real computers and compute things relevant to a real, physical world. They are part of larger systems and we need to be able to discuss how they are connected and embedded in a physical setting. To interact appropriately with an external world, computers must be able to reason about it and also be able to represent aspects of it with symbols. It is for worldly settings that Newell and Simon's physical symbol system hypothesis was developed and in such settings the concepts of knowledge, reference and representation are of interest.

An **embedded computer system** is one that is integrally part of a larger system. Examples of such larger systems include electronic ignition systems devices, electronic banking systems, inventory and manufacturing systems, aircraft carrier information management systems, electromechanical systems in a troubleshooting context, medical systems for patient monitoring, sales and inventory systems at point of sale terminals, and communications networks. The boundary of what constitutes the larger system depends on the purposes of our analysis. It could include machines or even people in a social organization. All computer systems can be seen as embedded systems.

Our dictionary definition of symbol says that symbols represent things. We now turn our attention to what it means to represent something.

When we talk about representation, we need to identify three things: the symbols, the situation, and an observer. As suggested in Figure 1.3, the observer is an agent, that is, someone or something that perceives both the symbols and the situation. The observer uses the symbols as a model of the situation. When the observer perceives the situation, he organizes his understanding of it in his mind in terms of different elements, often referred to as objects. These objects have

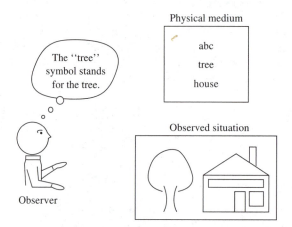

FIGURE 1.3.   Designation is in the mind of an observer. It is a mapping between elements he perceives in the situation and symbols in the physical medium.

different relations to one another. For example, the observer might view a *car* in a situation as being *on the driveway*, or a *car door* as being *part of* a *car*. The observer uses symbols to stand for objects in the situation. When an observer picks some set of perceived objects in the situation and makes symbols for them, we say that he **reifies** them. When he associates symbols with objects in the situations, we say that the symbols **designate** the objects. The relation indicating what symbols stand for is called **designation**, or equivalently, **denotation**.

This brings us to an important point about symbolhood and defining designation: the need for an **observer**. The problem is that giving an account of what symbols represent requires a vantage point, usually outside of the symbol system. In most cases, the things that symbols stand for have been perceived by somebody. What a symbol stands for is not determined by a symbol's encoding or by its location. Restated, designation is not a physical property of the markings. Designation is assigned by and relative to an observer.

We introduce a distinction between a symbol system and its **environment** as shown in Figure 1.4. The boundaries that define the symbol system and environment depend on a point of view. The boundary around a symbol system delimits where the symbols are for particular purposes of analysis. A symbol system is contained in its environment and often its symbols refer to parts of that environment. We use the term *domain* or **symbol domain** to refer to a elements of interest in the environment.

In Figure 1.4, the observer of the computerized heating and cooling system says that "the 'reading' symbol stands for the room's temperature." From a cognitive science perspective, we may imagine that the observer's mind may itself have separate symbol structures: one standing for the reading symbol in the computer, one standing for the room's temperature, and another standing for the designation relation between the first two.

Exactly what do we mean when we say that the "temperature reading of 20" designates the room's temperature? There may be many symbols equal to 20 at various places in the computer's memory. For example, another 20 may be used by the computer to keep track of the number of heat vents in the building. We do not mean that every 20 pattern in the computer's

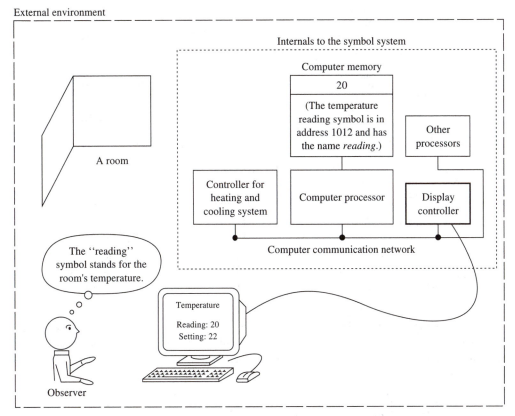

FIGURE 1.4. Designation is in the mind of an observer, who can give an account of both the symbol system and the manner in which its symbols designate aspects of an environment.

memory "stands for" the room's temperature. We probably associate a particular register in the machine as the "temperature variable." There must be some way for an observer to access a symbol. Two observers discussing the meanings of symbols must assure each other that they are referring to the same elements of the physical symbol system, such as by agreeing on the use of a particular addressing scheme. They might say that the symbol that is stored at memory location 1012 designates the temperature of the room.

Names are not the only means for identifying particular symbols. When a computer user looks at a display as shown in Figure 1.5, the display renders symbols and presents them for perception, identification, pointing and manipulation. A user interacts with a computer using the display and various keyboards or pointing devices. The picture elements or pixels in the display surface provide a view of information stored elsewhere in the computer, updated and maintained by a display controller. Thus, a user can identify a symbol by pointing at it, not just by naming it.

Figure 1.5 decomposes the process of designation for a variable into three steps. First an addressing scheme (memory address 1012 or "reading") is used to locate the variable or storage element. Then its value is determined (20). Then that value is assigned a referent in the environ-

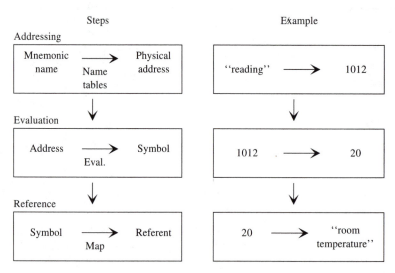

FIGURE 1.5. Designation for a variable involves addressing, evaluation, and mapping to some referent in the environment.

ment ("room temperature"). The addressing scheme provides each symbol with a unique address and supplies a reliable means for accessing the symbol through that address. In effect, the address is a name for the symbol. Computer languages often provide various external names that are mnemonics for referring to addresses.

1.1.3 *Causal Coupling*

All of the action of designation is in the mind of the observer. If an observer changes his mind about what a symbol refers to, that need not have any observable effect on the symbol or the environment. We now consider a more active relation where changes to the symbols or the environment can have effects.

Consider the heat-regulation system in Figure 1.6, which includes a thermocouple, a computer, and heating and cooling units controlled by the computer. In this system the electronics have been arranged such that the computer can access a symbol in its memory that it interprets as a reading of the temperature of a room on a numeric scale. The value of the temperature symbol is determined by a physical process starting with an interaction between the air in the room and a sensor. Electrical voltages corresponding to temperature are converted to digital signals by an analog-to-digital converter. The particular operating principles of the sensor and communication devices do not matter for the purposes of this example. The components are arranged so that when the temperature changes, a series of physical events follows, causing the temperature symbol — the contents of computer memory at address 1012 — to change. This kind of connection beween phenomena at one place and a distant symbol is called **causal coupling**. The term *causal coupling* can be expanded to include cases where all of the changes take place inside a single system, rather than just interactions between symbols in the system and entities in the environment.

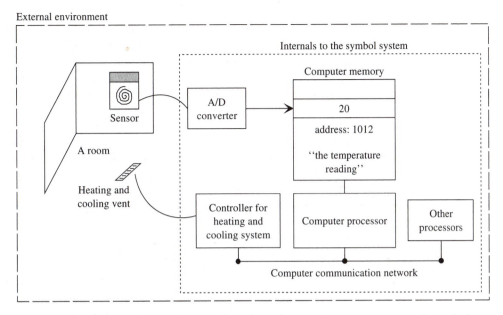

FIGURE 1.6. Causal coupling: In this example, a change in room temperature causes a change in the "temperature symbol" in a computer memory. Causal coupling can go from outside to inside as when a change in the sensor causes a change to a register in the computer's memory. It can also go from inside to outside, as when changing a register in the computer causes a setting to change in a heating vent. The key notion is that a phenomenon or a change in something causes a change in a symbol elsewhere.

There are always propagation delays between the time of the cause and the time of the corresponding change to a symbol. In large distributed systems, these propagation delays can be crucial in determining the dynamic behaviors of the systems. However, in the following examples, we will assume that the delays are negligible for the purposes of our analysis.

Causal coupling can go from outside a symbol system to inside such as from a sensor to a register in the example in Figure 1.6. It can also go from inside to outside, as when a change in a symbol in a controller in Figure 1.6 causes a change in the setting of a heating and cooling vent that controls the distribution of air. These two directions correspond respectively to sensing and motor control. Causal coupling can go between two symbols inside the computer such as when the system transmits a reading between different parts in order to decide whether to vent cool air into a room. Copies of the reading may be transmitted periodically along a computer communication network to various environmental control units in the building.

Causal coupling from an environment to symbols inside a computer is a very simple case of **machine perception**. In more sophisticated examples of machine perception, the effect on symbols is mediated by a potentially complex interpretation process. For example, consider a machine vision system that interprets digitized images from video cameras. The required computational process involves many levels of automatic analysis, and has many ambiguities and uncertainties associated with the sensor readings and the interpretation process. For example, the recognition of a person in a scene can involve processing of thousands of individual picture elements, recognition of edges and regions in the image, clustering of regions into larger images, comparing images from the sensor to stored images of objects expected in the scene, and so on until finally the image on the camera is associated with an identification symbol.

Causal coupling and designations are independent relations. A symbol may be causally connected to an object in an environment but not designate that object for some observer; similarly, a symbol may designate some object in the environment for an observer but not be causally connected with it. For example, suppose that the wire in Figure 1.6 becomes broken. In this event, the reading inside the computer probably will be incorrect and the tokens communicated to other systems will not be tied causally to the temperature of the room. The internal reading now contains misinformation. The neighboring systems may respond correctly, but based on misinformation. Indeed, reasoning about such disconnections illustrates an example where we need to reason separately about the two relations. Even though the wire is broken, we still want to say that the symbol "stands for" the temperature. Because the wire is broken, the mechanism is not operating correctly and the symbol may be wrong.

1.1.4   *Cognitive and Document Perspectives of Symbols*

Symbols in computational systems play two distinct and important roles: the document role and the cognitive role. When we are interested in the use of symbols to communicate with another person, we are taking a **document perspective**. In this role we are interested in symbols as **presentations**, that is, in the way that they can be used to explain things. Knowledge systems share properties with paper and electronic documents. They use symbols, they mediate communication, they are often constructed by groups of people, and people come to agreement about what the symbols mean.

When we are interested in the use of symbols for automated reasoning in the computer, we are taking a **cognitive** or **"mentalist" perspective**. In this role, we are interested in symbols as **representations**, that is, in the way that they model a situation, the properties of the symbols as the computer manipulates them in various ways to carry out reasoning, and in how we can use resulting symbols to infer things about the situation.

Figure 1.7 shows two users interacting with a graphical representation of scheduled temperature changes over time. In this case, the graph and various interactive menus for changing it constitute a user interface. They are external symbols that the users can see and talk about.

The situation in Figure 1.7 is representative of the context in which knowledge systems are created and used. Multiple people interact around a display. They create, discuss, share, and modify symbols that appear on the display. The symbols on the display are causally connected to symbols internal to the machine and perhaps to symbols on other machines. Part of the discussion is used to agree about meanings of the symbols. This is necessary in case multiple people are making changes to the system.

Sometimes we distinguish **model symbols** or domain symbols, such as the temperature reading symbol, from **view symbols** that represent and are causally coupled with presentations on the display. There are often many different kinds of view symbols, engaged in different parts of the process of rendering an appropriate image and supporting interactions with it.

Suppose two users are talking about the temperature control system, and one of them points to a display and says, "This is the room's temperature." He is interested mainly in the symbol structure on the display and probably means that it designates the room's temperature,

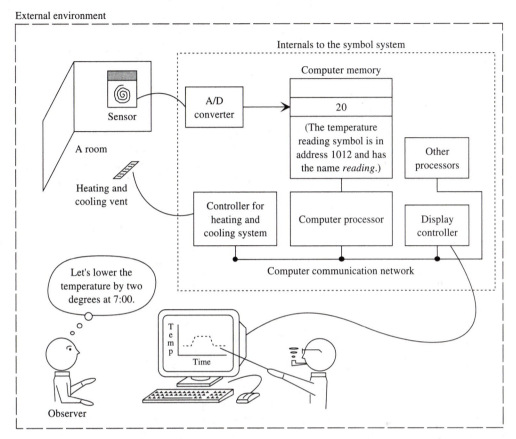

FIGURE 1.7. Two people having a discussion about the planned control of room temperature over time. The mechanisms of the system including the sensing of room air temperature, the formatting of the display, the interactions with the user interface, and the control of the heating and air conditioning through the controller can be explained in terms of causal coupling. The assignment of meaning to symbols is described by the concept of designation.

that he expects the other party to be able to read and understand it, and that the indication it provides is up to date because of causal coupling. If the second person is a designer of the system, he might be concerned with many internal symbols. He or she would be familiar with all of its internal connections and mechanisms, could refer variously to a symbol on the display, a symbol used to construct the image rendering of the display, the reading symbol in computer memory, the "symbol" that is the digital electrical pattern at the output of the analog-to-digital converter, the symbol that is the analog voltage on the output line from the sensor, or even the symbol that is the configuration of bent metal inside the temperature sensor? To the designer all of these symbols play a role in the overall mechanism. When there is a chain of causal connections between symbols in a symbol system, it is sometimes convenient to ignore the differences between them in informal conversation.

1.1.5 *Summary and Review*

We began with a dictionary definition of symbols that says symbols are markings that represent things. This definition leaves open issues about the nature of markings and the nature of representation, leading us ultimately to introduce both a recognizer and an observer into our account of symbols.

We define markings relative to a recognition process. Symbols are physical patterns that can be read, recognized, and written by a recognizer. The identification of a set of markings as constituting a symbol is called registration. Symbol structures (or expressions) are arrangements of symbols in a physical medium. There can be multiple copies of a pattern or symbol in a symbol system. This gives rise to the terminological distinction between types and tokens. Types are classes of equivalent symbols in the alphabet of the recognizer; tokens are individual symbols in a medium.

We make few computational requirements on the physical patterns used for making symbols. The patterns must persist long enough for the workings of the symbol system and there must be a means for reading and writing the symbol structures.

We define representation relative to an observer. An observer is able to look both at the symbol system and a situation, and determines which elements of the situation are referred to by the symbols. This kind of meaning is a semantics of reference, and is called designation or denotation. The term "symbol" is sometimes used casually by computer professionals to mean roughly the same thing as "term" in propositional logic, or roughly, what we called a "marking." However, when more precision is warranted, symbolhood requires specifying both a recognizer to identify the markings and an observer to assign meanings to them.

An environment is a setting that contains a symbol system. Computer systems are embedded in larger systems. Causal connections link symbols to their environments in such a way that a change in the environment causes a change in the symbol or a change in a symbol causes a change in the environment. Our heat control system provides an example of this kind of connection, where changes in room temperature lead to changes in a reading.

We distinguish two perspectives on symbols in symbol systems. The document perspective emphasizes the observer's use of symbols for communication in presentations. The cognitive perspective emphasizes the computational use of symbols as representations.

Exercises for Section 1.1

■   **Ex. 1**   [CD-05] *Warmups.* The following questions about symbols were raised early in this section. Indicate the answers with yes or no. If the question is ambiguous, explain briefly.
     (a) *Yes or No.* Is any marking a symbol?
     (b) *Yes or No.* Can the marking for a symbol be an electronic or biological encoding?
     (c) *Yes or No.* Can we determine from a symbol itself what it represents?
     (d) *Yes or No.* Can two people disagree about what a symbol represents?
     (e) *Yes or No.* Can a symbol represent itself?

   Ex. 2   [CD-05] *Recognizers and Observers.*
     (a) Briefly, why are symbols (themselves) defined relative to a recognizer?
     (b) Briefly, why is designation defined relative to an observer?
     (c) Briefly, what is the difference in concerns between part (*a*) and part (*b*)?

Ex. 3   *[05] Designation for Symbols on a Computer Display.* Consider the following story.
Two accountants are using a spreadsheet program to make financial projections about rental property. As is typical for spreadsheet models, they have defined variables that stand for things like rental income, utilities costs, mortgage payments, depreciation and so on. One of the two accountants points to a place on the screen and says, "The utility cost estimate for this month is too low because the tenants will probably run the air conditioner during the summer." Later they discuss whether monthly cashflow variables should include projected tax payments or depreciation.

In this chapter, we described a process of designation of program variables in terms of three steps: addressing, evaluation, and designation. Do these steps show up in the activities of the two accountants? Explain briefly.

Ex. 4   *[CD-05] Terminology.* For each of the following statements indicate whether it is true or false. If the statement is ambiguous, explain briefly.
(a) *True or False.* An embedded computer system is a computer that is hidden inside a larger system.
(b) *True or False.* In machine sensing, causal coupling means a change in the environment causes a change of a symbol or symbol structure.
(c) *True or False.* In machine control, causal coupling means a change of a symbol or symbol structure causes something to change in the environment.
(d) *True or False.* We define both types and tokens with respect to a recognition process.
(e) *True or False.* The document perspective of symbols in a knowledge system requires that symbols (or displays of them) need to be readable by observers who can discuss their meanings.

■   **Ex. 5**   *[!-15] Storyboards and the Role of Assumptions in Understanding Narrative.* Several projects in AI have sought to create computer systems that understand stories, that is, that give summaries of stories and answer questions about them.

This open-ended exercise shows how the translation of natural-language sentences into formal representations requires knowledge about the situations that the sentences describe.

Consider the following two-sentence story about Paige and Morgan, a girl and her brother.

> Paige rolled the ball to Morgan.
> Morgan threw it back to Paige.

(a) A storyboard, such as is used in making movies and cartoons, is a sequence of scenes, each of which is a snapshot of the story world.

Imagine a sequence of scenes representing the sequence of events in the story. Fill in information for the intermediate scenes that would be represented in a storyboard for our sample story.

> *For all scenes.*
> Paige is a person.
> Morgan is a person.
> There is a ball.
> Paige and Morgan are in a play area.
> They are playing together.
> (Various implicit facts about orientation, mass, roundness of balls, gravity, air, that are not really mentioned in the story.)

Scene 1
Paige has the ball.
She starts to roll it to Morgan.
(Various implicit facts about Paige's feet being on the ground, how she moves, etc.)

Scene 2
The ball is in motion, rolling from Paige to Morgan.
Paige no longer has the ball.
Morgan is paying attention to the arrival of the ball.

Scene 3

. . .

Scene 6
Paige catches the ball.
Paige has the ball.

(b) In the sample two-sentence story, does the story say explicitly who has the ball at the end? What assumptions might you use to answer the question? How does understanding the second sentence rely on understanding the first one?

Ex. 6   [*!-10*] *Assumptions and Nonsense.* The sentences we use for efficient human communication can be remarkably brief. This is possible because we use many clues from the context to understand what is being said. In doing that, we also make many assumptions. Consider the following answer that one person gave another when asked if he could have a ride to the airport.

1.   I could give you a ride.
2.   Except that my car is being fixed at the garage.
3.   But it should be ready by now.
4.   Except I don't have any money to pay for the repairs.
5.   But I can borrow some from Dan.
6.   Except Dan isn't around right now.
7.   But he should be right back.

(a) Describe what a normal, competent and rational listener would believe about the availability of a timely ride to the airport after hearing each of these statements.
(b) What does this tell us about inferential processes for understanding stories.

Ex. 7   [*T*] *The Knowledge Representation Hypothesis.* Brian Smith (1982) proposed the knowledge representation hypothesis, which follows:

> Every intelligent physical symbol system includes symbol structures that we as external observers can take to be a propositional account of the system's knowledge. These symbol structures play an essential and causal role in determining the system's behavior. Furthermore, the system's behavior is independent of our account of its internal structures.

Smith does not require a trivial mapping of one symbol structure to one proposition, and the symbol structures can be graphs, arrays, or distributed symbols. The encoding process could be arbitrarily complex. For example, in a particularly perverse security robot the symbols could be recorded using an encryption algorithm, which presumably would make the "mentalese" elusive or computationally intractible to decipher. Thus, the knowledge representation hypothesis covers a wide range of representational approaches.

(a) Briefly, compare the knowledge representation hypothesis to the physical symbol system hypothesis. What does the knowledge representation add, if anything, to the physical symbol system hypothesis? How does Smith's notion of a propositional account differ from Newell and Simon's notion of designation?

(b) What does the knowledge representation hypothesis guarantee about an observer's ability to make sense of "mentalese"? What does it predict about the correspondence between symbols used by the observer and symbols in the observed system?

(c) Why is it useful to ascribe levels in representational theories of mind?

(d) Are these hypotheses the subject of extensive inquiry in artificial intelligence research? Of what use are they to the study of knowledge systems?

Ex. 8   [CD-05] *Defining Symbols*. The dictionary defines a symbol as a written or printed mark that stands for or represents something. In this section we have argued that there are several practical issues about this definition.

(a) Briefly, what issues does the registration problem raise about the dictionary definition of symbols?

(b) In defining designation, the text claimed that designation is not a property of the symbol itself. Why not? Briefly, what issue does this point about designation raise about the dictionary definition of symbols?

1.2   *Semantics: The Meanings of Symbols*

The term *semantics* is used to describe both natural language and computer languages. It is often contrasted with syntax and is popularly understood to refer to the meaning of symbols and expressions in languages. "Getting the semantics right" is a goal often lauded in computer science.

In this vein, Hayes (1974) and others have argued for principled and systematic design of semantics for representation languages used in computers. As he put it, representation languages ought to have a semantic theory. Later in this section we consider in more detail what Hayes meant by this. For now we note that proposals like this have taken on broader appeal as the knowledge bases being proposed have increased in size and as it has seemed worthwhile to be able to combine knowledge bases that were developed separately.

There are many pragmatic issues in developing semantic theories for knowledge systems. The problem is not just principled versus "sloppy" semantics. More fundamentally, there is confusion about what kinds of semantics are needed.

A **semantics** is an approach for assigning meanings to symbols and expressions. Different kinds of semantics differ in the kinds of symbols considered and the kinds of meanings they assign. In the following we will consider several kinds of semantics that are relevant for understanding knowledge systems.

We begin by reviewing the most studied approach to semantics, the declarative semantics used for the predicate calculus. We then broaden the discussion by considering some historical examples of how AI researchers assigned meaning to expressions in representation languages and graph structures. For this it is convenient to establish some terminology and notation for graphs and trees. The terminology introduced here will be sufficient to carry us through the first three chapters of this book. Finally, we consider how different kinds of semantics are needed for different purposes. We compare several kinds of semantics that are relevant to knowledge systems.

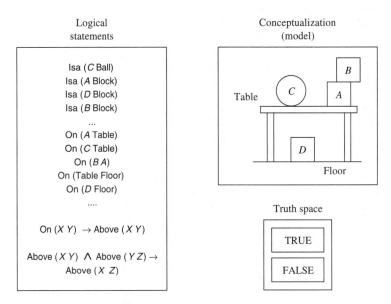

Logical statements / Conceptualization (model)

Truth space

FIGURE 1.8.   The elements of a declarative semantics for logic.

1.2.1 *Model Theory and Proof Theory*

We begin with the semantics developed for formal logic. We use this to establish a vocabulary and a basis for comparing other kinds of semantics. Our presentation is brief, since the goal is to summarize the concepts of semantics used with the predicate calculus.

Constants, Variables, Interpretations, and Models

Predicate calculus has two kinds of symbols: constants and variables. Constants are used to name elements in a special set known as the **universe of discourse**. In other words, this set includes terms for all of the things we are talking and reasoning about. Object constants name the objects in the set. Function constants are used to designate functions on members of the set. For example, arithmetic operations would be defined as functions. Relation constants name relations on the set.

Variables are used to describe properties of objects in the set without naming them. The predicate calculus includes relations for the logical operators $\wedge$ (AND), $\vee$ (disjunctive OR), and the usual others as well. A first-order predicate calculus includes universal and existential quantifiers on objects, but not on functions or relations.

Here is an example of an expression in predicate calculus in the example in Figure 1.8:

On (Ball Table)

In this example, On is a relation constant. Ball and Table are object constants. Another is

Above ($X\ Y$) $\wedge$ Above ($Y\,Z$) = >Above ($X\,Z$)

These statements are also called **axioms** in the model. Statements like these are what we write when we "axiomatise" a domain.

The first part of the semantics of predicate calculus is essentially the same as the semantics of reference from Section 1.1. We assume there is a memory or database of statements in the calculus. There is an observer and the observer has in mind a conceptualization, analogous to what we have called an environment. Designation in the mind of the observer associates the object, function, and relation constants with their counterparts in the conceptualization. In the terminology of logic, a mapping from the statements to the conceptualization is called an **interpretation**. Unfortunately, this is one of those words which has many different meanings in computer science.

For any term, we define its **extension** to be the elements in the conceptualization that it designates. Thus the extension of the term *C* would simply be the ball sitting on the table. A term like Block refers to a class of objects, whose members include the blocks *A*, *B*, and *D*. Similarly, an indefinite node might correspond to a variable whose referent has not yet been precisely determined, but that is perhaps limited to be some member of a class. So far we have not related the meaning of such terms to the inferences carried out on the model. To build a working system, claiming that terms refer to something does not signify much if the system does not reason with them. To formalize such reasoning, we need to add semantics of truth and semantics of proof.

The next part of the semantics involves the assignment of truth to logical statements. The basic idea is quite simple. First we consider ground statements or ground literals, which are ones that can be tested quite simply in an interpretation. For example, the statement that "*C* is a ball"—Isa(*C* Ball)—and the statement "*A* is on the table"—On(*A* Table)—can be readily checked. We say that they are satisfied in the obvious or intended interpretation of Figure 1.8. For a different interpretation they might not be satisfied. In Figure 1.8, the statement On(*B* Floor) is not satisfied. **Truth semantics** gives us a way of assigning a truth value to logical statements relative to an interpretation.

If an interpretation satisfies a sentence for all variable assignments, then it is said to be a **model** of the sentence. For example, the following sentence is satisfied by the intended interpretation of Figure 1.8 for all assignments to the variable *X*.

$(\forall X)$ Isa $(X$ Ball$) \lor$ Isa $(X$ Block$) \Rightarrow$ Above $(X$ Floor$)$

Variable assignment has no effect if there are no variables. Any interpretation that satisfies a ground sentence is a model of that sentence. A sentence is satisfiable if and only if there is some interpretation and variable assignment that satisfy it. An interpretation is a model for a set of sentences if it is a model for every sentence in the set.

The Meanings of Expressions

Much of the utility of predicate calculus arises from the systematic rules for assigning truth values to new expressions in the language. For example, if we are given that both of the following statements are true,

Isa(Block *A*)
Isa(Block *B*)

then we can conclude that the conjunctive statement is also true.

Isa(Block *A*) ∧ Isa(Block *B*)

The rules for this, which are learned by every beginning student of logic, are what people refer to as the well-founded semantics of logic. For another example, suppose we are asked whether the following formula is true.

(Isa (Block *A*) ∧ Isa (Block *B*))∨ Isa (Block *C*)

We can assign

X = Isa (Block *A*)
Y = Isa (Block *B*)
Z = Isa (Block *C*)

In our standard interpretation, we have

X = True
Y = True
Z = False

The next step is to determine the truth value of the expression.

(*X* ∧ *Y*) ∨ *Z*

One way to do this is with a truth table as in Table 1.1. In this table, we build up the values for the total expression from the truth values of the subexpressions. This is exactly the sort of property that Hayes requested of a semantic theory, that is, an account of how the meaning of a whole symbol structure is built up from the meanings of the parts. Of course, in complicated expressions there are often shortcuts and it is not usually necessary to write out a complete truth table. Nonetheless, at least in the propositional calculus, this is an approach than can be followed in case of doubt.

TABLE 1.1.   A truth table.

X	*Y*	*Z*	(*X* ∧ *Y*)	(*X* ∧ *Y*) ∨ *Z*
T	T	T	T	T
T	T	F	T	T
T	F	T	F	T
T	F	F	F	F
F	T	T	F	T
F	T	F	F	F
F	F	T	F	T
F	F	F	F	F

Formulas that are always true, regardless of the truth or falsity of their terms, are said to be **valid**. Such formulas are called **tautologies**. In propositional logic, truth semantics gives us a very simple and automatic way to determine whether a formula is valid. We simply compute its truth table and check whether every combination of truth assignments yields true for the formula.

Continuing with our example, if we have the statements

On (*A* Table)
On (*B A*)

then we can establish that the following statements are true without any further consultation with the model.

Above (*A* Table)
Above (*B* Table)

We can also ask questions about the truth of a statement without associating it with a particular interpretation. Some sentences are true for every possible interpretation. For example, the left statement below implies the right statement for all possible interpretations. In such cases, we say that the sentence on the left "logically implies" the sentence on the right.

$(\sim A \wedge B) \Rightarrow A \vee B$

The semantics of logic also deal with what is called provability. Predicate calculus provides prescriptions for establishing the truth or falsity of expressions, either from axioms or from expressions already established. Sanctioned inferences are described by **rules of inference,** which can be used to deduce new facts from old ones. The best known rule of inference is **modus ponens,** which says that if we have a fact p, and that p implies q, then we can deduce q. In the concise notation of logic, we would say

modus ponens: $A \wedge (A \Rightarrow B) \vdash B$

where the turnstyle figure means "proves." Figure 1.9 gives an example of the use of modus ponens to deduce that Felix is a member of the artificial intelligentsia. Roughly speaking, a **proof** is a sequence of statements where each successive statement follows from the preceding ones by some rule of inference, and the last statement is the "proved" conclusion.

A second important rule of inference is **universal instantiation**. It says that if something is true of everything, it is true of any particular thing. In logical notation, we would say

universal instantiation: $(\forall x) A(x) \Rightarrow B(x), A(a) \vdash B(a)$

Figure 1.10 shows how universal instantiation can be used to deduce that Ken is brilliant.

Truths, Proofs, and Decidability

The related ideas from truth theory and proof theory can be written using special symbols as follows. The following is a predicate calculus statement read as "*A* implies *B*."

$A \Rightarrow B$

Given the rule	
Can-pronounce (Student "heuristic")	;**IF** a student can pronounce *heuristic*
=> Member (Student	;**THEN** he is a member of the
Artificial-intelligentsia)	;artificial intelligentsia
And the fact	
Can-pronounce (Felix "heuristic"	;Felix can pronounce *heuristic*
Use modus ponens to deduce	
Member (Felix Artificial-intelligentsia)	;Thus, Felix is a member of the
	;artificial intelligentsia

FIGURE 1.9.   A logical deduction using modus ponens.

By itself this expression is neither true nor false. It is satisfied relative to an interpretation and variable assignment if and only if A is not satisfied (true) or B is satisfied in the interpretation. This rule is from truth theory. If such an implication is true for *every* interpretation and variable assignment, then we say "A logically implies B" and write the following.

$$A \vDash B$$

Note that this is not a statement *in* the predicate calculus, but rather, is a statement *about* predicate calculus statements. Similarly, we write the following if B is a tautology.

$$\vDash B$$

Finally, if there is a formal proof from A to B we write the following.

$$A \vdash B$$

Assuming the rule	
∀(Student)	;For all students
Undergraduate (Student)	;**IF** the student is an undergraduate
∧ Institution (Student Cal-Tech)	;at Cal Tech
=> Brilliant (Student)	;**THEN** the undergraduate is brilliant
And the facts	
Undergraduate (Ken)	;Ken is an undergraduate
Institution (Ken Cal-Tech)	;Ken goes to Cal Tech
Use universal instantiation to deduce	
Brilliant (Ken)	;Ken is brilliant

FIGURE 1.10.   A logical deduction using universal instantiation.

A proof of a sentence is a finite sequence of sentences in which each element is a sentence chosen from a set, a logical axiom, or the result of applying a logical rule of inference. An important result of mathematical logic states that whenever a set of sentences implies another sentence, then there exists a finite proof of that sentence. For this reason the predicate calculus is said to be **decidable**.

Such proofs offer us yet a third possible semantics for logic, called a proof semantics. A **proof theory** determines whether a given expression is valid, that is, derivable, from a given database of facts. It is valid if there is a proof. For a given statement, there may be many possible proofs or no proofs at all. A **proof semantics** can be defined to associate a statement with a proof, or more simply, with "valid" or "not valid."

Proof theory establishes a standard of reasoning. It brings sense to many examples of confusing and illogical reasoning. For example, consider the following.

Given:	All fleas like some dog.	
	No fleas like any swimmer.	
Conclude:	No dogs are swimmers.	(1)

Even if we suppose that the first two sentences are true relative to some interpretation, the conclusion does not follow. For example, all fleas could like the same nonswimming dog. Proof semantics provides a careful and systematic account of when deductions are justified, that is, what follows rightfully from what. Reasoning that follows the appropriate logical principles is said to be sound. Sound is used here as a technical term to describe systems or methods that derive no more than can be supported according to explicit rules of logic. Thus, the conclusion in (1) is not sound. In contrast, the conclusion in (2) is sound but bogus. Bogus is not a technical term. The fault lies not in the inference but in the nonstandard interpretation.

Given:	Some fleas like all dogs.	
	No fleas like any swimmer.	
Conclude:	No dogs are swimmers.	(2)

But how can we tell which inferences are sound? The approach in logic is to characterize sound inferences systematically as those that follow from specified rules of inference.

In summary, there are three parts to the semantics of predicate calculus, the semantics of reference, the semantics of truth, and the semantics of proof. Each is a mapping from symbols and expressions to some kind of meaning, where the meaning may be elements in a model, the symbols *true* and *false*, or a proof. These are related respectively to model theory, truth theory, and proof theory. Sometimes this whole approach is called a **declarative semantics**.

1.2.2 Reductionist Approaches for Composing Meanings

A **language** is a set of expressions. In natural languages, a conventional unit of expression is the **sentence**. In English, sentences contain subjects and predicates. Crucial to the notion of a language is that there is a way of deciding whether any particular arrangement of symbols is a sentence in the language. In written and spoken natural languages, grammars are sets of rules that determine which arrangements of symbols are sentences. Thus, the expression "Shoe blue knob five running." is not a sentence and "He runs in blue shoes." is a sentence.

One remarkable fact about natural language is that indefinitely many linguistic expressions have meaning for people. Consider the following sentence:

The pink mouse flew her helicopter downtown to the opera.   (3)

We have no trouble attributing a meaning to this silly sentence, even though it is unlikely that any reader of this book ever encountered it before reading it here. How can this be so? It suggests that the experience of understanding a sentence that we have never seen before is akin to the process of (say) adding two numbers we have never seen before or driving a car we have never seen before. We can do the addition because we view the numbers in terms of their smaller pieces, such as the digits in the ones column, the digits in the tens column, and so on. We have an algorithm that takes account the significance of the decimal representation and the rules for combining 1-digit numbers.

By this analogy, we expect it to be the case that there is a systematic way of interpreting expressions in natural language. This is a structural approach to composing meanings. Sometimes we call it a **reductionist** approach because the meaning of the whole sentence derives from the meanings of its parts.

The truth and proof semantics of predicate calculus both follow a reductionist approach in that the meaning of an expression is determined in a systematic way from the meanings of its parts. For example, the truth value of the expression $A \wedge B$ can be determined systematically from the truth value of A, the truth value of B, and the usual definition of $\wedge$.

It turns out that a reductionist view of the composition of meaning is not quite adequate for sentences in natural language. Consider the sentence "Is there any salt?" Asked of an environmental scientist measuring water quality, this sentence is probably a request for information about the results of his measurements. Asked of a waiter at a restaurant, the question would be interpreted as an indirect request to bring a salt shaker to the table. Part of the problem is that the sentence is not always the right unit of analysis. Context is provided by other sentences. Another problem is that this account of meaning fails to take into account the role of the speaker, the listener, and the situation.

For all of the shortcomings of a structural approach to semantics in natural language, this approach is important for systematic computer representations. We need to know how the meaning of an expression depends on the meaning of the terms in the expression. An account of the composition of meaning should draw on regularities in the arrangement of symbols. Restated, regularities in meaning should be reflected by regularities in symbol structures.

Computer systems use many different kinds of representations, not just sentences from a predicate calculus. Consider the following paragraph:

When I write at home, I often look out the window at some of California's giant redwood trees. This morning on one such tree, I saw some branches high above a hammock outside where age and neighboring growth have combined to cause them to turn brown and die. Sometime in the months ahead these branches will come crashing down. I remembered that I should phone a tree surgeon to tend to them before they land in the hammock.

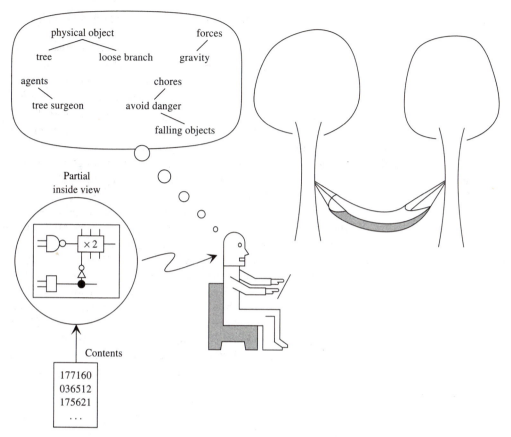

FIGURE 1.11. Deciphering the "mentalese" of the Mark-1 writing robot. This is analogous to trying to figure out how a computer works from the circuit diagram but without the operations manual.

According to Newell and Simon's physical symbol system hypothesis, the cognitive parts of this story—writing, observing trees, and planning activities—can be accounted for in terms of the processing of symbols, that is, marks in a memory and a processor that can read and manipulate those marks. Let us suppose for the purposes of this discussion that the agent in the previous paragraph is actually a manufactured physical symbol system, a "Mark-1" writing robot. As suggested in Figure 1.11, somewhere inside the Mark-1 there is a memory medium with marks that we expect correspond to "home," "giant California redwood trees," "hammock," "tree-surgeon," "phoning" and so on for whatever knowledge and beliefs the robot may be said to possess. In a well-ordered system we would also expect to find symbol-processing machinery that causes the anticipation of falling branches and the phoning of a tree surgeon. It is not necessary that the Mark-1 itself be able to tell us about the location and encoding principles for the underlying symbol system. However, if we as observers can discover the "mentalese" of the Mark-1, we expect to find symbols and processors that are causally connected with the behavior of the robot.

In artificial intelligence and cognitive science these expectations about symbols in memory and their connection with intelligent behavior are at the core of **representational theories of**

mind. In the context of knowledge systems, the emphasis shifts from deciphering mentalese to the systematic use of symbols in a computational knowledge medium.

By a **semantic theory** Hayes means an account of the way that particular configurations of symbols in a representation scheme correspond to particular configurations of the external world. By calling it a "theory," Hayes demands more than just allowing observers to assign arbitrary meanings to symbols. He wants a systematic approach for indicating how sentences in the language represent the subject matter. The grammar rules that determine whether a set of words is a sentence should also help us to determine what the sentence means. The regularities of this explain how we make any sense out of the sentence about the pink mouse in the helicopter.

Seeking a semantic theory shifts the focus from a concern with interpreting or decoding the symbol structures of a particular robot to the design of representation languages of adequate power for which we can give a principled account of what symbols written in them mean. The goal of this revised enterprise is technical: It is the development of engineering principles by which we can design symbol structures and knowledge systems whose properties are predictable and understood. In both cases—mentalese languages of the mind or representation languages—what we seek is a systematic way of assigning meanings to expressions.

Returning to our analogy about the understanding of natural language, we would like to ask questions about the meaning of symbols and to derive answers using a computational process on the symbol structures in memory. So far, the declarative semantics of predicate calculus satisfies the requirements we have listed. Later in this section, we discuss why additional kinds of semantics have been developed to satisfy additional requirements. First, however, we will look at further examples of representational structures and at some of the approaches for assigning meanings to them that are in the same spirit as the declarative semantics although they are usually less-thoroughly developed.

1.2.3 *Terminology for Graphs and Trees*

Graphs are made up of two kinds of elements usually called **nodes** and **arcs**. Figure 1.12 gives several examples of graphs. The nodes are the circles and the arcs are the lines connecting them. When the nodes or arcs have distinguishing labels the graph is called a **labeled graph**. It is common in depictions of knowledge representations to use graphs with labels on the arcs and the nodes. Graphs are also distinguished as being either **directed** or **undirected**. Directed graphs have directed arcs, meaning the two ends are distinguishable. Directed arcs have an orientation, meaning that they start at one designated node and end at another. They are usually represented visually as arrows as shown in Figure 1.12.

A graph is **cyclic** if there is a path, starting from one of its nodes, that leads along the arcs from one node to another leading back eventually to the starting node. For directed graphs, the path must follow in the direction of the arcs. An acyclic graph is a graph with no cycles. Figure 1.13 gives examples of cyclic and acyclic graphs. Directed acyclic graphs are called **dags**.

We define **trees** as directed acyclic graphs in which every node (except the root node) has exactly one ancestor. The **root node** is the unique node in the tree having no ancestors. Sometimes the term **forest** is used to refer to a set of trees.

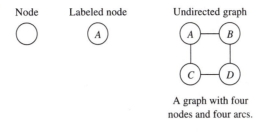

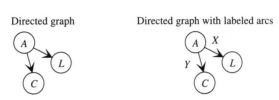

FIGURE 1.12. Some basic terminology about graphs.

Trees are a very important special case in graph theory and computer science. As is apparent from the reference to "ancestors" and "root node" in the definition, trees have their own special terminology, which we will now make more precise. For trees, the directed arcs are also called **branches**. Directionality of the arcs point is important. Borrowing familiar language from family trees, we say that branches directly connect **parent nodes** with **children nodes**. Conven-

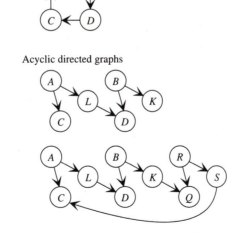

FIGURE 1.13. Examples of cyclic and acyclic directed graphs.

Tree
(directed graph version)

uag "Tree"
(undirected graph version)

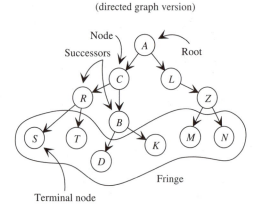

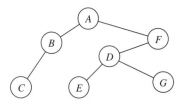

No unique root.
No differentiation between node and successors.
No terminal nodes or fringe.

FIGURE 1.14. Comparing two definitions of trees.

tionally, arcs point from parents to children. **Ancestor** and **descendant** nodes are defined in the obvious way. Mathematically inclined writers often prefer to use the term **successors** to refer to children nodes. Nodes with no successors are called **terminal nodes**.

Trees can be generated or drawn a little at a time. In this case, the term **leaf node** is used to refer to terminal nodes or to any other nodes showing no successors, even if further generation may potentially cause more successors to be presented. The set of nonterminal nodes is collectively called the **interior** and the set of leaf nodes is collectively called the **fringe**. In reasoning problems we often consider trees that are expanded incrementally. In these cases, the terms leaf node and terminal node are sometimes used to refer to nodes that have no successors yet, although they may later. We use the terms **dynamic fringe** or **frontier** in such cases to refer to the set of the deepest nodes in the tree that have been explored so far.

The term **branching factor** refers to the number of successors of a node. Often for the purposes of analysis, it is convenient to assume that all of the interior nodes in a tree have the same branching factor. When different nodes have different numbers of successors, we sometimes use an average branching factor for a set of nodes.

Before leaving this discussion of terminology, we note that although our definition of *tree* is the one most commonly used in computer science, it differs from the definition of *tree* most used in mathematics. In mathematics, trees are usually defined for *undirected* graphs rather than *directed* graphs. There are several equivalent definitions for trees as undirected graphs. (1) A tree is a graph that is connected and that has one more node than arc. (2) A tree is a connected, acyclic graph. Undirected trees are called "uags" or undirected, acyclic graphs.

Figure 1.14 compares trees based on directed and undirected graphs. In uag trees, there is no privileged node that stands for the root, no nodes are characterized or terminal or in the fringe, and there is no orientation to links differentiating nodes and their successors. It has been said that you can "pick up" a uag tree from any node so that the rest of it "hangs down." The directed version of trees is commonly associated with linked data structures in computer science and with search processes that have a starting place.

1.2.4 *Graphs as Symbol Structures*

In the following we will consider examples of a graphic descriptive language often called a **semantic network**. The term *semantic network* arises from Ross Quillian's Ph.D. thesis in which he used them as network models of information. Semantic networks are used for different purposes, are assigned meanings (semantics) in different ways, and are depicted by figures with nodes and directed arcs.

Since Quillian's thesis semantic networks have been used to model all sorts of non-semantic things such as propositions in logic, the physical structure of objects, and the behavior of devices. At some time, virtually every one of these representations has been called "semantic" by someone. In AI and knowledge engineering, the term *semantic network* refers generally to a wide class of informal and formal symbolic representations. What these representations have in common is that they are all made of links and nodes. In hindsight, it is clear that this definition is indistinguishable from that of a **graph**. Graphs and graph structures have many useful properties as representations. However, *there is nothing fundamentally "semantic" about graphs.*

Graphs can mean things in just the same way that sentences in a language can mean things. We choose graphs as examples of representations simply because so many representations in knowledge systems are graphs. The issues are much the same whether the representations are graphs, grammatical sentences, or bitmaps.

When we use the term *semantic network*, we draw on vocabulary from the AI literature. We develop several informal variations of semantic networks in the following, using them to show why we need principles for systematic representation languages.

Consider the sentence:

Willy threw a ball to Morgan. (2)

Figure 1.15 shows one way to represent the information stated in this sentence using a graph. The syntax of our graph is simple. **Nodes**, depicted here as ovals, stand for various kinds of **objects** and **links**, depicted here as arcs with arrowheads and labels, stand for various kinds of **relations**. Arcs naturally have two ends, so they are most useful for representing two-part or binary relations. Relations involving more than two parts (*n*-ary relations) can be represented as nodes. Thus, in addition to the nodes that correspond to physical objects (Willy, Morgan, a ball) there are nodes that stand for relations. For example, the verb *throw* is represented as a particular 3-ary relation called a "throw event." The binary relations include did-action, thrower, thrown-to, and object-thrown.

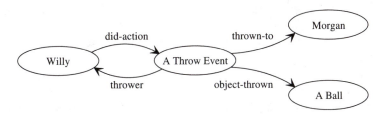

FIGURE 1.15. Example of a semantic network.

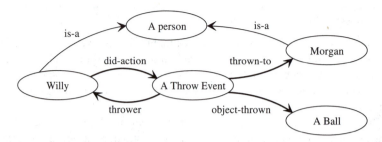

FIGURE 1.16. Extended example of the semantic network from Figure 1.15, showing some assumed relations (thin lines).

For such symbol structures to be useful in knowledge systems, there must be a way to structure knowledge in expressions and there must be a systematic way to determine the meanings of expressions from the individual terms and the structure of the network. Given the network in Figure 1.15, we could ask:

■ Was something thrown?
■ Is the ball a baseball?
■ When did the event take place?
■ Is Willy a person?

From Figure 1.15, we might guess that the presence of a "throw event" indicates that something was thrown. There is no indication at all of the kind of ball; nor is there any explicit indication that the kind of ball has not been determined. The form of the verb *threw* in (2) suggests that the event took place in the past. Unless the binary relation did-action indicates when the event took place, however, nothing is known about the time of the event. There is no explicit indication that Willy is a person, although this is a reasonable inference to make from the use of capitalization in the English sentence in (2). In a revised version of the semantic network in Figure 1.16, the graph is augmented with some thin-line arrows, intended to represent other relations, not stated in the sentence, but perhaps inferred from some context. The revised figure indicates (loosely speaking) that Willy and Morgan are people.

Unfortunately, this is much too glib. The history of representation languages in AI shows that it is easy and misleading to ascribe unwarranted knowledge and power to representations when we must use human intelligence to interpret them. A simple experiment demonstrates this. Consider how unintelligible the network becomes in Figure 1.17 when we substitute numbered symbols ("gensyms") for names: g0001 for is-a, g0002 for Willy, and so on. The loss of intelligibility reveals the amount of background that we unconsciously use to interpret drawn semantic networks. In effect we make guesses about what an interpreter would do. Changing the natural language symbols to gensyms removes the (possibly misleading) clues that guided our guesses.

Continuing this example, Figure 1.18 shows two sentences together with semantic networks that are intended to represent their contents. In this example, three elements take part in the across relation: Willy's *dwelling* is across the *street* from the speaker's *dwelling*. This three-part relation is expressed by the relation node with three binary relation arrows (across-object,

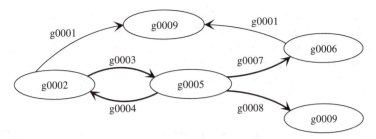

FIGURE 1.17. Semantic network of Figure 1.16 substituting numbered symbols ("gensyms") for names. The difficulty of making sense of this figure shows how easy it is to overlook the knowledge that people can bring to bear in interpreting semantic networks.

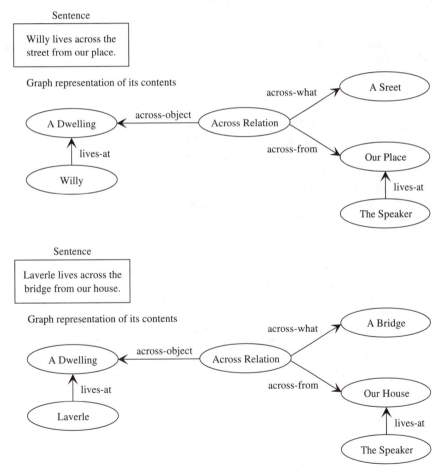

FIGURE 1.18. Sentences with similar meanings should be represented by similar symbol structures.

across-what, across-from) pointing to the other boxes. Such a representation provides specific predetermined places for putting expected kinds of information.

In summary, one of the requirements of having a semantic theory is that we give a detailed account of how meaning is ascribed to representations by their interpreter. For good engineering, the assignment of meaning should be systematic so that representations with similar meanings should have similar structures.

1.2.5   *The Annotation Principle and Metalevel Notations*   ADVANCED

In the following, we illustrate a sequence of semantic issues using semantic networks. In this sequence, we retrace some of the history of ideas in the development of representation languages in AI.

We begin by considering a symbol system intended to reason about characters in old cartoons. Tweety the bird and Sylvester the cat are favorite cartoon examples traditionally used at least once in all AI texts. Just for fun we will treat objects from such cartoons as our domain or "world" in the following examples. Presumably the system would need to represent the fact that birds and cats are animals, that birds have feathers and can fly, that canaries are birds, that Tweety is a neighbor of Sylvester and so on. One attempt to represent these facts in a simple semantic network is shown in Figure 1.19.

In describing such a representation, we must give an account of the processing that the system will carry out on the symbol structures in the course of its reasoning. For example, we expect the symbol system to infer that Tweety can fly. A common idea in such representations is that general information ought to be stored as high in a generalization hierarchy as applicable and inherited by nodes below it by means of a search process. This idea was motivated by psychological studies of human memory response. If more general properties are stored higher up in a generalization hierarchy, one would expect it to take more time for a subject to affirm a statement like "Tweety eats" than one like "Tweety is yellow."

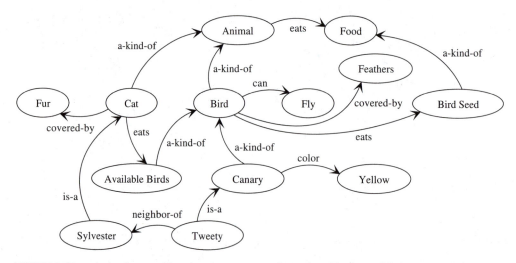

FIGURE 1.19.   A simple semantic network to represent facts about Tweety and Sylvester.

One account of the inferential processing in an inheritance model follows:

> The link from the bird node represents that birds can fly. The canary node is linked to the bird node, so that the processor can add that canaries can fly. Continuing this process, the processor infers that Tweety can fly because the Tweety node is linked to the canary node.

This naive argument and organization captures some of the logical structure of the domain. We know that a bird is an animal and the answers to questions about birds will often be derived through general properties of animals. Semantic networks treat these deductions specially, leading to economies of computation for common cases.

However, from the same network we could give an analogous account showing how the processor would infer that Tweety has fur, as follows:

> The link at the cat node represents that cats have fur. The Sylvester node is linked to the cat node, so that the processor can add that Sylvester has fur. Continuing this process, the processor infers that Tweety has fur because the Tweety node is linked to the Sylvester node.

The silliness of the latter account derives from the last step, where the "fur" inference is implausible because Tweety is not a cat. More precisely, the implied processing acts as if we can infer that y has a property if y is linked to x by an arc and x has the property. This inference is too broad. The problem is that the network does not explicitly indicate which links convey inheritance of properties and it is clear that not all of them do. Being a neighbor of somebody does not usually imply that one has the properties of that person. Neighbor-of means something different from is-a and a-kind-of, so the processor needs to treat these different relations differently. But they are all represented in the same way in the graph, as directed arcs, albeit with different names. This brings us to the annotation principle.

> **The Annotation Principle.** Differences in intended processing should be reflected by differences in symbol structures. If two symbol structures are intended to be treated in different ways by a processor in a symbol system, the processor must be able to distinguish among some of the properties of the symbol structures. If two symbol structures are intended to be processed in the same way by a processor, then some of their relevant properties should appear the same to the processor.

The annotation principle makes explicit a structural approach to systematizing the composition of meaning. It is simple and perhaps obvious, but it comes up in many different guises in the design of symbol systems. The term *annotation* refers to the use of auxiliary symbols that are used to modify the interpretation of other symbols. These annotation symbols typically do not have the same kinds of meaning as the symbols that they annotate. For example, they usually do not designate objects in the environment.

Annotations are also called **metalevel notations** and **metadescriptions**. They are the basis for many of the representational frameworks and declarative notations used in knowledge representation languages. They are called *metalevel* because they do not refer to the same environ-

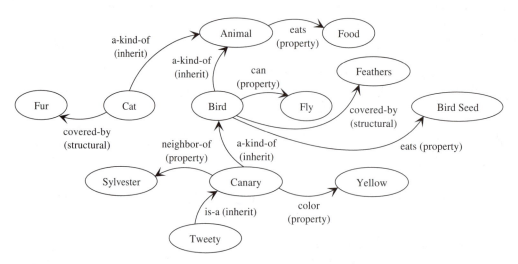

FIGURE 1.20. Augmenting the semantic network of Figure 1.19 with notations on arcs to guide processing.

ment that the cartoon characters in our example inhabit. Rather, they guide a processor in its processing of the symbol structures.

Programming and representation languages sometimes provide special mechanisms for adding annotations to symbol structures. For example, **metaclasses** in object-oriented languages are often used to define how the system instantiates classes or allocates storage. In this same vein, some languages provide ways of embedding structures within notations in a way that is invisible to programs using normal methods for accessing memory. Representation languages provide annotation mechanisms to simplify the design and development of interpreters or symbol structure processors. In this section, we will consider several examples of annotations. Many of these examples are drawn from problematic cases that were noticed by developers of early semantic networks.

In the example of the neighbor-of arc versus the is-a arc in Figure 1.19, we could modify our approach so that that the processor would differentiate among the arcs on the basis of their relation names. This would require that the processor have information for each different relation. An alternative is to augment the network with annotations.

In Figure 1.20, we extend the semantic network with additional annotations indicated by parenthetical labels associated with the arcs. This is a first step toward an engineering practice of developing taxonomic descriptions of relations. Such taxonomies characterize relations. For example, annotations can indicate which relations are used for inheritance, that is, for the propagation of properties from nodes that designate general classes to nodes that designate more specific ones. In Figure 1.20, is-a and a-kind-of are annotated as **inheritance** links. By such propagation the representation can serve to represent that canaries can fly and that Tweety is yellow. The amount of processing required to propagate properties is determined by the branching factor of the network and the depth to which the information must be propagated. To provent looping, inheritance networks are generally required to be acyclic.

Annotations can indicate which relations are **structural**, that is, which relationships describe information about physical structure in terms of subcomponents. In our cartoon example, cats have fur. If more detail were required we could show nested structural relations: Cats have paws, and paws have claws, and so on. As we make a representation more detail, we sometimes find it useful to increase the number of symbols used to represent the elements of a situation. Initially, it might be adequate to treat (say) properties of a cat's claws as properties of the cat. For example, we might just represent the cat's claws as being sharp. Later, however, we might need to represent claws on two different feet. Some claws are dulled and some are sharp. Furthermore, we may find that we want to reason in a similar way about bird claws and cat claws. At some point, however, the overall complexity of the representation may be reduced if we separate the representation of claw properties from cat properties, that is, if we reify the claws as separate objects with their own properties. Then the overall represent becomes a composite consisting of a cats, legs, paws, claws, and any other reified parts that are convenient. This makes it possible to simplify the overall hierarchy of classes into reusable representational elements.

Finally, some links could indicate information about nodes used for **documentation** by a database maintenance routine. Examples of this are the relations creator and date-created, which would connect nodes to representations of the knowledge engineer who created them and the dates that they were created. Such relations are used for purposes of bookkeeping and updating and can be ignored by a processor concerned strictly with the subject matter of cartoons.

These examples show how annotations enable an interpreter to distinguish cases for a small number of different annotations corresponding to **relation types** rather than a large number of different relation names. In particular, it opens up the possibility of defining classes of relations with common behavior. In our first account of processing in Figure 1.19, we assumed that the processor knew the names of the different relations in order to decide how to process them. With annotations, a symbol processor can treat is-a and a-kind-of as identical for the purposes of inheriting properties. Exercise 7 considers an alternative processing architecture for realizing this same effect. Regularities in the ways that symbols are to be interpreted can be exploited in terms of regularities in annotations and in the architecture of their processors.

Annotation in a semantic network can guide not only the processing of arcs but also the processing of nodes. How can the processor determines which objects designate things that can appear in a cartoon? Clearly, Sylvester and Tweety can appear and both are shown in the network as nodes. But canary is also a node. Does it make sense to say that "canary can appear in a cartoon" or "canary can appear in the node animal"? When we say that "Canaries are yellow," we do not refer to any particular canary. We referred to a **class** of small yellow birds. A class does not correspond to bounded physical entity in the world. You cannot "see" a class of birds. A class is a cognitive artifact that we use in organizing our thinking.

Making the meaning of classes such as "canary" philosophically and genetically precise requires more work. Does the class include ancestral birds from the age of the dinosaurs that differ increasingly from today's canaries? The value of precision in sorting out and representing such matters depends on the expected uses of the symbol system.

Figure 1.21 adds node annotations shown as parenthetical labels to indicate whether nodes designate classes or individuals. Even so, this is not yet enough to answer our question about what nodes designate things that can appear in the cartoons. For example, the network shows that cats eat available birds. What is this strange node available-birds? Again, it seems to describe a

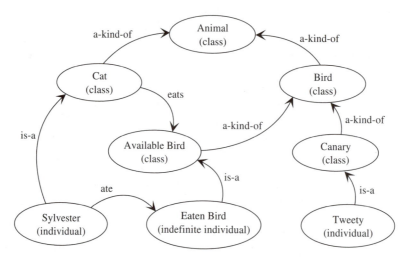

FIGURE 1.21.   Augmenting the semantic network of Figure 1.19 with notations on nodes to guide processing.

class. Early developers of semantic networks were quite free in defining such nodes, but lax in characterizing precisely what they meant. The issue here is not that such nodes have no place in a semantic theory. Rather, the issue is that there is a fair amount of work required to be precise about what such nodes are intended to mean, and also work in arranging that the operations of a system are correct relative to the intended meaning of such representations.

We consider one more example. It would be convenient to be able to refer to particular birds that have not yet been identified with known individuals. For example, we might see a grinning Sylvester in the cartoon with yellow feathers in his mouth. We may want to reason about the fate and status of the unfortunate consumed bird, without knowing whether it was Tweety. Mystery stories make much use of this kind of reference. They tell us about a murderer, before telling us whether the foul deed was committed by the pretty maid, the spoiled son, the spinster aunt, the wily lawyer or the sinister butler. Figure 1.19 introduces *indefinite individual* nodes to refer to concepts such as the unknown eaten canary or the unidentified murderer.

What these notations about nodes have in common is that they are all about reasoning about the identity of individuals. We assumed without saying so that distinct nodes refer to distinct things. Class nodes refer to classes of objects. In our simplest examples, we have one node for Sylvester and another node for Tweety. The indefinite nodes change the way an interpreter reasons about identity. If we have a node for "the murderer" and other nodes for the maid, the spoiled son, and so, then later inferences about the possible identity of the murderer may leave us with more than one node referring to the same thing. If the system infers that the butler did it, then we would say that the butler node and the murderer node are **co-referential**.

More generally, two representations are said to be co-referential if they refer to or designate the same thing. For example, the symbols "the first U.S. president" and "George Washington" would usually be co-referential. Technically, the question of whether two representations are co-referential must be determined relative to an observer. Annotations can be used to support reasoning about identity and co-referentiality. Thus, our example of indefinite individual annotations for nodes support such reasoning. In addition, some representation languages include specific co-reference relations intended to indicate where different symbols are known to be co-referential. Examples of such annotations and reasoning with them are given in the exercises.

1.2.6 *Different Kinds of Semantics*

We have now established the background to consider different approaches to semantics. A semantics assigns meanings to symbols. Different kinds of semantics differ in the kinds of symbols considered and the kinds of meanings they assign.

To understand the different approaches it is useful to understand the goals of people who use them. Following Woods' discussion of semantics in Woods, 1975, we compare these approaches using caricatures of different points of view. The first set of caricatures is concerned with assigning meanings to symbols in programs and representation languages. These include the Logician, the Programming Language Designer, the Systems Engineer, and the Representation Language Designer. The second set of caricatures is concerned with assigning meanings to symbols in natural languages. These include the Computational Linguist, the Social Linguist, and the Social Scientist. These caricature names do not fully characterize the different fields. They are intended to exemplify some of the different kinds of issues that are relevant when people create semantics.

Semantics for Programs and Representation Languages

The Logician is concerned with specifying the meaning of a formal notation. To this end she is usually concerned with a formal definition of truth in a set theoretic model, sometimes called a Tarskian semantics. She wants a systematic way to determine when expressions in the notation are "true" propositions, when they are false, and what follows from what. For example, she wants to know how the truth of an expression like "(Socrates is a man) and (Socrates is short)" depends on the truth assignments of the two parenthesized expressions and the conjunction *and*. In the previous section described the semantics of the predicate calculus in terms of a **reference semantics**, a **truth semantics**, and a **proof semantics**.

The predicate calculus by itself does not embody any computational process. Programming languages and practical knowledge representation languages, however, need to specify processes for computing and reasoning. To accommodate this, additional kinds of semantics have been proposed.

The Programming Language Designer is interested in providing a formal specification of computation in programming languages. He wants to be clear about how syntax indicates what computation is to be performed, so that he can build reliable and portable compilers and compiler-compilers. He prefers formal specifications so that the omissions, contradictions, and ambiguities typical of informal language specifications may be avoided. His semantics describe how the output and final states of a program depend on its inputs and input states. There are different approaches to specifying this.

The idea that a proof system can give meaning to a programming language, and hence to programs, is due to Hoare. This enterprise is sometimes called the **axiomatic semantics**, although it is more commonly called the **denotational semantics**. This differs from the usual sense of semantics in logic. Ordinarily, the formal semantics of a proof system is given by relating it to a model theory defined in set-theoretic terms. Here, a proof system is used to specify the semantics of a programming language or a class of its implementations.

The **denotational semantics** involves three interpretation functions. One interpretation function maps programs onto mathematical functions that relate inputs to outputs. A second maps language expressions and program states onto values. A third maps commands in the language onto state transition functions. The details and variations of this approach are intricate and beyond the scope of this section. The main point is that the semantics map syntax onto descriptions of a computation.

The Systems Engineer is also a computer scientist, but she is chiefly concerned with aids to building and maintaining large computer programs. She is concerned with how a large program is built up from many subprograms and hardware subsystems. Big programs are written by groups of people, used by different people in constructing their own subprograms, and modified as needs change. She wants to be able to modify her subprograms without changing the programs that use them. She also wants to be able to use subprograms without knowing the details of how they work. The semantics useful to a Systems Engineer are about the requirements of subprograms. She is interested in external data representations, subprogram parameters, control regimes, and computational resources required by subprograms. Generically, we say that such approaches are concerned with **interface semantics**. In practical examples this involves a mixture of informal and formal descriptions.

The Representation Language Designer is interested in the reasoning phenomena that arise when people gain new information while working on a problem. People make assumptions about defaults and about what events and values are possible and likely. They change their minds in the light of new information, sometimes retracting things they believed earlier. The Representation Language Designer would like to have ways of describing computational methods and goals that could guide such nonmonotonic reasoning in computers. To the extent that they effect the operation of an interpreter, he is also interested in distinctions such as those discussed earlier in this section between class nodes, individual nodes, and so on. He may characterize this as knowledge for control or metalevel reasoning. He does not want to hide this knowledge inside a "black box" interpreter or to intermingle it with the domain knowledge. He wants to enter the statements declaratively and have the interpreter find them and use them when it decides what to do next in the reasoning process. Generically, we call the association of such knowledge with domain symbols a **reasoning control semantics**. This semantics maps statements in the representational language to computational processes for reasoning. The semantics for programming and representing languages are summarized in Table 1.2.

Semantics for Natural Languages

We now turn to semantics for natural languages. The Computational Linguist is concerned with the translation of sentences in natural languages into formal representations of their meanings. She is interested in characterizing how the same sentence can sometimes mean different things and that some sentences mean nothing at all. She would like to find an unambiguous notation in which to express the different things that a sentence can mean. Thus, the Computational Linguist is concerned with the translation of sentences and expressions from natural language into formal notations such as predicate calculus or a well-defined semantic network. We call this approach a **logical language semantics**. Note that this approach maps sentences in one language to sentences in another.

TABLE 1.2. Different semantics for programming and representation languages.

Kind of Semantics	Used for	Symbols	Meanings
Reference semantics	Identifying how symbols in a computer refer to things in an observer's environment.	Symbols and expressions in a physical symbol system or in a representation language.	Designation. A description of things known to an observer.
Truth semantics	Identifying what terms and expressions are true.	Symbols and expressions in logical formulae with a given conceptualization.	True or false.
Proof semantics	Identifying what terms and expressions are valid.	Symbols and expressions in logical formulae with a given database of formula.	Valid or not, as supported by a proof.
Denotational semantics	Characterizing how the syntax in a programming language specifies a computation.	Symbols and expressions in the syntax of a programming language.	A characterization in terms of mathematical functions indicating how final states and output are determined by initial states and input.
Interface semantics	Characterizing the operations and requirements of modules in a computer program.	Program modules.	Abstractions described as protocols, arguments, types, and operations.
Reasoning control semantics	Characterizing how symbols should be treated in a nonmonotonic reasoning process.	Symbols and expressions in a representation language.	Reasoning processes for default reasoning priorities, and so on.

Before passing on, we note in passing that is not generally adequate to consider sentences one at a time when assigning meanings. Consider the following two pairs of sentences.

(1) It is 12:30. Morgan is out to lunch.

(2) His memos never make sense. Morgan is out to lunch.

In this example, the first sentence gives us an important clue about an idiomatic interpretation of the second sentence. Thus sentences do not necessarily provide independent chunks that can be analysed or processed independently to determine their meaning. Natural language requires a context to determine meaning. This is in striking contrast to the truth and proof semantics of logic, and contrary to the suggestion that the meaning of an expression in a representation language be determined by the meaning of its parts.

Returning to our tour of kinds of semantics, the Social Linguist recognizes that many sentences uttered in conversation are chosen for their effect on the listener rather than to communicate statements about an external situation. For example, the English statement, "The car is almost out of gas" may be uttered as an indirect request to a driver to stop at the next gas station. Even statements that seem to contain logical operators often have unusual meanings. Only a perverse sense of humor would allow one to answer "yes" to English question "Are you left-handed or right-handed?" This is a request for information. One of the expected responses is "right-handed." The Social Linguist refers to the semantics studied by the Computational Linguist as merely the "literal meaning." He classifies statements as kinds of "speech acts," whose purpose in conversation is to indicate agreements, disagreements, commitments, priorities, goals, understandings, and other aspects of the communication and negotiation process involving the agents. We call this approach **action semantics** because the meanings of the sentences are actions intended to have certain effects.

The Social Scientist is also concerned with the use of symbols in human interactions. She is interested in how it is that people come to agree about the meaning of terms that they use together in speaking and writing. She recognizes that people do not immediately understand each other's terms and that they develop models of each other and their use of language. She focuses on phenomena related to the change and elaboration of meaning. She characterizes the meaning of terms as being socially constructed and negotiated, as people sharpen or broaden what they mean by words. The point here is not the need for another kind of semantics, but rather, a need to focus on different properties of meaning. In our previous discussions of meanings, we acted as though meanings were fixed and unchanging. In contrast, the Social Scientist studies the evolution and convergence of meaning.

Before leaving these examples of kinds of semantics, we note that the list is not exhaustive and that there are many further variations. In the 1890s, the philosopher Frege, who invented the declarative semantics of logic, was also concerned with the relation between equality and the designations of terms in natural language. He proposed two natural language sentences, which have often been cited as perverse examples.

(1) Necessarily, the Morning Star is the Morning Star.
(2) Necessarily, the Morning Star is the Evening Star.

In these sentences, the term *Morning Star* refers to a bright star observed near the sun at sunrise. The term *Evening Star* refers to a bright star observed near the sun at sunset. From an astronomical point of view, the two terms refer to the same physical object, usually the planet Venus. From Frege's point of view, however, the first sentence is true and the second false. The two terms do not have the same "meaning."

People still argue about exactly what Frege meant with this example. Some people relate Frege's idea to the idea of transformational grammars. These grammars transform sentences to either a standard form or a logical statement. This approach is similar to the logical semantics described earlier. In this account, the terms *evening star* and *morning star* have different meanings because there are no rules for transforming them to the same form. The reason that the two terms are not made equivalent is that the transformational rules involve knowledge about variations in syntax but presumably not knowledge of astronomy.

A different explanation of Frege's point is based on consideration of the term *intensional* which means "of the senses." In this view, the semantics of *evening star* and *morning star* refer to the process by which they are perceived. They are perceived differently because one is seen in the morning and the other in the evening. This approach can be seen as a more sophisticated view of a reference semantics. It focuses on the operations, processing, and interpretation of the senses. We cannot simply refer to "the world" as though it were something that we necessarily all

TABLE 1.3. Kinds of semantics for natural languages.

Kind of Semantics	Used for	Symbols	Meanings
Logical language semantics	Characterizing what sentences in natural language mean.	Example sentences and expressions from natural language.	Sentences in a formal notation, such as predicate calculus.
Action semantics	Characterizing how sentences in natural language are used to cause action.	Example sentences and expressions from natural language.	The goals, agreements, and commitments of agents in a conversation.
Intensional semantics	Characterizing how terms in natural language refer to things that are perceived.	Terms in natural language used in writing and speech.	The operation, processes, and interpretations of the senses.

see the same way. We must say more about how we go about perceiving and understanding it. We call this approach **intensional semantics**. Table 1.3 summarizes approaches for assigning meaning to sentences in natural language.

Other philosophers take intensions to correspond to concepts, ideas, or things that can be imagined. Further discussion of related topics such as the semantics of necessity and intensional logic would take us too far afield.

1.2.7 Summary and Review

A semantics is a way of assigning meanings to symbols. There is no single "true" meaning or true way of assigning meanings, at least in the academic fields. Different fields have different traditions for assigning meanings. We considered examples of semantics for programming and representation languages and also for natural languages.

Looking back over the different examples of semantic theories, we can group them roughly into three families. First is the **referential family** of semantic theories. In this family, meaningfulness comes in the relations of symbols to objects of different kinds. Members of this family include the reference semantics, the intensional semantics, and perhaps the denotational semantics of programming languages where the "objects" are mathematical.

Next is the **cognitive family** of semantic theories. Meaningfulness arises from the systematic ways that subject matter is mentally and computationally represented and how reasoning processes are sanctioned over those representations. This family includes the truth semantics, proof semantics, operational semantics, reasoning control semantics, and interface semantics.

Third is the **social family** of semantic theories. This family emphasizes communication. In this approach, meaningfulness derives from the ways that agents use symbols in their interactions with each other. This family includes the action semantics.

These approaches to semantics are complementary. In discussing knowledge systems we draw on different approaches for different purposes. When we think of knowledge systems as embedded systems whose symbols refer to the world we draw on the referential family. When we

argue about the conclusions that knowledge systems should reach and their computational characteristics we draw on the cognitive family of semantic theories. Finally, when we interact with
people to incrementally define symbols to be used in a knowledge system that they will use and
when we consider the interactions of knowledge systems in a human organization, we draw on
the social family of semantic theories.

Exercises for Section 1.2

Ex. 1   [05] *Identifying Graphs and Trees.* Classify each of the following graphs as (1) directed or
undirected, (2) labeled or unlabeled, (3) cyclic or acyclic, and (4) graphs, trees, or forests.

(a)

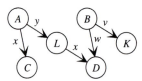

(b)

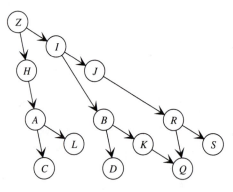

(c)

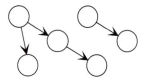

(d)

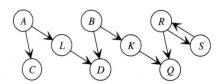

Ex. 2   [05] *Terminology*. For each of the following statements indicate whether it is true or false. If the statement is ambiguous, explain briefly.

(a) *True or False*. The main thing that different so-called semantic networks have in common is that they are composed of nodes and links (possibly labeled). This is the same as a definition of a kind of graph and there is nothing inherently semantic about graphs.

(b) *True or False*. A reductionist and structural approach to the meaning of a representation says that the meaning of an expression is determined by the meaning of its terms and by the pattern of their arrangement. Restated, the meaning of an expression composed of terms is a composition of their meanings.

(c) *True or False*. The annotation principle says that formal representations should be decorated with informal annotations that help people to understand them.

(d) *True or False*. Two nodes in a graph representation are defined to be coreferential if they both have arcs that point directly to a common node.

(e) *True or False*. The declarative semantics of predicate calculus consists of a reference semantics, a truth semantics, and a proof semantics.

Ex. 3   [05] *Terminology*. For each of the following statements indicate whether it is true or false. If the statement is ambiguous, explain briefly.

(a) *True or False*. A cyclic graph is one in which there are two directed arcs leading to the same node.

(b) *True or False*. In reasoning by inheritance, properties are propagated from general nodes to more specific ones.

(c) *True or False*. In drawings of is-a hierarchies, the arcs point in opposite the conventional direction for trees. That is, they point from specialized nodes to generalized nodes.

(d) *True or False*. The annotation principle is intended to make the design of interpreters simpler for systematic representation languages.

(e) *True or False*. The usual definition of a tree in computer science is equivalent to a dag.

■ **Ex. 4**   [CD-!-10] *Reasoning about Identity*. Indefinite-individual nodes are used to refer to individuals whose identity has not yet been established. They provide a notation to express incremental reasoning about identity. One proposed framework defines two kinds of relations for reasoning about such nodes: **anchor** relations, which link an indefinite-individual node to an individual node, and **co-reference** relations, which link two indefinite nodes to each other. In the usual interpretation, different individual nodes designate different objects in the environment, anchor relations mean that an indefinite designates the same object in the environment as the individual node it is linked to, and co-reference relations mean that two indefinite nodes designate the same object in the environment even if it has not been identified yet.

(a) Consider a semantic network with individual nodes Huey, Duey, and Louie representing duck characters in a cartoon story and indefinite nodes for dessert-eater and brown-coat-wearer. Draw a semantic network to indicate that the dessert-eater and the brown-coat-wearer are known to be the same individual.

(b) Describe appropriate processing on this representation that would infer who ate the dessert, given that the brown coat was worn by Huey.

(c) Suppose that in a different situation, the processor had anchored dessert-eater to Huey and brown-coat-wearer to Louie. In what sense would it then become semantically inappropriate for the processor to put a co-reference link between the two indefinite-individual nodes?

■ **Ex. 5** [CD-!-15] *Closed World and Other Assumptions.* In murder mystery stories, the closed (or locked) room scenario is one in which all of the possible suspects are locked together in the same room (or train), so that no one could enter or leave during the crucial period when the foul deed was done. Furthermore, in detective stories, there is a kind of "fair play" assumption amounting to a contract between the author and a reader, which says that it must be possible for the reader to solve the mystery from the evidence given. Introducing a revenge-seeking cousin in the last scene or aliens with special powers from outer space is not considered fair play in the genre.

Similarly, in AI systems the **closed-world assumption** means that all of the objects of interest are described in the database. Usually many assumptions about interpretations influence modeling and representation.

In this exercise we consider an adventure of the three cartoon character ducks Huey, Duey, and Louie, nephews of Donald Duck. The three ducks were locked alone in a room with the dessert, so that none of them could escape and no one else could enter. Suppose also that the dessert could only be eaten by a duck, and that the dessert disappeared while they were in the room.

(a) How could a knowledge system infer who ate the dessert, given that neither Duey nor Louie wore the brown coat and that the brown-coat-wearer ate the dessert? Show how this requires the use of a closed-world assumption?

(b) Professor Digit says, "Although we can use quite simple reasoning models to infer the answer to problems like this, real world (and cartoon world) possibilities are quite endless. How do we know that the dessert did not simply evaporate? There are many different assumptions about the world that a system could make in solving problems like this." Do you agree with Digit? If yes, give some examples.

(c) In everyday reasoning, we are able to imagine a wide range of possibilities, and yet we are not overwhelmed by them on simple problems. Briefly, describe an approach for knowledge systems that provides this capability.

■ **Ex. 6** [15] *Representing Physical Parts.* Representations are designed for a purpose and the adequacy of a representation is judged relative to that purpose. In this exercise, we consider representations of physical parts. We are given the following statements:

A Buick is a kind of automobile.
All automobiles can be driven.
A Skybird is a kind of Buick.
The body of a Skybird is a sport body with an asymmetric shape.
The particular Skybird with serial number 100 has a red body.
A Skybird body has a left door and a right door.
The right door of a Skybird body is a passenger door.
The left door of a Skybird body is a driver door.
A driver door is shaped as trapezoid pattern 1.
A passenger door is shaped as trapezoid pattern 2.
A car door has a handle.
The engine of a Skybird is a model 600.
A model 600 engine has four cylinders.

(a) Assuming that you will use a graph representation, discuss how you distinguish between the following:

Representations of part relations versus representations of other relations

Representations of classes versus representations of particular objects

(b) Suppose that our task is to compute the list of parts of an object, from the largest part down to the smallest one.

In a rigorous discussion of what it means to be a part, we would need to define more what it means to be a part. For example, coatings such as paint are not considered to be parts. Substances used to make up materials such as metal alloys are also not considered to be parts. There is also a practical issue of granularity. Are we really interested in listing the lock washer on the bolt that holds the hand to the door shaft? Assume for this problem that the granularity of interest corresponds to the granularity in the network.

Show a systematic graph representation for the statements above.

(c) Describe your method for computing the list of the parts of a Skybird, using your graph representation as the database.

(d) Describe your approach for inheriting part descriptions. Specifically, explain how your approach includes door handles for both the passenger and driver door in the inventory.

Ex. 7 [!-40] *Partitioned Semantic Networks.* In 1975, Gary Hendrix observed that semantic networks were clumsy when compared with predicate calculus for representing quantified statements. He proposed a mechanism (Hendrix, 1975) for partitioning semantic networks into "spaces" that contained nodes and links and that were convenient for indicating the scope of quantified relations. Spaces are well suited for this purpose in that the node and arc variables encoding information within a space look exactly like the representations of specific facts. Furthermore, such variables are effectively isolated from constant information by partition boundaries.

Although interest in using semantic networks for representing statements in predicate calculus has been rather limited, notations for partitioning networks have provoked more interest as general representational mechanisms. Partitions are used for delineating clusters and defining boundaries for information hiding. For example they have been used to represent contexts, alternative worlds, and plots.

(a) Figure 1.22 represents the statement "Every dog has scratched a flea." The partitions in this figure are SA, the outermost space, and S1, the space that indicates the form over which the variable *d* is scoped. Arcs labeled with an *e* indicate element-of relations for the sets to which they point. Similarly, arcs labeled with an *s* indicate subset relations. The presence of each node and arc within a space are interpreted as implicit statements of exis-

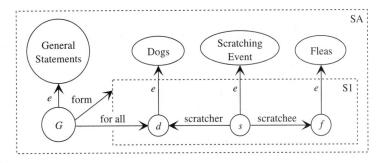

FIGURE 1.22. Roughly, "Every dog has scratched a flea."

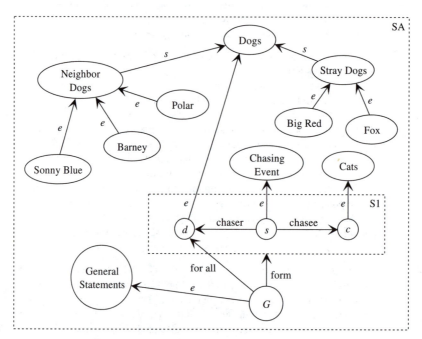

FIGURE 1.23.   The "invisibility" of the contents of spaces.

tence about objects and their relations. Thus, the nodes in the figure assert that the following:

> There are dogs.
> There are fleas.
> There are scratching events.
> Every dog, *d,* has participated in a scratching event, *s,* in which it was the scratcher and some flea, *f,* was the scratchee.

In the same network, there are some metalevel statements, the details of which we will be a bit vague about.

> *G* is a general statement.
> It has a form (the space S1) and a universally quantified variable within that form (*d*).

Use this same graph and boundary notation to express the statement: "Every dog has visited every fire hydrant." Assume that both quantifications are part of the same general statement.

(b) In Hendrix's scheme, partitions determine what nodes are *visible* to a routine search. We do not detail Hendrix's particular approach here. In this exercise, we assume that if a space is contained in another space, the contained space can "see" everything in the containing space, but the contents of the contained space are invisible to the containing space. We assume further that the spaces are organized in a strict containment or subset hierarchy.

For example, in Figure 1.23, a search for instances of **dog** would find Polar and Barney and Sonny Blue, but not *d.* What other mechanisms discussed in this section could serve to distinguish variables from constants?

FIGURE 1.24. Semantic network representing "Sylvester left the room."

(c) Two philosophers, Dr. A and Dr. B, have gotten together to discuss partitioned networks as presented in this exercise. After several minutes of deep thought, Dr. A exclaimed, "Eureka! Partitioned nets are not so strange. The partitions function just like parentheses in predicate calculus notation." Dr. B thought about this, and countered, "No. They are just notations for grouping network elements into sets. They could be used for other purposes, too."

What feature of partitions enables them them to do more than delimit sets?

(d) Explain how partitions are more flexible for representing sets than parentheses in a linear notation, assuming the usual rules for well-formed expressions?

Ex. 8   [*!-20*] *Modeling Beliefs of Multiple Agents.* Sometimes it is useful for representation languages to indicate when to "escape" to alternative interpretations. We consider this starting with an example, drawn from the cartoons. Tweety is a bird, Sylvester is a cat, and they play tricks on each other.

(a) Consider the sentence:

"Sylvester left the room."

Using the notation from this section, we could represent this in a semantic network as in Figure 1.24.

Consider now the revised sentences:

"Sylvester was hiding in the room."
"He knew that Tweety believed he had left the room."

What is at issue in semantics if we use the same representation as before to indicate what Tweety believed?

(b) Professor Digit says he can always distinguish beliefs by inventing new relations. For example, to represent the example from part (a) he proposes relations like knows, believes, and believes-that-another-agent-believes. Why is this approach problematic?

(c) Propose an approach that would distinguish what Tweety believes from what Sylvester believes. Describe some of the requirements for interpreting symbols in your approach. Will your approach extend to cover the situation where there is deliberate deception because Tweety really saw Sylvester hiding and acted as if he did not see him in order to fool him. (Hint: See preceding exercise.)

Ex. 9   [*10*] *Kinds of Semantics.* The following cases refer to the kinds of semantics described in this section.

(a) What is the difference in concerns between a naive reference semantics and an intensional semantics? Why might a social scientist find a reference semantics naive?

(b) Programming formalists who want guarantees of the correctness of systems advocate the decoration of programs with annotations describing expectations and invariants. What approach to semantics would they use?

(c) What kind of semantics is called the "literal meaning" of natural-language sentences?

Alternative #1—Chinese Restaurant

Pro Arguments
Chinese food is healthy.
A variety of food is available.

Con Arguments
Chinese lunch is expensive.

Alternative #2—Hotdog Stand

Pro Arguments
Hotdogs are prepared quickly.
Hotdogs are inexpensive.

Con Arguments
Hotdogs contain a lot of fat.
No place to sit down.

Alternative #3—Ice Cream Parlor

Pro Arguments
Ice cream is available quickly.

Con Arguments
Ice cream, by itself, is not satisfying.
Ice cream, by itself, is not healthy.

FIGURE 1.25.   Some arguments for lunch alternatives.

(d) What kind of semantics is most relevant to computer-aided software engineering (CASE) tools, that is, tools for coordinating the programming activities of a programming team?

(e) What kind of semantics is relevant for describing a reasoning process based on assumptions and defaults with different probabilities ?

Ex. 10   [*CD-!-30*] *Argumentation versus Proof.* It is often observed that arguments are not always won by "logic." This exercise considers ways that argumentation may be characterized in a way that is meaningful and computational, but which requires elements beyond those of the usual semantics of logic.

In this exercise, we consider three people who are discussing where to have lunch. We will call the lunchers A, B, and C. They have identified three possible restaurants: a Chinese restaurant, a hot dog stand, and an ice cream parlor.

(a) The three lunchers agree to write out arguments for and against the different alternatives. They come up with a chart like that in Figure 1.25.

One of the three lunchers, who is studying logic, observed that the process they were going through was quite different from the process of proving a theorem. It was not much like writing down a theorem "Chinese food is the best lunch" and then trying to prove it. Do you agree? If yes, explain the essential ways in which the process differs from proof.

(b) Once the arguments were written down, the lunchers then decided that some of the arguments depended on various assumptions. They wrote down a list of dependencies including those shown in parentheses in Figure 1.26.

Alternative #1—Chinese Restaurant	*Assumptions*
Pro Arguments Chinese food is healthy.	(Depends on assumption that the vegetables are fresh and not overcooked.)
A variety of food is available.	
Con Arguments Chinese lunch is expensive.	(Depends on assumption that they order separately. It is cheaper if they share a couple of main dishes.)
Alternative #2—Hotdog Stand	
Pro Arguments Hotdogs are prepared quickly.	(Depends on the assumption that they get there before the usual large lunch crowd.)
Hotdogs are inexpensive.	(Depends on whether the low-cost vendor is there today.)
Con Arguments Hotdogs contain a lot of fat. No place to sit down.	(Depends on the assumption that they are unwilling to sit at the fountain on the patio.)
Alternative #3—Ice Cream Parlor	
Pro Arguments Ice cream is available quickly.	(Depends on the assumption that they get there before the large lunch crowd.)
Con Arguments Ice cream, by itself, is not healthy.	

FIGURE 1.26.   Some arguments for lunch alternatives, showing supporting assumptions.

Reflecting on this process, one of the lunchers noted that the process was taking on some of the elements of deduction. Do you agree? Explain briefly.

(c) As the lunchers pondered the assumptions, they noticed that they didn't believe all of them.

Luncher A believes all of the assumptions except three. He does not believe that the low cost hot dog vendor will be there today. He does not believe that sharing main dishes in the Chinese restaurant will reduce costs. He also does not believe that they can get to the ice cream parlor before the lunch crowd does.

Lunchers B and C also have different beliefs in the truth of the assumptions.

At this point, one of the lunchers notices that their process has a kind of "truth theory," but that it is different from that of logic because it admits assumptions. Briefly, explain the significance of this difference.

(d) After the different beliefs in the assumptions were tallied, the lunchers noticed that there was still more they wanted to discuss before drawing a conclusion. For example, luncher A noticed that he believed the pro argument "Chinese food is healthy" and also the con argument "Chinese lunch is expensive." However, he cared about the former argument more than the latter because the amount of money he spends on lunch has never been significant to him. Similarly, the other lunchers evaluate the arguments in their own ways.

How does this part of their decision process require concepts beyond the declarative semantics of logic? Explain briefly.

Note: This exercise is based on the idea of an **argumentation spreadsheet**, as described in Stefik et al, 1987, which was part of the Colab project at Xerox Palo Alto Research Center (PARC).

Ex. 11 [!-L-*15*] *Graphs and Logic as Representations.* In many graph representations, an account of the meaning includes an account of processing by the physical symbol system. For example, a process might specify how information associated with one node can be propagated to other nodes to which it is linked in particular ways.

(a) Create a graph representation (semantic network) for the following three sentences. Referring to the elements of your graph representation, describe how you would infer that "Bill can fly":

> All birds can fly.
> A pelican is a kind of bird.
> Bill is a pelican.

(b) Instead of using the semantic network representation, translate these statements into formulas of the predicate calculus. Give a short proof that "Bill can fly." Indicate the rules of inference that (such as modus ponens and universal instantiation) you use in the proof steps.

■ **Ex. 12** [CD-*05*] *The Changeable Mind of the Observer.* Professor Digit is disturbed by the idea that the meaning of symbols is in the mind of an observer.

For example, suppose in a medical domain about infectious diseases that some of the microorganisms responsible for the disease "sniffleitus" develop a resistance to a particular antiobiotic treatment. In that case, doctors and other medical practitioners would extend the symbol sniffleitus to include the new dominant variant of the disease and would also prescribe a different treatment for it.

Professor Digit is concerned about the philosophical consequences of this, especially in the case that the knowledge system itself is not modified. He asks: "When people change their use of some symbols used in a knowledge system, does that change what the program means?"

(a) Briefly, show how the answer to the professor's question depends on our choice of semantics. Compare the answers for reference and denotational semantics.

(b) Suppose that the knowledge engineer now updates the program so that it prescribes a different treatment for sniffleitus, respecting its acquired resistance. Again, does this change the meaning of the program for denotational and reference semantics?

(This exercise was inspired by an example from William Clancey.)

1.3 *Modeling: Dimensions of Representation*

Like many computer programs, a knowledge system is a computational model of something, where the "something" is the domain or the situation. For example, a knowledge system for diagnosis and repair of radios would typically include a model of the physical parts of a radio, a model of the functions of the parts and of their electrical operation, a model of how the components can fail, a model of the diagnosis task, and a model for the repair task. For each model, representations are required and the representations must satisfy particular properties in order to be adequate.

The design of representations is a central concern in building computational models, involving many considerations and sometimes several changes until appropriate designs are found. In talking about the suitability of representations, we are concerned not only with the properties of the symbols themselves, but rather with their properties as *representations*. In the previous section, we discussed representational properties involving reference semantics, truth semantics, and proof semantics. These properties are concerned mainly with identity and inference.

In this section we broaden our discussion of representational properties, including many that bear on the computational use of representations. We discuss fidelity and precision, abstractions and implementations, primitive and derived propositions, explicit and implicit representations, canonical forms, use of multiple representations, space, time and structural complexity, and the broad implications of parallel processing for efficient manipulation of symbol structures. These dimensions arise in the design of all kinds of computational models.

The concepts introduced in this section are typical of an engineering approach to system design. For example, we ask about the adequacy of representations for making particular distinctions. We ask about the efficiency of particular operations on symbol structures. We ask how that efficiency differs according to different assumptions about the nature of the computational processing elements.

If you have had programming experience, many of the representational properties discussed in this section will be familiar. A programmer must design representations, making sure sure that they cover the cases of interest, that all of the important distinctions can be represented, and that computations run in reasonable time and space. These practical concerns are inherent in building knowledge systems and are encountered by everyone who builds computational models.

1.3.1 *Fidelity and Precision*

Fidelity refers to the correctness of statements or predictions about the world. When applied to representations, it refers to the correctness of the meaning that we ascribe to them. Another term for fidelity is accuracy. **Precision** refers to the degree of detail in predictions about the world. Similarly, the precision of representations refers to the degree of detail in the meanings that we ascribe to them. For example, a computation that is given to ten decimal digits is more precise than one that is given only to six digits. In a circuit diagnosis system, a representation that predicts that voltage will rise to "eight volts plus or minus one" is more precise than one that simply predicts that voltage will rise.

Representations can have fidelity with little precision or have great precision without fidelity. For example, the statement "The sun will rise tomorrow morning and set in the evening" has fidelity, but little precision. It does not give the precise time of the sunrise or say anything about its path across the sky. In contrast, the statement that there are 1,456,853,123 molecules of air in a tiny bottle in my study has great precision but is not accurate.

Different tasks have different requirements for accuracy and precision. Consider in Figure 1.27 two representations of a chemical structure for different tasks. The first representation presents molecules as topological structures, characterized by nodes (atoms) and arcs (bonds) be-

Topological representation:

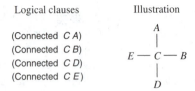

Three-dimensional representation:

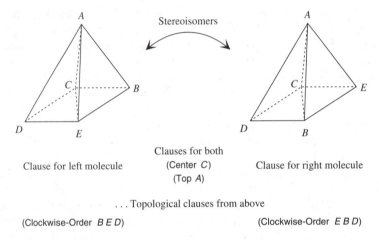

FIGURE 1.27. Stereoisomers are mirror-image molecules. They have the same atoms and the same corresponding chemical bonds, but they are distinguished by their shape.

tween them. A topological representation describes which atoms are connected. It is adequate for determining the chemical composition of a molecule in terms of its individual atoms.

However, a representation of a molecule limited to topology is inadequate for reasoning about molecular interactions. Molecules can have the same topological properties and yet differ in their three-dimensional structures. For example, organic enzymes must fit against other molecules and their interactions depend on the particulars of their three-dimensional structures. When two molecules are mirror images of each other, they are called **stereoisomers**. Stereoisomers have the same topology but act differently in some chemical reactions.

Precision and fidelity are not usually independent considerations. Representations that are correct but imprecise often lead ultimately to incorrect predictions. Continuous systems are ones in which a small change in the initial conditions leads to a small change in the final conditions. In continuous systems, small compromises in precision typically cause few problems in fidelity, if the results are not extrapolated too far. Chaotic systems, however, are ones in which arbitrarily small changes in the initial conditions can lead to large changes in the results. Even with great computational precision, there is little confidence in the fidelity of predictions for such systems.

Fidelity and precision reflect a tension between our representational goals and limitations when we use computational models. There are usually trade-offs in representations involving efficiency, fidelity and precision. Typically, an increase in precision requires a decrease in efficiency.

Practical knowledge systems employ multiple representations with different trade-offs in precision. In a diagnostic reasoning system, representations with low precision may be adequate for making coarse predictions about circuit behavior. For the purpose of isolating and identifying a faulty component, this may be enough to rule out major blocks of the circuit. More precise representations may then be called on to make a more detailed analysis on selected parts of the circuit. For this reason, the design of a computational model sometimes involves a suite of complementary representations with degrees of precision suitable for different purposes.

1.3.2 *Abstractions and Implementations*

Abstractions are high-level descriptions that say what a representation must do but not precisely how it must do it. Abstractions are essential in large programming projects. Abstractions are sometimes explicit as the "exported interface" of a program. When one subprogram refers to another and depends only on its exported interface, then implementations of the called program can be changed without changing the calling program. This facilitates the use of alternative implementations. **Implementations** are specific data structures and associated methods for storing information and carrying out operations relative to a given computational interpreter.

Unfortunately, the word *abstract* is misleading. All representations are abstract in that they leave out some features. In the terms of the previous section, all practical representations lack something in their precision, so they are necessarily "abstract."

The terms *abstraction* and *implementation* are better understood as describing relations between representations. When the relation between two representations is akin to the relation between high-level specifications and low-level and detailed descriptions, then we call the former abstractions and the latter implementations. This distinction is common in programming methodology and software engineering. Figure 1.28 suggests how an object-oriented language could specify abstractions in terms of "message protocols" that an implementation must include. In this context, an implementation is a description of how it carries out the required protocol. In idealized programming practice, we first build specify abstract models and then develop implementations. Typically, however, these processes are intertwined.

We define abstractions in terms of a set of features with meaning, a set of operations that change the features or return information about them, and a set of invariants on the features that must be preserved by the operations. This style follows object-oriented approaches to programming. For example, we could define an abstract representation of a figure as an entity with a shape, an origin and dimensions, certain computable properties such as area that are related to its dimensions, and operations for changing its dimensions, moving it about, and determining whether it covers arbitrary points in the plane. In this example, there are several invariants. The dimensions and shape of a figure do not change when it is moved. However the origin of a figure is not an invariant; it changes when the figure is moved. A complete characterization of the abstractions should characterize the required precision of the representation as well.

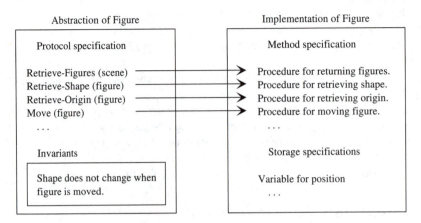

FIGURE 1.28.   Abstractions and implementations.

To make the abstraction/implementation distinction concrete we define an abstraction for figures and then compare three implementations of it. Our abstraction of "figure" requires the following specific operations:

- Get-Shape (figure): Retrieve a description of the shape of the figure, one of square, circle, triangle, and spiral.
- Get-Origin (figure): Retrieve the origin of the figure.
- Get-Area (figure): Retrieve the area of the figure.
- Move (figure): Move the figure to a new location.
- Overlap (figure 1, figure 2): Determine whether two figures overlap.
- Get-Overlapping-Figures (figure-set): Find all of the figures in a set that overlap a given figure.

We now consider three alternative data structures for representing a scene with figures. We think of these data structures as alternative implementations. We illustrate these data structures with example representations of a square.

A Binary Array Representation for Figures

Figure 1.29 shows a two-dimensional binary array (bitmap) representation of the square. Each position in the bitmap corresponds to a square picture element or pixel in the scene. A 0 in the bitmap indicates that the position is unoccupied, and a 1 indicates the presence of some object at the position. Movement of an object is represented by appropriately shifting the bits representing the object to new positions in the bitmap.

Figure 1.30 shows how a stack of such bitmaps can represent a scene containing several two-dimensional objects. Each object is represented by a separate bitmap and the composite scene is visualized by sighting through the stack of bitmaps, performing a logical OR of the bits corresponding to the same location on the plane.

```
0 0 0 0 0 0 0 0 0 0 0 0
0 0 0 0 0 0 0 0 0 0 0 0
0 0 0 0 0 0 0 0 0 0 0 0
0 0 0 0 1 1 1 1 0 0 0 0
0 0 0 0 1 0 0 1 0 0 0 0
0 0 0 0 1 0 0 1 0 0 0 0
0 0 0 0 1 1 1 1 0 0 0 0
0 0 0 0 0 0 0 0 0 0 0 0
0 0 0 0 0 0 0 0 0 0 0 0
0 0 0 0 0 0 0 0 0 0 0 0
```

FIGURE 1.29. A two-dimensional binary array representation of a square.

Figure 1.31 summarizes how the operations of the figure abstraction could be carried out in this implementation.

This representation has inherent limitations in precision. Consider the program that implements the shape recognizer. For large enough figures it is clear that the imprint on the bitmap will be different for squares, circles, triangles, and spirals. However, for cases where the size of the image is close to the size of a pixel, the images can be indistinguishable. For example, a 2-pixel-by-2-pixel square and a circle with a radius of 1 pixel have the same rendering. Similarly, in deciding whether two figures overlap, protocol must report that they do if they are within one pixel of each other. In a real task, we need to be specific in describing the required precision for the protocols in order to determine whether the bitmap implementation would be adequate.

A Property List Representation for Figures

Figure 1.32 proposes another representation of a square in terms of a coordinate table with property lists. This representation indexes figures through a table according to the coordinates of their origins. For each figure, there is a property list of features indexed through the table. For example, in a square, the value of the shape property would be "square." Also for a square, the value

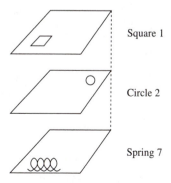

Square 1

Circle 2

Spring 7

FIGURE 1.30. A stack of bitmaps. The composite scene would be obtained by sighting through the stack.

- Get-Shape: A recognition program analyzes a bit image in a plane to infer a shape and its parameters.
- Get-Origin: A computation is performed on the image. For example, to find the origin of a square the location of the leftmost and bottom-most corner must be determined.
- Get-Area: A computation must be performed on the shape parameters returned by Get-Shape: For a square, the length of a side is multiplied by itself.
- Move: The property list is shifted to a new cell in the array.
- Overlap: A computation must be performed on the two shape descriptions.
- Get-Overlapping-Figures: A search is made through the list of planes, iteratively invoking the Overlap method.

FIGURE 1.31.   Implementing the operations for the bit image implementation of a figure.

of the side-length property would be a number indicating the length of the square's side. The origin of the square is determined by the indices of its description in the array. Thus, the lower left corner of the square is located in the scene at position (4, 3) and is indexed in the array through the cell at position (4, 3). If two figures have the same origin, then the coincident cell contains a list of pointers to the figure descriptions.

Figure 1.33 describes one way that the figure operations could be implemented. The operation of Get-Shape is simpler than in the pixel representation since it is only necessary to retrieve the value of the shape property. In contrast, the Overlap operation is made more difficult. Different computational approaches are possible. One approach, equivalent in precision to the bitmap approach, is to project the figure onto a temporary bitmap and then check whether any of the corresponding pixels are both on. An alternative approach is to solve the intersection problem analytically. To determine whether a square intersects a circle, we would need to compute the inter-

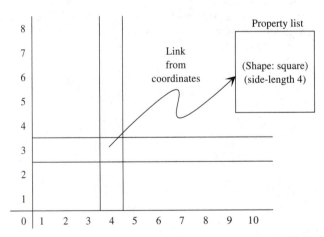

FIGURE 1.32.   A feature-oriented representation of a square in a table. The property list description of the square is located at index (4, 3) in the table.

- Get-Shape: Retrieve a token naming the shape from the property list.
- Get-Origin: Return the indices in the array to the property list.
- Get-Area: Perform a computation on the shape parameters. For a square, the length of a side is squared.
- Move: Shift the property list to a new cell in the array.
- Overlap: Perform a computation on the shape. This may be done by intersecting the boundaries of the two figures or by computing a projection for each figure onto a plane and then intersecting those projections.
- Get-Overlapping-Figures: Search through the list of planes for those that overlap the given figure.

FIGURE 1.33. Implementing the operations for the property list implementation of a figure.

section of a circle and a line. If all of the figures are rectangles or polygons, the latter approach can be quite efficient.

A Graph Representation for Figures

Our third candidate representation for figures is a graph representation as in Figure 1.34. This data structure has a unique node called the head node that represents the figure as a whole. In Figure 1.34, the head node has an is-a link to the class Square. The head node has part links to designate relations to each of the four lines that make up the sides, and other nodes representing such information as the position. Moving the square in this representation amounts to changing the position nodes to link to different coordinates. A set of figures is represented as a list of such graph representations.

  Figure 1.35 summarizes how the different operations of the figure abstraction could be carried out on the graph representation. As in the case of the property list representation, the shape of the figure is determined by a retrieval operation except that instead of returning the value of a property the procedure must follow an is-a link and return the name of a class. Retrieving the origin of a square requires traversing through the nodes representing the parts of the square to

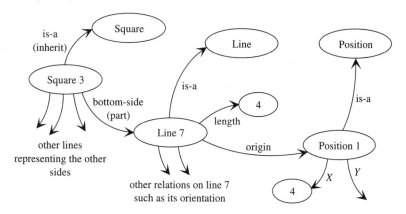

FIGURE 1.34. A graph representation of a square.

- Get-Shape: Starting at the head node, follow the is-a link to its class and return the name of that class.
- Get-Origin: Starting at the head node, follow the bottom-side link to a line, the origin link to a position, and then return the values of the *x* and *y* relations on that position.
- Get-Area: Perform a computation on the shape parameters. For a square, the length of a side is squared.
- Move: Shift the property list to a new cell in the array. All of the positions of all of the lines in the figure are updated to reflect new coordinates
- Overlap: The computation is analogous to the case of the property-list representation.
- Get-Overlapping-Figures: Search through the list of figures to find those that overlap.

FIGURE 1.35.   Implementing the operations for a graph representation of a figure.

obtain the origin of the bottom side. The computation of overlap is analogous to the property list case.

Comparing Representations for Figures

The bitmap, property list, and graph all support the same abstraction. We can compare their performance for carrying out the prescribed operations. For example, consider the retrieval of the origin of a square in a scene. In the property-list table, retrieval of the origin requires that the processor be able to determine the indices of the entry in the table containing the square's description. To retrieve the square's origin in the graph representation, the processor must traverse the graph to retrieve the coordinates of the line representing the bottom side of the square. In the bitmap representation, retrieving the origin (at least for a "Manhattan square") involves stepping through the bitmap to locate the lowest and leftmost bit that is 1 and then returning the indices of that bit. Thus, to present the same abstraction, the three implementations must employ radically different processes with different amounts of time and space for the operation. Table 1.4 crudely compares the speeds of the operations on the three representations.

As shown in Table 1.4 there are trade-offs in the choice of implementations. One implementation is better for some operations, and another is better for others. If the objects are rectangles aligned with the coordinate axes, the computation for determining overlap requires only a few arithmetic operations given the positions and sizes of the rectangles. In the absence of special hardware, using bitmaps to decide whether such rectangles overlap would be fast enough for small figures but inefficient for large ones. If, however, the shapes of objects are irregular and nonrectangular and the bitmap logical ANDing operation was limited to tight regions containing

TABLE 1.4.   Partial table of trade-offs for the three alternative implementations of a square.

Implementation	*Return Origin*	*Compute Overlap*	*Name Shape*
Pixel arrays	Slow	Fast for small figures	Slow
Property-list table	Fast	Depends on shapes	Fast
List graph representations	Medium	Depends on shapes	Fast

the objects, the bitmap representation could be made simple and efficient for determining the area of overlap. If we want to find the set of figures in a scene that overlap a given figure, then searching through the lists and tables and computing intersections can be a nontrivial computation for both the graph and feature representations.

1.3.3 *Primitive and Derived Propositions*

Reviewing the comparison of representations of figures, it is striking that, for each kind of query we considered, the favored data structure was one in which the required information was directly accessible.

Hector Levesque calls such representations **vivid** (Levesque, 1986). Others have called these analogical and direct. Vivid representations have the following characteristics:

- For every kind of object of interest in the world, there is a type of symbol.
- For every simple relationship of interest in the world, there is a type of connection among the symbols.
- There is a one-to-one correspondence between the symbols and the objects that they designate in the world.
- There is a one-to-one correspondence between the connections and the relations that they designate in the world. That is, the relation holds among the objects in the world if and only if the connection exists among the symbols in the knowledge base.

In considering vividness, we should not treat the notion of a "connection" among symbols too narrowly. Pointers in data structures are the simplest case of connections, but, as Levesque suggests, the notion can be extended to mean that two symbols are connected if they jointly satisfy some predicate that can be computed in bounded time. The tighter that the bounds are on computation, the better.

The terms *vivid, analogical,* and *direct* draw on a perceived similarity of the structure of a representation to the structure of the things designated.

An example of a vivid representation is given in Figure 1.36, which shows a line drawing of a chemical structure; Figure 1.37 shows a graph that could be used to represent the same structure. The similarity of both representations is apparent: There is a node for each atom of the molecule and a link for each chemical bond. The graph in Figure 1.37 shows a pair of links for each chemical bond, leading from each participating atom to the other.

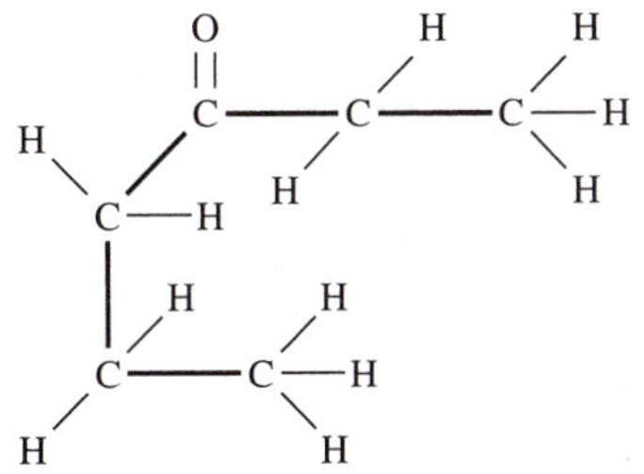

FIGURE 1.36. Line drawing of a chemical molecule.

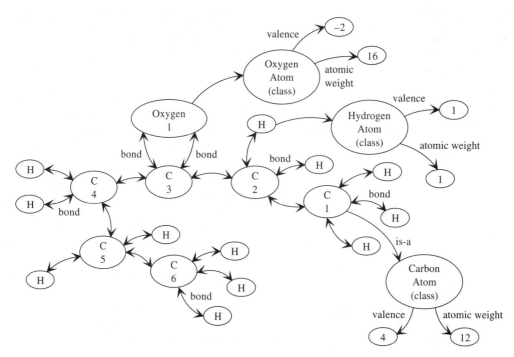

FIGURE 1.37. Semantic network and analogical representation of a molecule.

Analogical representations are like scale models. An often cited example of a direct representation is the representation of spatial relations in a room by maps. A map is called direct because of the similarity between the two-dimensional plane of the paper and the two-dimensional plane of the floor of the room. The paper is a direct homomorph of the room. Map and room have the same sort of structure (two-dimensional Euclidean space) and thereby admit the same sorts of operations such as sliding, rotation, and measurement. Naturally, the map is simpler than the actual room, in that various properties and relations such as texture, color, or a third dimension are missing from the map.

From another perspective, however, these concepts add nothing to the concepts of abstractions and implementations from the previous section. The "real world" does not present itself to us in terms of specific categories, objects, and relations. These concepts are all invented by us and we use them to describe what we perceive. To say that the line drawing of the chemical model is vivid is to say that it shares particular desired properties with the abstraction we want to use. The concepts of atoms and bonds are invented by people. In this regard, the notion of vividness is rather naive. Since designation depends on an observer, the directness of the representation depends on the distinctions already made by the observer. Thus, the world does not present itself to us in terms of objects and relations. Those are properties of how we think about the world, rather than intrinsic properties of the world itself. Thus vividness has to do with the correspondence of a representation with a favored model of the world, rather than a correspondence with the world itself.

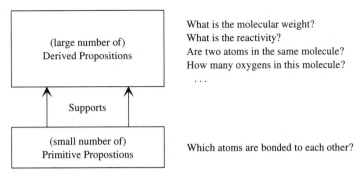

FIGURE 1.38. A small number of primitive propositions can support a much larger number of derived ones.

This argument brings us to a different way of understanding and appreciating what is important about vivid representations. Much of the appeal of a vivid representation arises from the astute selection of primitive and derived propositions. **Primitive propositions** are those modeled directly in the representation. **Derived propositions** are other propositions about the objects that can be determined by a computation based on the primitive ones.

The primitive propositions in Figures 1.36 and 1.37 are the representations of atoms and bonds. An example of a derived property is the connectedness of atoms in molecules. To determine whether carbon 1 is in the same molecule as carbon 6, one can simply follow the bond links starting from carbon 1, searching for a path to carbon 6. If no path can be found, the atoms are in separate molecules. Another derived property is the molecular weight, which can be computed by summing the atomic weights of all the connected atoms in a molecule.

Figure 1.38 illustrates a common strategy in the design of knowledge systems that exploits this distinction between primitive and derived propositions. A large number of propositions can be derived from a small number of primitive ones. Derived propositions are computed on demand. In our representation of a chemical molecule, we had explicit representations indicating which atoms are bonded to their neighbors. These bonds were the basis for other computations on the graph, such as computing the molecular weight, computing the number of instances of any particular kind of atom in a molecule, computing the distance of separation of atoms of a particular type in a molecule, and so on.

The disciplined separation of intrinsic and derived properties can simplify the process of verifying that **invariants** are satisfied. To verify invariants in a design that segregates primitive and derived operations, it is enough to check the effects of operations on the primitive propositions. For example, assuming that interactions with air or other environment sources of atoms are properly accounted for, the making and breaking of chemical bonds in organic chemistry does not change the weight of the compounds or the number of atoms present. In building a computational model of chemical reactions, we might demand that our model preserve the same invariants.

To take an example, if the links representing chemical bonds between carbon 3 and carbon 4 are broken, no further changes to the underlying representation are needed to indicate consistently that carbon 1 is no longer part of the same molecule as carbon 6. No further changes are needed to prepare for the computation of the molecular weight of the molecule containing carbon 1. In effect, the "conservation of atoms" that chemists ascribe to the real world is captured faithfully by the "conservation of nodes" during the operations that make and delete links between nodes. For another example, if carbon 1 were bond linked to carbon 6 to form a ring molecule, and then the bond link between carbon 3 and carbon 4 was deleted, then with no further computational work the representation would correctly show that the molecule remains intact. In summary, the design of a vivid representation involves not only deciding which properties to make explicit, but also which properties to compute from a small set of primitive symbol structures, manipulated by the operations of frequent interest.

1.3.4 Explicit and Implict Representations

Advocates of early representation languages developed in AI often characterized them as having explicit representations. But what is the difference between an explicit representation and an implicit one and what are the advantages of explicit ones? In this section we define what it means for a representation to be explict and compare some example representations along this dimension.

What It Means for a Representation to be Explicit

A representation is **explicit** or **declarative** to the extent that it has the following properties:

- ■ *Modularity.* The representation is self-contained and autonomous. In other words, there is an identifiable and bounded set of symbol structures that make up the representation, they are distinct and separate from the interpreter programs that use them, and there is a well-defined and narrowly prescribed interface by which other parts of the system access the representations.
- ■ *Semantics.* The representation must have well-understood semantics. As usual, different kinds of semantics are appropriate for different situations. A denotational semantics or interface semantics is required to describe what behaviors correspond to different representations. If the interpreter draws inferences from the representation, the semantics include a reference semantics, a truth semantics, and a proof semantics. When the representation is used in reasoning with limited resources defeasible reasoning, then the semantics must include a reasoning control semantics.
- ■ *Causal Connection.* For the representation to have any effect on the system from which it is separated, there must be a causal connection such that changing the representation causes the system to change its behavior in a way that is appropriate for the change to the representation and its semantics. This causal connection provides the basis by which the representation governs reasoning and behavior of the system.

A representation is said to be **implicit** if it is not explicit.

Explicit representations are important in knowledge systems. Their value does not rest on performance characteristics of the representations, since explicit and implicit representations are the same with regard to performance. Their value rests on the practical leverage that they provide for parameterizing the control of complex knowledge systems.

The importance attributed to explicit representations in knowledge systems reflects the concern of the field to the processes of updating of knowledge bases and reuse of knowledge systems. The combination of modularity, causal connection, and semantic correspondence makes it easier to change explicit representations than implicit ones. The semantics are understood and the interface is narrowly prescribed. These representational properties provide part of the interface to a knowledge system as a computational model.

The success of explicit representations in facilitating reuse and change depends on the extent to which the system's designers correctly anticipate the nature and extent of the different situations in which the system must operate, and which can be provided for by declarations. In this way, the design of explicit representations amounts to a bet about the likely dimensions needed for use and for change.

Comparing the Explicitness of Representations

We now consider two pairs of examples of representations to compare and discuss whether they are explicit. Figure 1.39 shows two approaches for organizing representations of facts about chemical elements in a reasoning system. In both organizations, particular parts of the systems are concerned with reasoning about molecular weights, chemical reactions, and printing reports about chemical structures.

In the first approach, facts about the elements are scattered throughout the system. For example, statements about the weight and valence of the element carbon are located in separate parts of the program, perhaps several times. To add a new chemical element to the system or to change the facts about an existing one requires finding all of the places where it may be encoded.

In the second approach, a single table of chemical facts is stored separately from the reasoning methods. Whenever a fact about the elements is needed, the program invokes a database retrieval interface to retrieve the required information. To update the facts used by the system requires only updating the table.

Which of these approaches use explicit representations? First we consider the requirements for semantics and a causal connections, which the two approaches have in common. Both representations in Figure 1.39 have a semantics described by a characterization of atomic numbers, valence, and molecular weight. These amount to what chemists call a "ball-and-stick" model of molecules or roughly "labeled graphs." The operational semantics of the representation of chemical reactions or the computation of molecular weight are easily described in terms of primitives for making and breaking of bonds and appropriate graph operations and conservation laws. In summary, both representations satisfy the second and third requirements of being an explicit representation.

However, the first approach does not satisfy the modularity requirement. The database interface for the second approach has a quality of modularity that is lacking in the first. The representations of chemical facts in the first approach are scattered throughout the program that uses them. In contrast, the symbols making up the representation in the database are identifiable and separable from their interpreter. The database symbols are stored in a separate database, and are accessible from the program by a retrieval interface to the database. Thus, the database is declarative or explicit, but the first approach is not.

Figure 1.40 shows two approaches for defining the term *father* in a reasoning system. The first approach defines the term *father* using a set of predicate calculus statements. These state-

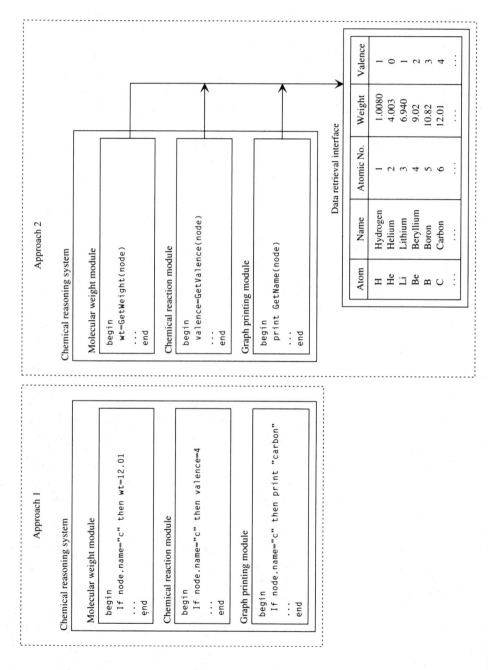

FIGURE 1.39. Two representations of facts about the elements in a chemical reasoning system.

Approach 1
    Parent(x) => Person(x)
    Child(x) => Perrson(x)
    Parent(x) => HasChild(x)
    Parent(x) => NumChildren(x)$\geq$ 1
    Father(x) => Parent(x) $\wedge$ Male(x)

Approach 2
Parent
    Superclasses: Person
    Children: [Value: a Person]
    Cardinality: Minimum 1

Father
    Superclasses: Parent, Male

FIGURE 1.40.   Two representations for defining the term *father* in a reasoning system.

ments enable a reasoning system to answer questions about fathers, noting that fathers have the properties of people, parents, and males and that they have at least one child. In the first approach, the relevant statements can be part of a large base of facts. The second approach in Figure 1.40 draws on concepts from object-oriented and frame-representation languages. A parent is defined as a person who has at least one child. The term *father* inherits the properties from male and parent.

We now consider the explicitness of the two approaches for defining *father*. Again, both approaches have semantics and both approaches have a causal connection. What is at issue is whether either or both representations satisfy the requirement of modularity.

It is sometimes argued that any representation in predicate calculus is explicit because the sentences in a logic language are identifiably separated from their interpreter. However, sentences about growing pumpkins can be mixed up with ones about conducting international affairs. There is nothing in the representation that makes evident the extent of interactions, especially if one assumes a complete theorem prover. Thus, without boundaries in the representation, there is only a limited sense of modularity.

In contrast, the frame representation is designed so that all of the symbols that make up the definition of father are clustered together in a unit. The interpreter of a frame language is limited to making certain kinds of inferences involving inheritance, subsumption, mutual exclusion, and so on. In this way, the interface between different concepts is more narrowly prescribed, according to the rules of the particular frame language. Furthermore, the interaction with and through the interpreter are narrow because the operations of the interpreter in a frame language are fewer and more directed than those in a complete theorem prover.

In summary, explicit representations must be modular, must have well-defined semantics, and must have a causal connection between the representation and the behavior of the system. Explicit representations are used in knowledge systems to provide convenient interfaces for controlling the behavior of the system. A design that makes some representations explicit makes assumptions about what aspects of the systems behavior need to be controlled and parameterized for ease of reuse.

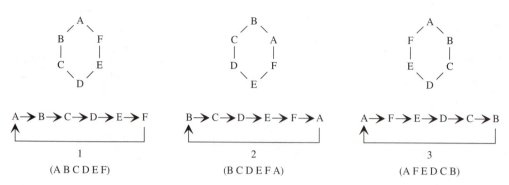

FIGURE 1.41. Three graph representations of a chemical molecule, equivalent under rotation and reflection.

1.3.5 *Representation and Canonical Form*   **ADVANCED**

The design of symbol structures with structure-building primitives often leads to questions about the equivalence of descriptions. Figure 1.41 shows three graphs representing chemical molecules. Each letter stands for a unique bivalent piece of the molecule, and the links indicate chemical bonds between the pieces. Below each drawing is a picture of a linked list, showing how the descriptions of the pieces might be arranged in a data structure. Thus, in the first molecule, the first element of the linked list is A, the second is B, and so on to F, corresponding to the last piece of the molecule, which is linked back to A.

The three graphs in Figure 1.41 are topologically equivalent; that is, they are made up of the same kinds of pieces connected in exactly the same ways. Graph 2 is like graph 1 except that it has been rotated, so that it starts with B rather than A at the top. Graph 3 is also like graph 1 except that it has been reflected: Reading graph 1 clockwise instead of counterclockwise would yield the linked list shown for graph 3. A computer program that could generate all six of the rotated versions of this data structure, as well as the corresponding six reflections, potentially would have to deal with 12 distinct graph representations for the same kind of molecule.

The graph in Figure 1.42 is made of the same pieces as the three we have considered. However, it designates a distinct class of molecule because it is topologically different. The positions of B and C have been exchanged in the graph. No combination of rotations and reflections will yield a data structure like those in Figure 1.41.

To simplify the testing of equivalence in such representations, it is convenient to define canonical forms and canonical functions. Canonical functions transform expressions into canonical or standard forms. For example, we define the canonical form for these graphs as the list structure that is earliest in an alphabetical order reading left to right.

Given a canonical function, there is a test for deciding whether two expressions are equivalent: Apply the canonical function and test whether the resulting canonical expressions are equal. Thus, a **canonical function** is a procedure c that transforms any expression e into a unique equivalent expression $c(e)$ such that, for any two expressions $e1$ and $e2$, $e1$ is equivalent to $e2$ if and only if $c(e1)$ is equal to $c(e2)$. The resulting expressions, $c(e1)$ and $c(e2)$, are called **canonical forms**. The canonical forms induce equivalence classes on the set of expressions. For each equivalence class, the canonical form is a distinguished representative of the class.

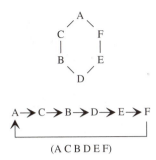

(A C B D E F)

FIGURE 1.42. A data structure representing a molecule that has the same pieces as that in Figure 1.41, but that is not equivalent.

In the circular molecular graphs example, rotation and reflection are equivalence-preserving transformations because they do not change the identity of the graph. Without a canonical function, testing for equivalence would require searching for a chain of equivalence-preserving transformations connecting two expressions. Given a canonical function, we need only compute the corresponding canonical forms and compare them for equality.

For circular lists like these, it is easy to define a canonical form. We need to determine a starting node and an orientation for traversing the graph. One approach is to pick the linear representation that would come earliest in an alphabetic ordering. Thus, the representation (A B C D E F) comes before (B C D E F G) and also before (A F E D C B). Because the linked list for graph 1 in Figure 1.41 is in canonical form, and is different from the linked list in Figure 1.42, which is also in canonical form, the two data structures must designate different kinds of molecules.

The basis of canonical forms comes partly from graph theory and partly from the domain model. Thus, the same issues that we considered in the representation of molecules arise in the representation of electrical circuits. Are two given circuits equivalent? Does a large circuit contain a subcircuit equivalent to a known one? For sufficiently rich domains, the simple assumptions of pattern-matching languages are inadequate for answering these questions.

In many cases, there is no general function for efficiently computing canonical forms. Chapter 2 shows that the issue of equivalence testing arises in the design of systems that systematically generate symbol structures as candidate solutions to a problem. Not paying attention to canonical forms in such systems can result in the unwanted generation of variant and redundant representations of the same solutions. What is important to remember is when our models are rich enough to represent things in more than one way, determining equivalence classes can be a crucial part of designing efficient approaches to reasoning.

1.3.6 *Using Multiple Representations*

All this attention of designing a suitable symbol structure and interpreter as a representation may have left the impression that a knowledge engineer must find a single best representation and stick with it. An important alternative to this is the use of multiple representations. Multiple representations make it possible to combine the advantages of different representational forms. In multiple representations, more than one symbol structure designates something in the environment.

```
Molecule:      A03
Molecular-     Wt: 58 [cached]
Structure:     <pointer to semantic network representation of the molecular
               graph>
```

FIGURE 1.43. Caching molecular weight using multiple representations.

Suppose we had a knowledge system that reasoned about interactions between molecules. Suppose it occasionally reasoned about breaking bonds, but very frequently needed to access the molecular weight. You will recall that in our example of a graphical representation of a molecule, molecular weight was computed by traversing the graph that represents the molecule and summing the individual atomic weights. If molecular weight was used for many inferences, it would be expensive to traverse the graph and recompute it everytime it was needed.

An obvious alternative is to cache the computed molecular weight as part of the representation of the molecule as in Figure 1.43. The cached molecular weight is redundant to the molecular weight computed by traversing the molecular structure.

Whenever multiple representations are used, measures must be taken to keep them synchronized. In this case, whenever any operation is performed that changes the graph representing a molecule, the cached molecular weight could become invalid. This issue is inherent in the use of multiple representations and is called the **stale data problem**. To preclude the accidental use of stale data in a computation, we need to extend our concern with the operations and invariants of abstractions to include multiple representations rather than just primitive propositions. As in the example of caching molecular weight, cached values need to be invalidated whenever the assumptions behind their caching become invalid. Specifically, the cached molecular weight should be invalidated whenever operations make or break chemical bonds.

It is worthwhile to approach the stale data problem in two parts. To preclude inferences using invalid derived data, it is enough to mark the cached and derived representations as invalid whenever the underlying primitive representations are changed. This is known as invalidating the cache. Typically, an additional bit or a special value associated with the cache is used to indicate when the cache is valid. A separate question is when to recompute the derived value. If the primitive values could change several times before the derived value is requested, it is wasteful to recompute the cache every time that the primitive data change. A more efficient alternative is to recompute the derived value only on demand, that is, when the value is requested and the cache is not valid.

For another example of the use of multiple representations, we return to the three implementations of the figure abstraction that we considered earlier. Suppose that a typical scene contained tens of thousands of figures and that a common operation was to find all of the figures in a given region that overlap with a given figure.

Each of the proposed implementations is potentially expensive for this operation. In the pixel representation, we need to compare (or AND) the planes of pixels for every figure. This operation is proportional to nd^2 where where n is the number of figures and d^2 is the number of pixels per plane. For the property-list representation, the table indicates the origins of the figures but not their sizes. Because figures can have arbitrary sizes, figures whose origins are arbitrarily

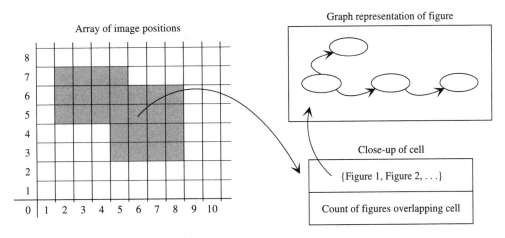

Array of image positions

Graph representation of figure

Close-up of cell

{Figure 1, Figure 2, . . .}

Count of figures overlapping cell

FIGURE 1.44. Combining representations.

distant could still overlap. Thus, information about origins does not let us weed out figures that potentially overlap and we need to compute the overlap of the figure of interest with every possible figure. For the graph representation, the computation is similar.

Figure 1.44 shows an approach to making this computation more efficient by combining multiple representations. In this example, each figure is represented in detail by a graph representation. From this graph representation, the coverage on the plane is then projected back onto a coarse map. We call this projection the figure's "shadow." Each cell in this coarse map has a count of the number of figures that cover that cell, wholly or partially, and a list of pointers to those figures.

The advantage of this representation is the way that it provides a coarse but inexpensive filter that makes it unnecessary to perform detailed overlap computations for most figures. To find the figures that overlap a given figure we procede as follows. First we find the shadow for the figure of interest. Then we collect all of the figures which have common elements in the shadow. These are the figures that "potentially" overlap the given figure. This eliminates from detailed consideration all of those figures whose shadows do not overlap. When there are tens of thousands of figures and all but a few of them are eliminated, the savings can be considerable.

As always with multiple representations, we must consider how operations could invalidate the cached values. Thus, when a figure is moved, the projection is recomputed and the old counts in the coarse array of image positions are decremented under its shadow. If any cell has a count of zero, then it's accumulated shadow is zeroed out. Then the origin of the figure is updated and a new projection is computed, the shadow is ORed into the coarse array, and the cell data are updated.

The coarser the shadow array, the less expensive it is to maintain. At any resolution, the shadow overlap is accurate in that it never misses a potential overlapped figure. Precision depends on the coarseness of the map. Lack of precision shows up as a false positive: Two figures may seem to overlap if they actually cover disjoint parts of a cell.

In summary, multiple representations create new options when there are unacceptable trade-offs among fidelity, precision, and efficiency. Whenever multiple representations are used, the concern with consistency and invariants must be extended to include not only primitive propositions but also multiple representations.

1.3.7 *Representation and Parallel Processing*   ADVANCED

In a conventional (von Neumann) computer architecture, one processor operates on symbol structures in a passive memory. As alternative computer architectures become available, we should consider the opportunities for parallel and distributed computation. The efficiency of operations on a representation depends both on the data structure and the capabilities of the computer.

Figure 1.45 shows an example of a parallel computer architecture: a simplified picture of a connection machine (Hillis, 1985). A connection machine links together thousands of extremely small processors and memories. The first generation of these machines contains up to 64,000 small processors. The sequence of operations carried out by the small processors is determined by the front-end processor, which broadcasts instructions to them. Figure 1.45 shows communication links from the cells to each of their four neighbors and to the front end processor. In the actual computer there is also a packet switching network that makes it possible to send information simultaneously between arbitrary pairs of processors.

A connection machine can perform discrete simulations of fluid flow, as shown in Figure 1.46. The hexagon-shaped cells correspond to small regions of space. Within a cell, particles move about according to specific interaction rules. For example, a particle in motion will continue to move in the direction it started unless it collides with another particle or with some obstacle in the space. In the figure, an obstacle in a cell is indicated by a solid rectangle and a moving particle is indicated by an arrow.

The wind in a wind tunnel does not blow over one square centimeter of an airplane model at a time. It blows across the whole model at once, showing the engineers how the flow in one

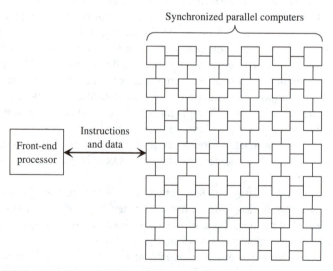

FIGURE 1.45.   Architecture of a connection machine.

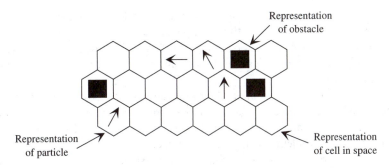

FIGURE 1.46.   Part of a simulation of fluid flow on a connection machine.

section interacts with the flow in another. If we simulate the wind in parallel, that is, simulating the flow of air particles through all of the space at once, the results can be computed more quickly. This approach has been called "data-level parallelism" (TMC, 1986).

With data-level parallelism, the simulation can be carried out by representing each cell with a processor in the connection machine. At each time step, every cell updates its state by checking all of its adjoining cells for particles that are heading in its direction. The cells then update their state according to the interaction rules. A connection machine is capable of modeling approximately 1 billion cell updates per second. These results are averaged to predict macroscopic effects accurately, providing a computational alternative to a wind tunnel.

This approach to simulating fluid flow would be almost unthinkable on a conventional computer. Data-level parallelism makes it practical by providing enough processor power to assign a computer to each region of space. The representation is analogous to a computational view of the universe in which small regions of space are seen as computational elements that communicate with their nearest neighbors. This point of view has some subtle advantages over steady-state modeling. For example, the analogical representation naturally and faithfully predicts the emergence of turbulence; that is, the unstable and chaotic swirls that develop as fluid flows across complex surfaces. This is an important aspect of reality that is not captured by the differential equation models typically used.

The main point of this example is that the efficiency of a representation depends both on the data structure and the capabilities of the computer. When we say that computers are "good with numbers," this is a result of the built-in hardware for efficiently performing arithmetic operations on binary representations of numbers. A connection machine is good for data-level parallelism because of the many built-in and interconnected processors supporting massive parallelism. As new computer architectures become widely available to knowledge engineers, the design of appropriate representations will need to encompass not only the selection of data structures, but also the selection of effective computer architectures.

1.3.8   *Space and Time Complexity*   ADVANCED

So far in this chapter we have referred rather loosely to symbol structures and their interpreters as being efficient or not. In this section we present notation and concepts for quantitatively characterizing the complexity of computations.

The amount of storage that an algorithm uses is called its **space complexity** and the amount of time that it uses is called its **time complexity**. In the broadest sense, the efficiency of an algorithm involves all the various computing resources needed for executing it. Time requirements are typically the dominant factor in determining whether or not a particular algorithm is efficient enough to be practical.

Time and space requirements of an algorithm can often be expressed in terms of a single variable, the "size" of the problem instance. For example, the size may be "the number of elements to be sorted" or "the number of cities to be visited." This is convenient because we expect the relative difficulty of problems to vary with their size.

For idealized computations, we assume that accessing any storage element in memory requires unit time, meaning that each access takes the same amount of time. Similarly, in computing time complexity, it is common to count the number of times that the steps are performed, where each step must be executable in constant time. In computing space complexity, it is customary only to account only for space actually accessed by the algorithm. There is no charge for memory that is not referenced during execution. If the algorithm requires that a large data structure be initialized, then we have to be clear about whether we are counting the initialization time and usually we should. Thus, the time complexity of an algorithm is always greater than or equal to its space complexity, since every an instruction can either reuse an element of memory or allocate a new one.

Asymptotic Complexity

In the theory of algorithms, the "big-oh" notation is used to indicate asymptotic measures of complexity. The notation $O(f(n))$ refers to a numeric quantity that is within a constant factor of $f(n)$ where f is a function of the integer n, which is some parameter of the method being analyzed. More precisely, we say that

$$x_n = O(f(n)) \tag{1}$$

when there is a positive constant C such that

$$|x_n| < C \, |f(n)| \tag{2}$$

for all n greater than some initial integer, n_0. For example, if the time complexity of some algorithm is precisely

$$6n^2 + 43n + 16 \tag{3}$$

we could say simply that it was $O(n^2)$ since, for large enough n, the running time is dominated by the squared term. This is called an **asymptotic complexity** because it need only hold for large enough n. In this way, the big-oh notation leaves out the details of a complexity measure while presenting enough information to get the main point of a comparison. It is often the case that minor variations in algorithms do not change the way that they scale, and thus, do not require changes to estimates of asymptotic complexity.

A	X	D	E	G	B	S	M	/

FIGURE 1.47. Entries in an unsorted, linear list. Search time is proportional to the length of the list.

In addition to the big-oh notation, there are two other conventional shorthands—little oh and omega notations—that summarize related asymptotic conditions. These notations are defined in equations (4) through (6).

$$g(n) \text{ is } O(f(n)) \qquad g(n) \leq C f(n) \text{ for } n > n_0 \qquad (4)$$
$$g(n) \text{ is } o(f(n)) \qquad \lim g(n) / f(n) = 0 \text{ as } n \to \infty \qquad (5)$$
$$g(n) \text{ is } \Omega(f(n)) \qquad g(n) > C f(n) \text{ for } n > n_0 \qquad (6)$$

Algorithms can take different amounts of time for different classes of starting data. If we talk about the time complexity of the algorithm, we have to specify whether we are referring to the exact time for particular data of size n, the worst-case time for data of size n, the average time for all possible data of size n, or the typical time for data of size n. In general, the worst-case times are the easiest to compute and at one time these were the ones most often used to characterize algorithms. However, worst-case times are not always usefully indicative of the performance of algorithms. Today it is considered more appropriate to give several characterizations of the time complexity of an algorithm, including not only worst-case and average times, but also typical times for well-characterized classes of cases.

To give an example of the use of the order notation for comparisons, we will compare three algorithms for searching a symbol structure for an entry. In the first case, the entries are kept in an unsorted linear list, such as that in Figure 1.47. Figure 1.48 presents pseudocode for searching this list. It iterates down the list starting at the beginning, comparing each list element in turn with the target entry. If a matching entry is found, it returns "yes" together with some auxiliary data. If the algorithm encounters the end of the list as indicated by the entry with a slash in it, it returns "no."

If there are n items in the list, the algorithm will execute the steps in the loop n times. We can treat this loop as a unit of time or otherwise normalize it to the instruction time for the steps in the loop. Of course in doing this, we need to be sure that no step in the loop requires a time that depends on n. In such cases, we need to account how much time each step takes.

```
To search a list:
  1. Procedure(target, list)
  2. do begin
  3.      item := pop(list)
  4.      if name(item) = name(target) then return "yes" with data(item);
  5. end until end-of-list (list);

     /* Here if target not found. */
  6. return "no"
```

FIGURE 1.48. Method for searching an unsorted, linear list.

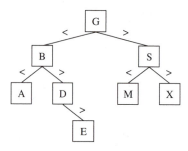

FIGURE 1.49.   Entries in a balanced tree. Search time is proportional to the depth of the tree.

How long does our algorithm take to run? In this problem, the worst-case time complexity is $O(n)$, where the algorithm searches to the end of the list and then fails. But what is the average time to find an entry? To answer this question, we need to make some assumptions about the list. Suppose, for example, that that the desired item will almost never be found in the list. In this case, the algorithm usually searches to the end of the list and then fails.

On the other hand, suppose that the target is usually found in the list. Again, to make the estimate we need to make assumptions about the position of the data in the list. Suppose that there is an equal probability that the target will be at each point in the list. It is easy to see that on average the method will search half of the list before matching the target. Since "half" is a constant factor, once again we have that the average time complexity is $O(n)$.

Different symbol structures and algorithms can support the same abstractions but with different efficiencies. Figure 1.49 gives an alternative tree representation of a set to be searched. For now, we assume that each entry in the tree has two links called "more" and "less." The data are arranged so we have a three-way test at each entry. If the entry equals the target, the search is done. Otherwise, if the target is alphabetically less than the entry, the algorithm follows the "less" link and checks the entry there. If the target is alphabetically greater than the entry, the algorithm follows the "more" link and checks the entry there. Eventually, the algorithm either finds the target or reaches the edge of the tree. This algorithm is presented in Figure 1.50.

```
To search a tree:
 1. Procedure(target, tree)
 2. begin
 3.        item := root(tree)
 4.       do begin
 5.             if name(item) = name(target) then return "yes" with data(item)
 6.             elseif lexical(target) < lexical(item) then item := less(item)
 7.             elseif lexical(target) > lexical(item) then item := more(item)
 8. end until null(item);

    /* Here if target not found. */
 9. return "no"
```

FIGURE 1.50.   Method for searching a tree.

length = 8	A	B	D	E	G	M	S	X

FIGURE 1.51.   Entries in a sorted, linear list. Search time is proportional to the length of the list.

Once again, we ask about the time complexity of the algorithm. To analyze the time we need to make assumptions about the shape of the tree. Suppose we know that this is a balanced tree, in the sense that the subtrees on either side of a node are of nearly the same size. As the algorithm proceeds, it marches down a path from the root or top of the tree. The maximum number of times the algorithm must execute the loop is the depth of the tree, that is, the number of steps in a path from the root. The length of such a path for a balanced tree is the ceiling or next integer greater than $\log_2(n)$. Thus, the worst-case time complexity of this method is $O(\lceil \log n \rceil)$. Readers interested in more details about operations on balanced trees can consult a basic textbook on algorithms and data structures, such as Knuth, 1973.

Before leaving this searching example, we note that achieving an $O(\log n)$ time on it does not necessarily require having a tree structure. Figure 1.51 gives a tabular representation of the list where items can be reached by indexing them in array. Unlike the previous list example, this one assumes that the items are kept in the table in alphabetical order. This sorted data structure lends itself to a binary search, where the first item checked is one halfway through the list. If an item does not match, the search then proceeds in a manner analogous to the method in Figure 1.50. It focuses its search to either the elements greater than or less than the item just searched and tries again at the middle of an unsearched portion of the list. At each comparison, the region left to search is approximately halved. A binary search considers the same items in the same order as the tree search. It trades arithmetic operations on indices for link-following operations in a tree. Once again, the average and worst-case time complexities are $O(\log n)$. Updating the table to add or delete an element takes time $O(n)$.

Different algorithms have different asymptotic complexity functions. What is efficient enough depends on the situation at hand. However, one widely recognized distinction is between polynomial time algorithms and exponential time algorithms. A **polynomial time algorithm** is one whose time complexity function is $O(p(n))$ for some polynomial function p, where n is used to denote the input size. An algorithm whose time complexity function is greater than this for all fixed polynomials is called an **exponential time algorithm**.

The distinction between these two types of algorithms is particularly significant when we compare the solution of large problems, since exponential functions grow so much faster than polynomial ones. Because of this growth property, it is common practice to refer to a problem as intractable if there is no polynomial time algorithm for solving it.

Space and Time Complexity for Parallel Algorithms

When multiple or parallel processors are engaged in a computation, it is appropriate to express time complexities in a way that takes into account the number of processors. In some cases, we can assign n processors to problems of size n although this option is often not realistic.

Using k processors can not reduce the asymptotic time complexity of a problem by more than a factor of k. This is not to trivialize the value of multiprocessing. After all, applying 64,000

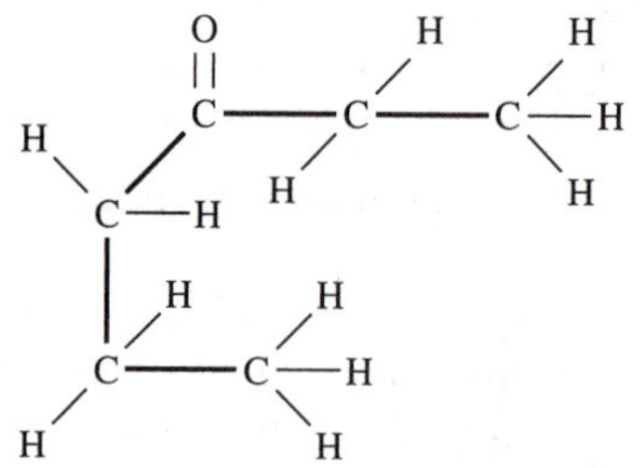

FIGURE 1.52.   The weight of a molecule is the sum of the weights of its constituent atoms.

processors to achieve a constant speedup by a constant factor of 64,000 can be very dramatic and practically significant.

Our earlier simulation example of fluid flow showed that when multiple processors are available, there can be an opportunity for radically rethinking an approach to a problem. Discovering different ways to partition problems can be very challenging and does not always lead to dramatic speedups. A recurring issue as parallel processing becomes more available is finding ways to partition problems.

In the fluid flow problem, the dramatic speed-up was largely due to the fact that the problem could be divided into a set of local computations. Each processor represented a small region of space. All of the data required for its computation was contained in the processor itself or could be obtained from its immediate neighbors. Such computations are called **local computations**. This is important because it is often the case in massively parallel computers that communications instructions beyond local neighbors require much more time than other instructions.

In contrast, **global computations** involve combining data from distant processors or aggregating over a large set of processors. In such computations, some serialization of processing is often required. For example, consider our earlier problem of computing the total weight of a molecule given a graph representation of its structure.

Figure 1.52 gives an example of a molecule. Suppose we assign a processor to every atom in the molecule. Each processor has a table of addresses of the processors that represent adjacent or chemically linked atoms in the molecule. An algorithm for computing the total weight must include the weight of each atom exactly once.

Roughly, one way to proceed is to start at one atom and have it ask each of its neighbors in turn to send it their weights for summing. The process iterates until each atom had contacted its previously uncontacted neighbors. The resulting partial sums are accumulated as they approach the starting atom. We can visualize the process in terms of two waves. The first wave is a request for weight sums. It moves out from the processor representing the starting atom. The second wave is the returning wave, containing the partial sums. Unfortunately, in spite of the fact that this approach uses n processors, it still runs in $O(n)$ time in the worst case, such as when the starting atom is at the end of a long linear molecule.

To speed up the process we would need to engage more processors at once. There are many ways to do this and specialized languages for different computer architectures. The details of this are beyond the scope of this section, but one way to understand it is to imagine that we superimpose a summing tree over the molecule as in Figure 1.53. There are 19 atoms in this figure, but they are linked in a tree with only 5 levels. All of the atoms linked together at the first

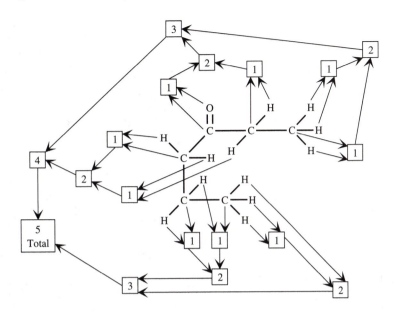

FIGURE 1.53. The weight of a molecule is the sum of the weights of its constituent atoms. Heavy links correspond to chemical bonds. Arrows indicate data flow to summation points for computing the total weight.

level of the tree (labeled 1) are performed on the first cycle. These partial sums are then combined at the second level of the tree on the next cycle. Those partial sums are combined at the next level. After each phase, only half as many processors are active as on the previous phase. The total sum is aggregated in time proportional to the ceiling of the depth of the tree, that is, in $O(\log n)$ time.

Complexity Distributions

It is well known that for some algorithms the worst-case complexity is much worse than the average complexity. But the average case can also be misleading.

Consider the distribution of computation times in Figure 1.54. In this example, there is a population of possible inputs to the algorithm and the time to perform the computation on the input varies drastically. Thus, there is a small set of elements for which the time is $O(x^1)$, and a few more where the complexity is $O(x^2)$. The largest set of elements has complexity $O(x^4)$. The curve drops off so that there are only a few elements where the complexity is $O(x^n)$.

In this example, the worst-case time complexity is $O(x^n)$. Perhaps surprisingly, the mean time complexity is still $O(x^n / n)$. That this is the case can be seen by considering equation (7).

$$\text{mean complexity} = (1/N) \sum_{i=1}^{N} x^i \tag{7}$$

Thus the mean complexity is dominated by the largest term.

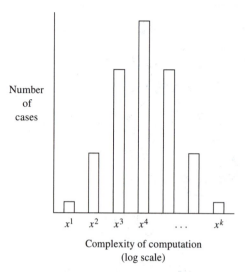

FIGURE 1.54.   Distribution of cases with different complexity orders.

What this shows us is that the mean complexity is also not necessarily representative of typical complexity. Referring back to Figure 1.54, most of the elements in the set will result in computations that are $O(x^4)$. Thus, the mode of the distribution is much less than the mean. This example suggests that providing a distribution of complexities may in many cases be a more meaningful way of conveying expectations about running time than either a worst-case or mean-case analysis.

Phases, Phase Transitions, and Threshold Effects

The previous section characterizes expected running times of algorithms in terms of their performance on populations of structures. In this section we consider phenomena that can arise when populations are characterized by possibly critical values of variables. The terminology of these phenomena—**phases**, **phase transitions**, and **threshold effects**—is drawn from physical chemistry. The analyses are drawn from statistical mechanics.

Phase transitions are familiar from everyday experience. Most substances have characteristic melting points and boiling points. As temperature is raised or lowered at constant pressure near these points, materials undergo phase transitions—from solid to liquid or from liquid to gas. Underneath this abrupt, qualitative change at the macroscopic level is a small change at the microscopic level. Temperature is a measure of the vibrations of atoms in a substance. As temperature is increased, these vibrations become more energetic. Increased temperature causes a substance to expand because the vibrations increase the average separations between atoms. Usually small changes in temperature cause small changes in vibration and small changes in the size of an object made from the material.

However, at certain critical points such as the melting point and boiling point, small changes in temperature result in gross changes at the macroscopic level. At these points, the actual energy and separations of the vibrating atoms changes only slightly it but results in a qualitative softening as vibrations become vigorous enought to enable atoms to slide past each other.

To a first order approximation, phase transitions are very sharp. Below the melting point, the substance is a solid and above it is a liquid. Such sharp transition points are called thresholds. If we view the area around the transition point in fine detail, the story is usually more chaotic. As ice forms, sometimes crystals form and then melt and then form again. Liquids sometimes exist in "superchilled" states for periods of time without making the transition. Mathematical models show both phenomena—the relatively sharp macroscopic transition points as well as fine-grained chaotic behavior in the immediate vicinity of the transition.

For a simple example of this phenomenon in the context of algorithmic complexity, we consider again algorithms that operate on trees. Suppose that we have a population of trees characterized by an average branching factor, b. We use the term **cluster size** to refer to the expected size of a tree drawn from the population. We will consider several such algorithms in Chapter 2 that search trees. For now it is enough to know that our algorithm visits every node in a cluster.

To determine the time complexity of such an algorithm, it is useful to know how many nodes there are in a cluster. To count the nodes, we start at the root of the tree. On average, there are b nodes immediately adjacent to the root. Then there are b^2 nodes immediately adjacent to these one level down. For a tree of infinite extent, the cluster size, $C(b)$, is given by equation (8).

$$C(b) = \sum_{i=0}^{\infty} b^i = 1 / (1 - b) \tag{8}$$

For trees of finite depth, d, the cluster size is given by equation (9).

$$C(b) = \sum_{i=0}^{d-1} b^i = (1 - b^d) / (1 - b) \tag{9}$$

Figure 1.55 shows cluster size as a function of the average branching factor for trees of different depth. For a potentially infinite tree, an average branching factor less than one leads to a finite-size cluster. However, when the average branching factor reaches 1, there is a singularity in the graph as number of nodes connected to the root on average suddenly becomes infinite. This singularity is an example of a **threshold**. It marks the existence of a phase transition characterized by an explosive increase in cluster size as the threshold is approached from below. For any fixed polynomial of b, the time complexity of our node-visiting algorithm exceeds the polynomial as b approaches the critical point.

The signature of the phase transition for potentially infinite trees is still visible for trees of finite depth. The other curves in Figure 1.55 show the expected cluster size for trees with several fixed depths.

Phase transitions show up in many kinds of computations. For example, they show up in the analysis of search methods where the number of nodes explored along a false "garden path" corresponds to the cluster size in this example. They also show up in analyses of algorithms that work over more general graph structures than trees. Again in these cases, the cluster sizes of graphs undergo phase transitions as the number of connections between nodes increases.

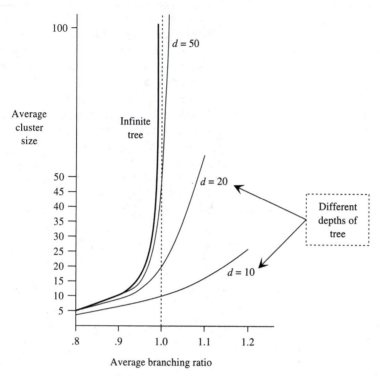

FIGURE 1.55. Cluster size for trees with finite depth, d, as a function of the average branching factor, b. (Adapted fom Huberman, B. A., and Hogg, T. Phase transitions in artificial intelligence systems. *Artificial Intelligence* 33, 1987, pp. 155–171.)

1.3.9 *Structural Complexity*   ADVANCED

Space and time complexity are properties of algorithms as applied to populations of different possible data structure inputs. Sometimes the running time of an algorithm over a particular data structure depends a great deal on its particular properties. For example, an algorithm to reverse the order of a list depends on the number of elements in the list. Algorithms that search trees depend on the particular depths and branching factors of the trees.

Measures of the properties of a structure are called **structural complexities**. In this book we use several different measures of structural complexity for different kinds of structures and different purposes, as suggested by Figure 1.56. In this section we develop and study two examples of such measures. First, however, we discuss generally what it is that measures of structural complexity are good for.

Measures of structural complexity provide scales for comparing structures. Suppose that we are given a set of structures $\{S_1, S_2, S_3, \ldots, S_n\}$ and a complexity measure C. If $C(S_1) > C(S_2)$ then we say that structure S_1 is more complex than S_2. We can use the scale to identify the simplest members of a set.

Suppose further that there is a computation, F, that we can perform on various members of the set, and that the time complexity of $F(S_k)$ depends in a known way on $C(S_k)$. In this case, the

Measure	Remarks
Number of elements	Same as space complexity.
Depth of tree	Can be used to compute space and time complexities for tree searches.
Branching factor	Can be used together with depth to compute space and time complexities of tree searches.
Hierarchical diversity	Measure of the diversity of structures in unlabeled trees.
Width of constraint graph	Measure of complexity of labeled graphs, such as constraint graphs. Related to time complexity for solving constraint satisfaction problems.
Bandwidth of constraint graph	Measure of complexity of graph structures. Related to time complexity for solving constraint satisfaction problems.
Shannon information entropy	Measure of the sharpness of a distribution of probabilities. Used in diagnostic systems to select probe sites most likely to reduce the number of competing hypotheses.

FIGURE 1.56. Examples of measures of structural complexity.

structural complexity measure can be useful for partitioning the set of structures into families whose time complexities for F are equivalent. For example, suppose that the time complexity relates to the structural complexity as follows:

time complexity $(F(S_k)) = O(m^{C(S_k)})$ for some constant m.

That is, the time complexity for computing F on S_k is polynomial in the structural complexity of S_k. In this case, C gives us a means for dividing $\{S_1, S_2, \ldots S_n\}$ into easy and hard problems. The more complex the structure, the longer it takes to compute F on it. In this way, measures of structural complexity can provide useful alternatives to nonrepresentative worst-case estimates of time complexity over large populations of data structures. The alternatives are either to measure $C(S_k)$ so as to get a better estimate of the time complexity of $F(S_k)$ or to identify S_k as belonging to a subpopulation where the range of $C(S)$ is much narrower and thereby more representative.

To be concrete, we now consider a particular complexity measure for unlabeled trees. This complexity measure is called **Huberman-Hogg complexity** or **hierarchical diversity** (Huberman & Hogg, 1986). Huberman and Hogg were struck by examples of structures in physics and computational systems. In physics, both crystalline materials and gases are considered to be relatively simple when compared with amorphous structures. Crystalline structures are considered simple because their molecular structures are repetitious. Gases are simple because the molecules are randomly located and do not aggregate. On the other hand, amorphous structures have a mixture of molecular structures of different sizes and are considered complex. Similarly in linguistics, random strings are viewed as simpler than sentences produced by the grammars of formal and natural languages. Huberman and Hogg sought a measure of structural complexity that would reflect these intuitions. They wanted to quantify the regularities and hierarchical structure of trees.

We first consider some examples of hierarchical structures. Figure 1.57 shows three unlabeled trees, $\{T_1, T_2, T_3\}$. Intuitively, what should be the relative complexities of the three trees? Most people would agree that T_1 is the simplest, that is,

$C(T_1) \leq C(T_2)$
$C(T_1) \leq C(T_3)$

However, what is the relation between $C(T_2)$ and $C(T_3)$. Because T_3 has more nodes than T_2 we might classify it as more complex. On the other hand, T_3 is very symmetric. All of the subtrees of T_3 are identical at each level, making it very simple.

Hierarchical diversity is intended to measure the diversity of a structure and to reflect the number of interactions among nonidentical elements. For this reason, it counts T_2 as the most complex of the three trees in Figure 1.57. In fact, the tree T_3 can be extended to balanced binary trees of arbitrarily large size without increasing its hierarchical diversity.

We are now ready to define hierarchical diversity. The hierarchical diversity of a tree, $D(T)$, is defined recursively. The diversity of a node with no subtrees is just 1. The diversity of a node with subtrees is the made up of two terms. The first term counts the number of non-isomorphic subtrees of the node. We refer to each set of identical subtrees as a cluster. At each level, there are k clusters of identical subtrees. We are interested in counting the number of different interactions at each level, so all identical subtrees count as 1. Specifically, we multiply together the diversities of the clusters at the lower level. This product is then multiplied by N_k, the number of ways that the k different clusters can interact as given in equation (8).

$$N_k = \binom{k}{1} + \binom{k}{2} + \binom{k}{3} + \ldots + \binom{k}{k} = 2^k - 1 \tag{8}$$

Combining these factors we obtain equation (9)

$$D(T) = (2^k - 1) \prod_{j=1}^{k} D(T_j) \tag{9}$$

where j ranges over the k nonisomorphic subtrees.

Figure 1.58 gives examples of computing hierarchical diversity. The number in the box for each level of the tree gives the structural diversity at that node. The diversity of T_1 is trivial, since the node has no subtrees. Because the subtrees of T_3 are identical, there is only one cluster at each level. Thus, the diversity of T_3 is 1 and is less than the diversity of T_2. In T_4 and T_5, the magnitude of the diversity is much higher, because the product of the diversities at lower levels is higher.

It is easy to see that Huberman-Hogg complexity does correspond to the intuitions about physical complexity by comparing the values it yields for different trees. We have already ob-

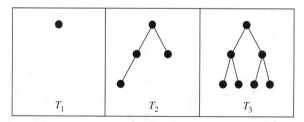

FIGURE 1.57. Some examples of hierarchical structures of differing complexity. By the hierarchical complexity measure, T_2 is the most complex of the three trees.

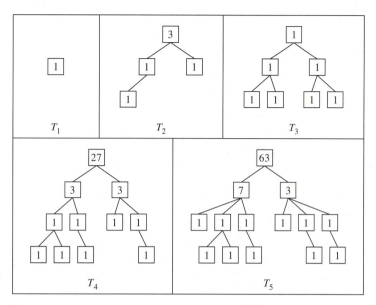

FIGURE 1.58. Examples of computing the hierarchical diversity of trees. The trees T_1, T_2, and T_3 are repeated from Figure 1.57, with the points indicating nodes replaced by boxes containing the diversity at that node in the tree.

served that it has a low value for trees with much symmetry, because the number of non-isomorphic subtrees of a node will be low. Indeed, for complete trees with uniform branching factors like T_3, it is easy to show that $D(T) = 1$. Similarly, hierarchical complexity is low for trees of trivial depth. It is highest for trees like T_4 and T_5, where there is substantial asymmetry. As Huberman and Hogg put it, the measure is optimum at a place midway between order and disorder. Although this goes beyond the scope of this section, Huberman-Hogg complexity and some variants of it are involved in hypotheses about the complexity of systems that are adaptable and are relevant to the study of machine learning systems.

In summary, the point of a structural complexity measure is to summarize intrinsic properties of structures on a scale so that we can compare them. When structural complexity measures are mathematically related to the time complexity of algorithms that run over the data structures, they can be used to partition the space of data structures into cases of graded difficulty.

1.3.10 *Summary and Review*

This section surveys computational issues in the design of representations. It introduces a vocabulary of dimensions for comparing alternative representations for computational models.

We compared symbol structures and their interpreters for representing a square: a pixel array, a property list, and a graph representation. These representations provide alternative implementations of a common abstraction for figures, with operations for such things as retrieving size and position, moving figures, and computing overlap of figures. Different implementations can have dramatically different computational requirements for time and space.

When we design representations, we decide which propositions to make primitive and which derived. This theme pervades our discussion of vivid and analogical representations. Thus directed graphs model the topology of molecules or the connectivity of circuits. Maps, like other scale models, have the same kinds of structures as their domains, that is, two-dimensional Euclidean spaces.

Representations are explict when they are written in a declarative language. This means that they are modular, that they have well-characterized semantics, and that there is a causal connection between the representation and the system that interprets it. The declarative quality of a representation depends not only on the symbols themselves, but also on the people who need to understand it and the complexity of what is described. Explicit representations are widely used because they afford advantages for making changes to systems.

When computational models are sufficiently expressive, they may admit several expressions of the same thing. In such cases we need to consider canonical functions and canonical forms.

It is not necessary to select and use a single representation in knowledge systems. When different implementations offer trade-offs in efficiency, multiple representations can be usefully combined. This requires maintaining an appropriate causal connection between symbol structures, and careful accounting to invalidate and recompute caches at appropriate times.

Parallel computing architectures offer opportunities to include both structure and process in analogical and direct representations. In the wind flow example, not only is the structure of the data similar to structure of the domain, but also the activity of the processors is similar to the activity in spatial regions of the domain.

Finally, we introduced the big-oh notation for summarizing asymptotic space and time complexity. The worst-case complexity is often the easiest to compute but need not be representative of the average complexity. Indeed, even average complexity can be misleading about the expected complexity if the average is skewed by a small number of cases of very high complexity. A more meaningful presentation of expectations is sometimes given by a distribution of complexities over a population of structures. A structural complexity measure is any measure based on the size or organization of a symbol structure. Measures of structural complexity are closely related to measures of time complexity for algorithms that run on the structures.

Exercises for Section 1.3

Ex. 1   [*CD-05*] *Systematic Representations.* Professor Digit was fascinated when he learned about the physical symbol system hypothesis, and dashed off to build several computer programs that he called "minimal symbol systems." He later exhibited these to his colleagues. The first minimal symbol system was a single instruction which compared two bits ("the input bits") in memory and then set a bit ("the output bit") in computer memory from 0 to 1 depending on the results. When his colleagues asked what his program did, he told them that it was an ultrafast multiplication program: When both of the input bits were 0, they represent the numbers 3141592653589793238462643 and 987654321987654321. In that case, the program sets the output bit to 0, indicating the product of the two numbers. If either of the two input bits is one, the program sets the output bit to 1 meaning that it does not know the input numbers and cannot compute the product. His colleagues were puzzled (flabbergasted?) by this, but he assured them that this his interpretation was reasonable because a bit can designate anything whatsoever.

(a) How many input and output states does his program have?

(b) In what way is Professor Digit's account unsatisfactory? (*Hint*: What do we reasonably require of a computer program that reasons about operations on numbers?)

Ex. 2 [*CP-10*] *Computing about Rectangles.* In this chapter we considered examples of representation where the choice of primitives or symbol structures was intended to make some inferences computationally effective. Manhattan rectangles are rectangles whose sides are parallel to either the x- or y-axes in the real plane. Such rectangles can be represented as a record with the fields (left, bottom, width, height).

Two rectangles are said to overlap if their areas have at least one point in common. Describe an algorithm for deciding efficiently whether two rectangles overlap. (*Hint*: It is possible to consider area-overlap in terms of x and y components.)

Ex. 3 [*CP-15*] *More Computing about Rectangles.* The Manhattan separation between rectangles can be defined as the minimum length of a segmented Manhattan line between the closest edges of the rectangles, where the edges of the line are confined to integer coordinates.

Briefly, sketch an algorithm for deciding whether two rectangles are within a Manhattan separation of k units.

Ex. 4 [*CD-!-CP-30*] *Parallel Computing about Rectangles.* The claim that bitmaps are inefficient for determining whether two Manhattan rectangles overlap depends on several assumptions about the rectangles and the capabilities of the computer.

Suppose we have a bitmap processing computer (called SAM for "synchronous active memory"). Each processor has 16 bits of addressable memory, a 1-bit accumulator, and 1-bit wide communication lines to each of its four neighboring processors. The instructions can communicate with a host computer. The host computer can select arbitrary combinations of rows and columns of the bitmap processors. All the selected bitmap processors perform the same instruction at the same time, as broadcast by the host computer. The processors have the following instruction set:

Load and store instructions
```
store <bit>        <bit>:=Acc
load <bit>         Acc:=<bit>
```

1-bit operations
```
clr—               Acc:=0
and <bit>          Acc :=Acc and <bit>
gt <bit>           Acc:=Acc greater-than <bit>
lt <bit>           Acc:= Acc less-than <bit>
xor <bit>          Acc:=Acc xor <bit>
or <bit>           Acc:=Acc or <bit>
nor <bit>          Acc:=Acc nor <bit>
cmp <bit>          Acc:=Acc equals <bit>
not <bit>          Acc:=not <bit>
ge <bit>           Acc := Acc greater-than-or-equals <bit>
inv—               Acc:=not Acc
le <bit>           Acc:=Acc less-than-or-equals <bit>
nand <bit>         Acc:=Acc nand <bit>
set—               Acc:=1
```

Neighbor communication operation
```
dot <mask>          Acc:=Mask₀Nbr₀+Mask₁Nbr₁+Mask₂Nbr₂
                    +Mask₃Nbr₃+Mask₄Acc
```

Host communication operations
```
read-               Host-Data:=Acc (ored over selected cells)
write-              Acc:=Host-Data (for all selected cells)
```

Note: The dot instruction is a kind of dot product. Each mask bit indicates which neighbor's accumulators are included in the result. For example,

    dot (0 3)   means to OR together the accumulators from neighbors 0 and 3 and save the result in the accumulator.

    dot (1 2 4)   means to OR together the accumulator values from neighbors 1 and 2 together with the accumulator of self and save the result in the accumulator.

(a) Suppose the initial data in bitplanes 1 and 2 for a 4x4 SAM array are as follows:

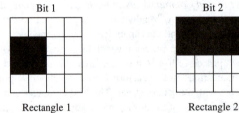

      Rectangle 1   Rectangle 2

The following algorithm computes the intersection of the rectangle stored in bit 1 (across the entire block) with the rectangle stored in bit 2.

```
load 1
and 2
read
```

Illustrate the action of this algorithm using matrices to show the state of bit 1, bit 2, and the accumulator at each step. How does the value read on Host-Data depend on the rectangles?

(b) Suppose that bit 0 in an 8x8 SAM memory is initialized with a large filled-in rectangle as follows:

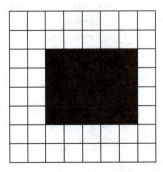

Trace the execution of the following program.

```
load 0
inv
dot (0 1 2 3 4)
inv
xor 0
```

Explain how this is an edge-finding program, finding those points at the outer limits of the rectangle. *Hint*: Consider de Morgan's laws.

Note that the bits in the mask of the dot instruction correspond to the directions of the neighbors with 0=North, 1=East, 2=South, and 3=West. Cells at the edge of the array always return 0 when they try ask for data beyond the array.

(c) Is the computation in part (*b*) an example of a local computation or a global computation? Explain briefly.

(d) Write a SAM program to compute whether rectangles stored in bit 1 and bit 2 are at least 1 unit of Manhattan separation apart. Does your program depend on the shape of the figures (that is, must they be rectangles)?

Ex. 5 [*10*] *Canonical Forms*. Each of the following data structures represents a circular linked structure of six items.

1. (a f b c e d)
2. (b c e d a f)
3. (b f a c e d)
4. (d e c b f a)
5. (c e d a b f)

(a) Suppose the interpreter is supposed to treat rotation and reflection is equivalence-preserving operations. The canonical form for these lists is defined as the list that is earliest "alphabetically" starting with the left-most term. In other words, the leftmost element of the canonical form of the lists is its alphabetically earliest one. In the event of a tie, then the second element is considered following the simplest rules of dictionary order.

Give the canonical form for each structure.

(b) Indicate which of the structures are equivalent to each other. How many distinct structures are represented here?

Ex. 6 [*05*] *Terminology*. Determine whether each of the following statements are true or false. If a statement is ambiguous, explain your answer briefly.

(a) *True or False*. Fidelity and precision refer roughly to the accurateness and detail of a representation in its use in making predictions.

(b) *True or False*. There is usually exactly one best way to implement a given abstraction.

(c) *True or False*. In most inferential systems, a large number of propositions can potentially be derived from a small number of primitive ones.

(d) *True or False*. One of the advantages of using multiple representations is that such systems need not contend with the stale data problem.

(e) *True or False*. In a system that is implemented in multiple layers, the implementation at one level of description may in turn be an abstraction for the next level down.

Ex. 7 [*05*] *More Terminology*. Determine whether each of the following statements is true or false. If a statement is ambiguous, explain your answer briefly.

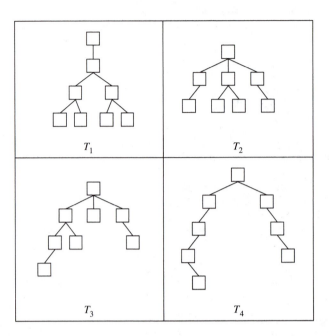

FIGURE 1.59. Three trees.

(a) *True or False*. When a system has two representations for the same thing and one is derived from the other by a long computation and the derived result is referenced more frequently than the primitive one is changed, it is appropriate to cache the derived representation.

(b) *True or False*. To prevent stale data problems, a cache should be invalidated whenever its value is retrieved.

(c) *True or False*. It is appropriate to recompute a derived and cached value whenever an operation changes a primitive value on which it depends.

(d) *True or False*. One problem with the bitmap representation of figures is that for low enough precision or resolution of the bitmap, the shapes of some figures are indistinguishable.

(e) *True or False*. If the running time of a computation is $56m^2n^3 + 37m^3n + 60m^2n + 3n + 30$, then we can characterize its time complexity as $O(m^2n^3)$.

Ex. 8 [05] *Even More Terminology*. Determine whether each of the following statements is true or false. If a statement is ambiguous, explain your answer briefly.

(a) *True or False*. Explicit representations offer advantages over implicit ones in knowledge systems that must be modified over time.

(b) *True or False*. An implicit representation is one whose utility rests on unstated assumptions.

(c) *True or False*. A bitmap is an implicit representation of shapes.

(d) *True or False*. An explicit representation usually requires a declarative semantics.

(e) *True or False*. The declarative semantics (including reference semantics, truth semantics, and proof semantics) are the only semantics needed for defining a declarative representation.

Ex. 9   *[05] Asymptotic Superlinear Speed-ups.* Is it possible to achieve more than a factor of *k* order speed-up on a problem by applying *k* processors instead of one, assuming that all processors are equivalent? If yes, give a brief example. If not, present a brief argument.

Ex. 10   *[05] Space versus Time Complexity (True or False).* The asymptotic time complexity of an algorithm for a single processor is always greater or equal to its asymptotic space complexity. Explain briefly.

Ex. 11   *[08] Hierarchical Diversity.* Figure 1.59 gives four unlabeled trees of eight nodes each. Compute the hierarchical diversity of each tree.

1.4 *Programs: Patterns, Simplicity, and Expressiveness*

Whenever we build computational models, we express them in programming languages or representation languages. Observably, some languages are better than others for particular programs in that the programs are generally more concise, easier to understand, and easier to extend. But what makes some languages and representations better than others in this way?

In the previous section on representational properties, we considered the use of programming abstractions. Programming abstractions are used to build systems in levels, so that the most abstract level gives a concise description of a program in terms of appropriate primitives.

In this section we consider two additional methods for achieving simplicity of expression: metalevel factoring and the use of epistemological primitives with a large base of shared knowledge. We introduce these concepts through a sequence of increasingly sophisticated examples. Along the way we consider basic ideas widely used in building knowledge systems: production rules, pattern matching, and logic programming.

1.4.1 *Using Rules to Manipulate Symbols*

Our first example is quite elementary for anyone who has written many computer programs. It is a starting point for comparisons.

Figure 1.60 depicts a traffic intersection where a farm road crosses a highway. The right-of-way at this intersection is indicated by a traffic light, which has a sensor to detect traffic entering the highway from the farm road, assuming that traffic drives on the right-hand side of the road.

Figure 1.61 depicts two internal symbol structures for the controller of the traffic-light system. There is a cell or storage element named `farm-road-light` that designates the traffic light facing the farm road. This cell contains one of three symbols `red`, `yellow`, or `green`. Similarly there is another cell, `highway-light`, designating the traffic light facing the highway. It is convenient to think of these cells as program variables, and the symbols in the cells as the values of the variables.

Symbol systems change symbol structures dynamically. Our account of the traffic-light controller is a **simulation**. That is, it uses a running computer program to model another (usually more complicated) system that we call its "world." The values in the program variables correspond to a snapshot of the world at some instant of time. As the program runs, its program actions model world actions that would change it over time. An observer could watch the simulation just as he might watch the world, seeing the traffic light on a highway turn yellow, and then red, and then a light on a farm road turn green.

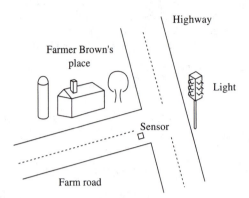

FIGURE 1.60.   Traffic light at an intersection of a highway and a farm road.

Figure 1.62 illustrates four computational "rules" that specify the behavior of a traffic-light controller. The particular syntax for the rules in this figure and others in this section is not important. Many variations are possible in programming languages.

The rules in our simulation example make use of two external timers called `light-timer` and `traffic-timer`, which can be started and tested to see whether an allotted time is up, and a sensor, which can be tested to determine whether a car is present at the end of the farm road. The code and variables for the simulated timers and sensor are not shown.

The rules in Figure 1.62 are examples of **production rules**. Each rule has two major parts, called the if-part and the then-part. The if-part of a rule consists of conditions to be tested. In the first rule, the conditions test whether the highway light is green, whether a car is waiting, and whether time is up on the traffic timer. If all of the conditions in the if-part of a rule are true, the actions in the then-part of the rule are carried out. In the idiosyncratic terminology of production rules, we say that the rule is "fired." The then-parts of these rules consist of actions to be taken. In the first rule, these actions turn the highway light to yellow and start the light timer. The parts of a production rule are sometimes called by different names. The if-part is also known as the situation part, the conditional or the antecedent. The then-part is also known as the action part or the consequent.

In our program, after the first rule is tried, the second, third, and fourth rules are tried in order. The program then starts over again with the first rule. The complete simulation program would have representations of cars and rules for modeling traffic. Cars could speed up, slow down, or turn. No two cars could occupy the same space at the same time (we hope!). The simulated sensor would occasionally indicate that a simulated car is present. Then the timers would perform their measurements of simulated elapsed time and the rules of our traffic-light controller

FIGURE 1.61.   Symbol structures in the traffic-light controller.

```
do                                              ;infinite loop
begin

    begin                                       ;Initially ...
        farm-road-light := 'red                     ;turn the farm-road light red
        highway-light := 'green                     ;turn the highway light green
        start (light-timer)                         ;start the light timer
        start(traffic-timer)                        ;start the traffic timer
        start (sensor)                              ;start the sensor
    end


    ;rule-1
    if      highway-light = 'green          ;IF the highway light is green and
            and car-waiting? (sensor)       ;and the sensor shows a car waiting
            and time-up?(traffic-timer)     ;and the traffic timer shows time up
    then    highway-light := 'yellow        ;THEN turn the highway light yellow
            start (light-timer)             ;and start the light timer.


    ;rule-2
    if      highway-light = 'yellow         ;IF the highway light is yellow
            and time-up?(light-timer)       ;and the light timer shows time up
    then    highway-light := 'red           ;THEN turn the highway light to red
            farm-road-light := 'green       ;and turn the farm road light to green
            start (traffic-timer)           ;and start the traffic timer.


    ;rule-3
    if      farm-road-light = 'green        ;IF the farm road light is green
            and time-up? (traffic-timer)    ;and the traffic timer shows time up
    then    farm-road-light := 'yellow      ;THEN turn the farm road light to yellow
            start (light-timer)             ;and start the light timer.


    ;rule-4
    if      farm-road-light = 'yellow       ;IF the farm road light is yellow
            and time-up? (light-timer)      ;and the light timer shows time up
    then    farm-road-light := 'red         ;THEN turn the farm road light to red
            highway-light := 'green         ;and turn the highway light to green
            start (traffic-timer)           ;and start the traffic timer.

end
```

FIGURE 1.62 Rules in the traffic-light controller.

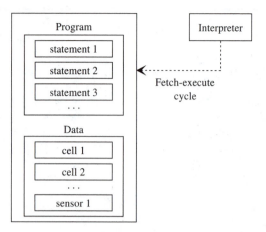

FIGURE 1.63.   Program and interpreter for the traffic-light controller.

would cycle around, switching the lights to control the simulated flow of traffic at the intersection.

Production rules take many different forms. The rules shown in Figure 1.62 are similar to IF statements available in most programming languages. In this example, the selection of which rule to fire next is quite trivial. The program specifies exactly what to do, step by step.

Variations on production rules can admit many kinds of additional information, different syntaxes, and different methods for controlling execution. They are used to model simulation and also to model reasoning. Later in this section we will consider production rules that are based on pattern matching. Production rules are an important representation in knowledge-based systems because they directly represent how actions depend on conditions. Production rules are sometimes called **situation-action rules**.

Figure 1.63 shows the organization of the traffic-light controller system. There is a program made up of a set of statements—the rules from Figure 1.63. The statements in this program are retrieved and executed by an interpreter. This architecture is essentially the same as that of a von Neumann computer where the program is represented as instructions in computer memory and the interpreter is the processor which carries out a fetch-execute cycle. The difference in this case is that the statements are rules and the interpreter executes the rules. Nonetheless, the interpreter is still quite simple, in that the rules are executed in sequential order. The bottom part of the figure corresponds to data read or written by the program. The data are the program variables that store the state of farm-road-light and highway-light. The reading from the sensor is also included in data. These data are read and sometimes written as the program runs. By design, the program never directs its interpreter to decode the data as instructions.

1.4.2   *Treating Programs as Data*

The representation of programs as symbol structures is related to the **stored program concept**: the storing of computer instructions in memory in the same manner as data. Different codes are recognized by the processor as different instructions. Storing programs in memory has the practi-

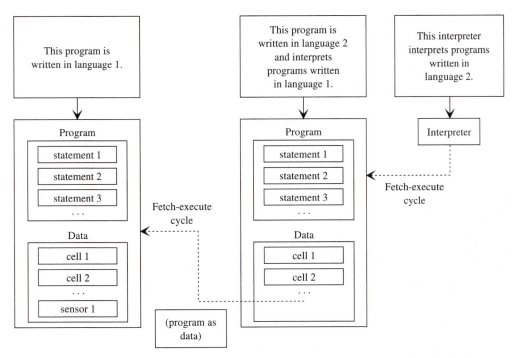

FIGURE 1.64. Universal computation, in which one computational process emulates another by interpreting its instructions as data.

cal advantage of making it easier to arrange for computers to run different programs. This is the major contribution of the von Neumann architecture for computers.

That programs on one computer can interpret symbolic instructions of a different computer is the **universal computation** concept. The "universal" part of this refers to the ability to simulate the instructions of *any* computer. A universal computer can be programmed to carry out the instructions of a different computer, even though its instruction codes are different. The basic idea as shown in Figure 1.64 is that the universal computer maintains a table to look up sets of instructions in its memory that simulate the instructions written for the other computer.

Universal computation places few constraints on the representations that are used in the two computers. The instruction sets on the two computers could be identical or very different. The symbols can have structural similarities or be very different. Let $\{s_1, s_2, \ldots, s_k\}$ be symbols on the simulated computer, representing either instructions or data, and $\{S^1, S_2, \ldots, S_k\}$ be symbols on the simulating computer. There must be a mapping, M, between the two sets of symbols, stated as $M: \{s_k\} \rightarrow \{S_k\}$. Similarly there must be a mapping, P, between the processing steps or instructions on the two computers. Suppose that $\{i_1, i_2, i_3, \ldots, i_n\}$ is a sequence of descriptions of the symbols in the memory of the simulated computer when its interpreter is run. Universal computation requires that when the simulating computer runs, that it yields a sequence of states, such that M holds between corresponding symbols in each of the states in order.

As suggested by Figure 1.64, universal computation divides an interpreter into layers. This layered approach is not limited, say, to simulating obsolete computers that are no longer manufactured. It is widely used in knowledge systems to partition programs into simpler layers. At each layer, interpreters make much use of symbol manipulation operations for recognizing patterns, extracting parameters, and carrying out parameterized action.

In the following sections, we see concrete examples of how symbol manipulation languages provide symbol manipulation primitives and thereby layers of interpretation that can simplify the writing of programs.

1.4.3 *Manipulating Expressions for Different Purposes*

The layperson's view of computers is that they are good with numbers, that is, they are able to do arithmetic rapidly. In contrast to arithmetic, algebra and calculus involve much richer symbol manipulation. For example, a typical exercise in an introductory calculus course is to differentiate a polynomial like that in expression (1) to yield its derivative (2).

$$\text{function: } f(x) = (2/3)x^3 + 7x^2 + 12x - 8 \tag{1}$$
$$\text{derivative: } f'(x) = 2x^2 + 14x + 12 \tag{2}$$

The function in (1) can be represented indifferent ways, such as the LISP computer language, as shown in (3). The advantage of LISP in the following examples is that the patterns are simpler because the program syntax requires no parsing.

```
(defun f (x) (+ (* (/ 2 3) (expt x 3))
               (* 7 (expt x 2))
               (* 12 x)
               (- 8)))                              (3)
```

Equation (1) could also be expressed in a graph notation, as shown in Figure 1.65. In either case, a symbol system (such as a standard LISP interpreter) can be made to compute the value of the polynomial given a value for x. A LISP interpreter would evaluate the equation in (1) to yield that $f(0) = -8$, $f(1) = 11.666667$, and $f(.508517) = 0$. A different program, a *differentiator*, could accept the definition of f as input and produce as output a symbolic expression $f1$ representing its derivative:

```
(defun f1 (x) (+ (* 2 (expt x 2))
               (* 14 x)
               12))                                 (4)
```

This expression (4) is a full-fledged LISP program, as is the original function definition in (3). It could be executed or further differentiated.

Looking at the equivalent semantic network representation in Figure 1.65, it is easy to see how a differentiation program could work, that is, how it could symbolically differentiate a polynomial. A differentiation program needs to create a second linked structure of terms, computing the coefficient and exponent relations of the new terms from corresponding relations on the old terms. For each term, it creates a new term node, linking it to a new coefficient node, a new exponent node, and a new next-term. Each new coefficient is computed by multiplying the old co-

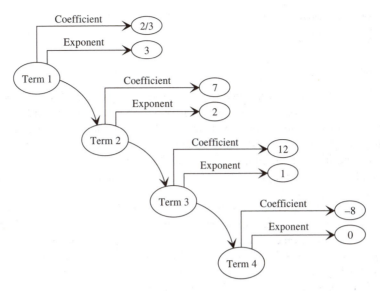

FIGURE 1.65. Graph representation of a polynomial.

efficient by the old exponent; the new exponent is the old exponent minus one. The new terms represent the new polynomial with the values as shown in (4). Thus, the differentiation process builds a new polynomial representation as it traverses the original polynomial representation, computing the parameters of each new term from the parameters of the old terms. It must walk through the graph and create a new graph whose properties are computed from those of the original graph.

Furthermore, different computations can be done on a single representation. Another symbolic manipulation program, a quadratic root finder, could be written to take the roots of a second-order polynomial such as (4). For this, we view a polynomial as fitting the following pattern

$$f(x) = ax^2 + bx + c \qquad (5)$$

and then apply the quadratic equations

$$\text{root1} = (-b + \text{sqrt}(b^2 - 4ac))/2a$$
$$\text{root2} = (-b - \text{sqrt}(b^2 - 4ac))/2a \qquad (6)$$

A quadratic root finder steps through the terms of a polynomial and extracts values for the parameters a, b, and c. Given these parameter values, computing the roots as in (5) and (6) requires another modest procedure, not much more complicated than the preceding polynomial functions.

In summary, radically different computations can be performed on a representation. The polynomial representation can be used to yield specific evaluations for different values of x. Alternatively, a differentiator program operate on the same representation to produce derivatives.

Similarly, a root finder can use the representation as a template for extracting parameters for computing quadratic roots.

1.4.4 Pattern Matching

In the examples of the last section, the symbol-manipulating operations included traversing graphs, extracting information, and creating new expressions. Because structure recognition and parameter extraction are so fundamental, people have designed computer languages that provide these operations as primitive computational mechanisms. Such mechanisms are widely used in production-rule and logic programming languages. This section uses these operations to give concrete examples of how appropriate symbol manipulation primitives can simplify the expression of programs.

There are two main variations on pattern matching, notably one-way pattern matching and two-way pattern matching (unification). In one-way pattern matching, a pattern with variables is matched against an expression containing constants. At the end of the operation, the variables in the pattern may take on values corresponding to parts of the constant structure. In **unification**, patterns with variables are matched against other patterns with variables. Variables in both patterns may take on values at the end of the matching operation.

Figure 1.66 shows a simple example of a pattern and the results of matching it against an expression. A key element in the syntax of pattern matching is the specification of **pattern variables**. In the following, there are three pattern variables to be matched: a, b, and c. In the following examples, we indicate that terms are variables to be matched by preceding them with question marks at the parts of the pattern where matching is to take place. Other terms are assumed to be constants in the matching process. When a pattern variable appears again later in a pattern-matching rule it need not be preceded by a question mark. The value of the variable is required to match the corresponding datum in the matching expression.

Matching a pattern against an expression requires aligning the corresponding parts of the pattern with the expression and then extracting values for the pattern variables. Thus, the pattern matching process assigns values $a = 2$, $b = 14$, and $c = 12$.

```
Matching the pattern
      (+ (* ?a (expt x 2))
         (* ?b x)
         ?c)

to the expression
      (+ (* 2 (expt x 2))
         (* 14 x)
         12))

yields values for the pattern variables
      a = 2, b = 14, c = 12
```

FIGURE 1.66.   An example of pattern matching.

```
if-part: {pattern to be matched}
    (if (match test-expression                    ;IF the test expression matches
            (+ (* ?a (expt x 2))                  ;a quadratic polynomial
            (*    ?b x)
                ?c))

then-part: {actions to be carried out}
    (then (setf root (/ (+ (- b)                  ;THEN compute a root
                        (sqrt (- (* b b)
                                (* 4 a c))
                (* 2 a))
```

FIGURE 1.67.   Pattern-matching rule for computing the discriminant of a second-order polynomial.

Figure 1.67 shows an example of how pattern matching can be used with a production rule. If the pattern matches the test expression, then the parameter values are extracted and a root of the polynomial can be computed.

To simplify programming, many production-rule languages and logic-programming languages provide an automatic way of searching for candidate expressions. The job of the interpreter is deciding how to traverse a database to find candidate expressions for possible matching. For example, the following three production rules do most of the work for differentiating polynomials:

```
rule 1: (deriv (* ?a (expt x ?n))) -> (* n a (expt x (n-1)))
rule 2: (deriv (+ ?u ?v)) -> (+ (deriv u) (deriv v))
rule 3: (deriv (- ?u ?v)) -> (- (deriv u) (deriv v))
```

These rules are examples of a rewrite or **substitution language**. In such a language, there is a working memory containing one or more expressions. Patterns are matched against these expressions. If they match, then the rule replaces the expression with a new one. Multiple rules correspond to different possible patterns in memory, treated as distinct cases. For rules in this format, the if-part is often called the **left side** and the then-part is called the **right side**.

Figure 1.68 dissects the first rule for our analysis. Given an appropriate interpreter, this rule specifies how to differentiate a single term in a polynomial: Create a new term such that the coefficient is the coefficient of the matching term times its exponent, and the exponent is the exponent of the matched term minus one.

```
if-part: {pattern to be matched}
    (deriv (* ?a (expt x ?n)))      ;IF there is an expression matching ?a $x^{?n}$

then-part: {rewrite actions to be carried out}
    (* n a (expt x (n-1)))          ;THEN replace it with na $x^{n-1}$
```

FIGURE 1.68.   Rewrite production rules combine pattern matching and action with search.

Initial expression
```
(deriv (+ (* (/ 2 3)(expt x 3))
          (* 7 (expt x 2))
          (* 12 x)
          (- 8)))
```

Step 1: Apply rule 2 to the sum of terms
```
(+ (deriv (* (/ 2 3)(expt x 3)))
   (deriv (* 7 (expt x 2)))
   (deriv (* 12 x))
   (deriv (-8)))
```

Step 2: Apply rule 1 to the first term
```
(+ (* 2 (expt x 2))
   (deriv (* 7 (expt x 2)))
   (deriv (* 12 x))
   (deriv (-8)))
```

Step 3: Apply rule 1 to the second term
```
(+ (* 2 (expt x 2))
   (* 14 x)
   (deriv (* 12 x))
   (deriv (-8)))
```

After a few more steps we have the derivative
```
(+ (* 2 (expt x 2))
   (* 14 x)
   12)
```

FIGURE 1.69.   Rule applications in the differentiation of a polynomial.

Figure 1.69 shows how these rules could be applied in the differentiation of a polynomial. In the first step, rule 2 is applied to change the derivative of a sum to the sum of some derivatives. Our single-step application of the rule operates on all of the terms at once. Alternatively, rules could be written that convert a sum of *n* terms into one term plus the sum of the remaining terms. In the second step, rule 1 is applied to differentiate the first term. This process continues until no more rules match and the polynomial is completely differentiated. For simplicity we have omitted some intermediate rules and steps for simplifying terms. For example, in addition to the steps in Figure 1.69, (expt x 1) is reduced to x, and (* 2 7) is reduced to 14.

Pattern-matching languages enable us to write very short programs. The first advantage is that the program does not need to specify in detail how to extract information. It need only specify the patterns to be matched and the use to be made of the extracted information. Much of the programmatic detail is supplied by the language interpretation program, which searches the graph, matches patterns against expressions, extracts parameters, and builds new structures with substituted information.

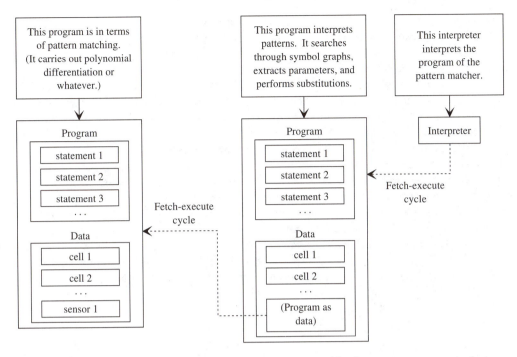

FIGURE 1.70. An example of metalevel factoring. In pattern-matching languages, programs can be terse because much of the work of graph search, matching, parameter extraction, and substitution is done automatically.

This approach in pattern-matching language shows an important way that conciseness can be achieved in programming: metalevel factoring. This conciseness is possible due to the partitioning of interpretation into two levels. As illustrated in Figure 1.70, one level of interpretation is carried out by the rules in pattern matching. This process differentiates polynomials, finds roots, and so on. The symbolic description of this program is simple, largely, because so much of the work is done by the next interpreter: the processor that interprets the pattern-matching rule program. That processor selects which rule to fire, locates candidate symbolic expressions to consider, tests candidate expressions to determine whether they match the patterns given in the if-parts of rules, extracts the values of pattern variables, and rewrites expressions according to the actions in the then-parts of the rules.

1.4.5 *Expressiveness, Defaults, and Epistemological Primitives* `ADVANCED`

The preceding discussion of symbol manipulation languages emphasizes simplicity of expression. In this section, we extend the discussion from programming languages to representation languages. The boundary between programming and representation languages is not sharp since many ideas that started out as part of representation languages are now part of programming languages and conversely. Roughly, representation languages represent facts in a way that enables their use for many different possible purposes. A **representation system** includes a database containing facts expressed in the representation language plus an interpreter that provides answers to queries. In this section, we consider what it means for representation languages and query languages to be expressive.

Our perception of the simplicity of computational models depends on being able to describe them in simple terms and on being able to leave many things unsaid. We begin with a characterization of representation in terms of predicate calculus and then consider other well-known languages.

In 1985, Hector Levesque and Ronald Brachman (Levesque & Brachman, 1985) called attention to what they described as a tradeoff between tractability and expressiveness. They asked: What is the appropriate service to be provided by a knowledge representation system? They offered a strawman proposal. A knowledge representation (KR) system manages a knowledge base and presents a picture of the world or an environment based on what it represents. Given a knowledge base, they required that a KR system be able to determine, given a sentence, Z, whether that sentence is believed to be true. More precisely, assuming that the knowledge base is a finite set of sentences and that KB stands for their conjunction, they wanted to know whether KB => Z. Determining this generally requires not just retrieval capabilities but also inference.

Their strawman proposal was to use the first-order predicate calculus as the exemplary representation language. This has the advantage that

$$KB \vDash Z \qquad \text{iff} \qquad \vdash (KB => Z)$$

That is, if Z is true then it is derivable from the sentences in the knowledge base. Unfortunately, this requirement also has the effect of ensuring that the strawman service as described cannot be provided.

The difficulty of providing this service follows from its generality. No theorem prover can always determine the answer for arbitrary sentences in reasonable time. Completeness requires generality and brings a price of intractability. This is not to say that finding a proof or counterexample is intractable for every sentence. For most theorem provers there are classes of problems that are easy. Many theorem provers also have worst cases that are much more time-consuming than the average cases and the easy ones. If theorem provers are complete then it follows that some classes of problems are intractable.

Knowledge systems use a wide range of representations with different expressiveness. One dimension along which representations differ is the degree to which they can leave things *unsaid* about a model. There are different ways that a language can be incomplete in what it can say.

Consider the logic sentences in Figure 1.71. The first sentence says John is not a female without saying what he is. The second sentence says that either Jack or Monica is a parent of Steve, but does not specify which. Nor does it say that some other person might not be a parent of Steve, since nothing has been said about a person having exactly two biological parents. The third sentence says that Steve has at least one male parent but does not say who that parent is. The fourth sentence says that all of Steve's neighbors own pets without saying who those neighbors are, who their pets are or even whether there are any neighbors. These examples show that first-order logic can leave many kinds of details unspecified. It avoids representing details that may not be known. Indeed, this ability to not specify details is quite remarkable. It reflects the original intended use of predicate calculus to formalize infinite collections of mathematical enti-

> ¬ Female (John)
> Parent (Steve, Jack) ∨ Parent (Steve, Monica)
> ∃ x Parent (Steve, x) ∧ Male (x)
> ∀ x Neighbor (Steve, x) => ∃ y Owns-Pet (x y)

FIGURE 1.71.   Example sentences with different kinds of incomplete information.

ties. This use emphasizes different requirements from typical applications of knowledge systems where domains are often finite and many of their details are explicitly represented.

Following the exposition in Levesque and Brachman, 1985, we consider incomplete knowledge and inference for a relational database, a logic program, and a semantic network. As we consider KR systems based on these languages, we will see not only that they cannot perform the strawman KR service, but also that they necessarily must perform different though related services. Our goal in the following is not to give a thorough characterization of relational databases, logic programming, or semantic networks. Rather, it is to sketch them briefly and compare them to reveal general issues about the expressivenesss of representations.

Representation and Inference Using a Relational Database

Databases store facts. In this section we consider examples from a relational database to show limitations that the format imposes on the kinds of incompleteness in represented facts. In principle, it might be argued that a database imposes no limitations on information because it is a general storage medium. In this argument, the interpretation of symbols is entirely open-ended. For example, we could use a database to build exactly one table that would just be addresses and memory contents for an arbitrary computer program. However, this misses the intent of the mechanisms provided with databases.

Databases have mechanisms for matching and retrieval and these mechanisms are used in a well-defined way by the query language. These are similar in purpose to the pattern-matching operations we discussed earlier for symbol-manipulation tasks. When we speak of using a database and having a "natural" or "standard" interpretation, we presume to make the most use of the query language and the retrieval mechanisms.

Figure 1.72 lists some entries from a relational database.

To characterize in first-order logic the information in these sentences, we can use a collection of function-free atomic sentences such as the following:

> Course(CS131)   Course(CS112)   Enrollmen (CS131, 60)
> Days(CS112,TTh)   Days(CS228A, TTh)   Cross-Listin (CS275, Ling120)

The expression of incompleteness is much more limited than in our earlier examples from predicate calculus. For example, we have no sentences like the following.

> ¬ Time(CS228A, 11)   Days(CS112, TTh)∨ Days(CS112, MWF)

Course	Name	Days	Time	Enrollment	Instructor	Cross-Listing
CS131	Applied Linear Algebra	MW	11	60	Golub	
CS275	Computational Linguistics II	TTh	3	10	Kay	Linguistics 120
CS112	Computer Organization	TTh	11	40	Gupta	
CS228A	Intro to Knowledge Systems	TTh	4	50	Stephic	
CS237A	Advanced Numerical Analysis	MWF	10	40	Staff	
CS260	Concrete Mathematics	MWF	9	35	Knuth	
	. . .					

FIGURE 1.72.   Example entries from a relational database.

Furthermore, the standard interpretation of a database contains more information than is typical of a collection of sentences from first-order logic. Suppose we were to ask the question,

"How many courses are offered at 11 o'clock?"   (7)

Assuming that the database includes only courses in the Computer Science Department, question (7) might be answered by a query (8) such as

Count c in Course where $c.Time = 11$ (8)

This query asks about the entries in the database. The relation between those entries and the world is in the mind of the questioner. It is also supported by various assumptions that the query system makes in its processing.

Returning to question (7), a logical account of what the query should return must use information not explicitly stored in the database. For example, it must determine which literal atoms correspond to distinct course names. In the simplest case, unique atom names correspond to unique courses. To indicate this with theorems would require us to add a statement expressing explicit inequality for every pair of constants. Such theorems are not represented explicitly in the database. However, even if we did that, it would not quite work in this case. Course CS275 is cross-listed between the departments of Linguistics and Computer Science, resulting in two course numbers for the same course. Thus, the rule for determining unique courses would need to be expanded to something like "unique atoms declared to be courses correspond to unique courses unless declared otherwise by an explicit Cross-Listing relation." Another important assumption used in answering query (8) to the database is that all of the courses that are offered are listed in the database. This is an example of a **closed-world assumption** (CWA). By embodying these assumptions, the query system is able to answer a question about the world using a computation on its database.

An important issue in processing queries is in finding answers quickly. In the context of databases this topic is called query optimization. Suppose we wanted to answer the following question:

"How many courses in the Computer Science Department are offered at 11 o'clock
by graduates of MIT who also teach in the medical school?"   (9)

In searching for an answer to such a query there are several choices about how to search the database. Should the system first identify all of the instructors of 11 o'clock classes in the Computer Science Department? Alternatively, it could identify all instructors who graduated from MIT or all instructors who teach both at the medical school and in the Computer Science Department. Query optimization employs a computational model of a database based on the times required by different database operations. Query optimization is concerned with the order that different fields are indexed and the size of sets on which various operations are performed. Although a discussion of the methods of query optimization is beyond the purposes of this section, we notice that such concern with the efficiency of answering a particular query is an important practical concern. Unfortunately, it is also outside the scope of the strawman KR service. Knowledge about query optimization is another example of knowledge we like a knowledge system to have but that we would not need to specify. In this case, the knowledge is unsaid and is unsayable in the knowledge base because it is handled by the query optimizer, which is a separate program. Beyond trivial problems, knowledge about how to make inferences efficiently is crucial.

In summary, inference is carried out by database operations and accessed through a query language. Normally, a query language makes certain assumptions about the way that symbols are used to represent the world. Knowledge for making inferences efficiently is held in the query system.

Representation and Inference Using Logic Programming

In this section we give a short introduction to logic programming to show how it fits in this sequence of representations with different expressiveness.

In logic programming a knowledge base is a collection of first-order sentences. They have the form:

$$\forall\; x_1\; x_2\; \ldots\; x_n\; [P1 \wedge \ldots \wedge Pm => P_m{+}1]$$
where each P_i is atomic and $m \geq 0$. $\hspace{3cm}$ (10)

Sentences in this form are called **Horn clauses**. Horn clauses are more general than sentences in a relational database. In the case where $m = 0$ and the arguments to the predicates are all constants, this reduces to the form of a relational database.

Figure 1.73 gives some examples of sentences in PROLOG. Each sentence ends with a period. The first six sentences are function-free atomic sentences as with the relational database examples. They say that "Paige is female" and "Morgan is male" and so on. The next four sentences are similiar except that they involve a 3-ary predicate.

The second to the last sentence defines brother as a **derived relation**. Roughly, it says that "someone is my brother if he has the same parents that I have and he is male and he is not me." In comparison with the previous syntax for Horn clauses, PROLOG elides the universal quantification symbols, replaces the conjunction symbols with commas, and replaces the implication symbol with :-. The \= means "roughly not equal," although we will discuss some subtleties of this later. A PROLOG rule consists of a head and a body, connected by :-. The head of the last rule in Figure 1.73 is brother(Self, Sibling). The head describes what the rule is intended to define. The body of the rule is the implied conjunction parents(Self, Mom,

```
                      female(paige).
                      female(mabel).
                      female(ellen).
                      male(morgan).
                      male(stan).
                      male(mark).

                      parents(mabel, paula, peter).
                      parents(stan, paula, peter).
                      parents(paige, ellen, mark).
                      parents(morgan, ellen, mark).

   brother(Self, Sibling) :- parents(Self, Mom, Dad), parents(Sibling, Mom,
           Dad), male(Sibling), Sibling \= Self.

   likes(polar, Person) :- has_food(Person), pats(Person, polar).
```

FIGURE 1.73.   Example sentences from PROLOG.

Dad), parents(Sibling, Mom, Dad), male(Sibling), Sibling \= Self. The body
describes a conjunction of goals that must be satisfied, one after the other, for the head to be true.
The body and head in PROLOG are in the reverse order that we defined them for the Horn clause
in (10).

In PROLOG, atoms that begin with capital letters are taken to be variables and atoms that
begin with lowercase letters are taken to be constants. The last sentence means roughly that
"Polar likes anyone who pats him and has food." In this sentence, polar is a constant corresponding to my neighbor's dog and Person is a variable. (Curiously, English conventions for
capitalizing names is at odds with PROLOG syntax in this example.)

The analog in PROLOG to processing a database query is interpreting a PROLOG program. Figure 1.74 illustrates some steps in processing the statement brother(paige, Sibling), which translates roughly as "Who is Paige's brother?" The process begins by retrieving
the rule that defines brother and binding Self to paige. This value for the Self variable is
kept for the subsequent matches in the sentence. The interpreter then steps through the clauses of
the rule. In the first clause, unification binds Mom to ellen and Dad to mark. After a few more
steps, a consistent binding is found and the answer morgan is returned.

This example is a very simple case. Only one step of backtracking was required, when the
matching routine binds both Self and Sibling to paige.

Figure 1.75 gives another example of running the same program, except that a different
query is answered because a different argument is made constant. In this case, the query
brother(Self, morgan) translates roughly as "Who is Morgan the brother of?" This ability
to use definitions in more than one kind of computation is one of the interesting features of logic
programming. It exemplifies what is meant when people say that logic programming makes it
possible to say *what* a program should compute without saying *how* it should compute it. This is

A Query
```
?- brother(paige, Sibling)
```

Trace of the matching process
Match brother(paige, Sibling) against the database.
This retrieves the definition of brother:
```
parents(Self, Mom, Dad), parents(Sibling, Mom, Dad), male(Sibling), Sibling
   \= Self.
```
bind Self to paige.
Match parents(paige, Mom, Dad) against the database.
bind Mom to ellen.
bind Dad to mark.

Match parents(Sibling, ellen, mark) against the database.
This first match is with parents(paige, ellen, mark)
bind Sibling to paige.

Match male(paige) against the database.
This fails and there is no method for proving male. So the matcher starts to unwind.

It looks for another match to (Sibling, ellen, mark) in the database.
It matches parents(morgan, ellen, mark)
bind Sibling to morgan.

Match male(morgan) against the database.

Test that morgan /= paige.

Return: morgan, that is, brother(paige, morgan)

FIGURE 1.74.   Processing a PROLOG query using the program in Figure 1.73.

also called a "declarative reading" of a logic program. For this query, the program returns the answer paige.

However, reading and executing a program in more than one way is not without costs. A PROLOG interpreter proceeds through its generation and backtracking process in a predetermined order. In logic programming languages, common practice is to write programs to be efficient for one expected use.

In our example of the brother predicate, it is assumed that the most common computation is to find the brother of Self. The way the predicate is written prescribes how the computation in that case is carried out as follows. First the Mom and Dad of Self are determined. Then the system generates candidates in the database having the same Mom and Dad as parents. Then candidates that are not male are eliminated. Finally, a check is made that the candidate is not equal to Self. The backtracking interpreter enables the program to answer other questions, but at a cost of more search. For example, when brother is asked how to determine whose brother Sibling

Another Query
```
    ?- brother(Self, morgan)
```

Trace of the matching process

Match `brother(Self, morgan)` against the database.
This retrieves the definition of brother:
```
parents(Self, Mom, Dad), parents(Sibling, Mom, Dad), male(Sibling).
```
bind `Sibling` to morgan.

Match `parents(Self, Mom, Dad)` against the database.
The first match is with `parents (mabel, paula, peter)`.
bind `Self` to `mabel`.
bind `Mom` to `paula`.
bind `Dad` to `peter`.

Match `parents (Sibling=Morgan, Mom=paula, Dad=peter)` against the database.
This fails. The interpreter backtracks.

Match `parents (Self, Mom, Dad)` against the database.
The next match is `parents (stan, paula, peter)`.
This fails in the same manner as the previous.

Match `parents (Self, Mom, Dad)` against the database.
The next match is `parents (paige, ellen, mark)`.
bind `Self` to `paige`.
bind `Mom` to `ellen`.
bind `Dad` to `mark`.

Match `parents(morgan, ellen, mark)` against the database.
This succeeds.

Match `male(morgan)` against the database.
This succeeds.

Test that `morgan /= paige`.
This succeeds.

Return: `paige`, that is, `brother(paige, morgan)`

FIGURE 1.75.   Another PROLOG query: "Who is Morgan the brother of?"

is, it begins by generating candidates for `Self` that have a `Mom` and `Dad`. The process is sound, but inefficient.

Logic programming extends the capability for determining whether a sentence is true beyond that of a relational database because it includes instructions for performing inferences that can determine the truth of derived relations. Thus, unlike the case of a relational database, some of the knowledge about the order in which to try inferential steps is in the knowledge base (database) and under the control of the programmer as expressed by the ordering of clauses.

In performing its inferences, the PROLOG interpreter makes several assumptions. It assumes that unique atoms refer to unique individuals. This assumption is reflected in the way that unification works. Obviously, the only constants it considers are those in the database. This is the closed-world assumption. It also assumes that something it cannot prove must be false. This explains the rationale behind the backtracks in Figures 1.74 and 1.75. This is called a "failure-as-negation" (FAN) assumption.

PROLOG is not a complete theorem prover. It is based on a resolution theorem prover for Horn clauses. The particular strategy that it uses is a form of linear input resolution. The inference process is split into two parts: a retrieval part that extracts atomic facts from a database by pattern-matching and a search part that tries to use non-atomic Horn sentences to form the inferences. There are many details that could be discussed about how PROLOG goes about deciding what clause to consider next and how this relates to more general theorem provers, but discussing them would take us beyond our current purposes.

However, it is interesting to note that the kinds of incompleteness of knowledge that logic programming can represent are similar to those in relational databases. For example, there are no clauses like the following:

$$\neg \, male \, (paige) \qquad parents \, (paige, ellen, mark) \vee parents \, (paige, ozma, wizard)$$

PROLOG has predicates for NOT and disjunction. However the predicate NOT(B) does not declare that B is false. Rather, it tests whether the negated clause *can be proven*. It succeeds if the negated clause cannot be proven. The status of this kind of statement is different from the others that we have discussed. For example, its effect depends not only on the contents of the knowledge base but also on the power of the theorem prover.

On one hand, including NOT in a language undermines its proof semantics. Characterizing what inferences are true becomes quite difficult. On the other hand, statements involving not can be quite useful for modeling certain kinds of human reasoning about defaults that resist formalization using standard semantics of logic. They allow the language to say "assume x if you cannot prove otherwise."

Within PROLOG, negation and disjunction can be used in rules, but they cannot be included as ground statements since all ground statements must be atomic. Similarly, there are restrictions on the $\neq$ predicate. Different versions of PROLOG treat it differently, but in most common ones it can only be used if the terms have already been bound. It succeeds only if the terms are different.

In summary, logical languages express several things. Like a relational database, they describe a space of possibilities. This is reflected in focusing on the terms in the database coupled with the closed world assumption. We can find all possible candidates for Paige's brother in the database. Restricting the kinds of incomplete knowledge in the language limits the work required of the inference machinery. Unlike a relational database, logical programming makes it possible to represent derived propositions. At the same time, the way that the statements for deriving propositions are expressed determines the efficiency of the search strategy for each kind of query. Clauses are considered in a predefined order so that logic programs implicitly embody expectations about what queries will be asked in terms of how a computation is performed. In

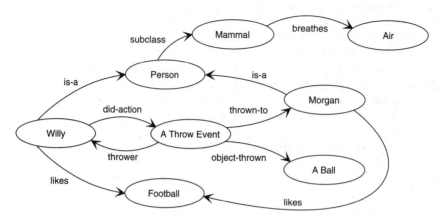

FIGURE 1.76. A simple semantic network.

other words, the way that a program is written makes some inferences more efficient than others. Finally, the inclusion of facilities like NOT can express metalogical knowledge. They make it possible to advise the inferential process about how to carry out default reasoning, a concept that is not part of standard logic.

Representation and Inference Using Frame Languages

We now revisit semantic networks as introduced earlier. Since there is no single language of semantic networks, we will concern ourselves with some features that have been common to a wide range of frame languages.

Figure 1.76 presents a semantic network representation similar to ones we considered earlier in this chapter.

One of the things to notice is that a semantic network provides different ways to handle predicates of different arity. Unary relations are called types or classes. They are organized in a taxonomy. For example, the relation

   Person(Willy)

is represented using the is-a link between the nodes Willy and Person. Binary predicates are represented by arcs. For example, in Figure 1.76, the binary relation meaning "Willy likes football," represented in logic by

   Likes(Willy, Football)

shows up in the semantic network as the arc labeled likes connecting the nodes Willy and Football. Binary relations are sometimes called attributes. Higher-order relations are represented by creating special objects. For example, the predicate

   Threw(Willy, Ball, Morgan)

is represented in Figure 1.76 with a special kind of object called a "throw-event."

Inferences in frame languages about classes take several forms. In the simplest case, all members of a class have some common property. The characterization of the property A is given at the level of the class class, but is interpreted as being a property of its instances.

$\forall x \, (\text{is-a} \, (x \, \text{class}) => A(x))$

We called such reasoning from classes to instances inheritance reasoning. In Figure 1.76, we infer that "Willy breathes air" from the facts that Willy is a person, person is a subclass of mammal, and all mammals breath air. By placing an attribute high in a taxonomy, one can allow many instances below to inherit that property. This kind of reasoning lends itself to a graph search where one starts with the node in question and searches up the taxonomy to find a node defining the property. It also lends itself to certain intuitive approaches for default reasoning. For example, if nodes at different levels of a taxonomy indicate different values to be inherited, then the search process can be used to either specialize or override the values of attributes of nodes at different levels.

There are other variations on information about inheritance. Predicate calculus provides no knowledge or epistemological primitives for organizing a knowledge base. In contrast, many frame languages provide primitives for expressing certain commonly used relations for organizing the terminology of a KS. These include such relations as subclasses, specifications for defaults, and primitives for defining the structure of objects in terms of their parts. These primitives are a beginning of a theory of semantics.

A simple example suffices to give the flavor of such expressions as they relate to the inheritance relations discussed so far. Figure 1.77 defines Plant-Part as a class for large structural elements of growing plants.

One of the properties of a plant part is that it has a color. In a frame language, we can indicate that all parts have some color by establishing a description involving a color link from the class. This is the link labeled "value specification" in Figure 1.77. That link indicates a closed-world specification. In particular, it indicates that the color of an instance of Plant-Part must be some instance of the Color node and that in the absence of other information we can assume that the color of a plant part is brown. In frame languages, such an instance of Color must be a **filler** of this role in an instance of Plant-Part.

Another node in the figure is the Tree node. The Tree node illustrates some notions for structuring inheritance relations. Frame languages incorporating such notions are called **structured inheritance languages**.

The Tree node defines a property of trees called foliage. The notation in Figure 1.77 is supposed to indicate the following: Trees have foliage. Foliage is a relation indicating a part of a tree. The value or filler in a foliage relation of an instance of a tree must be an instance of a plant part. Like all plant parts, tree foliage has a color. Its color, however, is limited to red and green rather than the full range of colors. Furthermore, the default color of foliage is green rather than brown. The dashed links in Figure 1.77 are intended to suggest this web of relations, so that the plant-part description for foliage of trees is related to the general description of plant part and overrides some of its elements.

This richer set of links conveys an important shift in style of representation. This style recognizes the awkwardness of representing objects, especially objects with structure, in terms of flat propositions associated with a single node. In this style, an individual is represented by a

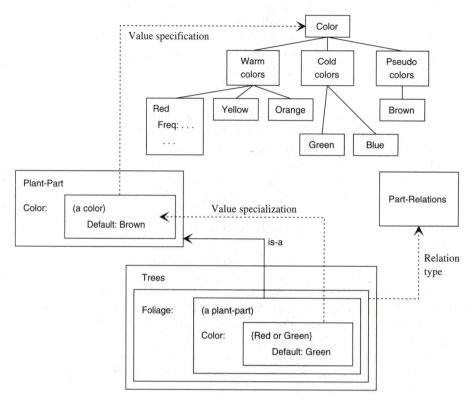

FIGURE 1.77. Example of structured inheritance in a frame-based representation language.

cluster of nodes where some nodes and links, primitive to the interpreter, are used to define the mutual roles. Within such representations, single is-a links are inadequate for capturing the many relations between the bundled parts. The richer set of connections opens up the possibility of specializing subconcepts of generic ones by restricting some of the subparts of the description embodied by the generic concept.

With the usual but important caveats about efficiency of inference and reasoning with incomplete knowledge, the meaning of everything we have said here about frame languages is similar to what we said about relational databases and logic programming in that it can be characterized by predicate calculus statements. What is extra is the set of knowledge primitives and guidelines for representation. Such guidelines are sometimes called the epistemological level for characterizing frame languages because they introduce primitives for knowledge used by the interpreter. In practical knowledge base tools, which emphasize the process of building KSs incrementally, such characterizations are also useful for limited forms of type checking as new concepts are added to the KS.

The appeal of the graphical nature of semantic networks has led to many forms of reasoning that are not well understood. Historically, developers of semantic networks have been lax in characterizing the semantics of the representations. As many formalists have lamented, it is unfortunately much easier to develop algorithms that seem to reason over structures of a certain kind than it is to characterize the behavior of those algorithms carefully or to justify the reasoning that is carried out.

Referring back to our earlier examples of a relational database and logic programming, frame languages are intermediate in terms of how they embody inference. As with relational databases, inference is carried out by an external interpreter that makes various assumptions about the network. Unlike logic programming, there is no way to express derived propositions. The main example of inference for semantic networks is reasoning about inheritance of properties. As in the case of NOT in logic programming, computations of default values have provided examples of reasoning that are said to model human reasoning but that are not characterized easily in terms of truth or proof semantics.

1.4.6 *The Symbol Level and the Knowledge Level*

The *what-to-how* spectrum ranks programming languages in terms of expressiveness. Programs written in languages at the "how" end of the spectrum describe what to do in many, simple steps. At the "what" end of the spectrum, languages provide integrated sets of powerful primitives. Because many of the details of what to do are represented in the interpreter, the programs written in these languages are shorter.

A representation system is expressive to the extent that it makes it possible to leave things unsaid, both in the language and in queries to the representation system. A striking aspect about this characterization of expressiveness is that the prescription of what an interpreter can bring to bear to process either a program statement or a query is extremely open-ended. Interpreters can be categorized according to what they bring to bear in processing queries.

In the design of knowledge systems, it is useful to distinguish between two levels of analysis known as the symbol level and the knowledge level. The **symbol level** is concerned with manipulating patterns of symbols. It is not concerned with what the symbols designate in an external world, that is, it is not concerned with their reference semantics. The **knowledge level** is concerned with particular tasks and, for that reason, with what symbols mean. At the knowledge level we are concerned with what knowledge is needed to carry out a task and how that knowledge can be used.

Most of the examples of expressiveness in this section have been about the symbol level. Analysis at the symbol level is concerned with the structural complexity of symbol structures. It is concerned with space and time complexity of algorithms over symbol structures, independent of what the symbols mean.

The advantages of expressiveness provided by pattern-matching languages are entirely due to operations at the symbol level. That is, the knowledge that pattern-matching interpreters use to make programs simpler is all about the symbols themselves. The interpreters know about pattern matching, they know about the extraction of parameters during matches, they know about substituting constants for variables, and they know about backtracking search. A theorem prover, a pattern matcher, or a query-processing program could be said to have knowledge, but what they know is about the structure of the symbols that they manipulate. They know about efficient indexing of their tables. They know how to reliably traverse a graph. They can carry out a search for solutions using such information.

When we analyze the complexity of various kinds of algorithms over graphs and relate their running time to properties of the graphs, we are working at the symbol level. Symbol-level analyses are of broad interest in computer science. Similar computational phenomena arise when similar procedures run over similar symbol structures.

The knowledge that an interpreter may use to interpret a statement in a program, representation language, or query, however, can also include knowledge and assumptions about the world. In our examples of the expressiveness of representation languages, we referred to closed-world assumptions and failure as negation assumptions. These examples are at the knowledge level because they are concerned with what symbols mean.

More broadly, an interpreter can gain further expressive leverage in query processing by effectively solving problems. In this way it moves beyond what we call a representation system toward what we call a knowledge system. The knowledge employed includes methods for finding solutions and knowledge for guiding that search. Chapter 2 discusses problem solving and the use of search methods as ways to find solutions. An analysis of a task at the knowledge level characterizes the use of world knowledge in terms of its effect in guiding the search of a space of possible solutions.

Looking further ahead, Chapter 3 discusses fundamentally what knowledge is and where it comes from. It extends our discussion about the construction of knowledge systems beyond the symbol-level manipulations in the computer to the social situations in which knowledge systems are created and used.

1.4.7 *Summary and Review*

In this section we considered the expressiveness of programming and representation languages. One indicator of expressiveness is what things need not be stated explicitly. In pattern-matching languages, the simplicity of the programs results because some operations are performed automatically by the interpreter of the language. Some of the complexity is factored out of the program and placed in the interpreter. In several example programs we saw how the expression of the differentiation program was made simpler when many of the details of graph search, parameter extraction, and substitution were handled by the interpreter of the pattern-matching language. This approach is called metalevel factoring.

Representations differ what they can express easily and the things they express at all. For example, all of the representations we considered were less capable than predicate calculus in expressing certain kinds of incompleteness of knowledge, such as ground literals involving negation and disjunction.

In the relational database example, the language is equivalent to function-free terms with constant arguments and the interpreter is the query system. We saw that a practical query language actually depends on additional assumptions, such as closed-world assumptions, and also that it needs to be concerned about the efficiency of query processing.

In the logic programming example, the representation is in terms of Horn clauses and the interpreter is that for the language. We required closed-world assumptions as well as failure-as-negation assumptions for use in the search for solutions.

In the structured inheritance networks, we saw that epistemological primitives can be used to organize clusters of nodes into larger coherent structures. These languages provide prescriptions for organizing representations, including specialized closed-world assumptions and knowledge about defaults. This idea has been extended to the design of specialized representation shells for specific tasks and to the approach of building large knowledge bases with many potentially reusable representations and compositional primitives. Such approaches are on the edge of current research.

Exercises for Section 1.4

Ex. 1 [00] *Pattern Matching.* Assume the following symbol structures:

> (and (likes Fido Bonzo)(feather-brained Fido))
> (and (likes Rover Lucky)(feather-brained Lucky))
> (and (likes Spot Sperald)(feather-brained Lucky))
> (or (likes Sport Dizzy)(feather-brained Dizzy))

What values would be assigned to the pattern variables by matching the following pattern against each of the symbol structures?

> (and (likes ?dog ?person)(feather-brained ?person))

Hint: Some of the expressions do not match at all.

■ Ex. 2 [15] *Common Sense and the Database.* Consider a database of family relationships. Suppose there are predicates for brother, father, mother, sister, and surname. For example, the database may contain several thousand facts like the following:

(brother Joe Mike)	(brother Mike Azel)	(brother Ed Joe)
(father Joe Pete)	(father Fred Sam)	(father Andy Nick)
(surname Mike Smith)	(surname Sam Stevens)	

You may assume for the purposes of this exercise that the personal names used in these relations are unique identifiers for individuals. In addition, there are some rules for inferring surnames:

> *Rule 1: "A father and a son always have the same surname."*
> If (father ?fath-1 ?son-1) and (surname ?fath-1 ?sur),
> then (assert (surname ?son-1 ?sur))

> *Rule 2: "Two brothers always have the same surname."*
> If (brother ?bro-1 ?bro-2) and (surname ?bro-1 ?sur),
> then (assert (surname ?bro-2 ?sur))

(a) In what way is rule 1 weaker than the common-sense meaning of the corresponding natural language statement? Discuss briefly.
(b) Does rule 2 have the same problems as rule 1? How does the answer to this question depend on the properties of the pattern-matching process of the rule interpreter?
(c) Give two additional rules similar to the ones above that would extend the situations for inferring the surnames of brothers, fathers, or sons. Briefly discuss any relevant properties of the matching process of the rule interpreter.
(d) Would it be appropriate to add a notation saying that the brother relation is commutative? (*Hint*: This is a trick question. The given database is missing entries for some crucial kinds of people in families.)

Ex. 3 [CD-00] *Simulation versus Deduction.* After staring at several production-rule programs, Professor Digit exclaimed, "Eureka! Simulation and deduction are just the same thing! All of these programs use production rules and some control structure or other! It's all just if–then or pattern matching." Do you agree with Professor Digit? Explain briefly.

Ex. 4   *[L-05] Representation Using Predicate Calculus.* Sometimes the naive translation of statements into the predicate calculus can be misleading. Consider the following statement:

```
Every person knows someone who has a feather-brained dog.
```

(*a*) Represent this statement in predicate calculus.
(*b*) Is the logical interpretation of the statement realistic? Give an example of what else a program would need to know to make realistic use of such a statement.

Ex. 5   *[!-15] Control in Production Systems.* In production-rule systems, it often happens that more than one rule matches the data in the working memory. When this happens and it is desired to fire only one rule, some means must be found for selecting among the rules. The set of rules that match the data at a given cycle is called the **conflict set**. A method for choosing which rules in a conflict set to fire is called a **conflict-resolution strategy**.

Suppose the following set of rules is used for recommending choices of food for patrons in a restaurant. The left sides are conjunctions of terms that must be in the memory, and the right sides list foods to be recommended.

For example, rule 3 can be translated roughly as "If it is breakfast time and the patron is overweight, then recommend cereal."

```
rule-1: breakfast-time -> (eggs bacon)
rule-2: breakfast-time hungry -> (eggs bacon waffles)
rule-3: breakfast-time overweight -> (cereal)
rule-4: breakfast-time hurried -> (juice toast jelly)
rule-5: breakfast-time overweight hungry -> (fruit cereal)
rule-6: breakfast-time kids -> (milk pancakes)
rule-7: breakfast-time runner -> (yogurt fruit)
rule-8: breakfast-time kids hungry -> (pancakes eggs juice)
rule-9: breakfast-time hungry runner -> (fruit cereal)
rule-10: kids -> (pizza)
rule-11: lunch-time kids -> (burgers fries shakes)
rule-12: lunch-time overweight -> (salad)
rule-13: runner -> (sportDrink)
```

(**a**) A rule is in the conflict set if all the terms on the left side of the rule are present in the working memory. What is the conflict set for each of the following cases?

```
working memory-1: kids
working memory-2: hungry runner
working memory-3: lunch-time
working memory-4: lunch-time kids
```

Note: The conflict set can be large or small, depending on how many rules match. Remember that every element on the left side of the rule must match an element in working memory.

(**b**) Suppose instead that the interpreter uses a "most specific rule" strategy. Again, the conflict set is made up of all of the rules that match the data. The winning rule is the one that matches the most terms in the data. In the event of a tie, the earliest rule in the sequence dominates. For each of the following cases, give the conflict sets, the match scores, and the winning rules.

```
working memory-1: kids
working memory-2: breakfast-time hungry kids
working memory-3: hungry runner
working memory-4: breakfast-time seniors
```

(c) Suppose that we change the interpreter of the rules so each cycle proceeds in two passes. First all of the rules are matched against all of the data. Then the most specific rule/data match (determined by the maximum number of matching terms) is identified and that rule is fired. After a rule fires, the data it matched are removed from the working memory and the process is repeated. In the event of a tie, the rule with the lowest index numbers is done first. Conflict sets are recomputed at each cycle. Briefly, describe the actions of the interpreter given the following initial working memory.

```
working memory: breakfast-time kids hungry runner
```

Ex. 6   [*10*] *Rule Interpretation Example*. Use the traffic-light controller rules in Figure 1.62.
(a) Describe the behavior of the traffic-light system when there is no traffic on the farm road. (Focus on the case where there has been no traffic there for a long time.)
(b) Describe the behavior of the traffic-light system when the farm road and the highway are both crowded with traffic.
(c) Describe the behavior of the traffic-light system if the sensor is jammed, so that it always indicates "car-waiting" even when there is no traffic on the farm road.

■   **Ex. 7**   [*!-20*] *Forward and Backward Chaining*. When the firing of rules is driven by matching the left sides of the rules against data, we say that the rules are driven by **forward chaining**. Consider the following rules:

```
(Rule-1
  (if (mother ?mom ?kid))
  (then (parent mom kid)))

(Rule-2
  (if (father ?dad ?kid))
  (then (parent dad kid)))

(Rule-3
  (if (and (parent ?gran ?par)
           (parent par ?kid)))
  (then (grandparent gran kid)))

(Rule-4
  (if (and (brother ?unc ?mom)
           (mother mom ?kid)))
  (then (uncle unc kid)))

(Rule-5
  (if (and (brother ?unc ?dad)
           (father dad ?kid)))
  (then (uncle unc kid)))
```

```
(Rule-6
  (if (and (sister ?an ?mom)
           (mother mom ?kid)))
  (then (aunt an kid)))

(Rule-7
  (if (and (sister ?an ?dad)
           (father dad ?kid)))
  (then (aunt an kid)))
```

(a) Suppose the interpreter fires the rules using forward chaining. The rules are matched against the data in the working memory. When more than one rule matches, the first rule is fired first. The interpreter uses an audit table to keep track of which rules have been fired on which data. Each rule is fired exactly once on each combination of matching data. More specifically, every combination of data is considered for each rule and no rule is fired more than once on the same data. When a rule is fired, the then-part adds new data to the working memory which may then be processed by other rules. The process stops when no more rules match any new data.

Write down the resulting data given that the working memory initially contains the following:

```
(mother Mary Ellen)
(father Virgil Ellen)
(brother Karl Ellen)
(sister Paula Ellen)
(sister Julie Ellen)
(mother Ellen Paige)
(mother Ellen Morgan)
(father Mark Paige)
(father Mark Morgan)
(brother Eric Mark)
(brother Mike Mark)
```

(b) Considering what you observed in part (a), is the answer sensitive to the order in which the rules are fired? Explain briefly.

(c) When the firing of rules is driven by matching the right sides of the rules against goals, we say that the rules are driven by **backward chaining**. For example, we could use backward chaining on the rules to find all of Morgan's aunts. We would first find the rules that conclude that somebody is an aunt, in this case, rules 6 and 7. Proceeding first with rule 6, we examine the left side. If the rule is satisfied, we can apply the rule at once. Otherwise, we can make new goals from the left side and try again. In this case, we can infer that Paula and Julie are Morgan's aunts.

Show how backward chaining can be used to determine Paige's uncles starting from the initial state of the working memory.

(d) Give the trace of backward chaining for determining Paige's grandparents.

(e) In backward chaining to compute Paige's grandparents, and expanding the clauses in rule 3,

```
(and (parent ?gran ?par)
     (parent par Paige)))
```

why is it probably more efficient to consider the clause about Paige's parents first?

(f) Briefly, what would happen if we use this approach to determine Ellen's grandparents?

Ex. 8 *[!-10] From Explicit Representation to Machine Learning.* Upon understanding the operation of a universal Turing machine and the von Neumann architecture, Professor Digit was struck by a sense of profundity. He gathered his graduate students together and announced that there were three main principles that should forever change the way they view computation and machine learning:

☐ Symbol structures are dynamic and changeable in physical symbol systems.
☐ Programs are prescriptions for changing symbol structures.
☐ Programs themselves are represented by symbol structures and can be interpreted by other programs.

From these, Professor Digit concluded that we have the key for building learning systems. Programs could just reason for a while, see how they are doing, and then use symbol processing to modify themselves to be better. Programs could be self-organizing, using the powerful pattern-matching ideas discussed in this section. For example, when a pattern in a rule (the manipulating rule) matched part of another is that simple!

Do you agree? Explain briefly.

Ex. 9 *[CD-CP-16] "Predicate Calculus as Assembly Language."* John Sowa sometimes remarks that predicate calculus (PC) is to a representation language (RL) what assembly language (AL) is to a high-level programming language (HL). Noting that the analogy is not exact, he observes that characterizing what a representation language means in terms of predicate calculus requires an increase in verbosity not unlike the increase in the size of a program description when a program in a high-level language is compiled. This exercise explores some questions inspired by this analogy.

In the following, RL, AL, and HL all correspond to classes of languages. For the purposes of discussion, choose whatever instances of these classes are appropriate.
(a) What semantics is relevant for comparing PC and RL? What semantics is relevant for comparing AL and HL?
(b) What expectations does the analogy about HL:AL create about the relative computational efficiencies of PC and RL? Briefly explain how the analogy is misleading with regard to efficiency.
(c) What things can you express in AL that you cannot say in HL? What kinds of things can you say in HL that you cannot say in AL?
(d) What things can you express in PC that you cannot say in RL? What kinds of things can you express in RL that you cannot say in PC?

Ex. 10 *[05] Basic Concepts.* Determine whether each of the following statements are true or false. If a statement is ambiguous, explain your answer briefly.
(a) *True or False.* Pattern-matching languages tend to provide simple expressions of programs because the detailed operations of matching, parameter extraction, substitution, and backtracking need not be explicitly described in the program.
(b) *True or False.* Requiring that it be possible to tell whether a sentence follows from a database of sentences is intractable even if we limit the class of sentences that can be expressed and tested. (*Note*: The sentence tested and the sentences in the database are *not* arbitrary but are limited to some restricted class. The question is whether proof must be intractable even so.)

(c) *True or False*. Failure as negation is seldom used as a policy in logic programming because there is no fixed upper limit on the amount of time needed to construct a proof.

(d) *True or False*. Horn clauses are more general and expressive than the atomic sentences used in a relational database.

(e) *True or False*. Compared with logic programming languages, structured inheritance languages tend to be strong on expressing inference and weak on providing epistemological primitives.

1.5 *Quandaries and Open Issues*   `ADVANCED`

This chapter concentrated on symbols, symbol structures, and physical symbol systems as fundamental concepts for understanding knowledge systems. In this section, we step back from this broad development to ask how our attitudes about symbols and traditional formal systems can be misleading. We consider results and speculations from cognitive science and philosophy. We briefly discuss theories of cognition that build upward from nerves and others that build downward from intelligent agents. These theories enrich our perspectives about the role of symbols in both computation and communication.

The Physical Symbol System Hypothesis, Again

We begin our consideration of open issues with the hypothesis with which we opened this chapter, the physical symbol system hypothesis by Newell and Simon (1975).

> **The Physical Symbol System Hypothesis**. A physical symbol system has the necessary and sufficient means for general intelligent action.

By this, Newell and Simon meant that an analysis of any system exhibiting general intelligence would show that the system is a physical symbol system and that any physical symbol system of sufficient complexity could be organized to exhibit general intelligence. By *general intelligent action*, they meant the same order of intelligent and purposeful activity that we see in people, including activities such as planning, speaking, reading books, or composing music.

The hypothesis proposes that intelligence follows from the organization of physical systems and that it obeys natural laws. It also suggests that human intelligence follows directly from our organization as physical symbol systems and that, in principle, it is possible to build artificially intelligent systems by creating symbol structures that have the right properties.

Throughout most of this book, we skirt around the question of what constitutes "intelligence." This issue leads to many debates within artificial intelligence, but the arguments have tended to be rather sterile in the context of knowledge systems, where the focus is on the construction of systems with task-specific performance criteria.

Within AI the hypothesis has received a mixed reception. Some researchers consider it obvious and tautological, given that physical symbol systems are capable of manipulating and interpreting symbols. They believe that **mind** is an emergent phenomenon from the right kind of computation. Others find the hypothesis fundamental, but not obvious and potentially wrong. Another argument is that the physical symbol hypothesis is vague and trivial. It begs the important questions of just what kinds of organization are necessary for intelligence, and what kinds of mechanisms are needed for processing the symbols. Supporters of this view argue that the essence of intelligence is in the details. They argue that vague hypotheses are of little use scientifically because they are not testable by experiment. Still others consider the hypothesis circular, turning on definitions of symbol, action, and intelligence that preclude normal kinds of scientific testing.

One of the most extreme positions on this was presented by Rodney Brooks when he argued that intelligent systems need not have representations (Brooks, 1991). Brooks' paper was based on ideas explored building simple robotic creatures called "insects," "mobots," or "animats." He argued that AI has relied too much on the study of representations. He proposed an approach wherein increases in functionality come from a layering of systems, each of which connects perceptors to effectors without symbolic intermediaries. In the same issue, Kirsh (1991) argues that the potential of Brooks' seemingly symbol-free approach is overstated and that the example systems embody symbols anyway.

The status of the physical symbol system hypothesis now is like the status of the axiom of choice before set theory was made rigorous. For many years, set theory was informal. Its theorems were considered obvious and not worthy of careful attention. Then, some puzzling examples were found in strangely constructed infinite sets. This led to the formalization of the seemingly ingenuous axiom of choice in mathematics. This axiom says that the Cartesian product of a nonempty family of nonempty sets is nonempty. Restated more simply, given a set, it is possible to select an element from it. At first nobody recognized that the axiom was needed. Then, after the axiom was made explicit, it was not at all clear what its consequences were. Set theory now includes branches of study with and without this axiom. In just this way, research on artificial intelligence now debates whether symbols are necessary for intelligence.

The debate about the role of symbols takes place in the context of models of mind. Since the time when he first proposed the physical symbol system hypothesis, Newell and others have gone on to develop much more elaborate hypotheses and models of mind. Although reviewing these is beyond the scope of this section, the interested reader is referred to Newell, 1991. The next few sections show how these debates are concerned both with the nature of intelligence and the nature of symbols.

Symbols in Natural Minds

Symbols in computer languages and memories are compact, discrete markings. Critics of computational models of cognition have argued that because symbols in computer systems are digital, they are irrelevant to the operation of memories in living brains. Our concern is with the converse. How do studies of brains or memory offer insights about the design of knowledge systems?

At the time of this writing, progress in understanding how memory in a brain works has been quite limited. Experiments on the biological mechanisms of memory have focused on animals with extremely simple nervous systems. These experiments study small parts of small nervous systems and raise many new questions. Are the mechanisms for memory in one part of the nervous system the same as mechanisms for other parts? What storage and retrieval mechanisms are universal across different species? Are the same mechanisms used for short- and long-term memories?

Beyond the issue of how memories work are larger questions about how minds and brains work. The organization of brains and nervous systems is being studied on many fronts. Within that context, the most crucial property of symbols is their use in causing action at a distance in space or time. Many kinds of actions are possible, such as triggering a specific external activity by the symbol system or evoking larger symbol structures. Symbols can cause action at a distance in space because they can be copied and transmitted to distant processors. Whenever they are presented, symbols cause a processor to carry out a reproducible action. Symbols can cause action at different times because they can be stored in memories and recalled for later use. This "action at a distance" property explains how memories stored in one part of a brain can be used to cause actions, controlled by a distant part of the brain.

The biological memories studied so far employ local, chemical, and physical changes during learning. Chemical traces of brain activity also provide data on how different areas of the brain have specialized functions; detailed timing studies of linguistic and problem-solving activities provide data on how much parallelism must be employed for various mental tasks. Combining these kinds of data for a unified understanding of brain function is a long way off.

Connectionism, Signals, and Symbols

Most of our discussion of the operation of physical symbol systems was based on architectural concepts from Turing and von Neumann machines, in which the processor is separate and distinct from the memory that retrieves symbols, interprets them, and causes operations to be carried out. In these models memory is a passive structure, capable of storage and retrieval but little else. Inspired by models of neural networks, there is an active and vigorous school of thought in cognitive science called connectionism that challenges these basic assumptions about symbols and information processing. Connectionists argue that von Neumann computational models are irrelevant to the operation of a brain.

Connectionist systems are networks of large numbers of simple but highly interconnected units. Each unit is assumed to receive signals along its input lines, either excitatory or inhibitory or both. Typically the individual units do little more than add the signals, perhaps combining them with an internal state. The output of a unit is a simple, nonlinear function, such as a threshold function of the sum. The connectionist framework gives us "distributed symbols," colorfully described as "symbols among the neurons." These distributed symbols have many of the essential properties of the symbols described in this chapter: They are material patterns, recognizable by complicated processors. However, connectionism mixes memories and processors together so much that one cannot draw a neat boundary between them. Connectionism challenges the notion that memory and processors are separable.

One mystery in cognitive models is how it is that slow nerves can compute so quickly. The massively parallel connectionist models have much appeal in explaining this. Related mysteries potentially drawing on massive parallelism include how people can recognize enormous numbers of patterns and how brain function continues without catastrophic failure even when the brain has sustained damage.

How do new symbols and expressions acquire their meanings? Connectionists look toward repeated patterns in the orderliness of the world and in the repeated structure of routine tasks. In this view, the meaning of symbol structures is intimately tied to their creation and use. From the beginning, symbols are linked to perception and action.

Agre and Chapman (1988) have argued that information-processing theories of intelligence presuppose a substantial and implausible amount of mental processing machinery. For example, they propose an "indexical functional" theory of representation rather than having unique symbols that stand for unique objects in the world. Illustrating their ideas in a video game player, they would have an indexical symbol standing for "the bee on the other side of the block in the direction I am moving" rather than having a bee-064 symbol. Roughly, the patterns of interaction between the symbols reflects the patterns of interaction between the observer and the environment. This moves much of the inferential load into the representation and even into the environment. By defining terms indexically, it may also reduce the number of symbols needed.

Fodor and Pylyshyn (1988) argue that a crucial point of difference between connectionist and classical models of mind is that the meaning of a unit in a connectionist account is not a rule-based composition of the meanings of the units to which it is connected. In this chapter we saw that this reductionist view that the meaning of an expression is composed from the meanings of its parts is a property of truth semantics of most representation languages such as the predicate calculus. It is also a property of denotational semantics that describe the operation of programming language, and it is useful in explaining concepts such as recursion.

In a connectionist graph, a link between unit x and unit y means that states of node x causally affect states of unit y. Fodor and Pylyshyn argue that this particular aspect of connectionism disqualifies it from providing a complete basis for a theory of cognition. They favor a classical information-processing model. For example, they observe that people can understand sentences that they have never heard before and that are structured quite differently. Similarly, people carry out wide classes of inferences that they have never made before. In the information-processing model, much of the power comes from pattern matching and **recursive processing** of symbol structures. In the grammar case, rules of grammar and rules of interpretation can be applied recursively in processing long (previously unheard of) sentences. Such recursive processing seems essential to the process and is missing from the connectionist account.

For Fodor and Pylyshyn, the connectionist models are more compelling for explaining low-level perceptual processes than high-level symbol manipulation processes in intelligent systems. From the perspective of knowledge systems, we would like to understand the computational limitations of models built in either way. This is an area in which much basic work remains to be done.

Although the physiological elements of a brain can be reduced to smaller elements, the basic notion that the meaning of the whole is a function of the meanings of the parts becomes less tenable as the parts become as small as individual nerve cells. More important in this realm are patterns of interactions. Marvin Minsky addresses this issue extensively in his book *The Society of Mind*. He describes many kinds of mental phenomena, processes, and possible constructs. One interesting aspect of Minsky's theory is that its elements range from being implementational in nature to being psychological in nature. In this vein, Minsky sees "symbolness" as a matter of degree rather than as a sharp issue. Comparing connectionist and symbolic formalisms for computing in terms of their capabilities and computational resources, Minsky (1990) argues that mental architectures need both kinds.

This notion that representations can have different degrees of a symbol-like character is also in line with computational models of perception. One of the ubiquitous concepts in research on perception is the **signal**. Examples of signals include acoustic waveforms, visual images, or the output of various other sensor arrays. Signals have extents in space and time. We can talk about changes in a signal over a second and can analyze the structure of a signal across both large and small intervals. Signal processing includes developing analyses of signals and various abstractions of them. For example, we can say that a signal has a particular frequency in some interval, or that its amplitude is increasing, or that it is periodic. Analyses of one-dimensional signals on time can attribute particular properties to arbitrary points in time; analyses of two-dimensional images can attribute abstractions to arbitrary points in a plane. When an abstraction is attributed to all of the points of a signal, the abstraction itself is said to be a signal-like representation. We can reasonably ask whether mental representations are more like signals or more like symbols.

Within architectures of cognition, it is now common to refer to subsymbolic processing. As experimentation with neural networks continues, such terminology and methodology will probably find its place in the design of knowledge systems.

Cognition and Levels

It would be nice to have theories of cognition that explain mental activities all the way from the firing of nerves to emotion and reason. Returning to our discussion of the ongoing dialog between information processing psychology and connectionism, Fodor and Pylyshyn suggest that instead of providing a comprehensive architecture for cognition, connectionism may provide a computational account of how nerves work, or rather the physical mechanisms of memory and low-level computation. Thus, although connectionist architectures may be unsuitable as a complete basis for explaining cognition, they are appropriate for *implementing* other levels of cognition. Many cognitive scientists suggest that systems should be understood in terms of **levels** of cognition and representation. Levels also lead to insights about different kinds of symbols, what they are used for, and how they fit into different kinds of theories.

Cognitive scientists characterize two levels of description above the raw physical encodings of memory. The memory itself is called either the **physical level** or the biological level. Above that Newell distinguishes the **symbol level** from the **knowledge level** (Newell, 1982); other cognitive scientists have used the corresponding terms *functional level* and *semantic level* (Pylyshyn, 1984), respectively. The symbol level is a description in terms of symbols (tokens and terms), expressions, and the deterministic interpretation of them. A symbol theory does not refer to the physical properties of a system but only to the way that the system operates. It is concerned with how the behavior of a system can be explained in terms of processes on symbols. In representational theories of mind, a system's behavior is explained not only in terms of the sensory inputs from its immediate environment, but also in terms of its internal state encoded in symbols. The symbol level is concerned with the manipulation of these symbols.

In theories of intelligence, the knowledge level is concerned with the representational content of the symbols. The knowledge level describes systems as agents, having goals, actions, and physical embeddings. An agent selects actions to achieve its goals. Newell's knowledge level is intended for predicting and understanding behavior without having an operational model of the processing actually done by the agent at the symbol level and below. To predict the behavior of an agent at the knowledge level, an observer ascribes to the agent principles of **rationality**. These principles provide constraints on the role and interpretation of symbols, but they are a much less complete description of behavior than a problem-solving process. More detailed accounts of behavior are possible at the symbol level. For example, at the symbol level one could predict which state-to-state transitions are likely to occur in a system, corresponding to rational decisions. Methodological approaches based on taking protocols of people solving problems and comparing these with computer traces (Newell, Simon, & Shaw, 1963) have shown how computer programs can predict and model in considerable detail the steps that human problem solvers take in solving problems. Such experiments provide evidence supporting the validity both of computational models of problem solving and for representational theories of mind.

The terms *symbol level* and *knowledge level* are used somewhat differently for knowledge systems. In the context of knowledge systems, we use the term *knowledge level* to refer to analyses of a task in terms of the knowledge that is needed for a task and how it is used. We use the term *symbol level* to refer to physical representations.

The Semantics of Existential Quantifiers

Terms in natural language routinely refer to states of affairs that are contrary to fact. The following phrases are all problematic in the analysis of their designations: "the current king of France," "the Wizard of Oz," "justice," "the common cold," "the unexplored regions of Africa," "the way things could have been," and "the average American." A well-known aphorism, attributed to Korzibski, comes to mind: "The map is not the territory." One should not confuse symbols with their designations. Linguists collect such odd examples of referring expressions. These examples reflect issues that a coherent theory for reference semantics must deal with. A larger set of such examples gathered from many sources can be found in Chierchia and McConnell-Ginet, 1990.

Graeme Hirst (1989) has analyzed such examples in a challenge to the semantics of existential and universal quantifiers in logic as used to represent the meanings of sentences in natural language. His examples range from sentences about things that aren't there ("I don't own a dog"), events that never happened, existence ("the existence of carnivorous cows"), fictional characters, things at different times, and things that might have been. His examples show that if we want a reasonable account of common sentences about existence, nonexistence, and nonexistent objects then we need more than one notion of existence.

Hirst's work makes it possible for us to see more clearly the assumptions behind our formulations of truth and proof semantics. In our discussion in this chapter about different kinds of semantics, we saw how some linguists use formal language semantics to represent the meaning of sentences. Hirst turns this around. He notices that most logics and knowledge-representation languages base their semantics of universal and existential quantifiers on the ontological assumptions of Russell and Quine. These examples show that these semantics are inadequate for capturing subtleties of meaning in natural language.

How Is Communication Possible?

The interaction between natural language and thought has been a topic of interest of many years. In the 1930s, Benjamin Whorf, an insurance company fire inspector, teamed up with an anthropologist Edward Sapir to explore the influence of language on thought and culture.

According to legend, Whorf developed his interest in language when he saw how frequently verbal misunderstandings led to fires. For example, he noted that people smoke and then thoughtlessly toss their spent matches into "empty" gasoline drums. Because gasoline fumes are highly flammable, empty does not mean safe.

The Sapir–Whorf hypothesis holds that language molds the form and texture of thought. As Whorf puts it, "We dissect nature along lines laid down by our native tongues. . . . We cut nature up, organize it into concepts, and suscribe significances as we do, largely because we are parties to an agreement to organize it this way—an agreement that holds throughout our speech community and is codified in the patterns of our language."

Language influences thought in several ways. It provides the words we use for expression, it determines what is routinely included in sentences, and it determines what is easy and difficult to express. This highlights the role of the social context in an analysis of the meaning of language. Children both learn about the environment and learn language in a social setting. Language shapes learning and perception and arguably thought.

When we communicate with each other through language, we routinely leave things out in the interest of efficiency in speech. This is why communication requires more than translation to internal symbols. To communicate effectively one needs not only only to translate or change the form, but also to fill in the missing information, to make plausible inferences, to integrate new knowledge with previous knowledge, and to signal understandings and possible misunderstandings with the other communicants.

There are deep questions about how these processes might actually work. What is really happening when two people believe they have achieved mutual understanding about the meaning of a word and how do they create a basis for convergence? Faced with such questions, Lakoff and Johnson studied examples of ordinary conversation. Lakoff is a linguist who was struck by the pervasive use of metaphor in everyday language and thought. Johnson is a philosopher who was struck that traditional philosophical views permitted little role for metaphor in understanding the world or mental life. Their book (Lakoff & Johnson, 1980) is a rich source of examples of how metaphors enable us to comprehend one aspect of a concept in terms of another. Consider the sentences "It's hard to *get* that idea *across* to him" and "Your reasons *came through* to us." Both sentences make use of a *conduit metaphor* for communication and meaning. "That boosted my spirits." "I'm feeling up." These sentences use an up/down metaphor, where happy is up and sad is down. Perhaps this is based on common human experiences related to posture. Drooping posture typically goes along with sadness and an erect posture with a positive emotional state. Lakoff and Johnson believe that metaphor enables new symbols and statements to draw on presumably familiar situations, imbuing symbol structures with meaning that relates to commonly shared experiences. Metaphors carry hints about the construction of meaning. This work is exciting because it suggests basic ways that communications can carry meaning, enabling a listener to construct meaning about experiences that he or she did not have with his own senses.

Pieces of Mind

Imagine that we are observing a team of people working together. As outside observers, we could try to model the group as a single symbol system. Of course, there are some immediate quibbles about the persistence of symbols. When someone speaks, the "speech symbols" are heard, recorded, and processed by the participants. One point of view is that the group of people functions as a single physical symbol system, or as an organization as having a **collective intelligence** or group mind. This attribution of agency to a group is not uncommon. Committees, companies, and even nations are often described anthropomorphically as having goals, personalities, strengths, and emotions.

Minsky (1986) has proposed modeling a mind as a society of agents, composed of simpler agents all the way down. In this model, new agents are created and specialized as a mind develops. In comparison with connectionism, which tries to extend upward from essentially nerve models, Minsky's **society of mind** tries to extend downward from powerful abstract agents to simpler ones. Symbols enable remote access. Symbols correspond to activations of "k-lines" that cause various parts of the brain to become active. There are many things yet to be understood about the power of this model of cognition. Indeed, it is difficult to tell at this stage whether various models of cognition are distinguishable experimentally. As a challenge, try to design an experimental psychological test under which the society-of-mind model and some different one would yield different signatures.

The society of mind blurs together all of the issues about communication and computation. Suppose we as observers have a wonderful "symbol-scope" for looking into the activities of a brain housing a mind. In a society model the interactions among high-level agents may be more akin to **communication** between separate beings while symbolic interactions between low-level agents may be more akin to **computation** or message passing as in a programming language. We can imagine looking at a robot who is looking at a scene. Suppose the robot is reaching for a block. As outside observers, we may see early visual processors creating scene descriptions. The early-perception agents may reduce these symbols to descriptions passed along to scene-interpretation agents, which have access to their previous interpretation of the scene a few moments ago, as well as to other scenes. They may identify changing parts of the picture and update an indexical representation of the "current scene." Elsewhere in the mind, we may see some high-level agent describing the place to put the block in terms of other constructions it has made before, possibly using "metaphor" in its communications. Of course, this scenario is very speculative. We just don't know how all this processing is done in the human brain. We can now build robots to carry out parts of it.

Minsky has been a critic of the assumption that there is a useful and crisp division between symbolic and nonsymbolic systems. The society model challenges another sharp distinction, between symbols used externally between agents (natural language) and symbols used internally between agents that form a mind.

Active Documents

People build knowledge bases collaboratively. They discuss and agree about the meanings of symbols in the knowledge bases. They design the behavior of the systems around the agreed upon meanings of the symbols. Viewed this way, knowledge systems are like blackboards or paper. They are a place for writing symbols. They augment human memory and processing with external memory and processing. Like scratch pads or calculators, knowledge systems augment our short-term memories. Like books in a library, they augment long-term memory. Like mail, speech, and blackboards, they augment various media for human communication. As we talk about this, it is curious how we begin to mix cognitive and document perspectives. In any social situation in which knowledge systems are built and serve a group of people, they necessarily must function as **electronic documents**, used for communication among those people.

Knowledge systems are not just passive media for recording and retrieving writings. We expect them to carry out rational processes using the symbols. This brings us back to the cognitive perspective on the meaning of symbols. In knowledge systems, we often use the same language to serve both cognition and documentation. For example, the same production rule language may be used for inference and as elements of explanations of the behavior of a system; the concepts acquired in knowledge acquisition are the same as the concepts used in problem solving. In programming terms, this is akin to the advantage of a "source language debugger," which makes it unnecessary to know a lower-level machine language (the target language for the compiler) when debugging a program. There can be several layers of symbol interpretation and compilation between the symbols that users see and the ones that are used in the rational processes of symbol manipulation. The advantage is that computations can be more efficient when the source language is compiled. To have it both ways, systems need to be able to translate back and forth between external (source) and internal (compiled) languages.

Returning to the discussion of the role of symbols, knowledge systems straddle the distinction between internal and external symbols. The psychological models of symbols are useful for describing the reasoning processes that knowledge systems engage in. The communications models for symbols are most useful for describing how separate knowledge system can interact, and for describing how knowledge systems can interact with people.

About Foundations

Although speculations about evolution, communication, and rationality are fascinating, they are far beyond the concepts that are applied routinely in knowledge engineering. Brian Smith (1986) wants to develop a theory of correspondence explaining the intricate relations among representation, specification, implementation, communication, and computation. Understanding these relations may provide insights about building knowledge systems. Symbols are deeply rooted not just in the methods of knowledge engineering and AI, but also in psychology, mathematics, computer science, and logic. The open issues in this section show that we have not yet heard the last word.

Knowledge systems are not built entirely on firm and securely established foundations. As is the case with even such fields as physics, astronomy, and mathematics, the foundations are subject to inspection, reexamination, and occasional challenges. We make progress in the absence of entirely satisfactory answers. Practitioners depend more on their native ability to communicate than on having a fundamental grasp of the connections between communication and computation. They draw insights from cognitive architectures without insisting that knowledge systems be modeled closely after human minds; they draw on insights from logic without insisting that a knowledge system use strictly logical principles.

It is important to adopt an appropriate attitude toward foundations. In physics and astronomy, new theories of elementary particles and cosmology provide insights about foundations. But only slowly does this work yield knowledge that changes what applied physicists do. In mathematics there have been revolutions in theories of measure and sets, but basic mathematics stays the same. For example, there have been no changes in the tables of integration and differentiation used in calculus, even as the foundations of measure theory have shifted. The subject matter of these fields depends on stable properties that are emergent from the properties of the foundations. For example, a sense of connection and coherence about topics in biology is mostly independent of foundations in chemistry, and a sense of connection and coherence in chemistry is mostly independent of foundations in physics. Although knowledge engineering is newer, there is a sense of connection and coherence about our theories of symbols, knowledge, and search that we expect to persist even as the field expands at its edges.

In considering the foundations of mathematics, Bertrand Russell once remarked that we judge the veracity of our axioms by their implications for our theorems, not our theorems by the axioms. We might say that we judge our symbols by what we can compute with them. This reflects a confident experimental and flexible attitude about foundations: They are important, but subject to change. The details become less relevant with increasing distance. This section conveys that spirit, as well as an engineering attitude about the use of symbols in the design of knowledge systems.

This chapter discusses how symbol systems solve problems. Search provides both computational models and an explanatory framework. This chapter presents basic search methods. The concepts of search are required background for Chapter 3, on knowledge.

2

Search and Problem Solving

Methods for solving problems are central to knowledge engineering. Chapter 1 discussed how symbol structures represent things in the world and how symbol systems can manipulate symbols. This chapter relates symbols to problem solving. It characterizes problem solving in terms of search problems. Problem solving as search rests on five basic ideas:

Symbol structures can stand for solutions to problems. If the problem is to find the best route from Stanford University to the San Francisco airport, a symbol structure describing a sequence of instructions about roads and turns could be a candidate solution. An example of such a symbol structure would be "Turn east on Page Mill and go to the Bayshore freeway. Then turn north on Bayshore freeway and go to the airport exit."

Physical symbol systems can generate symbol structures for alternative candidate solutions. Continuing the airport example, an alternative candidate solution program would be "Turn west on Page Mill and go to Highway 280. Then turn north on Highway 280 and go to Highway 380. Then turn east on Highway 380 and go to the Bayshore freeway. Then turn south on Bayshore freeway and go to the airport exit."

Physical symbol systems can perform tests on candidate symbol structures, to compare the quality of the symbol structures as solutions. For example, given a database about road distances and delays, a program could compare different routes and select the one expected to get us most quickly to the airport.

The processes of search can be described by methods. Methods are essentially programs for carrying out the steps of problem solving. A search method for getting to the airport could specify how to link highway segments from a map, creating a route that leads from a starting place to a destination.

> *Search methods can be informed by and improved by knowledge.* Knowing about alternative airports enables considering a wider range of alternatives. Knowing how traffic patterns at different times of the day affect highway congestion enables better predictions and comparisons of solutions.

In summary, search is a process of creating and comparing symbol structures that designate solutions to problems.

Much effort can be spent and wasted in search. A program could generate many useless symbol structures before finding the right ones. Why not just generate the right solution at once and be done, rather than bothering with the other candidates? The difficulty with this suggestion is that being able to recognize a good solution is not the same thing as being able to construct it or find it. Suppose the problem is to find the square root of 1,225. If we have a direct method, we can apply it. If we do not have a direct method, we can search for a solution. In either case, finding the solution involves more than simply checking whether a given answer of 35 is correct.

Search need not be random. In many situations a system can use knowledge to focus on (or construct) likely candidate solutions. In special cases like the computing of square roots there can be very direct methods of solution that involve very little search. General problem solvers can also follow direct paths to solutions, when they have access to special case knowledge. In the airport route example, a program could pay attention to the main highways and travel generally in a direction that reduces the distance to the airport. Search modified to use such knowledge is called **heuristic search**. The term *heuristic* refers to the art of good guessing; heuristic knowledge is knowledge that guides. Much of the practice of knowledge engineering is concerned with effective ways to incorporate such knowledge into reasoning systems.

This brings us to another important hypothesis by Newell and Simon, presented in the same paper as their physical symbol system hypothesis (Newell & Simon, 1975).

> **The Heuristic Search Hypothesis**. The solutions to problems can be represented as symbol structures. A physical symbol system exercises its intelligence in problem solving by search—that is, by generating and progressively modifying symbol structures until it produces a solution structure.

With this hypothesis, Newell and Simon place heuristic search in a central place for AI, as a framework for organizing physical symbol systems for intelligent action. As with the physical symbol system hypothesis, the reception to this hypothesis has been mixed. Some consider it obvious. Others consider the hypothesis trivial and circular, saying that any kind of reasoning process can be viewed as search. Later in this chapter we consider alternative frameworks (such as deduction) for understanding problem solving and the use of knowledge.

Whatever the case for intelligence, a thorough understanding of search methods is central to the design of knowledge systems. Search provides the basis of a conceptual framework for understanding how to formulate what knowledge systems should do and how knowledge should be employed.

2.1 *Concepts of Search*

Knowledge systems perform a great variety of tasks, such as diagnosis and trouble shooting, signal interpretation, computer configuration, job-shop scheduling, and synthesis planning for

Diagnosis: Find a set of malfunctions that explains the observable symptoms and is consistent with previous knowledge.

Interpretation: Find a set of situations (or interpretations) that explains the observed data and is consistent with what is known.

Configuration: Find a complete and workable arrangement of components consistent with the specifications, given partial configurations and component constraints.

Job-Shop Scheduling: Find a workable plan for coordinating shop tasks and parts delivery that is consistent with goals, given partial plans and constraints.

Synthesis of Organic Compounds: Find a sequence of chemical reactions that will produce a desired compound with acceptable yield, using available compounds.

FIGURE 2.1.   Tasks characterized in terms of search.

organic compounds. It might seem at first unlikely that search could provide a means for solving problems so varied. Figure 2.1 presents these tasks and tries to answer the question: How can these tasks be cast as search?

Figure 2.1 characterizes these tasks as symbol processing tasks in which symbol structures are found and then evaluated according to given goals and constraints. These characterizations are a beginning. They show us how to formulate and compare different tasks using the terminology of search.

We should not take the task definitions of Figure 2.1 as the end of the story. Formulated in terms of search, the tasks look more similar. However, this comparison is too shallow and glib because the tasks now look *too* similar. The level of generality in this characterization washes out many of the differences between the tasks. Tasks with the same name have a wide range of variations. In later chapters of this book, we analyze some of these tasks to illuminate what kinds of knowledge they need and how they use that knowledge. Doing that will require a framework for talking about search and search spaces. This framework is the subject of the next section.

2.1.1   *Solution Spaces and Search Spaces*

Central to automatic problem solving is the idea of searching a set of symbol structures to find solutions. In the parlance of problem solving as search, the term **search space** refers to the set of symbol structures that a program can consider as candidate solutions. The term **solution space** refers to the set of solutions, whether or not a program is able to consider all of them.

As suggested by Figure 2.2, a solution space can contain elements not in the search space either (1) if there are possible solutions that are not expressible in the language of symbol structures used in the system or (2) if there are valid symbol structures that for whatever reason may not be considered by the symbol system. A search space also can include elements not in the solution space, such as when a program needs to weed out structures that are systematically generated but that lie outside the set of acceptable descriptions of solutions. These exceptional situations aside, the terms *solution space* and *search space* are often used interchangeably when talking about search processes.

It is convenient to characterize the distribution of solutions in search spaces qualitatively, as suggested by Figure 2.3. We say that a solution space is **sparse** when only a minuscule frac-

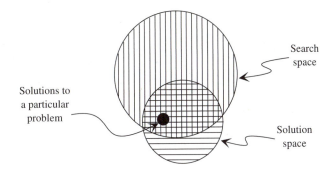

FIGURE 2.2.   Search spaces and solution spaces.

tion of the possible expressions correspond to solutions. We say that it is **dense** if a large fraction of expressions correspond to solutions. We also may characterize the solutions as coming in **clusters** if there is some metric on the space such that solutions tend to be found in groups that are close together, separated by regions where there are few or no solutions.

In the following we use an automobile diagnostic task to illustrate search spaces and solution spaces. Our purpose is to show concrete examples of how a search space can be used and created. This presentation of a diagnostic example is much simpler than the more practical examples of diagnostic tasks and representations that are presented in later chapters. In this formulation of diagnosis as search, to solve a problem is to identify a set of causes for system malfunctions, showing how the causes explain the observable malfunctions.

The first issue is how a program can find the set of possible causes. The simplest suggestion is that the program could have a built-in list of symbol structures that designate every possible cause. For diagnosing a broken car, this could be a list like (1).

```
{flat-tire, broken-axle, clogged-tail-pipe, dead-battery,
 no-gasoline, ...}
```
(1)

Each cause in the list could have an associated list of expected symptoms. The symptoms for a flat tire could be that the car leans to one side and makes a thumping noise when driving, that the tire will have a characteristically flattened shape, and that punctures may be visible in the tire. Diagnosis could then be cast, in part, as a process of going down the list of possibilities, eliminating those candidates that fail to account for the given symptoms.

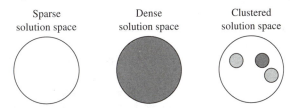

FIGURE 2.3.   Sparse, dense, and clustered solution spaces.

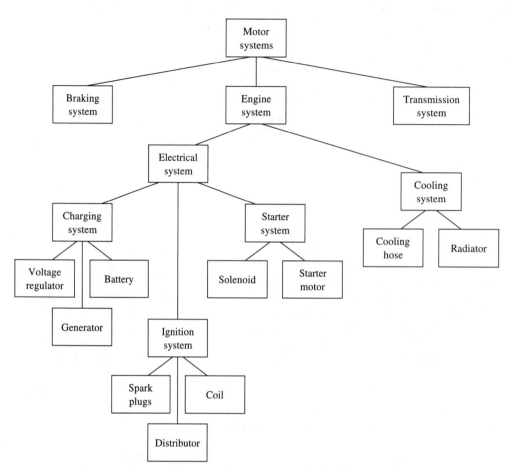

FIGURE 2.4. A hierarchical organization of diagnostic hypotheses following the functional decomposition of an automobile. This organization of the search space makes it possible to narrow the search to focus on those possibilities that bear on the observed malfunctions.

Actually, there is more to diagnosis than this. In most cases it is unreasonable to make all of the possible observations, since there can be a lot of them and some of them may be difficult, expensive, or hazardous. Typically, one wants to collect more information after a partial investigation. If we were told that the car would not start, just going down a list like (1) and soliciting new data ("Is the tire flat? Is the car leaning?") would seem pretty random.

Another approach is to organize the set of fault hypotheses according to functional subsystems as in Figure 2.4. This divides the description of an automobile into subsystems such as the braking system, the engine system, and the suspension system. Subsystems in turn are further subdivided into smaller systems (e.g., pistons, rings, sparkplugs) until reaching the smallest unit of description necessary for diagnosis. Diagnostic and symptomatic criteria for considering subcomponents and descriptions of possible fault modes are associated with the descriptions of subsystems at all levels. For example, Figure 2.5 shows a representation for a starter-motor. A

```
subsystem-name:    starter-motor
supersystems:      starter-system
symptoms:          (engine-does-not-turn-over)
fault-modes:       (worn-out-brushes, shorted-windings,
                    bad-ground-connection, bad-solenoid-connection, ...)
```

FIGURE 2.5. Explicit fault modes for a subsystem. In a functional description, this representation gives an explicit list of the ways a functional subsystem can fail. A program can then search a space characterized by different combinations of these possible faults. For example, the symptom "the engine does not turn over" is associated with faults including "the starter system has shorted windings."

starter-motor is a part of a starter system and should be considered when the engine doesn't turn over. It has several **fault modes**, such as shorted windings.

This reformulation of diagnosis does not necessarily change the set of diagnoses or symptoms that a diagnostician would consider, but it does change the effectiveness with which the search space would be considered. A functional organization of fault hypotheses has several advantages over the previous linear organization of the search space. This approach enables a system to focus its effort on broad categories of closely related hypotheses. For example, the possible faults of the starter-motor need not be considered at all if the electrical system can be ruled out. If a car will not start and it is known that there is no gasoline or no charge in the battery, then there would be little sense in disassembling the starter. The hierarchical structure makes it possible to screen out general diagnostic hypotheses when they are subsumed by more specific ones.

Not all hierarchical organizations are equally useful for organizing a search space for diagnosis. The alphabetically ordered tree in Figure 2.6 is hierarchical and it could be used for finding a node quickly given its alphabetic name, since at every node, all nodes of lower alphabetic order are on the left and all nodes of greater alphabetic order are on the right. However, this alphabetically ordered hierarchical organization confers little leverage for diagnosis. For example, it does not help much to know that *distributor* is the parent of *cooling system* in the organization: One cannot rule out problems in the cooling system when the distributor is known to be fault-free.

In the previous examples, the search space was organized as an explicit structure, prior to problem solving. Alternatively, the search space can be generated dynamically. Figure 2.7 suggests how we can use a components and behavior model of a starter subsystem to generate possible hypotheses as solutions. This figure combines a model of the structural and functional characteristics of an automobile engine with general characteristics. This model can be used for simulating and reasoning about the engine. It represents that power must come from the battery and go through the starter switch, solenoid, and intermediate cables to reach the starter.

Using this network together with models of faults, alternative hypotheses can be constructed. Hypothetical faults of particular power and control cables could be generated by applying fault models from the class of cables. Observables could also be predicted. For example, the descriptions of cables could include their physical layout. A generator of plausible faults and observables could use the fact that short circuits caused by frayed wires or stray blobs of solder are more likely between wires that are physically close. In this approach, a substantial part of the inferential work of diagnosis goes into guiding the generation of possible faults. The advantages

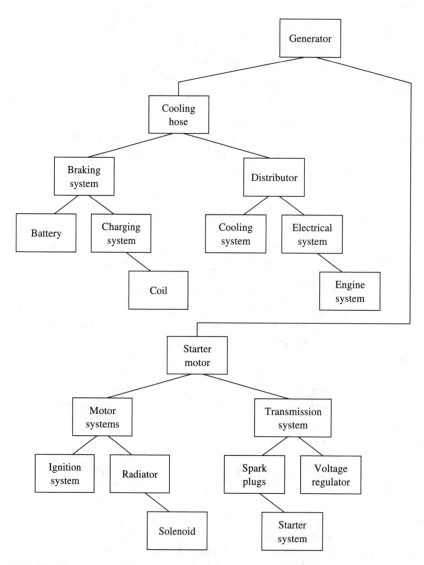

FIGURE 2.6. The diagnostic hypotheses of Figure 2.4 are reorganized here as a tree reflecting alphabetical order. Although this organization of the search space is hierarchical, it does not lend itself to reasoning about functionally related faults, similar symptoms, or families of subsystems. For example, ruling out the malfunctions of a node in this tree does not generally have any consequences for its successors. Consequently this organization is not particularly useful for guiding the search for a diagnosis.

of this systematic approach are increasingly important when there are many possible faults and subsystems.

Our examples of representations of a diagnostic search space are intended to illustrate variety: lists of symptoms, hierarchies of functional subsystems, simulation models. There are always many different options for describing a solution space. Solutions can be listed ahead of

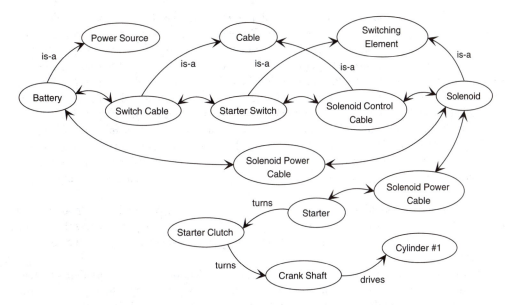

FIGURE 2.7. Figure showing some elements in an analogical model for a starter subsystem. Unlabeled links stand for electrical connections. Is-a links connect with classes that describe generalities. Search programs can generate fault hypotheses about such systems by considering a set of possible faults wherever they could apply in the causal part of the network.

time or they can be generated. Whatever representations are used, there must be a well-defined mapping from the representations to the solutions of interest.

2.1.2 *Terminology about Search Criteria*

The term **heuristic search** is often used to describe knowledge-based search methods. Historically, the term *heuristic* has been used to refer to the "art of good guessing." In this context, heuristic search programs employ methods that may work with great efficiency but that are not guaranteed. In current usage, the term *heuristic search* refers to any search method that uses domain knowledge to guide the search process. Such knowledge could be reliable and exact.

Search methods differ in the thoroughness of their search. A search method that always finds a solution in the solution space whenever there are any solutions is said to be **complete**. Restated, if a candidate is a solution, a complete search method can find it. A complete search method would never quit and report failure if there are any solutions to the problem. A search method that may potentially miss some solution in the space is said to be **incomplete**.

Exhaustive, Satisficing, and Optimizing Search

The four broad kinds of solution criteria for search are exhaustive, satisficing, optimizing, and resource limited. These correspond to finding all solutions, finding one solution that is good enough, finding the best solutions, and finding the best solutions that we can within limited computational resources.

An **exhaustive search method** returns all possible solutions. For example, chemical analysis tasks typically require exhaustive search. These tasks are also called structure elucidation tasks. They determine the structure and identity of chemical samples from their properties. Medical and scientific actions may hang crucially on the results: Is this animal hormone exactly the same as the human one? Is this the deadly or the beneficial version of the drug? It is not enough to find one candidate solution consistent with the data. It is important to determine whether any other solutions are possible that would work as well. If there are, further measurements will be needed to distinguish the results. In these analytic tasks there can easily be millions of variations on the possible molecular structures. Nonetheless, the measurements of chemical properties are often so precise that all but a few of the possible structures can be eliminated. It is sometimes possible to establish confidence in such systems by demonstrating that a search algorithm is exhaustive.

Completeness should not be confused with exhaustiveness. A complete method is merely capable of finding any solution; an exhaustive search method actually returns all solutions that exist. Any method that is exhaustive must also be complete. However, a method can be complete without being exhaustive.

Searches that stop when they find one good enough solution are called **satisficing** systems. If the task is to design a house, the number of possible ways to arrange the rooms, windows, doors, and counters and the number of possible choices of materials are quite large, and many of the variations are uninteresting. In tasks like this there is often no clear sense of optimality and little to be gained by considering systematically all of the combinations of choices. A designer generates one design, or perhaps a representative sampling of candidate designs, one of which will be chosen. Although a satisficing search need not be complete, it can be complete if it can be shown that if a solution exists, the search will find it.

In some problems we want the best solution and have a way of characterizing what we mean by *best*. This is called **optimizing**. Examples include finding the fastest route or the least expensive combination of parts.

There is a duality between satisficing and optimizing methods. A satisficer knows how good a solution needs to be but does not find out how good it could be. An optimizer does not know how good a solution needs to be, but it searches to find out how good the solution could be.

Resource-Limited, Anytime, and Due-Process Search

All search methods consume time and space resources. When constraints in these resources limit the activities of the search process, we say that the search is **resource limited**. Resource-limited searches are used in cases when there are budgets for searching for solutions or when the number of solutions is so large that a complete search is not possible. Sometimes search methods do not explicitly test for resource limits, but rather they carry out a reasonable search and are known to stop without consuming excessive computational resources.

There can be a trade-off between the value of the solution and the cost of finding it. Systems operating under real-time constraints must respond withing a fixed time. In some cases, failing to respond with a solution within the deadline is less desirable than responding with a poor solution. To this end, approximation methods guarantee somewhat weaker results than optimization methods, but do so with more tightly bounded resource requirements. An algorithm is called $\in$ -approximate (or "epsilon-approximate") if it produces a solution that is within fraction

$\in$ of being optimal. For example, a method is 5 percent approximate if it returns a result within 5 percent of the optimum. Roughly, a practical search strategy should somehow balance the amount of time spent and the quality of the solution found.

Further trade-offs are possible. For example, some algorithms typically find solutions, but may sometimes return a wrong answer or none at all. Combining these trade-offs, some algorithms usually find answers that are approximately correct. Such algorithms are called "**PAC**" for "probably approximately correct." These algorithms are of increasing interest in cases where the guarantees of completeness and accuracy are practically impossible.

Anytime algorithms are search methods that return some solution for any allocation of computer time and are expected to return better solutions when given more time. For some anytime algorithms, it is known that they will find an optimal solution if they are given enough time. In some cases we can characterize the performance profile of these methods in terms of a trade-off profile that guarantees different qualities of solutions for different amounts of time and other resources.

There are also many worthwhile search methods whose performance has not been quantitatively determined. When resource-limited searches are trusted as being reliable because experience with them has generally led to reasonable and acceptable results, we call them **due-process searches**. The term *due process* is drawn from the terminology of the criminal justice system and is intended to convey the sense that although no method is perfect, reasonable and informed people would approve the given method for a particular domain. Examples of due-process searches are:

1. A search method divides a space into subregions. For each subregion it returns all candidates that evaluate over threshold T_1. If ten candidates in a row are encountered in a subregion whose values are below threshold T_2, the search abandons the subregion.

2. A route-finding system considers only routes confined to major highways. The system returns the best solution it finds.

3. A configuration system may consider only candidates containing up to a fixed number of parts. Subject to that limitation, it returns as the solution the best candidate it finds.

4. A search method builds a description of a solution incrementally and uses local optimization criteria for each choice.

These searches are not necessarily complete. Thus, the first search is not strictly exhaustive and the other searches are not strictly optimizing. Whether these methods are complete for a given domain depends on properties of the domains. The first method is complete only if the threshold criterion, sampling method, and traversal order together establish for the domain that there are definitely no more solutions to be found in a subregion. The second method is complete only if it is known that any route using side roads cannot be optimal. The third method is complete only if no candidate containing more than the fixed number of parts can be optimal. The fourth method is complete only if local optimization implies global optimality. Typically, due-process methods are not complete. In using due-process and other resource-limited searches, it is useful to have a standard of comparison that characterizes the quality of the results of an average search relative to those of a complete search.

Search methods can be combined with a **sensitivity analysis** to check whether any drastically better solutions exist nearby. Sensitivity analysis involves making minor perturbations on the parameters of a solution to see whether it can be improved relative to the optimization criteria. These perturbations are intended to uncover improvements to the candidate solutions at hand, without the expense of exhaustive generation.

Nondeterministic Search

All of the search methods discussed in this chapter are **deterministic**, meaning that they carry out an identical and predictable series of operations every time when they are presented with the same data. Another kind of search method, **nondeterministic search**, is interesting from a theoretical point of view but has little application in knowledge systems. A nondeterministic search is essentially nonpredictable. Such searches can be approximated with suitable random number generators. In effect, they wander around in a search space, performing a "drunkard's walk" among possible candidates. Random search programs have the desirable property that they will eventually find any solution, and they require very little storage even for large search spaces since they do not keep track of where they have been. However, they get these properties at a price. The search is eventually complete for a suitable generator, but there is no way to be sure when the entire space has been searched. Furthermore, a nondeterministic search carries out a **redundant search** in that it may visit some nodes many times even before searching some other nodes at all. For these reasons, random and nondeterministic searches are usually unsuitable for problem-solving systems.

2.1.3 *Representing Search Spaces as Trees*

Figure 2.8 illustrates a search space represented as a tree. The root node is labeled *A*. The terminal nodes are labeled *M, N, O, P, Q, R, K*, and *L*. There are ten nonterminal nodes in the tree with an average branching factor of 1.7. By convention, we draw the root node at the top and the terminal nodes at the bottom. In drawing trees that represent search processes, it is common practice to leave off the arrowheads pointing to successors, even though the graph is directed.

Tree diagrams differ in the ways that they relate solutions to the nodes of the trees. In some presentations, candidate solutions correspond to nodes in the tree. Any node could be a solution whether it is a terminal or a nonterminal node. This is suggested by the heavy circles in Figure 2.8, indicating that the *P* and the *E* nodes are solutions. Alternatively, in some diagrams only terminal nodes can be solutions.

Figure 2.9 shows another variation in which solutions correspond to **paths** through the tree and nonterminal nodes correspond to intermediate steps in constructing descriptions of solutions. In this figure, the two paths *S-P-E-C-K* and *S-P-A* correspond to solutions. To understand a tree diagram we need to determine which kind of presentation is being used.

In our discussion of search methods we sometimes speak interchangeably of searching for a solution node and searching for a path to a solution node. Although this distinction is important in writing programs, it is of little theoretical significance because one can find a node from the path to it or, alternatively, one can encode a path in the data associated in the nodes. Much of what we have to say about the performance of different search methods is the same for both approaches.

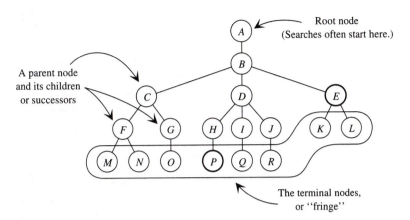

FIGURE 2.8. A search space represented as a tree. In this diagram, any node could be a solution. The heavy circles indicate that nodes E and P correspond to solutions.

2.1.4 *Preview of Search Methods*

Search is a very general framework for understanding how to solve problems, and search theory includes many different methods. A small number of behaviors have been widely observed in problem solving and used in AI programs. Cast in general terms, these methods constitute an important and enduring part of what has been learned in AI. These methods are useful and show up in all kinds of AI systems.

The terminology of search methods varies somewhat in AI textbooks. Nilsson (1971) calls them **problem-solving methods**. Newell (1973) calls them the **weak methods**. The term *weak* was intended to suggest their generality and to contrast them with special-purpose algorithms, such as those commonly found in numerical analysis or scientific programming. Winston (1984) calls them **search procedures**. There are also variations in the taxonomies and terminology of individual methods. Our purpose in the following is to present the main ideas and a guide to variations rather than a final or even complete taxonomy of search methods. However we classify

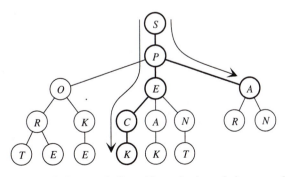

FIGURE 2.9. In this diagram, solutions are indicated by paths through the tree and nonterminal nodes correspond to intermediate steps in constructing candidate solutions.

How does a solution correspond to a search tree?
Solutions can be any nodes.
Solutions must be terminal nodes.
Solutions are paths through the tree.

When does a search method stop?
Satisficing: when it finds one solution.
Exhaustive: when it has considered all possible solutions.
Optimizing: when it has found the best solution.
Resource limited: when it has exhausted its computaitonal resources.
Due process: when it has searched with a method that has proven adequate for most cases.

How is search directed?
Blind: systematic search through possibilities (Section 2.2).
Directed: heuristics used to guide the search (Section 2.3).
Hierarchical: abstract solutions used to organize search (Section 2.4).

How thorough is the search?
Complete: If there is a solution in the search space, the system will find it.
Incomplete: The system may miss some solutions.

FIGURE 2.10.   Common dimensions in search methods.

search, we need to be able to answer certain basic questions about the methods suggested in Figure 2.10.

Search methods are often presented in terms of families. The major division in this chapter is between the **blind search** methods in Section 2.2 and the **directed search** methods in Section 2.3. Directed search methods differ from blind ones in that they impart a sense of direction in the search. There are very close cousins for many of the methods, such as methods that differ only in the first two dimensions above. In real applications, the methods are mixed and composed in different ways.

2.1.5   *Summary and Review*

The heuristic search hypothesis is that a physical symbol system exercises its intelligence by solving problems and that its problem-solving behavior is governed by search and guided by knowledge. This hypothesis is based on five basic ideas:

1. Symbol structures can stand for solutions to problems.
2. Symbol systems can generate alternative symbol structures as candidate solutions.
3. Symbol systems can perform tests on candidate symbol structures, to compare their quality as solutions.
4. The processes of search can be described by methods.
5. Search methods can be informed by and improved by knowledge.

It is useful to characterize the problem-solving behavior of a symbol system in terms of search spaces and solution spaces. Metaphorically, a search space is where a system looks for solutions. More precisely, it is the set of possible symbol structures designating candidate solutions that a system can consider. For any particular problem, the set of solutions is called the solution space. Usually the search space is much larger than the solution space.

Search processes must decide when to stop searching. We considered four major stopping criteria for search. Exhaustive search seeks all solutions. Satisficing search seeks one solution that is good enough. Optimizing search seeks the best possible solution. Due-process searches use methods that are known to stop after a systematic but relatively short exploration. Resource-limited search seeks the best solutions that can be found using limited resources, such as computation time or space. To make the results of such searches meaningful, there must be some theoretical basis or empirical standard for determining the quality of the results.

Exercises for Section 2.1

Ex. 1 [05] *Warm-ups.* Determine whether each of the following statements is true or false. If a statement is ambiguous, explain your answer briefly.

(a) *True or False.* Although the terms *search space* and *solution space* are often used interchangeably, they do not always mean the same thing.

(b) *True or False.* In representing search spaces as trees, the solutions correspond to terminal nodes.

(c) *True or False.* An optimizing search knows how good a solution can be but does not know how good it needs to be.

(d) *True or False.* A search process is heuristic if it uses knowledge as a guide.

(e) *True or False.* A PAC algorithm is a goal-directed producer-consumer algorithm, in which agents attempt to gobble tokens quickly while evading detection.

■ **Ex. 2** [CD-05] *Kinds of Search.* Determine whether each of the following statements is true or false. If a statement is ambiguous, explain your answer briefly.

(a) *True or False.* All exhaustive searches are complete.

(b) *True or False.* All complete searches are exhaustive.

(c) *True or False.* A satisficing search process for a clustered solution space should probably focus its search on the clusters.

(d) *True or False.* A satisficing search knows how good a solution needs to be but does not necessarily determine how good it could be.

(e) *True or False.* A due-process search is one specially designed for legal reasoning about case law in the criminal justice system.

Ex. 3 [05] *More Terminology.* Determine whether each of the following statements is true or false. If a statement is ambiguous, explain your answer briefly.

(a) *True or False.* A search that terminates when it has found the first solution that satisfies the given criteria is called a satisficing search.

(b) *True or False.* The union of the nodes in the fringe with the nodes in the interior includes all of the nodes in a search tree. (Assume that the root is included in the interior and that all of the nodes of the tree are expanded.)

(c) *True or False.* A blind search is one that does not distinguish between terminal and nonterminal nodes.

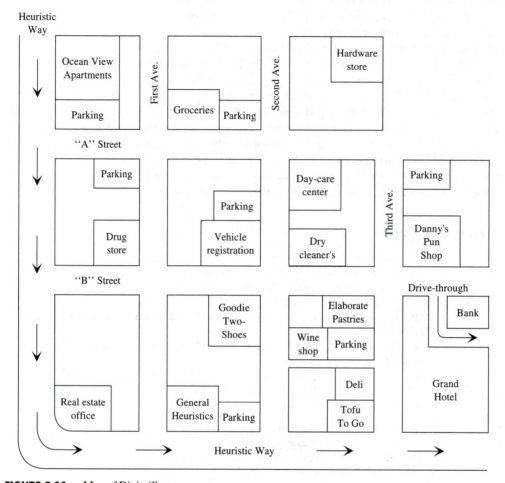

FIGURE 2.11.   Map of Digitville.

(d) *True or False.* In the context of problem solving, a heuristic search is one that relies on knowledge to guide the search.

(e) *True or False.* A heuristic search is an incomplete search.

Ex. 4   [*CD-!-15*] *Opportunistic Search.* Figure 2.11 shows a map of a section of the hypothetical city of Digitville, used in this exercise to illustrate aspects of the task of errand planning.

Suppose that Barbara works at General Heuristics and lives in the Ocean View Apartments. On the way home from work Barbara intends to carry out several errands: getting groceries, picking up the kids at the day-care center, picking up some clothes that are ready at the dry cleaner's, and perhaps picking up some treats for company that evening.

For simplicity, assume that each task takes 10 minutes to perform, that parking can only take place at designated parking lots and takes 2 minutes, that driving from point to point takes 2 minutes per block, that walking takes 3 minutes per block, and that Barbara needs to be home 75 minutes after she leaves work. Also assume that walking a partial block or crossing a street takes no time at all and that the time to "unpark" is included in the 2 minutes for parking. Other constraints are that groceries are too heavy to carry farther than the grocery-store parking lot and that the young kids will fuss too much if they are taken on more than one errand.

(This exercise was inspired by one used by Barbara and Frederick Hayes-Roth in testing cognitive models of planning by human subjects. It is a variation of the traveling salesman problem. This exercise is intended to promote discussion on human strategies of search for a familiar task.)

(a) Find a route home for Barbara that enables her to accomplish all of her primary tasks and as many of her secondary tasks as possible. The primary tasks are picking up the kids at day care, getting groceries, and picking up a prescription for the kids at the drugstore. The secondary tasks are picking up some forms at vehicle registration, getting cash at the bank, getting a widget at the hardware store, picking up some pastries at the Elaborate Pastry Shop, and picking up the clothing at the dry cleaner's. Present your solution showing the elapsed trip time after each leg of the trip.

(b) How would you characterize your solution process as a kind of search (e.g., optimizing, satisficing)? Explain how opportunism can play a role in the elaboration of solutions. How would you change your search characterization if the task included assigned priorities to errands?

Hint: A solution accomplishing three primary tasks and no secondary task is still adequate, or satisficing.

(c) Sometimes the data structures used by a problem solver are inadequate for representing all possible solutions. Suppose now that Barbara is married to Rick and that they drive home together from General Heuristics. Whenever they park, it is possible for each of them to run a separate errand and then to meet back at the car. How does this change the search process? How would you modify the representation used by a search program (or your thinking in part a to consider solutions for this revised problem?

Ex. 5 [05] *Search and 20 Questions*. There is a guessing game called 20 Questions in which the game master picks a kind of object in the world (typically an animal, mineral, or vegetable) and the questioner tries to determine the object's identity by asking up to 20 questions that can be answered by "yes" or "no."

(a) Give an example of a decision tree for determining whether a domesticated animal is a dog, cat, cow, or horse by asking such questions as "Does it make a barking sound?" "Does it carry riders?" and so on.

(b) Professor Digit claims that a program that carries out a decision tree as in part a does not really use search to solve problems. Is this correct? Explain your answer by identifying a correspondence between decision trees and a search space.

Ex. 6 [10] *Efficient Decision Trees*. An intuitively efficient questioning strategy is one that divides the set of remaining solution candidates in half with each question.

(a) Consider the 20 Questions game of Exercise 5. As before, up to 20 questions can be asked. Each question can be answered only by "yes" or "no." The 20 questions for any case can be drawn from a large set of possible questions. How many particular solutions can be differentiated (at most) by 20 questions?

(b) An alternative approach is to represent each candidate solution by a set of attributes. For example, for the set of domestic animals we might have the following symbol structures:

```
(dog    (sound bow-wow)
        (size small)
```

```
            (eats dog-food)
            (lives-in house))
(cat    (sound meow)
        (size small)
        (eats mice)
        (lives-in house))
(horse  (sound neigh)
        (size large)
        (eats hay)
        (lives-in barn))
(cow    (sound moo)
        (size large)
        (eats hay)
        (lives-in barn) )
```

Construct an efficient set of yes/no questions based on these attributes for differentiating among the four animals.

(c) Can a decision tree for this problem be built using only questions about the `size` and `lives-in` attributes? Explain.

■ **Ex. 7** [*!-12*] *Searching through Cause-Effect Rules.* In diagnostic tasks, requests for data to identify the malfunctions can be generated by backward chaining through cause-effect rules. In this exercise we use the term *cause-effect rules* to describe rules in which each condition of a rule is a necessary condition (or cause) for some effect predicted in the rule's conclusion. The complete set of rules comprises a model that can be used in simulating and troubleshooting a system.

Suppose an engine-starting system is represented in terms of production rules as follows:

Rule 1
```
IF      (1.1) there is power to the starter, and
        (1.2) the engine is warm, and
        (1.3) the starter is operational,
THEN    (1.4) the starter will turn over.
```

Rule 2
```
IF      (2.1)  there is power to the activation connector of the
               solenoid, and
        (2.2) the cable from the solenoid to the starter is
              intact, and
        (2.3) the cable from the battery to the power connector
              of the solenoid is intact,
THEN    (2.4) there is power to the starter.
```

Rule 3
```
IF      (3.1) there is power to the starter switch, and
        (3.2) the starter switch is on, and
        (3.3) the cable from the starter switch to the
              activation connector of the solenoid is intact,
THEN    (3.4) there is power to the activation connector of the
              solenoid.
```

Rule 4
IF   (4.1) the battery is charged and
       (4.2) the cable from the battery to the starter switch
           is intact,
THEN (4.3) there is power to the starter switch.

Rule 5
IF   (5.1) the battery is charged and
       (5.2) the cable from the battery to the light switch is
           intact,
THEN (5.3) there is power to the light switch.

Rule 6
IF   (6.1) there is power to the light switch, and
       (6.2) the bulb is not burned-out, and
       (6.3) the light switch is on,
THEN (6.4) the light will glow.

(a) Assume that our model of diagnosis enumerates "malfunctions" as a failure of any of the "causes" or "effects" mentioned in the rules. When rules are composed together, a single clause might be used as a cause in one rule and an effect in another. We refer to a cause as any clause mentioned in the antecedent (if-part) of a rule. Complete the following list of causes referred to by the first two rules:

(1.1) power to starter
(1.2) engine warm
(1.3) starter operational
. . .

Do not include deeper causes in other rules.

(b) Professor Digit has developed an approach to diagnosis that involves searching for most basic causes. He starts with a given effect and then traces backward using the rules to find a prior cause. His approach is to find the earliest cause that he can. If there is a malfunction, his system finds a rule that names the possible causes of the effect. It then asks about each of the causes in order. If one cause fails, his system looks for a rule that would give prior causes.

Suppose Professor Digit's system is given the malfunction "the starter does not turn over." Suppose further that the first clause his system encounters in each rule fails, which means it indicates a deeper malfunction. Show the order of rule retrieval and list the sequence of numbers of examined clauses that would be visited by backward chaining on the rules to show when the program could ultimately ask whether the battery is charged.

(c) Explain how the process in part b amounts to a search by identifying the search space and classifying the search method.

Note: In later chapters we consider more realistic techniques for building diagnostic systems. This exercise uses a rather naive model of troubleshooting to demonstrate concepts of search.

■   **Ex. 8**   [CD-!-15] *Search and the Mutilated Chessboard.* Mutilated chessboard problems have often been used in AI to demonstrate the power of reformulating a problem. In this exercise, we use the example to illustrate several ideas about search.

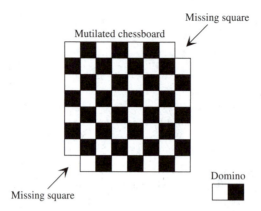

FIGURE 2.12. A "mutilated chessboard" with diagonal corner squares missing.

Figure 2.12 shows a chessboard from which diagonal corners have been removed. Also in the figure is a domino that is exactly the size of two squares of the chessboard. The question is whether it is possible to completely cover the chess board with dominoes such that the black square in each domino covers a black square on the board, the white square in each domino covers a white square on the board, and no domino hangs over the edge of the board.

(a) Briefly, describe a way of using search to determine whether the board can be completely covered by dominoes.

(b) Is there a way of answering the question by reformulating it? (*Hint*: Count white and black squares separately.)

(c) Upon seeing a proof like part b, Professor Digit announced that it illustrates the power of down-to-earth mathematics. He drew several morals from the example. First, search is bad. The argument in part b is much more effective than the procedure in part a. Second, one should deal with all elements of a set by ignoring individual elements and working with the set's definition.

Briefly, do you agree with Professor Digit? What does the example show in general about the avoidability of search in problem solving? (*Hint*: Are there other possible mutilations of the board for which your reformulation is no help?)

Ex. 9   [05] *"The Last Candidate Considered."* Dissatisfied about his apparent lack of luck and foresight, Profesor Digit once complained that "it always seems like the solution is the *last* candidate I look at." Although Professor Digit may have been referring to bad choices in putting candidates in an order to consider, his graduate student, Sam, thought about the literal meaning of the statement and decided that it would often be silly for a search method to consider further candidates after a solution has been found. For each of the following kinds of search, indicate whether the last candidate a method would consider is the solution it finds. Assume that the methods consider just one candidate at a time. Explain briefly.

(a) Satisficing search

(b) Optimizing search

(c) Anytime search

(d) Due-process search

2.2 *Blind Search*

The simplest search methods are those that proceed step by step, with no special knowledge to guide the traversal of the search space. These are called **blind search methods**. The only knowledge they use is the bookkeeping required to traverse the space systematically.

In the following presentation the blind search methods are illustrated both by example and by giving pseudocode for the methods. Although the methods for blind search are simple, they are important to understand because they are the basis for the more elaborate search methods. We use the term *method* to mean roughly the same thing as *algorithm*: a procedural description that says clearly and unambiguously what to do. The term *method* connotes a somewhat looser description, reflecting that methods are often parameterized by knowledge.

2.2.1 *Depth-First and Breadth-First Search*

Two of the simplest methods for blind search are depth-first search and breadth-first search. These methods are similar, but they have different characteristics, especially in their requirements for memory space. In the following we present and compare these methods. For simplicity, we begin with the simplest case where the search spaces are finite trees with branching factor *b*. The exercises present several variations of the methods.

In a **depth-first search**, the processor descends through the search tree starting at the root node and picking an alternative branch at each intermediate node until it reaches either a solution or a terminal node. Restated, it begins at the root and then visits the first successor of the root, and then the first successor of that node, and so on. At each level, it visits child nodes before visiting sibling nodes. If the processor reaches the end of a path without encountering a solution, it backs up in the tree to take an alternative branch at the nearest ancestor node with untried children. This is called depth-first because it plunges quickly downward into the search space.

Figure 2.13 illustrates the path of a depth-first search through a tree. The numbers adjacent to the nodes indicate the order in which the nodes are visited. The arrows suggest how the path is constructed. When the arrow returns to node 4 (*R*) after visiting node 5 (*T*) en route to node 6 (*E*),

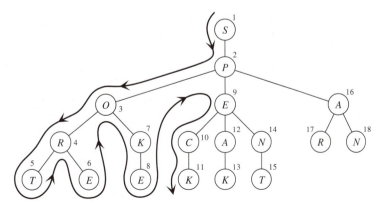

FIGURE 2.13. A depth-first search. The numbers on the node indicate their order of visitation in the search. The arrows suggest how the path is determined.

To carry out a depth-first search:
```
   1. Form a stack consisting of the root node.

   2. While the stack is not empty do
   3. begin
   4.       Pop a node from the stack.
   5.       If solution-tester(node) then exit with success reporting
            the node;
   6.       Else push the node's successors (if any) onto the stack.
   7. end

      /* Here if all nodes have been searched but no solution was found. */
   8. Exit with failure.
```

FIGURE 2.14.   Method for a satisficing depth-first search on a finite search tree. Every node is a solution candidate.

this does not mean that node 4 is visited again, but rather that the search has returned to get the next successor of node 4. By convention in this figure and in many others in this text, the left-to-right order of siblings in the figure indicates the relative order in which siblings are visited.

For simplicity in our presentation of search algorithms, we represent search spaces as trees. In some cases, search spaces are presented in terms of networks that contain cycles. In these cases the bookkeeping in the algorithms for searching them must include additional instructions to avoid looping. This modification is discussed in the exercises.

Figure 2.14 presents a method for a satisficing depth-first search. In this version of the method, solutions can appear anyplace in the tree. The method uses a stack for keeping track of its progress in the search. Depth-first search requires two auxiliary programs: a **generator** of successors and a **solution tester**. The solution tester determines whether a node is a solution.

We also call these auxiliary programs **knowledge interfaces** because they connect search methods to the data structures and knowledge with which the methods operate. Search methods as described in this chapter are intended to cover a wide range of possible programming styles and representations, imposing few requirements.

There are many variations of depth-first search. The method in Figure 2.14 satisfices and admits any node in the search as a potential solution candidate. Figure 2.15 gives a variation of the method that tests only leaf nodes as candidate solutions. This version avoids applying the solution test on interior nodes of the tree. This variation is useful if the solution test is time-consuming and solutions are known to be limited to the fringe. Like the version in Figure 2.14 this version stops when it finds its first solution.

A **breadth-first search** looks for a solution among all of the nodes at a given level before checking any of the children on the next level. Figure 2.16 illustrates a breadth-first search for our sample tree. Note that in contrast with depth-first search, breadth-first search finds the solution at node 4 (corresponding to the path *S-P-A*) before it would find the deeper solution corresponding to the path *S-P-E-C-K*. Figure 2.17 gives a method for a satisficing breadth-first search.

To carry out a depth-first search for leaf node solutions:
```
    1. Form a stack consisting of the root node.

    2. While the stack is not empty do
    3. begin
    4.        Pop a node from the stack.
    5.        If the node has successors, then push them onto the stack;
    6.        Else if solution-tester(node) then exit with success reporting
              the node.
    7. end

       /* Here if all nodes have been searched but no solution was found. */
    8. Exit with failure.
```

FIGURE 2.15. Another satisficing method for a depth-first search. This version considers only leaf nodes as candidate solutions.

As opposed to depth-first search, breadth-first search uses a queue rather than a stack to keep track of its processing. Another way to express the difference is that depth-first uses a **last-in-first-out (LIFO)** approach in deciding what node to expand next and breadth-first uses a **first-in-first-out (FIFO)** approach.

To compare the performance of depth-first and breadth-first search, we start with some extreme cases. Suppose that all of the solutions are relatively shallow in the tree, but that the tree contains some paths of great depth. If these deep and fruitless paths happen to be the first ones explored by depth-first search, then the method will slip past the levels at which the solutions appear and waste time exhaustively exploring parts of the tree lower down. Thus, a bad decision high up in the tree leads to useless thrashing down below. On the other hand, if all of the solu-

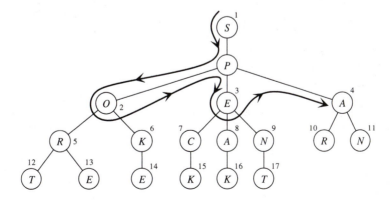

FIGURE 2.16. A breadth-first search.

To carry out a breadth-first search:
```
  1. Form a queue consisting of the root node.

  2. While the queue is not empty do
  3. begin
  4.       Pop a node from the front of the queue.
  5.       If solution-tester(node) then exit with success reporting the
           node;
  6.       Else put the node's successors (if any) onto the back of the
           queue.
  7. end

     /* Here if no solution has been found. */
  8. Exit with failure.
```

FIGURE 2.17.   Method for a satisficing breadth-first search. This version stops when it has found its first solution node. In this version of the method, every node in the tree is a solution candidate.

tions are relatively deep in the tree, a breadth-first search spends much time carefully checking all of the close-in nodes before getting to the levels at which the solutions begin to appear.

Our main purpose in this section is to compare search methods. To this end we leave out most programming considerations. However, a few general points about implementation of search methods are useful. The methods we have given for depth-first and breadth-first search put all of the successors of a node onto a stack or queue when a node is rejected. These successors reside there until they are popped, tested, and possibly replaced by their own successors.

Figure 2.18 illustrates two versions of the stack during successive states of a depth-first search of a tree. The stack on the left represents all of the nodes on the stack individually, as assumed in the method in Figure 2.14. The first cycle starts with node A, the root of the tree. If none of the nodes in this trace is a solution, node A is replaced on the stack during the second cycle with its successors $B,X,Y,$ and Z. Similarly, when node B is rejected, it is replaced by the nodes $C,L,$ and P. For a tree of constant branching factor, this puts up to $d(b-1)+1$ nodes on the stack where b is the branching factor and d is the depth of the tree. For simplicity in the following, we sometimes approximate this quantity as $O(bd)$.

On the right the stack contains **choice points** or **stubs**, rather than representing each of the nodes individually. A choice point is a representation of the choices that can be made at a point in a search process. In the example in Figure 2.18, the choice points represent the remaining successors that can be chosen for a node in depth-first search. The notation N–i represents a choice point for the node N where the i-th successor will be the next one to be considered. For example, A–1 refers to the first successor of node A, which is node B. D–3 refers to the third successor of node D, or node G. When the successors of node A are generated, the choice point cycles through A–1 for B, A–2 for X, A–3 for Z, and A–4 for Y. After A–4 there are no more successors and the choice point is removed from the stack. The choice-point approach has the advantage of requiring less stack space, essentially dividing out the branching factor from the requirement.

A choice-point version of depth-first satisficing search is given in Figure 2.19. This method retrieves successors in order from a choice point, popping the choice point from the

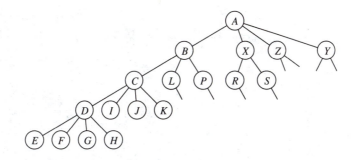

	Stack showing	Stack showing
Cycle	each node individually	choice points
1	A	Root—Maker-1
2	B X Y Z	A-1
3	C L P X Y Z	B-1 A-2
4	D I J K L P X Y Z	C-1 B-2 A-2
5	E F G H I J K L P X Y Z	D-1 C-2 B-2 A-2
6	F G H I J K L P X Y Z	D-2 C-2 B-2 A-2

FIGURE 2.18.   A choice-point representation of state reduces the stack space required for depth-first search. The number in the choice point indicates the successor that will be generated next.

stack when all of the successors have been retrieved. This version assumes that the interface to a choice point includes two functions. The function Next-Successor retrieves the next successor from the choice point and causes the choice point to update its internal state accordingly. The predicate Empty returns *true* if the choice point has no more successors to deliver. This predicate does not change the internal state of the choice point.

In the worst case where the only solution is the last terminal node to be visited, breadth-first search generates all nodes up to depth d, or $b + b^2 + b^3 + \ldots + b^d$ where b is the branching factor and d is the depth of the search. Using the order notation, the space complexity is $O(b^d)$. For depth-first search, space complexity is $O(b^d)$ or $O(d)$, depending on whether a choice-point representation is used. Assuming that b is a constant, we say that the space requirement is $O(d)$ in either case, although it is somewhat more informative to characterize the space requirement of the non-choice point approach as $O(b^d)$ to indicate how it depends on the branching factor of the particular problem.

These complexities are the same in the worst case for either a satisficing search or an exhaustive search. Note that the complexity of the average case for either space or time is just half of the worst-case complexity, which does not change the order. Thus, breadth-first search has a higher storage overhead than depth-first search.

The worst-case time complexity for all of these variations of depth-first and breadth-first search, $O(b^d)$, arises in the case that the last node in the tree is the only one that is a solution or

To carry out a depth-first search using a stack of choice points:

```
1. Form a stack consisting of the choice point that makes only the root
   node.

2. While the stack is not empty do
3. begin

        /* Get the next node. */
4.      Let node := Next-Node(stack).
5.      If solution-tester(node) then exit with success reporting the
        node;
6.      Else create a choice point for the node's successors and push it
        onto the stack.
7. end

   /* Here if no solution was found. */
8. Exit with failure.



1. Procedure Next-Node(stack)
        /* Get the choice point at the top of the stack without
        removing it from the stack.*/
2.      Let choice-point := Top-Element(stack).
3.      Let node := Next-Successor(choice-point).
4.      If Empty(choice-point)
5.          then pop the choice point from the stack;
6.      Return node.
```

FIGURE 2.19. Method for a satisficing depth-first search. This version saves space on the stack by storing choice points rather than individual nodes.

when there are no solutions at all. When solutions are restricted to being the leaf nodes of the search tree, depth-first search will reach a solution candidate before breadth-first search.

Depth-first and breadth-first search are so basic that they are part of almost every search method. Some search methods combine elements of depth-first and breadth-first expansion. Figure 2.20 summarizes some characteristics of depth-first and breadth-first searches. Exercises 4 and 5 present **depth-limited search** and **depth-first iterative deepening** as variations on these methods that combine features of depth-first and breadth-first searches to improve their worst-case behavior.

A fundamental problem for both methods, however, is that when the search order of nodes in the tree is random and the tree is very large, neither approach is particularly good. Search can be much better if there is guidance about which direction to go. Providing a means for heuristic knowledge to give such guidance is the idea behind the directed search methods in Section 2.3.

Blind Method	Depth-first search	Breadth-first search
Bookkeeping	Stack	Queue
Knowledge interfaces	Solution tester	Solution tester
Worst-case space	$O(d)$	$O(b^d)$
Worst-case time	$O(b^d)$	$O(b^d)$
Example bad cases	When solutions are shallow in the tree, but come after deep and fruitless paths	All solutions are deep in tree
Thoroughness	Complete search	Complete search
Some Variations		
How much to search	Satisficing / exhaustive/ depth limited / iterative deepening	Satisficing / exhaustive (not recommended for exhaustive search)
Where are solutions	Any node / leaf node	Any node / leaf node
Topology of space	Tree / directed graph	Tree / directed graph

FIGURE 2.20.   Summary of characteristics and variations for depth-first and breadth-first search methods.

2.2.2   Top-Down and Bottom-Up Search: A Note on Terminology

`ADVANCED`

The descriptions of depth-first and breadth-first search start at a place called the top of the tree and end up at a place called the bottom of the tree. While this is a simple way to define and visualize the searches, the terminology comes in conflict with that of other parts of computer science and computational linguistics, such as in grammars for parsing language, because it confounds the **direction of search** with the **order of node expansion**.

It is sometimes convenient to characterize the nodes of a search tree in terms of multiple generators, typically expressed as production rules. For example, a node might be

(Noun-Phrase)   (1)

and the children nodes in the search might be generated by rules such as

$$\begin{aligned}
\text{Noun-Phrase} &\rightarrow \text{Noun} \mid \text{Article Noun-Phrase} \\
&\mid \text{Adjective Noun-Phrase} \qquad\qquad\qquad (2)\\
\text{Adjective} &\rightarrow \text{Color-Adjective} \mid \text{Quantity-Adjective} \qquad (3)\\
\text{Color-Adjective} &\rightarrow \text{red} \mid \text{blue} \mid \text{green} \qquad\qquad\qquad (4)\\
\text{Noun} &\rightarrow \text{wagon} \mid \text{toy} \mid \text{ball} \qquad\qquad\qquad (5)\\
\text{Article} &\rightarrow \text{the} \mid \text{a} \mid \text{an} \qquad\qquad\qquad\qquad (6)
\end{aligned}$$

where the | symbol is used to separate alternatives. A left-to-right expansion of these nodes would expand the leftmost tokens first. A left-to-right, depth-first search from the node in (1) would first generate children nodes like

    (Noun)   (7)

and then (8) through (10) as follows:

    (wagon)   (8)
    (toy)   (9)
    (ball)   (10)

However, a left-to-right, breadth-first search starting with the node in (1) would also generate (10) and then (11) and (12).

    (Article Noun-Phrase)   (11)
    (Adjective Noun-Phrase)   (12)

This characterization of depth-first and breadth-first search takes the order of traversal as defined in the previous section and applies it to the generation of the nodes.

Using the terms *top* and *bottom* in the previous section to define depth-first and breadth-first search conflicts with other terminology for describing the way the production rules can be used to generate child nodes in a search. When the production rules are used in backward chaining, the search tree is said to be searched in a **goal-driven** manner and a parse is said to be constructed **top-down**. When the rules are used in forward chaining, the search tree is said to be searched in a **data-driven** manner and the parse is said to be constructed **bottom-up**. In this case, the rules are sometimes called **reduction rules**.

Figure 2.21 shows a graph over which we can apply depth-first search. It is not strictly a tree, so we assume that we have a version of depth-first search that does not visit any node more than once (see Exercise 2). In the previous section, we started a depth-first search at the root. In Figure 2.21, we have extended the graph superficially by connecting all of the nodes at one end to a node called *Top* and by connecting all of the nodes at the other end to a node called *Bottom*. A depth-first search starting at *Top* might visit the first few nodes in the order *Top-A-D-I-O-T-Bottom-P-U*. A breadth-first search starting at *Top* might visit the first few nodes in the order

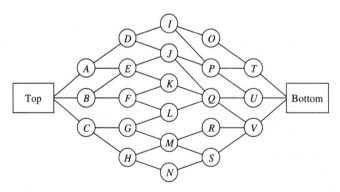

FIGURE 2.21.   A depth-first method.

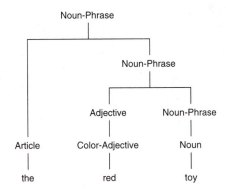

FIGURE 2.22. A parse tree for "the red toy." A search tree would show additional nodes and links corresponding to other paths that were tried. A top-down search tree would show additional downward links, such as from Adjective to Quantity-Adjective or from Noun to wagon. A bottom-up search tree would show additional upward links.

Top-A-B-C-D-E-F. A depth-first search starting at *Bottom* would visit the first few nodes in the order *Bottom-T-O-I-D-A-Top-P*. A breadth-first search starting at *Bottom* would visit the nodes *Bottom-T-U-V-O-P-Q*. This example shows that the direction of search is a separate consideration from the order of node expansion.

Another source of confusion arising in parsing examples is that both the search process and the solutions can take the form of trees, which means there can be both a search tree and a parse tree. A search tree shows all candidates that are tried. A parse tree shows all the intermediate productions that describe the parse or solution path for a particular candidate. In ambiguous grammars, there can be more than one parse for a given sentence. A parse tree shows a single parse. Figure 2.22 shows a parse tree for the phrase "the red toy."

In summary, the essence of depth-first search is that it generates its first alternative for a successor node, then the first alternative for the successor's successor, and so on. Breadth-first search generates all of the successors of a given node before starting on the next generation. The terms *top-down* and *bottom-up* refer to an orientation relative to a tree; the terms *depth-first* and *breadth-first* refer to an order by which nodes are expanded. Goal-driven (top-down) and data-driven (bottom-up) searches can be either depth-first or breadth-first.

2.2.3 *Simple and Hierarchical Generate-and-Test*

The term **generate-and-test** refers to a basic but important kind of search method. In this section we consider two of its variations: simple generate-and-test and hierarchical generate-and-test.

Simple Generate-and-Test

Simple generate-and-test requires two auxiliary programs: a generator of candidates and a solution tester. The output of the generator is the input to the tester. If the test is successful, it exists successfully with a solution; otherwise the generator must produce another candidate. If the gen-

To carry out a simple generate-and-test search:
```
   1. While the generator is not empty do
   2.        If solution-tester(generator(candidate)), then exit with
             success reporting the candidate.


          /* Here if no solution has been found. */
   3. Exit with failure.
```

FIGURE 2.23. Method for simple generate-and-test.

erator fails to produce a solution, the failure exit is taken. Figure 2.23 presents this method in all of its simplicity.

If we compare this method with typical algorithms from mathematical programming, we are struck by its general nature. Generate-and-test methods provide little knowledge of their own. Everything they know about generating candidates is in the generator, which could be anything from a co-routine employing a simple depth-first search to a comprehensive knowledge system. Everything they know about judging candidates is in the solution tester. Figure 2.24 presents a simple schematic of this method.

The strict separation of the generator from the solution tester and an interface that exchanges complete solutions leads to the main problem with simple generate-and-test: It is very inefficient. The generator needs to put together symbol structures representing complete solutions before any testing can be done, and there can be a lot of candidates. Consider the task of opening a combination safe without knowing the combination. In a simple generate-and-test method, the generator must offer complete combinations, one at a time. Suppose a combination requires three numbers between 0 and 19 as in Figure 2.25. This means the generator could create the 8,000 combinations (0-0-0, 0-0-1, . . . , 19-19-19) one at a time, and offer them up to the tester. If the lock were somewhat larger, such as five numbers of 100 possible values, the number of combinations goes up to 10 billion. Even if we could dial the safe at the unprecedented rate of one combination per second, it would take 317 years of nonstop dialing to try all the combinations.

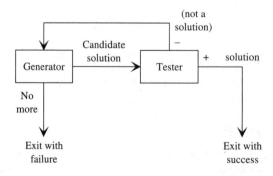

FIGURE 2.24. Schematic of simple generate-and-test.

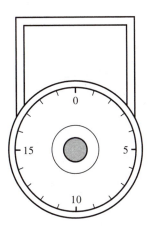

Possible
combinations

0-0-0
0-0-0
· · ·
1-1-1
1-1-2
1-1-3
· · ·
3-3-1
3-3-2
3-3-3
3-3-4
· · ·
19-19-19

FIGURE 2.25. Example of an exponential problem for simple generate-and-test: finding the combination for a safe.

Hierarchical Generate-and-Test

To improve the efficiency of simple generate-and-test, it is often advocated that some of the tests should be "moved into the generator." This may seem counterintuitive; after all, just moving code from one place to another does not make it run any faster. The gain in efficiency actually occurs when tests can be applied (perhaps with some alterations) to *partially specified* solution candidates. When the interpretation of partially specified structures is bound up in the control (and control stacks) of the generator, moving tests to the generator can be a convenient organizational expedient. However, any organization that applies tests to partial descriptions can help.

The value of applying tests to partially specified candidates can be illustrated continuing our combination-safe analogy. A safecracker in the movies always has his ear (or stethoscope) up against the safe to listen for the tumblers falling into place. ("Turn slowly to the right. Click! Aha, the third number must be 17.") Each test in this example rules out entire subtrees of combinations.

This approach in which a test can rule out an entire class of candidates is known as **hierarchical generate-and-test**. The viability of its hierarchical pruning turns on two things: Given a partially specified candidate the test must be computable, and it must be the case that when the test rules out the candidate all of its descendants can also be ruled out. One might say that the key idea behind hierarchical generate-and-test is to "prune early and often." This approach exploits the fact that many candidates can be eliminated for the same reasons.

Figure 2.26 shows a search tree for hierarchical generate-and-test. In this figure all solutions and other complete candidates are terminal nodes. Interior nodes represent partial descriptions. When an interior node is pruned, none of its successors needs to be generated.

A satisficing method for hierarchical generate-and-test is shown in Figure 2.27. Candidates are constructed incrementally as the tree is traversed. Each nonterminal node in the tree is a partially specified candidate. Figure 2.28 gives a simple schematic of hierarchical generate-and-test.

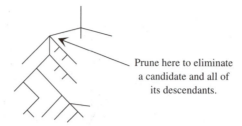

Prune here to eliminate
a candidate and all of
its descendants.

FIGURE 2.26.   Tests in hierarchical generate-and-test can eliminate entire classes of candidates.

Figure 2.29 suggests another way to visualize the difference between the operation of simple and hierarchical generate-and-test in terms of search spaces. The search spaces in this figure are partitioned into concentric rings. The outermost ring contains fully specified candidates, shown as black-shaded circles. Candidates in the inner rings are less fully specified. They are portrayed with decreasing darkness of shading, corresponding to decreasing completeness of specification.

The left ring in Figure 2.29 portrays simple generate-and-test. Since it only tests fully specified candidates, no pruning can take place until the generator reaches the outermost ring. Consequently, every "black-shaded circle" in the figure must be generated before it can be eliminated.

In contrast, hierarchical generate-and-test rules out portions of the search space with each evaluation. The right ring in Figure 2.29 portrays the hierarchical approach. It starts in the center of the circle. When it rules out a partially specified candidate, it also rules out all of the more

```
To carry out a hierarchical generate-and-test search:
  1. Initialize the generator to the root candidate.

  2. While the generator is not empty do
  3. begin
  4.        Get a candidate from the generator.
  5.        If the solution-tester(candidate) then
  6.        begin
  7.                If the candidate is complete, then exit with success
                    reporting it;
  8.                Else tell the generator to consider the candidates's
                    successors.
  9.        end
 10.        Otherwise discard the candidate (and its successors).
 11. end

     /* Here if no solution has been found. */
 12. Exit with failure.
```

FIGURE 2.27.   Satisficing method for hierarchical generate-and-test.

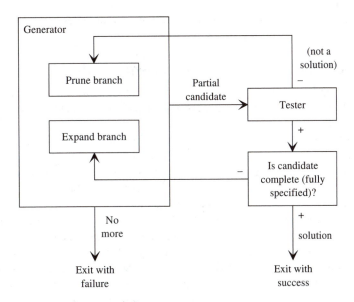

FIGURE 2.28. Schematic of hierarchical generate-and-test.

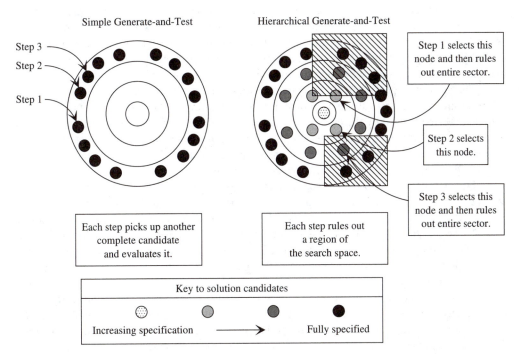

FIGURE 2.29. Simple versus hierarchical generate-and-test. Each step in the hierarchical method rules out regions of the search space.

fully specified candidates that extend it. Thus, each pruning eliminates pie-shaped wedges in the figure, representing regions of the search space.

Predicting the Efficiency of Hierarchical Generate-and-Test

Early pruning is the key to the efficiency of hierarchical generate-and-test. But how accurate must the candidate tester be on pruning decisions for partial candidates? Overzealous pruning will render the search incomplete.

In the following we develop a model for analyzing the performance of this method. For simplicity, we assume that the method need find only one solution and that there is exactly one solution at a leaf node in the search tree. The method is complete, which means it will always find the solution. The search tree has depth d, and for simplicity, it has a uniform branching factor, b. The generator uses a satisficing depth-first search.

First we look for bounds on the number of nodes visited for the best and worst cases. Given that the solution is a terminal node at depth d in the tree, the smallest number of nodes that could possibly be visited by a satisficing depth-first search is d, namely, all the nodes on the unique path from the root to the solution. Restated, we cannot find a solution by visiting fewer than $O(d)$ nodes, and we cannot under any circumstances expect to do this well or better on average. In the worst case, there is no early pruning and the solution node will be the last node in the tree to be visited. In this event, the time complexity is $O(b^d)$. Average and typical performance must lie somewhere between these linear and exponential bounds.

Our analysis follows an approach introduced in Chapter 1 where we are interested in the performance of generate-and-test on a population of problems. To model the population, we use probabilities in the search tree. We assume that the candidate tester will eliminate an unproductive branch with probability $(1 - p)$. Restated, the tester will wastefully tell the generator to continue searching successors of an unproductive branch with probability p.

The use of probabilities in our model does not mean the candidate tester is nondeterministic on a given case. The probability is a measure of the *average adequacy* of the domain knowledge used by the candidate tester to decide from a partial specification whether a branch is potentially part of a complete solution. Thus, if $p = 0$, the tester has perfect knowledge. Unproductive branches will always be pruned and the search for the solution will be quite focused. If $p = 1$, it has no knowledge and can never prune early.

Figure 2.30 counts nodes visited on average at different levels in a search tree. In this figure we assume that exactly one solution exists, portrayed without loss of generality as the leftmost terminal node. At level 1, there is only the root node to visit. There are b successors at level 2. The unique node that is on the path to the solution is kept. We assume that on average one-half of the remaining unproductive $(b - 1)$ nodes and their successors must be searched before trying the solution path during the satisficing search. The other nodes will not be searched because the method will stop when it finds the first (and unique) solution.

We now count the nodes visited at level 3, first considering the successors of the remaining nonsolutions from level 2. With probability $(1 - p)$, some of these nodes are eliminated by the solution tester at level 2. The remaining $p(b - 1)/2$ nodes will each have b successors to be tested at level 2. Also at level 3, we have the successors of the node on the solution path. The case here is analogous to the relation of the root node to the nodes at level 2. Thus, $1 + (1/2)(b - 1)$ successors of this node are searched at level 3.

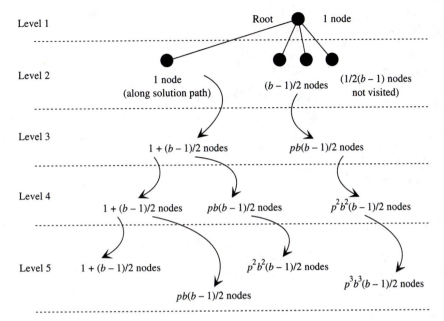

FIGURE 2.30. Counting the nodes visited on average by a satisficing depth-first version of hierarchical generate-and-test. Without loss of generality, we portray the actual solution node as the leftmost leaf of the tree. At each level, we assume that the depth-first generator visits half of the siblings along the solution path.

Continuing to level 4, the process repeats. Again, fruitless branches are eliminated by the tester with probability $(1 - p)$ and the remaining nodes have b successors to be tested at level 3. In this case, there are several sources of these nodes as shown by the accounting in Figure 2.30.

For N_j, the number of nodes searched at level j in the generate-and-test search tree, equations (13) and (14) give a recurrence relation and enumeration, respectively.

$$N_j+1 = N_j + p^{j-1} b^{j-1} (b - 1) /2 \tag{13}$$

$$N_j = 1 + 1/2 (b - 1) \sum_{k=0}^{j-2} p^k b^k = 1 + \tfrac{1}{2} (b - 1)(1 - p^{j-1} b^{j-1})/(1 - pb) \tag{14}$$

Equation (15) gives a somewhat simpler formula for N_j, substituting $z = pb$, and equation (16) gives an expression for the total number of nodes visited in the search.

$$N_j = 1 + 1/2 (b - 1) (1 - z^{j-1}) / (1 - z) \text{ where } z = pb \tag{15}$$

$$\text{Total}(d) = \sum_{k=1}^{d} N_k = d + [(b - 1)/(2(1 - z))] (d - (1 - z^d/(1 - z))) \tag{16}$$

Figure 2.31 shows effect of different values of the product pb. Even for a tree of only depth 4 and branching factor 5, the difference between perfect early pruning and no early pruning is enough to change the number of candidates generated from 10 to 80.

Pruning Knowledge	p	pb	Avg. N_4	Avg. Total (4)
Perfect	0	0	3	10
Almost perfect	.01	.05	3.11	10.2
Half right	.5	2.5	20.5	33.4
One percent	.99	4.95	62.4	78.88
Ignorant	1	5	63	80

FIGURE 2.31. The number of candidates generated by hierarchical search depends critically on its ability to prune fruitless candidates early. In this chart, we consider various values for p for the case where $d = 4$, $b = 5$. For trees of greater depth and branching factor, the exponential effect is much greater. N_4 is the number of nodes searched at level 4.

Looking back at the form of equations (15) and (16), we see that as $z = bp$ approaches 1 from below, there is an explosive increase in the number of candidates visited both at level N_j for large j and in total over all levels through d. This is made somewhat easier to see by rewriting equation (16) for the total in terms of constants as shown in equation (17).

$$\text{Total}(d) = A + \frac{B}{1-z}\left[\frac{C}{1-z} + D\right] \tag{17}$$

As z approaches 1, there is a sudden transition from linear to exponential search. Thus, in a large search problem, a small change in the local effectiveness of the pruning test has a major impact on the complexity of a large search.

It might be argued that the model underlying this prediction of a phase transition is unrealistic. For example, in a real generator the branching factor may not be uniform and pruning might not take place at a uniform rate. Furthermore, pruning of various branches might not be random if different partial specifications are pruned for the same reason. Williams and Hogg (1991) argue that the predictions from this simple model are robust across substantially weaker conditions.

Summary of Generate-and-Test Methods

Figure 2.32 summarizes the generate-and-test (G&T) methods. Hierarchical generate-and-test is more efficient than simple generate-and-test because the former is able to prune families of solutions. For the hierarchical method to be workable, the generator must partition the search space in ways that admit early pruning and the solution tester must be applicable to partial candidates.

2.2.4 A Sample Knowledge System Using   ADVANCED
         Hierarchical Generate-and-Test

In this section we pause in the elaboration of different search methods to consider a sample application of one of them. In doing this we introduce our first example of a knowledge system. We show how it is organized around the use of hierarchical generate-and-test. We show how the knowledge of the task domain connects with the method through its generator and tester. We also

Blind Method	Simple G&T	Hierarchical G&T
Knowledge interfaces	Generator	Generator
	Solution tester	Solution tester
What to evaluate	Whole candidates	Whole and partial candidates
Thoroughness	Depends on completeness of generator	Depends on completeness of generator and correctness of pruning rules
Some Variations		
Based on	Depth-first or breadth-first search	Depth-first or breadth-first search

FIGURE 2.32. Summary of characteristics and variations for simple and hierarchical generate-and-test search methods.

discuss how some of the representation issues from Chapter 1 arise in the search process, specifically the use of canonical forms.

The techniques in this example were also used in the well-known DENDRAL program, which determined the structures of organic molecules from mass spectrometry (and other) data. In our example, we choose a simpler structure elucidation program, GA1, that illustrates the basic points about hierarchical generate-and-test programs using a class of simple, linear molecules (Stefik, 1978).

To describe the molecular segmentation-structure elucidation problem (or "segmentation problem" for short), it is easiest to begin with an example solution. Figure 2.33 illustrates a circular DNA structure. Each number represents the size of a segment in the structure. The labels (such as "Eco RI") represent enzyme recognition sites, which are places where the molecule would be cut by the named enzyme. For example, Bam is the name of an enzyme and there are two Bam sites on the given structure. In Figure 2.33, one piece of the circular molecule is shown to the right. This piece would be freed from the larger molecule if the enzymes Hind III and Eco RI were used in combination. When a molecule is cut, it is customary to label its ends with the names of the enzymes that cut there. An "answer" to a segmentation problem is an ordered sequence of alternating sites and segment lengths.

An analogy may help you to visualize the problem-solving task. The segment lengths may be likened to lengths of chain and the recognition sites may be likened to locks with keys, as suggested by Figure 2.34. In these terms, the solution to the sample problem has six locks and three different keys (B, H, and E). Our data are provided by a quiz master, who has the necessary keys and several copies of the complete chain (whose structure is unknown to us). The quiz master uses different combinations of keys on the chain and reports the results back to us.

If we know the molecular structure, it is easy to predict what size pieces we would get back from any enzyme digestion. Figure 2.35 shows the pieces that would result from digestion by Eco RI. The diagram shows the interior enzyme sites on the pieces. Further digestion by a second enzyme would cut the pieces into still smaller ones at the indicated sites.

This shows how the enzyme-cutting operation works. Our task, however, is in some sense the opposite of this. The problem is to infer the *original structure* of the chains (molecules) given only the data about the pieces as exemplified by the sample data shown in Figure 2.36.

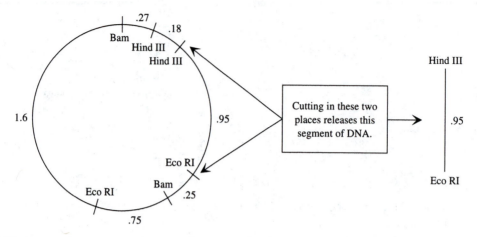

FIGURE 2.33. DNA molecule that is a solution to the segmentation problem. The numbers indicate masses of the DNA segments measured in megadaltons. The labels (Bam, Hind III, Eco RI) show the recognition sites for enzymes.

The candidate solutions for this problem can be visualized as the possible ways to fill in a template. Figure 2.37 shows a template for the sample problem. A complete candidate has segment weights and enzyme labels filled in for all of the corresponding parts of the template. In a given problem we know what enzymes are used, so those can be used to fill in the sites in the template. We use the union of the pieces from the double-enzyme digests as the list of possible

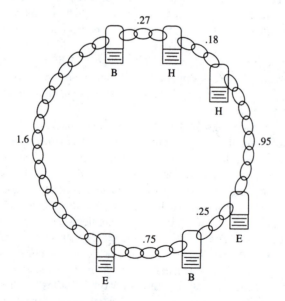

FIGURE 2.34. Locks and chains analogy to the segmentation problem.

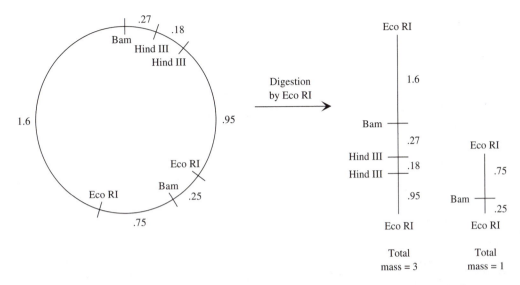

FIGURE 2.35. DNA molecule that is a solution to the segmentation problem. The numbers indicate masses of the DNA segments measured in megadaltons. The labels (Bam, Hind III, Eco RI) show the recognition sites for enzymes.

segments. This includes every possible segment because every segment must be cut on one end by some enzyme. However, a segment from a two-enzyme digest can include some internal sites. For example, in the sample problem some of the segments from the double-enzyme digest data have interior sites from the third enzyme. In this problem, a triple-enzyme digest provides data for a shorter list of candidate segments for filling in the template. If n enzymes are being used, an n-enzyme digest will provide the shortest list of starting pieces for the generator.

The number of ways to place any of the enzyme sites and segment weights into the template is about 1.3 billion. However, from the input data to the sample problem it is possible to infer that each segment can appear at most once in the template and that each enzyme appears in exactly two sites. This reduces the number of possibilities to just over 2 million distinct candi-

Enzymes	Weights of molecular segments observed after cutting by enzymes
Hind III	3.82, .18
Bam	2.35, 1.65
Eco RI	3.0, 1.0
Hind III and Bam	2.35, 1.2, .27, .18
Hind III and Eco RI	1.87, 1.0, .95, .18
Bam and Eco RI	1.6, 1.4, .75, .25

FIGURE 2.36. The input data to the segmentation problem.

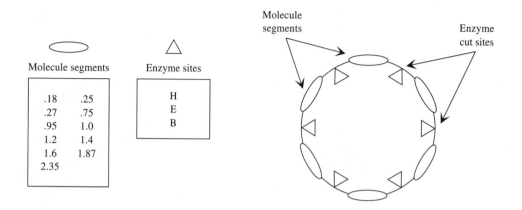

FIGURE 2.37.   A template for generating solutions. The candidate segments come from the double-enzyme digests.

dates. By applying additional candidate consistency rules in hierarchical generate-and-test, GA1 is usually able to reduce the number of candidates to six or fewer.

Figure 2.38 presents a hierarchical generate-and-test method for solving segmentation problems. It is a version of the hierarchical generate-and-test method presented earlier, specialized for segmentation problems. At each cycle in steps 3 through 14, the generator adds alternately an enzyme site or a segment. In this way it incrementally fills the template to create a description of a partial candidate. The tester is represented by rules that consider the partially filled template. The method performs an exhaustive search, accumulating a list of all the solutions.

An important addition is the test for canonical form in step 6. Canonical forms are discussed in Chapter 1. They are needed here because there are several distinct ways to fill in the template, each of which yields different symbol structures representing the same DNA structures. This difficulty is not unusual in generate-and-test problems, and failure to attend to it can be a source of redundancy and inefficiency. Generators are said to be **nonredundant** when they appropriately generate structures with unique designations. Because GA1 must find all of the solutions consistent with the data, it requires a nonredundant and complete generator.

The canonical form rules are run on partially specified solutions for the same reason that the pruning rules are. By applying canonical form rules early and often, the generate-and-test method can rule out entire classes of (noncanonical) candidates and thereby achieve greater efficiency. An example of a **canonical form rule** is:

> If circular structures are being generated, only the smallest segment in the list of initial segments should be used for the first segment.

To solve a segmentation problem:
```
    1. Initialize by acquiring and checking the data, clearing the solution
       list, and computing parameters for the rules.
    2. Form a stack consisting of the root node (or null candidate).

    3. While the stack is not empty do
    4. begin
    5.         Pop a node (candidate) from the stack.

               /* Apply canonical form rules. */
    6.         If the candidate is in canonical form then
    7.         begin
                   /* Apply data consistency rules. */
    8.             If the candidate is consistent then
    9.             begin
   10.                 If the candidate specification is complete,
                       then add it to the list of solutions;
   11.                 Else push the candidate's children onto the
                       stack. (Child nodes alternately add segment
                       weights or enzyme sites to the candidate's template.)
   12.             end
   13.         end
   14. end

   15. Return the list of solutions (if any).
```

FIGURE 2.38. The organization of GA1: exhaustive hierarchical generate-and-test.

This rule eliminates some of the symbol structures that are not in canonical form. It will not cause solutions to be missed because the exhaustive generator will generate the canonical form eventually.

An example of a **pruning rule** is:

> If an enzyme site is about to be placed and the neighboring segment did not appear in one of the two-enzyme digests for this enzyme, then this branch can be pruned.

This rule eliminates structures that are not consistent with the input data. It is based on the observation that a segment has exactly two ends. Thus, every molecular piece must appear in some two-enzyme digest. If a segment has been placed in the template, then only those enzymes consistent with the enzyme-digest data should be placed next to it.

Figure 2.39 shows part of the search tree for the sample problem. As marked in the figure, branches can be eliminated for violating canonical form rules or data-based pruning rules. For example, the partial description ".18 H .25 H" is pruned because all molecules containing this

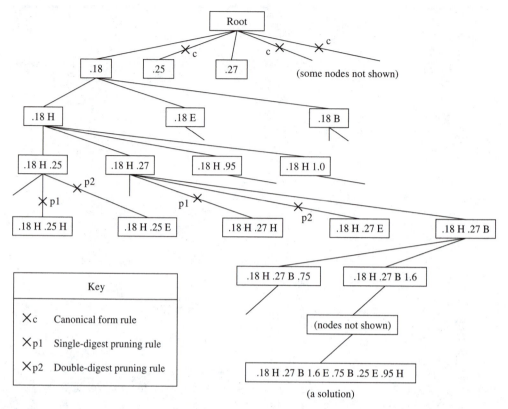

FIGURE 2.39. The organization of GA1: exhaustive hierarchical generate-and-test. These branches are pruned as soon as they violate any of GA1's rules.

segment should have a segment of length .25 megadaltons in the Hind III (H) digest. Similarly, the partial description ".18 H .25 E" is pruned because all molecules containing this segment should have a .25 megadalton segment in the Hind III/Eco RI (H/E) digest. Since the data show no such segments, these classes of molecular structures can be pruned early.

Altogether, GA1 used 16 pruning rules, 6 canonical form rules, and 20 rules that exploited redundancy to check and correct the input data. These different categories of rules show the "conceptual coatrack" provided by hierarchical generate-and-test for applying different kinds of knowledge. Using these rules to prune the space of possibilities, GA1 was able to solve the sample problem above in about 3 seconds and could solve most larger problems in less than a minute (using a PDP-10 computer in the late 1970s).

At the end of the generation phase, GA1 had a subsequent evaluation phase that applied some additional rules. This illustrates a final point about the use of hierarchical generate-and-test: When pruning rules are complex and specialized, there is sometimes a trade-off between including them in the program and applying them afterward on a short list of remaining candidates. Most of the pruning rules in GA1 use very localized information in the molecule and can be efficiently included in the inner loop. The more complex rules consider properties that depend on larger portions of the candidate symbol structures; they are difficult to code correctly in a loop that alternates between sites and segments and expensive to apply in the inner loop. In such cases it can be simpler and more efficient to use these rules in a simple evaluation at the end. The final evaluation phase of GA1, like that of DENDRAL, uses the candidate structure to predict the ideal data that should have been produced by the segmentation process. The data predicted for each candidate structure are then compared with the given data and scored. The overall match is used to rank candidates.

In summary, GA1 is a knowledge system whose search for solutions is organized around hierarchical generate-and-test. It assembles candidate solutions incrementally using a template. Partial candidates can be checked against the input data to see whether the candidates correctly predict the pieces that should appear in the enzyme digests. If the predictions are wrong, then the partial candidate cannot be a part of a larger solution and an entire branch of the search tree is pruned. The domain knowledge is used to set up the initial template and starting pieces as well as in the rules used to prune the candidates when they fail to match digest data or are not in canonical form.

2.2.5 *Simple and Backtracking Constraint Satisfaction*

The last category of blind search methods presented here is based on a formulation of search called **constraint satisfaction**. Figure 2.40 illustrates the general idea for the task of ordering dishes for a Chinese meal. In this example, several people have come together to have dinner and have agreed to order and share several large dishes. The meal must be varied and differences in taste and diet need to be taken into account. The selection of what to order can be formulated as a process of choosing dishes (depicted as circles) that satisfy a set of constraints (depicted as boxes connected to the circles). Thus, a chicken dish and a vegetable dish must be chosen such that neither includes peanuts. A pork dish and a seafood dish must be chosen such that no more than one of them is spicy hot. The total cost summed over all of the dishes must not exceed 30 dollars, and so on. The key element of this formulation is that the choices are not made independently.

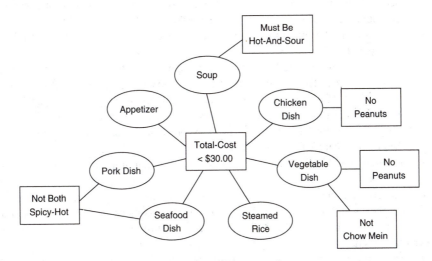

FIGURE 2.40.   A constraint network for ordering a Chinese meal.

An example constraint:
```
1. procedure not-too-hot(pork-dish seafood-dish)
2. begin
3.       If spicy-hot(pork-dish) and spicy-hot(seafood dish)
4.       then return (True)
5.       else return (False)
6. end
```

FIGURE 2.41.   A procedural representation of a constraint.

Choices are related by explicit constraints, creating a **constraint network** of interconnected decisions. A solution, an order for the meal in this example, must satisfy all of the constraints.

A more formal characterization of a constraint satisfaction problem is that there is a set of variables $\{x_1, x_2, \ldots, x_n\}$ and a set of constraints on subsets of these variables limiting the values that the variables can take on. In the terminology of constraint satisfaction, the set of possible or candidate values for a variable is often referred to as the variable's **domain**. Many different kinds of domains are possible. The domains most studied in AI consist of a finite number of discrete values. These are called **finite domains**. A solution is an assignment of values from the variable's domains to the corresponding variables that satisfies all of the constraints. A constraint can be unary,or a relation on values for a single variable; binary, or a relation on values for a pair of variables; or *n*-ary, meaning that it simultaneously limits the values of *n* variables. Constraint satisfaction problems are sometimes referred to as CSPs.

The Chinese meal example includes the variables `pork-dish` and `seafood-dish`. Values for `pork-dish` might include {sweet-and-sour-pork, twice-cooked-pork*, shredded-pork-in-garlic-sauce*, mu-shu-pork, bbq-pork-with-broccoli, pork-kidney-in-garlic-sauce*}, and values for `seafood-dish` might include {sizzling-rice-prawn, prawn-with-snow-pea, curry-prawn, prawn-in-lobster-sauce, szechuan-prawn*, kun-bau-prawn*, lover's-prawn, scallop-in-garlic-sauce*, crab-with-green-onion-and-ginger-root}, where the asterisk indicates that the dish is spicy hot. One of the constraints in the problem was that the selected pork dish and the selected seafood dish not both be spicy hot.

Constraints can be represented in various ways. One direct way would be as a procedure, such as that in Figure 2.41. The function `not-too-hot` is used as a predicate whose arguments correspond to variables of the constraint satisfaction problem. It makes use of an underlying primitive test that enables it to determine the properties of a variable, such as whether a particular dish is "spicy hot." Testing the constraint in this representation amounts to invoking the procedure with appropriate values for its arguments.

As with other search tasks, there is a range of possible solution criteria. An exhaustive search requires finding all of the solutions (that is, value assignments) that satisfy the constraints. A satisficing search requires finding one of them. In most cases, modifying a search method to do one or the other is a simple matter. When a set of constraints admits no solutions at all, the problem is said to be **overconstrained**. When there are multiple solutions, a problem is said to be **underconstrained**.

We begin with the two simplest search methods for constraint satisfaction: simple constraint satisfaction and backtracking constraint satisfaction. These methods are variations of

To carry out simple constraint satisfaction:
```
1. While the generator is not empty do
2. begin
3.      Generate (combinatorially) the next set of possible values
        for the variables.
4.      Test whether the values satisfy all of the constraints.
5.      If yes, exit with success. (The candidate is a solution.)
6. end

   /* Here if no solution has been found. */
7. Exit with failure.
```

FIGURE 2.42.   Satisficing method for (too) simple constraint satisfaction.

methods we have already discussed for blind search. The first of these, **simple constraint satisfaction**, is shown in Figure 2.42. Simple constraint satisfaction is just a paraphrasing of simple generate-and-test such that the generator is a program that delivers all possible combinations of value assignments for the variables and the solution tester is a program that checks whether these assignments satisfy all of the constraints.

As with simple generate-and-test, the problem with simple constraint satisfaction is that it is too inefficient, except for the most trivial of problems. Combinations of possible values can mount up very quickly. If there are 10 variables with 20 possible values each, this approach may test all 20^{10} of them in its search for a solution.

By analogy with hierarchical generate-and-test, we can improve this by moving some of the tests into the generator. This method, which is called **backtracking constraint satisfaction**, is illustrated in Figure 2.43 and 2.44. Backtracking involves the sequential assignment of values to variables. Assigning a value to a variable from its domain is also called **instantiating** a variable. When all the variables of a constraint have been instantiated, the constraint is tested. Since any particular constraint may reference only a subset of the total set of variables in a solution, testing a constraint amounts to testing a partial solution.

If the constraint is satisfied, the process of assignment and testing continues. If the constraint is not satisfied, the last variable assigned that has untried values is retried with its next value. Because of the way this approach always withdraws the most recently made choice on discovering a failure, it is also known as **chronological backtracking**. Although this approach is hierarchical, it turns out that there are several other formulations also involving hierarchies that improve the performance of constraint satisfaction methods. Rather than calling a particular one of them **hierarchical constraint satisfaction**, we prefer to use more specific names for each of them.

The search operation in backtracking constraint satisfaction is illustrated in Figure 2.43. This example has four variables $\{x_1, x_2, x_3, x_4\}$ with three possible values for each as shown. The first step instantiates the x_1 variable with the possible value a. Before instantiating any other variables, the search immediately collects all of the unary constraints on x_1 and tests them. If these constraints are not satisfied, no further combinations of variables involving $x_1 = a$ will be tried and the program will pursue the branch $x_1 = b$. In the other branches to the right, the pro-

Variable	Possible values
X_1	$\{\, a, b, c \,\}$
X_2	$\{\, d, e, f \,\}$
X_3	$\{\, g, h, i \,\}$
X_4	$\{\, j, k, l \,\}$

The first steps of backtracking constraint satisfaction

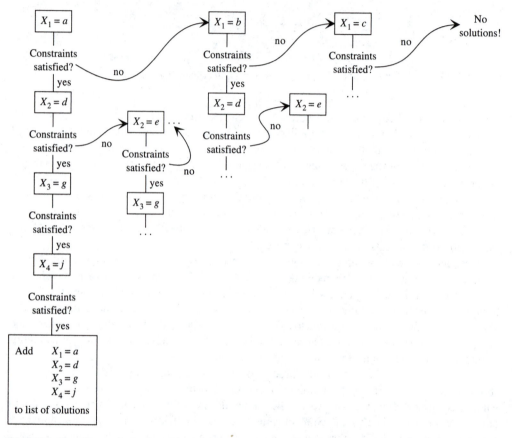

FIGURE 2.43.   Trace of a backtracking method for constraint satisfaction.

gram considers $x_1 = c$. If that branch also fails, no assignment of x_1 satisfies all of the constraints and the search process can be determined to be overconstrained after only three tests.

Returning to the first branch of the search, if all the unary constraints (if any) on $x_1 = a$ are satisfied, the program goes on to instantiate variable x_2 to d. Once more we retrieve the applicable constraints, which means all the unary constraints on x_2 and the binary constraints on x_1 and x_2. If any of these are not satisfied, we branch off to the right to try $x_2 = e$ and so on. If these constraints are satisfied we instantiate the next variable x_3 to g, and later, in like manner, x_4 to j. If all

To carry out a (chronological) backtracking constraint satisfaction:

```
  1.          Initialize the list of solutions to the empty list.
  2.          Reset generate-next-value for all the variables (no assignments).
  3.          Set the current variable index k to 0.
  4. next:     Extend the set of variable assignments. (Increment k)
  5.          If there are no more variables (k > n), then backtrack.

  6.          Retrieve all of the untested constraints for variables
              through k.
  7. gen:     Generate the next value for variable k.
  8.          If there are no more values for variable k, then backtrack
              to try the next candidate.

  9.          For each of the retrieved constraints do
 10.          begin
 11.              Test the constraint on the values of variables 1 to k.
 12.              If the constraint is not satisfied, discard all further
                  extensions of this set of value assignments and try the
                  next value for the last variable instantiated (go to
                  gen).
 13.          end

              /* Here if all the retrieved constraints have been
              satisfied. */
 14.          If all values have been instantiated in this value assignment
              (k = n), then add this set of value assignments to the list of
              solutions.
 15.          Prepare to generate next candidate (go to next).
```

To backtrack during constraint satisfaction:

```
  1. backtrack:   If all values of all variables have been tried, then
                  exit with the list of solutions;
  2.                  Otherwise decrement k until reaching the first
                      previous variable with untried values.
  3.                  Reset generate-next-value for all variables
                      greater than k.
```

FIGURE 2.44. Chronological backtracking method for constraint satisfaction. This version of the method finds all solutions.

of the constraints at this stage are satisfied, we can add the value assignment $\{ x_1 = a, x_2 = d, x_3 = g, x_4 = j \}$ to the list of solutions.

The method for backtracking constraint satisfaction is presented in Figure 2.44 with four auxiliary programs: generate-next-value, which produces the next value to be tried for a given variable and which can be reset to start over again to produce all the possible values for that variable; `retrieve-untested-constraints`, which retrieves all the constraints involving variables 1 to k that were not retrieved for variables 1 to $k-1$; `test-constraint`, which tests whether a constraint is satisfied for the assigned values of the variables; and `backtrack`, which unwinds the search to the last variable that was instantiated and starts a new branch. Of these, only `generate-next-value` is a parameter to be specialized for a particular problem.

This version of the method is organized as a depth-first search. However, instead of using an explicit stack to keep track of its place in the search tree, the search uses an index to the variables (k) and computes a tree of variable instantiations from x_1 to x_n.

To achieve efficiency in exploring a search space, hierarchical generate-and-test must be able to apply pruning rules early, on partial solutions. In the specialized formulation above, the pruning rules correspond to the constraints, and a value assignment to a *subset* of the variables corresponds to a partial solution. Since a solution must satisfy all the constraints, any assignment of values to a subset of the variables that violates even one constraint cannot be part of a larger solution. Backtracking constraint satisfaction exploits this fact for early pruning by applying constraints as soon as their variables are instantiated. Thus, substantial subspaces of the generate-and-test search space (the Cartesian product of all of the value assignments to variables) are eliminated from further consideration by a single failure.

Backtracking constraint satisfaction is generally a much more practical approach than simple constraint satisfaction. Although it is less efficient than some of the methods discussed in later chapters, it is easy to program and does not depend on special properties of the constraints or special properties of the domain values.

The version of the algorithm in Figure 2.44 finds all solutions. Even in the satisficing version, the worst-case time complexity is exponential in the number of variables because the only solution may be the last combination tried. In more typical cases, the time complexity is much better with backtracking constraint satisfaction than with simple constraint satisfaction because of the hierarchical pruning.

A variation of the method enables it to perform satisficing search (stopping after finding one solution) rather than exhaustive search. For this a slight modification to steps 12 and 13 is all that is needed. With satisficing search the worst case occurs when no solution exists solely because of an inconsistency between x_n (the last variable instantiated) and the other variables. In this case the number of tests is still exponential—depending on the number of elements per domain (a) and the number of constraints (c). For problems with only binary constraints, this is sometimes given as e, the number of edges of the graph. Thus, the worst-case time complexity of constraint satisfaction for satisficing is the same for both simple and backtracking methods, $O(ca^n)$.

The characteristics of simple and backtracking constraint satisfaction are summarized in Figure 2.45. The practical efficiency of backtracking constraint satisfaction depends on the efficacy of early pruning, and thereby on which constraints are tested first. In general, it is best to organize the variables so variables that are most connected to each other by constraints are closest together in the ordering.

Because of their simplicity of formulation and apparent generality, constraint satisfaction problems have been studied in detail, and special cases continue to be of theoretical interest. The complexity arguments we proposed here make no assumptions about the structure of the constraint graph. In later chapters we return to CSPs and see how insights from graph theory lead to more efficient methods of solution in special cases.

Blind method	Simple constraint satisfaction	Backtracking constraint satisfaction
Knowledge interfaces	The constraints	The constraints
	The domain values	The domain values
Worst-case space	$O(a^n)$	$O(a^n)$
Worst-case time	$O(a^n)$	$O(a^n)$
Thoroughness	Complete search	Complete search
Example bad cases	Exponential number of solutions	The only solution is the last tried
Based on	Simple generate-and-test	Hierarchical generate-and-test
Some variations		
Solution criteria	Exhaustive/satisficing	Exhaustive/satisficing
Efficiency	Some variations that exploit the topology of the constraint graph, the domain values, or other properties are considered in Chapter 7	

FIGURE 2.45. Summary of characteristics of simple and backtracking constraint satisfaction.

2.2.6 *Summary and Review*

This section presents blind search methods, which are basic approaches for searching a space of solutions using only bookkeeping knowledge about the traversal of a tree of candidate solutions.

In depth-first search the processor descends through a search tree, starting at the root node and selecting one alternative branch at each successor node until reaching either a solution or a terminal node. Breadth-first search is similar, except that it looks for a solution among all the nodes at a given level before advancing to successors at the next level. Because the breadth-first method carries multiple solution paths in parallel, it has a greater worst-case space complexity than depth-first search, the greater amount depending on the branching factor. However, if there are deep and fruitless paths in a search tree, depth-first search can waste much time thrashing uselessly in the depths of the tree. Neither approach is particularly good on average, since they are blind (by definition) to the use of heuristic knowledge to guide the search process.

Two versions of generate-and-test were considered, simple and hierarchical. In simple generate-and-test, the solution tester is applied on whole candidate solutions provided by the generator. This approach can be very inefficient, generating and then retesting the same large symbol structures repeatedly on minor variations in solution candidates.

Hierarchical generate-and-test achieves greater efficiency by assembling candidates incrementally and applying the solution test to partially specified solution candidates. This enables ruling out a family of candidates using a single test on the symbol structure common to the whole family, without taking the time to generate each family member explicitly. An additional auxiliary program keeps track of whether a candidate solution is completely specified. The efficiency of hierarchical generate-and-test depends crucially on the effectiveness of the candidate tester at pruning partial solutions. As the probability of pruning an unproductive branch for a partial solution drops in a population of problems, there is a phase transition in expected time complexity from linear to exponential in the depth of the search tree.

The advantage of the hierarchical version over the simple version was illustrated in the context of a program to figure out the combination to a lock. It was also illustrated with a sample application, the GA1 program for inferring the segment structure of DNA molecules. This application gave us a concrete example of the embedding of domain knowledge in the rules used by the generate-and-test process. This example also shows how several kinds of knowledge—expressed as data-checking rules, pruning rules, and canonical form rules—can be combined in the context of search.

Constraint satisfaction is a variation on generate-and-test in which the solutions are specified in terms of values assigned to variables and constraints on the compatible combinations of values. Our example of the Chinese meal problem illustrated CSPs with finite domains, problems in which the values assigned to variables are drawn from a finite set. Other variations of CSPs are discussed in later chapters.

Simple constraint satisfaction corresponds to simple generate-and-test. It is inefficient because candidate solutions are tested only when they are complete. Backtracking constraint satisfaction is a special case of hierarchical generate-and-test where the generation of partial solution candidates corresponds to assigning values to a subset of the constraint variables and the testing of partial solutions corresponds to the testing of constraints on those variables to which values have been assigned. The method we presented is called chronological backtracking because the search process always withdraws first the combination of values most recently assigned. Backtracking constraint satisfaction is generally a much more practical approach than simple constraint satisfaction.

Exercises for Section 2.2

Ex. 1 [10] *Space Requirements of Breadth-first Search.* Professor Digit says that as a practical matter, a breadth-first search of most problem spaces will exhaust the available memory in a computer long before an appreciable amount of time is used. Suppose that a 32 megabyte (MB) computer generates a million nodes per minute in a search using breadth-first search, that it requires 4 bytes per node, that the programs themselves occupy negligible amounts of storage, and that the nodes must be kept in memory or discarded. (For the purposes of this exercise, we ignore the possibility of using a large virtual memory.)
(a) Assuming that it does not find a solution first, how long could a breadth-first search program run before memory was exhausted?
(b) How many levels of the search tree could be completely searched before exhausting memory, assuming a uniform branching factor of 4?

Ex. 2 [CP-15] *Searching Graphs Containing Cycles.* The algorithms for depth-first and breadth-first search presented in this section require that the search space be organized as a tree. A more general formulation of these methods would allow them to work in cases where the search space is a directed graph. A directed graph includes cases where nodes connect back to their ancestors to form cycles in the graph.
(a) How would the method in this section for depth-first search fail when the search space is a graph with cycles?
(b) To avoid the problem in part a, the method in Figure 2.46 keeps records of which nodes have been noticed—either by setting a bit associated with the node or by putting a pointer to the node in a table. Marking node a means that they are successors of some node

To carry out a satisficing depth-first search on a cyclic graph:

```
 1.     Initialize the records of noticed nodes to empty.
 2.     Form a stack consisting of the root node.

 3.     While the stack is not empty do
 4.     begin
 5.         Pop a node from the stack.
 6.         If solution-tester(node) then exit with success reporting
            the node
 7.         Else
 8.         begin
 9.             For each of the node's successors do
10.                 If the successor is not marked as noticed, then
                    begin
11.                     Mark it as noticed.
12.                     Push it onto the stack.
13.                 end
14.         end
15.     end

        /* Here if no solution has been found. */
16.     Exit with failure.
```

FIGURE 2.46.   A version of satisficing depth-first search that works on cyclic graphs.

and have been placed on the stack, although they may not have been tested as solutions yet. What is the space complexity of the method?

(c) Does the order of traversal generate a spanning tree on the graph?

Ex. 3   [*CD-CP-20*] *Searching Graphs Containing Cycles, Again and Again*. This exercise discusses two approaches for reducing the space requirements of depth-first search on a graph containing cycles.

(a) In a search space we assume that all the nodes are reachable by some path that starts at the root. Suppose that cycles are rare in the graphs of interest and that fewer than one node in 1,000 has multiple parents. Suppose further that there is an easy way to tell whether a node has multiple parents and that this can be determined when the node is generated.

(i) Briefly, describe a method that exploits these properties to reduce storage requirements for searching graphs containing cycles.

(ii) What is the worst-case space complexity of this method?

(iii) Does the method perform a complete search?

(iv) Does the method test every node once and not more than once? If not, explain briefly.

(b) Another approach to searching a graph with cycles was proposed by Robert Tarjan. His method, shown in Figure 2.47, does not allocate any additional data structures for

```
/* To carry out a satisficing depth-first search on a cyclic graph: */
1.    Initialize the records of noticed nodes to empty.
2.    Form a stack consisting of the root node.
3.    While {node := Get-Node(stack)} is not nil do
4.    begin
5.            If solution-tester(node) then exit with success reporting the
              node;
6.            For each of the node's successors (if any) do
7.                    If the successor is not already on the stack then push
                      it onto the stack.
8.    end

      /* Here if stack empty. No solution found. */
9.    Exit with failure.


/* Retrieve the next node from the stack. This is a more complicated */
/* "pop" operation that avoids removing a node from the stack until its */
/* ancestors have been explored.*/
1. Procedure Get-Node(stack)
2.     begin
              /* Here to flush nodes on the stack whose successors have
              been processed. */
3.            While the top node of the stack is marked as noticed do
4.            begin
5.                    Discard the noticed records for the top node of the
                      stack.
6.                    Pop the top node from the stack and discard it.
7.                    If the stack is empty, return NIL.
8.            end
9.            Set node to the new top node of the stack.
10.           Mark node as noticed.
11.    Return node.
12.    end
```

FIGURE 2.47.   Tarjan's method for a satisficing depth-first search that works on cyclic graphs.

marking "noticed" nodes. Instead, Tarjan's method avoids looping on cycles in the graph by noticing when a successor is already on the stack.

    (i) What is the worst-case space complexity of this method ?

    (ii) Does it perform a complete search?

    (iii) Does it test every node once and not more than once? If not, explain briefly.

(c) Professor Digit wants a method that performs a complete satisficing, depth-first search on finite graphs containing cycles. He also wants the worst-case space complexity of the method to be no more than $O(d)$—ignoring constant factors. Finally, he wants the method to search each node in the search space no more than once. Do either of the methods in this exercise satisfy all of Professor Digit's goals? Explain briefly.

Ex. 4   [*CD-!-CP-20*] *Depth-limited Search.* One problem with depth-first search is the possibility that it will go past the levels at which solutions are found to systematically explore vast and barren parts of the solution space. One modification of the method intended to address this problem is to provide a parameter that provides a cutoff for maximum depth of the search.

(a) Present a method for **depth-limited, depth-first search (DLDFS)** for trees.

(b) Is a depth-limited search appropriate for a satisficing or an exhaustive search? Briefly, in what situations would a fixed-depth cutoff be a bad approach?

(c) Professor Digit says the DLDFS can also be used for searching graphs with cycles when it is known that all solutions are within a given depth. He claims that in this case the method avoids infinite looping and has only $O(d)$ space complexity. Is Professor Digit correct?

■   **Ex. 5**   [*CD-!-CP-20*] *Depth-first Iterative Deepening.* Breadth-first search has time complexity $O(b^d)$ to find a solution where b is the average branching factor and $O(d)$ is the depth at which the first solution is found. Unfortunately, the search also has space complexity of $O(b^d)$. Depth-first search has space complexity of d, but if solutions are shallow in the tree it can spend too much time fruitlessly exploring deep regions. If an arbitrary cutoff depth is used as in the previous exercise, no solution may be found since d is rarely known in advance.

These drawbacks can be remedied by a procedure known as **depth-first iterative deepening (DFID)**, which performs a series of depth-first searches starting with a depth cutoff of one and incrementing the depth cutoff by one for each iteration until a solution is found.

(a) Present a satisficing DFID method. For simplicity, you may assume that the search space is over a tree or an acyclic graph.

(b) What are the worst-case space and time complexities of DFID?

(c) Suppose a solution exists at depth $d = 5$. How many times will the method consider nodes at $d = 2$?

■   **Ex. 6**   [*!-20*] *Backward Chaining as Search.* It is illuminating to view the execution of production rules as the traversing of a search tree. For example, the diagnostic rules below represent cause-and-effect relationships in the parts of an ignition system.

Rule 1
```
IF    (1.1) there is power to the starter, and
      (1.2) the engine isn't frozen, and
      (1.3) the starter isn't broken,
THEN  (1.4) the starter will turn over.
```

Rule 2
```
IF    (2.1) there is power to the activation connector of the
            solenoid, and
      (2.2) the cable from the solenoid to the starter is
            intact, and
      (2.3) the cable from the battery to the power connector
            of the solenoid is intact,
THEN  (2.4) there is power to the starter.
```

Rule 3
```
IF    (3.1) there is power to the starter switch, and
      (3.2) the starter switch is on, and
      (3.3) the cable from the starter switch to the activa-
            tion connector of the solenoid is intact,
THEN  (3.4) there is power to the activation connector of the
            solenoid.
```

Rule 4
```
IF    (4.1) the battery is charged and
      (4.2) the cable from the battery to the starter switch
            is intact,
THEN  (4.3) there is power to the starter switch.
```

Rule 5
```
IF    (5.1) the battery is charged and
      (5.2) the cable from the battery to the light switch is
            intact,
THEN  (5.3) there is power to the light switch.
```

Rule 6
```
IF    (6.1) there is power to the light switch, and
      (6.2) the bulb is not burned out, and
      (6.3) the headlight switch is on,
THEN  (6.4) the headlight will glow.
```

(a) Draw a graph showing the nodes and branches implied by Rules 1 through 6 where each element of state (such as "there is power to the light switch" or "the battery is charged") corresponds to a node and the rule is represented by an AND-tree. Annotate the nodes with the numbers of the rule clauses that refer to them.

Hint: Some nodes will have more than one label.

(b) The order that nodes are visited in a search for solutions depends on the traversal strategy used by the rule processor. Given that the rule processor uses backward chaining starting from clause 1.4 and that the first successor of a node is the clause with the lowest index number, list the first ten nodes in the order of visitation if a depth-first approach is employed.

(c) Suppose these rules are used in a system that asks the user for information only in the case where there is no given way of computing the answer. In graphical terms, this means the user will be asked a question for exactly those nodes where there is no incoming link. Following this approach for a depth-first search, what are the first three questions that would be asked of the user (assuming that he or she always answers "yes")? What would be the first three questions if a breadth-first approach were employed?

(d) The three questions generated in part c would probably seem pretty strange to a practiced diagnostician and not very helpful to a driver unfamiliar with how an engine works. A more useful first question to ask would be, "Do the lights turn on?" since important subsystems could be verified as working by this simple test (e.g., that the battery is charged). Describe briefly an approach that would lead to questions like this being asked first. What knowledge does your approach use that takes it beyond blind search?

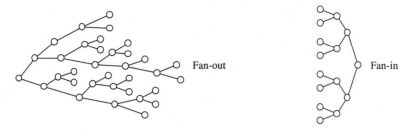

FIGURE 2.48. Fan-in and fan-out.

Ex. 7 [*10*] *Fan-in and Fan-out for Search Trees*. The shape of a search space can determine whether forward chaining or backward chaining is more efficient for determining which conclusions are supported from data. Figure 2.48 classifies two trees as fan-in and fan-out.

(a) Assuming that the nodes on the left are initial states (or data) and that the nodes on the right are goal states (or conclusions), in which direction would forward chaining go? Which direction would backward chaining go?

(b) The number of nodes visited is a measure of efficiency in search. To determine whether a particular conclusion is supported by available data, one could use forward chaining from the data or backward chaining from the conclusions. Which would be more efficient for a fan-out tree and which for a fan-in tree?

(c) Under what circumstances would it make sense to use both forward and backward chaining?

Ex. 8 [*05*] *Terminology*. What is the relationship between forward and backward chaining and depth-first or breadth-first searches? That is, can forward chaining be either depth-first or breadth-first? What is the relationship between backward and forward chaining and exhaustive or satisficing search?

■ **Ex. 9** [*30*] *Generation and Canonical Forms*. The issue of multiple possible representations of a solution and the use of canonical forms comes up often in generate-and-test and other search problems. Figure 2.49 is an example of what we will call a *cross-graph*.

This graph has a main track drawn horizontally. It also has one or more side tracks, drawn vertically. Thus, *d-e-f-g* is a side track that crosses the main track at node *e*. We assume that cross-graphs correspond to patterns in data and that it is important to determine when we have seen them before. The track data are always in graphs, but the graphs differ in appearance even when they are equivalent in the sense of having the same labeled nodes and the same corresponding connections.

$$
\begin{array}{ccccccccccccccc}
& & & & d & & & & j & & & & & \\
& & & & | & & & & | & & & & & \\
\text{Main} & & a-b-c-&e&-h-i-&k&-n-o-p & \\
\text{track} & & & & | & & & & | & & & & | & \\
& & & & f & & & & l & & & & q & \\
& & & & | & & & & | & & & & & \\
& & & & g & & & & m & & & & &
\end{array}
$$

FIGURE 2.49. Track data in canonical form.

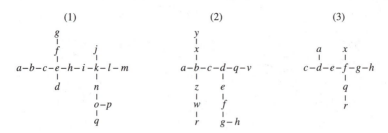

FIGURE 2.50.   Track data graphs not yet in canonical form.

(a) To make recognition of track data easier, Professor Digit has proposed a canonical form for track data, based on the observation that side tracks never have side-side-tracks. He proposes the following guidelines for drawing tracks in canonical form:

   1. Any node with more than two neighbors must be on the main track.
   2. In the event of ties for determining which of two nodes is on the main track, the one whose label is first alphabetically goes on the main track.
   3. In the event that a node can be placed either on the main track or on a side track, it is placed on the main track. (Roughly, the main track is "as long as possible.")
   4. The main track is drawn with the alphabetically earliest end node on the left. (This does not require that the entire main track be in alphabetical order.)
   5. Side tracks should be drawn with the longest part down.
   6. In the event of ties in rule 5, side tracks should be drawn with the alphabetically earliest end node up.

Using these guidelines, put Figure 2.50 into canonical form.

(b) After using this method for several years, Professor Digit came upon the idea of using a linear notation for representing cross-graphs. The following is the linear notation for the first cross-graph in this exercise:

$$(a\,b\,c\,(d\,e^*f\,g)\,h\,i\,(j\,k^*\,l\,m)\,n\,(o^*\,q)\,p)$$

In this notation, the side tracks are parenthesized, and the main track node that intersects the side track is followed by an asterisk (*). The left-to-right order of the main track is written left to right, and the top-to-bottom order of the side tracks is written left to right.

Put each cross-graph of Figure 2.50 into linear canonical form. What advantages does the linear form have for computer manipulation?

(c) One day Professor Digit was given the following cross-graph puzzle:

There are five nodes in the cross-graph $\{a, b, c, d, e\}$.
The following pairs of nodes are known to be connected: $\{a\text{-}b,\ c\text{-}d,\ e\text{-}b\}$.
The following pairs are known not to be connected: $\{d\text{\textasciitilde}a,\ c\text{\textasciitilde}a\}$.

Find all possible cross-graphs that satisfy these constraints and present them in linear canonical form. *Hint*: Use a generate-and-test approach.

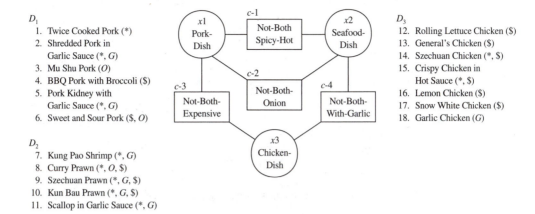

D_1
1. Twice Cooked Pork (*)
2. Shredded Pork in
   Garlic Sauce (*, *G*)
3. Mu Shu Pork (*O*)
4. BBQ Pork with Broccoli ($)
5. Pork Kidney with
   Garlic Sauce (*, *G*)
6. Sweet and Sour Pork ($, *O*)

D_2
7. Kung Pao Shrimp (*, *G*)
8. Curry Prawn (*, *O*, $)
9. Szechuan Prawn (*, *G*, $)
10. Kun Bau Prawn (*, *G*, $)
11. Scallop in Garlic Sauce (*, *G*)

D_3
12. Rolling Lettuce Chicken ($)
13. General's Chicken ($)
14. Szechuan Chicken (*, $)
15. Crispy Chicken in
    Hot Sauce (*, $)
16. Lemon Chicken ($)
17. Snow White Chicken ($)
18. Garlic Chicken (*G*)

FIGURE 2.51. More variations on the Chinese meal problem.

Ex. 10 [*15*] *A Chinese Meal Problem.* Figure 2.51 shows another version of our Chinese meal task. As before, * means spicy hot, *G* means garlic, *O* means onion, and $ means expensive.

(a) Often the dishes on a menu are numbered as suggested above. Suppose you are to pick one each of the three categories of dishes, satisfying the constraints of the problem. Which of the following are among the solutions?

   3-9-12   4-7-16   2-11-15

(b) Suppose we add the constraints that there be no more than two expensive dishes altogether and that at least two of the dishes be spicy hot. List all the solutions to the problem. (Do not limit your consideration to the candidates in part a.)

Ex. 11 [*10*] *Exponential Time Complexity in Constraint Satisfaction Problems.* Constraint satisfaction problems, like other kinds of search, are subject to combinatorial explosions. Suppose we are given a set of constraints on *n* variables, where each variable has a domain of size two. The task is to find all combinations of values for the variables that satisfy the constraints. Assume worst-case analyses for this problem.

(a) For 10 variables, how many candidates are there to consider in the search space?

(b) For 25 variables, how long would it take to look at all the possibilities one at a time at the rate of 1 million per second?

(c) Sometimes it is suggested that massive parallelism will make computers so fast that combinatorial explosions will not be an issue. Suppose we had a computer with 10 million processors in parallel, each able to look at 1 million million possibilities per second. Show that it could still take about 4,000 years to consider all the possibilities for only 100 variables.

Ex. 12 [*CD-10*] *Constraint Satisfaction.* Some variations on a three-variable constraint satisfaction problem are given in the following. In each case, the variables are *x*, *y*, and *z*. The domains are shown as sets in brackets. The relations indicated by the arcs are always "not-equal."

(a) What are the solutions to the following constraint satisfaction problem?

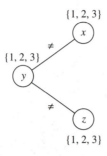

(b) How many solutions are eliminated when the constraint between x and z is added?

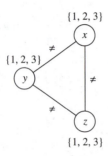

(c) How many solutions are there if the domains are just $\{1, 2\}$?

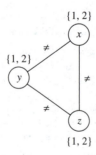

Ex. 13   [CP-15] *Simple Variations on Basic Search Methods.* The terms *depth-first search* and *breadth-first search* are used to describe families of methods including several simple variations. In this exercise we consider the algorithmic changes necessary for some variations.
(a) Present a method for exhaustive depth-first search in which every node is a candidate solution.
(b) Present a method for exhaustive depth-first search in which only leaf nodes are considered as solutions.
(c) Present a method for satisficing depth-first search in which only leaf nodes are considered as solutions.

Ex. 14 *[CD-10] Digit Does It Again.* Upon learning about how the space requirements of depth-first search are reduced by the judicious use of choice points, Professor Digit hit upon the idea of using choice points with breadth-first search. He reasoned that since the storage complexity of breadth-first search was worse, the effect would be even more dramatic. After scribbling a few notes in the margin of an early draft of this book, he cried "Eureka! The space complexity of BFS was a snare and a delusion. With choice points it is now competitive with DFS."

(a) Using the example and notation from the example of depth-first choice points in the text, show the successive versions of the queue through the first four cycles of a BFS method using choice points.

(b) Is Professor Digit correct? That is, are the space requirements now $O(d)$?

Ex. 15 *[CD-05] Terminology.* For each of the following statements indicate whether it is true or false. If the statement is ambiguous, explain briefly.

(a) *True or False.* Depth-first search uses a LIFO protocol on a stack.

(b) *True or False.* Early pruning refers to the process of premature aging found among those who search for solutions fruitlessly past all expectation of success.

(c) *True or False.* Chronological backtracking for constraint satisfaction is a specialized version of hierarchical generate-and-test.

(d) *True or False.* Breadth-first search is a blind search method and uses a LIFO protocol on a queue.

(e) *True or False.* The expected complexity of hierarchical generate-and-test ranges from linear in the depth of the search tree to exponential depending on the probability that the tester eliminates fruitless branches.

2.3 Directed Search

The blind search methods in the previous section traverse a search space systematically without benefit of knowledge about where solutions are expected. They can tell when they have found a solution, but not when they are getting near. In contrast, the **directed search methods** in this section try to aim the search toward solutions. There are different ways to impart directionality to a search, but they all influence the selection of nodes from which to search next.

Historically, directed search methods have been the central examples of heuristic search. Although the term *heuristic* is now used to mean any kind of knowledge used in search, historical usage of the term focused more narrowly on the evaluation functions used to rank different alternatives in a directed search.

An important concern in any discussion of search is the performance of the methods. For directed search methods, performance depends not only on the method and the search space, but also on the properties of the heuristic knowledge used to guide the search. In other words, although directed search methods are written so the knowledge that they use is separate from the method proper, the performance of the "method" is by no means independent from the heuristic knowledge. Any characterization of performance must also make explicit the properties of the heuristic knowledge on which it depends. In this section, we defer most analysis of this dependency until we reach the A* algorithm, which has been extensively studied.

Directed search methods use a formulation of search called **state-space search**. In this formulation the nodes of the search tree are called **states,** or more precisely, state descriptions. A set of **operators** is available that can change one state into another. These functions take state

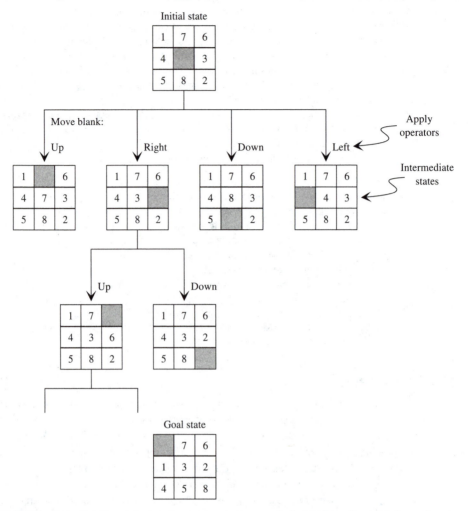

FIGURE 2.52.   Example of an eight-puzzle as a state-space search. In this formalism, the alternatives in the search tree are characterized in terms of the applications of the available operators. One operator can change several properties in the space at once.

descriptions for their domains and ranges. At each step of a state-space search, choosing a branch involves choosing an appropriate operator and applying it to the current state to bring the search closer to (or make it more like) a goal state.

Following Nilsson (1971), we use the eight-puzzle in Figure 2.52 to illustrate a state-space search. An eight-puzzle is a tray containing eight square tiles numbered from 1 to 8. The space for a ninth tile is vacant, leaving an empty square in the tray, as shown. The goal is to put the tray of tiles into a specified configuration by sliding the tiles. We can move a tile by sliding it vertically or horizontally into the empty square. In state-space search we formalize this movement concisely in terms of operators by viewing the empty square as an object that can be moved in any of four directions. In operator terminology, there are four operators—up, down, left, and right—that can be applied to a state of the tray to yield another state. Under specified circumstances in state-space search, particular operators are inapplicable. In the eight-puzzle, an operator is inapplicable when the empty square is on the edge of the figure and the proposed operator would move the empty square off the tray.

The operator formulation provides a convenient way of generating next-states when the states are relatively complex and when there is a small number of applicable operators. An operator may change several properties of a state at once. In this case, the search tree is compactly expressed in terms of operator applications. In the eight-puzzle, we could specify a particular search path as "up, left, left, up . . ." or a search tree as in Figure 2.52 but without the intermediate tray descriptions.

Without the operator formulation, the specification of branches for the eight-puzzle would be more complex because we would need to specify the locations of each of the eight tiles for each node in the tree. The operator formulation simplifies the specification of successor nodes because new states are completely determined by the sequence of applications of the four operators. For contrast, consider the safecracking example we used to illustrate the generate-and-test method in the previous section. Although we could formulate the safecracking task in terms of state-space operators, it would not help much because the states of a combination lock are already so simple and there are only two operators that must be applied alternately—spin left and spin right.

In programs that perform state-space search, virtually any data structure can be used to describe states. These include symbol strings, vectors, two-dimensional arrays, trees, and so on. For the eight-puzzle task above, an array representation analogous to the structure of the eight-puzzle itself might make a good representation of state.

The simplest method for directed search is **match**. Like generate-and-test, match is a general search method. Three variations of match are presented here: simple match, means-ends analysis, and hierarchical match.

2.3.1 *Simple Match*

Simple match has two auxiliary programs as parameters: a comparator, which compares two states and produces a description of the difference, and an operator selector, which selects an operator that can be applied to a state to remove a given difference. Simple match starts with an initial state and a goal state. At each step, it compares the current state with the goal state and tries to apply an operator to remove the difference. If the comparator reports that there is no difference remaining, the comparator exits with success. If at any step no operator can be found to remove the difference, the comparator exits and reports failure. The method for simple match is presented in Figure 2.53.

Figure 2.54 gives a rather contrived example of a travel domain where match can be used. A traveler starts at a starting point on the map and makes his way to the goal. We assume in this problem that the traveler is only prepared to travel in the unshaded hiking region and that he must avoid the snowy region, desert, and so on. The difference to the goal is expressed in x and y distances. The operators correspond to the four major compass directions.

The operator selector chooses the operator that reduces the largest outstanding distance, unless immediately blocked by an unpassable region. In that case, it repeats, trying the direction

To carry out a simple match:
```
    1.      Initialize the current-state to be the starting state.
    2.      While differences := comparator(current-state, goal-state) do
    3.      begin
    4.              operator := operator-selector(differences)

                    /* Here to go to next state in search space. */
    5.              If an operator is found, then current-state :=
                        Apply-Operator(operator, current-state)

                    /* Here if no place to go. */
    6.              Else exit with failure.
    7.      end

            /* Here if there are no more differences. */
    8.      Exit with success. (The current state is a solution.)
```

FIGURE 2.53.   Method for simple match. Although this method is extremely simple, it is the starting point for most of the directed search methods.

with the next largest outstanding distance. If all the operators with outstanding distance are blocked, the operator selector fails to find an operator. If the hiker starts at starting point A, this method will follow the dashed trail to the goal as noted.

Consider what happens if the traveler starts at starting point B. The simplistic approach of marching toward the goal takes him to the deadly swamp. In this example, the method will get stuck, unable to reach the goal.

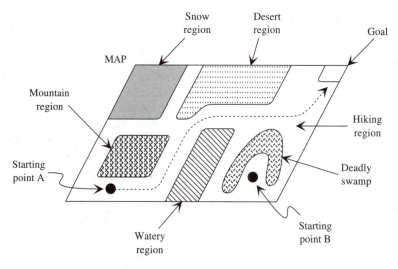

FIGURE 2.54.   Example of a simple traveling puzzle formulated in terms of match.

Simple match is not an optimizing method. It does not look for the shortest or least costly path. Rather, it just looks for some path. The operator selector picks an operator that reduces the difference. In the sample domain, we assume that it does not matter what path the traveler chooses as long as he reaches the goal. Match will propose different solutions for different starting points.

Because of its plodding approach that gets closer to a goal with each step, we say that match performs a **monotonic search.** More precisely, we distinguish two different ways that a problem solver can be monotonic. A problem solver is **monotonic in its decision space** if it never revises a decision it has made. In match, making decisions corresponds to choosing operators. Match is monotonic in its decision space because it never backtracks on its sequence of operator choices. A problem solver is **monotonic in its metric space** if it never retreats from its goal, that is, if it uses a metric to compare its current state to its goal state and never picks an operator that takes it further from the goal than its current state. Simple match incorporates a metric in that it chooses operators that reduce the differences between the current state and a goal—so the metric is the number of differences. Thus, simple match is monotonic both in its decision space and in its metric space.

Some problems cannot be solved satisfactorily without retreating from a goal in order to reach the goal. Figure 2.55 sketches such a problem. The goal in this problem is to construct an arch as shown in the goal state, using the blocks from the initial state. The operators allow us to pick up and move a block into position, rotating the block as needed.

Two additional requirements make the problem more difficult. First, the operations are carried out by a one-armed robot, so that only one block can be grasped at a time. Second, the intermediate structures must be stable under gravity. As suggested by the figure, the problem of constructing the arch is readily solvable, using block C as scaffolding to support the top of the arch until blocks D, E, and F are in place. Once the top of the arch is assembled, the scaffolding can be removed.

The point of the problem in Figure 2.55 is not that there is something mysterious about building arches. Nor do we claim to have carefully modeled or analyzed the forces and masses in a civil engineering sense to identify the conditions under which the arch can be built and will stand. Rather, the point is that incorporating the scaffolding is a necessary and strategic retreat *away* from the goal. It appears in neither the initial state nor the goal state and the method of taking differences will not reveal it. Simple match, applied in a straightforward way, fails in problems where it is necessary to make a strategic retreat from a goal in order to satisfy the goal.

Other examples of problems in which an apparent retreat from the goal is necessary include maze problems, where we must increase Euclidean distance from a goal location to reach a strategic passageway, or a problem to remodel a building in which we may need to remove walls and then put them back again to make other changes possible. In chemistry, many of the best paths for synthesizing compounds involve the use of molecular scaffolding.

In such cases, there may be ways to recast the problem by putting more knowledge in the comparator so differences conditionally emphasize different properties. Stated differently, a comparator with a different notion of distance may recast an operation so the operation no longer looks like a retreat. Although this approach can overcome the problem in specific situations, it does so at the expense of a more complex comparator. The revised comparator would need to perform a context-sensitive comparison that takes into account what operations have been performed already, what goals are outstanding, and perhaps what interactions there are between

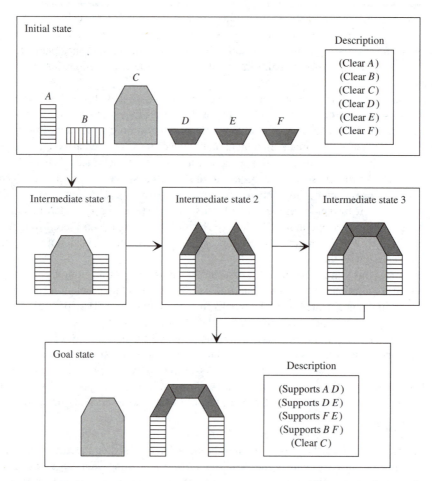

FIGURE 2.55.   A tough problem for simple match. A one-armed robot wants to build an arch-like structure. This structure cannot be built by first placing block *D* on top of block *A*, because gravity will cause
Block *D* to fall over. The solution above uses block *C* as scaffolding, which must be removed at the end of
construction. This solution violates the assumptions of simple match because inserting the scaffolding
moves the state away from the goal.

operators and goals. The next search methods, which we discuss shortly, provide better alternatives.

    As with generate-and-test, simple match has little knowledge of its own. Everything it
knows about comparing candidates is in the comparator. Everything it knows about picking
operators is in the operator selector. The strict separation of the comparator from the operator
selector leads to problems with simple match, just as the strict separation of the generator from
the tester led to problems with simple generate-and-test. Another way to characterize this is in
terms of modularity and interfaces. The narrow interface between generating and testing or
between comparing states and selecting operators is the problem.

Directed method	Simple match
Bookkeeping	none—remembers only current state
Knowledge interfaces	comparator
	operator selector
	operators and state descriptions
Directionality	difference computed between current state
	and goal state
Worst-case space	constant
Worst-case time	$O(b^d)$, but a more realistic estimate is typically $O(d)$ where
	d is the length of a plan
Example bad cases	(1) When there is no reliable and unambiguous
	basis for selecting operators
	(2) When the appropriate next steps
	cannot be determined from the immediate
	and apparent differences
	(3) when it is necessary to make a strategic retreat from a goal
Solution criteria	satisficing
Thoroughness	incomplete search, unless we can
	use properties of the domain to prove
	that a monotonic search will always succeed
Variations and related methods	
Selection of operator	(1) forward chaining
	triggered by contents of current state
	rather than by difference to a goal
	(2) hill climbing
	based on evaluation function
More flexible control	means-ends analysis
	recursion to satisfy operator conditions and
	backtracking to alternative operators

FIGURE 2.56.   The characteristics of simple match.

In simple match there is no explicit provision for dealing with situations in which there are many differences between a state and a goal; the comparator must summarize it all as a single difference description that can be reduced by some operator.

Figure 2.56 summarizes the characteristics of simple match. Several features are mixed together in simple match.

1. The search space is formulated in terms of operators and states.

2. The operator is selected using a computed difference between the current state and a goal state.

3. The search process modifies a current state without possibility of backtracking to a previous state or operator.

Many variations on simple match are possible. Simple match does not specify how the operator selector works. In principle it could be anything from a simple table for looking up operators to an extensive knowledge-based search program. Another source of variability is the range of requirements for sophistication on the representation of operators. Forward chaining of rules is similar to simple match in the way that it proceeds by applying one rule at a time to a single current state. Forward chaining differs from simple match in that forward chaining determines the next operation using pattern matching on the contents of the current state rather than on the differences between the current state and a goal state.

Simple match is too simple an approach for most problems. Like forward chaining, it finds application in small parts of large systems. In many cases the search performed by simple match is incomplete. To show that a particular application of simple match is complete, we need to show that the comparator and operator selector cannot accidentally go around or go past the goals.

Means-ends analysis is a much-studied specialization of simple match that improves on feature 3 above, enabling the match to recover in some cases after selecting a wrong operator. Means-ends analysis is presented next.

2.3.2 *Means-Ends Analysis*

Means-ends analysis is a more elaborate version of match that has had a profound influence on artificial intelligence. In Newell and Simon's experiments with the General Problem Solver (GPS) system reported in *Human Problem Solving* (Newell & Simon, 1972), means-ends analysis emerged as a powerful tool for explaining protocols of human problem solving in depth. Many of the newer search methods can be understood as incremental improvements of means-ends analysis.

A Travel Planning Example

Following Winston's example (Winston, 1984), we introduce means-ends analysis by showing its use in a task of travel planning. This example is substantially more demanding than the eight-puzzle example we used earlier to illustrate state-space search. Means-ends analysis employs more knowledge and richer symbol structures than simple match and requires a more challenging example to illustrate its operation. It solves basic planning problems and introduces many features that have been carried over to more sophisticated problem-solving methods. Even so, our modest travel planning example is somewhat too demanding for a completely adequate treatment by means-ends analysis.

Figure 2.57 illustrates our traveler's task of planning a trip to a conference. In a state-space representation, the initial state is that the traveler has finished at work one evening and the goal is to attend a conference in a distant city the next day. A set of operators can be applied. Some of them refer to forms of transportation such as driving a car, using a taxi, or taking a plane. Some refer to other preparations for the trip such as picking up clothes and getting money at the bank. Others refer to making arrangements such as registering at the hotel and registering at the conference.

Figure 2.58 shows several of the operators for the travel task. Each operator has specific **preconditions** that must be satisfied before the operator can be used. For example, to apply the take-plane operator we must be located at the airport, have money for our ticket, and have our luggage ready. Each operator also has a **transformation function** that describes what changes it

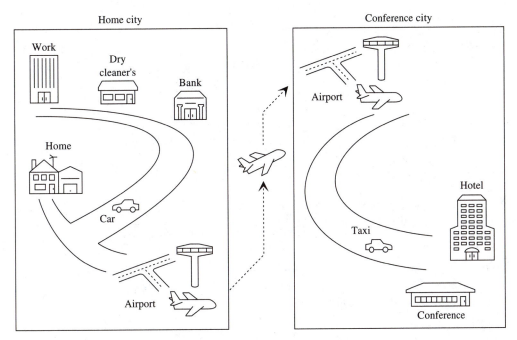

FIGURE 2.57. Planning a trip to a conference: a task for means-ends analysis. In this example an agent must develop a plan for getting ready for a trip, packing and getting money, arranging transportation and accommodations, and arranging for meals.

makes to the current state. The take-plane operator delivers the traveler and her luggage to the destination airport in exchange for a fare. The take-bus operator takes the traveler (but in this formulation, not her luggage) to the destination city for a fare. The register-at-hotel operator obtains for the traveler a place to sleep in exchange for a fee. Many complexities of a real travel task such as reservations for the hotel or preregistration at the conference are omitted, leaving in just enough to show how means-ends analysis works.

In developing operator descriptions for the travel problem, we need to express a rationale for choosing between the operators take-bus and take-plane. In Figure 2.58, we do this by noting that take-plane reduces distance, providing that the distance is greater than 500 miles. In a more realistic model, one can take planes for shorter trips and there are other factors involving scheduling and price. It may seem strange that the distance requirement is not simply modeled as a precondition.

As will become clear below, placing the 500-mile criterion as a precondition would open means-ends analysis to looking for a way to move the airport closer! This example shows two issues about representation of tasks. First, the design of a model for domain knowledge must reflect its use by the problem-solving method. Second, there are often trade-offs in generality and complexity. Having our problem solver propose moving the airport or building a new one is silly, but it is also a first step toward a system that could then realize why the step is silly. Practical knowledge engineering always involves choices about the value of building models of different coverage and to different depths. In the travel model, we have sacrificed generality and coverage

The Take-Plane Operator
Differences reduced: Distance of traveler to conference city (if > 500 miles).
                                   Distance of traveler's luggage to conference city (if > 500 miles).
Preconditions: Have fare for ticket ($500).
                                   Traveler located at airport.
                                   Luggage is ready.
Transformation function: Ticket money is spent.
                                   Traveler taken to airport at destination city.
                                   Traveler's luggage taken to airport at destination city.

The Take-Bus Operator
Differences reduced: Distance of traveler to conference city (if $20 < x < 500$ miles).
Preconditions: Have fare for ticket ($100).
                                   Traveler located at bus station.
Transformation function: Ticket money is spent.
                                   Traveler taken to bus station at destination city.

The Register-at-Hotel Operator
Differences reduced: Place to sleep obtained.
Preconditions: Have fee for registration ($100).
                                   Traveler located at hotel.
                                   Traveler's luggage located at hotel.
Transformation function: Hotel fee is spent.
                                   Hotel room is reserved as a place to sleep.

The Pack-Clothes Operator
Differences reduced: Clothes to wear packed.
Preconditions: Clean clothing located at home.
                                   Traveler located at home.
                                   Traveler's luggage located at home.
Transformation function: Pack clothes to wear in luggage.
                                   Luggage is ready.

The Attend-Conference Operator
Differences reduced: Traveler has not attended conference.
Preconditions: Registered at conference.
                                   Have place to sleep.
Transformation function: Traveler attends conference.

FIGURE 2.58.   Some operators for the travel task. Each operator has several effects as described by its transformation function.

for simplicity in illustrating how means-ends analysis works. We consider more representation issues from the travel domain in the exercises.

As with simple match, each operator for means-ends analysis has a description of the **differences** reduced. Means-ends analysis uses differences to decide which operators to apply at a given time. The method organizes its knowledge of how to pick operators given differences in an **operator-difference grid** as shown in Figure 2.59. This grid summarizes which differences are reduced by each operator. In addition, the ordering of differences in the rows and of operators in

Operators

Differences	Take-Plane	Take-Bus	Drive	Taxi	Register-at-Hotel	Register-at-Conference	Pack-Clothes	Pick-Up-Dry-Cleaning	Attend-Conference	Use-Credit	Get-Cash
No place to sleep					X						
Luggage not ready							X				
Clothing not at home								X			
Not registered at conference						X					
Distance 1<X<20 mi. Traveler and luggage			X	X							
Distance >500 mi. Traveler and luggage	X										
Distance 20<X<500 mi. Traveler only		X									
Not attending conference									X		
Need money										X	X
Preconditions	Have plane fare; Traveler at airport; Luggage ready	Bus fare; Traveler at bus station	Have car	Have taxi fare	Have hotel fee; Luggage at hotel	Have conference fee; Traveler at conference	Traveler at home; Clothes at home; Luggage home	Cleaning fee; Traveler at dry cleaner's	Registered at conference; Have place to sleep	None	At bank

FIGURE 2.59. Operator-difference grid for the travel task. Means-ends analysis determines which of the current differences to consider by taking the first one it encounters moving down through the rows. It then goes across the rows to pick the first operator with an X in a column. Finally, it chooses a subgoal based on the preconditions of the operator.

213

the columns determines which operator is applied when more than one operator could reduce the differences. Given a list of differences to be reduced, means-ends analysis searches top to bottom through the rows to determine which is the most important difference. Then it searches left to right through the operator columns to find the first operator that will reduce that difference. Finally, it checks the bottom of the grid for the preconditions that must be satisfied for the operator. The order that preconditions are given for an operator is irrelevant to this process. By adjusting the difference table to favor choices most likely to be right, we can reduce the expected amount of backtracking on problems.

A Method for Means-Ends Analysis

A method for means-ends analysis is given in Figure 2.60. To a first approximation it prescribes a combination of depth-first search and simple match. From depth-first search it gets a stack and backtracking; from simple match it gets operators, a goal node, and the idea of comparing the current state with a goal state and computing differences. The loop from step 1 to step 15 is the depth-first search loop. It uses a stack to keep track of its traversal of state nodes in the search tree, with the deeper elements on the stack being closer to the goal state. Means-ends analysis selects successor states in much the same way as simple match. A comparator is invoked to compute the differences from the goal state. The analysis then selects operators using the difference grid.

An important feature of means-ends analysis (notably missing in simple match) is subgoaling, which is the creation of subgoals. This takes place in steps 13 and 14. The basic idea is that means-ends analysis can select an operator to remove a difference even when the preconditions for that operator are not satisfied by the current state in the search tree. It can then create a subgoal to satisfy those preconditions and recursively invoke means-ends analysis to reach the intermediate goal. This capability enables means-ends analysis to solve problems in which a "strategic retreat" is required, taking it beyond the capabilities of simple match.

Subgoaling is so general and important that it has been incorporated in several programming languages. In Chapter 1 we saw that subgoaling is often part of the basic execution cycle of production-rule languages and logic programming languages. In these languages the goals say what to do, and the match process helps to decide how to do it. This use of goals to separate what from how is an important source of expressive power in these languages.

In the pursuit of its goals, means-ends analysis can back up from a bad choice. For this, it provides a mechanism for backtracking from depth-first search. This is another difference from simple match. In depth-first search, the selection of successor nodes is a primitive action and backtracking need only be concerned with the unwinding of choices about children nodes. In means-ends analysis, the branching process is divided into three stages: the computing of differences, the selection of operators, and the application of operators to reach new states. Although the stack contains the state nodes, the operators cause all actions. For this reason we extend the representation of nodes on the stack to be steps—with initial states, goals, pointers to the next steps, and untried operators. The stack-popping operation ensures that no step node is discarded until either an operator that could satisfy its preconditions has succeeded or all of the relevant operators have been tried.

We note in passing that the method does not pop a step from the stack until it has exhausted the set of possible operators for that step. This use of steps on the stack representing operator/

state combinations is an example of a **choice-point** such as we discussed earlier in the context of depth-first search.

Planning versus Reacting Interpretations

There are two interpretations of means-ends analysis, which we refer to as the planning interpretation and the reactive interpretation.

The **planning interpretation** of means-ends analysis models an agent who uses it to create a plan for later action. As the agent uses means-ends analysis, she records all the steps in a plan structure. Steps to achieve subgoals precede the steps that spawned the subgoals. The agent simulates the steps so the method can complete a plan. If a sequence of steps does not work out, the agent erases the sequence from the plan and backtracks. After the plan is completed, the agent may analyze the plan structure and optimize it in various ways. In the simplest case, she saves the plan for later execution, where steps are executed in an order that reflects the preconditions of the plan. When the ordering of steps leaves multiple choices about what must be done next, we assume arbitrarily that steps that were planned first are carried out first.

The **reactive interpretation** models an agent who uses means-ends analysis to guide his moment-to-moment activity on a task. Whenever he determines what steps to do, he immediately carries them out. This interpretation intermixes planning and action. Plan steps are not "simulated," but rather are carried out "in the world." If a sequence of steps ultimately does not work out, the agent must undo them not only in his plan, but also in the world in which he is engaged. Another difference in the reactive interpretation is that the agent can rely more on the world to keep track of the changes in state. After each step, the agent can query the world about state rather than relying on his capabilities for memory and simulation. In this way, the agent is better able to react to good and bad surprises caused by other agents in an environment.

The original development of means-ends analysis was described largely in terms of the reactive interpretation. However, whenever a task requires subgoaling, then some steps are deferred until their preconditions are satisfied. The planning interpretation is pedagogically interesting because it introduces basic issues and plan network representations relevant to more modern treatments of planning.

Details of the Travel Plan Example

Figure 2.61 illustrates some initial steps of means-ends analysis in the travel task. In the initial state the traveler is at work and his traveling clothes are at the cleaner's. In the final and goal state, he is attending the conference. Each solid box in Figure 2.61 represents a step, which is the application of an operator. The dashed boxes indicate preconditions for the adjacent operators. Two numbers are associated with each step. One number, located at the upper-right corner of the box, shows the order in which the steps were proposed in means-ends analysis.

We now consider some of the first detailed steps of means-ends analysis for the travel problem. In the first pass through means-ends analysis, the only difference is that the traveler is "not attending the conference." Searching through the difference table for an operator yields only the attend-conference operator. However, the operator has preconditions that need to be satisfied before it can be applied to the current state. Thus, a subgoal must be created to satisfy the preconditions, which means a goal state must be created between the initial state and the current state in which we have a place to sleep and are registered for the conference. Means-ends analysis is then invoked recursively, the two differences are noted by the comparator, and no place to sleep is the

To carry out means-ends analysis (MEA):

```
1.    Form a one-element stack consisting of a step whose initial state
          is the initial state and whose goal is the goal state.

          /* Main loop to reduce differences. */
2.    MEA: While the stack is not empty do
3.    begin
4.        Let the current-step be the top element of the stack. (But
          do not pop it yet.)

          /* Compute the difference. */
5.        differences := comparator(step:initial-state, step:goal-state)
          /* If there is more than one difference, the comparator
          selects the one that appears in the highest row of the
          difference table. Several passes through this loop may be
          needed to remove all the differences. */

6.        If there is no difference, then exit with success.
          /* A path to the solution is now known through the trace of
          operators that have been applied. */

          /* Pick an operator to reduce the difference. */
7.    Pick-Operator:
8.        If there are remaining untried operators for this step then
9.        begin
10.           Get the next operator in order from the difference table
              and mark it as tried.
              /* If the operators have not already been retrieved for
              this state, then cache records for all the operators
              from the difference table. */

              /* Recur on MEA if preconditions of operator are not
              satisfied. */
11.           If the preconditions for the operator are not satisfied,
              then
```

FIGURE 2.60. Means-ends analysis method used in the General Problem Solver. This method combines the state-space search ideas and operators from simple match with a capability for backtracking and recursion from depth-first search (continued next page).

highest difference in the difference table. The only operator that reduces this difference is register-at-hotel, so this operator is proposed next and the attend-conference operator is suspended, pending satisfaction of its preconditions. Similarly, the register-at-hotel operator has a precondition that the luggage be at the hotel, leading to subgoaling to the take-plane operator. This suspending of operations and chaining through subgoals continues all the way to the operator pick-up-dry-cleaning, whose two subgoals have no unsatisfied preconditions of their own.

```
12.               begin
13.                        Define a new step before the current-step whose
                           goal is to satisfy the preconditions, whose
                           next-step is the current step, and whose
                           initial-state is as given. Push the step onto
                           the stack.
14.                        Recursively call MEA;
                           /* If MEA succeeds, the current state has been
                           advanced to where the operator is applicable.
                           If MEA fails, the operator is not applicable. */
15.               end
16.          end

                 /* Apply the operator to reduce the difference. Apply-Operator
                 also updates the initial-state of the next-step to reflect
                 state changes caused by the operator. */
17.          If the operator is applicable, then
18.          begin
19.               Apply-Operator(operator, current-step)
20.               Pop the current-step from the stack.
21.          end

                 /* Here if the operator is not applicable. */
22.          Else if there are more untried operators, then go to
             Pick-Operator.

                 /* Here if there is no operator to reach the goal from
                 current-step. */
23.          Else pop the current-step from the stack and discard any
             previous steps taken to reach it.
24.     end

             /* Here if did not reach a goal state. */
25.     Exit with failure.
```

FIGURE 2.60.   (continued)

At this point, the difference between the reactive and planning interpretations of means-ends analysis becomes evident. The subgoals of pick-up-dry-cleaning are drive-to-dry-cleaner's and use-credit. In the reactive interpretation, the operators for these subgoals can be carried out immediately because their preconditions are satisfied. In the planning interpretation, these steps are not executed at once, but are arranged in a graph like Figure 2.61. Later, when the plan is to be carried out, the interpreter could begin at any step whose preconditions are satisfied. By con-

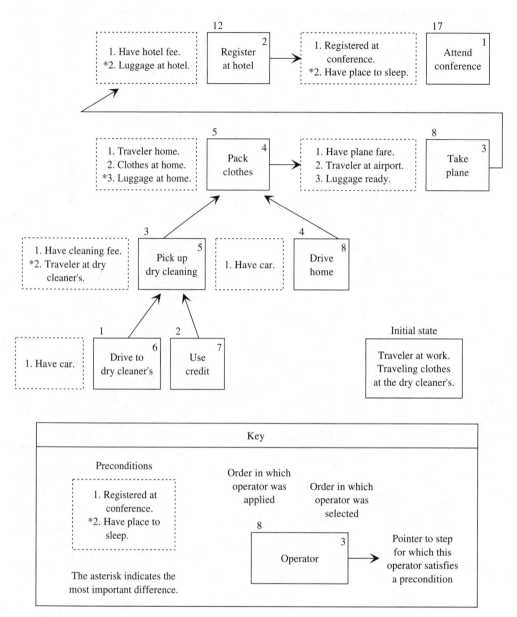

FIGURE 2.61. Detailed trace of means-ends analysis on the first few steps of the travel task. The trace shows preconditions and intermediate goals as conceived in the planning interpretation of means-ends analysis.

vention in this section, we assume that whenever there is a choice of which step to do next, the step that was planned first is chosen. The number above the upper-left corner of each box indicates the order in which the plan steps might be carried out in a planning interpretation of the trace.

Continuing the example, after the pick-up-dry-cleaning step is done, the system unwinds to the pack-clothes step and encounters the precondition that the traveler be at home. It then subgoals to the drive-home operator. The graph resulting from continuing this process is shown in Figure 2.62.

This analysis and example glosses over some representational issues. We have assumed that the comparator had access to world facts not made explicit in the discussion, such as the fact that initially the luggage would be found at home. In addition, the structure of the difference table was contrived to disguise some of the subtle difficulties of travel planning in particular and planning problems in general. If the use-credit operator had not preceded the visit-bank operator in the operator-difference table, the plan would have been cluttered with several side trips to the bank every time the traveler needed more money.

The method for means-ends analysis uses only a stack to keep track of the order relations between plan steps. A stack is not really an adequate representation for reasoning about plan structure. More realistic approaches to planning represent relations and interactions among the steps explicitly and use these representations to guide decisions about the order of steps in the plan. Some approaches for this are explored in the exercises.

Summary of Means-Ends Analysis

Figure 2.63 summarizes the major characteristics of means-ends analysis, showing it to be a marriage of depth-first search and simple match. Like depth-first search, means-ends analysis uses a stack for its bookkeeping. Directionality to the search is imparted by comparing the current state with a goal state and striving to reduce the differences. When there is more than one difference to reduce or more than one possible operator, preferences are determined by the order in the operator-difference table. Means-ends analysis stops when it has found one solution to the problem.

The match method in the previous section is difficult to make complete unless the domain lends itself to a monotonic search, which is a search without backtracking. Means-ends analysis is more amenable to complete search because it is capable of revisiting earlier decisions. It uses the order in the difference table to establish preferences, but if any choice fails, it will eventually try all of them. However, for completeness it does require that the difference table not preclude any solutions in the search space. Means-ends analysis will not find a solution if the path to that solution is not indicated by the differences computed by the comparator. The filtering provided by the comparator over the choice of operators is not open to reconsideration; if the solution requires stepping outside the possibilities indicated by the disciplined use of the difference table, then the solution will not be found by means-ends analysis.

In the next section, we consider how to modify match methods to take larger steps in plans, akin to macro-steps that can be treated as a group.

2.3.3 Hierarchical Match and Skeletal Planning

Even with subgoal creation, means-ends analysis plans all at one level, taking small steps toward a goal. In the travel plan example, if no room had been available at the hotel, an alternative operator for reserving a place to sleep, such as staying with friends, could be tried. Unfortunately, in backtracking and then selecting an alternative operator, means-ends analysis could discard unnecessarily much of the planning work it had done so far. For example, in choosing to stay

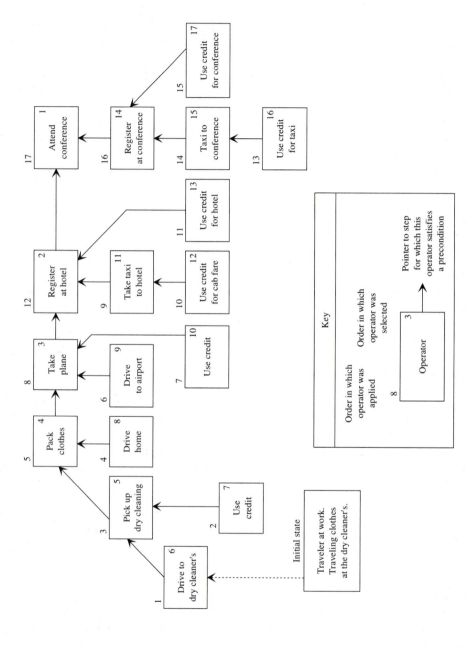

FIGURE 2.62. Trace of means-ends analysis on the travel task, showing both the order in which operators are proposed and the order in which they are applied. The arrows indicate that a step was proposed to satisfy a precondition of a later step.

Directed method	*Means-ends analysis.*
Bookkeeping	Stack.
Knowledge interfaces	Comparator, difference table, operators and state descriptions.
Directionality	Difference computed between current state and goal state, and preference imposed by the order of operators and preconditions in the difference table.
Built on methods	(1) Depth-first search for recursive application to satisfy preconditions. (2) Simple match for comparator and state-space search.
Worst-case space	O(length of longest plan).
Thoroughness	The search is generally expected to be complete, so every reasonable solution can be found eventually through backtracking. However completeness actually depends on the correctness of the difference table and operator descriptions.
Example bad case	When a problem cannot be solved with a fixed and constant set of preferences of operators and differences.
Solution criteria	Satisficing.

FIGURE 2.63.   Summary of characteristics of means-ends analysis.

with friends, it would discard all the planning work that it did to get to the hotel, and thus would need to replan all the steps for taking the plane, picking up the dry cleaning, and so on.

What is needed is a principled way to reason about bigger steps, analogous to the way that hierarchical generate-and-test takes bigger steps than simple generate-and-test by using hierarchical pruning. Hierarchical pruning takes big steps in search by eliminating whole families of candidates at once for a common reason. The viability of this method depends on the ability to tell from a partial description of a candidate solution whether all the ways of completing that solution could be ruled out. Typically, the partial description is a solution fragment.

A Travel Planning Example and Method

Unfortunately, hierarchical pruning cannot be used directly with match or means-ends analysis. The difficulty is that we cannot reliably tell from a solution fragment whether it is part of a satisfactory whole solution. Given the starting steps drive-to-dry-cleaner's, pay-for-dry-cleaning, pick-up-clothes, there is no way to rule out all the descendant plans; that is, there is no reliable evaluator of partial plans used as solution fragments.

The operator concept lends itself to another way to take big steps via abstract operators. We could describe an abstract solution to the travel planning problem in terms of four **abstract operators,** or steps, as in Figure 2.64. Traversing a plan with abstract steps is like taking big steps in the search space. Planning with abstract steps is a way of leaving some of the details until later.

The method of using an abstract plan to guide problem solving has been reinvented and renamed several times. Applied to match it is called **hierarchical match**. Applied to means-ends

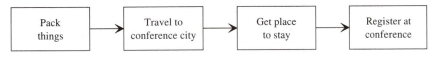

FIGURE 2.64.   Abstract plan for the travel task.

```
To carry out a hierarchical match:
    1.   For each abstract step in the given abstract plan do
    2.   begin
                /* Set up interface to next detailed level. */
    3.           Initialize the subproblem (with the subproblem-initializer),
                 providing an initial state and a goal state.

                /* Recursively invoke search for the next more detailed
                 level. */
    4.           Plan (with the subproblem-solver) between the initial state
                 and the goal state.

    5.           If solution-tester(subproblem) reports failure, then exit
                 with failure.
    6.   end
    7.           Exit with success (reporting the solution).
```

FIGURE 2.65. Method for hierarchical match. This method assumes that we are given an abstract plan. Its job is to fill in between the abstract steps using a subproblem solver, based on a method such as match.

analysis it is called **skeletal planning**. The term *skeletal* suggests how an abstract plan acts as a kind of skeleton of a detailed, complete plan. Skeletal plans are also called **scripts**. In this method, problem solving proceeds by filling in the detailed steps between the given abstract steps. The output state of each abstract step is treated as the initial state for the next one. In Section 2.4, we consider hierarchical planning, another variant of this approach that admits the problem-specific generation of abstract plans and the use of more than one intermediate level. For simplicity in this section, we ignore the differences between match and means-ends analysis and use the single term *hierarchical match* to refer to a hierarchical version of either search method.

Figure 2.65 gives a method for hierarchical match that starts with a given fixed linear plan. This version of hierarchical match depends on three auxiliary programs as parameters: a subproblem initializer, a subproblem solver, and a subproblem tester. The subproblem initializer sets up an initial state and a goal state for the subproblem solver. In practice it is useful to provide other knowledge, parameters, or constraints as well. The subproblem solver can be based on any version of match. It plans the detailed steps between the initial state and the goal state that it is given. The subproblem tester checks to see whether the plan created by the subproblem solver correctly reached the goal state.

Figure 2.66 shows hierarchical match at work between the first two abstract steps. The abstract steps divide a problem into smaller problems that can be solved separately. Thus, hierarchical match depends on the notion of divide and conquer, using a fixed abstract plan to partition the problem. This approach depends on being able to divide one large problem into a set of independent smaller ones. No abstract step is taken in hierarchical match before all the information required to take the step with confidence is available. Without backtracking in the abstract steps, no previously made decisions can be changed.

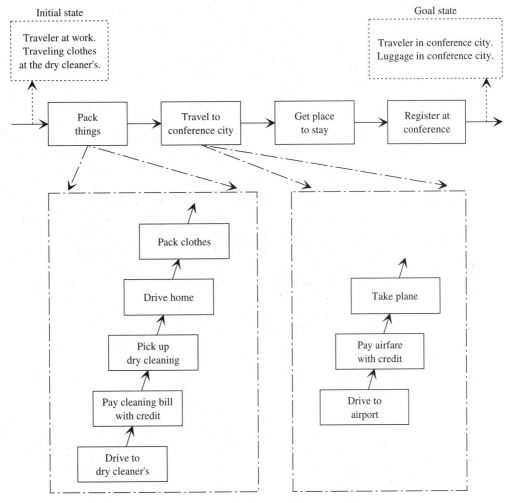

FIGURE 2.66. Using hierarchical match to refine a subproblem. In this figure hierarchical match has filled in between the first two steps of the abstract plan.

Analyzing Hierarchical Match

Hierarchical match splits a large planning problem into a sequence of smaller subproblems. To what extent does this reduce search complexity? Figure 2.67 shows a 20-step plan. The intermediate steps are called **planning islands**. In Figure 2.67 the problem has been divided into five equal parts by five abstract operators, resulting in four planning islands.

The value of planning islands has been understood in AI for a long time. Minsky (1961) gave the following account of how planning islands divide a search space to allow independent solution of subproblems and later combination of results:

In a graph with 10 branches descending from each node, a 20-step search might involve 10^{20} trials, which is out of the question, while the insertion of just four . . . sequential subgoals might reduce the search to only 5×10^4 trials, which is within reason for machine exploration. Thus it will be worth a relatively enormous effort to find such "islands" in the solution of complex problems. Note that even if one encountered, say, 10^6 failures of such procedures before success, one would still have gained a factor of perhaps 10^{10} in overall trial reduction. (pp. 441–442)

In general, the decomposition of a problem into independent subproblems whose solutions can be combined reduces the complexity of finding a solution from $O(b^d)$ to $O(b^k)$, where k is the size of the largest subproblem. This reformulation changes the time complexity of the overall problem to the sum of the complexities of the subproblems, rather than their product.

This transformed problem is analogous to the situation faced by a hiker trying to get across a stream. The hiker does not care so much about the length or width of the stream; what really matters in determining the difficulty of crossing is the largest jump between two successive stepping stones. In this analogy, the largest jump corresponds to the maximum subproblem size.

This example analysis assumes that the branching factor for operator choice is constant across a problem, that the length of a solution is known, and that the abstract plan is free because it is given. In such a case, the worst-case complexity of the search is reduced from $O(b^d)$ to $O((n + 1)b^{d/n})$—drastically reducing the exponent. In effect, the large search tree of depth d is replaced by $n + 1$ search trees of depth d/n. Although this analysis is idealized, it does clarify

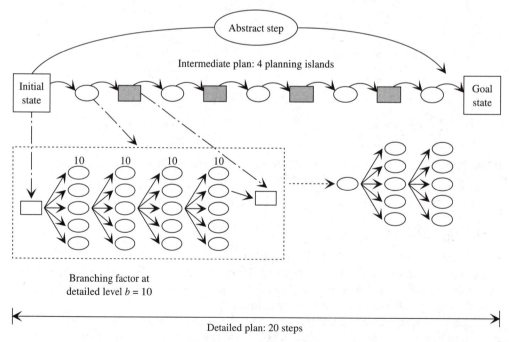

FIGURE 2.67. Organization of a search space using intermediate planning islands. In this analysis the search is reduced from 10^{20} to 5×10^4.

Directed method	Hierarchical match (skeletal planning).
Bookkeeping	Depends on subplanner.
Knowledge interfaces	Subproblem initializer, subproblem solver, subproblem tester.
Directionality	An abstract plan is given as input. Directionality is imparted between the steps of the abstract plan by the subproblem solver.
Built on methods	Simple match.
Worst-case space	$O(d)$—length of plan
Worst-case time	$O((n + 1)\, b^{d/n})$ for evenly spaced planning islands $O(b^n)$ for pessimally placed islands
Example bad case	When the problems cannot be solved as elaborations of a fixed abstract plan. For example, some problems may necessarily require iterative solutions.
Solution criteria	Satisficing.
Variations	
Multiple levels	Hierarchical planning employs intermediate abstraction levels, creates them dynamically, and is capable of backtracking. It is presented in Section 2.4.
Matching	Another variation would use means-ends analysis instead of simple match to fill in between the abstract steps.

FIGURE 2.68.   Summary of characteristics of hierarchical match.

how the use of planning islands reduces complexity. Section 2.4 gives more detailed models and applies them to analyzing hierarchical planning.

Summary of Hierarchical Match

Figure 2.68 summarizes the characteristics of hierarchical match. In Section 2.4 we return to hierarchical match to characterize its complexity.

Abstract plans are usually intended for use over many particular situations. Thus, the abstract travel plan is potentially applicable to many different trips. In any particular trip, it may turn out that there are no cabs at the airport late at night, or that limousines have much better fares than cabs, or that there is no airport close to the city, or that the conference is being held at the hotel. For such reasons, a plan that is too detailed cannot be used without change across many situations.

One strategy is to use an abstract plan to represent the expected common parts of solutions. Then for any particular situation, we add details to the description. We might add that the conference is at the hotel or that the only mode of local transportation at the airport is rental cars. This requires adding some capabilities to the subproblem initializer. Some psychological evidence from cognitive science indicates that people use such plans in repetitive situations.

2.3.4   Hill Climbing and Best-first Search

One important feature of match that distinguishes it from blind search and generate-and-test is that it computes differences between the current state and a goal state to bring a sense of direc-

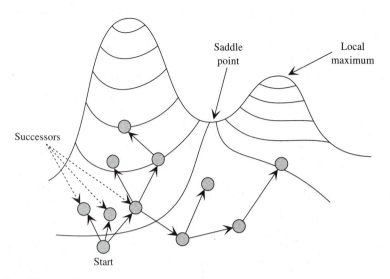

FIGURE 2.69. Visualization for terminology of hill climbing.

tion to the search process. **Hill climbing** is another way to provide a sense of direction to search. It uses an **evaluation function** to assess the best successor to follow from the current state. In contrast with blind search methods, hill-climbing methods tend to explore fewer nodes in their search for a solution.

Hill climbing gets its name from a visualization of the technique in which the nodes and their successors are viewed as being on a surface whose height is given by the evaluation function. Figure 2.69 presents an example of such a view. The filled circles correspond to nodes and the arrows point to their successors.

This visualization makes it easy to understand some problems faced by hill climbing. Hill climbing performs an incomplete, monotonic search and suffers from the same problems as simple match. It can be misled by local optimum points. To make an analogy with the terrestrial terrain, hill climbing will charge up a small, steep foothill if the foothill happens to be closer than a mountain that is farther off. For this reason hill climbing is also called a steepest ascent method. It can also wander about hopelessly on a flat plain and can get confused on ridges around mountains; that is, on regions where adjacent values of the evaluation function are about the same.

Nilsson (1980) gives an example of an evaluation function that could be used with hill climbing to solve the eight-puzzle:

$$f(n) = d(n) + W(n) \tag{1}$$

where $d(n)$ is the depth of the node n in the search tree and $W(n)$ counts the number of misplaced tiles compared to the goal. The term $d(n)$ is intended to favor solutions that minimize the number of moves. The term $W(n)$ is intended to characterize the similarity of the current state to a goal state. Figure 2.70 illustrates the use of this evaluation function for an eight-puzzle problem. This example is a variation of hill climbing ("valley descending"?) in which the next successor cho-

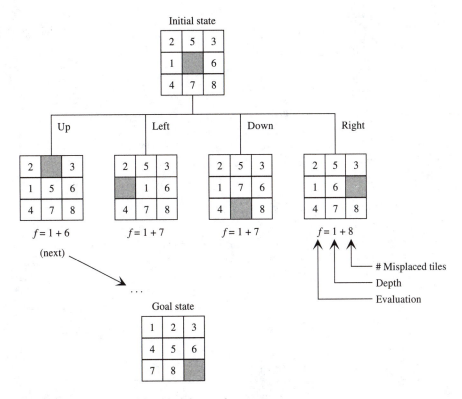

FIGURE 2.70. Evaluation of nodes for the eight-puzzle.

sen is the one with the smallest value of the evaluation function. The first move of the blank tile would be up.

Simple Hill Climbing

There are many variations on hill-climbing methods. We begin by considering two of them: simple hill climbing and backtracking hill climbing. A method for **simple hill climbing** is given in Figure 2.71.

Simple hill climbing uses two auxiliary programs as parameters: an evaluation function and a solution tester. The evaluation function computes numeric measurements for each of the successors. It uses the solution tester to determine whether any node it has reached is a solution. At each step, simple hill climbing considers a node and quits if it has found a solution. If not, it generates successor nodes, measures them with the evaluation function, and pursues the successor with the highest value.

There are several minor variations of simple hill climbing. One variation has no solution tester and just searches for a node that optimizes the value of the evaluation function. This variation cannot differentiate between cases where a local maximum is a solution or not. Other varia-

```
To carry out simple hill climbing:
    1.      Initialize the current node to the root node.
    2.      While node is not nil do
    3.      begin
    4.              If solution-tester(node) then exit with success reporting
                    node.
    5.              node := Pick-Highest(node)
    6.      end

            /* Here if no solution is found. */
    7.      Exit with failure.


1. Procedure Pick-Highest(node)
2. begin
3.    If there are no successors then return nil.
4.    Let highest be the successor with the highest rating by the
      evaluation function.

5.    If rating(highest) ≥ rating(node) then exit with success returning
      highest.

      /* Here if stalled on a local optimum. Successor's value is lower
      than that of the current node. */
6.    Else return nil.
7. end
```

FIGURE 2.71.   Method for a simple satisficing hill climb.

tions use operators to generate the next nodes, as in a state-space search, or search for minimum values instead of maximum values.

Simple hill climbing performs an incomplete, monotonic search. It can be trapped at local optimum points. The problems with simple hill climbing arise because it has no way to recover from a bad choice. It only follows the highest-rated successor of a node. An alternative version of hill climbing, called **backtracking hill climbing**, keeps a stack of successors and backtracks to them rather than giving up when its first-chosen path fails. The method for this is given in Figure 2.72.

Backtracking Hill Climbing

Like simple hill climbing, backtracking hill climbing uses an evaluation function and a solution tester. At each step, backtracking hill climbing considers a candidate and quits if it has found a solution. If not, it generates successor nodes, measures them with the candidate evaluator, and puts them on the stack so they will be considered in order of decreasing value. Because of its use of the stack, backtracking hill climbing performs a complete search. It can still be distracted by

To carry out backtracking hill climbing:

```
1.      Form a stack consisting of the root node.
2.      While the stack is not empty do
3.      begin
4.           Pop a node from the stack.
5.           If solution-tester(node) then exit with success reporting node.
6.           Else
7.           begin
8.                Measure the successors with the evaluation function.
9.                Sort them into decreasing order.
10.               Push the successors onto the front of the stack (so the
                  node on top of the stack is the successor with the
                  highest evaluation).
11.          end
12.     end

        /* Here if no solution has been found. */
13.     Exit with failure.
```

FIGURE 2.72.   Backtracking method for satisficing hill climbing.

local optima, but if it does not find a solution there it will eventually explore other parts of the search space. Thus, although backtracking hill climbing moves first in a direction of greatest progress or steepest gradient, it is not a monotonic search method.

Backtracking hill climbing has similarities to both depth-first and breadth-first search, but it differs from both of them. Like depth-first search, it puts the successors of successor nodes on the front of a stack. Although it does not expand all the nodes at one level before moving down to the next level like breadth-first search, it does examine all of the nodes at a level by applying its evaluation function on them and then sorting them.

It is typical in hill-climbing domains for the solution to be at the top of a hill. However, all the methods we have presented so far have a separate solution tester and evaluation function. They use the evaluation function to determine which successor to try next and they apply the solution tester to every point. This arrangement makes it possible to find a solution if that solution is on the path to a peak, without necessarily being at the top. In domains where the only solution is at the highest peak, an alternative formulation simply optimizes the value of the evaluation function.

One problem with backtracking hill climbing is that the number of nodes visited can become large if there is a great deal of branching and the search is deep. In the most obvious implementation of backtracking hill climbing, space complexity is $d(b-1)$ where d is the depth of the search tree and b is the branching factor. As we discussed for depth-first search, it is possible to reduce the space requirement to $O(d)$ by representing the stack with choice points. One complication for hill climbing, however, is that it needs to evaluate all the successors of a node before choosing one. This presents an implementation trade-off between the time cost to reevaluate the remaining nodes in the choice point and the space cost of remembering the evaluations of the remaining nodes or at least their relative ordering. Some considerations for a choice-point implementation are discussed in the exercises.

Another version of hill climbing, called beam search, uses two queues of fixed size. This is discussed in the exercises. Beam search may fail to find some solutions.

Best-First Search

If the evaluation function used for hill climbing is ill behaved, then the successors of the best-ranked node may have lower evaluations than the node's siblings. Unfortunately, in such cases backtracking hill climbing buries the sibling nodes below the more recently generated successor nodes. Best-first search addresses this problem by merging the successor nodes with all the other nodes in the list. This slows the main loop of the method because more nodes are potentially visited to determine their total ordering, but the best-ranked node is always tried first.

Restated, backtracking hill climbing explores the best successor next, but best-first search explores the best next node found anywhere on the dynamic fringe. Figure 2.73 compares the order of nodes on a sample list for hill climbing and best-first search. A method for a satisficing

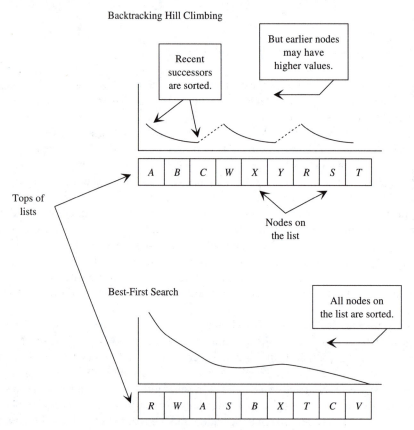

FIGURE 2.73. A comparison of the patterns of values of nodes on the stack for backtracking hill climbing and best-first search.

To carry out a best-first search:

```
 1.    Form a list consisting of the root node.
 2.    While the list is not empty do
 3.    begin
 4.        Pop a node from the list.
 5.        If solution-tester(node) then exit with success reporting
           the node.
 6.        Else for each successor of node do
 7.        begin
 8.                Measure the successor with the evaluation function.
 9.                Merge the successor node into the list of all
                   nodes, so the list is in decreasing, or
                   nonincreasing, order.
10.        end
11.    end

       /* Here if no goal has been found. */
12.    Exit with failure.
```

FIGURE 2.74. Satisficing method for best-first search.

best-first search is given in Figure 2.74. Because of the need to merge recently visited nodes with older ones, we use a list instead of a stack to keep track of the nodes under consideration.

The worst-case storage requirements for best-first search are the same as for breadth-first search: $O(b^d)$. For example, the worst-case space arises when all nodes at level k evaluate better than all nodes at level $k + 1$, resulting essentially in an inefficient breadth-first search. The best case arises when a well-behaved evaluation function leads to behavior essentially like "smart" depth-first search with space requirements of $O(b^d)$. The exercises discuss techniques for reducing the storage overhead by sacrificing completeness of search using a fixed-size list. This variation of best-first search is called width-limited best-first search. The characteristics of simple hill climbing, backtracking hill climbing, and best-first search are summarized in Figure 2.75.

There are two ways to characterize the role of an evaluation function in hill climbing and best-first search, and this is sometimes a source of terminological variance.

- An evaluation function can be viewed as measuring the quality of a candidate solution. Any point in the space can be a solution. From this point of view, hill climbing is an optimizing procedure, used to search about in a space for the highest or lowest point. The process is based on the assumption that the evaluation function is smooth, which means high points are near other high points. The nodes all correspond to complete solution candidates on which the evaluation function is computable. In this view, hill climbing is for situations in which there are adjustable parameters and a way of measuring the quality associated with any particular set of values for the parameters.
- An alternative view of the evaluation function is that it measures the distance of a candidate to a solution. In this characterization, solutions are paths to leaf nodes. The search is

organized at each step to choose the node that brings us closest to a solution. This process is based on various assumptions about the measurement and estimation of distance, such as that distance accumulates additively and that distance-estimating functions are smooth.

When solutions are paths to the leaf nodes, the goal is to find a minimal path. Incremental methods for problems of this kind are the subject of the next section.

2.3.5 *Shortest-Path Methods*

An important kind of hill-climbing task is the finding of shortest or **optimal paths**. There are two major variations of this task: finding the shortest path that visits all the nodes in a graph and finding the shortest (or minimum cost) path from the initial state to a final state. The first variation is called the traveling salesman problem and is known to be intractable in the worst case.

In the following, we consider only the latter and more tractable version: finding the shortest path to a goal node. In a graph representing the problem such as the one in Figure 2.76, each arc between nodes has a positive number corresponding to a cost or distance. The starting node and goal node are marked. Sometimes the starting node is called the origin or the root.

To develop intuitions about these problems we step through part of the search for a solution of the example in Figure 2.76. Node *A* is the root or starting node and node *H* is the goal. In this example, the branching factor per node is relatively low. Six of the nine nodes connect to

Directed method	Simple hill climbing	Backtracking hill climbing	Best-first search
Bookkeeping	Ordered list.	Ordered list.	Ordered list.
Knowledge interfaces	Evaluation function, solution generator, solution tester.	Evaluation function, solution generator, solution tester.	Evaluation function, solution generator, solution tester.
Directionality	From eval function.	From eval function.	From eval function.
Built on methods		Simple match and depth-first search.	Simple match and depth-first search.
Worst-case space	$O(1)$	$O(b^d)$	$O(b^d)$
Best-case space	$O(1)$	$O(b^d)$	$O(b^d)$
Worst-case time	$O(b^d)$	$O(b^d)$	$O(b^d)$
Example bad cases	(1) When siblings have higher ratings than the best successors. (2) Local optima.	When siblings have higher ratings than the best successors.	When siblings have higher ratings than the best successors.
Solution criteria	Satisficing or due process.	Optimizing.	Optimizing.
Thoroughness	Incomplete search.	Complete search.	Complete search.
Variations			
Limited list		Beam search.	Width-limited best-first search.
Minimizing	Seek minimum value rather than maximum.	Seek minimum value rather than maximum.	

FIGURE 2.75. Summary of the characteristics of hill climbing and best-first search.

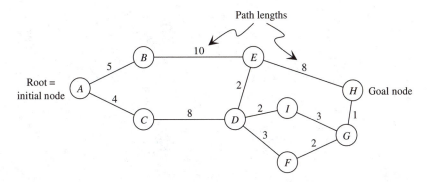

FIGURE 2.76. Example of an optimal path problem.

only two neighbors and no node has a branching factor of greater than 4. The obvious approach is to develop paths incrementally, starting from the root on the left and moving to the right. The process is familiar to anyone whose has planned a trip, taking a car, bus, train, or plane through intermediate cities to a final destination. Starting from the root and taking one step we can reach either node B or node C, with distances of 4 and 5, respectively. From those nodes we can go to node E or D, with cumulative path lengths of 15 or 12, respectively. At this point, we notice that we could get from D to E in only two more units. This gives us two paths from the root to E. The path A-B-E has length 15 and the path A-C-D-E has length 14. Since we are only interested in the shortest path, the path A-B-E can be discarded. We continue in this manner, advancing through the nodes and recording at each node the shortest path to it.

Because this simple method considers each arc in the graph exactly once, its time complexity is $O(N)$ where N is the number of arcs in the graph or $O(n^2)$ for a complete graph of n nodes. For graphs shaped as balanced trees, another way to express this is as $O(b^d)$ where b is the branching factor and d is the depth. One advantage of this latter formulation is that it provides a way to view the time complexity in terms of the solution length. The length of a solution path in the balanced tree is d. Since any method for finding a solution must visit each node in the solution, a lower bound on time complexity is d. To summarize, the time complexity for a shortest-path algorithm lies somewhere between d and b^d. These bounds are sometimes called the linear and the exponential cases, expressed in terms of solution length.

In this section we consider two methods for shortest-path search. Both methods have the same worst-case time complexity as the upper bound already discussed. The first method is easier to understand and prove correct. The second method is more closely related to methods that use more information that we consider next.

Dijkstra's Method

Dijkstra's method associates labels with the nodes of the graph. At each stage of the computation some labels are designated as permanent and the others as tentative. A permanent label represents the known length of a shortest path from the starting node to that node. A tentative label represents the least length known so far, an upper bound on the distance from the starting node. The arc length from node i to node j is given by a_{ij}.

To carry out a shortest-path search using Dijkstra's method:

```
        /* Initialize. */
1.      u₁ := 0
2.      Mark node 1 as "permanent."
3.      for node j from 2 to n do
4.      begin
5.              dⱼ := a₁ⱼ
6.              Mark node j as "tentative."
7.      end

        /* Designate next permanent label and test for completion. */
Designate:
8.      Find the tentative node, k, with the least uₖ.
9.      Mark node k as permanent.
10.     If node k is the goal node, then quit.

        /* Update bounds on tentative nodes. */
11.     For each node j marked as tentative
12.     begin
13.             If node j is connected to node k
14.             then uⱼ := min {dⱼ, dₖ + aₖⱼ}
15.     end
16.     Go to Designate.
```

FIGURE 2.77. Dijkstra's method for finding the shortest path.

At the beginning, the starting node is given the permanent label $d_1 = 0$. Each of the other nodes is given the tentative label $d_j = a_{1j}$, which is the length of the arc connecting it with the origin, if any. Nodes not connected to the starting node are given the label ∞. In the general step, tentative labels are progressively and systematically decreased. At each iteration, we first find the node, k, with the smallest tentative label. If there is a tie, it is broken arbitrarily. The label d_k is then marked as permanent. Then for each tentative node connected to node k, we compare d_k with $d_k + a_{kj}$, which is the cumulative distance from the starting node through node k to node j. If the route to node j through node k is smaller, then d_j is updated. This process continues until all nodes are permanently labeled or the goal node is reached. The pseudocode for Dijkstra's method is given in Figure 2.77.

The correctness of the method can be proven using induction. At each stage in the process the nodes are divided into two disjoint sets—those that are labeled permanently and those that are labeled tentatively. Suppose that the permanent nodes are labeled with the shortest paths from the starting node and that the tentative nodes are labeled with a shortest path with the restriction that each node in the path (except the last one itself) is permanently labeled. In this case, the tentatively labeled node k can be marked as permanent because if a shorter path from the starting node existed, it would have to contain a first node, m, that is tentatively labeled.

However, such a node m must be farther away from the starting node than k since its label is bigger than that of node k.

To determine the time complexity of Dijkstra's method, we count comparisons and additions. The first time the designation steps (8 through 10) are executed, $n - 2$ comparisons are called for, the second time $n - 3$, and so on. In the worst case of a complete graph the goal node is the last temporary node, leading to a total of $(n - 1)(n - 2)/2$. The updating steps (11 through 16) first call for $n - 2$ comparisons and the same number of additions. The next time $n - 3$ comparisons and additions are called for. Overall, there are again $(n - 1)(n - 2)/2$ comparisons and additions. In summary, the method has complexity $O(n^2)$.

Figure 2.78 shows a trace of applying Dijkstra's method on a sample problem. The shaded nodes are the ones whose labels have been marked as permanent. Labels on the arcs are the path lengths from the a_{ij} relation. Node labels are shown above or to the right of them. The label "inf." refers to infinity. Each step in the figure refers to a complete cycle through the method.

A Second Shortest Path Method

The second method for finding the shortest path to a goal is called SP-2 and is given in Figure 2.79. SP-2 is similar to best-first search, with a few differences. Each item processed by this method represents an arc from a source node to a destination node. The arc adds incrementally to a total path length. The total path length for a node is the shortest known path back to the starting node. The method is initialized with a zero-length path from the root node to itself and builds paths incrementally. An evaluation function is used to compute the incremental increase in path length when a new node is added to a path.

SP-2 systematically explores a search space and cannot stop simply because it has found a single solution. Before stopping, it must determine that there are no unexplored paths shorter than the ones already found. If SP-2 computed all possible paths then it would do more work than is needed. If it stopped after finding one path, there might still be unexplored paths that could turn out ultimately to be shorter. The stopping condition is to terminate when the length of the shortest incomplete path is greater than the length of the shortest complete path to the goal. This condition avoids computing all possible paths while ensuring that no shorter path remains undiscovered.

Figure 2.80 gives a trace of SP-2 on the same example as we considered for Dijkstra's method. The label above a node is a path length, when that is known. Nodes are shaded when they have been visited. In the fourth step of the trace, there are two possible nodes on the choice list both with path lengths of 11. In the trace, one of these is chosen arbitrarily, resulting in the assignment of a path of 20 to the goal. It remains for the next cycles of the method to discover that this is not the minimum path length.

Several variations have been studied and are an important part of operations research. For example, the test in step 8, which discards redundant longer routes to intermediate nodes, was discovered separately from the original formulation. In Figure 2.80 there are two paths from the initial state to node E. Only the shorter path need be saved. This idea of keeping only the minimum distance path to nodes is called the **dynamic programming principle**. This principle improves the efficiency for graphs in which there are paths of different lengths to nodes. Step 16 in the method applies the same concept to paths to goal nodes.

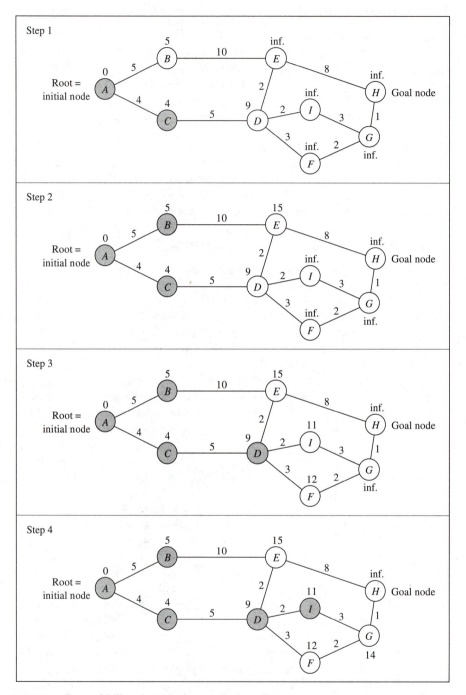

FIGURE 2.78.   Trace of Dijkstra's method on a sample problem.

To carry out a shortest-path search:

1. Initialize the variable best-solution with a distinguishable placeholder item whose path length is the longest possible path.
2. Form a list, consisting initially of the zero-length path from the root node to itself.
3. While the list is not empty do
4. begin
5.   Pop an item from the list.
6.   If the destination node is a goal node then
7.   begin
8.   If the total path length of the node is less than the total path length of best-solution, set best-solution to the new node.
9.   end
10.   Else for each successor of the destination node do
11.   begin
12.   Measure the incremental path length from the node to the successor with the evaluation function.
13.   Compute a total path length for the successor that is the sum of the lengths of the total path length to the node and the extension to the successor.
14.   If no previous path to the successor is known, or if the new total path length to the successor is less than a previous one, then
15.   begin
16.   Assign the new total path length to the successor.
17.   Record that the node is the "preceding node" for its successor, so we can reconstruct the path later.
/* Continue the search for further successors unless the path is already longer than some path to a solution.*/
18.   If the total path length of the successor is less than the total path length of best-solution, then merge the successor into the list (so the list is in increasing, or non-decreasing, order).
19.   end
20.   end
21. end

22. If best-solution contains the placeholder node, exit with failure.
23. Else exit with success returning the path associated with best-solution.

FIGURE 2.79. SP-2 method for finding the shortest path (with dynamic programming). This method begins at an initial state and incrementally extends paths in search of a path to the goal state. The search is directed only by its focus on short paths from the initial state.

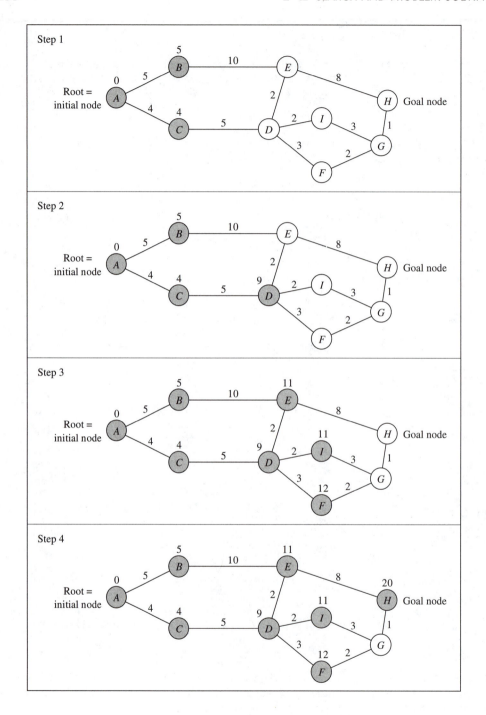

FIGURE 2.80.   Trace of SP-2 method on a sample problem.

Comparison of Shortest-Path Methods

We now compare the two shortest-path methods. Both methods build solution paths from the root incrementally. Both methods attempt to follow shortest overall paths by selecting nodes that seem to have the shortest paths so far. Both methods incorporate a version of the dynamic programming principle. Nonetheless, they differ in the selection of nodes and arcs to extend. Dijkstra's method maintains a distinction between tentative and permanent labels and extends its path bounds in a way that uses only the nodes with permanent labels. Whenever it reaches the goal node, it can stop because no shorter path can be found. In contrast, SP-2 does not make this distinction. Even if it reaches the goal node, it must continue exploring paths until all remaining paths are longer than the shortest known path to the goal. On the other hand, it proceeds by extending the shortest path in sight rather than by extending a set of known shortest paths. The proofs of completeness and complexity are somewhat more direct with Dijkstra's method.

The methods differ in trivial ways. Arc lengths in SP-2 are expressed in terms of an evaluation function rather than simply as an array a_{ij} as in Dijkstra's method. These are equivalent for our purposes. The evaluation-function formulation is more similar in structure to A* in the next section. Both methods must associate a path length with each node visited and an arc length for each arc. SP-2 explicitly stores back lengths so it can reconstruct the path at the end.

Neither method dominates the other in performance. It is possible to find problems such that Dijkstra's method explores fewer nodes than SP-2. It is also possible to find methods such that SP-2 explores fewer nodes than Dijkstra's method. The worst-case time complexity for both methods is $O(b^d)$ or, equivalently, $O(n^2)$.

SP-2 is complete in that it will find a solution if there is one. However, it is not exhaustive. If there are multiple equivalent solutions, SP-2 will return just one of them. To return all equivalent solutions would require only simple modifications.

Figure 2.81 summarizes the characteristics of the two shortest-path methods. It is ineffective when there are many paths of almost the same length. In these situations, its expansions of the shortest paths first does not reduce its time complexity much from an exhaustive search. SP-2 is also ineffective in cases where the right path at first appears to be a long path, as when the right path consists of a few big steps near the initial state. In such cases, SP-2 will spend most of its time expanding other paths made up of short steps before it gets around to the right one. A deeper analysis of the search behavior is possible. We develop such an analysis in the next section for the A* algorithm, which is closely related and somewhat more powerful.

2.3.6   A* and Related Methods   ADVANCED

The only source of information that guides the shortest-path methods of the previous section in their search for minimum-cost paths is the set of lengths of the paths tried so far. In this section we consider heuristic methods that extend this approach by using additional information to guide the selection of nodes to expand.

The A* Algorithm

The simplest heuristic method that we consider is the **A* algorithm** (Nilsson, 1971). A* seeks a minimum-cost or minimum-length path and uses the dynamic programming principle. The heuristic knowledge that A* employs is an estimate of the remaining distance to a goal. A* evaluates

Directed method	Dijkstra's method	SP-2
Bookkeeping	Sets of permanent and tentative labels.	Ordered list.
Knowledge interfaces	a_{ij} array for path length.	Evaluation function for path length generator of incremental steps.
Built on methods	Best-first search to node with shortest path to root.	Best-first search to successors of shortest path.
Worst-case space	$O(b^d) = O(n^2) = O(N)$	$O(b^d) = O(n^2) = O(N)$
Worst-case time	$O(b^d) = O(n^2) = O(N)$	$O(b^d) = O(n^2) = O(N)$
Example bad cases	Inefficient when there are many paths of the same length.	(1) Inefficient when there are many paths of almost the same length. (2) Finds the right path late when it involves only a few steps close to the initial state, but those steps are longer than many smaller steps along fruitless paths.
Solution criteria	Optimizing.	Optimizing.
Thoroughness	Complete search.	Complete search.
Variation		
Directionality		A* search method uses an estimate of the remaining distance to the goal to guide the selection of paths.

FIGURE 2.81.   Characteristics of two shortest-path methods.

a candidate node, n, for extending a path as the sum of the cost or distance along the path so far, $g(n)$, plus a heuristic estimate of the *remaining cost or distance to a goal node*, $h(n)$. The evaluation function, f, is the total shown in equation (1).

$$f(n) = g(n) + h(n) \tag{1}$$

In a variation of A* known as **weighted heuristic search**, numeric weights are assigned to g and h as in the two approaches shown in equations (2) and (3).

$$f(n,w) = (1 - w) g(n) + wh(n) \tag{2}$$
$$f(n,v) = g(n) + vh(n) \quad v > 0 \tag{3}$$

These variations have been used in studies of the effect of changing the weighting of the contributions in the evaluation to emphasize either contributions from the path length so far or the heuristic function. In some variations, the weights are changed during the course of a search. Equations (4) and (5) show the relation between the two forms of the weighted heuristic.

$$v = w / (1 - w) \tag{4}$$
$$w = v / (1 + v) \tag{5}$$

These formulations of the weighted heuristic are discussed further in the exercises. They are equivalent to each other in that scaling the evaluation function does not change the order in which nodes are considered.

Figure 2.82 presents the simple A* search method for arbitrary graphs. For simplicity, provisions for weighting the heuristic function are not included.

We denote by $h^*(n)$ the ideal function yielding the actual distance from an arbitrary node, n, to a goal node. If $h(n) = h^*(n)$ for all nodes we say that h is **perfect**. In typical situations, h^* is not known and h is the best estimate available. The performance of A* depends on the properties of h.

Completeness is an example of a performance property where the determination for A* depends on the properties of h. A heuristic function, h, is said to be **admissible** if it satisfies equation (6).

$$\forall n, h(n) \leq h^*(n) \tag{6}$$

In other words, h is admissible if it never overestimates the actual distance or cost to a solution. Thus, h never misleads A* to discard a node on the mistaken belief that the path from it to a goal is too long. If $h(n)$ is admissible, then the search carried out by A* is complete and A* will eventually find an optimal solution. Although it is possible for A* to be complete with an inadmissible heuristic function or even to frequently find the optimal solution, it is easy to construct cases where A* with an inadmissible heuristic function is incomplete.

The complexity and performance of A* has been studied both empirically and theoretically. The best performance is when A* unerringly finds a direct path to a goal. In this case its time complexity is $O(N)$, where N is the number of nodes on the solution path. We call this the **linear case**, since complexity is linear in the path length. In the worst case, or **exponential case**, the behavior of A* is $O(b^N)$, or exponential in the path length. Studies show that the time complexity of A* depends on the accuracy of the heuristic function—tending toward the exponential worst case unless the heuristic is highly accurate. We develop this result more precisely below.

That the performance of A* varies with h can be illustrated by considering extreme cases. If h is perfect, that is, if $h = h^*$, then A* explores only nodes lying along optimal paths. Perfect information yields the linear case with a time complexity of A* of $O(N)$. At the other extreme where $\forall n, h(n) = 0$, A* reduces to SP-2. In this case, h is admissible but ineffective. A* explores all nodes that do not increase their path lengths beyond that of the best-known solution. If A* with $h(n) = 0$ is applied to a tree of depth d and branching factor b, every node could be explored—giving us the exponential case. Realistic cases lie between these two extremes.

A* expands every frontier node satisfying inequality (7).

$$g(n) + h(n) < C^* \tag{7}$$

where C^* is the cheapest or shortest known path to a goal node, or some arbitrarily large constant used by the A* method if no path is yet known. In the method of Figure 2.82, C^* is the value of the `best-solution` variable. For various heuristic functions, h, the higher the admissible value that it returns for n, the fewer nodes that will be less than C^* and the fewer paths that will be explored.

To carry out an A* search:

1. Initialize the variable best-solution with a distinguishable placeholder node whose path length is the longest possible path.

2. Form a list, consisting initially of the zero-length path from the root node to itself.

3. While the list is not empty do

4. begin

5. 　　Pop an item from the list.

6. 　　If the destination node is a solution (that is, the path reaches a goal), then

7. 　　begin

8. 　　　　If the total path length of the node, g(n), is less than the total path length of best-solution, set best-solution to the new node (as associated with the computed path length and source node of the item as the preceding node).

9. 　　end

10. 　　Else if the total estimated path length of the destination node, f(n), is less than the total path length of best-solution, then for each successor of the destination node do

11. 　　begin

12. 　　　　Measure the incremental path length from the node to the successor.

13. 　　　　Compute a new known path length, g(successor), that is the sum of the lengths of the current path and the extension to the successor.

14. 　　　　If no previous path to the successor is known, or if the new known path length to the successor is less than a previous one, then

15. 　　　　begin

16. 　　　　　　Assign a total estimated path length to the successor, f(successor), that is the known path length, g(successor), plus the estimate of distance remaining to the goal, h(successor).

17. 　　　　　　If the estimated total path length of the successor, f(successor), is less than the path length of best-solution, then merge the successor into the list. (The list is in increasing, or non-decreasing, order based on the estimated total.)

18. 　　　　end

19. 　　end

20. end

21. If best-solution contains the placeholder node, then exit with failure.

22. Else exit with success returning the path associated with the best-solution.

FIGURE 2.82.　Method for A* search.

Characteristic Error Functions

A key to estimating the quantitative performance of a heuristic method is to relate the expected error in the heuristic estimate to an expected number of nodes to be explored. In the following we express different expectations about error in terms of different characteristic error functions. We then consider quantitative results relating error in the heuristic function to the time complexity of search.

The simplest specification of error for a heuristic function h is **constant-exact absolute error**. This case is defined by equation (8) where c is a positive constant.

$$\forall n,\ h*(n) - h(n) = c \tag{8}$$

This case is nearly ideal but not realistic. An exactly constant error is too predictable, being as informative as the case of no error at all. Since all that matters in best-first searches such as A* is the ranking of candidates, a constant error will never disturb their relative ordering. Consequently, A* using a heuristic function with constant absolute error will visit exactly the same nodes in exactly the same order as A* with a perfect heuristic function, resulting in a time complexity of $O(N)$.

A more reasonable model of error is where the heuristic function h has **constant-bounded absolute error** as characterized by equation (9). This case is also called **constant absolute error** or **bandwidth error**.

$$\forall n,\ h*(n) - h(n) \le c \tag{9}$$

This case is more difficult. If we assume the error for a given candidate is distributed within the given bandwidth, then differences in errors of the heuristic function for different nodes can cause A* to rank nodes out of the optimal order. In other words, the heuristic function can be seen as a noisy source of information. Figure 2.83 shows evaluations of four "next" nodes, considered as alternatives for extending a path in a search. The top of the bar corresponding to each node shows the value that would be reported by a perfect heuristic function. The shaded area shows bounds on the error. The actual error associated with each node could be anywhere within the shaded box. In this example, node n_1 is the actual lowest-cost choice. However, if the error in evaluating node n_1 is larger than the error in evaluating node n_3, then n_3 could be mistakenly chosen next, causing some nodes to be explored unnecessarily. The path corresponding to the expansion of n_4 would not be explored because it is greater than C*.

Typically, expected error is not independent of the distance of a node from a goal. The simplest specification of distance-dependent error is **constant-exact relative error** as defined by equation (10).

$$\forall n,\ \frac{h*(n) - h(n)}{h*(n)} = c \tag{10}$$

The error is called relative because it is normalized by the estimated cost. Thus, relative error is a fraction of the distance. As in the case of constant-exact absolute error, constant-exact relative

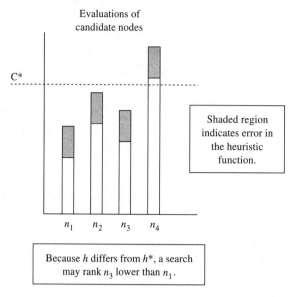

FIGURE 2.83. A set of candidates for the next node to consider in a heuristic search. Each bar corresponds to the evaluation of a candidate. The top of each shaded bar is the perfect evaluation that would be obtained by using h^*. The shaded area in each case indicates bounds on errors in the evaluation from the available heuristic function. The white bar indicates the underestimate. (If the heuristic function overestimated distance, it would be inadmissible.) The bar that extends above C^* corresponds to a node that would not be expanded, because it corresponds to a path length greater than some known path to the goal.

error is too predictable to be true. It is easy to show that if the error is exact the heuristic function is essentially as informative as a perfect heuristic function; that is, that a search program similar to A* can unfailingly make the best choice. (See the exercises.)

Again, a more realistic variant of relative error is **constant-bounded relative error** as defined by equation (11). This case is more simply called **constant relative error**.

$$\forall n, \frac{|h*(n) - h(n)|}{|h*(n)|} \leq \epsilon \tag{11}$$

Typically, the error function is more complex than a constant. Gaschnig (1979) studied the performance of A* for heuristic functions that were admissible and that tended to increase in value for greater distances to a goal. For such functions, the time complexity of A* can be analyzed in cases depending on the properties of *err*, a function of the distance, d, to a goal node. In Gaschnig's formulation, the characteristic error function, $err(d)$, is multiplicative with distance as in equation (12).

$$\text{error} = h*(n) - h(n) \leq err(d) * d \tag{12}$$

In this multiplicative formulation of the error of the heuristic estimate, several cases are possible. Given that $h^*(n)$ is the distance, d, of a node to a goal, equation (13) is just a restatement of the case of constant relative error.

$$err(d) = c, \text{ where } c \text{ is a constant.} \tag{13}$$

Equation (14) is equivalent to the case of constant absolute error. Equation (15) presents an intermediate case.

$$err(d) = c/d \tag{14}$$
$$err(d) = c(\log d)/d \tag{15}$$

Another formulation of the error function is used to represent arbitrary errors that grow at a slower than linear rate. This approach is called ø-normalized error as defined by equation (16).

$$Y(n) = \frac{h(n) - h^*(n)}{\phi[h^*(n)]} \tag{16}$$

In this formulation, $Y(n)$ is called the ø-normalized error and ø is a normalization function that increases monotonically with its argument and satisfies equations (17) and (18).

$$\lim_{x \to \infty} \phi(x) = \infty \tag{17}$$

$$\lim_{x \to \infty} (x)/x = 0 \tag{18}$$

Equation (19) relates this formulation to the multiplicative formulation:

$$err(d) = \phi(d)/d \tag{19}$$

When ø is the identity function, the error $h^*(n) - h(n)$ is proportional to $h^*(n)$. A lower order of ø implies greater accuracy of h. When the typical error $h - h^*$ grows like $\phi(h^*)$, the typical relative error grows like $\phi(h^*)/h$. In other words, if the typical absolute error grows at a slower than linear rate, the typical relative error possesses a limiting distribution that converges to zero as $h^* \to \infty$. A heuristic function satisfying equations (13) and (14) is said to be **informative**. In the following we consider some quantitative results that relate these different formulations of error in the heuristic function to the performance of A*.

Worst-Case Complexity of A* as a Function of Heuristic Error

Gaschnig (1979) studied the performance of A* for heuristic functions that were admissible and that tended to increase in value for greater distances to a goal. He modeled A* as a search of a tree where b is the branching factor, depth is unbounded, there is exactly one solution, that solution is at level N, and N is not known before the search is done. Gaschnig used the weighted heuristic form of A* with $w < 1$. This analysis is more restrictive than the cases covered by the

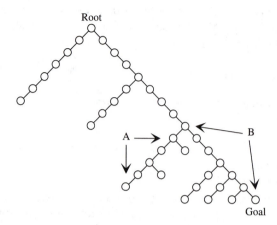

FIGURE 2.84. A* chooses which nodes to expand in a search. If it expands the node marked "A" to substantial depth, this is called "pursuing a garden path" because there are no solutions there.

method in Figure 2.82 in that there is exactly one goal and one path to it and, therefore, no concern with conditions under which the path to a goal is of minimum length.

Each possible heuristic function causes different subtrees to be expanded in the worst case, where a subtree of expanded nodes begins at some node on the solution path. Figure 2.84 shows an example of such a tree, where all paths start at the root and there is a single goal node, shown without loss of generality as the terminal node of the rightmost branch of the tree. The branch A is sometimes called a **garden path**, meaning that the search is misled into taking it because of errors in the heuristic function. The garden path A is expanded if the maximum value of the evaluation function, f, over its nodes is less than the maximum value of f over the nodes of subtree B.

For a while, the value of f may increase more slowly along a garden path than the solution path. A* may even pursue a garden path A to a depth greater than N. However, since f is monotonically increasing including the contribution of the g term, the evaluation along A must eventually pass that of B. The longer such garden paths are, the more nodes that are expanded in the search.

Gaschnig's analysis measures the time complexity of A* in terms of the number of nodes that are visited in the search. This approach assumes that the cost of computing the heuristic function is insignificant or is the same for each node. Gaschnig limited his analysis to heuristic functions that he called "IM-never-overestimating," which means roughly that h is admissible and that the value of h increases in magnitude with distance from the goal.

One result of the analysis is that the distance to which the search can extend from the solution path, or the maximum length of a garden path, is a fraction of the relative error of the heuristic. Suppose node n on the solution path is at depth k and the solution is at depth N. Equations (20) and (21) express some relevant relations.

$$g(n) = k \tag{20}$$
$$h^*(n) = N + k \tag{21}$$

The heuristic function, h, is admissible so that it may underestimate h^* by a little.

$$h(n) = (1 - \epsilon)\, h^*(n) = (1 - \epsilon)\, (N - k) \tag{22}$$

This gives us an expression for C^*. In particular, every node satisfying equation (23) will be explored.

$$f(n) = g(n) + h(n) = k + (1 - \epsilon)\, (N - k) < N \tag{23}$$

An estimate of the number of nodes explored follows in equation (24).

$$\text{nodes explored} = b \left\lfloor \frac{N\epsilon}{2 - \epsilon} \right\rfloor - 2 \tag{24}$$

where N is the length of the unique solution path and b is the branching factor of the tree.

In Gaschnig's formulation of this, ϵ is replaced by the characteristic error function delta. Using these results, he sought delta functions for which the number of nodes explored grows at most linearly, polynomially, or exponentially in N. That is, he determined how much relative error in the heuristic distance estimates could be tolerated and still guarantee a cost function that grows within certain bounds. The time complexity of A* can be grouped into cases depending on the properties of the characteristic error function *err*.

The worst-case complexity analysis of the following cases is illustrative:

1. Constant absolute error: If $err(d) = c/d$, then the worst-case time complexity of A* is $O(N)$. Restated, if the heuristic function has bandwidth error, then the time complexity is linear in the length of the solution path.

2. Logarithmic absolute error: If $err(d) = c(\log d)/d$, then the worst-case time complexity of A* is $O(N^{\log b}) = O(N^k)$. This case gives conditions for polynomial time complexity.

3. Constant relative error: If $err(d) = c$, where c is a constant, then the worst-case time complexity of A* is $O(b^{cN})$. In other words, if the relative error of the heuristic function is bounded by a constant, then the worst-case complexity of A* is exponential in the length of the solution path.

These estimates suggest that the precision complexity trade-off for A* is fairly inelastic. Very precise heuristics must be used if the search complexity is to be kept manageable. As Gaschnig expressed it:

These "limits to growth" results are somewhat sobering: A* must be given a heuristic function whose absolute accuracy decreases but slightly with distance from the goal node in order to guarantee good performance in the worst case. . . . even relative error that is constant with distance from the goal still causes exponential growth in cost. (p. 101)

Directed method	A*
Bookkeeping	Ordered list.
Knowledge interfaces	Metric for path length, generator of incremental steps, estimator of distance to goal.
Directionality	From eval function.
Built on methods	SP-2.
Worst-case space	$O(b^k)$ where b is the branching factor and k is the number of levels.
Worst-case time	$O(b^k)$, unless highly accurate heuristic function is available.
Average-case time	Depends on the accuracy of the heuristic.
Solution criteria	Optimizing.
Thoroughness	Complete search if heuristic function is admissible.

FIGURE 2.85.   Characteristics of A* and related methods.

Mean Complexity of A* as a Function of Heuristic Error

Worst-case complexity results can be misleading if they are overly conservative. Pearl (1984) generalized Gaschnig's worst-case results to the average case. We first present the complexity results and then a sketch of how they can be derived. Pearl was interested in quantifying the precision complexity trade-off. Using the ø-normalized formulation of error, Pearl showed that the mean complexity of A* grows as in equation (25).

$$\text{mean complexity of A*} = O(N \exp (C \, ø \, (N))). \tag{25}$$

The details of this analysis are beyond the scope of this section. Roughly, however, Pearl was interested in bounding the normalized errors. A typical error is defined as one where it is probable that the ø-normalized error is bounded both above and below by given constants. As in the worst-case analysis, a necessary and sufficient condition for maintaining a polynomial search complexity is that A* be guided by heuristics having logarithmic precision, such as $ø(N) = (\log N)^k$.

Figure 2.85 summarizes the properties of A*. A*'s complexity is very sensitive to the accuracy of the heuristics used. A small change in the accuracy of the heuristic estimator can lead to a large change in the number of nodes explored and therefore to a large change in the time-complexity of a search—changing the search complexity the linear to the exponential case.

The analysis of the time complexity of A* is another example of threshold effects as discussed in Chapter 1 and in the context of hierarchical generate-and-test. The "garden paths" that can dominate the running time of A* correspond to incorrect branches uselessly pursued. The phase transitions in A* are the changes from linear to exponential time complexity and the parameter that passes through a threshold represents the accuracy of the heuristic function. The analyses of A* were probably the first in AI to demonstrate threshold effects, although the terminology of phase transitions and threshold effects was not used in computer science at the time.

2.3.7   Summary and Review

In contrast with the blind search methods of Section 2.2, directed search methods use heuristic knowledge to guide the search process. Directed search methods are based on the state-space for-

Search method	Approach	Directionality	Where discussed
Simple match	Reducing best difference	State comparator	Section 2.3.1
Means-ends analysis	Subgoaling search	State comparator	Section 2.3.2
Hierarchical match	Two-level match	Abstract steps	Section 2.3.3
Hill climbing	Following best successors	Evaluation function	Section 2.3.4
Beam search	Limited hill-climbing	Evaluation function	Exercise 2.3-3
Best-first search	Follow best open node	Evaluation function	Section 2.3.4
Width-limited best-first search	Limited best-first search	Evaluation function	Exercise 2.3-4
Shortest-path methods	Shortest path	Path length computation	Section 2.3.4
A*	Shortest path	Remaining distance estimator	Section 2.3.6

FIGURE 2.86. Brief summary of directed search methods.

mulation of the search space, in which the nodes are states and operators change one state into another. The use of operators is advantageous when states are complex because the generation of new nodes can then be described simply in terms of small changes to existing nodes.

Figure 2.86 lists the directed search methods that are discussed in this section. Many more specialized methods for directed search are part of the subject matter of operations research and numerical analysis. Different methods depend on different assumptions about the nature of evaluation functions. For example, linear programming depends on linearity assumptions about the function being optimized and assumptions about the search space being bounded by polygons. Other numerical methods depend on assumptions of differentiability and convex or closed and bounded search spaces. The methods of this section tend to be used for searching spaces where we make weaker assumptions.

The simplest methods for directed search are the match methods. Simple match uses two auxiliary programs: a comparator and an operator selector. In simple match, the comparator computes a difference between the current state and a goal and then the operator selector selects an operator that removes that difference, bringing the current state closer to the goal. Simple match admits no backtracking. It is analogous to forward chaining, in that it advances a step at a time, choosing operators based on properties of the current state. Forward chaining and simple match differ in the way they select operators. Forward chaining depends only on properties of the current state, where as simple match makes use of differences between the current state and a goal state.

Means-ends analysis combines the features of simple match with depth-first search. From simple match it gets operators, a goal node, and the taking of differences. From depth-first search, it gets backtracking. Like simple match, means-ends analysis uses a comparator to determine the difference between the current state and a goal. However, means-ends analysis admits the possibility that there can be multiple differences. It employs an operator-difference table to determine which differences to reduce first and which operators to apply.

Means-ends analysis is similar to backward chaining. The retrieval of operators from a difference table to achieve goals in means-ends analysis is analogous to the retrieval of rules that potentially satisfy goals in backward chaining. Both methods set up intermediate subgoals.

Means-ends analysis sets up subgoals when operator preconditions are not satisfied; backward chaining sets up subgoals when conditions on the left sides of rules are not satisfied.

Hierarchical representations can be used to make match more efficient. Hierarchical match (also called skeletal planning) uses an abstract plan to indicate big steps on the way to a solution, dividing and conquering the search space. Problem solving between the abstract steps is carried out by simple match or means-ends analysis. In hierarchical match, the abstract plan itself is fixed. A natural extension to hierarchical match is to permit multiple levels of abstract plans, themselves created by the program. This is called hierarchical planning and is discussed in Section 2.4.

Another way to impart direction to search is to be guided by measurements of the current node. The simplest direct search method using this approach is called hill climbing. In hill climbing, the measurement is carried out by an auxiliary program called an evaluation function. An evaluation function can be used either to measure the distance of an intermediate node to a goal or to measure the quality of a candidate node as a solution itself. We considered two versions of hill climbing. Simple hill climbing is an incomplete, monotonic search method that always tries to advance from its current node. Backtracking hill climbing is a complete search that maintains a stack so that it can backup from a misguided choice.

Hill-climbing problem solvers act inappropriately when the successors of the current and best-rated node are rated less than its sibling nodes. Hill climbing always pursues the highest-rated successors of the current node. Backtracking hill climbing pushes the successor nodes in sorted order onto the end of a stack. An alternative is to merge the successors with the entire list so far. That variation is called best-first search.

Related to hill-climbing methods are those for finding shortest paths in a graph from a start node to a goal node. These methods build candidate paths piecewise, using the dynamic programming principle to prune all but the shortest path to any node. We considered two methods for this, Dijkstra's method (SP-1) and SP-2. Both methods have worst-case time N, where N is the number of arcs. For trees (such as spanning trees of graphs), this is sometimes expressed as b^d where b is the branching factor of the tree and d is the depth. For SP-2, the best-case time is d, the length of a solution.

The A* algorithm is a shortest-path algorithm that uses a heuristic function to estimate the remaining distance to a goal. It produces optimal solutions if the estimate of distance remaining to a goal can be guaranteed to be a lower bound on the actual distance. The complexity of A* is exponential in the worst case. However, both the worst-case and mean time complexity of A* can be much better if the error in the heuristic function is very small. As error in the heuristic function increases, the performance of A* undergoes a phase transition in complexity from linear to exponential in the length of a solution.

Determining the best direction is a key issue in all of the directed search methods. The issue is akin to one that people often face in their own problem solving. We say that people are shortsighted when they are distracted by the local situation at the expense of the bigger picture. A shortsighted evaluation function cannot see past a local hill to the greater mountain beyond. In the match methods, the issue arises in the comparison of states to yield differences. An example of this was the arch-making problem that showed why focusing on the immediate differences can be counterproductive. We sometimes need to retreat from a goal to find a better approach to that goal.

Building robust and adequate models is hard work, and in many cases, we do not yet know how to do it. In the later chapters, we will see that some harder problems yield better to approaches that enable us to represent and reason using multiple models. Hill climbing and related methods are unsuitable for doing the whole job, but they can be well suited for specialized parts of it. Returning to our visual metaphor, the fix is not just new glasses to fix our short-sighted methods, but rather multiple pairs of glasses that give us several perspectives on the problems. Seldom does a single search method provide an adequate problem-solving framework for a complex task. More often, the solving of large problems can be divided into the solving of a heterogenous set of subproblems. The basic search methods described in this section are often useful for solving specialized parts of larger problems.

Exercises for Section 2.3

■   **Ex. 1**   *[CD-05] Warm-up Exercises about Directed Search.* Determine whether each of the following statements is true or false. If a statement is ambiguous, explain your answer briefly.

(a) *True or False.* A method for exhaustive, backtracking hill climbing wastes computational resources. (Assume that solutions need not occur only on the highest peak.)

(b) *True or False.* Except in domains with special properties, simple hill climbing, like simple match, performs an incomplete search.

(c) *True or False.* At each cycle, best-first search expands the highest-rated successor of the current node.

(d) *True or False.* In general, tree search methods that use only a constant amount of storage (independent of problem size) perform incomplete searches.

(e) *True or False.* The dynamic programming principle is that once a path to a node is found, all longer paths to it can be discarded in the search.

Ex. 2   *[CD-05] More Warm-up Exercises.* Determine whether each of the following statements is true or false. If a statement is ambiguous, explain your answer briefly.

(a) *True or False.* Simple hill climbing and other local optimization approaches can prematurely reach a solution from which no further optimization can be achieved, even though more time is available.

(b) *True or False.* A* is an anytime search method.

(c) *True or False.* The worst-case complexity of A* is linear if the heuristic function has constant absolute error.

(d) *True or False.* The worst-case complexity of A* is exponential if the relative error of the heuristic function is bounded by a a constant.

Ex. 3   *[CD-15] Beam Search.* One problem with hill climbing is that the number of nodes can become unmanageable if there is a great deal of branching and the search is deep. **Beam search** is intended to cope with such situations.

Figure 2.87 presents a method for beam search. This method employs two lists. A list of size w is used to hold the best w successors at the next level. The search space is assumed to be a tree. (If the search space is a graph, then additional provisions must be made to prune nodes that have been visited previously.)

(a) If w is the beam width, b is the branching factor of the tree, and d is the depth of the tree, what is the maximum number of nodes evaluated with the evaluation function at each level? What is the maximum number of nodes evaluated in the entire search tree for beam search?

To carry out a satisficing beam search:

1. Allocate two lists of w elements, called the current list and the successor list.

2. Initialize both lists with placeholder nodes, which are distinguishable nodes that give the lowest possible value for the evaluation function.

3. Replace the first element of the current list with the root node.

4. Search: Until the current list is empty or the first element is a placeholder node do

5. begin

6.   Pop a node from the front of the current list.

7.   If solution-tester(node) then exit with success returning node.

8.   Else for each of the node's successors do

9.   begin

10.   Measure the successor with the evaluation function.

11.   Merge the successor in decreasing order into the successor list. (If the list is full, the last member is lost. This ensures that the successor list never contains more than w nodes.)

12.   end

13.   end

14. If the successor list contains only placeholder nodes, then exit with failure.

     /* Here to swap lists and repeat the process for the next generation of the beam. */

15. Replace the current list with the successor list.

16. Reinitialize the successor list with placeholder nodes.

17. Go to Search—start the search of the next level of the tree.

FIGURE 2.87.   Method for satisficing beam search.

(b) Compare beam search with best-first search. Specifically, describe how their operations are similar and different. Then compare the thoroughness of the two methods and their space complexities.

(c) Would an exhaustive version of beam search be a good idea? Why or why not?

Ex. 4   [*!-CD-20*] *Width-limited Best-first Search.* The space requirements for the stack in best-first search can become quite large if the search tree has a high branching factor.

(a) A satisficing method for carrying out width-limited best-first search (WLBFS) is presented in Figure 2.88. Explain briefly what the method does. How does its operation differ from simple best-first search?

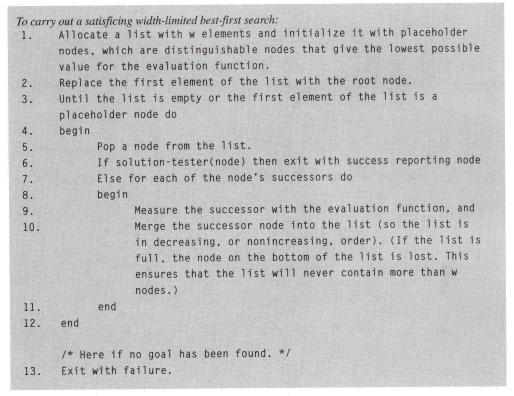

To carry out a satisficing width-limited best-first search:
1. Allocate a list with w elements and initialize it with placeholder nodes, which are distinguishable nodes that give the lowest possible value for the evaluation function.
2. Replace the first element of the list with the root node.
3. Until the list is empty or the first element of the list is a placeholder node do
4. begin
5.   Pop a node from the list.
6.   If solution-tester(node) then exit with success reporting node
7.   Else for each of the node's successors do
8.   begin
9.   Measure the successor with the evaluation function, and
10.   Merge the successor node into the list (so the list is in decreasing, or nonincreasing, order). (If the list is full, the node on the bottom of the list is lost. This ensures that the list will never contain more than w nodes.)
11.   end
12. end

    /* Here if no goal has been found. */
13. Exit with failure.

FIGURE 2.88. Satisficing method for width-limited best-first search.

(b) What is the space complexity of width-limited best-first search? Why does this method reduce both the space complexity and the time complexity for best-first search?

(c) Could width-limited best-first search terminate without finding the optimal solution? If yes, describe briefly the conditions under which this would occur.

(d) Briefly, compare the operation of WLBFS with beam search. Will the two methods always find the same results? If not, describe a case in which they would get different results.

Ex. 5 [10] *Shortest Path.* Figure 2.89 defines a shortest-path problem.

(a) What path will SP-2 find from Piglet's house to Christopher Robin's house? (*Note:* Just present the results in the form of path showing the nodes in order on the shortest path found and its total length without showing all the intermediate computations.)

(b) Are there any other paths of equal length? If yes, why does the method not find them?

■ **Ex. 6** [CD-CP-20] *The A* Algorithm.* A* uses the estimate of total path length (the length of the path plus an estimate of remaining distance) to order the choice of which nodes to expand next in the list.

(a) Which step(s) in the A* method embody the dynamic programming principle? Which steps embody the use of an estimate of remaining path length?

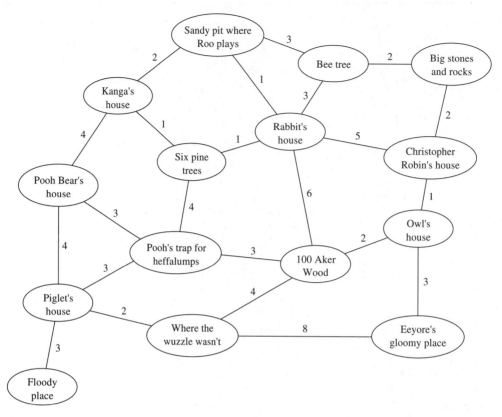

FIGURE 2.89. Map showing paths near where Winnie-the-Pooh lives.

(b) Figure 2.90 gives a minimum-path problem. Nodes are identified by their labels. Numbers along the arcs indicate incremental path lengths; numbers in parentheses indicate estimates of the distance from a node to the goal state *H*.

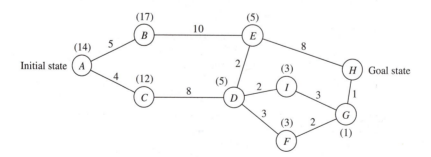

FIGURE 2.90. Sample problem for A*. The numbers in parentheses are estimates of distance to the goal state.

The following table traces the operation of A* on the sample problem. Fill in the missing entries (marked by xxx) until the method terminates.

Cycle	Node			List
	Successor	Accum. Dist.	Estimated Total	
1	A			C B
	B	5	22	
	C	4	16	
2	C			D B
	D	12	17	
3	D			I F E B
	xxx	xxx	xxx	
	xxx	xxx	xxx	
	xxx	xxx	xxx	
4	xxx			xxx
	xxx	xxx	xxx	
5	G			xxx
	xxx	xxx	goal	
6	F			xxx
	xxx	18 (too long)		
7	xxx			xxx
	xxx	xxx (too long)		
8	xxx			
	E	xxx		

(c) List the nodes along the minimum length path from *A* to *H*. How long is the path?

(d) Which is better in A*, underestimating or overestimating remaining path length? Why? Under what circumstances will A* find a solution with the minimum-length path?

■ **Ex. 7** [*15*] *Means-ends Analysis.* Figure 2.91 shows an operator-difference table for guiding the behavior of a hungry but strangely robotic agent.

(a) The agent starts in the state of being hungry, without money but having credit, and being in the office. Roughly, his goal is to have a meal. The only property of the goal state that matters is not being hungry. Present a diagram of the plan showing both the reactive and planning interpretations; that is, showing the order that operations are planned as well as the order that they would be carried out later by the agent. Leave in any redundant steps such as for unneeded travel that might be removed later by a plan optimizer. Pay attention to the left-to-right priority order of operators in the table.

(b) The difference table has no provisions for getting a snack from a canteen machine. Create two new operators: eat-snack and buy-snack. The eat-snack operator should have the prerequisite of having a snack and should remove the difference "being hungry." The buy-snack operator should have the prerequisite of having change and should remove the difference "need snack."

(c) In what way does the placement of the two operators of part b in the difference table matter? How do alternative placements influence the plans that the agent will make?

Ex. 8 [*CD-10*] *Limitations of Means-ends Analysis.* Although means-ends analysis can be used for simple planning tasks, its facilities for representation are primitive compared with what is used in newer planning systems. For example, in means-ends analysis the plan itself is not represented explicitly in a way that enables the problem solver to analyze dependencies and other relationships between goals and steps. Rather, a plan simply unfolds as means-

Difference	Eat-in-cafeteria	Get-Utensils	Buy-lunch	Buy-soft-drink	Get-change	Use-money-machine	Walk
Hungry	X						
Need utensils		X					
Need food			X				
Thirsty				X			
Need change					X	X	
Need money						X	
Not at right location							X
Prerequisites	In cafeteria Have food Have utensils	In cafeteria	Have lunch money In cafeteria	Have change In cafeteria	Have money At change machine	Have credit At money machine	

FIGURE 2.91.   Operator-difference table for the lunch task.

ends analysis runs; even saving the plan requires an additional recording process. In this exercise, we consider some inadequacies of means-ends analysis for planning tasks.

(a) In the travel planning example, the take-plane operator has preconditions that the luggage be ready. Given that some trips do not require any luggage and some traveling can be done by other means than planes, this appears to be a bug in the difference table. Briefly, what issues related to dimensions of representation are problematic in this formulation from a knowledge-engineering point of view?

(b) In real activities things go awry, so that replanning is required. Suppose in the conference travel example that the traveler arrived and discovered that there was no room at the hotel. Suppose further that the traveler had friends locally and was able to make arrangements to stay with them. Briefly, explain some reasoning that a traveler could use to switch accommodations without flying home and back again (as backtracking in means-ends analysis would seem to require).

(c) The difference table for the conference travel task was organized so a credit card would be used in preference to a trip to the bank. However, some travelers prefer not to use credit, and some expenses (such as a taxi) cannot typically be paid with a credit card. What if the get-cash operator withdrew only enough funds from the bank for the immediate purpose? Explain why the traveler could even become stranded or make unnecessary taxi trips. Give examples of additional heuristics and planning tactics a traveler should use to avoid these problems.

Ex. 9   *[CD-!-15] Nonlinear Planning.* Much of the planning research in AI in the 1970s was based on reasoning in very simple domains. Figure 2.92 illustrates a problem in "Blocks World" about rearranging blocks. In this problem, the emphasis is on the use of knowledge about the interactions among plan steps to guide planning. There are two operators: put-on and clear-top. Put-on puts one block on top of another one and has the precondition that the tops of both blocks must be clear. Clear-top removes a block from the top of another one

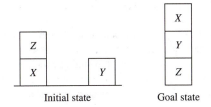

Initial state   Goal state

FIGURE 2.92. A Blocks World problem.

and puts it at some empty place on the table. It has the precondition that the block it moves must itself be clear.

In carrying out any plan for solving this problem we assume that the agent will ultimately perform one step at a time and therefore will carry out the instructions in some linear order. However, during the planning process an appropriate linear ordering of steps is usually not known at the onset. One strategy is to organize the steps in a partial ordering—linearizing the plan only as indicated by an analysis of the interactions among the steps. Thus, a network of ordering relations is an intentional representation of a class of possible plans.

Following this approach, the first elaboration of the plan is given in Figure 2.93. The fan-out (or fork) node at the beginning and the fan-in (or join) node at the end are used to anchor the partial ordering relations.

(a) Refine the structure by filling in steps with the operations to achieve these goals and also steps for satisfying their preconditions. Indicate the weakest ordering relations among the steps that are necessary. (In other words, impose no more order than is needed.) Omit steps to satisfy preconditions that are already satisfied in the initial step.

(b) A next step in planning is to look for interactions among the steps. How do the two steps (put-on *X Y*) and (put-on *Y Z*) interfere with each other? Why should (put-on *Y Z*) be done before (put-on *X Y*)?

(c) What further interactions are there among the partially ordered plan steps? What further candidates for ordering relations are there? Briefly, analyze the interactions. Is there a linear ordering that does not undo preconditions or undo the work of the plan steps? Show your resulting plan.

■ **Ex. 10**   *[CD-!-CP-10] Using Choice Points with Hill Climbing.* One key to reducing the space requirements of depth-first search is to represent nodes on the stack in terms of choice points rather than in terms of extensional lists.

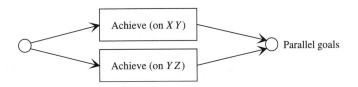

FIGURE 2.93.   First version of the nonlinear plan.

(a) Under what circumstances would this implementation technique be of little value for backtracking hill climbing?

(b) One complication for backtracking hill climbing is that the method needs to extract the individual successor nodes from a choice point in an order that depends on their evaluations. This requires some way of determining which nodes in a choice point have already been pursued. How might this be done without incurring a worst-case storage cost per choice point that is proportional to the branching factor?

Ex. 11 *[CD-!-CP-10] Using Choice Points with Best-First Search.* In best-first search the next node to be taken must be the highest-rated node still on the stack.

(a) Briefly explain how a method could determine which choice point to open next.

(b) There are three required operations on the choice points in best-first search. One operation (discussed in part a) is to find the choice point with the highest next node to pursue. The second operation is to extract the highest-rated node from the choice point. The third operation is to insert the choice point back into some data structure for the next cycle.

Briefly describe a data structure for organizing the choice points that makes it unnecessary to search through all of them when a node is selected and that does not incur the cost of sorting the choice points after a node is expanded.

Ex. 12 *[05] Strategic Retreat.* In many real problems, a strategic retreat is sometimes necessary. One must seem to move away from a goal (overriding some simple comparator or evaluation function) in order to achieve the goal. Consider the problem of finding a path to a room that is the goal state. The goal room is locked and the key to the room is located in some distant room. The goal of the problem is to be inside the goal room, as suggested by Figure 2.94.

Possible operators for the problem are as follows.

MOVE (from.position to.position)
OPEN (unlocked.door)
PICKUP (object at.position)
UNLOCK (locked.door key)

(a) Briefly, in what way does this problem present representation or solution difficulties for simple match? What difficulties does it present to simple and backtracking hill climbing? (*Note*: Do not describe a solution in detail. Just describe the main issues.)

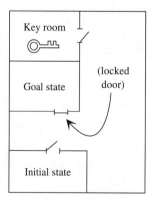

FIGURE 2.94. Strategic retreat.

(b) What provisions does means-ends analysis have for this kind of problem? Briefly describe the salient issues in encoding the operators and difference table to enable a strategic retreat to fetch the key.

Ex. 13 [10] *Weighted Heuristic A**. This section presents two formulations of numeric weighting for altering the effects of the contributions of g and h in the weighted heuristic version of A*.

(i) $f_1(n,w) = (1-w) g(n) + wh(n)$
(ii) $f_2(n,v) = g(n) + vh(n)$, $v > 0$

Show that these are equivalent. Explain your answer, briefly.

Hint: It is enough to show that for each possible assignment of a value to w (or v), there is an assignment to v (or w) that causes the same search behavior. Your argument should be independent of n.

Ex. 14 [10] *Weighted Heuristic Search with Constant-Exact Relative Error*. Professor Digit claims that the weighted heuristic formulation of A* has complexity linear in the length of the solution path when the heuristic function has constant-exact relative error.

Specifically he claims that if h has constant-exact relative error c, where $c < 1$, then the weighted heuristic version of A* will expand only nodes on an optimal path if

$$v = 1 / (1-c)$$

(a) Is he correct? Briefly prove the theorem or give a counterexample.
(b) Assuming that the theorem is correct, is it significant? Explain briefly.

Ex. 15 [M-10] *Bounds on A* Search*. The time complexity of A* search depends on the error of the heuristic function. This exercise considers some examples of bounds on it.

Suppose we are given that

$$h^*(n) - h(n) \leq d \, N^{1/2}$$

where d is the distance to the goal and N is the depth of the solution. Give a bound on the worst-case time complexity of A* in this case. Briefly explain your result.

2.4 *Hierarchical Search*

The qualifier *hierarchical* as applied to search methods means the method divides the search into subproblems recursively. This section revisits and unifies results about hierarchical search from earlier sections and extends these results to develop models of hierarchical planning.

Search Trees and Sub-Exponential Search

The time complexity of a search method is estimated by counting the number of nodes the method visits in a search tree. The counting approach is suitable for either of the two interpretations of search trees: either that solutions are a subset of the terminal nodes or that solutions are paths from the root to such a terminal node.

For simplicity we assume that a search tree has a uniform branching factor of b, is balanced, and has a depth of d. In these circumstances the best case is when the search takes a direct no-miss route to a solution yielding a search complexity of $O(d)$. The worst-case arises when every node in the tree must be visited before reaching a solution, yielding a search complexity of

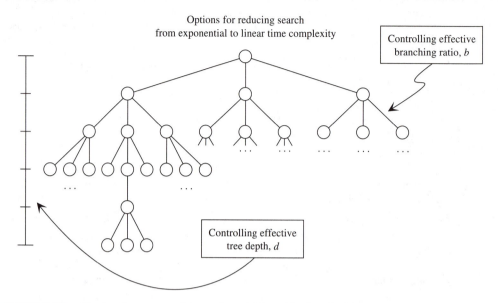

FIGURE 2.95. Confronting exponential searches with logarithmic reductions. To reduce search complexity, we can reduce the effective b, reduce the effective d, or reduce both.

$O(b^d)$. We refer to these extremes as the **linear** and the **exponential** cases, meaning linear in the depth of the tree or exponential in it. We try to arrange matters so performance of a search tends toward the linear case rather than the exponential one.

A useful way to think about search reduction is that fast methods counter exponential complexity by reducing the two search tree parameters of Figure 2.95: the effective branching factor, b; the effective depth, d; or both. Figure 2.96 summarizes how different search methods in this chapter reduce complexity by controlling the effective values of these parameters. These parameters determine how the worst-case time of the methods scale. The whole point of hierarchical methods, however, is to sidestep the worst-case exponential performance using heuristic knowledge. Each method has an **order parameter** that governs the quality of the heuristic knowledge.

To review briefly the approaches in Figure 2.96, we begin with A*. The performance of A* is determined by the error characteristics of its heuristic estimator as discussed in Section 2.3. This error is the order parameter that governs performance. The best case is where there is perfect knowledge, that is, when $h = h^*$. In this case the search complexity is $O(d)$. In the case where $h = 0$, A* is still admissible but it reduces to SP-2 with exponential worst-case performance. The trade-off between the precision of h and A*'s complexity is **inelastic**. If the error $h^* - h$ is bounded by a constant c, then the complexity is $O(b^{cd})$. Search can be contained to the linear case if error is no more than inversely proportional to the distance from the goal. Thus, a small change in error yields a large change in complexity so performance is subject to phase transitions leading from linear to exponential complexity. These results have been shown to apply both to worst-case and average analysis of A*. To summarize in the terms of Figure 2.96, A* achieves efficiency by controlling b—the effective branching ratio. If the error in h is too great, the search includes many "garden paths" and its complexity becomes exponential.

Relatively Slow Method	Faster Method	Tree Parameters Controlled	Order Parameters
SP-2	A*	b	Error $|h - h^*|$
Simple G&T	Hierarchical G&T	b	p—probability of not pruning early
Simple match	Hierarchical match	d	Number of well-spaced planning islands
Means-ends analysis	Hierarchical planning	b, d (k—expansion ratio, l—number of levels)	p—probability of not backtracking between levels

FIGURE 2.96.   How particular search methods fend off exponential complexity. Hierarchical planning is analyzed later in this section.

Although the hierarchical generate-and-test and A* are very different methods, the complexity results take the same form. Hierarchical generate-and-test is called hierarchical because of its ability to reason about classes of candidates corresponding to branches of the search. Search reduction is achieved when early pruning eliminates large subtrees. The order parameter governing performance is the probability that the method prunes fruitless branches. As this parameter approaches $1/b$, the search becomes exponential. Without early pruning, hierarchical generate-and-test degrades to simple generate-and-test. Our analysis showed that its performance varies from exponential to linear search, depending on the probability of early pruning.

In contrast with A* and hierarchical generate-and-test, hierarchical match limits the number of nodes visited by controlling d rather than b, or by controlling effective depth rather than effective branching ratio. As discussed in Section 2.3, hierarchical match is given an abstract solution that it uses to generate planning islands. The effective value of d is reduced because these islands divide the tree into sections that are searched separately. In this way the large search tree of depth d is replaced by $m + 1$ search trees of depth d/m, reducing complexity to $O((m + 1)b^{d/m})$.

If planning islands are a good idea at one level, they may be an even better idea at multiple levels. This leads to **hierarchical planning**, which we consider next. As explained in the following, the key control parameters for reducing the exponential search are the expansion ratio and the number of levels and these relate directly to b and d. The quality of the abstraction can be characterized by the probability of backtracking across levels, and this, then, is an order parameter of the method.

Hierarchical Planning

Hierarchical planning extends hierarchical match. Both methods reduce the complexity of planning by building from intermediate planning islands. Two features distinguish hierarchical plan-

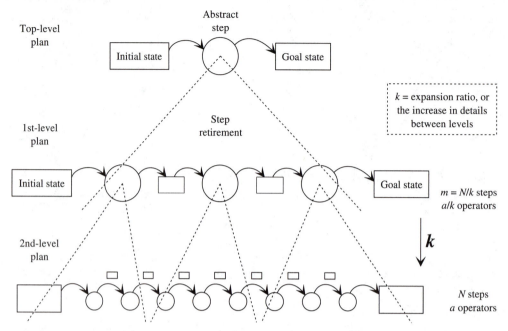

FIGURE 2.97.   Planning tree for two-level hierarchical planning. The circles indicate intermediate steps, at which operations are performed. The squares indicate states. The dashed lines indicate refinements in the plan. Hierarchical planning expands a plan by dividing it into subproblems, which it solves (mostly) independently. This figure shows one intermediate level of hierarchical planning. The approach can be applied with many intermediate levels.

ning from hierarchical match. First, in hierarchical planning the abstract plans are generated and progressively computed from goals, whereas in hierarchical match the abstract plans are given as fixed skeletal plans. Furthermore, hierarchical planning can use multiple levels of abstraction whereas hierarchical match is limited to only one.

A word about different kinds of tree diagrams for hierarchical planning is appropriate at this point, because the shift in notation is often misunderstood. Figure 2.97 is a **planning tree**. A planning tree is orthogonal to a search tree such as the one in Figure 2.95 where we used the terms b and d. The root node in Figure 2.97 represents a **universal plan** and is a technical convenience. The **detailed plan** at the bottom of Figure 2.97 corresponds to search tree of Figure 2.95. Assuming that planning proceeds from the earliest to the latest step, the root of the tree in Figure 2.95 corresponds to the leftmost node in this detailed plan. The branches of that search tree are not shown, except for those along a successful path. Thus, this interpretation of Figure 2.95 treats a solution as a path to a terminal node, where failed branches off the successful path are not shown. The branching ratio, b, corresponds to the number of possible operators, a, of the planning tree. The depth, d, of Figure 2.95 corresponds to the length of the plan, N, in Figure 2.97. Translating our terms for the linear and exponential cases of Figure 2.95 to hierarchical planning, a solution in time $O(N)$ corresponds to the linear case and a solution in time $O(a^N)$ corresponds to the exponential case.

To carry out hierarchical planning:
```
 1.     For each level of abstraction do
 2.     begin
 3.             For each step in the plan at this level except the last one do
 4.             begin
 5.                     Refine an initial state for the next (more detailed)
                        level.
 6.                     Refine a goal state corresponding to the prerequisites
                        of the next step.
 7.                     Retrieve the appropriate operators for the next level.
 8.                     Using means-ends analysis, search for a plan at the next
                        level to fill in detailed plan steps up to the next goal
                        state.
 9.                     If the goal is not reached, then exit with failure.
10.             end
11.     end
12.             Exit with success. (A solution has been found.)
```

FIGURE 2.98.   A simplistic method for hierarchical planning. This version is strictly top-down, length-first, with no provision for backtracking between levels.

Figure 2.98 sketches a method for hierarchical planning. It conveys the essentials of a simple, top-down length-first approach. This treatment is generalization of means-ends analysis. However, the details of the search method are not crucial to the analysis.

After formulating a complete plan at the most abstract level, hierarchical planning augments the state and operator descriptions and fills in the details between the abstract steps. This is called **plan refinement**. The problem of filling in the gap between two abstract operators is called a **gap subproblem**. The method in Figure 2.98 assumes that the individual gap subproblems can be solved without significant interaction and that there is no backtracking across levels. Subsequent search creates a complete plan corresponding to the bottom-level plan in the figure, which has more detail than the top-level plan. This process continues through successive levels of abstraction until a complete and sufficiently detailed plan is formulated.

To summarize, three important assumptions are made by this method:

- Downward refinement: There is no backtracking across abstraction levels.
- Subproblem independence: Gap subproblems can be solved without significant interactions.
- Monotonicity: The work done at an abstract level is not undone during refinement.

Unless otherwise stated, these assumptions are made by all the hierarchical planning methods in this section.

The amount of detail increases with each level of the plan. In the ideal models of hierarchical planning that we develop in the following, we use the term k to refer to an **expansion ratio** representing the increase in the amount of specification between successive layers.

There are several key questions about hierarchical planning. How many planning islands should there be in a level? Is there an optimal number of islands? How many levels of abstraction should there be? To what extent can we reduce search complexity by controlling these factors? How much does search complexity increase if we allow some backtracking across levels of abstraction or some interactions in solving plans for separate gap subproblems?

In following sections, we use variations of the method in Figure 2.98 to develop models for predicting the performance of hierarchical planning. The methods vary in terms of whether the number of operators (corresponding to b) is uniform across levels of abstraction. The methods also vary in whether backtracking between levels is permitted.

2.4.1 *Two-Level Planning*   ADVANCED

In hierarchical planning and matching, each node at the abstract level expands to a larger number of nodes one level down. We begin with the case where there is one intermediate abstraction level as in Figure 2.97. This special case is called **two-level planning**. Conventionally, the one-step universal plan at the top is kept as a technical convenience but is ignored in the counting of levels.

Given a fixed space to search, is there an optimal place to locate the abstraction level? Phrased differently, is there an optimum expansion ratio relating the complexity of the abstract level to the complexity of the detailed level? In the following, we develop three analytical models for hierarchical planning to gain quantitative insights about the complexity of hierarchical planning.

The HP-1 Model

We call our first model of hierarchical planning the **HP-1 model**. We assume there is one intermediate abstraction level. The top-level description of the problem contains only the initial state, the goal state, and one step. We call the three levels the top level, the abstract or intermediate level, and the detailed level. There are N steps in the detailed level. This case where there is one intermediate level is similar to the case of hierarchical match, except that a planner must search to create the intermediate level.

We define k as the expansion ratio between the bottom two levels. There are $m = N/k$ states (planning islands) in the intermediate space. There are a operators in the detailed space and a/k operators (but at least 1) in the abstract space. Our goal is to determine whether there is an optimum value for k. The terms for our analysis are summarized in Figure 2.99.

We begin by computing the planning work at the abstract level, w_a. The planner tries each possible operator in turn, performing an exhaustive search of all possible plans that are m steps long. Assuming that the planner must try every possible plan before finding one, this gives us a worst-case estimate as in (1).

$$w_a = (a/k)m = (a/k)(N/k) \tag{1}$$

Similarly, the work at the detailed level of planning consists of refining each of the steps that connect the planning islands. If the islands are equally spaced, the work is divided into m gap

N	Number of steps in the detailed plan.
m	Number of steps in abstract plan.
k	Expansion ratio, $k = n/m$.
a	Number of operators at the detailed level.
w_d	Planning time at the detailed level (detail work).
w_a	Planning time at the abstract level (abstract work).
w_t	Total planning time, $w_d + w_a$ (total work).

FIGURE 2.99. Summary of terms for the analysis of the work in a hierarchical plan with one intermediate level of abstraction.

subproblems, each of which requires n/m detailed steps involving choices among a operators. Thus, the work at the detailed level is given by (2).

$$w_d = m(a^{N/m}) = (N/k)(a^k) \tag{2}$$

This estimate assumes that subproblems are independent. If r gap subproblems interacted, we would have to search for a plan that solves all of them simultaneously. Such a plan would be of length $O(rN/k)$. As this approaches N, the complexity would approach $O(a^n)$, the same as non-hierarchical search. Without independence of subproblems, the abstraction hierarchy does not decompose the problem effectively. Since we assume that the gap subproblems can be solved independently, the total work of planning is the sum of the work at the abstract level and the work at the detailed level, as in (3).

$$w_t = w_a + w_d \tag{3}$$

Our goal is to determine whether there is a value of k that minimizes the total work. Figure 2.100 presents a computation of the total work for a detailed plan with 50 steps and 20 possible operators. This chart is also displayed graphically in Figure 2.101 using a logarithmic vertical scale. In a later section, we analyze these equations directly.

The figures and graph suggest that there is an optimal value for k when there is one intermediate level. The x-axis in Figure 2.101 is in terms of m, the number of steps at the intermediate level. Since k is inversely proportional to m, k decreases going to the right in this presentation. In our sample problem the total planning work, w_t, is minimized when there are approximately 11 intermediate steps or 10 planning islands. This occurs when $m = 11$ and $k = 4.5$.

Looking back over the equations, we can see that that w_d decreases as m increases because the work per subproblem decreases drastically as the exponent $k = n/m$ decreases. For low values of m and thereby very high values of k, however, there are so many planning islands that very little work is left to do at the detailed level. For example, with $k = 3.3$, finding the planning islands requires the combinatorial construction of a 15-step plan, which vastly dominates the complexity of constructing of 15 approximately three-step plans. In effect, this low value of k promotes most of the work of hierarchical planning to the abstract level.

			$N = 50, a = 20$	
m	k	w_t	w_a	w_d
2	25	6.7×10^{32}	1	6.7×10^{32}
3	17	1.4×10^{22}	1.7	1.4×10^{22}
4	12.5	7.3×10^{16}	6.5	7.3×10^{16}
5	10	5.1×10^{13}	32	5.1×10^{13}
6	8.3	4.2×10^{11}	1.9×10^{2}	4.2×10^{11}
7	7.1	1.4×10^{10}	1.3×10^{3}	1.4×10^{10}
8	6.3	1.1×10^{9}	1.1×10^{4}	1.1×10^{9}
9	5.6	1.5×10^{8}	1.0×10^{5}	1.5×10^{8}
10	5.0	3.3×10^{7}	1.0×10^{6}	3.2×10^{7}
11	**4.5**	**2.1×10^{7}**	**1.2×10^{7}**	9×10^{6} ← minimum w_t
12	4.2	1.5×10^{8}	1.5×10^{8}	3.1×10^{6}
13	3.8	2.0×10^{9}	2.0×10^{9}	1.3×10^{6}
14	3.6	3.0×10^{10}	3.0×10^{10}	6.2×10^{5}
15	3.3	4.7×10^{11}	4.7×10^{11}	3.2×10^{5}

FIGURE 2.100. Work in hierarchical planning with one level of abstraction for 50 detailed states and 20 detailed operators. The total work, w_t, is the sum of the work at the abstract level, w_a, and the work at the detailed level, w_d.

The Courier Model

To facilitate finding a closed-form complexity analysis of two-level planning we now simplify the model. This second model of planning is called either the **courier model** or the **macro model**. This model follows Korf (1987). The courier model rests on somewhat different assumptions about the work of planning. It plans with macro-operators.

In the courier model, the states in the abstract space are a subset of the states in the detailed space. Figure 2.102 illustrates this model graphically. We can think of it as a model of a travel planning problem for an overnight package delivery service. The abstract states correspond to big cities, connected by major routes. These are shown as the large spots in Figure 2.102, connected by thick arcs. The thick arcs correspond to abstract operations, going from one abstract state to another. All of the abstract states are reachable, but not necessarily in a single step from another one. The detailed states correspond to smaller cities portrayed as smaller spots in Figure 2.102. They are connected by smaller arcs, which also connect them potentially to the abstract states.

More formally, the abstract states are *distributed uniformly* among the detailed states. There are n_s detailed states and m_s abstract states. We distinguish n_s, the number of states in the space, from n_p, the expected number of steps in a plan. This latter term, n_p, corresponds to n in the analysis of HP-1. We define the state expansion ratio, k_s, as the ratio of states in the bottom two levels as follows:

$$k_s = n_s / m_s \qquad (4)$$

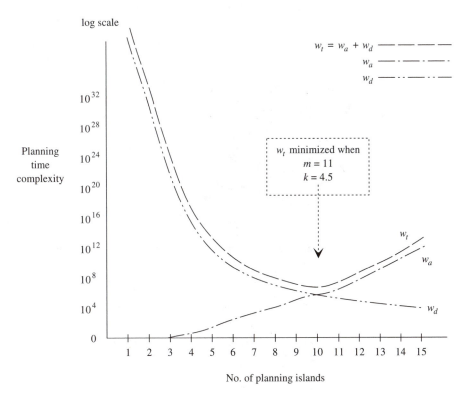

FIGURE 2.101. Work in hierarchical planning with one level of abstraction for 50 detailed states and 20 detailed operators. The total work of hierarchical planning in this example, w_t, is minimized when $m = 11$ and $k = 4.5$.

Planning in this model involves the following steps: planning from a detailed initial state to some abstract state (S_1), planning from the detailed goal state to some abstract state (S_2), and searching in the abstract space between S_1 and S_2. By analogy with a package delivery service, this corresponds to three stages: getting the package from the sender to the airport, flying it to the closest major city, and then delivering it from the closest airport to its ultimate destination.

The courier model differs from HP-1 in the way that it accounts for the work of planning. The courier model assumes that the refinement of the plan at the detailed level is limited to the two ends of the plan. A planner must find a route from the detailed initial state to one of the abstract states and from the goal state to one of the abstract states. The intermediate steps do not need to be refined, and the path joining them can be confined to operations at the intermediate level. By contrast, in the HP-1 model there is also planning work to be done at the detailed level between each of the abstract states. The terms of analysis for the two-level courier model are given in Figure 2.103.

A second simplification from HP-1 is that we dispense with accounting directly for the number of operators, a. In the courier model, we account for work simply in terms of the number

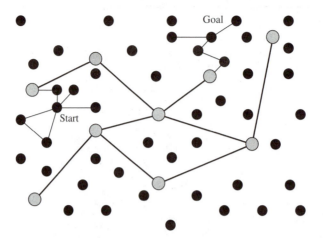

FIGURE 2.102.   A simpler, alternative model for analyzing the optimal value of k for one intermediate level in hierarchical planning.

of states we expect to visit in a random search. When we plan a move to another state at the detailed level, the probability that that state is a member of the intermediate space is simply $1/k_s$. This tells us that the expected number of states generated in a random search of the detailed space before encountering an abstract state is k_s. The work at the detailed level is the work to search from the detailed initial state to S_1 plus the work to search from the detailed goal state to S_2. Thus, the average w_d is given by equation (5).

$$w_d = 2k_s \qquad\qquad\qquad (5)$$

At the abstract level, we need to find a path between the two abstract states nearest the initial state and the goal state. As before, the work is the number of states the planner expects to visit. We assume the search is random so that on average a planner must search through half of the abstract states. There are n_s/k_s abstract states. This work is given by equation (6).

n_s	Number of possible states in the detailed space.
n_p	Number of steps in the detailed plan.
m_s	Number of possible states in the abstract space.
k_s	Space expansion ratio, $k_s = n_s/m_s$.
S_1, S_2	The detailed initial and final states, respectively.
w_d	Planning time at the detailed level (detail work).
w_a	Planning time at the abstract level (abstract work).
w_t	Total planning time, $w_d + w_a$ (total work).

FIGURE 2.103.   Summary of terms for the analysis of the work in the two-level courier model of planning.

$$w_a = (n_s/k_s)\,(1/2) = n_s\,/\,(2k_s).\tag{6}$$

As in the HP-1 model, the total work, w_t, is given by the sum of w_d and w_a as shown in equation (7).

$$w_t = w_a + w_d = n_s\,/\,(2k_s) + 2k_s = (n_s/2)\,k_s^{-1} + 2k_s\tag{7}$$

Again we come to the question of what value of k will minimize w_t. In this case, we can determine where the derivative dw_t/dk_s is 0 as in (8) and (9).

$$dw_t/dk_s = -(n_s/2)k_s^{-2} + 2\tag{8}$$
$$dw_t/dk_s = 0 \text{ when } k_s = (1/2)\,n_s^{1/2}\tag{9}$$

Thus, the courier model says the value of k_s that minimizes total work is roughly half of the square root of n_s, when there is one intermediate abstraction level. For this value of k_s, the total work is given by equation (10).

$$w_t = w_a + w_d = n_s\,/\,(2k_s) + 2k_s = 2\,n_s^{1/2}\tag{10}$$

Thus, by optimizing the value of k_s for the courier model we greatly reduce the total work, but not quite to the linear case. In terms of our search trees where $n_s = b^d$, we have reduced the complexity to $O(b^{d/2})$ but not to $O(d)$.

The HP-2 Model

Knoblock (1991) proposed another model of hierarchical planning that we call HP-2. It is closer to HP-1 in its formulation but it is amenable to an analysis drawing on the one we used for the courier model. Again, we focus on the case where there is one intermediate abstraction level.

Unlike the courier model, HP-2 accounts for the work of mapping between the abstract solution and detailed solutions at every step in the plan. Unlike HP-1, it does not assume that the number of possible operators at the abstract level (and thereby the branching ratio in planning) is reduced by k. The terms of analysis for HP-2 are summarized in Figure 2.104.

The expansion ratio k is taken as the *ratio of the solution lengths*, which is the ratio of the length of a solution in the detailed space to the length of a solution in the ground space. Thus, N/k is the length of a solution in the abstract space.

The planner maps a given problem into the most abstract space by deleting information from the initial state and goal that are not relevant to the abstract space. Next it finds a solution to the abstract problem, using the same operators as in the detailed space. Each of the intermediate states in the abstract plan serve as planning islands or goals for subproblems at the lower level in the abstraction hierarchy.

The work in the abstract space, w_a, is the size of the search tree in the abstract space and is given by equation (11).

$$w_a = \sum_{i=1}^{N/k} a^i\tag{11}$$

N	Number of steps in the detailed plan.
$d(S_j,S_j+1)$	Number of steps in the detailed plan between abstract step S_j and S_j+1.
k	Ratio of solution lengths: length of detailed solution / length abstract solution.
k_1, k_2	Two guesses of the value of k at which w_t is minimized. They are $N^{1/2}$ and $.5\,N^{1/2}$, respectively.
w_d	Planning time at the detailed level (detail work).
w_a	Planning time at the abstract level (abstract work).
w_t	Total planning time, $w_d + w_a$ (total work).

FIGURE 2.104.   Summary of terms for the analysis of the work in the two-level HP-2 model of planning.

Each step in the abstract space is used to guide planning at the detailed level. These steps define N/k subproblems at the detailed level. Work at the detailed level amounts to planning between the planning islands, as given by equation (12).

$$w_d = \sum_{j=0}^{N/k-1} \sum_{i=1}^{d(S_j,S_{j+1})} a^i \tag{12}$$

The greater the spacing of two adjacent islands—$d(S_j, S_j + 1)$—the greater the work of planning between them—$O(a^d(S_j, S_j + 1))$. In the best case, the islands are equally spaced and the sub-problems are of equal size, so that the abstract solution divides the problem into N/k planning subproblems each of length k.

The total work is the sum of the work at the abstract level and the detail level. In the ideal case of evenly spaced islands w_t is given by equation (13). Equation (13) also shows the dominating terms—$a^{N/k}$ for w_a and $(N/k)a^k$ for w_d—leading to an expression for the order of the overall complexity.

$$w_t = w_a + w_d = \sum_{i=1}^{N/k} a^i + N/k \sum_{i=1}^{k} a^i = O(a^{n/k}) + O\left((N/k\,)a^k\right) \tag{13}$$

The values of the two terms act differently for increasing k. Work at the abstract level decreases with increasing k, and work at the detailed level increases for increasing k. This observation is analogous to our graphical analysis of HP-1, which led to the prediction of a value of k that minimized total planning work.

By analogy with our analysis of the courier model, the next step would be to differentiate the expression for w_t, seeking a value of k at which the derivative $dw/dk = 0$. Unfortunately, the expression for w_t is more difficult to differentiate for HP-2. However, following Knoblock, we observe that k is bounded by 1 and N. We can try any intermediate value in this range as an estimate for the minimum point. In the analysis of the courier model, the optimum was found at half the square root. By analogy in this model, we first consider the complexity of HP-2 at the square root, or when $k = N/k$, as in equation (14).

$$\text{first guess of minimum point: } k_1 = (N)^{1/2} \tag{14}$$

Although this approach does not guarantee that k_1 achieves the absolute minimum for w_t, it enables us to estimate the order of the complexity at a near-minimum point. Looking at the high-order terms, w_d for this value of k is

$$O(N^{1/2}a^{N^{1/2}})$$

as in equation (15).

$$O(w_d) = O(a^{k_1}) + O(k_1 a^{k_1}) = O((k_1 + 1)\,a^{k_1}) \cong O(N^{1/2}\,a^{N^{1/2}}) \tag{15}$$

This is a substantial reduction from the original complexity of $O(a^N)$. We can perform exactly the same process for another estimate of the minimizing k as in equation (16).

$$\text{second guess of minimum point: } k_2 = .5(N)^{1/2} \tag{16}$$

Again, looking at the terms from equation (15) we have

$$O(w_d) = O(a^{4k_2}) + O(4k_2 a^{k_2}) \cong O(N^{1/2}\,a^{N^{1/2}}) \tag{17}$$

which is the same order estimate discarding constant factors.

To bring us full circle back to our original model for hierarchical planning, HP-1, the same estimates can be tried again. Again we use equations (1) and (2).

$$w_a = (a/k)^m = (a/k)^{(N/k)}$$
$$w_d = m(a^{N/m}) = (N/k)(a^k)$$

Developing an order estimate for this near-minimum point for equations (1) and (2) gives us essentially the same complexity estimates as in equations (15) and (17). It is interesting to compare these numerical estimates with the graphical ones from Figures 2.100 and 2.101. The graphically determined minimizing point of $k \cong 4.5$ lies between $k_1 = (50)^{1/2} = 7.07$ and $k_2 = .5\,(50^{1/2})$, or 3.53.

To summarize, all three models predict a substantial reduction in complexity when an intermediate abstraction level is used to guide planning. In all three models, the total work, w_t, is the sum of the work at the abstract level, w_a, and the work at the detailed level, w_d. With increasing k, w_a increases while w_d decreases. The models predict that there is an intermediate value of k that minimizes w_t. Assuming there is no backtracking across levels, the worst-case complexity for the more realistic models HP-1 and HP-2 occurs near where $k = N^{1/2}$ and the reduced time complexity is $O(N^{1/2}a^{N1/2})$. Under these assumptions, using just one intermediate abstraction level reduces the complexity of planning substantially from the exponential case, although it does not reduce it as low as the linear case where planning time would be $O(N)$. Next we consider the use of multiple levels of abstraction.

2.4.2 *Planning with Multiple Abstraction Levels* ADVANCED

So far our analysis of hierarchical planning has assumed only one intermediate level of abstraction in planning. If the planning island advantage is good for one level, it could be even better to

w_t	Total work across all levels.
j	Number of levels.
k	Expansion ratio across adjacent levels.
n_s	Number of elements in space at most detailed level in courier model.
N, n_p	Number of plan steps at most detailed level in HP-2 and the courier model, respectively.

FIGURE 2.105.   Summary of terms for the analysis of the work in a hierarchical plan with multiple levels of abstraction.

have multiple levels. How many levels should there be? Just as there can be too many intermediate planning islands, perhaps there can be too many levels. In the following we derive quantitative answers for this question from the models.

The Multi-Level Courier Model

In the analysis of two-level planning, the courier model was less realistic than the other two models but more tractable for analysis. A closed form expression of complexity was found for the courier model. We used its closed-form solution to estimate a minimum point for the more complex models. The same situation holds for the analysis of multiple-level planning. The courier model provides us with a simple enough framework to answer directly our question about the optimum number of levels.

Figure 2.105 summarizes some of the terminology for our analysis of multiple abstraction levels. The task at each level is to find a path from the initial and goal states to a state in the space above; at the top level, we assume for simplicity that the task is to find a path to a single intermediate state. Let k_i be the expansion factor from level k_{j-1} to k_j. The total work, w_t, is the sum of the work at all of the intermediate levels of abstraction as given by (18).

$$w_t = 2k_1 + 2k_2 + \ldots + 2k_j = \sum_{i=1}^{j} 2k_i \tag{18}$$

We omit the term for $w_a = n_s/(2k)$ from the case of one abstraction level because there is only one intermediate state at the top level. The k_j terms represent the ratios between the number of states between levels and n_s is the total number of states.

Given that there is only one state at the upper level, the product of these ratios must equal the number of states, n_s. From (18) we see that w_t is minimized when the sum of these factors is minimized.

$$n_s = \prod_{i=1}^{j} k_i \tag{19}$$

Next we show that for the minimum value of w_t, the ratios k_j must be equal. Suppose we have two variables, k_1 and k_2, with sums and products such that:

$$P = k_1 k_2 \tag{20}$$
$$S = k_1 + k_2 = k_1 + k_{1-1\,P} \tag{21}$$

where P is a constant. Then,

$$dS/dk_1 = 0 \text{ when } k_1^2 = P \text{ and } k_1 = k_2 = P^{1/2} \tag{22}$$

Thus, the terms must be equal.

We now extend this result to the case of several levels. The proof is by contradiction. Suppose that for the minimum $w_t = 2k_1 + 2k_2 + \ldots + 2k$, two factors k_l and k_m were not equal. We know that the product of the k_j terms must be n_s. We can replace k_l and k_m by $k' = (k_l k_m)^{1/2}$. Using equation (22), we have that $2k' < k_l + k_m$. So w_t was not minimal. So in the minimum w_t, all of the k_j must be equal. The number of levels, j, that minimizes w_t is given by (23) and (24).

$$n_s = k_1 k_2 k_3 \ldots k_j = k^j \tag{23}$$
$$\log_k n_s = j \tag{24}$$

As in our analysis of two-level planning, we compute the minimum total work by taking derivatives. Total work, w_t, is minimized with respect to k when $dw_t/dk = 0$.

$$w_t = 2k_1 + 2k_2 + \ldots + 2k_j = 2kj = 2k \, (\log_k n_s) \tag{25}$$
$$w_t = 2 \, (\log n_s) \, k/(\log k) \tag{26}$$
$$dw_t/dk = 2 \, (\log n_s) \, (\, (\log k)^{-1} - k^{-1} \, (\log k)^{-2}) \tag{27}$$

The minimum occurs when $dw_t/dk = 0$.

$$(\log k)^{-1} = (\log k)^{-2} \tag{28}$$
$$\log k = 1 \tag{29}$$
$$k = e \tag{30}$$

where e is the natural logarithm or approximately 2.71. Finally, the total work in this case, w_t, is given in equation (31).

$$w_t = 2e \log n_s \tag{31}$$

If the number of states in the search space is an exponential function of the number of steps in a plan,

$$n_s = a^{n_p} \tag{32}$$

(where a is the number of operators at the detailed level). Then we have that the time complexity of hierarchical planning in the courier model is $O(n_p)$. In short, by equation (33), we see that this set of circumstances achieves the linear case for hierarchical planning, assuming there is no backtracking across levels.

$$w_t = 2e \log (a^{n_p}) = 2e(\log a)n_p = O(n_p) \tag{33}$$

We cannot do better than this, since even printing out the steps in a plan requires time $O(n_p)$.

In practical domains, the assumptions of this model—such as the availability of evenly spaced abstraction levels and macro-style planning—may not be appropriate. Nonetheless, the result demonstrates in principle how a hierarchical approach can lead to a dramatic decrease in time complexity and suggests how the linear case can be within reach.

The Multi-Level HP-2 Model

We now return to a more realistic model of hierarchical planning to see whether it also admits the reduction to the linear case. In the analysis of the courier model for multiple levels of abstraction, w_t was minimized when k was constant across levels and when the relation between k and j is as given previously in equation (34).

$$\log_k n_s = j \tag{34}$$

Equation (35) suggests an analogous relationship in HP-2 where we substitute N for n_s. Again following Knoblock (1991) and the same strategy as in our analysis of two-level planning for HP-2, we do not prove that this equation necessarily gives the minimum value for w_t. Rather, we use the equation to estimate the values of k and j at which w_t is minimized and use that estimate to compute the order of the complexity in HP-2.

$$\log_k N = j \tag{35}$$
$$k^j = N \tag{36}$$

The estimated near-minimum point from equations (35) and (36) leads to an estimate of w_t. Equation (37) gives an expression for w_t based on counting the search steps for all the levels of abstraction.

$$w_t = \sum_{i=1}^{k} a^i + k \sum_{i=1}^{k} a^i + \ldots + k^2 \sum_{i=1}^{k} a^i + \ldots + k^{j-1} \sum_{i=1}^{k} a^i \tag{37}$$

We ignore the most abstract space containing only one step. The first term in equation (37) accounts for the search in the next most abstract space, which has exactly k steps. Each successive term accounts for the search at successive levels of abstraction. Thus, after a plan is found at the first level of abstraction, planning must take place between each of the planning islands to find a solution at the next level down. There is one term for each of the j levels of hierarchical planning. From equation (37), the order of the complexity of planning follows in equation (38).

$$O(w_t) = O((1 + k + k^2 + k^{j-1})\, a^k = O((1 + k + k^2 + k^{\log k}(N) - 1)\, a^k) \tag{38}$$

Since

$$1 + k + k^2 + \ldots + k^j = (k^{j+1} - 1)\,/\,(k - 1) \tag{39}$$

we substitute in equation (38), yielding

$$O(w_t) = O(\,(k^{\log k(N)} - 1)\,/\,(k - 1)b^k) \tag{40}$$

Simplifying, we have

$$O(w_t) = O((N-1) / (k-1) \, b^k) = O(N) \qquad (41)$$

Given that b and k are constant for a given planning space, we have that time complexity is $O(N)$, which again is the linear case where time is proportional to the length of the plan.

2.4.3 *Planning with Imperfect Abstractions*   ADVANCED

In the preceding analytical models of hierarchical planning, we assume that the abstractions are "perfect." Perfect abstractions yield reliable planning islands as abstract steps from which detailed plans can be constructed unfailingly. With perfect abstractions, the planning islands themselves never come into question. It is never necessary to backtrack from a failure in the planning of detailed steps to the replanning of the abstract steps. Another way to say this is that backtracking need never occur across abstraction levels. This is sometimes called the **downward refinement property (DRP)**.

With perfect abstractions, the preceding methods for hierarchical planning reduce the complexity of planning from $O(a^N)$ to $O(N^{1/2} a^{N1/2})$ for one abstraction level and to $O(N)$ when there are enough abstraction levels. In some planning regimes such as the ideal macro-operators of the courier model, once a plan has been found in the abstract space the existence of a detailed plan is guaranteed. What happens to the complexity of planning when the abstractions are not completely reliable?

Following Williams (1992), we now consider probabilistic models of **imperfect abstraction**. By relaxing the assumption of perfect abstractions, we acknowledge that decisions based on abstraction levels necessarily use incomplete and potentially inadequate information. Under such conditions, hierarachical approaches can suggest the outline of a solution in terms of planning islands but cannot guarantee that the islands lead to solutions. The interested reader can also consult Bacchus and Yang (1992) for an alternative analysis of a probabilistic model, different in particulars but leading to similar results.

For simplicity in the following, we limit our analysis to two-level planning. We are given the probability, p, that each step in the abstract plan can be successfully expanded in the detailed plan. This probability is called the **reliability** of the abstraction. Figure 2.106 summarizes the terms of our analysis of hierarchical planning with imperfect abstractions.

In the terms of our analysis, there are r abstract plans of length s in the abstract space and each step can be expanded successfully with independent probability p. Ideally, the abstract proofs are uncorrelated and each succeeds with probability p^s and fails with probability $1-p^s$. The probability that at least one of the abstract proofs leads to a successful plan is given by equation (42).

$$p_{succ} = 1 - (1 - p^s)^r \qquad (42)$$

Consider the case where $s = 7$ and $r = 5$. Even for p as low as .9, p_{succ} is approximately .96. In short, the probability that an abstraction provides useful guidance can be very close to 1 even though the abstraction is imperfect.

p	Probability that each step in the abstract plan can be successfully expanded at the detailed level ("reliability").
N	Length of a plan (number of plan steps) at the detailed level.
s	Length of a plan at the abstract level.
k	Expansion ratio across adjacent levels, $k = N / s$.
r	Number of plans proposed at the abstract level ("provability").
a	Number of operators at the detailed level.
T	a^k. Average size of the search tree generated for each step of an abstract plan expanded in the detailed space.
$1 \le <q> \le r$	The average trial, in a successful plan at which an abstract plan can be mapped successfully to a detailed plan.
$1 \le <f> \le s$	The average number of steps in a failing trial at which the detailed proof fails.

FIGURE 2.106. Summary of terms for the analysis of the two-level planning with imperfect abstractions.

The Complexity of Planning with Imperfect Abstractions

In Figure 2.107 we consider examples of the garden paths that can arise in two-level planning with imperfect abstractions. This figure shows 4 abstract steps in a completed plan, $A1$ through $A4$, and 20 detailed steps, $d1$ through $d20$. During planning, the tree is incomplete and the search process tries to find a sequence of steps that satisfies the requirements. Following our sketch of hierarchical planning in Figure 2.98, we assume the process is top-down so that the abstract plan $A1$ through $A4$ is completed before any planning at the detailed level is begun. Planning at the detailed level then commences to fill in between the planning islands. Four separate searches are required at the detailed level, corresponding to the four separate five-step groups.

Suppose the search fails during the construction of step $d12$. At this point, the planner has done all of the work of constructing the abstract plan $A1$ through $A4$ as well the detailed plan so far, $d1$ through $d12$. We are given that there are r possible plans at the abstract level. At this point in processing, one of them has failed and another needs to be generated. Different generation

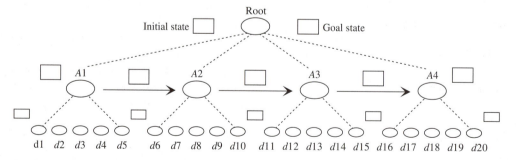

FIGURE 2.107. Examining a point of failure during hierarchical planning with imperfect abstractions. In this example, $A1$ through $A4$ constitutes an abstract plan with $s = 4$, and $d1$ through $d20$ constitutes a detailed plan with $N = 20$. The expansion factor $k = 20 / 4 = 5$.

processes are possible. A simple and general approach would be to start over again at the abstract level and replan to versions of $A1$ through $A4$. In other cases, it would be possible to generate a new abstract plan that preserves abstract steps $A1$ and $A2$ but that makes different choices for $A3$ and $A4$. The main point is that failure at the detailed level can trigger backtracking at the abstract level.

Carefully estimating the time complexity of different variations of hierarchical planning with imperfect abstractions requires a fairly complex counting argument. Our purpose in the following is to sketch the argument—the details are not crucial and the results are qualitatively similar across a wide range of assumptions. Readers with an interest in a detailed derivation can refer to Williams (1992).

There are two extremes in hierarchical planning: the cases where $p = 1$ and $p = 0$. The case where $p = 1$ corresponds to perfect abstraction where the previous $O(N^{1/2}a^N)$ complexity results for two-level planning hold without change. The case where $p = 0$ corresponds to where the abstractions do not help at all. Here the planner must resort to $O(a^N)$ exhaustive search in the detailed space. Realistic planning lies between these extremes. As p ranges from 0 to 1 the complexity of hierarchical planning should range from exponential to the quasi-quadratic limit for two-level planning. By analogy, in multiple-level planning the complexity ranges from the exponential case to the linear case. What remains in the analysis is to determine the complexity of the intermediate points.

We can sharpen our expectations about intermediate points by considering results from the methods in Figure 2.96. For A*, complexity is extremely sensitive to the magnitude of errors in the heuristic estimator, h. For extremely small errors complexity stays near the linear case . As errors grow, there is a rapid phase transition toward exponential complexity. Qualitatively, the same phenomena hold for hierarchical generate-and-test. For small degradations in the probability of early pruning, its complexity quickly transitions to the exponential case. What goes wrong in both methods is that time is wasted going down garden paths, or pursuing fruitless branches in the search. If hierarchical planning follows the same pattern, there should be a threshold in probability, p_{crit}, such that for $p > p_{crit}$ there is an advantage to using even imperfect abstractions. For $p << p_{crit}$, the search cost with imperfect abstraction should be worse than direct search in the detailed space. In the vicinity of p_{crit} a small improvement in probability should significantly reduce the complexity of search.

We now present without proof some of the conclusions of Williams's analysis. Equations 43–45 give the equations for average complexity, which depend on both C_{succ} and C_{fail} where C_{succ} is the average cost of a two-level search and C_{fail} is the average cost of an unsuccessful search. In equation (44) these terms are decomposed further into components of work at the detailed (ground) and abstract levels.

$$C = p_{succ}\, C_{succ} + p_{fail}\, C_{fail} \tag{43}$$
$$C = p_{succ}\, (C_{grd,succ} + C_{abs,succ}) + p_{fail}\, (C_{grd,fail} + C_{abs,fail}) \tag{44}$$

Equation (45) gives a more detailed expression for complexity in this model.

$$C = [((<q> - 1)<f> + s)T + (<q>/r)(a^{s+1} - 1)/(a-1)]\, p_{succ}$$
$$+ [r<f>T + (a^{s+1} - 1)/(a - 1) + (a^N - r)/(2a^N)\, (a^{N+1} - 1)/(a-1)]\, p_{fail} \tag{45}$$

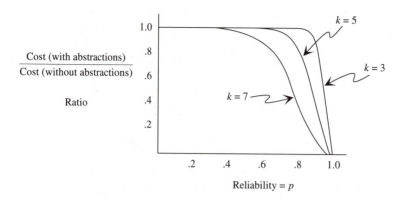

FIGURE 2.108. Ratio of the cost of planning with abstraction to the cost of planning without abstraction relative to reliability, p. The cost is shown for three values of the expansion ratio: $k = 3$, $k = 5$, and $k = 7$ (dark to light). (Adapted from Williams, C., personal communication)

A graphical interpretation as shown in Figure 2.108 illustrates predictions of the model. As expected from our discussion of extreme points, as abstractions become more reliable planning complexity approaches that for perfect abstractions. However, the transition is not gradual. Rather, there is a dramatic reduction in search cost for abstractions above a **critical reliability**. For higher values of k, the reduction in cost happens at somewhat lower values of p. In short, there is the same kind of threshold effect that we have seen for other hierarchical search processes. Relatively small errors in reliability lead to large penalties in planning complexity.

At the time of this writing, interest in the combinatorics of planning with abstractions, particularly with regard to variations in expansion ratios and number of abstraction levels, has been mainly of theoretical concern. In particular, there have been few systematic experiments from which useful data about realistic planning have been available. The development of the theoretical models in this section sets the stage in that it suggests things to look for, control, and measure in such experiments.

Complexity under Realistic Scaling

Before we leave the topic of planning with imperfect abstractions, there is one more matter of interest on the parameters in the models. In using derivatives to estimate the minimal cost, we have implicitly held the reliability (p) and provability (r) constant while varying the expansion ratio (k). In short, we assumed that the probability of needing to backtrack is independent of the strength of the abstraction.

Williams (1992) has observed that this violates intuitions. Rather, one would expect reliability and provability of an abstraction to decrease with its strength. Figure 2.109 shows possible ways that reliability might decay with increasing expansion ratios. It can be shown that when such decays are introduced into the model, the cost of the search is seen to be minimized at some optimum value for the expansion ratio.

Without such a correction to the model, the "optimum" value for an expansion ratio predicted using equation (45) wanders out to very large values. With the correction, the optimum

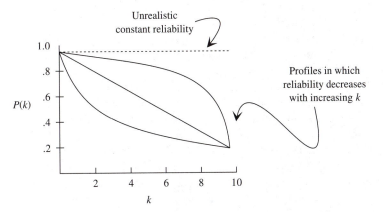

FIGURE 2.109. Possible decay profiles for reliability. (Adapted from Williams, C., *Imperfect Abstraction*, Figure 7.)

stays localized. We can understand this in terms of a competition. If an abstraction is reliable but weak ($p = .9$, $k \cong 1$), the size of the abstract space is comparable to that of the ground space. Thus much of it might need to be searched before a detailed plan can be found. Similarly, if the abstraction is strong but unreliable ($k >> 1$, $p << 1$) it is almost certain that the search will backtrack from many garden paths—leading to an exhaustive search of the ground space. In this way, the decay in probability stabilizes the predictions of the model. The parameters of this decay would be important to determine in an empirical model.

2.4.4 *Summary and Review*

Search trees are characterized by two parameters: their branching factor, b, and their depth, d. The number of nodes in a balanced tree is given by

$$\# \text{nodes} = 1 + b + b^2 + b^3 + \ldots + b^d \tag{46}$$

When finding a solution requires visiting all the nodes of a tree, the complexity is $O(b^d)$. This is called the exponential case. Hierarchical search methods control search by using heuristics that limit the effective values of b and d in the search. The branching factor is limited by the use of heuristics that are highly selective in choosing paths to explore. Depth is limited by heuristics that establish planning islands in the search.

In the beginning of this section we reviewed several basic search methods and their hierarchical counterparts. Whether the hierarchical methods can achieve linear complexity depends on their parameters. We recalled that for A* and hierarchical generate-and-test, there is a critical value of a parameter at which small changes in the value leads to large changes in complexity. If the parameter is above the critical value, performance tends toward the exponential case. Below that value performance tends toward the linear case.

The main part of this section was a presentation and analysis of hierarchical planning. Hierarchical planning extends hierarchical match by using planning islands recursively, so solutions can be created by introducing islands one level at a time. In this way, hierarchical planning limits complexity by controlling both b and d.

We used several different models to analyze the complexity of hierarchical planning. They differ somewhat in their exact assumptions about the work of hierarchical planning and in the tractibility of closed-form analysis, but they are ultimately very similar in their qualitative results. In each model, we showed that when there is one intermediate level (that is, two-level planning), the complexity can be reduced to roughly $O(N^{1/2}a^{N^{1/2}})$, where N is the number of steps in the detailed plan, assuming there is no backtracking across levels. Furthermore, when multiple levels of abstraction are allowed, minimum total work results when levels are spaced evenly for a particular value of k, the expansion ratio of detail between levels. For an optimal value of k, the total work is reduced to $O(N)$, assuming there is no backtracking between levels.

Our next step was to relax the assumption that there is no backtracking across abstraction levels. We modeled the amount of backtracking probabilistically. The revised model exhibits the full range of complexity from the linear case to the exponential case. As in other search problems, the complexity is critically dependent on a model parameter. For hierarchical planning, the crucial parameter is the probability of backtracking. The model predicts that there is a critical probability that demarks a phase transition in the complexity of the search.

Technically, the model is flawed in that it predicts that the optimum value of k rises to higher levels as p is increased. This result is a consequence of a counterintuitive assumption built into the model that the probability of backtracking remains constant with k. When we correct the model to have the probability of backtracking decrease with k, the model stabilizes. This suggests that the decay of p with respect to k is an important additional model parameter.

Exercises for Section 2.4

Ex. 1   [05] *Hierarchical Search Concepts.* For each of the following statements indicate whether it is true or false. If the statement is ambiguous, explain briefly.

(a) *True or False.* Hierarchical methods achieve efficiency by controlling the effective branching factor of the search tree, the effective depth of the search tree, or both.

(b) *True or False.* In the context of search, the term *garden path* refers to a twisting or curved path from the root of the search tree to a solution that is longer than the optimal path.

(c) *True or False.* The "linear case" in hierarchical planning refers to the case where the complexity of the search is linear in the length of a detailed solution, that is, $O(N)$.

(d) *True or False.* The complexity of two-level planning is optimally linear when the abstractions can be shown to be perfect.

(e) *True or False.* In our models for two-level planning, total complexity (w_t) is the sum of the work at the detailed level (w_d) and work at the abstract level (w_a). In general, as the expansion ratio k increases, w_a increases and w_d decreases.

Ex. 2   [CD-10] *Explaining the Basic Phenomena.* This exercise asks you to explain the phenomena that arise in hierarchical search. Please limit your answer to each part to two to three sentences.

(a) Briefly, how do hierarchical methods reduce search at all?

(b) Briefly, how do hierarchical methods fail? That is, why do they not always achieve the linear case of complexity?

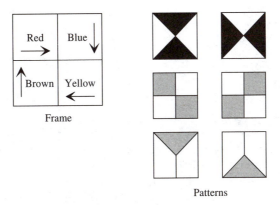

Frame

Patterns

FIGURE 2.110. Patterns for Professor Digit's textile design generator.

(c) Briefly, why is there often a critical value or threshold in the values of a parameter governing hierarchical search, such that small changes in the parameter near the critical value trigger large changes in complexity ?

Ex. 3 [15] *Generating Weaver Patterns*. After visiting and misunderstanding an exhibit on Native American art, Professor Digit took a keen interest in the systematic generation of geometric designs for use in textiles. He has devised an approach based on the use of rotating color applications and a fixed number of patterns for progressive tiling.

For example, in one of his series of designs, he used the four colors red, blue, yellow, and brown. An initial square is divided into four quadrants. Each color is assigned to a quadrant as shown in Figure 2.110. The pattern creation process proceeds in levels, as described shortly. At each cycle, the colors are rotated clockwise among the four top-level quadrants.

The designs in the series are composed by overlaying painted patterns. Six patterns are shown in Figure 2.110. At the top level, one of the six patterns is chosen randomly for each quadrant. Depending on chance, the same pattern might be used in more than one quadrant.

The design is completed by a recursive process. Each quadrant is itself divided into four subquadrants, and again a pattern is selected and dyed. The resulting color at a point is a blend depending on all the colors applied to that point at every step in the process, which means the resulting color is not just the last color applied. This process is repeated through five levels in a composition. Figure 2.111 presents Professor Digit's method.

(a) How many different designs could be generated using this scheme? Give a recurrence relation relating the number of designs at level k to the number at level $k - 1$.

(b) After looking at many such patterns, Professor Digit determined that there were simple aesthetic principles that governed whether particular combinations of patterns would be pleasing to him. In particular, he devised a number of what he calls pattern-compatibility rules. Given a pattern assigned to a quadrant, these rules determine which combinations of four patterns can be overlaid in its subquadrants. (Thus, the rules take effect starting with the second level.) On average, these rules reduce the number of immediate refinements of a quadrant from 6^4, or 1,296, to 5.

Given these rules, how many "pleasing" patterns are there? Show the recurrence relation you used to derive your answer.

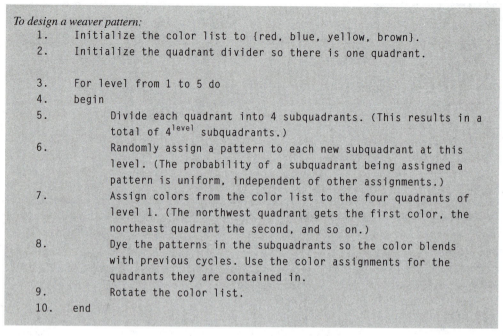

To design a weaver pattern:
```
   1.     Initialize the color list to {red, blue, yellow, brown}.
   2.     Initialize the quadrant divider so there is one quadrant.

   3.     For level from 1 to 5 do
   4.     begin
   5.             Divide each quadrant into 4 subquadrants. (This results in a
                  total of 4^level subquadrants.)
   6.             Randomly assign a pattern to each new subquadrant at this
                  level. (The probability of a subquadrant being assigned a
                  pattern is uniform, independent of other assignments.)
   7.             Assign colors from the color list to the four quadrants of
                  level 1. (The northwest quadrant gets the first color, the
                  northeast quadrant the second, and so on.)
   8.             Dye the patterns in the subquadrants so the color blends
                  with previous cycles. Use the color assignments for the
                  quadrants they are contained in.
   9.             Rotate the color list.
  10.     end
```

FIGURE 2.111.   Professor Digit's method for generating weaver patterns.

(c) Is the process of part b suitable for a hierarchical generation scheme? Explain your answer briefly.

Ex. 4   [CD-!-10] *Hierarchical Shortest Path.* Professor Digit has suggested that it would be useful to have a hierarchical method for route-planning applications. The search method is motivated by the observation that long-distance driving involves planning over distances on different scales. For example, in planning a route from Los Angeles to New York City, one would proceed by planning first a highway route through the major stops along the way. Later one would plan the exact street routes for lodging each day.

Figure 2.112 presents a hierarchical method for planning a trip using this approach. SBBS is a procedure for simple branch-and-bound search. It extends a route incrementally, keeping track of the total path lengths. The route information is given by two databases, highway data and streetmap data, that are appropriately coordinated and detailed.

(a) List some assumptions about routes and cities that this method depends on. Briefly explain some circumstances under which the method would fail.

(b) Briefly describe how the method oversimplifies a real trip planning task.

(c) Briefly, how might a "reactive planning" approach improve the utility of this method?

Ex. 5   [20] *Hierarchical Planning.* Hierarchical planning is useful in situations where the ultimate number of steps in a plan becomes large. In this exercise, an adventure game is used to illustrate some of the issues facing a planner.

Professor Digit has found the explorer's map shown in Figure 2.113. It illustrates an underground system of caves and rivers. He believes the treasure room contains the long lost "jewel of knowledge."

To carry out a hierarchical branch-and-bound search on the trip planning problem:

```
     /* First plan the highway route. */
1.      SBBS(start-city, goal-city, highway-data).

2.      Mark off day-travel distances on the map, indicating the farthest
        city as a stopping point that can be reached in each day's travel.
3.      Mark off fuel-tank distances on the map, indicating the farthest
        city as a stopping point that can be reached without running out of
        fuel.

4.      For each stopping-point city along the route do
5.      begin
6.          If the stopping point is for fuel, select a gasoline station
            as a destination
7.          Else select a hotel as a destination.
            /* Plan a street route to the destination. */
8.          SBBS(location, destination, streetmap-data).
            /* Plan a route from the city destination to the highway
            entrance. */
9.          SBBS(destination, highway-entrance, streetmap-data).
10.     end
```

FIGURE 2.112. Hierarchical branch-and-bound method for the trip planning task.

Anything not on one of the paths, passages, rivers, or rooms is presumed to be solid and impassible. The goal for Professor Digit and his student team is to survive the adventure, recover the jewel, and return with it.

Several obstacles make the journey difficult. The smoldering gas fires are impassible; the odds of getting lost in the maze are very high; the treasure room is locked; explorers are allowed to bring no supplies or tools with them.

(a) Professor Digit is known to be very methodical and demanding of his graduate student crew. He tells them he has considered three possible routes to the treasure, called the land route, the passage route, and the water route.

He requests that team members prepare high-level plans specifying the following three operations:

Walk(from-point, to-point)

Row-Boat(from-point, to-point)

Carry-Boat(from-point, to-point)

The plan should describe how to get to the treasure room. It need not describe specifically how to return. He insists that the team not concern itself with details about provisions, sleeping, keys, or other matters. They should focus only on transportation.

Describe the three different paths to the treasure room in terms of these high-level operators. Indicate which paths are the most plausible. (A route is not plausible if the explorers are likely to die using it.)

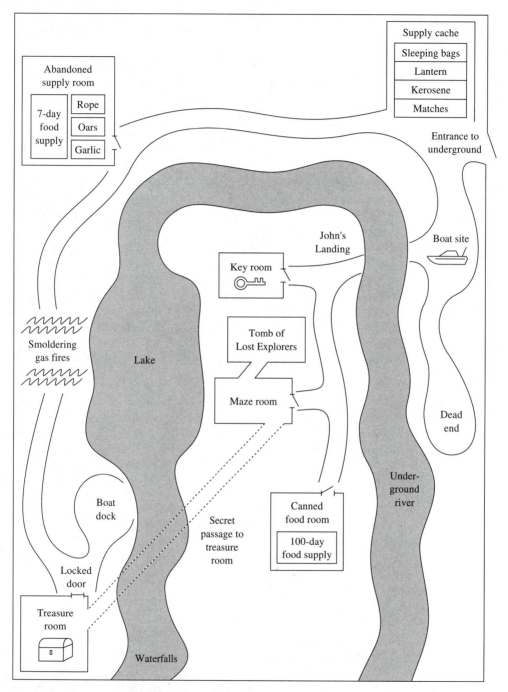

FIGURE 2.113.   A planning problem for an adventure game. The objective is to get from the entrance to the treasure and back.

(b) In hierarchical planning, it is important to introduce details as needed at the appropriate level.

Professor Digit next reveals more details about the quest. The boat cannot be used without oars. The key to the treasure room is in the key room. Travel from point to point takes a day (not counting locations in the same room). Explorers need to eat, and it would be prudent to take food for about 30 days altogether. The work is exhausting and explorers need to sleep. If the boat is left unattended in the water, it will drift away unless it is secured with rope. The journey is underground, and beyond the supply cache it will be impossible to see without a lantern. The team is allowed to begin with a map, but no other supplies and equipment.

Why is it helpful to ignore these conditions and operators during the first level of planning?

(c) Professor Digit indicates that he prefers the water route. He tells his students they should consider the following operators.

> Pickup-Object(object)
> Open-Door(door)
> Unlock-Door(door, key)
> Fill-Lantern(lantern, kerosene)
> Light-Lantern(lantern, matches)
> Secure-Boat(boat, rope)
> Ready-Boat(boat, oars)
> Eat-Food(food)
> Sleep

He suggests that a wise explorer does not overplan. Briefly, which of these operators would you leave out of the plan at the second stage of planning? Why?

(d) Make a more detailed plan for getting the treasure using some of the operators from part c. You need not specify the steps in the return trip with the treasure, but your plan should make a return possible.

(e) How does the need to return influence your travel plan to the treasure?

■ **Ex. 6** [CD-!M-20] *Hierarchical Constraint Satisfaction.* One appeal of constraint satisfaction as a problem-solving framework is the simplicity it affords for combining problems. We can cause two constraint satisfaction problems to interact by interconnecting the constraint networks with additional constraints. However, the complexity of a combined problem can be much greater than the complexities of the original problems.

Hierarchical constraint satisfaction attempts to extend constraint-satisfaction ideas to work on larger problems.

(a) Suppose a composite constraint-satisfaction problem of n variables is created out of two separate constraint-satisfaction problems of i and j variables, respectively, such that $n = i + j$. For simplicity, we assume that there are a possible values in the domains of each variable. What are the worst-case time complexities for the three problems? For simple and backtracking constraint satisfaction, how does the complexity of the composite problem depend on the time complexities of the original problems?

(b) In a more realistic Chinese menu scenario, diners can disagree about the importance of various constraints. Some might favor seafood dishes, and others might not. One diner might propose that there be no more than two spicy-hot dishes. Another diner might be allergic to certain ingredients or request a selection of dishes that provides variety. Another

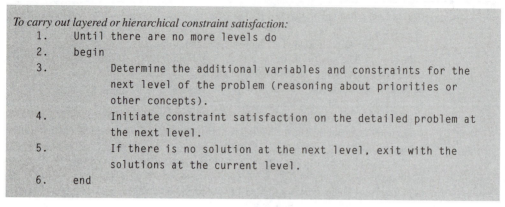

To carry out layered or hierarchical constraint satisfaction:
1.   Until there are no more levels do
2.   begin
3.   Determine the additional variables and constraints for the next level of the problem (reasoning about priorities or other concepts).
4.   Initiate constraint satisfaction on the detailed problem at the next level.
5.   If there is no solution at the next level, exit with the solutions at the current level.
6.   end

FIGURE 2.114.   Method for exhaustive hierarchical constraint satisfaction.

might request only vegetarian dishes. The diners may argue about which dishes to choose or what criteria to apply. In what way does modeling this scenario imply actions outside the scope of ordinary constraint satisfaction?

(c) Figure 2.114 presents a method for hierarchical constraint satisfaction. Roughly, this method introduces a sequence of constraint-satisfaction problems, where each successive problem introduces additional constraints. The algorithm stops either when there are no more levels or when the problem is overconstrained. Could this method be used in the scenario of part b? Explain your answer.

(d) The method in Figure 2.114 does not specify precisely how the candidate solutions from one level are used in determining the solutions for the next level. In the simplest (silly) version, they are not used at all and the constraint-satisfaction process starts over from scratch at each level. What is the complexity of the method in this simplest case?

(e) In another variation, extensive records are kept of the variables and of the combinations of satisfying value assignments at each level. Suppose that in this case, the problems of interest are such that the dominant computational work at each level is to determine values for the additional variables. If in the overall problem there are n variables in total, k levels, and m new variables introduced at each level such that $n = k\,m$, what would be the time complexity for the overall problem? Compare this to the worst-case time complexity for a nonhierarchical formulation of the same problem.

Ex. 7   [60] *Closed-form Value for Optimal* k. What value of k minimizes w_t?

(*Hint*: Differentiate w_t with respect to k and solve for k where the derivative is zero. If you have spent 15 minutes on this and still do not see, consult the answers at the back of the book.)

Ex. 8   [!-05] *Idealizations in Optimizing Expansion Ratios*

(a) The models of hierarchical planning described in this section assume that planning between planning islands can be carried out independently. Which equations depend on this assumption? How does the computation of w_t depend on this?

(b) In some hierarchical design methods there is a vocabulary shift between levels of abstraction. For example, in digital-circuit design, terms such as *shift register* are used at one level, stick diagrams indicating the assignment of materials and wires are used at another level, and precise material placements are specified for constructing the circuit devices at a third level. Is the assumption valid that there is a single number k for describing both the expansion in the number of states and expansion in the amount of detail per state (the number of operators) appropriate in cases like this? Explain your answer briefly.

2.5 *Quandaries and Open Issues*   `ADVANCED`

In this section, we step back from this development to ask, how could search be wrong? This section asks this question in the context of several topics in cognitive science and AI. It proposes alternative frameworks to search for modeling problem solving and offers examples where the model appears to break down. To answer how search could be "wrong," we need to be specific about the role of search in our account of knowledge systems.

Search and Cognition

One criticism of search is that it is inadequate for explaining intelligence. An account of intelligence just in terms of problem solving seems impoverished. Among other things, humans grow, learn, communicate, deceive, plan, have emotions, remember, combine what they know, and set their own objectives. While each of these may have parts that can be formulated in terms of search, and while search methods can be combined, this is not to say that we understand how they could be combined so as to constitute an intelligence.

An answer to the criticism that search explains too little about intelligence is that we should not expect so much from problem solving and search. The criticism presumes too large a role for search in our theories. The major focus of knowledge engineering has been design of specialized assistants and the creation of systems to build knowledge systems that solve particular classes of problems. This is a more limited ambition than building systems with general intelligence. It does not address any requirements for autonomous behavior or generality of ability.

This chapter focused on the use of search and search methods for explaining problem solving. In the rest of this section, we consider some alternative accounts and criticisms. The first alternative is ancient and the next two are more recent.

Problem Solving and Memory

In Plato's *Book of Meno*, Socrates questioned a boy about several geometry problems involving relationships between the lengths of sides and the areas of figures. According to the boy's master, Meno, the boy had no prior training in geometry. Whenever the boy answered incorrectly, Socrates questioned him further, asking more focused questions that (incidentally) served to direct the boy's attention and also break the large problem into several smaller problems. Eventually, under questioning, the boy came to realize his mistakes and then confidently gave the correct answers.

To explain how the boy managed to solve the problems without prior training, Socrates suggested that he had merely "remembered" the correct answers, retrieving them from his immortal soul that knows things from many past lives. In this view, problem solving and learning are nothing but recollection. Today, this account seems quaint in its apparent naiveté about how communication and teaching can take place through careful questioning. Socrates may not have given the answer directly to the boy, but his questions were effective in illuminating a search path toward a solution. From a perspective of more than 2,000 years, "remembering" as a model of problem solving is not so much a legitimate alternative to search as much as it is an indication of how far the scientific thinking on this subject has progressed.

Problem Solving and Deduction

Other accounts of problem solving come from logic. Because of its long and successful tradition, logic has had a strong appeal for many researchers in AI. Almost every knowledge system draws on models of rational inference and consistency in defining tasks and in modeling reasoning. At issue here is not whether logic and inference are important, but rather determining their role in formulating solutions to problems.

Exploring logic's role in problem solving and computing is an active area of research, especially in the design of theorem provers and of logic programming languages. One account that has provoked much discussion at AI conferences in recent years is that the core of problem solving is **logical deduction**. In such discussions, the term *deduction* is not used in a broad and general sense to mean clever reasoning á la Sherlock Holmes. Rather, it refers to the use of specific rules of inference in logic, or even more narrowly to the use of modus ponens as discussed in Chapter 1.

Periodically, when new programming languages involving logic are invented or when there is some success in speeding up theorem provers, a confusion about logic and reasoning seems to reappear. In its most naive form, the idea is that the ultimate problem solver *is* a theorem prover. One need only give a theorem prover the appropriate facts and questions and let it run. After a while, the right answers will pop out. From a perspective of search, there is a fundamental computational problem with this suggestion. Although logic can be used to justify how various assumptions and a line of reasoning lead to a result, it provides no guidance for *finding* a result.

In Chapter 1 we considered a hypothetical knowledge representation (KR) service that would represent facts about the world. You can state these facts to the KR service. You can tell the KR service which facts you assume to be true. Then you can ask whether some other sentence, call it Z, is true. In short, you can ask whether $KB \vDash Z$. We considered the case where predicate calculus is used as the representation language. The good news is that this choice leads to a very clear and specific notion of what a KR should do, as per the following well-known theorem of mathematical logic:

$$KB \vDash Z \text{ if and only if } \vdash (KB => Z)$$

Succinctly stated, the question of whether or not Z is true reduces to whether or not it is provable. Now comes the bad news. Deciding whether a sentence of first order logic is a theorem is unsolvable, or rather computationally intractable.

The difficulty is that theorem proving says nothing about how to search, and how to search is a crucial consideration in problem solving when very flexible representations are used that leave open an extraordinarily large number of possibilities. By its nature, logic is not concerned with the space and time complexities of the process of getting a solution. However, effective problem solving must be. These complexities are fundamental quantities that characterize the performance of search methods.

Recognizing such problems, McDermott (1987) has raised the question of whether logic could be extended to provide an appropriate account of reasoning. He suggests that deduction ought to be modified by use of a metatheory, which guides a deductive process. The meta-theory would provide the knowledge to focus a theorem prover so it could be efficient in solving problems. In short, the intuition is that the logical description need only be modified a little bit. We state the relevant problem facts in sentences in a logical formalism, and then just add a few more special sentences in a metalevel formalism saying how to carry out a search. The goal is to preserve the purity of logic with only a little heuristic contamination for guidance.

But McDermott despairs that the result is not really just a little contamination. One needs to make the connections between subtheories and search through the facts of these theories in order to generate any particular conclusion. At issue is the complexity of the "**metatheory**." McDermott says:

> There is nothing to say in general about the meta-theory idea; and for any given case there is too much to say . . . this study will dwarf the meta-theory framework. You will have to construct a very complex and detailed model to make any progress. (p. 154)

So metatheories need to be rich and knowledge intensive.

McDermott's conclusion brings us right back to search again. The metatheory is supposed to *guide* deduction; the knowledge in these theories is knowledge about searching for solutions. Viewed in this way, metatheories become candidate frameworks for embodying the search methods.

Ultimately, McDermott's proposal is concerned with two specific areas: efficient computational models for problem solving and languages for expressing these models appropriately as metatheories. Interfaces of appropriate modularity should connect metatheories to ground theories. In this way, the concerns of this approach become those of good programming practice and software engineering. Just as with search methods, we move from logic to programming. To the extent that we further divide the concerns of the metatheory into concerns at the symbol level and concerns at the knowledge level, then we take on the concerns of knowledge engineering.

Power versus Generality in Search

A different kind of challenge to search is not whether search is a good model for problem solving, but rather why programs need to "search" at all. Why not just use direct methods? For example, we could use decision tables for making particular kinds of decisions, root finders for finding roots, linear equation solvers for solving linear equations, and so on. Indeed, it is often said in AI circles that much of AI about ways to eliminate search.

On the surface this hardly sounds like a vote of enthusiasm for search, but actually it is. One way to understand this is to consider the task of going into a room to get an object. If you know exactly where the object is, you can walk directly there and get it. If you don't know exactly where it is but do know what part of the room it is in, you can confine your search to that part of the room. If you don't know anything about the room but know something about the object, such as that it is very large and that it must be out of direct sunlight, then you can still focus your search by looking in likely places such as in closets and big containers. If you don't know exactly what the object looks like or exactly what it is—it may be "the murder weapon" of a mystery story—then you have to hunt around for likely candidates and try them out. In this sequence of cases, the more you know the less you need to search.

The problem with direct methods is that they are inflexible. To a first approximation, when a method exploits knowledge of a situation so it does not have to look in certain places for solutions it abandons the ability to find solutions there. In other words, there is often a tension between power and generality in problem solvers. Most programs, such as a quadratic root finder, gain their power from having special case knowledge, such as knowledge about polynomials, coefficients, and root finding. Unfortunately, root finding is a narrow task and it is the only task a root finder can do.

The inflexibility problem is deep. The quadratic root finder is not easily extendible to use more knowledge or to do more tasks. Most quadratic root finders are programmed in such a way that they cannot make use of extra useful facts such as "the roots in this problem are all prime numbers less than 25." Nor can they be easily extended to find cubic roots, even if we have the mathematical knowledge in hand. The knowledge about cubic roots has to be programmed in, too, probably separately from the knowledge about quadratic roots. If we program it in the usual fashion, we will end up with a system that can either do quadratic roots or cubic roots. In effect, there is just a big switch for doing one kind of problem or the other. Furthermore, there may be little carryover in extending the system to do higher-order roots.

Our dissatisfaction with inflexible and direct methods of programming does not arise from their inadequacies for solving problems. Direct methods often perform their particular kind of problem solving quite satisfactorily. Rather, the dissatisfaction arises out of concerns about managing the knowledge. We not only want systems that can perform problem solving in a narrow area; we also want systems to be able to make use of extra information. We want them to be extendable to related tasks with little work, reusing all the existing knowledge that is applicable. We want systems that find solutions efficiently when they have special case knowledge, but we also want their performance not to degrade catastrophically. They should degrade gracefully by using (less efficient) searches when special knowledge is not available.

One idea is to divide the process into two stages: compilation and search. In the compilation stage, we gather information about the problem space and construct a specialized problem solver that exploits the available hardware and is efficient for searching for solutions. The second stage is to run that problem solver. Such architectures are at the frontier of current research.

These considerations take us beyond the computational issues of problem solving and more deeply into issues of design of knowledge systems. Search methods by themselves do not provide much architectural guidance for building knowledge systems with all these properties. Indeed, the generality of the search methods derives largely from the looseness of the requirements that they impose on knowledge representation. Search methods tell us little about the engineering concerns for providing modularity in organizing knowledge. They tell us little about how to use or characterize general knowledge. In the following chapters, we look at ways to exploit the structure of particular task domains to bring regularity to some of the pervasive issues about search and the use of substantial bodies of knowledge.

Summary

It is important to have appropriate attitudes and expectations about foundations. Although search concepts and methods for problem solving come from information-processing psychology, they are not adequate for or intended as architectures of intelligence. Search is a framework for describing processes for solving problems.

Many important problems require the use of special case knowledge to solve them efficiently. This chapter shows how this phenomenon arises, why it seems counter-intuitive, and what the implications are for creating knowledge systems.

Knowledge and Software Engineering

In the summer of 1973, Patrick Winston gave the Computers and Thought Award lecture at the International Joint Conference on Artificial Intelligence at Stanford University. In this lecture he spoke of his experience teaching MIT undergraduates about the workings of an AI program, MACSYMA, that could integrate and differentiate expressions from the real calculus. The problems that the program solved were the same kinds of problems that are given in first-year calculus courses. Sample problems for the program included the differentiation and integration of trigonometric functions, polynomials, exponentials, and compositions of them.

According to Winston, the pedagogical sequence usually worked out in the same way. The students were familiar with numerical approximation methods for integration and differentiation and with computer programs that used these methods. They were surprised and impressed, however, that a program could perform integration and differentiation *symbolically*. In their view, such a program had a pretty good claim on being intelligent. The next part of the course explored how the program worked. The students learned that the program was organized around search. It had a collection of rules for differentiation and integration. It matched these rules against situations to decide which ones to apply. When the students understood that the AI program used the basic differentiation and integration rules taught in an introductory calculus course, their perception changed. A typical response was: "That program is not so smart! It integrates the same way I do."

In retrospect, it is not clear what Winston's students expected to find inside the integration program beyond knowledge (the integration and differentiation rules) and the search methods. Their surprise at finding these ingredients at the core of the system suggests that they were prepared culturally for something quite different, something awesome and mysterious. In all fairness, the students' surprise when they understood the workings of the integration program was tracking a shift that was spreading throughout the field of AI at the same time. AI was shifting from the pursuit of powerful search and reasoning methods toward a recognition of the role of special case knowledge—in this case the transforms of calculus. As Goldstein and Papert (1977) put it four years later in an often-quoted paper, there had been a shift of paradigm in AI from a technique-oriented theory of intelligence to a knowledge-oriented theory of intelligence:

> The fundamental problem of understanding intelligence is not the identification of a few powerful techniques, but rather the question of how to represent large amounts of knowledge in a fashion that permits their effective use and interaction. (p. 85)

This chapter is about the formulation and formalization of knowledge for knowledge systems. It attempts to bridge the gap that separates our everyday human understanding of how we discover, use, and articulate knowledge from our technical understanding of how we can incorporate knowledge in computational models.

3.1 *Understanding Knowledge Systems in Context*

We begin by discussing terminology that is widely used for describing knowledge systems. To illustrate issues in developing knowledge sytems, we then consider a sequence of settings in which knowledge systems are developed and used.

3.1.1 *The Terminology of Knowledge Systems and Expertise*

Since the 1970s when the term *expert system* came into use, terminology has shifted to reflect a deeper understanding of issues and distinctions. This section discusses the terminology, the shifts, and the reasons for the shifts.

What Knowledge Is, According to the Dictionary

Since the beginning of knowledge engineering, the term *knowledge* has been controversial when it is used as a description of something that computers can represent and use. Much of the struggle in making sense of knowledge engineering is in dealing with this word. In ordinary usage, the term *knowledge* is used imprecisely and sometimes synonymously with other words such as *data*, *information*, and *truth*. Within technical literature, however, there is potential for confusion and controversy. To illustrate this, consider the simpler word *information*. The term *information theory* is routinely applied to concepts for encoding bits for efficient transmission over communication channels. Information theory is about noisy signals, compact encodings, redundancy, bandwidth, and so on. Perhaps surprisingly, information theory has nothing to do with what information *means*. This is confusing because in common discourse the term *information* is used broadly, leading us to expect much more from a theory with that name.

Philosophers distinguish several kinds of knowledge, such as knowledge about what we perceive. Mathematical theorems are arguably formalized knowledge. There is knowledge about natural laws. There is knowledge about social, legal, and regulatory constraints. There is knowledge about effective reasoning in particular contexts.

Webster's New Twentieth Century Dictionary of the English Language (second edition) provides evidence of the broad usage of the term *knowledge*. This dictionary was published in

1968, very near the time at which knowledge engineering was getting started. This dictionary definition of knowledge does not say explicitly that knowledge can be held only by people, but it does not mention computers or even books. It offers the following seven meanings relevant to our purposes:

1. a clear and certain *perception* of something; the act, fact, or state of knowing; understanding.
2. *learning*; all that has been perceived or grasped by the mind.
3. *practical experience*; skill; as a knowledge of seamanship.
4. *acquaintance* or familiarity such as with a fact or place.
5. *cognizance*; recognition.
6. *information*; the body of facts accumulated by mankind.
7. *acquaintance with facts*; range of awareness, or understanding.

We begin with meaning 1, about perception. The term *perception* connotes the certainty provided by reliable sensory perception as portrayed by the expression "seeing is believing." Perception provides evidence about an external reality. All models of knowledge formulation rely on external evidence somehow. Knowledge system development includes feedback loops that ultimately involve the sensory abilities of the system developers and others. However, a strict reliance on perception is too confining and overstates the reliability of the senses. What did the magician really do? The senses can be fooled. Such strict reliance also ignores the utility of communication for conveying knowledge of distant events. For example, we all know a bit about great historical figures from the past even though none of us has seen them; nor have we seen the integers of mathematics. From a perspective of knowledge engineering, perception is a *basis* for knowledge. Perception plus prior knowledge plus rationality gives a basis for action. But perception should not be confused with knowledge itself.

Meaning 2 is about learning. This can refer either to academic learning, as in references to a learned scholar or to more mundane forms of everyday learning. ("Everyone makes mistakes, kid. Now tell me, what you have learned about playing baseball near windows?") The academic meaning is too restricted for knowledge engineering because academic concerns at any given time are only a subset of human concerns. The more mundane interpretation of learning encompasses methods for acquiring information through processes of abstraction, generalization, and model building. In knowledge engineering, machine-learning techniques formulate experience as knowledge. But computers can represent and use knowledge obtained from other agents, without having direct experiences themselves and without generalizing from cases themselves.

Meaning 3 is about practical experience. Experience is what knowledge is about and is essential for the creation of knowledge. But one must reflect on the experience to gain knowledge. The seamanship example conveys the idea that to be considered knowledgeable, a person must have a breadth of practical experience. The implication is that a person who has been at sea often enough will probably have encountered enough situations to acquire whatever he needs to know.

Meaning 4 refers to acquaintance or familiarity with a fact. Colloquially, we contrast someone who has "book knowledge" with others who have practical experience. A medical intern with book learning may be a riskier candidate for treating a patient than a seasoned doctor. The former's experience is less complete than that of the latter. From a perspective of knowledge engineering, acquaintance and familiarity refer to degrees of knowledge, but should not be confused with the nature of knowledge.

Meaning 5, about recognition, refers to a shallow degree of knowledge. If we recognize a face but cannot remember much about the person, we "know" the person but not very well. Recognition is often thought to be easier than generation, as in the case of people who can roughly understand a foreign language without being able to speak it. This meaning of the term *knowledge* is similar in status to meaning 4.

Meaning 6, about information accumulated by humankind, suggests that knowledge can be accumulated. This meaning of information is not the same as in information theory. It suggests that knowledge is somehow encoded.

Meaning 7 is about acquaintance with facts. We attribute knowledge to those who demonstrate broad competence. This meaning has some of the same force and limitations as meaning 3. It suggests that part of the work of knowing something is being able to apply that knowledge to a range of situations. We must reason in new situations using what we have acquired in specific ones. This implies an ability to infer and to generalize. For example, if an automobile driver knows that he is driving in a school neighborhood where children are playing, he is expected to drive his vehicle slowly and cautiously. Suppose something unusual happens in a driving situation, such as a wagon load of children's toys rolling into the street. The driver's handbook probably does not mention this precise situation. Nonetheless, if a driver fails to slow down and ultimately injures someone, a court of law will not accept excuses about the "incompleteness of a mental theorem prover" or claims that the driver never had exactly that experience before. As in meaning 3, having knowledge implies broad competence.

Looking back over these dictionary meanings of knowledge—perception, recognition, learning, experience, competence—it is noteworthy that they are all about relations and processes involving agents and their environments. Knowledge is not characterized by such properties as weight or extent. Knowledge is not a substance or a quantifiable property. It is not simply an encoding. What seems to matter and what we are inclined to describe when we characterize knowledge are the expectations it creates between environments, agents, and their rational actions. This stance on the meaning of the term *knowledge* is consistent with usage of the term in technical discussions about knowledge systems.

Defining Knowledge in Terms of Situations, Action, and Agents

Knowledge, as the word is used for knowledge systems, refers to the **codified experience** of agents. The experience is the source of the information for solving problems. By *codified*, we mean that the knowledge has been formulated, recorded, and made ready for use. This statement connects the practical intuitions of those who build knowledge systems, the theoretical foundations of knowledge as embedded representations to guide action, and the issues and problems that are driving the development of the field. The formulation as codified experience acknowledges that such experience is generally hard-won and valued.

Thinking about experience and isolating what is new in it is hard work. Experience must be articulated to become explicit knowledge, and in our sense, that requires more than just a listing of facts, such as the price of eggs or the postal addresses of the founders of AI. Codified experience must be organized and generalized to guide future action. We can formalize the process of knowledge creation in terms of the scientific method. Knowledge is that which is justified by our experience, or more formally, it is what we have learned from our experiments.

It is easy but misleading to overlook the roles of agents with respect to knowledge. When we refer to an "experience," some agent must interact with the world to have the experience. Usually this agent is assumed to be a person. When we refer to the codification of experience in symbols, some agent must conceive the symbols. We can say that books contain knowledge, but when we do so, we tacitly assume that there are people who can make sense of the writings in the books.

Agents are also involved when we consider written representations of knowledge. One of the insights in the past few years about the nature of knowledge and knowledge systems is that when meaning is attributed to systems and symbols there is necessarily an **agent**. As discussed in Chapter 1, symbols do not have meanings inherently; they are assigned meanings by an observer/agent and the assignment of meaning is in the mind of the observer.

If we say that "Computer system X knows that meningitis causes fever," we imply that from the perspective of some observers (such as ourselves), the computer system has representations of meningitis and fever; has representations of the relations between them; can form judgments about this situation based on generalizations of other situations; and can render and communicate its judgments involving the situations, meningitis as an infectious agent, and fever.

Thus, knowledge cannot be isolated from its creation or use. Experience involves agents in particular situations working on particular tasks with their own background assumptions. For example, a doctor seeing a patient with particular symptoms may quickly propose an explanation of why the patient is sick, knowing that there has recently been well-water contamination in the area. Such knowledge is particular to experiences of the time and place.

Knowledge as a "Transportable Substance"

Within AI and knowledge engineering, the term **knowledge acquisition** refers to any technique by which computer systems can gain the knowledge they need to perform their tasks. For newcomers and also those who have thought deeply about knowledge, the term is problematic. The term *acquisition* is odd because it suggests that knowledge is like a substance. In this view, knowledge is delivered using a transportation process from someone or somewhere and the crucial step in building a knowledge system is to "get" the knowledge.

The metaphor of knowledge as a "transportable substance" has long been used in informal English conversation. For example, books and teaching are said to "convey knowledge"; elders "pass along" knowledge to the next generation; knowledge and secret information sometimes "leak out." These metaphors reflect a truism. During education, knowledge becomes known by additional people. Knowledge systems themselves are sometimes thought of as knowledge distribution systems. However the process of spreading and knowing involves more than transportation.

The substance and transportation metaphor implies that knowledge starts out in a domain expert's head and that the object is to get the knowledge into a computer. This sounds like a simple matter that involves asking a few questions of an expert followed by some programming. Unfortunately, on this simplistic line of thought, many knowledge systems projects have floundered in months of misguided attempts at knowledge acquisition that never converge. Some projects fail utterly.

The transportation metaphor ignores the processes of knowledge creation and use. It does not consider that knowledge must somehow originate. It does not consider that knowledge can be implicit in the interactions of an agent with an environment. It does not consider that communication is at least two-way, involving the cooperative activity of agents that need to agree on spoken or written symbols and behaviors.

To emphasize the constructive and comparative aspects of building knowledge bases we prefer the term **knowledge formulation**. The formulation of knowledge includes identifying it, describing it, and explaining what it means. To emphasize aspects of writing and the choice of representation, we say that knowledge is **codified**. This suggests that besides transportation, the process of building a knowledge base also involves articulating essential elements of experience and preserving them in writing.

Knowledge often goes through stages of refinement in which it becomes increasingly formal and precise. Part of this process involves identifying the conditions under which the knowledge is applicable, and any exceptional conditions. It also involves organizing the representations so they can be used by a problem solver or other interpreter. To convey these meanings, the term **knowledge formalization** is used. This term helps us to characterize what happens as we progress from informal notes to formal computational models.

As knowledge systems are built, it is often the case that participants achieve greater insights about how to carry out the task. These insights come from the careful examination of particular cases and the search for better generalizations. This suggests that the knowledge that goes into knowledge systems does not simply originate from finished mental representations that already express all the information. Experts sometimes can give only vague accounts of their thinking. But they do know how to make their thinking more precise through experiments. In this experimentation process, knowledge is often created or discovered.

In summary, the process of developing a knowledge base involves more than transportation of facts. Historically, the process has been called knowledge acquisition. Recognizing other dimensions of what is needed helps us to make sense of the process and the methods by which people approach it.

Expert Systems and Knowledge Systems

The terms **expert system** and **knowledge system** were invented in the context of artificial intelligence research and partly in reaction to it. The term *intelligence* has always been problematic because there is no widespread agreement about exactly what intelligence is.

In this context, the developers of the first expert systems were interested in what they saw as practical problems. They took scientific reasoning and practical problem solving as their central examples of intelligent behavior. They adopted interview techniques, protocol analysis, and other methods of information-processing psychology to investigate the nature of these task domains. As they built computational models, they were struck by the amount of special case knowledge that was brought to bear in solving the problems efficiently. This difference dominated the character of the programs and was the context for the "knowledge and expertise" terminology.

An **expert system** is a computer program whose performance is guided by specific, expert knowledge in solving problems. The problem-solving focus is crucial in this characterization. The knowledge of central interest in expert systems is that which can guide a search for solutions. The term *expert* connotes both narrow specialization and substantial competence. Having a narrow focus is essential to the feasibility of a system. Although the term *expert* has been loosely applied in some cases, it is intended to describe systems that solve problems that are otherwise solved by people having substantial training and exceptional skill. Thus the standard of performance for expert systems is in human terms, by comparison with people carrying out a particular kind of task.

The first expert systems were characterized as **expert-level advisors** or **consultants**. Expert systems are now being used in a wide range of different interactive roles. To the consultant metaphor, we now add other metaphors describing the role and interactivity of a system: the smart spreadsheet, the intelligent patient monitor, the financial advisor, the scheduling assistant, the therapy critic, the cognitive coprocessor. These terms suggest different ways of thinking about the split of initiative and responsibility between knowledge systems and their users. In whatever role we employ expert systems, those systems require knowledge to be competent.

Even in the most successful applications where expert systems outperform human experts in their reliability and consistency of results, expert systems have less breadth and flexibility than human experts. This has created confusion about the suitability of the term *expert*, often resulting in unproductive arguments about the quality and boundaries of expertise.

The term **knowledge system** is a shorthand for the term *knowledge-based system*. A knowledge system is a computer system that represents and uses knowledge to carry out a task. As the applications for the technology have broadened, the more general term *knowledge system* has become preferred by some people over *expert system* because it focuses attention on the knowledge that the systems carry, rather than on the question of whether or not such knowledge constitutes expertise.

The Parts of a Knowledge System

The classical formulation of a knowledge system is shown in Figure 3.1. This formulation has become somewhat frayed around the edges, and we offer alternative formulations shortly. Nonetheless, familiarity with it is worthwhile because the terminology is still widely used.

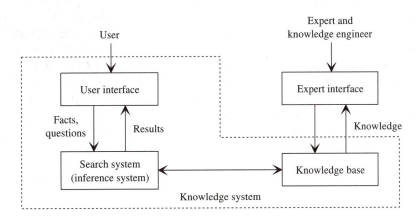

FIGURE 3.1. The classical characterization of a knowledge system.

The classical formulation includes a knowledge base, two human-computer interfaces, and a search or inference subsystem. The **knowledge base** is the repository for the knowledge used by the system—the rules and hints for guiding the search for solutions. The knowledge base is updated periodically to reflect changes or extensions to the domain knowledge.

The **user interface** is the part of a knowledge system that interacts with the system's primary users. It is responsible for all communications in the system's role as a consultant for solving problems in its domain, such as asking questions about the problem at hand, answering queries, and displaying results.

The second human-computer interface in the classical formulation is the **expert interface**. This is the interface by which knowledge is entered into the system. The expert interface is used by a knowledge acquisition team consisting of an expert and a knowledge engineer. The expert interface provides access for updating, testing, and debugging a knowledge base, including tools for examining the contents of the knowledge base. By implication, not all users can update a system's knowledge base. That responsibility is assigned to a smaller group that oversees and approves changes and takes into account effects across a wide range of situations. In personal knowledge systems or in knowledge systems that allow personalizing a knowledge base, the responsibilities and interfaces may be partitioned differently.

The inference subsystem is the part that reasons its way to solutions of problems, with its search guided by the contents of the knowledge base. Traditionally, colorfully, and colloquially, this part has been called the **inference engine**. This part of a knowledge system must include provisions for setting goals, representing and recording intermediate results, and managing memory and computational resources.

These terms—*knowledge base*, *search system*, *expert* and *user interfaces*—all name parts of a program or computer system. However, an inventory of program parts is not the best way to understand a knowledge system. Systems for different purposes and based on different approaches look too much alike by these top-level categories. Nor does further decomposition into smaller parts necessarily help us to understand how different systems work or what their limitations are.

Another problem with this classical formulation of expert systems in terms of their parts is that the formulation does not say precisely what the roles of the different parts are. Consider the knowledge base. In some systems the knowledge-base subsystem does no more than manage a collection of data structures, perhaps providing some search facilities. In others, the knowledge-base subsystem performs inference on the representations. With such variations in the architectural components, the terms give us little guidance for developing or understanding systems.

To make sense of knowledge systems and the knowledge that they carry, we need to step back and observe more than the apparent organizational structures of the programs. We need to look at a knowledge system both in its problem-solving context and in the social and organizational contexts in which knowledge is created, communicated, and reinterpreted. We begin by defining some terms about knowledge and work settings. In the next section, we consider a sequence of scenarios that provide contexts for understanding the processes by which knowledge and knowledge systems can be developed. First, we introduce terms about knowledge and activity.

Bodies of Knowledge

A **domain** is a body of knowledge. The subject matter of a domain must be recorded or carried somehow. It may be recorded in written literature or carried by people and conveyed verbally or by apprenticeship training. The term *domain* does not connote anything about the amount of knowledge included. Often a domain is either a field of academic study or a professional area. Internal medicine, health care, diets for diabetics, agriculture, law, civil engineering, and force transducer design are all examples of domains. Different domains have different degrees of specialization. For example, estrogen chemistry is more specialized than organic chemistry, which is more specialized than general chemistry.

A **task** is a kind of job that is done. In the context of knowledge systems, a task involves solving a kind of problem. Tasks can be described at different levels of generality. Very general tasks include such things as diagnosis, configuration, design, planning, and scheduling. An example of a very specialized task would be "inferring DNA segmentation structure from restriction enzyme digest data."

When we refer to **domain knowledge**, we mean the general terminology and facts of a domain without a focus on a particular task. For example, we might refer to a general corpus of facts about chemistry without considering whether the task was to plan a chemical synthesis or to interpret the data from an instrument. When we use the term **task knowledge**, we refer to the terminology, computational models, and facts associated with carrying out a kind of task, without necessarily focusing on a particular domain. For example, we might consider the knowledge and models about a scheduling task, without regard to whether it was job-shop scheduling for a manufacturing plant or course and classroom scheduling for a university.

The term **task domain** combines these ideas. A task domain is the knowledge, assumptions, and requirements associated with doing a particular task in a particular domain. The term is usually used in the context of a particular set of people doing a specialized task. "Diagnosing infectious diseases" is an example of a task domain. A **problem** is a particular instance of a task. It consists of a particular set of input data together with the accepted answers. A **case** is an example of a problem that includes the given information, the methods used, and the results obtained.

3.1.2 *Knowledge Systems and Document Systems: Five Scenarios*

Putting knowledge into computers raises many foundational questions. What is knowledge? Where does it come from? How is it created? How is it held by computers? In the context of particular knowledge systems, these questions tend to have concrete and immediate answers. We now present five scenarios in which knowledge systems are developed and used.

Personal Knowledge Systems

The first scenario is a **personal knowledge system** as illustrated in Figure 3.2. In this scenario a person has a sample situation or device in mind. It might be a radio, an electronic circuit, or a billing and inventory system. The task might be to fix the radio, to design the circuit, or to develop a purchasing schedule that reduces warehouse costs. Carrying out the task is framed in terms of a search for solutions. We refer to the person who builds the knowledge system as the system builder.

There are several motivations for creating personal knowledge systems. For example, the system builder may want the knowledge system to solve routine problems or routine parts of problems so he can focus on harder and more interesting ones. Alternatively, he may want to use the knowledge system to improve his productivity, check his work, or extend his methods to larger problems than he can solve by hand. He can rely on the tirelessness of an automatic system

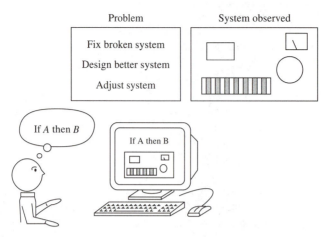

FIGURE 3.2.   A personal knowledge system.

to work systematically on large cases. Typically, the system builder determines what knowledge and methods are to be used in the system by reading books or by introspecting on his own problem-solving behavior.

Another important use of a personal knowledge system is as a computational and experimental medium for expressing, testing, and extending a theory. The computational medium offers unique advantages for exercising and testing a theory of problem solving. A system builder with this goal uses an operational knowledge system to understand knowledge and competence at diagnosing engines, playing chess, or managing cash flow and inventory.

Test cases are a key to refining a system. Alternative bodies of knowledge can be tested against the same cases to see which versions perform the best. Test cases also can be used to check stability of performance as a system is updated. After a system builder extends a knowledge system to perform on new cases, she can test whether the changes introduce bugs on older cases.

A knowledge system is usually constructed for use in a particular situation. Suppose a personal knowledge system was designed to fix FX-89 radios. If we later wanted to use the system to fix FX-90 radios, some changes would be necessary. Some of the changes would not become evident until we tried to use the knowledge system to fix an FX-90 radio. When the system failed in some way at that time, we would discover various ways the knowledge system relied on assumptions about the FX-89 or the context of fixing it. These assumptions are like "invisible links" to the situation in which our knowledge system was embedded. They are invisible in the sense that they would have no explicit representation in the knowledge base. For example, the knowledge base might not say explicitly that it assumed that tuning was accomplished by analog circuits rather than being digitally controlled. It might not say that speakers were assumed to be attached to the radio itself rather than located remotely, or that the radio was controlled by switches mounted on the radio rather than being controlled by one or more persons using separate handheld units. These assumptions might be bound up in the representations of radio structure and reflected perhaps in the policies and methods of troubleshooting.

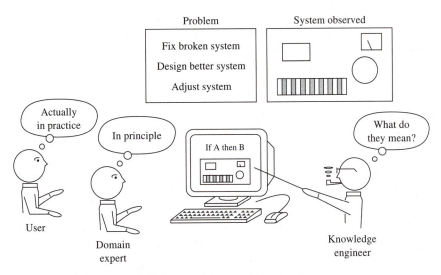

FIGURE 3.3. Knowledge system built by a participatory design team.

If we had designed the system initially to work on both FX-89 radios and FX-90 radios, or if the system used mostly general knowledge about the devices from which radios were constructed, then there would be a greater reusability of knowledge from one domain to the other. In practice, even situations that we think of as being static evolve over time. Knowledge systems cannot stand still. As a situation changes, knowledge systems need to accommodate with new behavior often based on new knowledge.

The scenario of the personal knowledge system is our simplest because it focuses on the activities of a single person. The system builder observes phenomena, designs symbol structures, and tests and uses the system. Even in this first simple scenario, there are some potentially subtle issues to be faced. How should it be determined whether the program solves problems correctly? The developer might compare the answers that a system gets with answers worked out manually. A developer could increase confidence in this approach by analyzing answers to the smaller sub-problems. A developer might compare the program's answers to published answers, or check the answers for internal consistency. These different approaches honor different "gold standards" or measures of the quality and performance of the knowledge and the knowledge system.

Participatory Design

Our second scenario is a knowledge system developed by **participatory design** as shown in Figure 3.3. This scenario is more complicated than the first because it involves several participants in its development and use. We distinguish three main roles for participants: the user, the domain expert, and the knowledge engineer. The difference we imply between the expert and the user is in the degree of experience. In any real situation, the user and the domain expert may be the same person or people may have overlapping roles. For simplicity, we assume that the user is also the customer. In a large project, there may be a division of technical responsibility between a knowledge engineer, a software engineer, and other programming staff. In such cases the team leader is often a software engineer. However, for simplicity in describing this scenario, we combine the technical roles into the single role of knowledge engineer. The key issue is that the system is built by a collaborative team, working together. This is why the approach is called participatory.

There are two primary motivations for developing a knowledge system for a group of users: replicating access to otherwise scarce expertise and standardizing high-quality work methods. For example, a knowledge service may make it possible to bring the best or most current diagnostic reasoning to a dispersed team of technicians or may make medical expertise quickly available to an emergency response team. In complicated or tiresome tasks, a knowledge system may enable a consistency of performance that ensures a standard high quality of the results.

The participatory design scenario differs from that for a personal knowledge system because it emphasizes communication among participants. A team approach is needed when there is a division of skills for building a knowledge system. The user or users understand what problem is to be solved. The domain expert has advice about how to solve it. The knowledge engineer understands the theory and technology of knowledge systems. The members of the team need to work to make sense of each other. The knowledge engineer does not understand the domain, and neither the users nor the experts have the skills or tools to build a knowledge system. The participants need to build a shared vocabulary.

Misunderstandings and disgreements may arise. For example, the user may believe that the domain expert is concerned with cases that are too idealized. The domain expert may find the user's accounts too ad hoc and unsystematic. Participants must make sense of each other's views and develop shared terminology and compatible goals. They will have many conversations and probably make extensive use of blackboards and project notes. They will use drawings and other notations to help each other to explain what the task is and what knowledge they use to understand and solve problems. Later in the process, they may use specific techniques to identify and articulate the knowledge to be represented explicitly in the system. Techniques for taking and analyzing problem-solving protocols are discussed later in this chapter.

Over time, the requirements of the knowledge system will change and new knowledge about the tasks will be discovered. In this regard, the need to accommodate change is the same as in the scenario of the personal knowledge system. Furthermore, when there are variations in the situations faced by users of the system, the goal to have the knowledge system work in multiple situations is more compelling than for personal knowledge systems. There can be corresponding variations in the knowledge used by different members of the community, and it may be useful to incorporate these variations in the shared knowledge base. Because of these variations and the need to accommodate change, participatory design does not end when a knowledge system begins to work. The system must evolve to reflect the changing needs of the community.

The participatory design scenario is the one most discussed in this chapter because it is widely used. It introduces the essential communication issues and is used for projects that are too big to be done by a single person.

Shared, Community Knowledge Bases

Our third scenario is the **shared, community knowledge base** as shown in Figure 3.4. In this scenario, a group of people agree to share the work of developing a common knowledge base. In the simplest version, there is a single repetitive task and several people plan to share the labor of developing a system and to build on each other's work. In more complex situations, they may want to solve different but related problems using a substantial common base.

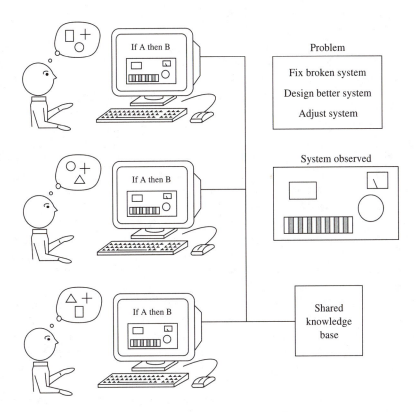

FIGURE 3.4. Developing a shared knowledge base.

Sharing in the building of a knowledge base is motivated by practical concerns about the ability to share knowledge, use common knowledge in closely related applications, and reduce the time or labor of encoding a body of knowledge. Systems of this kind are at the frontier of current research. As in the development of all kinds of software, there are difficult challenges in designing parts of a system to be usable in multiple contexts.

The primary motivation for this approach is that the participants believe there is a substantial corpus of knowledge that they want to use but could not develop for themselves. It may be that the common knowledge base requires that they each bring unique knowledge to the process. Alternatively, it may simply be that the scale of a project requires a joint effort.

Figure 3.4 shows three people developing a shared knowledge base. In practice, the participants may have somewhat different tasks and distinctions in mind, as suggested by the squares, circles, and triangles in the cartoon "thought balloons." These differences may be identified at the beginning of the project or they may surface during the process of building and using a knowledge system. Differences that are identified late in a design process may cause more difficulties than ones that are discovered early. In any case, the process of building a sharable knowledge base for overlapping but different tasks requires that the knowledge be tested against the range of tasks and problems. It challenges the developers to determine the generality and reusability of knowledge.

As with participatory design, the parties need to agree about terminology and distinctions in the knowledge base. In the participatory design case, the participants have different roles. Thus, in a discussion between a knowledge engineer and a domain expert, the roles usually reflect which person has the most experience for deciding any particular question. In the shared-knowledge-base scenario, there can be much more overlap among the roles and also much more differentiation, as when there are specialists for different bodies of knowledge.

When a knowledge base is shared, changes to it must be coordinated. This introduces further issues beyond the previous scenarios. First, multiple writers to the knowledge base must not accidentally delete each other's work. This issue is addressed by appropriate database-locking mechanisms and policies. Second, there is a tension between the need to extend and change the knowledge base and the need to keep parts of it debugged and usable. This issue is addressed by appropriate mechanisms and policies involving versions and releases. These are the relatively easy issues, although the management of multiple versions can be complex if there are many interdependent parts. The harder issue is the need to maintain a shared understanding and consensus on the nature of the desired changes to the knowledge base. This requires a continuing process among the developers of the system.

An important adjunct to the shared formal representations are the informal notes and discussions that explain the evolution of the knowledge base. In participatory design, informal discussion precedes formal representation. This suggests that the shared knowledge base should contain not only the formal representations that are end products of discussion and analysis, but also the notes and informal documents that make up the supporting and motivating material. The use of project documentation is discussed in more detail in Section 3.3.

Finally, as in any endeavor that involves sharing, there can be issues about rights and responsibilities. Policies and incentives will influence the degree of sharing. There are always costs for contributing to the knowledge base, maintaining it, generalizing it to cover new cases, and educating others. Some ideas bearing on this issue arise in the context of the next scenario.

Knowledge Services

Our fourth scenario, **knowledge services**, is projected beyond current practice. In this scenario several knowledge systems for different tasks are linked to do parts of a larger task. Figure 3.5 shows several knowledge systems that interact to design an automobile. One knowledge system designs engines. Another designs automobile interiors. Another designs automobile bodies. A top-level knowledge system that we call the contractor coordinates and integrates the designs of the different parts of an automobile.

The architecture of this scenario mirrors the way that complex projects are often carried out by specialists with different abilities. Different knowledge systems offer different specialized knowledge services. Each knowledge service performs an information-processing task and may be coupled with the other services. Some services may simply do database retrieval and others may do problem solving. The term **knowbot** is sometimes used to refer to such knowledge services, conjuring up an image of an automated agent that works over a computer communication network (Kahn & Cerf, 1988).

FIGURE 3.5. Knowledge services model.

As in the shared-knowledge-base scenario, this scenario emphasizes the possibility of shared and reusable knowledge. What is new is the principle for organizing sharing around separate knowledge systems that perform particular services. One motivation for this approach is that some problems require a breadth of expertise and a scale that preclude the use of a small, tightly coordinated design team. Each separate knowlege system can be built by a distinct team. A second motivation is that there may be distinctly different opportunities for amortizing the costs of development for each of the different domains. Each knowledge system may present different opportunities for reuse. In this example, the engine-design system may design engines for automobiles, trucks, heavy equipment, boats, or aircraft. Presumably knowledge about mechanics and materials and energy efficiency can be reused across these different applications. The approach also lends itself to the concept of creating services that make use of other services over a network by adding services of value. This leads to an arrangement of charging fees for knowledge services and for creating value-added services on a network.

For knowledge systems to interact with each other creates new challenges of generality and communication. What are the conditions under which a computational model for a task can be used across different domains? Do two approaches to diagnosis have the compatible representations for ranking diagnostic hypotheses? How much of the planning and scheduling knowledge developed for one application is reusable for another one? What differences are there between the terminologies used by a manufacturing organization and a field service organization? Different applications use different terminology and require different assumptions and approximations. In our previous scenarios, we discussed the need for members of a team of developers to make sense of each other. In this case the problem is compounded because the knowledge systems may be built by different organizations.

In Figure 3.5, interactions among the designers of the knowledge systems are organized around the specialized services that the knowledge systems will provide. The systems carry out prescribed subtasks. To carry out an overall task, the systems must communicate with each other. The division of labor suggests the use of standardized terminology and protocols for communication among the knowledge systems. For example, the engine-design knowledge system may use a specification language involving only information about the size, a desired power/speed curve, fuel, and temperature requirements of engines. Such standardization of language assumes that essentially the same kinds of problems are being solved repeatedly, albeit for somewhat different domains. This narrowness of channels of communication is indicated in the figure by drawing the connections between the knowledge systems as passing through narrow openings representing narrow interfaces. Each knowledge system has a relatively narrow channel for communication, akin to modular interfaces in all large programming systems.

The narrow channels attempt to simplify specifying what programs do. If different and specific protocols need to be developed for every application, the prospects for reusing knowledge systems and building value-added services are slim. Standards reflect a preunderstanding about requirements and their description in some language.

The new issues suggested by this scenario are the shift to arm's-length relations among the developers of the overall system and the need for communication among multiple knowledge systems. The shift to arm's-length transactions is one possible social response to the shift from a small team to a large team.

To illustrate the nature of arm's-length transactions, imagine there is an error in the final result. For example, the customer in our example may receive a sports car with a truck engine. One issue is the responsibility for the specifications and assumptions used in the design of the engine. Of course, the difficulties may be much more subtle than these. Perhaps the engine is not quite reliable enough for the intended use of the vehicle. The quality of the result depends on the interactions among different knowledge systems. Who is responsible when something goes wrong? Some means must be found to account for responsibility, reliability, and costs.

At the time of this writing, systems based on knowledge services and knowledge communication standards are a gleam in the eye of researchers, but the goal reflects a real need. In companies that have multiple computer systems including knowledge systems, there is often an urge to link these systems. For example, it would be desirable to make changes in one place about business practices and have these changes reflected appropriately in all the knowledge systems used by the organization.

The knowledge-services scenario extends the other scenarios. It provides the beginnings of an organizational approach for considering how bodies of knowledge might be organized. In so doing, it also gives a glimpse of the wide range of open issues there are in organizing large bodies of formal knowlege.

Documents and Information Workspaces

Our last scenario starts from the perspective of how people use documents in their work. We consider document use in three settings: a professional office, a point-of-sale terminal in a retail store, and a medical center.

We begin by considering documents in the office of a professional. The office could belong to an architect, a production manager, a lawyer, a hospital adminstrator, or an inventory clerk. Of course, each of these settings is different but they have many similarities. In each setting the people use many kinds of documents. The architect uses blueprints, specifications, notes from a client, site sketches, engineering reports, and billing reports. The lawyer has many different kinds of documents, briefs, contracts, and schedules.

All of these people refer to books and professional journals. They probably all have an in box and an out box to organize documents requiring different priorities for their attention. They use documents for multiple tasks and work on many tasks at once. Some documents may be in paper and others are online. Figure 3.6 suggests some elements of an office where documents in different media are used. One way to describe what professionals do is in terms of the **document work cycle**. In this cycle, people search for documents, process them, and write more documents. Of course, this level of description leaves out the goals and purposes of their work. It abstracts away the particular tasks that they do.

Another task-free characterization of work is an **information work cycle**. In this cycle, people search for information, process it, and create more information. This cycle is crucial for characterizing work steps that can be automated. It focuses on how documents serve as an external memory, conveying information among people.

In the following, we alternate between characterizing work in terms of a document work cycle and an information work cycle. The term **document base** or *document-oriented database* refers to computer files that store documents. The documents may be stored in a form that is editable using word processors and other programs, or they may be stored in the form of images. These files are linear in the sense that words have a linear order to form sentences, sentences have a linear order to form paragraphs, and other higher-order structures have linear orders, too. The term **database** or *information-oriented database* refers to organized data on files. Typically, such data are arranged in tables and are presumed to form a relational model of information used for an application. Typical examples would be tables of data about employees, an inventory of parts, or a history of repairs.

FIGURE 3.6. An office setting where documents of many different kinds are used to carry out several kinds of tasks.

Documents include both formal and semiformal representations. In the terminology of Chapter 1, a formal representation is defined with respect to an interpreter. The interpreter has a recognizer for the symbols. It can read and write symbols in the representation. It can draw useful inferences by combining different symbols. A **semiformal representation** is one that has some symbols that are interpreted by computers and other symbols that are not. The shift from informal to formal representations is in part a shift from documents to information and thereby a shift from humans as interpreters to computer systems as interpreters.

People do not just search for documents or information. Knowledge of a task guides the choice of what information or documents are sought and thereby guides the search process. Where is the phone number of the plumbing supplier? What is our current inventory of widgets? When did they say they could deliver the equipment? What was that warning notation scribbled on the blueprint next to the picture of the heating and cooling system of the new medical complex? What was the name of that person from the strategy office who visited last month? What did we do the last time we had a case like this? Can they test for helium leaks? The answer to each question is probably in a document somewhere. The relevant document might be in an in box, in the filing cabinet under "plumbing supplies," in the phone book, or in a notation on the side of a blueprint. The time and cost of locating relevant documents depends on how many documents there are, how they are organized, and how familiar we are with their organization.

People process information to accomplish a task. They combine facts to create new information. When people perform calculations on a scratch pad, they augment their working memories. They make decisions. They notice that some information will be useful for another task. They decide who else should see certain information.

Finally, people do not just write documents without a goal. They create documents to organize information for further work and to convey information to another time or person. They organize information in tables for ready comparison. Some documents bring together previously scattered pieces of information that are needed for a task. People organize documents to make them more useful as external memories. When a document is for a particular task, it presents the information needed for that task in a manner that facilitates use of the information. Returning to our cost characterizations of document and information processing, the document work cycle is often intended to reduce the cost of the next task by reducing the cost of accessing the relevant information.

Automating some of the document-processing steps often leads to increases in productivity. To illustrate this, we consider our second example. In the 1980s, a change began to sweep through retail outlets such as grocery stores. Point-of-sale terminals in many of these stores were equipped to scan the bar codes that are printed on products. A bar code associates a unique identifier with every kind of product. The information is scanned and routed automatically. The first economic advantage of the scanner is that it makes it possible to just mark prices in a database rather than marking individual items in the store. This enables stores to offer special prices on particular products for limited periods of time, without remarking all the prices on the unsold merchandise. Prices are shown to a customer by means of tags on the shelves and also on a detailed sales receipt showing items and their prices. A detailed database keeps track of when particular products need to be restocked on the shelves. The data can be used to guide the purchase of goods and to spot trends and changes in how goods are selling. In short, the introduction of bar-code scanners changed the way that people work in grocery stores.

We now consider several observations about documents, automation, and productivity. Continuing with the example of the grocery-store point-of-sale station, a bar-code recognizer interprets a symbol structure on a product. When a product is scanned, this is interpreted as meaning that the product has just been sold. In our terminology about representations, the label on a can of soup is a semiformal representation. Formal representations are a key to automating information-processing steps in the document work cycle. The work-saving steps at the point-of-sale terminal are a direct consequence of the assignment of bar codes to products and the reliability of the scanning process. The automation depends crucially on this recognition of symbols. It would not be possible if the computer system could not distinguish soup from nuts. The automation requires that the computer be able to combine symbols from different sources with reliability and precision.

Formal and semiformal documents can enable automation in a professional office, too. A spreadsheet file is a formal representation from the perspective of spreadsheet computations, but is semiformal if it includes uninterpreted comments. In contrast, a word processor does not interpret text according to its contents. Any productivity or quality gains around word processors are a result not of task automation, but of amplifying how people perform their work. Text processing is informal in that the processing involved in formatting and printing is trivial when compared with our human understanding of the words on a page. This is not to say that we can have no interpreters for text. Document retrieval systems search for patterns of words in text. They look for particular combinations of terms in paragraphs, sentences, or articles. They recognize synonyms and multiple linguistic forms of words. These processes tend to be broad and apply across a broad range of document- and information-processing tasks. Going beyond syntactic and grammatical knowledge to guide search, however, requires developing knowledge systems that have deeper models of what words mean.

Returning to our professional office example, a second observation is that the people in an office engage in many different activities in the course of a day. They do not just have one "task" to solve, but rather they have a collection of many different tasks. These tasks are related to each other and contribute to a large ongoing task of doing business. This contrasts with our discussion of tasks and problems in the other settings, where we focused on the building of a computational model for just one kind of problem. Sometimes much of the work in retrieving, processing, and creating documents involves the goal of making sense of a situation rather than solving a routinized problem. In short, not all of the work involving documents is easily characterized in terms of search and problem solving.

Our third scenario is about information processing in a medical center. There are documents about patient visits, documents about laboratory tests, and documents about medical policies and new treatment protocols. There are records of earlier diagnoses about a patient. In this complex of information sources, it is desirable to move documents and information easily from one place to another. A doctor and a nurse access many of the same documents. If a knowledge system is to become part of the environment, it is important that the system be integrated into the document and information databases that make up the work environment. If documents are semiformal and use standard codes such as unique patient identifiers, then some of the steps of searching and combining information can be automated. Much of the work in this setting is in combining documents—the middle step in our document and information work cycles.

This fact about combining information has several implications for introducing computer systems in general and knowledge systems in particular. Adding a new information-processing system to a medical center will save little work if people must manually transfer information to and from yet another kind of document. This means that adding a new word processor or adding an expert system may have little positive effect on the productivity of an organization if the new system does not connect gracefully with the other documents and systems.

Finally, we observe that there are trends both toward having more media and toward integrating them. This is not to predict the arrival of the "paperless, automated office." Indeed, for the immediate future, offices will use even more kinds of media than they use now—from paper, to computer files, to video files, and so on. However, in many settings more information is becoming routinely available online. As it does so, knowledge systems can make it possible to combine and reason with that information.

The previous scenarios emphasized knowledge systems as isolated problem solvers or as systems connected mainly to other knowledge systems. This active, document workspace scenario suggests that knowledge systems will increasingly inhabit a multimedia document and data space that includes information stored in many forms and at different degrees of formalization. People will continue to perform many different kinds of tasks using these media.

In summary, formal interpretation of symbols in documents is often a key to automation and the introduction of knowledge systems. For most organizations, automation plays only a small role, especially in the beginning. However, even in organizations where there seem to be few opportunities for automation, there is a continuing trend to integrate document and information services and knowledge systems can perform niche services that amplify parts of the document and information work cycles. Within any particular setting, there will be many different niches in which knowledge systems are used.

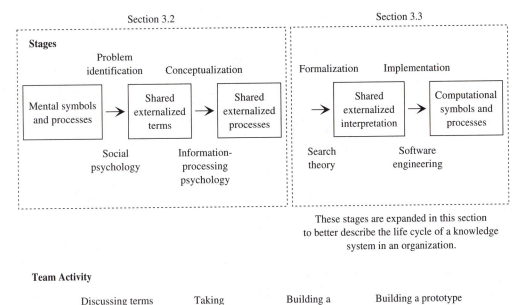

FIGURE 3.7. An overview of the transfer-of-expertise process. For simplicity, the figure leaves out feedback loops, which are part of iterative processes.

3.1.3 *Preview of Knowledge Acquisition Topics*

Figure 3.7 gives a preview of the topics in this chapter. The organization of topics loosely follows the development steps for a knowledge system in a plan of the kind associated with management practices. However, the presentation makes multiple passes in order to introduce important perspectives and foundations from different sciences. Competent practice requires that a knowledge-system builder use internal models of individuals (e.g., reasoning and problem solving) as well as models of the social and work practice setting in which knowledge systems are located and in which knowledge is used and created.

Section 3.2 is about the first stages of building a knowledge system using participatory design. It emphasizes concepts from social psychology and information-processing psychology. It is about individuals and how to get insights into their problem-solving activities. Section 3.3 is about the later steps in building a knowledge system, presenting concepts first from search theory and then from software engineering and ethnomethodology. It is concerned with the ways organizations themselves must evolve when they change their methods for creating, testing, and using knowledge.

3.1.4   *Summary and Review*

We began by discussing the meaning of the term *knowledge*. A dictionary provided us with seven meanings from common usage, involving perception, learning, practical experience, and competence. These meanings all focus on expectations that knowledge creates for a rational agent in an environment. We define knowledge as the codified experience of agents, where *codified* emphasizes that knowledge is written, *experience* emphasizes that knowledge is created and used in experiential situations, and *agents* have the experience. This definition is intended to illuminate what is involved in creating and using knowledge. To say that a human or computational agent has knowledge creates expectations about the agent's competence at some task.

The term *expert system* refers to a computer system whose performance is guided by specific, expert knowledge. The term *knowledge system* refers to a computer system that represents and uses knowledge to carry out a task. This term focuses attention on the knowledge that the systems carry, rather than on the question of whether or not such knowledge constitutes expertise. The term *domain* refers to a body of knowledge.

Knowledge systems are created and used in social and work contexts. Different settings have different requirements for developing knowledge systems. A personal knowledge system is the simplest kind of setting because it focuses on the activities of an individual. The participatory design setting involves several people in three roles: user, domain expert, and knowledge engineer. System development is participatory because all these people work together to develop a system. This is the most common setting in current practice and raises the essential issues about collaboration and communication.

In organizations, knowledge systems can function as active documents supporting people in many tasks, not just one. This positions knowledge systems as part of a working environment and information infrastructure in which there are many niches for incremental automation. This also creates opportunities for new kinds of knowledge systems and new approaches for building them because there are many different tasks to be performed and because there are practical advantages to having computationally expressed bodies of knowledge that can be shared.

Exercises for Section 3.1

■   **Ex. 1**   *[05] Terminology.* Indicate whether each of the following statements is true or false. If the statement is ambiguous, explain briefly.

(a) *True or False.* Transfer of expertise refers to a training process by which knowledge engineers train domain experts to build knowledge systems.

(b) *True or False.* An important advantage of a computational medium over a paper medium is that knowledge can be exercised and tested thoroughly on large cases. (For example, we can test whether a set of rules implies a particular conclusion by running the rules.)

(c) *True or False.* Participatory design refers to the ambition that knowledge systems should be able to participate in the design of newer systems that will eventually replace them.

(d) *True or False.* The major concerns of the shared-knowledge-base scenario are how multiple contributors can coordinate and negotiate changes to a knowledge base and how knowledge can be shared in closely related applications.

(e) *True or False.* The term *knowledge service* refers to a knowledge-based information-processing service. (Typically a knowledge service is part of a set of interacting services.)

Ex. 2   [05] *More Terminology.* Indicate whether each of the following statements is true or false. If the statement is ambiguous, explain briefly.

(a) *True or False.* Most of the issues about communication of knowledge do not arise in the development of a personal knowledge system because the system is developed and used by an individual.

(b) *True or False.* The document cycle refers to the chemical cycle of carbon oxidation and heat release as paper documents are created, used, shredded, and recycled into new paper products.

(c) *True or False.* A semiformal representation is one in which we have computational interpreters for some parts of the system but not others.

(d) *True or False.* Knowledge formalization refers to the process of writing knowledge in a medium.

(e) *True or False.* Knowledge refinement refers to an incremental process of extending and debugging a knowledge base using test cases.

Ex. 3   [05] *Even More Terminology.* Indicate whether each of the following statements is true or false. If the statement is ambiguous, explain briefly.

(a) *True or False.* The term *knowledge system* refers to a computer system that represents and uses knowledge to perform a task. The term is neutral about whether that knowledge constitutes expertise.

(b) *True or False.* The term *domain* is reserved for encyclopedic bodies of knowledge held in common by large groups of people.

(c) *True or False.* Usually, all the expert systems for a given application area use the same problem-solving architectures and computational models.

(d) *True or False.* A symbol level is a quantitative feedback mechanism invented by Charles Babbage for balancing the inferential loads in his analytical engine, roughly keeping the count (or level) of symbols even across different mechanical working memories.

(e) *True or False.* The ability to recognize and combine symbols is a key capability for automation in tasks involving documents.

Ex. 4   [CD-10] *Knowledge-System Scenarios.* This exercise considers some issues raised in the knowledge-system scenarios.

(a) In some cases of participatory design, the roles of users and domain experts are filled by different people. The domain expert might have an instructive role, such as briefing the users on new products in a configuration system. In this example, the users would be the ones who do configuration in their daily work and who would use the system to assist in their work. Briefly, in such a situation, why is it important to include a user in the participatory design team in addition to a domain expert?

(b) In the shared-knowledge-base scenario, multiple people can make changes to a knowledge base that they use in common. What issues does this raise beyond the participatory design case, where one knowledge engineer is responsible for updating the knowledge base? Why does common use involve issues beyond the "multiple-writers" problem, which is concerned with access mechanisms that preclude such problems as the accidental over-writing of files?

Ex. 5   [CD-10] *Information and Document Databases.* This exercise considers additional issues raised in the knowledge-system scenarios.

(a) What advantage does an information-oriented database such as a relational database of business data have over a document database for automating work processes? (A document database stores documents either as digital images or as editable files of text and graphics.)

(b) What advantages does a document database have over an information-based database for supporting activities in a work environment?

Ex. 6   [CD-10] *Digital Documents.* Professor Digit has become fascinated with the technology of character recognition systems for use in his office. After learning about the knowledge-system scenarios in this section, he declared that he would digitize all the documents in his office.

(a) A character recognition system is available to Professor Digit that recognizes alphabetic characters in a document image. The system scans an English-language document in a top-to-bottom and left-to-right order and presents the characters it finds as the resulting linear sequence. What information in documents is lost in this encoding? Briefly, what difficulties would arise in scanning stationery with institutional letterheads?

(b) Professor Digit has asked his beleaguered graduate student, Sam, to create knowledge systems to automate many of the mundane information-processing activities in his office. As an initial task, he proposes that Sam create a knowbot that will check all the scanned documents for new phone numbers. If a phone number appears that is not already in Professor Digit's files, the knowbot should create an appropriate entry for it in alphabetic order by the person's last name or the institution name. Briefly, describe two key issues that make this task difficult.

(c) Briefly, why would additional organizations of the scanned documents be useful for guiding a sequential key-word search?

3.2   Formulating Expertise

In this section we consider the first steps in developing knowledge systems using the participatory design approach. We focus on methods for identifying and articulating the knowledge used to carry out a task. Concepts and foundations are drawn from social psychology and information-processing psychology.

3.2.1   Conducting Initial Interviews

The participatory design approach begins with unstructured interviews during which a user, a domain expert, and a knowledge engineer try to ascertain the interest, needs, and possibilities for building a knowledge system. As before, we use these three roles to characterize different points of view and different aspects of the work that is involved. In any particular project, the roles may vary. More or fewer than three people may be involved.

Many questions arise at the beginning of a project. Is a knowledge system really needed? What exactly should it do? Who would use it? For whom would it have value? What value would it have? Who advocates creating it? What class of problems would it actually solve? Is a knowledge system for the task feasible at all? How would the required care and maintenance activities fit into the other activities of the organization? In short, the initial discussions are not only about the specialized knowledge of the task area, but also about the scope and feasibility of the project, as well as the organizational motivations and support for it. These context-setting questions are raised during an extended interview process. Most of the skills that we refer to are the seemingly ordinary skills of human conversation.

To understand the foundations of this process, we begin with a simple question. How is it that knowledge that starts out being held by one or more people comes to be held by others? One theory of communication holds that people learn by building on what they know already. When people converse about a new topic, they need to spend time developing terms of reference. They try to determine what concepts they hold in common so they can build a shared understanding from there. Their discussions consist of "communication acts" that help their colleagues in conversation to extend their understandings.

The base of knowledge that people hold jointly is called their **common ground**. The concept of common ground appears in many of the social sciences, such as social psychology, and in linguistic and psychological theories of communication, such as discourse theory. Knowledge formulation extends the common ground among users, domain experts, and knowledge engineers. At the beginning of a project, the user has an understanding of his job but may not have a clear notion how it could be affected or made more interesting with a knowledge system. The domain expert has experience solving problems in the domain and may have a sense of where automated knowledge processing would be helpful. The domain expert usually knows little about the creation of knowledge systems and has little initial basis for understanding what is required. The knowledge engineer presumably has experience building knowledge systems but knows little about the expert's domain. The user has a direct concern about how the knowledge system will fit into daily work, and may have mixed feelings about whether such a system would be helpful, threatening, or a nuisance. The user and domain expert have access to sample cases that illustrate the problems, the solutions, and solution methods.

The common ground of the participants includes knowledge from formal education and everyday experience. They need to decide whether a knowledge system would be useful, and whether building one is feasible. The project team needs to determine just what a knowledge system could and should do. This includes describing the task and the nature of the problems that a knowledge system would solve. In software engineering terminology, this is sometimes called the **problem identification stage**.

To understand what a knowledge system should do, a knowledge engineer needs to learn basic terminology from the task domain. For a medical domain, this may require extending a layperson's "folk" familiarity with diseases and laboratory tests to a more complete understanding of the medical concepts and terminology about disease agents, laboratory procedures, and medical interventions. It is normal in starting a project for this first part of the process to require several sessions. Providing a list of terms such as a medical dictionary is not enough because the knowledge engineer needs to understand which terms are important and how they relate to the task at hand. The domain expert and user need to help the knowledge engineer to learn enough concepts and terminology so that they can communicate efficiently about the characteristics of the task.

Automating and "Informating"

In knowledge systems we begin by identifying "problems to solve." This focus is typical of a knowledge engineering approach because it draws on its special methodologies and techniques that are intended for eliciting, formalizing, and representing knowledge about particular tasks and situations. Nonetheless, knowledge systems should not be thought of as if their only role was to provide software for automating some task.

The term "**informate**," in contrast with *automate* (Zuboff, 1988), is associated with computer technologies that give people computer-based access to the information needed for their work, especially when such technology gives them a larger degree of control in their work. This term directs our focus on some technical and social issues about designing computer systems, which we mention here briefly.

The first issues concern data interconnection. There are several social issues about connecting computers to share data, involving personal privacy and freedom that are beyond the scope of this chapter. In typical business knowledge systems, a more central issue is that a knowledge systems cannot function well as an isolated island in an organization. There are other computer systems and databases in use, dealing with such things as inventory, part descriptions, material constants, geographic temperature data, or whatever else might be relevant to the task at hand. Part of developing a knowledge system is to identify these other systems and to determine which ones it is appropriate to connect to. Developers of the knowledge system need to work with those who create and maintain these systems and databases. The technical issues involve the requirements for accessing the other systems. Identifying the connections is part of what is needed to understand the scope and context of a knowledge system.

All computer systems, including knowledge systems, change the organizations in which they are used. Change is brought about both by systems that informate and by those that automate. Thus, even the early stages of a project begin to take into account the role of a knowledge system in the organization and the possible effects on work practice. Rather than considering all these issues at once, we defer discussion of organizational issues until Section 3.3.

Today's organizations that get the most leverage out of their use of computers demand that their computer system give them the access, control, and seamless connectivity that they need. In this sense, all successful computer systems (including ones using extensive knowledge bases) must be informating.

Identifying a Task

It is essential early on to gather sample problems as cases. Cases can be supplied by both users and experts. They are used to focus discussion. Failure to collect sample cases is one of the common ways that knowledge-system projects fail. Indeed, an inability to collect sample problems and to agree on their solutions can usually be taken as evidence that an inappropriate task has been selected. At this stage, a knowledge engineer wants to understand what constitutes a task in terms of the input data, a sketch of a solution process, and acceptable answers.

General questions at this stage are used to gauge the difficulty of the task, the variability across problems, and the knowledge requirements. What is an example of a case? What are the input data? What is an answer? Are there multiple acceptable answers? Are different problems solved in the same way? Since important distinctions and purposes of these questions may not be established yet, the questions should be considered as tentative probes and the answers should not be taken as definitive. The questions are intended for early screening of impractically difficult domains and also to see how reflective the expert is about problem solving. The same questions will arise in more concrete form during the next stages of knowledge formulation using specific cases. At this stage they are useful in helping to determine whether there really is a well-defined problem for a knowledge system to solve and whether the expert has experience in solving it.

There may be no simple way to appreciate the scale of a project until later in the process. The informal questions and judgments at this stage do not substitute for the detailed knowledge-level analysis of a task that we will discuss later. They should be viewed as a screening exercise, useful for building a context and preliminary understanding of a project.

Is the Task Worth Automating?

A knowledge engineer is usually asked to estimate whether the knowledge for doing a task can be formulated and how long it should take. An even more fundamental question is whether a task is worth automating. Anyone who creates software for organizations needs to be careful about setting expectations. Unrealistic expectations established at the beginning about performance or the resources needed to create a system can make it very difficult later when a system is being evaluated.

People are sometimes driven by wishful thinking, hoping that AI technology will solve their hardest problems. ("Gee, this problem is *really* hard. Maybe if we just applied some artificial intelligence . . .") Much time can be saved by determining quickly that the initial expectations for a knowledge system are well beyond the state of the art, that the need for a knowledge system is insufficient to sustain the effort of building one, or that certain early goals for systems would lead to solving the wrong problems. Most successful knowledge systems automate tasks that are fairly routine and mundane for those who do them, rather than exotic and rare. In most commercially viable examples, the tasks are costly because they are performed frequently. This concern with the frequency of task performance is applicable whenever automation is considered.

Some tasks are too difficult to automate. Although there is no foolproof recipe for determining this at this stage of the process, some questions can give early indications. Who performs the task now? How often do they do it? How well do they do? How much training do they have? How long does it take to carry out the task? How much has the task changed over the past few years?

How long it takes to solve a problem can provide clues about how much knowledge is needed. A rule of thumb sometimes used by knowledge engineers is that a suitable task is one that takes an expert an hour or less, not counting the time spent on mechanical tasks such as looking up information, tallying numbers, or filling in forms. Tasks that take only a few minutes of expert time can probably be solved by simpler approaches or may not be worth automating at all. Tasks that require more than a few hours of expert time are often too difficult and unbounded in terms of the knowledge that they require.

These rules do not apply if the longer tasks are simply iterations of much shorter ones repeated several times in a session. As before, rules like these are useful for checking plausibility in a preliminary assessment of a task. Sometimes it is worth automating a short task, so as to achieve a consistently higher quality of results, and the task is complex enough to warrant formal knowledge engineering. A task may be worth automating even if it is very difficult if the economic arguments are strong enough.

If the people who carry out the task are highly trained, they may need their extensive education and experience to carry out the task. In this situation, formulating the knowledge will probably be time-consuming and expensive. If little training is involved, then the knowledge elicitation techniques may be unnecessary. If the task requires drawing on broad human experiences, then formulating the knowledge to automate the task may be problematic.

If the task is performed irregularly such as every few weeks, then it will be difficult to get a collection of test cases and there may not be enough commonality between cases. This may also be a clue that there is little value in creating a knowledge system that would automate the task. If solution methods are radically different for each problem, too much knowledge may be required to build a knowledge system. If the people who carry out the task do not do a good job now, then reliable expertise for the task may be difficult to locate. If the task changes rapidly, then the organization will need people who can keep the knowledge base up to date.

Knowledge engineers use common-sense judgments like these to help determine whether tasks are simple enough and valuable enough for automation. It is perhaps disconcerting that the question of whether a knowledge system can and should be built can not be determined by some elementary decision procedure. There are several reasons for this. First, the problems for which knowledge-system techniques can be usefully applied are not easily characterized. This prevents the domain expert from being able to answer the question right away. Second, understanding a task is complex. This prevents a knowledge engineer from answering the question right away. Third, the knowledge system itself may change the nature of the task. This complicates the user's assessment of the possibilities. In short, mutual ignorance among the user, domain expert, and knowledge engineer often precludes an accurate, immediate assessment.

Assembling a Project Team

After the initial sessions, additional users and experts may be added to the team. Sometimes the first expert selected to help build a knowledge system is not the right one. One or more experts and users are needed who deal with the task routinely as part of their job. They have the knowledge and experience to understand what the real problems are and to choose appropriate test cases. They should be available to work on the project for a significant portion of their time and must be able to articulate what they are doing when solving a problem.

It is not enough to have somebody with a theory about how cases like this should be handled or some good ideas about a new way to do things, or even an "eager and bright" beginner who will learn. Nor is it appropriate to try to use only a very senior domain expert who is unable to relinquish enough other responsibilities to have time for the knowledge acquisition process.

Representative users must be selected to adequately reflect the contexts of use. In later sections we return to this point to consider how the process involves not only knowledge engineering, but also social and organizational design because knowledge systems change the way that organizations work.

Conversational Skills

Most of the skills we have discussed for this stage of building a knowledge system might be called "conversational skills." Although describing and exemplifying those skills in detail is beyond the scope of this chapter, a few points deserve mentioning. It is typical in conversation generally (not just for knowledge acquisition sessions) for people to overestimate how well they understand each other (Nisbitt & Ross, 1980). Thus, at any point in the discussion the participants are likely to overestimate their agreement and common understanding. When there is a lot of new ground to cover, they must coach each other, moving concepts from individual intelligi-

DE1:   Okay, there are different ways that the driver springs can be implemented.
(Domain expert begins drawing a figure here.)
This is an idler shaft and this is a driver shaft and this is a section of sheet-metal side plate or something. The driver is usually fixed and there is some kind of shaft, and the guarder spring is linked around here somehow. To release paper jams, they just lift up the shaft providing an eighth inch clearance between the idler and the driver so that the paper can be pulled out.

KE2:   You mean you have to make the spring strong enough but not so strong that people can't pry them apart.

DE1:   Right.

KE1:   Basically you use the same spring mechanism to pry them apart.

KE2:   No, you have to counter back that spring mechanism to pry them apart.

DE1:   Right, you pull against the spring. The spring is bringing them together and you pull against it.

KE1:   Does this also mean that the guard rail pulls out when you open the baffle?

DE1:   That's just what I was getting to. This is one method. The other method that I have seen is essentially the same.
(Here the domain expert draws a second figure.)
Here's the top, the bottom, the driver, and some sort of side plate. Then you have a slat, and a spring anchor here, and here, a shaft, something like this. So when you close or open the baffle it will extend the spring.

FIGURE 3.8.   Edited transcript from a videotaped knowledge formulation session. This excerpt shows that much of the conversation is used by the participants to make sense of each other's ideas. This is a normal and time-consuming part of learning a new vocabulary. Statements in italics are comments and observations about the process added afterward.

bility to mutual intelligibility. Working on examples extends the common ground. To curtail rambling and focus the discussion, they can use conventional conversational techniques such as pausing to "summarize understanding so far."

Figure 3.8 presents a transcribed excerpt from a knowledge acquisition session from the PRIDE project (Mittal, Dym, & Morjaria, 1986), which built a knowledge system to assist in the design of paper-transport systems for copiers and printers. The intensive knowledge-formulation process for this project took place over a period of about six months. This transcription presents a few minutes from the fourth intensive knowledge-formulation session in the second month of the project. Much of the work in this session revolves around the definition of terms. The session centers around the meaning of new terms, such as *baffles*, *springs*, and *rollers* used in paper-transport systems, and the relations between these terms in the context of designing a copier. In a conversation like this, the domain expert has to work to make his concepts clear and the knowledge engineer has to test and demonstrate her understanding.

Domain experts often discover that these discussions cause them to reflect deeply on their methods. This is especially true in cases where they have never tried to organize or present their methods for these particular tasks before. This is consistent with the aphorism that "You never understand something fully until you have to teach it." Especially for a domain expert, these sessions are like interactive teaching sessions in which the "student" knowledge engineers play highly interactive and participative roles.

One danger in pedagogical sessions is to follow classroom teaching habits too closely and to oversimplify issues. A knowledge system cannot be completed by a team that discusses only abstractions, leaving out the details of practice. Unlike people, today's knowledge systems cannot learn the details on the job. For success, it is essential to get down to the nitty-gritty details, the special case facts, and the intermediate steps. This is the subject of the next section.

3.2.2   Taking Protocols

In software engineering jargon the next stage is called the **problem conceptualization stage**. During this stage the team begins to develop a detailed external representation of the problem-solving process for the task. In determining the scope of a knowledge system, there is a tension between pursuing depth and pursuing breadth. By pursuing depth, we refer to acquiring necessary step-by-step details for carrying out some part of the task. By pursuing breadth, we refer to a comprehensive identification of all of the subtasks that make up the whole. Metaphorically, to pursue depth is to use a microscope on a subtask and to pursue breadth is to develop a rough map of the territory.

The usual method for understanding a subtask in depth is protocol analysis. This section illustrates some of the practice of taking verbal protocols and briefly describes some foundations for this approach from information-processing psychology. The concepts and techniques for using verbal reports to develop symbolic models come from protocol analysis of information-processing psychology. The term **protocol** refers to recorded observations combined with verbal reports made by "subjects" who speak their thoughts as they solve problems. It is very common practice to record these sessions for later analysis, using audio and video recording equipment.

The taking of protocols contrasts with the less structured approach of the first stage, in which a knowledge engineer just asks a domain expert to explain what he does, among other things. The former request is too unfocused for gathering detailed and intermediate data about problem solving. It invites a domain expert to be pedagogical and to discourse broadly and abstractly about the task.

Verbal Data and Information-Processing Psychology

Within psychology, information-processing psychology arose in reaction to behaviorism, which focused on stimulus-response models for explaining behavior. Stimulus-response models elide all the intermediate steps between input and output.

Analysis of verbal protocols is a source of information about mental processes that take place between input and output. The goal of using protocol analysis in information-processing psychology is to gain insights about the nature of mental processing and mental machinery. When a psychologist uses protocol analysis to study a person playing chess, solving physics and algebra problems, or interpreting sentences, the psychologist may be interested in short-term memory, the nature of the errors made, the storage and chunking of memory elements, or in the time it takes to perform particular operations. The goal of using protocol analysis in knowledge engineering is to learn about the intermediate steps in solving a problem and to identify the knowledge that is used for them.

A crucial hypothesis is central to the use of protocols both in psychology and in knowledge engineering:

The Verbal Data Hypothesis. The information that is used during performance of a task is reportable in verbal protocols, and the information that is reported in verbal protocols is used in problem solving.

Within knowledge engineering, this is an operational hypothesis about human problem solving, seldom questioned or investigated. Within psychology, however, this has been a subject of theorizing as well as experimentation. There are several competing models of human cognition in psychology. For most questions about protocol analysis, the differences among them tend to be irrelevant because protocol analysis and the verbal data hypothesis impose few constraints on possible mental architectures.

Not too surprisingly, information-processing psychology models human cognition in terms of information processing. Within the problem-solving paradigm of information-processing psychology, a cognitive process modeled at the symbol level is roughly a sequence of **states** that are successively transformed by a sequence of information-processing **operations**. These states are stored in memory.

Psychology postulates that there are different memories having different capacities and accessing characteristics. The memories of shortest duration are the sensory stores. Then there is a short-term memory (STM) of limited capacity and intermediate duration. Finally, there is a long-term memory (LTM) with a large capacity and fairly permanent duration. The LTM has a much slower access time than the STM for both storage and retrieval. The problem-solving model postulates that there is a working memory, which contains the symbols in active use. The exact relation between the working memory, the STM, and the LTM is not entirely determined, and models differ on this point.

Protocol analysis uses search as its framework. In short, behavior is modeled as a search through a problem space, typically a state space with states and operators. During this search, the subject accumulates information about the problem situation. Each step is characterized as the application of an operator. There is presumed to be a relatively small set of operators specific to any task. The operators are assumed to apply to information held by the subject in the working memory. Application of an operator can bring new knowledge into the working memory and advance the problem-solving task to a new point in the problem space. Roughly, to analyze a protocol is to use the verbal data to build a cognitive simulation of problem-solving behavior in terms of states and operators.

Within this general model of mind many variations on cognitive models are possible. The working memory could be a separate and specialized storage medium or a specially and temporarily activated part of the LTM. The differences between these formulations are not important to our purposes here. The crucial relationships are those among verbal data, problem solving, and memories.

A Sample Protocol and Its Analysis

Figure 3.9 presents an example of a protocol taken of a subject solving a gas flow problem. The numbers have been added to the statements to simplify reference to them in the analysis that follows in Figure 3.10. Prior to recording a protocol like this, some psychologists recommend having subjects do warm-up tasks where the subjects provide a verbal protocol while doing some extremely simple task. The purpose of the warm-up is to familiarize subjects with the process of

Problem Statement

Nitrogen flows along a constant area duct. It enters at 40°F and 200 psi. It leaves at atmospheric pressure and at a temperature of –210°F. Assuming that the flow rate is 100 lb./min., determine how much heat will be transferred to the surroundings.

Protocol

1. Okay, the first thing I'm going to do is pick a system.
2. That is, the system will be the duct.
3. Okay, I draw that like this
4. and I'm going to write the first law on this duct
5. as Q plus Ws will equal m times $h2$ minus $h1$
6. where I'm ignoring the changes in kinetic and potential energy.
7. And this is probably a pretty good assumption.
8. Okay, I'm asked to determine how much heat will be transferred to the surroundings.
9. Okay, that will be the Q term here.
10. Since we have just a duct here, there will be no shaft work
11. so Ws will equal zero.
12. Q then will simply equal m times $h2$ minus $h1$.
13. Okay, m I know as 100 lb./min.
14. and $h2$ minus $h1$.
15. In order to determine that, I will need some physical properties for nitrogen.
16. So let me look these up.
17. Found these.
18. Okay, so let me put m is 100 lb./min.
19. Okay, $h2$, 2 is downstream,
20. so $h2$ is the enthalpy at one atmosphere and –210°F.
21. So let me look that up.
22. –210°, okay, this is in degrees Rankine, –210°, ah . . .
23. Okay, is 250° Rankine, this is $T2$.
24. While I'm at it, I'll just note that $T1$ will be 500° Rankine.
25. Okay, so 14.7 lb. f/cu. in.,
26. at a temperature of 250° Rankine.
27. I read h as 126.443 BTU/lbm, that's $h2$.
28. Now as $h1$ I have 200 psi and 500° Rankine.
29. Let me look that up
30. and I read $h1$ as 187.408 BTU/lbm.
31. Okay, I'm simply going to do the calculation.
32. I see that the pound masses cancel as they should
33. and my final answer will be in BTUs/min.,
34. which is what I'd expect.
35. Let me do the calculation now.
36. 126.443 – 187.408,
37. and when I multiply that by 100 I get –6096.5.
38. The negative sign is as it should be
39. because it indicates that heat is being transferred out of the system.
40. That's it.

FIGURE 3.9.   Transcript from a recorded session of a subject performing a heat flow problem. This session shows verbal protocol taken as the subject works on a problem. (From K.A. Ericsson and H.A. Simon, *Protocol Analysis*, MIT Press, page 307.)

thinking aloud, so they will remember to say enough when solving real problems. In psychological protocols, a subject is told that giving a protocol is different from having a conversation. During the warm-up exercises, subjects are coached to express their thoughts directly without explaining or interrelating the information. They should focus on what they are doing, without trying to reflect on or report about their thinking on the activity at some "meta" level. These issues and procedures are not as crucial or appropriate for the purposes of knowledge engineering as they are for modeling mental activity.

Several important questions arise about the analysis of protocols. Do the sequences of operations reported verbally actually correspond to the sequences of thoughts? Does speaking alter the thinking process? Under what circumstances are verbal reports more or less complete? Questions such as these have been the subject of debate and careful experimentation within information-processing psychology. Although a thorough discussion of the psychological evidence would go beyond our purposes, a few key points can be made.

Information-processing psychologists believe that various mediating processes intervene between attention to information and its verbalization. For example, intermediate processes translate internal information into a verbal form. In cases where a subject is asked to report on things he does not normally pay attention to, there may also be additional scanning or filtering processes. According to the model, such processes can change the sequence of operations because they require attention to additional information and thereby alter the working memory.

In controlled studies that minimize requirements for extra processing, such as attending to extra phenomena, there is no evidence that verbalization alters the course of thought processes.

Protocol Analysis for Problem
CHOOSE SYSTEM
　　　　The system is: (2) the system will be the duct.
　　　　Equation: (5) $Q + Ws = m (h2 - h2)$
　　　　The variables are: $Q\ Ws\ m\ h2\ h1$
COMMENT: (6–7) I'm ignoring the changes in kinetic and potential energy.
FIND Ws.
　　　　VALUE Ws: (11) 0
COMMENT: (12) now $Q = m (h2 - h1)$
FIND m.
　　　　VALUE m: (13) 100 lb./min.
FIND $h2$.
　　　　READ TABLE. (nitrogen tables)
　　　　VALUE $h2$: (16–17, 19–23, 25–27) 126.443 BTU/lbm
FIND $h1$.
　　　　READ TABLE. (nitrogen tables)
　　　　VALUE $h1$: (24, 28–30) 187.408 BTU/lbm
CHECK UNITS. (32–34)
SOLVE: (5) $Q + WS = m (h2 - h1)$
　　　　SOLUTION: (35–37) –6096.5
CHECK PLAUSIBILITY. (38–39)

FIGURE 3.10.　Protocol analysis for the session recorded in Figure 3.9. Numbers in parentheses refer to the steps in Figure 3.9. (From K.A. Ericsson and H.A. Simon, *Protocol Analysis*, MIT Press, page 307.)

Furthermore, in many cases verbalization does not substantially degrade performance on problems. It can, however, slow down performance when the mental operations are much faster than the corresponding speech so that the verbalizations need to be queued. Sometimes in an intense session a subject may stop verbalizing and need to be reminded. One explanation that has been offered for this is that verbalization stops when the task process requires a lot of working memory capacity.

Protocols of highly practiced activities are less complete. Psychologists believe that as processes become highly practiced, they become more fully automated and less accessible. This phenomenon may be analogous to executing a computer algorithm in compiled rather than interpreted form. Automation and compiling greatly speed up the process of doing a task. They also make the intermediate products inaccesssible. A theoretical explanation of why verbal reports of highly practiced tasks are less complete is that the intermediate products are not available to the working memory.

3.2.3 Characterizing Search Spaces

The **symbol level** and the **knowledge level** are two distinct levels for describing knowledge systems. At the symbol level we discuss algorithms and representations. At the knowledge level we are concerned with the characterization of the knowledge needed for a task and how the knowledge is used. To organize our understanding of task-oriented problem solving, we must describe the bodies of knowledge and the search spaces.

Several questions are addressed in a knowledge-level analysis. What is the overall problem being solved? What is a solution? What are the search spaces? How large is the space of candidates? What are the termination criteria? How does a search make progress? What phenomena make the task difficult? What are the subproblems? Which subproblems are the most difficult or challenging? Are the subproblems the same from one case to another? What knowledge is used in the subproblems? What knowledge is used in multiple subproblems? Do different subproblems require using knowledge in different ways?

Knowledge-level analysis precedes symbol-level analysis. In other words, before we try to implement a knowledge system we should first understand it at the knowledge level. The interview and protocol analysis activities provide data for the analysis.

Protocols are traces of problem-solving behavior. Protocols have three important roles for constructing a knowledge-level analysis. They provide an existence proof that some problems are solvable. They are a source of data about the use of knowledge. Collectively, they provide multiple cases for variations on a problem, providing data about what is constant across different problems and what varies.

In the following we consider a brief but concrete example of analyzing a task: troubleshooting electronic circuit boards from a telephone switching unit. Suppose we collect verbal and observational data about technicians performing the task. We observe technicians taking measurements and planning measurements. We observe them discussing which components they think are broken and which are working. We observe them removing components from the circuit boards and testing them. We observe them making predictions about how the measurements should differ if particular components are working or broken in known ways.

A great deal of data can be acquired in this way. Organizing the data is a major challenge. In this example we do not give an account of the process by which the data can be organized.

However, we do show how the analysis of the verbal protocol yields knowledge that could be used in the framework for diagnostic knowledge that is used in Chapter 9.

Figure 3.11 characterizes the troubleshooting and repair task in terms of three spaces: a data space, a hypothesis space, and a repair space. The three spaces correspond to three major categories of operations that would show up in the protocols: taking circuit data, inferring what components are broken, and replacing components.

The **data space** describes the data that can be collected. The input data would include various indicator lamps on the device, various information accessible through software controlling the board, and signal values measured by test equipment.

The **hypothesis space** characterizes what could be wrong with the circuit board. The basic elements of this space are candidate diagnostic hypotheses. A fundamental assumption in this formulation of the task is that if the telephone switching unit is not working then one or more of its parts must be broken. A solution candidate is a description characterizing which components of the circuit board are faulty and how they are faulty.

The **repair space** characterizes operations for replacing or adjusting components to bring the circuit board back into proper operation. The figure includes a separate **system model** that describes the structure and behavior of the device being diagnosed. The system model is referenced by operations in all three spaces.

Here are examples of statements from protocols that provide evidence of particular knowledge used in circuit board diagnosis:

- *Knowledge for data abstraction.* Example: "If the voltage at pin 56 is more than 5.3 volts then the carrier feedback voltage is too high." Such knowledge can be characterized as an operation that reduces raw data to abstracted data in a taxonomy in the data space.
- *Knowledge of system structure.* Example: "The polling unit has as its parts multiplexer M45, microprocessor MP16, ..." Such knowledge would be part of the component hierarchy in the system model and is referenced by operations in the repair and hypothesis spaces.
- *Knowledge for predicting behavior.* Example: "If adder 45 is working and its inputs are known, the output of the adder should be the sum of the inputs computed as 16-bit integers." Such knowledge would be part of the causal or behavior submodels of the system model.
- *Knowledge of fault behavior.* Example: "A stuck-at-1 fault in an inverter has prior probability .0001 and causes the output to be 1 if there is power to the inverter. This is independent of the input voltage." Such knowledge would be part of the fault submodel and referenced by hypothesis-forming operations.
- *Knowledge for hypothesis generation.* Examples: "A diagnostic hypothesis is a set of possible faults. If the output of the multiplier is faulty, then the multiplier may be malfunctioning or its inputs might be wrong. We rule out hypotheses that are not consistent with observed behavior. We consider the most plausible hypotheses first." Such knowledge controls the hypothesis-forming operations in the hypothesis space.
- *Knowledge for probe selection.* Example: "Select the probe point that results in the lowest Shannon entropy for consistent diagnoses." Other rules may bear on the relative ease, cost, or risk associated with alternative probes. Such knowledge is characterized as controlling the information-gathering operations in the data space.

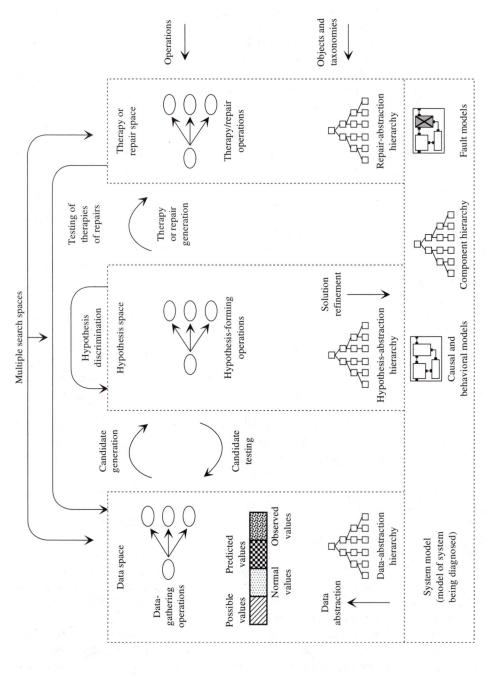

FIGURE 3.11. Some elements of a knowledge-level analysis of a diagnosis and repair task. These tasks are described in detail in Chapter 9.

The search spaces in Figure 3.11 locate each of these kinds of knowledge with regard to the problem being solved.

In the early stages of a knowledge-system project, the knowledge engineer and domain expert work together to create a map of the task and the knowledge used. The characterization in Figure 3.11 is an example of the kind of map that they create. Protocol data yield elements that they need to fit into their map. The map is organized so knowledge that is used together is located in the space. Knowledge that is used for several different problems is located in shared spaces, such as the system submodel in Figure 3.11.

Given a set of protocols, there is no single correct characterization of the search spaces. Furthermore, different experts may solve the same problem in different ways. The same expert may even solve the problem in different ways on different occasions. In such cases we can develop alternative models for organizing the knowledge and can compare the benefits of each.

As we analyze a task, we keep track of how different steps in solving a problem depend on each other. In doing this we may discover that the relative ordering of some of the steps in solving a problem is arbitrary. Thus, the characterization of the methods for searching the space need not duplicate human protocol data exactly. Different approaches may go through essentially the same steps but in different orders. As a model becomes more formal, we bring our experience with general search methods to the analysis.

To summarize, protocol data provide evidence about the steps used in a search method. To understand a task, we need to specify formally what a solution is. We need to identify input data, intermediate states, and any auxiliary conclusions. These data provide a basis for sketching out candidate search spaces. We then analyze the protocol data to see what knowledge is used in guiding the search. We look for dependencies in the steps in the protocols, so that we can separate which steps must come before others and for which steps the ordering is incidental. In the following, we look at some of the issues in carrying out this analysis.

3.2.4 *Adapting Protocol Analysis for Knowledge Systems*

The analysis of protocols raises many questions for knowledge engineering: How objective is the encoding of protocols? What demarks an intermediate step in the protocol? How should a set of operators be determined? How do we distinguish big steps from little steps? Does it matter how the little steps are aggregated into big steps and little steps, major and minor phases? How finely should the steps be recorded? Does the validity and usefulness of the analysis turn crucially on the vocabulary of operators? Can techniques be developed such that the encoding of protocols will be reliably repeatable across sessions, across subjects, or by different coders? Under what conditions do a coder's expectations bias the encoding of protocols? This potpourri of questions raises several methodological issues that have been the subject of investigation in information-processing psychology.

The questions are resolved in different ways for knowledge engineering because the goals of psychology and knowledge engineering are different. The goal of protocol analysis for information-processing psychology is to determine parameters of human cognitive performance. The goal of the analysis for knowledge engineering is to identify knowledge used for the task. Both fields use verbal data on cases to provide specific data about steps in a problem-solving process.

A crucial difference is that a knowledge engineering team views protocol analysis as merely an intermediate stage in its process of characterizing a task and identifying the knowledge that is used. Protocol analysis is one step along the way to building a workable, extendable, and maintainable knowledge system that performs a particular knowledge service usefully and reliably in a setting. Knowledge engineering is less concerned about whether verbalization itself alters the thinking process. It is less concerned about whether verbalization alters the validity of the knowledge elicited, and it employs additional tests of the organized knowledge to detect and correct inaccuracies.

A knowledge system is developed and tested using a *large set of cases*. In knowledge engineering, protocol analysis provides both an indication of what knowledge is needed and how that knowledge is used in context. A single protocol may provide useful indications of what knowledge is used and what constitutes correct performance. However, it is never used by itself. A knowledge system must ultimately perform correctly on additional cases that will be supplied and evaluated.

Since the goals of psychology and knowledge engineering differ, some aspects of the techniques for eliciting protocols are different. Techniques for improving effectiveness and reliability have overlapping but not identical concerns. For example, in both fields elicitation that relies entirely on retrospective answers to questions about prior behavior are suspect. In psychology, it is well understood that memory and recall can dramatically distort the record of a process because memory is selective and reporting is reformulative. In knowledge engineering, it is understood that when people construct accounts of how they do their work from memory they tend to abstract away essential details. In both fields, taking protocols helps to detect and avoid these distortions because they are real-time records of problem-solving behavior. However, in knowledge engineering retrospective analysis is used for fleshing out the details that can go by too quickly for discussion in a real-time problem-solving session.

The transcribed protocol of Figure 3.12 shows a knowledge engineer interrupting a domain expert to ask questions in the middle of a case. In information-processing psychology, psychologists prefer not to interrupt at all and only do so when it is absolutely necessary. They use interruptions mainly to remind an experimental subject to verbalize.

In contrast, knowledge engineers interrupt at any point at which they do not understand the expert's step. One reason for this difference is that knowledge formulation sessions can go on for much longer periods of time. A given session may last several hours, intermixing protocols and interviews, and the knowledge acquisition process may take place over several weeks or months. Some balance is needed to assure mutual intelligibility. One can interrupt too much and thereby derail a domain expert's train of thought. Recordings of sessions and organized notes can reduce the urgency of interruption by making it possible to return to an earlier point in the process.

The relationship between a knowledge engineer and a domain expert is quite different from that between an information-processing psychologist and an experimental subject. After all, a domain expert knows more about the domain subject matter than the knowledge engineer and they are working together in partnership. This changes the nature of protocol analysis in several ways. For example, the burden of categorizing and establishing the operation definitions need not rest solely with the knowledge engineer; rather, it is determined collaboratively and incrementally by the domain experts and the knowledge engineers together. Because the knowledge base evolves as it is tested on multiple cases, there is less emphasis on getting a single consistent protocol analysis at the beginning. In short, the purpose of the interview is quite different.

In the analysis of a protocol for a knowledge system, it is entirely appropriate to ask a domain expert the following questions: Do you always do this step? What if the data are not

> KE1: Are we done with the idler part now?
> (*At this point the knowledge engineers and domain experts refer to the outline of the notes so far.*)
> Or do you want to do the velocity check?
> DE1: No, once I've got this, we've got the normal force, shaft size, and selection. I think I'm worried about deflection here, because it's going to affect skew.
> KE1: Do you want to do skew now?
> DE1: Well, as long as I'm doing the idler normal forces I have enough information to do that now. Why I'm worried about deformation is that if the shaft deflects substantially we'll have uneven force distribution on the drive rolls.

FIGURE 3.12. Protocol from a knowledge formulation session. As in the heat flow problem, we see the domain expert verbalizing his reasons for doing particular steps. In this example, the knowledge engineer interrupts with questions.

available for this step? What else might have happened here? Such questions encourage the domain expert to think about additional cases. Figure 3.13, from a session of the PRIDE projects, shows an example of a domain expert realizing that the knowledge and examples previously articulated fail to take into account a special case in design. The expert then refines the knowledge by explaining an exception to the cases under which it should be used.

These suggestions illustrate again the difference in the role of a domain expert in knowledge formulation and the role of an experimental subject in a protocol experiment. In an information-processing psychology experiment, a psychologist probably would not ask the subject for his opinion in analyzing a protocol. In contrast, building knowledge systems is a team effort. It is common practice to draw on the background experience of the domain experts, who are familiar with cases and situations and can suggest appropriate abstractions and identify exceptional cases.

Finally, the expectation that a knowledge base will develop incrementally across many cases reduces the immediate pressure to codify every little detail from a case. Issues that are

> DE1: I want to back up for a moment. These two rules don't always apply. There can be interface requirements from neighboring subsystems (and I'm thinking particularly of VCS now) that create exceptions to the design rules.
> (*The domain expert pauses to draw a figure at this point.*)
> These are feed heads, that's a belt, that's a belt, . . . These feed heads have a corrugator so that when you acquire a sheet of paper by vacuum, it bends like this. When you try feed that paper into two sets of rolls it tends to track that corrugation.
> So what we recommend is that instead of two rolls, there is one roll lining up with the corrugation.
> That's the only exception that I know about.
> KE1: So you do that for all the rolls, or only the first roll?
> DE1: Only the first.

FIGURE 3.13. Edited transcript from a videotaped session showing the discovery and articulation of an exception. During a project, the limits of generality are modified incrementally as exceptional cases and families of cases are discovered.

important come up repeatedly in many cases. An expert can help in deciding which things are worth recording and remembering from a case. This conversational and collaborative character of working with protocol data would be completely out of place in a psychological study, since it would make the subject reflective about the task in a way that could distort subsequent data.

3.2.5 Summary and Review

This section introduces theory and practice for the first stages of the participatory design approach. The stages of knowledge-system development introduced in this section are called the problem identification stage and the problem conceptualization stage. The first stage requires that the users, domain expert, and knowledge engineer develop a preliminary understanding of the task using unstructured interviews. We discussed a theory of communication based on the notion of common ground from social psychology, as well as the use of project notes to organize the activity. The second stage uses particular cases and protocol analysis to reveal the intermediate steps in problem solving. Protocols provide a focus for identifying knowledge that would emerge very slowly in an unstructured interview process.

We discussed the differences in methodology between information-processing psychology and knowledge engineering in their use of verbal data and protocol analysis. A major difference is that in knowledge engineering, protocol analysis is one of many sources of evidence about the knowledge needed for a task. Ultimately a knowledge system must use the domain knowledge, but it need not closely duplicate the action sequence of a domain expert on a problem.

Exercises for Section 3.2

Ex. 1   [CD-10] *Accessible Expertise.* After reading a news report about expert systems, Professor Digit has decided to build one. His plan is to build a "voicewriter," that is, a knowledge-based typewriter that would print whatever he says into its microphone. The voicewriter should also accept simple spoken commands to control word processing.

His first step is to find some expert listeners and typists. Reasoning that secretaries sometimes have to take notes and then type letters and that a few of them can take dictation, he decides that they have the required knowledge. He solicits the aid of the secretaries of his department, to interview them about how they understand language and use a typewriter and to acquire their knowledge by taking protocols of them doing this task.

(a) What knowledge does Professor Digit need to access for representation in a voicewriter? Give your inventory in terms of an inventory of the following skills. For each skill, say briefly what its knowledge elements are, whether the secretary has them, and whether or how it is relevant to building a voicewriter.

> Typing skills
> Hearing skills
> Grammar, punctuation, and articulation skills
> Word processing skills
> Document layout skills
> Critiquing skills

(b) Do the secretaries have this knowledge? If yes, would the knowledge be accessible using interviews and protocol analysis? Explain briefly.

■ **Ex. 2** *[CD-10] Floundering in Knowledge Acquisition.* Many knowledge-system projects have floundered due to difficulties in knowledge acquisition. In this exercise we consider problems that are sometimes reported about projects that are not succeeding. For each problem, briefly analyze a possible cause and make a recommendation for fixing the problem or avoiding it.

(a) "The knowledge acquisition sessions fail to get specific."

(b) "The knowledge system is rejected by a subcommunity of users because its solution methods are not trusted by them."

(c) "The knowledge acquisition team wastes time by repeatedly going over the same material."

(d) "The domain experts are not able to provide test cases."

(e) "The knowledge system breaks down when tried beyond a small range of test cases."

Ex. 3 *[CD-12] Estimating Feasibility.* This section introduced several guidelines and criteria for estimating whether a knowledge system project is feasible. For each of the following guidelines, explain briefly (1) whether the guideline is useful, (2) what stumbling block or difficulty is the guideline trying to avoid, and (3) under what circumstances would the guideline be misleading (that is, when it might be appropriate to build a knowledge system anyway even if the guideline is violated).

(a) "A suitable task should take a domain expert an hour or two to perform."

(b) "Experts must be available who perform the task on a regular basis."

(c) "A suite of test cases must be available."

(d) "The solution methods should not be radically different for each problem."

■ **Ex. 4** *[CD-05] The Rationale of Protocols.* Verbal protocols of subjects solving problems are used both in information-processing psychology and in knowledge engineering. In both fields, protocols are valued more than retrospective accounts as data about problem solving.

(a) Why are retrospective accounts of problem solving suspect as data in both fields?

(b) Why is the attitude about interrupting a subject with questions during a protocol different in knowledge engineering than in psychological studies?

Ex. 5 *[10] Focus in Knowledge Acquisition Sessions.* Consider the following excerpt from a knowledge acquisition session.

DE1: I think that this approach we've been discussing will work most of the time, although there may be some nonstandard cases that require a substantially different approach.

KE1: That worries me, because we are going to be looking for a way to represent this knowledge. What we've seen so far are the nominal cases, which it seems can be represented in terms of rules and procedures. ... I'm worried that the methods and design rules you have been giving us may not scale up, if the nonstandard situations are too different.

DE1: I don't think we'll have trouble scaling them because a designer as such goes from this kind of design rules to start designing for new specifications. And he'll say, "I think that this rule is not going to be applicable because the rolls are too close now." ... It's only after he goes through the standard rules and discovers that it's not going to work that he moves away from the standard procedures.

KE1: You're making a very fundamental mistake here. Expert systems, even the best ones built today, don't have any sense of when the rules are not working. If you want a system that can reason about the applicability of its rules and which can back up when something fails, then you need a substantially different way of building an expert system. . . . We have to know how you know what the limits of the rules are, how you question them, how you find out what the exceptions are, and so on.

DE1: I don't know what to say.

[*This was followed by a 30-minute general discussion during which the knowledge engineer provided background about the state of the art of knowledge engineering.*]

(a) This was the first time the domain experts in this case had been involved in the creation of a knowledge system. They appeared to be confused and tired at this point in the conversation and not sure how to proceed. Do you think it was useful for the knowledge engineer to focus on the state of the art of knowledge engineering at this point? Discuss briefly.

(b) What major issue about the domain knowledge does the knowledge acquisition team need to consider at this time? Suggest some ways they could do this.

Ex. 6   [*05*] *Hypermedia and Knowledge Formulation.* A **hypertext** system is an information representation and management system built around a network of nodes containing text connected together by links. The term **hypermedia** is used when the nodes can contain other forms of information besides text, such as graphics, animation, video, or sound. Hypermedia systems are used for organizing and manipulating large amounts of irregularly structured information. (At the time of this writing, commercial and robust hypermedia systems are just becoming widely available.)

Briefly speculate about what properties of hypermedia systems might make them superior to text editing systems for taking and organizing notes from knowlege acquisition sessions. Explain your answers.

Ex. 7   [*10*] *Organizing Information in Hypermedia.* Suppose you were preparing a hypermedia publication of the book *The Wild Flowers of California*, a guide to identifying flowering plants native to that state.

Figure 3.14 gives an example of an article from this book. Describe briefly how the information might be organized for retrieval. How might you use links and nodes to structure the information in the article? What kinds of issues would guide your choices?

Ex. 8   [*10*] *From Retrieval Systems to Knowledge Systems.* Once knowledge is moved from a paper medium to a computational medium, it is possible to expand the capabilities beyond support for information retrieval.

(a) Briefly, what additional kinds of knowledge would be needed to provide a knowledge system for plant identification. Why could such a system be more flexible in its approach than the paperback version of the book?

(b) What would be some of the issues of integrating knowledge systems for different plant-related tasks in the book, such as knowledge systems for landscaping? For example, suppose the water requirements were represented (sporadically) in a text block in the plant database developed about plant identification. What requirements would the addition of an expert landscape system impose?

■   **Ex. 9**   [*30*] *Knowledge System for Checking Expense Reports.* Figure 3.15 presents excerpts from a transcript for a second session about a knowledge system to check expense reports. Expense reports are tabular documents that employees fill out in order to be compensated for their expenses on business trips. In the first session, the domain experts and the knowl-

Miner's Lettuce. Indian Lettuce.
Montia perfoliata, Howell. Purslane Family.

Smooth, succulent herbs. *Radical Leaves.* —Long-petioled; broadly rhomboidal; the earliest narrowly linear. *Stems.* — Simple; six to twelve inches high, having, near the summit, a pair of leaves united around the stem. *Flowers.* — White. *Sepals.* — Two. *Petals.* — Five, minute. *Stamens.* — Five. *Ovary.* — One celled. Style slender. Stigma three-cleft. *Syn.* — *Claytonia perfoliata*, Don. *Hab.* — Throughout California.

Though our Indian lettuce is closely allied to the Eastern "Spring Beauty," one would never suspect it from its outward appearance and habit. The little flower racemes look as though they might have pushed their way right through the rather large saucer-like leaf just below them. The succulent leaves and stems are eaten by the Indians, from which it is called "Indian lettuce."

Mr. Powers, of Sheridan, writes that the Placer County Indians have a novel way of preparing their salad. Gathering the stems and leaves, they lay them about the entrances of the nests of certain large red ants. These, swarming out, run all over it. After a time, the Indians shake them off, satisfied that the lettuce has a pleasant sour taste equalling that imparted by vinegar. These little plants are said to be excellent when boiled and well seasoned, and they have long been grown in England, where they are highly esteemed for salads.

FIGURE 3.14.   Sample article from *Wild Flowers of California*, by M.E. Parsons, 1914.

edge engineer decided that the knowledge system would be used by an accountant to look for errors in a submitted expense report.

(a) How is this session different from a protocol on a test case?

(b) A knowledge engineer needs to achieve a balance between guiding the conversation and letting the domain experts take the lead. Find the places in this session where the knowledge engineer needed to redirect the conversation. For each case, explain why you believe the knowledge engineer intervened.

(c) Sometimes domain experts give answers that are vague or couched in jargon that the knowledge engineer cannot understand. Identify places in this session where the knowledge engineer needed to ask questions in order to clarify the meaning of a concept or rule.

(d) The domain experts in this case consulted a rule book for clarifications. Why would the knowledge engineer not just use the rule book directly? What use would he have for the rule book?

(e) What advantages would there be for putting the rule book online? What reasons would there be for developing an integrated system that (1) puts the rule book online, and (2) provides an online knowledge system for checking expense reports, (3) provides a consulting/questioning mail service to reach policy makers and system implementers electronically, and (4) provides a facility for filing and mailing data about individual cases?

Ex. 10   *[CD-10] Multi-Organizational Knowledge Systems.* Sometimes tasks involve interactions with multiple business organizations. Developing knowledge systems in such cases involves understanding the roles of the different organizations, from both a perspective of their requirements for the knowledge system and the implications for knowledge formulation. This exercise considers some issues in the context of a knowledge system for supporting car repairs.

(a) Suppose the concept for the knowledge system was to support the logging, diagnosis, repair, and bill-writing aspects of the process. Given that repairs actually take place at the

1.	KE1:	Perhaps the best way to start is with some examples. If you have some expense reports that we can go over.
2.	DE1:	I found some that are very bad. Now this is a foreign trip that I pulled from the files. Here's one that someone typed and one that someone printed. See the difference?
3.	KE1:	(*pointing*) Is this one good because it's typed, or because it is valid?
4.	DE1:	Both.
5.	DE2:	Yes, both. See that the typed version has a lot of explanations on it that will be required later. Here's an exchange rate for foreign currency, which is missing from the other one. . . .
6.	DE1:	Okay, here's some incorrect forms that weren't very good. (*pause*) Do you understand why I'd find these difficult, and why I'd send them back so many times? I have to explain these reports to the auditors, and I can hardly read the handwriting.
7.	KE1:	Can we go over this, so you can point things out? How about if we look at what's allowed and what's not allowed in the expenses?
8.	DE1:	Those are the right kinds of questions. . . . This is an exception because the company has a policy for meals at meetings. Breakfast and lunch are $15 per person or a receipt is required. Dinner is $25 per person with receipt.
9.	DE2:	This is for a business meal.
10.	DE1:	So this is a dinner and they've spent $138.15. That was for five people. They still got paid for it, but it was an exception.
11.		(*Reaching for another report*) Let's see what this was an exception for. Ah, there was no original airlines bill. We had to go back to the travel agent. . . . Some of these I haven't audited yet so the items aren't circled yet.
12.	KE1:	Let's just take any one of them and go through the items and have you explain what you would do.
13.	DE1:	Okay, this is really a nice one. The secretary does excellent expense reports. Usually he (the traveler) waits until he gets back his American Express receipt so that he knows what the exchange rate will be.
14.		Now, the first thing I look for is the ticket. Unless the ticket looks pretty funny, I'm not going to question it.
15.	DE2:	Let's talk about that ticket.
16.	KE1:	What are the things you look for in that ticket?
17.	DE1:	Okay, being as he went to Tokyo I'm not going to check the class. That is, he went business class but I'm not going to get mad at him. On any flight over so many hours—eight hours—business class is okay. Usually, that's what I'll check on the ticket.
18.	DE2:	There are some exceptions, such as when a salesperson is traveling with a customer. But that's not applicable here.
19.	DE1:	Also I'm going to look at the times they left. That's going to be relevant when I get over to the meals, so I'm going to use this ticket twice. Let's see. The agency paid for it at $116.97 and the company paid for it on our charge. That's consistent with the expense report, so that's good. Next, I'll try to establish what receipts are what. Here's the expenses for each day. . . .
20.	KE1:	Could we stick with the ticket for a few minutes? The first thing you check is the length of the trip. Whether you have a receipt for the full amount, and the destination. Anything else?

FIGURE 3.15. Excerpts from a transcript of a first knowledge acquisition session about checking expense reports (continued next page).

21.	DE1:	Um, whether you paid for it or the company paid for it.
22.	KE1:	Now what things would you look for that you would not allow? Let's say that the trip amount and ticket amount were different.
23.	DE1:	I'd send it back and ask for an explanation.
24.	KE1:	What kind of explanation would you expect?
25.	DE2:	Say, for example, you had a ticket and there was a personal leg in there. Suppose the $50 was for your leg of the trip, and we didn't know that otherwise.
26.	DE1:	There's a place for additional information (*pointing to the form*)—see, right there.
27.	DE2:	You can't break a route without explanation. It's very difficult for us to tell whether you had to go from here to there on business. Sometimes people write in the wrong number. "Oh, I didn't mean to write in that number! It was a tax." So you go back and ask, why is that number there? The other implication is that a ticket may be exchanged for another ticket.
28.	DE1:	Like they changed the date of the trip, or whatever. . . . That's rare, but it's the kind of thing you occasionally see. . . .
29.	DE2:	Now the flight class shows on there. This one says "Y."
30.	KE1:	"Y" is economy.
31.	DE1:	Right.
32.	KE1:	(*Looking at an expense report*) What is "C"?
33.	DE2:	Let's see. There are codes for first class, business class, and economy. Sometimes there are special fares. (*consults manual*) . . . Business class has to be approved by a vice president, if you are going to use it for any extended period of time. . . . Business class can be used for the Far East, the Middle East, or Australia without prior approval. . . .
34.		Also we're talking about straight-through flights. If you fly to New York and stop in a hotel, you start over. That's another thing we look for. . . .
35.	KE1:	Let's go on to the next thing.
36.	DE1:	Taxis. The only time you don't need a receipt is if it's under $25.
37.	KE1:	Per day?
38.	DE2:	Per taxi.
39.	DE1:	Per day, I think.
40.	DE2:	(*consulting book*) Per taxi. But that's where the complication comes in. You can have 15 taxis at $10 each but you have to tell me that it's 15 taxis.
41.	KE1:	Oh, so someone uses 15 taxis but includes a footnote.
42.	DE1:	Right. Then I wouldn't mind.
43.	KE1:	So there's no limit to how many taxis you take in a day.
44.	DE2:	No. . . .
45.	DE1:	Also, it's $15 for parking without receipt.
46.	DE1:	Okay, the next thing on this is hotel or motel including tax. We want the figure as a daily rate. Most of the time I look for persons, to make sure that there were not two. If there are two people, we can only reimburse them for the single room rate.
47.	DE2:	Often on a hotel bill you'll have separate line items, for phone calls, meals, laundry, or whatever.
48.	KE1:	Is there a maximum amount a person can spend on a hotel?
49.	DE1:	Well, depending on the location.
50.	DE2:	In all cases, auditors are instructed to look for expenses that look strange.

FIGURE 3.15. (continued)

dealers' shops, why would an automobile manufacturing company be motivated to have a role in the development of the knowledge system? Why would a dealer be motivated to have the car company participate?

(b) Why would it be useful to have experts at the car company participate? Why would experts from dealer repair shops be important for establishing the problem definition for the knowledge systems?

3.3   *Collaboratively Articulating Work Practices*

This section extends our discussion of the participatory design of knowledge systems to consider later stages. We begin by discussing how the goals of the ongoing interview process change as the development of a knowledge system proceeds. Not all interview techniques yield the same information. We consider several dimensions of variation in the interview process and see how different variations are useful at different stages of development for obtaining different kinds of knowledge.

We then consider some pragmatic suggestions about the use of project documentation to organize system both knowledge acquisition and various aspects of development for projects that may span several months. Finally, we consider how automation, such as the use of knowledge systems, causes both systems and organizations to change. Not only must a knowledge system be developed to fit an organization, but also an organization must be fitted to a knowledge system. This is because automation changes the ways organizations work.

3.3.1   *Variations in Processes for Interview and Analysis*

The goals of the interview process change as progress is made in developing a knowledge system. Figure 3.16 repeats our rough map of the stages in developing a knowledge system, albeit without showing feedback loops. In the previous sections we discussed the problem identification stage and the conceptualization stage. Knowledge engineers do not abruptly stop interviewing at some stage in the process, but use interviews throughout the life cycle of a project. Interview techniques differ in the kinds of information that they are best for obtaining. Knowledge engineers shift to different techniques at different stages in the process as their needs change.

At the beginning of the project, what is needed most in participatory design is for the participants to gain a rough mutual understanding of the project goals and scope and what roles they will be playing. From the perspective of knowledge acquisition, the participants need to identify what problems need to be solved and roughly what is involved in solving them. By the problem conceptualization stage, they need more than a sketch of how problems are solved. Instead they need a much more detailed model of the task.

Once detailed task models have been developed, attention shifts to determining whether there are gaps in the model. Does the problem-solving model cover all cases that arise? As the model is further refined, the team can give more attention to refining the model and improving the quality of its solutions. Are there alternative solutions? Are some solutions better than others? Under what circumstances is one kind of solution preferred over another?

Four goals arise roughly in order: (1) establishing a rough understanding of the task, (2) developing a detailed symbolic model of problems and problem solving for the task, (3) identifying any classes of problems not covered by the model, and (4) improving the quality of the solu-

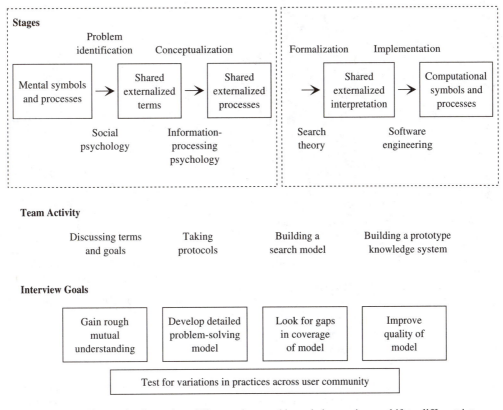

FIGURE 3.16. The needs of a project shift over time, and knowledge engineers shift to different interview techniques to get different kinds of information.

tions made by the model. Another goal in parallel with these is to determine whether there are variations in practice across the user community, such that solutions acceptable for some users are not acceptable for others.

Figure 3.17 gives four primary dimensions to interview processes: selection of the interview technique, selection of cases, selection of added constraints, and selection of experts and users. By varying their choices along these dimensions, knowledge engineers can tailor their interview processes to satisfy different goals, thereby obtaining the kinds of knowledge they need at different stages of the development cycle.

Selecting Interview Processes

The main kinds of interviews are unstructured interviews, structured interviews, protocol analysis, comparing scenarios, and circulating documents for comments. Figure 3.18 shows how these different interview processes satisfy different goals in the system development process.

In an unstructured interview, the knowledge engineer asks more-or-less spontaneous questions of the expert while the expert is performing or talking about a familiar task. As discussed already, these interviews can be more akin to conversations because the domain expert or user

Kinds of Interview
Unstructured interview
Structured interview
Protocol analysis on cases
Comparing scenarios
Circulating documents about knowledge, problems, and solutions

Kinds of Cases
Familiar or typical cases
Random cases
Extreme cases
Tough cases

Kinds of Added Constraints
No time limit
Limited time to solve problems
Withholding information

Kinds of Experts and Users
One domain expert (or user)
Pair: Domain expert and apprentice or novice
Pair: Two domain experts (or users)
Sampling: Cross-section of a community of users

FIGURE 3.17.   Dimensions of data gathering for knowledge acquisition.

may ask as many questions of the knowledge engineer. Many expert-systems developers have apparently relied almost exclusively on the use of unstructured interviews. Unstructured or loosely structured interviews are best suited for establishing common ground, as in the problem identification stage. Unstructured interviews are not very efficient for developing detailed problem-solving models in the problem conceptualization stage. This is where protocol analysis is used.

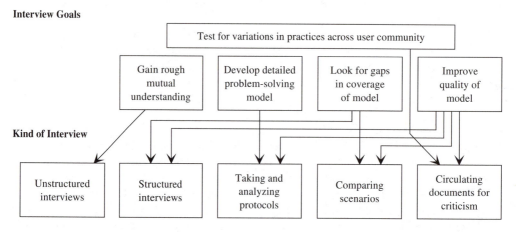

FIGURE 3.18.   Different kinds of interviews are best suited for obtaining different kinds of information.

If unstructured interviews are useful for establishing breadth, protocol analysis is useful for establishing details in depth. Protocol analysis, however, is too time-consuming to use for everything. The term *structured interview* refers to a case where a knowledge engineer makes a pass at a database and then goes over the results with an expert. This approach combines analysis with an interview. The database may be the results of a previous unstructured interview, or it may be obtained from recorded cases or texts. When an expert and a knowledge engineer work together on the analysis of protocol data, that would be called a structured interview. This can lead to the addition or deletion of entries, the qualification of entries, or the reorganization of the categorical structure of the data. The result of a structured interview is a second pass at analyzing data.

In the later stages where the goal is to identify gaps in the knowledge base or to compare alternative solutions in order to improve the quality of the knowledge base, the approach of comparing scenarios is appropriate. There are two important variations on the use of scenarios. One approach is for the interviewer to encourage the use of scenarios during the performance of a familiar task. This can evoke evidence about the expert's reasoning for scenarios of the given kind. Another approach is to compare scenarios to the current cases, probing for desiderata that have been missed. This is a structured interview aimed at comparing two cases.

Finally, the circulation of documents in the community of users and experts for suggestions and criticism can be an important source of information. Like the structured interview, this combines data collection and analysis. For example, documents can present sample cases and solutions. This provides an opportunity for people to comment on whether the cases are realistic or whether those solutions would be acceptable in their experience. Other experts can criticize knowledge inferred from cases by identifying situations where such knowledge would not work.

The circulation of documents is less personal than the other interview techniques, but it is more efficient for gathering feedback from a large number of people. It can also be helpful to the success of the development process because it makes more people feel that they had the ability to influence the project.

It is beyond the scope of this section to give a practical guide to all aspects of interviewing, but a few remarks about recording equipment may be helpful. It is increasingly common to record interviews using audio and video equipment. When possible, it is useful to conduct the interview in a small, quiet room. An exception to this is when it is important for the purposes of the interview to capture elements of the setting, such as machinery or other artifacts.

For video recordings, it is important to determine that the participants know the camera is present, to get their permission for using it, and to determine that they are not intimidated by it. If the camera is needed to pick up both people and writing surfaces, it is useful to have a separate person responsible for the camera who is not the same as the person asking the questions.

Selecting Cases

This brings us to a second dimension of interview processes, the selection of cases. In the following we consider the use of typical cases, random cases, extreme cases, and tough cases. In the problem identification stage, it is usually appropriate to focus on cases like those that are typically encountered. By their definition and selection, these cases are intended to reveal data and issues common to typical situations. If a knowledge system cannot handle typical cases, it is probably of little use at all. As shown in Figure 3.19, these cases are a good starting point both for problem identification and problem conceptualization.

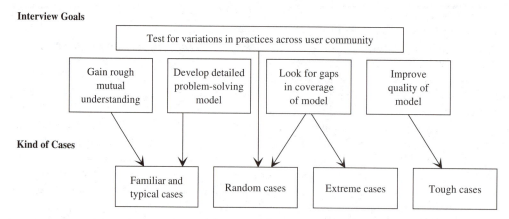

FIGURE 3.19.   Different kinds of cases are best suited for obtaining different kinds of information.

As an aside, it is important to ensure that cases are representative. There are sometimes systematic difficulties in the collection of cases. When cases are collected, experts and users sometimes choose cases that are ideal in the sense that they have complete or the most consistent data. However, if the knowledge system is expected to perform the task in the presence of faulty or missing data, too much idealization in case selection can be misleading and harmful to the system-development process.

Later in a project, the goal is not so much to establish the basic problem-solving framework as much as it is to determine whether the knowledge system covers the necessary range of situations. Knowledge that works for average cases may not be work well in extreme circumstances. For example, typical outdoor repair procedures for machinery may be different for average days as compared to extremely cold or stormy days. Knowledge for tuning a car for ordinary driving may not be suitable for tuning it for mountain driving or for race driving. For any given domain, one must identify the ways in which situations can be extreme. Data about extreme cases are useful for revealing hidden assumptions in the knowledge base and exceptions from typical cases. It is often useful to collect extreme cases and then carry out a systematic search for violated boundary conditions.

Figure 3.20 begins an example of an exception-finding process. This example was chosen because it seems trivial on the surface. Suppose we have taken protocols from a domain expert. The figure shows a statement from one of the protocols together with a representation of that knowledge in the form of a production rule. In this figure we presume that the task is to determine the proper temperature for rooms in a warehouse.

The issue in this example is to determine the boundaries of applicability of the rule. For example, we might ask: Is the rule applicable in both winter and summer? Should a summer refrigeration system attempt to cool a room to 5° C on a hot summer night, defeating the purpose of saving energy? Are there other situations beyond "occupancy" under which the lower temperature should be kept above freezing? Notice that although these factors may bear on the interpretation of the rule, they are not mentioned in the protocol. Part of the job in using protocols as data is to determine what additional conditions are implicit in the situation and not mentioned in the

---

Statement from protocol from some particular case:

DE: "I'll adjust the thermostat to 5° C since the room is not in use and energy costs are so high right now. This will prevent the water pipes from freezing."

Possible situation-action rule representing knowledge from the protocol:

IF   energy costs are high

          and the room is unoccupied,

THEN   set the room thermostat to have a minimum temperature of 5° C.

FIGURE 3.20. Example of a situation-action rule extracted from a statement in a protocol. A pervasive issue in such an extraction and generalization process is in determining the boundaries of applicability. Depending on factors not evident in the protocol itself, the conditions of this rule could be either too generalized or too specialized.

protocols. Figure 3.21 shows another version of the knowledge as it might be written after several more iterations of looking at cases and analyzing dependencies in them.

The process of characterizing a task in terms of search spaces is iterative. Exceptional conditions and assumptions are discovered piecemeal. At each iteration, new protocols may disclose more information about knowledge that is needed or limitations of the analysis so far.

A third kind of case is the so-called tough case. These cases need not be extreme in any dimension of the domain, and yet may be identified by experts as being tough. Tough cases are always rare. A case can be tough because it involves some unusual circumstance requiring special consideration. It can be tough because it involves a nearly balanced choice between different solution alternatives. It can be tough because it involves an unusual combination of features. Performance on tough cases often distinguishes differences between expert and novice behavior.

Situation: *Economy warehouse temperature rules*

Rule 1

IF   the room temperature is higher than the outside temperature

                    and the temperature control mode is "heating"

                    and the room does not contain cargo sensitive to low temperature

THEN   set the lower temperature limit of the room thermostat to 5° C.

RATIONALE: Use minimum energy to heat the room to prevent the freezing of water pipes.

Rule 2

IF   the room temperature is lower than the outside temperature

                    and the temperature control mode is "cooling"

                    and the room does not contain cargo sensitive to high temperature

THEN   set the upper temperature limit of the room thermostat to 40° C.

RATIONALE: Use minimum energy to cool the room to prevent overheating.

FIGURE 3.21. Hypothetical revised version of the rule in Figure 3.20. In this example, some of the implicit elements of the situations under which the rules apply have been made explicit in the "requirements." In addition, the rules themselves have been modified to reflect considerations that arose when more cases and factors were considered, beyond those that were mentioned in the initial case.

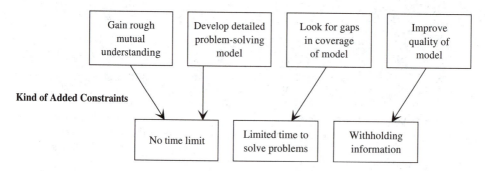

FIGURE 3.22.   Different kinds of cases are best suited for obtaining different kinds of information.

Identifying the desired behavior on tough cases is useful in establishing a standard high quality of performance for a knowledge system.

Finally, we come to the use of random cases. By random cases we mean real cases that are randomly selected from a case file. These cases are useful for guarding against unconscious biases in the selection process that may avoid certain kinds of difficulties. Thus, random cases are useful as checks for gaps in coverage. In addition, when the knowledge system is intended for a group of users, it is important that cases be drawn from across the community. This is important for ensuring that factors important for the situations faced by all of the users are taken into account.

Adding Constraints

Constrained processing tasks are ones that deliberately attempt to alter the reasoning strategies the expert uses. We consider limitations on the time to solve a problem and also the witholding of information about a case. Figure 3.22 summarizes how adding constraints in an interview process can provide different insights.

One approach is to limit the amount of time an expert has to solve a problem. This can provide insights into an expert's search strategy. It provides evidence about which desiderata are most meaningful.

Another approach is to limit the information available to an expert. In particular, it is possible to provide cases that leave out information that is usually available. For example, a doctor may want to have a patient's history before interpreting an x-ray. In this example, withholding the medical history can provide evidence about the extent to which the history data are used in the interpretation process. In general, this approach is used as part of a sensitivity analysis of the problem-solving knowledge and methods. By withholding data, it is possible to determine the extent to which problem-solving performance is robust over variations in missing or slightly distorted data. There are risks in using cases in which information is withheld. The further an altered task departs from the usual problem-solving situation, the less reliable it is as evidence about expert judgments.

A second problem is that an expert may feel uncomfortable and hesitant to make judgments in artificial situations. Potentially, some experts may feel as though such cases change the

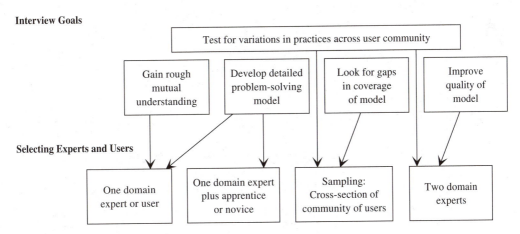

FIGURE 3.23.   Different combinations of experts and users can be involved in interviews. Different combinations are best suited for obtaining different kinds of information.

relation between collaborators, making them akin to rats in an animal psychology experiment. It is important to emphasize that the goal of the experiment is not to determine how clever the expert is, but rather to gauge the properties of the knowledge and problem-solving methods. One way to alleviate the problems of artificiality in cases where data are withheld is to engage experts in the design of artificial cases. They may have suggestions about cases where the data will be more or less meaningful and useful.

Selecting Experts and Users

Common practice in the problem identification and problem conceptualization stages is to interview one expert at a time. It can also be illuminating to involve a pair of experts on a case so they critique each other's methods, revealing subtleties not otherwise evident to a knowledge engineer. When a pair includes a novice or apprentice and an expert, the expert tends to take on a teaching role so as to illustrate subtle points to the novice. We often get more information than usual from this approach because of the pedagogical activities of the participants. Figure 3.23 summarizes ways in which the selection of different experts and users can be appropriate at different stages in the development of a knowledge system.

Interviewing multiple experts can be useful in cases where their expertise is specialized in ways that do not entirely overlap. Different experts may focus on different parts of a problem or on different kinds of cases. It is not necessary that the two experts be interviewed simultaneously. It is sometimes more practical to interview them separately on a case and then compare the steps and solutions.

Interviewing multiple experts is useful for satisfying interview goals that arise later in the development process. For example, it is useful in trying improve the quality of a model to have multiple experts critiquing a given solution. Naturally, in such situations, it is best to try to encourage constructive criticism, so the focus is on improving the quality of the solution rather than establishing the superiority of one expert over another.

DE1:   (*to DE2*) Are you familiar with these releasing nips?
DE2:   Yes. They are worried about static.
(*DE1 pauses for a moment with an "aha" look.*)
DE1:   That's a very important point. Someone asked earlier why these rolls were one inch wide.
         Well, one of the reasons is build-up of electrostatic charge. We want to minimize the contact
         area. There are two ways of eliminating static from the paper.
         One way is by use of a passive static eliminator. This is like Christmas tree tinsel that hangs
         down and eliminates it.
         The other way is by use of an active static eliminator. . . .
         As long as you limit the contact area, that is the roll size, the passive static eliminator can
         work and it is much cheaper.

FIGURE 3.24.   Edited transcript from a videotaped knowledge acquisition session showing interaction between experts during the session. In this case, the second expert was useful in bringing out some of the rationale behind a method.

When knowledge systems are being built for a community of users, it is important to interview a cross-section of the community. Different organizations may use radically different methods for solving problems or have subtly different notions of what constitutes a solution. Involving them early in the process makes it possible to take profiles of practice across the community.

One method for detecting divergent requirements and knowledge in a community is to take multiple protocols on the same cases from different representative experts. If their approaches and solutions are different, then there may be distinct subcommunities relative to practice and different knowledge may be required from the different communities. Alternatively, this process can reveal important areas where a consensus judgment is needed, although that judgment has not yet been made.

It is sometimes suggested that knowledge systems should only use one expert to avoid disagreements and contradictions. This strategy does not necessarily fix the problem of contradictions and can introduce other risks. If diversity arises because the expertise is plagued with uncertainty, then basing a knowledge base on one expert's performance may result in a knowledge system that is idiosyncratic.

It may give unreliable results without any indication whatsoever. When a knowledge system is constructed on the sole basis of interactions with one expert, there can later be surprises when users of the system complain that they do not trust the results because the system carries out the task in an unfamiliar or different way.

Figure 3.24 shows an example where discussion between two domain experts uncovered an underlying set of causes and motivations for some rules of design practice. In the discussion between experts, they realized that they had not explained to the knowledge engineer that it was necessary to take into account the build-up of electrostatic charge on the copier paper. Prior to this point on this case, neither expert had mentioned the phenomenon in the protocols or its bearing on design rules.

When a knowledge system will be used in a community of users, experts from different parts of the community may bring different opinions to bear. Disagreements and elaborations of knowledge are often discovered in face-to-face sessions working on a concrete case, but they can also be discovered when project working documents are circulated in a community. It is better to discover variability in the practices of a user community early in the development process, before systems and knowledge bases are constructed on an assumption of uniform community knowledge and goals. When diversity is exposed, there are several choices about what a system developer should do: One can try to combine the knowledge into a logically coherent whole; one can pick one of the approaches and discard the others; or one can have the system report all of the different conclusions, citing the source of the knowledge.

In summary, the goals of the interview process shift during the course of developing a knowledge system. To satisfy the initial goals of gaining a rough mutual understanding, it is appropriate to use unstructured interviews on typical cases. For the problem conceptualization stage, it is more efficient to use protocol analysis than unstructured interviews. In later stages where the goal is to identify gaps in the knowledge base and to improve its quality, it is useful to draw on multiple experts and to focus on extreme cases and tough cases. A knowledge engineer should be flexible, understand the dimensions of variation for these processes, and tailor interviews to acquire the different kinds of information that are needed at different stages.

3.3.2 *Documenting Expertise*

Documentation of interviews, protocols, agreements, and terminology is an important practical matter in knowledge-system projects. The amount of detail and unfinished business accumulates during a project. Documents provide a concrete basis for later discussion and analysis and often become important working tools for organizing a knowledge-system project. Documentation can be in passive media like blackboards or notebooks or active media like word processors, hypertext, or video. This section discusses some practical matters of using working notes for a project during these stages.

Project Notes as Artifacts for Organizing Activities

In our discussion of initial interviews, we introduced the term *common ground* from social psychology to refer to concepts that people hold in common. Publicly visible sketches and notes are an external symbol structure that can be shared in a project. They are a basis for a visible and **external common ground**. They are intermediate products in formulating, externalizing, and formalizing the knowledge of the task.

Operational or working definitions of terms need to be developed. Diagrams can be especially useful at this stage. There can be diagrams giving taxonomies of terms, diagrams showing the structure of domain objects, diagrams of the processes that the knowledge system could or should model, diagrams of social organizations that might use or interact with the system, diagrams of larger work processes in which the system would be involved, and diagrams of search spaces. Diagrams are important for visualizing relationships and testing understanding. People sometimes use diagrams to give the first level of a description about something. We use many such diagrams throughout this book to illustrate properties of knowledge bases and knowledge systems in action.

Figure 3.25 presents an example of a design **plan**, taken from the early documentation of the PRIDE project. To a first approximation, it is a description of a design process in terms of an ordered set of steps. Each step documents what design knowledge is needed and how it is used.

Design Process for "Paper Transport Using Pinch Rolls"
The design goes through the following main steps:
1. Examine input/output requirements for unusually tight specifications.

. . .

2. Examine interface requirements (requirements from the input and output systems) to obtain elaborate specifications and any unusual restrictions and requirements.

. . .

5. Consider velocity requirements.
> Case I. No change between input and output velocity.
> > NO PROBLEM. The critical buckle length (LB) should be taken as . . .
> Case II. Output velocity > input velocity.
> > NO PROBLEM. The critical buckle length (LB) should be taken as . . .
> Design rule: Spread the increase in velocity as follows . . .
> > *[NOTE: Coefficient for . . . not known yet. GR will supply . . .]*
> Constraints: If the speedup at any roller is greater than . . .
> Case III. Input velocity > output velocity.
> Design rule: Spread the decrease in velocity as follows . . .
> Calculate buckle length between each adjacent roll pair as follows: . . .
> > *[NOTE: MM says that this rule is pretty dubious. We need to . . .]*

6. Design the baffle: Gap and material.

. . .

7. Calculate the worst-case drive force needed for the pinch rolls.
> a. For the worst-case drive force analysis:
> > Consider the heaviest paper, the input curl, the . . . using the following formula . . .
> b. Check for stubbing.
> > Consider the largest baffle gap and the smallest . . . calculating as follows . . .
> c. Constraints
> > If the ratio of . . .
> > If the ratio is less than 1 then . . .

14. Calculate the required idler normal force and select shaft size.

. . .

FIGURE 3.25.   Excerpt from an intermediate document that was developed over several knowledge-formulation sessions on the PRIDE project. Such plans are developed incrementally from many protocol sessions on different cases.

Plans like this are developed from protocols of experts solving problems. In domains like that of PRIDE, it is possible to write down plans that summarize the problem-solving process used by experts over a wide range of problems.

Project notes like the plan in Figure 3.25 are used for organizing project activity. In this figure, there are several lines marked as "notes," indicating unfinished business in the project. For example, one note says that "GR" will supply a value for a coefficient that is needed for one of the steps. Thus, plan documents can contain more than protocol summaries. They also contain notes about what knowledge is incomplete or in need of further checking. In effect they are a summary of what has been discussed and is understood about the task so far. Documents can mix different kinds of instructions, equations, and diagrams.

DE1:	Now we need to compute the normal force.
KE2:	But didn't we already do that? Let's see, here in step 12-c when we did the driver force?
DE1:	Hmm. Yes, but that's just the "minimum total normal force" required. What we need to do now is to determine how that force is distributed over the rolls.
	What most designers do is just distribute it evenly. But what I do is go back to the computation of the driver force in step 7 and calculate the worst-case drive force required for the largest sheet of paper that will only be under two pinch rolls. And verify that the drive force supplied by those pinch rolls will handle that case.
KE2:	But I don't understand this loop. Why are we going back?
KE1:	Remember that in step 7 we have not yet established the number of rolls.
DE1:	Right, and the worst case is for the largest sheet of paper with the most possible curl.
KE2:	Oh.
DE1:	So we know that the total drive force exerted by the nips has to be greater than a certain amount. That's the worst case. What's the second worst case? A smaller size of paper, when it does not fall under the third roll. So, there has to be enough force from the first two rolls. To achieve this, we might want to distribute more normal force to the first two rolls.

FIGURE 3.26.   Edited transcript from a videotaped knowledge acquisition session. In this session, the knowledge acquisition team is working from a plan of a design process for paper-handling systems. This plan divides the process into discrete subproblems that can be done at different times. The knowledge acquisition team is scheduling and organizing its discussion around filling out knowledge about different parts of the plan, and revising the plan as the discussion uncovers steps that were left out in the first version.

Figure 3.26 presents an excerpt from a session where the knowledge acquisition team fills out more details in a design plan. The plan in this example was produced by generalizing from several cases. The participants are filling in details missed in earlier sessions. One of the knowledge engineers wanted to clarify why the plan returned to an earlier step in the process. Having an explicit plan in hand made it simple to indicate precisely which plan step was being repeated: "step 12-c." In other sessions, they might collaborate to reconcile variations in the problem-solving behavior from one case to another.

In the scenarios discussed at the beginning of this chapter, we noticed that informal drawings and project notes are important intermediate artifacts in a participatory design approach. Documents can be circulated for criticism and comment among the domain experts and knowledge engineers. They are a basis for common reference. The documents establish a standard for shared terminology. They support discussion about priorities in the project and can record unfinished business and agreements about work assignments. In the community knowledge base and knowledge services scenarios, such notes are an important addition to the formal knowledge bases shared in a project.

From Informal to Semiformal Notations

We say a representation is **formal** when its symbols are interpreted by a computer program that uses them to guide its activity in carrying out a task. In this sense, the symbols are akin to a computer program. We say a representation is informal or **nonformal** when the symbols are interpreted by humans, even if those symbols are stored in computer memory. Symbols manipulated by a

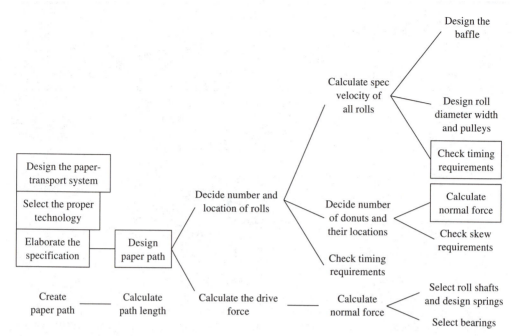

FIGURE 3.27.   Example of the formal plan notation used in the PRIDE system.

word processor are nonformal. In both cases, the symbols may be used for human communication. The term **semiformal** describes representations in which some of the terms are used by interpreters. In some cases the degree of computational interpretation varies over the course of a project.

Different notations and kinds of instructions may be used to record the processes for different parts of the task. The form of the instructions can range from an informal procedural language like that used for recipes in cookbooks, to rules for making inferences about parts of the problem, to flow diagrams of major phases of decision making.

Figure 3.27 gives another example of a representation of a plan. This example was taken from an interactive interface developed for the PRIDE project. This interface was used in developing the PRIDE knowledge base. It also served as an execution interface, showing the activity of the PRIDE knowledge system on different design cases. By our categories of notations, the PRIDE interface provides a formal notation since it is interpreted by the computer program when PRIDE designs a paper path automatically.

Increasingly, it is practical to use computer tools to manipulate knowledge using interfaces to informal, semiformal, and formal notations. In the past few years a new kind of software has been developed to support the work activities of groups. Such software is sometimes called **groupware**. Groupware introduces the notion of shared, computational workspaces. When such workspaces are accessible, visible, and manipulable by all members of a group at the same time, they are called WYSIWIS interfaces (for what you see is what I see). Such interfaces are a computational version of blackboards. Like all computational media, they provide capabilities for manipulation, copying, filing, retrieval, and interpretation that go beyond what is possible in passive media like blackboards and paper.

One advantage of a computational medium is that it is possible to integrate a wide range of interfaces to text, graphics, taxonomies, plans, and other structures. Systems that support extensive interlinking of data and interfaces are called **hypertext** systems.

Before leaving the topic of documentation, we note that protocol sessions can involve more than verbal data. An expert problem solver may use a tablet, blackboard, or even a computer for parts of the problem. In such cases, it is not adequate to record only the verbal data. We need to record the writings on external memories as well. As video and audio equipment have become less expensive and easier to use, some knowledge engineers are using such equipment to help record protocols. Although video equipment is improving rapidly, there are still many obstacles to using it routinely as a tool for documentation. It is often desired to record more activities than can easily be captured by a single fixed camera. Filming someone at a blackboard requires either that a camera operator follow the person around as he writes in different parts of the board, zooming in and out, or that multiple cameras be employed and sychronized. The visual resolution of current technology is not good enough to use a single fixed camera, postponing until later where to zoom for detailed viewing. Systems that combine video and computer, sometimes called **hypermedia** systems, are becoming available and make it possible to build up transcripts that combine video data, transcriptions, and notes. Such tools will come into routine use in the next decade.

In summary, the working notes of a project are useful for organizing project activity. They constitute a project knowledge base and are the basis for an externalized common ground. Different media can be used for taking and organizing notes in knowledge system projects. These media range from paper documentation to computational groupware or multimedia. As a project progresses, parts of the knowledge progress from nonformal to semiformal and formal notations. Thus, a project team can start out by sharing diagrams and text files and incrementally end up sharing and developing formal community knowledge bases. The next section discusses steps in formalizing protocol data in terms of symbols and search.

3.3.3 *Engineering Software and Organizations*

The term **software engineering** refers to engineering practices for developing software. Software engineering arose as a subject as it became desirable to control the development of software and as it became apparent that the methods and techniques that had been used in developing hardware were not appropriate for software. A practical difference between hardware and software is that most software is more "plastic" than most hardware, meaning it is easier to make changes. This is not to say it is always easy to make changes *correctly*. However, because the mechanics of change are simpler, changing software rather than hardware is the common approach when computer systems need to be adjusted to fit different or evolving situations. The accommodation of frequent change is one of the central issues that any successful approach to software engineering must take into account. Knowledge systems are among the most plastic of software systems.

In this section we focus mainly on the issues of developing knowledge systems in the context of human organizations, rather than on the technical issues of choice of implementations,

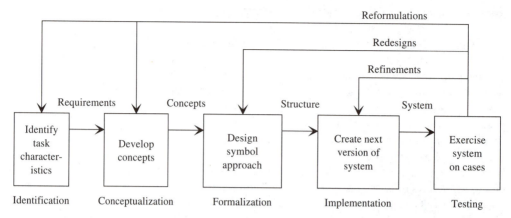

FIGURE 3.28. Stages in the development of knowledge systems. This diagram emphasizes the development of the knowledge in knowledge systems from a product-oriented point of view. It provides our initial map to the process, suggesting that knowledge is developed in stages as it is written down and debugged for active use in knowledge systems. In a product-oriented view, feedback from users begins only after a system has been implemented. (Adapted from F. Hayes-Roth, D. Waterman, and D. Lenat (eds.), *Building Expert Systems,* Reading, MA.: Addison-Wesley, page 139.).

which are covered elsewhere in this book. These issues are not unique to knowledge systems. Many of the issues are the same whenever new technology or new work practices are introduced. The issues in this section are less relevant for small organizations and perhaps irrelevant for building personal knowledge systems. However, most knowledge systems are built by and for organizations, which have the potential to change their work practices profoundly.

Stages in System Development

Our purpose in this section is to consider issues inherent in the development of software for organizations. Figure 3.28 sketches a traditional model of software development, showing processing steps in terms of information flow and sequencing. The steps in Figure 3.28 correspond to stages in participatory design of a knowledge system as follows:

■ The **identification stage** is where the project participants establish common ground and engage in conversations about their goals for a knowledge system and the necessary background. This stage includes the identification of users and domain experts. During this stage, the participants identify the general problem and begin to create a set of shared, externalized vocabulary for describing the task. This vocabulary is what we called the common ground. Theoretical foundations for this come from social psychology. The external symbols are nonformal project notes.

■ The **conceptualization stage** is where a broad framework for the task is developed. During this stage the participants develop a shared, external model of how the task is done, that is, the processes of problem solving. Theoretical foundations for this come from information-processing psychology. The external symbols may be semiformal.

■ The **formalization stage** is where protocol data and other evidence are used to develop a formal representation of the task. During this stage, the participants create a more complete model of the detailed steps. Theoretical foundations for this come from search theory.

■ The **implementation stage** corresponds to developing an operational prototype of a knowledge system. Implementation decisions are made. During this stage the participants develop a computationally based model of the knowledge of the task. Theoretical foundations for this come from computer science. The external symbols become formal.

Few successful projects actually follow this linear sequence of steps across all of the knowledge for a task. Furthermore, no projects should actually wait as suggested by Figure 3.28 until the end of the implementation stage before getting feedback from users. As we discuss in the following, this linear characterization of stages is a holdover from traditional software engineering. In the following, we discuss some more modern perspectives on the process.

Process versus Product

The perspective on system development as a sequence of stages as in Figure 3.28 is called a product-oriented view. A **product-oriented point of view** sees computer systems as delivered to users when they have been implemented. It regards software as a set of programs and documentation. In this view software is developed by a software development team to meet specifications and is then delivered. The software is then installed and stands on its own.

In the traditional product-oriented view, a software development task begins by gathering specifications. From these specifications, concepts for developing the system are developed, which in turn lead to a formal approach described in a design document. The system is then implemented and prepared for testing. Feedback in the product-oriented approach begins when a system has been developed and is ready for testing. Errors in implementation are corrected by refinements to the program. Redesign and reformulation can lead to changes in the requirements and revisions to the concepts for the system.

In contrast, a **process-oriented point of view** sees knowledge systems in terms of how they empower people and organizations in work, communication, and learning. The process-oriented view focuses on the interwoven processes of defining, creating, using, and maintaining them. The process perspective deemphasizes the idea of a strict linearization of stages. It leads to collaboration with users in developing and evaluating user interactions and system functions. The process-oriented view takes a longer-term perspective and is more in line with the participatory design approach.

The primary flaw with a strict product-oriented view is that feedback comes only after a system has been built and can be tested. This approach is too idealized for practical knowledge systems. It admits only a narrow channel for communication: the specifications at the beginning and the testing at the end.

Among other things, this idealization trivializes the process of determining what a knowledge system needs to do and understanding the knowledge that is required to do it. Getting the "specifications" is a major part of the job, as suggested already in our discussion of initial interviews, protocols, and formalization.

This emphasis on feedback and course correction is not just to promote a well-meaning theory of social involvement. The landscape is littered with failed attempts to build computer

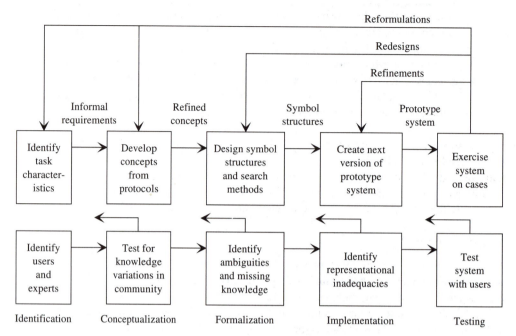

FIGURE 3.29. Augmenting the software development process of Figure 3.28 to emphasize greater participation by domain experts earlier in the process, as well as earlier mechanisms for feedback and revision.

systems without developing an understanding of what is needed. This is not an issue when people build knowledge systems to be used exclusively by themselves. However, it arises when they build knowledge systems for others and when organizations attempt to improve their productivity by introducing systems that deeply influence the way that they work. The examples we considered earlier of the use of informal specifications, project notes, and protocol analysis to elucidate task knowledge suggest that communication is hard work. Building a knowledge system requires more than meeting specifications: It requires creating specifications that make sense.

Figure 3.29 presents a first approximation to a process-oriented approach, emphasizing greater collaboration by domain experts and users. In this version of the process, feedback and correction begin to take place before a knowledge system is built.

- Feedback in the **identification stage** includes considering whether there is a real need for a knowledge system or any other computer system. It includes identifying the task and may lead to involving additional users and domain experts.
- Feedback in the **conceptualization stage** includes testing whether the community of users has a reasonably uniform view of the task and how it should be carried out. We have already discussed the use of multiple experts on cases and the circulation of cases as ways of getting feedback.
- Feedback in the **formalization stage** includes the identification of implicit assumptions and missing information. These are uncovered at this stage as the knowledge acquisition

team begins to analyze and compare protocols on different problems. This analysis enables them to identify and document many things that were covered only briefly in earlier stages.

■ Feedback in the **implementation stage** includes testing the viability and adequacy of the programmed symbol structures as representations. In a complex task, performance of the computer model on test cases is often a source of many detailed examples of forgotten assumptions and minor mistakes.

This shift to a model with participation and feedback at every stage contrasts strongly with the assumption in the product view that complete specifications can be acquired at the beginning. There are two main reasons that this shift is necessary.

First, the knowledge acquisition notes capture generalizations made by a user, domain expert, and knowledge engineer from a range of test cases. In generalizing from cases, the exceptional conditions are not discovered all at once. What is common sense to a domain practitioner may be news to anyone outside the field or local setting. During the formalization and implementation stages, a knowledge engineer needs to expose the system to cases where assumptions will be uncovered and a domain expert needs to identify the associations between the assumptions and situations. This continuing process uncovers areas of ambiguity. During the implementation stage, it is always necessary to explicitly "fill in" knowledge in the project notes.

Second, knowledge systems, like other computer systems that mediate work, have the power to change the ways that organizations work. In this regard they are like other computer systems that interact with an organization's work processes—ranging from inventory control systems to electronic mail systems and database systems. Some changes are difficult to anticipate. The users, domain experts, and developers will develop a better understanding of the changes that are possible and can discover as the project unfolds new areas to expand its role as well as unexpected areas where automation is more difficult than anticipated. Flexibility and participation in the system development process allow these insights to be incorporated into revisions of the project goals.

Assembling a Project Team, Revisited

In Section 3.2 we considered the need to assemble a project team and how additional users and experts may be added to the team after the project is underway. Our main concern in that discussion was in finding people who were able to articulate the knowledge needed to carry out the task and in getting a representative sampling of the community.

From an organizational perspective, there are many other considerations in organizing a team. Usually it is unworkable to invite everybody in the organization to participate in the discussions. This is unwieldy and it leads to a dilution of the sense of responsibility and participation that people have for the project. It is crucial, however, to identify a **constituency** for the project. This includes the domain experts, the users, the facilities people who will support the computers that run the system, the relevant executive personnel, customers, and others. It also includes groups that do not exist yet and will have to be created, such as trainers, staff for maintaining the system, and perhaps others.

Two roles often mentioned in a constituency are the project champion and the customers. A project champion is someone who is involved in shepherding the project through organizational roadblocks. A champion gathers support for the project, attends to its resources, and helps set reasonable expectations. In tough situations, the project counts on this person to understand what it takes to achieve a success and to have the energy to follow through where needed. The term *customer* is used in a more narrow sense than constituency. It usually refers to the person who is responsible for paying for the knowledge system. This person could be a user, a manager, or someone outside the organization. The focus on the customer is to ensure that this person is intimately involved in setting the project goals and priorities.

Identifying a constituency includes coming to understand what concerns and ideas they have. Again, this is not to say that even all of this constituency needs to be present at all discussions. Rather, it is important to understand what is at stake for them and to plan communications with them. For example, given that they may not understand the realities of system development, they may need to understand that an "impressive demo" is less than 10 percent of the work, that there is a life cycle to the development process, and that training of various kinds may be needed. To avoid surprises, they need to be kept up to date about progress and issues and need to understand that their suggestions are valued.

The acceptance of new systems involves not just the software itself, but also how it fits into the work. It involves reliability and efficiency. Studying the development and introduction of the XSEL program at Digital Equipment Company, Dorothy Leonard-Barton noted that new technologies face special problems caused by uncertainty on three fronts: untried procedures for incremental development, lack of clarity about technologies uses and users, and uncertain organizational impacts. She cited three major keys to the acceptance of new technology:

- Cultivating users as codevelopers
- Creating a support sytem, including a network of supporters and an adequate delivery system for users
- Organizational prototyping, or experimentation and planned learning about the integration of the new technology

These process-view suggestions are deceptive in their apparent simplicity. Exercise 8 considers these suggestions in the context of some example "war stories" about the introduction of expert system technology at Digital Equipment Corporation.

Rapid Prototyping and Representational Practices

The need to accommodate system changes throughout the design process creates value for approaches that make it possible to experiment and to reformulate a knowledge base flexibly. Such flexibility has been a goal and cornerstone of AI programming practice for many years, leading to development of programming languages and programming environments designed for making and testing changes quickly. Within the programming language community, this is called exploratory programming. In general engineering practice, this concept is called rapid prototyping. **Rapid prototyping** is the quick production of a demonstration model to obtain corrective feedback from experts and potential users.

The idea behind rapid prototyping is to build a complete though skeletal system. This enables the development team to search broadly for ways that the overall enterprise could fail. This is intended to help them to avoid the pitfall of concentrating all of their energy on one corner of the problem, assuming that the rest of it will work out. They may throw the first versions of the system away. Rapid prototyping helps to avoid building large systems that fail for obvious reasons.

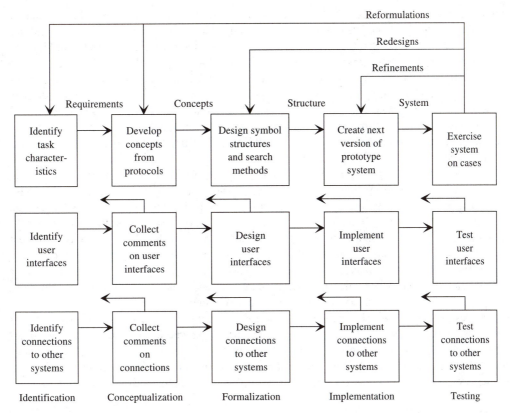

FIGURE 3.30. The development of knowledge systems involves connections to things outside the system, including the users and other systems.

In the product view a program is a formal mathematical object derived from specifications. "Correctness" can be established by proof with respect to the specifications. This attitude is useful in rigorously defining the operations carried out by a system and in understanding and characterizing its limits. This attitude is also a useful part of rigorous programming practice. However, it needs to be complemented by some means of checking the relevance of particular specifications. In the process view, this relevance checking comes from detailed feedback from the domain experts and users. Rapid prototyping does not replace a need for rigor, but it speeds the required cycle of communication and debugging between system developers and users. Participatory design places requirements on the practice of rapid prototyping and on software tools for doing it. In the most complete approach, anything that matters in the final system must be testable within the rapid prototyping environment.

Developing a knowledge system involves more than getting the knowledge right. Figure 3.30 identifies two other major activities that start early in the process and involve feedback along the way: user interfaces and external system interfaces. The prototype system is crucial for feedback from the constituency. A prototype makes it easier for users to visualize as concretely as possible what a system would do and how it would be used. Thus, the prototype includes an interface mockup that can be shown to potential users so they can be asked whether it is something they could use. Concreteness also includes things like the physical setting of the workstation. This could be a notebook computer, a laptop, or a desktop computer. Concreteness includes taking the computer to the field, to customer sites, to repair sites, or to wherever the knowledge system is expected to be used. This creates the context for raising many questions about the relation of the system to work practice. While the system is being used, will others such as customers be around who are not experts in its use? How will people use the system in practice? How will the knowledge system tie into other computer systems and documents used in the organization? A few weeks of effort can yield a clear demo that can be shown to various sections of the constituency enabling a great deal to be learned.

Part of the process of designing a knowledge system for an organization involves coming to understand the representational practice of the organization. People at work are not just solving problems; they are also creating and interacting with representational artifacts such as forms, equations, and diagrams. There are two reasons to be aware of these representations. The representations might encode organizing metaphors of the work that would be easy to miss from just the words in verbal protocols. Furthermore, it might be necessary for the knowledge system to traffic in these representations in its user interfaces, reasoning, and report generation. For example, the popular spreadsheet interface used in many accounting applications came roughly from putting representations from accounting practice onto computer screens.

Designing a keyboard interface for people who cannot or will not type is doomed to failure. Designing very busy and confusing interfaces for people who must use the computers under great pressure can also lead to problems in the reliability of the overall system, which includes the computer and its users. As computer systems evolve toward providing more integrated kinds of services, the design of interfaces between systems will play an increasingly important role.

Evolution versus Maintenance

Our last theme about system development is that a knowledge system is not finished until it is replaced. A strict product-oriented view characterizes the process as development followed by maintenance. Thus, a product view suggests a hand-off style of development in which a development team hands off a completed system to a maintenance team. The maintenance team adjusts and extends the system over time.

This **hand-off assumption** is usually counterproductive. It is more useful to think of the process as including a structured transition from a phase where the system is undeployed and definitely under development, through a phase where the system is deployed but still undergoing important changes in response to initial experiences, to a phase where the system is undergoing constant and sometimes large-scale evolution. Part of this transition process is a changing profile of personnel assignment. The problem with the naive hand-off conception is the idea that deployment means shifting all at once from a high-status development staff to a low-status maintenance staff. Instead, it is better to expand a project as it nears deployment, with some of the initial staff people moving on to other projects as the basics get settled in practice and staff numbers reaching a steady state of support, training, maintenance, knowledge-base evolution and growth, generalization to related or newly created tasks, and so on. This "steady state" can be anywhere from 2 part-time people in a small knowledge system to 10 or 20 people in a large one.

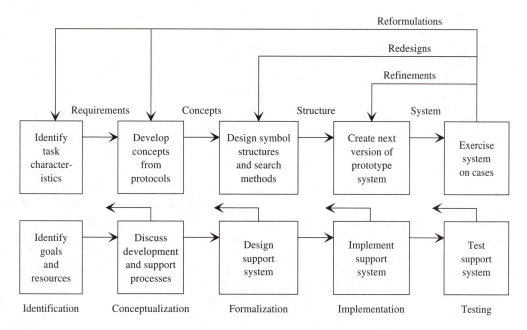

FIGURE 3.31. The successful use of knowledge systems in an organization depends on having an adequate support system, to guide the continuing evolution of the system as needs change. In some of the more successful systems, concern with the support process begins early in the cycle when goals and resources are discussed.

The process-oriented view embodies this more practical position. Figure 3.31 recasts the software and organizational engineering process so the issue of planning for ongoing support begins much earlier. Although recognizing that software needs to be maintained is a good start, it is only a first step. New systems themselves can change the nature of the work. Software succeeds if it works well with the work processes of an organization. Successful implementations of knowledge systems, like other new technologies, require an interactive process of incrementally altering the technology to fit an organization and simultaneously shaping the organization to exploit the potential of the technology. In the process-oriented view, this coevolution continues until the technology either is absorbed into routine use or is discontinued.

Collaborative Design and Articulation of Work Practice

A common thread in these organizational issues is that the development cycle is the collaborative articulation of work practice. Thus, a fielded knowledge system and its support network should embody an explicit articulation of a work practice that at the beginning of the design process was largely unarticulated. Every one of the backward arrows in our life-cycle diagrams can be viewed as a means of realizing that the provisional articulation of the work practice being modeled was mistaken in some way.

Thus, it is important to have the constituency involved in the loop from the beginning. Explaining the reasoning and search processes of prototype systems is a good way to evoke useful objections and qualifactions, as well as to provoke reflective thinking on what the work practice actually consists of. The "participatory" component of participatory design consists precisely of this collaborative activity of trying to characterize the whole work practice so as to decompose it and to realize some part of it in a knowledge system.

The design-as-articulation is naive if it does not consider work practice. Knowledge systems change existing practices. Adding a computer can transform the nature of the work in ways that are either positive or negative. This includes the reorganization of jobs, issues of training and support, and so on.

The oversimplification of the process of locating experts and identifying a "task" takes for granted that the existing division of labor before automation should be the same as the division after automation. However, knowledge systems can radically change the distribution of skills and patterns of communication in an organization. A knowledge system may make it possible to combine existing jobs, to shift responsibilities between jobs, or to carry out new jobs that were not economically feasible without automation. A project team should consider the opportunities to make their work and organization more effective, rather than limiting their thinking to automating an existing task. This means the design cycle should attempt not simply to articulate existing practice, but also to try to imagine and invent future practice.

3.3.4 *Summary and Review*

We reviewed several variations on the knowledge acquisition process and showed how they address needs that change as a system is developed. At the beginning of a project it is appropriate to use unstructured interviews with experts on typical cases. These cases help to define the core concepts and requirements for the system. Later in the process the emphasis shifts to defining the problem-solving process in detail, and then again to finding gaps in the coverage of task situations. Typical cases are useful at the beginning. Later, extreme and tough cases are useful for establishing a high level of performance and for establishing the boundaries of applicability for the knowledge.

Sessions can be designed to probe for variations in practice across a community of users. To resolve differences, different policies can be used, such as generalizing new coherent rules that cover the cases, letting one rule dominate, or reporting the different results of applying different knowledge. In any case, discovering variability early in the system development process can be important for avoiding surprises and difficulties of acceptance later on.

In the last part of the section we considered two perspectives from software engineering. A product-oriented view sees knowledge systems as products, implemented according to given specifications and delivered to users after they have been implemented. A process-oriented view sees knowlege systems as being developed in collaboration with their users, with the requirements unfolding as the systems are developed. The process view emphasizes the notion that "getting the specifications" is not a simple first step, but rather a major part of the collaborative development task requiring constant testing and refinement of the knowledge, the task, the user interfaces, the connections to other work processes, and the plans for ongoing support.

The software and organizational engineering issues do not arise in small projects, research prototypes, or student projects. They are most crucial for systems used by organizations over

```
To find the gcd of two given positive integers, m and n:
   1.     If m < n, then exchange m and n.
          /* Find remainder. */
   2.     GetRemainder: Divide m by n and let r be the remainder.

   3.     If r=0 then terminate successfully returning n as the gcd
   4.     Else
   5.     begin
                 /* Interchange. */
   6.              m := n
   7.              n := r
   8.              go to GetRemainder
   9.     end
```

FIGURE 3.32. Euclid's algorithm for finding the greatest common divisor that evenly divides both *m* and *n*.

extended periods of time. The same kinds of issues come up in the development of all large computer systems that mediate work and can change the way organizations go about their business.

Exercises for Section 3.3

Ex. 1 [CD-12] *What Makes Software Engineering Difficult.* A favorite introductory example in books about computer programming is the Euclidean algorithm for determining the greatest common divisor (gcd) of two given integers, *m* and *n*. An algorithm for this is given in Figure 3.32.

This exercise considers why knowledge systems require kinds of analysis and development processes that are radically different from what is illustrated in the Euclidean algorithm example. For each of the following, compare the approaches and requirements for the Euclidean algorithm versus a typical knowledge system. Use a knowledge system that you are familiar with as an exemplar. Limit your explanations to three or four sentences. Focus on the approaches and requirements that are different in important ways.

(a) Problem identification and specification.
(b) User involvement in the development process.
(c) Impact on the organization in the workplace.
(d) Maintenance requirements.

Ex. 2 [10] *Building an Expert System for Determining Task Feasibility.* Given the frustrations with the "knowledge acquisition bottleneck" and an apparent shortage of knowledge engineers, Professor Digit proposes to build an expert system for knowledge acquisition, focusing on the question of task suitability. Here is a sampling of some of the questions from Section 3.1. Briefly explain why the answers to these questions are likely to be problematic for the feasibility of his proposed project.

- How often do they do the task (that is, the determination of suitability of a task domain)?
- How long does it take to carry out the task?

□   How do the solution methods vary across different problems?
□   What is an example of a problem?
□   What are the input data?
□   What is an answer to the problem?

Ex. 3   [05] *Automating Knowledge Acquisition*. Beyond the task of determining task feasibility in Exercise 2, what other activities in knowledge acquisition are problematic from the perspective of trying to automate them with an expert system? Explain briefly.

Ex. 4   [05] *The Symbol Level and the Knowledge Level*. Professor Digit says most of the concerns of the formalization stage of particpatory design are at the symbol level. Do you agree? Explain briefly.

■   **Ex. 5**   [20] *Interpreting Protocol Data as Search*. In this exercise we consider some issues in developing a formal model from protocol data. Our example is based on the DNA segmentation problem from Section 2.2.4.

Figure 3.33 shows case data for a segmentation problem. Figure 3.34 shows an excerpt from a protocol.

(a) In step 3, explain the expert's logic when he concludes that there must be two restriction sites for each enzyme on the molecule.

(b) What knowledge is the expert using in step 4? Give rules for determining that the .18 segment is unique and what enzyme sites border it.

(c) How does the expert use summation evidence from the digest to suggest segment adjacency in the molecule? Propose a rule to explain the logic of step 5.

(d) Would the logic of steps 6 and 7 work if there were more pieces in the digests?

Ex. 6   [20] *Interpreting Protocol Data, Continued*. This exercise continues from the previous exercise, examining the protocol for the sample segmentation problem and the analysis of the task.

(a) Briefly explain what the domain expert is doing in step 8.

(b) A model-driven (or top-down) approach, such as the method described in Section 2.4, works from a model of the solution space. A data-driven (or bottom-up) approach attempts to propose only those candidates that are suggested by the data. The data-driven approach steps through the data space to propose hypotheses and the model-driven approach steps through the solution space, checking hypotheses against the data.

Which approach is the domain expert using in step 5? Which approach is he using in step 12?

Enzymes	*Weights of molecular segments observed after cutting by enzymes*			
Hind III	3.82	.18		
Bam	2.35	1.65		
Eco RI	3.0	1.0		
Hind III + Bam	2.35	1.2	.27	.18
Hind III + Eco RI	1.87	1.0	.95	.18
Bam + Eco RI	1.6	1.4	.75	.25

FIGURE 3.33.   The input data to the segmentation problem.

(c) Briefly, how does the domain expert make sure he does not miss any possible solutions? How does he make sure he considers each solution once? (*Hint*: This is a trick question.) What issue does this raise about knowledge-level analysis of this task in designing of a search method for the problem?

(d) In interpreting data, it is possible to make inferences from either the presence or the absence of data. (This is sometimes called positive data and negative data.) Reliability depends on what kinds of errors are common. If missing data are common, then negative data will be unreliable because they will be interpreted as negative data. If extraneous data are common, then positive data will be unreliable because extraneous data will be misinterpreted as positive data.

In the segmentation problems, missing data are much more common in these procedures than extraneous data. Furthermore, it is easy to design a generator that is relatively insensitive to the kinds of errors that appear in the data.

Assuming that the problem-solving goal is to find all solutions that are reasonably consistent with the data, what does this suggest about the choice of search strategy?

■ **Ex. 7** [30] *"War Stories" about Implementing Knowledge Systems.* Dorothy Leonard-Barton (1987) has argued that successful implementation of expert systems requires not only fitting the technology to the organization, but also fitting the organization to the technology. She cites several examples of difficulties encountered in the introduction of the XSEL program at Digital as illustrating a process she calls "integrative innovation." The following examples drawn from this study illustrate some issues of integrative innovation with examples of problems that arose in the development of XSEL and organizational measures that were tried.

XSEL was conceived as an interactive aid for the sales force that would help to catch errors in purchase orders for the configuration of computers. This fit into Digital's strategy of tailoring its computer products to customers' needs. There were two reasons that an expert system was wanted: (1) The number of potential computer configurations was increasing and (2) the sales force was increasingly composed of people with less technical training and experience than Digital's earlier sales representatives.

(a) Digital follows a model of participative design, reflecting a strong process-oriented point of view in which users aid not only in establishing system requirements at the beginning but also in reformulating them during development. In the XSEL project, the target users lacked expert knowledge about how to configure computers. This knowledge was best understood by the very senior sales representatives and people from field service. What recommendations would you make for the composition of a user group for designing the system? Why might there be a problem with too many or too few members?

(b) During meetings of the user design group, the inexperienced sales representatives recruited for the XSEL project tended to sit in the back of the room and say little. Nor did they stay with the project for very long. Over the first three years of the project, the more expert configurers on the development team dominated. They watched the system progress from about 50 percent to 90 percent accuracy. However, other sales representatives, equally expert but not involved in designing XSEL, tended to evaluate the system more negatively. The project team became concerned about a potential bias from working with the same small group of users. From what does the possibility of bias arise? Discuss some measures you would recommend to the design group.

(c) One measure was to add a "comment" facility to XSEL that allowed its users to append comments and suggestions that were then forwarded to team members and knowledge engineers. Why might this help?

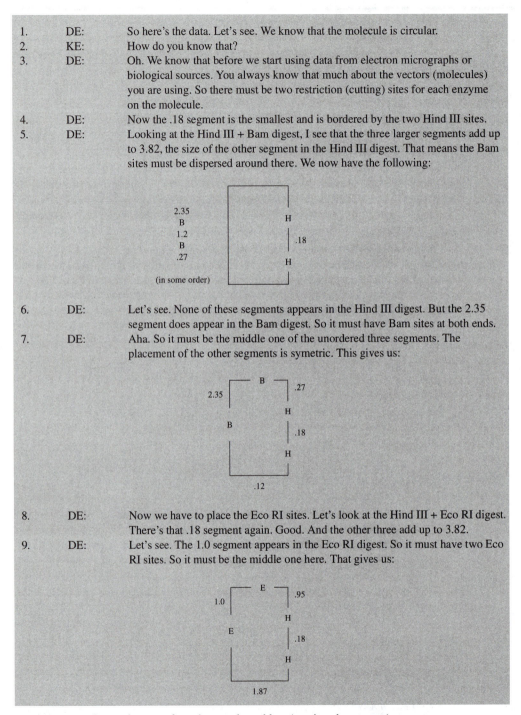

1.	DE:	So here's the data. Let's see. We know that the molecule is circular.
2.	KE:	How do you know that?
3.	DE:	Oh. We know that before we start using data from electron micrographs or biological sources. You always know that much about the vectors (molecules) you are using. So there must be two restriction (cutting) sites for each enzyme on the molecule.
4.	DE:	Now the .18 segment is the smallest and is bordered by the two Hind III sites.
5.	DE:	Looking at the Hind III + Bam digest, I see that the three larger segments add up to 3.82, the size of the other segment in the Hind III digest. That means the Bam sites must be dispersed around there. We now have the following:

6.	DE:	Let's see. None of these segments appears in the Hind III digest. But the 2.35 segment does appear in the Bam digest. So it must have Bam sites at both ends.
7.	DE:	Aha. So it must be the middle one of the unordered three segments. The placement of the other segments is symetric. This gives us:

8.	DE:	Now we have to place the Eco RI sites. Let's look at the Hind III + Eco RI digest. There's that .18 segment again. Good. And the other three add up to 3.82.
9.	DE:	Let's see. The 1.0 segment appears in the Eco RI digest. So it must have two Eco RI sites. So it must be the middle one here. That gives us:

FIGURE 3.34.   Protocol excerpt from the sample problem (continued next page).

10.	KE:	Umm. I don't see how you combine these structures. Aren't there two ways to superimpose these sites on the Bam and Hind III sites?
11.	DE:	Right. Let's see. Suppose the H .27 B segment overlays the H .95 E segment. That would give us a .68 segment in the Bam + Eco RI digest. Nope. Not there.
12.	DE:	So the .27 segment must be oriented the other way, over the 1.87 segment. That would give us a 1.4 segment in the Bam + Eco RI digest. That's it! That gives us:

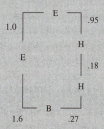

| 13. | DE: | So we still have one Bam site to place. The .75 and .25 segments from the Bam + Eco RI digest must overlay the E 1.0 E segment. But in what order? Maybe we can tell from the other digest. If the .25 segment is next to the .95 segment, then we should have a 1.2 setment in the Hind III + Bam digest. Aha. Got it. So the answer is: |

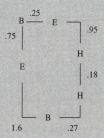

| 14. | DE: | Of course, we'd better check this to see if all of the digests come out right. We'd also better check whether any little variations give us the same thing. Pretty easy, eh? It's harder when there are more pieces. |

FIGURE 3.34. (continued)

(d) It is not unusual for highly placed managers to underestimate the amount of development left to be done on a project. For expert systems, the first prototype can seem very capable. Someone unversed in the technology can easily presume a far greater degree of technical readiness than is justified. One of the first and most visible advocates for XSEL at Digital was a vice-president who was impressed with an early prototype. In a September meeting he proposed that the development team aim to have XSEL on the desk of every sales representative by Christmas. Unwilling to admit their inability to meet the deadline, the team agreed to try. The sales organization then agreed to supply a computer for each sales region to run XSEL.

Unfortunately, preparing the system for the field actually took 12 months rather than 3. Thus, it was delivered 9 months after the promised date. What bad effects would this have? What could the team have done to prevent the problem?

(e) Because XSEL was not ready for the field until six months after the computers were in place, "reserved" space on them was often usurped by other software. It was difficult to expel these other programs when XSEL became ready. Each of the regional machines was controlled by a "systems manager," who regulated the allotments of file space and machine usage. During a period of about six months these "guardians" were especially critical to the dissemination of XSEL. One systems manager vociferously criticized XSEL as a "kludge." He programmed his computer to display the order in which the software invoked the rules needed to interact with the user. When he saw that these rules were activated in apparently random patterns, he concluded that the programming was inefficient.

Is the pattern of rule invocation unusual? Does it imply that the program is inefficient? How might the development team approach this manager?

Ex. 8   [05] *Terminology.* Please indicate true or false for each of the following statements. If the statement is ambiguous, explain your answer briefly and concretely.

(a) *True or False.* Common ground, in the context of knowledge systems, refers to a safe electrical ground for connections between the computer and its sensors.

(b) *True or False.* A process-oriented view of software engineering is concerned with the long-term effects of a system on the work practices of the organization.

(c) *True or False.* The formalization stage of software engineering for knowledge systems refers to the development of a rigorous but unimplemented model of a search process from case data.

(d) *True or False.* A common problem with the product-oriented approach to software engineering is that it admits too much user feedback before a system is implemented and ready to be tested.

(e) *True or False.* Many concerns of software engineering are irrelevant for personal knowledge systems developed for the exclusive use of one person.

■ **Ex. 9**   [CD-!-10] *Informating Systems and Organizational Change.* This exercise considers the relevance of the concepts and techniques in this chapter to automating even apparently mundane tasks. We use the scenario about point-of-sale terminals from Section 3.1.2 as our example.

(a) One task to be automated in this scenario is the look-up of prices at the point-of-sale terminal for the printing of sales receipts. Briefly evaluate the suitability of this task according to rules of thumb about the following:

- **(i)** Task frequency
- **(ii)** Required training
- **(iii)** Time needed to complete a task

(b) Store managers value point-of-sale product scanning systems for two main reasons. One is that the systems eliminate the need to mark prices on individual items in the store, including the need for marking them again when sale prices are in effect. Also, the systems reduce the demands on checkers to remember prices.

Briefly discuss two or three specific possible effects of automation on the organization of a store. How and where in the software engineering process would these factors be discovered and considered?

(c) Central to the notion of "informating" systems is the idea that automation ought to be used to empower people at work. In the case of the checkers and the managers, this suggests that rather than just buying an "off-the-shelf" scanner system, a store manager could consider the larger question of how the store might use automation to improve its processes and services. Imagine yourself participating in a "quality improvement task force" that includes the store manager, checkers, other store employees, store suppliers, customers, and software engineers. Briefly describe two or three specific possible services and automation that you would consider and their rationale.

Ex. 10   *[05] Variations in Knowledge Acquisition.* Please indicate true or false for each of the following statements. If the statement is ambiguous, explain your answer briefly and concretely.

(a) *True or False.* Unstructured interviews tend to be used at the beginning of a knowledge-system project. More structured interviews and protocol analysis then follow.

(b) *True or False.* The purpose of randomly selecting cases is to avoid unconscious bias away from cases with troublesome data.

(c) *True or False.* Tough cases are the first ones that should be considered, so a knowledge engineer can gauge the difficulty of a domain.

(d) *True or False.* When cases are created artificially by withholding information, the relation between the knowledge engineer and domain expert is purposefully changed to be like a psychological experiment.

(e) *True or False.* Extreme cases are useful for revealing assumptions in the knowledge and for problem-solving knowledge, thereby establishing boundaries of applicability of the expertise.

3.4 *Knowledge versus Complexity*

The preceding sections discussed approaches for developing knowledge systems. In this section we consider an example of a knowledge system in detail. Our goal is to give a concrete example of a knowledge system, discussing both its knowledge and its representations.

Using this example, we discuss the knowledge hypothesis (or the "knowledge principle"), which is treated as a tacit assumption in many projects. They hypothesis is that for most tasks, large amounts of specific knowledge are needed to achieve performance. We will see that although this is not a universal property of all tasks, it is often true and is an empirical question that can be asked about any particular task.

3.4.1 *MYCIN: Study of a Classic Knowledge System*

In this section we discuss the MYCIN system as an example of an expert system. MYCIN consults on the diagnosis of infectious diseases, especially bacterial infections of the blood. Its also makes therapy recommendations for patients with bacterial infections. MYCIN is a handy example because it is well understood and has been widely studied and imitated. Detailed studies of MYCIN are readily available for further reading (Buchanan & Shortliffe, 1984). This section presents examples of what MYCIN does and discusses the mechanisms and representations that enable its behavior.

When MYCIN was first reported, it was a startling example that was recognized as opening up a niche for a new kind of AI system. MYCIN's organization is no longer unique; it was the prototype for most of the first generation of knowledge engineering shells. Although it has since been superseded by other approaches for organizing knowledge systems, it is a good starting point for learning about knowledge systems. Many of the newer architectures can be understood in terms of how they go beyond some limitation of MYCIN's.

Describing MYCIN at the Knowledge Level and at the Symbol Level

To orient our discussion of MYCIN, we begin with some preliminary observations:

1. MYCIN's primary tasks are diagnosis and therapy. A knowledge-level analysis of MYCIN's task reveals three primary search spaces: a data space, a diagnosis space, and a therapy space.

2. MYCIN's diagnostic search is based on a heuristic classification model. In heuristic classification there are two spaces, called a data space and a solution space. Within the data space, raw data are abstracted to abstract data. Abstract data can be heuristically matched to abstract solutions. The set of possible solutions is finite and fixed for all problems. Chapter 7 discusses the heuristic classification model in detail. As suggested by Figure 3.35, MYCIN uses this model to map from data to diagnoses. The space of diagnoses corresponds to a predetermined set of infectious diseases.

3. MYCIN's therapy search is based on a configuration model. Configuration models select combinations of elements from a set and arrange them. The sets in MYCIN's therapy algorithm are sets of drugs, usually antibiotics. These are selected and arranged to satisfy various requirements, such as covering the most probable diagnoses and taking into account factors about a patient's condition. Chapter 8 discusses computational models for configuration.

4. MYCIN is implemented in terms of backward-chaining production rules. In discussing implementation, we move from the **knowledge level** to the **symbol level**.

In summary, we characterize MYCIN by its tasks (diagnosis and therapy), its computational models (heuristic classification and configuration), and its implementation (production rules and backward chaining).

A Dialog with MYCIN

Given these preliminary observations about MYCIN, we approach the system as it would be seen by a user. Figure 3.36 gives a sample of a user's dialog with the MYCIN system. In this dialog, MYCIN asks questions that bear directly on its search for an appropriate diagnosis and for therapy recommendations. The questions range over data from different sources—laboratory findings, questions about the patient's general state of health, and questions about clinical procedures.

When MYCIN was first demonstrated in the 1970s, a striking aspect was that its dialog was of the same kind one might expect from an expert human consultant. In particular, MYCIN did not ask a series of questions about probabilities and coefficients. It did not obviously ask questions about parameters of some mathematical model. ("Please enter fourth basis vector: . . . ") The interactions were in the terminology of medicine and cases. The overwhelming impression was that MYCIN reasoned about medicine in the same way that doctors did, that its reasoning was comprehensible and logical, and that it knew a lot about medicine.

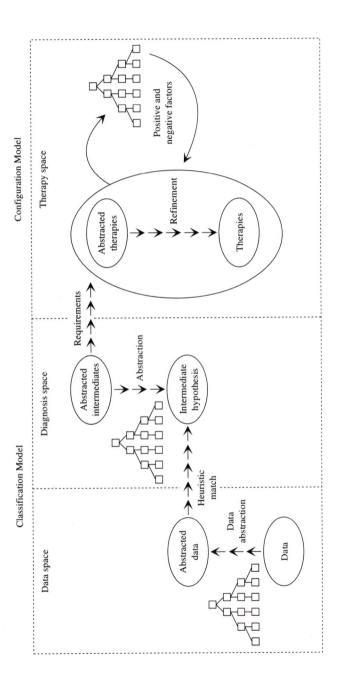

FIGURE 3.35. Search spaces and models used in MYCIN. MYCIN uses two models: a heuristic classification model that maps from a data space to a diagnosis space and a configuration model that proposes and evaluates therapies.

1)   Patient's name: (first-last)
**FRED BRAUN   *(Questions 1–3 request background patient data.)*
2) Sex:
** M
3) Age:
** 55
4)   Are there any cultures for Fred Braun which may be related to the present illness, and from
           which organisms have been grown successfully in the microbiology laboratory?
** Y

           CULTURE-1
5)   From what site was the specimen for CULTURE-1 taken?
** BLOOD
6)   Please give the date and time when CULTURE-1 was obtained.
         (mo/da/yr time)
** JUNE 20, 1977
The first organism isolated from the blood culture of 20-JUN-77 (CULTURE-1) will be
         referred to as:
ORGANISM-1
7)   Enter the laboratory-reported identity of ORGANISM-1:
** UNKNOWN   *(Typically identity is not yet known.)*
8)   The stain (gram or Ziehl-Neelsen acid-fast) of ORGANISM-1:
** NEG   *(Preliminary lab results give some clues.)*
9)   Is ORGANISM-1 rod or coccus (etc.):
** ROD

FIGURE 3.36.   Excerpts from a MYCIN consultation. Statements in bold after the double asterisks (**) are responses by the user. Comments in italics are not part of the actual interaction (continued next page). (From Buchanan and Shortliffe, 1984, page 69.)

Of course, any single dialog could be modeled simply by a trivial program. For example, one could imagine that MYCIN was implemented by a program such as the one sketched in Figure 3.37. Such a program would navigate through a decision tree whose nodes are questions and whose roots correspond to diagnoses and therapeutic recommendations. In that formulation, the questions to the user would be built in. The reasoning process would be determined by the program's structure, unfolding as the program executes. However, as we will see, MYCIN is not constructed in this way at all.

There are several practical difficulties with directly using a purely procedural knowledge representation as suggested in Figure 3.37. Although procedural languages are powerful and can describe very complex programs, they provide no separation of symbol-level concerns from knowledge-level concerns. At the symbol level, programs are very interconnected. Adding knowledge is a very complex task. For example, in the syntax of the `format` statement that controls the printing of prompts in interactions with the user, the relations between the patient, the cultures, the present illness, and the organisms are all linked in a programming constant (a string). Similarly, the use of the `putslot` and `get-new-object` statements mixes specifications about domain relations with specifications about the implementation of memory and choices of

10) What is the form of the individual organisms (e.g., lancet-shaped for cocci, fusiform for rods, etc.)?

** **FUSIFORM**

(. . . more questions follow in order to gather sufficient information to infer the identity and significance of the infecting organisms . . .)

23)   What is the suspected portal of entry of the gramneg rod from the blood culture of 20-JUN-77 (ORGANISM-1) into this sterile site?

** **GI** (6)   *(User indicates the uncertainty of his response.)*

24) Is Fred Braun a burn patient?

** **N**

25) Is Fred Braun a compromised host (e.g., alcoholic, sickle-cell disease, immunosuppressed)?

** **N**

26) Is Fred Braun febrile?

** **Y**

(. . . after about 50–60 questions, MYCIN prints the diagnostic hypotheses on which therapy will be based . . .)

My therapy recommendations will be designed to treat for organisms that are either very likely or, although less likely, would have a significant effect on therapy selection if they were present. It is important to cover for the following probable infection(s) and associated organism(s):

INFECTION-1 is BACTEREMIA

<ITEM-1> E.COLI [ORGANISM-1]
<ITEM-2> KLEBSIELLA [ORGANISM-1]
<ITEM-3> ENTEROBACTER [ORGANISM-1]
<ITEM-4> KLEBSIELLA-PNEUMONIAE [ORGANISM-1]

FIGURE 3.36.   (continued)

```
(setq patient-name(prompt-user "Patient's name: (first-last)"))
(setq patient-sex(prompt-user "Sex:"))
(setq patient-age(prompt-user "Age:"))
(setq reply(prompt-user(format nil "Are there any cultures for a which may
     be related to the present illness, and from which organisms have been
     grown successfully in the microbiology laboratory?" patient-name)))
(cond ((affirmative? reply)
   (setq culture(get-new-object 'culture))
   (putslot 'site culture(prompt-user(format nil "From what site was the
   specimen for ↑a taken?" culture)))
```

FIGURE 3.37.   Part of a program that could create the apparent dialog of Figure 3.36, but that would actually be unsuitable for representing the knowledge of MYCIN.

representation. Thus assumptions about choices of representation for cultures, sites, and the relations among them are embedded in the code repeatedly. If MYCIN had been coded directly in this way, there would be an ongoing programming burden for maintaining and updating the knowledge in the system. In practical terms, MYCIN would require the constant attention of a programmer who understands the medical domain, is familiar with the organization and conventions used in the knowledge system, and has the patience to track down all the parts of the program that need to be updated whenever a bug is found or a change is introduced. In the following we see how MYCIN works and what facilities it provides to simplify the addition of knowledge.

Inside MYCIN

As stated earlier, MYCIN is implemented in terms of production rules. Several examples of MYCIN production rules are shown in Figure 3.38. MYCIN translates these pseudo-English rules to and from an internal production-rule representation that is structured to enable easier interpretation. Figure 3.39 shows the internal representation of the first rule in Figure 3.38. The details of the translation processes are beyond the purposes of the present discussion. Briefly, the translation of a wide range of English sentences would have required a much more complex approach than was practical for MYCIN. Instead, MYCIN uses key words and templates to guide translation into internal symbol structures. To drive translation back to pseudo-English it uses recursive functions that combine pieces of text.

The **premise part** of each rule is a Boolean combination of clauses composed of predicate functions on elements of MYCIN's working memory, which are described later. There is a standardized set of predicate functions such as `same`, `known`, and `definite`. MYCIN uses several standard categories of objects such as `organism`, `culture`, and `drug`. In the jargon of this system, these categories are called context types. The **action part** of a rule indicates one or more conclusions that can be drawn if the premises are satisfied.

The set of context types used in MYCIN evolved as the system was further developed. They were used as a basis for indexing and organizing MYCIN's knowledge base. There were ten different context types in the 1975 version of MYCIN including (1) a current culture from which organisms were isolated, (2) an antimicrobial agent currently being administered to a patient, (3) an operative procedure the patient has undergone, and (4) an organism isolated from a prior culture.

During a consultation session, MYCIN builds a model of the patient, possible organisms, and so on by instantiating these context types and organizing them into a data structure called a context tree. Figure 3.40 shows an example of a context tree.

Context trees are used for several purposes. They represent some of the relations inferred by MYCIN's reasoning, some of which can be multivalued. For example, the tree in Figure 3.40 represents that Organism-1 came from Culture-1 and that both Organism-3 and Organism-4 came from Culture-3. The tree makes it simple to retrieve all the contexts in a particular relation to one another, such as all the cultures taken for Patient-1. The context tree is also used for internal indexing on the rules. MYCIN categorizes rules according to the context types to which they may be applied. Some rules may be applied to any culture, some only to the current culture, some only to organisms from prior cultures, some to any antimicrobial agent that has been administered to combat a specific organism, and so on.

```
RULE177
If         1) the infection is primary-bacteremia, and
           2) the site of the culture is one of the sterile sites, and
           3) the suspected portal of entry of the organism is the gastro-
                 intestinal tract,
Then there is suggestive evidence (.7) that the identity of the organism
     is bacteroides.


RULE037
If         1) the identity of the organism is not known with certainty, and
           2) the stain of the organism is gramneg, and
           3) the morphology of the organism is rod, and
           4) the aerobicity of the organism is aerobic,
Then there is strongly suggestive evidence (.8) that the class of the
     organism is enterobacteriaceae.


RULE145
If         1) the therapy under consideration is one of: cephalothin
                 clindamycin erythromycin lincomycin vancomycin, and
           2) meningitis is an infectious disease diagnosis for the patient,
Then it is definite (1) that the therapy under consideration is not a
     potential therapy for use against the organism.


RULE178
If         1) the identity of the organism is bacteroides,
Then I recommend therapy chosen from among the following drugs:
           1 — clindamycin           (.99)
           2 — chloramphenicol       (.99)
           3 — erythromycin          (.57)
           4 — tetracycline          (.28)
           5 — carbenicillin         (.27)
```

FIGURE 3.38. Examples of production rules from MYCIN. (From Buchanan and Shortliffe, 1984, page 82.)

```
premise:        ($and      (same cntxt infect primary-bacteremia)
                           (membf cntxt site sterilesites)
                           (same cntxt portal GI))
action:         (conclude cntxt ident bacteroides tally .7)
```

FIGURE 3.39. Internal representation of the first rule (Rule 177) from Figure 3.38.

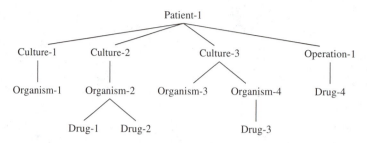

FIGURE 3.40.   A MYCIN context tree. This tree shows a sample patient with two recent positive cultures, an older culture, and a recent operative procedure. (From Buchanan and Shortliffe, 1984, page 84.)

In addition to the information in the context tree, MYCIN develops a body of information in its **dynamic database** or **working memory**. This database contains values of clinical parameters. A clinical parameter is a property of one of the contexts in the context tree, such as the name of a patient, the identity of an organism, the site of a culture, the dose of a drug, and so on. Clinical parameters are represented in data structures that include an **object** (the context), an **attribute** (a clinical parameter), and a **value**. Figure 3.41 shows examples of these data structures. The first 4-tuple indicates that the "site from which bacterial culture-1 was drawn was the blood." The second tuple indicates that "the identity of organism-2 is klebsiella." Thus, the 4-tuple representation can be understood in terms of objects (such as organism-2) with attributes (such as identity) and values (such as klebsiella). Some of these facts come from MYCIN's queries of the doctor and laboratory tests; others are derived or inferred by the rules from previously established facts in the database.

The fourth element of each data tuple is a number known as a **certainty factor**. Certainty factors are derived from and related to probabilities. MYCIN uses certainty factors in its approach to inexact reasoning. Certainty factors and other models for reasoning about belief and uncertainty are described in Chapter 4. These factors are used in tallying the weight of evidence for MYCIN's hypotheses, that is, for its statements of fact in its database. The value of every clinical parameter is associated with a certainty factor. For the purposes of this section, it is enough to know that a certainty factor is a number between −1 and 1 that reflects a degree of belief in a hypothesis. Positive certainty factors indicate there is evidence that the hypothesis is valid; negative certainty factors indicate there is evidence against the hypothesis. For example, the 1.0 certainty factor in the first tuple in Figure 3.41 indicates that it is certain that the site of

```
(site culture-1 blood 1.0)
(ident organism-2 klebsiella .25)
(ident organism-2 e.coli .73)
(sensitive organism-1 penicillin -1.0)
```

FIGURE 3.41.   Representations in MYCIN's dynamic database of facts about the world.

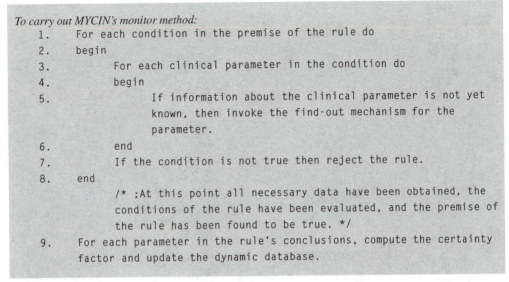

To carry out MYCIN's monitor method:
```
  1.    For each condition in the premise of the rule do
  2.  begin
  3.        For each clinical parameter in the condition do
  4.        begin
  5.              If information about the clinical parameter is not yet
                  known, then invoke the find-out mechanism for the
                  parameter.
  6.        end
  7.        If the condition is not true then reject the rule.
  8.  end
            /* ;At this point all necessary data have been obtained, the
            conditions of the rule have been evaluated, and the premise of
            the rule has been found to be true. */
  9.    For each parameter in the rule's conclusions, compute the certainty
       factor and update the dynamic database.
```

FIGURE 3.42. MYCIN's monitor method for rules. This algorithm describes how MYCIN decides whether a rule applies in the clinical situation. This is the first part of MYCIN's backward-chaining mechanism.

culture-1 is blood; the .25 certainty factor in the second tuple indicates that while the evidence is positive, it is only weakly suggestive. When MYCIN reaches a conclusion by executing a rule, the certainty factor assigned to the concluded clinical parameter reflects the certainty factors of the information used in the premise of the rule, any previous certainty factors for the parameter, and also the certainty factor associated with the strength of the rule itself. Later chapters consider the capabilities and requirements of several different models of inexact reasoning.

Given this background, we begin with a simplified discussion of how MYCIN solved problems. MYCIN's control structure is a goal-directed backward chaining of rules. At each cycle of the process, MYCIN has a goal to determine the value of a clinical parameter.

Figures 3.42 and 3.43 describe MYCIN's backward-chaining mechanism. The mechanism has two parts: the monitor method and the find-out method. The monitor method (shown in Figure 3.42) is used to analyze and process a rule. It iterates through the rule's conditions and through the clinical parameters in each condition. Whenever data are not yet known, the monitor method invokes the find-out method. After all the parameter values have been determined, the rule's premise is evaluated. The evaluation of the premise combines the certainty factors from the various hypotheses corresponding to the clauses in the premise. The details of the combinational procedure go beyond the purposes of this section, but the basic idea is that if the factors are high enough the premise is considered to be "true" and the rule is executed.

The find-out method determines whether a clinical parameter corresponds to laboratory data that it can obtain from the physician by asking. (MYCIN was not able to look up laboratory data from an online database.) Otherwise, it searches for other rules that could be used to infer the parameter from other parameters that are already known.

To carry out MYCIN's find-out method:

```
1.      If the parameter is a piece of laboratory data, then
2.      begin
3.              Ask the user for the value of the parameter.
4.              If the value of the parameter is known, return it;
5.              Otherwise call Find-Rules.
6.              Return;
7.      end
        /* Here if the parameter is not a piece of laboratory data. */
8.      Call Find-Rules(parameter).
9.      If the value of the parameter is known, then return it.
10.     Else ask the user for the value of the parameter.
11.     Return.


1.      Procedure Find-Rules(parameter):
2.      For each rule that concludes about the value of the parameter do
3.      begin       ·
4.              Retrieve the rule from the knowledge base.
5.              Invoke the monitor method for the rule.
6.      end
7.      Return.
```

FIGURE 3.43. MYCIN's find-out method for rules. This algorithm describes how MYCIN decides which questions to ask a physician user. This is the second part of MYCIN's backward-chaining mechanism.

Suppose that at one point MYCIN's goal was to determine the identities of the infecting organism (say organism-2). If the identity were known, that is, if it were already recorded in the database of tuples, MYCIN could just stop. Otherwise, MYCIN would retrieve from its knowledge base the rules needed to infer the identity of an organism. At this point, rules like the one in Figure 3.44 would be retrieved.

```
RULE177
If          1) the infection is primary-bacteremia, and
            2) the site of the culture is one of the sterile sites, and
            3) the suspected portal of entry of the organism is the gas-
               trointestinal tract,
Then there is suggestive evidence (.7) that the identity of the organism
is bacteroides.
```

FIGURE 3.44. Example of a production rule for inferring the identity of an organism. (From Buchanan and Shortliffe, 1984, page 82.)

To be able to apply this rule, MYCIN must be able to evaluate the elements in the rule's premise. This creates three more subgoals for the problem solver: (1) determining whether the infection is primary-bacteremia, (2) determining whether the site of the culture is one of the sterile sites, and (3) determining whether the portal of entry is the gastrointestinal tract. If the premise of the rule was found to be true, then MYCIN would modify its dynamic database by adding a tuple indicating its belief that the identity of organism-2 is bacteroides.

MYCIN's control mechanism is actually somewhat more complicated than what we have shown here. Exercise 4 considers some modifications to the methods to handle anomalies when references among clinical parameters form cycles in the knowledge base. One variation of the method uses forward chaining in special cases. This case arises when there is a chain of rules that concludes a value for a subgoal with certainty and whose premises are known with certainty. Such rules tend to be definitional, corresponding to inferences that would be obvious to a physician. To avoid asking silly questions, MYCIN first checks for a **unity path**, a chain of rules with $CF = 1$. If the rule monitor finds a unity path, then it has reached a conclusion with certainty and it is not necessary to try alternate rules. Since there are relatively few unity paths possible in the knowledge base, the amount of forward-chaining search tends to be small.

Mechanisms for Knowledge Additivity

Considering again the strawman procedural representation for MYCIN's knowledge suggested earlier, it should now be apparent how the production-rule representation, standardized database, and backward-chaining mechanism simplify the maintenance of the knowledge base by separating various programming concerns. In the procedural representation, adding a rule would involve finding the appropriate place in the program, taking into account the various representations that were used, and inserting new statements that modify the decision tree and update the internal representations. Finding the right place in the program is essential for ensuring that the rule will be used. In contrast, a backward-chaining system assumes much of the responsibility for indexing and locating the rules, guaranteeing that all the rules that bear on a clinical parameter will be found (by exhaustive search through backward chaining) and that they will be invoked only once.

The use of a standardized database and user interface simplifies updating the system because it avoids the widespread embedding of assumptions about representation in the code. That is, the rules themselves do not state how relations or objects are represented in the system. Different implementations of MYCIN could in principle use the same rules, and different relations could be recorded in different ways. The system has the responsibility for mapping externally expressed rules onto their implementations, through the actions of the translator and the rule interpreter. These implementation issues are typical in the design of knowledge systems.

Explanations from a Knowledge System in Context

The explicit knowledge base of MYCIN was used to advantage for other capabilities as well. Figure 3.45 shows another overview of MYCIN's organization, this time emphasizing the relation between the explanation program and the consultation program. In this perspective, the MYCIN system is made of three major programs. The **consultation program** interacts with a physician to obtain information about a patient. It generates diagnoses and recommends therapies. The **explanation program** answers questions, providing justifications and accounts of the

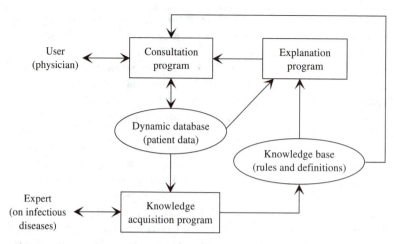

FIGURE 3.45.   Overview of the subsystems of MYCIN.

program's actions. The **knowledge acquisition program** is used by experts to update the knowledge base.

Explanation systems provide a mechanism whereby they explain or justify their conclusions. An explanation system can increase a user's confidence in a system. When MYCIN traces out its reasoning, it not only explains the knowledge that was used but also conveys a reassurance of a systematic process. Systems that explain their behavior in terms of the knowledge used are sometimes characterized as "transparent boxes," in contrast with "black boxes." This transparency also affects attitudes about responsibility for correctness, since it focuses attention on the knowledge a system uses rather than on the system itself. Figure 3.46 shows a sample of a MYCIN dialog illustrating the role of the explanation system in which a user asks questions of the system. In this dialog, the user asks how MYCIN came to particular conclusions and how particular data are used by the system.

MYCIN's explanation program is built from a collection of specialist subprograms, designed to answer particular kinds of queries. One specialist is used to provide answers to questions about the system's static knowledge base. The last question in Figure 3.46 is an example of a question. To answer questions about judgmental knowledge, such as the question, "What does GU manipulation tell you about the identity of an organism?" MYCIN makes use of two lists associated with each clinical parameter (attribute). One list contains every rule that uses the parameter in its premise; the other list contains every rule that concludes a value for the parameter. These lists are maintained automatically by the system and are updated when the knowledge base is changed. To answer the question in this example, the specialist can compute the intersection of the set of rules that refer to GU manipulation in the premise with the set of rules that refer to the identity of an organism in the conclusion.

MYCIN is also able to answer questions based on the dynamic data from a particular consultation. In doing this MYCIN makes use of a history tree, which it builds during a consultation. Each node in a history tree represents a goal and contains information about how the system tried to accomplish the goal. The tree structure reflects subgoals in the search process: Offspring for a node indicate which clinical parameters were traced during backward chaining for a goal. The

** IS ORGANISM-1 A STREPTOCOCCUS?

No. The identity of ORGANISM-1 IS e.coli (.74) bacteroides (.7) klebsiella-pneumoniae (.4) pseudomonas-aeruginosa (.22) enterobacter (.21) proteus-non-mirabilis (.19) serratia (.03) salmonella (.02)

**WHY DID YOU RULE OUT STREPTOCOCCUS AS A POSSIBILITY FOR ORGANISM-1?

RULE033 could have been used to determine that the identity of ORGANISM is streptococus. However, clause 2 of RULE033 ["the morphology of the organism is coccus"] was already known to be false for ORGANISM-1, so the rule was never tried.

**HOW DO YOU KNOW THAT CULTURE-1 WAS FROM A STERILE SOURCE?

I used RULE189 to conclude that this blood culture was taken from a sterile source. This gave a cumulative CF of (1.0). The last question asked before the conclusion was made was 7.

** WHAT DOES GU MANIPULATION TELL YOU ABOUT THE IDENTITY OF AN ORGANISM?

The rules listed below use:
    whether the patient has had a genito-urinary manipulative procedure
to conclude about:
    the identity of the organism
156, 163, 190
Which do you wish to see?

** 156

RULE156

IF: 1) The site of the culture is blood, and
       2) The gram stain of the organism is gramneg, and
       3) The morphology of the organism is rod, and
       4) The portal of entry of the organism is urine, and
       5) The patient has not had a genito-urinary manipulative procedure, and
       6) Cystitis is not a problem for which the patient has been treated
THEN: There is suggestive evidence (.6) that the identity of the organism is e.coli.

** IS BLOOD A STERILE SITE?

Yes. Blood is one of those sites that is normally sterile.

FIGURE 3.46.   An excerpt from an interaction with MYCIN's question and answering module.

history tree also indicates which rules succeeded and which failed. If a rule was tried but failed, the tree records why it failed. For example, when MYCIN is asked a question like, "How do you know that culture-1 was from a sterile source?" it recognizes that the value of a parameter can come from two sources: It can be inferred from rules or it could come from the response of a user to a question. Which of these sources of information was relevant to a particular consultation is recorded in the history tree. When MYCIN is asked why it ruled out a value for a parameter, it

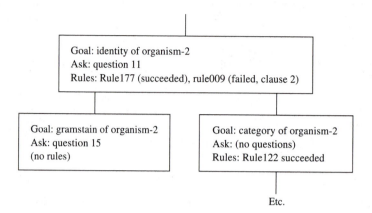

FIGURE 3.47.   A portion of a history tree built incrementally during a MYCIN consultation session. A history tree shows what goals were tried, what subgoals were pursued, what rules were tried, and what questions were asked. For rules that failed, a history tree records which clauses failed.

can consult its lists of rules for a parameter to find out which rules could have been used and then consult the history tree to find out what happened when each of these rules was tried.

It is instructive to compare MYCIN's explanation system with the discussion of the expressiveness of representation languages in Chapter 1. We considered a strawman proposal about what it means for a representation to be expressive in terms of the ability of an interpreter to answer whether a given sentence followed from a set of sentences in a knowledge base. We considered why this computation was intractable for predicate calculus and considered trade-offs in expressiveness and the ability to answer questions.

What is interesting about the explanation facility of MYCIN in this context is that the characterization of question answering in Chapter 1 misses the point of MYCIN's explanation facility because it focuses on the wrong kinds of questions. A user of MYCIN is not just interested in whether a statement is true or has been proven. Only the first question in Figure 3.46 is of this kind. "Is organism-1 a streptococcus?" is an example of a question about what was inferred from the data by the sentences in the knowledge base.

The second and third questions are about the nature of the proof. Here the user wants to know what support there is for a particular belief and how the system reached its conclusions. This brings us back to the notion of argumentation and the issue of what constitutes a proof. The user may at this point discard the conclusion in his own mind because he disagrees with a premise or does not believe or trust the data used by the system. Furthermore, this question requires that MYCIN keep a record of its reasoning activities. The notion of such a history goes beyond "truth" and "proof."

The fourth question is about the structure of the knowledge base and what is in it, rather than what it implies. The user wants to know what means the system has available for certain reasoning. Again, this provides information about the abilities of the system to make inferences.

Finally, the last question can be seen as providing information about the reference semantics for the symbols used by MYCIN. The physican user has a model of medicine. He asks, "Is blood a sterile site?" If MYCIN's answer does not match his expectations, then MYCIN does not model the world the same way that he does. If the dialog were between two people instead of a person and a knowledge system, we would say that the two conversationalists were establishing common ground. They were trying to establish a set of terms for communication and they were checking each other's models by a process of asking questions. When answers agree sufficiently, they judge that they are using the same terms to mean the same things. In the terms of Chapter 1, they are interested in reference semantics rather than truth or proof semantics. They are gathering information about the reference semantics of the terms in their shared language of discourse.

The interactive dialog also illustrates several examples of how conventional programming techniques would be inadequate as a substrate for representing the knowledge of MYCIN. To admit the dialog in Figure 3.46, the programming approach would need to be augmented by multiple representations of MYCIN's basis for reasoning. For example, to answer the question about ruling out streptococcus, MYCIN could maintain auxiliary representations to indicate the history of clauses that have been tried in the rules. To answer the question of how it was decided that culture-1 was from a sterile source, it would need auxiliary records about the kinds of conclusions that rules can reach. To answer the question about procedures for genito-urinary procedures, it would need a way of retrieving all of the rules that use that information to conclude about the identity of organisms.

MYCIN reflects a long-time goal in AI: the realization of systems that can take advice. By this we mean to suggest that the passing of advice among people seems simpler and less involved than programming because the "advice taker" assumes much of the responsibility for integrating the advice with what it knows already. MYCIN succeeds at this to an extent in its integration of new rules.

Redesigning MYCIN

Before leaving this example of a knowledge system in action, we pause to consider some of the symbol-level and knowledge-level issues in MYCIN. If MYCIN were being redesigned, alternative choices for implementation would be considered. For example, MYCIN's context tree represents several different kinds of relations. It mixes together different relations. The tree includes cultures obtained from a patient, organisms isolated from a culture, drugs that treat for an infection by an organism, and so on. Current practice would employ distinct symbols rather than uniform links for the different relations. This would make the interpretation of the context tree seem less ad hoc. Another possibility would be to combine MYCIN's two working memories: the 4-tuple database and the context tree. These could be unified in any of several representations, such as a relational database, a frame representation, or an object-oriented representation. These changes would make the assertions in the database more uniformly accessible.

Turning to knowledge-level issues, we begin by noting that the above examples of MYCIN's behavior suggest that its domain knowledge is well suited to a simple object-attribute-value representation. However, these examples do not include complex structures from anatomy or deeply nested part hierarchies. Hierarchical relationships are central for such reasoning and MYCIN lacks them. Its diagnostic model based on heuristic classification is not well suited for reasoning about cases where there can be multiple contributing causes. Indeed, MYCIN does not even model causal behavior. MYCIN does not reason in a substantial way about changes over time, leading to difficulties in reasoning about progressive diseases. In short, MYCIN reflected excellent trade-offs in complexity and feasibility for the state of the art in knowledge systems circa 1975!

To summarize, MYCIN was a particularly influential knowledge system. It provided an example of a system with an explicit knowledge base coupled to a simple search system. Although the architectural ideas of MYCIN are primitive by today's standards, the project established many important ideas, such as the value of capabilities for adding knowledge incrementally and for explaining conclusions in terms of the knowledge and data that were used. The most important point of this example for our purposes is that it reveals that MYCIN's behavior is a search for solutions and that this search is guided by its knowledge base. MYCIN's success in influencing knowledge engineering rests not so much on the enduring quality of its architectural choices as on the shift of emphasis toward methods for representing "large amounts of knowledge in a fashion that permits their effective use and interaction."

3.4.2 *The Knowledge Hypothesis and the Qualification Problem*

In this section we draw on the MYCIN example and others to consider the assumption that performing real-world tasks requires large amounts of case-specific knowledge.

Knowledge versus Complexity

In the AI community of the 1970s, MYCIN was a central example and seemed easy to understand. It was an expert system and it relied on a large knowledge base. Over the history of the MYCIN project, the capabilities of the system were extended many times to improve its performance at diagnosing infectious diseases and recommending therapies. In each case, the performance was improved not by improving its inference method, but rather by adding rules to its knowledge base.

This path toward increased functionality is not unusual. Figure 3.48 documents the similar increase in the number of rules used in the XCON program (McDermott, 1982) for configuring VAX computers. XCON's task is to recommend combinations of computer components to be assembled together so a computer can satisfy a set of customer needs. Components include such things as processors, memory options, storage media, and auxiliary peripherals, as well as the necessary cabinets, cables, and power supplies. XCON was developed over several years, starting with a research prototype that handled only a small subset of the product line and eventually scaling up to an online program integrated into Digital Equipment Corporation's regular business activities. During this time the breadth and complexity of the VAX line of computers has continued to increase, and knowledge about the more complex PDP-11 line of computers was added to the knowledge base.

The MYCIN and XCON experiences demonstrate a common view of the relations among the complexity of the world, the required functionality of applications, and the role of knowledge. The simple version of the story has three parts: The world is complex. Embedded systems that perform tasks in the world need to model that complexity faithfully. The more complex that a task and its environment are, the more knowledge it takes to model them. In essence, the idea is to pit the complexity of a symbol system against the complexity of the world. The more case-specific knowledge a system has, the more cases it can handle. As discussed in the quandaries section of this chapter, the count of the rules in a knowledge system is only a crude measure of its complexity. Nonetheless, the increase in the number of rules suggests that the program and the task became more complex.

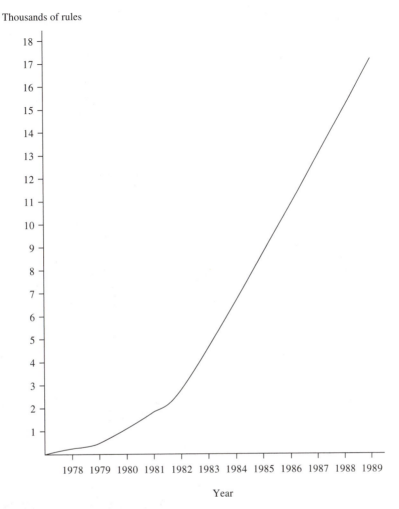

Thousands of rules

FIGURE 3.48. The main technique for increasing the breadth of functionality of the XCON system was to increase the set of rules used for reasoning about configurations.

These observations about the role of knowledge in the performance of expert systems were the driving examples behind the slogans of the late 1970s. Announcing a major shift for the field, advocates for a new style of building AI systems rallied around the phrase "Knowledge is power." The knowledge-is-power concept became such an integral part of knowledge engineering that Edward Feigenbaum (Lenat & Feigenbaum, 1987) has dubbed it the **knowledge principle**. In the following, we usually refer to it as the knowledge hypothesis.

The Knowledge Hypothesis. To achieve a high level of problem-solving competence, a symbol system must use a great deal of domain-specific, task-specific, and case-specific knowledge.

The knowledge hypothesis says that for a program to perform well, it must know a great deal about the task and domain in which it operates. As with the other very general hypotheses in the past two chapters, such as the physical symbol hypothesis, the heuristic search hypothesis, and the knowledge representation hypothesis, there is substantial debate about the centrality and power of this hypothesis for explaining the phenomenon of natural intelligence.

The observation that complexity increases when functionality increases is not limited to AI systems. Increasing complexity is characteristic of succeeding generations of many kinds of computer systems such as computer operating systems, database systems, and real-time control systems. Nor is the phenomenon limited to computer systems. Engines in automobiles have become more complex to enable them work with lower octane fuels without lead. Braking systems have become more complex to counteract skidding on slippery roads. Ride control systems have advanced from passive shock absorbers to active load-and-sway control. Automatic transmissions are changing from sensing a very limited set of mechanical data—engine speed, road speed, and the position of the gas pedal—to a set of 40 kinds of data. Furthermore, instead of just deciding whether to shift between gears, the new transmissions select among shifting patterns. These more sophisticated transmissions eliminate many of the unpleasant traits of the older automatics, such as undesired shifting back and forth between two gears or shifting when the car is going around a turn. In each of these cases, the increasing complexity in the structure of the physical system reflects an increasing awareness of its requirements as an embedded system and requires increasing amounts of knowledge about the task and the environment.

Computer systems are more readily changeable than (for example) brake systems or engines, and the tasks and environments are more diverse. Furthermore, engineering practice for knowledge systems in particular emphasizes the use of explicit and identifiable representations whose symbolic character is readily identifiable. By calling attention to the role of knowledge for coping with complexity, the knowledge principle has led to the shift in focus cited by Goldstein and Papert (1977) toward the development of techniques for reasoning with and managing large bodies of knowledge.

Where the Knowledge Hypothesis Fails

In the early 1980s when chess-playing programs were starting to compete in tournaments but fell far short of master-level performance, it was widely believed in AI circles that excellent chess play required large amounts of knowledge. It was estimated that grand-master chess players might carry 50,000 situations in their heads. That number was used to explain why chess players were better than "dumb machines." The path to making better chess programs was to put more knowledge in the programs.

Tidy as this example would be for the purposes of illustrating the knowledge hypothesis, it seems to be wrong. Since that time, considerable progress has been made at developing powerful chess programs, but some of the best systems have gotten most of their edge through faster computing on specialized parallel processors. The best of the current chess systems search more deeply than their predecessors. At least in tournament competitions, computational power has made the difference. At the time of this writing, a computer-based chess program, Deep Thought, has demonstrated the viability of this approach by beating all other computer-based chess programs as well as a human grand master. Does this mean the knowledge principle is wrong? Should we just build fast machines and not worry about knowledge formulation?

The chess example shows that the knowledge principle or hypothesis is not universal or precise as stated. However, it leads to a family of more specific scientific hypotheses, potentially falsifiable by experiment. Each hypothesis corresponds to a statement that *a particular class of problem-solving behavior requires a body of knowledge of some complexity to meet some performance standard.*

If the behavioral criterion is taken to be prowess at tournament chess, the success of those computer systems that rely on brute computational speed rather than special case knowledge disproves the knowledge hypothesis for that class of problem. In the same way, specific instantiations of the knowledge hypothesis can be defeated by demonstrating a system that exhibits intelligence without using much knowledge. The specific hypotheses differ in the criteria by which one defines performance and the measures one uses for knowledge.

We can turn the chess example around. The success of deep search tells us more about chess than about problem solving in general. It shows us that playing chess at some level of performance does not necessarily require much knowledge. In this regard, it suggests that the requirements for high performance at games like chess may be fundamentally different from requirements for high performance on less abstract tasks. Crucially, a chessboard and the rules of chess constitute a self-contained microworld. The game, unlike everyday life, is reduced to esssentials. For example, chess-game rules do not care about the shapes of the pieces or the habits of the players. Early advocates of the study of games in AI thought that study of games was an appropriate research strategy, because games provided substantial complexity of reasoning in its simplest form. A chessboard is neat, mathematical, and abstract when compared with everyday problems. Significantly, the knowledge principle arose from research on much messier situations, where it has not been possible to turn an order of magnitude improvement in computing speed by itself into a qualitative shift in performance.

The chess example also demonstrates that a human approach to reasoning need not be the only one. Suppose that human play of the game really does involve rapid indexing and use of 50,000 situations. The success of Deep Thought shows that a different approach can succeed on the same task. Different approaches may be necessary for different and specialized kinds of hardware. Humans play chess under different computational limitations than specialized parallel processors.

General Knowledge and the Qualification Problem

A basic question about building knowledge systems of greater competence is whether there are ways to get more mileage from the same knowledge, or alternatively, to get further using less knowledge or more general knowledge. To address these questions systematically and rigorously, we would need to introduce some measures of knowledge and complexity for which we have not yet presented the appropriate foundations. However, it is easy to see some of the general ideas by looking at examples of knowledge of different generality.

Perhaps the best known illustrations in AI about knowledge and generality are sentences about birds and flight. Figure 3.49 illustrates one way to organize some facts about flying birds, listing one fact about flying for each of 18 species of birds. According to the *Guide to Field Identification for Birds of North America*, by Robbins, Bruun, and Zim, there are approximately 8,600 species of birds in the world. Even though such a table may seem large, it is tiny when we consider that there are approximately 100 billion birds that populate the world.

(robins fly)	(Laysan albatrosses fly)	(gannets fly)
(crows fly)	(black-footed albatrosses fly)	(blue-faced boobies fly)
(common loons fly)	(Fulmars fly)	(great cormorants fly)
(red-throated loons fly)	(black petrels fly)	(red-faced cormorants fly)
(arctic loons fly)	(shy petrels fly)	(pelagic cormorants fly)
(western grebes fly)	(fork-tailed petrels fly)	(penguins don't fly)

FIGURE 3.49.   A complete table of this kind would require entries for approximately 8,600 species of birds.

Rather than extending this table, it would be simpler to represent most of the facts with a single symbol structure like the one in Figure 3.50 representing that birds of *all* species fly. The representational leverage in this example comes from reasoning about **classes**. Categorization is a very basic cognitive mechanism, making possible the sorting of objects, people, or events in the world. When we categorize, we treat different things as equivalent, responding to them in terms of their class membership rather than their individuality. Representing and reasoning about categories is fundamental to cognition and to knowledge engineering.

Continuing with the bird example, the statement reasons about categories in several ways. It treats all individuals of any given species as equivalent in answering questions about flying. It treats all species of birds as equivalent. It treats all situations as equivalent. In this way, it **overgeneralizes** the subject matter. It needs to be augmented to account for various exceptions. As stated in the last entry of Figure 3.49, penguins do not fly. To begin with, a more complete list of exceptions would need to include penguins and ostriches.

However, even with species-wide exceptions made explicit, this would barely begin to list the circumstances that actually determine whether individual birds can fly. Marvin Minsky had some fun with this point in an address at the 1985 National Conference of the American Association for Artificial Intelligence. He observed, for example, that "cooked birds can't fly." He also noted that a cooked bird that is served in flight as part of an airline meal "flies" according to a different sense of the term. Stuffed birds, frozen birds, and drowned birds cannot fly, nor can birds wearing concrete overcoats or heavy lead necklaces. Wooden birds such as duck decoys do not fly either. Birds that are pinned against a cliff by a 200-mile-per-hour hurricane cannot fly.

As the exceptions are enumerated, the amount of special case knowledge increases and apparently the set of symbol structures needed to represent the situations gets larger again. Minsky's remarks mention situations beyond what we have stated for the 100 billion birds so far. Whether any particular bird can fly is determined ultimately by its identity, its condition, and its situation; bird flight is influenced in some way by their health, physical encumbrances, and the local atmospheric conditions.

$\forall\ (x\ s)\ \text{species}(s\ \text{bird}) \wedge \text{inst}(x\ s) => (\text{flys}\ x)$

FIGURE 3.50.   Most of the facts about which species of birds can fly are captured in a single statement.

Once again, we can rely on reasoning by classes to reduce the complexity. We would like to make statements about what is usually the case separately from specific statements about what the exceptions are. General statements are just not right all of the time. John McCarthy has called the proliferation of the number of rules the **qualification problem**. Restated, we would like to organize our knowledge in terms of general statements about the usual cases and then to qualify those statements by describing their exceptions.

In the examples above, we could observe that "dead birds don't fly" and that "cooked birds are dead" and "drowned birds are dead" and "stuffed birds are dead" and so on. Thus we can factor the knowledge into models about how birds stop living and the fact that only living birds can fly. We can fill out our example models by observing that birds cannot fly when they are asleep, or when they are in a vacuum, or when they are under water, or when there is a severe snowstorm. Categories help us to simplify, whether we are reasoning about general categories of flying birds or categories of exceptions. Categories are used by symbol-processing methods to exploit the regularities of the world.

One approach proposed by McCarthy and others for formalizing such reasoning in a logical framework makes use of so-called abnormalcy predicates. For example, the following statement would mean roughly that birds fly unless there is something abnormal about them.

(bird x) and (not (ab1 x)) → (flies x)

Then other statements would be used to lay out the qualifications for the abnormal conditions. The next few statements delineate classes of birds that are abnormal and conditions for recognizing them.

(disabled-bird x) → (ab1 x)
(fake-bird x) → (ab1 x)

(wears x concrete-overshoes) → (disabled-bird x)
(dead x) → (disabled-bird x)

(drowned x) → (dead x)
(stuffed x) → (dead x)
(cooked x) → (dead x)

(wooden-image x) and (bird x) → (fake-bird x)

On the other hand, even fake or dead birds can "fly" as passengers or cargo on an aircraft. For a simpler semantics, we might use a different term such as *flies2* to mean carried by an aircraft in flight. In Exercise 13, we consider an argumentation strategy based on abnormalcy predicates for qualification problems.

The idea of classes and exceptional subclasses is illustrated graphically in Figure 3.51. By organizing the domain concepts according to regularities and exceptions, we introduce requirements for processing. This approach is analogous to the use of Taylor series of successive terms for approximating real functions: Just as each succeeding term is smaller in the approximating series, each subset is smaller in the sequence of approximating classes. The large outer set is the set of all birds, in which the default assertion is that birds can fly. In a smaller subset for birds

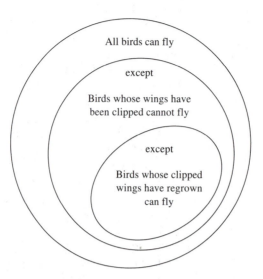

FIGURE 3.51. When there are regularities in the domain, special case knowledge can be organized into set descriptions. This requires that the interpreter be able to navigate through subsets and adjust the default assumptions accordingly.

whose wings have been clipped, the default assertion is that the birds cannot fly. In a yet smaller subset where the clipped wings have grown out again, the default assertion is that the birds can fly.

The separation of knowledge about typical situations from that of exceptional circumstances has certain benefits. It reduces the number of sentences and provides a framework that guides the introduction of new kinds of knowledge into categories. In building knowledge systems we want to focus on the representation and use of knowledge about critical cases and important differences. Thus, in the bird flying example, we do not want to be overwhelmed simply by the number of living birds or the number of species of birds. Rather, we want to be able to focus on categories of information that can be used to answer questions about bird flight.

These ideas concerning the separation of knowledge about typical conditions and exceptional ones are a small part of research in AI about practical and common-sense reasoning. Many different technical approaches have been developed, as discussed in later chapters on representation and reasoning. A basic goal in these approaches is to provide a systematic framework for systems that need to make assumptions. Thus **defaults** are statements that can be believed or assumed in the absence of contradictory information. The general statement about all birds can be restated in terms of defaults: "Unless you know otherwise for a particular bird, assume the bird can fly."

Figure 3.52 illustrates a simple way to organize the steps of an inferential process for determining whether a particular bird can fly. The top box consults general knowledge about most bird species: the statement that all birds can fly. The next box considers exceptions according to species. The bottom box considers exceptions to various situations, organized according to knowledge about the health of birds (birds that died for different reasons, birds with broken wings), local weather (snowstorms, vacuum), or physical encumbrances (concrete overshoes,

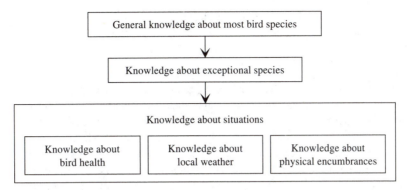

FIGURE 3.52.   Regularities in domain knowledge can provide a guide to the organization of a knowledge base. In this example, knowledge for reasoning about bird flight is organized according to categories. Furthermore, the interpreter can systematically consider the knowledge according to the categories.

heavy bracelets). For now, we can think of these boxes as being procedural "specialists" that are invoked to answer certain kinds of questions.

We should not trivialize the practical difficulty of knowing how to organize rich bodies of knowledge. Much of the subject matter of knowledge engineering is about techniques for organizing representation and reasoning. For now, however, the simple point of these examples is that there is more than one way to organize knowledge and that organizations can take advantage of *regularities* in a domain.

To understand how systems or people could make reliable inferences when they have unreliable and incomplete information, it is instructive to notice that people are often able to answer questions about situations that they have never encountered before. For a silly example, if someone were asked whether a bird could fly through a room that was completely filled with cotton candy, answering would be easy. A bird needs unobstructed air in which to fly. When we say that people know about flying, we assume that they know much more than how to spell it. Rather, people have a much richer model of what's going for flying, when it is possible, and what might preclude it. We can draw on a wide range of models when determining our best guess.

At this point it is clear that computer models of the world can never be finished in the sense of having complete fidelity over all possible situations. It may seem to follow that they can never be useful or reliable. After all, there may always be some circumstances bearing on the question of whether birds can fly that we would fail to make explicit in a knowledge base. There would always be situations for which our knowledge would be wrong or factors that it might not consider. However, this is not ultimately so discouraging. Knowledge systems are not the only "agents" in the world who don't know everything about everything; people don't either. We should not rely too much on any single fact to determine an outcome. All models of the world are partial; no process that reasons about a world can have perfect fidelity. Assumptions of omniscience for people or for any physical symbol system are just not sensible. Since it is not practical or theoretically sound to depend on getting all the facts right about everything, *reliability must come from some other source.* Reliable systems use checks and balances. This suggests that the theory of building reliable knowledge systems might be modeled in terms of additional agents that check on the plausibility of conclusions. Their job would be to wake up if the system attempts to take certain actions, even if those actions are plausible by some, presumably erroneous, line of thought. The crafting of large theories that require such architectures is an active research area.

Knowledge and Search, Revisited

Before leaving the discussion of the knowledge principle, it is worth revisiting the relationship between knowledge and search. One claim sometimes made about the construction of knowledge-based systems is that knowledge eliminates the need for search. This is an oversimplification, as illustrated by the example of adding knowledge to the DENDRAL program (Lindsay, 1980). The DENDRAL project began in 1965. Developed over several years, DENDRAL was the product of an interdisciplinary team from computer science, genetics, and chemistry. Its purpose was to infer the structure of chemical molecules from chemical data, especially mass spectrometry data.

Repeatedly confronted with difficult problems of chemical identification, DENDRAL was a test bed in which the action of knowledge could be observed. For example, most laboratories for chemical analysis employ a variety of different chemical instruments in identifying chemical structures. Mass spectrometers are among the most powerful instruments for chemical analysis, but there are other useful types of spectrometry including infrared, ultraviolet, and nuclear magnetic resonance. Different kinds of instruments provide complementary kinds of data about molecular structure. DENDRAL used a hierarchical generate-and-test search method (Section 2.2.3) and had a knowledge base of pruning rules that could make use of different sources of spectrometry data. Over the years of the project, thousands of chemical analyses have been performed by DENDRAL.

In general, the more knowledge DENDRAL is able to bring to a problem, the more definitive its analysis can be. One problem given to DENDRAL was to determine the possible structures of $C_{20}H_{43}N$. Using only topological reasoning, there are almost 43 million possible solutions. Knowledge of the valences of the different elements reduces this to about 15 million possible solutions. Using mass spectrometry data, which gives the composition of pieces of the molecule, DENDRAL was able to reduce this to 1.3 million possible structures. Given mass spectrometry plus nuclear magnetic resonance data, DENDRAL determined that there was only one molecular structure consistent with all the data. Of course, adding data would have been of no help if DENDRAL had lacked the knowledge of how to use the data. With the extra knowledge, DENDRAL was able to narrow the set of candidate solutions rapidly. In short, adding knowledge enabled DENDRAL to be more effective and to reduce its search.

DENDRAL exploits the mathematical regularities of chemical structures by representing the possibilities in a computational generator. It organizes its knowledge about structure identification according to sources of chemical measurements. These are coupled for an exhaustive search of the possibilities.

In summary, knowledge helped DENDRAL to prune its search. Knowledge reduces the time for search, but does not eliminate it. The DENDRAL example is essentially the opposite of the chess example with regard to the knowledge hypothesis. In the chess case, we could build a problem solver that relied on deep search but needed very little knowledge. In the DENDRAL case, the time complexity of search is greatly reduced by knowledge. The difference lies in the nature of the tasks and domains. Chess does not admit hierarchical pruning.

3.4.3 *Summary and Review*

In this section we began by presenting MYCIN as a concrete example of a knowledge system. We characterized MYCIN in terms of its tasks, its knowledge-level analysis, and its symbol-level implementation. We looked at examples of MYCIN's dialog, its knowledge, and its operation.

Given that background, we reconsidered the implicit assumption that we have made throughout this chapter that achieving adequate performance requires large amounts of task-specific and domain-specific knowledge. This is the knowledge principle or knowledge hypothesis. We interpreted this hypothesis as a strategy by which embedded systems use knowledge to cope with the complexity of the world.

We saw that the hypothesis is not true for all possible tasks, such as tournament chess. Rather, it is a hypothesis we can form about any task. If the hypothesis is disproved, that shows us that the task is easier (in a sense) than we thought. Finally, we looked at approaches for using general knowledge and came upon the qualification problem, which is the case where there is a proliferation of special case rules. We saw that systems can be organized to group defaults and rules into classes. These examples reflect thinking at the state of the art. They suggest that in some cases robust systems can be achieved by combining multiple models that balance and check each other's reasoning on cases.

Exercises for Section 3.4

Ex. 1   [*CD-00*] Expert systems are routinely developed over very narrow domains. Why is narrowness crucial to the practical success of early approaches to building expert systems?

Ex. 2   [*CD-00*] Goldstein and Papert (1977) characterized the challenge of AI (or knowledge engineering) as finding effective techniques for representing large amounts of knowledge in a fashion that permits the effective use and interaction of that knowledge. A key part of this in practical knowledge systems is in finding effective ways to build and maintain knowledge bases.
(a) An alternative way to formulate the MYCIN knowledge base would be as an explicit decision tree. In a decision tree, as in most programming languages, the position of a statement determines when it is used. How does MYCIN avoid requiring that a knowledge engineer specify places for locating rules in a knowledge base?
(b) Is MYCIN's technique more important for large knowledge bases than for small ones? Why?

Ex. 3   [*05*] Professor Digit has a company that designs the interiors of apartments. Unfortunately, his company does not know how to design liveable interiors for very small apartments, for which he sees a growing market. He has approached the Knowledge Systems Corp. to contract the building of an expert system for designing very small apartments, hoping to use a little "artificial intelligence" to increase his share of the apartment design market. What does the knowledge principle tell us about the merits of his proposal?

■ **Ex. 4**   [*CD-15*] *Knowledge Organization in Books.* In 1914, Mary Parsons published the book *The Wild Flowers of California* to provide a guide to identifying flowering plants native to that state. In the section "How to Use the Book," she lays out a method that is abbreviated below:

1. Collect a sample of the entire plant or parts from the entire plant, including roots, stem, leaves, flowers, buds, and fruit.
2. Sort the flowers into sets by color (white, yellow, pink, blue/purple, red, and miscellaneous).
3. For each flower in every color set do
4. begin
5. Write a short description of the flower. Use a magnifying glass or small dissecting microscope.

Note: There is a detailed discussion for naming roots (conical, napiform, fusiliform . . .), stems, leaves (with description sublanguages for venation, form, apex, margin, texture, and arrangement), and inflorescence (with sublanguages for the flower, stamen, pistil, and fruit).

6. Search for the most closely matching genus.
7. Search for the most closely matching species.
8. If no match is found or if it is difficult to determine to which color section a flower belongs, search in the other probable color sections.
9. end

(a) How does Parsons' design of the book reflect a basic concern of knowledge engineering: the organization of knowledge for use? Explain briefly.

(b) Suppose Parsons were publishing an updated edition of the book including several new plant species. How does the pattern of use for the book impose a pattern for updating it?

(c) At the beginning of the White section is a short table of flowers that are occasionally or partially white but that are not described in the White section. Similarly there is a table of exceptions at the beginning of each of the other color sections, an index of Latin names, and an index of common names at the end of the book. How do these complicate the process of updating the book?

(d) The color system divides the 500 or so kinds of plants into 6 categories described in 110, 86, 62, 80, 34, and 24 pages, respectively. Why is this better than a division into (say) 300, 50, 10, 10, 10, and 5 pages?

(e) In the 1970s Alan Kay coined the term *dynabook* to refer to a booksize portable computer. Suppose Parsons' book were to be republished on a portable computer medium. Explain briefly how that medium could support the following uses:

> Facilities for identifying or browsing plants organized by regions such as desert, woodland, marsh, meadow
> Facilities for identifying or browsing plants according to their height or month of blooming
> Additional material on the care, fertilizing, water requirements, and propagation of plants

Ex. 5   [05] *Knowledge and Search.* Conventional wisdom in AI has been that the more a system knows, the less it needs to search. However, Professor Digit built a system that used production rules to specify ways to generate candidate solutions. He observed that the more knowledge he adds to his system, the more time it spends searching by chaining through the rules. Believing he discovered a universal truth, he proposed calling this Digit's law: "The more you know, the more you need to search."

(a) Does Digit's law contradict the knowledge principle? Explain why Digit's law does not apply for DENDRAL.

(b) Under what circumstances does Digit's law correctly predict MYCIN's behavior after rules were added?

Ex. 6 *[05] Rule Bookkeeping.* How would multiple executions of individual rules violate design assumptions in MYCIN?

Ex. 7 *[15] Infinite Looping in Rule Execution.* For this problem we introduce the notation

$$(n)\, A => B$$

to indicate that the production rule (n) uses the clinical parameter A to draw conclusions about the clinical parameter B. Given this notation, consider the set of rules described by the following:

(1) $A => B$
(2) $B => C, D$
(3) $B, C => D$
(4) $D => A$

(a) Referring to the backward-chaining mechanism described in this section, what will happen if the monitor method is called to determine the value of the clinical parameter D?

(b) Show how the methods can be modified to avoid this problem.

(c) Show how a similar problem can arise in situations involving rules that conclude about multiple clinical parameters. How can the methods be modified to avoid that problem?

Ex. 8 *[10] Question Answering in MYCIN.*

(a) Under what circumstances does MYCIN ask a user for information even though there were rules for inferring the information?

(b) Why does MYCIN keep track of which clauses failed during rule invocation?

(c) What role does the history tree have in answering questions about changes to the static knowledge base?

Ex. 9 *[10] Backward Chaining, Again.* Suppose the third premise can be shown to be false in a rule having several premises. How could the goal-oriented approach be modified to notice this? Explain how this could lead to efficiencies in a program such as MYCIN.

Ex. 10 *[!-05] Default Reasoning in Rules.* An important issue in knowledge systems is the design of mechanisms for making assumptions in the absence of data. The approach for this used in MYCIN involved explicit rules in which the same parameter appears in both the premise and the action. For example, a rule could have the form:

IF a value for X is not known (after trying to establish one),
THEN conclude that the value of X is Z.

(a) Why should the control structure delay executing such rules until all other relevant rules have been tried?

(b) MYCIN's approach to default rules relies on a syntactic analysis of the rule content to determine whether the same variable appears on both sides. Suppose you had to design a reasoning system that distinguished among several kinds of rules: **default rules**, **initial value rules**, **typical-value rules**, **nonmonotonic revision rules**, **exception-checking**

rules, and so on. Would a rule-annotation approach be preferred over a syntactic analysis approach? Explain briefly.

(c) In some domains, information becomes available piecemeal and unpredictably during the course of solving a problem. In such a situation, information not available at the beginning of a session might become known before the end. Would the technique in part a for default reasoning be appropriate for such situations?

Ex. 11   *[CD-10] Manual and Automatic Knowledge Compilation.* One rule in the MYCIN knowledge base was

> IF the patient is less than 8 years old,
> THEN don't prescribe tetracycline.

(a) What kind of explanation would MYCIN generate if asked why tetracycline is not prescribed to a 7-year-old patients. Briefly, in what sense is this kind of explanation inadequate?

(b) Unstated in the MYCIN knowledge base was the rationale for the rule above: Children at that age are forming their adult teeth and if tetracycline is given it causes cosmetically objectionable discoloration in the new teeth. This information was not included in the knowledge base because it was judged not to be of clinical significance. That is, from the standpoint of performance at generating therapy recommendations, adding this information would not have improved the program's ability to suggest appropriate treatments for infections. Suggest a simple way that this knowledge could be incorporated in a system such as MYCIN.

(c) It is common in many domains to collapse inference steps. This collapsing process could be made an explicit part of a knowledge representation based on multiple levels of models. For example, the rules

$$A \rightarrow B \rightarrow C \rightarrow D \rightarrow E$$

might be collapsed into

$$A \rightarrow E$$

without any mention of *B*, *C*, or *D* unless questions were asked requiring the system to reconsider that part of its reasoning using a deeper model. Show a sequence of production rules for reasoning about tetracycline that could be compiled in this way to yield the single rule shown at the beginning of this exercise.

(d) Upon hearing about the idea of knowledge compilation as in part c, Professor Digit exclaimed that it is far too complex. As an alternative, he proposes that a reasoning system should simply maintain two separate sets of rules—r-rules for reasoning and e-rules for explanations. Briefly, what are some advantages and disadvantages of his proposal?

Ex. 12   *[!-L-12] The Qualification Problem and Argumentation.* Default reasoning is reasoning about beliefs held in the absence of contrary information. The AI literature includes many examples of such reasoning, including reasoning about the color of Clyde the elephant (he's probably gray) or about whether Tweety can fly (probably yes, since Tweety is a bird).

This exercise introduces an approach to default reasoning. The exercise is based on a note and suggestion by R.V. Guha and on the idea of "abnormal" predicates from John McCarthy. Our goal is not so much to define a rigorous approach as to give the reader an opportunity to see how reasoning might be nonmonotonic and yet systematic.

Several different approaches for modeling this have been proposed in the AI literature. These approaches differ in the ways they account for conflicts in these beliefs and in what they require for revising beliefs as new information becomes available. Many of the approaches make some use of the "failure as negation" idea introduced in this section in the context of logic programming.

In regular or monotonic logic, a proposition follows from a knowledge base (KB) if there is a proof of it from the KB. In this exercise, we generalize the usual definition of a proof or support structure to include assumptions. We call our generalized support structure an argument. A proposition can be justified (or not) by an argument. This approach does not use failure as negation.

The Argumentation Axiom
If $a1$ is an argument for $p1$ and
         a_1 is not invalid and
         if no valid argument a_2 is known for "(not p_1)"
then p_1 is justified by a_1.

(a) Given this background, consider the following statements.

bird(x) $\wedge$ ~ab$_1$(x) => flies(x)
bird(Tweety)

where

broken-wing(x) => ab$_1$(x)
dead(x) => ab$_1$(x)
heavy(x) => ab$_1$(x)
wears(x concrete-overshoes) => ab$_1$(x)

What can we now infer about Tweety? Explain briefly.

(b) Suppose we add the following statements to the KB.

penguin(x) => ab$_1$(x)
penguin(Tweety)

How does this change what we can infer about Tweety? Explain briefly.

(c) Suppose we add the following statement to the KB, including those of part b.

penguin(x) $\wedge$ ~ab$_2$(x) => ~flies(x)

How does this change what we can infer about Tweety? Explain briefly.

(d) Suppose we add the following statements to the KB, keeping those of the previous parts of this exercise.

aviator(x) $\wedge$ ~ab$_3$(x) => flies(x)
aviator(x) => ab$_2$(x)
aviator(Tweety)
lost-aviator-license(x) => ab$_3$(x)

Again, how does this change what we can infer about Tweety? Explain briefly.

3.5   *Open Issues and Quandaries*   ADVANCED

Today's knowledge systems fall short of human expertise, at least in breadth. We do not ascribe to them a substantial mental life. They know less than a young child, arguably less than most household pets. This suggests we should take care when referring to these systems as having substantial knowledge bases. Beyond this quantitative issue, there is also a qualitative issue. In the context of computers, some people find the term *knowledge* jarring. To paraphrase a typical complaint, "We may not be able to say exactly what knowledge is, but whatever it is, it is not the same as what is programmed in knowledge systems."

This attitude seldom arises in the context of concrete examples of knowledge systems. When a knowledge system is being used or demonstrated, the situation draws us to ask specific questions about the particulars of its problem-solving knowledge rather than general questions about the nature of a machine's ability to know. Why did MYCIN recommend this therapy? What are the side-effects of tetracycline? How do we know that the fever is not caused by meningitis? What does the system do if the doctors do not agree? In short, we do not challenge whether the system carries knowledge. Instead, we are interested in what determines its performance, and beyond that, in the social role the system plays and in the limits of its understanding.

This section is in the form of a dialog, where some common misunderstandings are put forth as challenges to be considered and questions to be answered. We begin with simple issues and misunderstandings. These are not really research issues, but rather confusions that involve attitude or confusions of terminology. After the easy issues, we move on to more subtle ones.

Simple Issues and Misunderstandings

The first challenges we consider are based on simple misunderstandings and are easily explained.

Misunderstanding: Knowledge is just information.

Discussion: Saying that "knowledge is just information" is like saying that "computer programs are just information" or that "a digital recording of a piano concerto is just information." From a certain perspective this is correct, but it is not particularly informative and it is dangerous to depend solely on such a view for understanding the nature and importance of knowledge, computer programs, or music.

The term *information* is most relevant to communicating and storing *representations* of knowledge. Information theory as invented by Shannon and others is about the efficient encoding of data for transmission along communication channels. It is concerned with the number of kinds of symbols to be transmitted and with minimal encodings that make it possible for a transmitter and receiver to differentiate among these symbols.

Information theory is not concerned with the use or meaning of the symbols. For example, the binary string 0101111011000011 could stand for an instruction on a computer for moving a memory word to register 3, part of a string of characters such as <control>-C used in describing a character type to interrupt processes in an operating system, or a representation of elapsed time in milliseconds in a counter in a wristwatch. Information theory does not care what symbols mean or how they are used.

Misunderstanding: Knowledge bases are the same things as databases.

Discussion: The distinction between knowledge and data eludes precise technical distinction, but very little of what we call data is akin to rules of behavior or knowledge about problem solving. If knowledge is "codified experience," it should be able to guide action in different situations. Breadth of experience and breadth of applicability matter. There is an important qualitative difference between, say, a single measurement using a scientific instrument and a thoroughly tested scientific theory. Both could be used to guide action, but the latter may be suitable for guiding action in many situations. A single measurement is "merely" data in that by itself it does not reflect a substantial body of experience. In this sense, data are less refined than knowledge.

A different question is whether the information stored in knowledge bases could be stored in databases. The answer is "Yes, of course!" This question confounds knowledge with the symbol structures that represent knowledge for an interpreter. Symbol structures can be stored in databases. General facilities for storing and retrieving symbol structures are useful for knowledge engineering. Databases provide storage and retrieval facilities that can be used for information for all kinds of things, whether the information is tables of facts or list structures or programs.

A third kind of question is whether the concerns of database research encompass the concerns of knowledge engineering. Database research is concerned with such matters as relational models, transaction processing, robust distributed storage, recovery from failures, and efficient access to mass storage. These are all important concerns for computer technology, but they are distinct from such theoretical issues as knowledge formulation, problem solving, and use. Thus, database research does not encompass knowledge engineering.

Misunderstanding: Building knowledge systems is just fancy programming.

Discussion: This complaint is about the inflation of terminology. According to this view, the processes of formulating, organizing, and representing knowledge are seen as just part of the art of programming. Formulation is just finding out what programs should do, representation is just choice of data structures, and organization is just consideration of modularity and other good programming practices. With tongue in cheek, we might say that making a wonderful chocolate eclair is "just cooking."

There are risks in letting the statement pass unchallenged. We begin by focusing on the word *just* in "just fancy programming." This word could be taken to mean (1) that there are no principles and no theory to guide the development of programs or knowledge systems or (2) that the essence of knowledge engineering is programming.

The first interpretation presumes that "programming" either requires no theory or has none and that fancy programming is more of the same. Some programming is done in the way of unprincipled hacking. For example, some children in first and second grade of elementary school can write programs. Some home appliances such as microwave ovens, timed water-sprinkling systems, and video recorders are programmable. It is all too easy to extrapolate from that that programming does not require much experience or intellectual depth. However, progress in computer science comes from the development of principles and questions that lead to better understanding. Reliable and powerful systems seldom arise from unprincipled hacking. Even those who work in areas where principles are not yet developed (and those who ignore principles that they should know) benefit from the use of well-designed computer systems, languages, compilers, algorithms, and so on. Thus, it is inappropriate to characterize programming as being without principles.

The second interpretation is that the essence of building knowledge systems is programming. The problem with this attitude is that it does not lend focus or direction to the field. For example, it does not guide the study of the properties of particular representations or search methods. It does not lead to introspection about the meaning of symbols, problem solving, or the use of knowledge. It does not lead to directions for research in machine learning. It does not lead to insights into the social processes of knowledge creation, validation, or propagation. Calling knowledge engineering programming does not call attention to either its principles or its unsolved problems. "Just fancy programming" is a terribly impoverished perspective.

Misunderstanding: Expert systems are really just areas where stupidity works, where just a little bit of knowledge is enough.

Discussion: We begin by separating the parts of this statement. Taking the second part first, we might ask whether it is the case that all expert systems use only a little bit of knowledge. If we compare the amount of knowledge in knowledge systems with the amount that most people have, the answer to this is unmistakably yes. On the other hand, because of the nature of the tasks to which knowledge systems are applied and the extensive knowledge formulation processes that are used, knowledge systems tend to have much more special case knowledge about solving problems than most conventional software.

Turning to the first part of the statement, we can ask whether expert systems work in areas where "stupidity" works. Again, given that all computer systems built to date are stupid when compared with people, this is correct. More specifically, knowledge systems and computer systems in general are often criticized as being too fragile, inflexible, and narrow. They violate our expectations of what communicating with an intelligent or knowledgeable agent should be like. When expert systems make mistakes, these mistakes can appear quite ridiculous in human terms. Many simple concepts widely regarded as common sense are simply beyond them: Big things do not fit through small holes. Water flows downhill. Expert systems lack what Hayes calls naive physics (Hayes, 1985).

This leads to the following research goals: understanding how to build knowledge systems that do not break down or fail on slight variations of problems just outside their area of expertise; understanding how to build knowledge systems that can reuse knowledge in similar, new situations; and understanding how to build knowledge systems that can flexibly integrate multiple kinds of knowledge and goals.

One idea is to try to build systems that can use very large knowledge bases in which many things could be found to apply in different situations. Lenat and Feigenbaum (1987) have called this the **breadth hypothesis**, believing that a broad knowledge base would provide the basis for metaphorical and analogical reasoning. Pursuing the naive physics example, we say that knowledge systems lack broadly applicable metaphors for reasoning, such as that things that perform work will run down unless their energy is replenished. For example, wind-up clocks need to be rewound or they will stop; cars will stop going if they run out of gas; left by themselves, hot things tend to cool. Starting with one of these examples, it becomes easier for us to understand the others. Knowledge is the lever for overcoming brittleness.

Quandaries and Methodological Issues

Beyond the simple misunderstandings raised already are deeper and perhaps more interesting issues that challenge our assumptions and analysis of knowledge systems.

Misunderstanding: The knowledge principle is not rigorous enough to pose testable questions because it does not say how to measure the complexity of a knowledge system.

Discussion: This is a serious challenge not only to the knowledge principle but also generally to the practice of knowledge engineering and the building of complex models of all kinds. Earlier in this chapter we illustrated the growth of knowledge for the XCON system in terms of the number of rules in its knowledge base. At the current state of the art of knowledge engineering, such figures can only be regarded as suggestive but not definitive for the very reason cited here: There are serious shortcomings in measuring the complexity of a knowledge system in terms of a count of its rules. Such a measure tells us nothing about the complexity of an individual rule; nothing about the interactions among the rules; nothing about generality or reuse of the rules across situations; nothing about redundancy in what the rules say; nothing about contradictions in the rules; nothing about parallelism, cycle time, and access time in the computer; and nothing about the time or space complexity of the search for solutions. Apparently there are many important and different properties to measure, but the field has yet to develop a coherent theory and practice of measurement.

Another reason for focusing on this complexity issue is that we need better means for understanding the issues in expanding a knowledge system. By measuring only the number of rules, we foster the misconception that it is sufficient simply to cram all the facts into a knowledge base. In contrast, it is widely recognized that the cost of sifting through a plethora of information can easily exceed the value of an answer. In short, there are always costs for finding and applying relevant knowledge. Just counting rules overlooks the fundamental organizations essential for retrieval and search in problem solving. Just adding facts can actually degrade the performance of a knowledge system.

Misunderstanding: The knowledge principle is counterintuitive and bad science.

Discussion: The argument is that the knowledge principle goes against the scientific attitudes that have led to the most progress in other areas of science, especially physics. In physics the simplest theories are usually the best. The physicist's goal is to find a few rules that describe many phenomena. As physics has progressed, large amounts of data have sometimes been replaced by a small number of rules. Famous physicists have summarized this by saying that Nature (you can almost hear the capital *N*) is simple and elegant. The creative leap is in uncovering the simplicities. One should not pride oneself in complexity. Those who cannot reduce their data to a small number of rules are probably wrong.

Continuing with the comparison with this standard, the argument is that the knowledge principle is wrong and wrong-headed. By advocating potentially large bodies of knowledge, knowledge engineering embraces complexity. From a physics perspective, this is bad science. It is like alchemy before there was chemistry.

One counterargument is that the statement misconstrues knowledge engineering's stance on the knowledge principle. Good knowledge engineering does not ignore Ockham's razor. For example, we would not prefer complex rules for describing the motion of the planets over a simpler heliocentric model. The issues of building appropriate models are as relevant to knowledge engineering as to other fields. As Einstein is reported to have said, "Everything should be made as simple as possible, but not simpler."

Interestingly, the so-called philosophy of science of the twentieth century has been characterized recently by several philosophers as merely the "philosophy of physics." To draw attention to the problems with extending a physics attitude to all other sciences, some scientific wits have started to refer to the silliness of "physics envy." Bartley (Radnitzky & Bartley, 1987) and others argue that many of the themes that are dominant within the philosophy of physics do not apply to biology or other sciences. In particular, the number and kinds of interactions in a biological system are much more complex than those in systems studied by physicists. For example, over time, biological systems have evolved many mechanisms for regulating the expression of genes. No amount of wishing by biologists or physicists will reduce that complexity to a single mechanism, and reducing the phenomenon to fundamental forces from physics results in no gain in predictive power and no real simplification because the systems then have too many parts to be tractable for reasoning. Citing many examples like this, philosophers argue further that the assumptions of simplicity are not strictly correct even within physics. This suggests that different attitudes and approaches are needed for progress in those fields where complexity is unavoidable.

Misunderstanding: The knowledge engineering community believes there is cheap knowledge out there to be mined. It's not knowledge that is out there, but the world. Advancement in knowledge comes solely from investigating the world. The knowledge engineer is incapable of doing that because he typically knows too little about the domain world.

Discussion: Before addressing the statement, it is worth looking at the main question behind it: Who should build knowledge systems: domain experts or knowledge engineers? The implication of the statement is that the people who build knowledge systems should be the domain experts, rather than knowledge engineers with a general education. Indeed, over the past few years the population of people building knowledge systems has shifted away from general knowledge engineers and toward people who specialize in an area. As the theory and practice of knowledge engineering becomes more accessible, more people whose specialization is outside of computer science are able to build their own knowledge systems. At the same time, as people aspire to build large and complex knowledge systems, there is a division of labor and many of those engaged in building the systems take knowledge systems and computer science as their primary subject matter.

The original statement contains several threads that deserve to be addressed separately:

■ The knowledge engineering community believes there is cheap knowledge out there to be mined.

One interpretation of this complaint is that the knowledge is just not "out there" at all. There are no experts who know the right things and knowledge engineers are wasting their time. For some tasks this is undoubtedly true. As some wit once said, "Ain't science wonderful. There's always something more to discover." The building of computer reasoning models is a relatively new enterprise, so there are many untried areas. The recommendation assumes that the greatest progress will be made by those who start fresh.

The trouble with grand, bold recommendations like this is that they are usually underqualified. Few of the big knowledge systems could have been built this way. XCON, the configuration system, could not have been built. Progress on that system depended crucially on tapping the experience of configurers and designers. MACSYMA was the same way. It drew on an established body of mathematics. So was DENDRAL, which drew on chemistry and a branch of graph theory. New things were discovered during the creation of all of these systems, but it would have been egotistical, impractical, and inefficient to ignore the expertise that was available. In many such cases, it takes a collection of people with different talents to succeed.

Every knowledge-system project must determine how and where most of the knowledge will be obtained. Sometimes the answer is to start from scratch. Sometimes it is to interview people who do it already, and sometimes the answer is to conduct experiments to gather the right knowledge. Knowledge engineering practice, like other scientific or engineering enterprises, begins by trying to ascertain what is already known. Otherwise, it would be almost impossible to make progress.

■ Advancement in knowledge comes solely from investigating the world.

Knowledge is created and arguably invented. It does not arise from the passive observation of nature. The idea of "just looking at the world" suggests a naive perspective about what activities one carries out in creating knowledge and what is necessary to generalize, test, and accumulate it.

The process of building knowledge systems, like the process of scientific discovery, is arguably a process of invention. Terms need to be established, representations and models need to be created, questions and processes need to be designed and tested. A knowledge system is an active entity that engages problems and proposes solutions. The creation of predictable processes that work reliably in this way is a significant exercise.

Most knowledge-systems projects are not started with the goal of advancing the state of knowledge. Rather, they are intended for mechanizing what is thought to be rather mundane and well-understood bodies of knowledge. Nonetheless, it often turns out that the requisite formalization and systematic testing leads to increased understanding in the domain. The crucial creative act in designing a knowledge system is to characterize the problem as a systematic and practical search of a space of possibilities. This creative step itself can sometimes be a contribution to the science of the domain, and it often exposes some elements of the domain that have escaped systematic and careful attention.

Misunderstanding: The transfer-of-expertise model is wrong because the knowledge is not accessible by asking questions of experts.

Discussion: This is an important line of argument, because it says there are fundamental restrictions on the kinds of tasks that can be automated by the interviewing of experts. To address the point, however, it is important to differentiate the different senses in which it is argued. We consider several possibilities.

1. Some kinds of knowledge cannot be communicated in words or writing. Examples of knowledge that cannot be communicated are easy to find. It is difficult to teach physical tasks, such as swimming, golf, or tennis, by just verbal instructions. The learning experience involves too much in the way of senses and motor skills. Of course, people do learn to swim, play tennis, and play golf. Instruction involves a richer modality of communication: The instructor moves the student's arm; students watch videos of good and bad swimming or good and bad tennis. These sports examples are real, but they lie outside the boundaries of the information-processing models used in knowledge systems.

   2. Some kinds of knowledge are not accessible by introspection. That some elements of competence are not accessible by introspection also relates to phenomena outside knowledge engineering. For example, we are all "experts" at listening to spoken language. But few of us can be articulate about how we discriminate among different sounds. A favorite example from speech recognition research is to say exactly how it is that we hear the difference between "how to wreck a nice beach" and "how to recognize speech." Such recognition processes take place at subconscious levels. Facial recognition is probably similar in its almost automatic or unconscious nature. As Pylyshyn describes it, such activities are not "cognitively penetrable." In trying to explain this, psychologists with a computational bent sometimes say that the activities are "compiled in."
   Such activities are probably carried out by brain centers only loosely connected with speech centers. Prospects are dim for finding out how to build a speech recognition system by interviewing, say, an experienced telephone operator. Progress in automating such tasks does not benefit from the interviewing techniques discussed in this chapter. Progress in machine recognition of speech depends instead on sciences ranging from signal interpretation to linguistics.

   3. What experts do is not the same as what they say they do. That domain experts sometimes "rationalize" their methods, saying they solve problems differently from the way they actually do, is a widely recognized methodological issue. The difficulty and distrust of retrospective accounts was discussed in Section 3.1. This is why the methods of protocol analysis stress "thinking out loud" on cases and why multiple cases are used and compared. These methods are intended to preclude the possibility of biased and selective rationalization.

   4. Some tasks that we automate are not carried out by any single expert. This issue arises in the construction of many kinds of embedded systems. Terry Winograd (1979) describes a hypothetical embedded system for scheduling and planning room use at a university. He started with a characterization of an initial computer system able to display building floor plans and various kinds of text another graphic data. The system kept track of current schedules. He considered the difficulty of extending that system so someone could give it a description of the courses scheduled for a future quarter and have it generate a proposed room assignment for all courses. It would consider factors such as expected enrollment, proximity of rooms to departments, and other matters. Building a system like this is not hard because of the intrinsic difficulty of the tasks, but in organizing and integrating all the elements starting with the initial system. In cases like this, knowledge about needs and knowledge about the existing systems is distributed in the heads of many people. The main challenge would be integrating this knowledge.

   5. Experts solve problems incorrectly and in unprincipled ways. When expert practice is imperfect or unprincipled, this can become apparent both to domain experts and to knowledge engineers part way through a project. In the DENDRAL project it became apparent that chemists did not have a precise model of how to generate hypotheses about possible molecules that would explain mass spectral data. What was missing was a general algorithm for producing all the ways to put molecules together from pieces. One could interview all the chemists in sight, but it turned out that although some of them realized this was an issue, none of them were able to do the generation task correctly all of the time. Furthermore, a mathematical breakthrough was needed to characterize the complex case with cyclical molecules.

Over a period of years, the problem yielded to a combination of insights from group theory and graph theory. DENDRAL was tested on several papers drawn from reviewed papers in scientific journals of organic chemistry. This showed that the publication review process in chemistry had been insufficient for validating all the experimental results that were published. DENDRAL, then (or the CONGEN program in particular), is an expert system, whose expertise is in a branch of mathematics applied to ball-and-stick models of chemical molecules. Transfer of expertise was not the main issue in building this system. Getting the molecular assembly model right was the main issue.

The more general point for knowledge engineering is that the transfer-of-expertise model is separate from the knowledge hypothesis. Both are main assumptions of common practice, and both can fail for different reasons. Knowledge-based systems can be built with or without using the transfer-of-expertise model.

In summary, this section considers several misconceptions about the nature of knowledge and information. Confusions about whether knowledge is mere information or whether knowledge bases are just databases reflect a lack of experience with the nature of knowledge systems. These perspectives focus on the writings of symbols without regard to their meanings. Such confusions tend to arise when the symbol-level perspective of a knowledge system is clearly in view but the knowledge-level perspective is ignored. Deeper issues about the knowledge principle or where knowledge comes from tend to arise in the absence of a concrete situation. Concrete situations make it easier to see the contexts of invention, formulation, and evolution of a body of knowledge. In this regard, knowledge engineering has created an explicit arena for investigating properties of human knowledge, at least in the small and focused areas where the engineering of a body of knowledge is practical.

THE SYMBOL LEVEL

4

Reasoning about Time

Engineers use different engineering models to solve different problems. Mechanical engineers use finite element models for structural analysis and thermal conduction and radiation models for thermal analysis. Different models answer different questions, have different requirements, depend on different assumptions, and use different approximations. Effective engineering requires choosing models and adapting them for particular situations.

The "engineering models" of knowledge systems are computational, consisting of representations and methods for reasoning with those representations. The most powerful models are domain and task specific. For the range of practical and recurring problems for which knowledge systems are most often applied, developing specific models is part of the design task. To this end, it is useful to be able to draw on experience with similar models developed previously, reusing such models either directly or as a guide in designing a specialized representation.

Many knowledge systems reason about processes such as the physical processes involved in the operation of physical devices or the work-flow processes of information work. Reasoning about processes requires representing time. A familiarity with models for time is a useful general background for building knowledge systems. What do temporal representations represent? As is often the case in understanding, the key to getting started is determining what questions to ask. Here are some fundamental questions about models of time:

Should time be represented as discrete or continuous?

This question could be taken as being about the nature of time, such as "Are there really time atoms?" In the following, however, we are concerned mainly with the nature of time representations. For example, if one is dealing with facts that vary in terms of days, then one can take the day as indivisible and use a discrete time model with the day as the unit, or "tick." Time is reported in discrete ticks in all digital clocks. Differences in this fundamental modeling choice—continuous versus discrete—lead to differences in models and also confusion for those unaware of the variety of models.

Should time durations be measured quantitatively?

The issue here is not whether time is measurable but whether reasoning about time is concerned with quantitative measurements. For some tasks, all that matters is a qualitative metric such as the ordering of events in time. For such reasoning it is enough to answer which event comes first, with little concern for what time it comes or how much time passes between two events.

What are the relevant properties of clocks?

Certain technical issues about the use of clocks are familiar to any world traveler or anyone who has daily business with people living in other parts of the world. For example, clock times and dates need to take into account world time zones and daylight savings time versus standard time. Even for computer systems in the same building, there are issues about the accuracy of different kinds of clocks and communication delays. There are fundamental physical issues for systems that travel at high relativistic speeds or for microscopic events of near synchronicity. For some applications that use clock times, it is necessary to incorporate pseudo-time information to assign an ordering to events when they occur closer together than the resoluti on of the reference clocks. For the most part, these physical issues are outside the scope of this section—either because they do not arise much in practical situations or because facilities for sampling time tend to have the required features built in.

Should time be represented as linear, parallel, or branching?

This question deals with the topology of time. One way to look at this question is that it is about the nature of the universe, as in, "Are there parallel timelines?" As before, however, our concern is with the nature of representations. Models of parallel and branching time can be used to reason about uncertain futures and uncertain pasts, such as is required in planning tasks or historical reconstruction. To this end, models of time adequate for supporting hypothetical reasoning about alternative courses of events typically incorporate temporal topologies other than a simple linear sequence of events.

Different tasks use different kinds of facts and require different kinds of reasoning. With representations of time, as with representations of other things, it is not the case that one size fits all. One step in understanding alternatives in temporal representations is to catalog the kinds of information that they need to represent, with attention to the fundamental questions already mentioned. Another is to quantify the scale, which is the amount of data. Another is to quantify the cost and profile of required operations. Variations in expressiveness, scale, and profile of operations lead to variations in the choice of temporal representations for particular applications.

Our discussion of temporal representations is organized as a sequence of cases. We begin with representations based on a timeline. This most basic category of temporal representation is used for describing situations in which the times of all events are known. The subsequent sections diverge from this basic case, introducing more powerful and complex representations.

4.1 *Temporal Concepts*

The simplest temporal representations index facts by times and dates. The difference between times and dates is generally just one of scale, and we will tend to use the term "time" to include cases where time is measured in days or larger units. Timeline representations are the mainstay of time-oriented databases, which are useful in applications where times can be assigned to every event.

When domain-independent computer databases were first developed as modular software systems, they did not incorporate temporal indices. In contrast with general-purpose databases, medical databases and banking databases have always needed to keep a record of past events, both to avoid inappropriate medical or banking procedures and to satisfy various legal requirements. Long audit trails are kept in banking to ensure traceability of errors and fraud and to ensure that corrections can be made as needed.

The dropping price of storing information has supported a movement toward more widespread use of temporal databases. Many of the concepts and terms from time-oriented databases carry over to more sophisticated representations, and indeed, several representational issues are already evident in this case. This section presents the concepts used in these representations, the kinds of questions they are expected to answer, and the semantic and computational issues that arise.

4.1.1 *Timeline Representations*

Timeline representations, also called **date-line** representations, assume that whenever something happens a time can be assigned to it. Fundamental to this capability is the idea of a **timestamp**, which associates temporal domain values with events or objects being described. A timestamp could be a string such as "September 15, 1992 10:08:54 PDT," which is a representation of a moment at which I looked at a clock while writing the first draft of this section. The key requirement is that the temporal ordering of two timestamps must be computable by simple operations. Timeline systems are mathematically grounded in either the integers or the real numbers, where increasing numbers correspond to later times. Of the two choices, the real numbers are more expressive because they admit dividing regions of time into arbitrarily small subunits.

The primary function of a temporal database is to index facts in time. Restated, for any propositional fact F that may be true of an entity x at time t, the database maintains a record $F(x, t)$. Given a banking database, we can ask for the balance of Fred's account last Tuesday. The proposition is the "balance." Temporal databases provide facilities for storing and retrieving time-indexed facts.

The term **proper historical database** refers to temporal databases with a complete historical record. Every intermediate time in the range of the history has exactly one value for every attribute of every object, including possibly a notation meaning that the value of the attribute is unknown. This property ensures that it is possible to determine a snapshot of the state of all the objects for any given time.

The term **event** refers to something that happens in time. Events are somewhat more problematic to define than facts. In many domain models, events are associated with changes in facts. For example, in the "blocks world" of early AI planners, a *block-moving event* would represent the application of a *move* operator to some *block* and would result in changes to the facts representing the block's position.

It is not generally satisfactory to define events in terms of fact changes. Consider the example "John ran around the track three times." At the end of three loops around the track, John's position is the same as it was in the beginning. Some facts have changed—John sweated, time passed, and there were footprints on the track—but these facts are not definitional of the event. For this reason we define events in terms of characteristic *patterns of activities* located in time. Events change temporal facts, but they are not just defined in terms of the facts that they change. For example, the event of driving a car would be defined as a characteristic activity located in time, such as over an interval from 1:00 P.M. to 2:00 P.M. The activity would involve sitting in the driver's seat of a car, watching traffic, and using the vehicle's controls to direct its course along a route. Carrying out the activity would cause various facts to change, especially the location of the vehicle, the driver, and any cargo. An entry in a temporal database is an assertion that the pattern of activity occurred at a particular time.

Different temporal models support different ways of mapping events to time. A model of instantaneous events assigns events to points in time. Other models could assign events to intervals or sets of intervals.

The term **transaction** refers to an atomic event. An atomic event cannot be interrupted and stopped part way. It is either finished or aborted. The term arises from database systems. Typically a transaction includes several primitive events that are bundled together to make the atomic event. An example of a transaction is when someone receives cash by withdrawing ten credits from a checking account. In this example, there are three main primitive events: the balance is checked, the cash is delivered, and the balance is debited. The cash should not be delivered without the balance of the account being reduced; nor should the balance be reduced without the cash being delivered. The atomicity of transactions together with the ability to serialize them assures the integrity of database algorithms.

Atomic events may have temporal duration or may be modeled as being instantaneous. The temporal treatment of the transaction as instantaneous is a convenient legal fiction that describes a simultaneous exchange of ownership and credits. It is also a reasonable temporal approximation for applications in which change is a rare or short-lived event. A cumulative record of transactions is known as a **log** or **journal**.

4.1.2   *A Discrete Model of Transactions in the Balance of an Account*

Figures 4.1 and 4.2 depict the balance of a bank account as various deposits and withdrawals are made. Although the example is mundane, it is useful for introducing concepts of temporal models. The vertical axis is the number of credits in the account and the horizontal axis is time in days. On day 0, the beginning of the period in the graph, 20 credits are in the account. On the third day, a deposit of 10 credits is made, raising the balance to 30 credits. Similarly, on the fifth day, 10 more credits are deposited.

On the eighth day, there is a deposit of 5 credits and a withdrawal of 30 for a net debit of 25 credits. At this point, the discrete nature of the time model is unmistakable. If the accounting process kept more precise records of time, we would see a rise in the balance when the 5 credits were deposited and a drop in the balance when the 30 credits were withdrawn. The shape of the shaded area in Figure 4.1 would be different depending on which came first. Ignoring the usual

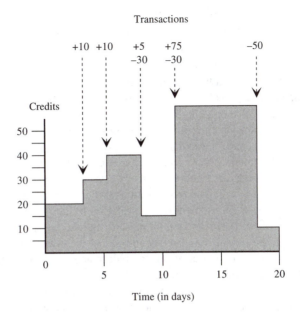

FIGURE 4.1. Graph of the balance of a bank account for Mac's Art Studio. In this application, changes are modeled in terms of instantaneous and atomic events. Between these events, the balance is constant. Time is recorded according to a discrete clock whose unit tick is one day.

delays for electronic clearance after the deposit of a paper check, this kind of daily record is typical of banking practice. The use of the day as the unit of discrete time simplifies the computation of interest and the minimum balance of an account. Another characteristic of Figure 4.1 and most banking applications is that the balance line is constant over each segment and is punctuated by abrupt changes at the period boundaries.

In summary, the time model in the banking example makes temporal approximations. Transactions are instantaneous. The long-term time record of the balance is indexed according to a discrete clock whose unit tick is one day.

Day	Check No.	Amount	New Balance	Description
0	—	—	20.00	Initial balance
3	30	10.00	30.00	Sell painting
5	31	10.00	40.00	Sell painting
8	32	5.00	45.00	Sell stained glass window
8	100	–30.00	15.00	Purchase potter's wheel
11	33	75.00	90.00	Sell statue
11	101	–30.00	60.00	Business license renewal
18	102	–50.00	10.00	Buy clay supplies

FIGURE 4.2. Transaction log of the data in Figure 4.1 for Mac's Art Studio.

4.2 *Continuous versus Discrete Temporal Models*

In the banking example, the model has both discrete states (integer amounts of credit) and discrete times. Queries about values in discrete models ask "What is the value at a given tick?" A tick has a duration lasting from the end of the previous tick to the beginning of the next one. There is no accounting about what happens between ticks. This does not say anything about the reality of ticks in the physical world. At issue here is the discrete nature of this *model* of time.

Discrete models are relatively impoverished. Consider the process of turning on a light-bulb. Imagine that we monitor the current flowing through an incandescent lightbulb and also its luminosity for a few milliseconds immediately after a switch is thrown connecting it to a direct-current power source. We could observe gradual increases in luminosity as the bulb brightens—changes that we might regard as continuous. This suggests the alternative of modeling the brightness of the bulb as a continuous real-value function over the real numbers.

Figure 4.3 illustrates two time models of turning on a light. The first model has discrete values and two discrete times. In this model, there is an interval during which the light is off followed by one in which the light is on. The second model is continuous and assigns values of luminosity to points. There is a point at which the bulb reaches half the expected luminosity—where we might arguably say that it is "half on."

Continuous models invite us to be concerned with lights that are half on and gradual changes. For such descriptions it is necessary and reasonable to ask not only about values over intervals but also, more fundamentally, about values at points. A basic theorem from real analysis, the **mean-value theorem**, states that a continuous function passes through all intermediate values. Continuous motion or continuous activity can be modeled with discrete ticks or intervals only in those circumstances where the intermediate values are of no interest.

We identify three dimensions of variation in time models. The time axis may be discrete or continuous, meaning time can be measured in ticks or in terms of real numbers. The two other

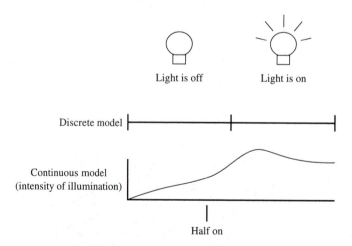

FIGURE 4.3.   Illustration of a bogus argument about the meaningfulness of time points and intervals.

dimensions are concerned with how values are assigned. In discrete-value models, a discrete set (either a finite set or a set corresponding to the integers) of values can be assigned. In real-value models, any real number can be assigned as a value. In either case, values either can be assigned to points or held constant over intervals. Modeling a continuous real-value function over the reals corresponds to having a continuous time axis with real values assigned to point. The account balance example corresponds to an opposite extreme in which discrete values are assigned to intervals whose endpoints fall on discrete ticks.

There are advantages and limitations of each kind of model. In discrete-time, discrete-value models, values are constant over some interval: The light is on, the man is in the room, or the account has 50 credits in it. This simplifies the description of logical combinations of states. Thus we can intersect intervals to find the ones during which both the light is on and the man is in the room. If property P_A holds over interval A and interval B is contained within interval A, then P_A holds over interval B. Thus, time containment or *during* relationships can be used to define a hierarchy of intervals in which propositions can be inherited. The straightforward simplicity of this arrangement is the basis of many temporal logics and almost all time-oriented databases.

4.3 *Temporal Uncertainty and Constraint Reasoning*

Consider the following sentences:

1. I had lunch at noon.
2. I ate lunch from 12:00 to 1:00.

In the first sentence, *noon* refers to a precise moment at which lunch began. This sentence exemplifies a **point-based event model**. In the second sentence, lunch starts at the beginning of the interval and finishes at the end, lasting an hour. This sentence exemplifies an **interval-based event model**. So far, the temporal concepts expressing the meaning of these sentences are drawn from concepts we have discussed already.

3. I left for lunch sometime between 12:00 and 1:00.
4. I took 20 minutes for lunch sometime between 12:00 and 1:00.

The third and fourth sentences introduce a different issue: temporal uncertainty. The third sentence uses a point-based event model but expresses incomplete knowledge about the time of the event. The leaving for lunch took place at some moment during the hour between 12:00 and 1:00. The sentence expresses lower and upper bounds on the moment. The fourth sentence shows that intervals can be used to express inexact knowledge in interval-based event models. Lunch began and ended sometime between 12:00 and 1:00 and took 20 minutes, but we are not sure of the exact times of lunch. What we know is that lunch began sometime after noon, that it finished before 1:00, and that it required 20 minutes. Thus we distinguish between the case where an event requires an hour to complete and the case where an event takes place at some unspecified time during an hour. In models with no explicit representation of uncertainty, these different interpretations of intervals are sometimes confounded.

4.3.1 *Partial Knowledge of Event Times*

We now consider examples of reasoning with various kinds of incomplete knowledge about the times of events. We maintain the foundation that event times could *potentially* be known, but we relax the requirement that all event times *are* known. Consider the following story:

> *Driving Story*
>
> It was 4:00 A.M. and Joe could not sleep. He went for a drive along the coast. During his drive he bought gasoline for his car and also some office supplies. He watched some surfers. Later, he drove to work and prepared some materials that he took to his 9:00 A.M. meeting.

Given this story, consider the following questions about it.

1. Which happened first: buying gas or preparing materials for the meeting?
2. Did Joe drive to work before 3:00 P.M.?
3. Which happened first: buying gas or buying office supplies?
4. Did Joe prepare materials before 7:00 A.M.?

What we seek in this example is a representation of the facts in the story and an accompanying approach to reasoning appropriate for answering the questions. We prefer a method that is sound and complete, which means that it should provide answers only to the questions that can be answered and that the answers it gives should be correct.

Figure 4.4 shows a representation of the facts of the story in terms of constraints about the times of events in the story. From this figure it is straightforward to determine which questions can be answered and to determine their answers. We model events as taking place over intervals and depict the events with labeled boxes. The first event is "Joe wakes up." The left side of an event box in the figure corresponds to its starting time and the right side corresponds to its ending time. Dashed lines represent constraints on the times that can be assigned to endpoints of the intervals. The dashed line between the event "Joe wakes up" and the event "Joe drives along the coast" means Joe finished waking up before he started driving. The beginnings of events occur before their ends—these internal event constraints are implicit in the diagram. A dashed line from an end time of an event to the time axis below indicate that the time is known and what it is. The figure shows all the constraints stated in the driving story.

Consider now the first question. Rephrased, which event came first: event G: Joe prepares materials or event C: Joe buys gas? Tracing backward in the figure, we see that Joe bought gas before he prepared materials. More formally, Figure 4.5 shows a sequence of operations on the time representations for deriving this answer. The sequence of derivations in Figure 4.5 works backward from the boundary points of interval G, following < (before) point relations and invoking transitivity. We use the suffixes – and + to indicate beginning and ending points of intervals, respectively. Thus, F+ is the ending point of interval F. Step 6 in Figure 4.5 converts from point relations to interval relations.

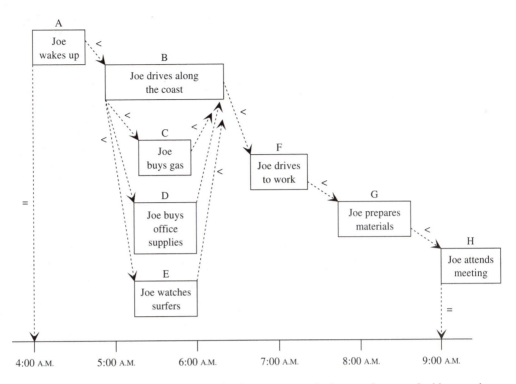

FIGURE 4.4. A graph showing time constraints between events in the story fragment. In this example, events are modeled as taking place over intervals and constraints are given in terms of the endpoints of the events.

Question: *What is the relative order of event C and event G?*

Derivation
1.   F+ < G−   (given)
2.   F− < F+   (definition of interval: internal constraint)
3.   B+ < F−   (given)
4.   C+ < B+   (given)
5.   C+ < G−   (transitivity of <, steps 1, 2, 3, 4)
6.   C < G   (definition of < for intervals)
      → Joe buys gas before he prepares materials.

FIGURE 4.5. Example sequence of reasoning steps for determining whether event C precedes event G in the events of Figure 4.4.

In a similar way, we could answer the second question. By transitivity, Joe drove to work before 9:00 A.M., so by transitivity he drove to work before 3:00 P.M. In contrast, consider questions 3 and 4.

3. Which happened first: buying gas or buying office supplies?
4. Did Joe prepare materials before 7:00 A.M.?

The buying-gas event and the buying-office-supplies event have no constraints connecting them, even indirectly, so we have no basis for determining their order. This indeterminacy in the constraint graph corresponds to an ambiguity in the story. Similarly, actual clock times are known for only two events in the story: when Joe wakes up and when he attends the meeting. In the absence of any other times or duration information, we have no basis for determining exact times of any other events in the story. Thus, we cannot answer the fourth question either.

In summary, this example illustrates a case of reasoning from incomplete information about event times. The interval-based model of events accommodates the difference in times between the beginnings and endings of events. Inequality constraints represent relative orderings of endpoints and equality constraints represent assignments of endpoints to points on the time-line. Because all the queries in the example are about relative orderings, the constraint model expresses the facts precisely. It also reflects the ambiguities in the story. Ambiguous event orderings in the story correspond to indeterminacies in the constraint system.

4.3.2 *Arc Consistency and Endpoint Constraints*

The preceding example used constraint satisfaction to reason about time. In this example we see that even partial satisfaction of constraints can be useful in temporal reasoning.

Figure 4.6 gives the results for composing two endpoint relations over three points. Given $A\ R_1\ B$, and $B\ R_2\ C$, the table lists the possible consistent relations between points A and C. For example, if $A < B$ and $B = C$, the table says we can conclude $A < C$.

Suppose we are given the set of intervals and point relations in Figure 4.7. Using Figure 4.7, we now ask questions like those in Figure 4.8. Each derivation in Figure 4.8 is just two steps long—the composition of two relations in the graph. The labels in the answer represent the relations that can hold between the points after the derivation. The first example in Figure 4.8 is a case of least information in which all three labels are present in the answer.

			R_2	
		<	=	>
	<	<	<	Any
R_1	=	<	=	>
	>	Any	>	>

FIGURE 4.6. Composed relations for three points. We are given $A\ R_1\ B$ and $B\ R_2\ C$. The table gives the possible relations between A and C.

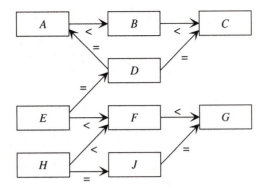

FIGURE 4.7. Examples of reasoning with composed endpoint relations from Figure 4.6.

This label propagation process can be carried out for all pairs of labels, deriving answers for all such questions. At each cycle, the composition of the relations is performed using the information in Figure 4.7. This often reduces the labels between other intervals. The process continues until a cycle is completed and no more labels are changed.

This process is a variation of what is called an arc-consistency algorithm. The problem of determining the relations between the two intervals is a rephrasing of a constraint satisfaction problem (CSP). The relation arcs correspond to the variables of a standard CSP and the possible relation labels correspond to their domains. The limited consistency test from the table in Figure 4.7 and subsequent removal of inconsistent labels correspond to achieving arc consistency. The labels remaining when the process completes are the ones that are arc consistent.

The idea of using an arc-consistency method to provide a partial solution of the CSP in temporal reasoning was first proposed by Allen (1983). Allen's particular proposal differed from the example here in that he computed relations between entire intervals rather than relations between their endpoints. He showed that 13 possible relations between two intervals can be derived from the 3 ordering relations on their endpoints. Allen's relations were intended to characterize the temporal inferences about time that people appear to make automatically or effortlessly during a dialog, story comprehension, or simple problem solving. As in the example

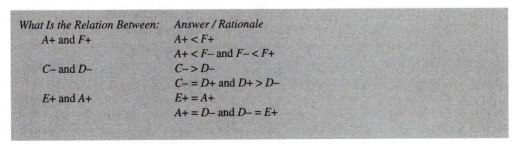

What Is the Relation Between:	Answer / Rationale
$A+$ and $F+$	$A+ < F+$
	$A+ < F-$ and $F- < F+$
$C-$ and $D-$	$C- > D-$
	$C- = D+$ and $D+ > D-$
$E+$ and $A+$	$E+ = A+$
	$A+ = D-$ and $D- = E+$

FIGURE 4.8. Examples of reasoning with composed endpoint relations from Figure 4.7.

above, Allen's approach involved inferences over two steps—again analogous to arc consistency. Because his relations involved two intervals rather than two endpoints, his variation of arc consistency goes twice as deep. Like all approaches to arc consistency, it stops short of checking all the constraints in a CSP and does not notice those nonsolutions that cannot be ruled out in two steps. See the exercises for more details about Allen's approach.

4.3.3 *Time Maps and Scheduling Problems*

In planning and scheduling tasks, the problem of handling queries concerning temporal facts is exacerbated by several sources of uncertainty. Our knowledge concerning the occurrence of events is generally inexact even with respect to events that are under our control. This occurs because commitments about the choice and ordering of steps are often made incrementally. In addition, our knowledge changes over time as our plans evolve and as we move about in the world gathering information. Hence it is necessary to keep track of the validity of the information returned in response to a query.

Figure 4.9 gives an example of a very simple planning problem. Our interest in this problem is not in planning methods per se. Rather, it is in the nature of requirements that planning and scheduling tasks impose on temporal representations. The goal in this problem is to complete operation D and its prerequisites before a given deadline of 20 minutes. The prerequisites of each operation are printed above it. D's prerequisites are either B or C, and both B and C require completing operation A as a prerequisite.

The planning in Figure 4.9 proceeds in steps. In this example, the planner first commits to operation D in step 1. It cannot tell whether operation D can be completed on time. That depends on whether D's prerequisite operations can be completed soon enough. In step 2, the planner commits to operation B. It still cannot tell whether the operation will be completed in time. In step 3, it commits to operation A. There is now a complete plan. To answer the question of whether D can be completed in time amounts to adding the durations of the chain of prerequisite steps and comparing the result with the deadline. Doing this shows that the plan completes in 20 minutes, satisfying the goal.

Suppose that sometime later the planner encounters some other constraints and revises the plan. For some reason, it decides to substitute operation C for operation D. With this change, there is still a complete plan to carry out operation D. However, the total time for the plan is now 25 minutes and the deadline goal is no longer satisfied.

The parts of Figure 4.9 are visual presentations of plans in a temporal database. At each step, the presentation lays out what is known about the past, present, and future. Moving from one instant to another does not require running a simulation backward or forward; it requires only moving about in the database. The term **time map** is sometimes used to emphasize that by scanning different parts of the map one can view activities at different times.

4.3.4 *The Interface between a Scheduler and a Temporal Database*

A temporal database stores facts and provides a temporal index to them. In this it handles the addition of new information, the removal of outdated information, and the detection of inconsistencies. It provides a query language that enables application programs to construct and explore hypothetical situations. In practice, it is useful to extend the functionality of temporal databases

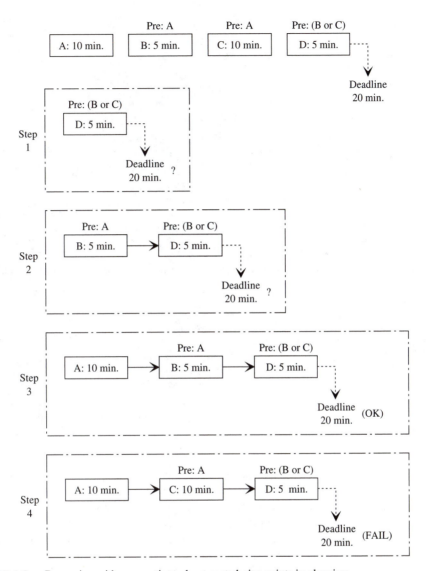

FIGURE 4.9.   Reasoning with assumptions about past choice points in planning.

to provide a modular interface to planning and scheduling programs. We consider this in the following, starting with a language for temporal queries.

The following two kinds of queries are the most basic:

1. Given what is known, is it possible that P is true at time T?
2. Given some temporal boundaries, find an interval such that the conjunction ($\land P_1 \ldots P_n$) is true throughout the interval.

```
(&    (tt ?begin ?end (production-status conveyor1 idle))
      (tt ?begin ?end (production-status ?lathe idle))
      (tt ?begin ?end (operational-status ?lathe in-service))
      (instance-of ?lathe turning-lathe)
      (throw ?lathe (>= (turning-radius ?lathe) 12))
      (attached-fixture ?lathe spray-weld)
      (tt ?begin ?end (production-status ?grinder idle))
      (tt ?begin ?end (operational-status ?grinder in-service))
      (instance-of ?grinder (>= (turning-radius ?lathe) 12))
      (elt (distance ?begin ?end) [1 ,*pos-inf*])
      (elt (distance *now* ?begin) [0 ,24]) )
```

Paraphrase: Find an interval ?begin to ?end and objects ?lathe and ?grinder such that:
- *conveyor1* is idle throughout the interval
- *?lathe* is both idle and in service throughout the interval
- *?lathe* is an object of type *turning-lathe* and has a maximum turning radius of no less than 12 inches
- *?lathe* has a spray-weld attachment
- *?grinder* is idle and in service throughout the interval
- *?grinder* is an object of type *cylindrical-grinder* and has a maximum turning radius of no less than 12 inches
- the interval *?begin* to *?end* begins sometime in the next 24 hours

FIGURE 4.10.   Example of a queries from a time management system. In the language of this example, *tt* is a temporal predicate meaning "true throughout." (Adopted from Dean, 1984, Figure 3, page 134.)

The first kind of query uses a temporal analog of universal quantification, requiring that a temporal predicate be true for all times in an interval. This version of the query implies that some inference may be needed in answering the question. A simpler variation of the first query would ask whether it is trivially known that P is true at time T, that is, whether the database stores that fact directly. The second kind of query uses a temporal analog of existential quantification, requiring that there is some interval in the range such that the temporal predicate is satisfied. In both examples the quantifiers range over a linear time axis. Figure 4.10 gives an example of the second kind of query from a job-shop scheduling system.

Beyond storing and retrieving time-indexed facts, several reasoning functions are associated with temporal databases used in planning and scheduling applications. To emphasize the reasoning functions created around such a database, the term **time-map management (TMM)** is sometimes used. For example, on the basis of data in the database, the user can make forward inferences or predictions, which are stored in the database and marked as depending on their antecedent conditions. A TMM can monitor the continued validity of conditional predictions. If the assumptions supporting a prediction are changed, further planning activities can be triggered.

It is useful to distinguish concepts having to do with time from concepts having to do with an underlying constraint system and concepts having to do with scheduling per se. Figure 4.11

Example Situation	*Related Temporal Database Concepts*

1. He drove from 7:00 A.M. until 9:00 A.M.

   Duration: An interval over which a fact is true or an event takes place. The boundary points represent known starting and stopping times.

2. There are between 2 and 4 hours after lunch and before dinner.

   Temporal Distance: The boundary points represent minimum and maximum distances between the end of the lunch event and the beginning of the dinner event.

3. The meeting will occur 30 minutes after his arrival on Monday.

   Dependency and Temporal Projection: Dependencies provide a way of indicating that some events in the database are predictions or temporal projections based on other events. If the traveler reschedules to arrive on Tuesday instead of Monday, then the assumptions behind this schedule are violated.

4. Reserve the lathe from 6:00 A.M. until 8:00 A.M. for maintenance.

   Protection: A duration for reserving the lathe. The term *protection* is intended to indicate that a triggering mechanism is involved. The maintenance task requires that the lathe be available. If further commitments are made that compromise lathe availability during that period, a notification action is triggered to initiate various planning and scheduling actions.

FIGURE 4.11. Sorting out the terminology of interactions used in scheduling programs and temporal databases.

presents terminology from temporal databases. The term **duration** refers simply to interval-based facts. Temporal **distances** are also expressed in terms of intervals, where the endpoints refer to lower and upper bounds on an unknown distance. The term **dependency** refers to a marking in the database that certain conclusions—events or facts—depend on others. Such markings can be by mechanisms that trigger actions when assumptions are violated.

In constraint systems, the basic concepts are variables and domains. In a problem-solving context, we distinguish between variables that are bound and those that are not. In terms of constraints, the duration in the first sentence of Figure 4.11 is understood in terms of bound variables.

1. He drove from 7:00 A.M. until 9:00 A.M.

We can represent this statement with one variable that takes an interval as its compound value. Equivalently, we could represent it with two bound variables corresponding to the starting and stopping times. The main points are that the variable or variables are completely determined and that any further constraint reasoning should take that into account.

2. There are between 2 and 4 hours after lunch and before dinner.

In constraint terminology the temporal distance of the second example is a constraint on two variables. The variables refer to the ending time of lunch and the beginning time of dinner. The constraint bears on the difference between the values of the two variables and requires that this distance be between 2 and 4. How this constraint can be used depends on which variables are bound. If the values of both variables are known, a constraint system can simply test whether the constraint is satisfied. If the value of only one variable is known, then bounds on the value of the other variable can be computed.

3. The meeting will occur 30 minutes after his arrival on Monday.

In constraint terminology the dependency is also expressed as a constraint on two variables: the end of the arrival and the beginning of the meeting. When we are given the time of arrival, the time of the meeting will be determined. If the arrival time shifts by a little, then so does the meeting time. To cope with the possibility that the arrival may slip to Tuesday, however, we need more than constraints. We need some means to characterize defaults, expectations, and dependencies. The expected situation with the derived meeting time depends on a Monday arrival. If this assumption is violated, then further reasoning will be needed. The reasoning in the fourth example also requires us to go beyond constraint satisfaction.

4. Reserve the lathe from 6:00 A.M. until 8:00 A.M. for maintenance.

This example requires scheduling concepts such as **commitments**. When a scheduler reserves the lathe, it is committing to perform roller maintenance at that time. That means that the scheduler will take actions to make this happen and that if something precludes its fulfilling the commitment, the scheduler should be prepared to take suitable action.

This is not to say that reasoning about commitments does not involve constraints, bound and unbound variables, and a search process. Rather, it is to say that sensible reasoning about commitments typically depends on more than simple backtracking. Sometimes commitments are made when it is very likely that the commitment can be honored, but before enough data are available to guarantee this. Suppose that after a scheduler plans an action, another urgent task comes up that requires resources previously committed. If this happens then the scheduler may need to break its commitment. In deciding what to do, a scheduler traffics in concepts like priorities, preferences, and defaults. These are the concepts of scheduling and they are used to determine what commitments to make and which ones to break.

The example in Figure 4.11 uses **protections** to reason about commitments. A protection is a temporal testing mechanism that assures that a condition holds over an intended interval. Dependency relations are set up on all the assumptions on which the condition depends. As long as the assumptions do not change, nothing happens. As soon as the assumptions are changed and the conclusion can no longer be justified, the protection attempts to find alternative support. If this fails, the scheduler is alerted about the failed assumption.

Continuing with the lathe scenario from Dean (1984), we consider the query in Figure 4.10. Suppose that assembly-line conveyers require periodic maintenance. The query in Figure 4.10 corresponds to a request to reserve appropriate equipment during an interval so the required maintenance can be performed. In particular, a specially outfitted lathe is required to resurface worn rollers.

Suppose no interval satisfies all the constraints. The temporal database could simply report that no plan is possible, providing the scheduler with no data to guide its decision of what to do next. In contrast, suppose there is an interval that satisfies all the constraints except one—namely that the only free grinder is scheduled to be out of service for lubrication. One possible remedy is to reschedule the grinder for earlier lubrication. This points to the inclusion of dependency analysis in the interface between the temporal database and the scheduler. By analyzing the failed constraints for "near misses," the temporal database can provide data for replanning. For example, it may turn out that the grinder needs to be serviced, that the time of its servicing has not yet been determined, and that its service can be scheduled early enough without compromising other commitments. In this case, the original schedule can be repaired with little effect on other commitments.

In summary, the most basic interface between a scheduler and a temporal database should support queries about what is known at different times. It is the nature of the scheduling task to plan in a world with surprises, creating plans that may need to be revised. Replanning in the face of scheduling conflicts has a temporal dimension and involves failure analysis. The preceding examples suggest that dependency records and protections provide a useful basis for failure analysis, justifying the inclusion of protections and dependency records as part of the functionality of a temporal database. See the exercises for issues concerning the efficient implementation of such systems.

4.4 *Branching Time*

One main difference among models of time is whether they are linear or admit branches. The simplest models, such as those used in banking transaction systems, admit no branches. In these models time is a linear sequence of events. Other applications require representing branch points on which the course of the future crucially depends. A branch point could involve an event beyond the agent's control, data outside the agent's knowledge, or a decision for which the agent has not yet committed. A strictly linear temporal model cannot simultaneously express multiple possible futures beyond a branch point.

In principle, one can compare two alternative futures even with the restriction of representing only one future at a time. You make an assumption, x_a, about the outcome at the branch point; project future A; extract datum d_a from the projection; unwind back to the branch point, erasing the representation of future A; make assumption x_b at the branch point; project future B; extract datum d_b; unwind to the branch point; and so on, reconstructing futures A and B as necessary to complete the comparison.

However, a more attractive approach is to generalize the notion of a time map to express alternative possible futures past a branch point. The futures along these branches are called **possible worlds**. This approach trades storage for computation time, making it possible to move not only forward and backward in the map, but also sideways across possible worlds. Possible worlds group events into sets. Changes in sets of events in different possible worlds are isolated in the sense that the system does not infer consequences and inconsistencies across different worlds.

By using multiple worlds a scheduler can elaborate alternative plans, each of which satisfies some goals. Possible worlds allow a scheduler to consider several hypotheses independently, examining their costs, commitments, and trade-offs before actually choosing among them. Figure 4.12 shows a simple example of possible worlds. In this scenario the agent is driving to the airport to pick up a visitor. He parks the car and then checks the arrival time of the flights. This is where the first branch point appears. In the first possible world, the flight is on time and the visitor arrives. In the second possible world, the flight is delayed by one hour. In the third possible world, the flight is delayed by many hours. Branch points can form trees of possible worlds.

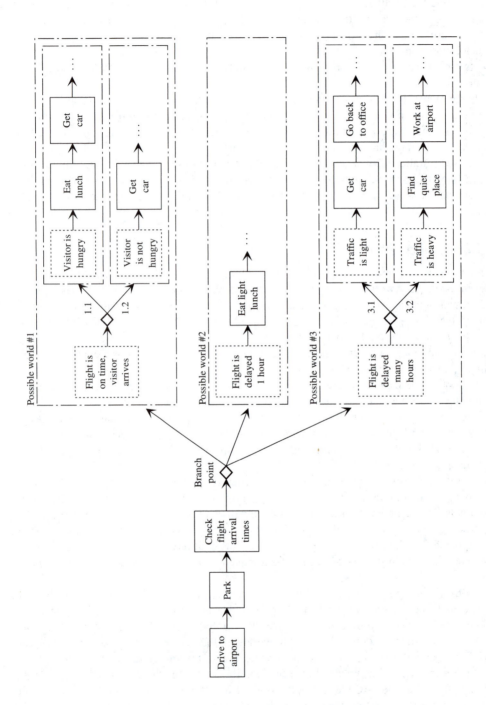

FIGURE 4.12. A plan showing choice points and multiple worlds.

Thus, the first possible world branches further into 1.1 and 1.2, depending on whether the visitor is hungry for lunch.

As the number of branches increases, the amount of planning and the number of possible worlds can increase exponentially. This phenomenon has long been recognized in game trees, where the first level of the tree represents the possible first moves of the first player, the second level represents the possible responses of the second player, the third level represents the answering moves of the first player, and so on. In games like chess, the number of possible games is so great that only an infinitesimal portion of such a game tree is expanded. The same combinatorial issue arises in the use of branch points to represent possible worlds in planning and scheduling. Thus, in the airport example of Figure 4.12, three major possible worlds are shown. In practi ce, there can be many possible outcomes at every branch point. For example, at the first branch point the weather could be bad and the plane could be rerouted to another city. In managing its reasoning resources, a planning or scheduling program can choose not to explore certain hypotheses if their probability is below some threshold. Thus, branch points express alternative futures, even though few branches are explored in depth and many are not represented at all.

Some models of time admit not only branching representations for reasoning about the future, but also branching representations for reasoning about the past. Again, the issue is not about whether the physical past is actually determined and unchangeable. The issue is to support reasoning about an agent's state of knowledge. Thus, an agent with incomplete knowledge of the past may consider different hypotheses about it. Such reasoning about multiple "possible pasts" is the standard fare of mystery stories, where a detective must gather clues from the present to rule out different hypotheses about the past involving the identity of a culprit and various aspects of a crime. The precise nature of the past is indeterminate from the detective's state of knowledge when the observed present could arguably have arisen from any of several possible histories.

In summary, temporal branches reflect limitations in an agent's state of knowledge. For different applications it can be appropriate to represent multiple possible futures or multiple possible pasts to support an agent's reasoning.

4.5   *Summary and Review*

Temporal representations must address several issues, depending on the application. All temporal representations must handle events and change, either discrete or continuous. The simplest temporal representations are the timeline representations that assign unique times to all events and retrieve events by their temporal indices. This representation is the mainstay of temporal databases, such as for modeling financial applications. Such models can use either point or interval event models.

Applications that reason with partial temporal information require the ability to represent quantitative relations among times and durations. In this section we saw how intervals can be used to represent persistences and also temporal uncertainty. As with most forms of reasoning with constraint systems, the time complexity is potentially exponential. Many temporal databases limit their temporal reasoning to computing limited forms of consistency in polynomial time.

Finally, some applications must be able to compare hypothetical courses of events. Time maps with branch points can be used to support reasoning about both uncertain futures and hypothetical pasts. The design of temporal representations in AI has been driven mostly by systems for planning and scheduling and by systems for interpreting natural language. In the quandaries section of this chapter we consider related work on temporal representation, including research on temporal logics, languages for parallel programming, and script languages for computer animation.

Exercises for Chapter 4

■ **Ex. 1** [05] *Terminology.* Indicate whether each of the following statements is true or false. If the statement is ambiguous, explain briefly.

(a) *True or False.* Discrete models of time always have a "tick" or "time atom," which is a smallest unit of time during which properties hold.

(b) *True or False.* An atomic event takes place in the smallest possible time.

(c) *True or False.* Intervals are impoverished representations for representing continuous change.

(d) *True or False.* Interval representations of temporal uncertainty are incompatible with interval-based event models.

(e) *True or False.* Branching time models are appropriate for representing multiple possible futures but have no role in representing the past because the past is already determined.

Ex. 2 [05] *More Terminology.* Indicate whether each of the following statements is true or false. If the statement is ambiguous, explain briefly.

(a) *True or False.* Once a time map is constructed, moving from one instant to another does not require cranking a simulation backward or forward.

(b) *True or False.* In temporal databases, the boundaries between possible worlds delimit the range of propagation for consistency-checking mechanisms.

(c) *True or False.* Possible-world models of time can describe unlikely and fictional situations.

(d) *True or False.* Job-shop scheduling, travel-time optimization, and resource management are generally assumed to be intractable problems. Temporal databases do not solve these problems.

Ex. 3 [30] *Allen's Interval Relations.* James Allen noticed that it is not necessary to record time relations among points, but rather that time relations over intervals can be used. Starting from the three point-based relations $\{<, =, >\}$ between their endpoints, he defined the interval-based relations as shown in Figure 4.13.

Is this set of relations complete? In Allen's approach we are given two intervals (X, Y), their endpoints $(X-, X+, Y-, Y+)$, and the three point relations $(=, <, >)$. Intervals are assumed to have positive length, which means $X- < X+$ and $Y- < Y+$.

Allen claims that exactly 13 possible interval relations express the valid combinations of the three relations among their endpoints. Do you agree? Explain your answer by showing a systematic list of the cases. Explain carefully the basis for your claim that the set is complete or incomplete.

Ex. 4 [20] *Complexity of Reasoning with Intervals versus Points.* Earlier in this section we gave a method for deriving consistent times that was equivalent to the arc-consistency method known as AC-3. The worst-case time complexity of AC-3 is $O(ea^3)$. In terms of the time model, e corresponds roughly to $n(n-1)/2$—or $n^2/2$ for our purposes where n is the number of intervals—and a corresponds to r, the number of possible relations.

Relation	Condition	Symbol	Symbol for Inverse	Example	Synonyms
X before Y	X+ < Y–	<	>	Y — / X —	Y after X
X equals Y	X– = Y– / X+ = Y+	=	=	Y — / X —	
X meets Y	X+ = Y–	m	mi	Y — / X —	X until Y / Y from X
X overlaps Y	X– < Y– / X+ > Y– / X+ < Y+	o	oi	Y — / X —	X leads Y / Y lags X
X during Y	((X– > Y–) and (X+ <= Y+)) or ((X– >= Y–) and (X+ < Y+))	d	di	Y ——— / X ——	Y spans X
X starts Y	X– = Y– / X+ < Y+	s	si	Y ——— / X —	
X finishes Y	X+ = Y+ / Y– < X–	f	fi	Y ——— / X —	

FIGURE 4.13.   Allen's relationships between two intervals.

(a) Allen's approach depends on a "transitivity table" or temporal relation composition table for three points at a time. In the interval-based version of the table, we are given three intervals $\{A, B, C\}$ and two relations between them $\{R_1, R_2\}$ such that $A \, R_1 \, B$ and $B \, R_2 \, C$. The table gives all the other interval relations from the set of 13 that are compatible with the data. A partial version of this table is given below with missing entries indicated by *xxx*. Fill in the missing entries.

	R_1		R_2	
	<	>	d	m
<	<	xxx	<, o, m, d, s	xxx
>	any	>		
d	<	xxx	xxx	<, m
m	xxx	xxx	xxx	xxx

(b) In the interval-based version of the consistency algorithm, the number of intervals is n and $d = 13$. In the point-based version in the text, the number of points is $2n$ and $d = 3$. Determine the order of the worst-case complexity for both methods.

(c) Suppose a fast variation of the time-consistency algorithm traded time for completeness of checking, limiting its consistency checking to the "most important checks" and finishing in worst-case time $r(n^2/2)$. Again, compare the worst-case times for interval-based and point-based approaches.

Ex. 5   [*00*] *Reference Intervals on the Timeline.* Consider the following paragraph:

> A month before admission, the patient first complained of fever and chills. He took medication and felt better. A week later the fever recurred, accompanied by anorexia. A few days later he developed jaundice. At admission, several lab tests were done including measurement of sugar level and blood pressure. The patient was found to have jaundice, pruritus, anorexia, severe abdominal pain, etc. Two months before admission he had eaten shellfish and had vomited a few times the next day. A few weeks later he had an attack of acute abdominal pain, but it subsided. Three days after admission his lab tests were. . . . Two days later he was operated upon for gallstones. A few days after admission he was all right and discharged. (Adapted from Mittal, Chandrasekaran, & Sticklen, 1984)

(a) For this purpose it is convenient to consider a group of related events, sometimes called an **episode**, and to record the times of most of the events relative to one or more **key events**. What is the key event in this description?

(b) An **event cluster** is a collection of events represented as occurring at a single point. Give an example of an event cluster from the case.

(c) Suppose reference intervals are used in a timeline model. In what way must the model be changed to accommodate the representational requirements of reference intervals? Explain briefly.

Ex. 6   [*15*] *Hierarchical Time Representations.* Figure 4.14 gives an example of a hierarchical time representation similar to the representations of hierarchical plans discussed in Chapter 2. Each box represents an interval during which the named event takes place. Vertical arcs are a shorthand meaning that the endpoints of the lower interval are wholly contained within the upper one. Horizontal arcs between interval endpoints mean that the endpoint at the beginning of the arrow precedes the one at the end. Although there are no examples in the figure, the representation could also include equality relations between endpoints.

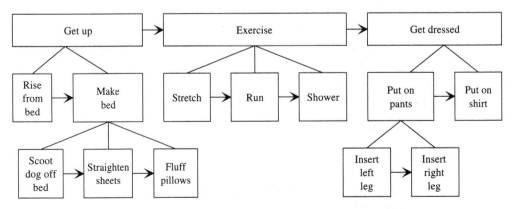

FIGURE 4.14.   A sample hierarchy of time intervals for some early morning activities.

(a) Briefly, what are the benefits of using a hierarchical representation for an arc-consistency computation of possible relations, and how must the computation be modified to exploit the hierarchy?

(b) Briefly, what reasoning is involved in showing that the actor straightens the sheets before inserting his right leg in his pants? Show this by completing the following derivation.

Derivation

1.	[Exercise]+ < [Get dressed]–	(given <)
2.	[Get dressed] – = [Put on pants]–	(given hierarchy)
3.	[Get dressed] – < xxx	(given hierarchy)
4.	[Exercise]+ < [Insert right leg]–	(transitivity)
5.		. . . (more steps)
Last.	[Straighten sheets]+ < [Insert right leg]–	*xxx*

4.6 *Open Issues and Quandaries*   `ADVANCED`

Representation is a vast topic. It is so vast that this chapter can provide only a sampling of approaches used in computer systems, even when restricted to techniques for representing time, space, and certainty. So ubiquitous are these topics that subfields in these areas have developed in many places in the scientific landscape. This section gives a high-level tour of portions of these subfields beyond the core ideas in the main body of the chapter.

Related Research about Time Representations

The Tensers and Detensers

Historically, one of the most important activities of mathematicians has been to give quantitative accounts of physical processes, which by their nature involve time. Time is represented traditionally as just another variable taking values from the real numbers. Physics follows this tradition. Time is important, but it is modeled like other dimensions.

For the philosopher Bertrand Russell, the truth or falsity of a proposition concerned both an entity and a time. He defined change as the difference in truth value between a proposition concerning an entity at a time, T_1, and a proposition concerning the same entity at another time, T_2. Specifically, a proposition has the form $f(x, t)$. This contrasts with describing a proposition as $f(x)$ at t where there are no terms referring to time. Thus, Russell treated temporal elements on a par with nontemporal ones. He saw no need to modify logic itself; that is, no need for a "temporal logic."

In many natural languages, notions of time are interwoven with syntax as exemplified by the tenses of verbs. Furthermore, natural languages employ relational temporal connectives such as {*when, while, before, after, since, until*} and adverbs such as {*now, then, always, sometimes, never, soon*}. Since Frege, philosophers have been interested in the language of logic and in its relation to natural language. Example sentences have motivated philosophers to develop logical formalisms that are closer in style and spirit to natural language.

In the 1950s, Prior constructed what he called a tense logic. Prior introduced logical notations for quantifying relations over time. For example, F*p* means "It will be the case that *p*"; G*p* means "It will always be the case that *p*"; P*p* means "It has been the case that *p*" and H*p* means

"It has always been the case that *p*." The Prior style of analysis of temporal discourse has come to be known as the modal approach to time, as distinct from the first-order approach typified by Russell, Quine, and others. Adherents of the modal approach are sometimes called "tensers," and those of the first-order approach are called "detensers."

Time and the Existential Inadequacy

Galton (1987) observed that the positions of the tensers and detensers revolve in part on different attitudes about the meaning of existential quantifiers. For a tenser using Prior's notation, there is a distinction between the following sentences:

1. $F(\exists x) f(x)$
2. $(\exists x) Ff(x)$

The first sentence means something like "It will be the case that there is something that is *f*" and the second means "There is something of which it will be the case that it is *f*." As Galton notes, the former sentence might be true if something that does not yet exist is later on going to exist and be *f*, whereas the latter can only be true if there already exists something that is later going to be *f*. For the detenser, these formulas come out something like:

3. $(\exists t)[\text{later}(t, \text{now}) \wedge (\exists x)[f(x, t)]$
4. $(\exists x)(\exists t)[\text{later}(t, \text{now}) \wedge [f(x, t)]$

These are equivalent in first-order logic, so for the detenser the distinction cannot be upheld. Restated, at least one difference in meaning revolves around the notion of existence: whether there can be transitory things whose existence begins and ends.

As we discussed in the quandaries section for Chapter 1, Graeme Hirst (1989) analyzed example sentences ranging from sentences about things that are not there ("I don't own a dog") to events that never happened, physical existence ("the existence of carnivorous cows"), fictional characters, things at different times, and things that might have been or could be. His examples show that if we want a reasonable account of common sentences about existence, nonexistence, and nonexistent objects, then we need more than one notion of existence. The tenser and detenser notations just considered reflect only a part of the existential inadequacy. They show how transitory objects are not adequately represented by the usual existential quantifiers of logic. What is needed, at least, is a notion of existence that is a function of time. Following in this vein, most of the different notions of existence cited by Hirst must also be functions of time.

Time Representations in Program Verification

Work on temporal logic in the theory of programs has been driven by the tasks of specifying, synthesizing, and verifying programs. The first of this work did not develop a temporal logic or explicit time representation as such, but it did set the stage for such work.

Floyd's landmark paper "Assigning Meaning to Programs" (Floyd, 1967) established the inductive assertion method, the first systematic approach to program verification. The method associates a propositional tag with each point in a program in such a way that it can be proved that if the tag at a given point is true when the program reaches that point, it is still true afterward. Proof of the correctness of an algorithm is established inductively. If the tag assigned to the start of a program is true—corresponding to conditions on the input specification—then the tag assigned to the end of the program will also be true. Other methods of proof are needed to show that programs actually terminate.

Seeking to use the methods of logic for reasoning about programs, Hoare (1969) extended this approach with a rigorous axiomatic system. He adopted a basic schema of the form $\{P\}S\{Q\}$, meaning that if assertion P is true when the program S is started, then Q will be true when it terminates. Hoare's influential paper led to the acceptance of the axiomatic semantics for programs, as discussed in Chapter 1. His initial axiomatization dealt only with assignment statements, sequential composition of statements, and the while statement. Over the years these ideas have been extended by many others to cover additional constructs such as procedures, recursion, and goto statements.

Owicki and Gries (1976) extended the Floyd–Hoare techniques to reason about parallel computation. As Galton (1987) characterizes this, one main conclusion to be drawn from that exercise is that Hoare's logic is not well suited for describing parallel programs. One outcome of this work has been that it inspired several other efforts to find better approaches—leading to several versions of temporal logics. In the following, we consider just a few of the mileposts of this subsequent work.

Burstall (1974) extended this method in a way that he characterized as "hand simulation with a little induction," or what is sometimes called "symbolic execution." In symbolic execution, a proof about a factorial program would reason with symbolic descriptions of variable values rather than actual numbers. With regard to temporal logics, the most significant part is that Burstall contrasted the implicit form of the statements in his proofs as

sometime (at L . . .)

with the form implicit in the Hoare and Floyd methods

always (at L . . .)

and observed that both types of statement can be seen as belonging to a modal logic. Manna and Waldinger (1978) followed up on this idea, characterized the latter as "intermittent assertions," and proved some properties about the power of such logics. Pnueli (1977) then systematized Burstall's logic as a temporal logic with future-tense operators corresponding closely to Prior's F and G.

The use of a branching time model for programs was considered by Lamport (1980). Ben-Ari and others developed the language UB for "unified system of branching time" (Ben-Ari, 1981). This language combines quantification over possible futures with quantification over individual times within a future. Since then, a number of branching-time languages have been proposed. A review of temporal logics with branching times is given by Emerson and Halpern (1983).

In conclusion, research on temporal logics related to the theory of programming has addressed many of the same temporal representation issues as research in AI. Despite this similarity, the two areas have evolved separately and researchers are generally unaware of each other's work. The AI research has tended to be more experimental and systems oriented whereas the programming theory work has been theoretical and mathematically oriented. For example, in the programming theory work there has been little attention to reasoning with defaults or any other approach to nonmonotonic reasoning. There is no analog of a temporal reasoning management system for reasoning with incomplete knowledge or incremental commitments in time. In contrast with AI, where much of the work has been driven by the needs of planning and scheduling tasks, the main focus in programming theory has been on program verification rather than on synthesis. On the other hand, the mathematical foundations employed by the programming theory researchers have been much more technically sophisticated than those used by the AI researchers.

Time Representations in Computer Animation

As computer technology for visualization has advanced, there has been growing interest in computer techniques for animation. The term *animation* brings to mind children's cartoon shows— and indeed, the use of computers to improve imagery and to speed production of special effects is one application of computer animation. Use of animation in advertising and in logos increased dramatically in television production in the 1980s. Interactive computer animation also became ubiquitous in video games. Beyond these pure entertainment uses, animation is increasingly incorporated in user interfaces to aid in visualization, where the persistence and motion of objects draws on the abilities of the human perceptual system in keeping track of relations and placements of objects.

The relevance of computer animation in this chapter is similar to that of languages for concurrent programming: the development of languages for representing actions in time. To explore the connections, we begin by describing some terminology from animation that derives from the earlier craft of filmmaking in studios.

The term *storyboard* refers to a film in outline form. It consists of a group of illustrations arranged in comic-strip format with directions as captions. A storyboard is a key representation for designing an animated story at the beginning and for coordinating the work of animators as work progresses. The illustrations in a storyboard are used to represent the key moments of a film. A sequence is a collection of illustrations that make up a specific action. Each sequence consists of a series of scenes that are defined by a certain location and set of characters. Scenes are divided into shots that are considered as picture units.

In animation there is a division of labor among animators. Typically, a lead animator draws the key frames. Often an individual animator is responsible for each specific character. "In-betweens" are the drawings that are placed between two key frames, which when displayed in sequence convey a sense of motion. Assistant animators draw some in-betweens and in-betweeners draw the remaining figures. A storyboard representation is basically equivalent to a timeline representation in which the events are ordered in a sequence and assigned times and durations. For computer animation, languages sometimes called scripting languages are used to describe the timing and coordination of actions.

One of the first scripting languages, DIRECTOR (Kahn, 1976), was based on the object-oriented notion of actors that can receive messages, send messages, remember state, and carry out various actions. This work was further extended by Reynolds (1978) and used to create some impressive animations. The temporal concepts in these languages include the usual sequential and iterative operators of conventional programming languages, and also statements for triggering and coordinating parallel events and delays. In this regard they are similar to CSP (Hoare, 1978). Indeed, it is interesting that both Hoare and Kahn had dual interests—in formalizing temporal models and in developing computer languages for describing such parallel processes. The term *script* is used to refer to a program in a scripting language. Typically, a script describes the coordinated action of several actors in the language. In this way, a script is a description from a choreographer's or director's point of view, in contrast to a description of what to do from the perspective of an individual actor.

An interesting difference between animation languages and programming languages is that the former tend to include primitives for lighting and rendering. For example, animation languages usually have provisions for describing the location and action of a special object: the "camera." Some animation languages have an explicit underlying unit of time, the "frames," corresponding to the individual pictures that are arranged in a sequence on film. To accommodate varying frame rates, other languages describe action in terms of neutral seconds and expect the rendering system to appropriately sample the image. One language issue in scripting languages especially for interactive graphics is the description of motions—especially accelerations and decelerations—in a manner that is independent of the rendering rates. This automation corresponds roughly to the traditional work of in-betweeners but depends on having computational descriptions of the movements of all the elements of a scene. A review of several scripting languages and other aspects of computer animation can be found in Magnenat-Thalmann and Thalmann (1985).

5

Reasoning about Space

When people discuss the breadth of human reasoning abilities, they usually include spatial reasoning. Spatial reasoning is ubiquitous in daily life. People remember where they keep things and put them away. They navigate from place to place. They fit jigsaw puzzles together. They design mechanical devices like engines, whose operation depends on the arrangement and motion of their deliberately shaped parts. Reasoning about space is central to all these activities. Within the context of computer systems, algorithms for machine vision, solid modeling, and robot planning are dominated by concepts of spatial and geometric reasoning.

Does spatial reasoning require specialized representations? In some cases, spatial reasoning can be carried out without a comprehensive model of space. In the folk tale *Hansel and Gretel*, two children do not know their way in the woods. They find their way home by retracing a trail of bread crumbs that they left behind. The environment records the memory of the trail for them; the children perceive the memory as they see and follow the crumbs back home. In this example, much of the reasoning work that might be done with an internal spatial representation is instead off-loaded to objects in the environment and the children's perception of those objects.

Not all spatial reasoning tasks lend themselves to relying on the environment as primary spatial memory. Controlled experiments, both with animals and people, suggest that internal spatial representations are used and perhaps necessary to do many common tasks efficiently, such as rats finding paths in mazes (Tolmen, 1948) or people identifying identical parts from different perspective views (Balsam, 1988).

So what do spatial representations represent? In the preface to his book *Computation and Cognition* (1984), Zenon Pylyshyn wrote:

> We conceive of space as a completely empty, infinite, three-dimensional, isotropic, disembodied receptacle distinct from the earth or any object that might be located on

the earth. . . . Such a strange idea was unthinkable before the seventeenth century; . . . not until Newton was the task of "geometrization of the world" completed.

This "geometrization" is the invention of what is sometimes called Euclidean space or the Cartesian coordinate system. It is the familiar characterization of space in terms of x, y, and z coordinates. Given that a simple coordinate system can represent space, what else is needed?

The representation requirements for spatial reasoning—like the requirements for any kind of reasoning—vary greatly with the particulars of a task. Reasoning about space can involve reasoning about volumes, surfaces, or distances. It can involve reasoning about shapes and intersection. Exactly what is involved is as open-ended as the tasks at hand. Choice of representation is important. Particular representations can make certain computations much more efficient than others. Different representations have different expressiveness. They have different efficiencies for particular kinds of reasoning and scale differently with the number of relationships being encoded.

In the following we consider a sequence of cases involving spatial reasoning. We have arranged the cases to provide a tour of considerations and approaches in supporting spatial reasoning. Our goal is not to provide a prescriptive set of representations. Rather, it is to illustrate fundamental choices one makes in designing spatial representations for knowledge systems.

5.1 *Spatial Concepts*

Euclidean space contributes several concepts that we employ in our discussion of spatial reasoning. We list some of these now, to be explicit about their role in our representations.

Points are atomic locations in space. Depending on the task, the space itself can be represented as being either two-dimensional (2-D) or three-dimensional (3-D). Points are referenced by their coordinates. As with temporal representations, the choice between real and integer coordinates depends on the application. The space as a whole is a set of points. Lengths are one-dimensional measures of distance in space, areas are two-dimensional, and volumes are three-dimensional. A **direction** can be defined as a point on the unit sphere, or a vector from the center of the sphere to some point on its surface. A **region** is a set of points. Two-dimensional rectangular regions, the set of points included in the edges and interior of a planar rectangle, are an important special case.

These spatial concepts are used in maps. For example, zoning regions for city planning are usually shown as superimposed over street maps. Office assignments and phone numbers in an office building are often shown as superimposed on two-dimensional maps of the floors of a building. Route planning is often illustrated in terms of selections over a map of highways and streets. Historically, maps have been sold as paper-based information products. Increasingly, map data are commercially available on computers. Not only are world and region maps available for computer-based browsing, but geographically organized databases also are widely available with which other data can be integrated.

Spatially indexed databases are databases in which location data are used to retrieve information about objects in the database. Such databases are analogous to the temporal databases discussed already, in which time information is used to retrieve information about events. In spatial databases, coordinate information is used to retrieve information about region properties or nearby objects. Spatial databases support spatially oriented queries characteristic of spatial problem solving and typically provide a visual user interface that displays images of the objects in their locations on a map.

In the production and interpretation of maps, certain conventions are used that determine what a map communicates to its users. For example, map data are supposed to be complete relative to the information types being displayed: A street map of a city is supposed to show all the streets. A room map of a building is supposed to show all the rooms. Such conventions support spatial versions of the closed-world assumption (CWA).

The nature and specification of these assumptions is especially crucial when maps are partial, dynamic, and under construction. Consider the construction of maps when people explore new territory or the dynamic world models created in systems for robot perception. In both cases, the maps represent the best-known interpretations of a scene at a given time. These dynamic cases require that the spatial representation include a means for characterizing ambiguity and incompleteness of information.

Here are some representational distinctions related to the closed-world assumptions that arise in maps:

1. *Data completeness:* Can it be assumed that the map shows every object that is in the real-world region represented by the map?

For example, in a map of new wilderness, if no potable streams are shown, does that mean there are none? Does it mean that there are no streams, or that streams are seasonal, or that their potability is in question? When a map is known to be incomplete, it can be useful to have a means to signify that some regions are known not to have certain kinds of objects. Without such notation, there is no way to distinguish the *known absence* of objects from the *absence of knowing* about any objects. Sometimes it is useful to indicate which regions have been explored and which have not. If the map is pieced together from parts by different explorers, then information about which explorers visited each region may be useful in determining what kinds of information may be complete or not in the map.

2. *Object uniqueness:* When can we assume that two separate object descriptions in the map correspond to two different real-world objects?

Suppose two explorers both report seeing ruins, but at somewhat different though close coordinates. Under what circumstances might we decide that they saw the same ruins?

3. *Object piecework:* If only separate parts of what might be one object have been perceived, how can their representations in the map be identified as being possibly (but not definitely) the same object?

Consider a situation where some mountains in one region have been explored by one group and mountains in another region have been explored by another group. Do the mountains make up a single range?

4. *Multiple levels of resolution:* Must all parts of a map present information to the same detail?

Travel maps are sometimes divided into sections with different levels of detail. A travel map for the San Francisco Bay area shows major highways for both sides of the bay and also detailed street maps for San Francisco, San Jose, and Oakland. The highway maps support planning routes between cities and the street maps support it within cities. Not only would a detailed street map of the entire Bay Area be unwieldy, but it also would present more complexity than is needed for planning highway travel.

The use of map sections with different levels of detail supports **hierarchical route planning**. In computer databases, multiple-resolution spatial representations are intended to serve similar needs. A **multiple-resolution spatial representation** is any representational technique that provides spatial information at more than one level of detail. Multiple-resolution representations can reduce the complexity of information that must be processed at the more abstract stages of reasoning, where too much spatial detail would be an unnecessary burden.

5.2 *Spatial Search*

Perhaps the simplest way to represent spatial data is to incorporate them into a relational database along with other data. Consider the following relational table of object names, colors, and coordinates.

Object	Color	Location	Width	Length
A	Red	(1, 5)	4	5
B	Blue	(3, 6)	3	10
C	Green	(2, 4)	6	9
. . .				

If the search to answer a query proceeds sequentially through the list, then the expected time is proportional to the length of the list. In a general-purpose relational database, spatial reasoning has no privileged position. Questions such as "Where is object A?" are answered in the same way as "What color is object B?" Questions such as "Does object A intersect object B?" require reasoning abilities beyond retrieval from the table. Relational and other general-purpose databases provide no particular support for spatial reasoning.

In contrast, suppose you are given a highway map of California and are asked to find the nearest city of more than 15,000 people near Santa Barbara. You would not start searching with Eureka, which is hundreds of miles away. You would probably first locate Santa Barbara on the map and then search through widening circles around its location until reaching a city of the required size.

In this way, the map supports reasoning about distance. Cities that are near each other in California are represented by dots that are near each other on the map. By searching in widening circles, we exploit the structure of the map to guide the search for a city. Computer searches through spatial databases that behave similarly are called spatial searches. A **nearest-first search** is one that considers candidate objects in order of increasing distance from a given object. Nearest-first search finds the closest object to the reference object that satisfies the search criteria. Some search methods approximate the nearest-first order of search.

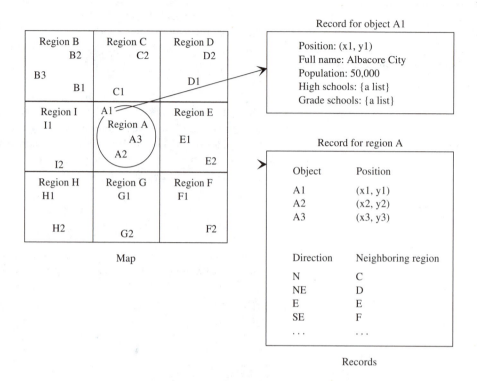

FIGURE 5.1.   A representation that divides space into uniform rectangular regions.

5.2.1 *Simple Nearest-First Search*

The following example illustrates one way to implement nearest-first search in a computer database. Figure 5.1 shows an area divided into equal-size, nonoverlapping regions shaped as Manhattan rectangles. Manhattan rectangles offer economies for representing their boundaries and for computing whether a given point is inside or outside a region. In Figure 5.1 regions are named by letters such as A, B, and C. Objects within the regions are given numbers. Thus A3 indicates an object in region A. The coordinates for each object correspond to its position in the figure.

Each **region** is represented by a record that gives its location, pointers to the records representing neighboring regions, and a list of all the objects contained within the region. One advantage of uniform-size Manhattan regions is that the region records can be kept in an array such that the index of a region record in the array can be computed easily from the region coordinates (see exercise 2). Each object in the region is represented by a record giving its attributes. To provide an efficient means for locating an object's record given the object's name, the names can be organized in records in a balanced tree, a hash table, or another data structure with appropriately low access times.

One way to approximate nearest-first search is to order regions to be searched according to their nearness to a point. Within each region, search through objects is exhaustive in any sequential order. There are two basic policies to be determined:

- What region should be searched next?
- When can searching be terminated?

To motivate the design of a search policy, let us first look at an example. Consider a nearest-first search out from the reference point (or "target") A1 in Figure 5.1. The closest object to A1 is C1 in the neighboring region. A1 is in the upper left quadrant of region A. Intuitively, it makes sense to search region B before searching region D. One way to show this is to observe that every point in the lower right quadrant of region B is closer to A1 (or other points in the upper left quadrant of A) than is *any* point in region D.

This example is suggestive of policies for simple, exhaustive, nearest-first search based on rectangular regions. The next region to be searched should be an unsearched region containing the closest points to the reference point. If no object has yet been found that satisfies the search criteria, then search does not stop until the database is exhausted. If a satisfying object has been found, search terminates when all the unsearched regions contain only points farther away from the reference point than the closest found object.

Figure 5.2 gives pseudocode for a method for simple nearest-first search, SNFS-1. This method is given a reference object and some criteria. It returns the closest object to the reference that satisfies the criteria. If more than one object at the same distance satisfies the criteria, SNFS-1 returns the first object it finds.

The method is similar to best-first search and related methods from Chapter 2. A key to its operation is the function Get.Unvisited.Region, which returns the closest region to the reference (if any) that contains any points closer to the reference than the closest object found so far. In practice, tables can be precomputed that list the nearest neighbor regions given coordinates of the reference point in the current region. For example, given that the reference point is in the upper left coordinate of a region, neighboring regions in the directions W, NW, and N could potentially contain the closest objects.

5.2.2 *Problems with Uniform-Size Regions*

The uniform-region representation in the preceding section divides the total space into nonoverlapping regions that can be searched separately. Spatial search is approximated down to the level of regions. To prevent the exhaustive search of each region from requiring excessive time, there must be enough regions to divide up the objects into small sets.

When an area is divided into uniform-size regions, nearest-first search forces a space/time complexity trade-off. If the objects of interest are distributed nonuniformly, then some regions may have many objects and others will have none at all. This leads to potentially wide variations in retrieval performance. On the other hand, if the entire space is uniformly subdivided to the greatest resolution needed to divide any region, then the representation of a clustered but sparse data set may result in allocating many empty regions. When objects are clustered or otherwise

```
1.    Method Simple.Nearest.First.Search (reference, Criteria)


      /* Initialize */
2.    closest.object := nil; object.distance := VeryBigNumber;
3.    current.region := Region-of(reference)


4.    While current.region do
5.    begin


      /* Search through the objects in the region. */
6.         For object in current.region do
7.           begin
8.             If Criteria(object) and
                    Distance(object, reference) < object.distance
9.             then begin
10.                  closest.object := object
11.                  object.distance := Distance(object, reference);
12.                end
13.   end


14.   Mark.as.Visited(current.region)


      /* Look for another region containing points
      as close as the closest object.*/
15.   current.region:= Get.Unvisited.Region(reference, object.distance)
16.   end


17.   Return(closest.object)
```

FIGURE 5.2.   Method for simple nearest-first search (SNFS-1).

deviate from a uniform distribution, there is a choice between allocating records to represent empty regions and having some regions with too many objects in them.

Another problem with uniform regions arises during updating. If the database is changed dynamically, then adding a few new objects to a region can increase its object population beyond the performance-preserving limit. With uniform regions, the choice again is between having a region with too many objects and reassigning the region boundaries across the entire area.

5.2.3 Quadtree Nearest-First Search

Quadtrees provide a useful alternative for indexing spatial information, accommodating uneven object density and reducing the cost of updating. Quadtrees are regular, recursive decompositions of space into equal-size regions, each of which can be potentially further divided into

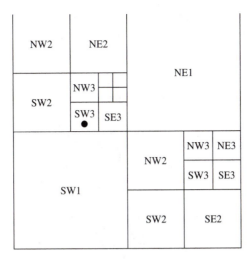

FIGURE 5.3.   A hierarchical quadtree representation that divides space recursively into quadrants. Sub-quadrants are created as needed, to keep the number of objects per region within specified bounds.

equal-size subregions down to some greatest resolution. In the standard 2-D approach, all the subregions are one-fourth of the area of their parent region and are referred to as **quadrants**. To avoid a proliferation of empty quadrants, the division is done only as needed. When the number of objects in a quadrant exceeds a threshold, then the quadrant is subdivided further into sub-quadrants through as many levels as needed to limit the number of objects per region. An example of a quadtree is given in Figure 5.3.

The labels of the quadrants in Figure 5.3 indicate the level of the quadrant and its position in the decomposition of its parent. We use this label notation to explain navigation operations on quadtrees. The four parts of a quadrant are labeled NW (northwest), SE, SW, and NW, corresponding to the directions of the compass. The number indicates the depth in the tree.

Sequences of these quadrant labels are used as addresses of nodes in a quadtree, with the most significant parts on the left. For example, NW1.SE2.SW3 corresponds to the subquadrant in Figure 5.3 with the black-filled circle in it. Although the level numbers are redundant in these strings, we retain them here for clarity. Navigation operations on these addresses are needed for traversing or browsing the quadtree. Here are examples of navigation in Figure 5.3:

    East (NW1.SE2.SW3) = NW1.SE2.SE3
    West (SE1.SE2) = SE1.SW2
    West (NW1.SE2.SW3) = NW1.SW2.SE3
    North (SE1.NW2) = NE1.SW2
    East (SW1) = SE1

Addresses in quadtrees have variable length because quadtrees have variable depth. The interpretation of these addresses in navigation requires handling exceptional cases that do not arise in fixed-length addressing schemes. For example, the length of the addresses returned by the navigation operations is always the same as the length of the given addresses. If the address is too long, meaning that the addressed quadrant has not yet been instantiated to that level, this would be detected while following the address by noticing that the parent has no successors. In that case, retrieval or other reasoning can take place using the larger parent quadrant. If the address is too short, meaning that the addressed quadrant has successors but the address does not specify one of them, then there are other choices depending on the needs of the method. For example, it may be appropriate to search all the successors. (See the exercises for methods for navigation and nearest-first search in quadtrees.)

In summary, quadtrees improve the space/time trade-offs of representing regions with sparse and clustered objects. Although we have discussed quadtrees here only for the case of representing two-dimensional spaces, the generalization to three dimensions is straightforward. In addition, it is possible to divide regions into numbers of subregions other than four, such as nine.

5.2.4 *Multi-Level Space Representations*

Maps sometimes portray different parts of a region in different amounts of detail. To plan a trip from a home in Palo Alto to a restaurant in San Francisco, a visitor might use a street map of Palo Alto to plan a route to the highway, a bay-area highway map to plan the middle part of the trip, and a street map of San Francisco to plan a route from the highway to the restaurant.

This use of different amounts of map detail for different levels in problem solving is a variant of hierarchical search as discussed in Chapter 2, but specialized to spatial representations. In this section we focus on abstractions related to space, such as approximations of location and distance. Figure 5.4 presents some fragments from a database, which is organized in multiple levels of detail. In this example we have a detailed database of the roads, buildings, and rooms in a section of a large city. The database is intended to help people find their way around in the city and may be implemented in portable computers or "personal digital assistants."

The top level of our hierarchical representation is a city street map. A portion of that map is shown in Figure 5.4. The city-street level divides the city area into a grid of regions. Object locations are represented only in terms of the regions in which they are contained. Thus, The New Curiosity Shoppe is in the lower left region. Shapes are not explicitly represented, except insofar as that bounding boxes can be inferred since they are listed in all the regions in which they extend.

The key point about this level is that it shows only the "main objects of interest" for the problems at hand. In our example, the map shows key buildings, key landmarks (such as Murky Lake), and main thoroughfares. Minor streets are not included. The conventions we have chosen in this example are similar to those in many city maps in that we do not show all the buildings, driveways, and so on. The amount of detail is presumably appropriate for the purpose at hand; to guide driving.

The intermediate level of our database, the block map, introduces more detail. The example in Figure 5.4 portrays the information in the block level for the shaded region from the city-street level. This level shows not only the main thoroughfares, but also the side streets, parking lots, and walking paths. The purpose of this level is to provide information to guide parking and walking to the building. All buildings are shown, including those of less immediate interest such as Convenience Pharmacy. Positions and shapes are also shown in more detail. Boundaries of objects are described in terms of bounding polygons. In addition, the data about buildings include height in terms of number of floors.

City Street Map

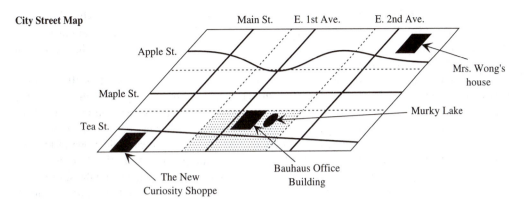

Block Map

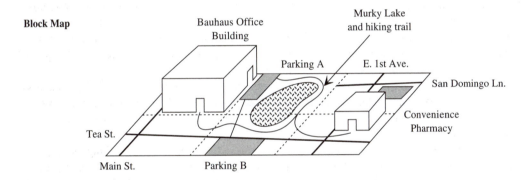

Third-Floor Map

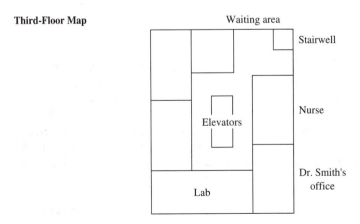

FIGURE 5.4. A multi-level spatial representation.

The most detailed level in our example database is the floor-plan level. Figure 5.4 shows the map of the third floor of the Bauhaus Office Building. This map shows the main places and routes that a visitor walking into the building would want to know about, such as the location of offices, stairways, and waiting rooms.

Consider a route-planning problem where Mrs. Wong is going to Dr. Smith's office for her first appointment. For all practical purposes, the city street map is enough to indicate that the Bauhaus Office Building is too far away for her to walk to it. It is also enough to plan a drive along East 2nd Street and then Tea Street. As Mrs. Wong approaches her destination, it becomes interesting to know about parking data on the intermediate level. She can select one of the two parking lots near the lake. Once she is inside the building, information from the floor-plan level becomes interesting, such as the location of Dr. Smith's office, the elevators, and the stairwell.

The use of multiple levels partitions the concerns of interest in spatial planning. Economy arises from being able to answer common questions using simple methods and "good enough" approximations, descending to greater levels of detail only as needed. In such an arrangement, the amount of detail facing a problem solver at different stages of the process remains roughly constant. When the problem solver is viewing the big map, many details are omitted so the number of objects in the view stays low. At each stage when the problem solver switches to a more detailed map, the region of interest is itself smaller so the total complexity stays low even though more details are shown in the smaller region. By reducing the area while increasing the detail, the problem solver manages the complexity of the view.

Multi-level representations require provisions for annotating the identity of objects across multiple levels. We need to know which symbols at different levels refer to the same physical object. It is sometimes convenient to omit information at a detailed level that has already been recorded at an abstract level.

Using a recursive region representation like a quadtree is not the same thing as having a hierarchical, multiple-level representation. The defining characteristic of a multi-level representation is that it represents different types of objects at each level. Typically, the highest levels in a multiple-level representation are the most abstract and the lowest are the most detailed. A quadtree representation provides a balanced way of allocating storage when objects are distributed unevenly. Each level in Figure 5.4 could be represented using a quadtree database.

5.3 *Reasoning about Shape*

So far our examples of spatial reasoning have emphasized maps and reasoning about routes. Within the context of maps, objects have been represented simply as being at located at points or as being contained within bounding boxes. We have not considered how object shapes could be described.

There is a vast literature about the representation of shape. We can give only a sketch of the ideas behind the main approaches. There are many possible representations of shape and the choice among representations depends, as usual, on the nature of the reasoning task. Figure 5.5 gives examples of four distinct approaches to the representation of shape:

■ *Volume sweeping*. In the first example, a three-dimensional shape is described as the volume swept out by moving a planar figure along a curve. The curves may be described in any number of ways, such as piecewise linear or polynomial expressions. This approach is elegant in its mathematical simplicity. Operations like scaling and translation are simple for this representation, whereas deciding whether figures intersect is potentially difficult.

■ *Volumetric*. The upper right example shows a volumetric approach to describing shape. Graphically, we visualize this one in terms of stacks of identical small blocks or cubes. In principle, the blocks can be arbitrarily small and the shape constructed from them can be quite complex. This representation provides quite simple means of computing volumes and intersecting two shapes constructed this way.

■ *Surface meshes*. The example in the lower left of Figure 5.5 is a surface mesh made of triangles. Meshes are most commonly constructed with triangles and rectangles, although higher-order polygons are sometimes used. Many of the surface points are common to different triangles, affording economies of representation that elide the redundant points. Surface meshes are commonly used in describing shapes to be rendered, as in engineering

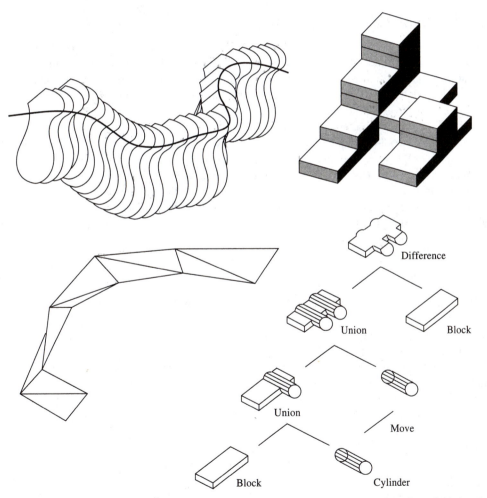

FIGURE 5.5. Examples of defining shape operationally in terms of volumes traced, surfaces folded, volumes integrated, and shapes combined.

design applications and digital special effects for movies. Thousands of mesh points might be used in describing a surface as complex as a human face.

■ *Constructive geometry.* The example in the lower right of Figure 5.5 shows how a shape can be described in terms of operations (union, difference, translation, scaling) on a set of primitive solids (cube, cylinder, cone). In this example, the shape of a pair of binoculars is roughed out. Variations of constructive geometric approaches are sometimes used for describing parts to be machined, especially when there is a simple mapping from the construction operations to machining operations.

Besides the general methods illustrated here, there are special methods for constructing shape descriptions from sampled points of physical objects and methods for transforming or deforming given shapes.

5.4 *The Piano Example: Using Multiple Representations of Space*

Several knowledge systems have been built that reason with space (Chen, 1990; Woodward, 1989), and spatially indexed databases are becoming easily available on personal computers. In comparing human spatial reasoning with current knowledge systems, one feature of human reasoning stands out prominently: flexibility. Computational systems tend to be specialized and quite limited in the questions they can answer. Computational systems tend to have a "competence cliff." If you take a computer system past the edge of its cliff to some slightly different requirements in spatial reasoning, competence falls off precipitously. In contrast, people tend not to have such abrupt cliffs. They manage to combine one form of spatial reasoning with another to approximate an answer. One key to such robust reasoning is the use and integration of multiple representations. In this section we consider an extended example of spatial reasoning about pianos, illustrating several different spatial models. Our purpose is twofold: to show different spatial representations of the same objects and to provide a context for discussing the integration of multiple spatial representations.

5.4.1 *Reasoning for the Piano Movers*

We begin with an example that combines reasoning with shape and route planning. Imagine that a delivery truck containing a piano has just arrived at the Steinway Apartment Building. The truck has a baby grand piano to deliver to Apartment 3-1, which is the first apartment on the third floor of the building. The piano is large and heavy.

Figure 5.6 shows the ground floor of the Steinway Apartment Building and Figure 5.7 shows the third floor. The navigation problem in this example is not particularly difficult. Assuming that the piano fits in the hallways and through the various doors, the movers presumably will just push the piano to the elevator and take it in the front door of the apartment. Figure 5.8 shows some steps in navigating a box around a corner. There is a kind of sliding back-and-forth motion that can be used, familiar to anyone who has parked an automobile.

As an example of human reasoning, the piano-moving example is quite simple. To expose the underlying issues and options for the spatial representation and reasoning, we now consider the steps in more detail.

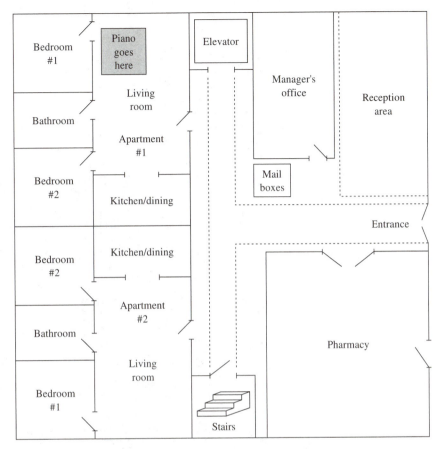

FIGURE 5.6. Floor plan of the ground floor of the Steinway Apartment Building.

In our example, we tacitly treated a baby grand piano as shaped like a box. We might choose a bounding box that is about 4 feet high, 54 inches wide, and about 6 feet deep. We could approximate the box as a little larger to allow room for maneuvering, dolly placement, and so on, as suggested by Figure 5.9. If a box this size fits easily down the hallways and through the doors, then there is little need to develop a more precise representation of the piano's shape. In tighter circumstances, however, the box approximations can be too conservative. For example, the elevator may be big enough to carry the piano but not big enough to allow for a person or dolly behind it. Since the movers do not need to move the piano around inside the elevator during the trip between floors, they could remove the dolly in transit. We could represent the spatial consequences of this by using two approximations of the piano shape: with and without the extra space for the dolly and maneuvering. But even a tighter box-shape can be too conservative. The front doors of apartments are rarely 4 feet wide. Typically, they are 3 feet wide or less. They are seldom less than 30 inches wide, since that is the width of many appliances.

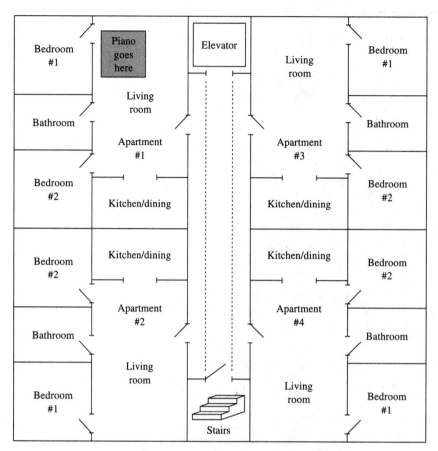

FIGURE 5.7. Floor plan of the third floor of the Steinway Apartment Building, showing where the piano should go.

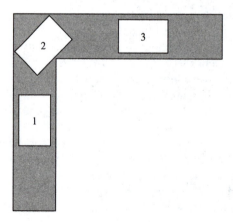

FIGURE 5.8. Getting a box around a corner.

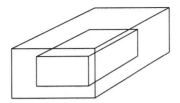

FIGURE 5.9.   Volume approximation of a 3-D region.

Fortunately, grand pianos are not solid from top to bottom. In many designs the body itself is only about 2 feet thick and rests on legs. Figure 5.10 suggests how a piano can be turned on its side and maneuvered through a doorway. A door can easily be removed from its hinges to gain additional space for maneuvering. A computer program limited to representing shapes in terms of bounding boxes would be unable to discover this solution for getting a piano through a doorway.

We now summarize and relate the piano-moving example back to the kinds of shape models introduced earlier. For reasoning about whether the shape of a piano can be maneuvered down a hallway, a volume-sweeping approach could be used, using a cross-section of the piano. However, this approach is not adequate for reasoning about moving a piano around corners or through narrow doorways. Specifically, the description of the shape of a piano does not benefit very much from this approach because the cross-section of a piano is not constant.

Bounding-box approximations provide a first approximation without the complexity of a richer representation of shape. They are conservative. If the piano fits according to the bounding-box approximation of its shape, then it will fit in reality because the actual shape is smaller and contained within the box.

For the part of the example where we fit the piano through a narrow door, as in Figure 5.10, we could use either a volumetric representation or a constructive geometry representation to represent the piano's shape. Either approach would require facilities for reasoning about the outer boundary of the composite shape, not just the separate shapes of the individual parts.

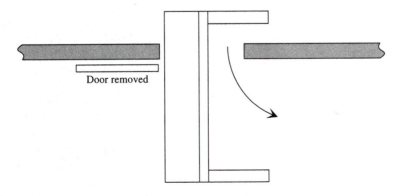

FIGURE 5.10.   Maneuvering a piano through a door.

Restated, it is necessary to be able to reason about the intersection of the outer boundary of the shape with the boundaries of potential containing volumes. It is also necessary to be able to rotate the shape to different positions, searching for a fit.

Throughout this example we implicitly assumed that various elements of commonsense knowledge were integrated with reasoning about shape. For example, we assumed that we could tell which objects were solid and therefore impenetrable and nondeformable. If doorways and walls were made of rubber sheets, different solutions would be possible. We assumed that we could tell which parts moved, such as doors and elevators. We assumed that we could tell which obstacles were removable, such as doors.

Finally, we note that many shape details were not included. The example did not require modeling anything about the insides of the piano, beyond assuming that the insides would not be damaged by rotating the piano. The example also did not require determining the visual appearance of the piano from its outer surface. These areas will be considered as we continue our spatial reasoning examples.

5.4.2 *Rendering a Piano*

We now sketch some of the space representation issues that arise when rendering objects. There is a vast body of literature on this topic, both in computer-aided design and in graphics and animation. As powerful graphics computers become more widely available, many programmers are able to produce 3-D renderings specifying only high-level rendering parameters. This is practical because increasingly the parameters for rendering are supported by special hardware and graphics software.

To begin, consider a view of a piano. Perhaps the most characteristic feature of a piano is its keyboard. There is much repetition in shapes of the white and black keys. In describing the shape of a piano, we are strongly motivated to exploit this repetition by developing a single description of a white key and then using that description for all 52 white keys. Actually, that won't quite work. It turns out that there are 4 different shapes of white keys in a standard piano keyboard. The shape of a white key depends on whether there is a black key to the left or right. All 36 black keys have the same shape.

Figure 5.11 shows a model of the surface of one type of white piano key. As we will see in the next example, there are other parts of a key that extend into the works of the piano. In most rendering systems, an image like this is composed of planar graphics elements. Thus, the top surface of the key is one graphics element. Each edge, side or bottom, is another. Depending on the approach being used, it may be necessary to divide each surface into separate triangles. In that case the top of the piano key would be described in terms of four adjacent, coplanar triangles as suggested by the dashed lines in Figure 5.11.

A typical description for a key like this would be a display procedure, named Draw-WhiteKey1. Consider an origin in 3-space. Each statement of the procedure would be a graphics call to render a surface element—triangle or other mesh shape—at specific coordinates relative to the origin. Thus, it might just be a call to draw a triangle as defined by the coordinates of three points. WhiteKey1 would be invoked by another procedure named DrawKeyboard. DrawKeyboard would call DrawWhiteKey1 once for each place that the key appears in the keyboard. It would call analogous procedures for the variant shapes of white keys and black keys.

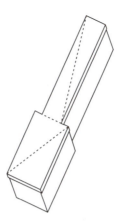

FIGURE 5.11.   3-D surfaces of a piano key.

Prior to each call, DrawKeyboard would reset the graphic origin in the space by pushing a transformation to the graphics transformation stack.

Figure 5.12 shows a picture of a piano. Imagine the appearance of the keys in an actual piano or a sophisticated rendering of one. Some surfaces of the keys are not visible. Many rendering systems have facilities (a "z-buffer") to automatically remove hidden surfaces. From a top-perspective view, for example, only the top of a key and two sides may appear. In a view of a keyboard, the closer surfaces of one key may occlude surfaces of an adjacent key.

FIGURE 5.12.   A piano. A computer program to compute an image like this would need to model not only 3-D space, but also reflections, texture, and shadow.

Even though many keys have the same shapes, differences in position and perspective result in differences in their exact appearance in the figure. One of the high-level parameters in a computer graphics system is the position of the observer, sometimes called the "camera." Thus, it is typical to be able to specify the camera in terms of its position, the direction it is aimed, and also the properties (such as focal length) of the lens that it uses in forming the image.

Another difference in the appearances of the keys is that they have different patterns of brightness and shadow depending on lighting and the images reflected in them. Current graphics systems allow a programmer to specify a range of high-level parameters that affect how these things get rendered, such as positions and brightness of various kinds of lights and reflectivity and transmission properties of all the surfaces. Lighting models interact with the basic shape representations in determining exactly how objects get rendered.

In summary, rendering models combine descriptions of the surfaces of objects with parameters about lighting, perspective, and material to create pictures of objects. The space models in such systems are often written as display procedures. These procedures are specialized spatial representations. They provide exactly the information needed by rendering systems, but they are not directly useful for spatial reasoning about object intersection or volume as in the piano-moving example.

5.4.3   *The Action of a Piano*

The last part of our spatial reasoning examples involving pianos concerns modeling the action of a piano. We use the diagram in Figure 5.13 and an accompanying explanation to discuss in simple terms how a piano works. This is the setup for the discussion that follows. There we consider the issues that arise around these diagrams, related diagrams, and computational representations intended to support reasoning about space and function.

Figure 5.13 gives a diagram of the action of a modern grand piano. The term **action** refers to the mechanical parts of the piano that move when a player depresses the piano keys, ultimately causing a note to sound. Figure 5.14 presents an explanation of a piano action. We now give a partial inventory of the information that is used in the explanation.

- *Solids.* Solid objects have shapes. Solids occupy space. When solids are brought together they push on each other, meaning that they do not interpenetrate. Examples: The end of the key rises and lifts the wippen. The L-shaped jack moves until it hits the regulating button. The hammer bounces off the strings.
- *Bearings and hinges.* Bearings and hinges are special connections on solids that enable them to rotate around a point. Hinges constrain two plane-shaped objects to rotate around a line. Bearings are shown as pins in the diagram. They are the basis for the flying hammer and the rolling roller.
- *Strings.* Strings vibrate at some main frequency when they are struck. The vibration dies down as the strings give off sound energy. Their vibration can be stopped by contact with a cushion, such as the damper.
- *Cushions.* Cushions are objects that deform to a limited extent when they are pushed against other objects. When solids are propelled against cushions, the motion of the solids is stopped. Examples: The padded hammer check prevents the hammer from bouncing back up to the strings. If the damper is not raised above the strings, they cannot vibrate.

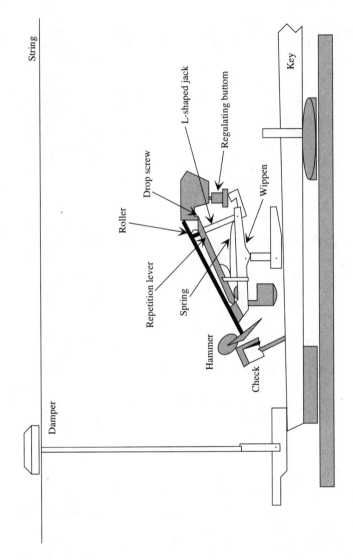

FIGURE 5.13. The action of a modern grand piano.

Explanation of a Piano Action

When a piano key is depressed, it starts a series of mechanical events that propel the hammer to strike the appropriate tuned strings, thus sounding a note. Besides sounding a note, the action also supports rapid repeated striking of a note in cases where there is no time for the hammer to return to its full-rest position.

The mechanical events are as follows: When a key is depressed, its back end rises and lifts the wippen. The wippen raises a pivoted L-shaped jack that slides along a small roller on the underside of the hammer shank, raising the hammer. When the back of the L-shaped jack touches the adjustable regulating button, the roller stops and the hammer flies free to strike the strings. Simultaneously, the upper end of the repetition lever rises until it is stopped by the drop screw. When the hammer rebounds from the strings, the roller falls back until it is stopped by the repetition lever. This enables the tip of the jack to return to position beneath the roller, even if the key is still partially depressed. If the performer restrikes the key before the key returns to rest position, the jack is ready to raise the hammer again.

Other motion is also controlled by the action. The padded hammer check prevents the hammer from bouncing back up toward the strings. Also, a separate lever at the extreme end of the key raises the damper above the strings, allowing them to vibrate.

FIGURE 5.14.   Explanation of the action of a modern grand piano.

▪ *Springs and weights*. Springs and weights are used to apply force. The figure shows a weight attached to the wippen, which is used to give the piano key a certain feel and to return the wippen and key back to their rest positions. Weights apply a constant downward force. Springs apply a negative force in the opposite direction from which they are pushed. This force increases linearly as a spring is pushed. Springs are shown between the various levers of the action, but their exact role is not discussed in the explanation.

This list shows that understanding the workings of a piano involves the interaction of spatial reasoning with mechanical knowledge. This knowledge can be expressed in computational engineering models, which express things such as tension, connection, vibrational frequencies, and so on. The relevant concepts for describing the piano action are part of the subject matter of the science of kinematics, the engineering of mechanics, and the practice of instrument design. Systems for reasoning with such objects, integrating spatial and physical properties, are at the leading edge of the state of the art.

5.5   *Summary and Review*

The most basic spatial representations are spatially indexed databases, in which location data are used to retrieve information about objects in the database. A spatial database is said to be complete in the sense of the closed-world assumption if every object in the real-world region of interest has a corresponding object in the database. To handle spatial data that change dynamically, databases need to distinguish between (1) absence of data about objects in a region and (2) data that objects are absent from a region. More generally, databases should include descriptions of their state of completeness.

Nearest-first search is a search method over databases that considers candidate objects in order of increasing distance from a given object. In the simplest arrangement, space is divided into equal-size regions. Records representing these regions comprise lists of the contained objects as well as pointers to neighboring regions. Uniform regions are inefficient when objects are unevenly distributed in space, such as when they are heavily clustered. For such regions, quadtree representations are preferred. Quadtrees are regular, recursive decompositions of space. Each region of a quadtree can be potentially further divided into equal-size subregions, down to some greatest resolution.

Multi-level spatial databases provide multiple levels of description, which means they present data at different levels of detail. Multi-level databases are effective with hierarchical spatial search because they filter the data, providing only the most relevant information at each stage of the search. Problem solvers can use this capability to control the complexity of their working memory, by increasing detail only as they shrink the area of the region of search.

Many of the choices that arise in representing time also arise in representing space. These choices include discrete versus continuous representations, quantitative versus qualitative metrics, and representations of ambiguity or incompleteness. Representation of shape, however, does not arise in the 1-D case and is a crucial requirement of many spatial reasoning tasks. Many different approaches for representing shape and volume are known, such as volume sweeping, volumetric integration, surface meshes, and constructive geometry. Each approach simplifies some computations but not others.

The piano examples showed how the design of spatial representations depends both on the kinds of spatial reasoning and on the combination of spatial data with other information. Thus the piano-moving example was concerned with operations by which objects occupy and move through space. Spatial reasoning was combined with information about the solidity or impenetrability of objects and also with information about which objects move. The piano-rendering example was concerned with describing the surface of the piano. This information was combined with information about camera position, lighting, and surface textures and reflectivity. Operations included removal of hidden surfaces and computation of lighting effects. The piano-works example described the shapes, locations, and connections of various parts. This was combined with information about materials as well as basic information about mechanics. Thus, although all three examples were about "a piano," there was little overlap in the spatial representations.

Exercises for Chapter 5

Ex. 1   [CD-05] *Terminology*. Indicate whether each of the following statements is true or false. If the statement is ambiguous, explain briefly.

(a) *True or False.* Spatial reasoning tasks inherently depend primarily on internal representations of space or shape.

(b) *True or False.* For nearest-first search over data distributed nonuniformly in space, quadtrees provide better efficiency guarantees than uniform rectangle representations.

(c) *True or False.* Spatially indexed databases are databases in which spatial coordinates are used to index information about objects.

(d) *True or False.* Nearest-first search is a kind of spatial search.

(e) *True or False.* In reasoning about map data, bounding boxes as minimum-enclosing rectangles are often a good first approximation of shape, for the purposes of reasoning about intersection and enclosure of seldom overlapping objects.

■   **Ex. 2**   *[10] Regions as Uniform Manhattan Rectangles.* For many mapping applications, it is convenient to divide regions into nonoverlapping Manhattan rectangles of uniform size. The following questions concern a computer database representing a map divided in this way. In the task at hand, we are given the coordinates of a point within the area and are asked to determine which region contains the point.

(a) Very briefly, describe your approach for representing regions and the data structures and search methods for retrieving the record for a region when given the coordinates for a point within the region.

(b) How does the complexity of your approach scale with the number of regions? (Assume your computer has as much memory as you need and ignore virtual memory effects.)

(c) Briefly, how do our provisions for region representation simplify this computation?

Ex. 3   *[!-15] The Optimality of Nearest-First Search.* After experimenting with a spatial database, Professor Digit began to get suspicious. He was working with queries of the form "Find the object X satisfying predicate P that is closest to reference object O1 in the database." He claims that it is not necessarily the case (even on average) that nearest-first search is the most efficient way to find X. Is he right? Explain your answer briefly with either a short proof or a sketch of a counterexample.

Ex. 4   *[15] Simplifying SNFS-1.* After staring at the pseudocode for SNFS-1, Professor Digit exclaimed, "This method works too hard! All the method needs to do is select regions in order of increasing distance from the reference object. It should search through the objects in those regions in order and quit as soon as it finds one that satisfies the criteria."

Is Professor Digit right? That is, does his revised method do less work and still reliably get the right answer? (If not, explain briefly with a counterexample. If there are ambiguities in his method description that matter, explain your assumptions.)

Ex. 5   *[M-10] Region-Splitting: Creating Subregions in a Quadtree.* Professor Digit is concerned that quadtree representations are inefficient on the grounds that the methods that add new regions to the representations unnecessarily create records representing empty subregions.

Suppose the data insertion method works as follows: When a new object is found, its coordinates are noted, a record describing it is created, and a pointer to the record is added to the quadtree in the region containing the coordinates. If adding the object to the region would bring the total number of objects in the region to greater than k, then the quadrant region is divided into four new subregions and the objects, including the new one, are spread among these subregions.

(a) Assuming the objects are uniformly distributed in the area of the region, what is the probability that k objects will be contained in no more than two of the subregions? Express your answer generally in terms of k, and also compute the numeric probability for the case where $k = 5$.

(b) What is the probability that at least one subregion will contain no objects? Express your answer generally in terms of k, and also compute the numeric probability for the case where $k = 5$. Repeat for $k = 20$. Is it likely that space will be saved by stingily allocating subregions for node splitting when 20 or more objects are in the region?

(c) Briefly describe how a quadtree-based spatial database could reduce the overhead of creating records for subregions. Given the results of parts a and b, under what circumstances would your change to the method be worthwhile?

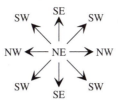

FIGURE 5.15.   Rewrite rules for moving from an NE node in a quadtree.

■   **Ex. 6**   *[15] Navigating in a Quadtree.* The recursive hierarchical structure of a quadtree lends itself to a set of move rules that apply at all levels. This exercise develops a quadtree navigation method that is independent of the node location in the tree and handles heterogeneous region sizes. The method uses a combination of neighbor rewrite rules and parent boundary classifications that are developed in the parts of this exercise. (The method in this exercise was adapted from Antony [1990].)

(a)   Figure 5.15 gives a set of eight nearest-neighbor rewrite rules for starting from an NE node. The rules describe the category of node that would be reached in a given direction if the tree were instantiated to the same level as the given node.

   Give the analogous nearest-neighbor rules starting from aN SE quadrant.

(b)   We now present a method for locating the nearest neighbor. Given a quadtree address and a direction, this method returns a quadtree address. The returned address specifies the resulting node to the same depth as the given node. In any particular quadtree, some nodes may not be expanded yet because they contain no objects. In that case, the excess specifications in the returned address can be discarded.

   Sometimes a move from a node in a quadtree not only leaves the region represented by the node, but also leaves the region represented by the node's parent or grandparent. Figure 5.16 classifies boundary penetrations by the direction of motion and the type of the node. A "null" classification refers to a situation where it is not possible to cross the boundary of a parent.

Direction	Boundary Penetration of Parent Node			
D	NE	NW	SW	SE
North	North	North	Null	Null
South	Null	Null	South	South
East	East	Null	Null	East
West	Null	West	West	Null
NE	NE	North	Null	East
SE	East	Null	South	SE
SW	Null	West	SW	South
NW	North	NW	West	Null

FIGURE 5.16   Classification of boundary penetrations for nearest-neighbor movement.

```
1.      Procedure(X, direction)
2.            For j from 0 to k do
3.            begin
4.                  If direction = null then Y₁₋ⱼ = X₁₋ⱼ
5.                  else begin
6.                        Y₁₋ⱼ := D(X₁₋ⱼ, direction)        /* node rewrite rule */
7.                        direction := P(X₁₋ⱼ, direction)  /* boundary rule */
8.                        end
9.      end
```

FIGURE 5.17. This method for movement in a quadtree returns the nearest neighbor $Y_{i-k} \ldots Y_i$ of node $X_{i-k} \ldots X_i$ in a given direction. Starting with the rightmost part of the address, the method computes a new part of the address with each cycle through the loop. The procedure D refers to the rewrite rules and P refers to the boundary penetration rules.

Using the method given in Figure 5.17, compute the result nodes for each of the following:

(i) West (NE1.SW2.SW3)
(ii) North (NE1.SW2.SW3)
(iii) East (NE1.SW2.SW3)
(iv) East (NE1.SW2.SE3)
(v) South (NE1.SW2.SW3)

■   **Ex. 7**   [*!-05*] *Nearest-First Search in a Quadtree.* In a nearest-first search of a single-level map, the procedure Get.Unvisited.Region takes as its arguments the reference object and object.distance, which is the distance to the closest matching object that has been found so far. Get.Unvisited.Region is called to return the next region to search, if any other regions need searching.

(a) In a flat representation, the criteria for terminating an exhaustive search are as follows:

> If no object has yet been found that satisfies the search criteria, then search does not stop until the database is exhausted. If a satisfying object has been found, search terminates when all the unsearched regions contain only points farther away from the reference point than the closest found object.

Professor Digit says that except for indexing issues in the quadtree, the stopping criteria for searching a quadtree are the same as the stopping criteria for searching a flat representation. Do you agree? Discuss briefly.

(b) Let region R0 contain the reference point. Let Nbrs = {R1, . . . , R8} be a set of regions adjacent to R0 at the same level, all of which are the same size as R0. Suppose further that some of the regions in Nbrs are subdivided into quadtrees to some depth and that others are not, as shown in Figure 5.18.

Suppose objects *w* and *x* are the only ones that satisfy the search predicate. Supposing that the search starts in region R1, which of the other objects would a quadtree search need to test explicitly before terminating? Explain briefly.

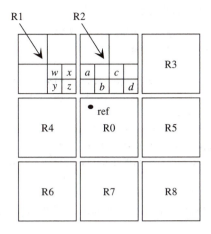

FIGURE 5.18. Quadtree describing a region.

Ex. 8   *[CD-05] "Extrapolating from 1-D."* In a moment of expansiveness in a lecture, Professor Digit turned to his students and said, "Actually, it is silly to treat representations of time and space separately. All we really need to do is take the concepts that arise in the one-dimensional concepts of time and write down the analogous concepts and operations for two- and three-dimensional space." Do you agree? Explain briefly.

    Hint: If you disagree, identify a key concept from spatial reasoning that does not arise in the one-dimensional case.

Ex. 9   *[10] Criteria for Approximating Shape.* Here are some criteria that describe the sense in which an approximation boundary for a shape corresponds to a real shape.

1.   The approximation boundary contains the real boundary.
2.   The approximation boundary is everywhere close to the real boundary.
3.   The real boundary is everywhere close to the approximating boundary.
4.   The areas or volumes of the symmetric difference between the two regions are small.

    For each case in Figure 5.19, indicate which of the criteria are satisfied. If the example is ambiguous, explain briefly. (This exercise is based on examples from Davis [1990].)

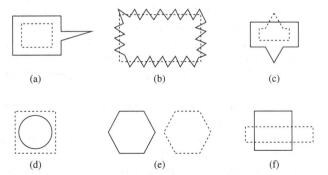

FIGURE 5.19. Real shapes shown with approximating boundaries superimposed. The real shapes are drawn with solid lines, and the approximating shapes are drawn with dashed lines.

5.6 *Open Issues and Quandries*   ADVANCED

In 1990, Jan Koenderink wrote a 700-page book, *Solid Shape*, about concepts for three-dimensional modeling. In the introduction he wrote:

> The subject of "shape" is too enormously varied to treat even superficially in a text like this. I had to be very selective. Some of the more interesting subjects that were left out—taken in random order—are

■ statistically defined shapes, such as textures or foams;
■ regular and quasiregular tesselations of space and surface patches, so-called patterns;
■ arborizations of all kinds;
■ thoroughly crumpled surfaces such as the by now well-known and even popular "fractals";
■ subjects of integral geometry, which are of considerable importance in integral geometrical methods of morphometry;
■ the venerable subject of regular polyhedra . . .

and so on. (p. 9)

The field of solid modeling is the successor to differential geometry. Koenderink was fascinated by all the different ways that shapes might be described, and his book covers many of them. Given that solid modeling is just one aspect of spatial reasoning, his remark about the vast number of topics is rather sobering.

Our broad consideration of spatial reasoning can be little more than a "whirlwind tour" of areas of study, not even a review of basic results. Given the myriad of spatial reasoning topics, to go further requires picking particular areas to focus on. All we can do is mention briefly some of the areas and provide starting points for accessing the literature.

One entry point for understanding spatial reasoning is psychology. Piaget & Inhelder (1967) studied the development of spatial concepts in children, providing an important classification of spatial knowledge into the categories of topological, projective, and Euclidean. A survey of this work and new proposals for the model was produced by Hart and Moore (1973).

Psychological studies of spatial reasoning also include studies of map use. Goldin and Thorndyke (1981) describe experiments including acquiring knowledge from maps versus acquiring knowledge from limited navigation, making spatial judgments from maps, and navigation from memorized maps. A review of human spatial abilities is given in McGee (1979). Kosslyn and Pomerantz (1977) review experiments and theories that relate performance in spatial reasoning to conclusions about internal spatial representations. Classic experiments discussing internal representations, or "cognitive maps," and based on experiments involving rat performance in mazes is reported in Tolman (1948).

Computer systems for spatial reasoning have long been used for computer-aided design. Work in this area ranges from systems that are essentially electronic versions of drafting boards, albeit with three-dimensional models, to programs that solve spatial constraints. Experimental systems performing aspects of automatic layout have been investigated by research architects. At the time of this writing, spatial layout tools capable of perspective drawings are becoming widely available on personal computers. Specialized programs for designing decks or kitchen cabinets are becoming available at hardware stores and cabinet-maker shops. In electrical engineering, spatial layouts of circuit design have been developed and compared, for both multilayer board designs and chip designs.

Computer systems capable of rapidly rendering complex, three-dimensional scenes have dropped in price substantially over the past few years. This has led to the use of such computers in entertainment for creating virtual realities. It has also led to their use in scientific visualization, for helping people to spot patterns in large data sets. Ultimately, interactive three-dimensionsal representations are leading back to psychological studies. Robertson, Card, and Mackinlay (1993) have created systems for information visualization, where a key idea in the design of user interfaces is to shift the "cognitive load" of the user out to his or her perceptual system. The information visualizer uses a number of 3-D presentations as well as animation techniques to help a user stay oriented in an interactive workspace and to make it easier to manipulate data and to find and recognize patterns of interest.

This chapter is about the systematic design
of spatial representations.

6

Reasoning about Uncertainty and Vagueness

Life's issues are not always exact and certain. People frequently and necessarily draw conclusions even when the available information is uncertain, vague, or incomplete. For example:

- A student is waiting to meet a friend for lunch. His friend is seldom late, but it is now 15 minutes later than their agreed-upon meeting time. He considers the lunch-hour traffic conditions and what he knows about his friend's schedule before deciding whether to go ahead and order lunch.

- A newspaper advertisement says that a car on sale has low mileage and looks "like new." A young driver interested in buying a sharp-looking car for less than the price of a new one decides whether to ignore the advertisement, to arrange to see and check out the car, or to phone for more information.

- A doctor is pondering choices in urgent treatment for a patient. Not all of the test data are available, but from what she knows she can recommend a treatment that will probably help and has little health risk.

- A commuter is driving home. He turns on his radio for the traffic report and learns that there is a "fender-bender" (minor accident) and traffic slowdown on his usual route. He has heard no news about traffic conditions for his two alternate routes. The highway turn-off for his first alternate route is just ahead and he will shortly make a choice.

These situations are not extreme or unusual. Every day, each of us draws conclusions and makes decisions without knowing everything relevant, but using the best of what we do know. Our conclusions are based not only on the facts at hand, but also on background and commonsense knowledge, which is knowledge about what is "generally true." Under these circumstances, conclusions are temporary and may be challenged by the arrival of new information.

These examples of reasoning defeat straightforward representation using classical logic because they introduce requirements for expressing vagueness, uncertainty, or incomplete and contradictory information. There are different sources of uncertainty. Here is a partial list:

■ *Unreliable data*. Data could be unreliable or errorful because the means for gathering them are limited or flawed in some way. For example, a measuring instrument may be biased or defective.

■ *Incomplete data*. We may be required to act on the basis of partial data, lacking data that would otherwise improve the reliability or optimality of our choices. For example, laboratory data may be late.

■ *Imprecise data*. The data may be known only approximately. For example, a signal may be sampled frequently enough only for a limited degree of precision.

In decision-making contexts, these issues are compounded when knowledge, goals, and evaluation criteria are also unreliable, incomplete, or imprecise. Thus, not only might the data be imprecise, but also the rules for drawing conclusions may be imprecise.

Knowledge systems in many domains require a means for reasoning with uncertain and inexact information, and much research has gone into formalizing different approaches. Different approaches make different assumptions about the sources and nature of the uncertainty.

Each approach represents something about what is known and what is unknown. Classical approaches such as logic represent what is known. Handling uncertainty requires representing something about the unknown. In the quandaries section, we will see that there are philosophical issues about what it means to "represent" the unknown. When specifics are not known, some generalities and bounds may still be known. By characterizing what is unknown, different approaches also change our sense of "what we know about what we know." They make different assumptions about the nature of what we know.

We next consider numerical methods based on probabilities and also on other approaches. Our goal is to present the basic concepts of the main approaches, discussing fundamentals but not all the variations. Rather than try to cover each approach in detail, we seek to present enough to give a sense of which kind of approach may be most relevant in a particular situation. Section 6.2 discusses fuzzy logic, which is used for representing vagueness rather than uncertainty. The quandaries section and references provide information for pursuing relevant approaches that we cannot cover here, mainly default and nonmonotonic logic.

6.1   *Representing Uncertainty*

We begin with basic concepts about representing uncertainty, and then discuss several of the most important approaches.

6.1.1   *Concepts about Uncertainty*

We now introduce terminology and concepts that underlie many approaches to reasoning with uncertainty. We give more technical definitions in the sections immediately following.

Knowing by Degrees

"Knowing" is not generally something that comes all at once as a kind of enlightened gestalt. We know things by bits and pieces. In knowledge systems, the bits and pieces correspond to separate statements about what we know.

Approaches to reasoning with uncertainty build on standard representational techniques. Some methods build on familiar concepts from logic such as propositions, predicates, quantifiers, and so on. For other approaches a formulation in terms of objects and their properties is preferred to express properties for classes as well as for individuals.

Object and logical representations represent facts and relations that are *visible and explicit* in the reasoning model. In contrast, representations of uncertainty, such as probabilities, represent facts and relations that are *invisible and implicit*, which means they represent unknown factors and exceptions. For example, when we say only that "It is April, so the chances of rain today are 60 percent," we are not saying what the forces are that determine rain—whether it has to do with warm air masses, moisture, or rain dances. From the perspective of someone looking at our representations, the "causes" are invisible. All that is present is a summary statement about belief and conditions. Most approaches to representing uncertainty start with standard representations and then modify and extend them to accommodate invisible and unknown background information.

The term **evidence** refers to the reasons that propositions are believed. Evidence per se is not a concept from logic. However, evidence plays a role in approaches to reasoning that honor the idea that truth can only be approximated through the gathering and combination of observations that support or defeat competing beliefs. A key step in increasing certainty or precision is to gather new relevant and discriminating evidence that can be combined with what is known already.

Issues in Defining Probability   ADVANCED

There is a philosophical debate about the meaning and interpretation of probabilities. Some argue that probability has nothing to do with the odds of the San Francisco Forty-niners winning their next game. Of course, people do attach numerical quantities to events to guide their betting behavior. Probabilities that represent an individual's beliefs are said to be **subjective**, as opposed to definitions based on mathematical objects, which are said to be **objective**. In the following we consider the definition of probability in terms of belief, relative frequency, and ratio. All three concepts have been called probability. Following Neapolitan (1993b), we begin by defining them separately here.

Definition 1: Ratios. Suppose there is a finite set Ω with n elements and that E is a subset of Ω with k elements. Then the **ratio** of the number of elements in E to the number in Ω is

$$r(E) = \frac{k}{n}$$

In the literature, ratios are sometimes called logical probabilities. The following properties of ratios follow from their definition.

$$r(\Omega) = 1$$
$$0 \le r(E) \le 1$$
$$r(E \cup F) \le r(E) + r(F)$$
$$r(E \mid F) = \frac{r(E \cap F)}{R(F)}$$

where $r(E \mid F)$ means the fraction of elements in F that are also in E. These properties are the same as the axioms of probability and the rule for conditional probability as developed by Kolmogorov. Ratios are objective in the sense that we can agree easily about their properties.

Definition 2: Converging Frequencies. Let an experiment be repeatable (at least in theory) an infinite number of times. Let E be a possible outcome of the experiment. The relative frequency of the occurrence of E is given by

$$f(E) = \lim_{n \to \infty} \frac{S_n(E)}{n}$$

where $S_n(E)$ is the number of times outcome E occurs in n repetitions of the experiment.

Suppose we repeatedly toss a coin. The outcome E can be the number of times the coin comes up with heads on top. The quantity $f(E)$ is the limiting value of the number of occurrences of heads divided by the number of coin tosses.

It is not necessarily the case that the relative frequency of an experiment will converge to a limit. For example, it could appear to approach one limit, and then shift to another, and then to another in a chaotic manner. A pragmatic approach is to note that the Kolmogorov axioms follow if we assume that the relative frequency converges and that the sequence generated is random, as suggested by Neapolitan (1990). In this way relative frequencies can be treated as objective. Restated, the use of relative frequencies about probability is not a philosophical constraint imposed on nature. Rather, the approach is applicable exactly when it works.

Suppose we perform an experiment. There may be great or little disagreement about whether a frequency stabilizes. Some might say that if we performed the experiment a few more times, some "destabilized" behavior might appear. In principle, there is no way to know. The sun might not rise tomorrow. In practice, however, after the experiment and careful analysis, some of us may believe strongly in a value for a relative frequency. In this way, the concept of **belief** enters the discussion. Ratios and relative frequencies do not themselves choose a course of action. They only describe physical phenomena. When we generalize the results of experiments and interpret the results using probability theory, we arrive at a belief to guide our actions. This brings us to the third definition.

Definition 3: Belief. Let E be a statement that is true or false or that will turn out to be true or false in the future.

$$b(E) = \text{"how strongly a person feels } E \text{ is true."}$$

For the moment, we assume that $b(E)$ is a function with a value between 0 and 1. This "belief function" approach has properties different from ratios and frequencies. For example, a belief is a property of a single event and a relative frequency is a property of an entire sequence of trials. Another difference here is that different persons can have different beliefs.

The term **certainty** refers to a **degree of belief** in something. For example, we may say that we believe (.5) that it will rain today. This statement does not mean we expect a half of a rainfall, such as a light or medium rainfall. Either it will rain or it won't. Uncertainty refers to the degree that we believe it will rain versus the degree that we believe it will not rain.

Exactly how a person obtains a belief or how a person's belief can be measured is a vast subject with many philosophical pitfalls. Some philosophers have argued for defining belief in terms of fair betting odds. Others object, saying that talk about betting diverts our attention to extraneous questions and social consequences of our actions. The "constructive" view involves the use of frequencies, even frequencies from "thought experiments" for unrepeatable experiments. The interested reader is referred to Neapolitan (1993b) for a discussion of the relation between the definition of belief and definitions of ratio and converging frequency.

Basic Concepts of Probability

Classically, probability is defined in terms of a set of mutually exclusive and exhaustive outcomes, Ω, called the sample space. A set of subsets of Ω, F, is defined such that

1. $\Omega \in F$
2. $E_1 \in F \wedge E_2 \in F \rightarrow E_1 \cup E_2 \in F$
3. $E \in F \rightarrow \sim E \in F$ where $\sim E$ denotes the complement of E

Restated, F is a subset of Ω closed under union and complementation. F is called a set of events relative to Ω. Finally, for each event $E \in F$, there corresponds a real number, $P(E)$, called the **probability** of E. From these definitions we can lay out some properties of probability. In some approaches, these properties are given as the defining characteristics of a probability distribution.

$$0 \leq P(A) \leq 1 \tag{1}$$
$$P(\text{certain event}) = 1 \tag{2}$$
$$P(A) + P(\sim A) = 1 \tag{3}$$

Together, the second and third rules tell us that the sum of the probabilities of all possibilities is 1.

In the following we consider basic concepts of probability. In our examples we use either converging frequencies or ratios, depending on what is convenient. To model decision-making behavior, we assume that subjective measures are available. For the most part we do not consider in depth how it is that one measures subjective beliefs, but merely assume that it is done in some appropriate and rational manner that follows the rules of objective probability.

Consider a pair of dice, each side of which is labeled from 1 to 6. When a fair die is cast a large number of times (N), the number of times that each side will come up will be close to $N/6$. Let A be the event that a die stops with 1 showing on the top. We say that the probability of event A, denoted $P(A)$, is 1/6. In the case of a die, this means that, on average, a side will come up one time in six throws. The probability that any of the other sides will come up instead is $P(\sim A) = 5/6$.

Let B be the probability that the die comes up 2. The probability in a given throw that either 1 or 2 comes up is $P(A) + P(B) = 2/6$. More generally, we have the additive law:

Additive law: $P(A \vee B) = P(A) + P(B) - P(A \wedge B)$ (4)

This additive law can be understood in terms of Venn diagrams. By itself, the expression $P(A) + P(B)$ would count twice those events where A and B are both present. The equation corrects for this by subtracting $P(A \wedge B)$. In the case of a die, the events A and B are mutually exclusive since only one side can come up on top. For mutually exclusive events, the term $P(A \wedge B)$ is zero.

When a probability space is created, we call the probabilities that are known based only on the initial information **a priori** or **prior probabilities**. The literal meaning of *a priori* is independent of experience. In practice, the term refers to probabilities based on the initial information for the population of events that are of interest. Probabilities based on additional information are called **conditional probabilities**.

Consider now events involving two different dice. Suppose, for example, that event A corresponds to die one coming up 1 and event B corresponds to die two coming up 1. We can ask what is the probability of getting both events A and B (or "snake eyes") when we throw the two dice. This is expressed by the multiplicative law as follows:

Multiplicative law: $P(A \wedge B) = P(A, B) = P(A) P(B)$ (5)
if A and B are independent

The notation $P(A, B)$ is just an alternative way of writing $P(A \wedge B)$. This special case is known as **marginal independence**. In the general case where A and B are not independent, the law is more complex as follows:

Multiplicative law: $P(A \wedge B) = P(A) P(B|A)$ (6)

where $P(B|A)$ means the probability of B given A, or the probability of A when B is known with absolute certainty. The quantities $P(A|B)$ and $P(B|A)$ are conditional probabilities. In traditional practice, these are defined as equation (7):

$P(A|B) = P(A, B)/P(B)$ (7)
$P(H|E) = P(H, E)/P(E)$ (7′)

Equation (7′) says the same thing but uses the common notation where H is a hypothesis and E is evidence bearing on it. Figure 6.1 illustrates equation (7) and the differences in odds between independent and dependent events. Figure 6.2 uses the equations to show how our estimates of conditional probabilities depend on what we know. Conditional probabilities are useful for organizing knowledge. In this interpretation, B stands for a context or body of knowledge and $A|B$ stands for the event A in the context B.

Bayes' Rule

The problem with the use of equation (7) as a diagnostic rule for determining $P(H|E)$ is that the probabilities $P(H, E)$ are often not available. Bayes' rule is an inversion formula that relates $P(H|E)$ to other probabilities:

Bayes' rule: $P(H|E) = P(H) P(E|H)/P(E)$ (8)

Case 1

We are given an urn with 5 red balls and 5 green balls. Two times we do the following: Pick a ball from the urn, note the ball's color, return it to the urn, and mix the balls in the urn.

What is the probability that we pick a green ball 2 times?

Solution:

This version of the problem is called "selection with replacement." Each event is independent. Each time we pick a ball from the urn, half the available balls are green, so there is a 0.5 probability that the selected ball will be green. The probability of doing this two times is:

P(picking 2 green balls) $= 0.5^2 = 0.25$

Case 2

We are given an urn with 5 red balls and 5 green balls. Two times we do the following: Pick a ball from the urn, note the ball's color, and lay down the ball next to the urn.

What is the probability that we pick a green ball 2 times?

Solution:

This version of the problem is called "selection without replacement." The events are not independent because the number of balls left in the urn is diminished each time. The probability of the first ball being green is the same as before:

P(selecting 1st green ball) $= 0.5$

Now there are 4 green balls and 5 red balls left. The probability of picking a second green ball at this time is:

P(2nd green ball) $= 4/9 = 0.444$

The probability of both events happening is:

P(picking 2 green balls) $= 0.5 * 0.444 = 0.222$

This computation reflects the multiplicative law:

Multiplicative law: $P(A \wedge B) = P(A) P(B|A)$

FIGURE 6.1.   Independent versus dependent events.

This rule states that the belief in a hypothesis H given evidence E is computed by multiplying the prior belief in the hypothesis, $P(H)$, by the probability $P(E|H)$ that E will happen if H is true. From the perspective of formal mathematics, equation (8) is a tautology derived from the definition of conditional probabilities in equation (7). To a Bayesian, however, equation (8) is more basic and fundamental: It is a rule for updating belief measures in response to evidence.

Some variations on this rule are useful in solving probability problems. These can be derived simply from the preceding equations (see the exercises).

$$P(E) P(H|E) = P(E|H) P(H) \tag{9}$$
$$P(E) = P(E|H) P(H) + P(E|\sim H) P(\sim H) \tag{10}$$

Case 3

We are given an urn with 5 red balls and 5 green balls. A ball is selected, its color is noted, and it is set aside. We are told that the ball is green.

What is the probability that the second ball we pick is green?

Solution:

$$P(\text{2nd ball green} \mid \text{1st ball green}) = P(B|A) = 4/9 = 0.444$$

Case 4

We are given an urn with 5 red balls and 5 green balls. A ball is selected, its color is noted, and it is set aside. We are not told what color the ball is.

What is the probability that the second ball we pick is green?

Solution:

There are two cases: Either the first ball was red or it was green. The probability that the second selected ball is green is the sum of the probabilities of those two cases.

$$P(\text{2nd ball green}) = P(\text{2nd green} \mid \text{1st ball red}) + P(\text{2nd green} \mid \text{1st ball green})$$
$$= \tfrac{5}{9} * (0.5) + \tfrac{4}{9} * (0.5) = 0.5$$

Note that the difference between cases 3 and 4 reflects the state of our knowledge. We simply do not know whether the first ball was red or not. Since the first ball could be red as often as it could be green, there are more possible outcomes that are not ruled out and the probability is higher.

FIGURE 6.2. Conditional probabilities.

Figure 6.3 gives an example of using Bayes' rule and these other formulas to answer some basic probabilistic questions. In many applications of Bayes' rule, data are gathered incrementally and pooled. Let $E = E_1, E_2, \ldots, E_n - 1$ correspond to the set of data collected so far and E_n be a new datum. One way to compute revisions in the belief in H, $P(H|E, E_n)$, would be to perform a global computation on the entire data set $\{E, E_n\}$. As n increases, the computation of $P(H \mid E, E_n)$ becomes increasingly complex (see the exercises). Under some circumstances the computation can be simplified by recursive and incremental updating as in equation (11).

$$P(H \mid E, E_n) = P(H \mid E) \, P(E_n \mid E, H) \, / \, P(E_n \mid E) \tag{11}$$

In this formulation, the old belief $P(H \mid E)$ for $n - 1$ assumes the role of a prior probability in the computation, since it summarizes the past experience.

Combining Evidence and Updating Beliefs

Many reasoning tasks require expressing and simultaneously considering a possibly contradictory set of beliefs or possibilities. From the given set of beliefs, others may be derived. Beliefs also may be revised as new evidence becomes available. The overall processes are called belief updating and evidence combination. The two parts to belief updating are revising propositional beliefs and revising the certainty information about those beliefs. Each approach to reasoning

Definitions

    $P(H)$ = the probability that a person has the flu

    $P(E)$ = the probability that a person has a fever

    $P(E|H)$ = the probability that a person has a fever given that he has the flu

    $P(E|\sim H)$ = the probability that a person has a fever given that he does not have the flu

Suppose we are given:

    $P(H) = .0001$ $P(E|H) = .80$ $P(E|\sim H) = .1$

Q1: What is $P(E)$?

That is, what is the a priori probability that someone has a fever?

    $P(E) = P(E|H)\ P(H) + P(E|\sim H) * P(\sim H)$

    $P(E) = .80 * .0001 + .1 * (1-.0001) = .00008 + .09999 = .10007$

Q2: What is $P(H|E)$?

That is, what is the probability that someone has the flu if he has a fever?

    $P(H|E) = P(H)\ P(E|H)/P(E)$

    $P(H|E) = .0001 * .80/.10007 = .0007994$

Q3: What is $P(H|\sim E)$?

That is, what is the probability that someone has the flu if he does not have a fever?

    $P(H|\sim E) = P(\sim E|H)\ P(H)/P(\sim E)$

    $P(H|\sim E) = (1 - .80) * .0001/(1-.10007)$

    $P(H|\sim E) = .2 * .0001/.89993 = .0000222$

FIGURE 6.3.   An example of using Bayes' rule.

with uncertainty provides a calculus, or **rules of combination,** for both propositional information and uncertainty information.

Decreasing the amount of uncertainty is a key goal in some tasks. For example, in selecting readings or tests in diagnostic tasks, the goal in a case is roughly to decrease the overall uncertainty in the diagnostician's knowledge of what could be wrong. This is done by selecting measurements or data that are most effective in reducing the overall uncertainty when combined with existing data. In these approaches, uncertainty or "information entropy" is measured in terms of the set of open diagnostic hypotheses.

Suppose we have two mutually exclusive propositions A and B in a domain, both supported by sets of evidence, A_E and B_E. Let E_{1a} and E_{2a} be two items of evidence that support A. Suppose we already know E_{1a}. When is it the case that obtaining E_{2a} decreases our uncertainty about whether A or B is true?

To make the issue of increasing or decreasing certainty concrete, consider the example in the domain rules of Figure 6.4. Suppose we learn that Jessie watched all the bowl games this season. Eliding some details, we might use Rule$_4$ to conclude that football is his favorite sport with certainty .7. If we are then told that he watched the Super Bowl, we could consider invoking Rule$_5$. Arguably, however, Rule$_5$ should not decrease our uncertainty because the information is redundant with what we already know. Restated, the Super Bowl is just one of the bowl games that we know that Jessie watched. Since we have not learned anything new, the certainty of the

---

Propositions
A: Jessie's favorite sport is baseball.
B: Jessie's favorite sport is football.

Rules
Rule 1:   If someone is observed playing a sport, then that sport is his favorite sport (.3).
Rule 2:   If someone is on the school team for a sport, then that sport is her favorite sport (.8).
Rule 3:   If someone always watches the World Series, then baseball is his favorite sport (.7).
Rule 4:   If someone watches all the bowl games near New Year's Day, then football is her favorite sport (.7).
Rule 5:   If someone watches the Super Bowl, then football is his favorite sport (.2).
Rule 6:   If someone announces her favorite sport, then her announcement actually is her favorite sport (.99).

FIGURE 6.4.   Possible propositions and judgmental rules for determining someone's favorite sport.

conclusion should not increase. The new information is **dependent** on the old information. In contrast, if we are told that Jessie is on the school football team or that he has told someone what his favorite sport is, that information is conditionally independent.

This distinction between dependent and independent sources of information arises in all approaches to uncertainty. For example, the notion of independence and nonindependence of events is inherent to probability theory. In probability theory, events are **independent** if knowledge about one of them has no bearing on our assignment of probabilities to the other. For example, in flipping a coin believed to be fair, knowledge of the results of the previous coin flip has no bearing on predicting the results of the next flip. Coin flips are independent. In contrast, consider picking cards from a fair poker deck of 52 cards. Suppose we are asked each time to predict the suit of the next card. As more cards become known, we know more and more about the next card. As an extreme, after we have picked (and somehow remember) 51 cards, we already know the identity of the remaining card even though we have not turned it over. Thus, these card-picking events are dependent.

The notion of independence is sometimes associated with a causal connection between the events. In diagnostic models, two measurements are treated as distinct and independent only if readings from them are significantly different in pruning the space of diagnostic hypotheses. In symbolic reasoning approaches, one proposition is dependent on another if the former is derived from the latter. Thus, there are several related notions of "dependence" grounded in different principles such as knowledge, causality, diagnostic pruning power, and derivability. Given these basic concepts and distinctions, we now consider particular approaches to reasoning with uncertainty or inexactness in more detail.

6.1.2   *The Certainty-Factor Approach*

Perhaps the most widely known approach to representing uncertainty in AI is the use of certainty factors (CFs) as developed for the MYCIN and Emycin systems (Buchanan & Shortliffe, 1984). This section presents the basic ideas of the approach.

Concepts of Certainty Factors

Certainty factors are used in two ways. Every hypothesis and intermediate parameter is stored with an associated certainty factor. The certainty factor associated with a hypothesis stands for the degree of belief, given all the evidence that has been used so far. The second use of certainty factors is in the rules. The certainty factor for a rule indicates the knowledge provider's degree of belief that the conclusion follows from the rule's premise. The following rule is representative:

> IF: 1) The stain of the organism is gram positive, and
>   2) the morphology of the organism is coccus, and
>   3) the growth conformation of the organism is chains
> THEN: There is suggestive evidence (0.7) that the identity of the organism is
>   streptococcus.

Roughly, this rule says that if the conditions about stain, morphology, and growth conformation are met, then we can be 0.7 certain about the identity of the organism. More precisely, the 0.7 is interpreted as information for updating belief rather than as a measure of absolute belief. In the following we will say more about the accounting of certainty and the assumptions of knowledge modularity underlying this approach, but for now we make a few orienting observations. The strength of a conclusion resulting from the execution of a rule reflects both the CF assigned to the rule and the determined degree of belief in the rule's premise. When several rules favor a single hypothesis, the resulting support is determined incrementally using combining functions described in the following.

The certainty-factor approach is explained in terms of a personal or subjective degree of belief in the hypothesis H, denoted $P(H)$. Following probability theory, this degree of belief ranges from 0 to 1. Observation of evidence E can change the expert's degree of belief. For example, $P(H|E)$ greater than $P(H)$ means that observation of E increases the expert's belief in H while decreasing his disbelief in it.

Three measures of certainty underlie the philosophical grounding of the certainty-factor approach: MB, MD, and CF. $MB(H, E)$ is a measure of increased belief in H resulting from E. $MD(H, E)$ is a measure of increased disbelief in H resulting from E. $CF(H, E)$ combines MB and MD into a single numeric measure, which ultimately is the only one used in the computational model. In equations (12) through (14), we first define these measures in terms of $P(H)$.

If $P(H) = 1$, $MB(H, E) = 1$.
Otherwise, $MB(H, E) = [\max[P(H|E), P(H)] - P(H)]/[1 - P(H)]$. $\quad\quad\quad$ (12)

If $P(H) = 0$, $MD(H, E) = 1$.
Otherwise, $MD(H, E) = [\min[P(H|E), P(H)] - P(H)]/[0 - P(H)]$ $\quad\quad\quad$ (13)

$CF(H, E) = MB(H, E) - MD(H, E)$ $\quad\quad\quad\quad\quad\quad\quad\quad\quad\quad\quad\quad$ (14)

From these definitions, we can see that both MB and MD range from 0 to 1 and that CF ranges from −1 to 1. If H is certain, then MB = 1, MD = 0, and CF = 1. If the negation of H is certain, then MB = 0, MD = 1, and CF = –1. When $P(H) \approx 0$, the a priori belief in a hypothesis is small. In this case,

$$CF(H, E) = MB(H, E) - MD(H, E) = [P(H|E) - P(H)]/[1 - P(H)] - 0 \approx P(H|E)$$

In other words, the CF of a hypothesis confirmed by evidence is approximately equal to its conditional probability on that evidence.

Combining Evidence and Updating Beliefs

Even though the certainty-factor approach is similar in many ways to a probabilistic approach, in most examples of its use the probabilities that would be needed are not available from formal studies. In practice, the CF numbers obtained from experts are assumed to be adequate approximations to the numbers that would be computed for MB and MD if the probabilities were known. Given that practice, there are further approximations in the method whose appropriateness depends on the domain being well behaved in certain ways. Suppose evidence E_1 and E_2 are encountered and that they confirm H. Using the definitions in equations (12) through (14), we have

$$
\begin{aligned}
CF(H, E) &= MB(H, E) - 0 = [P(H|E) - P(H)]/[1 - P(H)] \\
CF(H, E) &= [P(H|E_1 \& E_2) - P(H)]/[1 - P(H)]
\end{aligned}
\tag{15}
$$

It would be convenient at this point to compute $CF(H, E_1 \& E_2)$ from $CF(H, E_1)$ and $CF(H, E_2)$. Restated, we would like to compute $CF(H, E_1 \& E_2)$ from $CF(H, E_1)$ and $CF(H, E_2)$ that would "come close to what is needed if all the conditional probabilities were known." Unfortunately, there is no universal relationship for this that always works. One assumption would be that the events are independent. However, in principle, a domain could even include rules such that either E_1 or E_2 by itself confirms a given hypothesis but that their conjunction disconfirms it. There is a deep issue underlying this point, namely that the logic of confirmation has no inherent connection with the logic of probability. Thus, the combining functions depend on a domain being well behaved, which means that the events E_1 and E_2 can be treated as independent and that there are no aberrant rules. We return to this issue in the exercises.

We now turn to the certainty-factor combining functions that make up the approximations used in practice. A key feature is that the rules of combination are symmetric in their treatment of MB and MD and commutative with regard to the order that evidence is considered. This makes it unnecessary to partition evidence into positive and negative weights. Using this scheme, it is enough simply to store the cumulative CF and to combine it with new evidence as it becomes available.

We begin with equation (16), an expression for combining evidence from multiple sources. For simplicity in the expression, we let $X = CF(H, E_1)$ and $Y = CF(H, E_2)$. Roughly, this rule says that since a certainty factor represents a proportionate decrease in disbelief, the CF of a newly acquired piece of evidence should be applied proportionately to the disbelief still remaining. See the exercises for an alternative and earlier version of this function.

If both $X, Y > 0$:
$$\text{CF}(H, E_1 \& E_2) = X + Y(1 - X)$$
If one of $X, Y < 0$:
$$\text{CF}(H, E_1 \& E_2) = (X + Y)/[1 - \min(|X|, |Y|)]$$
If both $X, Y < 0$:
$$\text{CF}(H, E_1 \& E_2) = X + Y(1 + X) \tag{16}$$

Equations (17) and (18) give expressions for determining the certainty factor for a conjunction of hypotheses and a disjunction of hypotheses, respectively. Equation (17) says the measure of belief in the conjunction of two hypotheses is only as strong as the belief in the hypothesis least strongly confirmed. Equation (18) says the measure of belief in the disjunction of two hypotheses is as strong as the belief in the one most strongly confirmed.

$$\text{CF}(H_1 \wedge H_2, E) = \min[\text{CF}(H_1, E), \text{CF}(H_2, E)] \tag{17}$$
$$\text{CF}(H_1 \vee H_2, E) = \max[\text{CF}(H_1, E), \text{CF}(H_2, E)] \tag{18}$$

When rules are composed, the conclusions of one rule become the evidence for the next one in the chain. In these chains, the certainty associated with a piece of evidence must enter into the certainty equations for further conclusions. Let E_1 be a hypothesis supported by evidence E and H be a hypothesis that can be derived from E_1 by a given rule. If CF′ is the weight that would be used in the case that E_1 were known with certainty, then CF as given in equation (19) gives the revised weight. Restated, the CF of the rule is reduced simply by multiplying it by the known weight of the evidence. Figure 6.5 presents equations (16) through (19) in graphical form.

$$\text{CF}(H, E) = \text{CF}'(H, E_1) \max[0, \text{CF}(E_1, E)] \tag{19}$$

Figure 6.6 gives an example of the use of these rules, where the certainty of hypothesis D must be computed from that of evidence A and B, which is given as certain. Figure 6.7 gives another example, showing how the combination rules for conjunctions and disjunctions are combined with the strength of evidence rule in practice. In the certainty-factor approach, the accounting of certainty permeates all reasoning. The certainty factor of each rule is combined with certainty factors of the evidence used in the rule's premise to infer conclusions also annotated with certainty factors.

MYCIN incorporated a pragmatic 0.2 threshold to avoid pursuit of low-likelihood hypotheses. For example, evidence gathering in MYCIN takes place through backward chaining through rules that query the user for more data. This chaining is blocked, however, when the certainty of evidence cannot exceed 0.2. In that case, the results of this inquiry could have only a limited impact on the value of the current subgoal. Thus, this heuristic threshold was used to prune the expansion of chains of reasoning that could have little effect even if they were true.

Applicability of the Certainty-Factor Approach

As we noted earlier, the utility of probability theory for modeling reasoning with uncertainty is limited by practical difficulties. The main difficulty is the lack of sufficient data to accurately estimate the prior and conditional probabilities required to use Bayes' rule. The certainty-factor approach sidesteps these difficulties by using expert-estimated certainty factors in lieu of mea-

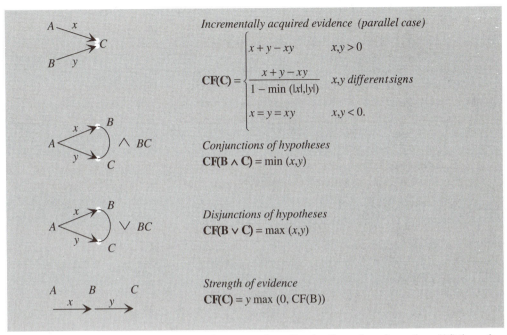

FIGURE 6.5. A summary of the certainty-factor equations. See the discussion of equations (16) through (19) for more details.

sured frequencies and by using a calculus of certainty combination that assumes conditional independence and requires far fewer numbers. This raises the following questions: What problems with the model have arisen? What limitations of its applicability are known? How well does the method work in practice?

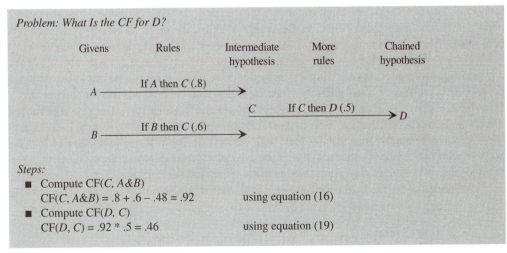

FIGURE 6.6. An example of using certainty factors.

Problem: What Are the CFs for W and Z?

Givens	Rules	Intermediate Hypothesis
A (0.7)	if $A \wedge B$ then W (.8)	

$\longrightarrow W$

| B (0.8) | If $B \vee C$ then Z (.7) | |

$\longrightarrow Z$

C (.09)

Steps:

■ Compute CF $(A \wedge B, A\&B)$
  CF$(A \wedge B, A\&B)$ = min$(0.7, 0.8)$ = 0.7   using equation (17)

■ Compute CF $(W, A \wedge B)$
  CF $(W, A \wedge B)$ = 0.7 * 0.8 = 0.56   using equation (19)

■ Compute CF$(B \vee C, B\&C)$
  CF$(B \vee C, B\&C)$ = max $(0.8, 0.9)$ = 0.9   using equation (18)

■ Compute CF$(Z, B \vee C)$
  CF$(Z, B \vee C)$ = 0.7 * 0.9 = 0.63   using equation (19)

FIGURE 6.7.   A second example of using certainty factors.

Early in the MYCIN project it was noticed that the method for combining evidence from multiple hypotheses causes cumulative CFs to increase, even for small CFs. No matter how small the CFs in the rules are, if there are enough rules the cumulative CF of their conclusion converges toward 1 (see the exercises). In applications where many rules are used in ways to derive conclusions, this leads to situations where too many conclusions seem to be derived. It has been suggested that certain ad hoc "damping factors" could be used to reduce this problem. Fundamentally, however, this problem is indicative of deep underlying assumptions in the model about modularity and independence. In the case of MYCIN, the model does not founder on this potential difficulty because its chains of reasoning are short and the hypotheses are simple.

If we look at the methods for combining certainty information, it is instructive that they apply to any two production rules in the knowledge base, without regard to what other rules are present. This property is called **locality**. Locality means that the methods of combination apply regardless of what else is present. Furthermore, any conclusions of a rule can be used in further inference. This property is called **detachment**. Detachment means that facts can be used for further inference without regard to how they were derived. In logic, the combination of locality with detachment constitutes **modularity**. In the certainty-factor approach, the modularity of the methods for combining certainty information mirrors the modularity of logic.

Suppose there is a rule like the following in the knowledge base:

IF: 1) The stain of the organism is gram positive, and
           2) the morphology of the organism is coccus, and
           3) the growth conformation of the organism is chains

THEN: There is suggestive evidence (0.7) that the identity of the organism is
  streptococcus.

Such a rule can be used whenever the conditions in its premise are satisfied. Furthermore, if the certainty of any of the premises of the rule is changed, then the combining methods can be used to recompute the certainty of the conclusion. These uses of the rule are not conditional on any other factors. No matter what else the knowledge base contains and no matter how the premises were derived, the rule can be used and the certainty computations can be revised.

This modularity in rule execution and certainty determination stands in sharp contrast to probability theory. Suppose we have a statement like $P(X|Y) = p$. What this statement means is that "if Y is true and that is the only thing you know, then we can assign probability p to X." The problem is that if we know other things, then our estimate of probability may change. Suppose we learn fact Z. We can then no longer use the rule. To estimate the probability of X, we would need to find a statement like $P(X|Y, Z) = p'$.

To understand this issue, consider the following example, suggested by Judea Pearl. Suppose we have the following rule:

Rule 1
IF: 1) The ground in front of my house is wet
THEN: There is suggestive evidence (0.7) that it rained.

From the principle of locality, this rule can be applied whenever the premise is satisfied. Once Rule 1 is invoked, it is not retracted. Given this, suppose we have the following possible and relevant facts:

Fact 1: "The neighbor's lawn is dry."
Fact 2: "The sprinkler was on last night."

A thorough model of the reasoning for the situation needs to account for the interactions between these possibilities. Neither of these facts necessarily indicates whether it rained on my lawn. Nonetheless, common sense tells us that either of these facts could reasonably be used to defeat the conclusion of Rule 1, since they undermine the value of the evidence.

In the certainty-factor approach as described in this section, there is no retracting of a conclusion once made. Within that framework, the only available option is preventing the conclusion from being made in the first place. Specifically, we could add "exception" or "screening" clauses to defeat the execution of the rule. This would give us variant Rule 1a:

Rule 1a
IF: 1) The ground in front of my house is wet, and
         2) the neighbor's lawn is not dry, and
         3) the sprinkler was not on recently
THEN: There is suggestive evidence (0.7) that it rained.

The disadvantage of this form of the rule is that the rule writer must pack together facts that may seem only remotely related to each other. This burden of anticipating and expressing the relevant facts in complex situations is another example of the **qualification problem** discussed in Chapter 3. Specifically, dependent pieces of data must be grouped into single rules. The certainty-factor approach would be unworkable in domains where large numbers of observations must be grouped in the premises of the rules to ensure their independence.

So how has the approach worked out in practice? Several studies of the MYCIN knowledge base were conducted to determine the quality of the medical reasoning and the sensitivity of the rules to small variations in certainty factors. In general, there is much empirical support that MYCIN has high competence in its area of medical expertise. It is important to note that these studies do not validate the certainty-factor approach in general. Rather, they validate its use in a particular medical domain as well as the quality of the encoding of the medical knowledge in that domain.

6.1.3   *The Dempster-Shafer Approach*   **ADVANCED**

The Dempster-Shafer (D-S) approach is a calculus for numerical degrees of belief. It was first described by Dempster in the 1960s and later extended by Shafer in his book *A Mathematical Theory of Evidence*. This approach attracted interest in the AI and expert systems communities because it sidesteps the requirements for completeness in probabilistic information in the form of prior and conditional probabilities and because it is compatible with formalisms of logic and database query languages. A key feature of the D-S approach in diagnostic reasoning tasks is its ability to model the narrowing of a set of hypotheses as evidence is accumulated. We now consider the concepts of the approach, its principles and methods, and finally its applicability.

Concepts of the Dempster-Shafer Approach

The main concepts of the D-S approach are the frame of discernment and the basic probability assignment. We describe these in the following.

The D-S approach defines a ground set of elements. The examples in the following focus on a common case where these elements correspond to diagnostic hypotheses. In general, these elements need not be hypotheses. When domain knowlege is encoded in a logical representational framework, the elements may correspond to any ground propositions.

The complete set of elements is called the **frame of discernment** and is denoted by θ. The elements in θ are assumed to be mutually exclusive and exhaustive. The set of subsets of θ is denoted 2^θ. Figure 6.8 shows 2^θ for $\theta = \{A, B, C, D\}$, where the letters correspond to distinct and mutually exclusive diagnostic hypotheses and the sets that include more than one element correspond to disjunctive hypotheses. For example, if A stands for "measles," and B stands for "chicken pox," then $\{A, B\}$ stands for "either measles or chicken pox." Elements not mentioned in a subset are not present. That is, the subset $\{A, B\}$ does not leave open the question of whether C is present. Rather, it means specifically that C is not present. Thus, it is straightforward in any group of subsets of 2^θ with assigned belief measures to identify the ones that include or exclude any particular element. Evidence against a hypothesis is regarded as evidence for the negation of that hypothesis.

The D-S approach uses a number between 0 and 1 to indicate a degree of belief. The assignment function, M, assigns a number $[0, 1]$ to every subset in 2^θ. All the other measures are

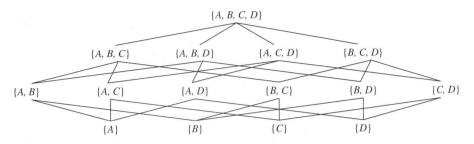

FIGURE 6.8.   The set θ and all of its subsets. Lines downward from a subset indicate its immediate proper subsets. The empty set, ϕ, is also one of the subsets in 2^θ, corresponding in the case where elements are diagnostic hypotheses to the situation where all the hypotheses are false. The set ϕ is not included in the figure.

based on M. M is sometimes called the **basic probability assignment**. The sum of the assignments over all subsets is 1, or

$$\Sigma\, M(x) = 1 \qquad \text{for } x \in 2^\theta \tag{20}$$

The null hypothesis, ϕ, is assigned 0. The quantity $M(\theta)$ is a measure of the total belief that is not assigned to any proper subset of θ. If $M(\{A, B\}) = 0.3$, then this portion of belief is not further subdivided among $\{A\}$ or $\{B\}$.

Figure 6.9 gives examples of how certainty can be assigned to subsets of 2^θ to characterize different situations. In each example, the certainty is apportioned to exactly those subsets for which it is known. Then $M(\theta)$ is assigned whatever is left over.

A basic probability assignment in the D-S approach plays a role in knowledge systems roughly analogous to a certainty factor in the CF approach. In the certainty-factor approach, the CF indicates the degree of belief that the conclusion of a rule follows from the rule's premises. Similarly, in the D-S approach, a basic probability assignment represents the degree to which belief in conclusions is altered by belief in the premises. Thus, a rule-oriented version of the D-S approach could have rules like

IF Premise_1 and Premise_2 and . . . Premise_n
THEN Conclusion_1 and Conclusion_2 and . . . $\text{Conclusion}_m\ (M_1)$

where M_1 is a basic probability assignment that affects the relevant conclusions. To complete the characterization of how this approach assigns probabilities, we need to specify how the probability assignments of different rules are to be combined. Restated, we need to characterize how evidence and beliefs are updated. That is the subject of the next section.

Combining Evidence and Updating Beliefs

Diagnostic tasks are incremental and iterative. They involve both conclusions from gathered evidence and decisions about what kinds of further evidence to gather. In this process, evidence

Example 1

Statement
Suppose we know that one or more diseases in $\{A, B, C, D\}$ is the right diagnosis, but we don't know enough to be more specific.

Probability Assignment
Assign 1 to $\{A, B, C, D\}$ and 0 to all other subsets.

Example 2
Suppose we have the following classifications superimposed upon the elements $\{A, B, C, D\}$ from Figure 6.8.

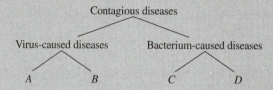

Statement
Suppose we know to degree 0.5 that the disease is caused by a virus, but we don't know whether it is disease *A* or *B*.

Probability Assignment
Assign 0.5 to Virus-caused Diseases = $\{A, B\}$ and 0.5 to $M(\theta)$.

Example 3

Statement
Suppose we know the disease is not *A* to the degree 0.4.

Probability Assignment
Assign 0.4 to $\{B, C, D\}$ and $M(\theta) = 0.6$.

FIGURE 6.9. Examples showing how belief measures can be assigned to reflect differences in beliefs. The examples are based on the elements in Figure 6.8.

gathered on one iteration must be combined with evidence gathered on the next one. In support of this the D-S approach has an evidence-combination rule. In the following we consider what the rule says and then the rationale for it.

Let M_1 and M_2 be two probability assignments. **Dempster's rule** computes a new M denoted $M_1 \oplus M_2$, for the combined effect. For every subset of θ Dempster's rule defines $M_1 \oplus M_2$ as follows:

$$M_1 \oplus M_2 (A) = \Sigma\, M_1(X)\, M_2(Y) \text{ where } X, Y \in 2^\theta \text{ and } X \cap Y = A \tag{21}$$

Because of the commutativity of multiplication, this rule yields the same value regardless of the order in which evidence is gathered and the functions are combined. Figures 6.10 and 6.11 give examples of the results of evidence combination using Dempster's rule. Figure 6.10 gives a par-

Statement
Given M_1 and M_2, compute $M_1 \oplus M_2$.

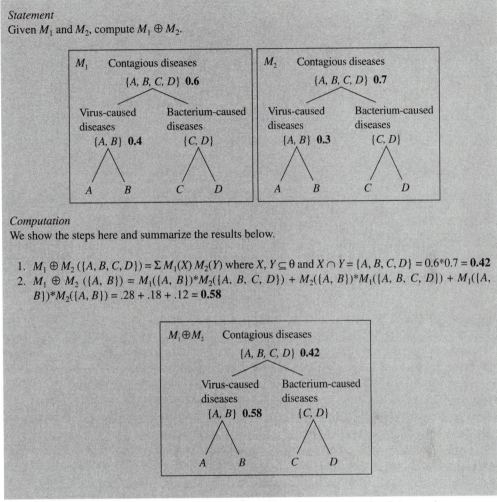

Computation
We show the steps here and summarize the results below.

1. $M_1 \oplus M_2 (\{A, B, C, D\}) = \Sigma M_1(X) M_2(Y)$ where $X, Y \subseteq \theta$ and $X \cap Y = \{A, B, C, D\} = 0.6*0.7 = \mathbf{0.42}$
2. $M_1 \oplus M_2 (\{A, B\}) = M_1(\{A, B\})*M_2(\{A, B, C, D\}) + M_2(\{A, B\})*M_1(\{A, B, C, D\}) + M_1(\{A, B\})*M_2(\{A, B\}) = .28 + .18 + .12 = \mathbf{0.58}$

FIGURE 6.10. Illustration of Dempster's rule of evidence combination. For simplicity, product terms that include zero are omitted.

ticularly simple case where both pieces of evidence provide data for exactly the same subsets of 2^θ.

Basic probability assignments have two key properties. One is that the probabilities assigned to all the subsets of θ must sum to 1. That is,

$$\Sigma M(X) = 1 \text{ where } X \in 2^\theta \qquad (22)$$

The second is that the probability assigned to the null set is 0, or

$$M(\phi) = 0 \qquad (23)$$

Statement

Given M_1 and M_2, compute $M_1 \oplus M_2$.

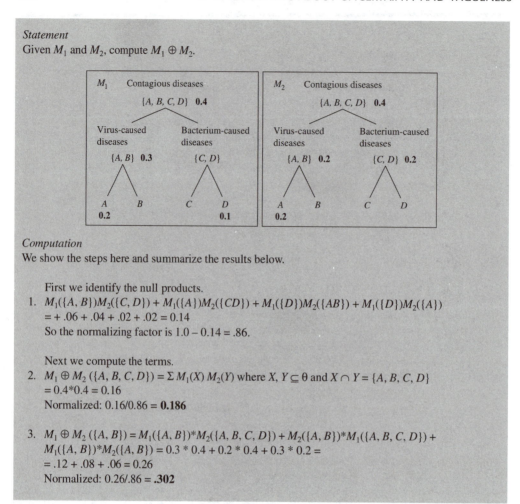

Computation

We show the steps here and summarize the results below.

First we identify the null products.
1. $M_1(\{A, B\})M_2(\{C, D\}) + M_1(\{A\})M_2(\{CD\}) + M_1(\{D\})M_2(\{AB\}) + M_1(\{D\})M_2(\{A\})$
    $= + .06 + .04 + .02 + .02 = 0.14$
    So the normalizing factor is $1.0 - 0.14 = .86$.

Next we compute the terms.
2. $M_1 \oplus M_2 (\{A, B, C, D\}) = \Sigma M_1(X) M_2(Y)$ where $X, Y \subseteq \theta$ and $X \cap Y = \{A, B, C, D\}$
    $= 0.4 * 0.4 = 0.16$
    Normalized: $0.16/0.86 = \mathbf{0.186}$

3. $M_1 \oplus M_2 (\{A, B\}) = M_1(\{A, B\}) * M_2(\{A, B, C, D\}) + M_2(\{A, B\}) * M_1(\{A, B, C, D\}) +$
    $M_1(\{A, B\}) * M_2(\{A, B\}) = 0.3 * 0.4 + 0.2 * 0.4 + 0.3 * 0.2 =$
    $= .12 + .08 + .06 = 0.26$
    Normalized: $0.26/.86 = \mathbf{.302}$

FIGURE 6.11.   Illustration of the use of Dempster's rule for combining evidence (continued next page).

When evidence from two different measures is combined in computing $M_1 \oplus M_2$, it sometimes turns out (as in the example of Figure 6.11) that there are subsets, X and Y, both of which have probability assignments but whose intersection is null. In such cases of empty intersection and in the absense of further arrangements, some of the probability mass in $M_1 \oplus M_2$ would be assigned to ϕ, violating equation 23. The Dempster-Shafer approach deals with this by renormalizing. In particular, $M_1 \oplus M_2 (\phi)$ is assigned to zero and the other terms of the product are increased proportionately. A procedure for doing this is illustrated in the example in Figure 6.11. This renormalizing process assures that probability is assigned only to noncontradictory subsets.

As we noted in the discussion of the certainty-factor approach, there is no universal relationship that relates certainties or probabilities of joint events to their individual certainties or probabilities. Restated, there is no general means for computing $P(H, E_1 \& E_2)$ from $P(H, E_1)$ and

4. $M_1 \oplus M_2 (\{A\}) = M_1(\{A\})*M_2(\{A, B, C, D\}) + M_1(\{A\})*M_2(\{A, B\}) + M_1(\{A\})*M_2(\{A\}) +$
    $M_2(\{A\})*M_1(\{A, B, C, D\}) + M_2(\{A\})*M_1(\{A, B\}) = .08 + .04 + .04 + .08 + .06 = 0.30$
    Normalized: $.30/.86 = \mathbf{.349}$

5. $M_1 \oplus M_2 (\{C, D\}) = M_1(\{A, B, C, D\})*M_2(\{C, D\}) = 0.8/.86 = 0.08$
    Normalized: $.08/.86 = \mathbf{.093}$

6. $M_1 \oplus M_2 (\{D\}) = M_1(\{D\})*M_2(\{A, B, C, D\}) + M_1(\{D\})*M_2(\{C, D\}) = .04 + .02 = .06$
    Normalized: $.06/.86 = \mathbf{.070}$

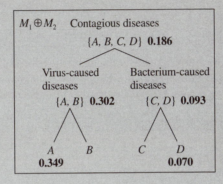

FIGURE 6.11.   (continued)

$P(H, E_2)$ because the logic of confirmation has no inherent connection with the logic of probability. Nonetheless, this is roughly what rules of evidence combination attempt to do.

It has been suggested that the rule reflects a natural pooling of evidence. In the discussion of the CF approach, we showed how this "natural pooling" embodies assumptions about independence of evidence and the absence of certain kinds of aberrant rules. In the special case where M_1 and M_2 assign probabilities to exactly one hypothesis, then $M_1 \oplus M_2$ reduces to the same rule of evidence combination as in the certainty-factor model (see the exercises). The D-S approach differs from the CF approach in the way it pools evidence for mutually exclusive hypotheses. Specifically, the bookkeeping of the D-S approach keeps track of weights assigned to all subsets of θ, not just weights for individual hypotheses. In a diagnostic setting, the D-S approach is better suited than the CF approach for expressing composite hypotheses.

Starting with the basic probability assignment, M, the Dempster-Shafer approach then goes on to define three other measures based on it as follows:

Bel   Assigns to every subset z of 2^θ the total belief assigned by M to z plus the belief assigned to all of its subsets. That is,

$$\text{Bel}(z) = \Sigma \, M(x) \text{ for } x \subseteq z.$$

D   The measure of doubt: $D(z) = \text{Bel}(\sim z)$.

Pl   The measure of plausibility: $Pl(z) = 1 - D(z)$. This measure is also called the upper belief function or the upper probability function.

Thus, $Bel(H)$ gives the toal amount of belief committed to hypothesis H, and $D(H)$ gives the amount of belief commited to its negation. $Pl(H)$ expresses the extent that the evidence allows one to fail to doubt H. These functions can be computed from the resulting M after all the evidence has been combined.

The following relationships hold among these functions (see the exercises for proofs):

$$Pl(A) \geq Bel(A) \tag{24}$$
$$Bel(A) + Bel(\sim A) \leq 1 \tag{25}$$
$$Pl(A) + Pl(\sim A) \geq 1 \tag{26}$$

The interval between $Bel(A)$ and $Pl(A)$ is sometimes called the belief interval in D-S theory. Working from a hierarchy as in the preceding examples, we see that the width of these intervals tends to decrease as evidence is added. Typically, further refinement of evidence leads to moving belief lower in the hierarchy.

For two hypotheses A and C such that $A \subseteq C$, the following hold:

$$Bel(A) \leq Bel(C) \tag{27}$$
$$Pl(A) \leq Pl(C) \tag{28}$$

Applicability of the Dempster-Shafer Approach

As in our discussion of the CF approach, we begin with probability theory as a basis for evaluating the D-S approach. The utility of probability theory for modeling reasoning with uncertainty is limited by the lack of sufficient data to accurately estimate the prior and conditional probabilities required to use Bayes' rule.

The D-S theory sidesteps the requirement for this data. It accepts an incomplete probabilistic model without prior or conditional probabilities. Given the incompleteness of the model, the D-S theory does not answer arbitrary probabilistic questions. Rather than estimating the probability of a hypothesis, it uses belief intervals to estimate how close the evidence is to determining the truth of an hypothesis. As with the CF approach, we raise the following questions: What problems with the model have arisen? What limitations of its applicability are known? How well does the method work in practice?

The D-S approach has essentially the same locality and detachment properties as the CF approach. When it is used in conjunction with a monotonic reasoning system, it has the same potential difficulty with the qualification problem. When used to model sources of evidence that are not independent, it can yield misleading and counterintuitive results (see the exercises). We discuss nonmonotonic approaches later in this section. For now it is enough to say that nonmonotonic approaches have provisions for retracting statements and that the D-S approach can be used together with nonmonotonic approaches.

There has been some debate about the viability of the D-S approach, especially with regard to the use of belief functions. One argument is simply that probability theory is the best basis for performing uncertain inference. Another is that mechanical applications of belief functions can lead to unacceptable results. In this debate, various alternative interpretations of belief functions have been offered, such as that they bound probabilities or that they express probability of provability. Shafer's defense of this has been that the criticisms are based on illegitimate applications of belief functions. Interested readers may consult Neapolitan (1993a). Neapolitan shows that belief functions use probability in the same way as the statistical tool, sig nificance testing. In significance testing, a conditional probability of certain observations is computed given the truth of the hypothesis of interest. If that probability is below a given level of significance, the hypothesis is rejected.

The popularity of the D-S approach stems from its ability to admit partially specified models, its convenience for formulating hierarchical refinement of hypotheses, and its compatibility with proof-based styles of inference. Its ability to account for composite hypotheses in a hierarchy ameliorates the qualification problem by providing more precise and powerful places for accumulating evidence; in the nonsingleton subsets of θ.

Roughly speaking, the most primitive clauses in a logical approach have direct evidence. Reasoning proceeds by combining primitive statements into larger ones by proof procedures. Rather than exploring all possible proofs, the reasoning system can be guided by the weight of evidence. The stronger the evidence for particular clauses, the more likely it is that a complete and acceptable proof (or hypothesis) will be assembled.

Provan (1990) and Kak (Kak et al., 1990) give examples of systems for machine vision that use the D-S approach for evidence combination. Both systems use evidence of plausibility to rank hypotheses. Hypotheses about the interpretation of large areas or objects of the scene are built from hypotheses of smaller ones. Hypothesis classes have ranking functions that give approximate ratings of plausibility from local information. Ranking data are used to guide the combination of smaller hypotheses, thus focusing the generation and evaluation of larger, composite hypotheses.

6.1.4 *Probability Networks* ADVANCED

There are many variations of probability networks, including Markov networks, influence diagrams, and various kinds of decision trees. This section focuses on two kinds of probability networks: **inference networks** (Duda, Hart, & Nilsson, 1976) and Bayesian **belief networks** (Pearl, 1988). Belief networks are also called **causal networks** (Neapolitan, 1990). These networks are well characterized and are intended for use in areas similar to the other formalisms that we have considered for reasoning with uncertainty. An influence diagram is a belief network augmented with decision nodes.

Quantitative approaches to certainty provide a means for updating beliefs that has less onerous data requirements than conventional probability theory. These approaches recognize that in most cases there is insufficient data to accurately estimate the prior and conditional probabilities required to use Bayes' rule. For example, a statement like $P(A|B) = p$ is insufficient for a reasoner using only probability theory. He must either find a statement like $P(A|B, C, D, \ldots)$ that accounts for every assertion ($B, C, D, \ldots$) in the knowledge base or else he must determine that other assertions in the knowledge base are irrelevant to A. Otherwise, the reasoner cannot tell whether the missing data are important and he cannot tell in any partially specified situation what inferences are permitted. In short, he is logically and computationally impotent.

All probability networks use probabilities to encode likelihood data and links in the networks to indicate relevance relationships. The links enable algorithms for belief propagation to work from network data. If a node is not indicated as relevant, then the reasoner need not take it into account in reasoning and need not be inhibited by the lack of specific rules for it. Thus, network representations make explicit the dependencies between beliefs.

Probability networks attempt to retain the theoretical framework of probability theory without acquiring an intractable computational burden. Suppose a reasoning system with a probability network is presented with a fact. The system begins by checking whether the fact is relevant to other facts, that is, whether the fact depends on other facts or whether other facts depend on it. Quantitative approaches such as the certainty factor and Dempster-Shafer approach assume that such tests are not necessary because facts are independent. Probability-network approaches allow facts to be dependent. However, rather than banning or ignoring dependencies, they attempt to make dependency testing efficient.

Inference Networks: An Early Approach

The best-known method for propagating probabilities in a network is the method of odds-likelihood ratios developed by Duda, Hart, and Nilsson (1976) for the Prospector expert system. Readers who are primarily interested in focusing on the best current techniques may want to skip ahead to the section on belief networks.

Although the inference-network method is now dated, it is a good starting point for illustrating the ideas, a simple transition from the methods we have discussed so far, and historically significant for stimulating research on methods for propagating probabilities in networks. We use the older term **inference network** to distinguish these networks from belief networks that we discuss later. The two kinds of networks differ in their treatment of nodes as variables.

This method assumes that inferences are carried out by rules of the form "if E then H." In the graphical presentation, propositional statements are represented as nodes and rules are represented as arcs. The truth values of the propositional statements are taken as probabilities. A collection of rules is represented as a graph, as in the example in Figure 6.12. In this figure, the H_i nodes at the top of the figure are hypotheses to be resolved and the E_i nodes below are supporting evidence. Evidence nodes play two roles. They provide supporting evidence for nodes above and they act as hypotheses to be resolved for nodes below. The rules have uncertainty numbers associated with them and the evidence used by the rules may also be uncertain. As in the CF approach, these numbers indicate degrees of belief, replacing the binary true/false of logic with numeric quantities.

Before presenting the approach, we define odds and conditional odds. These quantitities are central to the computations employed by the approach. We begin with the relation of odds to probability. There are many kinds of odds, but they are always defined the same way. If P is a "generic probability function," then O is the related "generic odds function" defined by equations (29) and (29′).

$$P = O/(O + 1) \tag{29}$$
$$O = P/(1 - P) \tag{29′}$$

Thus, odds and probabilities contain the same information. Using these two equations, we can translate back and forth between the two numeric formulations as needed.

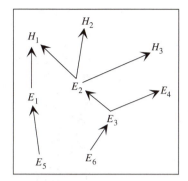

FIGURE 6.12. A simple inference network.

We now look at specific odds functions. Given a probability space and $H \in F$, the **unconditional odds** are defined by

$$O(H) = P(H)/(1 - P(H)) \tag{30}$$

If the probability is conditional, $P(H|E)$, then the **conditional odds** are defined analogously as in equation (31).

$$O(H \mid E) = P(H \mid E)/(1 - P(H \mid E)) \tag{31}$$

The case $O(H)$ is also called the prior odds, and $O(H \mid E)$ is called posterior odds. The **likelihood ratios** λ of E and $\bar{\lambda}$ of $\neg E$ are defined by

$$\lambda = P(E \mid H)/P(E \mid \neg H) \tag{32}$$
$$\bar{\lambda} = P(\neg E \mid H)/P(\neg E \mid H) \tag{32'}$$

Given these definitions, we can reformulate Bayes' rule to a multiplicative form. Equation (8), repeated here, gives the familiar form of Bayes' rule. Equations (33) and (34) give its odds-likelihood reformulations. (See the exercises for derivations.)

Conventional Bayes' Rule
$P(H|E) = P(H) P(E|H)/P(E)$

Multiplicative Odds Reformulation of Bayes' Rule
$$O (H \mid E) = \lambda\, O(H) \tag{33}$$
$$O (H \mid \neg E) = \bar{\lambda}\, O(H) \tag{34}$$

The quantities λ and $\bar{\lambda}$ have a role in the odds-likelihood approach that is analogous to the underlying measures MB and MD in the CF approach. Equation (33) says how to update the odds on H given the observation of E. A high value of λ ($\lambda \gg 1$) transforms low prior odds on H into heavy posterior odds in favor of it. Similarly, a large negative value of $\bar{\lambda}$ transforms prior odds on H into heavily negative posterior odds on it.

In the Prospector system, the users were asked to provide estimates of λ and $\bar{\lambda}$ for each rule. Although λ and $\bar{\lambda}$ must both be provided in a model, they are not independent of each other. With λ and $\bar{\lambda}$ defined as they are, we have equation (35).

$$\bar{\lambda} = \frac{1 - \lambda\, P(E \mid \sim H)}{1 - P(E \mid \sim H)} \tag{35}$$

Restated, the model is overspecified if λ and $\bar{\lambda}$ are both given, or $P(E \mid H)$ and $P(E \mid \sim H)$, or some other equivalent information. From equation (35), we have that $\lambda = 1$ exactly when $\bar{\lambda} = 1$. Furthermore, $\lambda > 1$ only if $\bar{\lambda} < 1$. To cope with this specification issue, various ad hoc adjustments are possible. We now have in hand most of the concepts for inference networks.

Figure 6.13 gives an example of the updating of probabilities in a network using the odds-likelihood approach. We have the prior probabilities, $P(Y)$ and $P(Z)$, that correspond to our beliefs in Y and Z in the absence of knowing about X. In the example, X becomes known, and the task is to compute $P(Y \mid X)$ and $P(Z \mid X)$. Restated, our goal is to propagate probabilities in the network to revise our degrees of belief in Y and Z. The first steps of this, computing $P(Y \mid X)$, are performed using equations (33) through (35).

The next part of the example is to compute $P(Z)$. This is where assumptions of independence first come in. We begin with equation (36), which defines a key relationship in a chain of probabilities.

$$P(Z, Y \mid X) = P(Z \mid Y, X)\, P(Y \mid X) \tag{36}$$

where X, Y, and Z are arranged in a chain as in Figure 6.13. What we need is a way of computing $P(Z \mid X)$. It follows from the axioms of probability that

$$P(Z \mid X) = P(Z, Y \mid X) + P(Z, \sim Y \mid X)$$

Transforming this with equation (37), we get

$$P(Z \mid X) = P(Z \mid Y, X)\, P(Y \mid X) + P(Z \mid \sim Y, X)\, P(\sim Y \mid X) \tag{37}$$

Next we assume that

$$P(Z \mid Y, X) = P(Z \mid Y)$$
$$P(Z \mid \sim Y, X) = P(Z \mid \sim Y)$$

Roughly, this means we assume that Z and X are independent. More precisely, we assume that when Y occurs and also when Y does not occur, the conditional probability of Z depends only on Y. Restated, all influence of X on Z is completely expressed by X's influence on Y. This assumption is not valid in networks in which there are multiple paths from the evidence to a conclusion. For example, if X is also evidence for Z along some other path, this assumption would not hold.

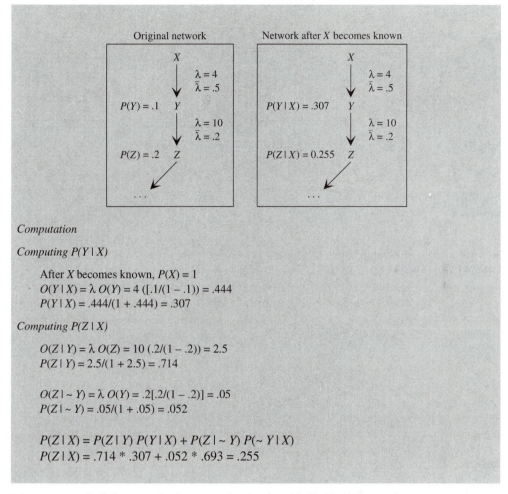

FIGURE 6.13. Belief propagation in a network using the odds-likelihood approach.

Given these independence assumptions we obtain equation (38) from equation (37).

$$P(Z \mid X) = P(Z \mid Y) P(Y \mid X) + P(Z \mid \sim Y) P(\sim Y \mid X) \ (\tag{38}$$

This is our first operational formula for propagating probabilities. Figure 6.13 shows these computations for the example. Thus we first compute $P(Z \mid Y)$ and $P(Z \mid \sim Y)$ using the odds-likelihood formulas and $P(Y)$. Then we use equation (38) to propagate probabilities given $P(Y \mid X)$ and $P(\sim Y \mid X)$. Note that $P(\sim Y \mid X)$ in the computation simply comes from the identity

$$P(\sim Y \mid X) = 1 - P(Y \mid X)$$

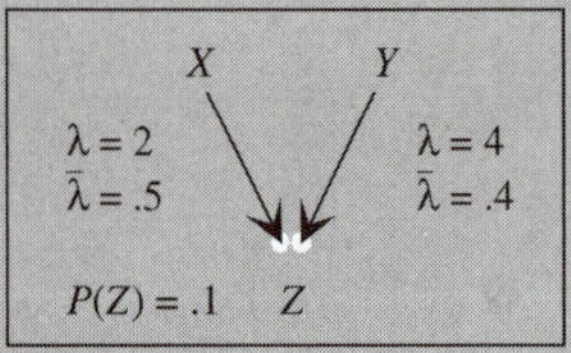

Computation

$$O(Z \mid X, Y) = \lambda_x \lambda_y \, O(Z) = 2(4)(.111) = .888$$

$$P(Z \mid X, Y) = O(Z \mid X, Y)/[1 + O(Z \mid X, Y)] = .888/1.888 = 0.470$$

FIGURE 6.14.   Using the odds-likelihood approach when evidence from multiple sources must be combined.

To summarize, if E is the premise in a rule and H is the conclusion, then the likelihood ratio method updates the belief in H when E becomes known to be either true or false.

Figure 6.14 gives an example of a network in a case where there are multiple sources of evidence for a hypothesis. Suppose in this example that both X and Y become known. To handle this case, we need to be able to compute $P(Z \mid X, Y)$. Assuming for $1 \leq i \leq n$ that the E_i's are conditionally independent, we obtain equations (39) and (40) (see the exercises for a proof).

$$O(H \mid E_1, E_2, E_3, \ldots, E_n) = \lambda_1 \lambda_2 \lambda_3 \ldots \lambda n \, O(H) \tag{39}$$
$$O(H \mid \sim E_1, \sim E_2, \sim E_3, \ldots, \sim E_n) = \overline{\lambda}_1 \overline{\lambda}_2 \overline{\lambda}_3 \ldots \overline{\lambda}_n \, O(H) \tag{40}$$

Figure 6.14 gives an example of using these equations and the relationship between odds and probabilities to compute the combined conditional probability for multiple sources of evidence.

Noting that the rules of multiple evidence for both λ and $\overline{\lambda}$ are multiplicative, it is convenient to define a combined or **effective likelihood ratio**. Suppose there is an arc from E to H and E' is all the evidence for A. The effective likelihood ratio is defined as:

$$\lambda' = O(H \mid E')/O(H) \tag{41}$$

This leads to the following result. Assuming for $1 \leq i \leq n$ that there is an arc from each of the E_i's to H, that E_i' is all the evidence for E_i, and that the E_i's are independent both when H occurs and when it does not occur, then equation (42) follows.

$$O(H \mid E_1, E_2, E_3, \ldots, E_n) = \lambda_1 \lambda_2 \lambda_3 \ldots \lambda_n \, O(H) \tag{42}$$

The odds-likelihood approach is a simple step away from the certainty-factor approach. It introduces the graphical presentation of the variables and inference rules. The method incorporates probability theory in its Bayesian updating scheme. However, when multiple variables as evidence bear on a single hypothesis, it presumes that the variables are independent. In the following, we extend these concepts to consider Bayesian networks with less restrictive independence assumptions.

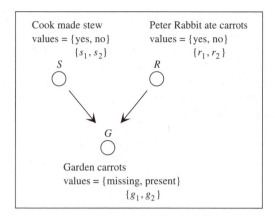

FIGURE 6.15.   A simple belief network. The three nodes are G, R, and S. G represents the question of whether the carrots are missing from the garden, R represents the question of whether Peter Rabbit stole the carrots from the garden, and S represents the question of whether the cook used the carrots in making stew.

Basic Concepts of Belief Networks

We now consider Bayesian **belief networks** (Neapolitan, 1990; Pearl, 1988). These networks are well characterized and are intended for use in areas similar to the other formalisms that we have considered for reasoning with uncertainty. At the time of this writing, belief networks are the preferred method for most applications of reasoning with uncertainty.

Belief networks differ from inference networks in the nature of variables in the network. In inference networks, each node represents a single proposition, typically a single cause in a diagnostic hypothesis. Two numbers associated with that proposition represent degrees of certainty. Nodes in belief networks are more like variables in constraint graphs in that they are assigned values from a set of mutually exclusive possibilities. Variables in a belief network are sometimes called **propositional variables**. They are assigned values from a set.

Figure 6.15 gives an example of a belief network. The three propositional variables are $\{G, S, R\}$, as shown. The network is from an example that we consider later in this section. Each variable has two elements in its domain. For example, S has the values $\{s1, s2\}$ meaning that "the cook made stew" or "the cook did not make stew."

More generally, we are given a set of n propositional variables $\{X_1, X_2, X_3, \ldots, X_n\}$ with finite domains. Let F' be "the set of all subsets of Ω" $= \{(X_1, X_2, \ldots, X_n)\}$ which is the set of all the ways to assign values to the propositional variables. Furthermore, let $P'(X_1, X_2, \ldots, X_n) = P(X_1, X_2, \ldots, X_n)$. The probability of each element in F' is the product of the probabilities of its elements.

We illustrate this definition and the assignment of probabilities using the example in Figure 6.15. Using the assignment set notation from constraint satisfaction problems, consider two of the possible complete assignment sets.

Assignment Set 1: $\{<S, s_1>, <R, r_1>, <G, g_1>\}$
Assignment Set 2: $\{<S, s_1>, <R, r_1>, <G, g_2>\}$

These particular assignment sets differ only in the value assigned to variable G. When we compute the probability of one of these assignment sets, its probability is the product of the probabilities of the individual variable assignments. For example, the probability of the first assignment set is the product of the probability that S is s_1, the probability that R is r_1, and the probability that G is g_1. Thus, the probabilities of the two assignment sets are computed by the same two first factors and differ in the factor representing the distinct probabilities for the assignments to G. The elements of the probability space—all of the possible assignment sets—are mutually exclusive and exhaustive. Furthermore, the sum of the probabilities assigned to all the complete assignment sets is 1. Such a distribution is called a **joint probability distribution**. If we hold one variable constant and sum the probabilities of all the other variables over all their values, then we obtain what is called a **marginal probability distribution**.

Conditional Independence

In a Bayesian approach, conditional probabilities guide the updating of beliefs by quantifying how it is that the estimated probability of one event depends on what is known about other events. Restated, we want to know how the realization of values by some propositional variables affects the probabilities of others. Probability networks support the computing of conditional probabilities by representing "conditional independencies" in networks. Conditional dependencies are indicators. They indicate where conditional probabilities need to be accounted for among variables. In this section we define conditional independency and consider several of its equivalent formulations. In the following sections, we relate conditional dependencies to structural properties of networks and define belief networks in terms of their representation of conditional dependencies.

Let U (a "universal" set of variables) be a finite set of variables with discrete values, and X, Y, and Z are three subsets of variables in U. Sets X and Y are **conditionally independent** given Z if

$$P(x \mid y, z) = P(x \mid z) \text{ whenever } P(y, z) > 0 \tag{43}$$

Roughly, this says that given z, the probability of x does not depend on y. For brevity, we use the standard notation $I(X, Z, Y)$ to indicate the conditional independence of X and Y given Z. Thus,

$$I(X, Z, Y) \text{ if } P(x \mid y, z) = P(x \mid z) \text{ whenever } P(y, z) > 0 \tag{44}$$

The following properties are equivalent to conditional independence (see the exercises).

$$I(X, Y, Z) \Leftrightarrow P(x, y \mid z) = P(x \mid z) \, P(y \mid z) \tag{45}$$
$$I(X, Y, Z) \Leftrightarrow P(x, y, z) = P(x \mid z) \, P(y, z) \tag{46}$$

Unconditional independence is denoted by $I(X, \phi, Y)$.

$$I(X, \phi, Y) \text{ if } P(x \mid y) = P(x) \text{ whenever } P(y) > 0 \tag{47}$$

- *Symmetry.* In any state of knowledge Z, if knowing Y does not affect the probability of X, then knowing X does not affect the probability of Y. More formally,

$I(X, Z, Y) \Leftrightarrow I(Y, Z, X)$

In graphical terms, symmetry states that if Z separates X from Y, then it also separates Y from X.

- *Decomposition.* If two combined items of information are irrelevant to X, then each separate item is irrelevant, too.

$I(X, Z, Y \cup W) \Rightarrow I(X, Z, Y) \wedge I(X, Z, W)$

Decomposition states that if Z separates X from the set $S = (Y \cup W)$, it also separates X from every subset of S.

- *Weak union.* If information W is irrelevant to X, then knowing W cannot make the irrelevant information Y become relevant to X.

$I(X, Z, Y \cup W) \Rightarrow I(X, Z \cup W, Y)$

Weak union provides conditions under which a separating set Z can be augmented by additional elements W and still separate X from Y. The condition is that the added subset W should come from the section of space that was initially separated from X by Z.

- *Contraction.* If W is found to be irrelevant to X after we learn irrelevant information Y, then W must have been irrelevant before we learned Y.

$I(X, Z, Y) \wedge I(X, Z \cup Y, W) \Rightarrow I(X, Z, Y \cup W)$

Contraction provides conditions for reducing the size of the separating set. It permits the deletion of a subset Y from the separator $Z \cup Y$ if the remaining part, Z, separates the deleted part, Y from X.

FIGURE 6.16. Equivalent characterizations of conditional independence. W, X, Y, and Z are disjoint sets of variables on a probability space. The proofs of these follow from the definitions of conditional probability and conditional independence (see the exercises).

Figure 6.16 gives four equivalent characterizations of conditional independence. In the explanations of these equivalent formulations, we sometimes call the known set Z a separating set. For now it is enough to understand Z's role in characterizing conditional independence. In the next section we look at the structural meaning of separation.

D-Separation: Dependencies and Graph Structure

We now relate conditional independence to graph structure. A chain is a sequence of nodes connecting two nodes. This is almost the same idea as a path in a directed graph except that it does not pay attention to the orientation of the arcs.

Following Neapolitan (1990), we define d-separation in terms of blocked chains. We are given a Directed Acyclic Graph (DAG), V, and a subgraph $Z \subseteq V$, and nodes x and y in $V - Z$. Restated, x and y are in V but not in Z. We are given further that there is a chain of nodes and

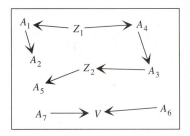

FIGURE 6.17.   Examples of nodes blocking a chain.

links between x and y. The question we ask is whether the chain is blocked by Z. The chain c between x and y is said to be **blocked** by Z if any of the following conditions hold:

1. There is a node $z \in Z$ on c such that the arcs that determine that z is on c meet tail-to-tail at z.

2. There is a node $z \in Z$ on c such that the arcs that determine that z is on c meet head-to-tail at z.

3. There is a node $v \in V$ for which neither v nor any of v's descendants is in Z. Node v is on the chain c such that the arcs that determine that v is on c meet head-to-head at v.

Figure 6.17 illustrates the conditions for defining blocking. The first blocking condition is satisfied by node Z_1 on the chain between A_1 and A_4. Therefore, Z_1 blocks A_1 and A_4. The second blocking condition is satisfied by Z_2 on the chain between A_3 and A_5. Therefore Z_2 blocks A_3 and A_5. Finally, the third blocking condition is satisfied by the set $Z = \{Z_1, Z_2\}$ for the chain $\{A_6, V, A_7\}$. In this case, V is the node with converging arcs and neither V nor any of its descendants is in Z. In this (perhaps counterintuitive) case, Z blocks the chain between A_6 and A_7.

We are now ready to define d-separation and to show how it relates to conditional independence. Let Z be a set of nodes in a belief graph V. Nodes x and y are nodes in $V -- Z$. Nodes x and y are **d-separated** by Z if *every* chain between them is blocked by Z. If X, Y, and Z are disjoint subsets of V, then X and Y are d-separated by Z if every $x \in X$ and $y \in Y$ are d-separated by some $z \in Z$.

Another version of the d-separation condition is given by Pearl (1988). If X, Y, and Z are three disjoint subsets of nodes in a DAG, then Z is said to d-separate X from Y if there is no chain between a node in X and a node in Y along which the following two conditions hold:

1. Every node with converging links is in Z or has a descendant in Z.

2. Every other node on the chain is outside Z.

Referring back to Figure 6.17, we see that the definition agrees for the three cases. That is, the set $Z = \{Z_1, Z_2\}$ d-separates $\{A_1\}$ from $\{A_4\}$; it also d-separates $\{A_3\}$ from $\{A_5\}$, and it d-separates $\{A_7\}$ from $\{A_6\}$.

We now come to the key result: D-separation amounts to **conditional independence**. More precisely, if X, Y, and Z are disjoint subsets of V such that X and Y are d-separated by Z, then X and Y are conditionally independent given Z. That is, $I(X, Z, Y)$. Readers interested in a proof of this result can consult Pearl (1988) or Neapolitan (1990).

To understand the significance of this result, consider the question of whether two variables in a network are dependent. Certainly if the variables are connected by dependency links, they are dependent. But they can also be dependent by virtue of an intermediate variable, as when some variable w affects some variable x that affects some variable y in a causal chain. In general, probability computations are simplest in the case where variables are independent. As we have just seen, the absence of a link between two variables in a network does not guarantee their independence. That is what the d-separation condition does. D-separation is a test for determining conditional independence. We are now ready to formally define belief networks.

Defining Belief Networks

Roughly speaking, Bayesian networks are directed acyclic graphs in which the nodes represent variables, the arcs (usually) represent dependencies, and the strengths of these influences are expressed by conditional probabilities. Directed arcs run from cause to effect, which means from parent to child. Given values for its parents, a node is independent of all nodes in the network except its children. This rough definition is not exactly right, as we will explain in the following, because there are some additional requirements on the parents.

Following Neapolitan (1990), we now give a more precise definition and illustrate it in Figure 6.18. Let V be a finite set of variables with a joint probability distribution. For each $v \in V$, $a(v)$ is the set of v's immediate parents (immediate ancestors) and $d(v)$ is the set of v's descendants. Let $nd(v)$ ("not descendants") be the set of all nodes in V excluding v and $d(v)$.

We now come to the crucial part of the definition. Let W be a subset of $nd(v)$: $W \subseteq nd(v)$. The DAG is a **belief network** if for every W, W and v are conditionally independent given $a(v)$. Restated in other notation, $I(v, a(v), W)$.

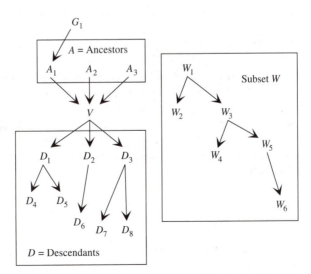

FIGURE 6.18. Illustrating the conditional independence condition in the definition of a Bayesian belief network.

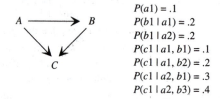

$P(a1) = .1$
$P(b1 \mid a1) = .2$
$P(b1 \mid a2) = .2$
$P(c1 \mid a1, b1) = .1$
$P(c1 \mid a1, b2) = .2$
$P(c1 \mid a2, b1) = .3$
$P(c1 \mid a2, b3) = .4$

FIGURE 6.19.   A nonminimal belief network.

Defining Minimal Belief Networks

We now revisit the definition of belief networks to consider minimal belief networks and a common variation on the definition of belief networks. Consider the belief network in Figure 6.19. In this belief network, B is not conditionally dependent on A, because the probability of the value of B does not depend on which value A has. Still, this is a valid belief network. Figure 6.20 shows what we get if we remove the arc from A to B.

The network in Figure 6.20 represents the same joint distribution as in Figure 6.19. Furthermore, we can remove no other edges and still represent the distribution. Such a representation is called minimal.

Suppose v is a node in a network with ancestors $a(v)$. The set of ancestors is **minimal** if there is no proper subset $U \subset a(v)$ such that $P(v \mid U) = P(v \mid a(v))$. Some authors define belief networks in a way that requires that the set of ancestors be minimal for each $v \in V$. Our definition follows Neapolitan (1990), and is more general. Defining a belief network as requiring that the set of parents be minimal for each node does have an advantage, however. In this case, the arcs represent dependencies. If we take the general definition of belief networks, which does not require minimal ancestors, then it turns out that there will always be a unique causal network containing a subset of the edges, having the same joint probability distribution, and for which the parent sets are minimal.

The construction of the minimal belief network depends on the following observation. Suppose that for some $v \in V$, $U \subseteq V$, and $W \subseteq V$ where $v \notin U$ and $v \notin W$, we have that $P(v \mid U) = P(v \mid W)$. In Figure 6.19, v corresponds to B, W corresponds to $\{A\}$, U corresponds to ϕ, and V corresponds to $\{A, B, C\}$. Under these conditions, $P(v \mid U \cap W) = P(v \mid U) = P(V \mid W)$.

Given a belief network, we can construct a minimal one (in principle) as follows. Given v, we find W, which is the set of all subsets of $a(v)$ such that $P(v|W) = P(v \mid a(v))$. We define a new set of parents, $a'(v)$, which is the intersection of all the sets in W. Repeatedly applying this, we eventually have $P(v|a'(v)) = P(v|a(v))$ for all v. We then eliminate from arcs all the arcs to v for vertices that are in $a(v)$ but not in $a'(v)$.

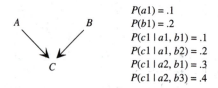

$P(a1) = .1$
$P(b1) = .2$
$P(c1 \mid a1, b1) = .1$
$P(c1 \mid a1, b2) = .2$
$P(c1 \mid a2, b1) = .3$
$P(c1 \mid a2, b3) = .4$

FIGURE 6.20.   A minimal belief network.

Finally, given a minimal belief network, we see its crucial properties, relating the structure of the DAG, the joint probability distribution, and conditional independences involving the DAG and the probability distribution. In a minimal network, every set of nodes and any other set of nodes not including descendants is conditionally independent given the node's parents. Restated: There are no hidden dependencies.

If $P(a(v)) > 0$, then at least one of the following holds:

$$P(v \mid a(v)) = 0$$
$$P(W \mid a(v)) = 0$$
$$P(v \mid W \cup a(v)) = P(v \mid a(v))$$

In a belief network, we can compute the joint probability distribution of each propositional variable given the variable's parents. That is,

$$P(V) = \prod P(V \mid a(v)) \qquad (48)$$
$$\text{for } v \text{ in } V \text{ and } P(a(v)) > 0$$

This can greatly reduce the complexity of determining the distribution. The single-connectedness condition guarantees that the information passed along any arc to a node is independent of information passed along any other arc to that node, so local updating will work.

Combining Evidence and Updating Beliefs for Polytrees

Each approach for reasoning with uncertainty has a method for updating certainties as new information becomes known. Many of the approaches keep this updating simple by making assumptions about independence of events. In belief networks, dependencies are represented explicitly. Furthermore, by their definition, we know that no dependencies are hidden. Roughly speaking, nodes that are not connected by some path are conditionally independent given the parents.

This suggests that when new information arrives, some computation involving the probabilities of the parents would be enough to revise probabilities by propagating information. It is worth noting, however, that nothing in the definition of belief networks precludes cycles. That is, nothing precludes causal loops. Loops introduce the complication of keeping track of nodes that have been visited, so that extra (or even nonterminating) visits do not inappropriately add up influences. We now consider restrictions on the topology of belief networks that make the updating computations more tractable.

Figures 6.21 and 6.22 give examples of a special DAG called a **polytree**. In a DAG there can be more than one path between nodes. Figure 6.21 shows an example of multiconnectedness in a DAG. Polytrees are a special case of DAGs. Like nodes in DAGs, nodes in a polytree can have more than one parent. However, the defining characteristic of polytrees is that they are singly connected, which means there is at most one path between two nodes. Figure 6.22 gives an example of a polytree.

In the following we consider an updating algorithm for belief networks that are polytrees. Each node in a polytree receives information from each of its parent and child nodes, representing all the evidence from the network beyond. The single-connectedness condition guarantees that the information passed along any arc to a node is independent of information passed along

FIGURE 6.21.   A DAG that is multiconnected.

any other arc to that node, so local updating will work. The time complexity of this approach is linear in the number of nodes.

The treatment here follows closely that developed in Neapolitan (1990). In the general case, nodes in polytrees can have multiple parents. For simplicity in the presentation, we present the method for the case where each node has exactly two parents. We refer to the method as "P3," for polytree probability propagation.

P3 is an algorithm that updates probabilities incrementally as information becomes known. Let A, B, and D be three nodes in the network with A and D being parents of B. The number of possible values for these nodes is n_a, n_b, and n_d, respectively. In these formulas, we refer to "messages" of information that are passed between the nodes. The information in these messages is obtained locally. For example, the $\pi_B(A)$ message is obtained from information about A and is meaningful at node B. The π message is passed from A to B and the λ message is passed from B to A. Figure 6.23 shows this configuration of nodes and messages graphically.

Before presenting the P3 method, we consider the meaning of the π and λ notations. Let W be a subset of instantiated variables in a network V, which is variables whose values are known. W_{B-} is the subset of W rooted at B, and W_{B+} is $W - W_{B-}$. Let $B \in V$ be some variable in the network. For $1 \leq i \leq n_b$, we define

$$\lambda(b_i) = \quad P(W_{B-} \mid b_i) \text{ if } B \notin W$$
$$1 \text{ if } B \in W \text{ and } b_i \text{ is the instantiated value}$$
$$0 \text{ if } B \in W \text{ and } b_i \text{ is not the instantiated value} \qquad (49)$$

The entire vector of values, $\lambda(b_i)$ for $1 \leq i \leq n_b$, is called B's λ value and is denoted $\lambda(B)$. Similarly, we define the π values.

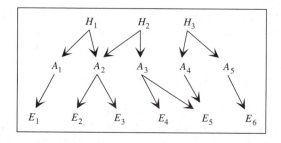

FIGURE 6.22.   A belief network shaped as a polytree, where nodes are singly connected.

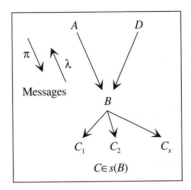

FIGURE 6.23. A belief network showing nodes and messages as they are named in the method, P3. Nodes A and D are parents of node B. The set $\{C \mid C \in s(B)\}$ contains the children of B. In the method, λ messages carry information about B to A, and π messages carry information about A to B.

$$\pi(b_i) = P(b_i \mid W_{B+}) \qquad (50)$$

As with the λ values, $\pi(b_i)$ for $1 \leq i \leq n_b$ is called B's π value and is denoted $\pi(B)$.

Thus, $\lambda(b_i)$ and $\pi(b_i)$ are incremental estimates of conditional probability. Roughly, the λ values are concerned with computing conditional probabilities of parents given probabilities of their children, and the π values are concerned with computing conditional probabilities of children given probabilities of parents. These can be understood as playing a loosely analogous role in the belief updating computation as the likelihood ratios λ and λ play in the odds-likelihood approach. In that approach, which assumed independence of variables, a multiplicative rule relates probabilities along a cause-effect chain so probabilities throughout the network can be computed from probabilities at the roots. Belief networks have a completely different interpretation of variable values than do inference networks and allow variables to be conditionally dependent. Nonetheless, the belief-updating computations make use of local information and propagate the effects of changes through the network.

P3 itself employs several formulas to compute probabilities. We give these formulas now so we can refer to them by label in the method. The λ message from B to A is given by equation (PT-1).

$$\lambda_B(a_j) = \sum_{k=1}^{n_d} \pi_B(d_k) \left(\sum_{i=1}^{n_b} P(b_i \mid a_j, d_k)\, \lambda(b_i) \right) \qquad \text{(PT-1)}$$

The π message from A to B is given by equation (PT-2).

$$\pi_B(a_j) = \quad \begin{array}{l} 1 \text{ if } A \text{ is instantiated for } a_j \\ 0 \text{ if } A \text{ is instantiated but not for } a_j \\ P'(a_j)/\lambda_B(a_j) \end{array} \qquad \text{(PT-2)}$$

where $P'(a_j)$ is the current conditional probability of a_j based on the variables instantiated so far.

For each variable B, $s(B)$ is the set of B's children. The λ value of B for $1 \leq i \leq n_b$ is given by equation (PT-3).

$$\lambda(b_i) = \prod_{C \in s(B)} \lambda_C(b_i) \text{ if B is not instantiated}$$

$\quad\quad$ 1 if B is instantiated for b_i

$\quad\quad$ 0 if B is instantiated, but not for b_i $\hspace{4cm}$ (PT-3)

The π value of B is given by

$$\pi(b_i) = \sum_{j=1}^{n_a} \sum_{k=1}^{n_d} P(b_i \mid a_j, d_k)\, \pi_B(a_j)\, \pi_B(d_k)$$

$\hspace{10cm}$ (PT-4)

Finally, $P'(b_i)$, the conditional probability of b_i based on the variables instantiated so far, is given by

$$P'(b_i) = \alpha\, \lambda(b_i)\, \pi(b_i)$$

$\hspace{10cm}$ (PT-5)

where α is a normalizing constant chosen so that $|P'(B)| = 1$. Figure 6.24 gives the P3 method.

Illustrating the Belief Network Approach for Polytrees

We now briefly consider an example. To minimize the number of computations required, we use a very simple example. Figure 6.25 shows a simple belief network. The nodes are intended to model a situation where we inspect a garden in the morning. Every morning we admire the growth of a fine patch of carrots. Every now and then some carrots are missing. Sometimes they are missing because the wily rabbit, Peter, has dug under the fence again and taken them. Sometimes they are missing because the cook has picked some carrots and prepared stew. (We assume further that, for some reason, nobody tries to catch Peter and the cook does not make rabbit stew.) The computations in this example follow those of an example in Neapolitan (1990, pp. 241–246), which contains a more detailed presentation of these methods and their proofs.

In principle, there is no causal relationship between the cook making stew and Peter Rabbit stealing carrots. Suppose, however, that we have noticed that some carrots are missing. We might start to get hungry for that stew. However, if we see a telltale hole under under the fence, we would decrease our belief that the cook made stew and conclude that the carrots are missing because Peter took them. Similarly, if the aroma of stew cooking is wafting out of the kitchen window, we might be less inclined to blame Peter or to inspect the ground near the fence for rabbit diggings. Thus, learning about either of these events would affect the probability we would assign to the other.

We now consider the initialization process for P3 on this example, before any variables are instantiated. Figure 6.26 gives the prior probabilities for the various events. The first step in the initialization procedure is to set all λ values, λ messages, and π messages to 1. Then in lines 2 and 3 of the method, for every root of the network, we set the π values to the prior probabilities.

```
               ;*** First initialize the polytree to compute prior probabilities.
     1.    Set all λ values, λ messages, and π messages to 1.
     2.    For every node A that is a root of the network do
     3.            for j from 1 to nₐ do π(aⱼ) = P(aⱼ).
     4.    For every node A that is a root of the network do
     5.            for each child B in s(A) do
     6.                    Post a new π message to B using PT-2.
                          ;*** This starts the propagation using the update
                          procedures.

                   ;*** Updating procedures, which are triggered when variables
                   are instantiated or when messages are received.

ON-INST:       ;*** On instantiation of a variable
     1.    When a variable B is instantiated for bⱼ, then
     2.    begin
     3.            Set P'(bⱼ)=1 and for i ≠ j, set P'(bᵢ) = 0.
     4.            Compute λ(B) using PT-3.
     5.            Post new λ messages to B's parents using PT-1.
     6.            Post new π messages to B's children using PT-2.
     7.    end

ON-LAMBDA:         ;*** On receipt of a λ message
     1.    When a variable B receives a λ message from one of its children,
           then if B is not instantiated
     2.    begin
     3.            Compute the new value of λ(B) using PT-3.
     4.            Compute the new value of P'(B) using PT-5.
     5.            Post new λ messages to B's parents using PT-1.
     6.            Post new π messages to B's other children using PT-2.
     7.    end

ON-PI:         ;*** On receipt of a π message
     1.    When a variable B receives a π message from a parent, then
     2.    begin
     3.            If B is not already instantiated, then
     4.            begin
     5.                    Compute the new value of π(B) using PT-4.
     6.                    Compute the new value of P'(B) using PT-5.
     7.                    Post new π messages to B's children using PT-2.
     8.            end
     9.            If λ(B) ≠ (1, 1, 1, ..., 1) then post λ messages to B's other
                   parents using PT-1.
     10.   end
```

FIGURE 6.24.   P3 is a method for propagating probabilities in polytrees, which means in singly connected networks. This method is based on Neapolitan, 1990, pp. 238–240.

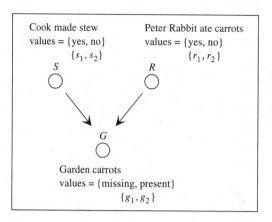

FIGURE 6.25.   A simple belief network. The three nodes are G, R, and S. G represents the question of whether the carrots are missing from the garden, R represents the question of whether Peter Rabbit stole the carrots from the garden, and S represents the question of whether the cook used the carrots in making stew.

This yields simply

$$\pi(R) = (.001, .999)$$
$$\pi(S) = (.01, .99)$$

Finally, in lines 4 through 6, we post new π messages to G from both R and S using PT-2.

$$\pi_G(s_1) = P'(s_1) / \lambda_G(s_1) = .01/1 = .01$$
$$\pi_G(s_2) = .99$$
$$\pi_G(r_1) = .001$$
$$\pi_G(r_2) = .999$$

As these messages are posted, the ON-PI updating procedure is invoked for G. We first consider the messages from S. Since G is not instantiated, step 5 is to compute a new value of $\pi(G)$ using PT-4. The first time the ON-PI message is received, $\pi_G(r) = (1, 1)$ because the initialization at node R is not yet complete.

$$\pi(b_i) = \sum_{j=1}^{n_a} \sum_{k=1}^{n_d} P(b_i \mid a_j, d_k) \, \pi_B(a_j) \, \pi_B(d_k)$$

Applying PT-4 for g_1, we have

$$\pi(g_1) = P(g_1 \mid s_1, r_1) \, \pi_G(s_1) \, \pi_G(r_1) + P(g_1 \mid s_1, r_2) \, \pi_G(s_1) \, \pi_G(r_2) + $$
$$P(g_1 \mid s_2, r_1) \, \pi_G(s_2) \, \pi_G(r_1) + P(g_1 \mid s_2, r_2) \, \pi_G(s_2) \, \pi_G(r_2)$$
$$\pi(g_1) = (.99)(.01)(1) + (.9)(.01)(1) + (.5)(.99)(1) + (.01)(.99)(1)$$
$$\pi(g_1) = .5238$$

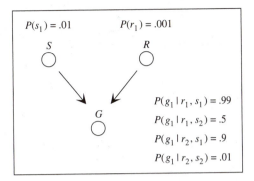

FIGURE 6.26.   Prior probabilities for the carrot example. We are given that there is a .01 chance that the cook made stew and a .001 chance that Peter stole carrots. It is also less than certain that we notice when carrots are missing. If both the cook and Peter took carrots, we'll notice this with probability 0.99. However, Peter is fairly sly in taking carrots and we'll notice his theft by itself only about half the time. If the cook took carrots, we'll notice it with probability 0.9. We'll falsely think that carrots are missing with probability .01.

Similarly,

$$\pi(g_2) = 1.4762$$

Next we use PT-5 to compute a new value of $P'(G)$:

$$P'(b_i) = \alpha\, \lambda(b_i)\, \pi(b_i)$$
$$P'(g_1) = \alpha\, \lambda(g_1)\, \pi(g_1) = \alpha(1)(.5238) = \alpha(.5238)$$
$$P'(g_2) = \alpha(1.4762)$$

Normalizing $P'(B)$, we get $P'(G) = (.2619, .7381)$. If G had children, the next step in ON-PI would be to send π messages to the children. Also, since $\lambda(B) = (1, 1, 1, \ldots, 1)$, no λ message is sent to G's parents.

The next event is to invoke ON-PI again for the π initialization message from node R. Again, the first step is to use PT-4. Because PT-4 is symmetric with regard to the two parents, this results in the same computation as before except that $\pi_G(R)$ is now initialized to (.001, .999) instead of (1, 1). Given this, we see that the order that the messages from parents are processed does not matter. The state depends on the last message processed, and the computation depends on the state of both parents. Continuing with PT-4, we have

$$\pi(g_1) = .019$$
$$\pi(g_2) = .981$$

Again, PT-5 is invoked to compute $P'(G)$. After normalization, we have $P'(G) = (.019, .981)$. Figure 6.27 gives the state of the belief network for the carrot problem after initialization is complete. Because no nodes have been instantiated yet, all l values are still 1.

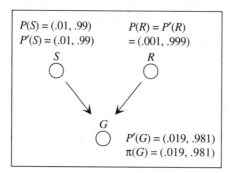

FIGURE 6.27.   State of the carrot-problem belief network after initialization.

We now have little expectation that any carrots are missing or that there will be stew for dinner. Suppose at this point that we are strolling past the garden and there is a noticeable gap in the carrot patch. In terms of the model, this means that variable G can now be instantiated to indicate that carrots are missing from the garden. Invoking ON-INST, we indicate this by setting

$$P'(G) = (1, 0)$$

In other words, we set the G variable to "carrots missing." We now compute $\lambda(B)$ using PT-3.

$$\lambda(b_i) = \prod_{C \in s(b)} \lambda_C(b_i) \text{ if } B \text{ is not instantiated}$$

$\quad\quad\quad$ 1 if B is instantiated for b_i
$\quad\quad\quad$ 0 if B is instantiated but not for b_i

$$\lambda(G) = (1, 0)$$

Next we compute λ messages for G's parents, S and R, using PT-1.

$$\lambda_B(a_j) = \sum_{k=1}^{n_d} \pi_B(d_k) \left(\sum_{i=1}^{n_b} P(b_i \mid a_j, d_k)\, \lambda\,(b_i) \right)$$

$$\lambda_G(s_1) = \pi_G(r_1)\, [P(a_1|s_1, r_1)\, \lambda\,(g_1) + P(g_2|s_2, r_2)\, \lambda\,(g_2)]$$
$$\quad\quad\quad + \lambda_G(r_2)\, [P(g_1|s_1, r_2)\, \lambda\,(g_1) + P(g_2|s_1, r_2)\, \lambda\,(g_2)]$$
$$\quad\quad = .001\, [.99(1) + .01(0)] + .999[.9(1) + .1(0)]$$
$$\quad\quad = .9$$

Similarly,

$$\lambda_G(s_2) = .01$$
$$\lambda_G(r_1) = .505$$
$$\lambda_G(r_2) = .019$$

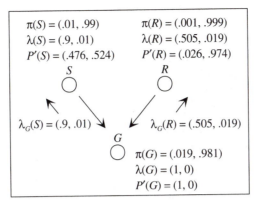

FIGURE 6.28.   State of belief network after carrots are noticed missing from the garden.

Figure 6.28 summarizes the λ messages sent from B to its parents. These λ messages trigger further computation via the ON-LAMBDA procedure for both nodes S and R. The result of these computations is shown in Figure 6.28.

We see now that our expectation of stew for dinner is almost 50 percent. It is still unlikely that Peter has been at work. The stage is now set for gathering further evidence. Using the procedures we have invoked so far, we could perhaps notice the appetizing aroma of stew cooking from the kitchen or, sadly, notice diggings around the garden fence. In P3, as in life, either kind of evidence would change our expectations of the corresponding belief and decrease our expectations of the other (see the exercises).

The revised estimates in the computation of P' in P3 reflect our use of the best available probabilities. In the beginning, our estimates are based on prior probabilities. When we learn that carrots are missing, we compute conditional probabilities reflecting that. Thus, the new version of P' corresponds to the conditional probability that we will have stew for dinner, given that carrots are missing and nothing else. If we subsequently see diggings by the fence, the algorithm cycles again. When it finishes, the new value for P' corresponds to the conditional probability of stew for dinner given both that carrots are missing and that Peter has stolen some carrots.

Applicability of the Belief Network Approach

The P3 method for polytrees uses a Bayesian updating scheme. Because there are no loops, the message traffic will always settle down. Because there is at most one path between any two nodes, no additional provisions are required to assure that evidence is only counted once. The approach does not make unwarranted assumptions of independency and is generally the preferred approach for applications requiring accuracy. The computational approach described in this chapter is drawn from Neapolitan (1990) and was originally proposed by Lauritzen and Spiegelhalter (1988).

Polytrees are a special case of network structures. This raises the question of methods for more general topologies such as the multiconnected network in Figure 6.29. Indeed, it is sometimes argued that most real networks are multiconnected, suggesting that more complex methods for updating are required.

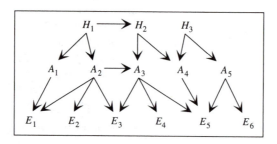

FIGURE 6.29.   Multiconnected belief network. This is a DAG, but not a polytree.

Although discussing more general methods for belief propagation goes beyond the scope of this section, a few summary remarks are in order. Pearl (1988) presents an approach to inference in multiconnected networks termed loop cutset conditioning. Selected variables are instantiated to cut open all loops. The resulting singly connected network is solved, and then the results of each instantiation are combined, weighted by their prior probabilities. This approach is similar to methods used for constraint satisfaction problems. A number of other reductionist approaches have been investigated and some of these have been shown to be equivalent. Several of these methods are surveyed in Henrion (1990) and compared in Neapolitan (1990).

At the time of this writing, the development of such methods is an active area of research. A major issue is that methods for the general case appear to be much more complex. Indeed, Cooper (1990) shows that the problem of determining probabilities in general causal networks is NP-hard. He shows that the problem of inferring probabilities in nonsingly connected belief networks is NP-hard.

6.1.5   *Summary and Conclusions*

Techniques for managing uncertainty fall into three categories: neo-calculist, neo-probabilist, and neo-logicist. The neo-calculist approaches use numerical representations of uncertainty but regard probability theory itself as inadequate. The Dempster-Shafer calculus and certainty factors fall into this category. The neo-probabilists use probability but augment the theory with new representations, primarily ones for rapidly ascertaining the independence of variables. The Bayesian probability network approach falls within this category. The neo-logicist approaches deal with uncertainty using nonnumerical techniques, such as default reasoning and nonmonotonic logic. We discuss neo-logicist approaches in the quandaries section of this chapter.

Of these approaches, certainty factors are still the most widely used, at least in the first generation of expert systems. This is because of the simplicity of their computational requirements and the smaller amounts of statistical data that they require. The weakness of the approach is the nonobvious interdependence restriction placed on the estimation of parameters by the assumptions of independence. The certainty-factor approach breaks down in domains where the reasoning chains are not short or where the hypotheses are compound, as in complex combinations of separately determined elements. Researchers in the field tend to characterize certainty factors as a primitive approach that eventually led to much better methods. Others argue that although the method is dated, it is still useful for projects with very modest demands for managing uncertainty.

The Dempster-Shafer approach is particularly convenient for formulating compound hypotheses hierarchically and refining them. It has gained in popularity. Like the CF approach, it admits partially specified models and is compatible with the proof-based style of logical inference. The Dempster-Shafer approach has essentially the same locality and detachment properties as the CF approach. It can be used together with nonmonotonic reasoning approaches.

Directed graphs provide a convenient notation for people to encode and communicate uncertain beliefs. The key idea in probability networks is to provide efficient methods for determining when parameters are independent. Much of the theory of probability networks is about the independence and dependence relationships among events that can be captured using probability or belief networks. This theory has led to a number of algorithms for performing inference on probability networks. These inference algorithms use local data within the network, but in general they must also have some way of globally integrating local computations. For example, in cutset conditioning the global part involves performing a summation over all the instantiations of the cutset nodes. The local part involves doing local propagation in a singly connected network relative to a given cutset instantiation.

The neo-logical approaches deal with uncertainty by extending the concepts and methods of logic but without introducing numerical measures of uncertainty. The most important of these methods are versions of nonmonotonic logic, of which many variants have been proposed. The problem with monotonic logic is that it lacks a device for handling conditionalization. Nonmonotonic approaches admit natural representations of multiple hypotheses. They represent dependency information and provide means for conditionally adding using defaults, conditionally retracting beliefs, and conditionally propagating changes to beliefs.

Completeness of Information, Accuracy, and Time Complexity

All these approaches to reasoning with uncertainty face fundamental trade-offs regarding completeness of information, accuracy of results, and time complexity. These trade-offs are not always understood or recognized. For example, the most commonly used rationale for the CF approach as compared with a probabilistic approach is that the data required to use Bayes' rule are rarely available. According to this argument, if reasoning is to proceed at all, even inaccurately, some nonprobabilistic approach to evidence combination must be employed. Without discounting the significance of this point, it is also the case that the rare-data argument by itself masks other deep and related issues of tractability and accuracy. In the following, we sketch some of these issues.

The CF and D-S approaches both assume that events are independent. By limiting its hypotheses to singletons, the CF approach extends its independence-assuming philosophy, since compound hypotheses tend to be correlated. For example, the two-element compound hypothesis {measles ∧ broken leg} connects with the one-element singleton hypothesis {broken leg}. The D-S approach provides a means for hierarchically organizing evidence and can handle compound hypotheses readily.

The probability-network approach takes a different tack. Rather than assuming that sources of evidence are independent, it uses explicit links in the network to indicate dependencies. Topologically based tests of the network detect whether events are independent. These tests and subsequenct compensating calculations are supposed to be fast. However, they are not necessarily fast for arbitrary networks. Indeed, the belief-updating algorithms are a variant of constraint satisfaction. The complexity of constraint satisfaction algorithms can undergo phase transitions on families of problems depending on their structural complexity as determined by graph structure and patterns of domain values. Restated, we can predict that if the density of dependencies in the network is high enough, there will be critically constrained sets of dependencies that demand massive propagations to be resolved. Specifically in the area of reasoning about uncertainty, it has been reported in the literature that probabilistic inference using belief networks is NP-hard.

Referring back to the CF and D-S approaches, we can now see that the independence assumptions of these approaches play two roles. One role is to enable reasoning to continue in the presence of sparse data. The other role is to keep the computation tractable, if not accurate. For accurate results in the CF approach when events are not independent, a designer must add "screening clauses" to rules to reflect dependencies among variables. Sometimes sets of rules must be replicated with minor variations to cover the different cases of interactions.

In summary, accuracy in complex situations admits no general escape from time complexity, and no method can be fast for all problems. If the characteristics of problem families for belief networks follow the characteristics of typical constraint satisfaction problems, then we can predict that the truly hard problems are rare—occurring only in the band of a phase transition.

The trade-offs around independence, uncertain reasoning, accuracy, and time complexity cross the boundaries between the symbol level and the knowledge level in the design of knowledge systems. In the next chapters we revisit these issues in the context of designing and analyzing knowledge systems for particular tasks.

Exercises for Section 6.1

Ex. 1   [CD-05] *Terminology*. Indicate whether each of the following statements is true or false. If the statement is ambiguous, explain briefly.

(a) *True or False*. The certainty-factor approach ignores prior probabilities.

(b) *True or False*. The certainty-factor approach assumes that evidence can be used without regard to how it was derived.

(c) *True or False*. The certainty-factor approach is strict Bayesian.

(d) *True or False*. When evidence combination involves conflicts, as in assignment to contradictory subsets, the D-S approach resolves such conflicts by renormalization.

(e) *True or False*. Like the certainty-factor and D-S approaches, probability networks assume that sources of evidence are independent.

Ex. 2   [CD-05] *Warmups*. Indicate whether each of the following statements is true or false. If the statement is ambiguous, explain briefly.

(a) *True or False*. In the D-S approach, two arbitrary propositions can be defined as being mutually exclusive or contradictory.

(b) *True or False*. Dempster's rule is commutative and can be used to pool evidence in any order.

(c) *True or False*. The statement $P(A|B) = p$ in the probability calculus permits us to draw conclusions about the probability of A only when the database entails B and no other information can affect A once we know B.

(d) *True or False*. The statement "If A then B (with certainty p)" in the CF calculus allows us to conclude B (with some probability) whenever A holds, regardless of what other information is in the database.

(e) *True or False*. In the graphical interpretation of $I(X, Z, Y)$, the removal of the Z nodes separates the X nodes from the Y nodes.

Ex. 3   [CD-05] *More Warmups*. Indicate whether each of the following statements is true or false. If the statement is ambiguous, explain briefly.

(a) *True or False*. In a dependency map, if two nodes are not connected then they are independent.

(b) *True or False*. The main problems with classical logic stem from its rigidly binary character.

(c) *True or False*. In the D-S approach the basic probability assignment plays an analogous role to certainty factors in the CF approach in that it indicates for a rule how to change degrees of belief if the premises are satisfied.

(d) *True or False*. In the D-S approach, if two pieces of evidence with the same basic probability assignment are combined, the resulting probability is the same. That is, $M_1 \oplus M_1(A) = M_1(A)$.

(e) *True or False*. The renormalizing process in the D-S approach ensures that probability is not assigned to contradictory subsets.

Ex. 4   [10] *Balls, Urns, and Conditional Probabilities*. In both the following questions, we are given an urn containing 5 green balls and 10 red balls.

(a) A ball is selected, its color is noted, and it is set aside. We are told the ball is green. What are the odds that the second ball we pick is green?

(b) A ball is selected, its color is noted, and it is set aside. We are not told what color the ball is. What are the odds that the second ball we pick is green?

Ex. 5   [05] *Variations on Bayes' Rule*. Briefly show that equation (10), restated here, is valid.

$$P(E) = P(E|H) * P(H) + P(E| \sim H)*P(\sim H)$$

Hint: $A = (A \wedge B) \cup (A \wedge \sim B)$

Ex. 6   [CD-25] *Using Bayes' Rule*. Let:

H = the event (hypothesis) that a person has measles
E = the evidence that a person has red spots

This exercise uses Bayes' rule to figure the relevant probabilities. For the purposes of this exercise, we are given:

$$P(H) = .001 \ P(E|H) = .99 \ P(E| \sim H) = .001$$

(a) What does $P(E| \sim H)$ mean in this case? Briefly, what would be involved in obtaining an estimate of this number?

(b) What is the probability that a person has measles, given that he has red spots?

(c) What is the probability that a person has measles, given that he does not have red spots?

(d) Suppose we have a statistically average sample of 1 million people. How many people are in each of the following categories:

- ☐ People with measles
- ☐ People without measles
- ☐ People with red spots
- ☐ People without red spots
- ☐ People with measles and red spots
- ☐ People with measles and no red spots
- ☐ People with no measles and red spots
- ☐ People with no measles and no red spots

(e) On considering the givens to this problem and the question in part b, Professor Digit reasoned intuitively as follows: "If a person has measles, then there is only a 1 percent chance that he will not have spots. Furthermore, only one person in a thousand will have spots and not also have measles. If you see spots, 99 times out of 100 that person has measles!" Briefly, what is the major flaw in Professor Digit's reasoning?

Ex. 7 [15] *Conditional Probabilities, Again.* This is essentially a repeat of Exercise 6 with different values for the probabilities. Let:

> H = the event (hypothesis) that a person has measles
> E = the evidence that a person has red spots

We are given: $P(H) = .01$ $P(E|H) = .90$ $P(E \sim H) = .01$

(a) What is the probability that a person has measles, given that he has red spots?
(b) What is the probability that a person has measles, given that he does not have red spots?
(c) Suppose we have a statistically average sample of 1 million people. How many people are in each of the following categories:

- ☐ People with measles
- ☐ People without measles
- ☐ People with red spots
- ☐ People without red spots
- ☐ People with measles and red spots
- ☐ People with measles and no red spots
- ☐ People with red spots and no measles
- ☐ People with no measles and no red spots

Ex. 8 [!-15] *Data Requirements for Pooling Evidence Using Bayes' Rule.* It is often said that the data requirements make using Bayes' rule impractical for diagnosis. In this exercise we determine how the data requirements scale with the number of kinds of evidence used and the number of diagnostic hypotheses entertained. Bayes' rule for a single hypothesis and a single datum is given by equation (8), restated here:

> $P(H|E) = P(H) * P(E|H)/P(E)$

(a) Generalize this expression of Bayes' rule to the case where k pieces of evidence are being used, $E_1, E_2, \ldots, E_k$.
(b) Sometimes data are not available. When data are missing, it is appropriate to use whatever data we have. However, this flexibility in using Bayes' rule comes at the price of having probabilities for whatever combination of data is being used. Considering all possible cases, how many different conditional probabilities must be known to pool whatever data are available?

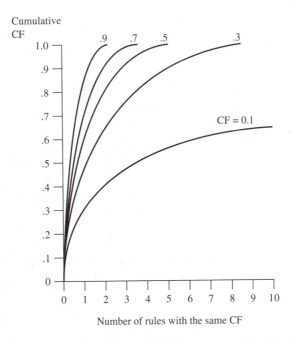

FIGURE 6.30. Family of curves showing how rapidly CFs converge. (From Buchanan and Shortliffe, 1984, Figure 10-1, page 213.)

(c) Suppose we know that the pieces of evidence are independent. How would this simplify requirements?

Ex. 9 [CD-10] *Convergence with Certainty Factors.* It is said that a difficulty of the certainty-factor approach for some problems is the rapidity with which CFs converge on the asymptote 1. Figure 6.30 relates the number of rules with a given CF providing evidence for a given hypothesis. Briefly describe domain conditions for which this would be a problem. How would the issue be addressed in a probabilistic approach?

Ex. 10 [15] *Variations in Combining CFs.* In the pre-1977 version of MYCIN, each hypothesis had both an MB and an MD stored with it instead of a single CF. The combining function was as follows:

> If $MD(H, E_1 \& E_2) = 1$, $MB(H, E_1 \& E_2) = 0$.
> Otherwise, $MB(H, E_1) + MB(H, E_2)[1 - MB(H, E_1)]$.
> If $MB(H, E_1 \& E_2) = 1$, $MD(H, E_1 \& E_2) = 0$.
> Otherwise, $MD(H, E_1) + MD(H, E_2)[1 - MD(H, E_1)]$
> $CF = MB - MD$

(a) Suppose ten rules all support a single hypothesis with CFs in the range 0.4 to 0.8. Using the equations above (and assuming that $MD = 0$), approximately what would be the cumulative MB in this case?

Hint: You can either work this out from a sample value or show an asymptotic limit for MB as evidence is accumulated.

(b) Suppose further that there is a single disconfirming rule with CF = –0.8 (that is, MD = 0.8). Using the pre-1977 combining rule, what would be the net support for the hypothesis?
(c) After 1977, the combination functions for MYCIN were changed as follows:

CF = (MB – MD)/[1 – min (MB, MD)]

$$CF_{combine}(X, Y) = \begin{array}{l} \text{if both } X, Y > 0, X + Y(1 – X) \\ \text{if one of } X, Y < 0, (X + Y)/[1 – \min(|x|, |y|)] \\ \text{if both } X, Y < 0, –CF_{combine}(–X, –Y) \end{array}$$

What would be the resulting value of CF for this revised combination function?
(d) How does the change in the definition of the combining function affect the following cases:

☐ There is a single piece of evidence (when MD or MB is zero).
☐ The evidence is either all positive or all negative.

Ex. 11 [*!-30*] *Mathematical Properties of CFs.* For each of the following criteria, show briefly that the CF method satisfies the property and explain briefly why the method is desirable. We use the notation e+ to refer to positive or confirming evidence and e– to refer to negative or disconfirming evidence. We use e_1 and e_2 to refer to two pieces of evidence where e_1 is encountered or observed before e_2. If additional assumptions are needed to carry out the proof, say what they are.
(a) MB(H, e+) increases toward 1 as confirming evidence is found, equaling 1 if and only if a piece of evidence logically implies H with certainty.
(b) MB(H, e_1&e_2) = MB(H, e_2&e_1)
(c) CF(H, e–) ≤ CF(H, e– & e+) ≤ CF(H, e+)

Ex. 12 [*05*] *More Mathematical Properties of CFs.* Show that the usual Boolean definitions of ∧ and ∨ follow from equations (17) and (18) for the special case where CFs are restricted to 0 and 1.

Ex. 13 [*10*] *Order of Evidence Accumulation with Certainty Factors.* One goal for evidence combination in the certainty-factor approach is that the order that evidence is considered should have no bearing on the results. Consider three pieces of evidence {x, y, z} whose CFs are {X, Y, and Z}, respectively. Using equation (16), show that the results are the same if the data are considered in the order x-y-z or z-x-y. For simplicity, just give the proof for the case where the evidence is all positive.

■ **Ex. 14** [*15*] *Example of Using CFs.* This exercise is based on the certainty-factor approach for uncertain reasoning. We are given:

Evidence: E_1, E_2, E_3 (all known with certainty)
Intermediate hypotheses: A_1, A_2, A_3, B_1, and B_2

And the rules:

Rule 1:   If $E_1 \wedge E_2$ then A_1 (0.6).
Rule 2:   If E_2 then A_2 (0.2).
Rule 3:   If E_3 then A_3 (0.4).
Rule 4:   If $E_1 \vee E_2$ then A_2 (0.3).

	***** *Number of Cases (out of 10)* *****		
Number of Intervals	***Same Organisms and Therapy***	***Different Organisms***	***Different Organisms and Therapy***
10	9	1	0
5	7	3	0
4	8	2	1
3	5	5	1
2	1	9	3

FIGURE 6.31. Results of CF sensitivity experiment. (From Buchanan and Shortliffe, 1984, Figure 10-3, page 219.)

Rule 5:   If $A_1 \vee A_3$ then B_1 (0.7).
Rule 6:   If $A_1 \wedge A_3$ then B_2 (0.9).
Rule 7:   If A_2 then B_1 (0.4).

(a) Using all the applicable rules and evidence, what are the CFs for A_1, A_2, and A_3?
(b) Using the results of part a and all the applicable rules and evidence, what are the CFs for B_1 and B_2?

■ **Ex. 15** *[CD-10] CF Sensitivity Analysis.* In 1979, Bill Clancey and Greg Cooper undertook an experiment to determine quantitatively how sensitive MYCIN is to changes in the CFs of the rules. In particular they were interested in determining whether MYCIN's behavior was sensitive to small changes in the CFs. The results of their study are given in Figure 6.31.

Clancey and Cooper took ten cases and modified the rules by mapping the CFs onto coarser scales. The original CF scale has 1,000 intervals from 0 to 1,000. Trials were run as shown collapsing the CF distinctions down to 10, 5, 4, 3, and 2 intervals. For example, when there are 5 intervals, the CFs are mapped onto 0, 200, 400, 600, 800, and 1,000.

(a) As the CF scale is made coarser, at what point does the performance seriously degrade?
(b) Does this sensitivity analysis primarily reveal a property of the CF approach in general, or of MYCIN's domain in particular? Explain briefly.
(c) Is reasoning in this domain highly sensitive to small changes in assignments of certainty? Explain briefly.

Ex. 16 *[CD-05] The Detachment Assumption and Evidence Combination.* The principle of detachment says that we can use evidence (or certainty information about evidence) without regard to how it was derived. Consider the following rules:

If a statement is reported in a major newspaper, then it is probably true (0.7).
If a statement is reported on a network TV news program, then it is probably true (0.6).
If a statement is reported on local radio news, it is probably true (0.5).
If a statement is reported on the BBC, it is probably true (0.8).

(a) Professor Digit is in the news. Suppose the statement "Famous movie star to wed obscure computer scientist" were reported in a major newspaper, on a TV news program, and on the local radio news. Using the methods of evidence combination for certainty factors, what would the resulting certainty for the statement be?

(b) Suppose later that we learn that all three stories were the result of a single report filed by a local reporter, who interviewed one of Professor Digit's students. Ignoring a priori doubts about the reliability of this particular source, should this new information increase or decrease our certainty of the conclusion? What does this show us about the certainty-factor approach? Explain briefly.

Ex. 17   [40] *Belief, Plausibility, and Doubt in the Dempster-Shafer Approach.* Show that the following basic relations hold:
  (a) Show $Bel(A) + Bel(\sim A) \leq 1$.
  (b) Show $Pl(A) + Pl(\sim A) \geq 1$.
  (c) Show $Pl(A) \geq Bel(A)$.
  (d) Given $A \subseteq C$, show $Bel(A) \leq Bel(C)$.
  (e) Given $A \subseteq C$, show $Pl(A) \leq Pl(C)$.

Ex. 18   [!-10] *Belief versus Doubt in the Dempster-Shafer Approach.* Which of the following statements is correct within the Dempster-Shafer approach? Explain briefly.
  (a) If $B(A) = 0$ then $D(A) > 0$.
  (b) If $D(A) = 1$ then $B(A) = 0$.

Ex. 19   [10] *D-S Evidence Conservation.* Show that $\Sigma\, M_1(X)\, M_2(Y) = 1$ where $X, Y \subseteq \theta$.

Ex. 20   [20] *D-S Evidence Combination.* We are given the probability assignments shown in Figure 6.32.
  (a) Compute $M_1 \oplus M_2$. (Present your answer in a graph as in Figure 6.32.)
  (b) Compute $M_2 \oplus M_1$.

Ex. 21   [!-15] *Evidence Combination: D-S versus CF.* Show that the Dempster-Shafer rule for combining evidence reduces to the certainty-factor rule for combining evidence in the case that M_1 and M_2 give support to exactly one and the same hypothesis.

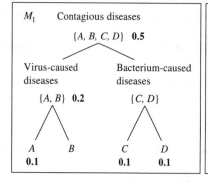
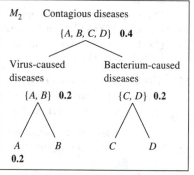

FIGURE 6.32.   Probability assignments.

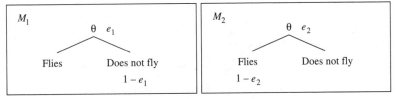

FIGURE 6.33.   Basic probability assignments for Rule 1 and Rule 2.

Ex. 22   [*!-CD-20*] *Common Sense and Renormalizing.* This exercise uses the old AI chestnut about Tweety following an example from Pearl (1988). Suppose we are given the following three rules:

Rule 1: $p \rightarrow\neg f(m_1)$ "Penguins do not (normally) fly."
Rule 2: $b \rightarrow f(m_2)$ "Birds (normally) fly."
Rule 3: $p \rightarrow b$ ($m_3 = 1$) "Penguins are birds."

In the following we let

$e_1 = 1 - m_1$
$e_2 = 1 - m_2$

Figure 6.33 illustrates the basic probability assignments for rules 1 and 2.
(a) Suppose we are given that Tweety is a penguin and that Tweety is a bird. Using the D-S evidence combination rule, compute $M_1 \oplus M_2$ for all possible outcomes. What does the approach give as the probability that Tweety can fly?
(b) Assuming that e_1 and e_2 are small, what does the D-S computation say about the probability that Tweety can fly when we learn that Tweety is a bird? Specifically, what does this predict if the proportion of nonflying birds is .01 and the proportion of flying penguins is .05?
(c) What is going wrong in this application of Dempster's rule? What role does renormalization play in the result? Briefly suggest ways to avoid the problem.

Ex. 23   [*!-CD-15*] *The Defective Coin Machine.* Suppose there is a defective coin machine that produces one-third of the coins with both sides heads, one-third of the coins with both sides tails, and one-third of the coins that are fair. We are given a coin produced by this machine but not permitted to examine the coin. Our assistant will toss the coin and tell us the results of the toss.
(a) The assistant is about to toss the coin for the first time. What odds should we give that the results of the toss will be heads? Explain briefly.
(b) Suppose the result of the first toss is heads. What odds should we give that the result of the next toss will be heads?
(c) Suppose the results of the next tosses are tails, heads, and tails. What odds should we give that the next toss will be heads?

Ex. 24   [*!-15*] *Numeric Definitions of Conditional Independence.* Show that each of the following properties is equivalent to the definition of conditional independence.
(a) $I(X, Y, Z) \Leftrightarrow P(x, y, z) = P(x \mid z) P(y, z)$.
(b) $I(X, Y, Z) \Leftrightarrow P(x, y \mid z) = P(x \mid z) P(y \mid z)$.

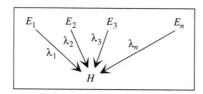

FIGURE 6.34.   Computing odds for multiple sources of evidence.

Ex. 25   [*!-20*] *Properties of Conditional Independence.* Show that each of the following properties follows from the definition of conditional independence.
(**a**) Show that symmetry holds, which means $I(X, Z, Y) \Leftrightarrow I(Y, Z, X)$.
(**b**) Show that decomposition holds, which means $I(X, Z, Y \cup W) \Rightarrow I(X, Z, Y) \wedge I(X, Z, W)$. The union symbol stands for the conjunction of events from the set union $Y \cup W$.
(**c**) Show that weak union holds, which means $I(X, Z, Y \cup W) \Rightarrow I(X, Z \cup W, Y)$.
(**d**) Show that contraction holds, which means $I(X, Z, Y) \wedge I(X, Z \cup Y, W) \Rightarrow I(X, Z, Y \cup W)$.

Ex. 26   [*!-10*] *Odds-Likelihood Rule.* Derive the odds-likelihood formulation of Bayes' rule:

$$O\,(H \mid E) = \lambda\, O(H)$$

Explain your proof, briefly.

Ex. 27   [*00*] *Odds and Probabilities.* It is sometimes said that the odds ratio and probabilities contain the same information, because they can be computed from each other. Show that

$$O = P/(1 - P)$$
$$P = O/(1 + O)$$

Ex. 28   [*00*] *Nonindependence of* λ *and* $\bar{\lambda}$. *Briefly show that*
(**a**) $\lambda > 1 \Rightarrow \bar{\lambda} < 1$
(**b**) $\lambda < 1 \Rightarrow \bar{\lambda} > 1$

Ex. 29   [*!-10*] *Odds for Multiple Sources of Evidence.* Figure 6.34 shows the general case of multiple sources of evidence. Using the odds-likelihood approach and assuming for $1 \leq i \leq n$ that the E_i's are conditionally independent, show that

$$O(H \mid E_1, E_2, E_3, \ldots, E_n) = \lambda_1\, \lambda_2\, \lambda_3 \ldots \lambda_n\, O(H)$$

■ **Ex. 30**   [*10*] *Multiple Sources of Evidence for Odds Likelihood.* Figure 6.35 shows a case of multiple sources of evidence. Compute $P(Z \mid W, X, Y)$, using the odds-likelihood approach and assuming that the E_i's are conditionally independent.

Ex. 31   [*CD-05*] *Spotting Conditional Independence.* For each of the following graphs, determine whether Y and Z are conditionally independent given X. Explain briefly. (This exercise is based on examples from Neapolitan [1990].)
(**a**)

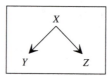

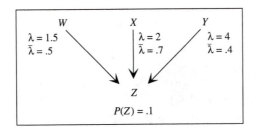

FIGURE 6.35. Combining evidence from multiple sources.

(b)

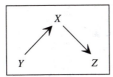

(c)

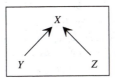

(d)

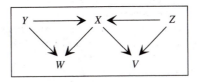

Ex. 32 [CD-05] *Polytrees.* Indicate whether each of the following graphs is a polytree. If it is not, explain briefly.

(a)

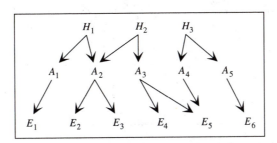

(b)

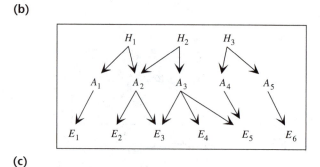

(c)

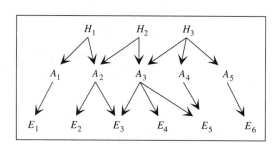

Ex. 33   *[30] Propagating Probabilities in Belief Networks.* This exercise continues the carrot problem from the text. The variable G represents the garden and has the value "carrots missing." There are two possible causes. Variable S represents the possibility that the cook has picked the carrots to make stew for dinner. Variable R represents the possibility that Peter Rabbit dug under the fence and stole the carrots. The prior probabilities for this exercise are given in Figure 6.36.

The current state of the problem is given in Figure 6.37. At this point, neither S nor R is instantiated, which means we do not know definitively why the carrots are missing. Suppose now, sadly enough, that we notice some fresh diggings around the garden fence, making it certain that Peter has paid a visit to the carrot patch. Show each of the following steps in the P3 method.

(a) What are the values assigned to $P'(R)$?

(b) Compute a new value of $\lambda(R)$.

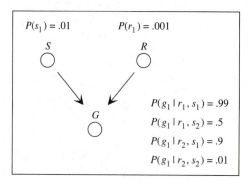

FIGURE 6.36.   Prior probabilities for the carrot example.

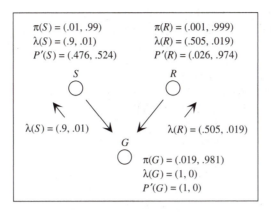

FIGURE 6.37. λ messages sent from *G* after instantiation.

(c) Compute new π messages to *R*'s children.

(d) At this point, the ON-PI procedure is activated for *G*. *G* is already instantiated. Compute the λ message from *G* to *S*.

(e) Node *S* now receives a new λ message from *G*, activating the ON-LAMBDA procedure. Compute the new λ values for *S*.

(f) What are the new normalized values of *P'(S)*?

(g) Briefly summarize how noticing Peter's diggings by the fence have affected our expectations of stew for dinner.

6.2 *Representing Vagueness*

In the preceding section we discussed representation of **certainty**, meaning a **degree of belief** in something. We considered uncertain statements about rainfall such as "We believe (.5) it will rain today." This statement does not mean that we expect a half of a rainfall, such as a light or medium rainfall. Either it will rain or it won't. Uncertainty refers to the degree that we believe it will rain versus the degree we believe it will not rain.

Fuzziness is another concept related to quantified degrees of knowing, but distinct from certainty. Fuzziness is about vagueness. Returning to the topic of rainy days, consider a spectrum of days with different amounts of precipitation. One day it may be misty all day long but never break into a shower. Another day it may rain for a few minutes, but then be sunny for most of the day. A third day there may be heavy showers all day long. Given these examples, consider the question "Was it a rainy day?" A day of showers is certainly rainy. The other two example days are rainy *to some degree*. Fuzziness is a way of defining concepts or categories that admits vagueness and degree. It has nothing to do with degree of belief in something and need not be related to probabilities. Restated, the source of imprecision in problems addressed by fuzzy set theory is the absence of sharply defined criteria of set membership, rather than stochastic processes.

The idea that people reason with shades of gray, not just black and white, has considerable appeal. Some writers have traced this notion in Western thinking back to early philosophers, and the mathematical foundations for it have many parents. Others have related it to Eastern belief systems, such as Zen Buddhism and Taoism. Interest in formal theories of fuzziness and their applications accelerated dramatically after Lotfi Zadeh published a paper on fuzzy set theory in 1965. Ordinary set theory is a theoretical foundation of much of mathematics (Halmos, 1960), and changing such a foundation creates significant ripples. Since 1965, there has been an expanding wave of theoretical results as one area of mathematics after another has been "fuzzified," building from the base of fuzzy set theory.

The range of theoretical results in the mathematics of fuzzy set theory has developed more quickly than it could be tested in a practical way. It also greatly exceeds what we can discuss in this section. Fortunately for the interested reader, good collections of papers on fuzzy sets are available, such as Dubois, Prade, and Yager (1993), which offers a selection of papers from many parts of the field, and Yager, Ovchinnikov, Tong, and Nguyen (1987), which collects many key papers by Zadeh. Graham and Jones (1988) have written a survey book on artificial intelligence that includes fuzzy concepts in the discussion of representation, logic, inference, and decision making.

6.2.1 Basic Concepts of Fuzzy Sets

In the following we introduce some basic concepts of fuzzy set theory and show simple examples of their use. Basic concepts include the definition of fuzzy set membership; operations on fuzzy sets such as union, intersection, and convex combination; fuzzy relations; fuzzy variables; and fuzzy inference.

Fuzzy Sets and Possibility Distributions

Fuzzy set theory was created for use in pattern classification and pattern matching. Fuzzy set theory introduces the idea of "gradual membership" in a set, or perhaps more precisely, a class. Suppose we are given a set of points or objects, X, meaning a universal set. A fuzzy set (class) A in X is characterized by a membership function, v_A, that assigns each point $x \in X$ a real number in the interval [0, 1], representing the degree or grade of membership of x in A. (In this book we use the symbol v to represent membership functions; it has the same meaning as μ, which is also used in the literature.) The notation f_A is also sometimes used to designate the characteristic function of the fuzzy set A.

Figure 6.38 graphs a possible characteristic function for determining when a person drawn from a population would be considered tall. In this example, any person x more than 6 feet in height is tall, with $v_A(x) \approx 1$, and any person under 4 feet in height is not very tall, with $v_A(x) \approx 0$. People whose height falls between these extremes are considered tall to an intermediate degree. A fuzzy set is a generalization of an ordinary set in that the characteristic function of an ordinary set would have only two values, 0 and 1, with no intermediate values.

In some applications of the fuzzy set approach it is convenient to use piecewise linear functions as characteristic functions. For example, Figure 6.39 shows three piecewise linear characteristic functions for the fuzzy sets "short," "medium," and "tall." It is also common to represent such functions using a vector notation in which each term has the form a_k/x_k, where a_k is the degree of membership and x_k is the x-coordinate at which that grade holds. The characteristic function for the fuzzy set "tall people" in Figure 6.39 would be as follows:

$$\text{vector}_{\text{tall}} = (0/4, 0/5, 1/6, 1/7)$$

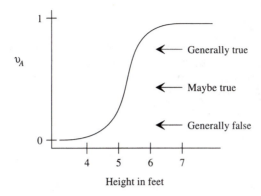

FIGURE 6.38. An example characteristic function for a fuzzy set representing "tall people." The function f_A indicates the degree to which individuals of different heights would be considered to be members of the fuzzy set of tall persons.

Figure 6.39 suggests more about the nature of fuzziness for related sets. Each characteristic function in this example corresponds to a term representing a height of a person. The set corresponding to the greatest height is called "tall." It has some overlap with "medium," which has some overlap with "short. In general, a fuzzy set provides a graceful transition across boundaries.

In the fuzzy approach, a variable like "height" is called a **fuzzy variable** or a **linguistic variable**. It can take on values like "tall," "medium," or "short" as in Figure 6.39. The important point is that a fuzzy variable takes on a fuzzy set as a value, whether it refers to that set by a name or some other means. Similarly, a fuzzy-variable temperature might take on values "steaming," "hot," "tepid," or "cold." The values in these variables are fuzzy sets described by characteristic functions. Fuzzy variables can be used in fuzzy rules with fuzzy inferences, as we discuss later.

Some additional vocabulary about characteristic functions is convenient. The **support** of A is the set of points in X at which υ_A is positive. A **crossover point** in A is a point at which υ_A equals 0.5.

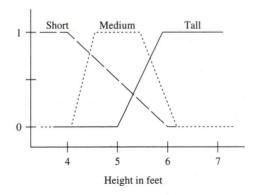

FIGURE 6.39. Three piecewise linear characteristic functions.

Continuing with the concepts for linguistic variables, fuzzy set theory tries to account for the use that people make of modifiers in their characterizations. We may say that a person is "very tall" or "slightly tall." Fuzzy set theory provides a mechanism called a **hedge** for modeling this. A hedge is a systematic modification to a characteristic function. Consider the effect of squaring the characteristic function. Since $0 \leq \upsilon_A \leq 1$, squaring has the effect of reducing the membership values of those elements that have smaller membership values. This particular operation is sometimes called concentration and is shown in equation (51).

$$\upsilon_{con(A)}(x) = (\upsilon_A(x))^2 \tag{51}$$

Performing the concentration operation on the characteristic function for "hot" may be appropriate for representing "very hot," or performing it on the characteristic function for "tall" may be appropriate for representing "very tall." Other hedge operations are discussed in the exercises.

Fuzzy sets and characteristic functions are used in two distinct ways. One way a characteristic function may be used is in estimating degrees of membership. Suppose we are given someone who is five and a half feet tall and we are asked to determine the degree to which this person is a "tall person." In the terminology of fuzzy systems, a specific value like "5.5 feet" is called a **crisp value**. According to the tall characteristic function in Figure 6.39, we would say the degree of membership is 0.5. Another way fuzzy sets can be used is in expressing possibilities in a situation where we have incomplete information. Suppose we are told that a person is of "medium height" but we do not know his exact height. In a case like this, the "medium" characteristic function in Figure 6.39 could be used to express preferences on possible values of a variable whose exact value is not known. This interpretation of a fuzzy set is called a **possibility distribution**.

If we are given an ordinary subset, the question often arises about the extent to which this subset is consistent with some fuzzy set. Suppose we are given the set of people {Joe, Bob, Ray} and are given that their heights are {5.5, 5.9, 5.6}, respectively. Now we are asked the extent to which our subset is consistent with them being "tall people."

Fuzzy set theory approaches this question with the **possibility measure**, $\prod(A)$. When A is an ordinary subset, $\prod(A)$ is defined as the maximum of υ_F over A. A related measure is the **necessity measure**, N(A). N(A) is defined as $1 - \prod(A')$, where A' is the complement of A. Thus, if we are given a set of objects for which we have incomplete knowledge about the value of some attribute, then $\prod(A)$ is a measure of the degree to which the set is possibly in A and N(A) is a measure of the degree to which the set is necessarily A.

Returning to our example subset of people, the maximum value of υ_{tall} occurs for Bob and has a value of about 0.9. Thus, $\prod(A)$ is 0.9. For all the characters not in our set, A', the maximum value of υ_{tall} is for someone 7 feet tall, which is 1. Thus, N(A) = 1 − 1 = 0.

Operations on Fuzzy Sets

The operations on fuzzy sets are defined as analogs to operations on ordinary sets. The analog of the empty set, ϕ, is the fuzzy set whose characteristic function is 0 on X. Two fuzzy sets, A and B, are equal if $\upsilon_A(x) = \upsilon_B(x)$ for all x in X. The **complement** of a fuzzy set A, denoted A', has as its characteristic function:

$$v_{A'} = 1 - v_A \tag{52}$$

Analogous to ordinary subsets, we define containment or subsets for fuzzy sets. If fuzzy set A is contained in fuzzy set B, we write this as follows:

$$A \subseteq B \Leftrightarrow v_A \le v_B \tag{53}$$

The **union** of two sets is defined as the smallest set that contains both fuzzy sets. This is equivalent to defining a set whose characteristic function is the maximum of the characteristic functions of the two sets as suggested by equation (54). Equation (54′) gives a variant syntax for this expression in which the logical OR symbol, $\lor$, is used to represent the maximizing operation. This variant syntax is common in papers about fuzzy sets.

$$v_C(x) = v_{A \cup B}(x) = \max[v_A(x), v_B(x)] \text{ for } x \in X \tag{54}$$
$$v_C(x) = v_{A \cup B}(x) = v_A(x) \lor v_B(x) \tag{54′}$$

Similarly, the **intersection** of two fuzzy sets is the largest fuzzy set that is contained in both A and B. The characteristic function for this minimizes the characteristic functions of the two initial sets, as suggested by Figure 6.40 and equation (55). (See the exercises for proofs of this and also for many of the other results in the following.) Equation (55′) gives a variant syntax where the logical AND symbol, $\land$, is used to indicate the minimizing operation.

$$v_C(x) = v_{A \cap B}(x) = \min[v_A(x), v_B(x)] \text{ for } x \in X \tag{55}$$
$$v_C(x) = v_{A \cap B}(x) = v_A(x) \land v_B(x) \tag{55′}$$

Figure 6.40 shows examples of the union and intersection operations on characteristic functions. Other basic properties of sets follow immediately from these definitions. For example, the two laws by **De Morgan** hold, as stated in equations (56) and (57).

$$(A \cup B)' = A' \cap B' \tag{56}$$
$$(A \cap B)' = A' \cup B' \tag{57}$$

In traditional calculus, a convex combination of two vectors f and g is a linear combination of them in the form

$$\lambda f + (1 - \lambda) g \text{ where } 0 \le \lambda \le 1$$

This mode of combining or interpolating vectors has an important generalization to fuzzy sets called **convex combination**. The convex combination of two fuzzy sets A and B is denoted $(A, B; \Lambda)$ and is defined by the relation

$$(A, B; \Lambda) = \Lambda A + \Lambda' B \tag{58}$$

In terms of characteristic functions, convex combination is given as in equation (59).

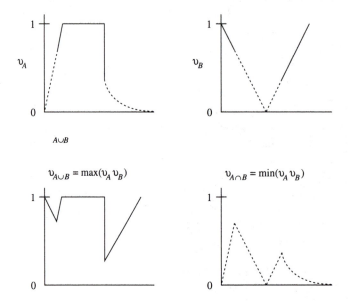

FIGURE 6.40. Characteristic functions illustrating the union and intersection of sets A and B. The highlighted portions of the graphs of f_A and f_B show the regions that are minimal and that therefore make up the profile of the intersection characteristic function.

$$\upsilon(A, B; \Lambda)(x) = \upsilon_\Lambda(x)\,\upsilon_A(x) + [1 - \upsilon_\Lambda(x)]\,\upsilon_B(x) \tag{59}$$

Roughly, convex combination creates another fuzzy set whose characteristic function is an interpolation between the characteristic functions of the two given sets. Equation (60) is an immediate consequence of this definition. Thus, convex set combination yields a fuzzy set in between the sets resulting from intersection and union for all λ and all $x \in X$.

$$(A \cap B) \subseteq (A, B; \Lambda) \subseteq (A \cup B) \tag{60}$$

Fuzzy Relations

In ordinary discourse we speak of relations as something that holds between two things or among several things. For example, we might say that Morgan is Paige's brother, which means he stands in the relation of brother to Paige. In this formulation, a relation is a mapping from one set to another. We can think of the relation as a set of ordered tuples. If Morgan, Lorgan, and Norgan were all brothers of Paige and Nick, Slick, and Mick were all brothers of Ryan, we could define the relation as the following set of pairs:

{(Morgan, Paige), (Lorgan, Paige), (Norgan, Paige), (Nick, Ryan), (Slick, Ryan), (Mick, Ryan)}

It is convenient to introduce names of relations. We could give the relation the name "brother" and use the notation "brother(Morgan, Paige)" to indicate an element of the relation. In conventional set theory, we can think of relations as having a truth value. Combining the use of names and truth values, we could indicate two elements of the relation as follows:

brother(Morgan, Paige) = true
brother(Morgan, Stanley) = false

meaning that Morgan is Paige's brother but that he is not Stanley's brother. A relation is binary if it takes two arguments, trinary if it takes three, and so on. If we have a cross-product of two sets, $X \times Y$, we indicate that a binary relation (such as R) is defined over the possible pairs of the cross-product with the notation $R \subseteq X \times Y$. Higher-order relations are defined over higher-order cross-products.

In fuzzy set theory, a **fuzzy relation** is a fuzzy set defined over a cross-product. Suppose that Morgan was a "stepbrother" to Nick and Ryan and that we choose to model this as ".333" on the fuzzy scale as a degree of brotherness. Then the fuzzy brother relation would include the elements

brother(Morgan, Paige) = 1
brother(Morgan, Stanley) = 0
brother(Morgan, Nick) = .333
brother(Morgan, Ryan) = .333

More generally, a fuzzy relation is represented by a characteristic function that associates a grade of membership with each element of the cross-product.

The composition of two fuzzy relations R and Q, or more precisely the **max-min composition**, is denoted $R \circ Q$. It is defined in terms of operations on characteristic functions. Specifically, if $R \subseteq X \times Y$ and $Q \subseteq Y \times Z$, then equation (61) holds. Equation (61′) gives a variant notation often used in fuzzy logic.

$$\upsilon_{R \circ Q} = \frac{\max[\min(\upsilon_R(x, y), \upsilon_Q(y, z))]}{y} \tag{61}$$

$$\upsilon_{R \circ Q} = \frac{\vee [(\upsilon_R(x, y) \wedge \upsilon_Q(y, z))]}{y} \tag{61'}$$

In the special case where piecewise linear characteristic functions for fuzzy sets are represented as vectors, the operations of composition can be expressed in terms of fuzzy matrix multiplication. For a matrix product of the form

$$B = A \circ M$$

each b_j is computed by

$$b_j = \max[\min(a_i, m_{ij})]$$

or equivalently, in the "logical" notation,

$$b_j = \vee[\wedge (a_i, m_{ij})]$$
$$1 \leq i \leq n$$

Thus, compared with conventional matrix multiplication, the product and sum are replaced with min and max functions, respectively. The compositional relation and the matrix formulation of it for piecewise linear characteristic functions are commonly used in fuzzy reasoning for max-min inference. The composition of fuzzy relations is a convenient way of representing fuzzy reasoning. We consider examples of this in the next section.

Many applications of fuzzy sets make use of a special kind of relation known as a **similarity relation**. A similarity relation is a generalization of an equivalence relation. Equivalence relations are relations that are reflexive, symmetric, and transitive. The first two requirements say roughly that an element x is equivalent to itself and that if x is equivalent to y, then y is equivalent to x. Transitivity means that if x is equivalent to y and y is equivalent to z, then x is equivalent to z. Equivalence relations are used to define equivalence classes.

Similarity relations are defined analogously except that they need to take into account the fuzziness of fuzzy sets. This shows up in the reformulation of the transitivity condition as in equation (62). Thus, it is not enough to say that elements are similar. There are degrees of similarity—and a chain of similarities needs to respect the possibility that the degree of similarity may lessen as we go down a chain of transitive similarities.

A similarity relation is a fuzzy relation that is reflexive, symmetric, and transitive. That is, for $x \in X$, a fuzzy relation S is a similarity relation if it satisfies the following properties:

- Reflexivity: $\upsilon_s(x, x) = 1$
- Symmetry: $\upsilon_s(x, y) = \upsilon_s(y, x)$
- Transitivity: $S \supseteq S \circ S$, or

$$\upsilon_s(x, z) \geq \frac{\max[\min(\upsilon_s(x, y), \upsilon_s(y, z))]}{y} \tag{62}$$

$$\upsilon_s(x, z) \geq \frac{\vee[\upsilon_s(x, y) \wedge \upsilon_s(y, z)]}{y} \tag{62'}$$

6.2.2 *Fuzzy Reasoning*

By itself fuzzy set theory is about representing vagueness. We now introduce concepts for reasoning with these representations. First we consider what it means to combine fuzzy evidence. Then we give an example of how these concepts can be combined in the architecture of a reasoning system.

Combining Fuzzy Evidence and Updating Beliefs

A fuzzy proposition is a statement that asserts a value for a fuzzy variable. For example, it might assert that "Joe's height is medium." In this case, "Joe's height" is the fuzzy variable and "medium," representing a fuzzy set, is a value for that variable. A fuzzy rule relates two or more fuzzy propositions. Like other inexact reasoning techniques, fuzzy inference must determine a belief in a rule's conclusion given evidence on the rule's premise. The two most common fuzzy inference techniques for doing this are max-min inference (corresponding to max-min composition) and max-product inference.

We begin with an example of **max-min inference**. The fuzzy rule is

If speed is normal
then braking.force is medium.

"Speed" and "braking.force" are fuzzy variables. The meaning of the rule is determined in part by fuzzy sets that define the values in the rules for the fuzzy variables. The characteristic functions for normal braking force and medium speed are piecewise linear functions defined by the following vectors:

speed:
Normal = (0/0, .1/20, .8/40, 1/60, .1/80, 0/100)

braking.force:
Medium = (0/0, .5/1, 1/2, 1/3, .2/4, 0/5)

Suppose now that we are given a value for the speed variable and are asked to determine the value for the braking force. The fuzzy value that we use in our example computation is

speed: S = (0/0, 0/20, .8/40, 0/60, 0/80, 0/100)

The given fuzzy speed in this example is equivalent to a crisp speed of 40. Given this value and the rule, what value should be assigned to the braking force? The answer to this question depends on the method of fuzzy inference that we choose. We now consider the results from using max-min inference.

When characteristic functions are piecewise linear, one way to carry out max-min inference is to define a matrix for the composition. The matrix M for compositional inference is defined so that

$$m_{ij} = \min(a_i, b_j)$$

The matrix for this example is as follows.

$$M = \begin{vmatrix} \min(0,0) & \min(0,.5) & \min(0,1) & \min(0,1) & \min(0,.2) & \min(0,0) \\ \min(.1,0) & \min(.1,.5) & \min(.1,1) & \min(.1,1) & \min(.1,.2) & \min(.1,0) \\ \min(.8,0) & \min(.8,.5) & \min(.8,1) & \min(.8,1) & \min(.8,.2) & \min(.8,0) \\ \min(1,0) & \min(1,.5) & \min(1,1) & \min(1,1) & \min(1,.2) & \min(1,0) \\ \min(.1,0) & \min(.1,.5) & \min(.1,1) & \min(.1,1) & \min(.1,.2) & \min(.1,0) \\ \min(0,0) & \min(0,.5) & \min(0,1) & \min(0,1) & \min(0,.2) & \min(0,0) \end{vmatrix}$$

Simplifying terms, we have the following.

$$M = \begin{vmatrix} 0 & 0 & 0 & 0 & 0 & 0 \\ 0 & .1 & .1 & .1 & .1 & 0 \\ 0 & .5 & .8 & .8 & .2 & 0 \\ 0 & .5 & 1 & 1 & .2 & 0 \\ 0 & .1 & .1 & .1 & .1 & 0 \\ 0 & 0 & 0 & 0 & 0 & 0 \end{vmatrix}$$

The braking force predicted by max-min inference is the fuzzy vector resulting from multiplying the matrix M by the input speed S:

braking.force = B = S ° M

The general term is given by

$$b_j = \vee_{1 \le i \le n} [\wedge(a_i, m_{ij})]$$

Thus, for the given speed vector, we have

$b_1 = \max[\min(0, 0), \min(0, 0), \min(.8, 0), \min(0, 0), \min(0, 0), \min(0, 0)] = 0$
$b_2 = \max[\min(0, 0), \min(0, .1), \min(.8, .5), \min(0, .5), \min(0, .1), \min(0, 0)] = .5$
$b_3 = \max[\min(0, 0), \min(0, .1), \min(.8, .8), \min(0, 1), \min(0, .1), \min(0, 0)] = .8$
$b_4 = \max[\min(0, 0), \min(0, .1), \min(.8, .8), \min(0, 1), \min(0, .1), \min(0, 0)] = .8$
$b_5 = \max[\min(0, 0), \min(0, .1), \min(.8, .2), \min(0, .2), \min(0, .1), \min(0, 0)] = .2$
$b_6 = \max[\min(0, 0), \min(0, 0), \min(.8, 0), \min(0, 0), \min(0, 0), \min(0, 0)] = 0$

B = (0, .5, .8, .8, .2, 0)

Equivalently, in the vector notation we have the following fuzzy representation for the braking force to be applied.

B = (0/0, .5/1, .8/2, .8/3, .2/4, 0/5)

This value for B is called an **induced fuzzy set**. For fuzzy control systems, such an induced value is typically "defuzzified" by techniques we consider shortly.

We now consider the effects of max-min inference. Notice that the induced fuzzy set in our example is a clipped version of the medium braking force.

Medium = (0/0, .5/1, 1/2, 1/3, .2/4, 0/5)
B = (0/0, .5/1, .8/2, .8/3, .2/4, 0/5)

Figure 6.41 graphs the effects of max-min inference for this example.

In the special case where the original set is a crisp value, the induced set can be determined by clipping. Thus, in the example, we get the same results as without constructing the composition matrix and performing max-min matrix multiplication.

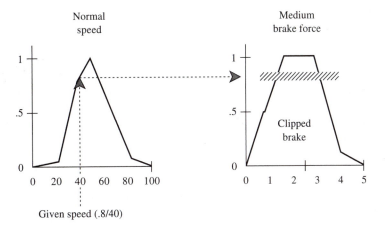

FIGURE 6.41. The effects of max-min inference.

$B' = [\min(.8, 0), \min(.8, .5), \min(.8, 1), \min(.8, 1), \min(.8, .2), \min(.8, 0)]$
$B' = (0, .5, .8, .8, .2, 0)$

Different inference methods in fuzzy logic yield different induced fuzzy sets. Another common inference method is **max-product inference**. Following the same example as before, the elements of the matrix are given by

$$m_{ij} = a_i b_j$$

The matrix for the example is as follows.

$$M = \begin{vmatrix} (0*0) & (0*.5) & (0*1) & (0*1) & (0*.2) & (0*0) \\ (.1*0) & (.1*.5) & (.1*1) & (.1*1) & (.1*.2) & (.1*0) \\ (.8*0) & (.8*.5) & (.8*1) & (.8*1) & (.8*.2) & (.8*0) \\ (1*0) & (1*.5) & (1*1) & (1*1) & (1*.2) & (1*0) \\ (.1*0) & (.1*.5) & (.1*1) & (.1*1) & (.1*.2) & (.1*0) \\ (0*0) & (0*.5) & (0*1) & (0*1) & (0*.2) & (0*0) \end{vmatrix}$$

Simplifying terms, we have the following.

$$M = \begin{vmatrix} 0 & 0 & 0 & 0 & 0 & 0 \\ 0 & .05 & .1 & .1 & .02 & 0 \\ 0 & .4 & .8 & .8 & .16 & 0 \\ 0 & .5 & 1 & 1 & .2 & 0 \\ 0 & .05 & .1 & .1 & .02 & 0 \\ 0 & 0 & 0 & 0 & 0 & 0 \end{vmatrix}$$

As in the example of max-min inference, we are given a value for the speed variable and are asked to determine the value for the braking force. The fuzzy value is the same as before:

speed: S = (0/0, 0/20, .8/40, 0/60, 0/80, 0/100)

Again, we compute the induced fuzzy set by composition.

braking.force = $B = S \circ M$

Thus, for the given speed vector, we have

b_1 = max[min(0, 0), min(0, 0), min(.8, 0), min(0, 0), min(0, 0), min(0, 0)] = 0
b_2 = max[min(0, 0), min(0, .05), min(.8, .4), min(0, .5), min(0, .05), min(0, 0)] = .4
b_3 = max[min(0, 0), min(0, .1), min(.8, .8), min(0, 1), min(0, .1), min(0, 0)] = .8
b_4 = max[min(0, 0), min(0, .1), min(.8, .8), min(0, 1), min(0, .1), min(0, 0)] = .8
b_5 = max[min(0, 0), min(0, .02), min(.8, .16), min(0, .2), min(0, .02), min(0, 0)] = .16
b_6 = max[min(0, 0), min(0, 0), min(.8, 0), min(0, 0), min(0, 0), min(0, 0)] = 0

B = (0, .4, .8, .8, .16, 0)

In the vector notation, we have the following representation for the braking force to be applied.

B = (0/0, .4/1, .8/2, .8/3, .16/4, 0/5)

In the special case that the input vector represents a crisp value, we can simplify the computation. The induced set is simply

Medium = (0/0, .5/1, 1/2, 1/3, .2/4, 0/5)
B = .8 * (0/0, .5/1, 1/2, 1/3, .2/4, 0/5)
B = (0/0, .4/1, .8/2, .8/3, .16/4, 0/5)

Of the two methods, max-min inference seems to be the most commonly used for discrete applications and the max-product inference is most commonly used for continuous control applications.

An Architecture for Fuzzy Reasoning

There is no single way that fuzzy logic is used to create a reasoning system, just as there is no single way that Boolean logic is used to create a reasoning system. However, in the following we show how the techniques we have described so far are typically combined to carry out fuzzy reasoning. First we show how to handle multiple premise rules; then we introduce the process of defuzzification, which creates crisp values from fuzzy values; and then we show one architecture for combining the results of several rules.

The examples of rules that we have considered so far all had a single premise. Consider the case where we extend the rule for determining braking force used in the earlier examples to take into account not only the speed but also the load:

> If speed is normal
> and load is light
> then braking.force is medium.

The input to the situation, then, would be two fuzzy sets representing a speed and a load. One approach, typically used in practice, is to assume a kind of independence of the two relations. We create a separate M matrix for each input premise, relating it to the conclusion. An inference method is used, yielding two induced fuzzy sets. These sets are then combined. Typically, if the premises are related by conjunction, the sets are combined by fuzzy set intersection. If the premises are related by disjunction, the sets are combined by fuzzy set union.

In control systems based on fuzzy logic, the outputs of a fuzzy computation need to be turned into some kind of crisp value for the device being controlled. There are two obvious candidates. The "maximum method" selects the point in the domain at which the maximum grade of the fuzzy set is found. The "moments method" or "centroid method" selects the point in the domain at which a line perpendicular to the x-axis would pass through the center of the fuzzy set. The latter is the most popular defuzzification method. The **fuzzy centroid** is defined in equation (63). This computes a kind of weighted average value depending on the characteristic function for the fuzzy set.

$$y_{centroid} = [\Sigma \, y_j \, \mu(y_j)]/\Sigma \, \mu \, (y_j) \tag{63}$$

Figure 6.42 illustrates the difference between choosing either of the two methods for picking a defuzzified value from the characteristic function of a fuzzy set. Similar to the choice of max-min and max-product inference, the maximum method is most commonly used for discrete problems and the centroid approach is found to give more stable results for continuous problems.

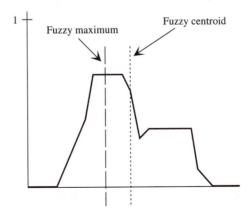

FIGURE 6.42. Two approaches to defuzzification. The fuzzy maximum approach just picks a point (perhaps a central point) at which the characteristic function achieves a maximum. The fuzzy centroid approach picks a place where there is equal weight on either side.

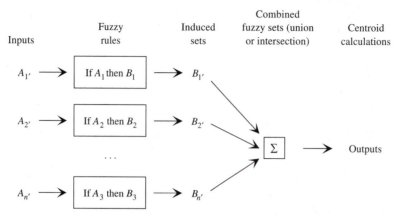

FIGURE 6.43.   A generic system architecture for reasoning based on fuzzy logic.

These elements of fuzzy reasoning can now be combined into a kind of architecture as shown in Figure 6.43. In this generic architecture, there are inputs to the system. If these inputs are crisp, they may be converted to fuzzy vectors by interpreting the corresponding fuzzy sets according to possibility distributions. Once the inputs are prepared, they are used in whatever fuzzy rules are appropriate. An inference method is used for the rules, such as max-min inference or max-product inference. Evidence from multiple premises is combined using fuzzy set union or intersection depending on whether the clauses are disjunctive or conjunctive. The output from multiple rules concluding about the same values is combined by union operations. Finally, the fuzzy set outputs of the system become crisp through defuzzification using centroid computations.

Applicability of the Fuzzy Set Approach

Fuzzy logic, as it has developed, is both a logic of gradual properties as well as a calculus for incomplete information. We have a general sketch of some basic concepts of the fuzzy set approach. We now face our usual questions about methods for reasoning with uncertainty and inexactness. What problems with the model have arisen? What limitations of its applicability are known? How well does the method work in practice ?

The most active area of applications of fuzzy concepts is fuzzy control theory. This area seems to have its greatest acceptance in Japan, where it is reported to be used in the computer control of a wide range of devices, including washing machines, elevators, video cameras, and braking systems. In this approach, expert knowledge is encoded in the form of fuzzy rules that recommend actions for situations described by fuzzy sets. The control system is supposed to recommend actions given the current situation. In this approach, the current situation is matched against two or more prototypical situations, sometimes ones that represent extremes of required behavior. A fuzzy control unit is invoked to match against these situations and to then recommend an action intermediate between the prototypes. The control unit uses an **interpolation function** to determine the required action. The difference between this and classical, discrete control theory is in the way the control law is found. In the fuzzy approach, the control is typically created starting with the experience of a human operator.

In control theory applications, the competing technology is typically some variant of linear system theories. What is often possible in fuzzy control systems is that the control is smooth across a wide range of inputs, even in cases where the fuzzy logic is approximating nonlinear relationships. Another advantage often cited for the fuzzy approach is that it is much easier to get the control knowledge from an expert human operator than it is to determine the optimum control theoretically. It is sometimes claimed that the systems are relatively easy to understand and adjust because they relate directly to performance indices (as represented by fuzzy variables).

Obviously, the success of any particular theory depends on the particulars of the situation. A recent collection of papers on fuzzy set theory (Dubois, Prade, & Yager, 1993) includes several research articles analyzing the properties of fuzzy logic and fuzzy systems, such as the stability of asymptotic behavior in closed loop systems (Tong, 1980). In addition, variations to the basic inference methods discussed here are evaluated according to various criteria about the nature of the results (Fukami, Mizumoto, & Tanaka, 1980).

Fuzzy set methods have been advocated for use in information retrieval systems. The key ideas are to admit elasticity in the query in the form of soft constraints, to retrieve items that partially match the query, and to use fuzzy set evaluations to order candidates that more or less satisfy the query.

6.2.3 *Summary and Conclusions*

Fuzzy sets are used to define concepts or categories that have inherent vagueness and degree. Fuzzy set theory is based on the idea of gradual membership in a set. A fuzzy set is characterized by a membership function, which relates a degree of membership on a scale of 0 to 1 to inherent properties of the objects.

Operations on fuzzy sets are defined in terms of operations on the characteristic functions. For example, the complement of a fuzzy set is the set whose characteristic function is 1 minus the original set's characteristic function at each point. The union operation takes the maximum of the characteristic functions of two sets; intersection takes the minimum. A fuzzy relation is represented by a characteristic function that associates a grade of membership with each element of the cross-product.

A fuzzy proposition is a statement that asserts a value for a fuzzy variable. It might assert that "The car's speed is slow" where slow is a value defined by a characteristic function. A fuzzy rule relates fuzzy propositions. A fuzzy rule might say

> If the car's speed is slow,
> then the required braking force is light.

The final part of this section showed how to define fuzzy inference. Using the example rule, suppose we are given a fuzzy value for a car's speed. A fuzzy inference specifies how to combine the fuzzy value with the rule so as to determine a new (fuzzy) value for the required braking force. The two most common forms of fuzzy inference are max-min inference and max-product inference. Max-min tends to be used for discrete operations and max-product is most commonly used for continuous control applications.

Exercises for Section 6.2

Ex. 1   [*CD-05*] *Terminology*. Indicate whether each of the following statements is true or false. If the statement is ambiguous, explain briefly.

(a) *True or False*. Fuzzy set theory is used to manage uncertainty.

(b) *True or False*. Fuzzy set characteristic functions must be continuous.

(c) *True or False*. A linguistic variable is a variable whose value is a fuzzy set.

(d) *True or False*. A hedge is a systematic modification to a characteristic function.

(e) *True or False*. An induced fuzzy set is a fuzzy set whose piecewise linear characteristic function is produced by induction on evenly spaced property values.

Ex. 2   [*16*] *Properties of Operations on Fuzzy Sets*. Fuzzy set theory defines operations on fuzzy sets that are analogous to operations on ordinary sets.

(a) Show that the union, C, of two fuzzy sets A and B has the characteristic function:

$$\upsilon_C(x) = \max[\upsilon_A(x), \upsilon_B(x)] \text{ for } x \in X$$

(b) Show that the intersection, C, of two fuzzy sets A and B has the characteristic function:

$$\upsilon_C(x) = \min[\upsilon_A(x), \upsilon_B(x)] \text{ for } x \in X$$

(c) Show that the first of De Morgan's laws holds:

$$(A \cup B)' = A' \cap B'$$

(d) Show that the second of De Morgan's laws holds:

$$(A \cap B)' = A' \cup B'$$

Ex. 3   [*!-CD-03*] *Hedge Operations on Fuzzy Sets*. Fuzzy set theory defines operatons on fuzzy sets that are analogous to operations on ordinary sets.

We are given three functions commonly used in fuzzy set applications as follows.

1. $\upsilon_{1(A)}(x) = (\upsilon_A(x))^2$
2. $\upsilon_{2(A)}(x) = (\upsilon_A(x))^{0.5}$
3. $\upsilon_{3(A)}(x) = (\upsilon_A(x))^3$

We are told that these hedges correspond to the three linguistic modifiers in the following. Which is which? Explain your rationale briefly.

(a) Which one corresponds to "somewhat"?

(b) Which one corresponds to "very"?

(c) Which one corresponds to "extremely"?

Ex. 4   [*06*] *Operations on Fuzzy Sets*. We are given three fuzzy sets, A, B, and C, defined with piecewise linear characteristic functions on the unit interval $x \in [0, 1]$.

$$\upsilon_A(x) = x$$
$$\upsilon_B(x) = 2 * |0.5 - x|$$
$$\upsilon_C(x) = 1 - 2 * |0.5 - x|$$

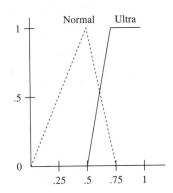
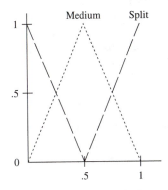

FIGURE 6.44.   The characteristic functions for the values of fuzzy variables A and B.

    (a) Draw a graph of the characteristic functions of the three fuzzy sets.
    (b) What is $A \cup B$? (Illustrate your answer with a graph.)
    (c) What is $A \cap C$? (Illustrate your answer with a graph.)

Ex. 5   *[15] Fuzzy Reasoning.* In this exercise we consider some basic operations in a simple fuzzy reasoning system. We are given the following two rules:

       Rule 1:
       If A is normal
       then B is medium.

       Rule 2:
       If A is ultra
       then B is split.

We are also given piecewise linear characteristic functions for the fuzzy variables as in Figure 6.44.
    (a) Give vector notation for the possible values for the fuzzy variables A and B. Give data at $x = \{0, .25, .5, .75, 1\}$.
    (b) Using Rule 1 and max-min inference, give the induced fuzzy set B' for the crisp input value of A of 0.25.
    (c) Using Rule 2 and max-min inference, give the induced fuzzy set B'' for the crisp input value of A of 0.25.
    (d) Compute the combined result of Rule 1 and Rule 2 using fuzzy union of B' and B''.
    (e) Compute a crisp value for output of the fuzzy system using the centroid method for defuzzification.

6.3   *Open Issues and Quandries*

Research on representations of uncertainty and vagueness is a very broad area with many special cases and areas of development for specific kinds of applications. In this chapter we characterized approaches as belonging in three broad categories: neo-probabilist (Shafer & Pearl, 1990), neo-calculist (Dubois, Prade, & Yager, 1993), and neo-logicist (Ginsberg, 1987). Publication in each of these areas has been extensive, including many research articles, books, and in some cases even specialized journals. The relationship between numeric and probabilistic accounts and symbolic ones has been the subject of some debate. The interested reader might consult the last chapter of Pearl (1988) for an account of intricate relationships, including an amusing dialog between a "logicist" and a "probabilist" on this open question.

On Nonmonotonic Logics

In symbolic approaches, it is often the case that if $A \rightarrow B$, then $A \wedge C \rightarrow B$. Restated, it is possible to add information without invalidating previously made conclusions. Systems that have this property, such as conventional uses of the predicate calculus, are said to be **monotonic**. However, many approaches for coping with inexactness, uncertainty, and incomplete information do not have this property. Logics in which new information can defeat previously made conclusions are said to be **nonmonotonic**. This issue of conflicts is not limited to derived information. We can ask whether it is always possible to incorporate new information without modifying the existing representations. We can ask whether a representation lends itself to later retracting a piece of information initially taken to be true, or perhaps to later adding qualifications on the conditions under which information is taken to be true.

In an effort to model salient features of commonsense reasoning, many extensions to classical logic have been developed. The breadth of approaches and differences among them is too great to survey here in detail. What we can do, however, is sketch some of the main approaches and offer suggestions about where the interested reader can learn more. Primary papers for most of the approaches can be found in a set of readings collected by Ginsberg (1987).

Sombe (a pseudonym for a group of French AI researchers) (1990) compares many of the approaches by representing variations of a single example across different approaches and comparing the results. As they note,

> Although they [the approaches] may seem to resemble one another, these various formulations will lead to logical systems whose behavior and results are sometimes highly differentiated. (p. 327)

In classical logic, the statement "all the A's are B's" is an example of what is easily expressed, such as "$\forall (x) \, x \in A \Rightarrow x \in B$." It is also a prime example of the kind of statement that many logics try to weaken in some way, to achieve greater generality. Sombe translates "all the A's are B's" for a variety of formalisms. The paraphrases of these translations are instructive in communicating some of the gist of the different approaches.

- Reiter's default logic is translated to "an A is a B, up to exceptions."
- Doyle and McDermott's nonmonotonic modal logic is translated to "if B is conceivable and if A, then B."
- Moore's autoepistemic logic is translated to "if a given A was not B, we would know it."
- McCarthy's circumscription is translated to "every A that is not abnormal is B."

- Besnard and Siegel's supposition-based logic is translated to "every A for which we assume B is B."
- Delgrande's conditional logic is translated to "typically the As are Bs."
- Stalnaker's logic of counterfactual conditionals is translated to "if it were an A, then it would be a B."
- Dubois and Prade's possibilistic logic is translated to "an A is almost certainly a B."
- Numerical quantifier logics are translated to "most of the As are Bs."

It is striking that these variations all deal in some way with the matter of what it is that we "know" at any given time and, furthermore, that the core of the question as it arises in logical formalisms often has to do with extension to the $\exists$ operator. Restated, it has to do with variations on the matter of existence, especially as existence relates to the matter of what we can assume in situations where we cannot reasonably expect to know or derive everything.

Many key examples and issues driving the development of nonmonotonic logic have been discussed in the earlier chapters at one place or another. In the following we summarize these ideas and also survey the way the nonmonotonic approaches build from them.

Chapter 1 introduced three ideas that are fundamental to nonmonotonic approaches:

Closed-world assumption (CWA). If some object is not listed in the database, then it is not in the world. More generally, if a fact is not in the database then the fact is not true.

For example, if a university course is not listed in the course catalog, then CWA licenses us to assume that no such course exists. The closed-world assumption is used in the interpretation of many representational systems. In the current chapter, we saw variations of CWA come up in the interpretation of maps and other spatial representations. One way to understand this assumption is that it "minimizes" predicates in the database. In the course example, suppose "CS 228C" is not in the database. By then assuming that no such course exists in the world rather than assuming that the course exists anyway, we minimize the extent of the "course" predicate.

Failure as negation (FAN). If some assertion cannot be proven, then it must be false.

Failure as negation extends CWA from the simple idea of "failure to find in the database" to "failure to derive from the database." Again, this can be understood as minimizing the extent of the corresponding predicate.

The qualification problem. The world is very complicated. There are limits to how much we can represent explicitly and how much a system can reason.

The computational response to the qualification problem is basically that reasoning must occasionally proceed on the basis of assumptions. The qualification problem first came up in the context of programs that reason about action. In that context, the question was whether some particular action changed some particular aspect of the world. But there are many aspects of the world, and descriptions of actions cannot mention all of them. Thus, actions were typically assumed to change only what they explicitly say that they change. If the action description did not mention some particular item or fact, then the action did not change that item or fact. Once more, we can see that this approach minimizes the extent of the effects of the operation. In this chapter, we have also seen manifestations of the qualification problem arising in competing numerical approaches for representing uncertainty, especially with regard to the difficulty of writing rules that are coupled with a monotonic reasoner.

We now illustrate these ideas, especially minimization, for some of the approaches in Sombe's list. A default logic is one that allows the drawing of conclusions in the absence of information to the contrary. In Reiter's default logic, a default rule takes the form

$$\frac{\alpha\,(x)\colon \beta(x)}{\Upsilon(x)}$$

in an expression where α is the precondition to the rule, β is a clause that must be checked for consistency with the database, and Υ is added to the database if β is consistent. Reiter's rules describe how to modify a database when drawing a default conclusion. In the same form,

$$\frac{\alpha\colon \alpha \to \beta}{\beta}$$

shows how to make a default inference. Within this framework, rules are applied both to make all the conclusions that can be made consistently and also to make no conclusion without reason.

The next two examples from Sombe are attempts to use modal logic to create a non-monotonic logic. McDermott and Doyle augmented logic with an M (or "maybe") operator. The statement

$$M\,p$$

means roughly "maybe p" or so long as p is consistent with everything that is known. In this framework, a default rule takes the form

$$b \wedge M\,p \to p$$

Since the sentence is itself a statement in the logic, we can write facts about default rules, defaults about default rules, and so on. Unfortunately, the semantics of this approach have been difficult to characterize adequately. Moore's autoepistemic logic replaces the "maybe" or "possibly" operator with a "necessarily" modal operator, L. In this, the statement p is possible only if $\neg p$ is not necessary. Thus, M p is equivalent to $\neg L\neg p$. The approach is nonmonotonic in that when new facts are added to a database, some old beliefs based on use of the modal operator will no longer be valid because the proof support for them will not hold.

The next example in Sombe's list is McCarthy's circumscription. The key idea in circumscription is that it attempts to minimize "abnormality." We considered examples of this earlier in exercises in Chapter 1. An example of this is the sentence

$$b(x) \wedge \neg\, ab_1(x) \to p(x)$$

This means that if $b(x)$ is true and x is not abnormal, then assert $p(x)$. A database contains a large number of statements like this. At any given time, the idea is to minimize the number of abnormal objects or facts, keeping only those that are known to be abnormal. A complication is that the circumscription approach requires the use of second-order logic, since it quantifies over predicates.

How are we to evaluate the wide range of approaches in nonmonotonic logic? At the time of this writing, it is possible to compare approaches but not to give enduring evaluations or prescriptions of use. We can ask which of a variety of approaches satisfy a variety of algebraic operations, such as transitivity or contraposition. We can ask whether they support conclusions about both individuals and classes. We can ask how they support revision of knowledge. Sombe (1990) provides such a comparison for the approaches mentioned in this discussion.

Nonmonotonic logic is an area of active research interest. Researchers are still in the process of gathering examples of human reasoning, some of which are expressed more conveniently in one approach than in another. Ginsberg (1987) has argued that much of the work on nonmonotonic inference can be unified formally with work on truth maintenance. The strength of the assumption-based truth maintenance work has been its attention to algorithms and complexity. It does not cover all the kinds of examples that motivate the creation of theories about how to reason nonmonotonically or with common sense. However, it does address a subset of these problems concretely and with a pragmatic orientation for the building of problem-solving systems (Forbus & de Kleer, 1993).

Existential Inadequacies in Representing the Unknown

Existential inadequacy is a recurring theme in representation. Earlier in this chapter we characterized representations of uncertainty as "representing facts and relations that are *invisible and implicit*, which means they represent unknown factors and exceptions." But what does it mean to represent the unknown?

One argument is that the unknown cannot be represented, at least not with a reference semantics. In a reference semantics, meaning is in the mind of the observer who sees both the symbol and the thing the symbol represents. If a thing is unknown, then an observer cannot observe it. That this argument is flawed is shown easily by a counterexample. The flaw is that an observer can observe something without knowing or recognizing it. Consider the familiar example of the closed-room murder mystery. We can have a symbol representing "the murderer," even though we do not know which of the characters did the foul deed. We know that the murderer must be one of the people in the room, but we do not know which one he is. In the exercises for Chapter 1 we considered approaches for representation in problems like this. Thus, a thing can be unknown and yet still observed.

Beyond this technicality about observation and recognition, however, are deeper problems in using a naive reference semantics for reasoning about uncertainty. Consider another case. Dan says, "I think something good will happen." Can we represent that? We can have a symbol that refers to "the thing that Dan said was good and that might happen." Technically, this is an **indirect reference**. We are referring to Dan's utterance rather than to the thing itself, and we trust that Dan has something identifiable in mind.

Although indirect references are not part of a reference semantics as we described the approach in Chapter 1, they are certainly part of our common practice in representation. Probably very few readers of this paragraph have visited Antarctica personally. Nonetheless, we all use the term *Antarctica*. We know that it is a large, icy continent at the South Pole. We rely on maps, photographs, and other observers and use the term in much the same way that we use terms about things that we have observed personally.

There are risks in using indirect references based on what other observers say. Just because someone uses a name does not guarantee that anything really exists. Consider the phrase "the current king of France." There is no such person. Here we have a symbolic expression but no actual king.

Returning to the issue of representing the unknown, the idea of symbols representing specific things is contrary to the way that most representations of the unknown are used, and this is a key to understanding the meaning of these representations. Representations of uncertainty do not need to represent specific unknowns. Their value is in characterizing what is known about *classes* of possibilities. For example, in troubleshooting, a priori probabilities of fault modes do not tell us what fault is actually present in a troubleshooting context. Rather, they measure expectations. They establish context that improves average efficiency of diagnosis.

In the next part of the book we consider how classification and diagnostic systems use representations of certainty. Diagnostic systems, whether based on certainty factors, the Dempster-Shafer calculus, probabilities, or nonmonotonic approaches, fundamentally deal with multiple possibilities. When these possibilities are circumscribed, much of the work of reasoning with uncertainty is in weighing the differences among the competing possibilities. Classification systems, which play a role in both diagnosis and perceptual tasks, accept data about unknown situations and create symbol structures to describe what they find. Roughly, they have a grammar that systematically relates regularities of observable features to classifications. Representations of uncertainty express degrees of ambiguity in the evidence for one class or another.

In summary, naive approaches to reference semantics have an inadequate notion of existence for understanding representations of certainty. We need to refer not only to what exists in some world, but also to what can possibly exist, in terms of both classes and individual elements. In the examples of this section and the following chapters, we consider tasks that represent the unknown as elements of search spaces, represented either as lists of explicit elements or in terms of a generative gr ammar. We use techniques from this section to represent the "unknown" in the sense that they characterize what is known or determined about classes in these spaces.

For fun, we now relate the representation of certainty and the unknown to everyday situations and to frontiers of AI research. Everyone faces the future without knowing exactly what is ahead. Two pieces of advice about facing the future are often attributed to mentors and counselors. The first piece of advice is to "visualize what you want as clearly as you can. If you cannot visualize it, you cannot create it or recognize it." The second piece of advice is to "make use of what comes your way. You cannot always expect things to show up exactly as you imagined them. Be flexible." These two pieces of advice relate in a direct way to what we have been saying about representing the unknown.

Can representations of certainty represent the "truly unknown"? We have shown that they carry information about circumscribed classes of things. The same could be said about advice for facing the future. How can we plan for the future without knowing what is ahead? The first piece of advice says that to imagine is to prepare. This is akin to the representation of possibilities, whether explicitly or implicitly in a generative grammar. The second piece of advice is to be prepared for differences and surprises. So returning to our idea of grammars, what can we do if something comes along that we never imagined before, something quite new and outside of the anticipated space? One thing to do is to extend the imagination (or the grammar) so we will be able to anticipate this new thing next time. Roughly, we can have rules not only for generating from a grammar, but also for extending a grammar to cover new kinds of things. This approach of actively extending the grammar shows more deeply how we can understand and represent the unknown. As before, representations of certainty are about classes in a space. But now we open the possibility of changing the grammar that generates the space.

It is exactly this notion of "extending the grammar" that lies at the core of Margaret Boden's account of exceptional creativity (Boden, 1992). What is it that makes something that one person does be judged as truly creative by a community of observers and peers? The newly created thing not only must be new, says Boden. It also must be new in a surprising way. She then goes on to characterize creativity in terms of search and, ultimately, to characterize what counts as a breakthrough in human creativity in terms of changes to fundamental generators of the search space in the community of practice. A famous example of a creative act is Kekule's explanation of the structure of benzene. His answer—resonating chemical rings—requires a shift in thinking about how molecules are put together and even a new notation to describe them. The chemical structure he proposed could not be expressed in conventional chemical notation because the electrons forming chemical bonds in his structure do not stay associated with the same pair of atoms all of the time—they resonate between different pairs of atoms. This change to the language for describing the structure of molecules has proven useful for many other structures. Resonance rings have since become a common feature in many chemical structures, such as steroids and the estrogen compounds.

Exceptional creators and inventors create not only new things, but also fundamentally new *kinds* of things. They don't just search a prescribed space. They find things that others have missed because they change the search space. Computer systems capable of such shifts are at the edge of research in artificial intelligence. Thus, the issues that arise in the representation of the unknown touch not only the frontiers of AI research, but also some of the curious depths of the human experience.

THE KNOWLEDGE LEVEL

This chapter describes classification as a process that selects solutions that match data. Classification models are used for a wide range of tasks in knowledge systems.

Classification

7.1 Introduction

To classify something—an unknown object, phenomenon, pattern, measurement, or anything at all—is to identify it as a member of a known class. For example, a field biologist might use several features such as shape, size, color, and so on to identify a species of plant or an animal. In this case, the sample plant or animal is the unknown thing and the species is a known class. **Classification problems** begin with data and identify classes as solutions. Knowledge is used to match elements of the data space to corresponding elements of the solution space.

An essential characteristic of **classification**, as we use the term, is that it *selects* from a predefined set of solutions. This does not mean that every set of data has a unique solution or even that every set of data has a solution at all in the solution set. It just means that the process of classification involves the matching of data to a fixed set of known possible solution classes. Some data match no solutions at all.

7.1.1 Regularities and Cognitive Economies

Classes express regularities. All members of a class share certain properties. For example, all diseases of a given class may be treatable in a common way or may have in common certain kinds of causes.

Classification affords economies in cognition. Cognitive scientists have noticed that much of our mental commerce with an environment deals with classes of things rather than with unique events and objects. For example, classifying symptoms as characteristic of a particular disease can be a crucial part of diagnosis. Classifying signal patterns can be a crucial part of signal processing, in which signal elements are identified. Classifying goals and requirements can be a crucial part of a planning process, for selecting individual actions or skeletal plans. In an order-entry task, customer orders may be classified prior to detailed processing. In knowledge engineering, classification models are used in many kinds of tasks.

To do any of these tasks an agent must reason about things that are different in their observable or given characteristics, but that can be clustered into categories for further processing. This factors a task into two steps: classify and process. Intuitively, the rules for reasoning about classes are simpler than rules about the myriad of instances.

Classes are defined in terms of necessary conditions. For example, we could define the class of "portable computers" to mean all computers that can be carried around with one hand by an average-size person. If we are presented with a computer and can pick it up easily with one hand and we are of average size, then it is portable by our criterion, even if it cannot be powered by batteries or does not fit into a briefcase.

Determination of an appropriate set of distinctions and categories is an important part of making sense of a domain and often a crucial part of building a knowledge system. However, determining the definitions of classes is not a part of classification itself. The identification of regular and meaningful patterns is a problem with its own methods, such as cluster analysis, and is outside the scope of this chapter. In classification tasks, a set of classes is given, together with necessary conditions for identifying them.

Over the past few years many knowledge systems have been built for which classification is central. Several of these systems work through recognizable phases of data abstraction, knowledge-based mapping to a taxonomy of pre-enumerated solutions, and refinement within the solution taxonomy. Each phase may have several steps, which means there may be multiple levels of data abstraction, multiple levels of associative mapping between data and intermediate solutions, and multiple levels of solution refinement. Figure 7.1 shows the flow of inferences for a bottom-up method starting with data. In other methods, the inferences are more mixed and may involve reasoning back from the solution space to the data space. Nonetheless, the description in Figure 7.1 is a useful starting framework from which we shall specialize a few variations in the following sections.

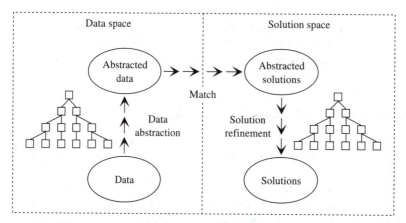

FIGURE 7.1.   An exemplar of a classification domain. There is a single data space and a single solution space, with abstractions in each. (Adapted from Clancey, 1985, page 296.)

The pattern of search spaces suggested by Figure 7.1 is called **heuristic classification** to emphasize the common use of imperfect and heuristic matching to assign data to classes. Some authors prefer the term **hierarchical classification**, to emphasize the importance of reasoning by levels as well as the computational advantages that arise from indexing actions over classes of situations rather than over individual situations. The term **heuristic selection** is used to emphasize the noncombinatorial nature of discrete choice. Our approach draws heavily on a formulation and analysis by Clancey (1985). For simplicity, we refer to the model as classification.

All classification models map data to a set of predefined solutions. Figure 7.2 shows a variation of the domain in which there is an intermediate space between the data space and the final solution space. There are two common ways to present **multistage classification models**. The **composed mappings view** emphasizes that the same relations of abstraction, match, and refinement occur in the different stages. This view presents those relations the same way in each stage, with abstraction indicated by up arrows, matching indicated by right arrows, and refinement indicated by down arrows. The **intermediate spaces view** emphasizes that classification can link intermediate spaces of different character. This view makes it easier to show the differences between the spaces. For example, the intermediate space may have a causal or time-based model. The intermediate spaces view also makes it easier to show how multiple elements in one space may map to the same element in another space. Diagrams like these are useful for visualizing particular classification tasks in terms of their search spaces.

The first two phases of classification in Figure 7.1—data abstraction and match—are themselves special cases of classification. Data abstraction is a simple form of classification in which the data space is a subset of the solution space. The features of the solution classes are a subset of the features of the given data. In data matching, the data and solutions can be in different spaces. This case arises when the given data are indirectly linked to the phenomena being classified. For example, in medical diagnosis the solutions may be disease states and the data may be patient history data, such as known prior diseases and treatments, and laboratory data, such as blood pressure or analyses of body fluids. The relations that link data to solutions may involve causal chains. Solution classes are conveniently arranged in a generalization taxonomy. In other variations, one or more of the phases may be missing, such as cases with no significant data abstraction or no solution refinement.

In characterizing classification, we usually exclude the case where the solution classes are known ahead of time but are generated rather than listed explicitly. However, when the generation process is trivial and the number of solutions is small, this issue is not so important. The generator approach is not called classification when it is more complex than the classification process, such as when the solution space is a power set of some basis set, made up of combinations of the basis elements. Models for configuration, an example of such problems, are taken up in Chapter 8. Similarly, many diagnosis problems involve more than classification because they require potentially combinatorial reasoning about composite hypotheses and determination of what additional data to acquire. These issues arise in the examples in this section and we mention some simple approaches. In general, computational models for combinatorial reasoning and for selecting data to discriminate among solutions are more complex than classification itself.

The following sections discuss variations on and specializations of classification. Section 7.1 analyzes classification domains. It presents a computational model of classification, asking what makes it difficult and what role different kinds of knowledge and assumptions play. Section 7.2 presents several examples of knowledge systems based on classification. The systems built

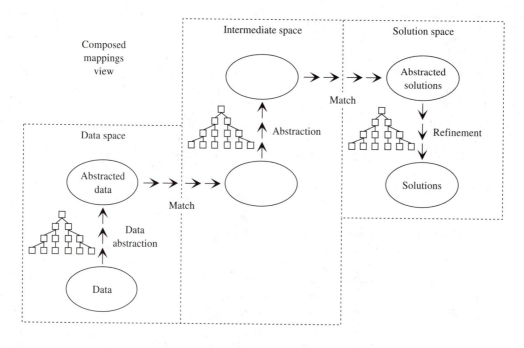

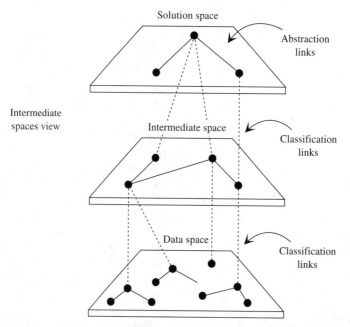

FIGURE 7.2. Two views of multistage classification models. The composed mappings view emphasizes the case where the same classification relations are used in each stage. The intermediate spaces view emphasizes the case where the intermediate spaces have different properties.

for the applications have both striking similarities and striking differences. Section 7.3 presents several specialized methods for classification, showing how they depend on different assumptions and use different knowledge.

7.2   *Models for Classification Domains*

In this section we consider more precisely what a classification model is, what makes classification tasks difficult, and what roles knowledge and various assumptions play.

7.2.1   *A Computational Model of Classification*

We begin by developing a simple finite set model for classification problems that we call a **conjunctive classification model**. This simple model is rich enough to illustrate the important phenomena of classification domains. In the following we also consider several simple extensions that do not violate the spirit of the simple model.

A conjunctive classification model has a **data space**, D, which is a finite set with elements $\{D_i\}$, and a **solution space**, S, which is a finite set with elements $\{S_j\}$. The $\{D_i\}$ can be assigned data values, representing the data to be classified in a particular problem instance. We are given values for some or all of the $\{D_i\}$. A datum can take values from the set $\{0, 1\}$. For convenience, we extend the data value notation by using $D_i =$ "?" to indicate that no value is known for the datum. We refer to the collective values for the $\{D_i\}$ as a data "vector." The $\{S_j\}$ stand for the predetermined solution classes that are candidate solutions for any particular problem.

For every solution candidate S_j in S there is a pattern that specifies necessary conditions for consistency of solutions with data. These patterns are defined by a covering relation defined as follows:

$C(S_j, D_i) = 1$ means $S_j \Rightarrow D_i = 1$
                            That is, S_j cannot be a solution if D_i is 0. It is consistent with $D_i = 1$.
$C(S_j, D_i) = 0$ means $S_j \Rightarrow D_i = 0$
                            That is, S_j cannot be a solution if D_i is 1. It is consistent with $D_i = 0$.
$C(S_j, D_i) = ?$ if the value of datum D_i is irrelevant to the consistency of solution S_j.

Given a covering relation, we can ask several different questions about a given pattern of data. For example, we can ask which solution classes are **inconsistent** with a given data vector. A solution candidate S_j is inconsistent with the data if at least one value is known to be inconsistent with it. A solution candidate S_j is **consistent** with the data if no known values are inconsistent with it. We say candidate S_j **covers** the datum D_i in either of two cases: (1) $D_i = 1$ and $C(S_j, D_i) = 1$ or (2) $D_i = 0$ and $C(S_j, D_i) = 0$. Note that a candidate is judged consistent when no data are known that bear on it one way or the other, or if only some of the relevant data are known and all known data are consistent with it. We say a candidate **matches** the data if all the data relevant to S_j are known and the values are all consistent with the candidate. If a candidate matches all of its relevant data, we also say that the candidate **explains** the data.

This model provides an explicit way to "rule out" a candidate. Specifically, a candidate can be ruled out if any data have been observed that are inconsistent with it. In the basic model, there is no way to "rule in" a solution.

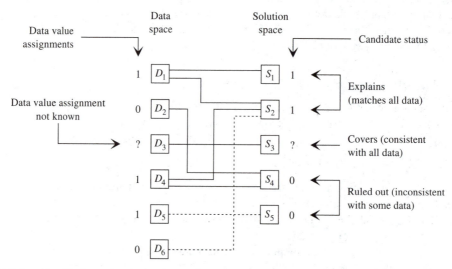

FIGURE 7.3.   Graphical notation for conjunctive classification problems. The D_i are elements of the data space and the S_j are elements of the solution space. A solid line from D_i to S_j indicates that S_j is consistent with $D_i = 1$. A dashed line from D_i to S_j indicates that S_j is consistent with $D_i = 0$.

It is convenient to define a graphical notation for describing conjunctive classification problems. In Figure 7.3, the D_i and S_j are indicated by boxes on the left and right, respectively. A solid line from D_i to S_j indicates that the candidate solution S_j is consistent with the value assignment $D_i = 1$. A dashed line from D_i to S_j, used less often in our examples, indicates that the candidate solution S_j is consistent with the value assignment $D_i = 0$. The absence of a line from D_i to S_j indicates that the data value is irrelevant to the consistency of candidate solution S_j, which means S_j is consistent with any value assignment to D_i.

The symbols to the left of the D_i boxes are the given values assigned to the data. The numbers to the right of the S_j boxes indicate the status of the solution candidate, where 1 means the solution class is consistent, 0 means the solution class is inconsistent, and ? means there is inadequate evidence to decide either way. In Figure 7.3, candidate solutions S_1 and S_2 match or explain the data, candidate S_3 is consistent with or covers some data but does not match them, and candidates S_4 and S_5 are inconsistent.

One feature of this notation is that the process of determining whether a candidate is consistent requires only propagating values from the data elements along the lines to the solution candidates. For solid lines, the data values are propagated as they are given. For dashed lines, the data values are inverted as they are propagated, which means 1 is changed to 0 during propagation and 0 becomes 1. For both kinds of lines, ? propagates to ?. The status of a solution candidate S_j can then be determined as follows:

If *all* values propagated to S_j are 1's, then S_j matches or explains the data.
If *any* value propagated to S_j is 0, then S_j is not consistent with the data and S_j is ruled out.
If *all* values propagated to S_j are 1's and ?'s, then S_j is consistent with or covers the data.

We use such diagrams in the rest of this section to illustrate classification phenomena.

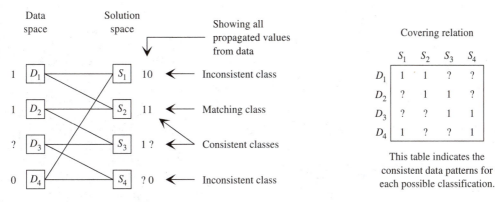

FIGURE 7.4. An example conjunctive-classification problem. All propagated values are shown. For the given data, only solution S_2 matches. The table to the right of the figure characterizes the data patterns that are accepted or recognized by each solution class. This table is a chart of the relation C and is equivalent to the graphical representation. It is constructed from the graph by placing a 1 in each row where there is a line from the solution to the datum and a ? in every other row.

Figure 7.4 presents another example of a conjunctive classification problem. You are encouraged to use this example to familiarize yourself with the propagation process and with judging which solution candidates are consistent. In this problem the data space and the solution space both have four elements. Each element of the data space is connected to two elements of the solution space, and vice versa.

7.2.2 *Model Variations and Phenomena*

Interactions between data patterns and the covering relations give rise to a variety of phenomena in classification problems. In this section we consider some of these phenomena and others that arise in variations of our basic model.

No Solutions, Multiple Solutions, and Composite Solutions

Given a covering relation, the prototypical situation is that a data vector matches a single class. However, it is also possible that some data vectors will match no classes at all, and other vectors may match more than one class. For the covering relation in Figure 7.5, every data pattern with more than two 1's matches more than one solution. For example, the data vector (1 1 1 0) matches S_2 and S_3. Every solution class in Figure 7.5 requires that two of the data values be 1. Therefore, every pattern with fewer than two data values of 1 matches no solution class. For example, the data vector (1 0 0 0) matches no solutions.

Many classes can match or be consistent with a given data vector. Some tasks based on classification models, however, make use of additional criteria in determining solutions. This raises the general issue about how multiple matches or multiple consistent classes are to be interpreted as solutions in a larger task. Consider a case in medical diagnosis where two of the diagnostic hypotheses are "measles" and "a broken leg." For this discussion, we assume that the symptoms of measles are fever and red spots on the body. The symptoms of a broken leg are

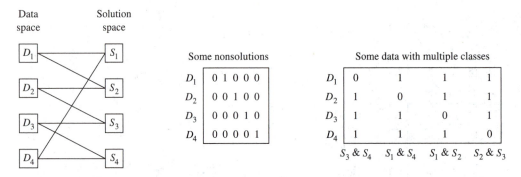

FIGURE 7.5. An example of a conjunctive-classification problem in which some data value assignments match no classes at all and others match more than one class. Every pattern with fewer than two data values of 1 matches no solution at all, and every data pattern with more than two 1's matches more than one solution.

localized pain and characteristic swelling of the leg. We presume that X-ray data are not available. It also is quite possible, if unlikely, that a patient could have both afflictions at the same time.

In this case, a natural diagnostic conclusion is that both afflictions are present. A solution in this case takes the form "*A* plus *B*," or "measles plus broken leg." We call such interpretations **composite solutions**. Composite solutions bundle multiple classes as single solutions.

Continuing the example, the symptoms "red spots and fever" might be accounted for not only by measles, but also perhaps by chicken pox, heat rash, mumps, or other diseases. Similarly, the symptoms "pain and swelling in the leg" might be explained by other specific afflictions, such as a torn muscle or various other strains not involving a fracture of a leg bone. Thus, the following are among the alternative or competing diagnostic hypotheses: "measles plus broken leg," "measles plus torn muscle," "chicken pox plus broken leg," "chicken pox plus torn muscle," "heat rash plus broken leg," or "heat rash plus torn muscle."

As long as the number of combinations to be considered stays small, the composite solution case seems like a small extension to classification. However, when a search must potentially consider *all* combinations of classes in a solution space, the process of generating the combinations of classes typically overwhelms a classification process. We discuss such models for diagnosis in Chapter 9.

Whether solutions are defined as single classes or as sets of classes is the first of several issues in interpreting the results of classification. Figure 7.6 presents alternative policies for data interpretation. Solutions can be singleton or composite, one or many solutions can be reported, and different rules can be used for evaluating candidates with regard to each other and the evidence. The list in Figure 7.6 is not exhaustive, but it does represent different classification policies.

Hierarchical Solution Spaces

When data are presented to a classifier, classes that are inconsistent with the data can be ruled out. When the data are very sparse, however, a data vector typically does not narrow the choices very much because we cannot rule out solutions as inconsistent on the basis of missing data. For

Form of Solutions	
Singleton solutions	Each solution is made up of exactly one class.
Composite solutions	Multiple classes can be combined as a set to form a single solution. This substantially extends and complicates the basic classification model.
Completeness of Search	
Satisficing search	Only one solution (singleton or composite) is reported even if multiple ones are possible.
Exhaustive search	All competing solutions (singleton or composite) are reported.
Termination Criteria	
Resource-limited search	Search ends when budgets for time, observations, expense, or risk are exhausted. Whatever candidates are under consideration are reported.
Inclusion Criteria	
Positive coverage	A solution is included if it covers some data and is not inconsistent with any data.
Conservative inclusion	A solution is included unless it is ruled out by evidence (even if it does not explain *any* data).
Complete explanation	To be included a solution must explain all the acquired data.
Probability threshold	To be included a solution must be consistent with observations and have a prior probability above some threshold.
Ranking Criteria	
Reasoning by elimination	A solution is accepted only when all other candidates have been ruled out by inconsistency with data.
Preponderence of evidence	One solution dominates another if the former covers more of the acquired evidence.
Minimal sets	If two composite solutions cover the acquired data and the set of classes included in one composite solution is a subset of the other set, then only the smaller composite solution is reported. This is also known as a parsimony rule.
Single-solution assumption	Solutions are mutually exclusive. Operationally, this means that once an explanatory solution is found, other solutions are immediately ruled out.
Ranked solutions	An additional function is used to rank alternative candidates, based on a priori information.

FIGURE 7.6.   Some goals for combining classes and evaluating solutions that can be imposed on classification models.

example, the data vector (? 1 ? ? ? ? ?) in Figure 7.7 is consistent not only with solution S_2, but also with all the other classes. Judgment depends on further data. In this case and also when there are more possible data than can reasonably be acquired all at once or at the beginning, the data can be acquired incrementally. In such iterative scenarios, it is sometimes possible to arrange the classes so data acquisition is systematic and exploits hierarchical relations among the classes.

Sometimes classes can be arranged so sparse data initially available are enough to determine rough classes and hierarchical elimination. When data are added, increased specificity is possible, corresponding to a descent through the levels of a hierarchy. Figure 7.7 illustrates a

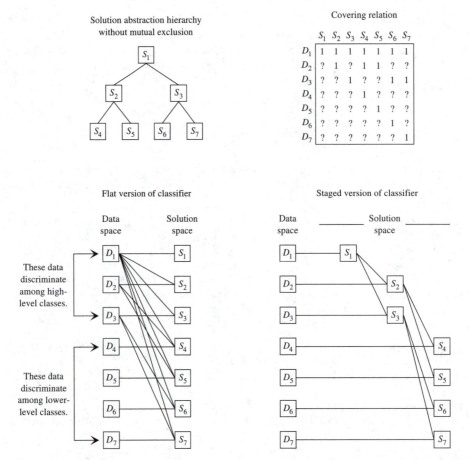

FIGURE 7.7. An example of data patterns for a hierarchical solution space. In a hierarchically organized solution space, the highest nodes designate the most abstract classes. The more specialized subclasses must satisfy all the criteria of their superclasses but can have additional criteria as well. In this example, the highest class, S_1, is characterized by a single data element, D_1. Subclasses S_2 and S_3, respectively, are differentiated by the data D_1 and D_2. In this way, the deeper nodes in the tree are differentiated by increasing amounts of data.

simple hierarchy of classes in which each successive subclass is distinguished from its superclass by requiring a match with an additional data element. By virtue of this arrangement, any data assignment that satisfies solution class S_5 must also satisfy S_2 and S_1. This nesting of superclasses can be reflected conveniently in the graphical notation by organizing the nodes and propagation in stages, corresponding to the levels of an abstraction hierarchy. The propagation rules need only be modified to keep propagating the values along all the connected arcs. Thus, in the example in Figure 7.7, the data vector (1 ? ? ? ? ? ?) is compatible with all the classes but can be summarized simply as S_1. More importantly, the data vector (0 ? ? ? ? ? ? ?) is inconsistent with all the classes and the data vector (1 0 ? ? ? ? ?) is consistent only with S_1, S_3, and all of S_3's subclasses.

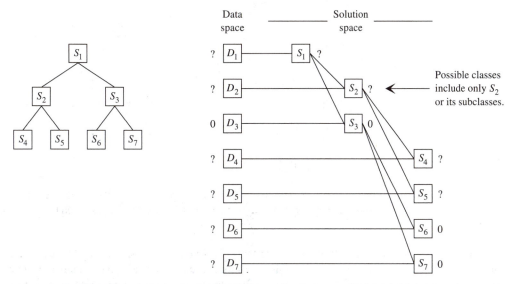

FIGURE 7.8. Hierarchical elimination in classification. The data vector (? ? 0 ? ? ? ?) is inconsistent with solution class S_3 and its subclasses. Assuming that all the members of S_1 belong either to S_2 or S_3, we can conclude that the only classes possibly consistent with the data are S_2 and its subclasses.

Pursuing the logic of hierarchical elimination a bit further, Figure 7.8 shows for the same classes as Figure 7.7 that the data vector (? ? 0 ? ? ? ?) is inconsistent with S_3 and all of its subclasses. Since S_2 and S_3 are the only subclasses of S_1, we would like to conclude that the classification must be S_2 or one of its subclasses. This hierarchical elimination relies not only on the topology of the solution hierarchy, but also on the requirement that *each solution classe designates the union of the designations of its subclasses*. In this case, since S_1 only has subclasses S_2 and S_3, if S_3 is ruled out only S_2 is left. This step would not be valid if there was an implicit set of "other" members of S_1 belonging to neither S_2 nor S_3. In the following we refer to class nodes satisfying this requirement in a taxonomy—class nodes that designate the union of the designations of their subclasses—as **encompassing class nodes**.

The links from the solution nodes to other solution nodes in Figure 7.8 imply that the nodes are all encompassing. This requirement on the interpretation of the graph could be built into the interpreter or indicated by additional annotations on graphs if an interpreter needed to reason with graphs with and without this meaning.

Reasoning by Elimination and Mutually Exclusive Solutions

In the basic conjunctive classification model, there is no way to "rule in" a solution. The only way to eliminate a solution is to observe a 0 where a 1 is required, or to observe a 1 where a 0 is required. In the following we consider a way to augment this with reasoning by elimination.

Consider a medical diagnostic case based on a classification model. Suppose simple tests can be performed that rule out all the diagnostic candidates but one. If we then conclude that the sole remaining candidate is the diagnostic solution, we have sanctioned reasoning by elimination. To paraphrase Sherlock Holmes, "Having eliminated the impossible, what is left must be the solution no matter how improbable."

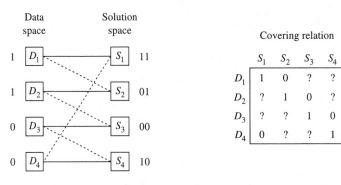

FIGURE 7.9. Mutually exclusive solutions. The classes S_1 and S_2 are mutually exclusive in this set. Every member of S_1 must have D_1 assigned to 1 and every member of S_2 must have D_1 assigned to 0.

In reasoning by elimination, negative evidence for one class is used as positive evidence for another. Mutual exclusion is a dual to this. With mutual exclusion, positive evidence for one class is used to rule out a second mutually exclusive class. In hierarchical networks such as that in Figure 7.7, evidence against a node like S_3 can be used to rule out all of its subclasses. If in addition we are given that S_2 and S_3 are mutually exclusive, then we could carry out additional reasoning by elimination. Mutual exclusion admits ruling out a class whenever a class mutually exclusive to the first class matches the data. For example, if S_4 matches the data then we can rule out S_5. Ruling in S_4 would admit S_2 by virtue of the hierarchy, which would then rule out S_3.

Some classes are mutually exclusive by virtue of their specific classification criteria, without adding any relations to the interpretation of the graph. In Figure 7.9 the solution classes S_1 and S_2 are mutually exclusive, as are S_2 and S_3, S_3 and S_4, and S_4 and S_1, respectively. Each mutually exclusive class places incompatible requirements on the data assignments.

Mutual exclusivity is not transitive. The data vector (1 0 1 0) in Figure 7.9 satisfies both S_1 and S_3, even though both S_1 and S_3 are mutually exclusive of S_2. In this model, whenever classes S_m and S_n are mutually exclusive, there must be some data value D_i such that $C(S_m, D_i) = 1$ and $C(S_n, D_i) = 0$. In models of classification with more flexible conditions relating data values to solution classes, the conditions for mutual exclusion are more general. There must be some combination of assigned values to data that is consistent with one class but not the other.

7.2.3 Pragmatics in Classification Systems

In this section we consider extensions to our basic classification model and some simple approaches for deciding what new data to acquire.

Generalizing Data Domains and Classification Predicates

Most of the example domains and knowledge systems in this chapter require extending the conjunctive classification model in two ways. First, the set of possible data values needs to be extended from the set {0, 1} to be a set of values appropriate for the domain and its instrumentation. Second, the way that conditions about data can be combined needs to be extended. In conjunctive classification, a class is matched if the first condition is satisfied *and* the second is satisfied *and* the third is satisfied and so on. That is why it is called conjunctive classification. There are other ways to combine data, such as by allowing disjunction or exclusive ORs. A very general approach is to allow the conditions on data to be combined by any logical predicate. Since the conjunctive classification model we have been using is a special case of the more general model, the phenomena we have discussed in the preceding section are properties of the general model as well.

Some applications use other extensions of the classification method beyond this. The most common variation is the addition of some means for incorporating estimates of prior probabilities, as in the MORE, MYCIN, and PROSPECTOR applications. Appropriate models of uncertainty are discussed in Chapter 6. In a classification context, the classification predicates determine which solutions match which data. The role of the probability estimates in classification processes is to sharpen the results of a match, using statistical knowledge to increase overall selectivity and establishing that some data or some solutions are unlikely when compared with others.

Data Abstraction

All the conjunctive classification examples we have considered so far assume that the matching criteria for selecting classes are expressed directly in terms of the raw data. As a practical matter, it is much more typical to abstract the data first. As suggested in the introduction to hierarchical classification, a data abstraction step is itself a special case of classification in that it abstracts combinations of data to "abstract data classes." These classes, however, differ from hierarchical solution classes in that they do not correspond to solutions to the larger classification problem. Abstracted data and raw data may be combined in matches for the "second" part of the classification model.

Figure 7.10 gives an example of a model having both data abstraction and solution refinement. It is a close-up illustration of the inside connections of a horseshoe diagram. In this example, some of the raw data are abstracted in one or more stages and some are used directly in the classification model.

In the simplest case, raw data elements are used directly in the classification problem. In Figure 7.10, R_{10} and R_{11} become D_6 and D_7. In contrast, abstraction changes the form of the raw data. R_7 changes its form to AD_4 before being used as D_3. An example of this from a medical domain might be that the raw data "white blood cell count is 2,000" is abstracted to "low WBC." A raw data element might change its form to more than one abstraction, depending on the measured value. The raw datum R_8 is abstracted to either AD_5 or AD_6 before being used. An example from a medical domain would be the abstraction of the raw datum "temperature reading" to either "normal temperature" or "fever temperature."

Multiple raw data elements can also be combined during abstraction. In Figure 7.10, abstract datum AD_3 combines two raw data elements, R_5 and R_6. In a real domain, the abstract datum might be "high pressure" and the two data elements might correspond to two different points of measurement.

Raw data can be abstracted through multiple levels. R_1 and R_2 are combined to form abstracted data AD_2, which is combined with AD_3 to form AD_1, which is then used directly as D_1. The combinators for data elements are not limited to conjunction. The point of this is that there is substantial variety in the forms of data abstraction used in different models.

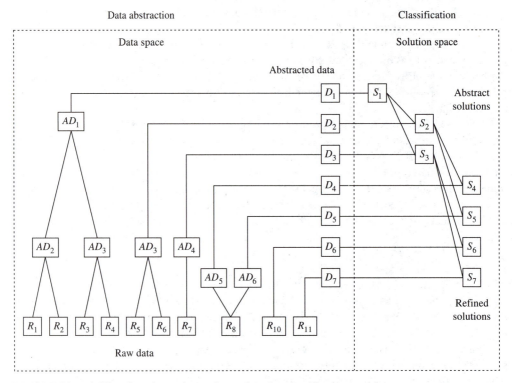

FIGURE 7.10.　Adding data abstraction to the conjunctive classification model.

Although we have distinguished data-space hierarchies from solution-space hierarchies, we note that the distinction is sometimes in the mind of the beholder. Another way to draw a front-end classification model is in terms of a multistage classification diagram in which the raw and abstract data form the first stage and the abstract and refined solutions form the second stage. In this redrawing, the topology of the links remains the same but the meanings of the links differ from our prototypical case.

7.2.4　Summary and Review

In this section we introduced a simple model for classification, conjunctive classification. This initial model allows binary values for data and simple conjunctive relations among data to match data with solution classes. Using examples based on this simple model, we illustrated cases where data matched no solutions, one solution, or many solutions.

We extended the model to admit reasoning by elimination and mutual exclusion. Reasoning by elimination uses negative evidence against one class to support another class. We considered variations on this idea in hierarchical organizations, which highlighted cases where entire branches of a taxonomy could be pruned at once. Mutual exclusion uses positive evidence for one class as negative evidence for another class.

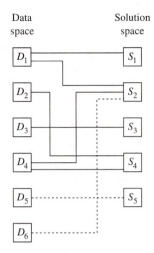

Data space   Solution space

FIGURE 7.11. A conjunctive classification graph.

Exercises for Section 7.2

■ **Ex. 1**   *[06] Conjunctive Classification.* This exercise considers some basic phenomena of conjunctive classification using Figure 7.11.

   (a) What data vectors are consistent with the class?

   Use the notation ? to mean that the datum is not known, and use the notation * to mean that the datum can match any of (0, 1, ?). For example, the notation {* (1 0) 1 ? 0 (0 ?)} means that the first element can be anything, the second must be 1 or 0, the third must be 1, the fourth is unknown, the fifth is 0, and the last can be 0 or unknown.

   (b) What data vectors would match class S_2?

   (c) Given the data vector (0 1 ? 1 1 ?):

   What solution classes are ruled out?
   What solution classes are consistent?
   What solution classes match?

   Ex. 2   *[05] Classification Hierarchies.* Figure 7.12 shows a flat graph of a conjunctive classifier. Redraw this graph as a hierarchical classifier with the same functionality but with a minimum number of links, moving some of the s-nodes to intermediate positions. Keep the same node numbering and vertical ordering in your figure.

   Ex. 3   *[10] Mutual Exclusion and Specialization in Classification.* Figure 7.13 shows a conjunctive classifier. As defined in the text, a solution candidate S_j is consistent with the data if no data elements with known values are inconsistent with the candidate. A candidate matches the data if all the data relevant to S_j are known and the values are all consistent with the candidate.

   We are told that when data are missing, we should interpret solution candidates using a mutual exclusion rule. Sibling classes, which are classes having a common superclass, are mutually exclusive. Top-level classes are also mutually exclusive. If a class matches the

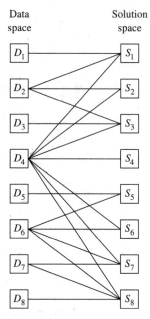

FIGURE 7.12.   A flat conjunctive classifier.

data, then at most one of its subclasses is expected to match. If a class and its subclass both match the data, only the more specific subclass is accepted as a solution. If one candidate matches and others are consistent but have data missing, the consistent ones with missing data are ruled out by mutual exclusion. If more than one candidate matches, the *problem* is inconsistent. Some data vectors may match no solutions.

For each of the following data vectors, indicate (1) the solution classes that are *consistent* with the data, (2) the most specific classes *matching* the data, (3) any classes ruled out by mutual exclusion, and (4) any apparent inconsistencies that arise in the problem specification.

Note: In listing classes ruled out by mutual exclusion, do not include classes that are ruled out by subclass dominance or those that are inconsistent with the data.

(a) $(0\,0\,0\,1\,0\,1\,0\,0\,0)$
(b) $(0\,0\,1\,1\,0\,1\,1\,0\,0)$
(c) $(?\,1\,1\,1\,0\,0\,0\,0\,0)$
(d) $(?\,1\,?\,1\,1\,?\,1\,0\,0)$
(e) $(?\,1\,?\,?\,1\,?\,1\,0\,1)$
(f) $(?\,1\,?\,1\,1\,?\,1\,0\,1)$
(g) $(1\,1\,1\,1\,0\,0\,0\,0\,0)$
(h) $(0\,1\,0\,1\,?\,?\,?\,?\,?)$
(i) $(0\,1\,0\,0\,?\,?\,?\,?\,?)$

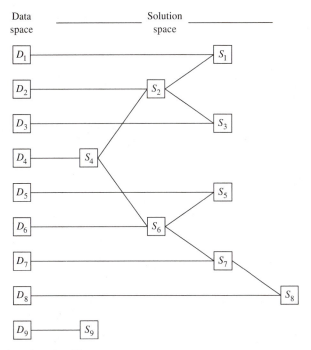

Data space ——————— Solution space ———————

FIGURE 7.13. A conjunctive classifier.

■ **Ex. 4** *[10] Mutual Exclusion and Data Consistency.* Professor Digit believes that mutual exclusion relations have no place in classifiers. He argues that the only way a mutual exclusion rule can be used is when some data are missing, and that its use in those cases is inappropriate. His argument is as follows:

> (1) If the classifier has all the data, then mutual exclusion rules are of little use because it is just as efficient to run the classification rules. (2) If data are missing, then using mutual exclusion rules makes it impossible to detect situations where the data themselves are inconsistent with the model. (3) Therefore, the data should not be used.

(a) Briefly explain whether you agree with Digit's first point.
(b) Do the same for his second point.
(c) Does Digit's conclusion follow? Explain. Would similar arguments apply for a single solution rule?

Ex. 5 *[10] The Use of Data.* In applications of classification, it is sometimes the case that the data that are routinely or initially available are insufficient for distinguishing among some of the possible solutions or hypotheses. Systems can be designed to request additional data that would be useful for differentiating among competing solutions. As usual in conjunctive classification problems, data can be 1, 0, or unknown.
(a) What data values could be acquired to rule out S_2?
(b) Suppose we had the data vector (1 0 ? ? 1 ?). What can we conclude about the solution? What use could we make of the single-solution assumption in this case?

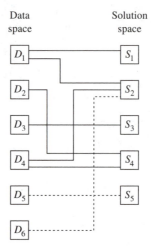

FIGURE 7.14.   Deciding what new data to acquire.

(c) Suppose we had the data vector (1 0 1 ? 1 ?). What can we conclude about the solution? What use could we make of the single-solution assumption in this case?

Ex. 6   [*!-20*] *Assumptions about Solutions and Data.* This exercise considers how the behavior of a classification system depends on what assumptions it makes and the solution criteria it uses. In the simplest approach, a conjunctive classification system reports all the classes that match the data. Beyond that, diagnostic systems can apply other criteria in generating, evaluating, and reporting solutions. In the following examples, we consider the variations on solution policies for classification shown in Figure 7.15..

Suppose there are several kinds of fever as follows:

Classification	*Symptoms*
Yellow fever	High temperature; feet turn yellow
Green fever	High temperature; hands turn green
Pink fever	High temperature; knees turn pink

We assume in this exercise that each specific fever always exhibits all of its symptoms and never exhibits the color-specific symptom of a different fever. We assume further that if a person has a normal temperature that he does not have one of these fevers.

(a) Without regard to the particular solution policies, list all possible solutions that could be considered in an exhaustive search. How many possible solutions are there?

(b) Suppose we are given a black-box diagnosis system whose solution criteria we do not know. We present this system with the data that the temperature is high and the hands are green. We are not given any other data. The diagnostic system concludes from the data that the diagnosis is simply "green hand fever."

For each solution policy listed in this exercise, indicate (yes or no) whether it is compatible with the data to support the diagnostic conclusion. If a solution policy is ambiguous, explain briefly. Of course, a real diagnostic system would have a policy that takes some position on each of the four groups of desiderata in Figure 7.15. For the purposes of this exercise, however, consider each element separately.

Form of Solutions

| Singleton solutions | Each solution is made up of exactly one class. |
| Composite solutions | Multiple classes can be combined as a set to form a single solution. This substantially extends and complicates the basic classification model. |

Completeness of Search

| Satisficing search | Only one solution (singleton or composite) is reported even if multiple ones are possible. |
| Exhaustive search | All competing solutions (singleton or composite) are reported. |

Inclusion Criteria

Positive coverage	A solution is included if it covers some data and is not inconsistent with any data.
Conservative inclusion	A solution is included unless it is ruled out by evidence (even if it does not explain *any* data).
Complete explanation	To be included a solution must explain all the acquired data.

Ranking Criteria

Reasoning by elimination	A solution is accepted only when all other candidates have been ruled out by inconsistency with data.
Preponderance of evidence	One solution dominates another if the former covers more of the acquired evidence.
Minimal sets	If two composite solutions cover the acquired data and the set of classes included in one composite solution is a subset of the other set, then only the smaller composite solution is reported. This is also known as a parsimony rule.
Single-solution assumption	Solutions are mutually exclusive. Operationally, this means that once an explanatory solution is found, other solutions are immediately ruled out.

FIGURE 7.15. Elements of policies for classification models.

(c) This case is just like part b except that we are given the additional data that the patient's knees are not pink and his feet are not yellow. Again, indicate (yes or no) which of the solution criteria listed in this exercise are sufficient with the data to support the diagnostic conclusion.

Ex. 7 [*!-10*] *Lamppost Bias.* Professor Digit is suspicious of the preponderance of evidence rule, which favors those candidate solutions that explain the most data. He argues that this is like the drunk who looks for his lost keys near the lamppost "because that's where the light is." This exercise addresses the issue briefly.

Suppose we have a covering relation for conjunctive classification as in Figure 7.16. Suppose also that the classification process routinely collects data for X, Y, A_1, B_1, and B_2.

(a) Assuming a random distribution of 1's and 0's over the data, which solutions are most likely to be ruled out by this process?

(b) If all the routinely collected data are 1, which solution would the preponderance of evidence rule favor? Would this be justified? Discuss briefly.

(c) How could the process be made less biased? Briefly discuss some issues and assumptions that bear on the use of the preponderance of data rule.

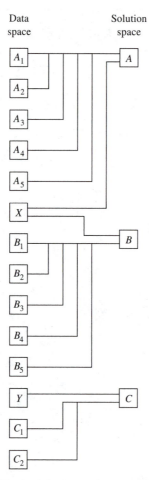

Data space

Solution space

FIGURE 7.16. Classification acquisition and the preponderance of data.

Ex. 8   *[05] Terminology and Concepts.* Answer true or false for each of the following. If the question is ambiguous, explain briefly.

(a) *True or False.* The single-solution assumption in classification problems holds that there is exactly one class that matches every pattern of data.

(b) *True or False.* In conjunctive classification graphs, the term *abstract data* refers to generalizations of observable data.

(c) *True or False.* Reasoning by elimination in a classification problem uses a closed-world assumption.

(d) *True or False.* In conjunctive classification, a satisficing search is incompatible with a "complete explanation" evaluation criterion.

(e) *True or False.* Technically, searches involving composite solutions do not fall within the definition of classification problems.

7.3 *Case Studies of Classification Systems*

In this section we describe several knowledge systems. The systems perform different tasks but all use classification as a model. We consider the search requirements of each task, the kinds of knowledge that are needed, how the knowledge is organized, and some issues of implementation. The systems from these case studies build on or extend the model of classification from the previous section.

In describing knowledge systems, there is always an issue about the choice of terminology. At the present state of the art, developers of different systems often use different terminology to describe the same things. Using the different terminologies of the developers makes it easier to give concrete examples of knowledge from the systems and to illustrate variations and particular features that they found important. However, unifying terminology across systems makes it easier to compare them. In this section, we acknowledge differences in terminology but emphasize a uniform terminology that we will use again in our later analysis.

7.3.1 *Classification in MYCIN*

MYCIN is a well-known system for diagnosing infectious diseases and recommending therapies. Because the MYCIN system was described already in Chapter 3, the discussion here is brief and limited to issues of classification. Historically, MYCIN's operation was explained at the symbol level in terms of its production-rule implementation. However, production rules per se provide little guidance about the organization of a classification task, and their behavior is essentially the same over a wide variety of tasks far removed from classification. To understand MYCIN's operation, the knowledge that it needs, and the limitations of its method, we need to approach it from a different level of description. What we seek is a knowledge-level perspective to clarify what knowledge MYCIN uses for solving a problem and how that knowledge is organized. The part of MYCIN of interest to us here is the part that determines whether a patient has an infectious disease and identifies the possible diseases using various medical data. Figure 7.17 presents a rule from MYCIN's knowledge base.

Screening clause:
```
     IF          (1) A complete blood count is available, and
```

Data-matching clause for heuristic classification:
```
                 (2) The white blood count is less than 2500,
```

Solution-mapping clause for heuristic classification:
```
     THEN        (3) The following bacteria might be causing infection: E. coli
                 (.75), Pseudomonas-aeruginosa (.5), Klebsiella-pneumoniae (.5).
```

FIGURE 7.17. Decomposition of a sample MYCIN rule. The first clause about the availability of blood-count data is used to prevent the rule's application in the event that the blood-count data are not already available. It is called a screening clause because otherwise the second clause would cause MYCIN's interpreter to request the data. The second clause is a heuristic test that is matched against lab data. As discussed in the text, the intermediate logic of the association is not represented explicitly in MYCIN. The third clause identifies plausible candidates in the solution space.

To explain this rule, we begin with the heuristic association at its core, fleshing out the intermediate logic of the situation. One kind of compromised host condition is the immuno-suppression condition, where the responsiveness of the body's immune system is suppressed by drugs, radiation, or an immune-system disorder. Pregnancy is another kind of compromised host condition. Leukopenia is a particular kind of immunosuppressed condition in which there is a deficiency of white blood cells. A rule of thumb is that the low-end threshold of blood count is 2,500. So far, this explains the first part of the intermediate logic starting from clause 2. To reiterate the logic in a progressive order: If the white blood count is less than 2,500, then the patient has leukopenia, which is a kind of immunosuppressed condition. Patients with an immunosuppressed condition are compromised hosts.

The next part of the intermediate logic matches the data to the solution space. When a patient has a compromised host condition, bacteria found normally in nonsterile sites in the body can cause an infection. There are several nonsterile sites in the body, including the skin, the upper airways, and the digestive tract. The most likely source of an infection is the gastrointestinal tract, which harbors the enterobacteriaceae as well as other bacteria such as *enterococcus*. In compromised hosts, the enterobacteriaceae are the most important pathogens to consider. Although *Proteus* is in this class, it is less likely than *E. coli*, *Pseudomonas*, and *Klebsiella* to invade the body from a gastrointestinal source. Compressing this logic to leave out intermediate steps, we could say that when a host is compromised, infections by these kinds of bacteria are likely.

The sequence of steps in this argument is diagrammed in Figure 7.18. This figure reiterates the basic stages of classification: generalizing data, matching to abstract solution classes, and refining solutions. The left side climbs through abstractions in the data space, the right side descends through specializations in the solution space, and the two spaces are linked by a match. MYCIN abstracts basic observations about patients to patient categories, which are heuristically linked to diseases and disease categories. In the overall process, MYCIN classifies an unknown organism from laboratory culture data and other patient data by matching against knowledge about its taxonomy of bacteria.

The uppercase labels on the arrows in Figure 7.18 indicate categories of relations. These categories are from Clancey (1985). For example, determining that a white-blood-cell count reading of less than 2,500 means that "WBC" is low is a qualitative abstraction, meaning that it simplifies quantitative data. Associating low WBC with leukopenia is a **definitional abstraction**, since this is how leukopenia is defined. Leukopenia is a kind of immunosuppressed condition, and an immunosuppressed person is in a compromised host condition, so the next links represent abstraction relations and generalizations. The link between a compromised host and infections by bacteria that colonize the nonsterile sites is a **heuristic association**, relating known properties of the world and known processes to likely conclusions. Although the only heuristic link shown is one that relates the compromised host to the identity of the *E. coli* infection, other factors are also considered in MYCIN such as the location, method of collection, and incubation of cultures taken from a patient and grown in the laboratory. For example, other heuristic associations could match against observations of organisms as being rod-shaped or reacting in particular ways with the gramstain technique.

Figure 7.19 shows two taxonomies that organize the classes in MYCIN's solution space. One taxonomy emphasizes subclass relations based on the measured response of bacteria to laboratory tests, such as their morphology or response to the gramstain test. A second taxonomy

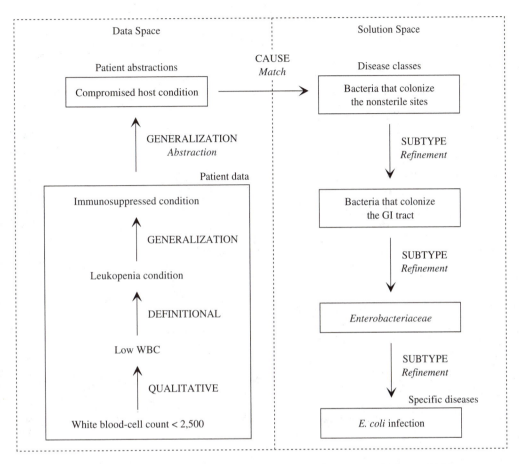

FIGURE 7.18.   The inference structure of MYCIN. (Adapted from Clancey, 1985, page 295.)

emphasizes subclasses of bacteria according to regions where they grow in a healthy patient. This second taxonomy reflects the reasoning of the case cited already.

All the parameter values in MYCIN's database have a numeric measure of the weight of the evidence. This weight is determined using a calculus of uncertainty and certainty factors associated with the rules. In this way, like many classification-based knowledge systems, MYCIN augments the use of necessary conditions and mappings in classification with an integrated means for reasoning about the uncertainty of evidence. There are many different approaches to this, and different systems use different ones.

MYCIN's knowledge base does not explicitly represent all the relations in Figure 7.18. The project did not have a comprehensive policy for determining what relations to represent distinctly and explicitly. Instead, the data abstractions, matches, and solution refinements were all mixed together in MYCIN's implementation with other kinds of rules. This analysis is about the knowledge that MYCIN depended on. MYCIN's backward-chaining interpreter performed classification, among other things.

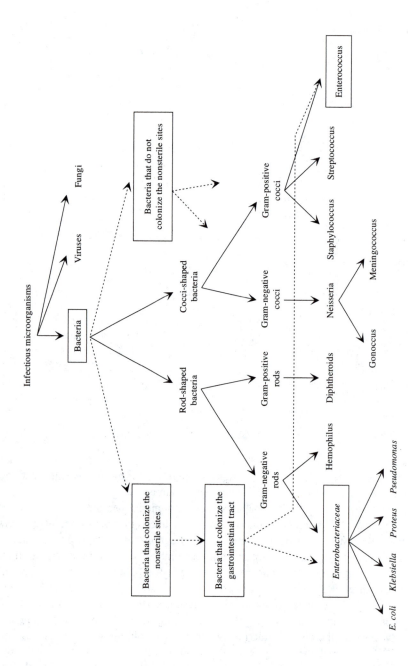

FIGURE 7.19. Two taxonomies showing MYCIN's classifications of bacteria. The solution space for MYCIN is organized by these taxonomies, with the most specific classes appearing as the bottom leaves. The taxonomy defined by the solid arrows represents classes of bacteria organized for reasoning from laboratory data, that is, from the results of the gramstain test and microscopic examination of morphology (shape of bacteria), which are readily available. Part of a second taxonomy is also shown with boxed labels and dashed links. This second taxonomy reflects classes of bacteria categorized according to where they grow in a healthy patient, as implicit in the reasoning stages of Figure 7.18. (Adapted from Clancey, 1985, page 293.)

Returning to the rule example in Figure 7.17, we note that the screening clause "a complete blood count is available" is outside the scope of our analysis of classification, since it is about when to acquire data. This reveals another interesting fact about how MYCIN's rules are constructed. The white blood count is one component of a complete blood count. If the complete blood count is not available, then the white blood count is not known yet and the clause prevents the system from asking for it. That is why we called this a screening clause: It prevents the normal action of the interpreter in invoking the rule. As a diagnostic system, MYCIN could have used this occasion to request additional laboratory data. However, the screening clause prevents this. In more recent diagnosis systems knowledge is used to guide the acquisition of new data and to focus the search on particular classes of solutions. As it stands, the MYCIN interpreter does not know that this is a "screening clause," and so it cannot use the clause in any focused reconsideration of which data to acquire. To summarize, MYCIN's task is the diagnosis of infectious diseases, its model is classification, and its implementation uses backward-chaining production rules.

7.3.2 Classification in MORE

MORE (Kahn, 1988) is an experimental task-specific shell used to develop knowledge bases to solve diagnostic problems. Like MYCIN, MORE uses a classification model in solving diagnostic tasks. The initial design of MORE was based on experience with diagnostic problems in a drilling-fluids domain. It was also used to develop prototype knowledge systems for the diagnosis of epileptic seizures, computer disk faults, and manufacturing defects in circuit boards. Figure 7.20 shows the search spaces of MORE's problem solver in terms of an example from the drilling-fluids domain. In this domain, MORE's data are symptoms from a malfunctioning drill unit and its environment.

The data space and the solution space in classification models determine what is observed and what is inferred. They are connected by heuristic mappings. In MORE's domain, the map-

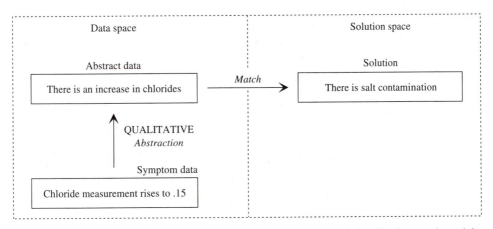

FIGURE 7.20. The inference structure of MORE. In this specialization of classification, a substantial part of the reasoning is involved in evaluating the confidence (or certainty) in both symptoms and diagnostic conclusions. Diagnostic significance is expressed as a quantitative certainty factor.

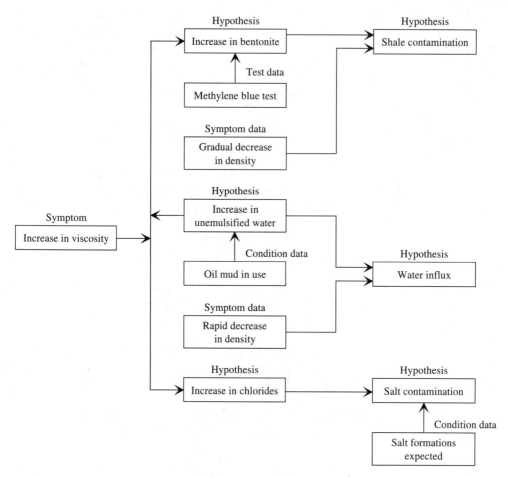

FIGURE 7.21.   MORE uses a directed graph of hypotheses, symptoms, tests, and conditions in its diagnostic problem solving. MORE's rules contain the situation-specific information for guiding the transitions in particular cases. The left-to-right arrows in this figure represent heuristic mappings from symptoms (data) to hypotheses (solutions). (Adapted from Kahn, 1988, page 20.)

pings are chained together through intermediate stages. Figure 7.21 suggests the inverted horseshoe pattern of classification, but with some variations. There is no step for refining solutions. There are several kinds of data, called symptom data, condition data, and test data, which are explained later. Still, the model satisfies the basic requirement that solutions be selected from a given set. The set of possible hypotheses or diagnostic conclusions is the same for every problem. Many of the associations between the data space and the solution space in Figure 7.21 correspond to causal connections. Causality flows in the opposite direction of the arrows, which means the arrows point from observables to solution classes representing possible causes. For example, a water influx would cause an increase in unemulsified water. Salt contamination leads to an increase in chlorides, which leads to an increase in viscosity, which can be observed.

MORE's creators call the spaces in Figure 7.21 an "event model." The term *event* refers to any node in the model. Transitions between nodes are governed by rules. MORE's use of its event model in carrying out diagnosis is guided by rules that are organized into families. The rules represent how patterns of evidence should be evaluated. Three types of rules are used in MORE's rule families.

Diagnostic rules represent an association between a symptom (datum) and a diagnostic hypothesis (solution). The following rule states a heuristic association between a symptom and a hypothesis:

```
If    there is an increase in chlorides <symptom>
and   the drilling fluid is undersaturated <symptom condition>
then  there is salt contamination. <hypothesis>
```

As more hypotheses are added, the rules become more specialized and informative. All diagnostic rules referring to the same symptoms and hypotheses are considered to be members of the same family. These rules perform the familiar class matching in classification.

Symptom-confidence rules represent the reliability of an observation about a symptom. The following rule would express the information that a measurement from a pH meter is more reliable than some less precise test for acidity, such as litmus paper:

```
If    there is an increase in pH <symptom>
and   this is known using a pH meter <test>
then  the reliability of the symptom should be treated as greater than
      normal. <confidence about symptom>
```

Symptom-confidence rules refer to symptoms but not to diagnostic conclusions. They can be applied whenever the evidential effect of a symptom needs to be appraised. All symptom-confidence rules referring to the same symptom are considered to be members of the same family.

Hypothesis-expectancy rules represent the likelihood of a particular diagnostic hypothesis. The following rule judges the likelihood of a hypothesis independent of any particular symptom:

```
If    salt contamination is hypothesized <hypothesis>
and   there is no known geological evidence for salt formations <frequency
      condition>
then  this reduces the expectation of encountering salt contamination.
      <confidence about hypothesis>
```

All hypothesis-expectancy rules referring to the same hypothesis are considered to be members of the same family.

MORE represents the degree to which particular symptoms support belief in particular diagnostic hypotheses. Possible influences include high pressures; high temperatures; contaminants; and inadequate treatments, such as improper use of chemical additives or of solids-removal equipment. The patterns of evidence are expressed using the kinds of rules discussed above. The invocation of the rules is controlled by the method shown in Figure 7.22.

To diagnose using MORE's method:

1.   Initialize the lists of symptoms, possible-hypotheses, hypotheses,
     and diagnostic rules to empty.
2.   Ask the user for the observed symptoms.

          /* Generate possible hypotheses */
3.   For each symptom do
4.   begin
5.   Set new-hypotheses to Retrieve-Hypotheses (symptom).
6.   Add the new-hypotheses to possible-hypotheses if they are
               not there already.
7.   end
8.

          /* Select diagnostic rules */
9.   For each hypothesis in possible-hypotheses do
10.   begin
11.   For each symptom associated with the hypothesis do
12.   begin
13.   Form a key from the hypothesis/symptom pair
14.   Set diagnostic-rule to Select-rule(key,
                    "diagnostic").
15.   Add the diagnostic-rule to the list of diagnostic
                    rules.
16.   end
17.   end

          /* Compute symptom confidence */
18.   For each symptom referenced by any of the diagnostic-rules do
19.   begin
20.   Set symptom-confidence rule to Select-Rule(symptom,
               "symptom-confidence")
21.   Apply symptom-confidence rule.
22.   end

          /* Apply diagnostic rules */
23.   Apply the chosen diagnostic rules to propose diagnostic
          conclusions and add these to the list of hypotheses. /* The
          certainty of the conclusion is computed using confidence
          factors associated with the symptom and the diagnostic rule.*/

FIGURE 7.22.   MORE's method for diagnosis. This method starts with reported observations. It then creates a list of tentative hypotheses and uses this to retrieve a set of diagnostic rules for proposing specific hypotheses. The confidence in the diagnostic conclusions is numerically weighted according to factors associated with the data and the conclusions. (*Note*: MORE was implemented in OPS-5, which does not support nested recursion or lists as a data type. The description here is intended to illustrate the essence of the approach, although it is not completely faithful to the implementation.) (Continued next page.)

```
          /* Adjust confidence for hypothesis expectancy */
24.       For each hypothesis referenced by the diagnostic-rule
25.       begin
26.             Set hypothesis-expectancy rule to Select-Rule(hypothesis,
                "hypothesis-expectancy")
27.             Apply hypothesis-expectancy rule.
28.       end

29. Report evaluation of candidate solutions and supporting evidence.
    Return.


          /* Subroutine for selecting one rule per family */
1.  Procedure Select-Rule: (key, rule-type)
2.  begin
3.        Retrieve the family of rules of the given rule-type related to
          the retrieval key.
4.        If the key is "diagnostic," then for every rule in the family
5.             If a datum mentioned is whose value is not yet known,
               then ask the user for its value.
6.        If there is a unique, most specific rule for the key in the
          family whose conditions are satisfied, then return it. /* A
          rule is subsumed when its conditions are a proper subset of the
          subsuming rule.*/
7.        Else if there are many applicable rules and one has the
          greatest confidence factor, then return it.
8.        Else choose an applicable rule arbitrarily and return it.
9.  end


          /* Recursive subroutine to return a list of all the
          hypotheses associated with a datum at any depth */
1.  Procedure Retrieve-Hypotheses: (datum)
2.  begin
3.        Using the event model, set local-hypotheses to the set of
          possible hypotheses associated with the given datum.
4.        For each hypothesis in local-hypotheses do
5.        begin
6.             If the hypothesis is an intermediate, then recursively
               invoke Retrieve-Hypotheses and append any new hypotheses
               to local-hypotheses if they are not there already.
7.             end
8.        Return the local-hypotheses.
9.  end
```

FIGURE 7.22.   (continued)

MORE's method begins with observations supplied by the user. It then determines a set of possible hypotheses from the event model, including possible immediate causes for the observed data as well as deeper causes for intermediate hypotheses. The possible hypotheses are then used to select diagnostic rules, which are used to determine the strongest competing hypotheses. In selecting among the diagnostic rules, MORE checks whether the rules depend on data not yet provided, and if so, it asks the user for the additional data. It then selects the most specific rule. In MORE's case, the most-specific rule is one whose conditions are satisfied, one that includes the conditions of all the other satisfied rules, and one that has at least one additional satisfied condition. If there is no most-specific rule, then the rule with the highest certainty factor is chosen. Otherwise, a rule is chosen arbitrarily.

Once the diagnostic rules are selected, MORE applies the symptom-confidence rules to adjust its confidence in the observed symptoms using knowledge about test conditions. These numbers are used in projecting confidence for the diagnostic conclusions. Finally, MORE adjusts the ratings of the conclusions using the hypothesis-expectancy rules.

MORE's use of rule families reflects important assumptions about evidence. In general, each family of rules is assumed to provide an independent source of evidence. Thus, the different symptoms are assumed to be independent, and the certainty factors associated with each rule family are combined in the evaluation. More than one rule may result from the search for the most specific one when there is no rule whose condition set is a superset of every rule in the family. This occurs primarily when the knowledge base has not been completed so that a rule with the combined condition set has not yet been written. Since all the rules in a family refer to the same symptom or hypothesis, they are treated as being redundant. Combining them would put too much weight on one piece of evidence. Accounting for the dependence of data is an issue that arises in many diagnostic systems.

One of the most striking aspects of MORE is the utter simplicity of its method. MORE makes all of its associations from data to solutions at once, using a data-driven approach. In broad strokes, MORE's method applies the three sets of rules in order, corresponding to three kinds of knowledge: symptom confidence, diagnosis, and hypothesis expectancy.

Compared with other diagnostic systems that we will consider, MORE's method is primitive. It makes no use of a data hierarchy or a solution hierarchy. Its reasoning about what data to acquire is determined by stepping through the clauses used in the rule families. It can unnecessarily request data for rules that could be subsumed by other logic. It does not reason explicitly about the discrimination among hypotheses, except indirectly in the selection of most-specific diagnostic rules.

In summary, MORE is a prototype shell whose task is diagnosis, whose model is classification, whose implementation is in terms of forward-chaining production rules, and whose interpreter is approximately the method as in Figure 7.22. MORE's method differs from the exemplar form of classification in that it does not refine solutions and it uses numerical confidence rules and measures to evaluate data and rank solutions.

7.3.3 *Classification in MOLE*

MOLE (Eshelman, 1988) is another shell for creating knowledge systems based on a classification model. MOLE's immediate predecessor is MORE. Like MORE, MOLE has been mainly used for building knowledge systems that perform diagnosis. In this section we draw on exam-

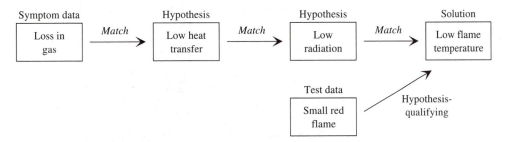

FIGURE 7.23. The inference structure of MOLE. A crucial feature of this specialization of classification is the use of multiple levels of association in its search for explanations. Depending on what hypotheses MOLE makes, it may seek additional data that may not have been reported as part of the initial symptoms. In this figure, the arrows point from symptoms to hypotheses, so causality flows generally from left to right.

ples of MOLE used with a knowledge base for diagnosing a power plant. For accuracy and clarity, we should probably refer to this system as MOLE/POWER PLANT. However, for simplicity, we simply refer to the system as MOLE.

Compared with MORE and MYCIN, MOLE seeks a specific causal interpretation for the data. It assumes that every abnormal finding has a cause. It attempts to differentiate among competing hypotheses, favoring single, parsimonious explanations when possible. MOLE performs two main actions called **cover** and **differentiate**. To cover is to find diagnostic hypotheses that explain observed symptoms. To differentiate is to seek data that will distinguish among competing hypotheses, some of which are presumably extraneous or redundant. In this section we focus on the kinds of knowledge used.

MOLE's knowledge is used to cover symptoms and to differentiate among hypotheses. As in descriptions of MORE, the creators of MOLE use the terms *event* and *event model* to describe the search spaces for data and hypotheses. Four types of knowledge are distinguished in MOLE's knowledge base: event descriptions, diagnostic knowledge, event-qualifying knowledge, and connection-qualifying knowledge. Figure 7.23 shows how the knowledge requirements for MOLE emphasize only the matching steps, and that it lacks both data-abstraction and solution-refinement steps. The matches, however, involve several levels of causal attribution.

Event descriptions represent events, which are the symptoms and hypotheses that MOLE reasons about. Symptoms and hypotheses are represented in almost the same way in MOLE, with symptoms being those events that require explanations. Events have names, such as HIGH-FLY-ASH-FLOW, FOULING, or EXCESS-AIR. During a problem-solving session, MOLE assumes that its database includes all possible events. For each event, MOLE has a small table of information, such as the following:

```
name:                EXCESS-AIR
values:              [HIGH NORMAL LOW]
method:              INFER
default value:       NONE
needs explanation:   YES
```

The choices of value for method are ASK and INFER, meaning that MOLE should ask the user to determine the value or use rules to infer the value indirectly. Most of the events are not directly observable. For many events, the values are simply YES and NO, meaning that the event is present or not. MOLE treats the values as mutually exclusive, so establishing one value precludes the others. The field for the default value indicates what value, if any, MOLE is to assume for the event in the absence of specific evidence. MOLE's representation allows some hypotheses to represent deeper causes than others. Such deeper hypotheses cover all the symptoms that intermediate hypotheses do, and can cover additional ones as well.

Diagnostic rules represent an association between a symptom (data) and a diagnostic hypothesis (solution), or between a low-level hypothesis and a higher-level hypothesis. These are represented as declarations or as simple matching rules:

```
If      there is a loss in gas <symptom data>
then    that symptom could be covered by a low heat transfer. <hypothesis>
```

Covering knowledge in MOLE is further qualified by other conditions expressed in the next two kinds of knowledge in MOLE.

Hypothesis-qualifying rules qualify the expectations for particular hypotheses. They are about the prior beliefs in the hypotheses, no matter what symptoms they are being used to explain. Hypothesis-qualifying knowledge takes two forms: definitive tests and preferences. For example, the following rule expresses the information that the presence of a small red flame is a definitive and reliable test for a low flame temperature:

```
If      there is a low flame temperature <hypothesis>
then    a small red flame must be observable. <test data>
```

In this example, a strong causal connection exists between the hypothesis and the symptom. If the hypothesis is correct, then the symptom must be present. If the symptom is missing, the hypothesis can be ruled out. In short, the rule expresses a necessary condition for the classification. In the terminology of the MOLE system, such knowledge is called **anticipatory** because it sanctions inferences from hypotheses to data. In terms of our conjunctive classification model, such rules just represent the usual necessary conditions.

In cases where strong causal reasoning chains are not possible, ranking of events can be expressed in terms of preferences. For example,

```
If      OXYGEN-READING is low <data>
then    prefer SMALL-PARTICLES over HIGH EXCESS-AIR as an explanation.
        <preference for hypothesis>
```

Hypothesis-qualifying rules can trigger an inquiry about observable symptoms that may not have been included in the initial data. All data, including data obtained after the initial symptoms, need to be covered by the explanations created by the program. Such supporting evidence can be used either to rule out the hypothesis of low flame temperature or to support it in competition with other hypotheses.

Connection-qualifying rules qualify the association between data and a particular hypothesis. They are about the dependability of the covering connection, which is the conditional belief in the hypothesis given the symptom. Such rules make explicit cases where particular symptoms are not interpreted independently. This admits a more fine-grained control over the reasoning about how hypotheses cover data than is possible with hypothesis-qualifying knowledge alone. Hypothesis-qualifying knowledge is used to support or reject a hypothesis no matter what it is being used to explain. Connection-qualifying knowledge is more specific. It makes it possible to support or reject a particular hypothesis depending on its use, as in the following:

```
If      FAN-POWER-IS-EXCEEDED needs to be explained <symptom>
and     there is NO LIGHT-LOAD <connection qualifier>
then    FOULING does not cover FAN-POWER-IS-EXCEEDED. <rule out connection>
```

Even when the connection from the FOULING hypothesis to FAN-POWER-IS-EXCEEDED is ruled out by this rule, the hypothesis could be used to cover some other symptom such as MISBALANCE-OF-CONVECTION. Connection-qualifying knowledge is used in circumstances where particular kinds of evidence are known to be unreliable in particular well-characterized situations.

In principle, the category of connection-qualifying knowledge is not necessary because any qualifiers used here could instead have been incorporated in the covering rules, making them more specific. MOLE's rules are not necessarily limited as to what kinds of terms can appear in them. For example, in this case, the conditions in the covering rule that said that FOULING covers FAN-POWER-IS-EXCEEDED could have been modified to discount the case where there is not a LIGHT-LOAD. Connection-qualifying rules were used in MOLE to augment declarations made in a simple language that linked symptoms to covering hypotheses but that was unable to express qualifying conditions.

In the same spirit of using a very simple and restricted language of description, the graph of events in Figure 7.24 shows links between nodes but cannot express the conditions that limit coverage. Thus, low flame temperature is a possible cause of low radiation. Usually, the desired solution is the deepest explanation—roughly, the earliest cause that explains the most data. In this figure, boxes with no arrows leading out of them correspond to observable data. Boxes with no arrows leading into them are primal or top-level causes. The other boxes correspond to intermediate states. For example, the observable symptom of high-bottom ash flow could be explained ultimately by fouling, grinder setting, or pulverizer malfunction.

MOLE's knowledge guides its search for alternative diagnostic conclusions. Hypothesis-qualifying and connection-qualifying knowledge are used by MOLE to help differentiate among candidates. MOLE attempts to explain all symptomatic data using hypotheses from its catalog of events. In ruling out hypotheses, it makes certain assumptions that simplify its search and the form of its conclusions. It prefers to find simple pathways converging on as few deep explanations as possible. These hypotheses tend to correspond to diagnostic conclusions that identify first causes that can be treated.

If there is independent evidence for one hypothesis (or explanatory pathway) and no evidence for another, MOLE assumes that the second candidate solution can be discarded. If MOLE has two hypotheses of different generality, it requests discriminatory data and eventually chooses the most general hypothesis that supports all the data. It uses hypothesis- and connection-qualifying knowledge to rank alternatives, to eliminate some alternatives directly, and also to eliminate hypotheses by default when there is support for some candidates but not for others. Although

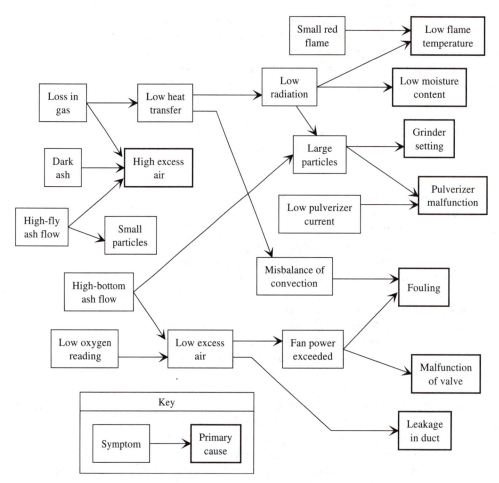

FIGURE 7.24. A causal network in MOLE. The goal is to find the most basic cause that covers all the data. Following the convention for displaying mappings between data and solutions in classification systems, the observable data are shown on the left and the solution classes (causes) are shown on the right. (Adapted from Eshelman, 1988, Figure 3-3, page 54.)

MOLE sometimes uses a single-class (or single-solution) assumption, in some situations it returns more than one hypothesis, as illustrated in Figure 7.25.

Figure 7.25 shows two cases that exemplify the domination of hypotheses according to MOLE's parsimony rules. The boxes with labels starting with D represent symptoms (data) and the boxes with labels starting with H represent hypotheses (solutions). Lines connecting hypotheses and symptoms are used to indicate which symptoms each hypothesis covers. A line connecting one hypothesis to another indicates that the deeper (rightmost) hypothesis covers the other, which means the deeper hypothesis covers all the symptoms covered by the other. Bold type indicates the dominating hypotheses. In the first case, hypothesis H_1 dominates hypothesis H_2 because it covers all the symptoms plus some additional ones. In the second case, hypothesis H_8

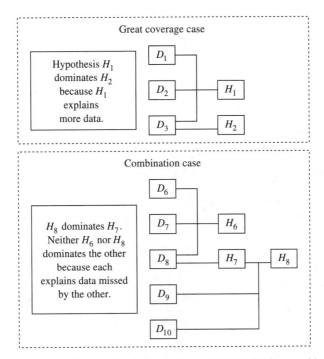

FIGURE 7.25. Parsimony rules for hypothesis domination in MOLE. The boxes with numbered D's in them stand for symptom data. The boxes with numbered H's in them stand for hypotheses.

dominates H_7 because it is more general and covers a superset of symptoms. However, neither H_6 nor H_8 dominates the other because each covers some symptoms not covered by the other. Just because a hypothesis is higher in the tree does not automatically mean that hypothesis dominates. A dominating hypothesis must also explain more symptoms.

The striking feature about MOLE's method in Figure 7.26, different from the methods of the previous examples, is its search for a deepest explanation. The deep explanations combine several intermediate explanations to yield a smaller number of root causes of interest for its diagnostic task. Typically, the solutions that MOLE reports are the causes that can be treated or modified to fix the malfunctioning system.

MOLE's method also differs from MORE's in that it is iterative. MOLE does not expect necessarily to get all the symptomatic data at once. Users of the system sometimes neglect to report an important symptom. MOLE can request data that it needs to differentiate among competing hypotheses. MOLE must keep track not only of which hypotheses are being considered, but also which hypotheses are strongly supported by the evidence.

MOLE does not represent definitional abstractions or generalizations. All the relations used in the reasoning process are heuristic associations, representing either how one event covers another or how data can be used to differentiate among hypotheses. MOLE uses preferences rather than numeric measures to compare competing hypotheses.

In summary, MOLE's task is diagnosis, its approach is based on a classification model, and its method includes both reasoning about coverage and reasoning about acquiring new data. As

To diagnose using MOLE's method:

```
 1.    Initialize the lists of symptoms, hypotheses, and symptom-hypothesis
       connections to empty.


       /* Propose hypotheses that will cover the initial findings */
 2.    Ask the user for the set of initial findings or symptoms.
 3.    For each symptom do Cover(symptom) (invoking the subroutine below).


       /* Seek deeper hypotheses */
 4.    Next-Pass: For each hypothesis Cover(hypothesis)


       /* Apply rules to rule out or prefer hypotheses or data-hypothesis
       connections. This may cause more data to be obtained. */
 5.    For each hypothesis do
 6.    begin
 7.         Retrieve the relevant hypothesis-qualifying rules.
 8.         For each rule in the set do
 9.         begin
10.             Request any prerequisite data or test results for the
                rules that have not yet been obtained.
11.             For each new datum do Cover(datum).
12.             Apply the qualifying rules to rule out or mark as
                preferred any hypothesis.
13.         end
14.         Retrieve the set of connection rules for disqualifying any
            hypothesis-symptom pair.
15.         For each rule in the set do
16.         begin
17.             Request any prerequisite data or test results for the
                rule that have not yet been obtained.
18.             For each new datum do Cover(datum).
19.             Apply the connection rules to rule out or mark as
                preferred any hypothesis-symptom connection.
20.         end
21.    end


       /* Favor hypotheses having independent support over those having no
       support */
22.    For each symptom do
```

FIGURE 7.26. MOLE's method for diagnosis. It uses classification to determine which solutions cover data. It then tries to differentiate among the solutions to find a small set that accounts for all the findings. The method presented here is a simplified version of the one actually used in MOLE, in that it does not incorporate any provisions for backtracking (continued next page).

```
23.    begin
24.        Let competing-hypotheses be the set of all remaining
           hypotheses that cover the symptom.
25.        For each pair of competing-hypotheses do
26.        begin
27.            If there is support from the qualifying rules for one
               hypothesis but not the other, rule out the unsupported
               hypothesis.
28.            If there is support from the connection rules for one
               hypothesis-symptom pair but not the other, rule out the
               unsupported connection.
29.        end
30.    end

       /* Eliminate redundant hypotheses and low-level hypotheses that are
       dominated by higher ones */
31.    For each pair (hypothesis₁, hypothesis₂) of hypotheses do
32.    begin
33.        Let symptoms₁ be the set of symptoms covered by hypothesis₁
           and symptoms₂ be the symptoms covered by hypothesis₂.
34.        If symptoms₁ is a superset of symptoms₂ then eliminate
           hypothesis₂.
35.        Otherwise if symptoms₂ is a superset of symptoms₁ then
           eliminate hypothesis₁.
36.    end

37.    If the set of hypotheses has not changed since the last pass, then
       return the set of hypotheses. Else, iterate again going to Next-Pass.


       /* Subroutine to cover a new event, a datum, or an intermediate-
       level hypothesis.*/
1.     Procedure Cover:(event)
2.     begin
3.         Collect all the hypotheses that could potentially explain the
           event.
4.         Add these hypotheses to the list of hypotheses if they are not
           on it already and have not been previously ruled out.
5.         Connect the hypotheses (solutions) to all the data (symptoms
           or lower-level hypotheses) that they cover unless the
           connections have been previously ruled out.
6.     end
```

FIGURE 7.26. (continued)

in all classification systems, MOLE's design turns crucially on the assumption that its catalog of events is finite, exhaustive, and rapidly accessible. Determining the set of potential covering explanations for a symptom or intermediate hypothesis requires negligible time. Other routine operations include determining how many explanations there are for a symptom, which ones have support, which ones are preferred, which ones have specific qualifying connections to particular symptoms, and which ones are supported by default information. If the set of hypotheses for MOLE were combinatorially large, these queries could become quite expensive.

7.3.4 Classification in MDX

MDX (Chandrasekaran & Mittal, 1983) is a knowledge-based system for diagnosing liver diseases. Figure 7.27 illustrates an example of classification reasoning as performed by MDX. In this example, a blood sample from a patient is determined to have a higher than normal bilirubin count. The translation from a numerical measurement to the judgment that the reading is high is a qualitative abstraction. Bilirubin is an orange pigment. Having a high concentration of bilirubin is indicative of a suppressed liver function sometimes called jaundice. The term comes from the characteristic yellow coloring of the skin and eyes. Normal liver function includes filtering bilirubin from the blood. Cholestasis is a liver disorder where bile, which contains bilirubin, is not properly discharged from the liver. Blockage of bile flow can be due to problems in the liver (intrahepatic) or to problems outside the liver, such as mechanical blockages in the extrahepatic ducts. Figure 7.27 models the medical reasoning by mapping high bilirubin to jaundice as a general cause and then mapping jaundice to the more specific causes of cholestasis, extrahepatic (causes outside the liver), and bile stones.

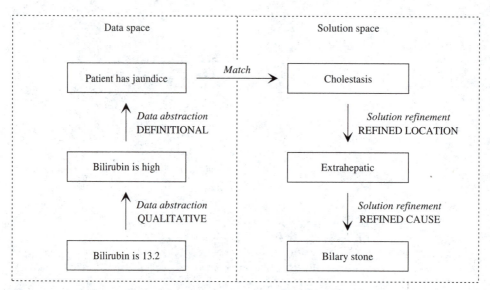

FIGURE 7.27.   An example of inference structure in MDX. In this model, the measurement of bilirubin is abstracted qualitatively to indicate that the bilirubin is high, a condition that defines jaundice. Jaundice is then matched heuristically with a possible cause, cholestasis. The cholestasis hypothesis is then refined first to extrahepatic causes and finally to the presence of a bile stone.

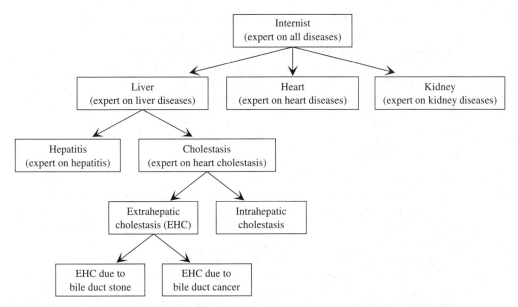

FIGURE 7.28. In MDX, the solution hierarchy is represented directly as a hierarchy of program modules, each of which is a specialist on establishing, rejecting, or refining the solution. This is a fragment of a solution/specialist hierarchy from MDX's medical domain.

Figure 7.28 illustrates part of the solution hierarchy for MDX. In MDX, this hierarchy is represented not as a network of static nodes, but rather as a hierarchy of interacting programs called "specialists." There is one specialist for each node in a tree of possible solutions. The top-level node stands for an "internist," which is an expert generalist that represents and "knows about" all diseases in the domain. Each successive level of the tree is more specialized. MDX's knowledge-level search method is distributed among the specialists in a program. Its overall behavior depends on the programming of all the specialists.

MDX's basic strategy, called establish-refine, is a top-down or goal-directed approach. It begins at the top level of the solution hierarchy. Once a specialist is established, it tries to refine its hypothesis by calling its subspecialists. Each subspecialist in turn may establish a more specific hypothesis and then call on still lower-level specialists. A specialist can request data and can also derive data abstractions from available data. At any level, a specialist may be rejected or suspended. Suspending a hypothesis means that it is unlikely but still remotely plausible. Compared with the other examples of classification systems discussed here, MDX is unique in its implementation as a knowledge system organized in terms of interacting specialists. This section does not advocate that particular implementation, but rather uses it to illustrate more of the range of implementation choices that are possible.

Another interesting aspect of MDX is the broad range of abstractions it uses for data and solutions. Besides the ones we have mentioned in our classification applications so far, MDX uses temporal, anatomical, and physiological abstractions. For example, if the data are in a series of measurements that rise and fall, MDX could characterize the data as intermittent. If the data are larger with each successive measurement, it could characterize the data as rising. Anatomical abstractions tend to model the body in terms of organs or systems having part-whole relations. For example, the liver is said to be malfunctioning if any part of it is malfunctioning. This variety derives from the wide range of kinds of evidence that MDX uses, including patient history, clinical examination, X-ray imaging, tissue examination or biopsy, and blood samples. In summary, MDX's task is the diagnosis of disease, its model uses classification emphasizing hierarchical hypotheses, and its implementation is based on a goal-driven hierarchy of specialist subprograms.

7.3.5 Classification in PROSPECTOR

PROSPECTOR (Duda & Reboh, 1984) is a knowledge system that classifies mineral exploration prospects. The project was started in 1976. Models for ore deposits continue to be developed and refined. Figure 7.29 presents an example of the inference paths in PROSPECTOR, showing how it uses intermediate hypotheses in classifying observational data. Solutions for PROSPECTOR are identifications for categories of ore deposits, numerically rated.

      After centuries of civilization and exploration, the odds of discovering new, economically viable ore deposits are low. Exploratory geology today depends on many clues from geochemistry and geophysics to augment conventional geological evidence about rock formations. Finding and identifying potential deposits involves trying to recognize and interpret evidence, even when

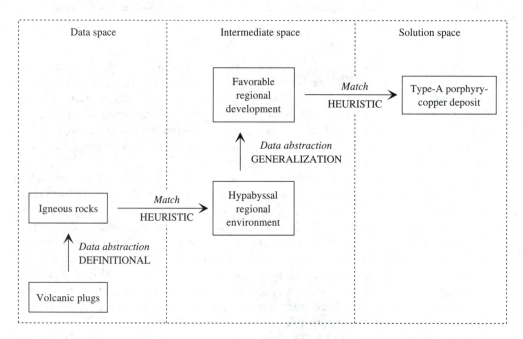

FIGURE 7.29.   This example of an inference in PROSPECTOR is typical in that it shows intermediate hypothesis spaces. Intermediate spaces were prolific in PROSPECTOR because of the many different kinds of data that were involved. Intermediate hypotheses corresponded to conclusions about such things as regional environment, kinds of rocks, kinds of intrusive minerals, kinds of alteration products, generalizations about texture, age of formations, and so on.

the clues may have been scrambled by subsequent geological events. To understand this, consider how a typical ore deposit is formed:

> A contemporary theory holds that . . . [Yerington-type or type-A porphyry-copper] . . . deposits were formed as a consequence of the subduction of an oceanic plate at the margin of a continent. The resulting heat and pressure led to the formation of magma that worked its way upward. If zones of weakness extended to the surface, the magma might erupt through volcanoes, such as those along the west coast of North and South America. Intrusive systems that did not reach the surface would cool slowly, forming large-grained crystals and various characteristic zones of altered rock. In favorable regimes of pressure and temperature, ore minerals would crystallize in characteristic sequences. Unfortunately, this ideal pattern is usually fragmented by such subsequent processes as uplift, faulting, erosion, leaching, and burial. Thus, one must read through such transformations to reassemble the pieces of the puzzle and recognize a possible deposit. (Duda & Reboh, 1984, p. 132.)

The task of rating candidates for possible mineral deposits is simplified by the results of detailed studies of the world's ore deposits, which suggest that almost all the economically important deposits fit in one of about 150 different classes. These classes are represented in PROSPECTOR as explicit and separate ore deposit models. PROSPECTOR contains models at different spatial scales—the prospect-scale models for individual deposits and regional-scale models for large geologic districts. Figure 7.30 provides statistics about the scope of PROSPECTOR's models in 1983. Each model is described in terms of production rules, linked into an inference network as shown in Figure 7.31.

Abbreviation	Description	Nodes	Rules
MSD	Massive sulfide deposit, Kuroko type	39	34
MVTD	Mississippi-Valley-type lead-zinc	28	20
PCDA	Near-continental-margin porphyry copper, Yerrington type	186	104
PCDB	Near-continental-margin porphyry copper, Cerro dePasco type	200	157
PCDC	Near-continental-margin porphyry copper, island-arc type	159	116
KNSD	Komatiitic-type nickel sulfide	127	72
WSSU	Western states sandstone uranium	200	148
ECSU	Epigenetic carbonaceous sandstone uranium	197	153
LCU	Lacustrine carbonaceous uranium	164	111
PCDSS	Porphyry copper drilling site selection	133	60
VCPMDSS	Porphyry molybdenum drilling-site selection, vertical-cylinder type	57	42
HPMDSS	Porphyry molybdenum drilling-site selection, hood type	76	48

FIGURE 7.30. PROSPECTOR's prospect-scale models for mineral deposits circa 1983. (from Duda & Reboh (1984), Table 2, page 136.)

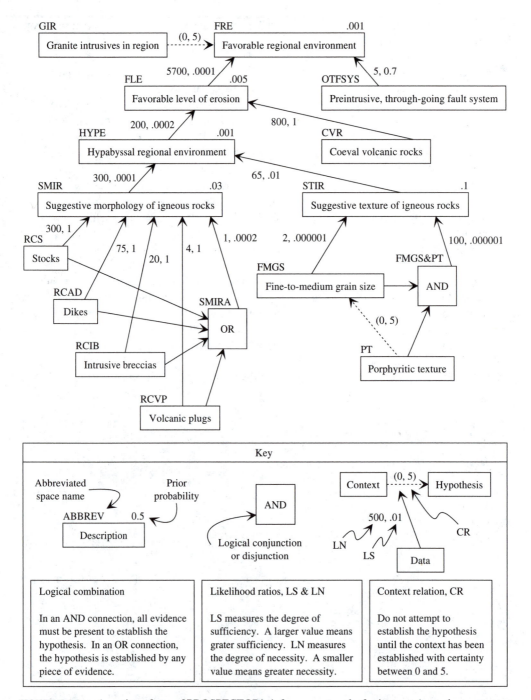

FIGURE 7.31. A portion of one of PROSPECTOR's inference networks for its type-A porphyry-copper model. These diagrams present in network form the rules and terms that PROSPECTOR uses to classify and rate candidate ore deposits. (Adapted From Duda & Reboh (1984), Figure 3, page 133.)

Among the knowledge-based classification tasks discussed in this section, PROSPECTOR is unusual in the relatively small size of the solution space combined with the relatively large amount of data that goes into evaluating a single-solution hypothesis. In PROSPECTOR, much of the system is devoted to weighing the contributions of different kinds of evidence in establishing the match of the models. The relatively small number of possible solutions leads to a straightforward strategy for typical consultations. In the first phase, data are gathered to determine which top-level or solution hypothesis to pursue. During this phase the user volunteers various data and PROSPECTOR provides feedback about the degree of match to various possible top-level hypotheses. This is called the antecedent mode because the data that the user provides (the antecedents) are used to trigger various rules, whose consequences are then propagated to establish weights for various intermediate and top-level hypotheses.

In the second phase, a top-level hypothesis is chosen. It may be the top-rated model or some other model chosen by the user. PROSPECTOR then enters its consequent mode. In this mode it searches the inference network of the active model seeking data by asking questions of the user. In deciding what question to ask next, PROSPECTOR uses backward chaining. It takes into account both what data are askable (some intermediate hypotheses are flagged as "unaskable" and are determined from other ones) and what data could have the greatest effect in establishing a rating for the current hypothesis. PROSPECTOR employs a fairly elaborate certainty calculus for combining and controlling the use of evidence. These factors are taken into account in ordering questions whose answers could change the current belief in the hypotheses.

Figure 7.31 presents a portion of PROSPECTOR's inference network for its type-A porphyry-copper model. The rectangles represent hypotheses and the links indicate inferential connections. The highest-level hypothesis is `favorable regional environment`. Near the bottom of the network, rectangles represent immediate data that can be acquired by asking a user, such as whether there are volcanic plugs. The logical connections between rule clauses appear in the network as logical connections between nodes. In general, nodes in the network initially have only prior probabilities. As data are acquired, various likelihood ratios are used to determine new estimates of the likelihood of connected hypotheses.

By themselves, the hypotheses and inferential connections did not provide enough information to the interpreter to guide the search for solutions or the acquisition of new data. An additional notation in the network called the context mechanism served both purposes. This notation informed the interpreter not to try to pursue a hypothesis until some other hypothesis ("the context") was established above a specified certainty. In Figure 7.31, it would not make geological sense to ask whether the igneous rocks have fine-to-medium grain size without knowing that they have porphyritic texture. But how sure must one be about the presence of rocks with porphyritic texture before asking about the grain size? In this particular example, the geologist decided that any positive evidence for the existence of phorphyritic texture was enough—hence the certainty scale from 0 to 5.

Another important task in mineral exploration is to determine the best sites for drilling, which are the locations where the drill bore will most likely intercept ore. The last three ore deposit models in Figure 7.30 were designed for evaluating drilling sites. The procedure for site selection is based on the idea of dividing the region into an array of smaller cells. Data about these cells are entered interactively on digitized maps. Once the data are entered, PROSPECTOR then runs its inference network on each of about 16,000 cells, storing the resulting evaluations for the drilling model on another map divided into corresponding cells. This map then presents a guide, highlighting PROSPECTOR's estimates for the most favorable drilling sites.

In summary, PROSPECTOR's task is evaluating candidate ore deposits, its model is classification, and its implementation uses a probability-based inference network. Its search exploits the fact that there are a relatively small number of recognized models for commercially viable ore deposits. Most of the work in PROSPECTOR is in weighing and combining evidence, to estimate the probability that a site matches a model. Some of prospector's models have been developed for selecting drilling sites. In this latter application, the network is executed in an efficient compiled mode so it can classify and evaluate thousands of potential drilling sites in a few seconds.

7.3.6   Summary and Review

To categorize is to group objects or events into classes, so as to respond to them in terms of their class membership rather than their uniqueness. Classification makes it possible to sort things from the world into functionally significant categories. The prototypical domain has a data space, a solution space, and mappings between them. The prototypical relations include data abstraction in the data space, matching from the data space to the solution space, and refinement in a hierarchical solution space.

In this section we reviewed five knowledge systems based on classification. Four of the systems performed diagnosis tasks, and one evaluated prospective mineral deposits. These systems differed in their specializations of the classification model and in their implementations. MYCIN used a uniform invocation of production rules for all phases of search. MORE and MOLE represented the knowledge in specialized kinds of rules that governed the event models. MDX was based on a hierarchy of specialist subprograms. PROSPECTOR was unusual in that it had a relatively small number of possible solutions and spent most of its computation weighing evidence. In the next section we develop a formal characterization of our model for classification and investigate the phenomena that arise in using it to model tasks.

Exercises for Section 7.3

Ex. 1   [05] *Terminology.* Answer true or false for each of the following questions. If the question is ambiguous, explain your answer briefly.

(a) *True or False.* The classification model requires that the particular set of possible solutions be fixed before a problem is solved.

(b) *True or False.* Classification involves three kinds of mappings: data abstraction, data-to-class matching, and solution refinement. However, not all classification problems use all three kinds of mappings.

(c) *True or False.* A screening clause in a production rule is a clause used to specify conditions of the context that determines when the rule should be activated.

(d) *True or False.* Parsimony rules give preference to low-cost solutions.

(e) *True or False.* The term *establish-refine* refers to a top-down approach to generating and testing solutions.

Ex. 2   [CD-21] *Diagnosis and Rationale in MOLE.* Figure 7.32 shows a small knowledge base with the kinds of relations used by MOLE. There are some bugs in the knowledge base and

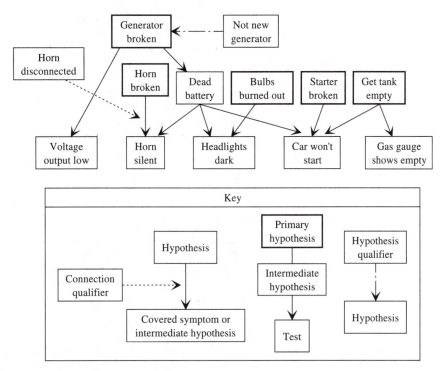

FIGURE 7.32. This sample knowledge base for MOLE shows potential hypotheses and qualifying knowledge. The bottom row of boxes corresponds to test data. These boxes correspond to the possible set of data reported as symptoms, tests, presenting data, and so on.

inadequacies in the representation. This exercise considers the shortcomings of the approach in the context of the operation of MOLE on sample data. Many of the issues that arise in this exercise motivate the systematic development of knowledge-level models of diagnosis in later chapters of this text.

(a) As defined in the text, presenting symptoms are symptoms reported when the diagnostic process is started. That a possible and possibly relevant symptom is not reported does not mean the symptom is not present, but rather that the observation was not made.

In this example the presenting symptom is that the horn is silent. According to Figure 7.32, what hypotheses could cover this?

(b) Continuing the example, suppose subsequent data are obtained that the headlights are dark, meaning that they won't switch on.

  (i) Now what hypotheses would be considered by MOLE?

  (ii) Which hypotheses would be favored? Assume that MOLE would request all relevant tests bearing on the active hypotheses.

  (iii) What test data would be requested and which would be useful to discriminate among the current hypotheses?

(c) *Yes or No.* Professor Digit says that from a practical perspective, the system should request checking the lightbulbs by touching the contacts to a battery. Given this knowledge base, would it?

(d) *Yes or No*. Professor Digit also says that because its causal model is naive, this knowledge base generally makes insufficient use of information about whether the horn is disconnected. Is he correct? Explain briefly.

(e) Continuing the case, suppose further that the event-qualifying knowledge was obtained that the generator was new. Assume that this means that the generator is unlikely to be defective or badly installed. How would that information be used by MOLE?

(f) *Yes or No*. Professor Digit says that the battery could be dead even if the generator is not broken and that the battery could be working even if the generator is broken. He complains that the network does not represent these possibilities. Is he correct? Explain briefly.

Ex. 3   [*10*] *Dependency-Directed Backtracking in MOLE*. The MOLE performance program for diagnosis is based on classification.

(a) What kinds of assumptions does MOLE make to simplify its search?

(b) What steps in MOLE's method could cause it to discover that its assumptions are wrong for a particular problem?

Ex. 4   [*10*] *Distributed Classification Specialists*. The MDX application illustrates an implementation of classification where there is a subprogram for every possible solution. Briefly, how could the modules be reorganized to admit a data-driven approach to classification?

Assuming that the system considers only those hypotheses that cover data that have been acquired, there are some control issues. Discuss one of them briefly.

Ex. 5   [*05*] *Knowledge Beats Search?* Professor Digit tries to explain the knowledge principle. He decides to use MYCIN as an example. As he says, "The key to better performance in MYCIN is more knowledge, not better search. Furthermore, no one would confuse MYCIN's inference methods (mostly backward chaining) with powerful and sophisticated approaches for search and inference. This proves that knowledge is more important than search."

(a) Why is it confusing to say that MYCIN's search method is backward chaining? Did MYCIN eliminate search?

(b) Briefly, what's wrong with Professor Digit's claim about the supremacy of knowledge over search?

7.4   *Knowledge and Methods for Classification*

In the preceding sections we considered several knowledge systems that use classification. We presented the basic conjunctive classification model and discussed the kinds of knowledge that are brought to bear in the example applications. This section refers back to our basic models for configuration and the case studies to show what is involved in knowledge-level and symbol-level analyses of classification domains. It then sketches and compares methods for classification tasks. Our goal is to show how variations in the requirements of classification can be accommodated by changes in method. The issues that arise in creating specialized methods for classification occur for other kinds of search. This section shows how general symbol-level and knowledge-level issues interact with the task requirements to shape the specialized methods for classification.

The methods for classification have two challenges: (1) They must provide a framework for organizing and maintaining the different kinds of knowledge that can be brought to bear in a task, and (2) they must accommodate different assumptions about classification, which are imposed by the larger tasks to which classification is in service. In the following, we introduce sketches of classification methods. Our goal is more to illustrate issues than to provide detailed algorithms. To simplify the presentation, we follow the approach of basic classification methods where solutions are made from singleton classes. That is, none of the methods handles composite solutions. We also assume that the search is exhaustive. Variations are left to the reader.

7.4.1 *Knowledge-Level and Symbol-Level Analysis of Classification Domains*

It is useful to distinguish between knowledge-level analysis and symbol-level analysis. Knowledge-level analysis is concerned with the kinds of knowledge required for a task. Symbol-level analysis is concerned with alternate implementations involving both representation and search.

Knowledge-Level Analysis

A knowledge-level analysis of a task domain describes the kinds of knowledge that are needed and how they are used. In this section, however, we are not interested in a single task domain, but rather in tasks modeled using classification. In our analysis, we draw on examples from the task domains described in our case studies. The key kinds of relations used in classification tasks are illustrated in the **horseshoe diagram**: relations that abstract data, relations that map abstract data to or from abstract classes in the solution space, and refinement relations in the solution space. We consider these three kinds of relations in turn.

In his characterization of classification, Clancey (1985) recognized three categories of **abstraction relations**. A **definitional abstraction** focuses on necessary and essential features of an abstraction of the data. ("If a bacterium can live in an environment where there is no free oxygen, then it is an anaerobic bacterium.") A **qualitative abstraction** reduces and simplifies quantitative data, such as by comparing it to an expected value. ("If the patient is an adult and white-blood-cell count is less than 2,500, then the white-blood-cell count is low.") A **generalization abstraction** reduces a description to a more general case in a subtype hierarchy. ("If the person is a father, then the person is a man.") Data abstractions can be about a wide range of kinds of data including temporal data, anatomical data, and physiological data.

Our categories of abstraction relations are not exhaustive or mutually exclusive. They do not cover all the abstraction relations that can be useful in hierarchical classification, and there are cases where the choice of which term to use in modeling is ambiguous. The categories are not a fixed part of classification theory or the epistemology of relations. Nonetheless, these categories of abstraction relations have a certain practical relevance because they exemplify broad ways of starting from data in problems that are grounded in the real world. These categories of abstraction relations are representative of relations established by knowledge-guided reasoning seen in many classification systems. What they have in common is that they map data from specific descriptions to more abstract descriptions and that they tend to be highly certain.

Class-matching relations are connections that relate available data to classes of solutions. In the most straightforward case, these are the heuristic matching relations that lead from observed data to solution classes. However, class-matching relations can be used in either direction. They can be used to validate hypotheses about solution classes, guiding the selection of data. They can also be used to match possible classes based on given data. The latter case applies when there are enough data for testing only a subset of the criteria associated with a class. If further assumptions are not allowed, a class cannot be established unless we know that all of its criteria are satisfied. Some of the methods in the next section often use matches on partial data to suggest "possible" solution classes, short of establishing the applicability of the classes.

Some regularities appear in the categories of matching relations that have been used in classification programs. A **causal association** explains data in terms of mechanisms involving causes and their direct effects. In an **empirical correlation**, the data and the solutions are often associated with each other in typical cases, but no causal mechanism is understood. For example, in a medical situation it may be known that people of a certain age or of a particular region are predisposed to having a particular problem. The utility of this knowledge is only statistical and not necessarily predictive for individual cases as more data are acquired. Empirical relations are not based on an understanding of mechanism, and in diagnostic tasks they may not suggest anything more specific than a symptomatic treatment. In intermediate cases, a direction of causality may be known but the conditions of the process may not.

As with our categories of abstraction relations, the categories of matching relations do not provide a solid epistemology for a theory of classification. Also as before, they have a certain practical value. They capture typical, useful connections for problem solving, organized to provide efficient indexing of solutions from available data. As a group, matching associations tend to be less reliable than the inferences about abstraction.

Refinement relations connect broad characterizations of solutions to more specific ones. These relations can be the inverses of abstraction relations, located in the solution space rather than in the data space. For example, a refinement mapping from *enterobacteriaceae* (bacteria normally found in the digestive tract) to *E. coli* (a kind of bacterium) is a subtype relation. Alternatively, refinement may trace a component hierarchy, following part-of relations to smaller system modules. Still other refinement relations may trace out increasingly localized areas of a physical or logical space. Still others may simply reason toward smaller sets, where there is a subset relation but no descriptive subtype relation beyond membership. What all refinement mappings have in common is a path toward greater specificity in determining solutions. Hierarchical solution spaces are composed through these relations.

Classification models are most typically used together with other models in characterizing a task domain. In an important special case, multistage classification models are used together to characterize a single task. Characterizing a classification model in terms of separate stages can increase clarity by partitioning both the spaces of interest and the kinds of knowledge that are used. In our earlier discussion we described two views of a multistage model. The composed mappings view emphasizes the idea that the same relations for abstraction, heuristic match, and refinement can occur in multiple stages. This view is especially useful for visualizing classification problems in stages where the solutions of one stage map to the data of the next.

Alternatively, the intermediate spaces view emphasizes how classification can link intermediate spaces of different character. Each space may have unique properties, and this view makes it easier to show the differences among the spaces. This latter view is helpful when intermediate spaces include additional kinds of reasoning beyond classification, such as temporal or causal reasoning. Chapter 9 discusses the CASNET/GLAUCOMA system among its case studies of medical diagnosis systems. The intermediate spaces view of CASNET is particularly useful in visualizing how it works.

Symbol-Level Analysis

A symbol-level analysis is about implementation. There are many possibilities for representing data and hypotheses in classification systems, including parallel processing approaches that compute solutions in parallel. Since representation and reasoning topics are discussed in detail in other parts of this book, we limit our discussion here to a few general words about how search can be governed in classification methods.

To be effective, all classification methods must routinely rule out most of the solution space. When a task is based on a classification model, it imposes a search model to the spaces that describe the domain. There are three basic approaches.

- A **data-directed search** starts with data and searches for possible solutions. It matches data against solutions, stopping when all relevant inferences have been made. This approach is also called bottom up where solutions and data correspond to the root and leaves of a search tree, respectively. The MORE and MOLE systems are largely data directed.
- A **solution-directed search** works back from possible solutions to explanatory data. This is also called top-down or goal-driven search. The MYCIN and MDX systems are mostly solution directed. The PROSPECTOR system starts out in a data-directed mode and then switches to a solution-directed mode.
- An **opportunistic search** works in both directions as information becomes available to trigger new inferences or to guide the search. New data can trigger a search for immediate abstractions. Heuristic rules can pose hypotheses, which are then tested under a focused hypothesis-directed search.

Given these basic variations in search, systems can make different assumptions about the data. In the simplest version of classification, all the classes that match the data are reportable as solutions and the others are not. Going beyond this simplest case brings us at once to more complex variations in implementation.

Some tasks assume that a complete listing of all relevant data is given as input at the beginning, implicitly discounting the possibility that data could be "missing." Other tasks assume that some data may be missed or left out accidentally. In this latter case, methods must seek additional data during the classification process or make assumptions about typical values for data.

Some tasks assume that all given data are reliable. Other methods assume that some data are more reliable than others. In the latter case, methods must evaluate the preponderance of evidence in classification.

All methods explicitly rule out classes when they violate the class criteria. Some rule out classes implicitly, based on mutual exclusion relations for classes for which there is positive evidence or by parsimony rules that weigh the preponderance of evidence. For example, on definitional grounds high blood pressure is enough to rule out low blood pressure. In many domains, such default and exclusion reasoning can lead to cases where there is an apparent contradiction in the interpretation of evidence. For example, there can be data supporting two classes that are supposed to be mutually exclusive. In another example, data acquired later may contradict the choice of classes suggested by applying parsimony rules to the data first acquired. In either case, these methods need to account for what to do in such cases, favoring one interpretation over another or simply reporting a contradiction. In the case where competing and possibly contradictory solutions need to be compared and reported, the system may apply techniques of truth maintenance or backtracking to keep track of competing alternatives.

7.4.2 MC-1: A Strawman Generate-and-Test Method

We begin in Figure 7.33 with an extremely simple "method" for classification, called MC-1, which is based on generate-and-test. The quotation marks around the term *method* are intended to emphasize that MC-1 is used more as a strawman to illustrate basic assumptions rather than as a practical method for typical applications. MC-1 simply steps through the set of possible solutions and tests whether any solution matches the data. It has a solution tester, which compares candidates against the data, rejecting ones that are consistent. MC-1 is formulated as **exhaustive generate-and-test**, with no ranking of multiple solutions. All the knowledge used by MC-1 is embodied in the predefined set of solutions and in the matching and evaluation criteria used by the solution tester. The solution tester itself may organize and represent the set of evaluation criteria for the classes in an explicit discrimination network or in any of a number of other ways.

MC-1 relies on several assumptions about classification. It assumes:

■ The set of solution classes is small enough to consider each class individually.
■ All the necessary data can be obtained at the beginning of the process.

The first assumption corresponds to the usual caveat about complexity for generate-and-test methods. The second assumption concerns the system's ability to reason from partial data. In MC-1, we do not postulate any mechanisms for providing default data or for acquiring data incrementally.

None of our example applications of classification uses MC-1 because none of the applications satisfies these simplifying assumptions. Other task requirements dominate the design of the specialized methods. MC-1 does not employ any knowledge about the major kinds of data abstraction or solution refinement relations cited in our analysis of the applications, nor does it exploit any hierarchical structure of the solution space. In the rest of this section, we relax the assumptions of MC-1 a bit at a time and consider how the methods can be modified accordingly.

To perform classification using MC-1:
```
    1.    Initialize the list of solutions to empty.
    2.    Obtain the data and abstract it.
    3.    For each candidate class do
    4.            If solution-tester(candidate, data) then add the candidate to
                  the list of solutions.
    5.    Report the solutions.
```

FIGURE 7.33. MC-1, an extremely simple method for classification based on exhaustive generate-and-test.

As the requirements become more realistic, the search control and the required knowledge for classification become more complex.

7.4.3 *MC-2: Driving from Data to Plausible Candidates*

Our next method, MC-2, is also quite simple. MC-2 reduces the amount of computational work when there is a large number of solutions. Instead of stepping through all possible solutions, MC-2 limits the number of solutions considered by evaluating only those that potentially explain the data. It also reduces the cost per candidate by keeping track of which candidates have been considered already and by evaluating each candidate exactly once. It depends on the same assumptions as MC-1 except that the first assumption is replaced with the following:

- There is an efficient procedure for retrieving all the candidate solutions that can potentially explain a data element and that are consistent with it.
- The given data are highly discriminatory, so that the set of candidate solutions is much smaller than the complete set of possible solutions.

The first assumption requires that there is a means of retrieving covering solutions from data. In MC-2, this is carried out by the candidate retriever. As discussed in Section 7.2, different policies are possible for the candidate retriever. For example, it could return all candidates that are consistent with the data or it could limit itself to consistent candidates that cover some of the data.

A data abstraction step is done before candidate retrieval. For example, a reading of blood pressure (a datum) may be abstracted to "high blood pressure." MC-2 uses a data abstractor and a solution tester as shown in Figure 7.34.

The data abstractor uses the abstraction operations discussed earlier in our knowledge-level analysis. It could use qualitative abstraction, temporal abstraction, spatial or part-whole

```
To perform classification using MC-2:
    1.    Initialize the list of solutions to empty.
    2.    Obtain the data.
    3.    Abstract the data using the data-abstractor.

          /* Find solutions that cover the data. Different policies are
          possible for the candidate retriever. */
    4.    candidates := candidate-retriever(data)

          /* Evaluate solutions on the full data. This is where knowledge for
          ranking candidates is used. */
    5.    For each class on the list of candidates do
    6.          If solution-tester(candidate, data) then add the candidate to
                the list of solutions.
    7.    Return the list of solutions.
```

FIGURE 7.34. MC-2 is a simple variation of MC-1 that requires an efficient and reliable means (the candidate retriever) for retrieving solutions that could potentially cover data elements.

abstraction, or definitional abstraction. The data abstractor is a small classification system in its own right. There are many implementation choices here. For example, in some applications it may be convenient to formalize a language of abstractions and to write a rule grammar for recognizing them. There may be more than one set of possible abstractions for a set of data.

The second assumption for MC-2 is that the candidate retriever greatly reduces the number of candidate classes to be evaluated. If it returns too few solution candidates, then MC-2 may miss a correct solution. If it returns too many, then MC-2 will show no improvement in performance over MC-1. After the initial set of candidates is acquired, then the solution tester must compare competing solutions. In the absence of acquiring more data, it must rely on some other measures of the solutions beyond their consistency with data. It may draw on information about prior probabilities of the candidates. It could employ a single-solution assumption or other knowledge for ranking candidates.

Like MC-1, MC-2 is simpler than any of the methods for the sample applications. Nonetheless, its revised assumptions are closer to the ones used in the example applications. The first set of method specializations that we discuss below all use more knowledge to cope with a large number of possible solutions.

The methods MC-1 and MC-2 are variations of simple generate-and-test. Neither of them takes advantage of hierarchical relations on the set of solutions. As discussed in Chapter 2, the usual way to extend a search method for larger spaces is to organize the search space hierarchically.

7.4.4 MC-3: Solution-Driven Hierarchical Classification

Method MC-3 uses a hierarchical generate-and-test approach to classification. MC-3 assumes that the possible solutions are arranged in a class hierarchy. It traverses that hierarchy, using a top-down, breadth-first search. At each level, it compares candidates to data, enabling it to rule out branches of the hierarchy. It may request additional data to discriminate among candidates. It then proceeds to the next level along those branches that are consistent. This version assumes that solutions are leaf nodes and that other classes higher in the hierarchy are partial descriptions of solutions.

This process is illustrated in Figure 7.35 for the first two levels of a solution hierarchy. The shaded boxes are the solution classes that have been visited. The black boxes represent solution classes that have been ruled out, together with their descendants. In the data space, the boxes outlined with heavy lines represent the data that have been acquired.

MC-3 depends on several assumptions beyond those of MC-2:

■ The solution classes are arranged in a superclass hierarchy or lattice that efficiently divides the classes of candidates.
■ There is a subset of data useful for discrimination at each level of the solution space.
■ The goal is to find the most-specific classes consistent with the data. (As in MC-2, additional evaluation criteria may be applied to rank competing candidates that are left after this.)

The first assumption is the key to MC-3's gain in efficiency. Subclasses are ruled out when their superclass is ruled out. If a class has multiple superclasses, it follows that the class can be elimi-

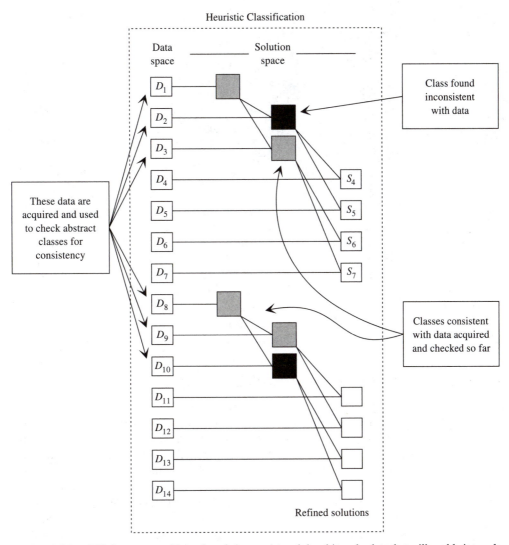

FIGURE 7.35.   MC-3 traverses a hierarchy of classes. At each level it seeks data that will enable it to rule out branches of the taxonomy.

nated when any of its superclasses is ruled out. The assumption admits the early pruning condition, crucial for all applications of hierarchical generate-and-test. For the taxonomy to be effective, each level must partition the remaining candidates into distinct classes.

The third assumption explains why the method does not just stop when it has eliminated competing solutions at a level. The search is for the most-specific characterizations of solutions. Figure 7.36 presents the method. MC-3 is vague about the process used for selecting discriminatory data. Some theoretical measures of information entropy can be brought to bear on this question, as discussed in Chapter 9.

To perform classification using MC-3:
```
     1.   Initialize the list of solutions to empty.
     2.   For each level of the solution hierarchy do
     3.   begin
     4.        Obtain the raw data useful for discriminating among the
              candidates at this level.
     5.        Abstract the data using the data-abstractor.
     6.        For each class at this level do
     7.        begin
     8.             If the ~ solution-tester(candidate, data) then discard
                   the candidate
     9.             Else if the candidate is incomplete, then remove it from
                   the list and add its successors
    10.             Else add the candidate to the list of solutions.
    11.        end
    12.   end
    13.   Rank the solutions and return them.
```

FIGURE 7.36.   The second stage of MC-3 is to map a subset of the data to initial "seed" classes. Many of these classes will prove inconsistent with the data, leading to a selection of further data.

7.4.5 MC-4: Data-Driven Hierarchical Classification

MC-3 comes closer to the methods used in the example knowledge systems in this chapter, but it is still simplistic. One major difference is that MC-3 starts every case by asking about the same data. In a troubleshooting application, for example, this would be silly. It would fail to make good use of highly focused initial data provided by an observer reporting faulty behavior. Similarly, in a medical setting it is more typical to reason from the presenting symptoms.

Like MC-3, MC-4 uses a hierarchical search space. Like MC-2, it uses a data-driven approach that draws on such data. MC-4 begins by establishing "seed classes" suggested by data offered by an external source. Like MC-3, it rules out classes that are inconsistent with the data, but it uses the data it is given to guide the search and rules out classes that are consistent with the data if those classes do not bear on the data. In a medical task, if MC-4 were given that the patient has a swelling in the ankles, it would not consider diseases that fail to explain those symptoms, such as "broken arm" or "measles."

In the following we introduce the method and its assumptions in stages. Figure 7.37 illustrates the first part of MC-4: data acquisition and abstraction. We assume that an initial subset of data has been preselected and that it is abstracted before further use. The data items highlighted with boxes indicate those that have been preselected. Abstractions are computed from these data to yield input data to the next part of the classification process.

The next part of MC-4 matches the data against high-level classes in the taxonomy of candidate solutions. We assume that there are many possible classifications and that fine discrimination requires a wide range of different data. MC-4 distinguishes data according to the classes that

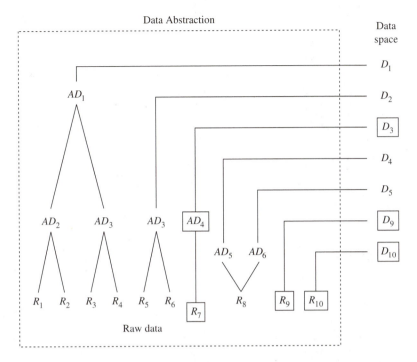

FIGURE 7.37. The first part of MC-4 is to abstract the raw data.

they match. The initial goal is to establish general classifications, based on a preliminary subset of the data.

In Figure 7.38, the data elements D_3, D_9, and D_{10} are matched against the most abstract classes in the solution space for which they are relevant. In the first pass, some abstract classes will be found to be inconsistent with the data. In the figure, the shaded boxes are consistent. These are the "seed" classes for further deliberations. The black boxes are inconsistent. The white boxes indicate data and solution classes that are not explicitly checked yet.

Figure 7.39 continues the process. Some of the possible data are now determined to be irrelevant, since they could only be used to rule out classes that have already been eliminated, either directly or indirectly because their superclasses have been eliminated. Discrimination among solution classes now moves down another level. In the figure, data elements D_6, D_7, D_{11}, and D_{12} are considered next. The next level of solution classes is checked against the data for consistency. The ones marked by black boxes are determined to be inconsistent at this stage. The ones marked by shaded boxes are consistent with the data.

The process recurs, dropping progressively to more detailed subclasses and acquiring and checking additional data. Other knowledge for ranking or ruling out candidates might be brought to bear. When there are many levels of subclasses, the hierarchical approach for pruning branches of the solution taxonomy can lead to substantial reductions in the amount of data that must be abstracted and matched.

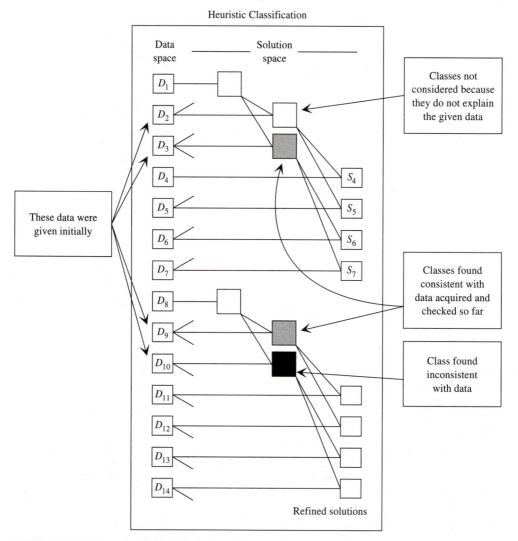

FIGURE 7.38.   The second stage of MC-4 is to map a subset of the data to initial "seed" classes.

MC-4 rests on the same assumptions as MC-3, plus an additional assumption: The initial selection of data determines the relevant classes to consider. Operationally, this means that classes that do not bear on or explain the initial data are ignored. No additional data will be explicitly requested to rule out these classes. This assumes a policy that implicitly rules out candidates if they do not explain any known data. However, such will be reconsidered if they are implicated by other data acquired to discriminate among other classes.

Figure 7.40 presents MC-4. The advantage of MC-4 over MC-3 is that the former does not burden the user by requesting irrelevant data. MC-4 assumes that the relevant data have been

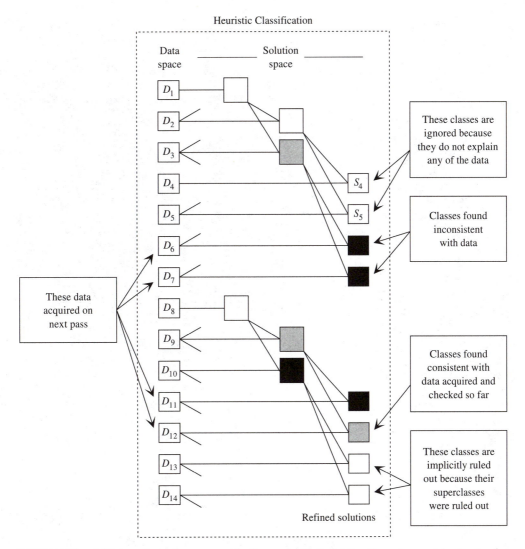

FIGURE 7.39. MC-4 continues the process of refinement and elimination through successive levels of the solution hierarchy.

reported and that it need only concern itself with discriminating among the candidates that could explain the reported data.

7.3.6 Method Variations for Classification

Methods MC-1 through MC-4 are simpler than the methods we saw for the example knowledge systems in Section 7.2. In this section we revisit those example systems briefly to compare their methods with the three simplified methods above.

To perform classification using MC-4:
```
    1.    Initialize the list of solutions to empty.

          /* This is where the initial raw data is given and seed classes are
          formed. */
    2.    Acquire the raw data selected by the observer.
    3.    Abstract the raw data.

          /* Form an initial list of seed candidates. As in MC-2, different
          policies are possible. */
    4.    candidates :=˙ candidate-retriever(data)

          /* This part of MC-4 is like MC-3 except that it proceeds from seed
          classes instead of from the top. */
    5.    For each level of the solution hierarchy below the seeds do
    6.    begin
    7.          Obtain the raw data useful for discriminating among the
                candidates at this level.
    8.          Abstract the data using the data-abstractor.

                /* The next step may require revisiting higher levels of the
                hierarchy. */
    9.          Add any new seed classes as needed, using the candidate-
                retriever over the new and old data.
   10.          For each class at this level do
   11.          begin
   12.                  If ~ solution-tester(candidate, data) then discard the
                        candidate
   13.                  Else if the candidate is incomplete, then remove it from
                        the list and add its successors
   14.                  Else add the candidate to the list of solutions.
   15.          end
   16.    end
   17.    Rank the candidates using the solution-tester.
   18.    Return the candidate solutions.
```

FIGURE 7.40.   MC-4 is a data-driven method for hierarchical classification.

MYCIN's method is implemented by the interaction of its knowledge base and its interpreter. The interpreter carries out backward chaining. It proceeds in the fashion described in Chapter 3, looking up the characteristics of the predicates in the rule clauses to determine whether to ask for data or to look for other supporting rules. MYCIN does not commit to any hierarchical search strategy like MC-3 and MC-4, although such strategies could be implemented by programming the rules in its knowledge base.

The MORE system uses an approach closest to MC-2. It differs from MC-2 in that much of its method and knowledge is concerned with computing "confidence" in the rules. It uses these confidence computations roughly as prior probabilities to rank data and solutions. To a first approximation, the diagnostic rules determine which solution candidates are consistent and then the confidence computations are used to rank competing candidates. MORE also differs from MC-2 in that it can request more data to discriminate among hypotheses implicated by the data it has so far.

The MOLE system uses a hierarchical approach closest to MC-4. It starts out with a set of raw data about symptoms observed by the user. MOLE maps this data to the most-specific hypotheses that it can in its solution taxonomy. It then switches to a goal-driven mode where it requests data to discriminate among these hypotheses. MOLE differs from MC-4 in that it explicitly incorporates a single-solution assumption and picks the highest classes in the solution hierarchy that explain the data.

The MDX system is closest to MC-3. Although MC-3 does not express the specialist- oriented organization advocated in the MDX system, MC-3 captures the essence of the establish-refine paradigm used by that system. It searches top-down and prunes subclasses hierarchically.

Like MC-4, the PROSPECTOR system switches from a data-driven to a solution-driven approach. Initially it works with whatever data are supplied by the user. PROSPECTOR is organized as a set of models, developed separately for different kinds of mineral deposits. Once initial data are evaluated, a top-level model is selected, and PROSPECTOR requests data to distinguish among the classes in that model. Like several of the other systems in this chapter, PROSPEC-TOR makes use of prior probabilities in ranking competing candidates. PROSPECTOR also makes use of annotations in its models to control more directly the acquisition of data and the pursuit of its hypotheses.

The matching process is at the core of classification. In the example knowledge systems, the complexity of this process ranges from almost trivial to moderately complex. The complexity comes not from any single small match or rule firing, but potentially from very large compositions of individual matches. The PROSPECTOR matches are probably the most complex in our examples, since they involve multiple models and each model is made up of hundreds of nodes and rules.

Following the arguments of cognitive psychologists in our introduction to this chapter, classification is central to cognition and permeates our mental life. This suggests that classification is central to many tasks that we might think of automating. To pick a somewhat exotic example, one could imagine creating a knowledge system that would recognize the text of fictional short stories as being in one of (say) a few hundred story types. In such a task the data abstraction and matching processes would need to reason not only with qualitative abstractions, which seem very simple and straightforward, but also about the different actions and interactions of actors over time. The matching process would need to represent and reason about characterizations of human situations. Such a system would require very large knowledge bases. In short, matching and classification can be a potentially very complex process, much more complex than the knowledge systems we considered. It is incorrect to judge processes based on classification as necessarily simple.

Figure 7.41 reviews some of the different goals and criteria that shape methods for classification. The simplest methods require that the number of solutions be small enough to be considered individually and that all of the necessary data are available at the beginning. Other methods

Favor consistent classes.
    Admit all classes that match over those that are merely consistent.
    Favor classes that have greater coverage of data.

When making assumptions, try the most plausible ones first.
    Assume domain-specific default values for missing measurements.
    Assume there is just one solution.
    Favor solutions having a preponderance of evidence.
    Favor deep causes over collections of shallow ones.
    Favor specific solutions over general ones.
    Favor common causes over rare ones.
    Trust measured data over default data.
    Distrust implausible measurements.

Try to reduce costs in acquiring data.
    Acquire no more data than is necessary.
    Acquire data that differentiate among competing solutions.
    Avoid expensive or dangerous measurements.

FIGURE 7.41.   Different goals and criteria for classification systems.

try to reduce search by focusing on only those subsets of solutions for which there is evidence, which means only those solutions that can potentially cover the data acquired so far. When solution spaces are larger, hierarchical approaches can be used to reason about families of solutions. As always, there are implicit requirements in these methods. Depending on what initial data are acquired, there can also be blind spots, which are possible solutions for which no data are acquired that the solutions could possibly cover. When it is not realistic to acquire all data at the beginning, methods can reason from initial data, look for ambiguities and inconsistencies, and then iteratively seek more data to resolve them. These methods can be more practical than methods that require that all the necessary data be acquired at the beginning. Such methods, however, raise many issues beyond those of just classification and are discussed in more detail in the chapter on diagnosis.

7.4.7 *Summary and Review*

To categorize is to group objects or events into classes, so as to respond to them in terms of their class membership rather than their uniqueness. Classification makes it possible to sort things from the world into functionally significant categories. In this section we considered methods for classification. We asked what classification is, what knowledge is required, and how that knowledge is used. We considered how differences in task requirements and also differences in the data and solution spaces lead to differences in knowledge-level methods for classification. Our knowledge-level analysis of classification models delineated three basic kinds of relations drawn from the horseshoe diagram: knowledge for abstracting data, knowledge for mapping data to solution classes, and knowledge for refining solution classes. Classification models are often used with other models and may be combined in multistage models.

What may be surprising is how simple (perhaps trivial) the classification methods are. The complexity for classification tasks is in the domain knowledge rather than the method that applies it. This is one reason classification tasks are well suited to knowledge-engineering approaches.

How can we tell when classification methods are suitable for a task? The answer goes back to our initial definition of classification: problems that involve the selection of solutions from a predetermined set. The analysis and methods we have discussed for classification have focused on a data space, a solution space, and mappings between them. When we analyze the patterns of knowledge use in a new task domain, we can look for the now familiar patterns of data abstraction, heuristic association, and solution refinement. To the extent that these patterns cover the patterns in the domain for selecting a solution class, the problem solving can use a classification model. In other cases, classification patterns are only a part of larger patterns of knowledge use.

Exercises for Section 7.4

Ex. 1   [05] *The Search Method of MC-2.* What search method from Chapter 2 does MC-2 specialize? Explain briefly.

Ex. 2   [00] Professor Digit says methods like MC-2 are so elementary that their foundations in terms of basic search methods convey little of interest. The main contribution from foundational search methods is the basic concepts. Argue this point of view briefly. What concepts from Chapter 2 are relevant?

Ex. 3   [05] Professor Digit says all the methods for classification in this section are much ado about nothing. Most classifiers are just discrimination networks. Discrimination networks are simply decision networks that map data onto classes.
(a) On what assumptions does Professor Digit's argument depend? What are the main issues? Explain briefly.
(b) If we take backward chaining as a search method, are we referring to the knowledge level or the symbol level?

Ex. 4   [10] *Classification and Search Methods.* In principle, classification models can be implemented using many different search methods, given domain knowledge appropriate to the method. For each of the following search methods from Chapter 2, explain briefly whether any of the methods for classification in this section are primarily based on it. (Do not count as a match those methods for which there is merely a superficial similarity for some of the features.)
(a) generate-and-test
(b) hierarchical generate-and-test
(c) hill climbing
(d) means-ends analysis
(e) constraint satisfaction
(f) branch and bound

Ex. 5   [10] *All-Encompassing Classes and Classification Methods.* Professor Digit has noticed that none of the methods in this section (MC-1 through MC-4) seems to depend on all-encompassing classes. That is, he expected to see the following assumption associated with hierarchical classification methods:

□   The designation of a class is the union of the designations of its subclasses.

(a) How can this assumption be used to rule out classes?

(b) What kinds of knowledge used in the example systems in this chapter might be productively combined with this assumption?

7.5   Open Issues and Quandaries

Cognitive psychologists believe classification is ubiquitous in mental life. A doctor recognizes that a patient's symptoms suggest liver failure. A geologist recognizes that a pattern of mineral data suggests an established kind of ore deposit. An editor recognizes that the situation unfolding in a short story is typical of a "closed-room mystery" format. By associating data with classes, we simplify our understanding of the world. Establishing a class enables us to employ previous learning in understanding the data.

This chapter presented several examples of knowledge systems based on a classification model. We discussed a computational model for classification as selection from a set of given classes. We carried out a general knowledge-level analysis based on several domains that use the model and discussed several search methods that can implement classification. We now step back from this development to look at rough edges. How could these ideas about classification be wrong?

Where Do Categories Come From?

Throughout this chapter we have accepted classes as given a priori. Determining an appropriate set of classes for a task was taken as outside the classification process itself. This position is comfortable from a pedagogical point of view because it enables us to focus on properties of the classification process. In contrast, opening the door to questions about what categories mean and where they come from exposes some slippery issues. In the following we open that door just a crack to get a sense of what is behind it.

All approaches to developing new categories require a feedback loop with observations of an environment. This is recognized by researchers in machine learning and neural networks. These researchers argue that the objects in the world that we perceive and interact with are unlabeled. They do not come from nature with predefined categories. Objects and situations can be unique and they can change over time. They argue that coping with this lack of predefined order is a crucial and fundamental function of living systems that is not explained by information-processing models of intelligence. This casts a cloud of suspicion about the incompleteness of any account of intelligence that depends on predefined categories or on symbol structures with fixed meanings. The issue is how mental patterns can become associated with an external reality.

This process of creating symbols for categories without predefined categories has been demonstrated in computer models and is a central theme in research on machine learning. There are many ways to do this involving feedback from sensors. For example, Gerald Edelman uses a two-stage connectionist system composed of a recognition component in series with an association component that retrieves properties that objects have in common. The feedback operation of the model is organized to select for patterns that enhance the overall well-being of a simulated organism. He explains the behavior in terms of evolutionary processes operating on a vast population of structures that result from the development of the organism. Other scientists with backgrounds in dynamic systems theory (Huberman, 1985) have observed the same kinds of phenomena in parallel computing structures. They model this behavior using a theory of dynamic systems involving mathematical concepts called fixed points and attractors. Alternatively, Fisher (1987) proposes a dynamic category utility theory based on statistical models that proposes and revises categories according to their value in clustering members into distinct classes.

Using Multiple Classifiers

There is a fundamental tension in using categories. Categories are a key to the economics of thought. However, every fixed set of categories imposes limitations. It blinds us to seeing the world in different terms. This tension plays itself out in everyday life and also in the sciences. Popular psychologists talk of techniques for achieving innovations by breaking through "mental blocks." We speak of finding ways to see past "old stereotypes." Futurists speak of using different kinds of "eyeglasses" for seeing the world in fresher ways, free of earlier preconceptions.

This issue of finding fresh and appropriate ways to interpret phenomena arises in methods of observation in the sciences. In sociology and anthropology, there is an issue in choosing the terms of analysis for understanding unfamiliar social structures and situations. Ethnomethodology is an approach to observation that seeks explanations of social structures in the terms used by the participants rather than in preestablished categories provided by professional observers. As the founders of ethnomethodology, Garfinkel and Sacks, put it, terminology about rules and institutions and the rest is not a "resource" for sociological theory. Rather, it is the phenomenon that sociology ought to be studying (Garfinkel, 1967). Rules and institutions do not come from a Platonic universe of social structures. Structures are invented. The invention or construction of rules and institutions, moreover, is not something one does only once. Instead it is, as they put it, a "continual accomplishment" of the members of any given social setting. This approach has now been used in studying activities in legal trials, office work, medical examinations, and other things. The relevance of this to classifications used in building knowledge systems is that there is value to identifying the categories used by the domain experts and user group. A well-meaning attempt to provide "more rational" categories in a task may well lead to problems with the acceptability of the model, if the group is not open to exploring new categories.

When Should Categories Be Revised?

Limitations of a classifier are imposed by the basics: what can be perceived, what the language can describe, and what use the categories have for further reasoning. Improvements in sensors sometimes reveal new differences and thereby the possibility for previously unnoticed categories. Scientific instruments that open up new phenomena have often led to advances in science: the telescope, the microscope, the radio telescope, the cloud chamber, the mass spectrometer. Blindness can come from intrinsic limitations either in the instruments or in our use of them. In 1990, a long-standing mystery about apparent long-distance coordination in herds of elephants became better understood. Previously, nobody had monitored the herds with detectors of very low-frequency sounds below the threshold of human hearing. Low-frequency sounds can travel great distances and are used by elephants. Unaided humans observing herd behavior are deaf to the very signals that are used for coordination.

Some sets of categories work better than others. For example, categories of objects are more useful when they can be determined from data observable about the objects. They are more useful if they have strong implications for further problem solving.

Suppose we have a program that classifies people. (This example was suggested by William Clancey.) One rule that our program might use follows:

```
IF    the client is a judge,
THEN  he is an educated person.
```

Such a rule is much like the ones for data abstraction and heuristic matching that we have seen in our examples. In a knowledge-level analysis of a task, we might ask about the role of the rule in a model. Does it express a data-type relation? Is it based on a causal model about the selection process for judges?

Such questions do not cover all the interactions of classifications with real situations. Judges are real people, with their own complex personalities and personal histories. What would it mean about our categories if we came across an "uneducated judge"? This atypical judge might have gained his or her position by some abridgment or irregularity of the intentions of the judicial system. A judge is supposed to be wise and educated.

Recognizing that categories are invented leads to the realization that they can be wrong and require revision. Revision of categories takes place at a slower rate than their use. A doctor classifying data about a patient's illness is not usually going to consider revising her model of bacteriology; a botanist in the field is not often going to change the taxonomies of the plant kingdom whenever he fails to identify a leaf. Practical and useful classifications arise over much longer periods of time.

Variations on Classification

Throughout this chapter we have presumed that classes are separate and discrete entities. This is fundamental to the way that we characterize classes, but it is not the only way it can be done. Consider the following remarks from a note from Richard Duda, one of the creators of PROSPECTOR.

> A . . . problem with PROSPECTOR that has always bothered me is PROSPECTOR's inability to recognize that ore-deposit models carve up a continuum. You may recall the three porphyry-copper models designated by PCDA, PCDB, and PCDC. If PROSPECTOR were used to match a given prospect against each of these models, it might come up with corresponding numbers such as .3, .2, .05. A standard interpretation would be that there are weak matches with *A* and *B*, and almost none with *C*. But perhaps the right interpretation is that the prospect shares some of the characteristics of *A* and *B*, and scores highly as an intermediate form between *A* and *B*. (private communication)

Duda's comment about PROSPECTOR can be seen as leading to more variations on the nature of solutions to "classification" problems. Earlier we considered the distinction between multiple solutions and composite solutions. Duda's example gives us yet another variation. What it leaves open is the issue of what one can do with solutions of this kind. Just what can we say about the properties of a prospect that is .3 PCDA, .2 PCDB, and .05 PCDC? To develop such characterizations into a useful computational model we would need to have ways to reason about the combination of properties of classes. In Chapter 6 we saw how fuzzy logic can be used to model this kind of reasoning.

Methods for identifying new classes have been studied for several years, especially statistically based methods used for recognizing regularities in noisy and complex environments. This work includes contributions from statistics, communication theory, switching theory, and operations research. Cluster analysis looks for patterns or groupings in data. Statistical methods are concerned with the distribution of values and about the reliability of certain decision-making procedures. Different methods rely on particular kinds of discrimination functions for determining classifications, such as linear boundaries. Discussion of these topics is beyond the scope of this book. A useful reference to the material continues to be Duda and Hart (1973).

Configuration

8.1 Introduction

A **configuration** is an arrangement of parts. A **configuration task** is a problem-solving activity that selects and arranges combinations of parts to satisfy given specifications. Configuration tasks are ubiquitous. Kitchen designers configure cabinets from catalogs of modular cupboards, counters, closets, drawers, cutting boards, racks, and other elements. Salespeople for home entertainment systems must design configurations from tape decks, optical disk players, receivers, turntables, and other units that can play recordings from different media, as well as from video screens, speakers, and other units that can present performances to people. Computer engineers and salespeople configure computer systems from various computing devices, memory devices, input and output devices, buses, and software. Dieticians configure diets from different combinations of foods. Configuration problems begin with general specifications and end with detailed specifications of what parts are needed and how they are to be arranged.

A definitional characteristic of configuration, as we shall use the term, is that it instantiates components from a predefined, finite set. This characterization of configuration does not create new parts or modify old ones. Configuration tasks are similar to classification tasks in that instantiation includes the *selection* of classes. However, to solve a classification problem is merely to select one (or perhaps a few) from the predefined set of classes. To solve a configuration problem is to instantiate a potentially large *subset* of the predefined classes. The search space of possible solutions to a configuration problem is the *set of all possible subsets* of components. This is the *power set* of the predefined classes. Furthermore, multiple instantiations of the same part may be used in a solution, and different *arrangements* of parts count as different solutions. Configuration problems are usually much harder than classification problems.

8.1.1 *Configuration Models and Configuration Tasks*

Custom manufacturing and mass manufacturing are often seen as opposites. Custom manufacturing tailors products to the specific and different needs of individual customers; mass manufacturing achieves economies of scale when high-volume manufacturing techniques make it possible to reduce the unit costs of nearly identical products. An industrial goal common to many kinds of manufacturing is to combine the flexibility of custom manufacturing with the economics of mass production. An important strategy for this is to create lines of products that can be tailored to a customer's requirements by configuring customer-specific systems from a catalog of mass-produced parts. This approach has been called an a la carte or build-to-order marketing and manufacturing strategy.

A la carte manufacturing requires special capabilities of an organization. For production, the required capabilities include the efficient means for managing of an inventory of parts, for bringing the parts together that are required for each order, for assembling the parts into products, and for testing the quality of the different assembled products. A well-recognized logistic requirement for this process is to accurately understand the customer's needs and to develop a product specification that meets those needs. This step, which actually precedes the others, is the configuration step. The success and efficiency of the entire enterprise depends on configuration.

Since flexible product lines can involve hundreds or thousands of different, configurable parts, there are many possibilities for errors in the configuration process. Errors in a configuration can create costly delays when they are discovered at assembly time, at testing time, or by a customer. An effective configuration process reduces costs by reducing level of inventory, reducing the amount of idle manufacturing space, reducing the delay before customers' bills are paid, and better ensuring customer satisfaction.

As these factors have been recognized, companies have sought automated and semi-automated configuration systems for routinely creating, validating, and pricing configurations to meet the differing requirements of their customers. One of the first and best known knowledge-based configuration systems is the XCON system for configuring VAX computer systems (McDermott, 1981). Knowledge-based systems for configuration tasks are being built by many organizations.

Configuration is a special case of design. In design the elements of the designed artifact are not constrained to come from a predefined set. They are subject only to the constraints of the manufacturing methods and the properties of the raw materials. The knowledge necessary for configuration tasks is more bounded than the knowledge for general design tasks. In general design tasks, the solution space is more open-ended. For example, designing a pickup truck from scratch is more open-ended than choosing options for a new one. In configuration tasks, much of the "design work" goes into defining and characterizing the set of possible parts. The set of parts must be designed so they can be combined systematically and so they cover the desired range of possible functions. Each configuration task depends on the success of the earlier task of designing configurable components.

From a perspective of knowledge engineering, configuration tasks are interesting because they are synthetic or constructive tasks. They are tasks for which combinatorics preclude the pre-enumeration of complete solutions. Just as not all classification tasks are the same, not all configuration tasks are the same. Configuration models can be used as a basis for different kinds of tasks, not necessarily involving manufacturing and physical parts. For example, "configuring" therapies can be a part of a larger diagnosis and therapy task. Configuring alternative combinations of steps for a plan can be an important part of a planning process. In such cases we refer to a **configuration model** for a task.

Knowledge-engineering techniques are suitable for classification tasks and configuration tasks because most of the complexity in specifying how to carry out the task is in the domain knowledge rather than the methods themselves. The knowledge-level methods define roles for different kinds of knowledge and these roles help to control the way that the bodies of knowledge interact and guide the search for solutions.

8.1.2 *Defining Configuration*

Selecting and arranging parts is the core of solving a configuration problem. Figure 8.1 presents an example of a configuration that is a solution to a configuration problem. In this example, the configuration has two top-level parts: Part-1 and Part-2. Each of these parts has subparts.

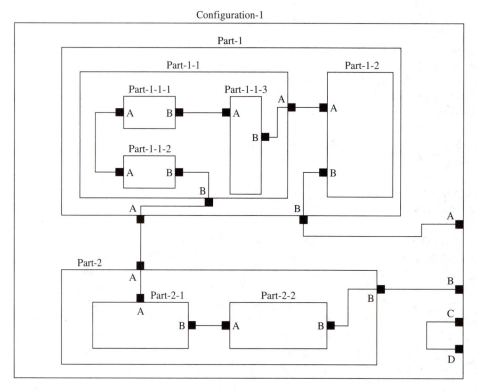

FIGURE 8.1. An example of a configuration using a port-and-connector model. In this figure, all components are shown as boxes and the top-level component is Configuration-1. It has two parts, Part-1 and Part-2. The arrangement of the configuration is indicated by the part-of hierarchy, displayed graphically by the containment of boxes and by the interconnections among parts. Each part has a number of ports, labeled A,B,C, or D. For example, the B port of Part-1-1-1 is connected to the A port of Part-1-1-3.

Configuration domains differ in their representations of arrangements. For example, Figure 8.1 represents arrangements using a **port-and-connector model**. The ports on each part correspond to the different roles that subparts can have with respect to each other. Like all models governing arrangements, a port-and-connector model constrains the ways things can be connected. Components can be connected only in predefined ways. Ports may have type specifications indicating that they can be connected only to objects of a particular kind. Each port can carry only one connection.

Variations in the search requirements and the available domain knowledge for different configuration tasks lead to variations in the methods. Nonetheless, certain regular patterns of knowledge use appear across many different configuration tasks. Configuration methods work through recognizable phases. They map from user specifications to abstract descriptions of a configuration, and they refine abstract solutions to detailed configurations specifying arrangements and further requirements. We distinguish between solution expansion and solution refinement phases, not to imply that they are independent, but to emphasize the distinct meanings of part requirement hierarchies, functional abstraction hierarchies, and physical containment hierarchies. Addition of required components is often a specialized process and can involve goals for both correcting and completing a specification. Refinements of specifications include the consideration of alternative arrangements as well as selection among alternative implementations. Configuration methods must mix and balance several kinds of concerns and different bodies of knowledge.

Figure 8.2 shows the relevant spaces for defining configuration problems. It is a useful starting framework from which we shall consider variations in the following sections. In some domains there is no separate specification language: Specifications are given in the language of

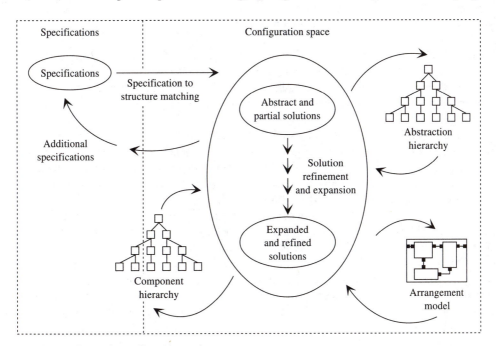

FIGURE 8.2.   Spaces in configuration tasks.

parts and arrangements and the task begins with a partial configuration. In that case, we omit the boundary in the figure between the specification space and the configuration space. The outer oval in the configuration space signifies that the representations for partial and expanded solutions are mixed together. Most configuration methods work incrementally on candidates, expanding the candidates to include more parts and refining the specifications to narrow the choices.

By analogy with names for classification methods, the pattern of knowledge use suggested by Figure 8.2 could be called **heuristic configuration** to emphasize the use of heuristic knowledge to guide the generation and testing of possible configurations. It could also be called **hierarchical configuration** to emphasize the importance of reasoning by levels, both component hierarchies and abstraction hierarchies. For simplicity, we just use the term *configuration*.

8.2 Models for Configuration Domains

This section discusses what configuration is and what makes it difficult.

8.2.1 Computational Models of Configuration

To understand configuration tasks we need a computational model of the search spaces and the knowledge that is used. Our model has the following elements:

- ■ A specification language
- ■ A submodel for selecting parts and determining their mutual requirements
- ■ A submodel for arranging parts
- ■ A submodel for sharing parts across multiple uses

We begin by describing these elements generally and simply. We then introduce the "widget" domain as a concrete instantiation of a configuration model. We use this domain to illustrate reasoning and computational phenomena in configuration tasks. Afterward, we draw on the domains from the previous section to extract examples of kinds of knowledge and the use of knowledge.

A **specification language** for a configuration task describes the requirements that configurations must satisfy. These requirements reflect the environment in which the configured product must function and the uses to which it will be put. A specification may also indicate which optimizing or due-process criteria should be used to guide the search, such as minimizing cost or space or preferring some possibilities over others. (See the exercises.)

A functional specification describes capabilities for desired behaviors. For example, rather than saying that a computer configuration needs a "printer," a functional specification might say that the computer needs to be able to print copies. The printing function may be further specialized with qualifiers about speed, resolution, directionality, character sets, sizes of paper, color or black and white, and so on. One advantage of describing systems in terms of functions rather than in terms of specific classes of manufactured parts is that functions can anticipate and simplify the addition of new classes of components to a catalog. When a functional specification language is used, the configuration process must have a means for mapping from function to structure.

A specification language is not defined independently of the other submodels. Some configuration models use the same language for describing specifications and for describing configurations. This approach avoids the function-to-structure mapping by associating each part with a list of key functions. The most common approach is called the **key-component approach**. This approach has two parts: (1) For every major function there is some key component, and (2) all the key components (or abstract versions of them) are included in the initial partial configuration that specifies a configuration. A specification is assumed to include all the key parts. To complete a configuration, a configuration system satisfies the prerequisites of all the key parts it starts with as well as the parts it needs to add to the specification, and it also determines a suitable arrangement for all the included parts.

A **submodel for parts** specifies the kinds of parts that can be selected for a configuration and the requirements that parts have for other parts. Some parts require other parts for their correct functioning or use. For example, computer printed circuit boards may require power supplies, controllers, cables, and cabinets. A part model defines required-component relations, so that when a configuration process considers a part description, it can determine what additional parts are needed. Required parts can be named explicitly or described using the specification language. Descriptions indicate which parts are compatible with each other and what parts can be substituted for each other under particular circumstances.

A **submodel for spatial arrangements** provides a vocabulary for describing the placement of parts and specifies what arrangements of parts are possible. Together, the arrangement model and the specification language form a basis for describing which arrangements are acceptable and preferred. They make it possible to determine such things as where a part could be located in an arrangement, whether there is room for another part given a set of arranged parts, and which parts in a set could be added to an arrangement. Arrangement models constrain the set of possible configurations because they govern the consumption of resources, such as space, adjacency, and connections. These resources are limited and are consumed differently by different arrangements. Arrangement models are a major source of constraints and complexity in configuration domains.

A **submodel for sharing** expresses the conditions under which individual parts can be used to satisfy more than one set of requirements. In the simplest case, part use is mutually exclusive. For example, a cable for one printer cannot be used simultaneously to connect to another printer. For some applications, mutual exclusion is too restrictive, such as with software packages that may use the same memory, but at different times. The following exemplifies a range of categories of use and sharing for configuration systems:

- *Exclusive use*: Components are allocated for unique uses.
- *Limited sharing:* Parts can be shared between certain functions but not across others.
- *Unlimited sharing:* A component can be allocated for as many different purposes as desired.
- *Serial reusability:* A component can be allocated for several different purposes, but only for one purpose at a time.
- *Measured capacity:* Each use of a component uses up a fraction of its capacity. The component can be shared as long as the total use does not exceed the total capacity. The electrical power provided by a supply is an example of a resource that is sometimes modeled this way.

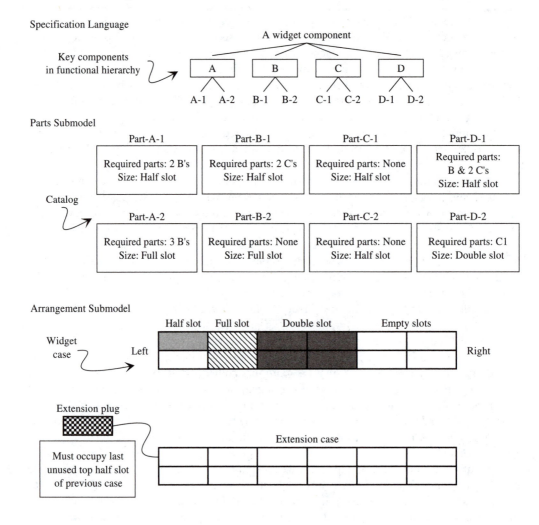

FIGURE 8.3.   The widget model, W-1, illustrates phenomena in configuration problems.

A particular domain model may incorporate several of these distinctions, assigning different characteristics to different parts. Sometimes these distinctions can be combined. One way to model how different software packages could share memory would be to post capacity constraints indicating how much memory each package needs. The system allocation for serial usage would be determined as the maximum capacity required for any software package. This approach mixes serial reusability with measured capacity.

In summary, our framework for computational models of configuration has four submodels: a specification language, a submodel for parts and requirements, a submodel for arrangement, and a submodel for component sharing. We return to these models later to describe variations on them and to identify the ways in which they use domain knowledge. In the next section, we instantiate our configuration model for the widget domain and use it to illustrate important phenomena in configuration tasks.

8.2.2 *Phenomena in Configuration Problems*

This section describes reasoning phenomena that arise in configuration problems. These phenomena are illustrated in the context of the sample domain in Figure 8.3. Figure 8.3 presents W-1, a model for configuring widgets. We use W-1 to illustrate configuration phenomena in the following discussion and in the exercises at the end of this section.

Widget requirements are specified in terms of the key generic components A, B, C, and D. The W-1 parts submodel provides a catalog with two choices of selectable components for each generic component. Thus, generic component A can be implemented by either A-1 or A-2, B can be implemented by B-1 or B-2, and so on. Each component requires either a half slot, a full slot, or a double slot. Figure 8.4 presents the rules for the widget model.

When components are arranged in the widget model, there are sometimes unavoidable gaps. When configurations are combined, these gaps are sometimes complementary. For this reason it is not always adequate to characterize the amount of space that a configuration takes up with a single number. Figure 8.5 defines several terms related to measures of space in the widget model. **Occupied space** refers to the number of slots occupied by components, including any required extension plugs. **Trapped space** refers to any unoccupied slots to the left of other slots, including slots to the left of or below an extension plug. **Space** (or total space) is the sum of occupied space and trapped space. The **minimum space** for a specification is the minimum amount of space required by any possible configuration that satisfies the specification.

Required Parts
Each part in a configuration must have all of its required parts, as shown in Figure 8.3.

Arrangement
Components must be arranged in alphabetical order (left to right and top to bottom). Parts with the same letter (e.g., C-1 and C-2) can be mixed in any order.
All identical components (components with the same letter and number) must be in the same widget case.
A full-slot component must occupy a single vertical slot. It cannot be split across slots. A double-slot component must occupy two adjacent full slots in the same widget case.
An upper half slot must be filled before the corresponding lower half slot can be filled.
No full-slot gaps are allowed, except at the right end of a case.
If a case is full, an extension case can be added but it requires using an extension plug in the last upper half slot of the previous case.
When an extension plug is used, no component can be placed in the half slot below the plug.

Sharing
The W-1 sharing submodel requires that distinct parts be allocated to satisfy each requirement.

FIGURE 8.4. Further rules governing the W-1 widget model.

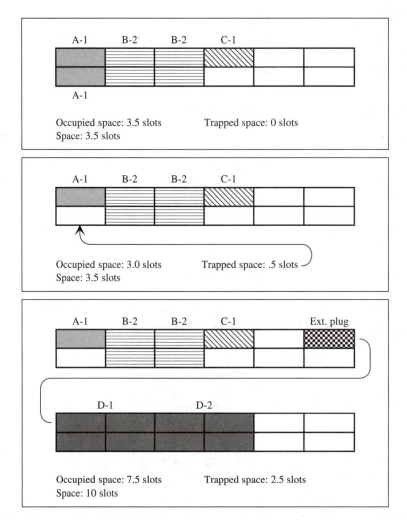

FIGURE 8.5.   Examples illustrating the terms total space, occupied space, and trapped space. For most problems, the key factor is the total space, which is called simply "space."

Configuration decisions are made incrementally. Figure 8.6 illustrates stages in a solution process, starting with the initial specifications {A, D}. Under the part-expansion phase, alternatives for required parts for A and D are considered. For requirement A, the candidates are the selectable parts A-1 and A-2. However, A-1 and A-2 both have further requirements. A-1 expands to two B's, which could be implemented as either B-1's or B-2's. If B-1's are chosen, these require C's, which themselves can be implemented as either C-1's or C-2's. This expansion of requirements shows why we cannot use a simple constraint-satisfaction method with a fixed number of variables and domains to solve the configuration task for the top-level parts. Depending on which alternatives are chosen, different required parts will be needed, and different fur-

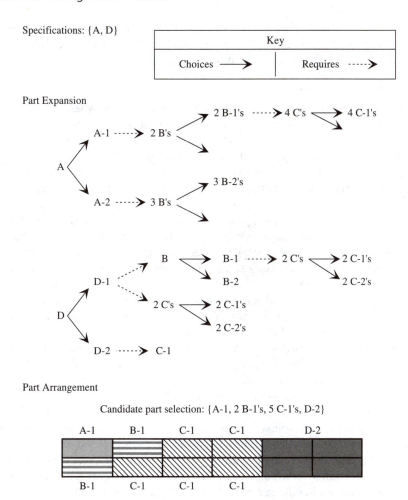

FIGURE 8.6. The dynamic nature of configuration problems. In this example, the initial specifications are {A, D}. The solid arrows indicate where there are alternatives for implementing a part. The dashed arrows indicate places where a part requires further parts. There are several possible solutions for the given specifications. One solution is shown at the bottom. This one fits within a single widget case.

ther requirements will be noted. This dynamic aspect of the problem suggests the use of dynamic and hierarchical constraint methods.

The arrangement model for W-1 lends itself to a sequential layout process, which first places the required A components and then the B components, C components, and D components in left-to-right order. If at any point all of the components of the same type cannot be fitted into the space remaining in a widget case, an extension case is required. If the number of required components of a given type is more than fits into a single case, then the candidate cannot be arranged according to the rules. Furthermore, when more than one case is required, there must be an available slot in the previous case for its extension plug. At the bottom of Figure 8.6 is one solution to the sample problem, which fits within a single widget case.

Threshold Effects

Configuration problems exhibit **threshold effects**. These effects occur when a small change in a specification causes candidates to exceed certain fixed thresholds, requiring discontinuous and potentially widespread changes to the candidate. For example, in computer configuration domains, overflowing the capacity of a cabinet requires the addition of not only an extension cabinet, but also various components for extending the bus and additional power supplies. In applications where parts have parameters to be determined by configuration, requirements for upgrading the size of components can have ripple effects, so that further parts need to be changed to accommodate changes in weight or size, resulting in shifts to different motor models. Depending on how the decision making is organized in a configuration system, threshold effects can occur in the middle of solving a problem if requirements discovered partway through the process exceed initial estimates of required capacity. In such cases, many early decisions may need to be revised (see Exercise 4).

Figure 8.7 illustrates a threshold being exceeded when the widget specification is changed from {A, D} to {A, 2 D's}. In the two solutions shown, the additional required components exceed the capacity of a single widget case. Furthermore, in the second candidate solution, some of the implementations for a C part were switched to C-2 (rather than C-1) to avoid violating the rule that identical parts must be placed in the same case and to avoid overflowing the extension case. The capacity of a case is a resource. Threshold effects can occur for different kinds of resources. Other arrangement resources include order and adjacency.

Global resources that can be exceeded in different configuration domains include size, power, weight, and cost. These resources present special challenges for allocation and backtracking. They are called **global resources** because they are consumed or required by components throughout a configuration rather than by just one component. In the cases cited, the consumption of the resource is **additive consumption**, meaning that requirements can be characterized in terms of numeric quantities. Requirements from different parts are summed together.

Horizon Effects

When configuration decisions are made incrementally, their evaluation criteria are typically applied in a local context, meaning that they recommend the best solution limiting the evaluation to a small number of factors. This due-process approach is called myopic because it does not try to take into account all of the entailments of a decision caused by the propagation of effects in the model. This leads to a phenomenon called the **horizon effect**. In nautical experience, the curvature of the earth defines a horizon beyond which things are hidden. To see things farther away, you have to get closer to them. In reasoning systems, the "visible horizon" corresponds to things that have been inferred so far. Partway through a configuration process, you cannot see all the consequences of the choices so far because some inferences have not yet been made and because some other choices have yet to be made. At best, you can make estimates from the decisions made so far.

In the idealized case where configuration choices are independent, locally optimal decisions yield globally optimal solutions. For example, if the total cost of a solution is the sum of

Specification {A, 2 D's}

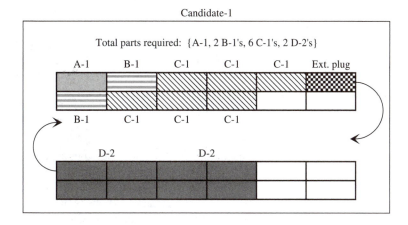

FIGURE 8.7. Threshold effects. This figure illustrates two possible solutions to a widget configuration problem with the specifications {A, 2 D's}. Both candidate solutions exceed the capacity of a single widget case. In more involved examples, exceeding one threshold can lead to a ripple effect of exceeding other thresholds as well, leading to widespread changes in a configuration.

the costs of the independently determined parts, then picking the cheapest part in each case will lead to the cheapest overall solution. If the choice of the next component can be determined by combining the known cost of a partial solution with an estimate of the remaining cost, and the estimate is guaranteed never to be too high, then the A* algorithm can be used as discussed in Section 2.3.

However, in many configuration situations and domains these conditions do not hold and myopic best-first search does not necessarily lead to a globally optimal solution. In each of the following cases, both part A and part B satisfy the local requirements. Part A costs less than part

B and would be chosen by an incremental best-first search that is guided by cost of the part. These cases show why a choice that is locally optimal need not be globally optimal.

> Case 1. *Undetected required parts.* The other parts required by part A are much more expensive than the parts required by part B, so the total cost of a complete solution is higher if A is chosen. The further requirements for parts A and B may involve constraints not yet articulated, choices dependent on situations not yet determined, or design variables not yet introduced.
>
> Case 2. *Unanticipated arrangement conflicts.* The parts required by part A consume slightly more of some resource than the parts required by part B. If A is chosen, a threshold will be crossed by later decisions leading to additional expensive cabinets, cases, or whatever. If B had been chosen, the threshold would not have been crossed and the overall solution would have been cheaper (see Exercise 4).
>
> Case 3. *Undetected sharability.* There are requirements not yet considered for a part that is compatible with B but not with A. If B is a sharable component, then choosing B at this stage will make it unnecessary to add parts later on, leading to an overall savings. This phenomenon is especially likely to occur in domains that include multifunctional components, such as multifunctional computer boards that incorporate several independent but commonly required functions (see Exercise 5).

All three cases exhibit the horizon effect. The local evaluation fails to lead to an optimal solution because the indicators fall past the "observable horizon" defined by the commitments and inferences made so far.

If computational complexity was not an issue, the effects of the first case could be mitigated by determining the problematic effects of the required components for a part before committing to a part. Thus, no commitment would be made to choose A until the effects of all of its required components are known. The second case could be mitigated by considering the effects on all resources consumed by a component. The effects in the third case could be mitigated by considering all possible sharings of a component before committing to the selection.

To summarize (with tongue in cheek), the effects of incremental decision making and myopic optimization can be mitigated by performing decision making as far past the immediate horizon as needed. Unfortunately, exponential computational resources are required to look so far ahead. In the following knowledge and symbol-level analyses, we discuss more realistic ways to cope with threshold and horizon effects.

8.2.3 *Summary and Review*

This section models configuration in terms of four elements: a specification language, a model for selecting parts and determining their mutual requirements, a model for arranging parts, and a model for sharing parts across multiple functional requirements. Parts models can be simple catalogs of parts. They can also include hierarchical relations based on functionality, required parts, and bundled packaging. Arrangement models express what physical arrangements of parts are possible and how some arrangements of parts preclude other arrangements. Arrangement models range from complex spatial models to simple named resource models where parts fit in any of a finite number of separately accounted spaces. Sharing models indicate when parts chosen to satisfy one requirement can be used to satisfy others as well. Variations in sharing include exclusive use, open use, metered use, and serial reuse.

Search spaces for configuration domains can be large. Configurations themselves are represented in terms of fairly complex symbol structures that indicate the selection, arrangement, and parameterization of their parts. Most configuration tasks are carried out incrementally, building up descriptions of candidate solutions from descriptions of their parts.

Although configuration domains differ in the complexity of their submodels and the degree to which decisions in each submodel are dependent on decisions in others, they typically exhibit threshold effects where small changes in local requirements can cause discontinuous effects when overall capacities are exceeded. These threshold effects can arise in any of the submodels. Threshold effects and horizon effects for large interconnected problems create a challenge in ordering and managing configuration decisions. The next section presents case studies of configuration systems.

Exercises for Section 8.2

Ex. 1   [*!-05*] *Global Resources*. Decisions about global resources are often problematic in configuration tasks.

(**a**) Why? What are some examples of global resources from the configuration domains in this chapter?

(**b**) Briefly describe some alternative approaches for making decisions about global resources.

Ex. 2   [*10*] *Skeletal Configurations*. Professor Digit is a consultant to a company that configures computer systems for its customers. He argues that the number of possible computer configurations may be high but that the number of "really different" configurations sought by customers is actually quite low. He proposes that a knowledge system for configuration would be simpler if it proceeded as follows:

1. Search a library of configurations and find the one closest to the initial configuration proposed for the customer, taking into account which components are key components.
2. Add new key components from the customer's initial configuration that are missing, and remove any extra key components and their required parts from the matching library configuration.
3. Revise the configuration to accommodate the customer's needs.

(**a**) Briefly describe the main assumptions about the configuration task on which the viability of Professor Digit's proposal depends.

(**b**) Sam, a graduate student working with Professor Digit, says this proposal creates a tension in the solution criteria for cases in the library between conservative and perhaps inefficient configurations that are easy to extend and ones that are minimal for a fixed purpose. Do you agree? Explain briefly.

(**c**) Suppose the computer configuration domain is subject to many threshold effects. Briefly, what are the implications for Professor Digit's proposal?

■ **Ex. 3**   [*25*] *Configuring Widgets*. The text defines a configuration model, W-1, for widgets. We assume that the following cost figures apply for widget parts.

Part	Unit Cost
A-1	$50
A-2	$20
B-1	$20
B-2	$40
C-1	$ 5
C-2	$10
D-1	$40
D-2	$20

(a) Find a minimal space configuration for the specification {A, B}. Use the standard widget model in which there is no sharing of parts across functions. If there is more than one configuration with the minimum space, choose the one with the lowest cost. Draw the final configuration, following packing constraints.

(b) Find a minimal cost configuration for the specification {A, B}, ignoring case costs. If there is more than one configuration with the minimum cost, choose the one with the lowest space requirement. Explain your reasoning. Draw the final configuration.

(c) Parts a and b use the same solution criteria but in a different order. Are the results the same? Why?

■ **Ex. 4**   [*30*] *Threshold Effects in Local Cost Evaluations.* This exercise considers threshold effects in a configuration task. It uses the same cost figures as Exercise 3.

(a) Complete the following table showing the configurations for the minimum costs and minimum space solutions for the specifications {A}, {B}, and {C}. Include trapped space in your computation of minimum space.

Specification	Minimum Cost	Minimum Space
{C}	$5 {C–1}	.5 {C–1} or {C–2}
{B}		
{A}		

(b) Find a minimal cost configuration for the specification {A, 2 B's}. Explain your reasoning. Ignore case costs.

(c) Suppose we are given the following costs for cases:

Widget case	$60
Extension case	$120

Find a minimal cost configuration for the specification {A, 2 B's} including the cost of the case(s). Draw your configuration and explain your reasoning.

■ **Ex. 5**   [*15*] *Estimates That Aggregate Space and Cost Constraints.* Professor Digit proposes that a simple and appropriate way to account for case costs would be to add to the cost of each component a fractional cost corresponding to the fraction of the slots that are required. He offers this as a method of reflecting case costs back into the decision making about individual parts. The purpose of this exercise is to evaluate this approach.

We are given the following costs for cases:

Widget case $60
Extension case $120

(a) Show the adjusted component costs by filling in the missing entries in the accompanying table. The case increment is the additional cost of the part accounting for the space the part requires in terms of a fraction of the case cost.

Part	Part Cost	Case Increment	Case-Adjusted Part Cost
A-1	$50	$ 5	$55
A-2	$20	$10	$30
B-1	$20		
B-2	$40		
C-1	$ 5		
C-2	$10		
D-1	$40		
D-2	$20		

(b) Using Professor Digit's adjusted case costs, complete the following table, showing the configurations with the minimum costs.

Specification	Minimum Cost Configuration
{C}	$10 {C-1}
{B}	$45 {B-1, 2 C-1's}
{A}	

(c) Briefly explain why Professor Digit's proposal is both fair and inadequate for guiding a search for a minimal cost solution.

(d) Using the above table as an evaluation function to guide the search for a minimum cost solution, what would be the minimum cost configuration that Digit's approach would yield for {A, 2 B's}? What is its estimated cost? What is its real cost? Explain briefly.

(e) What is the real minimum cost solution? What is its estimated cost and its real cost?

■ **Ex. 6**   [40] *Shared Parts.* In this exercise we develop the modified widget model W-S to enable limited sharing of parts. Suppose the functions for {A} and for {D} are never needed at the same time. We define A* to be the set of components including an A and all of its required parts. Similarly D* is the set including a D and all of its required parts. In W-S, sharing is permitted between A* and any D*, which means a single component can satisfy a requirement both for A and for D. No other part sharing is allowed, such as between two different D*'s.

(a) Fill in the following table of configurations, focusing on those requiring minimal space. For simplicity, leave specifications for C unrefined to C-1 or C-2 where possible.

You can use the results of previous exercises. You need only fill in the minimal space partial configurations.

Hint: You may find it useful in solving the later parts of this exercise to include other "near minimal space" partial configurations in your table as well.

Specification	*Minimum Space Configurations*			
	Configuration	*Space*	*Occupied Space*	*Trapped Space*
	{A-1, 2 B-2} {A-1, B-1, B-2, 2 C}	3	2.5	.5
{D}	{B-2, 2 C, D-1} . . . more		2.5	
{2 D}	{2 B-2, 4 C, 2 D-1} . . . more	5		

(b) Without sharing, what are all the minimal space configurations for {A, 2D}? Draw the configurations you find. Briefly explain your reasoning.

(c) With sharing, what are the minimal space configurations for {A, 2D}? Draw the configurations you find. Briefly explain your reasoning.

(d) What do the results of parts b and c tell us about optimizing in shared part models? Briefly describe the computational phenomena introduced to the optimization process when sharing is permitted.

Ex. 7   [05] *Widget Thresholds*. In the example of the widget configuration domain, how does the rule that all identical parts must be in the same case contribute to a threshold effect?

Ex. 8   [05] *Special Cases for Spatial Reasoning*. The following paragraph describes some requirements for spatial relationships in configurations of elevators:

> The counterweight is a piece of equipment made up of metal plates that are always 1 inch thick. The plates are stacked to get the total load needed to balance the weight of the elevator car, the car's load, attached cables, and other components. The plates can be ordered in varying lengths and widths. They are usually hung from the machine sheave that provides the traction that moves the elevator. The placement of the sheave and its angle of contact with the cable are critical to get enough traction to make the elevator move. Safety codes regulate the minimum clearance between the elevator car and the counterweight, between the counterweight and the shaft walls on its three other sides, and between the counterweight and the floor in its lowest position and the ceiling in its highest position. These code clearances, in turn, are calculated using values such as the weight supported, length of cables, height of the building, and other factors. The configuration must specify the position of the sheave, the length of hoist cable, the size of the counterweight in three dimensions, and actual clearances of the counterweight and any obstacle it might run into all along the elevator shaft.

(a) Is a general approach to spatial reasoning important for this example? If not, why not?

(b) Why was it appropriate to use a fixed structure for its parameter network to capture the reasoning above?

8.3   *Case Studies of Configuration Systems*

In this section we consider several knowledge systems and show how they solve configuration problems. Our purpose is to consider the search requirements of the task, the kinds of knowledge that are needed, the organization of the knowledge, and examples of implementation. The cases illustrate a range of approaches to configuration tasks.

8.3.1   *Configuration in XCON*

XCON (also called R1) is a well-known knowledge system for configuring computer systems (McDermott, 1982). XCON has a place among configuration systems analogous to MYCIN's place among classification systems. XCON was the first well-known knowledge system for configuration, and it was initially characterized in terms of symbol-level issues and basic search methods. Work on both MYCIN and XCON continued for several years and resulted in successor systems. Retrospective analyses of these systems have uncovered new ways of looking at them in knowledge-level terms. For MYCIN, the analysis has shifted from an account of backward chaining at the symbol level to models for classification at the knowledge level. For XCON, the analysis has shifted from forward chaining and match at the symbol level to search spaces and models for configuration at the knowledge level. In both cases insights from the analysis have led to new versions of the systems. For MYCIN the new system is called NEOMYCIN (Clancey & Letsinger, 1981); for XCON it is XCON-RIME (Barker & O'Connor, 1989).

We consider XCON together with its companion program, XSEL. Together, the two systems test the correctness of configurations and complete orders of Digital Equipment Company computers. Different parts of the configuration task are carried out by the two systems. XSEL performs the first step in the process: acquiring initial specifications. Neither XSEL nor XCON has a separate "specification language," but XSEL acquires a customer's order interactively in terms of abstract components. XSEL checks the completeness of an order, adding and suggesting required components. It also checks software compatibility and prerequisites. The output of XSEL is the input to XCON.

XCON checks orders to greater detail than XSEL. XCON adds components to complete orders. It also determines a spatial arrangement for the components, power requirements, cabling requirements, and other things. It considers central processors, memory, boxes, backplanes, cabinets, power supplies, disks, tapes, printers, and other devices. It checks prerequisites and marketing restrictions. It also assigns memory addresses and vectors for input and output devices. It checks requirements for cabling and for power. Figure 8.8 illustrates the knowledge and inference patterns for XSEL and XCON. For simplicity in the following, we refer to the combined system simply as XCON.

Although XCON does not have a functional specification to satisfy, it still needs to decide when an order is complete. It needs to detect when necessary components have been omitted, but it would not be appropriate for it to pad a customer's order with extra components, routinely inflating the price and the functionality of the configured system. Instead, XCON just adds what-

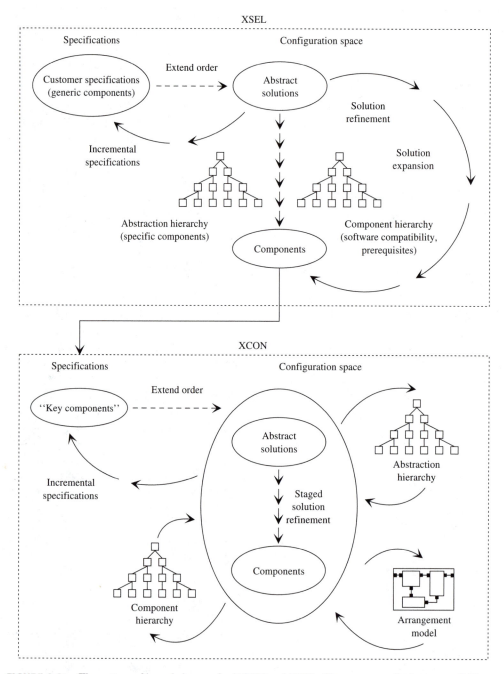

FIGURE 8.8. The pattern of knowledge use for XCON and XSEL. The systems split the responsibility, with XSEL performing the first steps and XCON performing a more detailed job. XSEL is concerned mainly with the completeness of a customer's order with regard to major system components ("key components") and software compatibility and licensing. XCON focuses on hardware configuration and considers power requirements, bus connections, cabling, and arrangement of components in the cabinets.

ever parts are necessary for the operation of the parts that have been specified already. XCON uses a key-component approach.

Crucial to the operation of XCON is its component database. This database has grown over time and in 1989 was reported to contain information on more than 31,000 parts. There were 40 types of parts and an average of 40 attributes per part. Figure 8.9 gives an abbreviated example of two component descriptions. The interpretation of the information in Figure 8.9 is approximately as follows:

> The RK711-EA is a bundle of components. It contains a 25-foot cable (70-12292-25), a disk drive (RK07-EA*), and another bundle of components (RK611). The RK611 consists of three boards (G727), a unibus jumper cable (M9202), a backplane (70-12412-00), and a disk drive controller (RK611*). Because of its interrupt priority and data transfer rate, the RK611* is typically located toward the front of the unibus. The module is comprised of five hex boards, each of which will start in lateral position "A." It draws 15.0 amps at +5 volts, 0.175 amps at -15 volts, and .4 amps at +15 volts. It generates one unibus load and can support up to eight disk drives. It is connected to the first of these with a cable (070-12292).

Other information includes requirements for boards and power and information about communications that will influence how the devices are connected to the computer's buses.

In addition to the component database, there is a container-template database that describes how parts can physically contain other parts. These templates enable XCON to keep track of what container space is available at any point in the configuration process and what the options are for arranging the components. They also provide coordinate information so XCON can assign components to locations in a cabinet. In XCON, arrangement includes electrical connections, panel space, and internal cabinet locations. XCON uses a model for spatial reasoning in which the possible locations are described in terms of "slots," places where boards can plug in, and nexuses, places where devices can be attached in cabinets. Figure 8.10 gives an example of a template. Part of the interpretation of this template follows:

> The components that may be ordered for the CPU cabinet are SBI modules, power supplies, and an SBI device. Up to six bus interface modules fit into the cabinet. The cabinet contains a central processor module and some memory. There are three slots for options that occupy 4 inches of space and one slot for an option that occupies 3 inches of space. The description "CPU nexus-2 (3 5 23 30)" indicates that the central processor module must be associated with nexus 2 of the bus interface. The numbers in parentheses indicate the top left and bottom right coordinates of the space that can be occupied by a CPU module.

Customer orders to XCON are highly variable. Although two system configurations may need most of the same kinds of actions to occur, even slight differences in the configurations may have broad consequences because of complex interactions between components. The knowledge for driving the configuration task in XCON is represented mostly using production rules. In the following we examine some rules from XCON and consider the kinds of knowledge they represent.

RK711-EA
CLASS: BUNDLE
TYPE: DISK DRIVE
SUPPORTED: YES
COMPONENT LIST: 1   070-12292-25
                      1   RK07-EA*
                      1   RK611

RK611*
CLASS: UNIBUS MODULE
TYPE: DISK DRIVE
SUPPORTED: YES
PRIORITY LEVEL: BUFFERED NPR
TRANSFER RATE: 212
SYSTEM UNITS: 2
SLOTS REQUIRED: 6 RK611 (4 TO 9)
BOARD LIST: (HEX A M7904)
                                (HEX A M7903)
                                (HEX A M7902)
                                (HEX A M7901)
                                (HEX A M7900)
DC POWER DRAWN: 15.0 .175 .4
UNIBUS LOAD: 1
UNIBUS DEVICES SUPPORTED: 8
CABLE TYPE REQUIRED: 1   070-12292 FROM A DISK DRIVE UNIBUS DEVICE

FIGURE 8.9. Two component descriptions from XCON's database. The attributes of a component are used in the configuration process to determine when other parts are needed, such as subsystems and cabling. They also describe parameters that influence the arrangement of parts and the power requirements. (Adapted from McDermott, 1982a, Figure 2.2, pp. 46–47.)

Parts require other parts for their correct operation. The initial specifications to XCON refer explicitly to key components, but not necessarily all the other components required to enable a configuration to function correctly. Figure 8.11 gives an example of a rule for adding a component.

Parts require other parts for a variety of reasons. For example, disk drives require disk controllers to pass along commands from the central processor. One disk controller can service several drives. All of these devices require cables to interconnect them. They also require power supplies to power them and cabinets to house them. The interlocking requirements are represented in XCON by a combination of rules and the databases about components and templates. Requirements for additional components are expressed locally, which means each description of a component includes specifications for other components that it requires. When XCON adds a component to a configuration, it needs to check whether the new component introduces requirements for other components.

XCON uses knowledge to govern the automated arrangement of components, as demonstrated in Figure 8.12. Several kinds of choices must be made about arrangements in XCON. A

CPU CABINET
CLASS: CABINET
HEIGHT: 60 INCHES
WIDTH: 52 INCHES
DEPTH: 30 INCHES
SBI MODULE SPACE: CPU NEXUS-2 (3 5 23 30)
                             4-INCH-OPTION-SLOT 1 NEXUS-3 (23 5 27 30)
                             MEMORY NEXUS-4 (27 5 38 30)
                             4-INCH-OPTION-SLOT 2 NEXUS-5 (38 5 42 30)
                             4-INCH-OPTION-SLOT 3 NEXUS-5 (42 5 46 30)
                             3-INCH-OPTION-SLOT NEXUS-6 (46 5 49 30)
POWER SUPPLY SPACE: FPA NEXUS-1 (2 32 10 40)
                             CPU NEXUS-2 (10 32 18 40)
                             4-INCH-OPTION-SLOT 1 NEXUS-3 (18 32 26 40)
                             MEMORY NEXUS-4 (26 32 34 40)
                             4-INCH-OPTION-SLOT 2 NEXUS-5 (34 32 42 40)
                             CLOCK-BATTERY (2 49 26 52)
                             MEMORY-BATTERY (2 46 26 49)
SBI DEVICE SPACE: IO (2 52 50 56)

FIGURE 8.10. An example container template from XCON. (Adapted from McDermott, 1982a, Figure 2.3, page 48.)

distinction is made between the CPU cabinet, the CPU extension cabinets, and the unibus cabinets. The CPU is the central processing unit and SBI modules are bus interface modules. Components whose class is SBI module are located in the CPU cabinet. There is only a limited amount of space in these cabinets, as indicated by the templates. XCON assigns components to locations incrementally. In placing objects in the unibus cabinet, XCON needs to account for both panel space and interior space. Modules that support each other need to be located either in the same backplane or in the same box. Another arrangement issue is the electrical order by which objects are located on the bus. This order affects system performance. Other arrangement decisions concern the allocation of floor space to cabinets, taking into account any known obstructions at the customer site.

```
Rule for adding parts
     IF:     The most current active context is assigning a power supply
             and a unibus adapter has been put in a cabinet
             and the position it occupies in the cabinet (its nexus) is known
             and there is space available in the cabinet for a power supply
             for that nexus
             and there is an available power supply
             and there is no H7101 regulator available
     THEN:   Add an H7101 regulator to the order.
```

FIGURE 8.11. A rule from XCON for adding required parts to a configuration.

Rule for arranging parts
```
   IF:        The most current active context is assigning a power supply
              and a unibus adapter has been put in a cabinet
              and the position it occupies in the cabinet (its nexus) is known
              and there is space available in the cabinet for a power supply
              for that nexus
              and there is an available power supply
              and there is an H7101 regulator available
   THEN:      Put the power supply and the regulator in the cabinet in the
              available space.
```

FIGURE 8.12.   A rule from XCON for arranging parts in a configuration.

Other rules add specifications to further guide the configuration process. The XCON rule in Figure 8.13 is an example of this. In other cases in XCON, the rules propose changes to the given specifications. For example, if there are components in the order that have incompatible voltage or frequency requirements, XCON tries to identify a minority set of components having the "wrong" voltage or frequency and replaces them with components of the right voltage and frequency.

Choices also must be made about implementation and arrangement. Some combinations of choices are incompatible with others. For example, there may be a tension between having optimal performance of the bus and still packing as many components into a single cabinet as possible. XCON can fall back to delivering a configuration that works without guaranteeing that performance is optimal.

The strategy taken by the designers of XCON was to organize it to make decisions in an order that would enable it to proceed without undoing the decisions it has made so far. XCON's decisions are organized into stages and subtasks. Stages correspond to large groups of subtasks,

Rule for extending the specifications
```
   IF:        The most current active context is checking for unibus jumper
              cable changes in some box
              and the box is the second box in some cabinet on some unibus
              and there is an unconfigured box assigned to that unibus
              and the jumper cable that has been assigned to the last
              backplane in the box is not a BC11A-10
              and there is a BC11A-10 available and the current length of the
              unibus is known
   THEN:      Mark the jumper cable assigned to the backplane as not assigned
              and assign the BC11A-10 to the backplane
              and increment the current length of the unibus by ten feet.
```

FIGURE 8.13.   An example of a rule for adding or changing specifications.

Stage 1	Determine whether anything is grossly wrong with the order, such as mismatched items or missing prerequisites.
Stage 2	Put the appropriate components in the CPU and CPU expansion cabinets.
Stage 3	Put boxes in the unibus expansion cabinets and put the appropriate components in those boxes.
Stage 4	Put panels in the unibus expansion cabinets.
Stage 5	Create the floor layout of the system.
Stage 6	Add necessary cables to the configuration.

FIGURE 8.14.   Stages for the XCON system. The grouping and ordering of decisions in these stages is arranged so that, for the most part, later decisions depend only the results of earlier decisions.

and subtasks can involve as little as a single rule. There are six stages and several hundred subtasks. We first discuss gross interactions among the stages and then the more complex interactions among subtasks.

XCON's stages are shown in Figure 8.14. These stages were not determined through a rigorous analysis of the configuration problem. Rather, the ordering was originally designed to reflect the way human experts performed the task. The ordering has evolved since then for XCON, based on the insights and measurements that have become possible with an explicit knowledge base. Nonetheless, the basic rationale of XCON's ordering of stages is straightforward. Component selection and component placement in boxes determines what cables are needed, and floor layout must be known to determine the length of cables. This is why stage 6 comes after stages 1, 2, 3, and 5. Any arrangement of components made before all the required components are known is likely to require rearrangements, because prerequisite components often need to be co-located. This is why stages 2 and 3 should come after stage 1. Any attempt to locate front panels for unibus devices on cabinets before it is known how many cabinets are being used and where devices are located would probably need some redoing. This is why stage 4 comes after stage 3. Ordered in this way, the later stages implicitly assume that the previous stages have been completed successfully.

The first stage adds missing but required components to the specification. The component descriptions characterize some components as requiring others for their operation and also characterize some components as coming in "bundles," which means they are packaged together for either marketing or manufacturing reasons. Adding required components is potentially recursive, since some required components require still other components. The first stage does not arrange components. In addition to adding components, the first stage detects any mismatched components in the order, such as components with mismatched power requirements as discussed already.

The second and third stages arrange components. The second stage locates SBI modules in the CPU cabinet. This stage can introduce additional components, but not ones that could themselves require revisiting decisions in the first stage or this stage. For example, stage 2 may need to add CPU extension cabinets if there are too many components to fit in the one containing the central processor. When all the relevant components have been placed, stage 2 puts a bus terminator in the appropriate place in the last cabinet and adds dummy or "simulator" modules to fill out any leftover slots corresponding to unordered options. Until these cabinets have been configured, it is not known whether these additional parts are needed. Because these parts do not compete for space with other components and because they have no further requirements, adding them does not trigger requirements for further parts.

The third stage is the most complex. This stage determines the parameters of three kinds of arrangements: spatial arrangement of boxes in cabinets, spatial arrangement of components inside boxes, and electrical arrangement of components on the unibus. For communication on the unibus, the relevant factors are interrupt priority level and transfer rate. In an optimal order, the components would be arranged in descending order of priority level (or more precisely, in nonincreasing order). Within components of the same priority, they should be ordered by decreasing transfer rate. XCON defines an "(almost) optimal unibus order" as one in which no pairs of components at the same priority level are connected so that the one with lower transfer rate comes before the one with the higher transfer rate. Below that, XCON characterizes any other ordering as suboptimal. The third stage uses an iterative approach in configuring the unibus expansion cabinets. It first tries to arrange the components in an optimal unibus order within the space available. If that fails, it then tries other rearrangements of the components that compromise the optimal unibus order but save space. Depending on what it can achieve, XCON may need to allocate new cabinets and try again. This leads to ordering further parts in addition to the cabinets, needed for extending the unibus across the cabinets. Within this stage XCON must sometimes backtrack to consider all the alternatives.

The fifth and sixth stages for XCON introduce no new theoretical issues. The fifth stage generates a linear floor plan for the computer system. The last stage generates cable assignments, using the interdevice distances that have been determined by the earlier stages. It is interesting to note that XCON's method does more than satisfice. Especially in stage 3, its ranking and iterative development of alternatives is a **due-process approach** that attempts to optimize the layouts using essentially a best-first generate-and-test method.

The next level down from stages in XCON is subtasks, implemented as one or more rules. In contrast to the simple and fixed ordering of stages, the determination of the order of performing subtasks is complex, situation specific, and governed by conditionals. XCON employs extensive look-ahead to detect exceptional situations and to check for possible future conflict before making decisions. Early subtasks check for interactions with later ones. One difficulty in XCON is that there are many potential long-range interactions. Restated, in spite of the task ordering, there are still many possible interactions among decisions that are scheduled in early tasks and those that are scheduled in later ones. Anticipating these interactions with conditional subtasks has yielded a knowledge base that has proven quite complex to maintain. In 1989, XCON had more than 31,000 components and approximately 17,500 rules (Barker & O'Connor, 1989). The knowledge base changes at the rate of about 40 percent per year, meaning that modifications are made to that fraction of it.

This maintenance challenge has led to the development of a programming methodology for XCON called RIME (Bachant, 1988; van de Brug, Bachant, & McDermott, 1986), which provides guidelines intended to simplify the continuous development of the system. RIME provides structuring concepts for rule-based programming. From the perspective of configuration problems, it institutionalizes some of the concepts we have seen already in the organization of XCON, especially in the third stage.

RIME advocates an approach based on concepts called "deliberate decision making" and "propose-and-apply." Deliberate decision making amounts to defining configuration in terms of small formal subtasks that are represented as explicit, separate processes. Examples of these processes in the RIME implementation of XCON include selecting a device, selecting a container for a component, and selecting a location within a container to place a component. These processes were distributed and sometimes duplicated among the rules of XCON. By naming these processes explicitly and representing them uniquely, RIME brings to XCON-RIME a concern for modularity at the symbol level.

Another part of the RIME methodology, called propose-and-apply, organizes subtask descriptions as a sequence of explicit stages that include proposing operators, eliminating the less desirable ones, selecting an operator, and then performing the operation specified. In the context of configuration tasks, this separates each subtask into three parts: looking ahead for interactions in the situation, selecting a best choice for part selection or arrangement, and then executing that choice. This bundling institutionalizes the way that XCON-RIME considers interlocked combinations of choices and backtracks on generating alternatives but not on making commitments.

Sometimes configuration choices cannot be linearly ordered without backtracking because the optimization requires a simultaneous balance of several different kinds of decisions. In XCON, this occurs most noticeably in the third stage, which resolves this issue by bundling decisions and generating combinations of decisions in an iterative approach. In particular, by generating composite alternatives in a preferred order, this stage generates some combinations of choices before committing to any of the individual choices about unibus order and spatial arrangement.

In summary, XCON is a knowledge system for configuring computer systems. Together with XSEL, it accepts customer orders interactively in terms of abstract parts. Using the key component assumption, functionality is specified in terms of a partial configuration. Decisions about the selection and arrangement of a part often interact with decisions about distant parts. XCON organizes its decision making into an ordered set of stages, but the detailed set of decisions is still highly conditional and must account for potential interactions. RIME is a programming methodology for a new implementation of XCON that organizes the configuration process in terms of small, explicit subtasks with explicit modules for look-ahead, generation of alternatives, and commitment.

8.3.2 Configuration in M1/MICON

M1 is an experimental knowledge system that configures single-board computers given a high-level specification of board functions and other design constraints. M1 is part of a larger single-board computer design system called MICON (Birmingham, Brennan, Gupta, & Sieworek, 1988). Single-board computer systems are used for embedded applications, in which computer systems are integrated in larger pieces of equipment. The limitation to single-board systems means M1 does not contend with spatial layout issues for components inside boxes and cabinets.

M1 configures systems that use a single microprocessor, memory, input and output devices, circuitry to support testing, and circuitry to enhance reliability. The output of M1 is a list of components for a design, the list of how these components are interconnected, an address map that defines where input and output devices are in memory, and some graphs detailing options and costs for enhancing reliability and fault coverage. Figure 8.15 sketches the main search

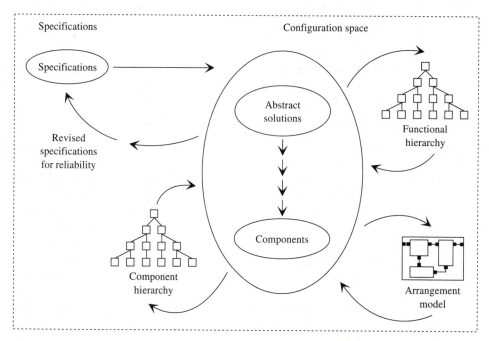

FIGURE 8.15.   The specification language for M1 is a list of key components, using M1's functional hierarchy. M1 also has a component hierarchy that describes required parts, which are supporting circuitry. Its arrangement model is based on ports and connections. Not shown in this figure is M1's knowledge for reliability analysis.

knowledge for M1. Like our exemplar of configuration systems, M1 has knowledge for mapping specifications to abstract solutions; knowledge for refining abstract solutions by selecting, adding, and arranging parts; and knowledge for adding specifications.

M1 represents a functional hierarchy of components, as shown in Figure 8.16. This hierarchy includes both abstract parts and physical parts. The abstract parts are developed by generalizing the functions of a class of parts. For example, the abstract part PIO-0 embodies a set of functions common to all the devices in M1's database for parallel input and output. An important purpose of abstract components is that they define a standard wiring interface called a "functional boundary."

M1 begins with an interactive session with a user to acquire specifications for the system to be configured. This session leads to a number of specifications about power, area, and the desired functionality of the system. Like XCON, M1 uses a key-component assumption for specifying functionality. The key components used by M1 correspond to the third level (the lowest abstract level) of its component hierarchy. For example, M1 asks the user whether a serial input/output device is required and represents what it knows about serial input/output devices in its description of the abstract class SIO-0, as shown in Figure 8.16.

Each abstract part has a set of specifications that characterize its function and performance. In 1989, the parts database described 574 parts, of which 235 were physical parts and the rest were abstract parts. The user's requirements for these are entered as a set of values. For example, the specifications for a serial input/output device allow the user to specify, among other things,

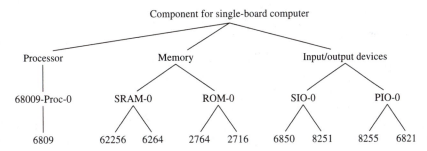

FIGURE 8.16. A functional hierarchy used in the M1 system. Some parts in this hierarchy represent abstract parts. These parts are developed by generalizing the functions of a class of physical parts. For example, the abstract part PIO-0 embodies a set of functions common to all parallel input/output chips in M1's database. SRAM-0 represents static random-access memory. ROM stands for read-only memory. SIO-0 and PIO-0 represent serial and parallel input/output devices, respectively. Parts like SIO-0 and PIO-0, at the third level of M1's component hierarchy, correspond to key components and are used for specifying functionality. They also define functional boundaries, which provide a framework for specifying how the more detailed parts should be connected. (Adapted from Birmingham, Brennan, Gupta, & Sieworek, 1988, Figure 2, page 38)

how many ports are needed, a chip type if known, an address, a baud rate, and whether the device should be compatible with RS232 output. The user requirements then become constraints to guide the initial selection of parts.

Once abstract parts are selected, M1 moves on to instantiate these parts and to arrange them. The main arrangement decisions for M1 are the electrical connections between the components. In contrast with the spatial arrangement subtasks in XCON, M1 produces a spatially uncommitted network list that is passed to commercial programs for layout and wire routing.

During the phase of part instantiation, M1 adds supporting circuitry. Figure 8.17 shows that a baud rate generator and RS232 driver are instantiated as parts of a serial input/output device. The templates are represented procedurally as rules, as suggested by the abbreviated English rule for connections in SIO-0 in Figure 8.18. In some cases the part expansion involves substantial expansion into individual parts. For example, individual memory chips are organized into an array to provide the required word width and storage capacity.

The next step in M1 is an optional analysis of the reliability of the design. If the analysis is requested, the user is asked about several more characteristics as well as a selection of reliability metrics such as mean time to failure and coverage of error detection. The user is also asked to provide relative weights for trading off total board area and monetary cost. M1 has a number of rules for determining sources of failure. These rules also guide it in making design changes, such as substituting parts, changing their packaging, or adding error-correcting circuitry and redundant circuitry. M1's method is summarized in Figure 8.19.

In summary, M1 has one of the simplest configuration tasks of the applications we will consider. Specifications include parameters about size and power as well as function. Functionality is represented in terms of key components, where key components are expressed as abstract parts in a component hierarchy. A weighted evaluation function is used to select among competing parts when there is no clear dominance. Part expansion is driven by templates represented as rules. No conflicts arise in expanding or arranging parts. Other than recomputations required

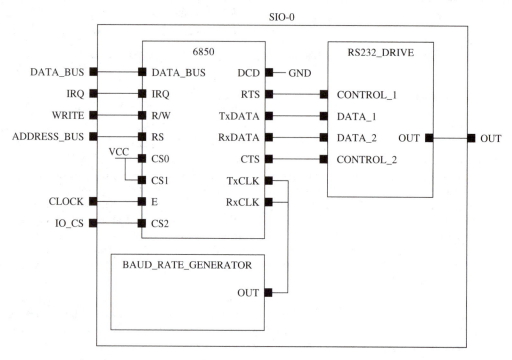

FIGURE 8.17. M1 uses templates and a port-and-connector model for describing the space of possible interconnections. The template in this figure is for the serial input/output device SIO-0. (Adapted from Birmingham, Brennan, Gupta, & Sieworek, 1988, Figure 4, page 37)

after the reliability analysis, M1 performs no backtracking. M1 uses a port-and-connector model for arrangements. The arrangement process does not compute an optimal layout. All topological arrangements are achievable, so no revision of component choices or specifications is required on the basis of connectivity constraints.

```
IF      the goal is assert_template and
        the part_name is 6850 and
        the abstract_part_name is 6850
THEN    get_part(RS232_DRIVER)
        get_part(BAUD_RATE_GENERATOR)
        connect_net(6850, d0, SIO_0, DATA_BUS)
        connect_net_VCC(6850, CS0)
        connect_net_GND(6850, DCD)
        connect_net(6850, TxCLK, BAUD_RATE_GENERATOR, OUT)
        ... (more)
```

FIGURE 8.18. Sample rule representation for template knowledge, specifying connections between the internal parts that make up an abstract component and the outer ports of the abstract part. These outer ports are called a functional boundary.

To perform M1's method for configuring single-board computer systems:

```
     1.   Get specifications.


          /* Initial part selection. */
     2.   Repeat through step 4 for each key function of the specifications.
     3.        Collect parts that satisfy the specification.
     4.        Select the part having the highest rating according to M1's
               feature-weighted evaluation function.


          /* Perform a reliability analysis if requested and make part
          substitutions. */
     5.   If a reliability analysis is requested, then repeat through step 9
          until the reliability specifications are satisfied.
     6.        Use an external program to predict mean time to failure, error-
               detection coverage, and reliability of individual components.
     7.        Report on reliability and acquire revised specifications.
     8.        Acquire weighting factors from the user to guide trade-offs
               between board area and cost.
     9.        Select parts, substituting more reliable components and adding
               redundant and error-detection circuitry as needed.


          /* Expand design for cascaded components. */
    10.   Repeat through step 11 for each cascadable part.
    11.        Invoke associated procedure to cascade the parts to the
               required sizes. (Generate arrays for memories or trees for
               priority encoding and carry look-ahead.)


          /* Connect parts using structural templates. */
    12.   Repeat through step 14 for each unconnected part.
    13.        Retrieve the template rule for this component.
    14.        Apply the rule to retrieve parts for ancillary circuitry and
               connect the ports of the parts as required.
```

FIGURE 8.19. The search method used by M1.

8.3.3 *Configuration in MYCIN's Therapy Task*

MYCIN is well known as a knowledge system for diagnosing infectious diseases. Its diagnostic task has been so heavily emphasized that its second task of therapy recommendation is often overlooked. The computational model for therapy recommendation is different from that for diagnosis. This section explains how therapy recommendation in MYCIN is based on a configuration model.

The term *therapy* refers to medical actions that are taken to treat a patient's disease. The most powerful treatments for infectious diseases are usually drugs, such as antibiotics. In

Example results from the diagnostic task

Therapy recommendations are based on the following possible identities of
the organisms:

<item 1>   The identity of ORGANISM-1 may be STREPTOCOCCUS-GROUP-D.
<item 2>   The identity of ORGANISM-1 may be STREPTOCOCCUS-ALPHA.
<item 3>   The identity of ORGANISM-2 is PSEUDOMONAS.

Example results from the therapy task

The preferred therapy recommendation is as follows:
In order to cover for items <1><2><3>
Give the following in combination
                1. PENICILLIN
                Dose: 285,000 UNITS/KG/DAY - IV
                2. GENTAMICIN
                Dose: 1.7 MG/KG Q8H - IV or IM
                Comments: Modify dose in renal failure.

FIGURE 8.20.   Therapy recommendation in MYCIN. (From Shortliffe, 1984, pp. 123, 126.)

MYCIN, a therapy is a selected combination of drugs used to cover a diagnosis. Figure 8.20 presents an example of diagnostic results and a therapy recommendation. The results are characterized in terms of items. The first two items correspond to alternative and competing identifications of the first organism. Medical practice usually requires that the therapy be chosen to cover both possibilities. A possible therapy is shown at the bottom of the figure, recommending a combination of drugs. In some cases, MYCIN ranks alternative therapies, each of which is a combination of drugs. By analogy with more typical configuration problems, the organisms that must be covered by the treatment correspond to specifications, drugs correspond to parts, and therapies correspond to configurations.

It would have been simpler in MYCIN if the same computational model could have been used for both diagnosis and therapy. However, there are several phenomena and considerations that arise in therapy recommendations that violate assumptions of the classification model that MYCIN used for diagnosis. The most basic issue is that the number of possible solutions based on combinations of drugs to cover combinations of diseases is too large to pre-enumerate. More problematic than this, the selection of drugs to cover one item is not independent of the selection of drugs to cover another. This follows from competing concerns in therapy. On the one hand, it is desirable to select therapeutic drugs that are the most effective for treating particular diseases. For the most part, this decision is based on drug sensitivities of different organisms. Tests are run periodically in microbiology laboratories to determine the changing resistance patterns of microorganisms to different drugs. On the other hand, drugs sometimes interfere with each other and it is usually desired to keep as low as possible the number of drugs simultaneously administered to a patient. Thus, the best combination of drugs to cover two different diagnoses might be different from the union of the best drugs to treat them separately. For example, it might be best to treat both possible infections with the same drug, even if a different drug might be selected by itself for either one of them.

Sometimes the risks associated with illness require that a doctor prescribe a treatment before time-consuming laboratory tests can be completed. For example, culture growths would narrow the range of possible diagnoses but may delay treatment for several hours. Other complicating factors include drug interactions, toxic side-effects, cost, and ecological considerations. An example of an ecological factor is when physicians decide to reserve certain drugs for use only on very serious diseases. In some cases, this measure is used to slow the development of drug-resistant strains of organisms, which is accelerated when a drug is widely prescribed. In medical jargon, all negative factors for a therapy are called "contra-indications." Patient-specific contra-indications include allergies, the patient's age, and pregnancy.

In the initial therapy algorithm for MYCIN (Shortliffe, 1984), therapy recommendation was done in two stages. A list of potential therapies was generated for each item based on sensitivity information. Then the combination of drugs was selected from the list, considering all contra-indications. This approach was later revised (Clancey, 1984) to make more explicit the mediation between optimal coverage for individual organisms and minimization of the number of drugs prescribed.

The revised implementation is guided by the decomposition of the decision into so-called local and global factors. The local factors are the item-specific factors, such as the sensitivity of the organism to different drugs, costs, toxicity, and ecological considerations. Global factors deal with the entire recommendation, such as minimizing the number of drugs or avoiding combinations that include multiple drugs from the same family, such as the aminoglycosides family. One variation is to divide the hypothesized organisms into likely and unlikely diagnoses and to search for combinations of two drugs that treat all of the likely ones. There are sometimes trade-offs in evaluating candidates. One candidate might use better drugs for the most likely organisms but cover fewer of the less likely organisms. In such cases, the evaluation function in the tester needs to rank the candidates. Close calls are highlighted in the presentation to a physician.

Figure 8.21 shows MYCIN's revised therapy method. Local factors are taken into account in the "plan" phase. Global factors are taken into account in the generate-and-test loop. Thus, the

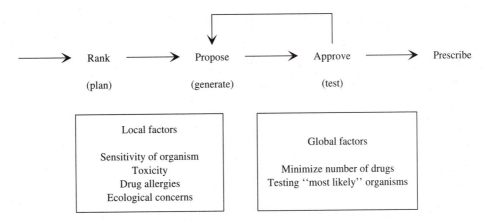

FIGURE 8.21. Therapy recommendation viewed as a plan, generate, and test process. (Adapted from Clancey, 1984, Figure 6-1, page 135.)

test step considers an entire recommendation. Patient-specific contra-indications are also taken into account at this stage.

In summary, MYCIN is a knowledge-based system that performs diagnosis and therapy tasks. The diagnosis task is based on a classification model and is implemented using production rules. The therapy task is based on a configuration model and is also implemented using production rules. A solution to the therapy task is a selected subset of drugs that meet both local conditions for effectively treating for organisms as well as global optimality conditions such as minimizing the number of drugs being used. MYCIN's configuration model involves selection but not arrangement of elements. As in all configuration problems, small variations in local considerations can effect the scoring of an entire solution.

8.3.4 *Configuration in VT*

VT is a knowledge system that configures elevator systems at the Westinghouse Elevator Company (Marcus, 1988; Marcus & McDermott, 1989; Marcus, Stout, & McDermott, 1988). VT searches for solutions by proposing initial solutions and then refining them. This is called a "propose-and-refine" approach. The search spaces for VT are shown in Figure 8.22.

Interwoven with VT's model of parts is a parametric model of elevator systems. Components are described in terms of their parameters. For example, a hoist cable may have a parameter for HOIST-CABLE-WEIGHT. Parameters can also describe aspects of an elevator system not associated with just one of its parts. For example, the parameters TRACTION-RATIO and MACHINE-SHEAVE-ANGLE depend on other parameters associated with multiple parts.

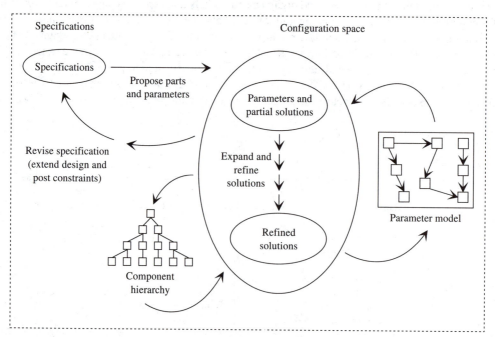

FIGURE 8.22.   VT uses a propose-and-refine approach.

Design methods involving such parametric models are sometimes called **parametric design**. Collectively, VT's parameters provide an abstract description of a solution.

VT starts with specifications of elevator performance, architectural constraints, and design drawings. Specifications of elevator performance include such things as the carrying capacity and the travel speed of the elevator. Architectural constraints include such things as the dimensions of the elevator shaft. VT's task is to select the necessary equipment for the elevator, including routine modifications to standard equipment, and to design the elevator layout in the hoistway. VT's design must meet engineering safety-code and system performance requirements. VT also calculates building load and generates reports for installing the elevator and having it approved by regional safety-code authorities. Data for VT come from several documents provided by regional sales and installation offices. There are documents describing customer requirements, documents describing the building where the elevator will be installed, and other design drawings. VT also accepts information about the use of the elevator, such as whether it is mainly to be used for passengers or freight, the power supply available, the capacity, the speed, the shaft length, the required width and depth of the platform, and the type and relative location of the machine.

VT's approach involves two separate phases. The first phase is for knowledge acquisition and analysis. During this phase VT uses a knowledge acquisition tool called SALT to develop a general plan for solving elevator configuration problems. SALT is not concerned with the specifics of a particular case, but rather with the acquisition and organization of knowledge for the range of cases that VT needs to solve. The concepts and analyses of SALT are discussed in the following. The second phase for VT is the solution of particular cases. This is where the propose-and-refine approach is applied. Roughly, VT follows a predetermined plan using knowledge organized by SALT to guide its decisions. VT constructs an elevator configuration incrementally by proposing values for design parameters, identifying constraints on the design parameters, and revising decisions in response to constraint violations in the proposal.

To explain the operation of VT we begin in the middle of the story, with its parameter network. This network is generated by SALT and used by VT on particular cases. Figure 8.23 gives an example of part of a parameter network. Each box represents a design parameter. The arrows show a partial order of inferences in which values of parameters at the tail of an arrow determine values of parameters at the head of an arrow. Solid arrows indicate how one parameter is used to compute values for another. Dashed lines indicate cases where values for parameters establish constraints on values for other parameters. We use this network to establish a vocabulary about kinds of knowledge used in VT's propose-and-refine approach. Afterward, we consider the analysis used by SALT to organize such knowledge.

Within a parameter network, knowledge can be expressed in one of three forms: procedures for computing a parameter value, constraints that specify limits on parameter values, and fixes that specify what to do if a constraint is violated. Figure 8.23 shows some of VT's knowledge for extending a configuration by proposing values for parameters. SALT expects to have a procedure for every parameter. The first rule in Figure 8.24 computes a value for a design parameter from other parameters. A rule like this is shown in a parameter network by arrows between boxes. In Figure 8.23, the rightmost pair of boxes connected by a downward arrow depicts this relation.

The second rule in Figure 8.24 selects a part from the database. Like M1 and XCON, VT has a database of parts that describes the pieces of equipment and machinery VT configures.

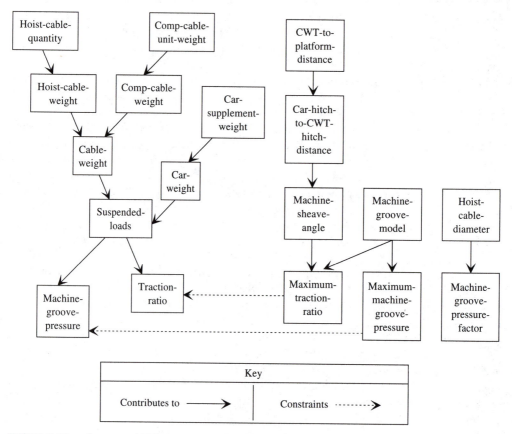

FIGURE 8.23.   Segment of VT's knowledge base showing relations among parameters. Each box represents one of VT's design parameters. Arrows between the boxes indicate a partial order for determining values for parameters. (Adapted from Marcus, 1988, Figure 4-5, page 102.)

There is a table of attributes for each kind of part, such as motors and machine models. The attributes describe functional restrictions, such as the maximum elevator speed or the maximum load, and other attributes, such as height or weight. Roughly speaking, VT first establishes values for certain key design parameters and then selects appropriate parts from the database.

Within VT's representational framework, the type of a part is itself just another parameter. The third rule in Figure 8.24 uses attributes from a database entry about a selected part to set values for design parameters. The domain for a given design parameter is the set of values obtainable from the relevant fields of the parts database.

Besides proposing values for design parameters, VT can post constraints on design values. Figure 8.25 gives an example of a constraint, expressed both in a tabular form and as a production rule. The precondition or conditional part of a constraint determines when the constraint is applicable, which means when it will be posted. VT uses its constraints to influence values in a directional way. The constraint in Figure 8.25 constrains a value of the parameter CAR-JAMB-

Computing a value for a parameter

IF: A value has been generated for HOIST-CABLE-DIAMETER, and there is no value for MACHINE-GROOVE-PRESSURE-FACTOR

THEN: Set MACHINE-GROOVE-PRESSURE-FACTOR to be 2 * HOIST-CABLE-DIAMETER.

Selecting a part from the component database

IF: A value has been generated for SUSPENDED-LOAD, and there is no value for MACHINE-MODEL

THEN: Search the database in the MACHINE table and retrieve the value of the MACHINE-MODEL field for the entry with the SMALLEST WEIGHT whose field value for MAX-LOAD is greater than the value of the SUSPENDED-LOAD parameter.

JUSTIFICATION: Taken from Standards Manual IIIA, page 139.

Using attributes from a selected part to set other parameters

IF: A value has been generated for MACHINE-MODEL, and there is no value for MACHINE-SHEAVE-DIAMETER

THEN: Search the database in the MACHINE table and retrieve the value for MACHINE-SHEAVE-DIAMETER from the value of the SHEAVE-DIAMETER field in the machine entry whose field value for MODEL is the same as the value for the MACHINE-MODEL parameter.

FIGURE 8.24. Examples of rules representing knowledge for extending a configuration. All three rules propose values for parameters. (Adapted with permission from Marcus, Stout, & McDermott, 1988, Figures 7 and 8, page 100.)

Tabular form

constrained value: CAR-JAMB-RETURN

constraint type: MAXIMUM

constraint name: MAXIMUM-CAR-JAMB-RETURN

PRECONDITION: DOOR-OPENING = SIDE

PROCEDURE: CALCULATION

FORMULA: PANEL-WIDTH * STRINGER-QUANTITY

JUSTIFICATION: This procedure is taken from Installation Manual I, page 12b.

Rule form

IF: DOOR-OPENING = SIDE

THEN: CAR-JAMB-RETURN MUST BE <= PANEL-WIDTH * STRINGER-QUANTITY

FIGURE 8.25. An example of a constraint from VT's knowledge base. (From Marcus, 1988, page 88.)

```
IF:     There has been a violation of the MAXIMUM-MACHINE-GROOVE-PRESSURE
        constraint
THEN:   (1) Try a DOWNGRADE for MACHINE-GROOVE-MODEL. (Level 1 effect:
        Causes no problem.)
        (2) Alternatively, try an INCREASE BY-STEP of 1 of HOIST-CABLE-
        QUANTITY. (Level 4 effect: Changes minor equipment sizing.)
```

FIGURE 8.26.   An example of a rule representing knowledge for selecting a part by performing a search of the database when enough of the parameters are known. When there is more than one possible fix for a problem, VT relies on an ordered set of effect levels, trying more drastic fixes only after the less drastic ones have failed.

RETURN, depending on values of the parameters PANEL-WIDTH and STRINGER-QUAN-TITY.

Figure 8.26 gives an example of the third form of knowledge used by VT, knowledge for revising a configuration after a violation has occurred. In this example, two alternatives are proposed to guide the choice of revisions when the constraint is violated. Constraint violations can be understood as conflicts over priorities. Viewed in the larger context of the entire elevator system, every procedure for proposing parameter values is a myopic best-first search. If the solution to the overall elevator configuration problem were made up of independent subproblems, then each parameter subproblem could be solved or optimized separately. Constraint violations correspond to antagonistic interactions between subproblems. To arbitrate in these cases, VT uses a scale for comparing the effects of changes. VT recognizes several different kinds of effects for making a change and establishes preferences among them. These effects are summarized in Figure 8.27. According to this list, the least desirable kind of fix is one that compromises the perfor-

Effect level	Effect of fix
1	Causes no problem
2	Increases maintenance requirements
3	Makes installation difficult
4	Changes minor equipment sizing
5	Violates minor equipment constraint
6	Changes minor contract specifications
7	Requires special part design
8	Changes major equipment sizing
9	Changes building dimensions
10	Changes major contract specifications
11	Compromises system performance

FIGURE 8.27.   Categories of effects from making a change in VT. When VT detects that a constraint has been violated and there are several different possible fixes, it prefers to make fixes with the least drastic consequences. This list enumerates the kinds of fixes from least drastic to most drastic. Every "fix" rule is assigned an effect level corresponding to an entry in this list.

mance of the elevator system. In weighing the costs of different changes, one-time difficulties in installation (#3) are considered less costly than ongoing increases in maintenance costs (#11).

To review briefly, VT distinguishes three main forms of knowledge about elevator design: knowledge for proposing parameter values, knowledge constraining parameter values, and knowledge about what revisions to make when constraints are violated. We next consider some of the analyses and considerations that go into VT's organization of such knowledge. The core of SALT's operation is the analysis and structuring of parameter networks.

Much of SALT's analysis is concerned with checking paths through the network. In the ideal case, there are unique paths through the network whereby all the elevator system parameters can be computed for any combination of input parameters. In the simplest case, VT would need only to invoke knowledge for proposing parameter values, without using knowledge for constraining parameter values or fixing values after constraint violations. The partial ordering represented by the network would allow VT to compute other parameter values from the given ones, continuing in a data-driven fashion until the elevator was configured. Such an ideally structured computation has not proven workable in practice. Analogous to RIME, SALT can be understood as a structured programming environment for building parameter networks that approach this ideal. It uses the equivalent of structured programming in the parameter network to yield behaviors that converge to optimal configurations given a wide range of input parameters.

SALT's analysis includes checking for a number of undesirable patterns in the parameter network, including ones involving loops. These patterns correspond to such things as race conditions, unreachable paths, and potential deadlocks as described in the following. For example, if one procedure is applicable for computing motor torque for speeds less than 300 and another is applicable for speeds greater than 200, then there would be two applicable procedures for the speed 250. This is a race condition because either procedure could be executed depending on the order of traversal used by VT's interpreter. Similarly, there might be combinations of conditions such that no procedure is applicable for some combination of parameters.

A deadlock condition is recognized when there are procedures for computing two parameters such that each procedure requires the value of the other parameter before it can be run. In a data-driven interpreter, this would result in an infinite delay while each procedure waits for the other. When it detects the possibility of a deadlock, SALT guides the builder of a knowledge base in adding procedures that estimate initial parameter values. When this results in multiple procedures proposing a value, SALT guides the user in converting some of the procedures to post constraints on values and in adding procedures that propose fixes when there is a conflict. In this way, SALT incrementally builds revision cycles into the parameter network. These revision cycles correspond to programming idioms. For example, a revision loop can incrementally increase the value of a parameter up to some limit. That idiom, implemented in terms of constraints and fixes, corresponds in function to an iterative looping construct in procedural programming languages.

SALT assumes that the procedures for proposing parameter values correspond to an underconstrained case reflecting local optimality. Potential fixes should be less preferred (locally) than the value originally proposed. The default strategy in VT is to try values in a best-first order. If the fixes for one constraint violation have no effect on other constraint violations, then this strategy guarantees that the first configuration found will be the most preferred. However, it is possible that fixes selected for one constraint violation may interact with values for other parameters in the network. A particularly pathological case of feedback between conflict-ing fixes is called thrashing. Thrashing occurs in scenarios of different complexity. In a simple scenario, a fix for one parameter value causes a new value to be computed for a second variable, which then violates a constraint, causing a fix to a third variable, which causes an opposing change in the first variable, violating the original constraint again. The term **thrashing** refers to any persistent looping behavior that results when antagonistic fixes undo and redo a repeating sequence of changes.

SALT uses syntactic techniques to analyze a parameter network for the possibility of these behaviors. A detailed consideration of SALT's syntactic analysis methods and the expressive power of the language is beyond the scope of this section. The tests built into SALT are intended to detect common errors of omission by builders of a VT knowledge base.

Given a SALT-created network, VT works on a particular case as follows. It starts with a forward-chaining or data-driven phase in which procedures extend the configuration by propos-ing parameter values. As it extends the design, VT records which parameter values were used to derive other ones using a truth maintenance system (TMS). Constraint violations are detected by demons, which invoke procedures to revise the network. The fix procedures then propose changes to values of individual parameters or to combinations of parameters.

The effects of the proposed change are investigated with limited look-ahead as follows. First VT verifies that the revised value violates no constraints on the changed parameter. Then it works through the consequences, verifying that there are no antagonistic changes to the proposed fix using a TMS. If a proposed change violates constraints, then the next alternative fix is consid-ered. The TMS keeps track of combinations of revisions it has tried so as not to repeat any. This process is a due-process approach. The prioritized list of effects in Figure 8.27 guides backtrack-ing to approximate a best-first search.

From a network perspective like that in Figure 8.23, many kinds of interactions in the search space can be visualized. The most common interaction among design parameters in VT is a rippling effect that follows when a constraint violation causes one piece of equipment to be upgraded, or increased in size. In this case, other pieces of related equipment may be affected and upgraded as well. Depending on circumstances, the initial fix may trigger a sequence of changes. For example, requiring more hoist cables than fit on the machine model selected may result ultimately in selecting a larger machine model and using larger sheaves.

The 1988 version of VT recognized 54 different kinds of constraint violations, of which 37 had only one known fix, meaning one parameter that might be revised. The remaining constraint violations also had a small number of fixes. Each possible fix provides directions of where to look next in VT's search for solutions. On an average case, however, VT needs to consider only a small number of fixes. In a typical run, VT makes between 1,000 and 2,000 design extensions and only about one-hundredth as many fixes to a design. In a typical case, VT detects 10 or 20 constraint violations and averages just slightly more than 1 fix per violation.

In summary, VT constructs an approximation to a solution and then refines it. VT's knowl-edge base is made up predominantly of three kinds of knowledge: knowledge for proposing design extensions, knowledge for posting constraints, and knowledge for revising the configura-tion when constraint violations are detected. VT's rules are applied in a data-driven fashion with limited look-ahead. VT's performance using this approach depends on the prior analysis by SALT, which identifies undesirable patterns and missing information in the network. In represen-tative runs, VT detects very few constraint violations, and the first fix tried almost always works.

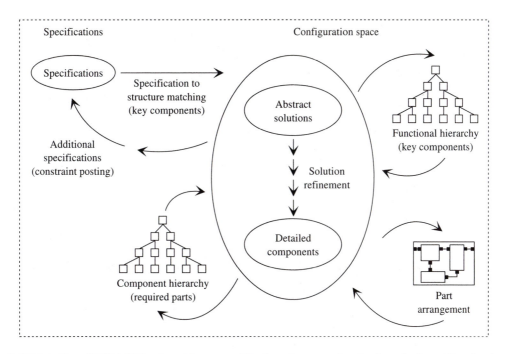

FIGURE 8.28. COSSACK begins with user specifications, in terms of evaluation criteria and functional specifications. The evaluation criteria are used to order candidates in component selection. Functionality specifications are represented using a key-component approach, where key components may be either hardware or software components.

8.3.5 *Configuration in COSSACK*

COSSACK (Mittal & Frayman, 1989) is a knowledge system for configuring personal computers that was developed at Xerox Corporation. Because Xerox stopped selling personal computers shortly after COSSACK became operational, the system never received substantial field testing. However, COSSACK is an interesting system from a technical point of view especially in its use of a **partial-choice strategy**.

Like the other computer configuration systems we have considered so far, COSSACK's process starts with customer requirements. These include evaluation criteria, such as minimum cost, expandability, early delivery requirements, and functionality requirements. COSSACK performs a best-first search, using the evaluation criteria to order candidates during component selection. Figure 8.28 shows the elements involved in COSSACK's search. Specifications are mapped onto abstract solutions. Abstract solutions are incrementally refined, making choices about component selection and arrangement.

COSSACK uses key components to express functionality specifications. It creates requirements in terms of specific components, such as an "Epson-LX80 printer," and also in terms of abstract component descriptions, such as a "letter-quality printer." Figure 8.29 presents a portion of COSSACKS's functional hierarchy. In this class hierarchy, each node represents a sub-

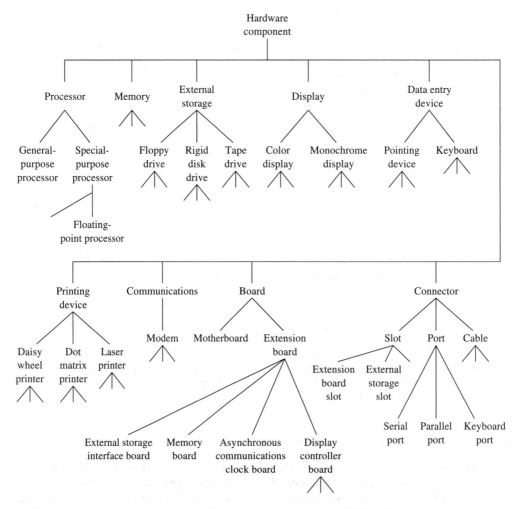

FIGURE 8.29. Portion of the functional hierarchy for components in COSSACK. Any component below the root can be a key component. COSSACK also considers software components in its configuration and has classes for word processors, accounting programs, spreadsheets, and operating systems.

class of its parent node. Any node lower than hardware component, the root, can be used to express a key component. Besides the classes of hardware components shown, COSSACK represents software components as well. In January 1987, COSSACK represented a total of 65 different hardware components and 24 different software components.

As in other configuration tasks, specifying a key component often leads to requirements for other components. COSSACK distinguishes two main relations for this, `subcomponent` and `required component`. The `subcomponent` relation indicates that other components are always included with the key component. This can reflect a manufacturing decision, as when multiple components are assembled as part of the same board. For example, the manufacturing

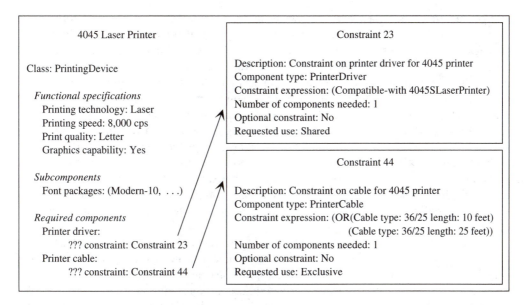

FIGURE 8.30. Frame representation of a component in COSSACK's functional hierarchy. This frame represents a 4045 laser printer. Frame slots are organized into groups: functional specifications, subcomponents, required components, and processing information. The functional specifications are used when matching this description against specifications using key words. Slots in subcomponents refer to other parts, both hardware and software, that are included or bundled with this component. The required-component slots describe other components, not bundled with this one, that are needed for correct operation. Constraints associated with those slots are used to narrow the choices.

group may package a clock, memory, and modem on one multifunctional board. Parts can also be bundled for marketing reasons. The `required component` relation indicates that other parts are necessary for the correct functioning of a part. As with XCON and M1, this indicates a range of requirements for auxiliary parts and cables. `Required component` relations are also useful for software components. For example, these relations can indicate how much memory or external storage capacity a particular software package needs to run.

Figure 8.30 gives an example of a frame representation of a component from COSSACK's knowledge base. The key component in this case is a 4045 laser printer. The slots grouped under "Functional specifications" are used for matching. For example, this printer would satisfy a specification for a letter-quality printer. The subcomponents include various other parts that are necessarily included. This example shows that various font packages are routinely bundled with a printer purchase.

Required components for the 4045 printer include a software driver for the printer and a cable. Like VT, COSSACK posts constraints to guide future decisions. In Figure 8.30 Constraint 23 indicates that any driver can be used that is compatible with the 4045 printer. Constraint 44 indicates that the cable must be of type 36/25 and can have a length of either 10 or 25 feet.

The two constraints in this figure illustrate a representational issue not dealt with in the previous configuration systems that we considered: the reuse or sharability of components across different requirements. When one component description presents a requirement for another component, can the second component be used to satisfy any other requirements? In Figure 8.30, the software module for the printer driver can be shared, meaning that, in principle, the driver can be used for other components as well, such as when a configuration includes multiple printers. Similar issues come up for required components for hardware. For example, can a modem and a printer use the same RS232 port? In contrast, constraint 44 indicates that the printer cable cannot be shared. It must be dedicated to the exclusive use of one printer.

Like VT, COSSACK does not organize its design subtasks in a fixed order for all subproblems. Also like VT, it has knowledge for extending a design by making choices and for posting constraints. COSSACK is able to retract component decisions, revisit preference-guided choices, and remove constraints that were posted as requirements when the retracted components were originally selected. Unlike VT, COSSACK does not use domain-specific knowledge for modifying a configuration when constraint violations are detected, but rather employs a blind search.

COSSACK uses a partial-commitment strategy to reduce backtracking. Figure 8.31 shows a simplified example of a case where partial commitment makes guessing and backtracking unnecessary. In this example, both the operating system and an accounting package are specified as key components. Neither component has any immediate constraints bearing on the other. We assume that no other preferences are known to guide the choice. At this point, a simple generate-and-test approach could arbitrarily select candidates for either one. Suppose it arbitrarily selected Accounting Package #1 and OS Version B. Then later, when it expanded the required components for Acounting Package #1, it would pick a rigid disk drive and discover that none of the satisfactory disk drives are compatible with OS Version B, leading to backtracking. The partial-choice approach enables it to generalize the requirements held in common by Accounting Package #1 and Accounting Package #2. This would result in the generation of a constraint specifying that whatever rigid disk was chosen, its operating system must be OS Version A.

Arrangement issues in COSSACK are not as complex as in XCON and are represented using constraints on a port-and-connector model. The main arrangement conflict is that personal computers have a limited number of slots. Components consume both slots and ports.

In summary, COSSACK is a knowledge-based system for configuring personal computers. It uses a key-component model for functionality, a preference model for selecting components in a best-first search, constraint posting to add specifications for related decisions, and partial commitment to reduce backtracking. It relaxes the notion that required components need to be dedicated to a single use by representing "sharable" components.

8.3.6 *Summary and Review*

A configuration is an arrangement of parts. A configuration task instantiates a combination of parts from a predefined set and arranges them to satisfy given specifications. The large size of configuration search spaces precludes pre-enumeration of complete solutions. Knowledge-based systems for configuration are important to manufacturers that customize their products for individual customers by configuring customer-specific systems from a catalog of mass-produced parts.

XCON is a well-known knowledge system for configuring computer systems at Digital Equipment Company. Together with its companion program, XSEL, XCON tests the correctness

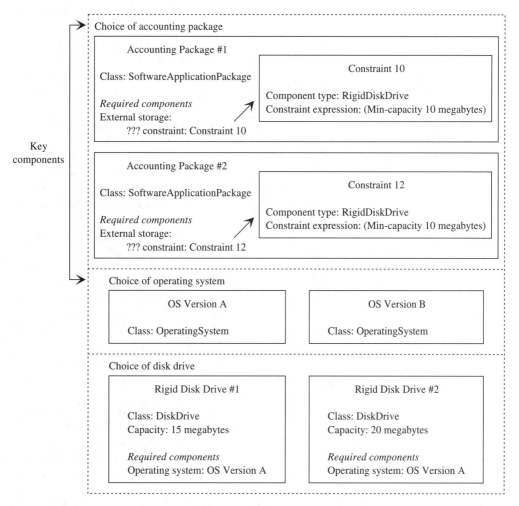

FIGURE 8.31.   Simplified partial commitment example from COSSACK. In this example, we assume that an accounting package and an operating system have been specified as key components. COSSACK notices that whatever rigid disk drive it chooses, the required operating system is OS Version A.

of configurations and completes orders for computers. Like all configuration systems, XCON relies on a component database and a body of rules that describes what combinations of parts work correctly together and how they should be arranged. The challenge of maintaining a large database about parts and a body of rules about their interactions has led to the development of a programming methodology for XCON called RIME. RIME organizes configuration knowledge in terms of small recurring subtasks such as selecting a device, selecting a container for a component, and selecting a location within a container to place a component. To a first approximation, these subtasks are local, explicit, and separate processes. To represent knowledge about the interactions among these subtasks, RIME organizes the subtask descriptions as a sequence of explicit stages that look ahead for interactions in the situation and select a best choice for part selection or arrangement before executing that choice.

M1 is an experimental knowledge system that configures single-board computers given a high-level specification of board functions and other design constraints. M1 represents components in a functional hierarchy. Like XCON, M1 relies on the use of key components to specify system function. It selects abstract parts and then instantiates them. Spatial layout is carried out by commercial programs for layout and wire routing.

In MYCIN, a therapy is a selected combination of drugs used to treat a patient for infectious diseases. This example shows that configuration can be used as a model for a task not involving manufacturing. The heuristic classification model that MYCIN uses for diagnosis is inadequate for characterizing therapy because the number of possible solutions based on combinations of drugs to cover combinations of diseases is too large to pre-enumerate. MYCIN's configuration model separates consideration of local factors, such as the sensitivity of the organisms to different drugs, from global factors that deal with the entire recommendation, such as minimizing the number of drugs.

VT is a knowledge system that configures elevator systems at the Westinghouse Elevator Company. Interwoven with VT's model of parts is a parametric model of elevator systems. VT's approach involves separate phases for knowledge acquisition and analysis and for solving particular cases. The analysis phase includes checking for race conditions, unreachable paths, and potential deadlocks. The case phase uses data-driven procedures to extend the configuration by proposing parameter values. VT's knowledge is organized within a parameter network in one of three forms: procedures for computing a parameter value, constraints that specify limits on parameter values, and fixes that specify what to do if a constraint is violated. Analogous to RIME, VT's analysis and knowledge acquisition facility can be viewed as a structured programming environment for building parameter networks.

COSSACK is a knowledge system for configuring personal computers. It begins with user specifications, in terms of evaluation criteria and functional specifications. The evaluation criteria are used to order candidates in component selection. Functionality specifications are represented in terms of key components. In describing how components require each other, COSSACK distinguishes between subcomponents that are always included and ones that must be added. COSSACK also distinguishes between different ways that components may be shared to satisfy multiple requirements. COSSACK uses a partial-commitment strategy.

Challenges in configuration tasks arise from the size of the search spaces and the complexity of individual solutions. Most configuration systems build descriptions of solutions incrementally. However, the acceptability of a configuration depends not only on local considerations. Following the threshold effect and horizon effect, interactions can propagate and be far-reaching. The next section considers how different computational methods used in these cases try to cope with these effects.

Exercises for Section 8.3

Ex. 1   [05] *Prefigured Configurations*. Professor Digit argues that very few of the possible VAX computer configurations are actually ever built. By his own estimate, no more than 1 in 1,000 of the configurations that are possible for VAXes will ever be ordered. He believes that all the effort in building knowledge-based configuration programs like XCON is unnecessary. He recommends instead that a table recording all actual configurations be kept and used to avoid refiguring them. This table would contain the input/output pairs from the history of configuration. It would show what configuration was used for every VAX system that has been ordered. The first column of the table would contain the specifications and the second column would describe the configuration.

(a) Briefly discuss the merits of Professor Digit's proposal. Is a reduction by a factor of 1,000 enough to make the table size manageable?

(b) Discuss advantages for building a knowledge-based configuration system over a "table system" even in cases where the determination of configurations is not computationally challenging.

Ex. 2 *[10] Due Process in Configuration Problems.* Several of the descriptions of the configuration systems mentioned optimization and best-first search.

(a) Which of the configuration systems discussed in this section perform exhaustive searches for solutions?

(b) Briefly explain the meaning of the term *due-process search* in the context of configuration problems, relating it to ideas for best-first search and optimization as discussed in this section. What are the implications of a high rate of turnover of knowledge in configuration domains?

Ex. 3 *[05] "Parts Is Parts."* This exercise considers limitations of a simple port-and-connector model for configuration as shown in Figure 8.32.

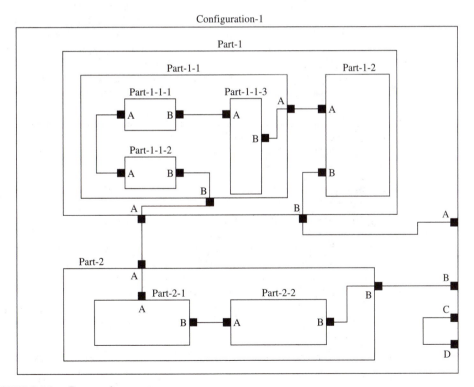

FIGURE 8.32. Ports and connectors.

(a) How many top-level parts are there in configuration-1? How many detailed parts are shown?

(b) Why is there a difference between subparts and required parts in configuration problems?

(c) Are cables parts? A port-and-connector model represents cables as mere connections between ports. Briefly, what are some of the practical issues in representing cables as parts? How could a port-and-connector model be augmented to accommodate this?

Ex. 4   [05] *Key Components*. The key-component approach is the technique of representing the functionality of a configuration in terms of essential components or abstract components in a partial configuration.

(a) Briefly, what representational issues does this approach seek to side-step?

(b) What is an advantage of this for the user interface in systems like XCON?

(c) Does the configuration model for therapy in MYCIN use a key-component approach?

■ **Ex. 5**   [*!-10*] *Thrashing in Antagonistic Subproblems*. Thrashing occurs in VT when fixes for constraint violations of one parameter lead to constraint violations of another parameter, whose fixes lead ultimately to further violations of the first parameter.

Here is an example of thrashing behavior for the parameter network in Figure 8.33: VT derives a value for machine-groove-pressure and maximum-machine-groove-pressure and finds that machine-groove-pressure is greater than the maximum. This triggers a fix that decreases car-supplement-weight. This decreases car-weight, which in turn decreases suspended-load. This decreases machine-groove-pressure, the desired effect, but also increases traction-ratio. An increase in traction-ratio makes it more likely for it to exceed its maximum. A violation of maximum-traction-ratio leads to the fix of increasing comp-cable-unit-weight, which in turn increases comp-cable-weight, cable-weight, and suspended-load. Increasing suspended-load increases machine-groove-pressure. Thrashing occurs if this scenario repeats.

(a) Annotate Figure 8.33 with directed arcs to show the operation of the fix operations to revise parameter values. Also annotate it with + and − to show the subsequent increases and decreases in parameter values.

(b) An antagonistic interaction is one where there are simultaneous contributions from different arcs in opposite directions to change the value of a parameter. At which nodes in the thrashing scenario are there antagonistic interactions? Briefly, what measures can be taken in systems like VT to deal with such interactions?

Ex. 6   [10] *Structured Programming Methodologies for Configuration Knowledge*. Several of the configuration projects discussed in this section have needed to face the classical knowledge engineering issue of providing support for acquiring, organizing, and maintaining a large knowledge base. In two of the cases that were described (XCON/RIME and VT/SALT), special languages or subsystems were developed for this. This exercise briefly compares the approaches taken for RIME and SALT.

(a) Both XCON and VT build descriptions of solutions incrementally. How is this reflected in the forms of knowledge that they expect?

(b) What is the distinction between local and global interactions in configuration problems? Why is this distinction important?

(c) Briefly compare propose-and-apply with propose-and-revise.

Ex. 7   [10] *Configuration Grammars*. Professor Digit says the knowledge representations used in configuration systems are excessively ad hoc. In particular, he advocates developing gram-

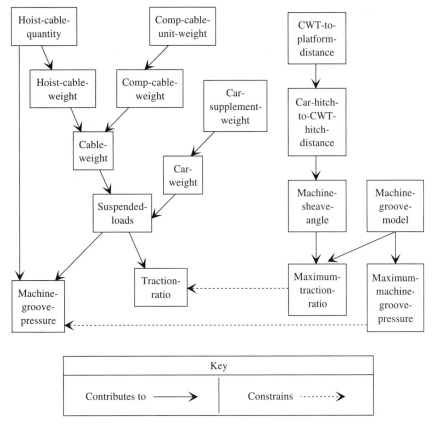

FIGURE 8.33. Interactions between antagonistic subproblems. (Adapted from Marcus & McDermott, 1989, Figure 5, page 18.)

mars for describing valid configurations analogous to those used for describing valid sentences in computer languages. He argues that standard algorithms from the parsing literature could then be used to carry out configuration tasks.

(a) Briefly list some of the kinds of domain knowledge needed for configuration tasks. What are some of the main problems with Professor Digit's proposal for using grammars to represent this knowledge?

(b) Is configuration essentially a parsing task? Explain briefly.

Ex. 8 [05] *Levels of Description.* Professor Digit can't decide whether XCON, the well-known rule-based computer configuration program, reasons forward or backward. On the one hand, the production rules used by XCON are interpreted by forward chaining. On the other hand, he has seen XCON described as working backward by setting up subproblems. Briefly, how can the apparent terminological confusion be resolved? Are either of these characterizations useful in understanding the main computational phenomena that arise in XCON's configuration task?

8.4 *Methods for Configuration Problems*

In the preceding sections we considered example knowledge systems for configuration tasks and developed a computational model to compare and analyze configuration domains. This section revisits our model of configuration to discuss knowledge-level and symbol-level analysis and then presents sketches of methods for configuration. Our goal in this section is not to develop an "ultimate" configuration approach, but rather to show how variations in the requirements of configuration tasks can be accommodated by changes in knowledge and method.

As in the case of classification tasks, most of the complexity in configuration tasks is in the domain-specific knowledge rather than in the search methods. Furthermore, most of the remaining complexity in the methods is in implementations of general search techniques. In this section the methods are stripped down to basics so we can see the assumptions they depend on in the configuration domain.

8.4.1 *Knowledge-Level and Symbol-Level Analysis*
of Configuration Domains

Knowledge about configuration is used by the submodels of our model. We begin our knowledge-level analysis by considering variations in the knowledge from the domains of our case studies. The submodels define major categories of knowledge for configuration in terms of its content, form, and use.

The Parts Submodel: Knowledge about Function and Structure

The parts submodel contains representations and knowledge about what the available parts are, what specifications they satisfy, and what requirements they have to carry out their functions. The simplest parts submodel is a catalog, which is a predetermined set of fixed parts. However, in most configuration domains the set of parts includes abstractions of them, organized in an abstract component hierarchy also called a functional hierarchy. Such hierarchies are used in mapping from initial specifications to partial configurations and in mapping from partial configurations to additional required parts. In most configuration domains these hierarchies represent functional groupings, where branches in the hierarchy correspond to specializations of function. In the last section we saw several examples of functional hierarchies in the computer configuration applications for XCON, M1, and COSSACK.

At the knowledge level an abstraction hierarchy guides problem solving, usually from the abstract to the specific. At the symbol level a parts hierarachy can be implemented as an index into the database of parts. There are several other relations on parts that are useful for indexing the database.

The determination of required parts is a major inference cycle in configuration. This process expands the set of selected parts and consumes global resources. The **required-parts relation** indicates what additional parts are required to enable a component to perform its role in a configuration. For example, a disk drive requires a disk controller and a power supply. These parts, in turn, may require others. These relations correspond to further requirements, not to specializations of function. In contrast, power supplies are required parts for many components with widely varying functions. Power supplies perform the same function without regard to the function of the components they serve.

We say that parts are **bundled** when they are necessarily selected together as a group. Often parts are bundled because they are manufactured as a unit. Sometimes parts are manufactured together because they are required together to support a common function. For example, a set of computer clocks may be made more economically by sharing parts. In other cases parts are made together for marketing reasons. Similarly, bundling components may reduce requirements for some resource. For example, communication and printing interfaces may be manufactured on a single board to save slots.

In some domains, parts are bundled because they are logically or stylistically used together. In configuring kitchen cabinets, the style of knobs and hinges across all cabinets is usually determined by a single choice. Parts can also be bundled for reasons not related to function or structure. For example, a marketing group may dictate a sales policy that certain parts are always sold together.

Some part submodels distinguish special categories of "spanning" or "dummy" parts. Examples of spanning parts from the domain of kitchen cabinets are the space fillers used in places where modular cabinets do not exactly fit the dimensions of a room. Examples of filler parts from computer systems are the conductor boards and bus terminators that are needed to compensate electrical loads when some common component is not used. Examples from configuring automobiles include the cover plates to fill dashboard holes where optional instruments were not ordered. Dummy and filler parts are often added at the end of a configuration process to satisfy modest integrity requirements.

Another variation is to admit parameterized parts, which are parts whose features are determined by the given values of parameters. A modular kitchen cabinet is an example of a parameterized part. Parameters for the cabinet could include the choice of kind of wood (cherry, maple, oak, or alder), the choice of finish (natural, red, golden, or laminate), and the choice of dimensions (any multiple of 3 inches from 9 inches to 27 inches).

Finally, parameterization can be used to describe properties of parts and subsystems, as in the VT system. Global properties of a configuration such as power requirements, weight, and cost are usually treated as parameters because they depend on wide-ranging decisions. In the VT system, essentially all the selectable features of the elevator system and many intermediate properties are represented in terms of parameters.

The Arrangement Submodel: Knowledge about Structure and Placement

The arrangement submodel expresses connectivity and spatial requirements. There are many variations in the requirements for arrangement submodels. Some configuration domains do not require complex spatial reasoning. For example, VT's elevator configurations all use minor variations of a single template for vertical transport systems. M1 uses a port-and-connector model for logical connections but its configurations are spatially uncommitted. Spatial arrangement of antibiotics is not relevant for MYCIN therapy recommendations.

Arrangements do not always require distance metrics or spatial models. In configuring the simplest personal computers, the slots that are used for different optional parts are referenced and accounted for by discrete names or indexes. A configuration task need only keep track of which slots are used without bothering about where they are.

Figure 8.34 illustrates several examples of specialized arrangement models. The simplest of these is the port-and-connector model. This model was used in the M1 and COSSACK appli-

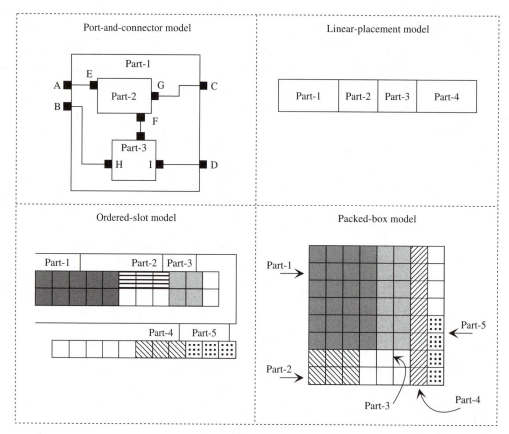

FIGURE 8.34.   Alternative models of arrangement for configuration problems. Different arrangement models lend themselves to different resource allocation strategies.

cations discussed earlier. In this model, ports are defined for all the configurable parts. Ports have types so that different kinds of ports have different properties. Ports are resources than can be assigned to at most one connector. COSSACK implemented a port-and-connector model in a frame language, combining its use for specifying the arrangement of parts with indexing on constraints that specified what parts were compatible or required. The linear-placement model organizes parts in a sequence. A specialization of this model was used in XCON for specifying the order of electrical connections on a computer bus. In that application, roughly speaking, it is desirable to locate parts with a high interrupt priority or a high data rate nearer the front of the bus. Location on the bus was a resource that was consumed as parts were arranged. The ordered-slot model combines a linear ordering with a spatial requirement. In the version in Figure 8.34, parts are ordered along a bus, starting with Part-1 and ending with Part-4. Parts in the first row can be up to two units deep, and parts in the second row can be only one unit deep. In this example, both space and sequence are resources that get consumed as parts are arranged. The packed-box model emphasizes the efficient packing of parts. In this model, space is a consumable

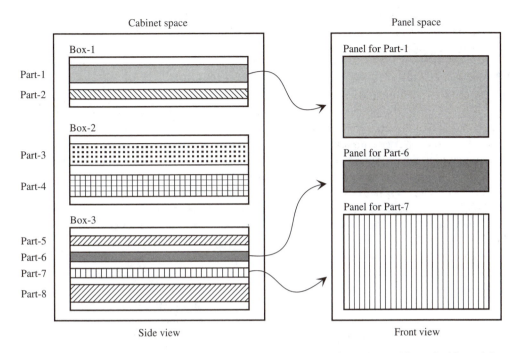

FIGURE 8.35. Another variation on models of arrangement for configuration problems. In this model, parts are arranged in boxes and boxes are arranged in cabinets. In addition, some parts require control panels and there is a limited amount of panel space. Panels for parts must be located on the cabinet that contains the parts. In this model, space in boxes, space in cabinets, and space for panels are all resources consumed during configuration. Because of the connections between parts and panels, the resource allocation processes are interdependent.

resource. Constraints on packing may also include requirements about certain parts being adjacent to one another.

All the variations in Figure 8.34 represent physical containment. **Physical-containment relations** form a hierarchy whose branches indicate which parts are physically contained in others. For example, a cabinet may contain a circuit board, which in turn may contain a processor and some memory. Contained parts do not necessarily carry out specializations of their container's function, nor are they necessarily required parts for their container.

COSSACK uses a port-and-connector model to account for the use of slots. It also keeps track of memory resources. XCON's arrangement models are the most complex in our example systems. Figure 8.35 illustrates another complication in arrangement models. In this example, there are three interlinked tasks in arrangement: the location of boards inside boxes, the location of boxes inside cabinets, and the location of panels on the front of cabinets. The tasks are interlinked because the control panels for particular boards need to be located on the cabinet containing the corresponding boards.

XCON also admits complex arrangement conditions and interactions with nonspatial resources. For example, a rule for allocating slots inside boxes says: "a box can accommodate five 4-slot backplanes; the exception is that a 9-slot backplane may not occupy the space reserved for the second and third 4-slot backplanes." This example combines electrical requirements with space allocation.

Knowledge about Decision Ordering and Interactions

The difficulty of configuration problems arises from a three-horned dilemma, where the three horns are combinatorics, horizon effects, and threshold effects. The combinatoric difficulty is that the number of possible configurations increases multiplicatively with the number of parts and arrangements. In the configuration domains discussed in this chapter, there are far too many possible configurations to instantiate them all in complete detail. Most decisions need to be made on the basis of partial information about the possible configurations. This is where the horizon effect comes in. At each stage of reasoning, some interactions are not yet visible either because not enough inferences have been made or because not enough commitments have been made. When information is partial, a natural approach is to rely on estimates. This is where the threshold effect comes in. A small difference in specifications or descriptions can lead to large, widespread changes. Because of their approximate nature, estimation functions can be off by small amounts. If these small errors are near critical thresholds, then the estimates may not be trustworthy.

To reiterate the argument in short form, there are too many configurations to develop them in detail. Making choices on the basis of partial information is subject to horizon effects. Estimates at the horizon based on partical information are subject to threshold effects.

The approaches that we consider for coping with these effects assume that there are predictable or typical patterns of interaction and that knowledge about these patterns is available. The following discussion is concerned with the dimensions of these patterns.

The first horn of the dilemma, combinatorics, is dealt with by two major techniques: abstraction and decision ordering. Thus, the use of functional abstractions in reasoning about configuration amounts to hierarchical search and has the usual beneficial effects. Controlling the order of decisions can reduce the amount of backtracking in search. In the context of configuration, knowledge-level justifications of decision ordering complement the symbol-level graph analyses. In XCON and VT, the reduction of backtracking is characterized in terms of dependent and independent decisions, where each decision is carried out only after completing other decisions on which it depends.

For example, XCON defers cabling decisions to its last subtask. Three assumptions rationalize this late placement of cabling decisions. The first assumption is that for any configuration, cabling is always possible between two components. This assumption ensures that the configuration process will not fail catastrophically due to an inability to run a cable. The second assumption is that all cables work satisfactorily, for any configuration. Thus, a computer system will work correctly no matter how long the cables are. The third assumption is that cable costs do not matter. Cable costs are so low when compared with active components that they will not influence an overall cost significantly. As long as these assumptions hold, XCON would never need to backtrack (even if it could!) from a cable decision and there is no need to consider cable issues any earlier in XCON's process. If there were some special cases where cables beyond a certain length were unavailable or would prevent system operations, a fix in terms of other component choices or arrangements would need to be determined and XCON would be augmented with look-ahead rules to anticipate that case.

Much of the point of the SALT analysis in the elevator domain is to identify patterns of interactions. VT's data-driven approach is a least-commitment approach and is analogous to constraint satisfaction methods that reason about which variable to assign values to next. Least commitment precludes guessing on some decisions when refinements on other decisions can be made without new commitments. Deadlock loops correspond to situations where no decision would be made. To handle cases where decisions are inherently intertwined so there is no ordering based on linear dependencies, SALT introduces reasoning loops in the parameter network that search through local preferences toward a global optimum.

The partial-commitment approach extends least commitment by abstracting what is common to the set of remaining alternatives and then using that abstraction to constrain other decisions. VT narrows values on some parameters, sometimes on independent grounds, so that components are partially specified at various stages of the configuration process.

In VT, such reasoning can amount to partial commitment to the extent that further inferences are drawn as the descriptions are narrowed.

All efforts to cope with the combinatorics of configuration encounter horizon effects. Since uniform farsightedness is too expensive, an alternative is to have limited but very focused farsightedness. Domain knowledge is used to anticipate and identify certain key interactions, which require a deeper analysis than is usual. This approach is used in XCON, when it employs its look-ahead rules to anticipate possible future decisions. The required conditions for look-ahead can be very complex. In XCON, heuristics are available for information gathering that can tell approximately whether particular commitments are feasible. The heuristics make look-ahead less expensive.

Finally, we come to techniques for coping with the threshold effect. The issue is not just that there are thresholds, but rather that the factors contributing to the threshold variables are widely distributed. Sometimes this distribution can be controlled by bringing together all the decisions that contribute. This helps to avoid later surprises. Knowledge about thresholds and contributing decisions can be used in guiding the ordering of decisions. In general, however, there is no single order that clusters all related decisions. One approach is to anticipate thresholds with estimators and to make conservative judgments. For example, one could anticipate the need for a larger cabinet. This conservative approach works against optimization. In XCON, many of the constraints whose satisfaction cannot be anticipated are soft. This means that although there may be violations, the softness of the constraints reduces the bad consequences. Thus, the extra part may require adding a cabinet, but at least it is possible to add new cabinets.

In summary, domain knowledge is the key to coping with the complexity of configuration. Knowledge about abstractions makes it possible to search hierarchically. Knowledge about key interactions makes it possible to focus the computations for look-ahead to specific points beyond the horizon. Knowledge about soft constraints reduces the effects of threshold violations.

8.4.2 *MCF-1: Expand and Arrange*

In this section and the following, we consider methods for configuration. In principle, we could begin with a method based on a simple generate-and-test approach. By now, however, it should be clear how to write such a method and also why it would be of little practical value. We begin with a slightly more complex method.

Figure 8.36 presents an extremely simple method for configuration, called MCF-1. MCF-1 acquires its specifications in terms of key components, expands the configuration to include all required parts, and then arranges the parts. Although this method is very simple it is also appropriate for some domains. MCF-1 is M1's method, albeit in skeletal form and leaving out the secondary cycle for reliability analysis and revision. It is practical for those applications where the selection decisions do not depend on the arrangement decisions.

MCF-1 has independent auxiliary methods get-requirements, get-best-parts, and arrange-parts. The auxiliary method get-requirements returns all the requirements for a part and returns the initial set of requirements given the token initial-specifications. Given a set of requirements, there may be different alternative candidate sets of parts for meeting a requirement. The method get-best-parts considers the candidate sets of new parts and employs a domain-specific evaluation function to select the best ones. Finally, given a list of parts, the method arrange-parts determines their best arrangement. A recursive subroutine, add-required-parts, adds all the parts required by a component.

MCF-1 relies on several properties of its configuration domain as follows:

■ Specifications can be expressed in terms of a list of key components.
■ There is a domain-specific evaluation function for choosing the best parts to meet requirements.
■ Satisfactory part arrangements are always possible, given a set of components.
■ Parts are not shared. Each requirement is filled using unique parts.

The first assumption is quite common in configuration tasks and has little bearing on the method. The second assumption says there is a way to select required parts without backtracking. An evaluation function is called from inside get-best-parts. The third assumption says that arrangement concerns for configurations involve no unsatisfiable constraints, even in combination. This is not unusual for configuration tasks that use a port-and-connector model for arrangements. In such domains, one can always find some arrangement and the arrangement does not affect the quality of the configuration. This assumption is crucial to the organization of MCF-1 because it makes it possible to first select all the required parts before arranging any of them. It implies further that the arrangement process never requires the addition of new parts. A somewhat weaker assumption is actually strong enough for a simple variation of the method: that part arrangement never introduces any significant parts that would force backtracking on selection or arrangement decisions. The last assumption means the system need not check whether an existing part can be reused for a second function. This method would need to be modified to accommodate multifunctional parts.

8.4.3   *MCF-2: Staged Subtasks with Look-Ahead*

Method MCF-1 is explicit about the order that configuration knowledge is used: first, key components are identified; then required parts are selected; and finally, parts are arranged. As discussed in our analysis of configuration, these decisions may need to be more tightly interwoven. Sometimes an analysis of a domain will reveal that certain groups of configuration decisions are tightly coupled and that some groups of decisions can be performed before others. When this is the case, the configuration process can be organized in terms of subtasks, where each subtask

To perform configuration using MCF-1:

```
        /* Initialize and determine the key components from the
        specifications. */
1.    Set parts-list to nil.

        /* Get-requirements returns specifications for required parts given
        a part. */
2.    Set requirements to get-requirements(initial-specifications).
3.    Set key-components to get-best-parts(requirements).

        /* Add all the required parts to the parts-list. */
4.    For each key component do
5.    begin
6.        Push the key component onto the parts-list.
7.        Add-required-parts(key-component).
8.    end

        /* Arrange parts in the configuration. */
9.    Arrange parts using arrange-parts(parts-list).
10.   Return the solution.


        /* Recursive subroutine to add parts required by a given
        part. When there are multiple candidates it selects the best one
        get-best-parts. */
1.    Add-required-parts(part)
2.    begin
3.        Set requirements to get-requirements(part).
4.        If there are some requirements, then
5.        begin
6.            Set new-parts to get-best-parts(requirements).
7.            For each of the new-parts do
8.            begin
9.                Push the new-part onto the parts-list.
10.               Add-required-parts(new-part).
11.           end
12.       end
13.   end
```

FIGURE 8.36. MCF-1, a simple method for configuration problems in which there is no interaction between selection and arrangement of required parts.

performs a combination of closely related decisions to refine, select, and arrange components. Subtasks cluster decisions so that most interactions among decisions within a subtask are much greater than interactions with decisions outside of it.

In some domains the partitioning of decisions into subtask clusters does not necessarily yield a decision ordering in which all later decisions depend only on early ones. To restate this in constraint satisfaction terms, there may be no ordering of variables such that values can be assigned to all variables in order without having to backtrack. To address this, knowledge for selective look-ahead is used to anticipate interactions. Such knowledge is domain specific and may involve conservative estimates or approximations that anticipate possible threshold effects. This approach can be satisfactory even in cases where the look-ahead is not foolproof, if the failures involve soft constraints.

This approach is followed in MCF-2. The method description given in Figure 8.37 says very little about configuration in general. Nonetheless, MCF-2 is the method used by XCON, albeit with its domain-specific particulars abstracted.

To perform configuration using MCF-2:

```
        /* Initialize and get the key components from the specifications. */
   1.   Set parts-list to nil.
   2.   Set requirements to get-requirements(initial-specifications).
   3.   Set key-components to get-best-parts(requirements).


        /* Conditionally invoke Subtasks. */
   4.   While there are pending subtasks do
   5.   begin
   6.           Test conditionals for invoking subtasks and choose the best
                one.
   7.           Invoke a specialized method for the subtask.
   8.   end
   9.   Return the solution.


        /* Each specialized method performs a subset of the task. It is
        responsible for refining some specifications, adding some parts, and
        arranging some parts. It incorporates whatever look-ahead is needed.
        */
   10.  Method-for-Subtask-1:


        /* Subtask-1: Look ahead as needed and expand some parts. */
        /* Subtask-2: Look ahead as needed and arrange some parts. */

   20.  Return.
   ...
   30.  Method-for-Stage-3:
   ...
```

FIGURE 8.37. MCF-2, a method for configuration problems in which part selection and arrangement decisions can be organized in a fixed sequence of subtasks. The method depends crucially on the properties of the domain. This method tells us very little about configuration in general.

This method is vague. We might caricature it as advising us to "write a configuration system as a smart program using modularity as needed" or as "an agenda interpreter that applies subtasks in a best-first order." Such symbol-level characterizations miss the point that the decision structure follows from an analysis of relations at the knowledge level. This observation is similar to the case of methods for classification. The particulars of the domain knowledge make all the difference. The burden in using MCF-2 is in analyzing a particular domain, identifying common patterns of interaction, and partitioning the decisions into subtasks that select and arrange parts while employing suitable look-ahead.

It is interesting to compare MCF-2 to the general purpose constraint satisfaction methods. One important result is that when the variables of a constraint satisfaction problem (CSP) are block ordered, it is possible to find a solution to the CSP with backtracking limited to the size of the largest block, which is depth-limited backtracking. Although there are important differences between the discrete CSP problems and the configuration problems, the basic idea is quite similar. Subtasks correspond roughly to blocks. When subtasks are solved in the right order, little or no backtracking is needed. (See the exercises for a more complete discussion of this analogy.)

As in MCF-1, MCF-2 does not specify an arrangement submodel, a part submodel, or a sharing submodel. Each domain needs its specially tailored submodels. In summary, MCF-2 employs specialized methods for the subtasks to do special-case look-ahead, to compensate for known cases where the fixed order of decision rules fails to anticipate some crucial interaction leading to a failure. The hard work in using this method is in the analysis of the domain to partition it into appropriate subtasks.

8.4.4 *MCF-3: Propose-and-Revise*

In MCF-2, there are no provisions in the bookkeeping for carrying alternative solutions, or for backtracking when previously unnoticed conflicts become evident. Figure 8.38 gives MCF-3, which is based loosely on the mechanisms used in VT, using the propose-and-revise approach. Like MCF-2, we can view MCF-3 as an outline for an interpreter of knowledge about configuration. It is loosely based on the ideas of VT and the interpretation of a parameter network. It depends crucially on the structure of the partial configuration and the arrangement of knowledge for proposing values, proposing constraints, noticing constraint violations, and making fixes.

The beauty of MCF-3 is that the system makes whatever configuration decisions it can by following the opportunities noticed by its data-driven interpreter. In comparison with MCF-2, MCF-3 is does not rely so much on heuristic look-ahead, but has provisions for noticing conflicts, backtracking, and revising.

8.4.5 *Summary and Review*

This section sketched several different methods for configuration, based loosely on the example applications we considered earlier. We started with a method that performed all selection decisions before any arrangement decisions. Although this is practical for some configuration tasks, it is not adequate when arrangements are difficult or are an important determinant of costs. The second method relied on look-ahead. Our third method triggered subtasks according to knowl-

To perform configuration using MCF-3:
```
      /* Initialize and obtain requirements. */
1.    Initialize the list of parts to empty.
2.    Set requirements to get-requirements(initial-specifications).
3.    Set key-components to get-best-parts(requirements).


      /* Apply the domain knowledge to extend and revise the configuration.
      */
4.    While there are open decisions and failure has not been signaled do
5.    begin
6.          Select the next-node in the partial configuration for which a
            decision can be made.
7.          If the decision is a design extension, then invoke method
            propose-design-extensions(next-node).
8.          If the decision is to post a constraint, then invoke method
            post-design-constraints().
9.          If there are violated-constraints, then invoke revise-design().
10.   end
11.   Report the solutions (or failure).
```

FIGURE 8.38.   MCF-3, a method based on the propose-and-revise model.

edge about when the subtasks were ready to be applied and used constraints to test for violations when choices mattered for more than one subtask.

Exercises for Section 8.4

Ex. 1   [*10*] *MYCIN's Method.* How does MYCIN's method for therapy recommendation fit into the set of methods discussed in this section? Is it the same as one of them? Explain briefly.

■ **Ex. 2**   [*R*] *Subtask Ordering.* After studying the XCON system and reading about constraint satisfaction methods, Professor Digit called his students together. "Eureka!" he said. "MCF-2 is really a special case of an approach to constraint satisfaction that we already know: block ordering. In the future, pay no attention to MCF-2. Just make a tree of 'constraint blocks' corresponding to the configuration subtasks and solve the tasks in a depth-first order of the tree of blocks."
(a) Briefly sketch the important similarities and differences between CSP problems and configuration problems.
(b) Briefly, is there any merit to Professor Digit's proposal and his suggestion that there is a relation between traversing a tree of blocks in a CSP problem and solving a set of staged subtasks in a configuration problem?
(c) Briefly relate the maximum depth of backtracking necessary in a CSP to the "no backtracking" goal of systems like XCON.

Ex. 3   [*10*] *Methods and Special Cases.* The methods for configuration are all simple, in that the complexity of configuration tasks is manifest in the domain-specific knowledge rather than in the methods. The methods, however, form a progression of sorts, in that they can be seen as providing increased flexibility.

(a) In what way is MCF-1 a special case of MCF-2?

(b) In what way is MCF-2 a special case of MCF-3?

(c) In what way could MCF-3 be generalized to use other techniques from the example systems in this chapter?

8.5   Open Issues and Quandaries

In the 1970s, folk wisdom about expert systems said that they might be developed routinely for "analytic" tasks but not "synthetic" tasks, which were too difficult. Analytic tasks were characterized in terms of feature recognition. Medical diagnosis was cited as an example of an analytic task. In contrast, synthetic tasks reasoned about how to put things together. Design was said to be an example of a synthetic task.

In hindsight, this dichotomy is too simplistic. Some problem-solving methods combine aspects of synthesis and analysis, to wit: "synthesis by analysis" and "analysis by synthesis." Large tasks in practical domains are made up of smaller tasks, each of which may have its own methods. In the next chapter we will see that even methods for diagnosis require the combination of diagnostic hypotheses.

However, the main point for our purposes is that synthetic tasks tend to have high combinatorics and require a large and complex body of knowledge. This made them unsuitable for the first generation of knowledge systems, which performed simpler tasks mostly based on classification. Design tasks are still more often associated with research projects than with practical applications. Ambitious knowledge systems for design tasks tend to be doctoral thesis projects.

Configuration tasks specify how to assemble parts from a predefined set. It could be argued that the "real" difficulty in configuration tasks is setting up the families of components so that configuration is possible at all. For computer configuration, this involves designing the bus structures, the board configurations, the bus protocols, and so on. If these standards were not established, there would be no way to plug different options into the same slot. There would be no hope of creating a simple model of functionality around a key-component assumption. Behind the knowledge of a configurable system, there is a much larger body of knowledge about part reusability in families of systems. This brings us back to the challenges of design.

The goal in both configuration and design is to specify a manufacturable artifact that satisfies requirements involving such matters as functionality and cost. Design can be open-ended. Will the truck ride well on a bumpy road? What load can it carry? What is its gas mileage? Can the engine be serviced conveniently? There is an open-ended world of knowledge about materials, combustion, glues, assembly, manufacturing tools, markets, and other matters.

Human organizations have responded to the complexity of designing high-technology products by bringing together specialists with different training. The design of a xerographic copier involves mechanical engineers concerned with systems for moving paper, electronical engineers concerned with electronic subsystems, and computer engineers concerned with internal software. But this is just a beginning. Other people specialize in particular kinds of systems for transporting paper. Some people specialize in printing materials. Some specialize in the design of user interfaces. Some specialize in different manufacturing processes, such as plastics, sheet metal, and semiconductors. Others specialize in servicing copiers in the field.

As the number of issues and specializations increase, there are real challenges in managing and coordinating the activities and in bringing appropriate knowledge to bear. Competition drives companies to find ways to reduce costs and to speed the time to bring products to market. In this context, a large fraction of the cost of producing a product is determined by its design. Part of this cost is the design process itself, amortized over the number of products made. But the main point is about the time of decisions. Many decisions about a product influence the costs of its manufacture and service. What size engine does the truck have? Does it run on diesel or gasoline? Can the battery be replaced without unbolting the engine? How much room is in the cab? How many trucks will be sold? Many of these decisions are made at early stages of design and cannot be changed later, thus locking in major determinants of the product cost.

To reduce costs we must understand them at earlier stages of design. Thus, products are designed for manufacturing, designed for flexibility, designed for portability, or designed for servicing. All these examples of "design for X" attempt to bring to bear knowledge about X at an early stage of design. In design organizations, this has led to the creation of design teams and a practice called "simultaneous engineering." The idea is to bring together specialists representing different concerns, and to have them participate all the way through the design process.

There are no knowledge systems where you "push a button to design a truck." The challenges for acquiring the appropriate knowledge base for such ambitious automation are staggering. Instead, the response to shortening product development times involves other measures. Many of these involve ways for moving design work online. Databases and parts catalogs are online. Simulation systems sometimes replace shops for prototyping. The controls for manufacturing equipment are becoming accessible through computer networks. Reflecting the reality that much of an engineer's day is spent communicating with colleagues, another point of leverage is more advanced technology for communicating with others. This ranges from facsimile machines and electronic mail, to online computer files, to devices that enable teams of engineers to share a "digital workspace."

Systems to support design need not automate the entire process but can facilitate human design processes, simulate product performance and manufacturing, and automate routine subtasks. The elements of new design systems include knowledge systems, online catalogs, collaboration technology, simulation tools, and visualization tools. These elements reflect a move toward shared digital workspaces. As the work practice and data of design organizations become more online, many different niches appear where knowledge systems can be used to assist and automate parts of the process.

Automation advances as it becomes practical to formalize particular bodies of knowledge. Inventory and catalog systems now connect with drafting systems to facilitate the reuse of manufactured parts. Drafting systems now use constraint models and parameterized designs to relate sizing information from one part of the system with sizing information from other parts. In design tasks such as the design of paper paths using pinch roller technology (Mittal, Dym, & Morjaria, 1986), it has been practical to systematize a body of knowledge for performing large parts of the task.

Conventional tools for computer-aided design (CAD) tend to be one of two kinds: analysis tools or drafting tools. An example of an analysis tool is one for predicting the effects of vibrations on structure using finite element analysis. An example of a drafting tool is a tool for producing wire-frame models of solids. Knowledge-systems concepts are beginning to find their way into CAD systems, joining the ranks of graphics programs, simulation systems, and visualization systems. As computer technology for computer graphics and parallel processing have become available, there has been increased development of tools to help designers visualize products and manufacturing, by simulating those steps and showing the results graphically.

In summary, configuration tasks are a relatively simple subset of design tasks. They are more difficult because specifications can be more open-ended and design can involve fashioning and machining of parts rather than just selection of them. Human organizations have responded to the complexities of modern product design by engaging people who specialize in many different concerns. This specialization has also made it more difficult to coordinate design projects and to get designs to market quickly.

Earlier chapters discussed diagnostic systems based on classification models. We now extend the discussion to include plan-based models, causal network models, and detailed physical models for diagnosis.

Diagnosis and Troubleshooting

9.1 Introduction

To diagnose is to observe a physical artifact that is malfunctioning or a person who is ill and then to determine what is wrong through reasoning and further observations. The term *troubleshooting* refers to the diagnosis of physical devices such as mechanical and electronic systems. Troubleshooting is sometimes characterized as the diagnosis and repair of devices that have stopped working. Different domains and situations place different demands on diagnosis and troubleshooting.

9.1.1 Diagnosis and Troubleshooting Scenarios

The following scenarios illustrate some similarities and differences among diagnostic and troubleshooting tasks.

- *Infectious disease scenario.* A patient comes to a doctor complaining of listlessness, fever, and aching joints. The doctor takes the patient's temperature, listens to his breathing, and takes a culture sample while examining his throat. She determines that the patient has a bacterial infection and administers a broad-spectrum antibiotic. Later she checks the results of the throat culture to verify that the given antibiotic should be effective.

- *Board troubleshooting scenario.* A computer maintenance technician receives a complaint that the mouse on a computer workstation does not work. He replaces the mouse with a spare one, but the cursor on the display still does not track mouse movements. He then opens the keyboard case where the mouse plugs in, probes the output of an oscillator with an oscilloscope, and decides that the oscillator is working. He probes an interrupt line on the output of a microprocessor chip and discovers that it remains stuck at five volts whether the mouse is stationary or moving. He probes several other points in the circuit and determines that one of the chips needs replacing. He turns off the system, replaces the chip, and tests the system again. The system works fine.

■ *Picnic scenario.* Late on a hot afternoon of a big picnic, several people experience nausea, vomiting, muscular weakness, and disturbed vision. A physician and a member of the local health department come to the scene. The officials ask people what they ate, take samples of different foods, and run tests on the samples. The picnickers are treated for food poisoning. Shortly thereafter, another picnicker reports the same symptoms. The doctor learns that the picknicker ate some of the potato salad and treats him for food poisoning.

■ *Communications box scenario.* A communications technician is notified that a communications switching controller is not working. She checks the lights on the front panels of the communications controllers and turns off the controller that has red lights glowing on the front panel. Inside the box are five identical circuit boards. She replaces the first board, turns on the unit, and determines from the red lights that the unit is still not working. She repeats this for the second board in the unit with the same result. She repeats it for the third board in the unit, and this time all the lights turn green and communications start working again. She places the original third board in a briefcase for broken boards and returns with it to her service van.

■ *Copier troubleshooting scenario.* A reprographics technician receives a phone call that a high-speed copying machine is making illegible copies. He comes to the machine and tries several test patterns, verifying easily that the copy quality is below specifications. He plugs a portable computer into the machine and discovers that earlier that morning the machine's internal print-quality feedback loop adjusted several of its parameters to extreme values. He looks at the maintenance log and notices that the toner was also replenished that morning. He examines the toner powder and discovers that someone has filled the toner reservoir with the wrong kind of toner for the machine. He vacuums out the improper toner from the machine, refills the reservoir with the correct toner, and verifies that the copy quality is within specifications.

These scenarios have much in common. In each case, the diagnostician (doctor or technician) gathers and selects information about the malfunctioning system and its environment and uses the information to determine a treatment or repair.

9.1.2 *Dimensions of Variation in Diagnostic Tasks*

There are substantial differences in the above scenarios, illustrating important variations in diagnostic and troubleshooting tasks.

■ *What can be a cause.* The scenarios differ in the nature of the causes of failure, such as broken components versus diseases versus environmental causes. In the board troubleshooting example and the communications box scenario, the technician's model of the malfunctioning system is expressed in terms of broken components. In that context, to diagnose a system is to determine which components need to be replaced. This contrasts with the infectious disease scenario, where the difficulty could be an externally introduced infection that spreads throughout the patient's body. In the picnic scenario and copier scenario, the causes are neither diseases nor component failures. In the picnic scenario the picnickers consumed toxins from spoiled food; in the copier scenario the machine was given a toner powder that did not meet its operating requirements. These scenarios implicate causes in the environment.

■ *Availability of intermediate diagnostic measurements.* The availability of diagnostic measurements varies in the scenarios. In the board troubleshooting example, a technician can probe any exposed wire in the system. To partition a diagnostic solution space efficiently, intermediate system data are needed. Because of the risk of complications, however, physicians prefer noninvasive techniques. Physicians usually have very limited options for obtaining or reasoning about internal data about a patient. Thus, there are differences across domains in the accessibility and usability of information about intermediate states in systems. Accessibility of state can change with improvements in instrumentation. Medical practice continues to become more sophisticated in its use of technology for imaging and measuring body function. At the same time, desire for large-scale integration and high density in manufacturing leads to compromises in provisions for accessing the internal states of electronic devices.

■ *Specificity of diagnosis.* Another variation in these scenarios is the required specificity of diagnosis. In the communications box example, the technician only needed to determine which of five identical boards had failed. She did not care which component in the board was damaged. In the parlance of field service, a board is an example of a field replaceable unit (FRU) and a chip is not. Diagnosis in field work need not be more precise than the possible repair options. Similarly, in the infectious disease case, the doctor did not establish a precise vector of infection, but rather treated the patient with a broad-spectrum antibiotic.

■ *Modifiability of system state.* The systems being diagnosed offer different opportunities for a diagnostician to put them into different states. In the board troubleshooting case, a diagnostician could have a special unit to arbitrarily drive the input of the board with different test vectors. This makes it relatively easy to put the system under diagnosis in a different state. In the copier scenario and medical scenarios, the systems (or people) have internal feedback loops that automatically compensate for changes in the external environment. Feedback loops make it more difficult to change the internal state.

■ *Steady state versus dynamic behavior.* Time-dependent behavior can substantially complicate diagnosis. In medical systems, some diseases have periodic symptoms and some diseases are progressive. Medical diagnostic systems differ in terms of whether they treat each diagnostic session as an isolated event or whether they can reason about multiple successive visits of a patient. Electronic and troubleshooting systems typically carry out different functions over time. Some faulty behaviors occur only when certain functions are being performed. Diagnostic and troubleshooting systems differ in whether they model systems as having steady-state or time-varying behavior and in whether they can reason about intermittent faults.

■ *Task overlap among diagnosis, testing, and treatment.* In many real applications, the useful tasks that people perform merge diagnosis with therapy or testing. In the communications box scenario, the technician replaces the boards one at a time until the controller works. In this case, observations of the operation of the controller before and after board replacement provide data about the possible cause. Repairs and therapy can be tried experimentally to determine whether they are effective. In such cases, therapeutic and repair actions also yield data about the system and its faults.

Similarly, testing is the process of certifying that a system is fully operational. In a manufacturing setting, testing is a procedure for systematically checking the operation of a large practical subset of a system's behavior. In a medical context, the analogous task is a multiphasic physical exam. In contrast, diagnosis is usually undertaken to remedy an identified misbehavior and does not necessarily include looking for other problems not yet detected. Nonetheless, although diagnosis does not necessarily imply a thorough checking of all possible conditions and behaviors, it is often expected that certain obvious and perhaps simple tests be carried out so the repaired system will not immediately fail again, albeit due to a different cause. In many real situations, diagnosis, repair, and testing tasks are combined.

9.2 Models for Diagnosis Domains

In this section we develop a general model for knowledge-based diagnosis. We consider the basic phenomena and then compare approaches. In this way we seek to understand what diagnosis is, what makes it difficult, and what roles knowledge and various assumptions play in it.

Search Spaces for Diagnosis

So far the discussion has focused mainly on how diagnostic tasks can differ. Figure 9.1 presents a framework for describing what they can have in common. It shows the search spaces and operations that underlie knowledge-based systems for diagnosis. The three main spaces for diagnostic reasoning are a data space, a hypothesis space, and a therapy or repair space.

The **data space** presents a finite set of possible measurements, also called probe points, probes, observations, observables, manifestations, findings, history items, laboratory data, and signs and symptoms. For diagnostic reasoning, we distinguish different kinds of values for each data variable, such as possible values, normal values, predicted values, and observed values. The possible values are the ones that can be considered at all in a given diagnostic model. Predicted values are those expected from a model and from what is known. Observed values are those reported by instruments coupled to the system in its physical environment. Normal values are those that can occur within the normal operating conditions of the device being modeled.

The **hypothesis space** represents diagnostic hypotheses about what could be wrong with the system being diagnosed. A hypothesis can involve multiple underlying faults, also called syndromes, diseases, or causes, depending on the domain. The **therapy** or **repair space** represents a set of possible actions to treat or repair the system.

Below all three spaces in Figure 9.1 is another box labeled "**System Model**." Roughly, a system model describes the structure and behavior of the system being diagnosed, including some elements of its environment. The three spaces and the system model reference many of the same representations and may usefully share common procedures and data structures in their implementations. For example, it is useful to be able to install hypothetical faults in the system model corresponding to faults postulated by diagnostic hypotheses and to predict resulting values in the data space. Similarly, we can install various repairs in a model and then predict the result-

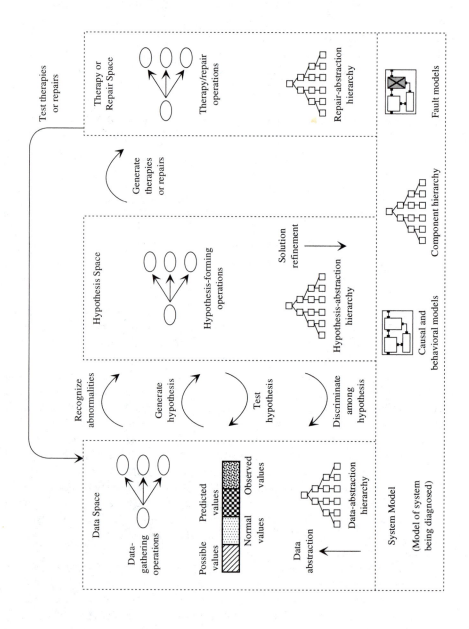

FIGURE 9.1. Search spaces and shared system models for diagnosis tasks.

ing changes in system behavior. In the following, we discuss the spaces and system model further to develop an informal definition of diagnosis.

All three spaces describe operations. Data-gathering operations carry out observations of the system under consideration. Therapy and repair operations in the therapy and repair space make changes to the system to fix the problem. The central operations in diagnosis tasks are the ones that manipulate diagnostic hypotheses. The operations in the hypothesis space include generating hypotheses and discriminating among competing hypotheses. These operations are carried out in recurring patterns of search and knowledge use. These patterns exemplify common elements characteristic of knowledge-based diagnostic systems.

All three spaces can have representations at multiple levels of abstraction. As in the horseshoe diagram for classification, a data space can include data abstractions that simplify mapping to fault or disease hypotheses. A qualitative abstraction may map a particular measurement of body temperature to "fever." Diagnostic hypotheses can be organized in terms of general and specific hypotheses. For example, the hypothesis that there is a fault in the "adder" is more general than the hypothesis that there is a "stuck at 1" fault in a particular chip that is part of the adder.

An Example of a System to be Diagnosed

Figure 9.2 gives an example of a simple (albeit fictional) system to be diagnosed, TS-1, that we use to illustrate concepts and issues in the following. In this example, the components A1 and A2 are hardware adders and M1 and M2 are multipliers. The data space in this example includes descriptions of values for the inputs and outputs of each component. For example, M1 has the values 3 and 2 on its inputs. Measurements can be taken on the input and output points for the system and also on the internal test points T1, T2, and T3.

A behavioral model indicates what the different components do. In our simple model, the adders add their inputs and deliver the results on their outputs. The multipliers multiply their inputs together and deliver the results on their outputs. Adders and multipliers have limited precision. In TS-1 the components use a 5-bit binary representation for positive integers. This representation accommodates numbers between 0 and 31, where any bits representing larger numbers are simply lost. Figure 9.3 presents behavior rules for the adders and multipliers in our example.

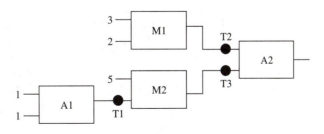

FIGURE 9.2. TS-1: An example of a system to be diagnosed, composed of two multipliers and two adders.

Behavior Modes for Adder

Mode	Probability	Behavior
w (working)	.9990	Out = (In1 + In2) mod 32
s (shorted)	.0003	Out = 0
d (drop MSB)	.0006	Out = (In1 + In2) mod 16
u (unknown)	.0001	—

Behavior Modes for Multiplier

Mode	Probability	Behavior
w (working)	.9990	Out = (In1 * In2) mod 32
s (shorted)	.0003	Out = 0
d (drop MSB)	.0006	Out = (In1 * In2) mod 16
u (unknown)	.0001	—

FIGURE 9.3. The behavioral modes of the components in our sample model, including the normal working mode, known fault modes, and a catchall unknown fault mode. The probabilities provided by the manufacturer are the prior probabilities that a given component is broken. The abbreviation MSB refers to the most significant bit.

The names In1 and In2 refer to the two inputs to the adders and multipliers. We use the convention in our circuit diagrams that In1 is the upper input and In2 is the lower one.

In Figure 9.1 the behavior and component specifications are both part of the system model. The other major part of the system model is the fault model, where a "fault" is what can go wrong in TS-1. As discussed earlier, fault models can include diseases in medical diagnosis systems or environmental effects. In TS-1, the fault model expresses how components can be broken. It specifies the behavior of specific kinds of faults and gives the prior probability that a component of the given type is faulted in that way. In practice, we assume there is a finite (and usually quite small) number of possible faults. Probabilities of faults can be determined by statistical testing, provided by the fictional manufacturer of components. Figure 9.3 lists the various behavior modes of the adder and multiplier in TS-1, including the normal working mode and a catchall unknown fault mode for both kinds of components.

The Main Subtasks for Diagnosis

The basic paradigm for diagnosis can be understood as the interaction of observation and prediction. Observation is based on what we can see or detect about a physical artifact, the system of interest. Prediction is based on a computational model of the system, which indicates what it is supposed to do under various circumstances. The model supports expectations about the system's behavior. When a difference or discrepancy is detected between between observations and predictions, we begin diagnosis. Presuming that its model is correct, a diagnostic system attempts to account for the discrepancy in terms of defects in the physical system, such as broken components or, in the case of medical diagnoses, diseases of various kinds.

The main subtasks in diagnosis are:

■ *Recognizing abnormalities and conflicts.* A diagnosis task usually starts when some data are presented indicating potentially abnormal symptoms or measurements. The first step in diagnosis is to determine how the data acquired so far conflict with expectations. This step identifies ways in which the data are abnormal, are inconsistent with each other, or are inconsistent with a model of the system being diagnosed.

■ *Generating and testing hypotheses.* The next step is to identify or generate hypotheses to explain the data conflicts. In a hierarchical approach, this step may involve refining general hypotheses. Testing means to determine which hypotheses are consistent with the data, which are inconsistent, and which are unresolved. In principle, generation could be a simple and systematic process for constructing alternatives, to be followed by a separate process for knowledge-based testing and ranking of the alternatives. In practice, however, diagnostic systems use similar knowledge to guide both.

■ *Discriminating among hypotheses.* This step reflects the goal of making a sharp diagnosis. It must gather new information about the system, such as by selecting a new probe point, by running tests, or by perturbing the system state and gathering new data. It determines what new information is needed to rule out hypotheses.

These three subtasks are our points of departure for comparing different approaches to building knowledge-based systems for diagnosis. For each subtask we explore the phenomena that arise and compare approaches.

Therapy or repair selection involves considerations beyond those for diagnosis itself, especially in cases where there are long-term treatments or progressive diseases. Analysis of the therapy or repair space and its associated operations is mostly outside the scope of this chapter. Chapter 8 includes a case study of the therapy model used by MYCIN, based on a configuration model.

9.2.1 *Recognizing Abnormalities and Conflicts*

In diagnostic practice, some evidence is used initially to determine whether to perform diagnosis. In a medical setting, the initial data are called the "presenting symptoms." In some domains the determination of whether the data indicate an abnormal condition is just a simple screening step preliminary to the main parts of diagnosis. Other diagnostic systems always perform a diagnosis, starting with whatever data the system is given. In the following we consider some of the issues that arise.

The task at this point is to determine whether the known data about the system indicate that the system is in an abnormal state, requiring diagnosis and subsequent repair or treatment. This is a smaller job than diagnosis. We do not need to determine exactly what is wrong. We need to decide whether to begin a thorough diagnostic process. This task includes making judgments about the signal or probe values at hand. For the present, we ignore systems that adjust themselves, such as self-adjusting equipment or homeostatic biological systems. In such systems, determining whether the system is in a "normal" state can be complex.

Figure 9.4 presents an example where an abnormality or conflict would be recognized for TS-1. In this example, we are given all the integer inputs to the circuit. The dashed boxes indicate predictions made using the behavior rules for TS-1. For each prediction, the components listed between braces are assumed to be working. In other words, the rule used to predict the value assumes that the component is in the normal working behavior mode. A conflict arises when the output of A2 is predicted to be 16 but is measured to be 0.

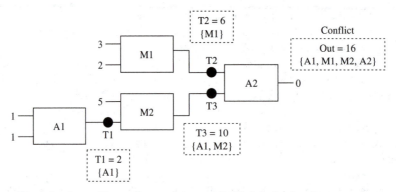

FIGURE 9.4.   Example of a conflict or abnormality noted in TS-1, indicating that some measured value is inconsistent with other measured values and the assumption that the components are all working. The numbers given next to inputs and outputs in the diagram are measured probe values. For example, the inputs to A1 are both 1. The values given in dashed boxes are values predicted by the system model assuming that the listed components are working.

Figure 9.5 presents a functional diagram of another, more complex system to be diagnosed. The figure is a block diagram for an electronic circuit, but in principle it could represent any kind of a system. On the left side of Figure 9.5 are shown a number of causes, input signals or "inputs." The question marks indicate signals whose values are not known. Effects or outputs of the system are also shown. These are the labeled lines on the right side of the figure. For example, the value of the output signal a is not known and the value of the output b is 1. In some systems, the distinction between inputs and outputs is not meaningful and the terminology of causes

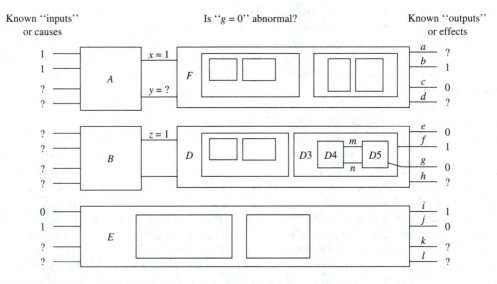

FIGURE 9.5.   Functional diagram of a system being diagnosed.

and effects is preferred. In a medical example, "heart rate," "temperature," and "nausea" might be examples of effects.

Given that the output g has value 0, we ask whether this value is normal or expected. Various properties of the system in Figure 9.5 can conspire to make this question less straightforward than it might seem. If we have a complete simulation model of the system, then in principle we can run the simulation given the inputs, predict the outputs or effects, and compare them to what is measured. Wherever the predictions are different from what has been measured, we note the conflicts.

This approach is not always feasible because it requires knowing so much. The process of computing a value for signals like g requires that we know values for other signals that may not be available. For example, if the value of g depends on the unknown values for the input signals to module B, then the simulation value for g cannot be determined.

Because of the clocking of signals and devices in digital circuits, a signal can usually flow only from inputs to outputs. An adder cannot be made to subtract by reversing the "flow" of its signals. However, this physical directionality is not a limitation for constraint propagation in diagnostic reasoning. Suppose we are given that the output of an adder in TS-1 has the value 10 and that one of its inputs has the value 6. Using its addition behavior in "reverse," we can subtract and predict that the value of its other input is 4. Rules for reasoning backward from component output values (effects) to input values (causes) are sometimes called **antibehavior rules**. Using such rules increases the number of predictions that can be made from limited data. In either case, predictions are of the form "g will have the value 1 if $f = 1$ and $D4$ and $D5$ are working." Contradictions have the form "given that $g = 0$ and $f = 1$, at least one of the components $\{D3, D4, D5\}$ must be broken."

Most approaches to prediction are logically incomplete. This leads to cases where additional analysis can be used in making predictions and in finding contradictions. For example, it might turn out that $g = 1$ for *all* possible combinations of inputs to module $D5$. In such cases, we can infer the output values even when the particular input values are not known. Given no values for signals m or n, one constraint propagation scheme might be stymied where another could determine that $g = 0$ is always abnormal, implicating components inside $D5$.

Figure 9.6 summarizes approaches for determining whether diagnosis is needed. These approaches differ in the form of analysis they carry out. On the right side are approaches that use system models to predict behavior using physical models and the assumption that components operate according to known rules.

Recognizing Abnormalities

Look for unusual data "Classification"		Look for differences "Conflict recognition"	
Table of thresholds	Classification network	Behavior propagation	Simulation model

Eclectic	Systematic
No structure to behavior mapping	Maps structure to behavior

FIGURE 9.6. Alternative approaches for recognizing abnormalities and beginning diagnosis.

On the left side are classification approaches that classify the data directly as normal or abnormal. A classification approach can be eclectic. Rules for identifying particular cases of abnormal data, which may be important but overlooked by systematic but incomplete constraint propagation strategies, can be added on a case-by-case basis. Classification approaches to detecting abnormalities can be implemented equivalently as decision networks or rule systems. In simple cases where the data are independent, classification may simply use separate tables for each signal.

9.2.2 *Generating and Testing Hypotheses*

A diagnostic hypothesis is an account of the causes of symptoms. Hypothesis generation involves reasoning from symptoms to diagnoses, which are explanations of what may plausibly have caused the symptoms. Hypothesis generation is a search problem, and there are many ways to approach it. In the ideal case, the search process tries to generate all possible diagnostic hypotheses. In practice, search methods prune low-probability diagnoses early.

To test a hypothesis is to compare predictions made on the basis of the hypothesis with observed data. When the predictions for a hypothesis do not bear out, the hypothesis is usually rejected. Because the reasoning and representation issues are so intertwined, we consider generation and testing together in the following.

Several themes are woven into our discussion of hypothesis generation and testing:

■ *Open-ended models of failure*. The simplest troubleshooting systems describe diagnoses in terms of specific kinds of component failures. But failures can result from many different kinds of interactions, some of which might not be included in a particular model. More powerful approaches to modeling expand the basis for plausible diagnoses incrementally in a systematic way.

■ *Singleton versus composite diagnoses*. The simplest diagnostic systems assume that the system being diagnosed has only a single fault or a single disease. This assumption greatly simplified the earliest diagnostic systems and is still widely used. Unfortunately, it is not generally valid and leads to incorrect results. A second approach is to assume that faults can be determined one at a time and then subtract away the corresponding symptoms, analyzing the "residue" for further diagnoses. This approach also leads to certain systematic difficulties. Better approaches use composite diagnoses, in which different combinations of possible faults or diseases are considered as a group. The challenge in this approach is to control the combinatorics.

■ *Hypothesis hierarchies*. The combinatorics of composite diagnoses and other considerations of efficiency lead to approaches to diagnosis based on hierarchical search. Typically, the hierarchies are based on abstraction and containment relations of functional subsystems.

■ *Independent versus interacting causes*. A basic issue in diagnosis is determining which evidence implicates which faults or diseases. Systems lacking models of how symptoms interact have inherent difficulties in assigning credit or blame to diagnoses.

We now consider these themes in more detail.

Models of Subsystem Failures and Interactions

The data space is about what is observable and the hypothesis space is about what is conceivable, meaning what can conceivably go wrong with a system. In the following we consider the variety of approaches that have been used in characterizing this. The most basic issue in defining a diagnostic hypothesis space is determining and specifying what can go wrong in the functioning of a physical artifact.

In the simplest troubleshooting systems a diagnosis is expressed in terms of faults of particular components. In TS-1, each component has four behavior modes. Besides the normal mode, there are three abnormal modes including one mode where the behavior of a component is not known. Diagnostic systems generally have some most primitive level of description for components. The space of possible diagnoses is determined by accounting for all the possible faults for the primitive devices. Thus, in TS-1 where adders have four possible modes, then either adder could be in any of these modes.

In the design of component models, much variability is possible not only in the level of description but also in deciding what constitutes a part and what faults are possible. Even in electronic domains, where there is a great deal of engineering practice to draw on, variations are possible. We illustrate this by considering the role of "wires" in models for electronic troubleshooting.

In many troubleshooting systems, a wire is not modeled as a device and is therefore not recognized as being capable of having a fault. This presents no difficulty so long as no "wire faults" occur in practice. However, in all electronic technologies, wires are conductors and are subject to faults. If a conductor gets too thin, its electrical resistance increases. If it is thin at a particular point or if too much current passes through a wire, it can melt, leading to an open circuit. Conductors are separated from other conductors by insulating material. Extraneous pieces of conductor material or holes in the insulators can result in unintended conductive connections. These shorts are called "bridging faults." If we want to predict whether a bridging fault is likely between two wires, then we need to take into account the physical layout and manufacturing techniques. In general, the likelihood of a bridging fault is greater if two wires are close together. There can also be interactions between conductors even when they are not connected. When current flows through a wire, it also sets up electrostatic and electromagnetic fields. If two wires are near each other, these fields can cause capacitive or inductive coupling of signals between the wires even if they do not touch. Such coupling usually corresponds to a design error but can also result when long cables are unintentionally moved close to power lines.

The point of this discussion about wires is that the "fault possibilities" that we build into our models reflect assumptions about what physical effects in the system are likely and important. Behavior depends on causal pathways, by which activity on one part can have effects on another. To answer the question "what can go wrong" in a system, we need to determine what mechanisms are present and what parts of a system can interact. In the process of designing an artifact, certain causal pathways are emphasized over others. Although the models we used in our diagnostic systems tend to emphasize the interactions that are planned in the design, there may be other interactions, too.

The notion of causal pathways also depends on identifying what interactions between components are possible. A diagnostic system explains malfunctions using only the terms and phenomena in its model. When some pathways of interaction are not included, the diagnostic system

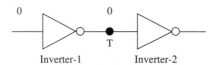

FIGURE 9.7.   If test point T is not 1, the determination of suspected components depends on which inter-actions are modeled. In the most common electrical model, only Inverter-1 is suspected. In a model that includes interactions through current flow, a failure of either inverter could cause the effect. (Adapted from an example in Hamscher, 1988, page 30.)

is blind to some of the possibilities. For example, Figure 9.7 shows a simple electronic circuit with two inverters in series. A common model of digital circuits says each node is driven to 0 or 1 by just one gate. According to this model, a discrepancy at testpoint T can only be caused by nodes upstream, that is, by Inverter-1. However, the gates also interact through current flow. It is possible for the second inverter to fail in such a way that it pulls down the voltage at the test point. In this case, the common digital model yields the wrong answer because it does not include a possible pathway of interaction.

Diagnostic systems make closed-world assumptions about the range of possible interac-tions. The issue here is not that models make assumptions. Indeed, simplifying assumptions are essential to keep models tractable. The issue is that the assumptions need to be identified and managed.

Recognizing the tension between the completeness or precision of a model and the need to constrain the diagnostic search, Davis and Hamscher (1988) proposed that candidate generation should be thought of in terms of causal pathways of decreasing probability. Experienced engi-neers know that some things are more likely to go wrong than others. As a result, they first attempt to generate solutions that employ simpler and more likely hypotheses. Only in the face of a contradiction do they fall back on more elaborate and less likely possibilities. Davis and Hamscher found three principles in the cognitive models used by engineers:

1. Engineers have a set of categories of what can go wrong.
2. There is an ordering criterion that indicates which categories of hypotheses to enter-tain first.
3. The categories are ordered but none is permanently excluded.

These principles embody an alternative to a fixed closed-world approach in the spirit of the con-centric models of exceptions discussed for the qualification problem in Chapter 3. At each stage, there is a search space of possible diagnoses. When nothing in the space amounts to a satisfac-tory solution, the space is expanded to include categories previously thought too implausible. Metaphorically, a single closed world is replaced by a series of concentric worlds, each repre-senting more pathways for interactions than its predecessor. Within each concentric world it is important to keep the search for hypotheses as constrained as possible. In the bridge-fault exam-ple, a system should not examine every pair of adjacent pins, but just the ones that could account for the observed discrepancies.

Diagnoses: Single Faults versus Multiple Faults

The most likely cause of misbehavior in many systems is the failure of a single component. Jumping from plausibility to certainty, many simple diagnostic systems assume in every case that there is at most one fault or disease. This simplifies the generation of hypotheses and enables reasoning by elimination.

Unfortunately, the single-fault assumption is not always valid in practice. Not only is it possible for multiple faults or diseases to co-occur, but also they are not always independent. For example, a failure of one electronic part may cause other parts of a circuit to become overloaded and subsequently to fail. Bad alignment of wheels in a car can cause tires to wear badly and to fail. A patient weakened by one disease is often more vulnerable to additional afflictions.

To simplify the accounting of multiple causes, some diagnostic systems adopt a sequential, or one-cause-at-a-time, approach. The basic idea is to order the symptoms in terms of importance and to iteratively identify which candidates explain the main symptoms. When the best-matching causes are selected, their symptoms are marked as "accounted for" and causes for the "residual symptoms" are then sought. This approach follows the ground rules of sequential decision making in which one decision problem must be resolved before its successor problems are started. Unfortunately, the complications of interactions among causes as discussed later make this approach unreliable.

An attractive alternative is to consider combinations of multiple faults at the same time. This is called a **set-covering** or **composite-diagnosis approach**. This technique goes back at least to Reggia, Nau, and Wang (1983). It was one of the most important advances in diagnostic systems over the past few years because it provides a systematic basis for reasoning about difficult diagnostic cases, where there are separate but potentially interacting effects of multiple faults or diseases.

The main advantage of this approach is that it provides a systematic basis for considering the interacting effects of multiple causes. The main challenge with the approach is that there are so many combinations of causes! Every combination of faults is a possible diagnostic hypothesis. The smallest set of components is the empty set, meaning there are no broken components. When the single-fault assumption common to many diagnostic programs is used, there are only n candidates involving one component each for a system of n components. However, in the general case, every component could either be working or not working, leading to 2^n combinations. Figure 9.8 illustrates a graph of these combinations, arranged according to the terms of the binomial theorem. The bottom row contains all combinations of single faults, the next row all combinations of double faults, the next row all combinations of triple faults, and so on. The lines connect sets in each row to their supersets in the next row above.

As shown in Figure 9.9, there are 32 combinations of faults for a system with 5 components. This exponential complexity is inherent in any approach that can consider all possible combinations of faults and is a major obstacle in realistic diagnostic problems. Even considering only one fault mode per component, there are a total of 2^{50}, or roughly 10^{15}, possible candidates in a 50-component system. The probability of individual candidates usually drops off rapidly as more faults are postulated. Nonetheless, a best-first search in a 50-component problem would contend with roughly 20,000 candidates of up to three faults. Suppose we consider larger and more realistic electromechanical systems of 500 components. As Figure 9.9 indicates, even limiting attention to candidates with no more than three faulty components, there are millions of can-

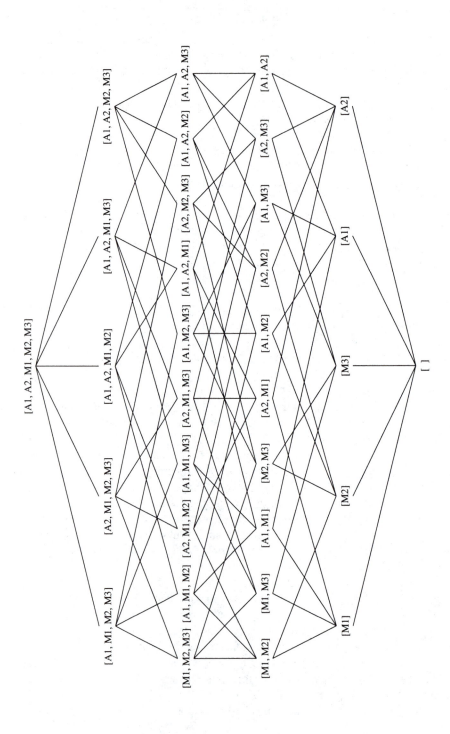

FIGURE 9.8. Sets and subsets of the five components, A1, A2, M1, M2, and M3. Each set corresponds to a diagnostic hypothesis, where the elements in the set are faulty and other components are working. The top row is the set where all components are broken and the bottom row is the set where no components are broken. Each row corresponds to a term in the binomial theorem, indicating the combinations of k broken components. Thus, there are 5 single-component sets, 10 double-component sets, 10 triple-component sets, 5 quadruple-component sets, and 1 set of 5 components.

684

Number of Components	Number of Possible Diagnostic Hypotheses for k faults			
	$k=1$	$k=2$	$k=3$	Total Over All k
5	5	10	10	$2^5 = 32$
10	10	45	120	$2^{10}=1024$
50	50	1,225	19,600	$2^{50}=1.1 \times 10^{15}$
100	100	4,950	161,700	$2^{100}=1.3 \times 10^{30}$
300	300	44,850	4,455,100	$2^{300}=2 \times 10^{90}$
500	500	124,750	20,708,499	$2^{500}=3.3 \times 10^{150}$
1,000	1,000	499,500	166,167,000	$2^{1000}=1.1 \times 10^{301}$
5,000	5,000	12,497,500	20,820,835,000	$2^{5000} = 1.6 \times 10^{1505}$

FIGURE 9.9. The number of candidate diagnostic hypotheses grows exponentially.

didates to consider. A goal of researchers working in this area is to diagnose systems with thousands of components. In the following sections we see how different system models affect diagnostic complexity and how different approaches seek to cope with it. Every diagnostic system that can reason about multiple faults needs to cope with this explosion by drastically narrowing the set of candidates.

You may wonder at this point whether handling multiple faults is important enough to warrant all this complexity. The importance of multiple faults depends a great deal on the situation. In medicine, the care of indigents often involves treating multiple infections and other problems. In electronic and mechanical systems, the failure of one component can cause other components to fail. In cases where reliability is a crucial or where troubleshooting and repair are expensive or inconvenient, an ability to diagnose and repair multiple faults has substantial value.

Figure 9.10 returns to our TS-1 model to present an example of computing candidates and their probabilities. In this figure we have the conflict or abnormal reading at the output of A2 as shown. One explanation for the conflict is that the component A2 is in mode d, meaning it has dropped its most significant bit. In the figure, this diagnostic hypothesis is indicated by the notation $[A2_d]$, which means A2 is in the d mode and all the other unnamed components are in working modes. The prior probability of this singleton candidate is the product of the probabilities that each component is in the mode indicated.

Figure 9.11 gives an example of a possible composite candidate, $[M1_s, M2_s]$, explaining the same conflict. This diagnostic hypothesis is that components M1 and M2 are both shorted, so that their outputs are zero. Figure 9.11 gives the prior probability of this candidate in the same fashion as before. From the example it is clear how the prior probability of a composite candidate is usually much less than the prior probability of a singleton candidate.

Hierarchies for Diagnostic Hypotheses

Hierarchical approaches reduce the combinatorics of search on large problems. The design and roles of hierarchies in diagnosis domains relate not only to hypothesis generation, but also to hypothesis testing and discrimination. As in hierarchical approaches to other kinds of problem solving, hierarchies provide a means of describing and reasoning about classes of solutions rather than just individual solutions. The effectiveness of a hierarchical approach depends on the

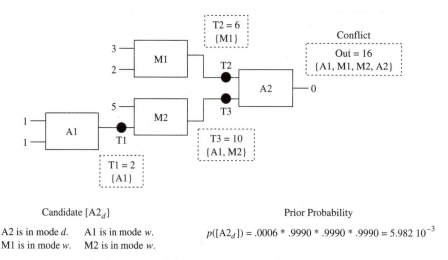

Candidate [A2_d]   Prior Probability

A2 is in mode d.   A1 is in mode w. $p([A2_d]) = .0006 * .9990 * .9990 * .9990 = 5.982 \ 10^{-3}$
M1 is in mode w.   M2 is in mode w.

FIGURE 9.10.   Example of a singleton candidate and its prior probability.

availability of knowledge and problem-solving operations that can exploit the class boundaries induced by the hierarchies. As usual, the strategy of a hierarchical approach is to divide and conquer.

Figure 9.12 presents a hierarchy for guiding hypothesis generation on a particularly simple system model. In case 1 in the figure, we begin with a single element, corresponding (say) to a single device like others in a system to be diagnosed. The behavior of element A is described relative to its four external connections. Case 2 connects 16 elements together. The resulting system has 16 external connections and 24 internal ones. Reasoning about the aggregate behavior requires that we compute the interactions of elements through all the viable combinations of states.

Case 3 suggests how four composed elements can be abstracted to a single "macro-element." In creating this abstraction we combine elements and connections together describing their aggregate behavior as a single element, but in less detail. Macro-connections are analogous to the aggregation of wires into buses that carry composite signals. In case 4 we compose four macro-elements together. Case 4 has the same number of primitive elements as case 2 but presents two smaller problems for diagnosis instead of one large problem. Using just one level of

Candidate [M1_s, M2_s]
M1 is in mode s.
M2 is in mode s.
A1 is in mode w.
A2 is in mode w.

Prior probability
$p([M1_s, M2_s]) = .0003 * .0003 * .9990 * .9990 = 8.982 \ 10^{-8}$

FIGURE 9.11.   Example of a composite candidate and its prior probability.

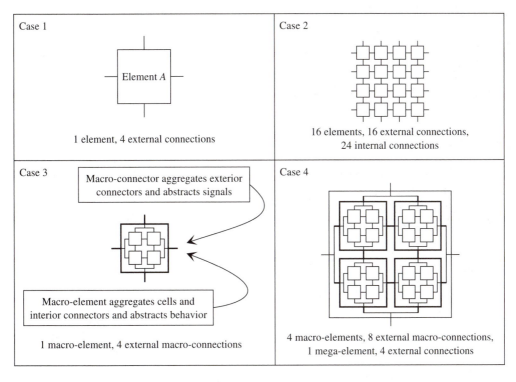

FIGURE 9.12. Abstraction is the key to reducing complexity in hypothesis hierarachies. Case 4 reduces the number of elements to be considered at once.

abstraction, the complexity of the outer description is reduced to four macro-elements and eight macro-connections. Recursively, we can introduce another "mega" level of aggregation and abstraction to bring us back to one mega-element with four mega-connections. Introducing multiple levels of abstraction transforms diagnosis to a sequence of smaller subproblems. In the exercises we consider how the time complexity of diagnosis depends on of the number and size of the subproblems.

Different kinds of elements and heterogenous mixtures of elements compose according to different rules. Typically, new abstractions are required for each level of aggregation. Still, the basic point about the combinatorics remains the same. The complexity of diagnosis can increase exponentially with the number of components. Abstractions extend the size of the systems that can be diagnosed. Most diagnostic practice uses **lumped-element models**, which are models that "lump" functionality into specific and separate elements rather than treating functionality as completely distributed in space. Describing such models requires abstracting both the elements and their connections.

All the hierarchical systems we considered have a bottom, most primitive level of representation. Higher levels of organization are defined by composition of the lower ones. Choosing a primitive level leads to three fundamental commitments. First, it makes some failures indistinguishable to the troubleshooting system. Every failure inside a primitive component will result in the same diagnosis. Second, it makes some failures representable only as failures in multiple components. For example, a short circuit between two supposedly noninteracting components would be diagnosed as a failure of the two components. Third, the lower the level of detail, the more work is involved in predicting behavior. This is not to say that one cannot add parts or even levels later, corresponding to building a new foundation or basement under an existing house. In some practical systems where size is an issue or where a mixture of technologies has been used, it may be appropriate to represent different parts of the system at different levels of detail.

The use of hierarchies to organize levels of hypotheses is not limited to diagnosis of human-made systems. In medical diagnoses, concepts about organs and functional subsystems such as digestive systems, immune systems, and circulatory systems are often used in organizing diagnostic hypotheses. The value of this is easy to see. Organs and other subsystems tend to carry out a single major bodily function: transporting materials in the blood, removing waste products, exchanging oxygen and carbon dioxide, destroying foreign substances, and so on. Any disease of that organ tends to diminish its effectiveness in carrying out that function, causing similar effects and symptoms.

This phenomenon also arises in digital subsystems. Some behaviorally complex digital components can have many different kinds of internal faults. At any particular level of behavioral abstraction, some set of faults will collapse onto a single misbehavior. In hardware design, current design practice tends to minimize the number of parts and to implement complex behavior using software or firmware for microprocessors, which use the same hardware components repeatedly for several steps in an overall computation. In these implementations, failures at one stage tend to cascade so that complex devices soon fail catastrophically. Thus, after testing subsystems on simple cases, experienced troubleshooters can reliably treat entire complex subsystems as very low likelihood suspects. Many complex systems either work completely or fail utterly.

Finally, hierarchies need not necessarily be based on models of physical faults. In medical domains the hierarchies can taxonomize infecting agents in terms of families of related microorganisms, microorganisms that respond to the same treatments, or microorganisms that result in some of the same symptoms. A taxonomy of diseases in medicine is also called a nosology. There is no single right way to construct a **nosology**. Such taxonomies can be based on anatomical locus such as diseases of the liver, caustative agent such as type of bacteria, or symptoms such as swellings. Multiple relations for categorizing can be combined in a single framework of specialization. To cite an example from ABEL (Patil, 1981), renal disease is defined to be a disease of the renal system (anatomical locus). Renal failure is then defined as a renal disease characterized by low urine output (physiological locus). Acute renal failure is renal failure with sudden and severe onset, and, finally, drug-induced acute renal failure is acute renal failure of chemically toxic etiology. Each step in the above definitions defines a disease that is further specialized by one of its primary characterizations.

Independent versus Interacting Causes

Accounting for which symptoms correspond to which diagnoses is crucial, in both generating and testing diagnostic hypotheses. Figure 9.13 summarizes some possibilities both for the ideal case and for complications. In this figure, C1 and C2 are two possible causes of misbehavior in a system being diagnosed. The function S is the set of symptoms that are visible given a set of causes.

Ideal case
- Single symptoms, $|S(\{C1\})| = 1$. Each cause has exactly one symptom.
- No overlap, $S(\{C1\}) \cap S(\{C2\}) = \emptyset$. Different causes have no symptoms in common.
- Independence of symptoms. $S(\{C1, C2\}) = S(\{C1\}) \cup S(\{C2\})$. The symptoms observed when there are multiple causes is the union of the symptoms that are seen when the causes are present individually.

Complications
- Multiple symptoms, $|S(\{C1\})| > 1$. A fault or disease can have more than one symptom.
- Overlapping symptoms, $S(\{C1\}) \cap S(\{C2\}) \neq \emptyset$. Different faults or diseases can lead to the same symptoms.
- Compensating symptoms, $S(\{C1, C2\}) \subset S(\{C1\}) \cup S(\{C2\})$. When two diseases or faults are both present, *fewer* symptoms may appear than in the union of their separate sets of symptoms because of compensating effects.
- Synergistic symptoms, $S(\{C1\}) \cup S(\{C2\}) \subset S(\{C1, C2\})$. When two diseases or faults are both present, there can be *more* symptoms than there are in the union of the sets of their individual symptoms.

FIGURE 9.13. Idealized and realistic relations between causes and symptoms. In this figure, C1 and C2 are two possible causes of faulty behavior and S is a function that maps a set of causes to the set of observable symptoms.

The first phenomenon, multiple symptoms, is no surprise. Diseases and component faults can change several aspects of a system's behavior, so it is not surprising that a routine sampling of observations often detects more than one symptom from a single disease. However, this has implications for diagnostic systems that implicate causes from the presence of symptoms. One issue is that different symptoms are not necessarily independent. When they are related to or caused by the same underlying disease state, they should not be counted as independent evidence. Approaches that add "evoking strengths" cumulatively and independently from whatever symptoms have been observed favor diagnoses with the most commonly observed findings.

The second phenomenon, overlapping symptoms, is also familiar in medical domains because some symptoms are common to multiple diseases. For example, fever is associated with most types of infections, many forms of cancer, blood abnormalities, cardiovascular disorders, and diseases associated with abnormal immune systems. One approach to accounting for overlapping symptoms is to represent and reason about intermediate pathophysiological states. These intermediate states represent the fact that disease states both share symptoms and lead to multiple observables. This representation goes beyond the metaphor of having fixed fingerprints or "symptom profiles" for different diseases. It provides a basis for factoring symptoms into interdependent sets. It enables a diagnostic program to attribute symptoms to causes while diminishing the influence of interdependent manifestations of a single disease.

The compensating symptom phenomenon occurs when two diseases exert opposite influences on some observable parameter. For example, electrolyte and acid-base systems in the human body are influenced by many factors. A patient with salmonellosis and vomiting may exhibit normal acidity. Vomiting causes metabolic alkalosis, which raises the pH, and salmonellosis causes moderate metabolic acidosis. which lowers pH. Together, the two effects on pH cancel each other leading to an almost normal pH in the presence of other symptoms. Diagnostic systems for reasoning about compensating systems must reason about the symptoms of a group of causes, rather than reasoning serially about the symptoms for individual causes.

Synergistic symptoms have also been noted in medical practice. The synergistic symptom phenomenon occurs when contributions are additive and cross a threshold. For example, a patient with mild heart disease and lung infection is likely to have dispnea, a shortness of breath. Neither of the two causes is usually sufficient by itself to cause the effect, but taken together they go over a threshold and cause an additional observable effect.

9.2.3 *Discriminating among Hypotheses*

With some exceptions, most diagnostic tasks are limited more by resources for gathering data than by resources for reasoning or computation. In this common situation, the key challenge is not efficient decision making or weighing of evidence, but rather efficient gathering of evidence. This focuses attention on alternative strategies for acquiring data to discriminate among hypotheses. Evidence available at the beginning provides only a partial description of the initial state of the diagnostic situation. While such "presenting signs and symptoms" can be suggestive of abnormal or pathological conditions, in most cases conclusive evidence concerning an underlying cause must be obtained by additional steps. Furthermore, it is seldom practical to routinely obtain all of the possible data. There are costs, delays, and other factors that constrain the use of data-gathering operations.

When is there enough evidence to establish a fault or disease in diagnosis? Roughly speaking, for most diagnostic programs the answer is "when all of the other plausible alternatives are ruled out." Diagnosis proceeds by elimination rather than by seeking more and more evidence for a favorite hypothesis.

One reason favoring this competitive elimination approach is the multiple symptom phenomenon cited previously. Faults and diseases can cause multiple observable symptoms. Observing more of them does not necessarily make a favored hypothesis more certain. Diagnostic problem solving is usually posed in terms of a competition between mutually exclusive hypotheses.

The basic issue in discriminating among hypotheses is determining what data to acquire next. In troubleshooting, this is usually formulated in terms of the selection of new probe points. Alternatively, it could involve creating new "input test vectors" that would drive the system into different observable states. It could be reformulated in terms of the selection of test programs to run to test a computer system. In medical domains, the probe points are analogous to biomedical laboratory tests, noninvasive scanning techniques, or exploratory surgery. The test vectors are analogous to medical interventions, such as administering a drug. Most research in diagnosis systems has focused on probe selection. Although knowledge systems for generating test vectors have been built (Shirley, 1989), discussion of that topic goes beyond the scope of this chapter.

The most straightforward and widely used technique for selecting probe points is called the **guided-probe approach**. This approach starts at a point where a discrepancy has been detected. The idea is to follow it upstream to components that influence the output of the one where the discrepancy was noted. The search process focuses on those elements whose outputs are also discrepancies. The search continues until a component has been identified as having an incorrect output but whose inputs are correct. If the component receives valid information but produces a bad result, it must be faulted.

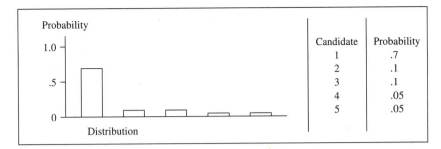

FIGURE 9.14.   An example of a distribution of hypotheses with different probabilities.

Although the guided-probe technique is simple, it often uses more measurements than are needed. The technique does not make much use of reasoning from a system model and it is possible to do much better. This is important because the most limited resource in many diagnostic tasks is the time to take measurements and observations.

Shannon Entropy

In the ideal case, diagnosis is complete when there is exactly one candidate with probability one, where a candidate may represent a set of multiple faults or diseases. This is the sharpest or most definitive diagnosis. A decidedly worse case is when there many candidates, all having minuscule probabilities. When there are competing candidates, further appropriate measurements are needed to discriminate among them. Figure 9.14 gives an example of a distribution of probabilities for competing candidates by charting the probabilities associated with different hypotheses. In this example there are five candidates. There is a dominant candidate with probability .7 and four lesser candidates with lower probabilities.

Probe points are sometimes compared according to the "sharpness" of the expected diagnosis, where the sharpness is a property of the expected distribution of candidate probabilities. In the ideal sharp case, there is exactly one candidate diagnosis of probability one. Figure 9.15 gives two more examples of candidate probability distributions. The first distribution in Figure 9.15 is further from the ideal case than the second one. Thus, a probe site with the second distribution is sharper than one with the first.

Many diagnostic systems described in this chapter use an evaluation function based on the Shannon entropy measure of information to measure diagnostic sharpness. **Shannon entropy** is defined as follows:

$$H = -\sum^{\text{all } i} p_i \log p_i$$

where the p_i are the probabilities of the candidate diagnoses that are not yet ruled out. Usually, entropy is computed using the natural logarithms. First we note that $\log(1)$ is zero and that $\log p$ is negative for all other p between 0 and 1. This shows that the qualitative behavior of H yields a value of zero for the ideal sharp distribution of a single candidate and higher values for cases having multiple candidates.

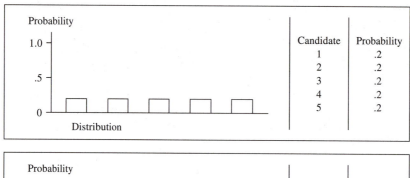

FIGURE 9.15.   The first distribution is further from an ideal than the second because we need find only one measurement to discriminate between its candidates and finish the diagnosis.

Several of the exercises in this section are intended to provide experience in reasoning about entropy and diagnostic sharpness. Exercise 2 provides a series of candidate distributions that demonstrate that entropy provides an intuitive measure of sharpness. Exercise 3 considers the appropriateness of entropy as a measure of diagnostic sharpness for certain simple cases. Exercise 4 shows how entropy estimates the number of future probes needed to reach a definitive diagnostic conclusion about the set of candidates.

Figure 9.16 uses our TS-1 model to present an example of computing the entropy of a set of candidates consistent with a probe value. We suppose again that a conflict has been detected at the output of A2. A generate-and-test procedure has created a set of candidates that is consistent with the fault data or symptoms. In this example, the generator has focused on single- and double-fault candidates. For simplicity in this example, we leave out candidates that include an unknown mode since they have very low probability anyway. There are two singleton candidates and one double-fault candidate. The distribution of probabilities is shown together with the entropy calculation that measures the sharpness of the distribution.

The Selection of Probe Points

The basic idea in selecting probe points is to pick those that are expected to increase the sharpness of diagnosis. So far in our example, we have shown how to compute the entropy given a complete set of candidates. However, at the time that we need to select a probe site, we do not actually know what value the probe will measure.

A common strategy for dealing with this issue is called **one-step look-ahead**. For each probe point there are several possible values. Each possible value is compatible with some of the diagnostic candidates and incompatible with others. Each candidate diagnosis assigns operating

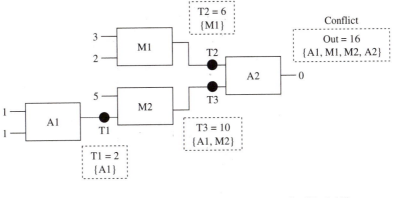

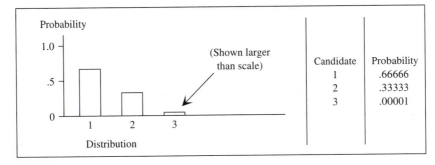

	Candidate	Prior Probability	Normalized Probability
1	$[A2_d]$	$5.982\ 10^{-3}$	.66666
2	$[A2_s]$	$2.991\ 10^{-3}$	.33333
3	$[M1_s, M2_s]$	$8.982\ 10^{-8}$	.00001

$$H = -\sum^{\text{all } i} p_i \log p_i = (.2703 + .3662 + .00011) = .6366$$

FIGURE 9.16. Example of computing entropy for a set of candidates.

modes to the components. By combining the modes with the known measurements, we can often predict what value would be measured at a probe point.

We can estimate the probability of each possible value at a probe point as the sum of the probabilities of all the candidates that are consistent with that value. We then compute the entropy of the distribution that would result if all the incompatible candidates were ruled out and their probabilities were redistributed among the remaining candidates. Because there are fewer candidates, the new candidate distribution would be sharper than the one we started with—measuring the increase in our information.

Following this approach, we estimate the expected entropy for a probe point t_i as follows:

$$H_e(t_i) = \sum_{k=1}^{m} p(t_i = v_{ik})\, H(t_i = v_{ik})$$

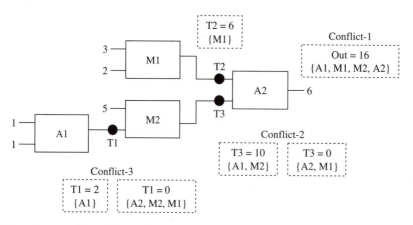

FIGURE 9.17.   An example requiring selection of a probe point.

where m is the number of distinct data values and $H(t_i = v_{ik})$ is the entropy resulting if t_i is measured to be v_{ik}. The estimated entropy of a probe point is the weighted average of the entropies of the distributions of candidates that result for all possible values that might be observed. The weight used for the entropy of the distribution of candidates for each possible value is the estimated probability of the measured value. Momentarily, we consider some complications in assigning these probabilities, but first we look at a simple example.

Figure 9.17 gives an example of a diagnostic situation for TS-1 in which the selection of a probe point is more interesting. In this example, the output of A2 is measured to be 6 antibehavior rules that are used to detect conflicts. Conflict-1 arises from the simulation of all of the components in TS-1. If we assume that M1 and A2 are working, we can use an antibehavior rule to predict that T3 must be 0. This prediction of T3 conflicts with the other prediction for T3 that assumes that A1 and M2 are working. If we further assume that M2 is working, we can work backward with antibehavior rules again to predict that T1 is 0. This conflicts with another prediction that T1 is 2, based on the assumption that A1 is working.

Figure 9.18 lists some candidates for explaining the conflicts in Figure 9.17. The only fault mode for A2 that explains conflict-1 is that A2 is in an unknown mode. The other modes—working, shorted, or drop most significant bit—simply do not explain the output. On the other hand, M2 or A1 could be shorted or be in unknown modes.

As the probabilities of the candidates decrease, we limit the search by imposing an arbitrary cutoff point. In this example, the cutoff point corresponds to the beginning of the double-fault candidates. Candidates below the cutoff point are ignored until higher probability candidates are ruled out. The column labeled "Prior Probability" gives the product of the prior probabilities that the components listed in the candidate are in the modes shown and that the remaining components are all working.

The column labeled "Adjusted Probability" shows the results of redistributing the probabilities proportionally, after ruling out candidates that are inconsistent with the measurement at the output of A2 and also after assuming that the candidates past the cutoff point can be ignored. This renormalization of probabilities is essential. The total probability associated with each possible value is computed as the sum of the prior probabilities of the candidates consistent with the

Candidate	Prior Probability	Adjusted Probability
[]	.9960	0 (inconsistent with measurement)
[A1$_s$]	2.991 10^{-4}	.3
[M2$_s$]	2.991 10^{-4}	.3
[A1$_u$]	9.970 10^{-5}	0 (ignored due to policy for unknown mode)
[A2$_u$]	9.970 10^{-5}	0 (ditto)
[M1$_u$]	9.970 10^{-5}	0 (ditto)
[M2$_u$]	9.970 10^{-5}	0 (ditto)

————————————cutoff

[A1$_s$, M2$_s$]	8.982 10^{-8}	0 (ignored because of cutoff)
...		
[A1$_u$, A2$_u$, M1$_u$, M2$_u$]	1.000 10^{-16}	0 (ignored because of cutoff)

FIGURE 9.18. Some candidates for explaining the conflicts in Figure 9.17. The adjusted probabilities redistribute the probabilities after discarding candidates that are inconsistent with the output of A2 or that are below the cutoff point in the analysis.

value. Typically, some low-probability candidates are ignored. In this case, it is necessary to renormalize the probabilities. After all, when the probe point is measured, *some* value will be found. Renormalizing allows us to fairly and rationally compare the expected entropies for the candidates under consideration.

The determination of whether candidates are consistent is problematic when they involve components faulted in the unknown mode. One interpretation of this mode is that we can make no predictions about the candidates' behaviors, so the unknown mode is consistent with *any* value that could be observed. On the other hand, if the unknown mode for a component is indistinguishable from the normal working mode, then it would be of little diagnostic interest.

Consider the case of candidate [M1$_u$]. The unknown mode is useful when the output of M1 is abnormal and different from what is predicted by its known abnormal modes. If M1 is working, the behavior rules predict that the value at T2 is 6. One way to try to get a conflict for T2 in this example is to use an antibehavior rule with the assumption that A2 is working. However, this does not quite work. The value for the output of an adder over the positive integers is always greater than either of its inputs (ignoring the mod 32 limit for the moment). In this case, if T3 is 10 and the output is 6, then A2 cannot be working and we should not apply the antibehavior rule. Consequently, we are left with no basis for predicting a conflict at T2. Similar issues arise for the unknown modes of the other components, since the shorted mode is capable of explaining all of the shown conflicts. This leads us to a special operational interpretation of the meaning of an unknown mode. An unknown mode is invoked only when all other modes fail to give an explanation of observed or predicted behavior.

Figure 9.19 continues the diagnostic process by determining the candidate distributions that can be expected for each possible value at each possible probe point. For each probe point, we list all the predicted values and list all the candidates consistent with each of the predicted values. The normalized probability is the probability of each candidate, assuming that the probe value is observed and that inconsistent candidates are ruled out. The entropy of each set of remaining candidates is given for each possible probe value. The weighted entropy gives the entropy of this distribution of candidates weighted by the probability of the given value for the probe point. Finally, the expected entropy of a probe is the sum of the weighted entropies for the distributions corresponding to each possible probe value.

Probe Site T1	
Candidates consistent with T1 = 2	
Candidate	$[M2_s]$
Probability of candidate	.3
Normalized probability	1.00
Probability of value	.3
Entropy	0
Weighted entropy	0
Candidates consistent with T1 = 0	
Candidate	$[A1_s]$
Probability of candidate	.3
Normalized probability	1.00
Probability of value	.4
Entropy	0
Weighted entropy	0
Expected entropy for probe site T1	0
Probe Site T3	
Candidates consistent with T3 = 0	
Candidate	$[A1_s]$
Probability of candidate	.3
Normalized probability	.500
Candidate	$[M2_s]$
Probability of candidate	.3
Normalized probability	.500
Probability of value	.6
Entropy	.6931
Weighted entropy	.4159
Candidates consistent with T3 = 10	
Candidate	$[A2_u]$
Probability of candidate	.1
Normalized probability	1.00
Probability of value	.1
Entropy	0
Weighted entropy	0
Expected entropy for probe site T3	.4159

FIGURE 9.19. Example of computing entropy for a set of candidates.

Looking over the computations in Figure 9.19, we have no estimates for test point T2 because no conflicts were computed for that point. The estimated entropies for T1 and T3 were averaged over the predicted values and computed as 0 and .4159, so that T1 gives us the lowest entropy. This result is also intuitively satisfying. Measuring a zero at T3 does not distinguish between either A1 or M2 being shorted, so this probe leaves ambiguities. At T1, a measurement of 0 is consistent with A1 being shorted and also explains the output of M2 and A2. If a measurement at T1 leads to a value other than 0 or 2, we would need to invoke an unknown mode for A1 and continue reasoning. We note that although the measurement at T1 is more definitive than the measurement at T3, it does not definitively rule out the possibility that both A1 and M2 are shorted, or that M1 and A2 are in unknown modes. However, these multiple-fault candidates are much less likely than the singleton candidate explanation that A1 is shorted.

We now return to some of the further complications in handling candidate diagnoses in entropy predictions. Different diagnostic systems have different policies with regard to this. Here are some of the cases of interest for a candidate Cj.

Case 1 Cj ruled inconsistent.   This is the case where Cj has been used to predict a value different from what has been observed. In this case, Cj should be ruled out or assigned a probability of zero.

Case 2 Cj predicts a value.   In this case, Cj should be included in the list of candidates for the probe value that it predicts. It is one of the candidates to be further discriminated among should that value be observed. The probabilities of the candidates in each such list can be normalized to sum to 1 for the purposes of computing the entropy of the probe point.

Case 3 Cj makes no prediction.   In this case, no probe value can be used to rule out the candidate. Such candidates are called **uncommitted candidates**. Adding them to the candidate lists for every value of a probe for which they make no prediction essentially spreads out their probability uniformly. However, adding the probability of the candidate to every value in computing the probability of the value is misleading. One approach is to divide the probability of the uncommitted candidate by the number of possible values before including it in the sum of candidates "consistent" with a given value.

Case 4 Cj has an unknown mode.   In this case, one or more of the components in the candidate is in an unknown mode. Some systems treat this as just another uncommitted candidate, in that no predictions about values can be based on the behavior of those components. In the above, we suggest distinguishing candidates with such components by not including them in lists where the component in the unknown mode would be indistinguishable in behavior from its working mode.

Figure 9.20 sketches the one-step look-ahead method that we just used in our example for selecting probe points. The method is given a set of candidates, a set of observed data, a set of probe points, and a set of possible data values for each probe point. The method calls upon a system model to determine which values are incompatible with the possible probe point values.

To select the next probe point:
```
 1.   Acquire a set of candidates (diagnostic hypotheses), a set of data,
      and a set of possible probe points.
 2.   For each possible probe point do
 3.   begin
 4.        For each possible value of the probe point do
 5.        begin
 6.             For each diagnostic candidate do
 7.             begin
 8.                  Given the candidate, invoke the system model to
                     make predictions about resulting data values.
 9.                  If there is a contradiction, reset the candidate's
                     context probability to zero in this context. (The
                     context is for this value of this probe point.)
10.             end
11.             Adjust the probabilities of the remaining candidates
                within this context (after eliminating those with zero
                probabilities and discarding those below a given
                threshold).
12.             Compute the probability of this value of the probe point
                as the sum of the probabilities of the viable candidates.
13.             Compute the value of the evaluation function (e.g.,
                entropy) for the distribution of remaining candidates
                given this value of the probe point.
14.        end
15.        Assign the probe point a total estimated evaluation that is the
           weighted average of the evaluations for each of its possible
           values. The weights are the probabilities of each value as
           computed from the probabilities of the consistent candidates.
16.   end
17.   Select the probe point having the lowest estimated evaluation.
```

FIGURE 9.20. Method for using a measure of a set of hypotheses in selecting a probe point. The evaluation function approaches 0 in the ideal case and increases for less satisfactory probe points.

In summary, the method plays a what-if scenario to predict an expected distribution of candidates for every possible data value that could be observed. It projects one step ahead to see which candidates would be inconsistent with each set of values. If a candidate credits a component as working but predicts a value that is not consistent with it working, then the candidate is ruled out. As described already, the probabilities of the remaining candidates are renormalized and the evaluation function is applied to the set of candidates. Each probe point is assigned an overall evaluation that is the weighted average of the evaluations for each of its observable values. Finally, the probe point with the lowest expected weighted average is selected.

Beyond Entropy

The entropy approach assumes that the only relevant property of probe sites is the expected information gain. For example, the cost of a measurement is assumed to be constant or not to matter. Risks associated with any probe are assumed to be equal. The delay involved in carrying out any measurement is assumed to be the same. Entropy does not measure the harm caused by uncertainty. All diagnoses are assumed to be of equal concern, whether the patient has the common cold or cancer. Entropy measures the cost of removing the uncertainty by querying an oracle, where all queries are assumed to cost the same. The point is that in many domains, it is necessary to combine an entropy measure with other relevant measures that reflect the other important desiderata of the task.

This issue about entropy is an example of a recurring issue in designing knowledge systems. Most tasks are characterized in terms of multiple search spaces. We have characterized the main search spaces of diagnosis as a data space, a hypothesis space, and a therapy or repair space. Probe selection also involves a minimizing search over the estimated entropies of sites. A deeper analysis for a particular domain could result in a probe search that takes more factors into account. One approach from decision theory is **information value theory** (Howard, 1966), which combines costs and entropy values in the evaluation function.

Some domains would require complex models to incorporate all of the factors. Figure 9.21 shows some rules for selecting a probe site. The first rule eliminates probes that risk disabling the patient unless the diseases are life-threatening. The second rule establishes a preference for noninvasive probes over invasive ones.

The issue of probe selection can even include human factors in cases where the "probe" data must be obtained by querying a human user. For example, a common assumption is that a

```
IF      none of the diseases is life-threatening
THEN    no probe that risks disabling the patient should be used.


IF      there are two competing probes and
        one of the probes (P1) is invasive and
        the other probe (P2) is affordable to the patient
THEN    P2 should be preferred over P1.
```

FIGURE 9.21. Example rules representing knowledge that might be employed in selecting probes in a hypothetical domain.

diagnostic or classification system should try to minimize the number of questions the user gets asked. A hallmark of a competent consultant is that it gets swiftly to the crucial questions. The designers of the PROSPECTOR system used a strategy of asking questions that was intended to maximize information gain. PROSPECTOR did not use an entropy measure in determining probe selection, so the comparison and conclusions are somewhat unclear. Nonetheless, PROS-PECTOR produced questioning sequences that struck its users as being disconnected and incoherent, no matter how well the questions could be justified post hoc. To keep the dialogs more focused, they introduced the notion of "contexts." Contexts mediated the question asking process by the requirement that question areas be sufficiently established by other ad hoc criteria before any of their subgoals could be investigated. Reportedly, this change resulted in much more acceptable questioning sequences. A similar phenomenon was reported in the NEOMYCIN reimplementation of MYCIN (Clancey & Letsinger, 1981). NEOMYCIN's creators observed that MYCIN only asks a question to evaluate a clause of a rule for the goal that it is pursuing. Its rules are not sorted by conclusion, so its questions appear to skip back and forth randomly among hypotheses. In contrast, NEOMYCIN's forward, nonexhaustive search of its hypothesis space provided a much greater sense of coherence and continuity. The human factors requirements for dialog are not well understood. However, just choosing the question that maximizes information gain can lead to a process that is perceived as jumpy and incoherent. Even though human factors are not the only issue in selecting probes, an information gain approach falls short because it does not take into account factors of risk, cost, and value that are important i some domains. In summary, information gain is just one of several factors for ranking alternative probe points.

9.2.4 *Summary and Review*

The introduction to this chapter presented five scenarios of diagnosis, including an infectious disease scenario, a board troubleshooting scenario, a picnic scenario, a communications box scenario, and a copier troubleshooting scenario. This chapter characterizes diagnosis as a knowledge-intensive task. Our goal has been to clarify the similarities and differences among these tasks and the basic concepts for designing knowledge-based diagnosis systems.

Our analysis of diagnosis is based on its search spaces and subtasks. We distinguish a data space, a hypothesis space, and a repair or therapy space. The main subtasks are recognizing abnormalities, generating and testing hypotheses, and discriminating among hypotheses.

Describing what can go wrong is fundamental to generating hypotheses in diagnosis. A component-oriented description emphasizes that a system is composed of elements that can fail and be replaced. A disease-oriented description emphasizes that failures can be widespread across components and that treatment may involve therapies specific to the malady but not specific to a particular component. More generally, failures can result from many different kinds of interactions, including interactions with things such as wires or elements of an environment that might not be counted as components of the system. Newer approaches focus on layered families of causal pathways.

A basic issue in diagnosis is determining which evidence implicates which faults or diseases. This determination is complicated by several phenomena. A fault or disease can have multiple symptoms and different faults or diseases can lead to indistinguishable symptoms. When two diseases or faults are present, there can be interactions leading to greater or fewer symptoms than the union of the symptoms that would appear from either alone.

Hypotheses are represented as combinations of faults or diseases. This leads to exponential increases in computational costs if all combinations of low-level faults are considered. The most direct way to address such combinatorics is to frame diagnosis as a hierarchical problem, using representation and search at multiple levels of abstraction. The greatest challenges in current work on diagnosis are in building appropriate models for representing the systems to be diagnosed.

Discrimination involves determining what additional information would differentiate between competing hypotheses. Shannon entropy measures the distance from a set of competing hypotheses to an ideal diagnosis, where there is exactly one hypothesis. Since this measures the value of information and excludes costs and risks of different probes, it needs to be augmented with other measures in many domains.

Exercises for Section 9.2

Ex. 1   [05] *The Size of Diagnostic Search Spaces.* Many diagnostic approaches (including those based on heuristic classification, linear discriminant analysis, and statistical decision theory) assume that diagnosis selects from a given set of diagnostic possibilities. In internal medicine, a practicing clinician knows approximately 10,000 disease entitites.

(a) Why is the number of possible hypotheses required to categorize patients greater than the number of disease entities?

(b) Assuming an upper bound of 10 for the number of concurrent disease processes in a patient, approximately how many diagnostic categories would be required to classify arbitrary patients?

(c) If there are n possible disease entities (or faults), how many distinct diagnostic hypotheses are possible? How large is the complete set of disease hypotheses?

Ex. 2   [00] *Search Spaces and Fault Modes.* Suppose the behavior model for a system to be diagnosed is based on device models. It has n devices altogether, and every device has one operational mode and two failure modes. How many diagnostic hypotheses are possible allowing for the possibility of multiple simultaneous failures?

Ex. 3   [05] *Corroboration.* Noticing that any component involved in a discrepancy is a suspect, Professor Digit supposes that any component involved in a corroboration must be innocent. More precisely, suppose we are given a system S, a set P of parts from S, $P_1, P_2, \ldots, P_n\}$, and a set of measurements, D. We are given a trusted set of rules about the behavior of the parts. Suppose further that we have run the rules on the data, that the rules describe the behavior of all of the parts in P, that the rules predict some new data, and that observations confirm those predictions. According to Professor Digit, all the parts in P must be working.

Do you agree with Professor Digit? Explain briefly. If you disagree, illustrate with a short example.

Ex. 4   [CD-20] *Shannon Entropy and Candidate Probability Distributions.* The goal in troubleshooting tasks is to determine the cause of the malfunctions. In the ideal case, diagnosis proceeds until there is a single diagnostic candidate, perhaps involving several components. This exercise considers several possible states of information about the probability distribution of diagnostic candidates. It is intended to demonstrate by example why minimum entropy is a plausible measure of the completeness of a diagnostic task.

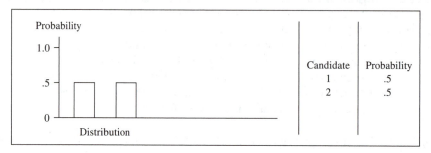

FIGURE 9.22.   A distribution of candidate probabilities with two candidates of equal probability.

In the following there are several different distributions of candidates and probabilities, such as might correspond to conclusions about a system at different points in a diagnostic process. In each example, there is a set of candidates whose probabilities sum to one, meaning that we are considering the complete set of candidates. For each distribution, compute the Shannon entropy using natural logarithms.

$$H = - \sum_{}^{\text{all } i} p_i \log p_i \quad \text{where log refers to the natural logarithms}$$

(a) What is the Shannon entropy when there are just two candidates of equal probability as shown in Figure 9.22?

(b) What is the entropy when there are five possible candidates of equal probability as shown in Figure 9.23? Briefly explain why diagnosis is less resolved in part b than in part a.

(c) Repeat the computation extending the situation in part b for the cases where there are 10 and 20 possible candidates of equal probability. Briefly explain why the entropy increases as the number of candidates increases.

(d) What is the entropy when there are two possible candidates, one of which is much greater than the other as shown in Figure 9.24? Briefly, why is the diagnosis sharper than in part a?

(e) What is the entropy when there is only one candidate of probability 1, as shown in Figure 9.25?

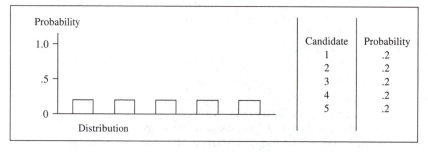

FIGURE 9.23.   A distribution of candidate probabilities with five candidates of equal probability.

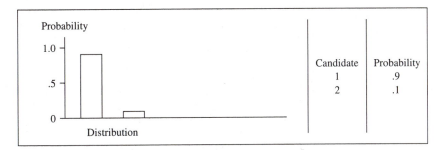

FIGURE 9.24. A distribution of candidate probabilities with two candidates at very different probabilities.

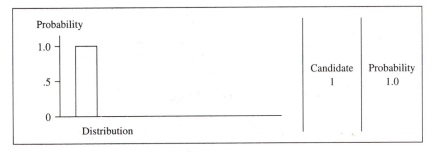

FIGURE 9.25. A distribution of candidate probabilities with one certain candidate.

(f) What is the entropy when there is one leading candidate and several other candidates of near zero probability as shown in Figure 9.26? Why does this case approximate part e more closely than does part d? Would the entropy increase or decrease if the five minor candidates were combined into one?

Ex. 5 [*!M-10*] *Using and Approximating Shannon Entropy.* The Shannon entropy for a set of probabilities (p_i) is defined as

$$H = - \sum_{i}^{\text{all } i} p_i \log p_i$$

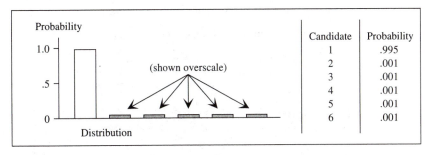

FIGURE 9.26. A distribution of candidate probabilities with one main candidate and five candidates of low probability.

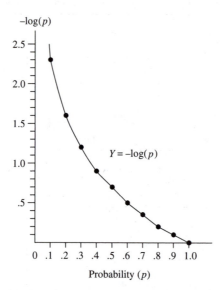

FIGURE 9.27. Negative logarithmic weighting of probabilities.

This exercise formalizes some of the properties desired for an evaluation function of diagnostic competeness and then demonstrates them for Shannon entropy.

(a) Briefly explain why $-\log_e (p_i)$ as shown in Figure 9.27 is a plausible weighting for evaluating candidates and sets of candidates of known probability. Why is it reasonable that the weighting factor should decrease as probability approaches 1?

(b) One rule that could be inferred from the examples for an evaluation function for diagnosis, E_D, is that

$$E_D(1) = 0.$$

Show that Shannon entropy satisfies this condition.

(c) Another rule is that

$$E_D(0) = 0.$$

Show that Shannon entropy satisfies this condition.

(d) The distance to a diagnostic conclusion is increased whenever a fixed probability is split among multiple candidates. This could be formalized as

$$E_D(p) < n\, E_D(p/n) \text{ where } n \text{ is a positive integer}$$

Is this satisfied by Shannon entropy?

(e) Show that the entropy function shown in Figure 9.28 using natural logarithms has a maximum at $p = 1/e$, where e is the base of the natural logarithms. What is the value of the entropy function at this point?

(f) Where is the maximum of the entropy function on the interval $[0, 1]$ if it is defined using logarithms of the base 2 instead of natural logarithms? (*Hint:* Trick question.)

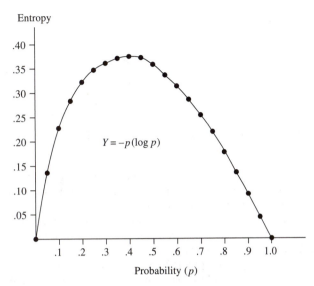

FIGURE 9.28. Shannon entropy versus probability of a candidate.

■ Ex. 6 [*!-10*] *Shannon Entropy as a Count of Future Probes.* It is sometimes said that Shannon entropy counts the number of measurements still needed before a diagnosis can be made. This exercise examines some of the assumptions behind that characterization.

(a) Using a $\log_2$ formulation for entropy,

$$H = -\sum_{i}^{\text{all } i} p_i \log_2 p_i$$

compute entropy for the following distributions of candidates:

(i) A single candidate with probability 1.0
(ii) Two candidates with equal probabilities of .5
(iii) Four candidates with equal probabilities of .25
(iv) 2^k candidates with equal probabilities of $1/2^k$

(b) Briefly relate the computation in part a to a search of a binary tree.
(c) Is it possible, on average, to do better than halving the number of candidates in a single measurement? If yes, relate this to required properties of the diagnostic situation.

Ex. 7 [*!-05*] *Deriving Shannon Entropy and the Expected Number of Probes.* This exercise considers the properties of an evaluation function for choosing probe points, E_D. The details of the device being diagnosed are not important for this exercise. Instead, we focus on the way the selection of probe points divides the search space of remaining possible diagnoses.

Figure 9.29 shows diagnostic candidates arranged in a balanced binary tree where terminal nodes correspond to diagnostic candidates and intermediate nodes in the tree correspond to sets of solutions representing the set of their successors.

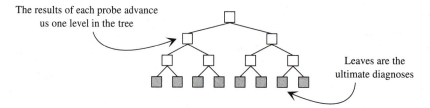

The results of each probe advance
us one level in the tree

Leaves are the
ultimate diagnoses

FIGURE 9.29.   Hypothesis space of diagnostic candidates arranged in a binary tree.

For simplicity, we assume that candidates have equal probability. $C(p)$ is the cost (in terms of the number of probes) of identifying a candidate of probability p. We are given that $C(1) = 0$. We take measurements one at a time.

(a) Suppose our selection of probe points is such that after each probe we advance exactly one level in a tree. Give an expression for the cost to isolate a diagnostic candidate when there are 2^k possible diagnoses.

(b) Show that $C(p) = -\log_2(p)$ reflects the conditions of part a.

(c) E_D is an evaluation function for probe points based on the probability of candidates (c).

$$E_D = \sum^{\text{all } c} p_c \, C(p_c)$$

Give an expression relating E_D to Shannon entropy. Assume that entropy is given in terms of logarithms of base 2 rather than natural logarithms.

(d) Based on part c, briefly explain the effect of each measurement on the size of the space of unresolved candidates facing the diagnostician. What is the ratio of the number of candidates remaining at probe_i and probe_{i+1} for $i < k$?

(e) Assuming that the p_c are renormalized after each probe so the sum of the probabilities of the remaining candidates is 1, relate E_D to the expected number of remaining probes before only a single candidate remains.

Ex. 8   [05] *"Precise Information."* Professor Digit says the idea of thinking about probe selection to gain information makes no sense at all. He argues that we could just as easily "gain information" by measuring the same probe point over and over.

(a) Why is it reasonable for the measured value of a probe to change slightly, even in cases where it is assumed that the system is static during a session of measurements?

(b) Do you agree that measuring the same probe point repeatedly gains information? Briefly, is it the right kind of information?

(c) Briefly explain whether change in entropy measures the relevant information.

Ex. 9   [M-15] *Complexity Estimates for Hierarchical Diagnosis Methods.* This exercise considers a hierarchical approach to diagnosis.

Figure 9.30 repeats our example from the text for dividing a system into subsystems. We use the system in the figure as a concrete example and then generalize the results. Not shown is case 5, the recursive next step after case 4. Case 5 has 4 mega-elements and 64 basic elements. Only cases 3, 4, and 5 have more than one level of organization.

(a) Disregarding the five cases momentarily, suppose we are given a system of n parts to be diagnosed. Suppose our fault model says that each part has two modes: working and

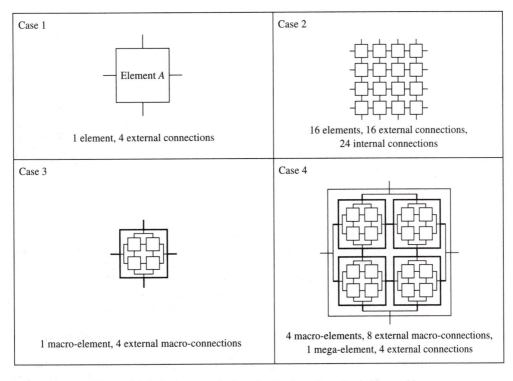

FIGURE 9.30. Abstraction is the key to reducing complexity in hypothesis hierarachies.

broken. If we make a single-fault assumption, what is the maximum number of hypotheses? How many hypotheses are there if we assume that there are two or fewer faults?

(b) Suppose we are given a diagnosis method (DM) whose worst-case complexity measured in terms of the number of possible hypotheses is $C(n)$, where n is the number of hypotheses. We define a top-down hierarchical method, HDM, which applies DM on the outermost abstract description. We assume that a complete diagnostic process is performed at this level, including probe selection and further reasoning. For the purposes of our analysis, we assume that this always identifies a single subsystem at a level, most likely to be faulty. HDM then recursively expands the description of the identified subsystem to the next more detailed level of description and applies HDM again.

Briefly, what are some of the basic assumptions behind HDM? Does it rely on a single-fault assumption? If yes, describe briefly how it could be modified to admit multiple faults.

(c) Fill in the missing entries in the following table for the complexity of HDM applied to the cases in Figure 9.30. $C(n)$ refers to the complexity of DM. Thus, the first column where $C(n) = n$ refers to a single-fault situation and the last column where $C(n) = 2^n$ refers to all composite diagnoses. The middle column is intermediate and near the case where there are up to two faults. The entries in the table count the number of hypotheses considered by HDM summed over all levels of its analysis.

Case	$C(n) = n$	$C(n) = n^2$	$C(n) = 2^n$
1	1	1	2
2	16	—	—
3	4	—	—
4	$4 + 4 = 8$	$16 + 16 = 32$	32
5	12	—	—

Briefly, what does this table tell us about the relative performance of DM and HDM?

(d) Give a general expression for the complexity of applying HDM where k is the number of elements in a diagnostic group at one level (e.g., four in a macro-element), $C(k)$ is the number of hypotheses considered at one level, and m is the number of levels. Assume that k is constant across levels.

Ex. 10   [15] *Reasoning about Fault Modes and Candidates.* This exercise considers some of the basic computations for identifying conflicts and candidates and in computing the probabilities of candidates.

Consider a device with three components, as shown in Figure 9.31. For the purpose of this exercise, we assume that chips are primitive and are the only components that can fail.

Components B and C have two behavior modes: w (for working) and f (for unknown fault). Component A has three behavior modes, $w, f,$ and i (for inactive).

The output signal of each device depends on its mode and its input signals. The correct output signals are generated only if components are in mode w. All connections are shown.

(a) Suppose the initial symptom is that the output of C is wrong. What is the initial conflict set, expressed in physical components?

(b) Present the complete set of minimal diagnostic hypotheses consistent with bad output from C. The minimal hypotheses all assume that at least one of the devices is in some mode other than working.

(c) Suppose we are given the following prior probabilities for components being in particular modes:

Prior Probabilities for Different Modes

	w (working)	f (faulty)	i (inactive)
Component			
A	.9899	.0001	.0100
B	.9998	.0002	—
C	.9950	.0050	—

Fill in the values for all the x's in following table of candidate prior probabilities. Adjusted probability is the probabilities normalized to add up to 1, after discounting any candidates already known to be inconsistent with observations. (In this exercise, we consider only singleton candidates.)

Candidate	Computation	Prior Probability	Adjusted Probability
$[A_i, B_w, C_w]$	$p(A_i) \times p(B_w) \times p(C_w)$	.009948	.65
$[A_w, B_w, C_f]$	$p(A_w) \times p(B_w) \times p(C_f)$	.004949	xxx
$[A_w, B_f, C_w]$	$p(A_w) \times p(B_f) \times p(C_w)$	xxx	xxx
$[A_f, B_w, C_w]$	xxx	xxx	xxx

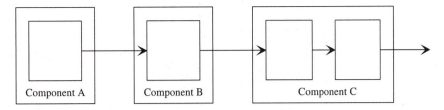

FIGURE 9.31.   Some components in a system being diagnosed.

Ex. 11   [20] *Entropy and Probe Selection.* The one-step look-ahead approach selects a probe point using the values predicted by candidates to estimate the expected entropy or information gain for different outcomes. In this approach, a list is made of all the possible values that could be measured at each probe point. The probabilities for each value are determined. Then the expected entropy is computed for each probe point. This exercise steps through one such computation.

In Figure 9.32, three possible probe sites are identified and numbered. The behavior model predicts that the signal at points one, two, and three should be "changing" at a given frequency if all the components are in working mode. If any component is in a fault mode, all downstream signals will be constant instead of changing. There are no antibehavior rules.

(a)   We are given that the signal at probe site three has been observed to be not changing. The next step is to compute the expected entropy at each of the probe points, given the information so far. Fill in the values for the x's in the following tables to compute the expected entropy for measurements at each of the two remaining probe sites. Limit consideration to the four single-fault candidates shown.

For each probe site, x_i, we need to compute the expected entropy

$$H_e(x_i) = \sum_{i=1}^{m} p(x_i = v_{ik}) \, H(x_i = v_{ik})$$

In the following tables we use the term *weighted entropy* to refer to a term in this sum, that is, the entropy computed for a given probe value, $H(x_i = v_{ik})$, weighted by the probability of that value, $p(x_i = v_{ik})$.

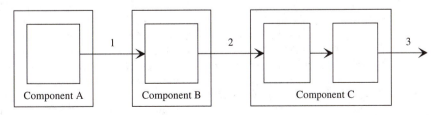

FIGURE 9.32.   Some components in a system being diagnosed. The numbers in the circles indicate competing probe sites.

Probe Site 1

Candidates consistent with the "signal is changing"

Candidate	Probability	Normalized probability
$[A_w, B_w, C_f]$	.33	.96
$[A_w, B_f, C_w]$	.013	xxx

Probability of value .34   *Entropy* xxx   *Weighted entropy* .0578

Candidates consistent with the "signal is constant"

Candidate	Probability	Normalized probability
$[A_i, B_w, C_w]$	xxx	xxx
$[A_f, B_w, C_w]$	.0065	xxx

Probability of value .651   *Entropy* xxx   *Weighted entropy* xxx

Expected entropy for probe site 1 xxx

Probe Site 2

Candidates consistent with the "signal is changing"

Candidate	Probability	Normalized probability
xxx	.33	1.00

Probability of value .33   *Entropy* 0   *Weighted entropy* 0

Candidates consistent with the "signal is constant"

Candidate	Probability	Normalized probability
xxx	.013	.01
xxx	xxx	xxx
xxx	xxx	xxx

Probability of value xxxx   *Entropy* .117   *Weighted entropy* xxx

Expected entropy for probe site 2 xxx

(b) Which probe site should be selected? Does it make a big difference in this case which probe point we select? Briefly argue the logic of the result and whether it makes sense.

Ex. 12 [20] *Beyond High-Probability Hypotheses.* To simplify entropy computations, some diagnostic systems focus on the most probable diagnoses and ignore the less probable ones. This exercise shows that this can be suboptimal, even in simple cases.

Figure 9.33 has three components, A, B, and C. All three components are buffers, meaning that their outputs equal their inputs when they are working. There are four possible probe sites: in-1, out-1, out-2, and T-1. We are given that in-1 is 0 and out-1 is 1.

In this exercise we assume that a component can be working or broken. When a component is broken, we make no predictions about its behavior. Following the usual rules of diagnosis, a component can never be exonerated. The diagnostic process involves ruling out those diagnostic hypotheses that inconsistently state that some component is working.

(a) First we consider only single-fault hypotheses. As usual, we use the notation [A] to represent the hypothesis that component A is broken and the others are working. In other

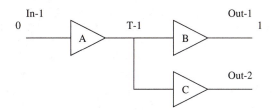

FIGURE 9.33.   Selecting a probe site. (From de Kleer, 1989, Figure 3, page 7.)

words, this example does not use detailed fault models with behavioral rules. Fill in the following chart showing which single-fault diagnostic hypotheses are either possible (consistent with the evidence so far) or ruled out for values that might be measured at each probe point.

Probe Point	Predicted Value	Consistent Candidates	Inconsistent Candidates
T-1	0	[B]	[A]
	1		
Out-2	0		
	1		

Considering only single-fault hypotheses, which probe site is best?

(b) List all the possible double-fault hypotheses for this circuit.

(c) Fill in the table again, showing only the double-fault candidates.

Probe Point	Predicted Value	Consistent Candidates	Inconsistent Candidates
T-1	0		
	1		
Out-2	0		
	1		

Considering these additional hypotheses, which probe site is best?

(d) Briefly, what is the significance of the example?

9.3 *Case Studies of Diagnosis and Troubleshooting Systems*

In the following we consider seven knowledge systems developed for diagnostic and trouble-shooting tasks. In comparison with configuration systems, there has been much more experience and experimentation with different approaches for diagnostic programs.

Research on diagnostic knowledge systems has been sustained for many years, especially in medical diagnosis and electronic troubleshooting domains. Medical diagnostic systems using different approaches have been developed since the mid-1960s. There has been a substantial industry in electronic test systems since the 1940s.

Because so many knowledge systems have been built for diagnosis, it is not possible to review even all of the major systems that have been developed. Instead, a selection of systems representative of the major approaches has been chosen. For each system in the following, many alternative systems could have been chosen as well. These examples provide a representative sampling of the ideas and illustrate concepts and patterns of knowledge use that are at the core of diagnosis in many domains. The seven systems illustrate the major approaches to knowledge systems ranging from plan-based approaches to systems based on device models. In some cases, we consider closely related systems to illustrate the development of ideas.

9.3.1 *Diagnosis in DARN*

DARN is a plan-based knowledge system designed to guide an inexperienced technician in a diagnosis and repair task (Mittal, Bobrow, & de Kleer, 1988). DARN was developed for use in diagnosing failures in a workstation's disk controller and was later extended to represent fault-isolation procedures for copier repair. DARN is representative of a large number of diagnostic and repair programs, modeled after the diagnosis and repair procedures and decision trees used in repair manuals in training technicians for repairing mechanical and electrical equipment. Similarly, flowcharts and plans for medical diagnosis and therapy appear regularly in medical texts, especially in treatment protocols. Plan-based knowledge systems have been developed for specialized areas of medical diagnosis and treatment.

The key to DARN and systems like it is the diagnosis and repair network. This network is essentially a flowchart, as shown in Figure 9.34. It represents a repair procedure that technicians are expected to follow. Different kinds of nodes in the chart represent diagnostic tests, diagnostic observations, diagnostic actions, subplans, and ordered sequences of repairs to try. Test nodes correspond to data-gathering steps. In the case of disk diagnosis and repair, carrying out a test can involve taking an electronic measurement, visually inspecting a mechanical part, or running test software to exercise a disk and display the results on a maintenance panel. Observation nodes represent choice points, responding to particular results from the tests. For example, in Figure 9.34, there are observations corresponding to maintenance panel codes such as "MP 151." Action nodes represent repairs or adjustments to the system. In Figure 9.34, these are usually steps for replacing a component.

Systems like DARN provide a graphical interface for diagnosis and repair and for extending the knowledge base of plans. The execution interface interacts with a technician who is following the procedure. For example, following the plan in Figure 9.34, DARN begins by asking the technician to "boot" the computer. The interface prints a message, highlights the corresponding node in a display of the network, and provides further information as needed about how to boot the computer under test. Then it asks the technician what code appeared on the maintenance panel display. If the code is 151 or 149, it asks the technician to run the diagnostic program E1 Disk. If that leads to the maintenance code 1192, then it tries a sequence of steps in order. First it recommends replacing the HSIO board and then running E1 Disk again. If code 1192 persists, DARN recommends checking and possibly replacing the cooling fan. If the cooling fan is okay or its replacement does not fix the problem, DARN recommends checking the voltage at the processor.

One view of a plan-based approach is that it provides a specialized and structured programming environment for diagnostic procedures. There are many variations in the language and

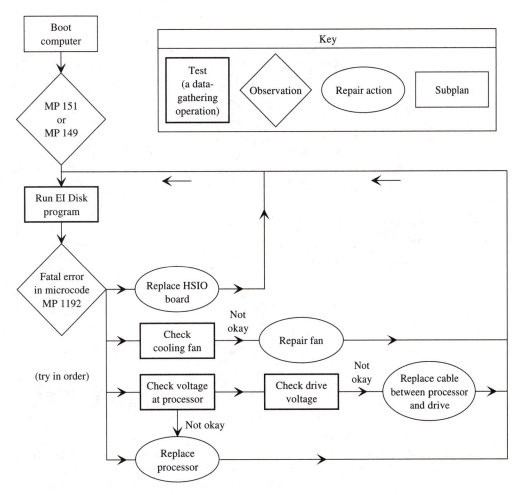

FIGURE 9.34. Fragment of a diagnosis and repair network in DARN. This network is essentially a flow-chart, describing an algorithm that a technician is expected to follow in diagnosing a device. (Adapted from Mittal, Bobrow, & de Kleer, 1988, Figure 1, page 62.)

debugging features that can be employed. Space does not permit discussing here the differences and trade-offs among them.

Once we accept the adequacy of a plan-based approach, there are several advantages of a computational medium over a paper medium. The main advantage is that a computational medium is interactive. Repair steps and part replacements can be automatically logged as a plan is followed. User interfaces can display the progress and history of a troubleshooting session. For example, they can make it easier to locate the next steps in a plan by avoiding the need to thumb through a manual.

A second advantage is that a computational medium is easier to update than paper. Computer-based plans can be updated and distributed electronically without going through a cycle of

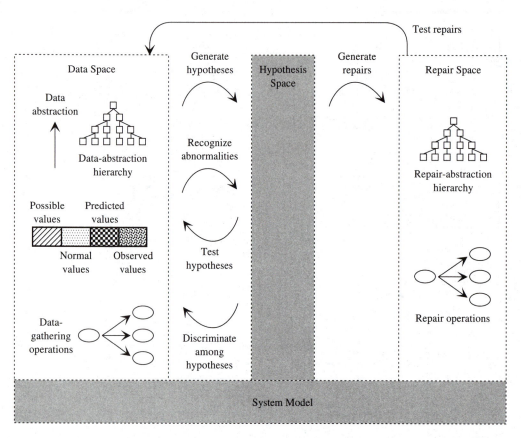

FIGURE 9.35.   Search spaces in DARN. The hypothesis space and system model are shaded in this figure to indicate that they are only minimally represented in DARN. The diagnostic hypotheses in DARN
are represented by the program counter of an interpreter traversing the diagnosis and repair network.
DARN does not have an explicit model of the system's components or their behavior. It represents the
names of specific faults but characterizes them only in terms of their presenting symptoms.

printing, binding, and mailing repair manuals. According to the experience with DARN and similar projects, the browser puts the development and distribution of the plans into the hands of the
senior technicians rather than technical writers. The senior technicians working with DARN
found it easy to update and distribute new versions of repair plans. In multimedia presentations
of diagnosis and repair plans, photographs of machines and their parts and videos of disassembly
and repair procedures can be integrated in a plan network. This makes it easier to illustrate tricky
assembly procedures and what a diagnostician should look for, such as characteristic patterns of
wear that are difficult to convey in words or sketches.

Figure 9.35 shows the main relations and search spaces of DARN. DARN's task combines
diagnosis and repair. DARN has explicit representations for the data space in the observation and
test steps in its plans. It also represents the repair space explicitly in the action steps of its plan.
However, unlike other knowledge systems for diagnosis that we consider later, DARN does not

have explicit representations for its diagnostic hypotheses and has no explicit hypothesis-manipulating operations in its plans. DARN engages hypotheses implicitly as it executes the associated nodes in a plan. It generates a report of hypotheses that it has considered.

DARN also has no structural or behavioral model of the system it is diagnosing. The behavioral model is represented only implicitly in the layout of the network. For example, if there are two voltage tests on opposite ends of a cable and one of them indicates that the voltage is correct and the second indicates that it is zero or too low, then the repair action may be to replace the cable. A model of current flow and broken cables is implicit in the flowchart arrangement of tests and repair actions. Thus, DARN only represents a diagnosis and repair *plan*. Recognizing this lack of explicit representations for hypotheses, system structure, and behavior is a key to understanding both DARN's flexibility and also its limitations.

In summary, DARN is a knowledge system for diagnosis and repair. It captures diagnosis and repair knowledge in the form of plans, which are generalized from protocols of expert behavior. Repair plans and fault-isolation procedures are familiar forms of documentation that have been used in paper form for many years.

Plan-based approaches are difficult to build and maintain. Every time something is added to the plan or changed in it, the interactions in it change. For example, adding a test early in the plan may mean the system being diagnosed is no longer in the same state for some later test. A diagnostic plan would need to be revised to reflect these changes.

Even for static systems, there are fundamental difficulties with plan-based approaches. Most plan-based approaches employ diagnostic tests for discriminating among individual faults, meaning they make a single-fault assumption. To handle the possibility of multiple interacting faults, plans would need to be much more complex. In principle, a plan maker would need to anticipate all possible interactions among all possible combinations of multiple interacting faults and to create a plan for discriminating among them. In practice, most plan-based approaches consider only the most likely combinations of faults. Such plans simply fail when some other combination of faults arises and provide no guidance for such cases.

9.3.2 *Diagnosis in INTERNIST*

INTERNIST is a knowledge-based system for diagnosing disorders of internal medicine. It is well known because of the extensive coverage of its knowledge base and its substantial testing. The research on this project has continued for many years and has spawned several generations of systems for knowledge-based diagnosis. The project started as an exercise in understanding the logic of diagnosis. The first system was known as DIALOG (Pople, Myers, & Miller, 1975) and covered approximately half the diseases known by a practicing clinician in internal medicine. Experience with the system led to new generations INTERNIST-I, INTERNIST-II (Miller, Pople, & Myers, 1984; Pople, 1977), and CADUCEUS (Pople, 1982). In this section we draw on examples from different generations of the system to illustrate the evolution and rationale for variations in the architecture and patterns of knowledge use. Following the practice of its creators, we refer to the operational system as INTERNIST-I and to the evolving new system as CADUCEUS.

From the begining of this project the strategy was to represent and reason explicitly about diagnostic hypotheses. Diagnostic hypotheses corresponding to disease categories were organized in specialization taxonomies. As in the classification methods of Chapter 7, INTERNIST-I

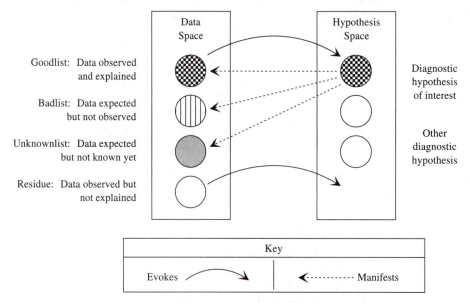

FIGURE 9.36.   Relations between data and hypotheses in INTERNIST-I.

reasons about associations between a data space describing disease manifestations and a hypothesis space describing disease categories. As we will see, INTERNIST-I extends classification to reason about composite diagnoses using an incremental approach that considers one disease at a time.

Two relations were defined corresponding to the two possible directions for mapping between the spaces. The `evokes` relation associates manifestations with diseases, meaning it maps from data to diagnostic hypotheses as solutions. For example, the symptom `pallor` may evoke hypotheses of iron deficiency or anemia. The `manifest` relation indicates which elements of the data space would be expected for a given diagnosis, which means it maps from diagnostic hypotheses to data. For example, the hypothesis `biliary cirrhosis` would manifest the symptom `jaundice`.

Every diagnostic hypothesis partitions the data space into four categories: data (or manifestations) observed and explained by the hypothesis, data predicted by the hypothesis but contrary to observations, data predicted for the hypothesis but about which nothing is known, and data observed but not relevant to or explained by the hypothesis. These four categories, summarized in Figure 9.36, are crucial for explaining INTERNIST-I's focus of attention.

The association between data and hypotheses is looser in INTERNIST-I than in the basic conjunctive classification model. In conjunctive classification, the associations represent strict necessary conditions. INTERNIST-I's knowledge base is a network that quantifies its associations using the scales shown in Figure 9.37. These scales are used in explicit places in INTERNIST-I's method, which is shown in Figure 9.38. In 1984, INTERNIST-I represented approximately 3,550 different manifestations (symptoms) and about 500 different diagnostic hypotheses. Approximately 2,600 different links between hypotheses were represented, and there were 6,500 relations of all kinds.

$L(D_i/M_a)$	The likelihood relative to other causes of M_a that diagnosis D_i is its cause. Measured on a scale from 0 to 5 where 0 refers to a nonspecific symptom such as fever and 5 refers to a highly specific (or "pathognomonic") symptom.
$F(M_b/D_j)$	Estimate of the frequency with which patients with D_j will display M_b. Measured on a 1 to 5 scale, with 1 indicating that M_b occurs rarely in D_j and 5 indicating that it always occurs.
Import	Estimate of how readily a symptom can be ignored as irrelevant.
Type	Combined estimate of risk and benefit of a symptom to a patient. A type rating places each symptom on a scale of three levels indicating a rough level of expense for and danger to the patient.

FIGURE 9.37.   Numeric scales in INTERNIST-I.

Characteristic of INTERNIST-I is its relative scoring of hypotheses, which is the notion of choosing hypotheses that are the best of several competing hypotheses rather than being those above some threshold on an absolute scale.

INTERNIST-I's method is a specialization of the classification methods in Chapter 7. Like MOLE's method and MC-2, this method creates an initial set of seed hypotheses from the initial or "presenting data." Also like MOLE, INTERNIST-I ranks hypotheses according to how well they explain symptoms.

One interesting property of the method in Figure 9.38 is that the number of competing hypotheses can grow or shrink during the diagnosis and candidate discrimination process. INTERNIST-I enters different "modes," depending on the number of hypotheses on its master list. When there are five or more hypotheses, it enters a mode to try to rule many of these hypotheses out. When there are between two and four hypotheses, it focuses on the top two candidates and acquires data to discriminate between them. If there is one leading candidate but it does not quite dominate the others yet by an adequate amount according to the scoring functions, INTERNIST-I seeks further data to "confirm" the candidate, by widening the difference between the scores of competing candidates. During this process, it always reappraises the candidates as it acquires new data, and occasionally the results of this reappraisal cause candidates to be added. This behavior is characteristic of best-first searches and of the due-process decision criteria associated with diagnosis.

Figure 9.39 shows the inference paths in INTERNIST-I in the terms of our example diagnostic system. In those terms, INTERNIST-I has an explicit data space and an explicit hypothesis space. INTERNIST-I does not make recommendations about therapy. Finally, INTERNIST-I lacks a system model in that it has no model of anatomy (system structure) or medical cause or time (behavior). Indeed, INTERNIST-I's inability to reason anatomically or temporally has been identified by its creators as indicating the direction for further development in the follow-on system, CADUCEUS. For this subsequent research, INTERNIST-I serves as a point of departure. Because many of the reasoning and representation extensions posed for CADUCEUS are explored in the other knowledge systems in this section, we consider them only briefly in the following paragraphs.

One difficulty with INTERNIST-I in evoking and evaluating diagnostic hypotheses is that it does not recognize when symptoms are interdependent. That is, symptoms related to the same internal state count the same as independent data. This can lead to an overemphasis by

To diagnose using INTERNIST-I's method:

```
1.    Initialize the master list, deferred list, and DoneFlag to NIL.

      /* Phase I—Entry of presenting symptoms */
2.    DATA-ENTRY: Ask the user for the set of initial findings or symptoms.
3.    For each symptom collect a list of evoked-hypotheses do
4.          For each evoked hypothesis do invoke UPDATE-
            HYPOTHESIS(hypothesis).

      /* Phase II—Control loop */
5.    Until DoneFlag is signalled do
6.    begin
7.          Recompute the master list evoking PARTITION.
8.          If num-candidates > 4 then invoke RULEOUT, else
9.          If 1 < num-candidates < 5 then invoke DISCRIMINATE, else
10.         If num-candidates = 1 then invoke PURSUE.
11.   end
12.   Return and report results.

1.    UPDATE-HYPOTHESIS(hypothesis):
2.    For each symptom do
3.    begin
4.          Collect a list of evoked-hypotheses
5.          For each evoked hypothesis do
6.          begin
7.                Update the data observed and explained (goodlist), data
                  observed but not explained (residue), data predicted but
                  not observed (badlist), and data predicted but about
                  which nothing is known (unknownlist).
8.          end
9.          Add the hypothesis to the master list.
10.   end

      /* Compute a score for each hypothesis. */
1.    INTERROGATE:
2.    For each hypothesis compute a score as follows:
3.    begin
4.          Add an amount based on a nonlinear scale indexed by the
            combined evoking strengths of the data on its goodlist.
5.          Discount an amount for all the data on its badlist, weighted
            according to a scale based on its IMPORT.
6.          Discount an amount for all the data in its residue, weighted
            according to a scale based on F(Mb/Dj).
7.    end

      /* Partition the diagnostic hypotheses into two lists: master and
      deferred list. */
```

FIGURE 9.38.   Method for diagnosis in INTERNIST-I (continued next page).

```
1.    PARTITION:
2.    begin
3.        Move all hypotheses back from the deferred list to the master list.
4.        Recompute scores for the hypotheses using INTERROGATE.
5.        Sort the master list.
6.        Pick the hypothesis with the top score.
7.        Compute the "remaining residue" as the residue left over after
          removing data explained by previously confirmed hypotheses.

          /* Include competing hypotheses on the master list, but discard
          other hypotheses less powerfully supported. */
8.        For each hypothesis on the master list do
9.        begin
10.               If the remaining residue is a subset of the remaining
                  residue of the top hypothesis, or vice versa, then the
                  hypotheses are "competing." Add the hypothesis to the
                  master list.
11.               Otherwise, if its score is below a relative threshold
                  from the top score, move it to the deferred list.
12.       end
13.       Set num-candidates to be the number of top entries on the
          master list.
14.   end

1.    RULEOUT: ...
      /* Ask about manifestations with very high frequency of occurrence in
      the hypotheses. These questions stand a good chance of eliminating
      one or more of the hypotheses. The level of questions is incremented
      via "type" and stops when the level reaches laboratory procedures. */

1.    DISCRIMINATE: ...
      /* Select the top two hypotheses for discrimination. Data are
      requested that count heavily for one hypothesis while counting
      heavily against the other.*/

1.    PURSUE:
      /* Select data that would strongly support the top hypothesis. The
      system continues in this mode until either the initial spread reaches
      a criterion or the top hypothesis no longer stands alone on the
      considered list.*/

1.    CONCLUDE:
      /* If the distance between the top models reaches a threshold,
      conclude that the disease corresponding to the diagnostic hypothesis
      is present. Remove from future consideration all observed
      manifestations that are explained by the diagnosis. If there are no
      significant unexplained data, then set DoneFlag. */
```

FIGURE 9.38.   (continued)

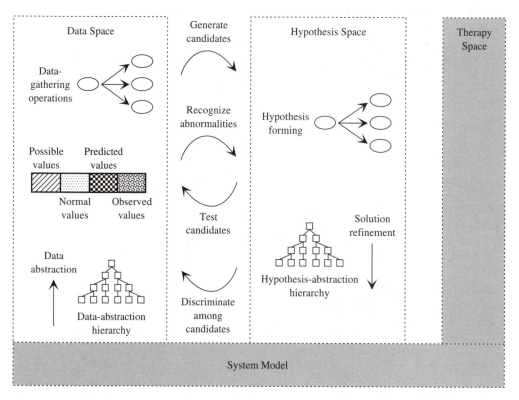

FIGURE 9.39.   Search spaces in INTERNIST-I. Compared with plan-based systems like DARN, INTER-NIST-I has an explicit hypothesis space. It has no explicit model of system behavior and function.

INTERNIST-I on disease hypotheses that have many easily observable but interdependent symptoms. For example, persons with elevated conjugated bilirubin levels in their blood usually have bilirubinuria. At present, the evoking strengths of each finding count redundantly toward any diagnosis that can explain them. Creation of a causal network of internal or pathophysiological states, interposed between observable manifestations and top-level diagnoses, could be used to lessen the combined influence of interdependent symptoms.

A related problem in INTERNIST-I arises from the need to isolate the effects of multiple diseases, which INTERNIST-1 considers one at a time. When INTERNIST-I concludes a diagnosis, that diagnosis is used to explain any observed manifestations that are listed on its disease profile. Once a datum has been explained, INTERNIST-I no longer uses it to evoke new disease hypotheses or to participate in the scoring process. The creators of INTERNIST-I noticed some problems with this approach, especially in cases where more than one disease process is active in a patient. In a case involving obvious liver and gastrointestinal involvement, the singular focus of INTERNIST-I favors those liver diagnoses that also exhibit gastrointestinal symptoms and those gastrointestinal disorders that exhibit liver symptoms. This preference behavior is an artifact of the one-at-a-time rating scheme, which considers each disease individually as though it were the sole cause. A more realistic weighing of diagnoses would compare different composite diagnoses involving combinations of diseases.

To address these problems, research on CADUCEUS has augmented the knowledge base with a causal network and also with a disease taxonomy. Both measures are intended to guide the aggregation of diagnostic hypotheses. Figure 9.40 presents a portion of a causal network developed for CADUCEUS. Nodes in this graph represent findings, treatable causes, and diagnosable intermediate conditions. The arrows indicate which states cause others. When there is more than one arrow leading to a node, any of the preceding nodes can lead to that state. We refer to such networks as **disjunctive causal networks**. This figure follows the conventions of the CADUCEUS developers, in which causes drawn on the left lead to symptoms drawn on the right. Note that this convention is the opposite of that used in Chapter 7 for drawing associations in classification.

This causal characterization of medical conditions represents disease mechanisms only in very abstract terms, since it has no detailed representation either of anatomy or of the duration of disease processes. Nonetheless, the identification of common causal nodes provides a starting point for recognizing when two pieces of data are independent, and also a guide for aggregating elements in a differential diagnosis and selecting intermediate hypotheses and measurements. For example, the first decision suggested by the causal network for determining the cause of jaundice is to discriminate between conjugated and unconjugated hyperbilirubinemia. These disease states are characterized by the presence of conjugated or unconjugated bilirubin in the blood, respectively. A finding from a blood test known as the "indirect-to-direct ratio" can be used to determine which kind of bilirubin dominates in causing jaundice. Similarly, if conjugated bilirubin is found to dominate, the next decision suggested by the network is between cholestasis and hepatocellular dysfunction. For this purpose, assays of liver enzymes obtained on routine blood screening may settle the issue.

This causal network can be augmented with a disease taxonomy that includes generalizations of the disease states that can be identified by simple clinical observations, as shown in Figure 9.41. A state abstraction need not be treatable, but it is more useful for discrimination if there are tests for confirming or disconfirming the state. Very high level state abstractions are organized around body organs, such as the heart, liver, and so on. This approach works because organ systems are specialized to carry out limited functions. Different diseases of an organ system result in the loss of function for the organ, producing many common symptoms.

By convention, when there is a causal link from an abstract cause to some other state, all specializations of the abstract cause are assumed to inherit the link. In this example, a finding of *caput medusae* can be taken at once as evidence for the abstract state portal hypertension. Portal hypertension, in turn, could be caused by fibrotic hepatocellular involvement or hepatic vascular involvement.

A diagnostician plans a strategy for resolving more detailed causes incrementally and in a way that takes into account the availability and cost of tests. This overlay reformulates the diagnosis process as a **hierarchical search**. The search through the network for causes can be staged to begin first at an abstract level, eliminating the complexity of detailed causes until whole sections of the network have been ruled out. Given the hierarchical network in Figure 9.41, a finding of *caput medusae* permits the conclusion of portal hypertension, although it gives no basis for discriminating among its subtypes. To resolve the subclassification requires the use of an inva-

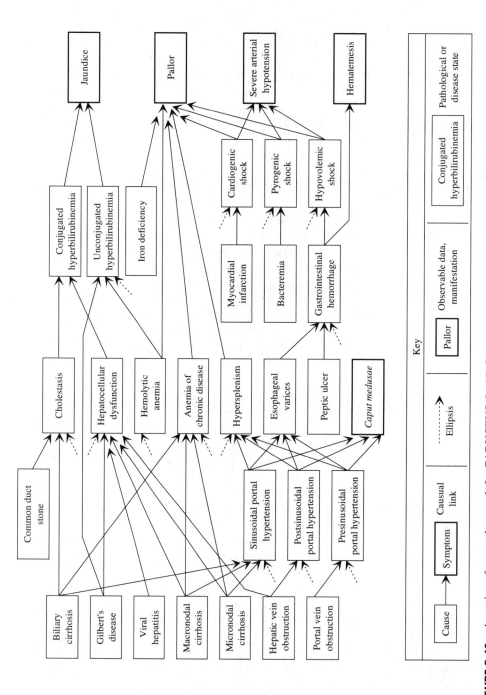

FIGURE 9.40. A portion of a causal network for CADUCEUS. In this figure, causal relations are indicated by directed causal links. Boxes with outgoing arrows represent causes and intermediate disease states. Symptom boxes are drawn with wide borders. Dashed arrows indicate where links and states have been elided. (Adapted from Pople, 1982, Figure 2, page 152.)

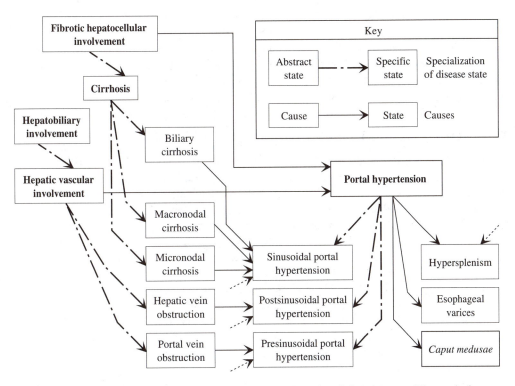

FIGURE 9.41. Extending the causal network to include a hierarchy of disease states. (The particular kinds of relations shown in this figure have been simplified from the ones proposed for CADUCEUS.)

sive procedure, the hepatic vein wedge pressure test measures the venous pressure inside the liver by means of a catheter wedged into the hepatic vein. Because of the complexity of this test, it may be easier for the diagnostician to resolve the cause, for example, by choosing some means for discriminating between fibrotic hepatocellular involvement (a cirrhosis) or hepatic vascular involvement. This example shows how grouping the interacting causes reasoning reduces the complexity of hypothesis discrimination.

Reflecting back on INTERNIST-I, a main source of difficulty is its pursuit of diagnostic hypotheses one at a time, leading to a style of reasoning that does not adequately account for the coverage of evidence by hypotheses when a patient has multiple diseases with overlapping symptoms. CADUCEUS is intended to consider diagnostic hypotheses that combine multiple possible causes, including causes for which there is no direct evidence. The problem-solving process for CADUCEUS is designed to carry multiple composite hypotheses at once, and to generate, compare, and evaluate these composites in a relative fashion.

In summary, INTERNIST-I and its successors are knowledge systems for diagnosing diseases of internal medicine. INTERNIST-I is unusual among knowledge-based diagnostic systems in medicine because it has a very wide coverage of diseases. It has served as a test bed for several different approaches to managing the generation and testing of diagnostic hypotheses. INTERNIST-I considers hypotheses one at a time. Several recognized shortfalls in INTERNIST-

I's performance have led to proposals for a follow-on system known as CADUCEUS. The key proposals for CADUCEUS involve the use of a hierarchical causal network admitting a hierarchical approach to diagnosis. CADUCEUS employed a disjunctive causal network augmented with abstract states, explicit refinement relations, and causal relations among the abstract states. Several elements of the CADUCEUS proposal are used, albeit in much narrower domains, in the other knowledge-based systems for diagnosis discussed in the following.

9.3.3 *Diagnosis in CASNET/GLAUCOMA*

CASNET/GLAUCOMA is a knowledge-based system to aid in the evaluation and treatment of patients with glaucoma (Kulikowski & Weiss, 1982; Weiss, Kulikowski, Amarel, & Safir, 1978). The term *glaucoma* refers to a number of sometimes chronic conditions of the eye. Glaucoma is a leading cause of blindness in the United States. Irreparable loss of vision can easily occur if glaucoma is not treated properly. Glaucoma is a subtle disease and physicians often refer their most complex cases to specialists. The CASNET/GLAUCOMA system is a consultation program intended for use by physicians. For simplicity, we refer to it as CASNET in the following.

Figure 9.42 presents a view of the kinds of knowledge used by CASNET. In the terminology of multistage classification, this is an intermediate-spaces view. This presentation emphasizes how the intermediate states in the causal network connect observations with diagnostic hypotheses. The links between the observations and pathophysiological states are established by conjunctive classification rules with weights measuring confidence in the association. These states are linked with disease categories, which are arranged in a generalization hierarchy. Figure 9.43 presents some examples of rules that map observations to states.

These rules can combine multiple observations or tests. Observations are taken as true, false, or uncertain. The confidence factors in the rules are combined to compute a confidence measure for the associated disease state. Negative confidence measures in the rules indicate that the rule provides evidence against the state, thereby disconfirming the state. An accumulative confidence that a patient's eye is in a particular state is derived from multiple associations from tests to states. According to thresholds, this confidence leads to an interpretation that a state is confirmed, denied, or undetermined. In the interest of brevity, we do not detail the rationale of CASNET's particular techniques for combining numeric weights for confidence.

Figure 9.44 illustrates a network of causal states and pathways describing the causes and course of glaucoma diseases. Again, our purpose is to sketch the approach rather than to explain or argue about its details. **Root causes** in the network are those for which no antecedent causes have been represented. Root causes are assigned prior frequencies, analogous to prior probabilities. Transitions between states are assigned weights called "causal strengths" or **transition frequencies**. These weights reflect the frequency that a disease will transition from one state to the next. The frequency for transitioning from a node is assumed to be independent of the path taken to reach that node. In short, the network is much like a Markov network (Breiman, 1969), except it is not strictly based on probabilities. In 1978, CASNET's knowledge base for glaucoma represented 400 tests, 100 states, 75 sets of rules for classifying observations and tests, and 200 statements about treatments.

A treatment plan in CASNET consists of an ordered list of statements like those shown in plan T4 in Figure 9.45. The list is ordered by preference, so the first treatment is tried before the second, the second before the third, and so on. Thus, the plan represents a prototypical sequence

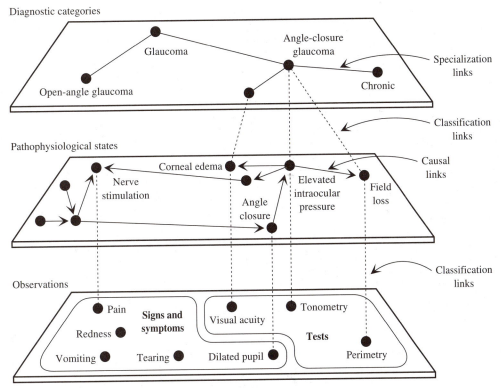

FIGURE 9.42. View of CASNET as a multistage classification system. (Adapted from Kulikowski, & Weiss, 1982, Figure 4, page 31).

of treatments for patients in a given diagnostic category. This ordering can be changed in response to particular observations about an individual patient. CASNET computes a preference factor for each treatment using rules like that shown in Figure 9.46. Contributions from multiple rules are combined in a manner similar to the way that confidence factors are combined from

```
IF    the ophthalmoscopy C/D test is greater than .6,
THEN  there may be damage to the optic nerve (.3).

IF    there is no arcuate scotoma,
THEN  there should be no visual field loss (-.3).

IF    the tension of the eye is greater than 18 mm of HG
      and peripheral anterior synechias (adhesions between the iris and
      the trabecular meshwork) are observed by gonioscopy,
THEN  there have probably been repeated episodes of angle closure (.6 to
      .8).
```

FIGURE 9.43. Examples of CASNET rules for mapping from observations to pathophysiological states.

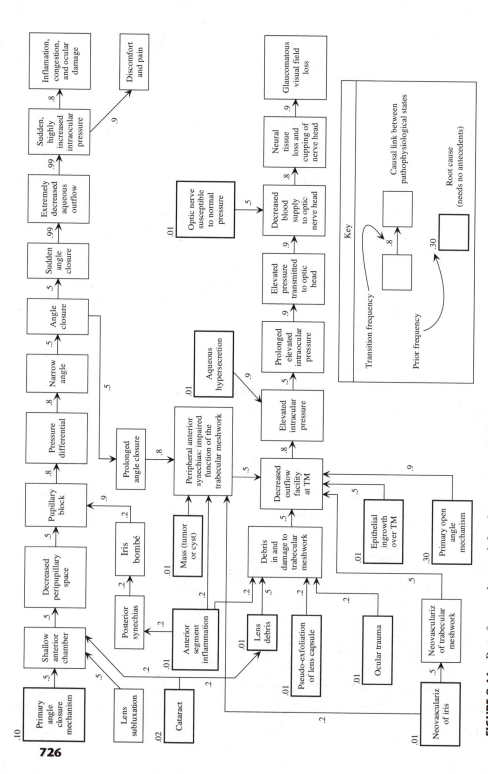

FIGURE 9.44. Part of a causal network for glaucoma from CASNET. Boxes stand for physiological states. In this figure, time and causality (indicated by the arrows) flow generally to the right. The arrows represent the order that states can appear in time as a disease develops. States corresponding to "initial causes," which are states with no antecedents represented, are shown in bold boxes and have prior frequencies associated with them. The numbers on the links are a measure of the transition frequencies with which glaucoma develops from one state to the next. (From Weiss, Kulikowski, Amarel, & Safir, 1978, Figure 2, page 149.)

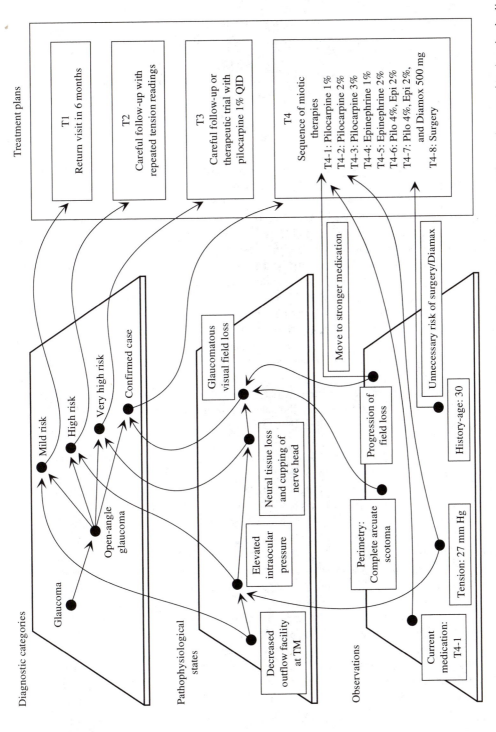

FIGURE 9.45. Examples of treatment plans and their relation to observations, pathophysiological states, and diagnostic categories. A patient's clinical status must be reevaluated on successive visits. New factors may need to be considered, the effectiveness of the current medication must be assessed, and new conditions may be detected that were missed at a previous visit. In this figure, we see how rules for selecting treatments in CASNET can draw on observations (such as current medication), as well as diagnostic categories. (From Weiss, Kulikowski, Amarel, & Safir, 1978, Figure 4, page 166.)

```
IF    the patient is thirty or older,
THEN  prefer other treatments over surgery (because it entails unnecessary
      risk) (-.7).
```

FIGURE 9.46. Example of a rule from CASNET for prescribing a treatment. Such rules are used to modify the preference factors associated with particular treatments. In this example, the negative preference counts against surgery as a treatment.

multiple observations to yield a confidence for a pathophysiological state. The rules with the highest preference are identified. From these, the earliest treatment in the plan is selected.

A common complaint about medical diagnostic systems is that they are unable to reason about the course of a disease or to advise on the treatment of patients over multiple visits. Although CASNET does not solve these problems comprehensively and lacks a quantitative model of time, it took some initial steps in recognizing and addressing the issues. In glaucoma treatment, the effectiveness of medication must be assessed while a patient is undergoing treatment. New factors must be considered, such as side effects, complications of the disease for which the current therapy is not effective, and conditions not detected during previous visits. Figure 9.45 shows how the selection of a therapy makes use of information from the other spaces. Although CASNET does not represent measurements of time, its causal network characterizes how diseases progress through a sequence of states. In a sequence of visits, a patient's condition may improve with treatment or worsen to the point where changes in therapy are required.

All diagnostic systems must determine what data to acquire. The techniques used in CASNET are not as systematic as others we will discuss for discriminating among multiple composite candidates. However, we describe them briefly because they illustrate several issues about test selection in a medical setting.

CASNET computes two sets of weights for nodes in the causal network of disease states that are used in guiding test selection. These are the so-called forward weight and the inverse weight. The **forward weight** of a node summarizes the weight of evidence carried from its antecedent causes. The **inverse weight** summarizes the weights of the confirmed states that are its consequences. Both weights rest on a concept of admissible paths. An **admissible path** from node a to node b is a sequence of intermediate causal states leading from a to b such that none of the intermediate nodes in the path has been disconfirmed. The weight of an admissible path between two nodes is defined as the product of their transition weights. If more than one node has been confirmed along a path, the weight of the path is computed from the nearest confirmed node. When none of the nodes has been confirmed, CASNET uses the prior frequencies of the root causes. The total forward weight of a node is the sum of weights from the admissible paths to it. The inverse weight of node a along an admissible path to node b is defined as the forward weight along the path normalized by the ratio of the weights of a to b. The total inverse weight of a node is defined as the maximum of its inverse weights along all of its admissible consequent paths. The **total weight** of a node is defined as the maximum of its forward and inverse weights.

Given these weights and costs associated with all of the available tests, CASNET can use different strategies for selecting measurements. Data are selected to rule out or support pathophysiological states. The weight computations group together and summarize evidence for particular causal pathways. Because of the connections among states, evidence for or against one node can influence the evaluation of other nodes to which it is connected. Thus, test selection involves choices of observable data for all the nodes along a path. One strategy is to select a test that has the maximum weight-to-cost ratio. Another is to select the test that has the maximum weight within a range of costs. In contrast with our TS-1 model, none of these weights measures the information value of a probe in terms of the probability distribution of the remaining competing hypotheses.

CASNET has been used as a test bed for experimenting with strategies. Some strategies take into account medical practice of clinicians. For example, history questions are asked before the physical examination, which precede the laboratory tests. After that, the clinician is usually concerned with determining the most likely root cause of the disease.

Figure 9.47 redraws CASNET's data space, hypothesis space, and therapy space in the format we have used for the other diagnosis systems. Comparing this with the multistage classification view, the observation plane becomes the data space, the causal network of pathophysiological states becomes the system model, and the plane of hierarchical diagnostic categories becomes the hypothesis space. The multistage view does not include the treatment plans in the therapy space. CASNET is the first knowledge system for diagnosis that we have considered that has substantial representations for all three spaces as well as the system model.

In summary, CASNET/GLAUCOMA is a knowledge system for diagnosing and prescribing treatment for patients with glaucoma. Diagnosis in CASNET is based on a multistage classification model. Observations are classified first into pathophysiological states, which in turn are mapped to diagnoses at different levels of generality. As in CADUCEUS, a causal network is used to represent disease states intermediate between observations and diagnostic categories. The network models behavior explicitly, but not anatomical structure. It represents the progression of a disease through multiple physiological states. CASNET used this network for modeling the time course of a disease and the revision of therapies for patients over multiple visits. Like other diagnostic systems, CASNET decides what data to acquire next. Although CASNET did not have a single, comprehensive approach for this and did not compare the information value of alternative probe points, it served as a testbed for experimenting with strategies for selecting data.

9.3.4 Diagnosis in SOPHIE III

SOPHIE III (Brown, Burton, & de Kleer, 1982) is a system built for teaching troubleshooting skills about electronic circuits. SOPHIE III is the third of a sequence of systems, each of which was used to explore techniques not only for student modeling and computer-based tutoring, but also for the representation of expertise for troubleshooting. In this section we focus on its knowledge engineering aspects. SOPHIE III pioneered several ideas that have been explored further in subsequent troubleshooting systems. It provides examples of diagnostic practice in a clear and simple form, especially the use of device and fault models in troubleshooting systems and its hierarchical behavior model.

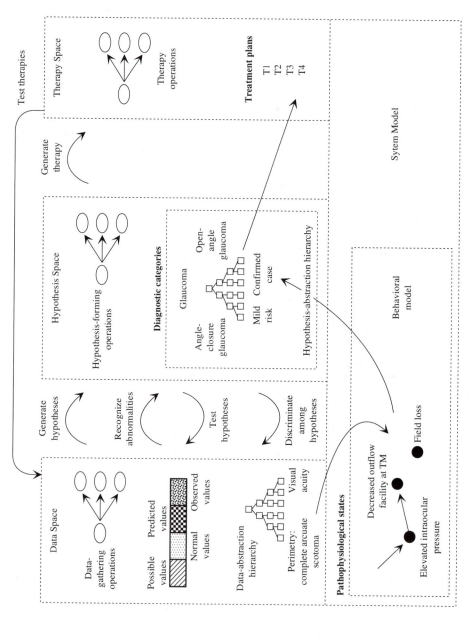

FIGURE 9.47. The search spaces of CASNET. In this figure, the pathophysiological states and the diagnostic categories are shown as separate subspaces. The "system model" overlaps with the three spaces, incorporating the causal model and the disease hierarchy.

An ambition of SOPHIE III's designers was to have the diagnostic system reason in a circuit-independent manner, as far as possible. As they put it:

> Many troubleshooters typically have great difficulty fixing familiar devices with unusual faults or unfamiliar devices for which they have had no specific training. This is not the kind of troubleshooter we wish to develop. (p. 229)

This pursuit of generality led SOPHIE III's creators to find ways to reason about function from information about structure, sometimes called **structure-to-function reasoning**. That is, SOPHIE III mostly used knowledge about components and their possible arrangements rather than knowledge about particular circuits. The developers sought principles of diagnosis that depended on knowledge of the devices from which circuits were constructed, but without further information about their intended functionality at a higher level. As it turns out, for efficiency in diagnosis SOPHIE III still needed to know about the intended function of its components. However, it was possible to separate SOPHIE III's knowledge into circuit-dependent and circuit-independent parts.

Figure 9.48 shows a piece of one of the circuits that SOPHIE III can diagnose. This circuit includes several different kinds of devices. For each kind of device, SOPHIE III has a behavior model and a list of its possible faults as shown in Figure 9.49. Systems like SOPHIE III are sometimes called "component centered" because so much of their knowledge is organized around classes of components.

SOPHIE III can carry out causal reasoning, analogous to the reasoning carried out by CASNET and CADUCEUS that used causal networks. In causal networks, the nodes of the network correspond to root causes, intermediate states, and observables or symptoms of the system being diagnosed. Reasoning in a causal network enables a diagnostician to answer questions

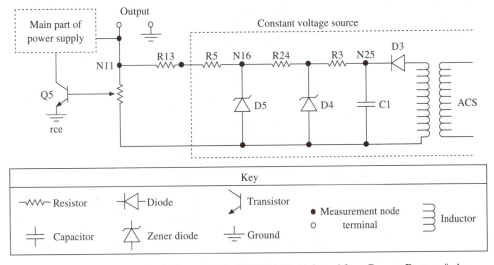

FIGURE 9.48.   An example circuit diagnosed by SOPHIE III. (Adapted from Brown, Burton, & de Kleer, 1982, page 258).

Device Parameters

```
    IMIN: the maximum allowable reverse current flow, -1 microampere.
    IMAX: the maximum allowable forward current flow, 1 ampere.
    VMIN: the minimum voltage across the diode, -50 volts.
    VMAX: the maximum voltage across the diode, .8 volts.
    IOFF: current for the diode OFF state, 1 microampere.
    ION: current for the diode's ON state, 2 microamperes.
    VOFF: voltage for the diode's OFF state, .3 volts.
    VON: voltage for the diode's ON state, .45 volts.
```

Behavior Rules

```
    Notation: V = voltage, I = current.

    GIVEN   A new voltage specified as a range, V = [VL,VH]
    IF      VH <= VOFF
    THEN    propagate the range I = [-infinity, ION].

    IF      VL >= VOFF
    THEN    propagate the range I = [ION, infinity].
```

FIGURE 9.49.   Example behavior rules from SOPHIE III's device model for diodes.

such as "what conditions could cause this symptom?" and "if the system is in this state, what other symptoms should be visible?"

In SOPHIE III, the ability to reason about states and causes depends on a simulation model and a fault model. The simulation model describes how the devices behave in SOPHIE III's electronics domain. Given the inputs to a device, the simulation model enables SOPHIE III to predict its output, among other things. Sometimes a single measurement can lead to the computation of many circuit values, propagated from component to component in the circuit. These computations make use of general electronic models, parametric device or component models, and demon interfaces ("watchpoints") that connect to higher-level behavior models that we discuss later.

The circuit laws describe relations among currents and voltages in a connected electrical system. For example, Kirchoff's current law says that the sum of the currents entering and leaving the terminals to a node must be zero. Kirchoff's voltage law states that if two voltages are known relative to a common point, the voltage between them is their (signed) sum. Ohm's law is one of the basic laws for resistors, saying that the voltage across a resistor is the product of the current through it and its resistance. These laws can be combined in a simple propagation theory to compute various other voltages and currents from known ones.

Figure 9.49 illustrates some elements of SOPHIE III's device model for diodes. We use the term *device* interchangeably with *component* to mean an electrical component with a characteristic behavior. The behavior rules interact with the general electrical rules, such as Kirchoff's laws.

The device fault model in Figure 9.50 provides a basis for describing primary causes of system malfunction. In the circuit fragment shown in Figure 9.48 there are 5 resistors, and therefore 20 possible resistor faults. There is 1 capacitor and therefore 2 possible capacitor faults, there are 2 zener diodes and therefore 4 possible zener diode faults, and so on. Faults are pre-

Device	Possible Faults
resistor	open, shorted, high or low
capacitor	shorted or leaky
diode	open or shorted
zener diode	breakdown-voltage high or low
transistor	beta-low, beta-high, sh/op/op, and others

FIGURE 9.50. Device faults in SOPHIE III. (Adapted from Brown, Burton, & de Kleer, 1982, page 263).

sumed to be mutually exclusive and exhaustive. The total number of diagnostic hypotheses would be much higher if multiple faults were considered in combination. SOPHIE III assumes that the only faults that can occur are of the known categories and that there is *exactly one* fault in the system. In short, SOPHIE III made the **single-fault assumption**. Given this limiting assumption, SOPHIE III uses the fault model as a basis for generating singleton diagnostic hypotheses.

SOPHIE III's troubleshooting activity is partitioned into what its designers called "passive troubleshooting" and "active troubleshooting." **Passive troubleshooting** refers to inferences about a circuit that are made about circuit values after gathering new information through measurements. **Active troubleshooting** refers to the deliberation of what new measurements to make in order to discriminate among competing hypotheses. Both processes of troubleshooting begin with a conflict, which is an unexpected value for a circuit parameter.

Figure 9.51 shows examples of passive troubleshooting rules from SOPHIE III's diode model. In SOPHIE III's component-oriented approach to troubleshooting, the goal is to rule out from consideration as many components and component modes as possible. Passive troubleshooting rules associated with the devices are used to rule out particular behavior and fault modes. For example, one of the rules says that if there is more current flowing through the diode than the shutoff current, IOFF, then the diode cannot be open. These rules enable SOPHIE III to accumulate increasing details about the state of the system being diagnosed as more measurements are taken. Passive troubleshooting involves propagating values and constraints through a description of the circuit. It works with inequalities using "range arithmetic" representations of predicted values for voltage and current.

Another useful approach in analyzing a circuit is to reason about it in terms of higher-level modules, whose behavior and interactions can be described more simply than that of their individual components. In SOPHIE III, the need for higher-level descriptions was rationalized in part by the need to be able to follow the reasoning of the students being tutored. The descriptions also provide the usual efficiency benefits of hierarchical problem solving.

Like primitive devices, modules are described in terms of their "modes" of operation. The bottom-level modules are built from primitive devices. These modules, in turn, are organized as still higher-level modules. In this way the behavior and structure of the overall system at several levels. Understanding the complete system is simpler at the top level because the number of interacting elements is greatly reduced.

The description of the behavior of a module in SOPHIE III has strong implications about the description of the behavior not only of its neighboring modules, but also of its parents and

Passive troubleshooting rules

```
IF      I_H <= I_MIN,
THEN    the diode must be open or I must be too low.

IF      I_L >= I_MAX,
THEN    the diode must be shorted or I is too high.

IF      V_L >= V_MAX,
THEN    the diode must be open or V is too high.

IF      V_L >= .1,
THEN    the diode cannot be shorted.

IF      I_L >= I_OFF,
THEN    the diode cannot be open.
```

FIGURE 9.51.   Example rules for passive troubleshooting from SOPHIE III's device model for diodes. As information accumulates from measurements and propagations, the passive trouble shooting rules eliminate device faults from consideration.

submodules. In particular, a knowledge engineer constructs a circuit-specific description of how each module's behavior contributes to the behaviors of its parents. Figure 9.52 gives an example rule describing how the behavioral mode of a parent module (IP-28) can be determined from the modes of its submodules.

SOPHIE III uses a model of strict subsumption in reasoning about faults in a behavior tree, enabling reasoning by elimination. If all of the faults of a node are eliminated, then none of its submodules can be faulted at any level. If a module is in a fault mode, then all of its parents must also be in some fault mode. Eliminating a module from consideration involves searching up and down the behavior tree for behaviors to eliminate. If a parent module is known to contain a fault, and all of its submodules but one are fault free, then the remaining submodule must be faulted. Figure 9.52 gives an example of the fault reasoning for the module IP-28 and its submodules REG and DCS. Reliable use of the behavior tree depends on completeness properties of the module descriptions.

When voltages and currents are discovered through measurement or propagation of values, rules can be triggered to propagate the passive troubleshooting process through the hierarchical module descriptions. SOPHIE III's propagator monitors values discovered by the low-level propagations. As in the diagnosis systems based on classification as discussed in Chapter 7, measurements of specific voltages are first abstracted to qualitative values (such as "voltage N14 is high"). These are then abstracted further to assertions about module behavior, triggering circuit-specific rules. Figure 9.53 shows an example of a propagation rule that operates at an abstract behavior description level involving modules and modes rather than voltages and currents. When there is more than one path to a point in a circuit, passive troubleshooting can provide values and constraints from each path. When the values predicted for a point are inconsistent with each other, there is a conflict.

Examples of propagator rules
```
    IF      the voltage (N11, N14) >= 31 volts,
    THEN    voltage (N11, N14) is high.


    IF      the voltage (N11, N14) is high,
    THEN    the variable voltage reference is high.
```

Rules for propagating behavior modes upward
```
    IF      REG is very-low or DCS is zero or DCS is very-low,
    THEN    IP-28 is very low.
```

FIGURE 9.52. Examples of rules that carry the propagation of electrical values to higher levels of module description. The first rule maps the quantitative voltage to a qualitative value. The second rule rule identifies a high voltage of a node with the variable voltage reference of the circuit. The third rule relates known fault modes of subcomponents with a fault mode of their parent.

Active troubleshooting refers to the process of deciding where to measure. SOPHIE III can request measurements at any exposed point in the circuit, on any terminal of any device. Measurements should be chosen that add information and thereby make it possible to rule out particular components or some of their fault modes. SOPHIE III reasons about this both in diagnosing circuits itself and in critiquing student performance at the task. The goal is to remove as many components from suspicion as possible. Toward this end, SOPHIE III relies on a probe evaluation function, which is used to score various alternative probe points for measurements. Figure 9.54 presents the elements of SOPHIE III in the format we have used for other diagnosis systems. Diagnosis programs that reason primarily from these models are sometimes said to use a "model-based" approach.

In summary, SOPHIE III is a knowledge system for diagnosing electronic systems. It pioneered several techniques that have been used in other troubleshooting systems, especially the combined use of a device fault model and a hierarchical behavior model. SOPHIE III reasons about both structure and function. SOPHIE III's structural knowledge indicates how components are connected. Its functional knowledge includes characterizations of component behavior in different conditions and their behaviors when they are faulted in various ways. The goal of this approach was to build a diagnostic system that could reuse much of its diagnostic knowledge on different circuits. SOPHIE III models each component of a given type in the same way, independently of its role in the circuit. This measure helps to ensure that SOPHIE III does not have hid-

Propagation rules for abstract module interactions
```
    IF      the voltage at N11 equals that at N14,
    THEN    eliminate the fault mode "sh/op/op" (collector open and base
            shorted to the emitter) for transistor Q5.
```

FIGURE 9.53. Example of a rule for reasoning about interactions between abstract modules in SOPHIE III. Such rules make it possible to take "big steps" in reasoning about interacting modules, without reasoning about all the detailed electrical implications.

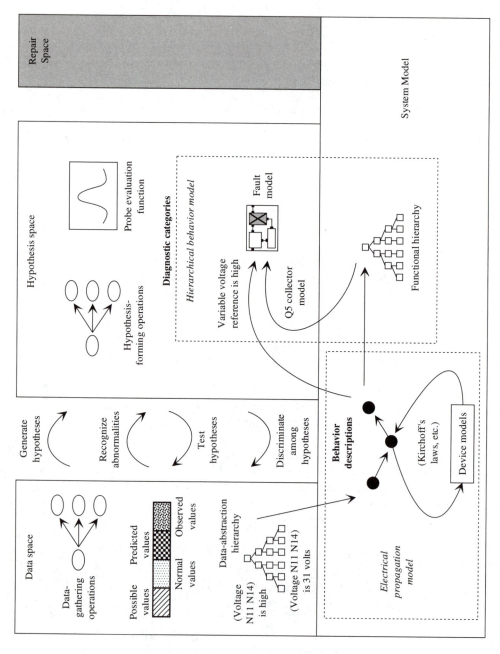

FIGURE 9.54. Main inference paths for diagnosis by SOPHIE III. Several of the models overlap between the hypothesis space and the system model. The repair space is shaded because SOPHIE III does not reason about repairs.

den assumptions about circuit functionality. The knowledge engineering strategy behind SOPHIE III's design recognizes that circuit diversity arises from the combinations and connections of a few kinds of parts. The complexity of SOPHIE's circuit-independent knowledge is determined by the small number of *kinds* of parts. To simplify its behavioral predictions and reduce its overall search, SOPHIE III relied on a hierarchical but circuit-specific model of its circuit modules.

9.3.5 *Diagnosis in GDE*

GDE (de Kleer & Williams, 1987) is a general system for troubleshooting. It exemplifies what is sometimes called **model-based diagnosis**. What GDE does not do well has served to define the open issues in diagnosis and troubleshooting. In this way, GDE has become a standard to which other diagnostic systems are compared. Much of the progress on knowledge systems for diagnosis has extended GDE's basic approach.

GDE extends ideas from SOPHIE III. In particular, it reasons from the structure of component-centered circuit models to predict behavior. It compares observations to predicted behavior and creates diagnostic hypotheses by reasoning about the differences. GDE is not a performance system with large knowledge bases developed for particular circuits or applications. It is of interest because it demonstrates systematic and principled techniques for handling multiple faults and for selecting probe sites.

Figure 9.55 gives an example of a digital circuit modeled by GDE, consisting of three multipliers interconnected with two adders. This circuit is a popular example for comparing how different troubleshooting systems work. The following discussion uses examples from de Kleer and Williams (1987). The behavior of the multipler M1 is modeled by a constraint relating its input values at A and C to its output at X. This constraint supports the prediction that the value at X is 6, given the input values shown in the figure. Then the value for X could be combined further with other predicted or measured values and constraints to make more predictions. For example,

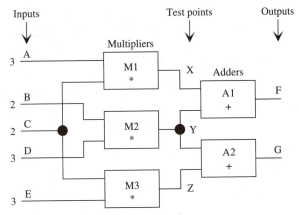

FIGURE 9.55. A digital circuit consisting of three multipliers and two adders. Each component is modeled by a behavioral constraint. For example, the behavior of M1 is modeled by the constraint that X = A * C. (From de Kleer & Williams, 1987, Figure 20, page 100.)

if we have that Y is 6, the values at X and Y could be used with an addition constraint for A1 to predict that the value at F is 12.

Constraint propagation can begin at any point in the circuit where a measurement has been taken. GDE uses both behavior rules and antibehavior rules. Using constraint propagation, GDE makes predictions by assigning values to many points in the system being diagnosed. The predictions provide a basis for noticing discrepancies with actual measurements. A symptom is indicated when two different values are predicted for the same point in the circuit. In other words, a symptom is any inconsistency in the predictions of values. For example, if a measurement indicates that the value at F is 10, this contradicts the chain of constraint propagations from circuit inputs, which predicts that the value for F is 12. Starting from such a symptom, GDE must infer the possible problems with the circuit.

GDE divides the diagnostic task into three phases: conflict recognition, candidate generation, and probe selection. Conflict recognition identifies symptoms in terms of contradictions between its predictions of values based on measurements. In our model of basic subtasks for diagnosis, we called this "recognizing abnormalities." Candidate generation creates diagnostic hypotheses. GDE's goal is to identify the set of candidates consistent with the measurements taken so far. Probe selection is the determination of the points for new measurements that will provide the most information for discriminating among the candidates.

In broad terms, conflict recognition begins with a set of components assumed to be good. De Kleer and Williams call such sets "environments." To avoid confusion with other meanings of that term in diagnosis, we use the term *good set* to refer to a set of components all of which are assumed to be working. Given a good set and a set of measurements, GDE uses constraint propagation to predict values for other points in the circuit. It maintains dependency records to keep track of the assumptions used to make predictions. These assumptions are the measurements and the components referenced by the rules used in constraint propagation. The prediction process need not be complete, in the sense of predicting all the values that could be derived from the measurements. The consequence of incompleteness is that some contradictions may not be noticed so the diagnostic system may take some additional measurements or fail to rule out some candidate diagnoses.

We now consider a simple example of prediction and conflict detection. We are given the inputs to the circuit in Figure 9.55. Assuming that M1 is working, GDE predicts that X is 6. Assuming that A1, M1, and M2 are working properly, it predicts that F should be 12. Suppose the value at F is measured to be 10 instead of 12. To explain the symptom, GDE assumes that there are one or more faults in the circuit, where a fault for GDE is a broken component. GDE uses symptoms to create **conflict sets** or, more simply, **conflicts**. A conflict for GDE is a set of components of which at least one is functioning incorrectly. Thus the set <A1, M1, M2> is a conflict set because at least one of these components must be faulted. We use angle brackets to indicate that a set is a conflict set.

For complex circuits, a single symptom can give rise to many conflicts. The set of conflicts must be represented and manipulated concisely to reduce the combinatorics of diagnosis. GDE assumes that every superset of a conflict set is also a conflict set. A **minimal conflict set** is a conflict set such that no proper subset of it is also a conflict set. In GDE, the goal of the conflict recognition phase is to identify the minimal conflict sets indicated by the measurements so far. Keeping the sets minimal helps to reduce the number of diagnostic candidates needed to cover them.

Step	Prediction	Good Set	Antecedent Steps	Comment
1	A = 3	{ }		In the following, we assume that the input values are measured and that they do not depend on any components working.
2	B = 2	{ }		Ditto.
...				
3	X = 6	{M1}		Predicting X = 6 depends on M1 working.
4	Y = 6	{M2}		
...				
5	F = 12	{A1, M1, M2}	3, 4	This prediction assumes 3 components are working.
6	G = 12	{A2, M2, M3}	...	
...				
7	F = 10	{ }		Suppose we measure that F = 10.
8	X = 4	{A1, M2}	4, 7	This prediction works backward from the addition constraint and components for computing Y.
9			3, 8	Conflict noted. Contradiction because multiple values are predicted for X.
10	Y = 4	{A1, M1}	3, 7	This prediction works backward from the addition constraint and components for computing X.
11			4, 10	Conflict noted. Contradiction because multiple values are predicted for Y.
12				Record minimum conflict set for F as <A1, M1, M2>. All these components are involved in the prediction that F = 12.

FIGURE 9.56. Steps in conflict recognition using examples from the sample circuit.

We now consider this operation in more detail. Suppose we are given the inputs to the circuit in Figure 9.55. GDE performs constraint propagation to compute values for all the labeled points in the figure. One of the values predicted is that F = 12. This prediction depends on the good set {A1, M1, M2}. Similarly, G = 12 depends on the good set {A2, M2, M3}. Figure 9.56 lists more of the intermediate steps in this computation and presents examples of computing other minimal conflict sets given more measurements. Sometimes a measurement will agree with one prediction and yet disagree with another. For example, if all the components in the sample circuit are working, the value predicted for G is 12. At the same time, the value G = 10 could be predicted from the observation that F = 10 and the subsequent derivation that Y = 4 in step 10. A subsequent measurement that G = 12 would agree with the first prediction but conflict with the second.

To reason systematically about minimum conflict sets, GDE begins with the empty good set and moves up through supersets. No set is explored until all of its subsets have been considered. At each step, GDE applies a constraint propagation process. If two different values are assigned to any cell, then the current good set is a conflict set. Whenever a good set is identified as a conflict set, no superset of that set is generated. This process generates only minimal conflict sets.

GDE uses several additional techniques to reduce the cost of conflict recognition. If old input values are kept constant as new measurements are made, then both the measurements and predictions based on them increase monotonically. GDE uses truth maintenance techniques to ensure that no inference is performed twice. Finally, good sets are not created unless there are some predictions that can be run. This last inhibition is GDE's main defense against a combinatorial explosion. The sets of components in circuits that tend to interact are the sets of components that are connected and whose signals interact. Circuits are typically designed so that the component interactions are quite limited. Consequently, the inference rules are also weakly connected, reducing the number of conflict sets generated.

To summarize, each conflict set generated by conflict recognition contains at least one faulty component. All the components in a conflict set are used in the predictions that led to the contradiction. To explain why a circuit is misbehaving, it is necessary to assume that at least one component in the conflict set is broken. The next step in GDE's diagnostic reasoning is to generate minimal diagnostic hypotheses, which are minimal sets of components that are adequate for explaining all of the symptoms. These sets are also called **minimal covering sets**. As noted in Section 9.1, the size of the search space of candidates is exponential in the number of potentially faulted components.

GDE assumes that candidates, like conflicts, have the property that every superset of a diagnostic candidate is also a candidate. Actually, this is not true when there are compensating symptoms, such that a second fault masks the effects of a given fault. Ignoring this issue for the moment, GDE generates new candidates incrementally. A candidate that does not explain the new conflict set is replaced with each of its immediate supersets. This is accomplished by replacing the old minimal candidate with a set of new tentative minimal candidates, each of which contains the old candidate plus one component from the new conflict set unless it contains one already. Any tentative new candidate that is subsumed or duplicated by another is eliminated. The remaining candidates are added to the set of new minimal candidates. This process ensures that each minimal candidate has a nonempty intersection with every minimal conflict set.

GDE begins with the empty set as the minimal candidate, meaning loosely that "everything is working." Actually, the exact interpretation of this minimal candidate is not that no component is faulty. Nor is the candidate generation and diagnosis approach based on the presupposition that every component is working unless proven faulty. Components can always be added to a minimal candidate to yield larger composite candidates. Rather, the interpretation of a candidate is that no smaller candidate containing a strict subset of components of the minimal candidates can explain all the known symptoms. As the diagnostic process continues, smaller minimal candidates are ruled out. Once ruled out, these discarded minimal candidates never reappear.

We now consider the candidate generation process starting with our sample circuit and the symptom F=10. As in Figure 9.56, the minimal conflict set for this is <A1, M1, M2>. The empty set is immediately ruled out because it fails to account for the symptoms. It is then replaced with three candidates, each specifying one of the components. Figure 9.57 shows additional steps in the candidate generation algorithm, where the minimal candidates are changed again.

Before leaving the discussion of candidate generation, we observe a few things about the meaning of minimal candidates for a diagnostic task. In this we return to some of the fundamental issues of candidate generating and testing discussed in our earlier analysis. Suppose that there

Step	Minimal Conflict Sets	Minimal Candidates	Comment
1	<A1, M1, M2>	[ ]	Given this minimal conflict set for F = 10, GDE begins with the empty set as its minimal candidate. Since the candidate is no longer valid, it must be replaced with its immediate supersets.
2	Tentative generation	[A1], [M1], [M2]	GDE generates minimal supersets as tentative candidates. Each of these by itself is enough to explain the discrepancy, so GDE stops.
...			
3	<A1, A2, M1, M3>	[A1], [M1], [M2]	This is another conflict from the observation that G=12. Old candidate [M2] does not explain all the symptoms, so it is no longer minimal.
4	Tentative generation	[A1, M2], [A2, M2], [M1, M2], [M2, M3]	[M2] is expanded by elements from the conflict set.
5	Elimination		Tentative candidates [A1, M2] and [M1, M2] are supersets of existing candidates and are eliminated.
6		[A1], [M1], [A2, M2], [M2, M3]	These are the new minimal candidates.

FIGURE 9.57.   Steps in minimal candidate generation using examples from the sample circuit.

is only one minimal candidate and that every conceivable measurement has been made. Even in this extreme case, there is no guarantee that replacing all the components mentioned in the minimal candidate or even every component in the system will fix the problem. That interpretation rests on further assumptions about the nature of faults, such as that all the components are being modeled, that environmental influences do not matter, and that faults are not intermittent. Furthermore, some components that are actually faulty might not appear in any conflict for several reasons. There may be undiscovered symptoms or some symptoms may be masked by multiple failures. Components that do not appear in conflicts will not appear in any minimal candidate. Nonetheless, the minimal candidates are valuable because they tell us that any diagnosis of faulty components must include all of the components in at least one of the candidates. In most situations the probability that misbehavior is caused by multiple faults—that is, larger candidates— drops off rapidly as the number of assumed faults is increased. Since minimal candidates are the smallest sets by construction, they are usually good indicators of the probable faults.

The remaining phase in GDE is hypothesis discrimination. The key decision in hypothesis discrimination is the selection of points to take new measurements. At each cycle of the diagnostic process there are several possible points to measure in the system. GDE assumes that taking a measurement does not affect the system being diagnosed and that all measurements have the same cost. Its goal is to select measurement points that provide the most information on average, for discriminating among the hypotheses.

GDE's compares probe points using Shannon entropy as a measure of their diagnostic completeness. GDE's approach to candidate discrimination is similar to the general one outlined at the beginning of this chapter. We discuss it in the following because GDE's method shows a way of making good use of available component information and because it differs from the approaches used by the diagnosis systems in our preceding case studies.

As GDE takes measurements, it finds out more about the state of the circuit at different points. Like SOPHIE III, it uses its model of the circuit to make predictions. If a prediction does not agree with observations, GDE concludes that there must be a fault in the circuit, meaning it identifies a conflict set. The probability of a specific diagnostic candidate is reduced to zero when its predictions are in conflict with measurements. For example, if a candidate states that a certain set of components is working and this leads to a contrary prediction, then the candidate is discarded in favor of ones that implicate more components. When GDE wants to select a probe point, it seeks those that are likely to yield a sharper distribution of candidate probabilities. For each measurement, there are a number of possible values. Depending on what value is measured, some candidates will be eliminated and the remaining ones will increase in probability. GDE compares alternative probe points by computing for each possible probe value the expected entropy of the remaining candidates. Probe points are favored that result in the lowest expected entropy for the remaining candidates.

We now consider GDE's approach to probe selection in more detail. The first issue is computing the necessary probabilities. Each component is assigned a prior probability of being faulted, typically obtained from the manufacturer or by independent testing. GDE assumes that components fail independently. The probability of candidate failing is computed from the probabilities of failure of its components. A candidate diagnostic hypothesis specifies for each component in the circuit whether it is working or faulted. The prior fault probability, p_i, assigned to a candidate, C_i, is the product of the prior probabilities of failure for each component, p_c, that the candidate designates as failed, times $(1 - p_c)$ for each component the candidate designates as working.

For each probe point or measurement, x_i, there are a finite number of possible values, v_{ik}. GDE is interested in which (multicomponent) candidates can be eliminated if x_i does not equal v_{ik}. These candidates are called the selected candidates. The other remaining candidates are called the uncommitted candidates.

As the diagnostic process continues, the probabilities of the candidates are adjusted to account for the results of measurements. This process uses Bayes' rule for computing conditional probabilities as follows where p_j' is the revised probability for candidate C_j given the measured result that $x_i = v_{ik}$.

$$
\begin{aligned}
p_j' &= p(C_l \mid x_i = v_{ik}) \\
&= p(x_i = v_{ik} \mid C_j) * p(C_j)/p(x_i = v_{ik}) \\
&= p(x_i = v_{ik} \mid C_j) * p_j/p(x_i = v_{ik})
\end{aligned}
$$

There are three cases for evaluating $p(x_i = v_{ik} \mid C_j)$, depending on whether the candidate has been previously ruled out and whether it makes a prediction about the value for x_i. Substituting back into Bayes' rule, we have:

Case 1 $p_j' = 0$ if C_j is already ruled out as a candidate because it predicts a value different from what has been observed.

Case 2 $p_j' = p_j/p(x_i = v_{ik})$ if C_j predicts that $x_i = v_{ik}$. That is, the probability for the candidate is revised by weighting it with the probability that $x_i = v_{ik}$.

Case 3 $p_j' = p_j/(mp(x_i = v_{ik}))$ if C_j is involved in no predictions about the value and m is the number of possible values for x_i.

What is still needed to perform these computations is a means of computing $p(x_i = v_{ik})$. GDE does this as follows:

$$p(x_i = v_{ik}) = p(S_{ik}) + p(U_i)/m$$

Thus, the probability has two components. The first part is just the total probability of the selected candidates, which are those candidates that predict that $x_i = v_{ik}$. Thus, the probability of any possible value is given by the candidates that predict the value. By itself, this term underestimates the probability because although the sum of the probabilities of all of the candidates must be 1, the uncommitted candidates make no predictions at all. To compensate for this, GDE adds back in a fraction of the probabilities of the uncommitted candidates. The approach assumes that the values predicted by the uncommitted candidates are spread uniformly over all possible values.

Thus, GDE computes probabilities for its candidates, estimates probabilities for different values, selects probe points, obtains new observations, and revises the candidate probabilities in light of the new information. The initial candidate probabilities are computed from the empirical data about prior probabilities. As new measurements are taken, the candidate probabilities are computed according to the three cases just discussed.

GDE's goal in probe selection is to identify the best candidate using a minimum number of measurements. To choose the best measurement, GDE computes an expected entropy for each possible measurement as follows:

$$H_e(x_i) = \sum_{i=1}^{m} p(x_i = v_{ik}) H(x_i = v_{ik})$$

where m is the number of distinct data values and $H(x_i = v_{ik})$ is the entropy resulting if x_i is measured to be v_{ik}. The exercises step through the probability computations for a simple circuit.

Several additional refinements and variations are possible. There are some computational shortcuts, such as computing incremental changes to entropy at each stage rather than computing new distributions. These details go beyond the scope of this section.

Another way to describe probe selection is in terms of interpretations. In other words, rather than focusing on candidates as minimal sets of components that are broken, we could focus on maximal sets of components that are assumed to be working. This is just the complement of a candidate relative to the set of all possible components. An interpretation is analogous in logic to what is called a possible world, which is a maximal set of statements assumed to be true. A probe provides data that can defeat an interpretation by contradicting some of the statements in it. In this perspective, the assignment of probabilities to a candidate is recast as an assignment to the prior probabilities of an interpretation.

In summary, GDE is an experimental system for troubleshooting that extends several ideas from SOPHIE III. GDE works from a component-centered model, where component behavior is expressed in terms of constraints. GDE explains misbehavior of a device in terms of broken components. It does not require or use specific models of kinds of faults. GDE's diagnostic hypotheses are expressed in terms of minimal sets of broken components, called minimal candidates. GDE uses an iterative method, which computes the sets of components involved in contradictions from measurements (conflict sets), minimal sets of components implicated in explaining the symptom (candidates), and selections of measurements that most fully discriminate among the candidates. GDE is representative of several experimental systems in diagnosis and troubleshooting, which are seeking generality and which are exploring the limits of simple but rigorously defined models.

9.3.6 *Diagnosis in SHERLOCK*

SHERLOCK (de Kleer & Williams, 1989) was developed as a next generation system after GDE. This section describes SHERLOCK briefly, to show how variations in the way systems are modeled can have significant implications for diagnostic strategy.

To understand the differences between SHERLOCK and GDE, it is instructive to revisit SOPHIE III as described previously in this chapter. SOPHIE III was one of the first diagnostic systems to use a circuit model to predict behavior and thereby to detect deviations from expected behavior. GDE differs from SOPHIE III in that GDE has no explicit model of how components could fail. This change was motivated by the observation that fault models were incomplete. A system that only looks for known kinds of faults cannot cope with unknown kinds of faults. GDE eschews fault models and represents components as either working or faulted. Not depending on models of faults, GDE determines that components are failing without knowing how they can fail. In this way it was hoped that GDE would escape limitations from the inevitable gaps in its knowledge about possible kinds of faults.

Unfortunately, giving up fault modes also means giving up important capabilities for diagnostic reasoning. Figure 9.58 illustrates the value of fault modes in modeling a simple circuit. In this circuit, B is a battery and there are three lightbulbs (L1, L2, and L3) connected in parallel. From the circuit we would predict that all three lightbulbs are lighted. Suppose, however, that we observe that lightbulbs L1 and L2 are off and L3 is on. Following GDE's approach, we would log the conflicts <B, L1> and <B, L2> for those components involved in the prediction. This would lead to the minimal candidates [B] and [L1, L2].

This brings us to the point about fault modes. It is silly for the battery to be a candidate. Either a battery is charged or it is not. If the battery is discharged (faulted), then there is no way it could still provide power to L3 *without also* powering L1 and L2. So the behavior of the circuit rules out the possibility of the battery being faulted. Unfortunately, when GDE identifies a component as broken, it makes no predictions about its behavior. To reason about the behavior of a faulty component requires modeling the component's fault modes.

This shortcoming did not pass unnoticed by the designers of GDE. In SHERLOCK they reintroduced models of how components can fail. SHERLOCK extends the approach of SOPHIE III in that it can also hypothesize that a component has failed, even when it does not know the mechanism of failure. Thus, SHERLOCK regains the ability to use information about what is likely to go wrong with a component and how components behave when they are faulted. This

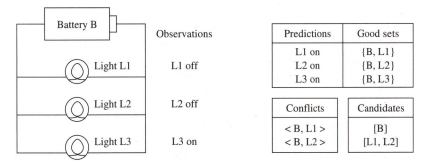

FIGURE 9.58. An example illustrating the value of modeling fault modes explicitly. (Adapted from Struss & Dressler, 1989.)

enables it to rule out implausible diagnostic candidates, which are derived from conflict sets but which do not realistically explain the particulars of the observed symptoms.

SHERLOCK reformulates its central task as identifying the correct and faulty behavioral modes of components. Figure 9.59 gives an example of a description of the behavior modes of a component. It describes the behavior of an inverter in terms of four modes including one good mode, two explicit fault modes, and one catchall fault mode for unknown behaviors. This multiple-mode formulation of diagnosis makes it possible to reason about multiple working modes as well as multiple faulty modes. Given this basic difference, we can now describe the operation of SHERLOCK.

Like GDE, SHERLOCK organizes its diagnostic process in three stages: conflict recognition, candidate generation, and probe selection. A conflict is a set of observations, inferred behavioral modes, and predicted probe values that is inconsistent. Like GDE, SHERLOCK computes minimal conflict sets. A good set (or "environment") for SHERLOCK includes values for the specific measurements that have been taken. SHERLOCK uses an incomplete prediction facility based on constraint propagation from device models.

A candidate for SHERLOCK assigns a behavioral mode to every component of the device. This contrasts with candidates for GDE, which simply designates each device as either working

Mode	Behavior	Comments
$G(x)$	$In(x) = 0 \rightarrow Out(x) = 1$	The good mode with correct behavior
	$In(x) = 1 \rightarrow Out(x) = 0$	
$S0(x)$	$Out(x) = 0$	A bad mode meaning "output is stuck at 0"
$S1(x)$	$Out(x) = 1$	A bad mode meaning "output is stuck at 1"
$U(x)$	No model	Catchall bad mode for unknown behaviors

FIGURE 9.59. Behavioral modes for an inverter. This model identifies four distinct behavioral modes. The G mode is the "good" mode. S1 and S0 are "stuck-at" modes for the output of the inverter. U is the unknown model, for which no behavior is predicted. The unknown mode covers all uncharacterized faults.

or faulted. Like GDE, SHERLOCK uses estimates of the probability of candidates in determining what measurements to take next. The probability of a candidate for SHERLOCK is the product of the probabilities that each of the components is in the designated mode.

Candidate generation is the area where SHERLOCK makes its greatest departure from GDE. The number of possible diagnostic hypotheses increases from 2^n for GDE to k^n for SHERLOCK, where k is the number of behavioral modes per component. SHERLOCK's creators wanted it to be able to consider all possible diagnoses without becoming burdened by accounting for all of them before the much smaller set of most probable diagnoses has been considered and eliminated. This goal led to the design of an approach that distinguishes **leading diagnoses** from nonleading diagnoses. SHERLOCK uses probabilities to guide the selection of which candidates to consider next. For SHERLOCK, a variable $k1$, nominally set to 5, determines the maximum size of the set of leading hypotheses. This set is extended as needed to include other diagnoses of equal probability. Consideration of candidates with probability less than $1/k2$ of the best diagnosis is deferred until later. The parameter $k2$ is nominally 100. Taken together, the diagnoses need not include more than the fraction $k3$ of the total probability of possible candidates, where $k3$ is nominally .75. In short, SHERLOCK performs a best-first search, guaranteeing that all unfound diagnostic candidates have lower probability than the ones that are tried.

For SHERLOCK, both the truth-maintenance system and the constraint propagator limit their reasoning to the leading diagnoses. No prediction is made unless its results hold in a good set limited to this focus. SHERLOCK uses the method described in Figure 9.60. There is a bootstrapping issue in the initialization because the leading diagnoses cannot be accurately identified without sufficient minimal conflicts. Furthermore, SHERLOCK's reasoning process cannot efficiently identify minimal conflicts unless there are leading diagnoses to focus on. The initialization sequence builds off the given observations and uses the most probable candidates to develop a list of leading diagnoses. Once the initial set of leading candidates has been determined, SHERLOCK enters the main loop of conflict recognition, candidate generation, and probe selection.

A useful insight from the method is that it is not necessary to normalize the probabilities of all the candidates in order to control the search. Since "unnormalized probabilities" are not probabilities, we switch terminology at this point to separate the notion of the probability of a candidate from the notion of an evaluation function for candidates used to control a best-first search. This description of SHERLOCK's method leaves out many details. For example, in the best-first search, candidates that are pruned as having too low a probability are not forgotten forever but are moved to another place from which they will not normally be retrieved.

SHERLOCK's approach to probe selection uses essentially the same probability computations and entropy concepts as GDE. However, given that there are potentially so many candidates, SHERLOCK characterizes the discriminating information by introducing diagnostic partitions, or **d-partitions**. A d-partition specifies that certain sets of modes are not to be discriminated. This groups together multiple candidates into larger equivalent sets whose probability is summed. It gives a way to assign a meaningful probability to a group of related modes without having to make strong commitments about their relative likelihoods. For example, it may only be important to discriminate between good and faulty behavior. In this case, the goal of identifying the most probable d-partition corresponds to identifying which components need to be replaced.

To find the initial candidates and minimal conflicts for SHERLOCK:

```
        /* Initially there are no measurements, conflicts, or candidates. */
        /* Loop to carry out the search for candidates and conflicts.
        SHERLOCK invokes this loop every time it gets a new measurement.*/
1.   AFTERPROBE: do until Done is signaled
2.   begin


            /* Extend the search incrementally. After a measurement,
            SHERLOCK looks at newly generated candidates and also leading
            candidates generated earlier. */
3.          Find the next best diagnosis given the conflicts so far.
4.          Focus the predictor on the new candidate, finding any
            predictions that have not been discovered earlier.
5.          If any contradictions are noted, describe them using minimal
            conflicts, eliminate the candidate, and go back to AFTERPROBE.
6.          Compute the probability of the new candidate using Bayes' rule
            by multiplying its probability by $1/m^n$ where n is the number of
            times the candidate fails to predict any of the measurement
            outcomes. (Actually, SHERLOCK ignores P(obs), treating it as a
            normalization factor.)
7.          Merge the new candidate into the list of leading candidates in
            order of decreasing evaluation.


            /* Check whether initialization is complete. */
8.          If the total evaluation of the set of leading candidates is k3
            or more, then signal Done.
9.          Eliminate any of the leading candidates that have evaluation
            less than 1/k2 of the leading candidate.
10.         If there are more than k1 candidates, prune candidates from the
            lower end of the list until it contains k1 candidates.
11.  end

     /* Here when Done has been signaled. */
12. Return the set of leading candidates.
```

FIGURE 9.60. Method for establishing SHERLOCK's initial set of leading candidates. The parameters *k*1, *k*2, and *k*3 are as described in the text.

To rank d-partitions efficiently while maintaining the desired focus on leading candidates requires some provisions and approximations. Whenever a diagnosis is found, all other candidates potentially in the same d-partition should be included in calculating its probability. In addition, there are other diagnoses beyond the leading candidates whose probabilities need to be included in the sum for the d-partition. Since predictions based on these diagnoses have not yet been run, SHERLOCK estimates their probabilities as the sum of the probabilities for the modes in the d-partition. This estimate is an upper bound.

This grouping of modes into d-partitions is especially relevant for describing multiple working modes. In particular, it is not meaningful to assign prior probabilities to component working modes in the same way that prior probabilities are assigned to component failure modes. Which working mode a component is in depends on the behavior and state of the system, not on the mechanisms of failure. D-partitions make it unnecessary to assign such modes. The XDE system described next uses a variant on this approach to describe working modes, by incorporating them in the descriptions of its behavioral model.

In summary, SHERLOCK is a knowledge-based troubleshooting system that extends ideas from GDE and SOPHIE III. Its main departure from GDE is that it models components as having multiple behavioral modes, including a catchall mode for unknown behaviors. The assignment of multiple possible modes increases the detail of the modeling of components and greatly increases the size of the search space. The advantage over GDE's approach is the ability to use knowledge about what kinds of faults are likely. This knowledge enables SHERLOCK to be more precise than GDE in deciding whether a candidate actually explains the observed measurements and discrepancies. SHERLOCK attempts to cope with its increased search space by focusing its computation on a set of leading candidates that explain the symptoms and have the greatest probability.

9.3.7 *Diagnosis in XDE*

Most component-based diagnostic systems have been exercised on circuit models that are small when compared with the practical working devices that diagnosticians actually troubleshoot. In contrast, XDE (Hamscher, 1988) is a knowledge-based system created to develop and test approaches for troubleshooting systems of realistic size and complexity. We include XDE in our set of diagnostic systems because it provides clear and cogent examples of knowledge that can be used for diagnosing such systems and because it provides an example of a modern hierarchical approach to the diagnostic task that makes realistic assumptions about what can be observed.

XDE diagnoses failures of the console controller board of Symbolics 3600 series computers, which has approximately 50 chips and 300 visible circuit nodes. In its reasoning, each chip is typically modeled as having several "chiplet" components. This greatly increases the combinatorics of search.

Interestingly, XDE uses many of the same diagnostic concepts as GDE and SHERLOCK. As its creator observes, XDE's abilities are not due to any major innovation in troubleshooting technology, but rather to innovations in constructing the device models it uses. Most of XDE's knowledge is in its model, which describes not only the structure, behavior, and common faults of the system, but also the kinds of signals that are easily observed. Crucially, XDE uses a **hierarchical diagnostic model** and hierarchical search strategy for its diagnostic task.

The majority of what is important about XDE is not actually embodied in XDE per se, but rather in the languages it uses to describe structure and behavior. For precision, we should probably reserve the name XDE to refer only to the domain-independent parts of the troubleshooting system. However, for simplicity in referring to these concepts and following our usage of the

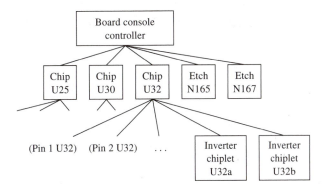

FIGURE 9.61.   Physical parts hierarchy. (From Hamscher, 1988, Figure 4.3, page 77.)

names like SHERLOCK and SOPHIE III, we use the term *XDE* to refer to the entire system, including the representation languages that it uses.

XDE's diagnoses are expressed in terms of components that can be replaced or repaired. XDE relates components using a strict physical-part-of hierarchy, whose smallest components in its electrical circuit domain are etches, pins, and "chiplets." An etch is a metallic strip and conductor on a circuit board, roughly the equivalent of a wire. A pin is a connector between a chip and a circuit board. A chiplet is an area of silicon inside a chip package. Chiplets are not individually replaceable, as are chips. They are defined in XDE to reflect the common engineering practice of co-locating several small functional units on a single chip. Figure 9.61 presents one such part hierarchy. Each candidate diagnosis specifies that each component is working normally, is faulty in some known way, or is faulty in some unknown way.

XDE represents the functional organization of a system hierarchically and describes the behavior of groups of components at multiple levels of abstraction. Thus, a functional characterization of a digital logic gate is easier to reason about than an equivalent collection of resistors and transistors. Similarly, it is easier to reason about the behavior of adders or shift registers operating on representations of integers than it is to reason about the detailed signals in the collections of logic gates that implement them. Figure 9.62 illustrates physical and functional part relations for a 4-bit adder. The physical parts form a strict hierarchy, starting with boards (board A and board B), chips (QA1, QA2, QX1, QX2, QO1), and chiplets (a1, a2, and so on). The functional part hierarchy has an *adder* at its root. We use italic labels here and in the figure to indicate functional units. The 4-bit *adder* is composed of two 2-bit adders (*tb1* and *tb2*). Each 2-bit adder is composed of two "full adders." The lower part of the figure superimposes the physical and functional part relations. From this we can see that the 2-bit adder *tb2* spans three chips and two boards. The other 2-bit adder *tb1* fits entirely on Board A. Although the physical-part-of relation is central to the troubleshooting task, the physical packaging of digital circuits can have an ad hoc nature. This is especially true in technologies where circuits are built using off-the-shelf chips, as in the adder example. In such cases, implementing the desired functionality requires sharing several functions in one package.

In the electrical circuit domain there is a much richer set of compositions of functional components than of physical ones. The reason for this is that there are many ways to connect

Functional part relations

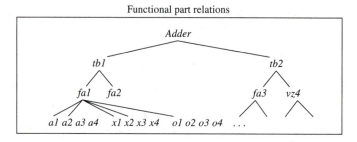

Physical part relations

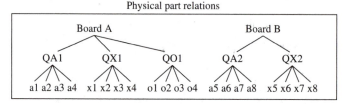

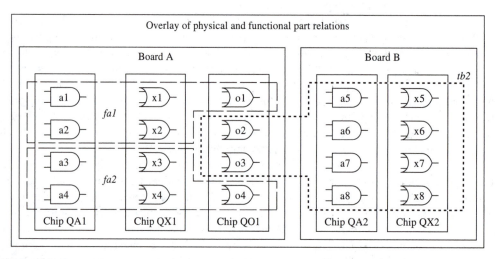

FIGURE 9.62. Physical and functional organizations of a 4-bit adder. (Adapted from Hamscher, 1988, Figures 7.4, 7.5, pp. 190–191.)

components together to provide different functions. A "flip-flop" is a simple circuit that holds a single bit of state. It can be combined with a transistor in different ways for different functionalities. For example, these same components can be connected to create a "toggle," which alternates between two binary states every time it is signalled. In another arrangement these components can form part of a clock generator.

XDE uses concepts based on ports and connectors to represent connections between components, both in the physical hierarchy and in the functional one. Such connections are essential for describing behavior, since they are the main paths for interactions among components. Functional ports and connectors are mapped to physical ones. The simplest correspondence relation is identity, meaning that a functional port or connector maps directly to a physical one. Functional ports and connectors can also correspond to concatenations of physical ones. This is how XDE represents computer busses and other pathways involving multiple connectors. For example, thinking back to the adder and multipler examples we considered for GDE, XDE can represent a binary integer in terms of successive connectors representing successive bits.

This brings us to the area where XDE gets most of its leverage: the description of abstract behavior. Figure 9.63 gives two examples of behavior rules for devices. These descriptions rest on an interval-based representation of time. The primitive statements in the time representation make it possible to assert that a signal has a particular value during a time interval, or that two signals have the same value. Behaviors are described in terms of functions that make reference to time intervals. We do not dwell the details of XDE's notations for behavior, and the figures leave out details such as backquoting and syntax for connecting to the truth-maintenance system. However, Figure 9.63 and later figures include some notes for making sense of the rules.

A behavior rule for an inverter

```
    IF      [isa ?i inverter]
    and     [thru ?l1 ?u1 (mode ?i) normal]
    and     [thru ?l2 ?u2 (num (in 0 ?i)) ?v]
    and     (overlap (?l1 ?u1) (?l2 ?u2))
    THEN    [thru (max ?l1 ?l2) (min ?u1 ?u2) (num (out 0 ?i)) (- 1 ?v)]
```

Translation

If the device is an inverter and is in the normal behavior mode on some interval, and if there is a value at its input port during a known interval, then the output of the inverter is a number whose value is 1 minus the input value.

A behavior rule for an adder

```
    IF      [isa ?a adder]
    and     [thru ?l1 ?u1 (mode ?a) normal]
    and     [thru ?l2 ?u2 (num (in 0 ?a)) ?v1]
    and     (overlap (?l1 ?u1) (?l2 ?u2))
    and     [thru ?l3 ?u3 (num (in 1 ?a)) ?v2]
    and     (overlap (?l1 ?l2 ?l3) (min ?u1 ?u2 ?u3))
    THEN    [thru (max ?l1 ?l2 ?l3) (min ?u1 u2 ?u3)
                  (num (out 0 ?a)) (+ ?v1 ?v2)]
```

Translation

If the device is an adder and is in the normal behavior mode on some interval, if there are numeric values to its input ports during known intervals, and if these intervals interlap, then the output of the adder during the interval intersection is a number whose value is the sum of its inputs.

Note on notation

[thru ?l ?u ?signal ?value] means that from the lower bound time ?l1 to the upper bound time ?u inclusive, ?signal had value ?value.

FIGURE 9.63. Behavioral descriptions for an inverter and an adder. XDE's behavior descriptions make use of an interval-based representation of signals over time. In addition, XDE has antibehavior rules that support constraint propagation in other directions and also rules that determine the modes of the devices.

XDE packages together many ideas about knowledge and its representation that we consider in the following. Perhaps the single most crucial insight is that even abstract and imprecise characterizations of behavior can be quite powerful for ruling out classes of diagnostic candidates. It is computationally expensive to model and predict the signals and transitions of circuit behavior in great detail. Furthermore, great precision is often not necessary for ruling out major fault categories, nor can typical instrumentation such as oscilloscopes routinely observe signals to great precision without great expense. This argument leads to characterizations of circuit behavior that take into account the kinds of observations that a practical troubleshooter can make. These characterizations help to define levels of abstraction at which to model the behavior of the device and its components. By representing the interactions of groups of components at appropriate levels of abstraction, predicting the behavior of a complex device from its physical organization can be greatly simplified. Use of multiple levels with their own vocabularies is crucial for XDE, since troubleshooting real digital circuits means reasoning about the behavior of components from resistors to microprocessors.

Figure 9.64 illustrates the general idea of a behavioral abstraction. In this example, the base-level behavior is simple addition and the abstract-level behavior is qualitative addition as defined by the table at the top of the figure. XDE requires that abstracting the predictions of base-level behavior should yield the same results (where it is defined) as applying an abstract-level prediction to abstractions of base-level inputs. In other words, if (QPLUS(Sign x)(Sign y)) is defined, then it is equal to (Sign(Plus x y)). The following example illustrates that the same result, +, is predicted by both approaches.

Abstracting the outputs
of base-level predictions = (Sign(Plus 4 5)) = (Sign 9) = +

Abstracting base inputs
and predicting behavior = (QPLUS(Sign 4)(Sign 5)) = (QPLUS + +) = +

Although reasoning about behavior at the abstract level leads to the same results, it can be not only less precise but also less complete than reasoning at the lower level. For example, QPLUS is not defined for the case where its arguments are of opposite signs. Thus, the abstract model makes no prediction for the abstract equivalent to the base-level case (Plus –5 4).

XDE's most powerful behavioral abstractions are its temporal abstractions. These include change, sequence, count, cycle, frequency, and sampling. The change abstraction indicates that a signal has changed its value over the last time interval. Abstractions related to the change abstractions on signals include indications that a signal crosses a value and the derivative of a signal. Given these abstractions, one can formulate questions about whether a signal changed during a known interval or how long a signal has stayed at the same value. The count abstraction counts the number of particular events in a time interval. The sequence abstraction indicates that a particular string of values has appeared contiguously on a signal. The cycle abstraction counts the number of occurrences of a particular set of values. The sampling abstraction returns the value that a signal takes on a certain moments, such as those determined by a clock signal.

Figure 9.65 gives two examples of signals. The distorted sine wave in the second signal is caused by a component malfunction. In this case, the number of zero crossings of the derivative is characteristic of a particular component failure and is easily observed by an oscilloscope.

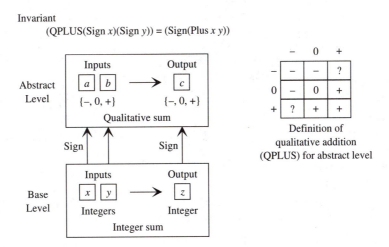

FIGURE 9.64. An example of a behavior and an abstraction of it. (Adapted from Hamscher, 1988, Figure 5.5, page 108.)

Using its abstract models, XDE can often make qualitative predictions about signals, leading to measurements that rule out major classes of diagnostic hypotheses.

Abstractions can be applied to any description of behavior. The XDE knowledge base includes rules for abstracted behavior. For example, Figure 9.66 shows how conclusions about frequency can be combined with behavior descriptions of an inverter. Two inverters are connected in series to implement a frequency buffer. The rule says that when this is done, the signals on the input and the output will have the same frequency. Similar rules are used to describe the behavior of oscillators, frequency dividers, and systems for synchronizing (clocking) digital logic. Such rules reflect the capabilities of typical equipment for measuring digital signals. Comparing the frequencies of two signals is a straightforward operation with an oscilloscope. These

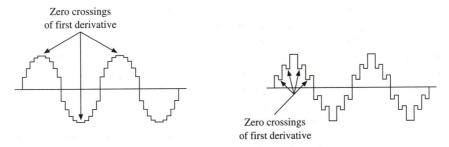

FIGURE 9.65. Examples of signals. Both signals represent digital approximations of sine waves. The lower signal is created by a faulty circuit. XDE describes the signals abstractly in terms of frequency, crossings of the midpoint value, and zero crossings of the first derivative. The signals can be distinguished by the too high number of zero crossings in the second signal. (Adapted from Hamscher, 1988, Figure 3.6, page 47.)

Rule predicting abstract behavior of a frequency buffer

```
IF      [isa ?d frequency-buffer]
and     [thru ?l1 ?u1 (mode ?d) normal]
and     Signal (fww ?w '(?a ?b) (l1 (in a ?d))) exists
THEN    [tsame ?l1 ?u1 (fww ?w '(?a ?b) (l1 (in a ?d)))
                        (fww ?w '(?b ?a) (l1 (out y ?d)))]
```

Translation

If the device is a frequency buffer and is in the normal behavior mode on some interval, and if the frequency of the input signal during the interval is known, then the frequency of the signal at the output is the same as the frequency of the signal on the input over that interval.

Notes on notation

`[tsame ?l ?u ?signal1 ?signal2]` means that at every time between the lower bound time `?l1` to the upper bound time `?u` inclusive, `?signal` has the same value as `?signal2`.

`(l1 ?port)` refers to the signal that is the logic level at some port.

`(fww ?windowsize ?sequence)` is the frequency abstraction function. It yields the frequency of a signal with respect to a window size and a particular sequence of values.

FIGURE 9.66.   This rule predicts the behavior of a frequency buffer in terms of the frequency of its signals, rather than in terms of the detailed signals as might be measured in its implementation as two inverters in series.

abstracted behaviors are not derived automatically but are coded as part of XDE's knowledge base.

Although XDE does not create abstract behavior descriptions automatically, the XDE methodology includes several standard classes of abstractions and principles for creating abstract behaviors. Reduction and encapsulation are two classes of abstraction used extensively by XDE. A **reduction abstraction** replaces a function of n-inputs with one of fewer inputs where the others are held constant. An **encapsulation abstraction** replaces a group of components with a single component, usually with fewer internal states and simpler behavior.

Figure 9.67 gives an example of a reduction abstraction. Reduction abstractions often make it possible to make predictions about device behavior in special cases where some of the inputs are not known and where they need not be known. For example, if all but one of the inputs to an AND-gate are held to 1, the gate acts like a buffer. In the two-input case, this means that as long as input `?n` is 1, the output is the same as the input. This case is interesting because the identity between the output and free input will have consequences for any abstraction of either signal, including temporal abstractions.

If one of the inputs to a working AND-gate is known to be zero, then the value of the other input does not matter and need not be known in order to determine the value of the output signal. Such abstractions are especially useful in diagnostic reasoning because they can be applied in cases where there is not enough information to make predictions at more detailed levels of description. This enables efficient use of probe data when ruling out major categories of faults.

Figure 9.68 illustrates a circuit for a reset hold counter and a three-state abstraction for it. The circuit, containing a 14-bit counter, has at least 2^{14} distinguishable states. However, its be-

Reduction: Rule for a two-input AND-gate with a constant input
```
IF      [isa ?x and2]
and     [thru ?l0 ?u0 (mode ?x) normal]
and     [thru ?l1 ?u1 (l1 (in ?n ?x)) 1]
and     (overlap (?l0 ?u0) (?l1 ?u1))
THEN    [tsame (max ?l0 ?l1) (min ?u0 ?u1)
                (l1 (in (- 1 ?n) ?x)) (l1 (out y ?x))]
```

Translation
If the device is a two-input AND-gate in the normal behavior mode on some interval, and if all but one of its inputs is held to 1, then as long as input ?n is 1, the output is the same as input.

Notes on notation
(in ?n x) refers to one of the inputs to AND-gate x. This is the one that is held to a constant 1.
(in (- 1 ?n) x) refers to the other input to AND-gate x. This is the one having the same value as the output y.

FIGURE 9.67. Example of a behavior reduction rule for a two-input AND-gate.

havior can be summarized by the three states in the right half of the figure. In the figure on the right, the counter starts in the reset state. Once the reset line is raised, the clock drives the counter. From then on, the counter is in the run state until either the reset line is dropped or the counter reaches 2^{13}. What makes this example work is that if you know that the clock frequency is constant, then you can reason about signal durations rather than individual counts. Again, the point of this example is that the reasoning about the counter can be greatly simplified for the purposes of troubleshooting the larger system. Furthermore, the output of the counter as described in the three-state figure characterizes signals that are useful for diagnosis and easily observable.

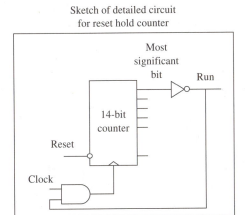
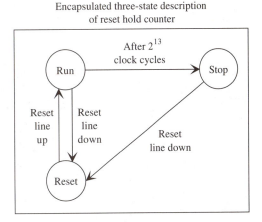

FIGURE 9.68. Functional organization of the audio decoder. (Adapted from Hamscher, 1988, Figures 5.11, 5.12, pp. 141–142.)

Encapsulation abstractions are used throughout XDE's knowledge base to model devices at many different levels of complexity. For example, microprocessors, which are fairly complex devices, are also represented abstractly as having only two unfaulted states: stop and run. Many of the most common internal failures of microprocessors cause them to fail catastrophically. The abstract model helps XDE to consider a microprocessor in the context of the whole circuit, without becoming prematurely concerned about the complex interactions of its parts before it has been determined that the microprocessor is a likely site of failure. For example, temporal abstractions are used to represent the behavior of programmed microprocessors in handling keyboard and mouse events. Without such abstraction, the inputs from the mouse and keyboard would be encoded at too low a level to be useful for troubleshooting—as can be observed in the action of human troubleshooters. Temporal abstractions map from the hardware up to rates of travel of the mouse in the x and y dimensions. Again, the abstractions translate detailed events in the hardware to events at a temporal scale that can be easily observed.

XDE uses essentially the same ideas for reasoning about faults as SHERLOCK. Components have failures, which are ranked by their likelihood. In XDE, failure rates are estimated from the number of breakable physical parts. In a more realistic model, other factors such as power dissipation of a chip would be included to give better predictions. The advantage of XDE's approach is that it affords workable estimates of failure rates directly from device structure as represented in available circuit diagrams. Figure 9.69 shows how likelihoods for component failure can be estimated in this way. There is a distinction between physical failure modes and observed behavioral failure modes. Since this table counts physical components, it makes sense only for estimating physical failures.

XDE represents some fault modes explicitly, especially those that are relatively common and those that result in drastically simplified device behavior. This involves keeping track of the status of subcomponents and associating different behavioral rules for different fault modes. These faults with explicit behaviors are called **syndromes**. Figure 9.70 shows examples of behavioral rules for components in faulted modes. Faults are represented explicitly in XDE in those cases where they represent a relatively high proportion of the probability mass for a component failing, and also in cases where they drastically simplify a component's behavior. XDE also implicitly represents the possibility of an "unknown" fault mode for components.

Component	Complexity	Probability of Working
Etch	1	$.9999^1 = .9999$
Chiplet	1	$.9999^1 = .9999$
Pin	2	$.9999^2 = .9998$
16-pin chip	33	$.9999^{33} = .997$
Oscillator chiplet	100	$.9999^{100} = .99$
Typical circuit board	2,000	$.9999^{2000} = .82$

FIGURE 9.69. Typical probabilities for various components. Complexity in this table is defined as the number of breakable physical parts. This table uses the number .0001 as the probability of failure for a single breakable part. That estimate and the first entries in this table overstate the actual probability of failure but provide a crude model of how the rate of failure increases with complexity. (Adapted from Hamscher, 1988, page 169.)

Behavior rule for a pin when the bonding wire is disconnected

```
IF      [conn ?pin (hole ?i ?e) ?port]
and     [status-of ?pin open]
THEN    [thru -infinity infinity (qci (hole ?i ?e)) 0]
and     [thru -infinity infinity (qci ?port) 0]
```

Translation

If there is a pin connecting a hole (connection point on a circuit board) to a port of the component, and if the pin is open, then the current through the hole and the current through the port are zero at all times.

Behavior rule for an oscillator circuit when the crystal is cracked

```
IF      [isa ?o oscillator]
and     [thru ?l1 ?u1 (mode ?o) inactive]
and     signal (fww ?w ?c (l1 (out 0 ?o))) exists
THEN    [thru ?l1 ?u1 (fww ?w ?c (l1 (out 0 ?o))) 0]
```

Translation

If the device is an oscillator and its mode is inactive, then the frequency of the output signal will be a constant 0 at all times. Another rule marks an oscillator circuit as being in an inactive mode when its crystal is cracked.

FIGURE 9.70.   Example of behavior rules for faulted components.

Like GDE, XDE has phases for conflict recognition, candidate generation, and probe selection. XDE extends this by two operations: decomposition and refinement. **Decomposition** supports hierarchical diagnosis. Whenever XDE performs decomposition, it expands the number of components it is attending to. Assumptions about the original parent component are made invisible and are replaced by assumptions about its subcomponents.

Refinement uses XDE's explicit fault models. For each component in the system, a diagnostic candidate asserts that the component is in a particular mode or "status." The prior probability assigned to a diagnostic hypothesis is the probability that the components have the status indicated by the hypothesis.

XDE uses a one-level look-ahead strategy for probe evaluation. The overall approach to troubleshooting used by XDE is sketched in Figure 9.71. The assignment of "repair weights" for components in step 8 is analogous to SHERLOCK's grouping of fault modes in d-partitions. XDE incorporates this repair consideration into its system model, where it can be used by the troubleshooting system.

In summary, XDE extends the troubleshooting techniques of GDE. It uses hierarchical models of system function to resolve as much of its diagnostic reasoning as it can at the simpler, abstract levels of description. In this way, it trades incompleteness of an abstract model for efficiency in ruling out diagnoses. Unlike GDE, XDE's does not model a circuit as being in a steady state. Its behavioral predictions consider the changing of signals over time intervals. Much of its power comes from its hierarchical model and its temporal abstractions. XDE's abstractions enable it to predict abstractions of signals that are relatively simple to measure. The results of these measurements enable it to focus quickly on subsets of the circuit that are most plausibly broken. Figure 9.72 summarizes the kinds of knowledge and innovative modeling techniques used in XDE.

To troubleshoot using XDE's method:

```
1.   Do until there is a dominant candidate.
2.   begin
3.   If there is a free observation, go to OBSERVE.

        /* Make predictions. */
4. TOP:
        Make predictions using behavior and antibehavior rules.

        /* Compute conflicts. */
5.      Compare predictions with observations. Compute conflict sets.
6.      If there are no conflicts, then quit, returning the leading
        diagnosis.

        /* Compute candidates. */
7.      Generate the set of diagnoses from the maximal consistent
        good sets.

        /* Assign weights to candidates. */
8.      Assign a probability to each diagnosis in a manner similar to
        SHERLOCK. This involves assigning zero probability to
        inconsistent candidates, and normalizing the remaining ones.
9.      Compute a repair weight for each component. The repair weight
        is the sum of the weights of diagnoses in which that component
        is broken.

        /* Refine candidates using fault model. This reallocates the
        probability of failure among the different syndromes. */
10.     For each candidate with weight > 10 % do
11.         If there is a refinement for the candidate, apply the
            fault model and go to TOP.

        /* Decompose candidate. This involves deciding whether to
        descend a step in the physical or functional hierarchy. In the
        physical hierarchy, assumptions are split. In the functional
        hierarchy, behavioral rules are run. */
12.     If there are decompositions, then descend into the hierarchy.
        Substitute more detailed model and go to TOP.

        /* Select probe. */
13.     Else select next probe using the minimal entropy one-level
        look-ahead strategy.
14. OBSERVE:
        Make next observation at probe point and go to TOP.
15. end
```

FIGURE 9.71.   Sketch of XDE's method for troubleshooting.

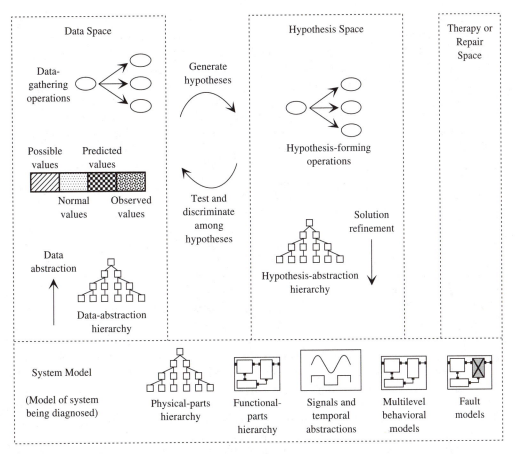

FIGURE 9.72. Search spaces and sources of knowledge in XDE.

9.3.8 *Summary and Review*

This section described seven example knowledge systems that perform diagnostic tasks. The DARN system is a plan-based system for diagnosis and repair. DARN's knowledge is embedded in a diagnosis-and-repair plan, which guides a technician though a series of measurements and part replacements. Plan-based systems are widely used both in medical and troubleshooting domains to represent repair procedures or treatment protocols in a computational medium. The plan-based approach is the most widely used approach for diagnostic systems. The knowledge base is essentially a flowchart, representing how to proceed but lacking explicit representations of the behavior, structure, or common faults of the system being diagnosed. This approach becomes unwieldy for tasks involving composite diagnoses.

The INTERNIST-1 system uses a classification model in solving diagnosis problems in internal medicine. INTERNIST-1 attempts to differentiate among diseases that have overlapping symptoms. It uses a one-at-a-time approach to reason about multiple diseases. CADUCEUS is a follow-on project to INTERNIST-1 that augments the knowledge base with anatomical knowledge and the ability to reason about the time course of diseases. CADUCEUS organizes its knowledge about diseases hierarchically. It uses a causal network to represent how some disease states lead to others. This provides a basis for modeling interactions among data elements.

CASNET/GLAUCOMA is a knowledge system for evaluating and treating patients with glaucoma. CASNET uses a multistage classification method for diagnosis that includes an intermediate level of interconnected pathophysiological states. The states are linked together in a causal network that represents prerequisites for disease and thereby the time course of diseases. CASNET explicitly represents behavior but not physiology. Transitions between disease states are assigned transition frequencies for when a disease will transition from one state to the next. Disease categories are represented in a taxonomy. CASNET also advises on treatment plans.

SOPHIE III is the first of the troubleshooting systems considered in this chapter to use an explicit model of a circuit in terms of the physical devices from which it is composed and the behavior of those devices. Components are represented as being in various behavioral modes, including different modes for different characterizable faults. SOPHIE III propagates information from measurements on some components to rule out modes for other components. It augments its device-level behavioral models with hierarchical functional models of the system. SOPHIE III uses a single-fault assumption to limit its search.

GDE is a system whose domain-specific knowledge is in its device models. It has no circuit-specific knowledge beyond the interconnection of devices in a circuit. GDE uses a systematic approach to diagnosing multiple faults, enabling it to discard the single fault assumption. A major challenge in all such systems is the need to focus diagnostic attention, so as to avoid becoming enmeshed in the exponential number of possible candidates. GDE selects probe points that will maximize the information gain. This computation is based on an entropy-based evaluation function of candidate sets, information about the failure rates of components, and Bayes' rule for computing the probability of candidates from the probability of the faults in the components they include. This technique is also used in SHERLOCK and XDE.

SHERLOCK is a next generation system to GDE. GDE's model of component behavior distinguishes only whether components are working or faulted. SHERLOCK models components as being in one of several different modes. This more precise domain modeling enables it to identify more specifically the symptoms expected for different kinds of faults. SHERLOCK also differs from GDE in that it conducts a best-first search through the most plausible candidates. This approach enables it to avoid generating the vast majority of implausible candidates.

The goal for XDE was to extend diagnostic techniques to realistically sized tasks. XDE uses essentially the same kinds of candidate generation schemes and techniques for probe selection as SHERLOCK. It differs, however, in that it uses a hierarchical model of the system being diagnosed, representing behavior and signals at multiple levels of abstraction. Much of XDE's ability comes from its use of temporal abstractions, which describe system behavior in ways that are easily measureable by available instrumentation.

These example knowledge systems differ in their models, problem-solving methods, and kinds and amounts of domain-specific knowledge. Nonetheless, they all confront similar phenomena that are inherent in diagnostic tasks. The next section develops submodels for the basic subtasks of diagnosis and discusses the phenomena that arise in them.

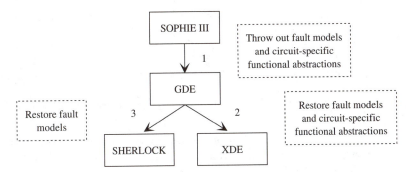

FIGURE 9.73. History of ideas in some electronic troubleshooting systems.

Exercises for Section 9.3

■ **Ex. 1** *[10]* *"Throwing Out the Baby with the Bath Water."* Consider the diagram in Figure 9.73 of the history of systems for model-based troubleshooting. According to this view of history, SOPHIE III had fault models and functional abstractions, both crucial for reasoning about large circuits. GDE threw out both things; subsequent work reintroduced them. This exercise considers some of the transitions in the approaches for these systems.

(a) Briefly, why did the creators of GDE throw out fault models?

(b) What were the major theoretical advances in GDE beyond SOPHIE III?

(c) The creators of SHERLOCK and XDE both included fault models to their diagnostic systems, but with an important difference from SOPHIE III. What was it?

(d) XDE also restored the idea of functional abstractions. In what ways did XDE carry this idea beyond SOPHIE III?

Ex. 2 *[05]* *Possible Candidates.* SHERLOCK and XDE both derive from GDE and both shift away from having a generator of all possible candidates. What are the key new ideas in the shift?

Ex. 3 *[05]* *Estimating Prior Probabilities of Failure.* Faced with competing hypotheses, diagnosis systems need to decide what observations to make. Most techniques depend on having estimates of the prior probabilities of diffrent faults. SHERLOCK requires that probabilities be supplied either by the manufacturer of components or by independent observations. The XDE system uses a weighting model that counts the number of components of different kids. Briefly compare the relative advantages of the two approaches.

Ex. 4 *[10]* *Diagnosis Using a Flat Causal Network.* In CADUCEUS, the causal network representation includes a graph of intermediate possible pathological states. This kind of description characterizes diseases only in very abstract terms. Although it has no explicit representation of anatomy or the time course of the disease processes, it can be used to guide a diagnostic process. This exercise considers some useful computations on the graph.

(a) Pople (1982) defines two kinds of differential diagnosis in terms of the causal graph. The "raw differential diagnosis" for a finding is defined as the complete set of disease entities (terminal nodes) that can cause it. The "refined differential diagnosis" is defined as the immediate set of causal predecessors for the finding in the network. Referring to Figure

9.40 (and ignoring ellipsis marks in the figure for the purpose of this exercise), what are the raw and refined differential diagnoses for jaundice?

(b) What are the next decision points suggested by the network if cholestasis has been determined as a cause for jaundice?

(c) Suppose the observed findings include both jaundice and pallor. What causes could explain both findings?

(d) Briefly compare the formalism and goals of a flat causal network in CADUCEUS with conjunctive classification.

Ex. 5   *[10] Diagnosis Using a Hierarchical Causal Network.* Hierarchical causal networks represent behavior using multiple levels of abstraction. This exercise considers some operations on the network in Figure 9.74.

(a) According to the network in Figure 9.74, what are the immediate general causes of pallor and jaundice?

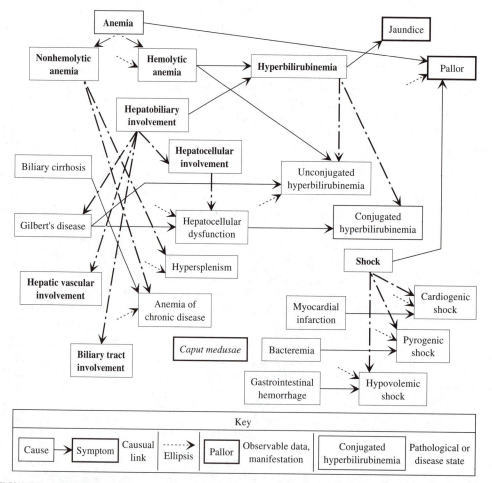

FIGURE 9.74.   A hierarchical causal network. (This network and exercise were inspired by CADUCEUS examples and are based loosely on them. However, the notation has been revised to be more similar to that used for other diagnostic systems in this book.)

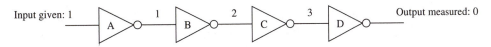

Input given: 1   A   1   B   2   C   3   D   Output measured: 0

FIGURE 9.75. This exercise is based on one suggested by Johan de Kleer (1989).

(b) Does conjugated hyperbilirubinemia cause jaundice? Does hypersplenism cause pallor? If yes, how are these relations indicated in the network?

(c) Suppose the patient exhibits both jaundice and pallor. (For the purposes of this exercise, ignore the seeming contradiction of a person appearing both yellow and white.) Why might hemolytic anemia be an attractive diagnostic hypothesis, over Gilbert's disease? Explain briefly.

Ex. 6   [24] *The Minimal Cardinality Principle.* When components fail with very small and independent probabilities, then every diagnosis with $k + 1$ faults or more has neglible probability compared to any k-fault diagnosis. This leads to an approach where on the first pass we consider only single-fault hypotheses. If no single-fault diagnosis is satisfactory, meaning no diagnosis explains enough of the symptoms, then we extend the set of diagnostic hypotheses under consideration to include composite candidates with two faults, and so on. Assuming that all components fail with equal probability, then the following very simple variation on the entropy computation can be used:

$$\$(\text{probe site}) = \sum_i c_i \ln c_i$$

where i indexes over the number of possible values $\{x_i\}$ at the probe site and c_i is the number of diagnoses of size k consistent with $x = v_i$.

(a) Consider a circuit of four inverters, as shown in Figure 9.75. We are given that the input to the device is 1 and the output is 0, indicating that there is a fault somewhere along the line.

Consider only single-fault candidates, where the notation $[X]$ means that component X is faulted and the other candidates are working. Fill in the x's in the following chart. Assume that the usual behavior and antibehavior rules are in effect.

Probe Point	Predicted Value	Consistent Candidates	Inconsistent Candidates
1	0	[B], [C], [D]	xxx
	1	[A]	xxx
2	0	xxx	xxx
	1	xx	xxx
3	0	[D]	xxx
	1	xxx	xxx

(b) Assuming a uniform prior probability of faults as .001, compute the expected (weighted) entropy for the three possible probe points. Consider only single-fault candidates and assume (for simplicity in this exercise) that these exhaust all possibilities. Use natural logarithms.

(c) Alternatively, compute $\$$ for the three possible probe points. Does the selection of the best probe point agree with part b?

(d) What important fault information used by SHERLOCK and XDE does this technique ignore?

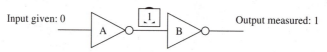

Input given: 0   Output measured: 1

FIGURE 9.76.   Diagnosing a two-inverter circuit. (Based on an example suggested by Johan de Kleer.)

Ex. 7   [15] *Supersets of Minimal Diagnoses.* A diagnosis must explain the symptoms. One complaint about the concept of minimal diagnoses is that not every superset of a minimal diagnosis is itself a diagnosis. Restated, a superset of a minimal diagnosis may not explain all
the symptoms that a subset explains. This exercise illustrates this point using a simple
example.

Let $AB(x)$ be the "abnormal" predicate that indicates when a component is broken.
We assume that a diagnosis is an assignment for every component c such that either $AB(c)$
or $\uparrow AB(c)$.

(a) Suppose that we have a circuit involving inverters and that we make observations at
different times. We require behavior of an inverter as follows:

Inverter(x) =>
$\neg AB(x)$ => $[In(x, t) = 0 \equiv Out(x, t) = 1]$

Give a second rule describing the behavior of an inverter when its input is 1.

(b) Suppose we are given the two-inverter circuit shown in Figure 9.76. Furthermore, we
are given the input value and the observed output value as shown.

Fill in the following table of possible diagnoses. Indicate which of these are minimal
in the sense used by GDE.

Diagnosis	Abnormal	Normal
1.	A	B
2.		
3.		

(c) Suppose we are given further that the inverters have two fault modes. Either the output is shorted to the input or the output is stuck at 0.

Stuck-at-0(x) => $[Out(x, t) = 0]$
Shorted(x) => $[Out(x, t) = In(x, t)]$

We are told that these are the only possible fault modes. Explain briefly whether all three
diagnostic candidates from part b explain the symptoms. What does this show about supersets of minimal diagnoses? Does your conclusion still hold if there could be additional but
unknown fault modes?

9.4   Knowledge and Methods for Diagnosis

The previous section reviewed several knowledge systems in detail. The computational models
used in these systems fall into four major categories: plan models, classification models, causal
models, and behavioral models. In the following, we compare these approaches to see how they
cope with diagnostic problems and to understand implications about their use of diagnostic
knowledge.

9.4.1 *Plan Models for Diagnosis*

Most knowledge systems for diagnosis are built around explicit representation of diagnostic plans or procedures. As shown in the case study of the DARN system, diagnostic plans are essentially procedures or decision trees. They are a way to write down a sequence of tests needed to guide diagnosis and repair.

There are several benefits to a plan-based approach. A plan-based approach places no constraints on the kinds of faults or repairs that can be described. This can be an advantage in large hardware-software systems, electromechanical systems, and living organisms where there are large gaps both in our understanding of such systems and in our ability to model their behavior. A plan-based approach makes no commitments about representation of function, structure, or faults. Furthermore, assuming that there are experts available who can diagnose the system of interest, the plan-based approach provides a representation quite close to easily collected protocols of problem-solving behavior. At least for systems of moderate size that are diagnosed on a routine basis, it is often quite straightforward to take protocols of diagnosis and repair strategies of expert technicians and to organize a plan around what they do on typical problems, without developing deeper models of system behavior. Paper-based plans for therapy or repair and diagnosis are commonly used in technical manuals for mechanical and electrical systems and in medical texts to present diagnostic procedures and treatment protocols. One appeal of such networks is that they can be extended incrementally to cover new diagnoses.

But the same simplicity that is the strength of plan-based approaches is also their weakness: they offer no demarcations of search spaces, no partitioning of subproblems, and no provisions for reusing diagnostic knowledge. Thus, although plan-based networks can be extended incrementally, they offer little leverage for making knowledge reusable. Similar knowledge used in different parts of a search tree is reentered for each part of the search to which it applies. A uniform extension to many parts of a model may require that decision nodes need be modified or inserted at multiple places in the network. Because they are extended in an ad hoc fashion, there is no easy way to determine the extent to which plan-based approaches cover their search spaces completely or systematically.

A plan-based approach for diagnosis works best in situations where there are relatively few competing diagnostic hypotheses. In cases where there are multiple interacting hypotheses, writing a diagnostic procedure to differentiate among all possible *combinations* can become quite complex, especially given the requirement that information-gathering operations should be done in an efficient order. Unfortunately, it is often in these complex situations that decision support is most needed.

The strength and weakness of plan-based approaches can be understood by considering their possible use in teaching about troubleshooting. Suppose most of our experience was based on troubleshooting a particular device. We might generate rules like "if the output voltage is between 33 and 35 volts, replace component C12." Such rules, while perhaps valid for repair of familiar equipment by average troubleshooters, do not teach concepts and do not generalize to other situations. If we change to a new device, few if any of the rules would be useful.

In summary, plan-based diagnostic systems provide representations for tests, observations, repairs or therapies, and machine states or pathophysiological states. Although this structure is close to concepts available from easily collected protocols, it does not provide much leverage for diagnostic domains where multiple competing hypotheses must be considered and where the col-

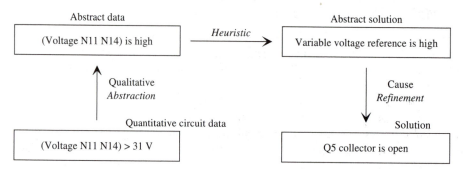

FIGURE 9.77. SOPHIE III characterized in terms of classification. This view of the system correctly characterizes some of the mappings of data to abstract data and also the use of SOPHIE's functional hierarchy in dividing the hypothesis space. However, since it leaves out crucial search spaces (such as probe selection) and processes (such as hypothesis testing), it gives a very incomplete characterization of diagnosis. (Adapted from Clancey, 1985, page 299.)

lection of probe data must be efficient. Because plan-based do not reason about test coverage, structure, or behavior of the system being diagnosed, the responsibility for organizing a plan to search the space of diagnostic hypotheses is left to the senior technician or knowledge engineer who creates the plans. Plans must be created anew for each system. Since function and structure are not usually represented explicitly, assumptions about the function and structure of the device are distributed in an unmarked fashion throughout the system. A small change to the system being diagnosed may require a major restructuring of the plan. One way of viewing the other models of diagnosis that follow is that they provide various strategies for computing a decision tree dynamically.

9.4.2 *Classification Models for Diagnosis*

As discussed in Chapter 7, classification systems provide a framework for organizing knowledge in tasks that fit the model. To illustrate some limitations of using this model for diagnosis problems, we recast the SOPHIE III system discussed earlier in this section in classification terms and see what is left out. Figure 9.77 characterizes SOPHIE III in terms of classification.

This characterization of SOPHIE III is correct as far as it goes, but it leaves out important search spaces and subtasks. It is correct in characterizing the qualitative abstraction of circuit data. It is also useful for characterizing the role of SOPHIE III's functional hierarchy and the refinement of hypotheses from abstract modules to individual components. However, by omission, it fails to describe the knowledge that SOPHIE III uses to generate and test hypotheses. For example, there is no discussion of knowledge for passive and active troubleshooting. The passive troubleshooting involves knowledge of device behavior, fault modes, and electrical laws. The active troubleshooting involves knowledge for probe selection.

This inadequate recasting of SOPHIE III in terms of classification shows how crucially knowledge-level analysis turns on identifying search spaces, and how leaving out a search space can apparently trivialize parts of a task. When we say that a system has diagnosis as a task and uses classification as its model, we are also emphasizing and deemphasizing certain functionalities. In this SOPHIE III example, classification is a part of the job but not the whole job. It associates symptoms and hypotheses but leaves out other parts of the reasoning.

9.4.3 *Causal and Behavioral Models for Systems*

Causal networks are multistage classification models that represent the states of the system being diagnosed and transitions between them. The network consists of nodes that stand for states and links that stand for transitions. The causal network explicitly represents disease (or failure) processes in terms of causes and intermediate stages. These networks have been used primarily for medical applications, such as CASNET, CADUCEUS, and ABEL.

Behavioral models are system descriptions in terms of functional and physical parts, part hierarchies, and behavioral rules. There are connections between the parts and statements about the interactions among parts. A central challenge is to reason from structure to behavior. Rules or working and faulted behavior are given for primitive physical parts. Behavior of larger functional units is described by composition of the primitive elements. These models have been used primarily for troubleshooting aplications, as in SOPHIE III, GDE, SHERLOCK, and XDE. Our TS-1 model is an example of a behavioral model.

To compare these two different styles of models, it is interesting to note that nodes stand for different kinds of things and that adjacency of nodes in the representation corresponds to very different things. In causal models, nodes stand for system states and adjacency in the representation means temporal adjacency with implied but unspecific cause. In the component models, nodes stand for components. System state, on the other hand, is expressed in terms of modes of components. Adjacency in the network represents spatial adjacency of components. Temporal adjacency is computed from structure-to-behavior mappings. The relative simplicity of such mappings in electronic systems and the lack of simple models for this in medical systems helps to explain the difference in modeling techniques across the two domains.

There are also differences in the degrees of aggregation for the systems being modeled. On the one hand, living systems have fewer repetitive structures than circuits at the level of diagnostic interest. Body diagrams do not have 32 replicated hearts or livers in the same sense that computers have multiple registers. Although replication and diversity at the cellular level defies the imagination, processes at the cellular level are seldom modeled as part of medical diagnosis. Another difference is that cells in the body participate in many different functions. The function of the "heart" is simpler than the function of the heart cells. Heart cells, like other body cells, need blood, metabolize glucose, produce waste products, can get cancer, and so on.

The key issues in building diagnostic systems are issues of modeling. Substantial work is involved in designing, building, and testing models. To put this in perspective, it is interesting that many of the electrical models involving such things as Ohm's law or Kirchoff's laws are based on theories for circuits that were discovered in the early 1800s. As we consider complex devices, with many interacting components and functions, we need to build more abstract and sometimes qualitative representations.

In comparing the recent causal network representation for diagnosis in medical domains (Patil, Szolovits, & Schwartz, 1981) and component-centered representations for troubleshooting domains (Hamscher, 1988), the convergence of representational issues is quite striking. Both medical and troubleshooting systems represent part and functional hierarchies. State-of-the-art systems in both general domains must deal with aggregations of components. The fundamental subtasks and phenomena of diagnostic reasoning are the same. It is not unusual to use simplifying state-space representations to represent aggregate behavior for higher functional modules. For example, recall the high-level representations of a counter by XDE, or imagine what representation would be appropriate for showing a set of processors in a "deadlock" situation. Both examples drive us toward state diagrams, as in the causal networks.

9.4.4   *Summary and Review*

To build a diagnosis model for a given class of systems, you have to ask: What goes wrong? What repairs can be made? What can be observed? How much is known about how the systems work? In this section we briefly reviewed and compared the main approaches to building diagnostic systems. The causal and diagnostic systems base their conclusions on device models and on explicit search processes for recognizing abnormalities, generating candidates, and selecting probe sites. Classification systems work on more shallow models, collapsing all the issues for identifying diagnoses in terms of a recognition task. Plan-based systems collapse all the search processes in a single, fixed network for performing tests and proposing repairs or therapies.

Figure 9.78 reviews goals and solution criteria, extending those that we considered for classification problems in Chapter 7. We now reconsider these in light of the four basic approaches to diagnostic systems. The choice of singleton or composite diagnoses corresponds to one of the major shifts in the design of diagnostic systems. Although plan-based systems require no stand on this issue, the practical difficulties of writing fixed plans for combinatorial searches mean that most plan-based systems are limited to singleton solutions. Similarly, classification systems are not suitable for a comprehensive treatment of candidates based on sets of solutions. In both plan-based and classification systems, composite solutions tend to be admitted in an ad hoc fashion for only the most common cases. In contrast, behavioral and causal systems automate the generation of diagnostic candidates, and this issue is central to the candidate generation subtask. Modern behavioral approaches provide a uniform strategy for generating composite candidates over the entire search space.

The choice of satisficing or exhaustive search tends to be problematic in plan-based approaches. Since decision networks stop in different places depending on the situation, they invite the creation of systems without a coherent policy on this issue. Classification systems vary on this issue, as discussed in Chapter 7. Typically, behavioral approaches are exhaustive, subject to the caveat that candidates whose probability falls below some threshold are ignored. The termination criteria listed above are most relevant for systems that include a repair process as part of the basic problem-solving task. Variations in these criteria illustrate some of the interplay between diagnosis and repair or treatment.

The policies for including solutions vary considerably. As before, plan-based systems tend to not enforce any uniform policy with regard to this. Behavioral systems incorporate considerations of positive coverage through the conflict recognition subtask and use probability thresholds to contain combinatorics in the candidate generation process.

On the policies for evaluating solutions, the same pattern occurs again. Plan-based systems typically take no coherent approach to this and may act differently depending on what symptoms are presented. As discussed in Chapter 7, classification systems also vary. Specific domain knowledge may make it appropriate to rank solutions or use preponderance-of-evidence rules. Behavioral systems also vary but tend to use a uniform policy across a search space.

Form of solutions

Singleton solutions	Each solution (a diagnostic hypothesis) is made up of exactly one cause.
Composite solutions	Multiple causes can be combined as a set to form a single solution.

Completeness of search

Satisficing search	Only one solution (singleton or composite) is reported even if multiple ones are possible.
Exhaustive search	All competing solutions (singleton or composite) are reported.

Termination criteria

Resource-limited search	Search ends when budgets for time, observations, expense, or risk are exhausted. Whatever candidates are under consideration are reported.
Treatment possible	Search ends when diagnosis is complete enough to enable a treatment that covers all of the symptoms.
Treatment successful	Search ends when the applied treatment or repair has eliminated all symptoms.

Inclusion criteria

Positive coverage	A solution is included if it covers some data and is not inconsistent with any data.
Conservative inclusion	A solution is included unless it is ruled out by evidence (even if it does not explain *any* symptoms).
Complete explanation	To be included a solution must explain all the acquired data.
Probability threshold	To be included a solution be consistent with observations and have a prior probability above some threshold.

Ranking criteria

Reasoning by elimination	A solution is accepted only when all other candidates have been ruled out by inconsistency with data.
Preponderance of evidence	One solution dominates another if the former covers more of the acquired evidence.
Minimal sets	If two composite solutions cover the acquired data and the set of classes included in one composite solution is a subset of the other set, then only the smaller composite solution is reported. This is also known as a parsimony rule.
Single-solution assumption	Solutions are mutually exclusive. Operationally, this means that once an explanatory solution is found, other solutions are immediately ruled out.
Ranked solutions	An additional function is used to rank alternative candidates, based on a priori information.

FIGURE 9.78. Some goals for combining classes and evaluating solutions that can be imposed on classification models.

Exercises for Section 9.4

■   **Ex. 1**   *[10]* *Model-Based Troubleshooting.* Hamscher used Figure 9.79 to summarize concepts and motivations behind the development of XDE. While accepting GDE's "model-based" framework for diagnosis, he believed that earlier programs had several inadequacies as suggested in the figure. This exercise considers the nature of these limitations.

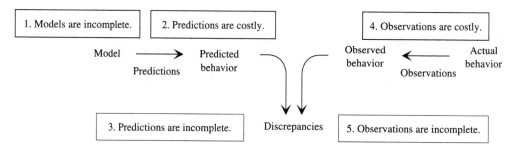

FIGURE 9.79.   Difficulties in troubleshooting from models for structure and behavior. (Adapted from Hamscher, 1988, Figure 1.2, page 3.)

(a) Briefly explain the basic framework for model-based troubleshooting illustrated by the diagram. (Your explanation should be general enough to cover the approaches used by SOPHIE III, GDE, SHERLOCK, and XDE.)

(b) For each of the following claims, briefly explain what the issue is and what XDE did to address the issue beyond GDE.

> (i) Models are incomplete.
> (ii) Predictions are costly.
> (iii) Predictions are incomplete.
> (iv) Observations are costly.
> (v) Observations are incomplete.

Ex. 2   *[10] Hidden Assumptions in Diagnosis Systems.* This exercise considers two assumptions that are ascribed to most of the knowledge-based systems for diagnosis in this chapter. For each assumption, discuss whether you believe XDE embodies this assumption. If so, state briefly how it is reflected in the system and how the system might act if the assumption were violated.

(a) Fixed-structure assumption: The structure of the system does not change during a diagnostic session.

(b) Non-intermittency assumption: Devices behave the same way over time.

Ex. 3   *[10] Cascading Faults.* In both troubleshooting and medical domains, one component failure or disease may predispose the system to have others. For example, a failure of one electronic part may cause other parts of a circuit to become overloaded and to fail themselves. For a medical example, a patient with a compromised immune system has increased risk of pneumonia.

(a) Briefly suggest how knowledge of such effects could be incorporated into a diagnostic system based on a classification model.

(b) Briefly suggest how knowledge of such effects could be used in a diagnostic system based on a component model.

Ex. 4   *[05] What's in a Method?* Professor Digit proposed the method in Figure 9.80 for use in a knowledge system for diagnostic tasks. He claims that it will work in any diagnostic domain.

Professor Digit says the method's sparseness is a virtue, since it reveals startling generality. Sam, his graduate student, disagrees. Sam says the method is about as general as

```
1.   Compute candidate hypotheses.
2.   Repeat through step 7 until Done has been signaled.
3.        If there is exactly one candidate, then stop. (Signal Done with
          success.)
4.        If there are no candidates, stop. (Signal Done with failure.)
5.        If there are multiple candidates, then generate a test.
6.        If no test is found, quit. (Signal Done with failure.)
7.        Execute the test (acquiring data as needed) and draw
          conclusions.
8.   Return the candidate.
```

FIGURE 9.80.   Digit's method.

the fetch-execute instruction cycle of digital computers and also about as informative for building knowledge systems.

(a) What is the fetch-execute cycle? Briefly, in what way is Digit's method like it or unlike it?

(b) Digit's method is a specialization of a well-known basic search method. Which one?

(c) Briefly compare Professor Digit's method with method MCF-2 for configuration in Section 7.2.

9.5 *Open Issues and Quandaries*

We now step back from our discussion of knowledge-based diagnostic systems to revisit basic questions and assumptions. What is a diagnosis? What is a causal explanation? What must we presume about the nature of systems that they be "diagnosable" at all? What are the immediate unresolved issues in building diagnostic systems? Our goal is to better appreciate that fuzzy boundary of practice and understanding that surrounds the state of the art.

Where Causal Models and Explanations Fail

A diagnostic hypothesis should *explain the cause* of misbehavior. This point has been made by many who have worked on diagnostic systems and who see an underlying and deeper requirement for diagnosis. Falling short of this goal, the first generation of medical diagnosis programs were merely **phenomenological**. These programs describe associations among phenomena but not the mechanisms underlying the observed associations. This shortcoming was not just limited to the systems. Rather, it also reflects the state of medical knowledge.

In contrast, current diagnosis and troubleshooting programs construct an account based on causes and effects. In a larger philosophical context, we can point to ambiguities and problems with concepts like cause and explanation. When is a cause "deep" enough? How must an explanation be organized to meet the needs of the listener? However, in troubleshooting, these issues are not treated as problematic. Causes are thoroughly grounded by the terminology of components, faults, and behavior. Explanations refer to causes. What needs to be taken into consideration is bounded by the repair and observation processes, and perhaps by considerations of later repairs. However, even though the issues of cause and explanation may seem so well understood in this context, there are situations where the mechanisms explored so far in diagnostic systems fail. This section considers some of these.

Most causal explanations are linear, constructed in chains that reflect the ordering of events in time. Thus, A causes B and B causes C, so D doesn't happen and E is observed. The elements of such an account include primitive events, subsequent events that cause other events later in time, and a theory of the interactions between events. This is not to say that only one thing can happen at a time. Certainly in a car engine, there are always many events going on at once. But many of the events are synchronized, and within the context of a subsystem we can often construct linear accounts, albeit with parallel strands.

A more complicated situation is where there are feedback loops. The human body sustains life by a number of homeostatic processes—feedback that maintains the functions of the body even in face of malfunctions. The output of systems with feedback can be correct even if the input is not. Feedback generally corrects small errors. For example, the cardiovascular system works to maintain sufficient pressure. There are feedback cycles that can signal to either increase or decrease the pressure. The immune system regulates the amount of antibodies produced by the body. Other systems regulate the balance of acid and base. In general these stay in balance, but it is possible for errors to exceed an adjustable range leading to catastrophic failure. Thus, in shock, the positive feedback in the circulatory system can dominate and lead to quite rapid decline and death.

Looking back at the examples of causal networks, none of those in this chapter could explain the behavior of feedback looks. Indeed, few of the systems had representations that were adequate to represent the control inherent in feedback links. In principle, state transition diagrams can be used to represent this detail but they become more complex. For example, to model a transition when a threshold is reached requires representing a quantity (state) that can change incrementally. An account of the behavior of the system needs to have ways to summarize the accumulation of effects.

So how does one organize causal explanations of feedback mechanisms? From the limited perspective of linear acounts, if any component in a feedback loop is implicated, then all other components are potentially implicated. Furthermore, the compensation reaction is often critical to understand in debugging the system. The situation is not limited to biological systems and is very similar in analog electronic or chemical systems that use feedback.

Beyond the issue of circularity and feedback are complex situations where behavior results from the interaction of many little influences. In most causal accounts, we seek to outline a "main thread of an argument." There is no simple account of the causes of behavior in complex situations, at least not in the same kinds of terms.

Finally, there are situations not only where the end behavior is dependent on many little things, but also where the ultimate behavior is extremely sensitive to small changes in the input. Such systems are called chaotic. Chaotic systems are another example of where the notion of a causal explanation is problematic.

Consider the behavior of a floating swimming-pool cleaner, which automatically bumps its way around a pool following an apparently random path. There are many ways these filters can be designed. Let us suppose that the direction of movement depends on the small variations in water currents created by several flexible hoses through which the pool water is pumped. Carefully observing the cleaner over several minutes might reveal to us that it does not repeat the same path twice around the pool. It moves like a self-propelled ball in a pinball game.

Suppose someone makes some unknown adjustments to the pool and cleaner after which we notice that the automatic cleaner tends to miss one area of the pool. We might then try to determine why the pool is no longer being thoroughly cleaned. Is the water level wrong? Have the hoses changed? Is a pressure setting wrong? In this case, analyzing the particular interactions that determine the path of the cleaner around the pool would be difficult because the interactions are so complex and the patterns never repeat exactly.

Alternatively, we could look for systematic pressures that would keep it out of the area in question. For example, there might be a water jet in the side of the pool that now systematically pushes the cleaner away more of the time. The point of this example is that the right frame of reference for a causal account may not be obvious at all from the set of objects and forces that are at work. Once again we come to recognize that the state of the art in building diagnostic systems is limited by the state of the art in describing models.

The same requirements and limitations that we face in diagnosing systems arise in designing them. Over the past few years there have been several movements in engineering practice that are concerned with designing systems that are diagnosable as well as being manufacturable and reliable. One example of an engineering methodology following this approach is known as FMEA, or failure mode and effect analysis. The analytic method is concerned with identifying potential modes of failure and relating those modes to causes, effects, and hazards. Furthermore, the modes are assigned priorities based on their probability, the severity of failure, and capabilities for detection. Thus we see that the notions of fault modes, cause, and effect arise not only in diagnosis, but also as part of the design cycle. They are part of how we come to understand how things work.

Dimensions of Variation in Diagnostic Tasks, Revisited

In the opening scenarios that we used to illustrate the meaning of diagnosis and troubleshooting, we identified several dimensions for identifying commonalities and differences among diagnostic tasks. These dimensions, which are given in Figure 9.81, are also useful for identifying some outstanding issues and technical problems in the design of diagnostic systems. Common to many of the open problems in building diagnostic systems is the relative weakness of current computational models of structure and behavior.

Closing Comments

In closing, recall our rough characterization of diagnostic search spaces: The data space represents the observable and the hypothesis space, the conceivable. It sometimes happens in diagnostic practice that a problem is outside the scope of the model. In the previous section, we discussed the suggestion that diagnostic possibilities should be organized in terms of decreasingly plausible pathways of interaction.

When they are stymied, diagnosticians must face the challenge of going beyond their models. More colorfully, they must find ways of seeing the unseeable and thinking the unthinkable. The truly open-ended nature of possibilities and human knowledge is illustrated by the following

What can be a cause. The scenarios differ in the nature of the causes of failure: broken components versus diseases versus environmental causes. A key issue in building diagnostic systems today is developing adequate computational models of structure and behavior, at several levels of abstraction.

Availability of intermediate diagnostic measurements. Although many current diagnostic systems do have entropy-based models of the information accessible through a probe, they do not combine this with rigorous measures of cost, risk, and reliability.

Steady state versus dynamic behavior. Time-dependent behavior can substantially complicate diagnosis. Most diagnostic systems do not use representations that are capable of adequately representing and reasoning about sequences of system states over time.

Modifiability of system state. There has been some work on the development of programs to develop automatic suites of test programs (Shirley, 1989), but there has been little integration of this work in troubleshooting programs. A key issue, again, is the development of adequate behavioral models.

Task overlap among diagnosis, testing, and treatment. Some repair actions provide diagnostic information. A common problem in formalizing troubleshooting is that some "tests," such as swapping components, are actually repair attempts. To handle these properly, a system needs a model of the actions involved in the repair attempt.

FIGURE 9.81. Some dimensions of variation in diagnostic and troubleshooting tasks, and the ways these relate to open issues in system construction.

story about the diagnosis of a simple but malfunctioning wood stove. In this scenario, creosote is a product of incomplete combustion. It condenses as a black liquid on cold parts of a chimney and hardens to a crystalline mass. If ignited, it can cause dangerous chimney fires. The correct adjustment of a wood stove includes provisions to reduce or eliminate creosote. The story is excerpted with permission from Busha and Morris (1982):

> We have adopted a Socratic method of assisting customers, emulating the technique of the Greek philosopher who taught his students by answering their questions with questions of his own. The trick is in knowing the right questions to ask, and as any veteran of the Vermont Castings Customer Relations staff will attest, the most important question is always the one left unasked.
>
> For example, a man from Long Island with an acute creosote problem patiently exhausted the resources of our most experienced experts. Everything seemed right—good installation, the right fuel—and yet every morning would see new rivulets of gooey black fluid appearing.
>
> The customer himself was cooperative and seemingly intelligent, and yet his stove resisted every proffered solution. Not until we actually saw his stove did the cause of his woes become obvious—there was a five-ounce fishing sinker attached to his air inlet damper which kept it permanently shut.
>
> A frustrated Customer Relations representative, who had spent many long hours educating the customer to the nuances of stove operation, called back to ask, "Why?" The customer replied that his wife had devised the sinker to eliminate the

slight clinking noise which occurred whenever the damper closed. The Customer Relations person could contain himself no longer and blurted, "Why didn't you tell us that you had a five-ounce lead weight on your air inlet damper?" The response was as simple as it was frustrating: "You never asked." (pp. 143–144)

Annotated Bibliographies by Chapter

A.1 Further Reading on Symbol Systems (Chapter 1)

The subject matter of this chapter is drawn from subfields that have evolved separately as cognitive science, formal computation, mathematical logic, knowledge engineering, and computer architecture. The references are separated into mainline references dealing with the material in the body of the chapter and quandaries references that discuss the more difficult questions raised in the "Quandaries and Open Issues" section. A few references are included because they are cited in the exercises.

Mainline References (Chapter 1)

Barr, A., & Feigenbaum, E. A. *The Handbook of Artificial Intelligence,* Volume 1. Los Altos, CA: William Kaufmann, 1981.
> This volume contains tutorial articles about artificial intelligence, including a chapter about knowledge representation.

Blank, T., Stefik, M., & vanCleemput, W. A parallel bit map processor architecture for DA algorithms. *ACM/IEEE Eighteenth Design Automation Conference Proceedings,* pp. 837–845, Nashville, Tennessee, June 29–July 1, 1981.
> This paper contains more information about the bitmap processor used in the exercises in Section 1.3 and a bibliography about related computers developed for image-processing applications.

Bobrow, D. G., & Collins, A. *Representation and Understanding*. New York: Academic Press, 1975.

> This edited book contains many first-rate papers bearing on the meanings of symbols, such as Bobrow's "Dimensions of Representation," which inspired the examples in Section 1.4. Other influential papers in this collection include Woods' "What's in a Link: Foundations for Semantic Networks" and Brown and Burton's "Multiple Representations of Knowledge for Tutorial Reasoning."

Brachman, R. J. On the epistemological status of semantic networks. In Findler, N. V. (ed.), *Associative Networks: Representation and Use of Knowledge by Computers,* pp. 3–50. New York: Academic Press, 1979. Reprinted in Brachman & Levesque (1985).

> This paper is in some ways a natural continuation of Woods (1975). It presents a survey of semantic network schemes and focuses on the primitive kinds of links that have been used in different representations. The paper is worth reading for the survey alone, which gives many illuminating examples from the development of semantic networks as motivated by psychological research on memory, linguistic research on sentence understanding, AI research on simulation and modeling of devices, and also research on learning. This paper fleshes out an earlier paper by Brachman titled "What's in a Concept," which appeared in the *International Journal of Man-Machine Studies* in 1977. It includes ideas that appeared in the KL-ONE network for structured inheritance languages that provide guidance for structuring knowledge and descriptions in terms of the primitives of the language.

Brachman, R. J., & Levesque, H. J. *Readings in Knowledge Representation*. Los Altos, CA: Morgan Kaufmann, 1985.

> This is a collection of reprints of important papers on knowledge representation. It includes Brachman's "On the Epistemological Status of Semantic Networks," Woods' "What's in a Link: Foundations for Semantic Networks," and Smith's "Prologue to Reflection and Semantics in a Procedural Language."

Ceccatto, H. A., & Huberman, B. A. The complexity of hierarchical systems. *Physica Scripta,* Vol. 37 (1988): 145–150.

> This paper extends the development of hierarchical complexity measures based on diversity discussed in Section 1.3. The measure in this paper gives a more local measure of hierarchical complexity, where the effects of interactions decrease with distance from the current level.

Chierchia, G., & McConnell-Ginet, S. *Meaning and Grammar: An Introduction to Semantics.* Cambridge: MIT Press, 1990.

> This textbook presents a broad introduction to issues in semantics. It explains and relates the contributions to theories of semantics by different philosophers and linguists, including Chomsky, Frege, Kripke, Montague, Tarski, and many others. The book requires little background in grammar, logic, or linguistics.

Clancey, W. J. The frame of reference problem in the design of intelligent machines. In van Lehn, K. (ed.), *Architectures for Intelligence: The Twenty-Second Carnegie Symposium on Cognition,* pp. 357–423. Hillsdale, NJ: Lawrence Erlbaum, 1989.

> Clancey's paper is about many of the themes developed in this chapter about symbols and meaning. At the time of writing this paper, Clancey was located at the Institute for Research on Learning, which is a multidisciplinary organization including many social scientists. Clancey's paper is a response to many philosophical arguments about cognitive science and AI. He is primarily interested in knowledge engineering as a practical engineering activity with distinct goals from artificial intelligence. His paper is an attempt to relate knowledge engineering practice to the philosophical issues, to integrate several perspectives from the symposium at which his paper was presented, and to reinterpret the idea of a knowledgel-level analysis from the relativistic perspective requiring an observer. Clancey draws on insights from the social sciences in developing a perspective similar to the documentation perspective of Section 1.1.

Davis, R., & King, J. An overview of production systems. In Elcock, E. W., & Michie, D. (eds.), *Machine Intelligence 8,* pp. 300–332. New York: Wiley, 1976.

> This is a very readable summary of different kinds of production-rule languages. It considers their syntax, applications, and assumptions behind their design. It clarifies both the unity and the diversity in this family of languages.

Hayes, P. J. Some problems and non-problems in representation theory. *Proceedings of the AISB Summer Conference,* pp. 63–79, University of Sussex, 1974. Reprinted in Brachman & Levesque (1985).

> This classic paper touches on many of the topics of this chapter, from the requirement for a semantic theory for representation schemes, to issues in the control of reasoning, to a discussion of several unsolved problems in representation.

Hendrix, G. G. Expanding the utility of semantic networks through partitioning. *Proceedings of the Fourth International Joint Conference on Artificial Intelligence,* Sept. 3–8, pp. 115–121. Tbilisi, Georgia, U.S.S.R., 1975.

> This paper describes a formalism for semantic networks that includes ways of grouping collections of nodes and links into partitions. It argues that these partitions can be useful for representing contexts, belief spaces, and the scope of variable quantification.

Huberman, B. A., & Hogg, T. Phase transitions in artificial intelligence systems. *Artificial Intelligence,* Vol. 33, 1 (1987): 155–171.

> This paper introduces the concepts of phases, phase transitions, and threshold effects to the characterization of large searches and proposes the use of concepts from statistical mechanics for analyzing many kinds of large-scale computations.

Kleene, S. C. *Mathematical Logic.* New York: Wiley, 1967.

> This is an introductory but thorough introduction to logic, including the propositional calculus and the predicate calculus. It is also very readable and often witty.

Knuth, D. E. *The Art of Computer Programming,* Volume 3: *Sorting and Searching.* Reading, MA: Addison-Wesley, 1973.

> This classic textbook and reference presents concepts about data structures, algorithms, and their complexity.

Levesque, H. J. Making believers out of computers. *Artificial Intelligence,* Vol. 30, 1 (1986): 81–108.

> A general review of symbols and logic, including the introduction of the term *vivid representation.* This was the invited Computers and Thought Award lecture at the International Joint Conference on Artificial Intelligence in 1985.

Levesque, H. J., & Brachman, R. J. A fundamental tradeoff in knowledge representation and reasoning (revised version). In Brachman, R. J., & Levesque, H. J. (eds.), *Readings in Knowledge Representation*, pp. 41–70. Los Altos, CA: Morgan Kaufmann, 1985.

> This "revised version" combines several earlier papers by Levesque and Brachman. Their analysis of inference versus calculation inspired some of the discussion in Section 1.4.

Tennent, R. D. The denotational semantics of programming languages. *Communications of the ACM*, Vol. 19, 8 (August 1976): 437–453.

> This is a tutorial introduction to the theory of programming language semantics as discussed briefly in Section 1.2. For the most part, the concepts and techniques of this approach have been impractical to apply in the design of knowledge systems because the systems have been too complex.

Williams, C. P., & Hogg, T. *Universality of Phase Transition Phenomena in A. I. Systems* (working manuscript). System Sciences Laboratory, Xerox Palo Alto Research Center, 1991.

> This paper extends the analysis of the conditions under which phase conditions can arise in search problems and shows that they arise under conditions much weaker than those used in Huberman and Hogg (1987).

Woods, W. A. What's in a link? Foundations for semantic networks. In Bobrow, D. G., & Collins, A. M. (eds.), *Representation and Understanding: Studies in Cognitive Science,* pp. 35–82. New York: Academic Press, 1975. Reprinted in Brachman and Levesque (1985).

> Until the publication of this paper, the meanings of semantic networks seemed to depend on the intuitions of the reader and on suggestive naming conventions. In this paper, Woods considers how this situation came about and discusses several approaches for defining meaning and also some of the inherent limitations of the (now) naive use of semantic networks.

Quandaries References (Chapter 1)

Agre, P. E., & Chapman, D. Indexicality and the binding problem. In *Proceedings of the AAI Spring Symposium Series, Parallel Models of Intelligence: How Can Slow Components Think So Fast?* pp. 1–9. Menlo Park, CA: American Association for Artificial Intelligence, 1988.

> This paper argues that some of the notions of how symbols and variables are used are implausible from a connectionist point of view.

Brooks, R. A. Intelligence without representation. *Artificial Intelligence,* Vol. 47, 1–3 (January 1991): 139–160.

> This paper argues that representations are overstudied in AI and that the field should progress from studying and modifying layers of simple behavior. It argues that many intelligent albeit simple behaviors do not require general symbol manipulation.

Fodor, J. A., & Pylyshyn, Z. W. Connectionism and cognitive architecture: A critical analysis. In *Cognition,* Vol. 28 (1988). Reprinted in Pinker, S., & Mehler, J. (eds.), *Connections and Symbols,* pp. 3–72. Cambridge: MIT Press, 1988.

> This paper explores the difference between classical and connectionist models of cognition, especially on the commitment to a symbolic representation of mental states. It presents many of the arguments about symbols and suggests that connectionism may pro vide an account of the neural or physical level in which higher-level cognitive architectures are implemented.

Garey, M. R., & Johnson, D. S. *Computers and Intractability: A Guide to the Theory of NP-Completeness.* San Francisco: W. H. Freeman, 1979.

> This is a well-written book about the mathematics of intractable problems. The book is widely used and cited.

Gazzaniga, M. S. *The Social Brain: Discovering the Networks of the Mind.* New York: Basic Books, 1985.

> This is a popular book by a noted brain researcher reporting in understandable terms about the methods and results in a range of split-brain experiments. This book discusses some of the best brain-based evidence for a modular architecture of mind, similar in some ways to that described in Minsky (1986).

Gazzaniga, M. S. Organization of the human brain. *Science,* Vol. 245 (1 September 1989): 947–952.

> This is a very readable overview of current knowledge about the human brain. The article describes how a correlation between brain structure and function is determined by various experiments, such as using nuclear magnetic resonance data from people who have brain lesions. The article concludes that there is much evidence for a modular organization and a high degree of functional specificity in the information transmitted over neural systems. The article also offers some perspectives on how special activities in the left hemisphere contribute to a sense of consciousness.

Ginsberg, M. L. (ed.). *Readings in Nonmonotonic Reasoning.* Los Altos, CA: Morgan Kaufmann, 1987.

> This is a collection of papers about the theory and applications of nonmonotonic reasoning. A well-organized collection with helpful introductions to collections of papers, it is highly recommended.

Hillis, W. D. *The Connection Machine.* Cambridge: MIT Press, 1985.

> This book contains Hillis's thesis on the connection machine as described briefly in Section 1.4.

Hillis, W. D., & Steele, G. L. Data parallel algorithms. *Communications of the ACM,* Vol. 29, 12 (December 1986): 1170–1183.

> A paper discussing data parallelism. The issue of CACM in which this appears contains several other articles about the programming of massively parallel computers.

Hirst, G. Ontological assumptions in knowledge representation. In *Principles of Knowledge Representation and Reasoning,* pp. 157–169. San Mateo, CA: Morgan Kaufmann, 1989.

> Most contemporary logics and knowledge representation languages base the semantics of the existential and universal quantifiers on the ontological assumptions of Russell and Quine. This paper considers the inadequacy of this approach for developing a logical semantics for natural language. The article is concerned with sentences that speak of existence, nonexistence, and nonexistent objects. In short, there is more than one notion of what it means to "exist." This paper shows why, with examples.

Huberman, B. A., & Hogg, T. Complexity and adaptation. In *Physica D,* Vol. 22 (1986): 376–384. Amsterdam: North-Holland.

> This paper proposes the hierarchical complexity measure discussed in Section 1.3. This measure of complexity is intended to indicate the diversity within a system while ignoring its detailed specification. It provides a quantitative measure for discrete hierarchical structures made up of identical elementary parts. This measure of complexity is maximal for systems that are intermediate between symmetric order and complete disorder. In later papers, Huberman and Hogg speculate that this measure provides an indicator for the potential of systems to adapt—roughly, that complexity is inherent in adaptable systems.

Kirsh, D. Today the earwig, tomorrow man? *Artificial Intelligence,* Vol. 47, 1–3 (January 1991): 161–184.

> This paper is a response to Brooks (1991). It argues that Brooks' "representation-free" approach is not really without a limited form of symbols and that its potential is overstated.

Kowalski, R. Algorithm = Logic + Control. *Communications of the ACM,* Vol. 22, 7 (July 1979): 424–436.

> This very famous early paper is about the concept of logic programming. It argues that a program is specified by a logic component that determines the meaning of an algorithm and a control component that determines problem-solving strategies.

Lakoff, G., & Johnson, M. *Metaphors We Live By.* Chicago: University of Chicago Press, 1980.

> This is a very readable account of the role of metaphor in the way that language carries meaning and enables communication. Lakoff and Johnson believe that the meaning of utterances in communication must be constructed. They see metaphor as an important conversational tool that provides hints in the construction of meaning, using meanings associated with one concept as a basis for focus and elaboration of meaning for another.

Miller, L. Has artificial intelligence contributed to an understanding of the human mind? A critique of arguments for and against. *Cognitive Science,* Vol. 2 (1978): 111–129.
> This is a general discussion of the contribution of artificial intelligence to the study of the mind.

Minsky, M. *Society of Mind.* New York: Simon and Schuster, 1986.
> Minsky's lucid account of an architecture of cognition based on groups of interacting agents. The book is at once playful, insightful, provocative, and easy to read. See also *Artificial Intelligence,* Vol. 59, 1991, for a set of four reviews of this book together with a response by Minsky.

Minsky, M. Logical vs. analogical or symbolic vs. connectionist or neat vs. scruffy. In Winston, P. H., & Shellard, S. A. (eds.), *Artificial Intelligence at MIT: Expanding Frontiers,* pp. 218–243. Cambridge: MIT Press, 1990.
> This article describes some fundamental differences between connectionist and symbolic computing, the strengths and weaknesses of each, and how the forms of computation can be combined.

Newell, A. The knowledge level. *Artificial Intelligence,* Vol. 18, 1 (1982): 87–127.
> In this paper Newell explains intelligence in physical symbol systems in terms of levels, introducing the symbol level (at which tokens are manipulated) and the knowledge level (at which meaning is ascribed).

Newell, A. *Unified Theories of Cognition.* Cambridge: Harvard University Press, 1991.
> This book presents Newell's most comprehensive account of the architecture of mind, with experimental evidence for mental phenomena at different levels of description. See also *Artificial Intelligence,* Vol. 59, Feb. 1993, for a set of eight reviews of this book together with a response by Newell.

Newell, A., & Simon, H. A. GPS, a program that simulates human thought. In Feigenbaum, E. A., & Feldman, A. J. (eds.), *Computers and Thought,* pp. 279–293. Mulabar, FL: Robert E. Kripp, 1981.
> This is a classic account of the early experiments with the General Problem Solver (GPS) in which Newell and Simon describe how closely the steps taken by their program model the steps taken by human problem solvers on the same problems.

Newell, A., & Simon, H. A. Computer science as empirical enquiry: Symbols and search. *Communications of the ACM,* Vol. 19, 3 (March 1976): 113–126.
> The is the Turing Award paper in which Newell and Simon articulated the physical symbol system hypothesis.

Pylyshyn, Z. W. *Computation and Cognition.* Cambridge: MIT Press, 1984.
> Pylyshyn presents evidence and arguments for a representational theory of mind, skillfully weaving together insights from cognitive psychology and computer science.

Radnitzky, G., & Bartley, W. W. (eds.). *Evolutionary Epistemology, Theory of Rationality, and the Sociology of Knowledge.* La Salle, IL: Open Court, 1987.

> This collection connects theories of knowledge and rationality with biological theory and the theory of evolution. As such, this volume makes accessible some perspectives on the emergence and nature of cognition that are outside the conventional thinking of AI. The volume includes contributions by Karl Popper, Donald T. Campbell, and several others.

Simon, H. A. *The Sciences of the Artificial*, 2nd edition. Cambridge: MIT Press, 1981.

> This collection of essays includes topics from AI and cognitive science. The essay, "The Architecture of Complexity," contains the often-cited parable of the watchmaker, with suggestions about the evolutionary advantages of nearly decomposable systems.

Smith, B. C. *Reflection and Semantics in a Procedural Language.* Massachusetts Institute of Technology, MIT-TR-272, 1982. Prologue reprinted in Brachman and Levesque (1985).

> Brian Smith's doctoral dissertation describes the design of a reflective Lisp called 3-Lisp. The prologue and first two chapters are recommended as a thoughtful account of why reflection is needed in computational systems and what some of the issues are in incorporating primitives for reflection in programming languages.

Stefik, M., Foster, G., Bobrow, D. G., Kahn, K., Lanning, S., & Suchman, L. Beyond the chalkboard: Computer support for collaboration and problem solving in meetings. *Communications of the ACM,* Vol. 30, 1 (1987): 32–47. Reprinted in Greif, I. (ed.). *Computer-Supported Cooperative Work: A Book of Readings,* pp. 335–366. San Mateo, CA: Morgan Kaufmann, 1988.

> This paper describes the concepts, goals, and technology of the Colab project, which ran at Xerox PARC from about 1985 to 1989. This project was inspired by the ways that groups use blackboards to organize conversations in face-to-face meetings. However, the goal was to create a new medium that was both interactive and computational. This paper introduces interactive computer systems for brainstorming sessions and also for argumentation. The exercise in Section 1.2 on an "argumentation spreadsheet" is based on the ARGNOTER system described in this paper.

Suchman, L. A. *Plans and Situated Actions: The Problem of Human-Machine Communication.* Cambridge, UK: Cambridge University Press, 1987.

> Suchman discusses the use and meaning of a man-machine interface through the eyes of an anthropologist. This book describes the use of plans, focusing on some experiments to simplify user interfaces to copiers by modeling and supporting plans of users. Traditional work on planning in AI assumes that plans are made ahead of time and used to guide action. Suchman presents an alternative account in which plans play a communication role and are used crucially in the construction of understanding. Suchman's book provides good examples of how the social sciences can provide important insights about computers, symbol systems, and human use as computers are increasingly used in the everyday world.

Tennant, N. Intentionality, syntactic structure and the evolution of language. In Hookway, C. (ed.), *Minds, Machines & Evolution*, pp. 73–103. Cambridge, UK: Cambridge University Press, 1984.

> Drawing on insights from biology and cognitive science, Tennant argues that languge and mind co-evolved.

A.2   *Further Reading on Search and Problem Solving (Chapter 2)*

Mainline References (Chapter 2)

Bacchus, F., & Yang, Q. The expected value of hierarchical problem-solving. In *Proceedings of the Tenth National Conference on Artificial Intelligence*, pp. 369–374. Menlo Park, CA: AAAI Press/MIT Press, 1992.

> An analysis of hierarchical planning, demonstrating the phase transition between linear and exponential behavior depending on the probability of backtracking across abstraction levels.

Barr, A., & Feigenbaum, E. A. *The Handbook of Artificial Intelligence*. Los Altos, CA: William Kaufmann, 1981.

> Contains tutorial articles about artificial intelligence, including a chapter about search.

Brown, H., & Masinter, L. An algorithm for the construction of the graphs of organic molecules. *Discrete Math,* Vol. 8 (1974): 227–244.

> An approach to the generation of molecular structures with cycles using the mathematics of double costs. This paper explains the basis of the generator for the Dendral program.

Buchanan, B. G., Sutherland, G. L., & Feigenbaum, E. A. Heuristic DENDRAL: A program for generating explanatory hypotheses in organic chemistry. In Meltzer, B., & Michie, D. (eds.), *Machine Intelligence 4*, pp. 209–254. Edinburgh, UK: Edinburgh University Press, 1969.

> A very readable description of the Dendral program, explaining its organization as a problem solver.

Chakrabarti, P. P., Ghose, S., & DeSarkar, S. C. Heuristic search through islands. *Artificial Intelligence,* Vol. 29, 3 (1986): 339–347.

> This research note investigates the properties of algorithms that search through islands. The problem is formulated in terms of finding an optimal path. This paper does not address the complexity of the algorithm but does show that it is admissible and expands no more nodes than A*.

Gaschnig, J. G. *Performance Measurement and Analysis of Certain Search Algorithms*. Doctoral dissertation, Department of Computer Science, Carnegie-Mellon University, 1979. (Available from University Microfilms International, 7925014.)

> Gaschnig's thesis is a detailed study of the performance of various search algorithms including A*. The thesis combines an analysis of the worst-case complexity with extensive experimental measurements of performance.

Hayes-Roth, B., & Hayes-Roth, F. A cognitive model of planning. *Cognitive Science,* Vol. 3, 4 (1979): 275–310.

> A discussion of the task of planning, analysis of the problem-solving behavior of people carrying out errand-planning tasks, and results of computer models that include heuristics for opportunistic search. (This article inspired Ex. 2.1-2 and explains more deeply the ideas introduced there.)

Huberman, B. A., & Hogg, T. Phase transitions in artificial intelligence systems. *Artificial Intelligence,* Vol. 33, 1 (1987): 155–171.

> This paper introduces the concepts of phases, phase transitions, and threshold effects to the characterization of large searches and proposes the use of concepts from statistical mechanics for analyzing many kinds of large-scale computations. The model of phase transitions in heuristic search as applied to hierarchical generate-and-test was suggested by this paper.

Knoblock, C. A. Search reduction in hierarchical problem solving. In *Proceedings of the Ninth National Conference on Artificial Intelligence—AAAI-91,* Vol. 2, pp. 686–691. Menlo Park, CA: AAAI/MIT Press, 1991.

> This paper presents an analysis of hierarchical planning essentially like Korf (1987), together with supporting empirical data.

Korf, R. E. Depth-first iterative-deepening: An optimal admissible tree search. *Artificial Intelligence,* Vol. 27, 1 (1985): 97–109.

> This paper introduces the DFID algorithm and demonstrates its properties.

Korf, R. E. Planning as search: A quantitative approach. *Artificial Intelligence,* Vol. 33, 1 (1987): 65–88.

> This paper develops some mathematical models of hierarchical planning and analyzes their complexity. It is the basis for much of the analysis of hierarchical planning in Section 2.4.

Lawler, E. L. *Combinatorial Optimization: Networks and Matroids.* New York: Holt, Rinehart & Winston, 1976.

> A classic textbook used in operations research and industrial engineering courses on combinatorial optimization.

Levesque, H. Taking issue: Guest editor's introduction. *Computational Intelligence,* Vol. 3, 3 (1987): 149–237.

> This is a special issue of *Computational Intelligence* organized by Hector Levesque. It begins with a well-known article by Drew McDermott, "A Critique of Pure Reason." Twenty-eight other articles by a variety of AI researchers then follow, expounding different perspectives on what logic is and what it is for.

Lindsay, R. K., Buchanan, B. G., Feigenbaum, E. A., & Lederberg, J. *Applications of Artificial Intelligence for Organic Chemistry, the DENDRAL Project.* New York: McGraw-Hill, 1980.

> A general overview and history of the Dendral project.

McDermott, J. R1: A rule-based configurer of computer systems. *Artificial Intelligence,* Vol. 19 (1988): 39–88.

> Description of the R1 system for configuring computer systems. This system was later renamed XCON, and has often been cited as the first commercially successful expert system. This paper is about the technical ideas behind the system and discusses its use of the hierarchical-match search method.

Minsky, M. Steps toward artificial intelligence. In *Proceedings of the Institute of Radio Engineers,* Vol. 49 (January 1961): 8–30. Reprinted in Feigenbaum & Feldman (1963).

> This classic early paper outlines basic concepts of artificial intelligence. It includes an example and analysis of the power of reasoning with abstractions.

Newell, A., & Simon, H. A. *Human Problem Solving.* Englewood, NJ: Prentice Hall, 1972.

> A classic book in which Newell and Simon examine psychological evidence that people use weak methods in a range of puzzle and problem-solving tasks.

Nilsson, N. J. *Problem-Solving Methods in Artificial Intelligence.* New York: McGraw-Hill, 1971.

> An early but comprehensive survey of problem-solving techniques in AI with many well-illustrated examples. Continued theoretical work on the search methods has been carried out largely by researchers in operations research.

Nilsson, N. J. *Principles of Artificial Intelligence.* Los Altos, CA: Morgan Kaufmann, 1985. (First published by Tioga Publishing Company, Palo Alto, California, 1980.)

Pearl, J. *Heuristics: Intelligent Search Strategies for Computer Problem Solving.* Reading, MA: Addison-Wesley, 1984.

> A clear and well-written text that introduces search concepts, provides an overview of heuristics in problem-solving situations, describes a taxonomy of basic heuristic search strategies, and analyzes basic properties of heuristics—including trade-offs between complexity and precision. This textbook is an excellent source book for understanding statistical methods for analyzing the performance of algorithms.

Stefik, M. Inferring DNA structures from segmentation data. *Artificial Intelligence,* Vol. 11 (1978): 85–114.

> A discussion of hierarchical generate-and-test and a comparison of methods for solving a combinatorial data analysis problem.

Williams, C. P. *Imperfect Abstraction,* working paper. Dynamics of Computation Group, Xerox Palo Alto Research Center, April 1992.

> An analysis of solving problems with abstractions. This paper departs from previous, simpler models in which it is assumed that backtracking across levels is not needed. Williams models the need for backtracking more realistically in terms of probabilities and shows that there is a threshold in such probabilities such that the time complexity of the search transitions from the linear to the exponential case.

Winston, P. H. *Artificial Intelligence,* 2nd edition. Reading, MA: Addison-Wesley, 1984.

> This introductory textbook for courses on artificial intelligence is well written and provides many examples for those seeking a general survey of this broad field.

Quandaries References (Chapter 2)

Hamilton, E., & Cairns, H. (eds.). *The Collected Dialogues of Plato*. Princeton, NJ: Princeton University Press, 1980.
> This edition includes a translation of the book of Meno referenced in the quandaries section. Socrates argues that the knowledge necessary to solve problems is available from former lives and can be remembered if we try hard enough.

Hayes, P. In defense of logic. In *Proceedings of the Fifth International Joint Conference on Artificial Intelligence,* pp. 559–565. Los Altos, CA: Morgan Kaufmann, 1977.
> A discussion of the role of logic in representation and problem solving and some of the limitations of ad hoc mechanisms in AI for control of inference.

Levesque, H. J., & Brachman, R. J. A fundamental tradeoff in knowledge representation and reasoning (revised version). In Brachman, R. J., & Levesque, H. J. (eds.), *Readings in Knowledge Representation*, pp. 41–70. Los Altos, CA: Morgan Kaufmann, 1985.
> This "revised version" combines several earlier papers by Levesque and Brachman. Of particular relevance to Section 2.5 is the discussion of why logic provides a good formal basis for a semantics of a representation language, why theorem proving provides a good basis for providing the service expected of a representation language, and why the combination is computationally intractable. As the authors put it, "The good news in reducing the KR service to theorem proving is that we now have a very clear, very specific notion of what the KR system should do; the bad news is that it is also very clear that *this service cannot be provided*." The authors then analyze what they call a trade-off between expresssiveness and computational tractability of providing the service. The related trade-off, implicit in this chapter, is between generality and efficiency in problem solving.

McDermott, D. A critique of pure reason. In Levesque (1987).
> A thoughtful paper by one of the most articulate proponents of deduction, about why deduction provides an inadequate framework for understanding intelligence or problem solving. This paper develops ten alternative ways to "fix up" deduction and then argues why they don't work. In the same issue are a number of responses by other authors in AI.

Newell, A. Artificial intelligence and the concept of mind. In Schank, R. C., & Colby, K. M. (eds.), *Computer Models of Thought and Language*. San Francisco: W. H. Freeman, 1973.
> Contains an essay by Allen Newell on "the science of weak methods" that argues that work in artificial intelligence has the character of the discovery and development of a set of methods.

Newell, A., & Simon, H. A. GPS: A program that simulates human thought. In Feigenbaum & Feldman (1963), pp. 279–293.
> An early paper showing how a computer program (GPS) can provide a detailed account of the steps of human problem solving in terms of means-end analysis.

Newell, A., & Simon, H. A. Computer science as empirical enquiry: Symbols and search, *Communications of the ACM*, Vol. 19, 3 (March 1976): 113–125.

> The Turing Award paper in which Newell and Simon articulate both the Physical Symbol System Hypothesis and the Heuristic Search Hypothesis.

Simon, H. A. Experiment with a heuristic compiler. *Journal of the Association of Computing Machinery*, Vol. 10, 4 (1963): 493–506.

> An account of Simon's experiments in the GPS framework with a program called the heuristic compiler. This included experiments in which GPS was organized in a layered control structure for tasks.

A.3   *Further Reading on Knowledge and Software Engineering (Chapter 3)*

Mainline References (Chapter 3)

Bobrow, D. G., Mittal, S., & Stefik, M. J. Expert systems: Perils and promise. *Communications of the ACM,* Vol. 29, 9 (September 1986): 880–894.

> Written for a general computer science audience, this paper provides an overview of the process of building expert systems. It illustrates the practice and some of the pitfalls through comparative case studies, proposing guidelines for choosing applications and managing the development process.

Buchanan, B. G., & Shortliffe, E. H. *Rule-based Expert Systems: The MYCIN Experiments of the Stanford Heuristic Programming Project*. Reading, MA: Addison-Wesley, 1984.

> An extensive account of the MYCIN project discussing the ideas, history, results and lessons of one of the most influential projects in knowledge engineering.

Conklin, J. Hypertext: An introduction and survey. *Computer,* Vol. 2, 9 (September 1987): 17–41.

> A readable overview and history of hypertext systems with examples.

Ericsson, K. A., & Simon, H. A. *Protocol Analysis: Verbal Reports as Data*. Cambridge: MIT Press, 1984.

> A comprehensive discussion of the theory and practice of protocol analysis. It summarizes the scientific basis for using verbal thinking-aloud protocols as data about mental processes.

Floyd, C. Outline of a paradigm change in software engineering. In Bjerknes, G., Ehn, P., & Kyng, M. (eds.), *Computers and Democracy: A Scandinavian Challenge*. Aldershot, UK: Avebury, 1987.

> This paper compares two perspectives on software engineering: a product-oriented perspective and a process-oriented perspective. The former regards software as a product standing on its own, consisting of a set of programs and related texts. The usage context of the product is presumed to be fixed and well understood, thus allowing software requirements to be determined in advance. In the process-oriented

perspective, software is seen in relation to human learning, work, and communication. The actual product is perceived as emerging from the interleaved processes of analysis, design, implementation, evaluation, and feedback. The author argues for adapting the latter perspective, which is much closer to the practice of rapid prototyping and knowledge engineering.

Goldstein, I., & Papert, S. Artificial intelligence, language, and the study of knowledge. *Cognitive Science,* Vol. 1, 1 (January 1977): 84–123.

Hoffman, R. R. The problem of extracting the knowledge of experts from the perspective of experimental psychology. *AI Magazine*, Vol. 8, 2 (Summer 1987): 53–67.
  This paper offers a working classification of methods for acquiring knowledge from experts, discusses differences in the data that such methods yield, and suggests criteria for selecting methods relative to the needs of the system developer. The article is intended as a practical guide for knowledge engineers. It was the inspiration for the discussion in Section 3.3 on dimensions of interview techniques.

Krauss, R. M. Mutual knowledge and communicative effectiveness. In *Conference on Technology and Cooperative Work*. Tucson, AZ: University of Arizona, 1988.
  An introductory overview of research on communication from the perspective of social psychology. In this overview communication is modeled as the exchange of information. This paper presents the basic concepts of "common ground" and the assumption that any communicative act rests on the basis of mutual knowledge, which means that one person can only tell another about something by making use of knowledge that they both have.

Leonard-Barton, D. The case for integrative innovation: An expert system at Digital. *Sloan Management Review* (Fall 1987): 7–19.
  A well-written and important case study of the development and introduction of an expert system in an organization. This study reports on the XSEL expert system at Digital Equipment Corporation. It discusses the philosophy of software engineering used on this system, which involved users from the first stages of design. It follows the gradual introduction of the system, the experiences in different parts of the company, and the changes that took place both in the system and in the organizations that use and support it.

Lindsay, R. K., Buchanan, B. G., Feigenbaum, E. A., & Lederberg, J. *Applications of Artificial Intelligence for Organic Chemistry: The DENDRAL Project*. New York: McGraw-Hill, 1980.

McDermott, J. R1: A rule-based configurer of computer systems. *Artificial Intelligence,* Vol. 19 (1988): 39–88.
  A description of the R1 system for configuring computer systems. This system was also called XCON and has often been cited as the first commercially successful expert system. This paper is about the technical ideas behind the system. See also Leonard-Barton (1987).

Mittal, S., Dym, C., & Morjaria, M. PRIDE: An expert system for the design of paper handling systems. In Dym, C. L. (ed.), *Applications of Knowledge-Based Systems to Engineering Analysis and Design.* New York: American Society of Mechanical Engineers, 1985.

> A general description of PRIDE, an expert system that aids in the design of paper-handling systems. PRIDE is an example of a system that combines search methods to carry out its problem-solving tasks.

Mittal, S., Dym, C. L., & Morjaria, M. PRIDE: An expert system for the design of paper handling systems. *Computer,* Vol. 19, 7 (July 1986): 102–114.

> PRIDE is a knowledge system for designing the paper-handling systems for copiers and printers. Several examples of dialog in knowledge acquisition sessions in this chapter were drawn from videotapes of early sessions on the PRIDE project.

Motta, E., Eisenstadt, M., Pitman, K., & West, M. Support for knowledge acquisition in the knowledge engineer's assistant (KEATS). *Expert Systems,* Vol. 5, 1 (February 1988): 6–28.

> Description of a software environment intended to provide support for a knowledge engineer beginning at the early stages of knowledge acquisition. Very little work has been done in this area.

Newell, A., & Simon, H. A. *Human Problem Solving.* Englewood Cliffs, NJ: Prentice Hall, 1972.

> The classic volume on models of human problem solving, GPS, and the use of evidence from protocol analysis to build information-processing models.

Schorr, H., & Rappaport, A. (eds.). *Innovative Applications of Artificial Intelligence.* Menlo Park, CA: AAAI/MIT Press, 1989.

> A collection of short papers on knowledge-system projects selected by AAAI as innovative in 1989.

Zuboff, S. *In the Age of the Smart Machine.* New York: Basic Books, 1988.

> Subtitled "The Future of Work and Power," this book is about the introduction of computers into the workplace. Zuboff is an associate professor in the Harvard Business School. The book is the result of several years of in-depth interviews with people in many different settings where computers are being introduced: paper-making plants, insurance companies, banks, a pharmaceutical company. Zuboff is interested in the transition whereby work becomes mediated by computers, and studies the effects on authority, control, and the quality of work. Her study focuses on organizations as they make the transition, since the participants at that moment are thoroughly aware of the differences between the old and the new. On the one hand, the technology can be a source of surveillance techniques. On the other, it can become a resource for a deepened sense of collective responsibility and joint ownership. The case studies in this book are interesting for and relevant to those who are building knowledge systems and other information systems.

Quandaries References (Chapter 3)

Feigenbaum, E., McCorduck, P., & Nii, H. P. *The Rise of the Expert Company.* New York: Times Books/Random House, 1988.

This is a collection of case studies about the development, role, and significance of knowledge systems in 20 companies. This book is written in a popular style. It does not explain how the systems worked. Rather, it focuses on the significance of the systems as perceived by the people who use them and reports on the obstacles that needed to be overcome before the systems could succeed. Subtitled "How Visionary Companies Are Using Artificial Intelligence to Achieve Higher Productivity and Profits," the book is written for business managers. It includes a catalog of expert systems by Paul Harmon.

Feigenbaum, E. A., Buchanan, B. G., & Lederberg, J. On generality and problem solving: A case study using the DENDRAL program. In Meltzer, B., & Michie, D., *Machine Intelligence 6,* pp. 165–190. New York: American Elsevier Publishing, 1971.
> This historic paper articulates the knowledge principle in the DENDRAL project.

Goldstein, I., & Papert, S. Artificial intelligence, language, and the study of knowledge. *Cognitive Science,* Vol. 1, 1 (1977): 84–123.
> This paper, which appeared in the first issue of *Cognitive Science*, discusses a shift of paradigm in artificial intelligence research, leading to a focus on methods for using and maintaining large knowledge bases rather than developing more powerful reasoning systems.

Halasz, F. G. Reflections on NoteCards: Seven issues for the next generation of hypermedia systems. *Communications of the ACM*, Vol. 31, 7 (1988): 826–852.
> Halasz views hypertext as a publishing medium and is keenly aware of the open opportunities and challenges that hypertext poses for organizing, browsing, and retrieving information. Halasz is particularly concerned about the issues that arise in the use of hypertext by groups of users, attempting to leverage the medium for coordinating their work. This paper lays out a series of challenges, some of which begin to bridge the gaps between nonformal and semiformal representations.

Hayes, P. J. The second naive physics manifesto. In Brachman, R. J., & Levesque, H. J. (eds.), *Readings in Knowledge Representation.* Los Altos, CA: Morgan Kaufmann, 1985.
> This engaging paper by Pat Hayes challenges the ways we think about the physical world and argues some consequences for knowledge representation.

Kahn, R. E., & Cerf, V. G. *An Open Architecture for a Digital Library System and a Plan for Its Development.* Reston, VA: Corporation for National Research Initiatives, 1988.
> This white paper discusses concepts for creating a digital library that would take advantage of improvements in technology for storing, retrieving, and transmitting documents and information. The article coins the term *knowbot* to refer to computational agents that can navigate in a network and perform services.

Kolodner, J. L., & Riesbeck, C. K. *Experience, Memory, and Reasoning.* Hillsdale, NJ: Lawrence Erlbaum, 1986.
> An edited volume of papers from the first annual workshop on Theoretical Issues in Conceptual Information Processing. These papers draw from a variety of disciplines in cognitive science. They share an interest in content-based theories of conceptual information processing and have in common the theme that knowledge is the product

of experience. These papers present cognitive science perspectives on learning, the indexing and organization of knowledge, and various working models of memory.

Lenat, D. B., & Feigenbaum, E. A. On the thresholds of knowledge. *Artificial Intelligence,* Vol. 47, 1–3 (January 1991): 185–250.

> This paper presents the knowledge principle and the breadth hypothesis and makes some predictions about the progress and leverage for building intelligent systems that the authors expect from natural language and machine learning.

Nisbitt, R., & Ross, L. *Human Inference: Strategies and Shortcomings of Social Judgement.* Englewood Cliffs, NJ: Prentice Hall, 1980.

> This book starts out with an apparent paradox: the contradiction between the triumphs and failures of the human mind. As the authors put it, "the same organism that routinely solves inferential problems too subtle and complex for the mightiest computers often makes errors in the simplest of judgments about everyday events." The book is an analysis of human behavior in formulating knowledge, or as the authors put it, the work of the intuitive and the professional scientist. It is about formal and heuristic strategies in knowledge acquisition; that is, people's failure to use the normative principles and inferential tools that guide formal scientific inquiry. It is also about people's readiness to apply simplistic inferential strategies beyond their appropriate limits. The book is relevant to knowledge engineering for its insights about knowledge formulation from a social psychology perspective.

Radnitzky, G., & Bartley, W. W. *Evolutionary Epistemology, Theory of Rationality, and the Sociology of Knowledge.* La Salle, IL: Open Court, 1987.

> An edited collection of papers on recent directions in the philosophy of science, influencing and influenced by an evolutionary perspective. Includes the interesting article, "Philosophy of Biology versus Philosophy of Physics." Bartley presents arguments relevant to the viability of the knowledge principle.

Smith, B. C. The owl and the electric encyclopedia. *Artificial Intelligence,* Vol. 47, 1–3 (January 1991): 251–288.

> A response to Lenat and Feigenbaum (1991). This paper takes issue not so much with the knowledge principle itself, but rather with a bevy of surrounding claims and proposals for a large project to "encode the knowledge of the world." Smith's paper outlines some preliminary requirements for a theory of "embedded computation," which he believes will address some shortcomings of the Feigenbaum and Lenat view of how to build a machine intelligence as well as the traditional logicist view.

Stefik, M. J., Foster, G., Bobrow, D. G., Kahn, K., Lanning, S., & Suchman, L. Beyond the chalkboard: Computers support for collaboration and problem solving in meetings. *Communications of the ACM,* Vol. 30, 1 (January 1987): 32–47. Reprinted in Greif, I. (ed.), *Computer-Supported Cooperative Work: A Book of Readings,* pp. 335–366. San Mateo, CA: Morgan Kaufmann, 1988.

> This paper describes the early stage of the Colab project, which created an experimental computer-equipped room for supporting face-to-face meetings. This paper asks how we can build an interactive medium for writings in conversation that is

more powerful than a conventional chalkboard. To this end it develops the concept of a shared, real-time, computational workspace. As such interfaces and large-screen devices become more widely available, they can be used by knowledge systems projects for formulating and formalizing knowledge. The book of readings in which this paper is reprinted contains several seminal articles on groupware.

Winograd, T. Beyond programming languages. *Communications of the ACM,* Vol. 22, 7 (July 1979): 391–401.

> This article was addressed to a computer science audience, which Winograd saw as primarily concerned with issues of program correctness and the design of programming languages. The paper argues that the crucial problems that were dominating the costs of building computer systems were not addressed by this research at all. The crucial problems stem from the fact that most applications are embedded systems and that they are subject to changes in requirements, changes in the hardware base, and changes in the environment with which they must interact. Winograd makes several recommendations about the need for an expressive, descriptive calculus capable of describing the knowledge that such systems must use.

A.4 *Further Reading on Models of Time (Chapter 4)*

Mainline References (Chapter 4)

Allen, J. F. Maintaining knowledge about temporal intervals. *Communications of the ACM*, Vol. 26, 11 (November 1983): 832–843. Reprinted in Weld, D. S., & de Kleer, J. (eds.), *Readings in Qualitative Reasoning about Physical Systems.* San Mateo, CA: Morgan Kaufmann, 1990.

> This is a widely cited and influential paper about interval representations for temporal reasoning. The paper introduces relations over intervals rather than points, as well as reference intervals, and anticipates later results on hierarchical arc consistency. The goal of this work was to provide a computational basis for representing the meaning of sentences in natural language.

Allen, J. F. Towards a general theory of action and time. *Artificial Intelligence,* Vol. 23, 2 (July 1984): 123–155.

> This paper presents Allen's interval-based model for reasoning about time.

Dean, T. Planning and temporal reasoning under uncertainty. In *Proceedings IEEE of the Workshop on Principles of Knowledge-Based Systems,* pp. 131–138, Denver, Colorado, August 1984.

> This short paper introduces time maps as modular facilities that can be used with systems that solve planning and scheduling problems.

Dean, T., & McDermott, D. Temporal data base management. *Artificial Intelligence,* Vol. 32, 1 (April 1987): 1–56.

> This paper introduces time maps as modular facilities that can be used with systems that solve planning and scheduling problems. This is a longer and more detailed report of the system described in Dean (1984), giving more notational details, implementation details, and proofs of correctness.

Galton, A. A critical examination of Allen's theory of action and time. *Artificial Intelligence,* Vol. 42, 2–3 (1990): 159–188.

> This piece presents an elaborate argument that the interval-based time models of Allen (1983) are not adequate for representing continuous change—essentially the same point that this chapter argues using the mean-value theorem. It then goes on to present a temporal calculus in which values can be ascribed both to points and intervals.

McDermott, D. A temporal logic for reasoning about processes and plans. *Cognitive Science,* Vol. 6, 2 (April–June 1982): 101–155.

> This paper offers a so-called naive theory of time, intended to provide a framework for programs to reason about time. McDermott models the timeline using the real numbers. Although he does not give time itself a branching structure, he does make provisions for reasoning about partially ordered future states.

Mittal, S., Chandrasekaran, B., & Sticklen, J. Patrec: A knowledge-directed database for a diagnostic expert system. *IEEE Computer* (September 1984): 51–58.

> An example of the use of a time-oriented database in a knowledge system. This system used a point-based representation of time with explicit range indications to indicate uncertainty in time.

Quandaries References (Chapter 4)

Burstall, R. M. Program proving as hand simulation with a little induction. *Information Processing,* Vol. 74 (1974): 308–312.

Emerson, E. A., & Halpern, J. Y. "Sometimes" and "not never" revisited: On branching vs. linear time. In *Proceedings of the 10th ACM Symposium on Principles of Programming Languages,* pp. 127–140. New York: Association for Computing Machinery, 1983.

> A tour and classification of the semantics of several temporal logics with branching time.

Galton, A. *Temporal Logics and Their Applications.* London, UK: Academic Press, 1987.

> A worthwhile and readable edited volume about logics for representing time. By a "logic," Galton means a formal calculus designed to specify, reason about, and represent programs and systems. The focus of this book is on the meaning of time representations, and not so much on the efficiency of any representation or its connection to any particular applications. The book includes reviews of temporal logic from several interdisciplinary perspectives. Galton's introduction to the volume gives a more complete survey of many of the topics mentioned in the quandaries section of this chapter and was an inspiration for much of that discussion.

Hawkings, S. W. *A Brief History of Time.* Toronto: Bantam Books, 1988.

> This popular book really does not have much to do with this chapter, but it is a fun read for those with an interest in the fundamental nature of time and space and the fate of the universe, such as can be known.

Hoare, C. A. R. An axiomatic basis for computer programming. *Communications of the ACM,* Vol. 12 (1969): 576–583.
> In this paper Hoare proposes the axiomatic semantics of programs.

Hoare, C. A. R. Communicating sequential processes. *Communications of the ACM,* Vol. 21 (1978): 666–677.
> One of the most influential of the early languages for parallel programming.

Kahn, K. *An Actor-based Computer Animation Language.* MIT AI Working Paper No. 120, 1976.
> Paper describing the Director language developed by Kahn as part of his doctoral thesis.

Kahn, K., & Gorry, G. A. Mechanizing temporal knowledge. *Artificial Intelligence,* Vol. 9, (1977): 87–108.
> This paper organized temporal data in three main ways: by date line, relative to reference events, and by chains of events ordered relative to reference events. This was one of the first temporal languages in AI.

Lamport, L. "Sometimes" is sometimes "not never": On the temporal logic of programs. In *Proceedings of the 7th ACM Symposium on Principles of Programming Languages,* pp. 174–185. New York: Association for Computing Machinery, 1980.
> This paper argues semantics for branching time models of temporal logics for describing programs.

Magnenat-Thalmann, N., & Thalmann, D. *Computer Animation: Theory and Practice.* Tokyo: Springer-Verlag, 1985.
> A readable survey of techniques for computer animation, included here because of its chapter on scripting languages. These languages have been developed to describe the movement of elements in animation, such as characters, objects, lighting, and camera.

Owicki, S., & Gries, D. An axiomatic proof technique for parallel programs. *Acta Informatica,* Vol. 6 (1976): 319–340.
> This paper is one of the immediate precursors to developing temporal logics for describing parallel programs.

Reynolds, C. W. Computer animation with scripts and actors. *Computer Graphics* (Proceedings of SIGGRAPH 1982), Vol. 16, 3: 289–296.
> Paper describing the scripting language developed by Craig Reynolds. At Symbolics, he used this language in developing a remarkable animated feature about birds and fish ("boids") known as "Stanley and Iris."

Richards, B., Bethke, I., Van der Does, J., & Oberlander, J. *Temporal Representation and Inference.* London, UK: Academic Press/Harcourt Brace Jovanovich, 1989.
> A technical book about issues in temporal logics written by philosophers (logicians) for philosophers. Much of this book is about issues in representing tenses, indexicals, and temporal connections in an interval-based framework known as IQ.

Shoham, Y. Temporal logics in AI: Semantical and ontological considerations. *Artificial Intelligence,* Vol. 33, 1 (September 1987): 89–104.

A review of foundations for temporal logics.

A.5   *Further Readings on Models of Space (Chapter 5)*

Mainline References (Chapter 5)

Antony, R. T. A hybrid spatial/object-oriented DBMS to support automated spatial, hierarchical, and temporal reasoning. In Chen, S., *Advances in Spatial Reasoning.* Norwood, NJ: Ablex Publishing, 1990.

This paper gives a detailed account of a multiple-layered spatial representation. The database described has a quadtree implementation for spatial indexing and objects for representing and classifying physical objects in the scene. The paper presents a good example of how to meet a variety of reasoning requirements by combining different representational approaches.

Balsam, P. D. Selection, representation, and equivalence of controlling stimuli. In Atkinson, R. C., Herrnstein, R. J., Lindzey, G., & Luce, R. D. (eds.), *Steven's Handbook of Experimental Psychology,* 2nd edition. New York: Wiley, 1988.

See especially pages 140–142 for a discussion of the use of representations.

Chen, S. *Advances in Spatial Reasoning.* Norwood, NJ: Ablex Publishing, 1990.

A two-volume edited collection with a range of examples of spatial reasoning in AI systems. The papers range substantially in the kinds of spatial reasoning they consider and the techniques they employ. Tasks include navigation, sensor positioning, and building of solid models from sensor data.

Davis, E. *Representations of Commonsense Knowledge.* San Mateo, CA: Morgan Kaufmann, 1990.

Samet, H. Hierarchical representations of collections of small rectangles. *ACM Computing Surveys,* Vol. 20, 4 (December 1988): 271–309.

Rectangles are commonly used to approximate other shapes, serving as minimum enclosing objects for them. This article is a tutorial survey of techniques for collections of different sizes and properties.

Woodward, J. (ed.). *Geometric Reasoning.* Oxford, UK: Clarendon, 1989.

All of these papers are about reasoning about shape. Topics range from applications to motion planning, part recognition, manufacturing, and design of human workplaces. Theoretical approaches range from shape algebras to use of constraints and other partial descriptions, connectionist models, and models of composition and tolerance. The papers are drawn from a workshop in the United Kingdom and the topics covered provide a good survey of active research. Each paper is followed by a transcription of the panel discussion that followed presentation of the paper at the workshop. These discussions make interesting reading for exploring limitations, alternatives, and context for each paper.

Quandaries References (Chapter 5)

Goldin, S. E., & Thorndyke, P. W. *Spatial Learning and Reasoning Skill.* Rand Note R-2805-ARMY, July 1981.
> This report summarizes two years of investigation at Rand on a variety of spatial reasoning tasks related to military training. The results of the report suggest that people learn differently from different kinds of spatial data, such as from maps, from short tours, and from verbal descriptions.

Hart, R. A., & Moore, G. T. The development of spatial cognition: A review. In Downs, R. M., & Stea, D. (eds.), *Image and Environment*, pp. 246–288. Chicago: Aldine, 1973.
> Survey of the literature on the development of spatial cognition in children.

Kosslyn, S. M., & Pomerantz, J. R. Imagery, propositions, and the form of internal representations. *Cognitive Psychology,* Vol. 1 (1977): 265–295.
> A review of results relating human performance in spatial reasoning to conclusions about internal spatial representations.

McGee, M. G. Human spatial abilities: Psychometric studies and environmental, genetic, hormonal, and neurological influences. *Psychological Bulletin,* Vol. 86 (1979): 889–918.
> A study of influences on performance in human spatial reasoning, showing also how widely people vary in their skills.

Piaget, J., & Inhelder, B. *The Child's Conception of Space.* New York: Norton, 1967. Originally published in French, 1948.
> Piaget's classic study about how children learn to reason about space.

Robertson, G. G., Card, S. K., & Mackinlay, J. D. Information visualization using 3D interactive animation. *Communications of the ACM,* Vol. 36, 4 (April 1993): 57–71.
> Description of the information visualizer system. This is a human computer interface that uses 3D images and animation to convey information to a user. The basic idea is that the human visual channel has enormous bandwidth. By appropriately exploiting human perceptual skills, the information visualizer seeks to simplify the understanding of information by shifting "cognitive load" to the perceptual system.

Tolman, E. C. Cognitive maps in rats and men. *Psychological Review,* Vol. 55 (1948): 189–208.
> Extensions of the ideas on cognitive maps and early experiments on human spatial reasoning.

A.6 Further Readings on Models of Uncertainty and Vagueness (Chapter 6)

Mainline References on Uncertainty (Chapter 6)

Buchanan, B. G., & Shortliffe, E. H. *Rule-based Expert Systems: The MYCIN Experiments of the Stanford Heuristic Programming Project.* Cambridge: MIT Press, 1990.
> This book conveys the experience, motivations, and conclusions from ten years of research on the MYCIN project. It includes four chapters on reasoning with uncer-

tainty that discuss the background, the certainty-factor model, a critique of the model, and the Dempster-Shafer theory of evidence.

Cooper, G. F. The computational complexity of probabilistic inference using Bayesian belief networks. *Artificial Intelligence,* Vol. 42 (1990): 393–405.
> Chapter 5 gives results on the distribution of hard problems. It is suspected that all of the NP-hard problems exhibit distributions of complexity, with threshold effects on key parameters. In this article Cooper shows that the problem of determining probabilities in causal networks is NP-hard.

Duda, R. O., Hart, P. E., & Nilsson, N. J. Subjective Bayesian methods for rule-based inference systems. In *Proceedings of the National Computer Conference,* Vol. 45 (1976): 1075–1082.
> A description of the method used in Prospector. This is probably the best known method for propagating probabilities in an inference network. This work stimulated much other research in the area.

Feller, W. *An Introduction to Probability Theory and Applications*, Volume 1. New York: Wiley, 1968.
> A standard and readable textbook on probability.

Henrion, M. An introduction to algorithms for inference in belief nets. In Henrion, M., Shachter, R. D., Kanal, L. N., & Lemmer, J. F. (eds.), *Uncertainty in Artificial Intelligence 5*. Amsterdam: North Holland, 1990.
> This edited volume contains collected papers on reasoning with uncertainty.

Kak, A. C., Andress, K. M., Lopez-Abadia, C., Carroll, M. S., & Lewis, J. R. Hierarchical evidence accumulation in the Pseiki system and experiments in model-driven mobile robot navigation. In Henrion, M., Shachter, R. D., Kanal, L. N., & Lemmer, J. F. (eds.), *Uncertainty in Artificial Intelligence 5*. Amsterdam: North Holland, 1990.
> Description of a machine vision system based on the Dempster-Shafer theory of evidence combination.

Lauritzen, S. L., & Spiegelhalter, D. J. Local computation with probabilities in graphical structures and their applications to expert systems. *Journal of the Royal Statistical Society B*, Vol. 50, 2 (1988): 157–224.
> This often-cited paper presents an efficient technique for performing inferences in polytree belief networks.

Neapolitan, R. E. *Probabilistic Reasoning in Expert Systems: Theory and Algorithms*. New York: Wiley, 1990.
> A very readable textbook discussing probability theory, graph theory, causal and belief networks, and algorithmic considerations bearing on the structure of belief networks. The book also discusses philosophical foundations of probability theory and implications for its use in knowledge and decision systems.

Neapolitan, R. E. The interpretation and application of belief functions. *Applied Artificial Intelligence,* Vol. 7 (1993a): 195–204.

This paper discusses the use of belief functions in the Dempster-Shafer approach. It shows that the belief functions use probability theory in the same way as the statistical tool, significance testing.

Pearl, J. *Probabilistic Reasoning in Intelligent Systems: Networks of Plausible Inference.* San Mateo, CA: Morgan Kaufmann, 1988.

A comprehensive and mathematically oriented book on probability networks and other methods for reasoning with uncertainty. Pearl's book discusses Markov and Bayesian networks, belief updating, decision and control theory, taxonomic hierarchies, and non-numeric approaches.

Provan, G. M. The application of Dempster-Shafer theory to a logic-based visual recognition system. In Henrion, M., Shachter, R. D., Kanal, L. N., & Lemmer, J. F. (eds.), *Uncertainty in Artificial Intelligence 5.* Amsterdam: North Holland, 1990.

Provan describes an experimental system for machine vision. This paper does not compare different models of uncertainty for the task and focuses on the use of a logic-based approach as opposed to design for performance. However, it does provide a simple and clear explanation of how the D-S approach can be used and integrated with an ATMS, using an evidence-ranking scheme to focus attention on the most plausible hypotheses.

Shafer, G. *A Mathematical Theory of Evidence.* Princeton, NJ: Princeton University Press, 1976.

An description of the Dempster-Shafer approach to reasoning with uncertainty.

Shafer, G., & Pearl, J. *Readings in Uncertain Reasoning.* San Mateo, CA: Morgan Kaufmann, 1990.

This broadly construed set of readings is about reasoning with uncertainty. It discusses probability, decision making, Bayesian approaches, belief functions, and also some non-numerical approaches. It does not cover fuzzy sets. See Ginsberg (1987) for a more extensive discussion of nonmonotonic logics.

Mainline References on Vagueness (Chapter 6)

Dubois, D., Prade, H., & Yager, R. R. (eds.). *Readings in Fuzzy Sets for Intelligent Systems.* San Mateo, CA: Morgan Kaufmann, 1993.

This sweeping collection of papers on fuzzy sets covers basic concepts, representations of uncertainty, use in control theory, and approximate reasoning.

Durkin, J. *Expert Systems: Design and Development.* New York: Macmillan, 1994.

This introductory, engineering-oriented text on expert systems includes a useful chapter on fuzzy-set techniques.

Graham, I., & Jones, P. L. *Expert Systems: Knowledge, Uncertainty, and Decision.* London, UK: Chapman and Hall, 1988.

A survey book on expert systems. An unusual feature of this book is that it discusses logical, probabilistic, and fuzzy considerations for databases; representation of uncertainty; inference; and decision making. A good introduction to techniques and mathematics for decision-making applications in expert systems.

Halmos, P. R. *Naive Set Theory.* New York: Van Nostrand, 1960.
A classic little text on basic set theory.

Yager, R. R., Ovchinnikov, S., Tong, R. M., & Nguyen, T. T. *Fuzzy Sets and Applications: Selected Papers by L. A. Zadeh.* New York: Wiley, 1987.
This collection was originally planned as a tribute to Lotfi Zadeh, on the twentieth anniversary of the publication of the first paper on fuzzy sets. It brings together many important papers that would otherwise be difficult to locate. See also Dubois, Prade, and Yager (1993) for papers by other contributers to this field.

Quandaries References (Chapter 6)

Boden, M. *Creativity: Myths and Mechanisms.* New York: Basic Books, 1992.
This is a book for a popular audience on the nature of creativity. Some of Boden's ideas are cited in the quandaries section because they bear on the question of how to represent "the unknown."

Forbus, K. D., & de Kleer, J. *Building Problem Solvers.* Cambridge: MIT Press, 1993.
The focus of this textbook is the design and programming of truth maintenance systems (TMSs). The book is oriented around programming examples in Common Lisp, with a sequence of designs for TMSs. At the time of this writing, this is the only textbook available that discusses the programming and practice of TMSs at a level sufficiently detailed to enable someone to build them.

Ginsberg, M. L. *Readings in Nonmonotonic Reasoning.* Los Altos, CA: Morgan Kaufmann, 1987.
This collection contains many of the important papers cited in the quandaries section on nonmonotonic extensions to classical logic. It also contains an extensive bibliography of the field in 1987.

Sombé, L. Reasoning under incomplete information in artificial intelligence: A comparison of formalisms using a single example. *International Journal of Intelligent Systems,* special issue, Vol. 5, 4 (September 1990). Republished as Sombé, L., *Reasoning Under Incomplete Information in Artificial Intelligence.* New York: Wiley, 1990.
This is an interesting book that surveys and compares the major formalisms being developed in artificial intelligence research in support of common-sense reasoning. To facilitate comparison of approaches, a single example is carried through and discussed for all the approaches. The book was written in French by a working group of nine people, including Philippe Besnard, Marie-Odile Cordier, Didier Dubois, Luis Farinas del Cerro, Christine Froidevaux, Yves Moinard, Henri Prade, Camilla Schwind, and Pierre Siegel. The name "Lea Sombé" comes from "les A sont B," which means "the A's are B's." The book was translated into English by Sandra A. Sandri.

A.7 *Further Reading on Classification (Chapter 7)*

Mainline References (Chapter 7)

Buchanan, B. G., & Shortliffe, E. H. *Rule-based Expert Systems: The MYCIN Experiments of the Stanford Heuristic Programming Project.* Reading, MA: Addison-Wesley, 1984.

> An extensive account of the MYCIN project discussing the ideas, history, results, and lessons of one of the most influential projects in knowledge engineering. MYCIN has been characterized as the "drosophila of expert systems" by the geneticist Joshua Lederberg, meaning it is the most familiar experimental subject and is used as a basis of comparison for much later work. Of special interest to this chapter are several articles by William Clancey on the construction of the GUIDON program, which was intended to reuse the MYCIN knowledge base for teaching medicine to medical students. More than any of the other MYCIN experiments reported in this book, the GUIDON work confronted basic issues about what knowledge MYCIN actually used and needed. Among other things, this work led to a critical reexamination and reinterpretation of the knowledge in MYCIN and to the articulation of heuristic classification as a knowledge-level model.

Chandrasekaran, B., & Mittal, S. On deep versus compiled approaches to diagnostic problem solving. *International Journal of Man Machine Studies,* Vol. 19 (1983): 425–436.

> This paper describes MDX and offers some thoughts on the representation and organization of expertise in terms of specialists.

Clancey, W. J. Heuristic classification. *Artificial Intelligence,* Vol. 27, 3 (December 1985): 289–350.

> This paper is a careful reexamination of several knowledge systems that shows how they all have a regular pattern of knowledge use.

Clancey, W. J., & Letsinger, R. NEOMYCIN: Reconfiguring a rule-based expert system for application to teaching. In *Proceedings of the Seventh International Joint Conference on Artificial Intelligence,* pp. 829–836. Los Altos, CA: William Kaufmann, 1981. Reprinted in Clancey, W. J., & Shortliffe, E. H. (eds.), *Readings in Medical Artificial Intelligence: The First Decade,* pp. 361–381. Reading, MA: Addison-Wesley, 1984.

> This paper describes NEOMYCIN, a reimplementation of much of MYCIN intended for use in the GUIDON system for teaching medical students. This paper examines the characteristics of MYCIN's knowledge base and explains how it fails to capture many crucial elements of a diagnostic process, as might be observed from protocols of clinician behavior. This paper begins a knowledge-level analysis of the additional kinds of knowledge that are needed.

Duda, R. O., Hart, P. E., Konolige, K., & Reboh, R. *A Computer-based Consultant for Mineral Exploration,* Final Report, SRI Project 6415, Grant AER 77-04499. Menlo Park, CA: Artificial Intelligence Center, SRI International, September 1979.

> One of the public reports about the PROSPECTOR project. These reports give detailed examples of the network models developed to guide mineral exploration with PROSPECTOR.

Eshelman, L. MOLE: A knowledge-acquisition tool for cover-and-differentiate systems. In Marcus, S. (ed.), *Automating Knowledge Acquisition for Expert Systems,* pp. 37–80. Boston: Kluwer Academic Publishers, 1988.
> This paper describes how the MOLE system uses a specialized version of heuristic classification to solve diagnostic problems. It also discusses how the method provides a framework for guiding knowledge acquisition.

Gaschnig, J. Application of the PROSPECTOR system to geological exploration problems. In Hayes, J. E., Michie, D., & Pao, Y-H (eds.), *Machine Intelligence 10,* pp. 301–323. New York: Wiley, 1982.
> A careful and detailed account of the knowledge representations used in PROSPECTOR, the reasoning methods, and the performance of the system, including sensitivity analyses.

Kahn, G. MORE: From observing knowledge engineers to automating knowledge acquisition. In Marcus, S. (ed.), *Automating Knowledge Acquisition for Expert Systems,* pp. 7–35. Boston: Kluwer Academic Publishers, 1988.
> This paper describes how the MORE system uses a specialized version of heuristic classification to solve diagnostic problems. It also discusses how the method provides a framework for guiding knowledge acquisition.

Quandaries References (Chapter 7)

Bruner, J. S., Goodnow, J. J., & Austin, G. A. *A Study of Thinking.* New York: Wiley, 1956.
> This book has been characterized by Clancey as the most significant work in psychology done on classification. Bruner was concerned with the nature of concepts and categorizes, how they were learned, and how they were useful for problem solving. He emphasizes strategies for selecting cues and examples—information-gathering strategies—and on hypothesis formation and strategies for avoiding errors in learning.

Duda, R. O., & Hart, P. E. *Pattern Classification and Scene Analysis.* New York: Wiley, 1973.
> A good overview of topics in statistical pattern recognition. This book provides a basic mathematical introduction to probability distributions, discrimination functions, and other topics from statistics, communication theory, and operations research.

Duda, R. O., & Reboh, R. AI and decision making: The PROSPECTOR experience. In Reitman, W. (ed.), *Artificial Intelligence Applications for Business,* pp. 111–147. Norwood, NJ: Ablex Publishing, 1984.
> A readable and comprehensive paper about the PROSPECTOR system, for classifying ore deposits.

Fisher, D. Improving inference through conceptual clustering. In *Proceedings of the National Conference on Artificial Intelligence, AAAI-87,* Seattle, Washington. Los Altos, CA: Morgan Kaufmann, 1987.

> Fisher uses a notion of category utility invented by Gluck and Corter. Basically, categories are formed because they are useful for classification. By quantifying this utility, an algorithm can be constructed to search for and dynamically maintain the most useful set of categories.

Garfinkel, H. *Studies in Ethnomethodology.* New York: Prentice Hall, 1967.

> A text introducing ethnomethodology, a branch of sociology that draws its terms of analysis from the participants in the social situation being observed.

Lakoff, G., & Johnson, M. *Metaphors We Live By.* Chicago: University of Chicago Press, 1980.

> This is a classic book, showing how metaphors shape our communications and arguing that they shape the way we think about the world. It is a rich sourcebook for those seeking examples of reasoning by analogy.

A.8 *Further Reading on Configuration (Chapter 8)*

Bachant, J. RIME: Preliminary work toward a knowledge-acquisition tool. In Marcus, S. (ed.), *Automating Knowledge Acquisition for Expert Systems,* pp. 201–224. Boston: Kluwer Academic Publishers, 1988.

> This paper discusses the programming methodology that was developed for XCON. Roughly speaking, it is a structured programming approach for rule-based systems.

Barker, V. E., & O'Connor, D. E. Expert systems for configuration at Digital: XCON and beyond. *Communications of the ACM,* Vol. 32, 3 (March 1989): 298–318.

> This is a review of XCON and several other systems developed at Digital Equipment Corporation for configuring computer systems. It describes the evolution of ideas and several systems. It also includes an embedded subarticle by Judith Bachant and Elliot Soloway that describes the knowledge engineering issues explored in the RIME reimplementation of XCON.

Birmingham, W. P., Brennan, A., Gupta, A. P., & Siewiorek, D. P. MICON: A single board computer synthesis tool. *IEEE Circuits and Devices* (January 1988): 37–46.

> This paper describes the MICON/M1 system for configuring single-board computer systems.

Clancey, W. J. Details of the revised therapy algorithm. In Buchanan, B. G., & Shortliffe, E. H. (eds.), *Rule-based Expert Systems: The MYCIN Experiments of the Stanford Heuristic Programming Project,* pp. 133–146. Reading, MA: Addison-Wesley, 1984.

> This paper explains the algorithm for "configuring" therapies for MYCIN. This is an expanded version of a paper originally appearing in the *Proceedings of the IJCAI* (1977).

Clancey, W. J., & Letsinger, R. NEOMYCIN: Reconfiguring a rule-based expert system for application to teaching. In *Proceedings of the 7th International Joint Conference on Artificial Intelligence,* Vancouver, B.C., pp. 829–836. Los Altos, CA: William Kaufmann, 1981.

McDermott, J. R1: The formative years. *AI Magazine,* Vol. 2, 2 (September 1981). Reprinted in Engelove, R. (ed.), *Readings from the AI Magazine,* Volumes 1–5, 1980–1985, pp. 93–101. Menlo Park, CA: AAAI Press, 1988.

> This paper presents one of the early and most accessible accounts of the R1 program for configuring VAX computers. It is a broad paper, discussing both the technical issues and the organizational issues, which almost precluded getting R1 launched.

McDermott, J. R1: A rule-based configurer of computer systems. *Artificial Intelligence,* Vol. 19, 1 (September 1982a): 39–88.

> This paper presents a comprehensive symbol-level account of the R1 system that configures VAX-11/780 computer systems. Several subsequent papers have documented XCON, RIME, and other successor programs to R1. Nonetheless, this paper contains some of the best documentation of the ideas and assumptions used in these systems, and it is a useful starting point for those interested in the evolution of systems and ideas about configuration tasks.

McDermott, J. XSEL: A computer sales person's assistant. In Hayes, J. E., Michie, D., & Pao, Y.-H. (eds.), *Machine Intelligence 10,* pp. 325–337. New York: Wiley, 1982b.

> A discussion of the XSEL program and its relation to R1/XCON. This paper describes the concepts for XSEL when it was at an early stage of development and shows the ways in which it was conceived differently from R1. Although this paper has little to add about theories of configuration per se, it does illustrate some of the nebulous boundaries of configuration as a real-world task.

Marcus, S. (ed.). *Automating Knowledge Acquisition for Expert Systems.* Boston: Kluwer Academic Publishers, 1988.

> This edited volume contains papers about several experimental knowledge systems and knowledge-system shells based on abstract methods. Although the presentations are more about particular tools than results, the collection provides a current overview of the work on this subject, focusing on projects linked to Carnegie-Mellon University.

Marcus, S., & McDermott, J. SALT: A knowledge-acquisition language for propose-and-revise systems. *Artificial Intelligence,* Vol. 39, 1 (1989): 1–37.

> This paper gives examples of knowledge used in the VT configuration system for elevators and describes SALT, the knowledge-acquisition system used to build it.

Marcus, S., Stout, J., & McDermott, J. VT: An expert elevator designer that uses knowledge-based backtracking. *AI Magazine,* Vol. 9, 1 (Spring 1988): 95–112.

> This paper presents the concepts behind the VT system for configuring elevators. It presents the basic methods used and compares the VT system with several other knowledge systems that perform configuration and design tasks, or that need to man-

age their reasoning about alternatives using various approaches to dependency-directed backtracking.

Mittal, S., & Frayman, F. Towards a generic model of configuration tasks. In *Proceedings of the Eleventh International Joint Conference on Artificial Intelligence*, pp. 1395–1401. San Mateo, CA: Morgan Kaufmann, 1989.

> This paper presents an analysis of configuration tasks. Two important assumptions are identified as underlying many applications: functional architecture and the "key component per function."

Mittal, S., Dym, C. L., & Morjaria, M. PRIDE: An expert system for the design of paper handling systems. *Computer*, Vol. 19, 7 (July 1986): 102–114.

> PRIDE is a knowledge system for designing the paper-handling systems for copiers and printers. Several examples of dialog in knowledge acquisition sessions in Chapter 3 were drawn from videotapes of early sessions on the PRIDE project.

Shortliffe, E. H. Details of the consultation system. In Shortliffe, E. H., & Buchanan, B. G., *Rule-based Expert Systems: The MYCIN Experiments of the Stanford Heuristic Programming Project*. Reading, MA: Addison-Wesley, 1984.

> This chapter describes the original approach to therapy selection in MYCIN before it was reworked to use a configuration model. It is condensed from Chapter 3 of Shortliffe's thesis, published as *Computer-based Medical Consultations: MYCIN* (New York: Elsevier/North Holland, 1976).

Tong, C. *Knowledge-based Design*. Doctoral dissertation, Computer Science Department, Stanford University, 1988.

> Tong built a computer system to explore issues in the design of digital circuits. His thesis explores issues in the use of multiple abstractions and the representation of knowledge about design trade-offs.

Van de Brug, A., Bachant, J., & McDermott, J. The taming of R1. *IEEE Expert* (Fall 1986): 33–39.

> This paper discusses the reimplementation of R1 to simplify the task of maintaining the knowledge base.

A.9 *Further Reading on Diagnosis and Troubleshooting (Chapter 9)*

Mainline References (Chapter 9)

Brown, J. S., Burton, R. R., & de Kleer, J. Pedagogical, natural language and knowledge engineering techniques in SOPHIE I, II, and III. In Sleeman, D., & Brown, J. S. (eds.), *Intelligent Tutoring Systems*, pp. 230–279. New York: Academic Press, 1982.

> SOPHIE III was a system for teaching troubleshooting of electronic circuits. As such it explored some of the practice of teaching and coaching and also knowledge engineering techniques for building robust circuit models and diagnostic practices. Several of the diagnostic systems considered in Section 9.3 build on this work.

Clancey, W. J., & Letsinger, R. NEOMYCIN: Reconfiguring a rule-based expert system for application to teaching. In *Proceedings of the Seventh International Joint Conference on Artificial Intelligence,* pp. 829–836. Los Altos, CA: William Kaufmann, 1981. Reprinted in Clancey & Shortliffe (1984) pp. 361–381.

> This paper describes NEOMYCIN, a reimplementation of much of MYCIN intended for use in the GUIDON system for teaching medical students. This paper examines the characteristics of MYCIN's knowledge base and explains how it fails to capture many crucial elements of a diagnostic process, as might be observed from protocols of clinician behavior. This paper begins a knowledge-level analysis of the additional kinds of knowledge needed in a tutoring situation.

Clancey, W. J., & Shortliffe, E. H. *Readings in Medical Artificial Intelligence: The First Decade.* Reading, MA: Addison-Wesley, 1984.

> An excellent collection of readings about clincical decision making and cognitive and knowledge engineering issues for medical applications of knowledge systems. Several medical diagnosis systems are reviewed in addition to the ones discussed in this chapter.

Davis, R. Diagnostic reasoning based on structure and behavior. In Bobrow, D. G., *Qualitative Reasoning about Physical Systems,* pp. 347–409. Cambridge: Bradford Books/MIT Press, 1985.

> This is a thoughtful essay on the nature of diagnostic systems and on directions for research. The paper is based on the experience of the hardware troubleshooting group at MIT. Several of the ideas for the analysis of diagnostic tasks in Section 9.3 have their origins in this paper, such as the discussion about paths of interaction and the notion of layered and prioritized categories of failure. Rather than advancing vague claims about the generality of an approach, Davis's paper takes a more refreshing stance. It looks for a way to uncover the assumptions on which models of cause, behavior, and diagnostic reasoning depend.

Davis, R., & Hamscher, W. Model-based reasoning: Troubleshooting. In Shrobe, H. E. (ed.), *Exploring Artificial Intelligence: Survey Talks from the National Conferences on Artificial Intelligence,* pp. 297–346. San Mateo, CA: Morgan Kaufmann, 1988.

> This is a survey article about troubleshooting systems. It is well written and covers the main ideas of knowledge-level analysis for diagnosis. The approach in Section 9.2 that divides diagnosis into hypothesis generation, testing, and discrimination was inspired by this article. The overview focuses mainly on approaches that make a single-fault assumption. It gives very little detail about considerations for selecting probe points to discriminate among candidate solutions.

de Kleer, J. *Using Crude Probability Estimates to Guide Diagnosis*, SSL P89-00056.

> This paper simplifies the techniques developed for GDE and SHERLOCK by considering all candidates of k faults at a time, without computing candidate probabilities.

de Kleer, J., & Williams, B. C. Diagnosing multiple faults. *Artificial Intelligence,* Vol. 32, 1 (April 1987): 97–130.

> This is the main paper about GDE, the general diagnostic engine discussed in Section 9.3. GDE is well known for its systematic approach to diagnosis with multiple possible faults, and also for its systematic approach to selecting optimal probe points.

de Kleer, J., & Williams, B. C. Diagnosis with behavioral modes. In *Proceedings of the Eleventh International Joint Conference on Artificial Intelligence,* pp. 1324–1330. San Mateo, CA: Morgan Kaufmann, 1989.

> This paper introduces SHERLOCK, the extension to GDE that models components in terms of multiple modes of behavior.

Hamscher, W. C. *Model-Based Troubleshooting of Digital Systems.* Massachusetts Institute of Technology, Artificial Intelligence Laboratory Technical Report 1074, 1988.

> This is Walter Hamscher's thesis, describing his methodology, representation, and program for troubleshooting digital circuit boards. Hamscher's research explores variations on most of the important ideas for knowledge-based disagnosis. This thesis is very clearly written, describing the concepts, the limitations, and the research directions.

Hamscher, W. C. Modeling digital circuits for troubleshooting. *Artificial Intelligence,* Vol. 51, 1–3 (1990): 223–272.

> A shorter presentation of Walter Hamscher's thesis, using the same examples.

Kulikowski, C. A., & Weiss, S. M. Representation of expert knowledge for consultation: The CASNET and EXPERT projects. In Szolovits, P. (ed.), *Artificial Intelligence in Medicine,* AAAS Selected Symposium 51, pp. 21–55. Boulder, CO: Westview Press, 1982.

> This is an overview paper about CASNET and the glaucoma diagnosis and treatment system. It was written for an audience with a scientific and medical background.

Miller, R. A., Pople, H. E., & Myers, J. D. INTERNIST-1: An experimental computer-based diagnostic consultant for general internal medicine. In Clancey and Shortliffe (1984), pp. 190–209.

> A readable account of the concepts used in the INTERNIST system for diagnosing diseases of internal medicine. This paper includes a condensed version of the results of a study that appeared earlier in the *New England Journal of Medicine,* describing the performance of INTERNIST-1 on some very difficult problems and comparing its performance with that of several physicians and specialized teams of physicians.

Mittal, S., Bobrow, D. G., & de Kleer, J. DARN: Toward a community memory for diagnosis and repair tasks. In Hendler, J. A. (ed.), *Expert Systems: The User Interface,* pp. 57–79. Norwood, NJ: Ablex Publishing, 1988.

> An example of a knowledge system for diagnosis based on a decision tree that models faults and tests.

Patil, R. S. Causal Representation of Patient Illness For Electrolyte and Acid-base Diagnosis. Cambridge: MIT Laboratory for Computer Science, Technical Report MIT/LCS/TR-267, October 1981.

> This is Ramesh Patil's doctoral dissertation. This dissertation is comparable to Pople's proposal for CADUCEUS (Pople, 1982). It differs in that Patil's contact with medical problem solving is much narrower than Pople's. However, the formalisms proposed for medical diagnostic problem solving seem to do the same work, albeit with simpler notations and mechanisms.

Patil, R. S., Szolovits, P., & Schwartz, W. B. Causal understanding of patient illness in medical diagnosis. In *Proceedings of the Seventh International Joint Conference on Artificial Intelligence*, pp. 893–899. Los Altos, CA: William Kaufmann, 1981. Reprinted in Clancey and Shortliffe (1984), pp. 339–360.

> This paper discusses several issues and techniques in representing medical knowledge for diagnosis. This work merges concepts from causal networks and lumped element models. It presents several examples of diagnosis in cases where multiple causes have compensating or synergistic effects.

Pople, H. E. The formation of composite hypotheses in diagnostic problem solving: An exercise in synthetic reasoning. In *Proceedings of the Fifth International Joint Conference on Artificial Intelligence,* pp. 1030–1037. Los Altos, CA: William Kaufmann, 1977.

> This paper proposes changes to INTERNIST-1 for handling hypotheses involving multiple diseases. The ideas are presented clearly, but they are largely superseded by further proposals in Pople (1982).

Pople, H. E. Heuristic methods for imposing structure on ill-structured problems: The structuring of medical diagnostics. In Szolovits, P. (ed.), *Artificial Intelligence in Medicine,* AAAS Selected Symposium 51, pp. 119–190. Boulder, CO: Westview Press, 1982.

> This is one of the most extensive papers about the INTERNIST-1 system for medical diagnosis and contains the best discussion of the shortcomings of INTERNIST-1 and the plans for CADUCEUS. It describes the methods and limitations of INTERNIST-1. In this paper, Pople considers the assumptions that underlie the methods for most medical diagnosis systems and finds that they bear little resemblance to the assumptions that pertain in real practice. He shows why the task of medical diagnosis is necessarily much more than differential diagnosis. This paper presents a fairly detailed proposal for CADUCEUS, in terms of its handling of multiple, composite hypotheses and its use of a hierarchical causal network.

Pople, H. E., Myers, J. D., & Miller, R. A. DIALOG: A model of dianostic logic for internal medicine. In *Advance Papers of the Fourth International Joint Conference on Artificial Intelligence,* pp. 848–855. Los Altos, CA: William Kaufmann, 1975.

> This is an early paper discussing the INTERNIST-1 diagnostic system (initially called DIALOG) for internal medicine. This paper provides examples of reasoning and also rules from the knowledge base. Most of the ideas for hypothesis discrimination in INTERNIST-1 are developed in this paper.

Reggia, J. A., Nau, D. S., & Wang, P. Diagnostic expert systems based on a set covering model. *International Journal of Man-Machine Studies,* Vol. 19, 3 (November 1983): 437–460.

> This is one of the first papers on diagnostic systems that had a systematic approach for diagnosing multiple faults.

Szolovits, P. (ed.). *Artificial Intelligence in Medicine,* AAAS Selected Symposium 51. Boulder, CO: Westview Press, 1982.

> An edited collection of papers on AI in medicine, based on a symposium held at the 1979 AAAS National Annual Meeting in Houston, Texas. Overall, this is an excellent sampling of papers on AI techniques for representation and reasoning applied in medical contexts. It includes several case studies of specific knowledge systems for diagnosis.

Weiss, S. M., Kulikowski, C. A., Amarel, S., & Safir, A. A model-based method for computer-aided medical decision making. *Artificial Intelligence,* Vol. 11 (1978): 145–172. Reprinted in Clancey and Shortliffe (1984), pp. 160–189.

> A comprehensive paper discussing the modeling techniques and methods used in the CASNET knowledge system for diagnosis and therapies of glaucomas.

Quandaries References (Chapter 9)

Bobrow, D. G. (ed.). *Qualitative Reasoning about Physical Systems.* Cambridge: MIT Press, 1985. Reprinted from *Artificial Intelligence,* Vol. 24 (1984).

> This is an edited volume with papers by several leading researchers on qualitative reasoning systems. The book contains two papers about diagnostic systems, and many of the other papers on qualitative reasoning were motivated by applications to diagnosis. As argued in Section 9.3, the construction of appropriate physical models is crucial in the design of diagnostic systems. The techniques for this are in flux, but this book gives several detailed examples of alternative approaches. A background in the approaches discussed in this book would be useful for building knowledge systems that must reason about or interact with the physical properties of the world.

Breiman, L. *Probability and Stochastic Processes: With a View Toward Applications.* Boston: Houghton Mifflin, 1969.

> There are many textbooks about probability theory. This particular one is intended to convey a working knowledge of probability and stochastic processes. It includes chapters on Markov chains and Markov processes, which provide a formal basis for the probabilistic causal models discussed in this chapter.

Busha, W., & Morris, S. (eds.), with contributions by the staff of Vermont Castings. *The Book of Heat: A Four-Season Guide to Wood- and Coal-Stove Heating.* Lexington, MA: Stephen Greene Press, 1982.

> An informative and amusing guide to the history, design, maintenance, diagnosis, trials, tribulations, and joys of having a wood stove and "speaking stove." This book condenses many of the lessons of "Stove School" used for factory training of all rep-

resentatives of Vermont Castings, Inc. This book is the source of an anecdote in the quandaries section of this chapter.

Howard, R. A. Information value theory. *IEEE Transactions on Systems Science and Cybernetics,* Vol. SSC-2, 1 (August 1966): 22–26.

This paper argues that Shannon's information theory is best used in problems involving efficient communication and that it is misapplied in many other cases. The basic argument is that no theory that involves just the probabilities of outcomes without considering their consequences could possibly be adequate in describing the importance of uncertainty to a decision maker. Information-value theory is an approach that deals both with the probabilistic nature of uncertainties and also with the economic impact the uncertainties have. This point is relevant in extending diagnostic systems to incorporate additional kinds of knowledge in probe selection.

Shirley, M. H. *Generating Tests by Exploiting Designed Behavior.* Doctoral dissertation, Massachusetts Institute of Technology, Artificial Intelligence Laboratory, Technical Report 1099, 1989.

This thesis describes Shirley's methodology, representation, and program for designing test patterns for digital circuits. To acquire more information about the possible faults in a circuit, the diagnostic systems discussed in this chapter select new places to "probe." This is generally not practical in a testing situation, where an assembly-line approach is needed for testing large numbers of identical circuits. The challenge faced by Shirley's program is the generation of testing patterns that provide adequate coverage of possible faults.

B

Selected Answers to Exercises

B.1 Chapter 1

Selected Answers to Exercises for Section 1.1

Ex. 1   **(a)** No. Some markings are not symbols. For example, the tracing left by the ocean tide and waves on the sand at the beach is a marking, but it is not taken to be writing. It does not contain individual symbols and it is not *about* something. In a strict definition, symbolhood requires both a recognizer of markings and an observer to assign meanings.

(b) Yes, if there is an interpreter—for example, if we can interpret sequences of DNA as genes that code for particular proteins and correspond to particular biological traits.

(c) No. Meaning is not part of the symbol. Meaning is assigned by an observer. There may be clues in a symbol's structure to the meaning assigned by some observer. For example, we can examine an English word to determine its roots in other languages. However, structural clues about meaning are not required for a marking to be a symbol.

(d) Yes. This happens all the time. For an extreme case, consider legal or religious debates about the meaning of written laws.

(e) Yes, although this is unusual. Arguably this is the case for the symbols T and NIL in Lisp.

Ex. 8   **(a)** The registration problem shows us that two different recognizers can parse a given set of markings differently. These different accounts of a mark or physical pattern are called *registrations* of it. This shows that the identification of markings is not a property of just the markings, but rather that recognition and identification must be defined relative to a recognizer. The issue with the dictionary definition is that it assumes that the parsing of symbols is evident; it does not acknowledge the need to define classes of markings relative to a recognizer.

(b) Two different observers may assign different meanings to a given symbol. This shows that designation is not a property of markings, but rather that it must be defined relative to an observer and a situation. The issue with the dictionary definition is that it assumes that a

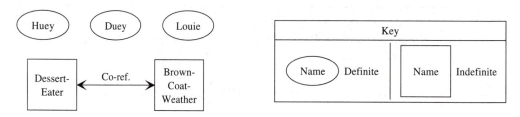

FIGURE B.1.   A semantic network with definite and indefinite nodes.

meaning is somehow inherently associated with a symbol; that is, that meaning is objective rather than subjective. It does not mention the need to define representation relative to an observer and a situation.

Selected Answers to Exercises for Section 1.2

Ex. 1   (a) Directed, labeled, acyclic graph.

(b) Unlabeled forest. Like all forests, it is directed and acyclic.

(c) Directed, labeled, acyclic graph. It is not a tree because node Q has two ancestors.

(d) Directed, labeled, cyclic graph. The cycle is between nodes R and S.

Ex. 4   (a) Figure B.1 shows one approach to creating a semantic network to represent the situation. The notation allows us to say that the two indefinite nodes are intended to refer to the same unique individual, even though the identity of that individual has not yet been determined.

(b) If the brown coat is worn by Huey, then the indefinite node for the brown-coat-wearer can be anchored to the definite individual node that represents Huey. Because of the co-reference link between the nodes for the dessert-eater and the brown-coat-wearer, the processor could then infer that Huey is the dessert-eater.

(c) The identity model here should follow the usual rules of equivalence relations. Given that the individual nodes are supposed to be unique, the transitivity operations along co-reference relations should allow nodes to have only one identity. Adding a co-reference link between two indefinite nodes already anchored to different definite nodes would violate the semantics by equating Huey to Louie.

Ex. 11   Examples analogous to this exercise have been at the center of many different arguments and ideas about representation and semantic networks. Section 1.6 lists several papers that deal with the inadequacy of naive approaches to representing quantifiers in semantic networks, especially Brachman (1979), Woods (1975), and Hendrix (1975). Computational approaches using parallel processing computers for propagating quantified properties expressed in semantic network representations are described in Hillis (1985).

(a) Models might be built in several ways that could have the properties required in this example.

Figure B.2 illustrates two approaches. Both approaches require that the interpreter have a graph-walking procedure for supporting the inheritance of properties.

To infer that "Bill can fly," the first approach assumes that the interpreter knows that properties are inherited along is-a and kind-of links. In short, to determine whether Bill can

Approach 1

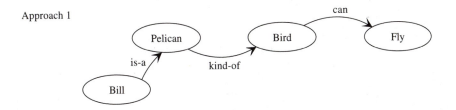

Approach 2

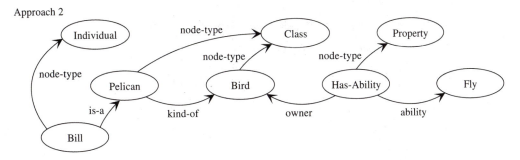

FIGURE B.2. Two of the possible graph representations.

fly, it walks up the is-a links and kind-of links searching for a node that has an arc labeled can leading to a node named fly.

The second approach is similar but makes use of node and arc annotations. In this approach, the nodes bird and pelican have node types called classes, Bill has a node type of individual, and has-ability has a node type of property. These node types are critical for determining the processing by the following algorithm. To determine whether an individual (e.g., Bill) has a particular property, the following algorithm is performed.

Starting at the individual node, collect all property nodes immediately connected to it. If a property node is found containing the sought property, return with that node's value. Otherwise, find the class node for the individual by following the is-a link.

For this class node collect all property nodes immediately connected with it. If the sought property is found, return with its value. Repeat for all superclasses found by following kind-of links from the class node. If the sought property node is not found by this procedure, then the individual is assumed not to have the property.

(b) *Background.* Modus ponens says that given a, and a implies b, we can infer b. In logic notation this is:

$$a,\ a \Rightarrow b \vdash b$$

Universal instantiation says that if we are given that for all x where $A(x)$ is true, that $B(x)$ is true, and also that if we are given $A(a)$, then we can infer $B(a)$. In logical notation, this is

$$(\forall x)\,A(x) \Rightarrow B(x),\ A(a) \vdash B(a)$$

Answer.
Here is one way to approach this problem using two applications of universal instantiation.

First we translate the statements as follows:

1. All birds can fly.

   $(\forall x)$ is-a $(x$ bird$) \Rightarrow$ can-fly (x)

2. A pelican is a kind of bird.

   kind-of (pelican bird)

3. Bill is a pelican.

   is-a (bill pelican)

We also assume the following definitional relationship between is-a and kind-of:

4. If y is a kind of z and x is a y, then x is a z.

   $(\forall x, y, z)$ kind-of $(y \quad z) \wedge$ is-a $(x\ y) \Rightarrow$
   is-a $(x\ z)$

Using universal instantiation with 3 and 4, we get

5. Bill is a bird.

   is-a (bill bird)

Using universal instantiation with 1 and 5, we get

6. Bill can fly.

   can-fly (bill)

Ex. 12   **(a)** There are different possible semantics for symbols in a knowledge system. In this answer we consider two of them: a reference semantics and a denotational semantics.

In a reference semantics, the "meaning" is in the mind of the observer. If the observers change their minds about what the symbols mean, then that changes what the program means. However, this is not as strange as it seems. We could re-paraphrase Professor Digit's question as a statement: "When people reinterpret what the symbols in a knowledge base mean, they also change their minds about what the program means." So for a reference semantics, the answer is "yes." The "sniffleitus" symbol refers to something different.

A denotational semantics is a description about what a program does. It is in terms of inputs, outputs, and internal states. If people change their minds about something without changing the program, this does *not* change the program's behavior. It will still carry out the same computation given the same inputs. So for a denotational semantics, the answer is "no."

More generally, in terms of the referential families of semantics, especially the reference semantics and the intensional semantics, the meanings change when people reinterpret what the symbols used by a knowledge system mean. Within the cognitive family of semantic theories, however, meaningfulness depends only on how information is computationally represented and reasoned about. The meanings do not change when an outside observer reinterprets the meaning of a symbol.

(b) The changes by the knowledge engineer have the opposite effect: They change the denotational semantics but not the reference semantics.

This exercise gives a concrete example of when it is important to be clear about what we mean by the "meaning" of a system.

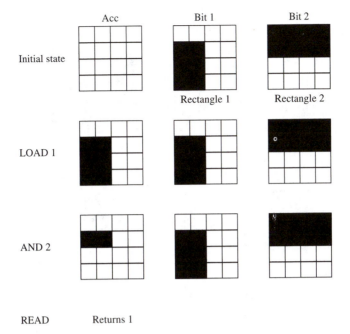

FIGURE B.3.

Selected Answers to Exercises for Section 1.3

Ex. 1 **(a)** The program seems to have only four input states (2 bits) and two output states (1 bit).

(b) Professor Digit's account is unsatisfactory in several regards. The main issue is its lack of generality. It is excessively narrow in its representation of numbers, arithmetic expressions, and the multiplication process. Thus, there is little basis for generalizing his representation of the expression of the product of 31415926535589793238462643 times 987654321987654321 as a single 0 bit.

For most representations of numbers we expect to give an account of how different numbers are represented, how large a number can be represented, and so on. For representations of arithmetic expressions, we expect to give an account of what operations are possible and how they are indicated. For multiplication, we expect to give an account of how the representation of the process interacts with the representation of expressions and numbers, whether it correctly yields representations of the product, and how long it takes. Professor Digit's system is so trivial that it is not clear how to systematically extend it to cover additional numbers and operations.

Another answer is that Professor Digit's account does not give a denotational semantics for his program. In other words, he does not really tell us how it performs the computation.

Ex. 4 **(a)** The action of the intersection algorithm is illustrated in Figure B.3. The algorithm assumes that the figures are stored in bit plane 1 and bit plane 2.

(b) Figure B.4 shows the trace of the execution of the program, including the contents of the accumulator.

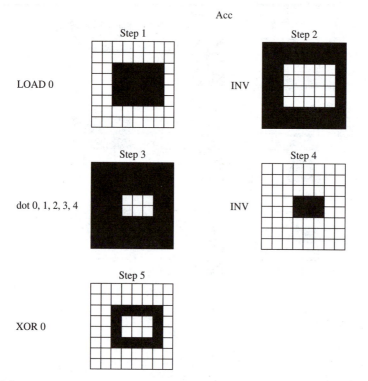

FIGURE B.4.

The program works by computing the interior of the rectangle and then subtracting it from the original rectangle.

```
load 0              ;load the rectangle into acc
inv                 ;compute the interior of the rectangle
dot (0 1 2 3 4) ;
inv                 ;
xor 0               ;subtract interior from rectangle
```

The computation of the rectangle's interior can be understood an an application of de Morgan's laws. The interior corresponds to the set of cells in the original figure that are on (that is, in which bit 0 is 1) and whose neighbors are off.

By de Morgan's law:

```
interior = (and self (not nbr0) (not nbr1) (not nbr2)
                     (not nbr3))
         = (not (or (not self) nbr0 nbr1 nbr2 nbr3))
```

which explains the operation of the middle three instructions in the program.

(c) The edge-finding computation in part b is local, because the results in each cell depend only on data in neighboring cells.

(d) One version of the program follows, based on the idea of exercise 4:

```
load 1          ;load rectangle-1 into acc
dot (0 1 2 3 4);expand rectangle-1 by one unit in
                all directions
and 2           ;intersect expansion with rectangle-2
read            ;return indicator of intersection
```

This program works for arbitrary figures, not just rectangles.

Ex. 10 True. The asymptotic time complexity of an algorithm is always greater or equal to its asymptotic space complexity. Suppose an algorithm uses m memory cells. The processor must visit each memory cell at least once. Therefore, its time complexity is at least $O(m)$.

Selected Answers to Exercises for Section 1.4

Ex. 1 Matching

(and (likes ?dog ?person)(feather-brained ?person))

with

(and (likes Fido Bonzo)(feather-brained Fido))

yields **no match** because person cannot be bound to both Bonzo and Fido.
Matching with

(and (likes Rover Lucky)(feather-brained Lucky))

yields **a match** with dog = Rover and person = Lucky.
Matching with

(and (likes Spot Sperald)(feather-brained Lucky))

yields **no match** because person cannot be bound to both Lucky and Sperald.
Matching with

(or (likes Sport Dizzy)(feather-brained Dizzy))

yields **no match** because and in the pattern does not match or in the expression.

Ex. 6 **(a)** When there is no traffic on the farm road, the traffic light system goes to its initial state with the farm-road light red and the highway light green.
(b) In this case, the light system cycles alternately, letting traffic proceed along the farm road and the highway. The flow of traffic at each iteration is controlled by the traffic timer, which determines how long the light stays green for each road. In this case, the rules fire in sequence: rule-1, rule-2, rule-3, and rule-4 where the time in each state is determined by the timers.
(c) The behavior when the sensor is jammed is the same as when cars are waiting at the farm road.

Ex. 7 **(a)** The rules fire to add the following clauses to working memory.

(parent Mary Ellen)
(parent Ellen Paige)
(parent Ellen Morgan)
(parent Virgil Ellen)

```
(parent Mark Paige)
(parent Mark Morgan)
(grandparent Mary Paige)
(grandparent Mary Morgan)
(grandparent Virgil Paige)
(grandparent Virgil Morgan)
(uncle Karl Paige)
(uncle Karl Morgan)
(uncle Eric Paige)
(uncle Eric Morgan)
(uncle Mike Paige)
(uncle Mike Morgan)
(aunt Paula Paige)
(aunt Paula Morgan)
(aunt Julie Paige)
(aunt Julie Morgan)
```

B.2 Chapter 2

Selected Answers to Exercises for Section 2.1

Ex. 1   **(a)** *True.* A search space can contain elements not in the solution space, such as when a program needs to eliminate structures that are systematically generated but that are in the space of acceptable descriptions of solutions. A solution space may include elements not in the search space if there are solutions not expressible in the language used by the search program.

(b) *Ambiguous.* There are different conventions for representing search processes in terms of trees. In one convention, solutions are terminal nodes. In other conventions, solutions can occur anyplace in the tree. In others, paths through the tree correspond to solutions. To understand such diagrams we need to know which convention is being used.

(c) *Generally True.* A satisficing search knows how good a solution needs to be. In practice, an optimizing search may incorporate such knowledge and report "no solutions" if the best candidates are not good enough.

(d) *True.* Historically, the term *heuristic* refers to "knowledge that guides."

(e) *False.* Pun based on Pac-man games. A PAC algorithm is one that gives answers that are *probably approximately correct.*

Ex. 6   **(a)** $2^{20} = 1,048,576$ for a balanced binary tree where every path to the leaves involves 20 questions.

(b) There are multiple ways to build the tree. Here's one:

```
("Is the size large?"
(Yes ("Is the sound Moo?"
        (Yes "It's a cow")
        (No "It's a horse")))
(No (Is the sound meow?"
        (Yes "It's a cat")
        (No "It's a dog"))))
```

(c) No—because these two attributes are exactly correlated. In this data set an animal is large if and only if it lives in a barn, and an animal is small if and only if it lives in a house.

Selected Answers to Exercises for Section 2.2

Ex. 1 **(a)** 32 MB ÷ 4 MB/minute = 8 minutes. (This computation assumes that the space for the fringe dominates.)
(b) In breadth-first search, stack space is assumed to be reclaimed when a node is popped from the stack. This means that we need only account for the space required by the fringe.

> max number of nodes = 32 MB/4 bytes per node = 8 MB nodes
> Number of nodes on fringe at depth $d = b^d = 4^d$
> $4^{11} = 4,194,304$
> $4^{12} = 16,777,216$

so that only 11 levels of the tree could be completely searched before exhausting memory.

Ex. 2 **(a)** It will enter an infinite loop on the first cycle it encounters.
(b) The revised method for this exercise avoids the problem of infinite loops, but at the cost of greatly increased space complexity. Even if it only allocates 1 bit for every node in the tree, it needs space for every node in the search space. Where b is the branching factor and d is the "depth" of the graph, the asymptotic space complexity is $O(b^d)$.

This complexity does not mean that the method is impractical for small enough search trees. Indeed, for search problems where the entire tree is kept in memory, an overhead of 1 bit per node may be trivial. However, when the search space is arbitrarily large, so is the space required by this method for keeping track of whether nodes have been visited.
(c) Yes—a tree of nodes whose order is just the order that nodes are visited. This is a spanning tree for the graph.

Ex. 9 **(a)** The three cross-graphs in Professor Digit's two-dimensional canonical form are shown in Figure B.5.

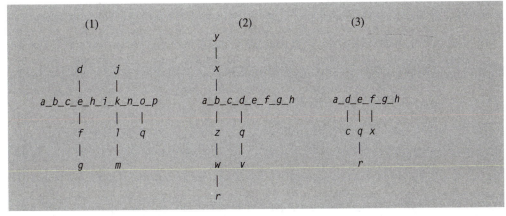

FIGURE B.5. Canonical forms for the three sets of track data.

(b) Here are the three graphs in canonical linear form.

```
(a b c (d e* f g) h i (j k* l m) n (o* q) p)
(a (y x b* z w r) c (d* q v) e f g h)
(a (d* c) (e* q r) (f* x) g h)
```

The linear form would be easy to manipulate with a list processing language.

(c) We are given a graph with two subparts:

```
(a b e)
(c d)
```

By the constraints, the second subpart cannot be connected to *a*, so it must be connected to either *b* or *e* in some order. If it is connected to *b*, then it will be on the main track and *e* will be on a side track, leading to the solutions:

```
(a (b* e) c d)
(a (b* e) d c)
```

If it is connected to *e*, the entire graph will be linear, leading to the solutions:

```
(a b e c d)
(a b e d c)
```

Selected Answers for Section 2.3

Ex. 1   **(a)** *True.* If the hill-climbing method is exhaustive, then it must tirelessly test every node to see whether each node is a solution. In this event, it gets no benefit from the directionality provided by the evaluation function and we might as well just use depth-first search.

Note that it is important not to confuse an exhaustive search with a complete search. An exhaustive search must return all solutions. A complete search is merely capable of finding any solution.

(b) *True.* Neither method keeps track of where it has been. As discussed in the text, sometimes it is possible to prove for a particular domain that the search will be complete. However, this is not true in general and requires places rather stringent constraints on the domain's search space.

(c) *False.* Backtracking hill climbing expands the best successor of the current node, but best-first search expands the best node from anywhere on its dynamic fringe.

(d) *Ambiguous.* Most of you will answer this as true. Actually, it is a bit of a trick question. Most of the search methods discussed in this section were not redundant, in that they visit each node once. Limiting consideration to searches like those in this section, this statement is true. However, a nondeterministic search method—such as one that selects nodes from a space using a uniform random number generator—will eventually perform a complete search. However, this search is **redundant,** which means it searches some nodes more than once. Another disadvantage of a nondeterministic search is that we never know exactly when it has finished searching the entire space. For these reasons, a nondeterministic search method is usually not satisfactory.

(e) *Ambiguous* (mainly *True*). The principle says that if there are multiple paths to a node, we can discard all but the shortest path to it. Furthermore, once a path to a solution is known, all longer paths to any node can be discarded.

Ex. 3   **(a)** The maximum number of nodes evaluated at each level in beam search is wb, rather than mb where m is the number of nodes at the next higher level. The maximum number of nodes considered altogether in beam search is wbd rather than b^d.

(b) Best-first search advances from the best open node so far, no matter where that node is in the tree. Beam search progresses through the tree one level at a time, advancing from only the best w nodes at each level.

Best-first search is complete. Beam search is incomplete. Depending on the properties of the evaluation function, beam search may fail to find some solutions (e.g., if they are located along paths whose initial nodes have evaluations lower than those of their sibling nodes). Best-first search is capable of finding solutions if they are anywhere in the search space.

Beam search has space complexity of $O(w)$. Best-first search has space complexity of $O(d)$ where d is the depth of the search tree. This depends on using a choice point implementation of the stack. (See Exercise 9.)

(c) No. The main point of using a limited list size is to trade completeness for space and time complexity. If the list were allowed to grow as needed, the method would lose its space-saving benefits and gain a greater time burden for the merge operation.

Ex. 6   **(a)** More than one step could be seen as embodying the dynamic programming principle. Step 8 updates the current best value for a goal and step 16 updates the distances to each goal in the paths developed.

(b) Here is the completed table.

Cycle	Node			List
	Successor	*Accum. Dist.*	*Estimated Total*	
1	A			C B
	B	5	22	
	C	4	16	
2	C			D B
	D	12	17	
3	D			I F E B
	E	14	19	
	I	14	17	
	F	15	18	
4	I			G F E B
	G	17	18	
5	G			F E B
	H	18	goal	
6	F			E B
	G	18 (too long)		
7	E			
	—	(Too long. Skip generating successors.)		
8	B			
	E	15 (too long)		

(c) The minimum path is ($A\ C\ D\ I\ G\ H$) and is 18 units long.

(d) Underestimating is better. If an incomplete path is discarded because the completion distance is overestimated, then the problem solver could fail to find the optimal solution to

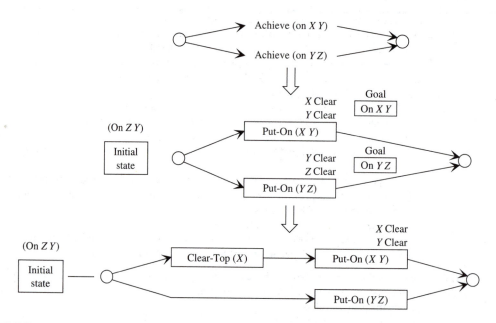

FIGURE B.6.   A Blocks World problem.

a problem. If the estimator never overestimates path length, then A* will find the optimal path. Underestimates cannot cause the minimal path to be overlooked. The closer an underestimate is to the correct distance the better A* will work, because it will correctly focus its attention on the shortest path. The condition that the evaluation function not overestimate the actual distance is sometimes called the "admissibility condition" for A*.

Ex. 9   **(a)** Figure B.6 illustrates preconditions, operators, goals, and ordering relations for the first steps in solving this problem.
(b) If the step (put-on X Y) is done before (put-on Y Z), then the preconditions for the second operator (a clear top on Y) will not be satisfied. We can use the analysis of this interaction to propse the additional ordering constraint that (put-on Y Z) be done before (put-on X Y). The resulting plan structure is shown in Figure B.7.

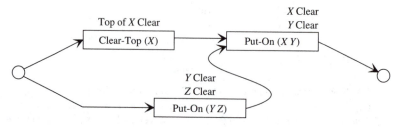

FIGURE B.7.   Refining the partial ordering.

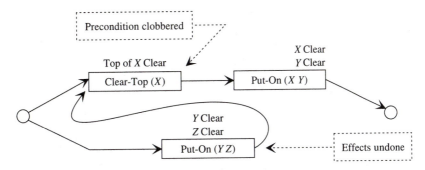

FIGURE B.8. A buggy-candidate plan refinement.

(c) So far, the plan imposes no ordering constraint on (clear-top *X*) and (put-on *Y Z*). However, if we perform (put-on *Y Z*) first, that leads to the plan in Figure B.8.

This has two problems. The step (put-on *Y Z*) interferes with the precondition of (clear-top *X*) that the block on *X* be clear. Second, if we add more steps to reestablish the preconditions of (clear-top *X*), we need to undo the work that (put-on *Y Z*) carries out.

The other alternative ordering is shown in Figure B.9. This linearization clobbers none of the goals or preconditions.

Note: The analyses we have discussed here are just a beginning in understanding how to linearize partially ordered plans. In more complex cases, the analysis can be extended to be explicit about regions of time over which certain conditions are assumed to hold. Research on such problems has been carried out in planning in AI, in automatic programming, and in compiler optimization.

Selected Answers to Exercises for Section 2.4

Ex. 1 **(a)** *True.*
(b) *False.* In the context of search, the term *garden path* refers to a candidate that is ultimately shown *not* to be a solution. Such candidates often have the property that their failure to be a solution cannot be discovered until much work is invested. In this regard, they are misleading and take the searcher "down a garden path."
(c) *True.*

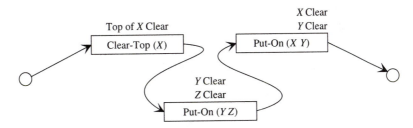

FIGURE B.9. A better plan refinement.

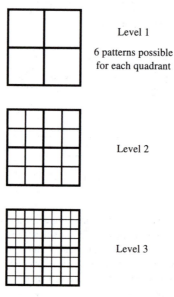

Level 1

6 patterns possible
for each quadrant

Level 2

Level 3

FIGURE B.10.   Quadrants for levels 1, 2, and 3.

(d) *False.* Algorithms for hierarchical planning with *linear* complexity generally require multiple levels of abstraction. The complexity of two-level planning is usually related to $N^{1/2}$. For example, the complexity of HP-1 is

$$O\left(N^{1/2}a^{N^{1/2}}\right).$$

(e) *False.* In general, as the expansion ratio k increases, w_a *decreases* and w_d *increases*.

Ex. 3   **(a)** As suggested by Figure B.10,

With 1 level there are 6^4 combinations.

There is a recurrence relation for determining the number of designs at each level. It is:

$$D(n) = D(n-1) * 6^{4^n}$$

Thus,

With 2 levels there are $6^{4^1} * 6^{4^2}$ combinations.
With 3 levels there are $6^{4^1} * 6^{4^2} * 6^{4^3}$ combinations.
With 4 levels there are $6^{4^1} * 6^{4^2} * 6^{4^3} * 6^{4^4}$ combinations.
With 5 levels there are $6^{4^1} * 6^{4^2} * 6^{4^3} * 6^{4^4} * 6^{4^5}$ combinations.

Because of the changing of colors in the outer quadrants, each assignment of a pattern yields a distinct design.

In total there are 6^{1364} = approximately $2.5 * 10^{1061}$ possible patterns.

(b) The total number of pleasing patterns at each level is determined as follows.

With 1 level there are 6^4 combinations, as before.

The reduction of choices then occurs between levels. There is a recurrence relation for determining the number of designs at each level. It is:

$$D'(n) = D'(n-1) * 5^{4^{n-1}}$$

Thus,

With 2 levels there are $6^4 * 5^{4^1}$ combinations.
With 3 levels there are $6^4 * 5^{4^1} * 5^{4^2}$ combinations.
With 4 levels there are $6^4 * 5^{4^1} * 5^{4^2} * 5^{4^3}$ combinations.
With 5 levels there are $6^4 * 5^{4^1} * 5^{4^2} * 5^{4^3} * 5^{4^4}$ combinations.
In total there are $6^4 * 5^{340}$ = approximately $5.3 * 10^{240}$ possible patterns.

This is a reduction of about 821 decimal orders of magnitude.

(c) There are different perspectives on answering this question. We start with the simplest answer.

Yes—the parent compatibility rules lend themselves to a hierarchical generate-and-test scheme because they can be applied immediately when the children of a node are generated in a depth-first generation process.

On the other hand, since the pleasing alternatives are already known, there is no point in generating the other and pruning them. We might as well just generate the pleasing ones—moving the "test" well inside the generator.

From a third perspective, there are still very many patterns. Professor Digit will not have enough time to look at them all.

B.3 *Chapter 3*

Selected Answers to Exercises for Section 3.1

Ex. 1   (a) *False.* Transfer of expertise is a general term referring to a process for transferring knowledge from a domain expert to a knowledge system. It does not say anything about the training of a domain expert about knowledge systems. As discussed in the text, transfer of expertise correctly conveys the notion that an expert's knowledge can often be tapped, but it understates the subtlety of the process by relying on a transportation metaphor.

(b) *True.* The longer-term computational knowledge medium is also used.

(c) *False.* Participatory design refers to an approach to building knowledge systems in which a user, a domain expert, and a knowledge engineer work collaboratively.

(d) *True.* This coordination and negotiation of changes is a central part of the work. In some cases, it may be possible to partition the knowledge for a problem into nearly independent topics. Even when that is possible, it is necessary to establish a shared vocabulary.

(e) *True.* Another term for knowledge service is *knowbot.*

Ex. 4   (a) It is important to include users in a participatory design group because they know many practical aspects of their work and have a direct interest in the quality of the design. Failure to include users in designing a system could lead to oversights and a lack of cooperation later when a system is being debugged and tested. This issue is discussed further in later sections. Another reason for including users is that a domain expert might have a good theoretical understanding of what is required, but might be too far removed from daily performance of the work to anticipate all the important, practical concerns.

(b) The problem of making changes to a shared knowledge base involves more than coordinating access to it. The access problem can be approached in terms of strategies for locking or protecting parts of a database or file system. The more difficult issue is that the different parts of a knowledge base need to be usable together. Different contributers may have different understandings about what the system should do. They may have different assessments about the value of stability and the need for change. They may not understand each other's terminology completely. The more tightly coupled the interactions in the knowledge base, the more important coordination and discussion become.

Selected Answers to Exercises for Section 3.2

Ex. 1 **(a)** The main task of the voicewriter is to recognize and transcribe speech. Professor Digit wants to access the knowledge that people use when they understand speech. He has chosen secretaries, reasoning that they perform this task regularly. By that criterion, a courtroom stenographer would be a better choice. In either case, however, his approach is seriously flawed. To see why, we begin by identifying some of the relevant skills.

> *Typing Skills.* The typing skills of secretaries are not relevant because a voicewriter would use a printer without having to find keys. That is, the knowledge about what keystrokes correspond to what printed characters is not relevant to a machine that generates printed characters from character codes (such as ASCII).

> *Hearing Skills.* Professor Digit hopes to access the skills for hearing and understanding that translate spoken language into written language. The skills involve both disambiguation among similar word sounds and correction of garbled sounds. They involve the parsing of such sounds into linguistic units. They also involve the translation of acoustic patterns (involving pitch and several classes of spoken sounds) into internal symbols. The skills also include knowledge of what words to omit, such as the nonsense, time-filling "um"'s and "uh"'s that litter so many people's speech. Although secretaries have such knowledge, there are issues of accessibility and relevance. The disambiguation and correction skills are both unconscious and extensive. The linguistic skills are possibly accessible—to the extent that we study them in school and explain them to each other—but they are likely to be extensive. The skills for translating speech into internal symbols are of less immediate value in building a voicewriter because it is not known exactly what internal symbols people use for sounds, or how those relate to representations that would be used in a voicewriter.

> *Grammar, Punctuation, and Articulation Skills.* Most secretaries have skills in creating grammatical sentences, using proper punctuation, and expressing thoughts clearly. The rules of the first two skills are extensive and documented in various writer's guides. However, the skills of clear expression are more difficult to articulate. In any given situation, a secretary probably draws on her knowledge of the speaker and the speaker's business and purpose in determining a good way to articulate those thoughts. It is likely that capturing such knowledge would be a very time-consuming process.

Document Layout Skills. Most secretaries have skills in designing documents. These include such things as knowing where to place dates and header information, use of forms of address, subtitles, use of emphasis indications such as italics and boldface, and so on. It includes choice of paragraph shape and line spacing. In some cases this knowledge is simpified by the use of standard forms for different purposes. Many secretaries have this knowledge and some of them could be articulate about it. Designers of voicewriters would need to decide whether incorporating such skills is part of their overall project.

Word Processing Skills. Most secretaries have word processing skills, which are skills at choosing and carrying out word processing operations such as inserting missing words and correcting spelling. However, depending on design decisions bearing on how elements of a document are pointed to and referenced by voice command, it seems likely that a voicewriter would have a built-in word processor rather than access a separate program.

Critiquing Skills. On the other hand, Professor Digit may discover that he wants a "smart editor" able to critique and improve a document. Unfortunately, this task is very open-ended. The latter skills are ones that secetaries might be articulate about, given test cases. However, the knowledge that secretaries bring to bear in doing this is based on broad experience and it would be very time-consuming to formulate and formalize that knowledge.

(b) Since the secretaries understand speech, type, and write letters, they clearly have and use much of the knowledge that Professor Digit hopes to put in his voicewriter.

Unfortunately for Professor Digit, the key processes of speech recognition—ranging from signal processing to word disambiguation in context—are not reliably accessible by introspection.

It is implausible that a secretary (or anyone else) could give a protocol showing how they do speech understanding or, introspectively, convey very much knowledge about how they do it. Such processes are said to be **cognitively impenetrable,** meaning that they are part of the unconscious mind that is not normally open to introspection. Protocol analysis would be of no use in accessing this knowledge and the verbal data hypothesis would not apply.

Ex. 4 **(a)** Retrospective accounts of problem solving are suspect in psychology because, by themselves, they have proven to be an unreliable guide to actual problem-solving steps that people use. Verbal data may be distorted by the value that the subject puts on them. Retrospective accounts do not preserve the temporal and sequential properties of a thought process. Accounts delivered "after the fact" tend to be rational reconstructions. Data and knowledge that were used may be forgotten so that the record is incomplete. Furthermore, memory is selective and retrospective accounts sometimes mix later insights with ones that were used at the time.

In knowledge engineering, retrospective accounts can distort data by omission. Purely retrospective accounts are avoided because of the difficulty of reconstructing the issues and concerns that were important at the time of problem solving, and because domain experts, like other people, tend to become too pedagogical and abstract when they are asked to explain how they did something.

(b) The goal of information-processing psychology is to gain insight into models of cognition. According to the theory, interrupting a subject with questions will change the contents of the STM and thereby change the course of problem-solving behavior. Interruptions are used routinely to remind a subject to verbalize. Interruptions could be used experimentally and systematically to test their effect on problem solving, but they are inappropriate when the goal is to gather the best trace of the steps of some mental process.

In knowledge engineering, results are gathered from multiple protocols. Protocols of multiple domain experts on multiple cases are taken and generalities are sought. Furthermore, the ultimate criterion for the acceptability of a problem-solving system is not the detailed reproduction of an expert's behavior on a case. Rather, it is the delivery of appropriate answers on a range of test cases. Because the knowledge base evolves as it is tested on multiple cases, there is less emphasis on any single protocol. A knowledge engineer is more likely to interrupt a domain expert in a conversational manner, in order to better understand what the expert is doing.

Selected Answers to Exercises for Section 3.3

Ex. 1   **(a)** Problem identification and specification.

Euclidean algorithm. The specification is clear at the beginning. There is little room for misunderstanding.
Knowledge system. Specifications are acquired incrementally. Formulating and refining the specifications is a major part of the task. Very often there are hidden assumptions and special case situations that are unnoticed until later stages.

(b) User involvement in the development process.

Euclidean algorithm. The program for this algorithm can be developed with very few consultations with users.
Knowledge system. Much feedback and collaboration with users is required.

(c) Impact on the organization in the workplace.

Euclidean algorithm. The Euclidean algorithm would probably be used deep in some mathematical application. People in an organization would not be immediately concerned with its workings, but only with the use of its results.
Knowledge system. Knowledge systems often must fit into an organizational environment. When knowledge systems are visibly involved in the work processes of an organization, much consulting is required in their design.

(d) Software maintenance requirements.

Euclidean algorithm. The Euclidean algorithm would probably need little and infrequent maintenance. For example, it may need to be recompiled when the underlying arithmetic hardware is changed.
Knowledge system. Knowledge systems would need to be improved and tuned throughout their life cycle.

Summary. From a perspective of knowledge systems, problems like the Euclidean algorithm are too idealized. They are misleading examples for judging the nature of the development process for a knowledge system.

Ex. 10   **(a)** *True.* Unstructured interviews tend to be used to develop common ground and goals. More focused techniques are used later for efficient knowledge acquisition.

(b) *True.*

(c) *False.* Typical cases are usually the first ones that should be considered. Tough cases are most useful later for establishing the quality of the decision making.

(d) *False.* When cases are created artificially by withholding information, it is important for a knowledge engineer to emphasize that what is being measured are properties of the knowledge and problem-solving methods rather than the cleverness of the domain expert. To preclude making the domain expert feel like an experimental subject, it is useful to engage his help in the design of the cases.

(e) *True.*

Selected Answers to Exercises for Section 3.4

Ex. 1   Tasks in narrow domains require less knowledge than tasks in broad domains. Because the acquisition and representation of knowledge in expert systems is usually a bottleneck, domains requiring very limited amounts of knowledge are more practical than domains requiring much knowledge.

Beyond this major point are some other factors as well. Narrow technical knowledge is less widely available than broad and general knowledge. This is why there is often a greater economic value to making a body of specialized knowledge available in a knowledge system than making a body of general knowledge available. Narrow domains also tend to have narrowly defined problems and solution criteria. Narrowness makes the formulation and testing of a knowledge system more tractable.

Ex. 7   **(a)** To determine the value of D, MYCIN will trace back for rules to determine the value of C, causing it to trace back to determine the value of B, causing it to trace back to determine the value of A, causing it to trace back to determine the value of D, resulting in an infinite loop.

(b) To avoid looping, some means of bookkeeping must be used to keep track of which rules have been visited. Algorithms for traversing graphs with cycles achieve this by labeling the nodes or edges as they are traversed. Analogously, the rules could be marked or labeled as they are tried.

An equivalent approach is to manage a list of "tracing parameters" to the find-out and monitor methods for MYCIN. This enables the system to keep track of all parameters currently being traced by the find-out method. The monitor method then simply ignores a rule if one of the parameters checked in its premise is already being traced.

Modified methods that incorporate this change are shown in Figures B.11 and B.12.

(c) Consider the rules described by the following sequence:

> **1.** $A \Rightarrow B, C$
> **2.** $B \Rightarrow D$
> **3.** $D \Rightarrow C$

In this case, if the system is asked to determine the value of C, rule 1 could be invoked twice. The problem can be avoided by refusing to permit the same rule to occur twice in a reasoning chain.

Ex. 12   **(a)** In this example, we combine

> bird(x) $\wedge$ ~ab$_1$(x) => flies(x)
> bird(Tweety)

To carry out MYCIN's monitor method:
1.   For each condition in the premise of the rule do
2.   begin
3.   For each clinical parameter in the premise do
4.   begin
5.   If this parameter is on the tracing-parameters list, then exit.
6.   If information about the clinical parameter is not yet known
                 then invoke the find-out mechanism for the parameter.
7.   end
8.   If the condition is not true then reject the rule.
9.   end
         ;At this point all necessary data have been obtained, the conditions
         of the rule have been evaluated, and the premise of the rule has
         been found to be true.
10.   For each parameter in the rule's conclusions, compute the certainty
      factor and update the dynamic database.

FIGURE B.11.   MYCIN's monitor method.

To carry out MYCIN's find-out method:
1.   Push the parameter description onto the tracing-parameters list.
2.   If the parameter is a laboratory datum, then
3.   Ask the user for the value of the parameter.
4.   If the value of the parameter is known, return it;
5.   If the value of the parameter is not known, then call Find-Rules.
6.   Pop the parameter from the tracing-parameters list.
7.   Return;

      ;Here if the parameter is not a laboratory datum
8.   Call Find-Rules (parameter).
9.   If the value of the parameter is known, return it.
10.   Ask the user for the value of the parameter.
11.   Pop the parameter from the tracing-parameters list.
12.   Return.

1.   Procedure Find-Rules:
2.   For each rule that concludes about the value of the parameter do
3.   begin
4.   Retrieve the rule from the knowledge base.
5.   Invoke the monitor method for the rule.
6.   end
7.   Return.

FIGURE B.12.   MYCIN's find-out method.

and the fact that there are no arguments (valid, invalid, or unknown) at all for ~flies(Tweety) to conclude

flies(Tweety)

or more formally

justified(<flies(Tweety)> a_1)

where a_1 is the assumption ~ab_1(Tweety).

(b) These new statements allow us to conclude

ab_1(Tweety)

This undermines a_1 so that flies(Tweety) is no longer supported. Furthermore, we have no basis for concluding

~flies(Tweety)

so the status of flies(Tweety) is now unknown.

(c) With the new sentence, we now conclude

~flies(Tweety)

from

penguin(Tweety)

penguin(Tweety) $\wedge$ ~ab_2(Tweety) => ~flies(Tweety)

or more formally

justified(<~flies(Tweety)> a_2)

where a_2 is the assumption ~ab_2(Tweety).

(d) With the new sentences, we can conclude

aviator(Tweety)
ab_2(Tweety)

we lose the justification for believing

~flies(Tweety)

Furthermore, we conclude again that Tweety flies from

aviator(Tweety) $\wedge$ ~ab_3(Tweety) => flies(Tweety)

assuming ~ab_3(Tweety). See Ginsberg (1987) for a collection of papers on the theory of nonmonotonic reasoning.

B.4 *Chapter 4*

Selected Answers to Exercises

■   **Ex. 1**   **(a)** *Ambiguous.* Time models can be "discrete" in either of two senses: time axis or property values. The former are *discrete-time* models and the latter are *discrete-value* (or *dis-*

crete-state) models. Thus discrete-time models always have ticks but discrete-value models do not necessarily have them.

(b) *False.* The defining characteristic of an atomic event (such as a transaction) is its all-or-none character. Either all of its actions are carried out or none of them are. In many applications it is convenient to describe transactions as being simultaneous, but that is not part of the definition of transactions or of atomic events more generally.

(c) *Ambiguous.* The statement is true in the simplest case where we assume that intervals have finite, positive, and nonzero length. To represent continuous functions adequately generally requires being able to assign values to points.

The answer is false if we allow intervals to have zero length. In this way, the real number line becomes a set of zero-length intervals on which continuous functions can be defined. A reconstruction of points from intervals is possible, although the arguments are longer than it is convenient to present here. Although such an arrangement is possible, it defeats the whole notion of interval so that it is essentially the same as the notion of a point.

(d) *False.* Interval representations of uncertainty can be used with point-based events or interval-based events.

(e) *False.* Branching time models can be used to represent uncertain knowledge about events of the past.

Ex. 3 Allen's enumeration is correct. There are 13 possible relations on intervals. We consider two demonstrations of this in the following. The first is a visual demonstration, which is perhaps the easiest to follow. The second systematically builds up relations between intervals from relations between their endpoints, eliminating combinations that are inconsistent.

First Approach—A Systematic Visual Presentation

Figure B.13 is organized by cases. The first column shows all the valid cases where $Y+ > X+$. In the second column, $Y+ = X+$. The five columns are mutually exclusive and account for all possibilities.

Each entry in a column moves $Y-$ to one of the possible lower values, ignoring situations where the intervals have zero or negative length. Necessarily, $Y- < Y+$ ans $X- < X+$. In this manner, all 13 cases are covered.

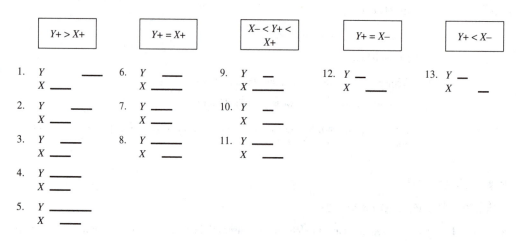

FIGURE B.13.   Thirteen possible relationships between two intervals.

Second Approach—A Counting Argument

Every relation between the intervals X and Y is ultimately defined in terms of relationships between their endpoints. The next two tables enumerate the relations from $X-$ and $X+$, respectively, to $Y-$ and $Y+$, indicating which pairwise combinations are valid.

Endpoint Relations Involving X+

	X+ R Y−	X+ R Y+	Valid?	Comment
1.	<	<	Yes	That is, $(X+ < Y-) \wedge (X+ < Y+)$ is possible.
−	<	=	No	That is, $(X+ < Y-) \wedge (X+ = Y+)$ is not possible.
−	<	>	No	
2.	=	<	Yes	
−	=	=	No	
−	=	>	No	
3.	>	<	Yes	
4.	>	=	Yes	
5.	>	>	Yes	

Endpoint Relations Involving X−

	X− R Y−	X− R Y+	Valid?	Comment
1.	<	<	Yes	That is, $(X- < Y-) \wedge (X- < Y+)$ is possible.
−	<	=	No	That is, $(X- < Y-) \wedge (X- = Y+)$ is not possible.
−	<	>	No	
2.	=	<	Yes	
−	=	=	No	
−	=	>	No	
3.	>	<	Yes	
4.	>	=	Yes	
5.	>	>	Yes	

To summarize, only five of the combined relations involving $X+$ are valid and the same is true of $X-$. To enumerate the relations on intervals, we need to put together entries from these endpoint tables to create combinations involving all four endpoints. The following table joins the valid entries, yielding 25 combinations. Combinations that fail to honor the constraints that $X- < X+$ or $Y- < Y+$ are eliminated. The 13 consistent interval relations are enumerated and Allen's names for them are given.

Enumeration of Consistent Combinations: The Possible Interval Relations

	X+ comb.	X− comb.	Valid?	X R Y	Comment
1.	1	1	Yes	<	$X < Y$
−	1	2	No		$(X+ < Y-) \wedge (X- = Y-)$ is not possible.
−	1	3	No		
−	1	4	No		
−	1	5	No		
2.	2	1	Yes	m	X meets Y
−	2	2	No		
−	2	3	No		

Enumeration of Consistent Combinations: The Possible Interval Relations

	X+ comb.	X– comb.	Valid?	X R Y	Comment
–	2	4	No		
–	2	5	No		
3.	3	1	Yes	o	X overlaps Y
4.	3	2	Yes	s	X starts Y
5.	3	3	Yes	d	X during Y
–	3	4	No		
–	3	5	No		
6.	4	1	Yes	fi	Y finishes X
7.	4	2	Yes	=	X = Y
8.	4	3	Yes	f	X finishes Y
–	4	4	No		
–	4	5	No		
9.	5	1	Yes	di	Y during X
10.	5	2	Yes	si	Y starts X
11.	5	3	Yes	oi	Y overlaps X
12.	5	4	Yes	mi	Y meets X
13.	5	5	Yes	>	X > Y

Note: Some readers have argued that Allen's "meets" relation is actually impossible. The argument turns on whether we think of the intervals as containing or not containing their bounding points. For purposes of argument, let us define the intervals as including their endpoints. In this case, the argument goes, that this should be included as a case of "overlaps." By distinguishing the "meets" special case as separate, we are giving special attention to the case where the overlap has zero measure. One rationale for keeping this case separate in the theory is that its consequences are stronger than those of "overlap" and that it is a common case.

B.5   Chapter 5

Selected Answers to Exercises

Ex. 1   (a) *False or Ambiguous.* This is usually true, but there are exceptions, such as the Hansel and Gretel example at the beginning of the section.
(b) *True.*
(c) *True.*
(d) *True.*
(e) *True.*

Ex. 3   Professor Digit is correct. The answer depends on several things:

□   How many objects are in the database
□   How many of the objects satisfy the predicate
□   How the objects are spatially distributed
□   What kinds of fast indexing are available in the database

In general, nearest-first search is most efficient when solutions are near the reference object.

Counterexample 1. Suppose there is a very large database, that objects satisfying *P* are extremely rare, *and that there is a fast method for retrieving objects satisfying P independent of the position of the objects.* For example, the objects could be sorted or indexed by color and the predicate could be a color test. A better strategy in this case is simply to exhaustively search through all the objects satisfying *P* (exploiting the index or the sort) and to pick the one closest to O_1. Given that the objects satisfying *P* are rare enough, this approach will examine far fewer objects in total than would be considered by proceeding out from O_1 until encountering one of them. That is, there are many objects near the reference object that do not satisfy the predicate and that it will not need to consider.

Counterexample 2. Suppose the predicate is "the object is at least 10 miles away" where this distance puts it on the distant fringes of the map. In this pathological case, searching in from the edges until the reference distance is less than 10 miles is better. For this predicate and object distribution, the reference point is almost the *worst* place to start searching.

Note: In answering this question it is not enough to simply propose a random, exhaustive, and nonspatial search. You have to show your assumptions about the distribution of objects, the order in which they would be searched, and how the search is exhaustive.

Ex. 7 **(a)** Yes, Professor Digit is correct. In quadtrees there are more neighbors and more potential neighboring regions at a given distance. However, the essence of the criteria is the same as with flat representations.
(b) After starting in R1, a quadtree search would need to test the various subquadrants. If it found *x* first, it would not need to test the region containing *w*. If it found *w* first, it would replace it with *x* as the nearest object. Given *x*, it would still need to test objects *a* and *b*, since those regions contain points as close to ref as *x*. It would not need to test the regions containing *c* and *d*, since even if the objects in those regions satisfied the criteria, they are farther from the reference point than *x*.

B.6   *Chapter 6*

Selected Answers to Exercises for Section 6.1

Ex. 1 **(a)** *True.* The certainty-factor approach does not explicitly use probabilities at all. Furthermore, the approach fundamentally assumes that the rules can be applied in any order. This property is called the detachment assumption.
(b) *True.*
(c) *False.* The certainty-factor approach is not Bayesian.
(d) *True.* When Dempster's rule for evidence combination is applied, all the "probability mass" that would be assigned to contradictory subsets of θ is instead redistributed proportionately.
(e) *False.* Quantitative approaches such as the certainty-factor and Dempster-Shafer approach operate on the assumption that facts are independent. However, probability network approaches allow facts to be dependent. Rather than banning dependencies, they test for independence and use network representations to make dependency testing efficient.

Ex. 6 **(a)** $P(E|\sim H)$ means the probability that a person has red spots (*E*) given that they do not have measles. A value of .001 means that in a large set of people who do not have measles, only 1 person in 1,000 will have red spots.

To obtain this probability statistically, we would need to have a representative and large enough sample of people and a definitive medical test (other than spots) for determining whether a subject has measles. We would use the medical test to eliminate all people who have measles. Then the ratio of the remaining red-spotters who do not have measles to the total number of people who do not have measles would be our estimate of $P(E|{\sim}H)$.

(b) What is $P(H|E)$—that is, the probability that a person has measles, given that he has red spots? By definition we have:

$$P(H|E) = P(H,E)/P(E)$$

and by Bayes' rule we have

$$P(H|E) = P(E|H) * P(H)/P(E)$$

We are given:

$$P(H) = .001 \quad P(E|H) = .99 \quad P(E|{\sim}H) = .001$$

To use either formula, we need $P(E)$.

$$P(H) = P(E|H) * P(H) + P(E|{\sim}H)*P({\sim}H)$$
$$P(H) = .99 * .001 + .001 * (1 - .001) = .00099 + .000999$$
$$= .001989$$

Using Bayes' rule, we have

$$P(H|E) = P(E|H) * P(H)/P(E)$$
$$P(H|E) = .99 * .001/.001989 = .4977375$$

(c) What is $P(H|{\sim}E)$? That is, what is the probability that someone has measles if he does not have red spots?

$$P(H|{\sim}E) = P({\sim}E|H) * P(H)/P({\sim}E)$$
$$P(H|{\sim}E) = (1 - P(E|H)) * P(H)/(1 - P(E))$$
$$P(H|{\sim}E) = (1 - .99) * .001/(1 - .001989) = .00001/.998011 = .00001$$

(d) Given a statistically average sample of 1 million people, the following number of people are in each of the designated categories:

☐ People with measles	1,000
☐ People without measles	999,000
☐ People with red spots	1,989
☐ People without red spots	998,011
☐ People with measles and red spots	990
☐ People with measles and no red spots	10
☐ People with no measles and red spots	999
☐ People with no measles and no red spots	998,001

(e) The exact logic of Professor Digit's account is pretty vague. Apparently, he fails to appreciate that the rarity of measles at a given time in the population means there are many more people who do not have measles than who do. A smallish rate of false positives applied to a big population is still a significant number. In part d, only 1,000 people of a million have measles, and of them, 990 have red spots. Meanwhile in the population, 999 people without measles also have red spots. This is why $P(H|E)$ is only .4977. For a more definitive diagnostic conclusion, we need to combine data about spots with other tests.

Ex. 11 **(a)** Show (1) that MB(H, e+) increases toward 1 as confirming evidence is found, and (2) that it equals 1 if and only if a piece of evidence logically implies H with certainty.

Let x, y be two CFs from successive confirming evidence, and z be the resulting CF, with $0 \le x, y \le 1$.

By the rules of combination, we have

$z = x + y(1 - x).$

First we show (1) that $z = 1$ if either x or y is 1.

Suppose $x = 1$.
Then $z = 1 + y(1 - 1) = 1$.

Suppose that $y = 1$.
Then $z = x + 1(1 - x) = 1$ (which proves (1)).

Now we show (2) that MB increases toward 1.
Suppose that $z = x$. (This is what we would get if x were the first piece of evidence encountered.) Now we need to show that z increases when y is encountered. That is, we need to show $x \le x + y - xy \le 1$.

$x \le 1$	Given
$xy \le y$	Multiply by y, which is positive
$0 \le y - xy$	Subtract xy
$x \le x + y - xy = z$	Add x

This shows that z increases.
Now we show that z stays less than 1.

$y \le 1$	Given
$y(1 - x) \le 1 - x$	Multiply by $(1 - x)$, which is positive
$y - xy \le 1 - x$	Distribute
$z = x + y - xy \le 1$	Add x

(b) Show MB(H, e_1&e_2) = MB(H, e_2&e_1)
Restated, we are to show that the order that evidence is encountered does not matter. Some assumptions are necessary for this. For example, we assume that the domain is consistent in that it is not the case that there is certain evidence confirming H as well as certain evidence disconfirming it.

By the proof of part a, if there is confirming evidence, then the order in which it is encountered does not matter for MB = 1. An analogous proof holds for MD.

Otherwise, the formula in effect for both MB and MD is

$z = x + y - xy$

It is evident that this formula is symmetric in x and y. Therefore, the order does not matter.
(c) Show CF(H, e–] $\le$ CF(H, e– & e+] $\le$ CF (H, e+).
The proof of part a shows that MB increases when given positive evidence. This is enough to show:

CF(H, e–) $\le$ CF(H, e– & e+)

A proof analogous to part a shows that MD increases toward 1 when given negative evidence. The proof of part b shows us that the order in which evidence is received does not matter. Combining these results we get the second half of the inequality.

Ex. 18   **(a)** Is it true that

If $Bel(A) = 0$ then $D(A) > 0$?

No, the statement is false.
   By definition, we have

$D(A) = Bel(\sim A)$ and
$Bel(A) + Bel(\sim A) \le 1$

However, it is entirely possible to have a domain in which (for example) $Bel(A) = Bel(\sim A) = 0$.

(b) Is it true that

If $D(A) = 1$ then $Bel(A) = 0$?

Yes, the statement is true.
   Again, by definition, we have

$D(A) = Bel(\sim A)$ and
$B(A) + Bel(\sim A) \le 1$

So if $D(A) = Bel(\sim A) = 1$ then $Bel(A) = 0$.

Ex. 26   Show: $O\,(H \mid E) = \lambda\, O(H)$

Proof

We begin with the regular form of Bayes' rule and its variation for $\neg H$.

$P(H|E) = P(H)\quad P(E|H)/P(E)$
$P(\neg H|E) = P(\neg H)\quad P(E|\neg H)/P(E)$

Dividing these we obtain

$P(H|E)/P(\neg H|E) = [P(H)\ P(E|H)/P(E)]/[P(\neg H)\ P(E|\neg H)/P(E)]$
$P(H|E)/P(\neg H|E) = [P(E|H)/P(E|\neg H)]\ [P(H)/P(\neg H)]$

Yielding by the definition of odds and of λ

$O(H \mid E) = \lambda\, O(H)$

Ex. 33   **(a)** The ON-INST procedure is triggered. It assigns

$P'(R) = (1, 0)$

meaning that Peter ate some carrots.

(b) Still running ON-INST, we use PT-3 to compute the new value of $\lambda(R)$.

$\lambda(b_i) = \prod \lambda_C(b_i)$ if B is not instantiated for $C \in s(B)$ (PT-3)
      1 if B is instantiated for b_i
      0 if B is instantiated, but not for b_i
$\lambda(R) = (1, 0)$

(c) Still running ON-INST, we use PT-2 to compute new π messages for G.

$$\pi_B(a_j) = 1 \text{ if } A \text{ is instantiated for } a_j \qquad\qquad \text{(PT-2)}$$
$$\qquad\quad 0 \text{ if } A \text{ is instantiated, but not for } a_j$$
$$\qquad\quad P'(a_j)/\lambda_B(a_j)$$
$$\pi_G(R) = (1, 0)$$

(d) The ON-PI procedure is triggered for G. We use PT-1 to compute new λ messages from G to S.

$$\lambda_B(a_j) = \Sigma\, \pi_B(d_k)\, (\Sigma\, P(b_i|a_j,\, d_k)\, \lambda(b_i)) \qquad\qquad \text{(PT-1)}$$
$$\qquad\qquad \text{for } k \text{ from 1 to } n_d$$
$$\qquad\qquad\qquad\quad \text{for } i \text{ from 1 to } n_b$$
$$\lambda_G(s_1) = \pi_G(r_1)\, [P(g_1|s_1,\, r_1)\, \lambda(g_1) + P(g_2|s_1,\, r_1)\, \lambda(g_2)]$$
$$\qquad\quad + \pi_G(r_2)\, [P(g_1|s_1,\, r_2)\, \lambda(g_1) + P(g_2|s_1,\, r_2)\, \lambda(g_2)]$$

Using the results of part c, we have

$$\lambda G(s_1) = (1)[(.99)(1) + (.01)(0)] + 0[(.9)(1) + (.1)(0)]$$
$$\lambda G(s_1) = .99$$

Similarly,

$$\lambda_G(s_2) = \pi_G(r_1)\, [P(g_1|s_2,\, r_1)\, \lambda(g_1) + P(g_2|s_2,\, r_1)\, \lambda(g_2)]$$
$$\qquad\quad + \pi_G(r_2)\, [P(g_1|s_2,\, r_2)\, \lambda(g_1) + P(g_2|s_2)\, \lambda(g_2)]$$
$$\lambda_G(s_2) = (1)[(.5)(1) + (.5)(0)] + 0[(.01)(1) + (.99)(0)]$$
$$\lambda_G(s_2) = .5$$

In summary, $\lambda_G(S) = (.99, .5)$

(e) The ON-LAMBDA procedure is triggered for S. We use PT-3 to compute new λ values for S.

$$\lambda(b_i) = \prod \lambda_C(b_i) \text{ if } B \text{ is not instantiated for } C \in s(B) \qquad\qquad \text{(PT-3)}$$
$$\qquad\quad 1 \text{ if } B \text{ is instantiated for } b_i$$
$$\qquad\quad 0 \text{ if } B \text{ is instantiated, but not for } b_i$$

Since there is only one child, the result is immediate.

$$\lambda(s_1) = \lambda_G(s_1) = .99$$
$$\lambda(s_2) = \lambda_G(s_2) = .5$$

(f) The ON-LAMBDA procedure is still running. We use PT-5 to compute $P'(S)$.

$$P'(b_i) = \alpha\lambda(b_i)\, \pi(b_i) \qquad\qquad \text{(PT-5)}$$
$$P'(s_1) = \alpha\lambda(s_1)\, \pi(s_1) = \alpha(.99)(.01) = .0099$$
$$P'(s_2) = \alpha\lambda(s_2)\, \pi(s_2) = \alpha(.5)(.99) = .495$$

Normalizing so that $|P(S)|=1$ yields

$$P'(S) = (.02, .98)$$

(g) The probability that we will have stew for dinner has now been changed through a sequence of events. When we learned that carrots were missing, we revised our estimate of the probability of stew to the conditional probability of stew given that carrots were missing. This raised the probability from .01 to .476. However, when we saw diggings by the fence, we had to revise our estimate again to take into account both that carrots were missing and that Peter had taken carrots. PT-3 tries to compute the joint probability from this. The estimate for stew now drops from .476 to a measely .02—still more than the prior probability, but now very low.

Selected Answers to Exercises for Section 6.2

Ex. 1   **(a)** *False.* Fuzzy set theory is used to represent vagueness, not certainty.

(b) *Ambiguous or False.* In principle, a characteristic function must take a value between 0 and 1, but it need not be continuous. However, in practice, characteristic functions are usually chosen to be continuous so that minor changes in property values do lead to abrupt changes in inference

(c) *True.*

(d) *True.*

(e) *False.* An induced fuzzy set is a fuzzy set produced when a fuzzy inference technique is applied to a fuzzy value.

Ex. 3   **(a)** Function 2 corresponds to "somewhat." This operation dilates the function by increasing the membership value of those elements of low degree more than those of high degree. It is sometimes called a "dilation" operation.

(b) Function 1 corresponds to "very." This operation reduces the degree of those elements of low degree. It is sometimes called a "concentration" operation.

(c) Function 3 corresponds to "extremely." This operation is a more potent version of the concentration operation.

B.7   Chapter 7

Selected Answers to Exercises for Section 7.1

Ex. 1   **(a)** Given the solution class S_2:

The data corresponding to $\{(1\ ?) * * (1\ ?) * (0\ ?)\}$ are consistent where "*" is $(1\ 0\ ?)$ and "?" means that the value of a datum is not known.

(b) The data corresponding to the pattern $(1 * * 1 * 0)$ match S_2.

(c) Given the data vector $(0\ 1\ ?\ 1\ 1\ ?)$:

The following classes are ruled out: S_1, S_2, S_5.
The following classes are consistent: S_3, S_4.
The following classes match: S_4.

Ex. 4   **(a)** It's impossible to answer absolute points about efficiency without specific examples, but often, the computations for deciding whether class matches data are quite trivial. Similarly, the computations for ruling out solutions are quite trivial. Neglecting very data-intensive problems such as those involved in machine perception, Professor Digit is probably right in his first point.

(b) Professor Digit is also right in his second point. A system cannot detect inconsistencies among data if the data are not observed at all. However, much of the point of mutual-exclusion reasoning is to be able to cover cases where data are missing.

(c) Professor Digit's third point does not follow. His complaint about data consistency would make sense in tasks where data are unreliable, so that redundancy of measurement is an important part of achieving system reliability. But this depends on the specifics of the task and instrumentation. In some cases, the costs, time, or risks associated with acquiring the additional data greatly favor the use of the logic of mutual exclusion of solutions.

Similar points could be made about other assumptions about the solutions, such as the use of a single solution assumption. For example, in many troubleshooting tasks, the probability of multiple independent failures is the product of the probabilities of single failures, so that solutions involving those are much rarer than solutions involving single failures.

Selected Answers to Exercises for Section 7.2

Ex. 1 (a) *True*. Classification requires that the set of solutions be fixed before a problem is solved. However, it does not require that it be determined before knowledge system is built or that the set cannot be changed over time.

(b) *True*. Some classification systems do not perform solution refinement and others do not perform data abstraction.

(c) *True*.

(d) *False*. Parsimony rules are rules that express preferences for simple solutions over complex ones.

(e) *True*. The term *establish-refine* refers to a top-down approach to generating and testing solutions.

Ex. 4 A data-driven approach invokes specialist modules directly from data. For example, there could be different specialists for different kinds of data. Another approach would be to organize the specialists to trigger off of a shared memory, as in a blackboard architecture. Typically, such an organization attempts to account only for hypotheses that are suggested by the data.

One issue here is that with a bottom-up approach, it may be discovered partway through diagnosis that additional data are needed to discriminate among candidates. However, new data may also implicate new possible hypotheses. Thus, the control structure would need to accomodate the addition of new hypotheses to explain the new data.

Selected Answer for Section 7.3

Ex. 1 (a) There are many possible answers to this exercise. Probably the simplest answer is "generate-and-test." Another answer is that MC-2 is a composition of two methods. The first method abstracts the data. This is a bottom-up or data-driven specialization of generate-and-test. The second part evaluates the candidates.

B.8   Chapter 8

Selected Answers to Exercises for Section 8.1

Ex. 1 (a) Reasoning about global resources is problematic because demands arise from many different parts in configuration problems. Almost every decision affects the requirements on global resources in some way. For example, in computing configurations, adding devices usually increases power requirements.

Power and cost requirements are global resources. Timing delays in a bus layout are another example. Many arrangement models are made up mostly of global resources in domains where almost any component could be placed almost anywhere.

(b) Here are some approaches to reasoning about global resources:

   (i) Make sure all commitments to them can be easily revised, since early estimates can easily be wrong.

   (ii) Make sure any early decisions are conservative. This is appropriate in cases where it is easier to scale back than it is to expand requirements.

   (iii) Delay decisions on global resources as long as possible, so estimates on requirements can be more realistic.

Ex. 3   **(a)** The rationale for the answer is as follows. In expanding B, there are two choices: B-1 and B-2. B-2 occupies a full slot. B-1 occupies only a half-slot, but requires two C's at a half-slot each for a total of 1.5 slots. This means that B-2 usually occupies less space than B-1. However, since B-2 requires a full slot, B-1 may effectively take no more space than B-2 in the case where it is preceded by an unusable lower half-slot left over from A-1. A-1 requires a half-slot plus two B's. A-2 requires a full slot plus three B's. This means that A-1 always occupies less space than A-2.

The specification {A, B} can be implemented using four slots in either of two ways as shown in Figure B.14. The C's can be implemented as either C-1's or C-2's with no difference in space.

(b) Following the cost table for this exercise, we can compute the minimum costs for various component descriptions. The description {C} can be implemented as either C-1 or C-2 with a minimum cost of $5 for C-1. The description {B} can be implemented as either B-1 or B-2. B-1, by itself, costs $20, for a total of $30 minimum if the two required C's are included. Although B-2 occupies less space, it costs $40. Finally, A-1 costs $50, but has a minimum total of $110 if the required B's and C's are included. Thus, the minimum total cost (not counting the case) is for {A-1, 3 B-1, 6 C-1}, for a total of $140.

Another alternative is to use the less costly A-2 instead of A-1. This results in the configuration {A-2, 4 B-1, 6 C-1}, which also costs $140 but requires more slots, as shown in Figure B.15.

(c) No, the results are different. The order that criteria are used in the search matters because it determines which criteria dominate.

Selected Answers to Exercises for Section 8.2

Ex. 1   **(a)** From the discussion of XCON in this section, we know that the database in 1989 included information on more than 30,000 parts of more than 40 types. The number of "possible" configurations based on the arrangement of parts from the power set is astronomical. Such a table size, even reduced by a factor of 1,000, would not be manageable. Professor Digit's proposal would require a much greater reduction of the search space than this.

(b) Even if the number of table entries were manageable, there are other benefits to building a knowledge-based problem solver that are overlooked by Professor Digit's proposal.

   1. *Quality assurance.* Building a formal and systematic knowledge base offers an opportunity for controlling the quality of configurations. It encourages the systematic recording of criteria for determining when systems are correctly configured. Quality control is important for all product-making organizations and is more diffi-

Specifications: {A, B}

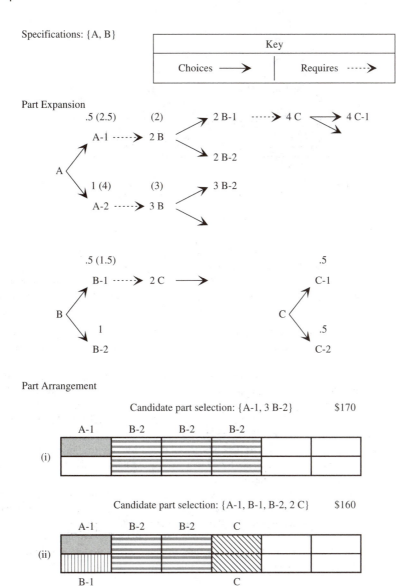

FIGURE B.14. The minimum space expansions of {A, B}. Configuration (ii) is the least costly of these.

cult to achieve in a custom-order business. A table built by ad hoc means could contain many errors and suboptimal solutions. Any mistakes in a case added to the table would be repeated every time the entry was used.

2. *Order checking*. Part of the task for XCON and XSEL is to check for inconsistencies in the specification. A table-driven approach, by itself, would not do that and could not make minor corrections to the specification.

Specifications: {A, B}

Part Arrangement

Candidate part selection: {A-1, 3 B-1, 6 C-1} $140

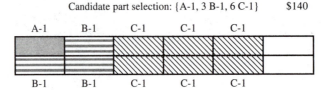

FIGURE B.15.   The minimum cost expansion of {A, B}. Configuration (i) is the most space-efficient
of these.

3. *New components*. As new components are added and system standards change,
the choice of the best configuations changes. A program based on a table would continue to offer the "old-style configuration" even after new possibilities became available. The table, itself, provides no basis for updating the procedures to accommodate
new possibilities.

Ex. 3   **(a)** There are two top-level parts in configuration-1: part-1-1 and part-1-2. A total of nine
parts are shown. The other five parts are part-1-1, part-1-1-1, part-1-1-2, part-1-1-3, and
part-1-2.
(b) The term subpart is usually used refer to parts that are packaged together. For example, multiple parts may be manufactured on a single board. In some systems, the term is
also used to refer to things that are always sold together, even if they have unrelated
functionalities. The term requires-component is defined to indicate what additional parts a
component needs to function correctly.
(c) Whether cables are parts depends on our definition of *part*. For example, if we define
a part as being a class of object found in a particular catalog or database, then some cables
may be parts and others may not.

The basic approximation in the port-and-connector model, however, defines cables
only as the connectors that go between ports. In most tasks, this approximation needs to be
augmented to respect the fact that there are different kinds of cables.

For example, specification of a cable could include such things as the number and
types of connectors, shielding, and length. In many cases, the representation of cables is
complex enough to warrant a detailed representation.

Selected Answer for Section 8.3

Ex. 1   MYCIN's method differs from the methods in this section in that it does not have an
arrangement submodel. Nonetheless, it does carry out a process of expanding and refining
its solution. As described in the text, it plans solutions using local factors and then ranks
and prunes its list of candidates using global factors. Clancey characterized the method
simply as plan-generate-and-test.

B.9 Chapter 9

Selected Answers to Exercises for Section 9.1

Ex. 1   **(a)** Because a patient can have multiple diseases.

(b) For an arbitrary patient, we must consider up to 10 different diseases (including "no disease process") from a set of 10,000 disease processes.

$$\text{Number of hypotheses} = \sum_{k=0}^{10} \binom{n}{k} \text{ where } n = 10^4 \text{ or roughly } 2.7 * 10^{33}$$

$k = 0$ corresponds to the case where the patient has no diseases.

Another way to figure this is to imagine that we are filling in a vector $\{d_1, d_2, \ldots, d_{10}\}$ for ten diseases including "no disease." There are 104 ways to select the first disease, and $10^4 - 1$ ways to select the second, and so on, for each of the ten concurrent diseases. This yields a total of approximately 10^{40} different vectors. However, the order of selection does not matter, so we need to divide out the 10! possible orderings of the elements in the vectors. This gives us the same answer as before.

(c) Since each disease (or fault) may be either present or absent, there are a total of 2^n possible diagnoses. The is $2^{10,000}$, or roughly $10^{3,300}$ diagnoses. This estimate is silly because it admits the possibility of diagnosing a patient having as many as 10,000 manifest diseases. Life is too short, both for the patient and the diagnostician!

Ex. 4   Entropy computations for this exercise were requested in base e. However, to accommodate those who insist on using base 2 and to simplify correcting exercises, the answers in base 2 are also given.

(a) .693 base e; 1.0 base 2.

(b) 1.61 base e; 2.32 base 2.

Part b has more entropy than part a because there are more unresolved candidates.

(c) For 10 candidates, 2.30 base e; 3.32 base 2.

For 20 candidates, 2.99 for base e; 4.32 base 2.

The entropy increases further because there is more diagnostic work to rule out the unresolved candidates . We can give a mathematical motivation for this as well. Given that entropy is

$$H = -\sum^{\text{all } i} p_i \log p_i$$

In this special case, each term in the sum is identical since all candidates have probability $p = 1/n$.

$$Hn = -n(1/n \log (1/n))$$
$$= -\log(1/n) = \log n$$

Since log is an increasing function, for $m < n$,

$$H_m < H_n.$$

Ex. 7   **(a)** $C(p) = k$.

(b) That is, show that $C(p) = -\log_2(p)$ satisfies the condition from part a.

$$C(p) = -\log_2 (1/2^k) = -[\log_2^1 - \log_2(2^k)] = -[0 - k \log_2 2) = k(1) = k$$

(c)

$$E_D = -\sum_{}^{\text{all } c} p_c C(p_c) = -\sum_{}^{\text{all } c} p_c \log_2 p_c = H$$

In other words, Shannon entropy is a sum of products for each candidate, where the contribution from each candidate is its probability times its expected identification cost.

(d) Under the conditions in part c, each probe divides the set of unresolved candidates in half.

(e) We are given that after each probe, the probabilities are renormalized so that

$$\sum_{}^{\text{all } c} p_c = 1$$

From this we have that

$$E_D = -\sum_{}^{\text{all } c} p_c C(p_c) = H = k$$

so that Shannon entropy as applied in this circumstance is a measure of the number of probes probably needed before the correct diagnostic candidate is isolated.

We note in passing that this derivation does not rely on a single-fault assumption. The diagnoses in the tree can be composite.

Ex. 11 **(a)** Here's the table filled in.

Probe Site 1

Candidates consistent with the "signal is changing"

Candidate	Probability	Normalized Probability
$[A_w, B_w, C_f]$	.33	.96
$[A_w, B_f, C_w]$	.013	.04

Probability of value .34   *Entropy .17*   *Weighted entropy .0578*

Candidates consistent with the "signal is constant"

Candidate	Probability	Normalized Probability
$[A_i, B_w, C_w]$	.65	.99
$[A_f, B_w, C_w]$	.0065	.009

Probability of value .6565   *Entropy .052*   *Weighted entropy .034*

Expected entropy for probe site 1 .091

Probe Site 2

Candidates consistent with the "signal is changing"

Candidate	Probability	Normalized Probability
$[A_w, B_w, C_f]$	.33	1.00

Probability of value .33   *Entropy* 0   *Weighted entropy* 0

Candidates consistent with the "signal is constant"

Candidate	Probability	Normalized Probability
$[A_w,\ B_f,\ C_w]$	.013	.01
$[A_i,\ B_w,\ C_w]$	.65	.97
$[A_f,\ B_w,\ C_w]$	.0065	.009

Probability of value .67   *Entropy* .117   *Weighted entropy* .078

Expected entropy for probe site 2 .078

(b) Probe site 2 has the minimum expected entropy.

Selected Answers to Exercises for Section 9.2

Ex. 1   **(a)** SOPHIE III modeled components as having explicit failure modes. In reasoning about behavior, it turned these models to advantage by being able to explicitly rule out certain failures if the circuit behavior was inconsistent with the particular component failure. However, it was not able to generate hypotheses to cover any failure for which it lacked an explicit model. In short, it could only cope with the specific kinds of component failures in its model.

GDE gained the ability to hypothesize faults for which it had no explicit model. All that it required was that the predictor be able to show that measurements dependent upon a suspect component were not consistent with the assumption that it was working properly.

(b) The following were important advances of GDE over SOPHIE III.

1. The ability to reason about multiple faults. SOPHIE III built in the assumption that there was only a single fault, and it used this assumption (zealously and incorrectly) to rule out certain hypotheses.

The idea of defining hypotheses in terms of covering sets was also reported earlier by Reggia, Nau, and Wang (1983).

2. A systematic way of reasoning about the information value of probe sites.

New in GDE was the integration of systematic generation of multiple-fault hypotheses with the minimal entropy idea.

3. The use of Bayes' rule to compute probabilities of expected failure for ranking candidates.

(c) The key idea was to allow the possibility of an "unknown" failure mode for every component. This mode could be hypothesized if the behavior of the component was inconsistent with its unfaulted behavior or any known fault mode.

(d) XDE carried functional abstractions beyond SOPHIE III in its development of temporal abstractions, which are abstract behaviors. Furthermore, it represented devices and signals at levels of abstraction that took into account what was reasonable to observe.

Ex. 4   **(a)** The *raw* differential diagnosis for jaundice is: common duct stone, biliary cirrhosis, Gilbert's disease, hemolytic anemia, viral hepatitis, macronodal cirrhosis, micronodal cirrhosis, and hepatic vein obstruction. The refined differential diagnosis for jaundice is conjugated hyperbirubinemia and unconjugated hyperbilirubinemia. These are illustrated in Figure B.16.

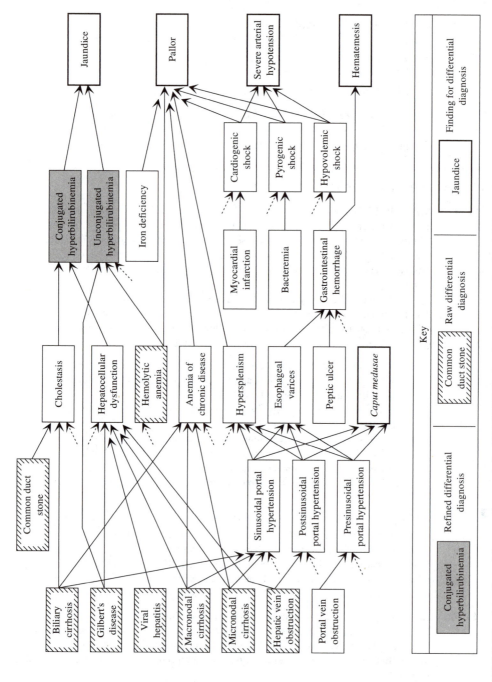

FIGURE B.16. A portion of the causal network for CADUCEUS, showing the raw and refined differential diagnoses for jaundice.

(b) The next determination after cholestasis is between a common duct stone and biliary cirrhosis.

(c) The diagnoses that explain *both* jaundice and pallor are the three cirrhosis nodes, hemolytic anemia, and hepatic vein obstruction. (See Figure B.17.)

(d) CADUCEUS's flat causal network is a *disjunctive* hierarchical-classification network. It is flat in the sense that it does not contain abstraction relations. (See Exercise 5.) However, the chains of causes form their own hierarchy similar in form to the hierarchical conjunctive classification systems in Chapter 7.

Another difference in thinking about causal networks is that the goals of diagnostic reasoning and classification reasoning are different. In diagnosis, we seek to eliminate unsupported, competing hypotheses. In classification, solutions either match or they don't. In particular, classification solutions are often not mutually exclusive.

Selected Answers to Exercises for Section 9.3

Ex. 1 **(a)** The basic paradigm of model-based troubleshooting compares the behavior of a physical artifact model with a model of it. When there is a discrepancy, model-based troubleshooting assumes that there is a defect such that the device fails to correspond to the model. It hypothesizes various defects, intended to explain the misbehavior.

(b) **(i)** "Models are incomplete." Models are always only a partial representation of a device. There is no single feature of XDE that ameliorates this difficulty. However, there is a general philosophy of making choices in modeling that gains something back when completeness is sacrificed. For example, when there are two components whose failures result in a single repair, they are treated as a single component. Another example is that unlikely failures need not be represented explicitly, but are treated as part of a single, aggregate, "unknown" failure mode.

(ii) "Predictions are costly." Predictions are costly when the models are complex. XDE addresses this issue by using hierarchical models that use abstract (and faster) predictions when possible.

(iii) "Predictions are incomplete." This refers to the fact that the process of making predictions from what is known is incomplete in that it does not make all possible predictions. The more abstract a prediction the less complete. Still, XDE recognizes that partial and abstract predictions are more valuable than none at all because they can allow more discrepancies to be detected and help rule out some diagnoses. By using a hierarchical approach, XDE can supplement abstract predictions with more detailed ones.

(iv) "Observations are costly." This refers to the fact that making observations is the most crucial resource in most diagnostic systems. XDE addresses this by making abstract predictions that correspond to things relatively easy to observe. In other words, its requests for data take into account the nature of the observational instruments that are available and what kinds of signal characteristics are easily observable.

(v) "Observations are incomplete." XDE takes into account the precision with which certain measurements can be made, thus bringing knowledge about ambiguities into the probe selection process. XDE also uses additional sources of information such as the relative failure rates of components in ranking hypotheses.

Ex. 3 **(a)** In a classification-based diagnostic system, one could incorporate such knowledge in terms of associations between elements of the solution space. These rules would become

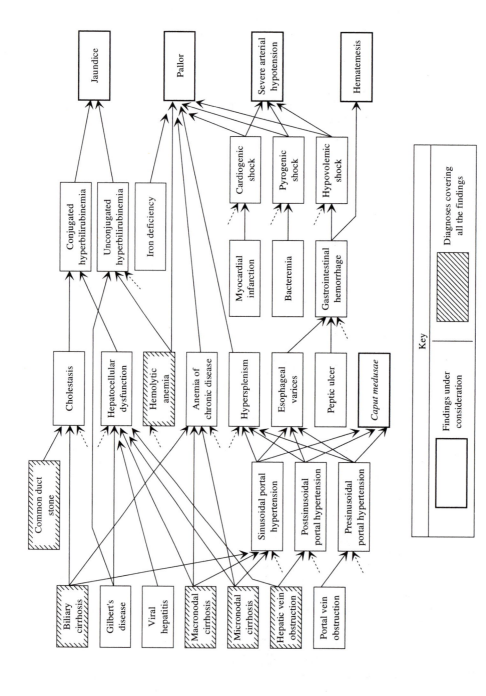

FIGURE B.17. Determining the set of causes that explain more than one diagnosis using a disjunctive causal network. The shaded nodes indicate those candidate causes that explain both jaundice and pallor.

active in the phase of the program that generates hypotheses. Simply put, these rules would use evidence of one cause (such as failure of one part) to implicate possible failure of the other part.

(b) In a model-based system, the knowledge could also be incorporated in the hypothesis-generation phase. Evidence for one fault could be used to increase the prior probability of another fault. This would make the prior probabilities of faults be conditional on beliefs about other faults. This would cause hypotheses that include both faults to have a higher probability than otherwise.

Index